SPORTS LAW

CASES AND MATERIALS

By

Robert M. Jarvis
Professor of Law
Nova Southeastern University

Phyllis Coleman
Professor of Law
Nova Southeastern University

AMERICAN CASEBOOK SERIES®

ST. PAUL, MINN., 1999

610 Opperman Drive
P.O. Box 64526
St. Paul, MN 55164–0526
1–800–328–9352

Printed in the United States of America

ISBN 0–314–23890–5

To H. Wayne Huizenga
For Bringing the Marlins and Panthers to South Florida

*

Preface

Our introduction to the field of sports law came in 1987 when our good friend and former dean, Roger I. Abrams, began teaching the course here at Nova using his own notes. At the time, there were no published materials available.

During the next few years, as law professors became more interested in the field, a number of sports law casebooks appeared. Although each was slightly different in format and organization, all viewed the subject as a subset of antitrust and labor law. As a result, their pages focused primarily on the application of these two disciplines to athletic endeavors.

Believing that sports law consists of much more than just antitrust and labor law, we have tried to write a different kind of book. In particular, we have sought to look at sports through the eyes of fans and to discuss issues as they affect those sitting in the bleachers.

Needless to say, we are very interested in receiving your thoughts about our book. Please direct your comments to:

Professor Robert M. Jarvis
Nova Southeastern University Law Center
3305 College Avenue
Fort Lauderdale, FL 33314-7721
Phone: (954) 262-6172
Fax: (954) 262-3835
E-mail: jarvisb@nsu.law.nova.edu

or

Professor Phyllis Coleman
Nova Southeastern University Law Center
3305 College Avenue
Fort Lauderdale, FL 33314-7721
Phone: (954) 262-6166
Fax: (954) 262-3835
E-mail: colemanp@nsu.law.nova.edu

*

Acknowledgements

All authors rely on others for help, and we are no exception.

First, we are thankful to Judith A. Jarvis and Susan Melian for their support and encouragement.

Second, we are grateful to our NSU colleagues Johnny C. Burris, Michael F. Flynn, Joseph D. Harbaugh, Lawrence Kalevitch, and Gail L. Richmond for their many helpful insights.

Lastly, we are indebted to the following publishers:

American Business Law Journal, for permission to reprint Kenneth L. Shropshire, Introduction: Sports Law?, 35 American Business Law Journal 181 (1998).

The Daily Oklahoman, for permission to reprint Scott Munn, Pop Goes the Market: Gone Are the Bubble-Gum Days of Card Collecting, The Daily Oklahoman, July 3, 1997, at 25 (Copyright © 1997 Oklahoma Publishing Company).

Sports Illustrated, for permission to reprint David Seideman, Caught in the Act of Forgery in Chicago: The FBI Breaks Up A Ring Trafficking in Fake Sports Memorabilia, Sports Illustrated, Oct. 20, 1997, at R8 (Copyright © 1997 Time Inc. - All Rights Reserved).

United Feature Syndicate, Inc., for permission to reprint the Peanuts cartoon strips of January 6-7, 1997.

*

Table of Cases

The principal cases are in bold type. Cases cited or discussed in the text are roman type. References are to pages. Cases cited in principal cases and within other quoted materials are not included.

*

Summary of Contents

Table of Contents

SPORTS LAW

CASES AND MATERIALS

*

Chapter 1

INTRODUCTION

A. OVERVIEW

In future chapters we discuss legal issues that arise in connection with different sports figures, including owners, players, agents, and coaches. In this chapter, however, our focus is more general. In particular, we are interested in exploring two questions: 1) what is meant by the term "sports law"?; and, 2) what ethical rules apply to sports lawyers?

B. DEFINITIONS

Since its emergence as a topic worthy of serious study, sports law has resisted easy characterization. The readings that follow explain why.

INTRODUCTION: SPORTS LAW?

Kenneth L. Shropshire
35 Am. Bus. L.J. 181 (1998).

What is sports law? One scholar provides the following broad definition of the field:

> Sports law is an amalgamation of many legal disciplines, ranging from antitrust to tax law. These disciplines are applied to facts arising from a sports context and are supplemented by case law nuances and a growing body of state and federal statutes specifically applicable to sports. Sports law, with its wide variety of legal aspects, probably encompasses more areas of the law than any other discipline. Sports law is also a dynamic field of the law with new issues arising on an almost daily basis due to court decisions, new legislation and regulations.

[Given the foregoing,] [s]hould this area of study be referred to as "sports law" or "sports and the law"? I believe the latter is more appropriately descriptive of this body of law. Sports law implies that there exists a unique substantive corpus that can be neatly categorized such as is the case with contracts, torts, or property, for example. There is little law that is unique to sports alone. Even the exemption to the antitrust laws with regard to its application to baseball might equally be characterized as antitrust law. The growing sports-only corpus is that of federal and state statutes impacting sports. Laws at the state level regulating boxing, for example, have long been with us. The number of sports agent regulatory statutes has grown to a fairly large number as well. And although federal statutes impacting sports are rare, they do exist and new, unlikely-to-be-passed legislation is introduced annually. Thus, what we normally mean when we say "sports law" is sports and the law that impacts that industry.

DAVIS v. COMMONWEALTH

564 S.W.2d 33 (Ky.Ct.App.1978).

VANCE, Judge.

Appellant Mary Crumes was indicted and convicted of theft by deception involving more than $100.00, a class D felony, and of criminal conspiracy to rig a sports contest, a class B misdemeanor.

Appellant Major Davis was convicted of complicity in theft by deception and with tampering with or rigging a sports contest.

All charges arose out of the promotion of a "Miss Black U.S.A." beauty pageant in Louisville. Appellant Crumes promoted the State of Kentucky pageant under a franchise granted by appellant Davis, the founder of the national pageant.

The charges, as they relate to theft by deception, concern the solicitation of a donation from the City of Louisville by the appellant Crumes. The solicitation was made by letter which read as follows:

> We are adults working with youths and their problems. This project will be promoted through all available channels: radio, newspaper, television, people and businesses beginning the first week of February. Young Black ladies from all areas of our city are seeking sponsorship. Donations toward our plan of procedure will be greatly appreciated. Portions of funds will be given to the sickle cell awareness foundation. The pageant's overall expenditures include: building, schoalarship, (sic), personality workshops, photos, advertising, trophies, band, program books, national franchise fee, transportations and lodging. All donations are tax deductable (sic). Please help us to meet these goals.

A donation of Two Hundred Dollars was made by the City of Louisville. A check was sent to appellant Crumes accompanied by a letter which stated the intended use of the funds and which required the return of an acknowledgement of receipt.

It is the Commonwealth's contention that theft by deception was committed because no monies were donated to a sickle cell awareness foundation and none was used for scholarships.

It is clear that the solicitation was made to defray the costs of putting on the pageant and was so understood by the city officials responsible for the donation. Those officials did not purport to have any knowledge that the donation was misused. There was no evidence that the pageant made any profit; in fact, the evidence indicates it was promoted at a loss. We do not believe the solicitation gave any basis for an impression that the donation would not be used in its entirety, if necessary, to defray the costs of the pageant.

As far as we can determine from the record, there is no proof that the donation was used in any different manner than intended by the donor. The evidence was insufficient to sustain a conviction and appellant Crumes' motion for directed verdict should have been sustained. The charge of complicity against appellant Davis must necessarily fall with the dismissal of the main charge against appellant Crumes.

The convictions for tampering with the outcome of a sports contest must be reversed because a beauty pageant is not a sports contest. KRS 518.060 provides as follows:

> (1) A person is guilty of tampering with or rigging a sports contest when, with intent to influence the outcome of a sports contest, he:
>
> (a) Tampers with any sports participant or sports official or with any animal, equipment or other thing involved in the conduct or operation of a sports contest in a manner contrary to the rules governing the sports contest in question; or
>
> (b) Substitutes a sports participant, animal, other than a horse, equipment or other thing involved in the conduct or operation of a sports contest for the genuine person, animal or thing.

A sports contest is defined by KRS 518.010(3) as any professional or amateur sport, athletic game or contest, or race or contest involving machines, persons or animals that is viewed by the public.

The Commonwealth contends that it was the intention of the legislature in enacting KRS 518.060 to make it a crime to tamper with the outcome of any contest, sport or otherwise, and that a beauty pageant is "a . . . contest involving . . . persons . . . that is viewed by the public" and thus fits the statutory definition of sports contest.

This contention ignores the word "sports" in the title of the act and also that the word "contest" in the definition section is clearly limited to professional or amateur sports, athletic games or races involving machines, persons or animals. We also note that KRS 518.060 is preceded in the statutes by KRS 518.040, sports bribery and KRS 518.050, receiving sports bribes and is followed by KRS 518.070, ticket scalping.

We think the proscription of KRS 518.060 was intended to be and is limited in application to sports contests as are normally understood by the usage of that term. If the general assembly intended the act to apply to all forms of contests, it certainly did nothing to make that intention clear by adding the words "sports" to the title and to the body of the act.

The judgment is reversed.

NEWMAN IMPORTING CO. v. UNITED STATES

415 F.Supp. 375 (Cust.Ct.1976).

WATSON, Judge.

Plaintiff seeks classification of its imported tents as sport equipment [Item 735.20 of the Tariff Schedules of the United States, as modified by T.D. 68–9, providing for duty at the rate of 12% ad valorem] instead of the classification assigned by the customs officials under a residual provision for articles of textile materials [Item 389.60 of the Tariff Schedules of the United States, as modified by T.D. 68–9, providing for duty in the amount of $25 per pound, plus 18% ad valorem].

Plaintiff claims these tents are designed for use in the sport of backpacking. Defendant argues that backpacking is not a sport and, even assuming it is, these tents are not used in the sport in the sense in which sport equipment must be used. Defendant also argues that these tents are not of the quality used in "serious" backpacking and further that a legislative intent existed to exclude tents from classification as sport equipment. This final argument relies on material from the Explanatory Notes to the Brussels Nomenclature (1955) and the Standard Industrial Classification Manual (1957). Since I detect no ambiguity in the term "sport equipment" there is no need to look for clues to legislative intent. Furthermore, I have strong doubts as to whether the language of the Brussels Nomenclature (Appliances, Apparatus, Accessories and Requisites for * * * Sports * * *) or the SICM (Sporting * * * Goods) is sufficiently similar to the term "sport equipment" to support any conclusions drawn from the former as to the scope of the latter.

Based on the testimony, I am persuaded that backpacking is a sport and that these tents are designed for use in the sport of backpacking so as to come within the meaning of the tariff term "sport equipment."

I have concluded from the evidence that backpacking is the activity of traveling on foot in relatively wild areas and maintaining oneself with supplies and equipment carried on one's back. This activity falls within my understanding of the term "sport." It possesses to a meaningful degree the same attributes of healthy, challenging and skillful recreation which characterize such acknowledged sports as scuba diving, skiing, horseback riding and mountain climbing.

I reject the government's contention that a sport must involve competition either between individuals or against the natural elements; although I would say that the activity of backpacking involves sufficient subjection to the forces of nature to qualify as a competitive sport in the second sense of the government's contention. In any event the element of enjoyment or recreation arising from the development or practice of individual skills, different from those involved in routine daily activities, is a better indication of a sport than competitiveness. See Sports Industries, Inc. v. United States, 65 Cust.Ct. 470, 474, C.D. 4125 (1970). See also David E. Porter v. United States, 76 Cust.Ct., C.D. 4641 (1976). In short, the common meaning of the word "sport" is not limited to competitive activities, a fact which can be generally confirmed by reference to the dictionary definitions.

From the testimony it is clear that the use of a shelter is a necessary and regular part of the prudent practice of backpacking, and the normal method of obtaining shelter while backpacking is to carry and utilize a specially designed, lightweight portable tent. On this essential point these tents are distinguished from the nets which were held not to be golf equipment in Nichimen Co., Inc. v. United States, 72 Cust.Ct. 130, C.D. 4514 (1974). The nets bordering the areas in which golfers practice their sport were not being used in the sport in anything approaching the sense in which these tents are used in backpacking.

At this point I note specifically that the use of a tent for shelter is part of the sport of backpacking, which encompasses not only the act of walking with a pack on the back but all the activities associated with the maintenance of the individual while away from "civilization." In this respect tents would be equipment even under the stringent view of equipment formerly prevailing and exemplified in Cruger's (Inc.) v. United States, 12 Cust.Appls. 516, T.D. 40730 (1925), which held equipment to be limited to objects ordinarily required for the proper and efficient playing of a sport or protection from its hazards. It would therefore seem certain that, under the modern view that sport equipment includes not only that which is "necessary" but also that which is specially designed for use in the sport, these tents are indeed sport equipment. See generally American Astral Corporation v. United States, 62 Cust.Ct. 563, C.D. 3827, 300 F.Supp. 658 (1969).

That these tents were specially designed for use in backpacking is not in doubt as is made plain by the testimony as to their design and the emphasis placed on their lightness, compactness and ease of assembly. Defendant's argument that these tents lack the quality to be used in "serious" backpacking was not supported by the evidence and was not persuasive. I see no indication that sport equipment must be of a quality required by the most demanding practitioners of a sport or that these tents are not of a sufficient quality to be used in the sport. Cf. New York Merchandise Co., Inc. v. United States, 62 Cust.Ct. 38, C.D. 3671, 294 F.Supp. 971 (1969). Consequently, since backpacking is a sport and these tents are equipment specially designed and even necessary for use in the sport, they should have been classified for tariff purposes as sport equipment under item 735.20 of the TSUS, as modified.

Judgment will enter accordingly.

Notes

1. For a further look at what constitutes "sports law," see Ross D. Petty, *The Impact of the Sport of Bicycle Riding on Safety Law*, 35 Am. Bus.

L.J. 185 (1998) (arguing the term should be expanded to include the legal consequences of such activities as bicycle riding and pick-up basketball games). *See also* James A.R. Nafziger, *International Sports Law: A Replay of Characteristics and Trends*, 86 Am. J. Int'l L. 489 (1992) (describing "international sports law" as a distinct legal field).

2. Can the decisions in *Davis* and *Newman* be reconciled? If not, which one do you find more persuasive? Frankly, we have problems with both opinions. With respect to *Davis*, it seems to us beauty pageants are sporting events because they pit skilled competitors against one another while the public watches and neutral referees enforce well-established rules. Conversely, in *Newman*, we have trouble viewing recreational activities such as backpacking, scuba diving, and mountain climbing as sports. Although Judge Watson says competition is not a prerequisite and a "sport" is any activity that involves "the development or practice of individual skills, different from those involved in routine daily activities," under his definition piano playing, painting, and basket weaving would all qualify as sports rather than as hobbies, pastimes, or leisure pursuits.

3. No "sport" provides more of a classification challenge than professional wrestling. For a useful article that traces the evolution of wrestling in this century from a true sport to a rigged (but wildly popular) entertainment spectacle, see Stephen S. Zashin, *Bodyslam from the Top Rope: Unequal Bargaining Power and Professional Wrestling's Failure to Unionize*, 12 U. Miami Ent. & Sports L. Rev. 1 (1994/1995).

Problem 1

While at a dance, a woman slipped and fell on the floor. When she sued the dance hall, its owner argued falling was a normal part of the sport of dancing and a risk the plaintiff had assumed. If she responds dancing is not a sport, how should the court rule? *See Bush v. Parents Without Partners*, 21 Cal.Rptr.2d 178 (Ct.App.1993).

C. PROFESSIONAL RESPONSIBILITY

No special ethical rules govern sports lawyers. Instead, as the cases that follow make clear, they are subject to the same standards that apply to other attorneys.

ARENA FOOTBALL LEAGUE, INC. v. ROEMER

9 F.Supp.2d 889 (N.D.Ill.1998).

PALLMEYER, United States Magistrate Judge.

Plaintiff, Arena Football League, Inc. ("AFLI"), filed this two-count action against Defendants, E. Guy Roemer ("Roemer") and Roemer & Featherstonhaugh, P.C., for legal malpractice and breach of fiduciary duty. In its first count, AFLI alleges that Roemer was negligent in advising AFLI employees that the AFLI's member teams could seek coverage under a single workers' compensation account through the State of Delaware and that he concealed material information regarding this application from the AFLI's Board of Directors. In its second count, the AFLI alleges that Defendants are liable for breach of fiduciary duty, both by providing negligent advice and by mishandling litigation that resulted from the negligent advice. Defendant has moved for summary judgment on both counts of the Amended Complaint. For the reasons set forth below, summary judgment is denied.

Factual Background

The following facts are drawn from the parties' Local Rule 12(M) and 12(N) statements, and pertinent submissions attached thereto.

The Parties

Plaintiff Arena Football League, Inc. ("AFLI"), a Delaware corporation, is a nonprofit membership organization and the successor to an Illinois corporation of the same name, which for the purposes of differentiation will hereinafter be referred to as "the League." The League was formed in 1987 for the purpose of holding indoor football games in various cities across the United States. (Defendants E. Guy Roemer and Roemer & Featherstonhaugh, P.C.'s Statement of Material Facts as to Which No Genuine Issue Exists ("Defs.' 12(M) Stmt.") p 1; Plaintiff's Response to Defendant's Local Rule 12(M) Statement ("Pl.'s 12(N) Stmt.") p 1.) This case arises in part out of state laws that required the various league teams ("member teams") to maintain workers' compensation insurance for their employees and personnel. (Defs.' 12(M) Stmt. p 6.)

Defendant E. Guy Roemer ("Roemer") is an attorney licensed to practice law in the states of New York and Florida and is a senior partner at the law firm of Roemer & Featherstonhaugh, P.C., also a Defendant in this case. (Defs.' 12(M) Stmt. p 2; Pl.'s 12(N) Stmt. p 3.) In 1991, the AFLI Board of Directors hired Roemer as general counsel to represent AFLI in all areas regarding its legal needs. (Additional Facts Warranting Denial of Summary Judgment ("Pl.'s 12(N)(3)(b) Stmt.") p 1; Deposition of Guy Roemer ("Roemer Dep."), Vol. 1, at 60–62.) Roemer & Featherstonhaugh, P.C. is and was at all relevant times a law firm organized as a professional corporation under the laws of the State of New York with its principal office located in Albany, New York. (Defs.' 12(M) Stmt. p 3.)

The Events

The parties agree that between 1987 and 1993—the relevant time period in this lawsuit—one of any team's largest operating expenses were its workers' compensation insurance premiums. (Defs.' 12(M) Stmt. p 6; Pl.'s 12(N) Stmt. p 6.) Between 1987–1990, each member team paid the same premium by virtue of the League's holding itself out as a "single-entity employer" located in Illinois. (Pl.'s 12(N) Stmt. p 7.) By holding itself out as a single-entity employer, the League "was able to retain a single carrier to provide workers' compensation and pay premiums which were lower than those charged in [the] home states of some of its members." (Id.)

In 1990, however, the National Council of Compensation Insurance ("NCCI") directed that the League's member teams cease this practice. The NCCI is the plan administrator for the assigned risk market in 23 states, including Illinois and the League's state of incorporation, Delaware. (Id.) According to the AFLI, the assigned risk market "is the involuntary insurance market where insurance is 'force-placed' randomly to insurance carriers that underwrite business in a certain state." (Pl.'s 12(N)(3)(b) Stmt. p 20; Deposition of Terrence Delehanty ("Delehanty Dep.") at 25–26.)

In a written decision, the NCCI ruled that the League was not a single-entity employer and therefore not entitled to coverage by a single carrier. (Id.) Instead, Plaintiff alleges, the NCCI concluded that the individual member teams, and not the League, employed the players (Plaintiff's Amended Complaint, Ex. A to Def.'s 12(M) Stmt., p 10); Defendants concede that this was the NCCI's ruling, but neither party has furnished a copy of the decision itself, nor has either side identified the date the decision was entered. The ruling effectively required each member team thereafter to apply for its own workers' compensation insurance coverage in the state of its home office. (Id. p 11.)

In response to the NCCI ruling, the AFLI [having reincorporated in Delaware in December 1991] hastily formed what it called the Ad Hoc Committee on Workers' Compensation and, assisted by Roemer (who had since been hired as the AFLI's general counsel) and Jardin Insurance Agency–Michigan, its insurance broker, attempted to devise a strategy to standardize premium costs for its member teams. (Id. p 13.) Roemer apparently believed that the most effective strategy would be simply to get the NCCI to reconsider its ruling; he wrote that agency at least two letters (one dated October 22, 1992 and the other dated December 14, 1992) asking them to do just that after the ruling was handed down. (Pl.'s 12(N)(3)(b) Stmt. pp 15–18; Letters From Roemer to NCCI Representative Pamela Tackett, Exs. 3, 6 to Pl.'s 12(N)(3)(b) Stmt.) That strategy ultimately proved ineffective, however; on February 3, 1993, the NCCI sent Roemer a letter affirming its prior ruling that the AFLI would not be considered a single-entity employer. (Pl.'s 12(N)(3)(b) Stmt. p 19; 2/3/93 Letter From NCCI Representative Pamela Tackett to Roemer, Ex. 7 to Pl.'s 12(N)(3)(b) Stmt.)

In early April 1993, the workers' compensation insurance carrier for two member teams, the Tampa Bay Storm and the Albany Firebirds, notified the respective owners of those two teams, Robert Gries and Glenn Mazula, that the teams' insurance premiums were being raised. (Defs.' 12(M) Stmt. pp 10, 12.) Tampa Bay's annual insurance premium was slated to be increased by at least $340,000—from $60,000 to between $400,000 and $500,000—and Albany's by almost $350,000—from $90,000 to $428,000. (Id.) Both owners promptly called then-AFLI Commissioner Joseph O'Hara and told him their respective teams would sit out the 1993 season if they could not obtain lower annual premiums. (Pl.'s 12(N)(3)(b) Stmt. p 23.)

There appears to be no dispute that the AFLI determined to attempt to obtain lower premiums for the Tampa Bay and Albany franchises. Neither does there appear to be any dispute that applying for insurance coverage in Delaware as a single-entity employer—this despite the fact that Delaware was a state "covered" by the NCCI's 1990 ruling—is the course of action the AFLI ultimately took in this regard. What the parties do dispute, and what ultimately is the subject of this litigation, is the extent to which Roemer participated in the decision to apply for coverage in Delaware.

Defendants' version first: Defendants assert that Mark Higley, the AFLI's director of business and financial affairs, came up with the idea of obtaining insurance coverage through the State of Delaware without any input from Roemer. (Def.'s 12(M) Stmt. pp 8, 16, 17; Deposition of Mark Higley ("Higley Dep.") at 7, 16, 33.) Higley testified that it was "[his] idea to investigate Delaware as well as several other states under the charge from [O'Hara] to secure or investigate insurance premiums that are affordable." (Higley Dep. at 33.)

After learning of this proposal from Higley, the story goes, Roemer advised the AFLI that to make the plan work it would have to establish a "presence" in Delaware as fully and as completely as possible. (Def.'s 12(M) Stmt. p 17; Roemer Dep. at 211.) Defendants further assert that it was Higley's responsibility, not Roemer's, "to make certain that Arena's presence in Delaware was established," (Def.'s 12(M) Stmt. p 18), relying for this assertion on Tampa Bay Storm owner Robert Gries's testimony that he (Gries) believed that to be the case. (Deposition of Robert Gries ("Gries Dep.") at 18.) Higley testified, moreover, that he did not view Roemer as an expert on workers' compensation insurance issues. (Def.'s 12(M) Stmt. p 18; Higley Dep. at 18.)

Defendants assert that the Board of Directors did in fact authorize the establishment of an AFLI office in Delaware. (Def.'s 12(M) Stmt. p 20; O'Hara Dep. at 80.) Pursuant to the Board's grant of authority, Higley prepared and signed an application for workers' compensation insurance through the State of Delaware on behalf of the AFLI—an application that Roemer testified he had no input on or even saw until after it was submitted. (Def.'s 12(M) Stmt. pp 21, 28; Roemer Dep. at 192, 201; Delaware Insurance Application, Ex. 30 to Pl.'s 12(N)(3)(b) Stmt.) It is undisputed that Roemer did not sign the application. (Defs.' 12(M) Stmt. p 21; Pl.'s 12(N) Stmt. p 21.) To corroborate Roemer's testimony, Defendants offer Higley's testimony to the effect that he did not believe the application was provided to Roemer for review prior to its submission. (Def.'s 12(M) Stmt. p 25; Higley Dep. at 23.) They also rely on the following colloquy between Higley and AFLI's counsel at Higley's deposition to bolster their position that Roemer did not advise Higley as to the contents of the application:

Question: And at any time before, during, or after the completion of those applications, did Mr. Roemer encourage you to make misrepresentations or state inaccuracies to either Travelers [the Delaware insurance carrier later assigned to AFLI], NCCI, or anyone else on the subject of workers' compensation issues?

Answer: No.

(Higley Dep. at 44.) Finally, Defendants, paraphrasing Commissioner O'Hara's deposition testimony, assert that "no member of Arena's Board of Directors ever told O'Hara that they relied on Roemer in making the decisions to procure workers compensation insurance in Delaware." (Def.'s 12(M) Stmt. p 35; O'Hara Dep. at 78.)

The AFLI, predictably, has a much different view of Roemer's involvement in the Delaware scheme—it asserts that Roemer played an active role in the decision to pursue the Delaware option. (Pl.'s 12(N)(3)(b) Stmt. pp 26, 27.) There is ample support for this assertion in the record. Donald Balmes, a Jardin employee who took part in Ad Hoc Committee negotiations, testified that he participated in several conference calls with Roemer in which the two discussed the possibility of obtaining coverage for the AFLI through Delaware. (Deposition of Donald Balmes ("Balmes Dep.") at 41.) He further testified that Roemer told him the AFLI "[was] a Delaware corporation, that all of the employees of at least these two teams were, in his mind, employees of the league, and if the application was filed under the name of Arena Football and they had established a business presence [in Delaware], that it should fly." (Id. at 46.)

The extent of Donald Balmes's involvement in preparing the Delaware application is unclear, but the AFLI asserts, responding to Defendants' intimation that Higley prepared the application singlehandedly, that Balmes "spoke to Roemer and Higley for advice and direction during the compilation and submission of the application." (Pl.'s 12(N) Stmt. p 21.)

Additionally, Balmes's signature appears underneath Higley's on the final application (Delaware Insurance Application, Ex. 30 to Pl.'s 12(N)(3)(b) Stmt.), and the AFLI asserts without dispute that Balmes was responsible for formally submitting the application. (Pl.'s 12(N)(3)(b) Stmt. p 34; Higley Dep. at 42.)

Members of AFLI's Board of Directors also recounted that Roemer participated in the decision to obtain coverage through Delaware. Board member Jerry Kurz, asked whether he knew who had been charged with filling out the Delaware insurance application, responded that "anything that was supposed to be done with insurance, the person in the league office was Mark Higley, and he was to work in conjunction and under the guidance of Guy Roemer being counsel for the league." (Deposition of Jerry Kurz ("Kurz Dep.") at 26.) Board member William Niro took it one step further, testifying that Roemer rendered legal advice to the AFLI on the Delaware issue:

> And I recall that there was some talk about at some point in time we may have to move the league offices and everything to Delaware and that would complete all of this and make everything all right and good and proper. And I remember there was a lot of questions about the propriety of this or the—you know, the workers' comp issues and single entities' [sic] employers and so on.
>
> And I recall that Roemer was on some sort of mission, if you want to call it that, a high priority research project, to come to grips with this issue and advise the league in the proper course of action. That was his charge. And I recall seeing legal memoranda on the subject.
>
> I remember Guy Roemer advising the board and answering questions from the board on various issues or things that they would raise.
>
> I recall the certainty with which he drew the conclusions that he drew as to whatever it was [we] did or didn't do.

(Deposition of William Niro ("Niro Dep.") at 21.) Niro also testified that Roemer, who had initially indicated to him that a relocation to Delaware would not be necessary, advised him only after the Delaware insurance application had been submitted that a relocation would be necessary. (Niro Dep. at 39.)

Finally, Higley provided damaging testimony about the extent of Roemer's involvement in preparing the Delaware insurance application. Higley testified that because he had only a "street-level understanding" of the single-entity employer issue, he relied on Roemer's legal expertise in preparing the Delaware insurance application. (Higley Dep. at 89, 90.) He further testified that O'Hara instructed him to defer to Roemer on "legal matters." (Id. at 91.)

In addition to presenting evidence that Roemer participated heavily in the decision to obtain insurance coverage through the State of Delaware, the AFLI has presented evidence that the AFLI's Board of Directors were not informed of the decision, allegedly made by Higley, Roemer, and Balmes, to submit the Delaware application. (Pl.'s 12(N)(3)(b) p 38.) Board member Kurz testified that he did not know until "after the fact" that the application had been filed. (Kurz Dep. at 28.) Likewise, Niro testified that he did not "remember" the Board ever approving the submission of the Delaware insurance application. (Niro Dep. at 11.) The AFLI also disputes Defendants' assertion that the Board authorized the opening of an office in Delaware, again relying on the testimony of Kurz and Niro. (Pl.'s 12(N)(3)(b) p 38.) Kurz, parroting his earlier testimony, testified that he did not learn about the move until "after the fact." (Kurz Dep. at 28.) Niro, meanwhile, testified that O'Hara presented the move to the Board in a purely "informational, this is what we're going to do" manner, the clear import of his testimony being that the issue was presented as if it were already decided. (Niro Dep. at 42.)

The parties agree that the application Higley prepared and ultimately submitted on behalf of the AFLI to the State of Delaware contained a number of material misrepresentations, particularly as to the status of the AFLI as a single-entity employer and the extent of the AFLI's "presence" in Delaware. (Pl.'s 12(N)(3)(b) Stmt. pp 35, 36, 37.) The application, for example, listed the application's insured as the AFLI despite the NCCI's ruling, applicable to Delaware, that the AFLI could not be considered a single-entity employer. (Pl.'s 12(N)(3)(b) Stmt. p 35; Delaware Insurance Application, Ex. 30 to Pl.'s 12(N)(3)(b) Stmt.) Further, the application listed as the AFLI's principal place of business 1013 Center Road, Wilmington, Delaware, an address which indisputably "was nothing more than a mere CT 'service office' designated to accept service of process, subpoena, and other documents." (Pl.'s 12(N)(3)(b) Stmt. p 36; Delaware Insurance Application, Ex. 30 to Pl.'s 12(N)(3)(b) Stmt.)

The State of Delaware initially overlooked those misrepresentations; it accepted the AFLI's application some time in late 1993 and assigned the AFLI's claim to Travelers Insurance Company, a private insurance carrier selected at random from its assigned risk pool. (Id. p 39.) After examining the AFLI's application more closely, however, representatives at Travelers began to suspect that the application contained inaccuracies about the AFLI's contacts in Delaware. (Id. p 40.) Travelers initiated a full-scale investigation, determined that the application was a sham, and brought suit against the AFLI in Delaware federal court to recover money it had paid out on claims during the pendency of the policy. (Id. p 51; Def.'s 12(M) Stmt. p 31.) The suit ultimately settled (neither party specifies when) for $224,578.66. (Pl.'s 12(N) Stmt. p 33.)

The parties dispute the extent to which Roemer participated in the Travelers litigation. Defendants assert that his participation was minimal, relying on O'Hara's deposition testimony to the effect that Roemer was only a "resource" to the attorneys hired by the AFLI to represent it in the Travelers litigation and that he (O'Hara) "believe[d]" Roemer was not the AFLI's counsel of record in that litigation. (Def.'s 12(M) Stmt. p 32; O'Hara Dep. 32–33.) O'Hara further testified that he believed Roemer's stance to be that the AFLI "[was] not going to win the litigation" and should settle. (Def.'s 12(M) Stmt. p 32; O'Hara Dep. at 37.) Finally, Defendants make the unremarkable, and unchallenged, assertion that the AFLI's Board of Directors was the ultimate decision-maker as to whether to settle or proceed with the litigation. (Def.'s 12(M) Stmt. p 32; O'Hara Dep. at 37.)

The AFLI concedes Roemer was not the counsel of record, but notes the testimony of John Parkins, who did act as counsel to the AFLI in the litigation, that from the beginning of the litigation he (Parkins) sent all pleadings, legal memoranda, and discovery requests to Roemer for his approval. (Pl.'s 12(N)(3)(b) Stmt. p 55; Parkins Dep. at 8–11, 43, 49, 56.) The AFLI further notes that Niro testified to Roemer's telling him he was "the person responsible for" conducting the Travelers litigation. (Pl.'s 12(N)(3)(b) Stmt. p 53; Niro Dep. at 50.)

As to Roemer's "forecast" for the litigation, the AFLI suggests Roemer went to significant effort to keep the AFLI in the dark about the precariousness of its situation. The AFLI alleges that Roemer's outlook as to the course the Travelers litigation would take was initially favorable. As proof, it points to a November 30, 1993 memorandum Roemer sent O'Hara, Mazula, Gries, Higley, Kurz, and Balmes on the heels of the AFLI's being served by Travelers, wherein Roemer opined that the Travelers suit was "winnable" and "defendable." (Pl.'s 12(N) Stmt. p 32; Roemer Memorandum of November 30, 1993, Exhibit 39 to Pl.'s 12(N)(3)(b) Stmt.) It also points to the testimony of Board member Niro, who recalled that in Board meetings Roemer was "animated about how Travelers had no case, how he had done everything absolutely appropriate ... he acted like he would lay down in front of a speeding train to assure the league that he done everything on the up and up." (Pl.'s 12(N)(3)(b) Stmt. p 36; Niro Dep. at 35–36.) Only after Travelers filed a motion for summary judgment, the AFLI alleges, did Roemer advise it that the case should settle. (Pl.'s 12(N) Stmt. p 32; Memorandum Letter From Roemer to Kurz, Ex. 45 to Pl.'s 12(N)(3)(b) Stmt.) The AFLI insists that had Roemer acted as a reasonably prudent attorney and researched the claim to determine Arena's actual chances of winning the suit, "he could have advised Arena to settle earlier and Arena would have avoided paying costly attorney fees incurred in litigating the case." (Pl.'s 12(N)(3)(b) Stmt. p 69.) The AFLI does not identify the point at which Roemer reasonably should have settled the case, but asserts that it lost in "in excess of $150,000" in attorney's fees over and above the settlement amount. (Id. p 68.)

In addition to being less than candid about the AFLI's chances of success in the Travelers litigation, the AFLI asserts that Roemer failed to notify the AFLI of discovery requests, with the result that sanctions were entered against the AFLI by the Delaware court. (Pl.'s 12(N)(3)(b) p 64.)

Defendant asserts that after the Travelers litigation was settled, the AFLI's member teams "reimbursed" it for the settlement loss and attorney's fees. (Defs.' 12(M) Stmt. p 34.) It further asserts that the AFLI "benefitted" from the Travelers ordeal because obtaining insurance coverage through the State of Delaware "permitted Albany, Tampa Bay, and the other Arena teams to play the 1993 season as scheduled." (Id. p 38.) Finally, it asserts, presumably as further proof that obtaining insurance coverage through the State of Delaware benefitted the AFLI, that "the most recent Arena team member franchise was sold for $2,000,000, and the Arena member teams in 1993 only had a value of approximately $250,000." (Id. p 39.)

The AFLI rejects the notion that the fact its member teams contributed toward the settlement means that the AFLI suffered no loss due to Roemer's conduct. The AFLI notes that it is a not-for-profit membership corporation and that "the individual teams were assessed a fee by Arena to cover any shortfall in the cost of the settlement." (Pl.'s 12(N)(3)(b) Stmt. p 72.) Thus, it concludes, "any assessment made by member teams is not and cannot be construed as any reimbursement to Arena because the assessed fee was an additional capital contribution made by the member teams to the general operating funds of Arena[.]" (Id.) The AFLI further asserts that "it was the sole defendant in the Travelers litigation and that it paid the settlement amount in full to Travelers" (id.), presumably before it assessed the "fee" to its member teams.

As to Defendants' claim that the AFLI benefitted from its pursuit of insurance coverage through the State of Delaware, the AFLI notes that O'Hara himself testified the 1993 season would not have been ruined if Albany and Tampa Bay had decided not to play (O'Hara Dep. at 76), and that in any event the "[n]egative consequences, if any, resulting to Arena by Albany and Tampa Bay sitting out the 1993 season were negligible in comparison to all damages incurred due to Roemer's negligent advice and failure to advise in procuring workers' compensation insurance in Delaware." (Pl.'s 12(N) Stmt. p 37.) Finally, regarding Defendants' veiled assertion that the selling price of the member teams increased dramatically as a result of the AFLI's obtaining insurance coverage through the State of Delaware, the AFLI "denies that Arena's success had anything to do with Albany an [sic] Tampa Bay participating in the 1993 season or the specious Delaware 'workers' compensation solution.' " (Id.)

Procedural History

On March 27, 1996, the AFLI filed a three-count Complaint against Roemer individually and Jardin Insurance Agency–Michigan. Count I of the Complaint charged Roemer with legal malpractice, claiming that he advised the AFLI to file the Delaware insurance application even though he knew or should have known the application contained information that he knew or should have known was false. The AFLI also claimed in Count I that Roemer failed to disclose the Delaware insurance scheme to the AFLI's Board of Directors, and that he "knowingly" allowed claims to be submitted to Travelers on behalf of players for the AFLI who, under the Delaware insurance policy that had been obtained, were uninsurable risks. Count II, directed at both the Roemer Defendants and Jardin, charged breach of fiduciary duty. It essentially repeated Count I's allegations of negligence, but omitted the "negligent advice" claim previously made against Roemer (that claim would be inapplicable to Jardin) and replaced it with the claim that both Roemer and Jardin failed to keep the AFLI's Board of Directors adequately apprised of the status of the Travelers litigation. Finally, Count III charged Jardin with negligent misrepresentation for its involvement in preparing the Delaware insurance application.

On September 10, 1996, the Honorable Elaine E. Bucklo granted Jardin's motion to dismiss the case as to it for want of personal jurisdiction. Less than a month later, on October 7, 1996, the AFLI filed an Amended Complaint dropping Count III of the original Complaint and adding the law firm Roemer & Featherstonhaugh, P.C. as a defendant. The case was transferred to this court by consent of the parties on

February 24, 1997, and on June 24, 1997, Defendants moved for summary judgment on both counts of the AFLI's Amended Complaint.

Discussion

Standard of Review

Summary judgment is appropriate whenever the pleadings, depositions, answers to interrogatories, and admissions on file, together with any submitted affidavits, fail to raise "a genuine issue of material fact[.]" Fed.R.Civ.P. 56(c). In considering a motion for summary judgment, the court accepts as true the facts set forth by the non-movant, and draws all justifiable inferences in that party's favor. Wade v. Byles, 83 F.3d 902, 904 (7th Cir.), cert. denied, ___ U.S. ___, 117 S.Ct. 311, 136 L.Ed.2d 227 (1996).

Analysis

In their motion for summary judgment, Defendants argue that the AFLI will be unable to establish causation or damages for its legal malpractice and breach of fiduciary duty claims. As to causation, Defendants' primary contention is that Roemer cannot be held liable for legal malpractice because Higley, not Roemer, filled out the Delaware insurance application. (Memorandum In Support of Defendants' Motion for Summary Judgment ("Mem.Supp.Mot.Summ.J.") at 4–5.) They buttress this argument by noting the additional undisputed fact that the AFLI's Board of Directors had ultimate decision-making authority to pursue the Delaware plan. (Id. at 5.) Second, Defendants contend that the AFLI's causation argument is defeated by the facts that: (1) the AFLI is guilty of fraud and is precluded, under the doctrine explained in Goldstein v. Lustig, 154 Ill.App.3d 595, 107 Ill.Dec. 500, 507 N.E.2d 164 (1st Dist. 1987), from seeking the court's assistance to relieve it of the consequences of its fraud; (2) Roemer was not the AFLI's counsel of record; (3) the AFLI had no chance of winning the Travelers litigation anyway; and (4) the AFLI's Board of Directors, not Roemer, made the ultimate decision to settle the case. (Id. at 5–8.) As to damages, Defendants argue that the AFLI incurred no damages from the Travelers litigation because the AFLI's member teams "reimbursed" it for the settlement loss. (Id. at 8.) For this reason, they conclude, to award the AFLI damages in this case would be to award it a "double recovery." (Id. at 10.) All of Defendants' arguments will be considered in turn below.

Defendants' argument that the AFLI lacks standing to sue concededly rests on their contentions that Plaintiff cannot establish causation and damages. As discussed below, however, this court concludes that Defendants have not established the absence of material disputes on these issues; accordingly, the court declines to dismiss the AFLI's claims for lack of standing.

1. *Legal Malpractice and Breach of Fiduciary Duty: The Elements*

The elements of a legal malpractice claim and a breach of fiduciary claim are essentially identical, and are not in dispute. To prove legal malpractice, a plaintiff in Illinois must establish: (1) the existence of an attorney-client relationship ("duty"); (2) a negligent act or omission on the part of the attorney ("breach"); (3) causation; and (4) damages. Serafin v. Seith, 284 Ill.App.3d 577, 587, 219 Ill.Dec. 794, 672 N.E.2d 302, 309 (1st Dist.1996). Similarly, a successful claim for breach of fiduciary duty in Illinois requires proof of: (1) the existence of a fiduciary duty, (2) breach of that duty, and (3) resulting damages. LaSalle Bank Lake View v. Seguban, 937 F.Supp. 1309, 1324 (N.D.Ill.1996). As the court's summary of Defendants' arguments indicates, Defendants' motion for summary judgment raises only the issues of causation and damages.

2. Causation

Defendants' arguments as to causation have no merit. As a general rule, causation is a question of fact for the jury in legal malpractice cases, Metrick v. Chatz, 266 Ill.App.3d 649, 652, 203 Ill.Dec. 159, 639 N.E.2d 198, 200 (1st Dist.1994), and this case is no exception. Consider first the questions of fact that abound with respect to the AFLI's claim that Roemer negligently advised it to prepare the Delaware insurance application. Contrary to Defendant's position that the undisputed facts in this case show that Roemer's involvement in the decision to pursue insurance coverage through the State of Delaware was at best minimal, the AFLI has presented evidence that: (1) Roemer spoke on numerous occasions with Jardin representative Donald Balmes about the possibility of the AFLI's obtaining coverage through Delaware; (2) at least one Board member understood Roemer to be broadly in charge of the AFLI's workers' compensation insurance issues; (3) Roemer participated heavily in discussions with the Board about the Delaware plan, and even advised the Board as to its feasibility; and (4) Higley relied on Roemer's legal advice in preparing the Delaware insurance application. In this court's view, this evidence justifies the inference Roemer negligently recommended to the AFLI that it apply for insurance coverage through the State of Delaware.

Defendants urge, however, that Roemer cannot be held liable for legal malpractice because it is undisputed both that Roemer played no part in filling out the misrepresentation-ridden application and that the AFLI's Board of Directors, not Roemer, ultimately made the decision to apply for insurance through the State of Delaware. (Defs.' Mem.Supp. Mot.Summ.J. at 4–8.) Neither fact is controlling. Defendants' reliance on the fact that Roemer did not himself fill out the application ignores completely the gist of the AFLI's claim: that Roemer negligently advised it to do so.

In Illinois, the law is clear that a plaintiff may assert a cause of action for legal malpractice when an attorney's pre-litigation advice causes the plaintiff to be sued. See Jackson Jordan, Inc. v. Leydig, Voit & Mayer, 199 Ill.App.3d 728, 733, 145 Ill.Dec. 755, 557 N.E.2d 525, 529 (1st Dist.1990) (observing, in a case where the plaintiff alleged his defendant attorney's negligent advice had caused him to be sued, that "[t]he entire litigation and concomitant expenses might have been avoided if [the defendant's] assertedly negligent advice had not been given") rev'd on other grounds, 158 Ill.2d 240, 198 Ill.Dec. 786, 633 N.E.2d 627 (1994); cf. Kerschner v. Weiss & Co., 282 Ill.App.3d 497, 504–505, 217 Ill.Dec. 775, 667 N.E.2d 1351, 1356–57 (1st Dist.1996) (holding that plaintiff's complaint, which alleged that "no competent lawyer, exercising a reasonable degree of care and skill" would have advised the plaintiff to withdraw from partnership, stated a claim for legal malpractice). Defendants' reliance on the allegedly undisputed fact that the AFLI's Board of Directors made the decision to apply for insurance through the State of Delaware is similarly unavailing. To begin with, the AFLI has presented evidence sufficient to create a dispute of fact on the issue of whether the Board authorized the Delaware plan. But even if it had not, Roemer would still not be entitled to summary judgment. Illinois law clothes all clients, in all cases, with decision-making authority on strategic decisions, County of Cook v. Patka, 85 Ill.App.3d 5, 11, 40 Ill.Dec. 284, 405 N.E.2d 1376, 1380 (1st Dist.1980), and so to accept Defendants' argument would be effectively to hold that attorneys are immune to suit. As Plaintiff points out, the logic of Defendants' position is that an attorney should have a rock-solid defense in nearly every case—that the client could ultimately have rejected his negligently given advice. A client is entitled to rely on the advice of her attorney, however, and Defendants provide no basis for the suggestion that Roemer's client should have known better than to accept Roemer's counsel.

Defendants appear to awaken to the nature of Plaintiff's claim in their reply brief, there clinging to Higley's testimony that Roemer never explicitly advised him to make misrepresentations on the Delaware insurance application. Their reliance on that portion of Higley's testimony is misplaced. Although Higley declined to take the position that Roemer specifically instructed him to make misrepresentations on the application, Higley did testify that he relied on Roemer's legal advice in preparing the application. That testimony rationally raises the inference that Roemer advised Higley that applying for insurance coverage through the State of Delaware was legally permissible.

The AFLI has also presented enough evidence to preclude summary judgment on its claim that Roemer mishandled the Travelers litigation and thereby cost it unnecessary attorneys' fees. According to the AFLI, first, Roemer "double-billed" it by directing the AFLI's counsel of record, John Parkins, to send all pleadings, legal memoranda, and discovery requests to him for approval. He compounded the double-billing problem, it asserts, by negligently handling the case—he asserted upon the AFLI's being served that the Travelers suit was "winnable" and "defendable" and only advised the AFLI to settle the case after reading Travelers motion for summary judgment, almost a full year later. In this court's view, this evidence rationally raises the inference of negligence, particularly when read in conjunction with the evidence that Roemer knew, at the time the Travelers suit was filed, that the NCCI had ruled the AFLI was not a single-entity employer.

Defendants' arguments to the contrary are unavailing. First, Defendants erroneously rely on Goldstein for the proposition that the AFLI is a fraudfeasor. Goldstein reaffirmed the general rule that Illinois courts "will not aid a fraud feasor who invokes the court's jurisdiction to relieve him of the consequences of his fraud." Goldstein, 154 Ill.App.3d at 603, 107 Ill.Dec. 500, 507 N.E.2d at 170. There, a dentist whose on-the-job fraud was discovered by his employer went to his attorney for advice. The attorney advised him to stand pat and wait to be fired, and then to file suit for wrongful discharge—this even though the dentist's employment agreement provided better post-termination benefits if he resigned of his own option. The dentist took the attorney's advice and brought suit against his employer upon being fired. The case ultimately settled, but for an unsatisfactory amount because the settlement amount did not include the termination benefits the dentist would have received had he resigned of his own option. The trial court dismissed the dentist's subsequent suit for legal malpractice and the appellate court affirmed, reasoning that the dentist's action was "an attempt to reduce the economic consequences of his fraudulent conduct" by recovering damages from his attorney "to which he was not entitled under his employment agreement." Id. at 602–03, 107 Ill.Dec. 500, 507 N.E.2d 164.

The problem with Defendants' Goldstein argument is that it assumes, incorrectly, that the facts surrounding the underlying fraud in this case are not in dispute. As discussed above, in this case there is evidence that Roemer advised the AFLI to commit the fraud that resulted in its being sued—indeed, that evidence forms the basis of the AFLI's separate "negligent advice" claim. In Goldstein there was no such evidence; the client had clearly committed the fraud on his own before he sought legal advice. Thus, Goldstein is inapposite.

Defendants' remaining arguments may be dismissed in relatively short order. First, although it is undisputed that Roemer was not the counsel of record in the Travelers litigation, the evidence Plaintiff has presented suggests that Roemer nevertheless played a key role in handling paperwork and formulating strategy.

Second, the fact that it is unlikely the AFLI would have prevailed in the Travelers litigation even if Roemer had performed flawlessly is irrelevant. It is true that in Claire Associates v. Pontikes, 151 Ill.App.3d 116, 104 Ill.Dec. 526, 502 N.E.2d 1186 (1st Dist.1986), the case relied on by Defendants for this argument, the Illinois appellate court observed that "no malpractice exists unless counsel's negligence has resulted in the loss of an underlying cause of action, or the loss of a meritorious defense if the attorney was defending in the underlying suit." Id. at 122, 104 Ill.Dec. 526, 502 N.E.2d at 1190. In that case, however, the plaintiff corporation specifically alleged that its attorney's negligence prevented it from prevailing in the underlying action. Id. at 121, 104 Ill.Dec. 526, 502 N.E.2d 1186, 502 N.E.2d at 1189. In this case, however, the AFLI is not claiming that "but for" Roemer's negligent performance it would have prevailed in the Travelers litigation; the AFLI claims that "but for" Roemer's negligent performance it would have incurred less in legal fees and would not have been hit with discovery sanctions. In Glass v. Pitler, 276 Ill.App.3d 344, 212 Ill.Dec. 730, 657 N.E.2d 1075 (1st Dist.1995), the Illinois appellate court explained that a plaintiff may sue her attorney for mishandling a prior case even where the prior case has settled, so long as the damages flowing from the alleged malpractice can be "factually established." Id. at 351, 212 Ill.Dec. 730, 657 N.E.2d at 1080. As noted above, Plaintiff has presented sufficient facts to raise the inference that, but for Roemer's negligence in handling the Travelers litigation, it would have accrued less in legal fees.

As for Defendants' final argument, the fact that the AFLI had the ultimate authority to settle the case does not help Defendants. As noted above, Illinois law clothes all clients, in all cases, with decision-making authority on strategic decisions. Patka, 85 Ill.App.3d at 11, 40 Ill.Dec. 284, 405 N.E.2d at 1380. In any event, as also noted earlier, the AFLI is not claiming that Roemer's mishandling of the Travelers litigation resulted in settlement losses that it otherwise would not have had to pay. Accordingly, this court rejects Defendants' arguments as to causation.

3. *Damages*

Defendants' arguments as to damages fare no better. Defendants' primary argument is that any damages awarded to the AFLI in this case would amount to a windfall or "double recovery" for it because the AFLI's member teams already reimbursed it for the settlement amount. As the AFLI argues, however, Defendants are barred from reliance on this defense by the "collateral source" doctrine. Under the collateral source rule, as it is called, "benefits received by the injured party from a source wholly independent of, and collateral to, the tortfeasor will not diminish damages otherwise recoverable from the tortfeasor." Wilson v. Hoffman Group, 131 Ill.2d 308, 320, 137 Ill.Dec. 579, 546 N.E.2d 524, 530 (1989). As the Supreme Court of Illinois explained long ago,

> [n]o injustice is done to a person negligently injuring another in requiring him to pay the full amount of damages for which he is legally liable without deduction for compensation which the injured person may receive from another source which has no connection with the negligence, whether that source is a claim for compensation against his employer, a policy of insurance against accidents, a life insurance policy, a benefit from a fraternal organization or a gift from a friend.

Stifle v. Marathon Petroleum Co., 876 F.2d 552, 560 (7th Cir.1989) (quoting Bryntesen v. Carroll Const. Co., 27 Ill.2d 566, 568, 190 N.E.2d 315, 317 (1963)). The "no connection" language in the Supreme Court's justification of the rule is important; for that requirement to be met, the allegedly independent source of the disputed payment must in no way have been responsible for causing, in whole or in part, the damages sought to be recovered by the party seeking to invoke the collateral source rule. See, e.g. Stifle, 876 F.2d at 560 (explaining that application of the collateral source rule is justified in the context of workers' compensation payments because those payments are made pursuant to statutory obligation, without regard to any negligence on the employer's part); Bryntesen, 27 Ill.2d at 568, 190 N.E.2d at 316–17 (same).

Application of the collateral source rule to the facts of this case is straightforward. Defendants have not alleged that the member teams were in any way responsible for causing the damages the AFLI seeks to recover in this case, and there is no independent evidence in the record to suggest that they were. Accordingly, the member teams have "no connection" to the alleged negligence that forms the basis of this lawsuit. Moreover, as members of the AFLI, the teams will presumably benefit from any recovery the AFLI may achieve in this litigation.

Defendants have made two arguments that the collateral source rule should not apply in this case, but both fall wide of the mark. Their first argument, that the member teams were "connected to the events and alleged negligence at hand" and thus are not wholly independent of Roemer, reflects, as indicated by the above analysis, a misunderstanding of the collateral source rule's "no connection" requirement. Of course the member teams were connected to Roemer's alleged negligence in the literal sense—the very purpose of Roemer's seeking insurance coverage through the State of Delaware was to benefit the member teams, in particular the Tampa Bay Storm and the Albany Firebirds. The problem with Defendants' argument is that the member teams can in no way be said to have caused the damages flowing from Roemer's alleged negligence.

Defendants' second argument that the collateral source rule should not apply is that the member teams may be the "real party in interest" in this case. The concern here, Defendants appear to argue, is not that the AFLI will receive a double recovery but that they (Defendants) will potentially be subject to double payment if the member teams decide to bring suit against them. At least one case has held the risk of double payment to be a valid consideration in determining whether to apply the collateral source rule. State Security Ins. Co. v. Frank B. Hall & Co., 109 F.R.D. 95, 97 (N.D.Ill.1985). Here, however, there simply is no danger that the member teams will sue Defendants separately. Indeed, it is difficult to conceive of a scenario in which the member teams would have standing to do so; the AFLI was the only named defendant in the Travelers litigation and thus the only party legally obliged to pay Travelers the settlement amount. Further, any attorney's fees wrongfully assessed by Defendants were assessed against the AFLI, not the member teams. Accordingly, summary judgment is denied on the damages element of the AFLI's legal malpractice and breach of fiduciary duty claims.

Defendants also argue that the AFLI should not be allowed to recover in this case because it actually benefitted from the Delaware scheme, first because obtaining insurance coverage through the State of Delaware "permitted" Albany and Tampa Bay to play in the 1993 season, and second because the AFLI's member teams have appreciated in value since the AFLI implemented the "workers' compensation solution." As to the first asserted "benefit," Defendants have failed to demonstrate that it would have been impossible to secure Tampa Bay's and Albany's commitment to play without resorting to fraud. Put another way, awarding the AFLI damages in this case cannot be construed as a "windfall" if proper legal advice would have put it in the same position as the negligent advice. As to the second asserted "benefit," it is sheer speculation on Defendants' part that the AFLI's member teams appreciated in value because the AFLI sought insurance coverage through the State of Delaware.

CONCLUSION

The court denies summary judgment on Counts I and II of the AFLI's Amended Complaint. Questions of material fact remain as to the causation and damages elements of Plaintiff's legal malpractice and breach of fiduciary claims.

PASSANTE v. McWILLIAM

62 Cal.Rptr.2d 298 (Ct.App.1997).

SILLS, Presiding Justice.

As someone once said, if you build it they will come. And by the same token, if you make a baseball card that can't be counterfeited, they will buy it. Which brings us to the case at hand.

In 1988 the Upper Deck Company was a rookie baseball card company with an idea for a better baseball card: one that had a hologram on it. Holograms protect credit cards from counterfeiting, and the promoters of the company thought they could protect baseball cards as well. By the 1990's the Upper Deck would become a major corporation whose value was at least a quarter of a billion dollars. Collecting baseball cards, like baseball itself, is big business.

But the outlook wasn't brilliant for the Upper Deck back in the summer of 1988. It lacked the funds for a $100,000 deposit it needed to buy some special paper by August 1, and without that deposit its contract with the major league baseball players association would have been jeopardized.

The Upper Deck's corporate attorney, Anthony Passante, then came through in the clutch. Passante found the money from the brother of his law partner, and, on the morning of July 29, had it wired to a company controlled by one of the directors. That evening, the directors of the company accepted the loan and, in gratitude, agreed among themselves that the corporate attorney should have three percent of the firm's stock. The rest is history. Instead of striking out, the Upper Deck struck it rich.

At this point, if we may be forgiven the mixed metaphor, we must change gears. No good deed goes unpunished. Anthony Passante never sought to collect the inchoate gift of stock, and later, the company just outright reneged on its promise. Passante sued for breach of oral contract, and the jury awarded him close to $33 million—the value of three percent of the Upper Deck at the time of trial in 1993.

The trial judge, however, granted a judgment notwithstanding the verdict, largely because he concluded that Passante had violated his ethical duty as a lawyer to his client. There was no dispute that Passante did not tell the board that it might want to consult with another lawyer before it made its promise. Nor did Passante advise the board of the complications which might arise from his being given three percent of the stock.

The board had a clear moral obligation to honor its promise to Passante. He had, as the baseball cliche goes, stepped up to the plate and homered on the Upper Deck's behalf. And if this court could enforce such moral obligations, we would advise the company even yet to pay something in honor of its promise.

But the trial judge was right. If the promise was bargained for, it was obtained in violation of Passante's ethical obligations as an attorney. If, on the other hand, it was not bargained for—as the record here clearly shows—it was gratuitous. It was therefore legally unenforceable, even though it might have moral force. We must therefore, with perhaps a degree of reluctance, affirm the judgment of the trial court.

Facts and Procedural History

The Upper Deck Company was formed in March 1988 to produce baseball cards with holograms. The initial directors were Paul Sumner, William Hemrick, Boris Korbel, Richard P. McWilliam, Angels' pitcher DeWayne Buice and Anthony Passante. Passante, who was already the personal attorney for Korbel and McWilliam, was appointed corporate attorney and secretary. McWilliam, an accountant with contacts to a number of investors, had the responsibility of obtaining start-up financing for the company. Passante made no investment in the company and owned no stock.

The Upper Deck needed $100,000 to put on deposit with an Italian paper company by August 1, 1988, so the paper would be available for the inaugural run of baseball cards planned for December. Without the paper, the company risked losing its license with major league baseball. However, as of July 26, 1988, the company had not obtained financing. To make matters worse, McWilliam was demanding more stock in return for the financing he was supposed to obtain. Board members instructed Passante to demand the return of McWilliam's stock if he would not change his demands.

When Passante found out that McWilliam would not be coming up with the money, he told his law partner, Andy Prendiville that "there was really no hope for the company to make it." Prendiville asked Passante if he should talk to his brother, who was a doctor and might be able to make a loan of $100,000. Passante told Prendiville to call his brother, who said that he "was in a position to loan the money and would do so." Both Passante and Prendiville spoke to Korbel concerning the availability of "those funds." They told Korbel "that the funds were available."

Korbel then requested that Passante come to a special board meeting to be held on the evening of July 29, 1988 "in order to talk to the other two shareholders about that loan." Korbel said he wanted the other shareholders to be a party to the loan. And, because the shareholders would be guaranteeing the repayment of the funds, Korbel "wanted to make sure that he had the agreement of his co-shareholders for that type of an arrangement."

Dr. Kevin Prendiville wired $100,000 to an account controlled by Korbel just a little after 11 a.m. on July 29, 1988, though Passante still understood that if the board did not approve the loan "it wasn't going to be made."

At the board meeting that evening, Passante told the assembled board members (assembled without notice to McWilliam) "about the availability of the funds." He asked them "if they would be interested in obtaining the money from Dr. Prendiville." The board members agreed.

The board members were "all quite excited about the availability of those funds." Korbel "brought up" the idea that the board should consider giving Passante some ownership interest if he got the loan, and Hemrick said, "Look, if you can get that money for us then I think you're entitled to three percent of the company." There was "general agreement" among the board members "that that would be the case." Passante said, "Okay. We'll do the loan," and then went back to his office.

Passante drafted a note which did not have an interest rate on it. However, at Korbel's insistence, an extra $10,000 was paid to Dr. Prendiville for the 90–day loan. The Upper Deck made its deposit.

The day after the deadline, the board members were "quite happy people." At a meeting held that day, the board members discussed how McWilliam's 11 percent would be divided; "it was determined" that Passante would receive 3 percent from McWilliam's 11 percent, and Korbel would receive the 8 percent balance. Passante's three percent, however, was "to be held by Boris Korbel." The idea was that Korbel would hold Passante's interest in the company until McWilliam returned his stock certificate, and, when a new investor was brought in and new certificates were issued, Passante would receive his stock.

But the Upper Deck still needed financing, and, after an unsuccessful attempt to enlist a New York firm, Korbel told Passante that maybe McWilliam should be brought back into the company after all. Passante told Korbel that he "should do whatever he thought necessary to make the company go forward."

What Korbel thought necessary was to contact McWilliam. On August 31, 1988, Korbel told Passante about Korbel's conversation with McWilliam. McWilliam, it seemed, was "extremely upset" at Passante "because of what had occurred at the end of July." Accordingly, McWilliam would only "invest in Upper Deck" on the condition that Passante "not participate as an owner of the company." Korbel told Passante that "in order to get the company going" Korbel would hold Passante's three percent for him and "we wouldn't tell Mr. McWilliam or any of the other shareholders about this interest." After McWilliam "cool[ed] off" and everything was "smooth again," Korbel would discuss Passante's three percent interest and either "get a stock certificate representing that interest from the corporation," or Korbel would at least make sure Passante "obtained the benefit of that three percent through him" by way of profit distributions from the company.

In early fall McWilliam came back into the company; McWilliam soon brought in Richard Kughn, a Chicago investor. As a result, the shares of the company were redistributed, leaving Korbel, McWilliam and Kughn each with 26 percent. After Kughn made his investment, Passante was fired as corporate attorney because Kughn wanted the company represented by a large law firm.

In 1988 and early 1989, Korbel told Passante that he need not be concerned about the three percent—that Korbel "had it" and he "would take care of it" for Passante. In November 1990, however, Korbel told Passante that he wasn't going to get his three percent. In essence, Kughn had been given Passante's three percent in the redistribution of stock occasioned by Kughn's investment.

The next month Passante filed this lawsuit. Andy Prendiville was also named as a plaintiff because Passante told him, after the August 2 meeting, that "because of his being so instrumental in obtaining the $100,000 loan" "half of whatever [Passante] got was his."

As set forth in his second amended complaint, Passante sued McWilliam for intentional interference with prospective advantage, negligent interference with economic relationship, bad faith, breach of fiduciary duty, bad faith denial of contract, conversion, intentional interference with contract, fraud, negligent misrepresentation, unjust enrichment, intentional fraudulent misrepresentation, and equitable estoppel. He sued the Upper Deck for negligent interference with economic relationship, bad faith, bad faith denial of contract, conversion, unjust enrichment, intentional fraudulent misrepresentation, and equitable estoppel. He sued Boris Korbel for negligent interference with economic relationship, bad faith, breach of fiduciary duty, breach of oral contract, bad faith denial of contract, conversion, fraud, negligent misrepresentation, constructive trust, unjust enrichment, intentional fraudulent misrepresentation, and equitable estoppel. Passante did not sue the Upper Deck for breach of oral contract.

All breach of fiduciary duty and intentional fraudulent misrepresentation claims were dismissed pursuant to sustained demurrers. The bad faith, fraud and negligent misrepresentation were dismissed pursuant to stipulation after the trial court refused, as a sanction for not having disclosed the identity of the witness during discovery, to allow Passante to present the testimony of Daniel Lybarger, a former controller of the

Upper Deck, who would have testified that McWilliam actually knew that Passante had been given three percent of the company's stock.

After the close of the plaintiffs' case, the trial judge granted nonsuit motions which eliminated all remaining claims against McWilliam, the Upper Deck, and Korbel except the 11th cause of action for breach of fiduciary duty and imposition of a constructive trust against Korbel only. However, the trial judge also granted Passante's request to add a claim for breach of oral contract against the Upper Deck.

The claim against the Upper Deck and the claim against Korbel went to the jury. The jury found for Passante and awarded him some $32 million against Upper Deck and $1 million against Korbel. The Upper Deck then moved for a judgment notwithstanding the verdict or, alternatively, a new trial; the trial court granted both. The trial judge also determined that the sole remaining claim against Korbel was equitable in nature and, in a tentative decision issued July 2, 1993, gave judgment for Korbel on that claim, finding that there was no transaction between Korbel and Passante "which could serve as a basis for imposing a constructive trust."

Two formal judgments were filed August 3, 1993, one in favor of both the Upper Deck and McWilliam, the other in favor of Korbel on the equitable cause of action. Passante then filed this appeal from those judgments.

DISCUSSION

In his opening brief Passante asserts that "[a]n enforceable contract requires only a promise capable of being enforced and consideration to support the promise." As framed, the assertion is incomplete. Consideration must also be given in exchange for the promise. Past consideration cannot support a contract. (See Leonard v. Gallagher (1965) 235 Cal. App.2d 362, 373, 45 Cal.Rptr. 211 ["It appears to be the universal rule throughout the United States that past consideration will not support a promise which is in excess of the promisor's existing debt or duty."].)

Cases relied on by Passante merely demonstrate the rule that the extinguishment of a preexisting obligation, or the rendering of past services with the expectation of future payment, constitute sufficient consideration for a contract. In Parke etc. Co. v. San Francisco Bridge Co. (1904) 145 Cal. 534, 78 P. 1065, the plaintiff was an agent of the defendant who had been clearly working with the expectation of payment all along. In Raichart v. Phillips (1953) 120 Cal.App.2d 645, 651–652, 261 P.2d 777, the appellate court was able to infer from the record the existence of a preexisting obligation and a clear expectation of payment. In Blonder v. Gentile (1957) 149 Cal.App.2d 869, 874–875, 309 P.2d 147, the appellate court stressed that the recital in a written agreement, "in consideration of the services heretofore rendered," was not conclusive because the "true consideration" was a promise made at the time, not the past services ostensibly referred to. Indeed, the Blonder court acknowledged that, "The general rule is that a past consideration is not sufficient to support a contract." (Id. at p. 874, 309 P.2d 147.)

As a matter of law, any claim by Passante for breach of contract necessarily founders on the rule that consideration must result from a bargain. (E.g., Simmons v. Cal. Institute of Technology (1949) 34 Cal.2d 264, 272, 209 P.2d 581 ["But the consideration for a promise must be an act or return promise, bargained for and given in exchange for the promise."]; Enslow v. Von Guenthner (1961) 193 Cal.App.2d 318, 14 Cal.Rptr. 231 [building contractor's promise to replace defective roof held unenforceable because not bargained for]; Dow v. River Farms Co. (1952) 110 Cal.App.2d 403, 410–411, 243 P.2d 95 [corporate resolution to pay executive $50,000 in consideration of past services rendered held unenforceable given absence of any expectation of payment when services were rendered].)

Thus if the stock promise was truly bargained for, then he had an obligation to the Upper Deck, as its counsel, to give the firm the opportunity to have separate counsel represent it in the course of that bargaining. The legal profession has certain rules regarding business transactions with clients. Rule 3–300 of the California Rules of Professional Conduct (formerly rule 5–101) forbids members from entering "a business transaction with a client" without first advising the client "in writing that the client may seek the advice of an independent lawyer of the client's choice."

Here it is undisputed that Passante did not advise the Upper Deck of the need for independent counsel in connection with its promise, either in writing or even orally. Had he done so before the Upper Deck made its promise, the board of directors might or might not have been so enthusiastic about his finding the money as to give away three percent of the stock. In a business transaction with a client, notes our Supreme Court, a lawyer is obligated to give "his client 'all that reasonable advice against himself that he would have given him against a third person.' " (Beery v. State Bar (1987) 43 Cal.3d 802, 813, 239 Cal.Rptr. 121, 739 P.2d 1289, quoting Felton v. Le Breton (1891) 92 Cal. 457, 469, 28 P. 490.) Bargaining between the parties might have resulted in Passante settling for just a reasonable finder's fee. Independent counsel would likely have at least reminded the board members of the obvious—that a grant of stock to Passante might complicate future capital acquisition.

For better or worse, there is an inherent conflict of interest created by any situation in which the corporate attorney for a fledgling company in need of capital accepts stock as a reward for past service. As events in this case proved out, had the gift of 3 percent of the company's stock been completed, it would have made the subsequent capital acquisition much more difficult.

Passante's rejoinder to the ethics issue is, as we have noted, to point to the evidence that the stock was virtually thrust at him in return for what he had done. The terms were totally dictated by the Upper Deck board. And that is it, precisely. There was no bargaining.

A close reading of the facts shows that the stock had not been bargained for in exchange for arranging the loan; Passante had already arranged the loan (even though the loan had not been formally accepted by the board) before the idea of giving him stock was ever brought up. There is no evidence that Passante had any expectation that he be given stock in return for arranging the $100,000 loan. Clearly, all of Passante's services had already been rendered by the time the idea of giving Passante some stock was proposed. As the court in Dow plainly stated, "if there was no expectation of payment by either party when the services were rendered, the promise is a mere promise to make a gift and not enforceable." (Dow, supra, 110 Cal.App.2d at p. 410, 243 P.2d 95.)

In response to the point that the loan had been, in actuality, made earlier that morning, Passante makes the distinction between merely putting money in an account controlled by Korbel (which happened about 11 a.m. on July 29) and the actual acceptance of the loan by the board later that evening. The distinction does not help him. Regardless of whether the loan is characterized as having been in the morning or the evening, the undisputed fact is that Passante had already done what the board wanted to reward him for—finding the money—by the time the Board proposed to give him stock for it.

Conclusion

The promise of three percent of the stock was not a reward contract; it was Passante who first told Korbel that "funds were available." It was simply, to use a phrase usually associated with life insurance contracts, an inchoate gift—that is, an unenforceable promise from a grateful corporate board. Like the corporate resolution in Dow, it represented a moral obligation. And like the corporate resolution in Dow, it was legally unenforceable. (See Dow, supra, 110 Cal.App.2d 403, 243 P.2d 95 [company executive rendered services without expectation of payment, thus subsequent promise by board to pay him $50,000 for those services as soon as the company became free of floating indebtedness was unenforceable].)

Our conclusion about the contract issue necessarily obviates all other issues in this appeal, including those involving any promise by Korbel to hold Passante's interest for him, all of which are predicated on the idea that Passante had a bargain with the Upper Deck. The judgments in favor of McWilliam, the Upper Deck, and Korbel are affirmed.

IN RE FELDBERG

862 F.2d 622 (7th Cir.1988).

EASTERBROOK, Circuit Judge.

A grand jury investigating agents who signed amateur athletes to undisclosed contracts issued a subpoena to World Sports and Entertainment in March 1987. The subpoena called for all contracts between World Sports and college football players. World Sports, as a corporation, had no privilege to resist disclosure. See Braswell v. United States, 487 U.S. 99, 108 S.Ct. 2284, 101 L.Ed.2d 98 (1988). Norby Walters, the president of World Sports, engaged Michael Feldberg, a partner of Shea & Gould, to represent both of them. Feldberg came into possession of 51 contracts (just how is the principal issue today) and turned them over to the grand jury on behalf of World Sports. All of these contracts were dated after the expiration of the athletes' collegiate eligibility. The grand jury was not satisfied; after it made a further request, Feldberg produced another seven contracts. Six of these pertained to athletes who held themselves out as eligible to participate in the fall 1987 college football season. The contracts had been post-dated to make it appear that they had been signed after the players' college careers ended; the disclosures revealed that World Sports made a practice of surreptitiously contracting with "amateur" athletes. Such contracts terminated the players' amateur status and made them ineligible to compete; the contracts also exposed the players' colleges to the risk that contests in which they participated would be forfeited. The post-dating came to light only because these contracts had been produced in advance of the date they bore. After receiving the post-dated contracts, the grand jury indicted World Sports and Walters for mail fraud. One of the players involved, Cris Carter (now a wide receiver with the Philadelphia Eagles), has pleaded guilty to mail fraud and obstruction of justice. Sports Illustrated 113 (Sept. 26, 1988).

I

The grand jury wants to know why it did not receive the second set of contracts in response to the subpoena. The prosecutor believes that there may have been obstruction of justice. Although the United States Attorney does not suspect Feldberg of wrongdoing, the grand jury summoned him to testify about how he obtained the initial batch of contracts. Feldberg is the obvious source of information, because Walters, if summoned, doubtless would invoke his privilege against self-incrimination. Curcio v. United States, 354 U.S. 118, 77 S.Ct. 1145, 1 L.Ed.2d 1225 (1957).

The subpoena put Feldberg in an uncomfortable position, because he had served World Sports in two capacities. He was on the one hand its agent, a delivery boy in connection with the documents; he was simultaneously the firm's attorney and undoubtedly had supplied legal advice to Walters and World Sports with respect to their obligations under the March 1987 subpoena. File clerks may be required to testify about their search for documents, but lawyers ordinarily may not be required to testify about facts they learned in confidence in the course of rendering legal advice.

Feldberg answered many questions but asserted the attorney-client privilege in response to the ones of greatest interest to the grand jury—such as who searched the files, and how. The prosecutor asked the district court to compel Feldberg to answer. Walters and World Sports intervened to protect their interests. The district court instructed Feldberg to answer; Walters and World Sports immediately filed this appeal.

The parties disagree about the application of the privilege to eight questions.

1. Q. Did you conduct a search of the files for purposes of gathering the information responsive to this subpoena? A. No. Q. Did you direct someone else to do so? A. [Invocation of privilege.]

2. Q. This [list of 51 names] was to your understanding a ... complete list of the players who were under contract to either Walters or World Sports & Entertainment, Inc.? A.... [T]hat is correct. Q. How did you come to that understanding? A. [Invocation of privilege.]

3. [After Walters received the subpoena, he talked for 15 minutes with Feldberg.] Q. And to the best of your recollection, what was said? A. [Invocation of privilege.]

4. Q. Prior to contacting the U.S. Attorney's Office [and offering to supply the contracts in response to the subpoena], you said that you represented World Sports Entertainment and would handle compliance with [the] subpoena that had been served. Did you have a conversation with anyone affiliated with World Sports Entertainment in which you told them that you were going to do that? A. [Invocation of privilege.]

5. Q. [I]t would be your intention to, at the instructions of your clients, not to answer any questions regarding conversations pertaining to the 51, or the contracts pertaining to the 51 athletes produced on April 6, 1987, is that right? A. Those are my instructions from my former clients. [Shea & Gould ceased representing Walters and World Sports after mid–1987, which is not important for current purposes.]

6. Q. Did you tell [Walters and an associate] that you were going to convey these contracts to the Government, with the representation that they were all contracts called for by the subpoena? A. [Invocation of privilege.]

7. Q. [D]id you direct anyone to produce such a list [of contracts] for disclosure to the Government? A. [Invocation of privilege.]

8. Q. Did you have a conversation in which you asked someone to give those [51 contracts] to you for disclosure to the Government? A. [Invocation of privilege.]

The prosecutor made two arguments in the district court: first, that there was good reason to believe (a "prima facie case") that Walters or World Sports had committed a crime during the course of the legal representation, making the attorney-client privilege inapplicable (the "crime/fraud exception" to the privilege); second, that because Feldberg gathered the documents in order to turn them over, neither lawyer nor client could have had a reasonable expectation that their discussions would remain confidential.

The district court summarily rejected the first argument, stating without explanation that "no prima facie case of fraud or obstruction of justice has been made out". The court did not discuss the second argument. It ordered Feldberg to answer all of the questions on the basis of an argument the prosecutor had not made: that there is a distinction "between communications relating to the act of production on one hand and communications relating to the general subject matter of the grand jury investigation on the other. The pending questions which Feldberg has refused to answer appear to be of the former type, and they should be answered." In this court the prosecutor not only reasserts the two arguments that did not persuade the district court but also defends the ground that court advanced for its decision.

II

We start with the question whether there is reason to believe that a crime occurred. At the time the district court ruled, the grand jury had not decided whether to indict Walters and World Sports for substantive offenses. Learning how the search had been conducted might have helped the grand jury decide whether to continue its investigation in the hope that there might be more documents where the second set came from. After the district judge's decision, the grand jury returned an indictment. The prosecutor is not entitled to use the grand jury after the return of an indictment to obtain discovery in the criminal case. So unless there is some prospect of demonstrating obstruction of justice, there is no need for Feldberg's testimony, and the case is moot.

III

Although the prospect of establishing obstruction of justice prevents the case from being moot and provides a potential basis for overcoming a claim of privilege, it does not supply a basis for affirming the decision, because the district court never subjected the prosecutor's claims to the test. The court's order rests on a different ground, a distinction between Feldberg's role as substitute for the corporate records custodian and his role as lawyer. Walters and World Sports contend that no such distinction is tenable. To the contrary, a distinction of this kind is essential if the privilege is to be limited to those disclosures related to legal advice. A business that gets marketing advice from a lawyer does not acquire a privilege in the bargain; so too a business that obtains the services of a records custodian from a member of the bar.

The attorney-client privilege has not been codified. But statements of that privilege from every perspective recognize a limitation to legal topics. Wigmore's treatise, which we quoted favorably in Radiant Burners, Inc. v. American Gas Ass'n, 320 F.2d 314, 319 (7th Cir.1963), says that the privilege applies "[w]here legal advice of any kind is sought from a professional legal adviser in his capacity as such, the communications relating to that purpose" (8 Evidence § 2292, internal numbering omitted). The Supreme Court's proposal in 1972, which treated the privilege as an exception to the rule of access and therefore one of limited scope, stated things this way: "A client has a privilege to refuse to disclose and to prevent any other person from disclosing confidential communications made for the purpose of facilitating the rendition of professional legal services to the client". Proposed Fed.R.Evid. 503(b), 56 F.R.D. at 236. The American Law Institute's Restatement of the Law Governing Lawyers (Tent. Draft No. 1, 1988), which contains perhaps the broadest privilege ever proposed in the United States, has similar language. A communication is privileged under the ALI's treatment if made for "the purpose of obtaining or providing legal assistance for the client", § 118(4), which the Restatement further defines as a communication that "relates to legal advice or other legal assistance that a lawyer is to render to a client", § 122(1). The comment adds: "the person consulted must be functioning in the professional capacity of a lawyer".

Most corporate records custodians are not lawyers. Answers to questions such as "where did you look for the documents?" will not reveal legal advice; recognizing the grand jury's right to ask such questions will not dissuade persons from obtaining legal advice. A grand jury may compel a corporate records custodian to testify about the nature of his search and the adequacy of the disclosure, In re Grand Jury Proceedings (John Doe Co.), 838 F.2d 624, 626 (1st Cir.1988). Such an inquiry may be essential to determine whether the grand jury has received the documents to which it is entitled. If the inquiry itself is legitimate, the addressee of the subpoena cannot put the subject off limits by having counsel turn over the documents. After all, the attorney-client privilege covers "only those disclosures necessary to obtain informed legal advice." Fisher v. United States, 425 U.S. 391, 403, 96 S.Ct. 1569, 1577, 48 L.Ed.2d 39 (1976). Since questions about the adequacy of the search do not entail legal advice, the topic is not off limits just because an attorney plays a role.

The privilege is not good in itself. The legal system needs information to decide cases correctly. See United States v. Nixon, 418 U.S. 683, 708–13, 94 S.Ct. 3090, 3107–10, 41 L.Ed.2d 1039 (1974). When the privilege shelters important knowledge, accuracy declines. Litigants may use secrecy to cover up machinations, to get around the law instead of complying with it. Secrecy is useful to the extent it facilitates the candor necessary to obtain legal advice. The privilege extends no further. Courts protect adverse information in the hands of counsel because counsel needs both favorable and adverse news to devise a strategy. It is not possible to separate adverse from favorable information in advance; a client, knowing this, would find disclosures of all sorts more costly if there were no privilege. See also Upjohn Co. v. United States, 449 U.S. 383, 101 S.Ct. 677, 66 L.Ed.2d 584 (1981). There is no need for a privilege to cover information exchanged in the course of document searches, which are mostly mechanical yet which entail great risks of dishonest claims of complete compliance. Dropping a cone of silence over the process of searching for documents would do more harm than good. It is easy for a firm such as World Sports to hire an attorney to render advice on all legal matters while hiring a clerk to look through the records. The categories would merge if the clerk should find a questionable document, leading the firm to inquire of the lawyer whether the document fell within the scope of the subpoena (and whether, if it did, it had to be produced). Perhaps some of the conversations in this case were of that character, and if so they are privileged. But a corporation may be required to disclose its books and documents to a grand jury, e.g., Consolidated Rendering Co. v. Vermont, 207 U.S. 541, 554, 28 S.Ct. 178, 181, 52 L.Ed. 327 (1908), and may not throw the veil of privilege over the details of how files were searched, and by whom, through the expedient of involving a lawyer in the process.

The distinction between the mechanical and advisory portions of Feldberg's role shows that the district court was right to compel answers to several but not all of the questions. Questions 1, 7, and 8 all deal with whether Feldberg, in his role as records custodian, directed someone to search the files; if so, who and how. The answers would not reveal legal advice rendered to the firm or confidential information received from it. Question 6 is similar, asking only whether Feldberg told World Sports that he was about to turn over the documents as the full reply to the subpoena. Question 4 concerns the scope of Feldberg's employment, a topic not privileged unless the extent of the engagement reveals confidential information—doubtful here, given that Feldberg's role in turning over documents is public knowledge. Question 3, however, likely called for some privileged information (assuming the fraud/crime exception is inapplicable). It required Feldberg to disclose the contents of a 15–minute conversation with Walters. This may have been limited to mechanical questions, but the prosecutor who put the question did not first attempt to identify its scope; the conversation could well have covered privileged subjects too. It was premature to order Feldberg to answer this question.

The remaining questions are not so easy to put in pigeonholes. The exchange we have identified as Question 5 is not a question but a statement of intent to invoke the privilege in response to a category of questions that might be asked. Question 2 (essentially, "how did you know the list of 51 contracts was complete?") calls for information that might be mechanical ("The person who did the search told me these were all he found.") or might be covered by the privilege ("After someone had found a lot of documents, I made a judgment about which were responsive to the subpoena.") or might be some mixture ("I gave legal instructions to the searcher based on a determination about the scope of the subpoena, and the searcher told me that he had found all documents fitting the description I gave him."). The district court could not properly order Feldberg to answer Question 2 without making a preliminary determination—after an in camera hearing, if necessary—about the kind of answer that would be forthcoming. And if the court meant to compel answers to every inquiry potentially within the category covered in Question 5, it acted rashly.

IV

Our analysis implies the need for a remand, so that the district judge may refine his directions about which questions must be answered and explore the crime/fraud exception. The prosecutor submits that further investigation is unnecessary because any disclosures were made to Feldberg for the purpose of relaying the documents to the grand jury. Information imparted to counsel without any expectation of confidentiality is not privileged. United States v. Weger, 709 F.2d 1151, 1154 (7th Cir.1983); 8 Wigmore at § 2292 (privilege applies only to communications "made in confidence"); Restatement § 118(3). World Sports knew that Feldberg would disclose what he received, so, the prosecutor concludes, the clients could not have anticipated confidence.

This line of argument confuses expectations about the documents with expectations about the communications. Rare is the case in which attorney-client conversations do not lead to some public disclosure. The criminal defense lawyer gathers information and formulates strategy in preparation for a trial; since the trial is public, does it follow that the antecedent communications are unprivileged? A lawyer writes a brief to be filed with the court; does it follow that the drafts of the brief are available to the adversary? A corporation prepares and publishes an internal report about "questionable payments" abroad; we know from Upjohn Co. that it does not follow that the government has access to the interviews underlying the published report. An accountant prepares worksheets underlying a tax return; we may infer from United States v. Arthur Young & Co., 465 U.S. 805, 104 S.Ct. 1495, 79 L.Ed.2d 826 (1984), that if there were an accountant-client privilege (there isn't) its domain would include these worksheets. None of the prosecutor's arguments suggests that Feldberg, Walters, and World Sports anticipated (or should have anticipated) the disclosure of their conversations.

The decision of the district court is vacated, and the case is remanded for further proceedings consistent with this opinion.

Notes

1. For other cases involving ethics and sports lawyers, see, e.g., *Herrick Co. v. Vetta Sports, Inc.*, 1998 WL 637468 (S.D.N.Y.1998) (in dispute over sale of athletic equipment business, previous opinions of defendants' ethics expert had to be turned over to plaintiffs), and *Peat, Marwick, Mitchell & Co. v. Los Angeles Rams Football Co.*, 394 A.2d 801 (Md.Ct.App.1978) (in accountant malpractice action growing out of sale of football team, motion to disqualify buyer's law firm denied because made on eve of trial).

2. Attorneys who wish to pursue a career in the sports industry have numerous resources to which they can turn for guidance. See, e.g., J.G. Ferguson, *Careers in Focus: Sports* (1998); Shelly Field, *Career Opportunities in the Sports Industry: A Comprehensive Guide to the Exciting Careers Open to You in the Sports Industry* (2d ed. 1998); William R. Heitzman, *Careers for Sports Nuts & Other Athletic Types* (2d ed. 1997); David M. Carter, *You Can't Play the Game If You Don't Know the Rules: Career Opportunities in Sports Management* (1994); Kenneth L. Shropshire, *Careers in Sports Law* (1990). *See also* Robert P. Garbarino, *So You Want to be a Sports Lawyer, or Is It a Player Agent, Player Representative, Sports Agent, Contract Advisor,*

Family Advisor or Contract Representative?, 1 Vill. Sports & Ent. L.F. 11 (1994).

3. The American Bar Association (ABA), headquartered in Chicago, Illinois, and the Sports Lawyers Association (SLA), located in Reston, Virginia, provide those interested in sports law with national networking, publishing, and continuing education opportunities. To learn more about these organizations, check out their web pages at *www.abanet.org/forums/entsports/home.html* and *www.sportslaw.org*. While surfing the net, the following sites also may be of interest:

Arena Football League: *www.arenafootball.com*

Major League Baseball: *www.majorleaguebaseball.com*

Major League Soccer: *www.majorleaguesoccer.com*

National Association for Stock Car Auto Racing: *www.nascar.com*

National Basketball Association: *www.nba.com*

National Collegiate Athletic Association: *www.ncaa.org*

National Football League: *www.nfl.com*

National Hockey League: *www.nhl.com*

United States Golf Association: *www.usga.org*

United States Olympic Committee: *www.usoc.org*

United States Tennis Association: *www.usta.com*

Women's National Basketball Association: *www.wnba.com*

Breaking Sports News: *cnnsi.com*, *espn.com*, and *www.sportsline.com*

Links to Other Sports Sites: *www.sportsquest.com*

Problem 2

To make her television advertisements more effective, an attorney plans to hire a famous sports FIGURE and have him say, "If you want to get on the winning legal team, you need this attorney!" Does her plan violate any ethical rules? *See Committee on Professional Ethics and Conduct v. Humphrey*, 377 N.W.2d 643 (Iowa 1985), *appeal dismissed*, 475 U.S. 1114 (1986).

Chapter 2

FANS

A. OVERVIEW

While fans are affected to some degree by every aspect of the sports they follow, certain matters resonate with special force. Four such issues are considered in this chapter: 1) what legal rights does a ticket confer?; 2) what responsibilities do stadium owners have to the public?; 3) what recourse do fans have when games are blacked out?; and, 4) what protections exist for collectors of sports memorabilia?

B. TICKETS

Although rarely given much thought (except when being sought after), the legal questions posed by tickets are among the thorniest in sports.

1. NATURE

A ticket is a license that grants the holder permission to use a designated seat during a particular game. Whether it also creates other rights is a hotly-contested question.

IN RE LIEBMAN

208 B.R. 38 (Bankr.N.D.Ill.1997).

BARLIANT, Bankruptcy Judge.

The Debtor has something greatly prized in the Chicagoland area: Season tickets to the Chicago Bulls basketball games. The question presented by the trustee's motion to sell "renewal rights" for those tickets is whether the holder of a season ticket has a property interest in the right to renew. The Chicago Bulls contend that he does not have any interest. He has, they argue, only an expectation of an offer to renew, and that is not property. This Court agrees with the Bulls and finds that the renewal priority afforded season ticket holders does not give rise to a property interest.

DISCUSSION

Property of the estate is broadly defined by § 541 of the Bankruptcy Code as including "all legal or equitable interests of the debtor in property as of the commencement of the case." "Property interests [however] are created and defined by state law." Butner v. United States, 440 U.S. 48, 55, 99 S.Ct. 914, 918, 59 L.Ed.2d 136 (1979). This court must therefore look to the law in Illinois to determine the nature of the opportunity to renew season tickets to sporting events. One Illinois court has addressed the issue. That court concluded that a season ticket is a series of revocable licenses, which, by definition, may be revoked at the will of the licensor, and the purchase of those licenses did not create an enforceable option to buy more in later years. Soderholm v. Chicago Nat'l League Ball Club, Inc., 225 Ill.App.3d 119, 167 Ill.Dec. 248, 587 N.E.2d 517 (1st Dist.1992).

Not surprisingly, since Soderholm is not a bankruptcy case, it arose out of slightly different facts. There the plaintiff had bought eighteen season tickets to Cubs games for six seasons. The Cubs heard rumors that the plaintiff had been "scalping" the tickets and refused to sell him more than six season tickets. The plaintiff filed suit to compel the Cubs to sell him the season tickets, arguing that his purchase of season tickets created an option contract. The court rejected this argument. In reaching this conclusion it considered similar cases from other jurisdictions. One of the decisions it relied upon specifically addressed the issue whether a property right was created by repeated sales of season tickets. See Soderholm, 225 Ill.App.3d 119, 123, 167 Ill.Dec. 248, 587 N.E.2d 517, discussing Kully v. Goldman, 208 Neb. 760, 305 N.W.2d 800 (1981).

Kully involved season tickets to University of Nebraska football games that had been purchased annually by the defendant for seventeen years, with an oral agreement to sell four of eight of the tickets to the plaintiff. The trial court concluded that there was an implied trust between the parties, but the Supreme Court of Nebraska reversed, "finding that defendant had no contractual right with the university to purchase the season tickets in the future, and, therefore, no property right existed which could be the 'res' of the subject matter of a trust." Soderholm, 225 Ill.App.3d 119 at 123, 167 Ill.Dec. 248, 587 N.E.2d 517. The Illinois appellate court found Kully and other decisions "persuasive" and concluded that the plaintiff had no option contract, no right of first refusal and no lease. Instead the court held that the season ticket holder had a revocable license.

The few bankruptcy opinions that have addressed this issue are divided. See In re Harrell, 73 F.3d 218 (9th Cir.1996) (Phoenix Suns season ticket holder had no property interest that could be sold by the trustee. Although they generally gave the season ticket holder an opportunity to renew, there was no guarantee, nor any legal right, that the Suns would extend the offer to renew); In re Tucker Freight Lines, Inc., Case No. HK83–02391, Adv. Pro. No. 84–0381 (Bankr.W.D.Mich. July 30, 1984) (Notre Dame's past practice of selling the debtor season tickets for over forty years did not create any contract). Cf. In re Walsh, 1994 WL 249249, 1994 U.S.App. LEXIS 14193 (4th Cir.1994) (season tickets to the Charlotte Hornets were property of the estate where the debtor was one of the original subscribers and had paid a $10,000 deposit for the right to purchase up to 100 tickets each year); In re I.D. Craig Service Corp., 138 B.R. 490 (Bankr.W.D.Pa.1992) (right to renew season tickets for the Pittsburgh Steelers was property of the estate that could be sold by the trustee over the objection of the Steelers, where the longstanding policy was to permit automatic renewal and transferability of season tickets).

The key factor that distinguishes the cases relied upon by the Bulls from the cases relied upon by the trustee is how the sports franchise treats the renewal rights of season tickets holders. The Bulls' policy is clearly stated in all pertinent material: The season ticket invoice states that "[s]eason tickets are offered on a one-year basis"; the playoff ticket invoice says that "[e]ach season and playoff ticket is a revocable license"; various letters sent to season ticket holders state that "[t]he Bulls reserve the right to review all accounts before offering season tickets for the [next] season." The Bulls also prohibit the transfer of season tickets except in very limited circumstances. The written policy provides: "NEW CONTRACTS ARE NOT TAKEN FOR PERSONAL ACCOUNTS. WE DO NOT CHANGE NAMES, ADD NAMES, NOR DO WE TAKE 'CARE OF' NAMES AND ADDRESSES. SEASON TICKETS ARE NOT TRANSFERABLE AND THEY ARE A REVOKABLE [sic] LICENSE. SEASON TICKETS ARE OFFERED ON A ONE–YEAR BASIS ONLY."

This policy is similar to that of the Cubs and found by the court in Soderholm to create only a revocable license. The Bulls treatment of its season ticket holders is in marked contrast to the Steelers', which permitted transferability of season tickets and the attendant right to renew and its policy of automatically renewing season tickets upon payment. In addition, the court in Craig Service (the Steelers' case) heavily relied upon and analogized to a case involving the right to renew a liquor license under a Pennsylvania statute. See In re Nejberger, 934 F.2d 1300 (3d Cir.1991).

The trustee places significant weight on the Bulls' practice of automatically renewing season tickets if the account was current and allege that the Bulls generally only revoked season tickets for misconduct, such as scalping. The expectation that the tickets would be renewed, however realistic, does not ripen into a property interest. See Soderholm, 225 Ill.App.3d at 124, 167 Ill.Dec. 248, 587 N.E.2d 517 ("[a] license is revocable at any time at the will of the licensor (citations omitted) and mere permission to use land does not ripen into a prescriptive right regardless of the length of time that such enjoyment is permitted." (Citation omitted)). See also Harrell, 73 F.3d at 220 ("[a]lthough season ticket holders are generally awarded the opportunity to renew, there is no guarantee that the Suns will extend the offer. Season ticket holders are powerless to stop the Suns from declining to do so.")

This Court finds that a Bulls' season ticket holder has nothing more than a license to purchase tickets, which the Bulls may revoke at any time. The expectation that the Bulls will offer a similar license in future seasons is not an interest in property under Illinois law. Accordingly, there is no property interest that is included in this debtor's bankruptcy estate and the trustee's motion to sell the "right to renew" the season tickets is denied. The money currently held in escrow will be returned to the successful bidder.

DOBBS v. DOBBS

N.Y. L.J., Feb. 6, 1998, at 26 (N.Y.Sup.Ct.1998).

DIAMOND, Justice.

There are two issues presently before this court: first, is a season subscription for four New York Knickerbocker basketball tickets and New York Rangers hockey tickets (the "tickets") acquired during the couple's 43–year marriage marital property? Second, if it is, is the disposition of the tickets governed by the parties' post-nuptial agreement?

The parties were married on August 30, 1953 and have three emancipated children. In or about June 1992, plaintiff commenced an action for divorce. In 1993, the parties decided to reconcile, the wife discontinued her divorce action, and the parties resumed living together. The parties, both of whom were represented by counsel, also executed a post-nuptial agreement (the "Agreement") which divided their property in the event their reconciliation was not successful. The attempted reconciliation failed and in or about September 1995 the husband moved out of the marital home. On January 10, 1996, pursuant to the Agreement, the husband notified the wife in writing that he intended to live separate and apart. Under the Agreement that date became the separation event that triggered a series of transactions enumerated in the Agreement.

The husband claims that the wife never showed any interest in the tickets, never attended games and never demanded tickets. The wife cries "foul" and claims that she expressed an interest in the tickets and attended some games. Contending that the tickets are marital assets, she seeks use of all four of the tickets for one-half of the home games so as to avoid attending games with the husband. The husband argues that since "the Knicks and Rangers season tickets were owned in my name alone as of the date of the Postnuptial Agreement and have been so owned for more than 25 years, by the Postnuptial Agreement, the tickets are my separate property." As support for this proposition, he points to an October 13, 1997 letter from Madison Square Garden which states that "you [husband] are the subscriber of record to the above Knicks and Rangers accounts since October 1, 1974." The husband argues that he does not have to share the tickets because he has sole title to them.

The threshold question of whether the tickets are marital assets is a slam dunk. With the enactment of [the] Equitable Distribution Law (Domestic Relations Law [''DRL''] Sec. 236[B]), New York went from a title jurisdiction, in which only jointly owned property interests were considered marital property, to a non-title state:

> The term ''marital property'' shall mean all property acquired by either or both spouses during the marriage and before the execution of a separation agreement or the commencement of a matrimonial action, regardless of the form in which title is held, except as otherwise provided in agreement pursuant to subdivision three of this part.

(DRL Sec. 236[B] [1] [c]; O'Brien v. O'Brien, 66 NY2d 576, 584–585 [1985]). Further, New York courts have characterized a wide and ever expanding variety of tangible and intangible interests as marital assets (O'Brien v. O'Brien, supra, 66 NY2d at 576 [professional degrees and licenses]; Majauskas v. Majauskas, 61 NY2d 481 [1984] [pension]; Elkus v. Elkus, 169 AD2d 134 [1st Dept 1991] [celebrity status], appeal denied 79 NY2d 851 [1992]; Smith v. Smith, 162 AD2d 346 [1st Dept 1990] [lottery winnings], appeal denied 77 NY2d 805 [1991]; Jolis v. Jolis, 111 Misc 2d 965, 974 [Sup Ct, NY County 1981] [personal property such as furniture, art objects, and jewelry], affd 98 AD2d 692 [1st Dept 1983]). While courts in other jurisdictions have treated season subscriptions to sporting events as marital assets (Wagner v. Wagner, 821 SW2d 819 [Ky Ct App 1992] [subscription to University of Kentucky season basketball game tickets]; McClerin v. McClerin, 425 SE2d 476 [SC Ct App 1992] [season tickets for Charlotte Hornets basketball games]), no such decision is reported in this jurisdiction.

Contrary to the husband's contention, title is irrelevant under the Equitable Distribution Law as long as the property in question is acquired during the marriage. The husband's claim that the tickets were acquired because of his efforts and that the wife played no role is also irrelevant (McDicken v. McDicken, 109 AD2d 734 [2d Dept 1985]). The tickets are indisputably marital assets.

The remaining issue is whether the Agreement covers their disposition (DRL Sec. 236 [B] [1] [c] and [3]) or whether a contribution analysis is necessary (DRL Sec. 236 [B] [5] [c] and [d]). The Agreement, executed as part of the parties' attempted reconciliation, equally divides their assets and liabilities as set forth in their respective Net Worth Statements (Agreement P 2.1, Exs B and C). Paragraph 2.1 further provides that:

> As a result of the division of assets, Leonard's assets and liabilities shall be as set forth on Exhibit ''I'' and Gloria's assets and liabilities shall be as set forth on Exhibit ''J''. For purposes of this Agreement, the assets set forth on Exhibit ''I'' shall be deemed Leonard's Separate Property and the assets set forth on Exhibit ''J'' shall be deemed Gloria's Separate Property. The parties warrant and represent that the assets and liabilities set

> forth on Exhibits "B" and "C" are the only assets and liabilities of the respective parties that are known to the respective parties.

The husband argues that the Agreement provides that the wife receive one-half of all the property listed on the parties' Net Worth Statements and since neither the Net Worth Statements nor the Agreement make specific reference to the tickets they are his separate property.

The principle is well settled that a separation agreement entered into by spouses is a contract subject to the principles of contract interpretation (Rainbow v. Swisher, 72 NY2d 106, 109 [1988]). Where the contract is clear and unambiguous on its face the intent of the parties must be gleaned from within the four corners of the instrument (Ibid.). The words and phrases used in an agreement must be given their plain meaning so as to define the rights of the parties (Tillim v. Fuks, 221 AD2d 642, 643 [2d Dept 1995]).

Whether a writing is ambiguous is a question of law to be resolved by the court (See, Wallace v. 600 Partners Co., 86 NY2d 543, 548 [1995]). Although the parties' assets and liabilities are set forth in their respective Net Worth Statements and the Agreement, there is no mention or specific reference to the tickets in either (Agreement P 2.1, Exs B and C). There is no mention of or specific reference to the tickets in either party's separate property schedule (see, Agreement, Ex. I and J) or the relevant section of the Agreement, which provides:

> 2.2 Leonard's Separate Property
>
> Except as otherwise provided in this Article, all property set forth on Exhibit "I" annexed hereto or hereafter acquired in either (a) Leonard's name alone, (b) in trust for Leonard or (c) in Leonard's name jointly with a person other than Gloria shall be and remain Leonard's Separate Property as to which Gloria shall make no claim of possession, use, right, title or ownership at any time. Leonard's Separate Property includes, without limitation, the property set forth on the annexed Exhibit "I", and Leonard's business (except for Gloren Associates, and Leonard Dobbs, Inc.), career, skills, celebrity status and any enhanced earning capacity, or any other tangible or intangible asset which he may have simultaneously with the execution of this Agreement, or acquire following the date hereof, and all income which he may receive simultaneously with the execution of this Agreement or acquire following the date hereof from Leonard's Separate Property.

Identical language is used to define the wife's separate property (Agreement P 2.3).

The clear language of paragraphs 2.1 and 2.2 provide that in order for the tickets to be the husband's separate property, they must be listed on Exhibit I, which they are not. The husband is skating on thin ice when he claims that the phrase "Leonard's Separate Property includes, without limitation, the property set forth on the annexed Exhibit 'I' or any other tangible or intangible asset which he may have simultaneously with the execution of this Agreement, or acquire following the date hereof'' means that the tickets are his. That language mandates that for the tickets to be his separate property the husband must have acquired them "simultaneously with the execution of this Agreement" or "following the date hereof'', which he did not.

The husband further argues that the wife waived her claim to the tickets because although she knew of their existence she failed to list them on either her Net Worth Statement or the Agreement, ignoring the fact that he did not list them either. This argument is misplaced. For the wife to have waived her claim to the tickets there had to have been a "voluntary and intentional abandonment of a known right which, but for the waiver, would have been enforceable" (Gen. Motors Acceptance Corp. v. Clifton–Fine Cent. School Dist., 85 NY2d 232, 236 [1995]). Although the husband indicates that the wife had knowledge of the tickets for decades, what is crucial is not knowledge of the existence of the tickets, but knowledge of the fact that the tickets were marital assets subject to equitable distribution and that the parties had knowingly agreed that he could keep them for himself. The Agreement and the record are devoid of any proof that the parties' negotiations addressed the tickets. Neither the Agreement nor the record point to clear affirmative conduct by the wife evincing an intent to waive her interest in this marital asset. The failure of both parties to list the tickets on their respective Net Worth Statements is puzzling, but not dispositive. It certainly does not, under the language of the Agreement, mean that they are the husband's separate property or that the wife waived her interest in them. The husband was the party who acquired the tickets, arranged for their payment, divided them among friends and business associates and used those not given away or sold. As between the parties, he is certainly required to disclose them as an asset on his Net Worth Statement for any waiver to be effective. This is particularly so in view of the Agreement which states that:

> The parties warrant and represent that the assets and liabilities set forth on Exhibit "B" and "C" are the only assets and liabilities of the respective parties that are known to the respective parties.

(Agreement P 2.1). Although not specifically referred to in the Agreement, the disposition of the tickets is nonetheless governed by its terms. Under contract principles, where the intent of the parties can be determined from the four corners of the written instrument, interpretation of the contract is a matter of law (Unisys Corp. v. Hercules Inc., 224 AD2d 365, 367 [1st Dept 1996]; American Express Bank Ltd. v. Uniroyal, Inc., 164 AD2d 275, 277 [1st Dept 1990], appeal denied 77 NY2d 807 [1991]). Here, the Agreement clearly evidences that the parties intended to fully discharge and settle all their rights and claims in each other's property by reason of their marriage (see, Whereas clause, Agreement at p. 2; Hatch v. Nyco Minerals Inc., ___ AD2d ___, 1997 WL 768348 [3d Dept

1997] [recital may have a material bearing on the construction of a contract]) and to equally divide all of their marital assets (see, Agreement PP 2.1, 2.5, 2.6, 2.10 [D] [2], and 3.1 [B], [C]). Further, since Gloren Associates (which under the Agreement is jointly held property [see, Agreement P 3.1]) used its funds to pay for the tickets during the marriage they should be treated in the same manner as the parties treated Gloren Associates and divided equally.

Accordingly, the wife is entitled to a one-half interest in the tickets. Each party shall pay for his or her tickets. Given the contentious, never-ending nature of these proceedings, it would be better for all concerned if the parties were not required to sit side-by-side at these games. Having gone their separate ways after 43 years, this court will not compel them to team up once again at courtside. The wife is entitled to tickets for all future even numbered games for the remainder of the basketball and hockey season. Commencing next season and thereafter, the husband shall be entitled to tickets for all even numbered New York Knickerbocker basketball tickets and all odd numbered New York Rangers hockey tickets. The wife shall be entitled to all odd numbered New York Knickerbocker basketball tickets and all even numbered New York Rangers hockey tickets. All playoff tickets shall be similarly divided.

Notes

1. As the foregoing cases make clear, the rights conferred by a ticket depend on the identities of the parties and the nature of the action. *See further Livingston v. Miller*, 28 F.Supp.2d 623 (D.Colo.1998) (judgment creditor entitled to garnish season tickets); *Sportsco Enterprises v. Morris*, 917 P.2d 934 (Nev.1996) (judgment creditor could execute on judgment debtor's rights in luxury sports box); and *Copland v. Summ*, 644 N.Y.S.2d 59 (App.Div.1996) (plaintiff did not suffer a compensable injury when defendant refused to continue sharing his season tickets).

2. At the time *Liebman* was decided, the Chicago Bulls had a waiting list of 25,000 names. *See* Phil Rosenthal, *Keeping Fans Happy is Top Priority for VP*, Chi. Sun–Times, May 10, 1998, at 9. Thus, it is little wonder the trustee believed he could obtain a sizeable amount of money for the debtor's tickets. For a further discussion of this point, see Susannah L. Baker, Comment, *It's All Fun and Games Until Somebody Declares Bankruptcy: A Debtor's Right to Season Ticket Holder Status*, 14 Bankr. Dev. J. 159 (1997).

3. The longest waiting list for season tickets, with 36,500 names, belongs to the Green Bay Packers. Because an average of only five names move up each season, it would take thousands of years to clear the current list. *See further* Roger Thurow, *The Longest Wait: Packers Fans Buy Seat After 32 Years*, N.Y. Times, Sept. 12, 1997, at B1.

4. Of course, a waiting list occasionally empties faster than expected. In 1979, for example, the Boston Celtics' list had 6,000 names. But after three losing seasons and relocation of the team from Boston Garden to the larger (and less charming) Fleet Center, the list shrank so much the club had to begin a campaign for new season ticketholders. *See First Pride, Now Fall: Celtics Tickets Available*, Wash. Post, Aug. 9, 1996, at D2.

5. The temporal legal nature of tickets has caused many fans to want something more permanent. Sensing a new opportunity to make money, a number of teams have responded by offering personal seat licenses. In exchange for a one-time payment (which can run as high as $15,000), PSL holders are guaranteed the right to renew as well as sell their seats. *See further* John Clayton, *Sitting Pretty: Personal Seat Licenses are the New Rage in the NFL*, Tacoma Morning News Trib., June 11, 1997, at C1.

Problem 3

Despite having a ticket, a woman was denied admission to a race track because she was thought to be part of an illegal gambling ring. In fact, she was innocent. If she sues, what damages can she recover? *See Marrone v. Washington Jockey Club*, 227 U.S. 633 (1913).

2. TERMS AND CONDITIONS

All tickets are sold subject to a variety of "terms and conditions." Although imposed unilaterally, these provisions will be upheld if they are reasonably designed, conspicuously noticed, and uniformly applied.

GANEY v. NEW YORK JETS FOOTBALL CLUB

550 N.Y.S.2d 566 (N.Y.C.Civ.Ct.1990).

TOM, Judge.

The issue raised in this action is what recourse does a holder of season tickets for a professional football team have when the tickets are lost.

Claimant purchased season tickets from defendant for the New York Jets football team in September 1989. Shortly after the football season began, claimant notified defendant that the tickets were lost and requested replacement tickets. Defendant informed claimant that the Jets' policy regarding ticket holders who have lost or misplaced their tickets is to allow the ticket holder an opportunity to purchase a new season ticket subscription for the same designated seats. There is no refund or replacement for the lost tickets, however, if the tickets are later found by the holder, the club would give a refund for the unused tickets.

Claimant then purchased two of his three season tickets and commenced this action for double billing and unjust enrichment. The causes of action for double billing and unjust enrichment are based on the theory that the two sales transactions represented one single contract, and that defendant charged the claimant twice for the same designated seats.

This argument cannot prevail since the two sales transactions made between the parties constituted separate and distinct contracts. Claimant originally purchased three season tickets for the New York Jets. The season tickets gave claimant the right and privilege to view home games of the New York Jets football team from the designated seats. The condition precedent in the contract provides that the ticket holder must present the ticket at the gate for admission. Claimant could not meet this condition and by his own conduct has caused his own inability to reap the benefit of the agreement. Defendant has fulfilled its end of the bargain between the parties. It is printed clearly on the ticket that, "Tickets cannot be replaced if lost, stolen or destroyed."

The subsequent sale and purchase of season tickets between the parties constituted a new and separate contract. Although defendant sold tickets twice to claimant for the same seasonal seats, the second sale was made at the request of claimant who could not fulfill his contractual obligation for admission under the first contract with defendant. Defendant was under no obligation to sell claimant new tickets for the same seats. However, the second set of tickets were offered for sale to claimant as an option which would permit him to attend the Jets' games. Claimant accepted the option by purchasing the new tickets. Defendant has also offered claimant a refund if the original tickets are found.

Defendant argues that the Jets' policy of no refund or replacement and the opportunity to purchase a new ticket subscription was made to balance two competing interests. On the one hand, the Jets do not want to deprive ticket holders who have actually lost or misplaced their tickets of the opportunity to attend and view Jets' games in their contracted seats. On the other hand, the Jets organization had to devise a procedure by which individuals who did not purchase Jets' tickets are prevented from entering the stadium which can cause serious security problems.

The Jets' present policy concerning claims of lost and misplaced tickets has been implemented for approximately 9 years. Prior to this policy, the Jets' organization learned that many season ticket holders would falsely claim to have lost or misplaced their tickets in order to obtain a new and free set of season tickets. The ticket holder would then give a set of tickets to friends, relatives or ticket scalpers who would use or sell them to gain improper entry into the stadium. This not only caused theft of services but also created a security problem which affected the safety and welfare of the other attendants. Often the intruders would sit in the seats of other fans which created arguments and possibly at times altercations. This situation resulted in a security nightmare for the Jets' organization. Defendant argues that since the implementation of this policy the claims of lost Jets' tickets have decreased by thirty percent.

The Court finds that the present policy of the Jets regarding claims of lost or misplaced tickets is not only sound but is a necessary precaution to insure the general safety and welfare of attendants who attend Jets' games. Defendant claims that most of the major metropolitan sports teams have the same policy including the Knicks, Rangers, Giants, Nets and the Devils.

Since the two ticket sales transactions made between the parties represented separate contracts, defendant could not be held liable for double billing or unjust enrichment as urged by claimant. (Sloame v. Madison Square Garden Center, Inc., 56 A.D.2d 92, 391 N.Y.S.2d 576, aff'd, 43 N.Y.2d 656, 400 N.Y.S.2d 815, 371 N.E.2d 533). The recourse of obtaining a free duplicate set of tickets from defendant for those bona fide ticket holders who actually lost or misplaced their tickets has been extinguished by the action of those unscrupulous fans who have abused the Jets' earlier policy of free replacement tickets to gain improper entry by others into the stadium.

Based on the foregoing, claimant's causes of action against defendant are dismissed.

Note

Although tickets vary from venue to venue, they almost always: a) specify disorderly fans will be ejected; b) disclaim liability for injuries; c) reserve the right to change the date or time of the game; d) state what will happen in the event the contest is cancelled; e) prohibit the ticket from being resold for more than face value; and, f) permit the use of the holder's likeness.

Problem 4

Following an excruciating loss, a fan returned to the parking lot to find her car vandalized. When she sued, the team pointed to the disclaimer printed on the back of her parking pass. Although it said what the club alleged, it was printed in type so small it could only be read with a magnifying glass. Given these facts, will a court enforce the release? *See Yates v. Chicago National League Ball Club, Inc.*, 595 N.E.2d 570 (Ill.App.Ct. 1992).

3. PRICES

As a general matter, teams are permitted to charge whatever they wish for tickets. Nevertheless, fans occasionally have challenged pricing policies.

CONIGLIO v. HIGHWOOD SERVICES, INC.

495 F.2d 1286 (2d Cir.),
cert. denied, 419 U.S. 1022 (1974).

KAUFMAN, Chief Judge.

Whatever else might be said about professional football in the United States, it does seem to breed a hardy group of fans who do not fear litigation combat. No fewer than five lawsuits have been instituted by football aficionados from Dallas to New England, each claiming that the respective defendant National Football League (NFL) team had violated the Sherman Act by requiring an individual who wishes to purchase a season ticket for all regular season games to buy, in addition, tickets for one or more exhibition or preseason games. In each case, including the instant one, the response of the district court has been the same: To dismiss the complaint upon the defendant's motion for summary judgment. Without passing upon the wisdom or desirability of this ticket sale modus operandi, we find the practice to be outside the ambit of even the broad reach of the Sherman Act. Accordingly, we affirm.

I.

Angelo F. Coniglio is a resident of Amherst, New York, a suburb of Buffalo. An employee of the New York State Power Authority, Coniglio's vocation is hydraulic engineering; his avocation—avid football fan and ardent rooter for the Buffalo Bills football team (Bills).

The Bills, owned and operated by Highwood Service, Inc. (Highwood), was a charter member of the American Football League (AFL), playing its inaugural season in 1960. From its inception, the Bills has been the only professional football team in Buffalo, indeed, filling a void of more than one decade's duration since the demise of the All American Conference in 1949.

Although Coniglio regularly attended the Bills home games from 1960 onward, he did not become a season ticket holder until 1964. With this new status, he gained a number of advantages over those who purchased tickets on an individual game basis, such as preferential seat selection, preferential call on post-season playoff tickets, and preferential seat selection for the following season. Coniglio repeated his season ticket purchase in 1965.

The year 1966 produced two events of some significance to Bills fans. First, the American Football League and its arch rival, the older National Football League, tentatively agreed to merge into one league, provided congressional approval, obviating a possible antitrust violation, could be obtained. Second, the Bills altered its season ticket sale policy by requiring the purchaser of a season ticket to also buy a ticket for one exhibition game.

In 1968, the Bills increased the number of exhibition games included in the season ticket package to two. And, two years later, in 1970, the season ticket holders were required to purchase tickets for three exhibition games. Whether because of this or perhaps because of the congressionally sanctioned merger between the AFL and the NFL, which was also consummated in 1970, the Bills that year saw the end of Coniglio as a season ticket purchaser. The record does reflect, however, that in 1971 Coniglio attended five of the seven regular season home games played by the Bills at Buffalo's War Memorial Stadium, by purchasing individual tickets for each game, and that Coniglio, in fact, had chosen not to attend the two remaining home games that year.

Disenchanted with the Bills's season ticket sale practice, Coniglio commenced an antitrust action against Highwood, the NFL, and its Commissioner, Pete Rozelle, by filing a complaint in the Western District of New York on September 9, 1970. He claimed that for the period 1966–1970, Highwood's policy of conditioning the purchase of season tickets to a requirement to buy exhibition game tickets constituted an unlawful tying arrangement in violation of Section 1 of the Sherman Act, 15 U.S.C. § 1. Moreover, he charged, it also constituted an abuse of the

Bills's monopoly power over professional football in the Buffalo area, in breach of Section 2 of the Sherman Act, 15 U.S.C. § 2. In addition, Coniglio alleged that the unlawful tie between season tickets and exhibition game tickets was the product of a conspiracy between Highwood, the NFL, and Rozelle, and that such conspiracy was a further violation of Section 1 of the Sherman Act.

Coniglio initially sought to maintain this suit as a class action, on behalf of approximately 750,000 season ticket holders of the Bills as well as a number of other NFL clubs, against a defendant class represented by Highwood. In this latter class Coniglio included all NFL clubs with season ticket policies mandating the purchase of exhibition game tickets. Following more than two years of pretrial discovery during which a substantial number of documents were produced by Commissioner Rozelle, the late Judge Henderson, on September 18, 1972, entered an order upon motion of the defendants limiting the plaintiff class to some 23,000 Bills season ticket holders, and denying Coniglio's motion to establish a defendant class.

On March 21, 1973, after additional discovery of documentary evidence and the completion of Coniglio's deposition—the only oral deposition taken by either side—the defendants moved for summary judgment. On August 1, 1973, Judge Henderson, in a brief opinion reported only in 1973–2 CCH Trade Cas. P74,795 (W.D.N.Y.1973), granted the motions and dismissed the complaint.

II.

We proceed directly to a consideration of the law applicable to the alleged Sherman Act violations. In Northern Pacific Railway Co. v. United States, 356 U.S. 1, 78 S.Ct. 514, 2 L.Ed.2d 545 (1958), the Court concisely defined a tying arrangement as:

> an agreement by a party to sell one product but only on the condition that the buyer also purchase a different [or tied] product....

Northern Pacific Railway Co. v. United States, supra, 356 U.S. at 5, 78 S.Ct. at 518. The Court further elucidated the subject by describing the basis upon which a tying arrangement would be found to be a violation of Section 1 of the Sherman Act.

> [Tying arrangements] are unreasonable [restraints of trade and commerce] in and of themselves whenever a party has sufficient economic power with respect to the tying product to appreciably restrain free competition in the market for the tied product and a "not insubstantial" amount of interstate commerce is affected.

Id. at 6, 78 S.Ct. at 518. Thus, using Northern Pacific as a springboard for our analysis, we can identify four factors essential in determining whether a particular sales practice constitutes an illicit tying arrangement:

(1) two separate and distinct products, a tying product and a tied product;

(2) sufficient economic power in the tying market to coerce purchase of the tied product;

(3) anti-competitive effects in the tied market;

(4) involvement of a "not insubstantial" amount of interstate commerce in the tied market.

It seems clear, at the outset, that the fourth factor is easily satisfied in this instance since, in 1970 alone, the total value of tied exhibition game tickets was approximately $483,000. In International Salt Co. v. United States, 332 U.S. 392, 68 S.Ct. 12, 92 L.Ed. 20 (1947), roughly $50,000 of interstate commerce was deemed sufficient. And see Fortner Enterprises, Inc. v. United States Steel Corp., 394 U.S. 495, 89 S.Ct. 1252, 22 L.Ed.2d 495 (1969).

We turn next to the second Northern Pacific prerequisite—the power to coerce purchase of the tied product—for the district judge rested his decision on the ground that the Bills lacked sufficient economic power in the season ticket [or tying] market to coerce purchase of exhibition game tickets. Judge Henderson concluded that since more than half of the 46,206 seats at War Memorial Stadium could be purchased on an individual game basis (as Coniglio himself did in 1971), "there is no tying problem even though the seller may offer a package of both season and preseason [exhibition] game tickets. See Northern Pacific Ry. v. United States, 356 U.S. 1, 6 (78 S.Ct. 514, 2 L.Ed.2d 545) (1958)." Although the question is indeed a close one, we believe that, despite the relatively large quantity of individual game tickets available here, the district court's conclusion, that as a matter of law the requisite coercive power was absent, is erroneous.

The district judge's reliance on Northern Pacific in the factual context of this case seems to have been misplaced. In Northern Pacific, the Court noted that "where the buyer is free to take either product by itself there is no tying problem even though the seller may also offer the two items as a unit at a single price." Northern Pacific Railway Co. v. United States, supra, 356 U.S. at 6 n.4, 78 S.Ct. at 518. Here, however, the buyer is not "free to take either product [season ticket or exhibition game ticket] by itself." Indeed, it is undisputed that a season ticket could not be purchased unless a certain number of exhibition game tickets, three in 1970, were purchased as well.

Appellee Highwood responds that a season ticket is no more than the sum of its parts—the individual regular season football games played by the Bills in Buffalo—and, therefore, the availability of tickets on an individual game basis eliminates the coercive tie under Northern Pacific. We have already referred to the advantages obtained through the purchase of a season ticket, principally the preferential seat selection accorded the season ticket holder. Although Highwood would thus have us characterize this suit as one to "guarantee every spectator a seat on the 50–yard line for the home games of the Bills," we are not inclined to take so disparaging a view. Rather, we are mindful of the test for coercive power announced by a unanimous Court in United States v. Loew's Inc., 371 U.S. 38, 45, 83 S.Ct. 97, 102, 9 L.Ed.2d 11 (1962):

> The crucial economic power may be inferred from the tying product's desirability to consumers or from uniqueness in its attributes.

That approximately 23,000 people were "willing" to purchase season tickets in a stadium that can seat only 46,000 is certainly some evidence of the "desirability" of these tickets, sufficient at least to persuade us that the existence of the requisite economic power is a triable issue of fact.

Highwood contends that in any event there is no tying arrangement, lawful or otherwise, because the first prerequisite—the separability of the tying and tied products—has not been satisfied in this case. See e.g. Times–Picayune Publishing Co. v. United States, 345 U.S. 594, 73 S.Ct. 872, 97 L.Ed. 1277 (1953). It argues that exhibition football games and regular season contents are substantially equivalent, each involving a struggle between two professional football teams fielding eleven-man units with the object of the battle being to get that pigskin across the goal line whether by brain or brawn or both. See Pfeiffer v. New England Patriots Football Club, Inc., 1973 CCH Trade Cas. P74,267 at 93,265. Coniglio answers that exhibition games are clearly inferior to regular season games. He argues cogently that the exhibition season is virtually conceded to be the time for experimentation with line-ups, plays, etc., during which the won-loss record is of distinctly secondary importance.

Product separability based on quality differentiation has been an essential ingredient in a long line of tying cases. See e.g. United States v. Loew's, Inc., supra (block sale of desirable and undesirable movies); American Manufacturers Mutual Insurance Co. v. American Broadcasting–Paramount Theatres, Inc., 388 F.2d 272 (2d Cir.1967) (block sale of television advertising for both desirable and undesirable television stations); Associated Press v. Taft–Ingalls Corp., 340 F.2d 753 (6th Cir.), cert denied, 382 U.S. 820, 86 S.Ct. 47, 15 L.Ed.2d 66 (1965) (block sale of desirable and undesirable wire services). To be sure, Highwood urges in response that quality is a continuum on which distinctions could be drawn between each regular season game as well. Although there is a measure of validity in Highwood's position, see Shayne v. Madison Square Garden Corp., 1974 CCH Trade Cas. P74,920 at 96,123 (E.D.N.Y. 1973), appeal dismissed, 491 F.2d 397 (2d Cir.1974), we believe that the distinction between exhibition and regular season contests is sufficiently sharp, at the very least, to render the factual determination of product separability more appropriate for a trial rather than for summary judgment. Grossman Development Co. v. Detroit Lions, Inc., 1973–2 CCH Trade Cas. P74,790 at 95,539.

With Coniglio having successfully traversed three quarters of the field, Highwood raises its final but insurmountable barrier. It contends that Coniglio failed, as a matter of law, to demonstrate an anti-competitive effect in the tied (exhibition football game) market. Quite simply, just as the Bills has a monopoly over the presentation of regular season professional football games in the relevant geographic market, which is Buffalo, so too does it have a monopoly over the presentation of exhibition professional football games—the tied product. Thus, Highwood is not using its economic power in the tying [season ticket] market to "restrain free competition in the market for the tied product," Northern Pacific Railway Co. v. United States, supra, 356 U.S. at 5, 78 S.Ct. at 518, for it is undisputed that, at the time this complaint was filed, there were neither actual nor potential competitors to the Bills in the professional football market. Accordingly, the tying arrangement attacked by Coniglio does not fall within the realm of contracts "in restraint of trade or commerce" proscribed by Section 1 of the Sherman Act, 15 U.S.C. § 1.

Coniglio tries strenuously but unsuccessfully to skirt this obstacle. He argues that the tying arrangement foreclosed competition in what could only be characterized at oral argument as the "general entertainment market in Buffalo." Support for this obviously vague assertion, moreover, is limited to a self-serving statement in Coniglio's affidavit in opposition to summary judgment which reads:

> There are alternative activities available on Friday and Saturday evenings [when the Bills's home exhibition football games were generally played] which are attractive to me, including movies, some live theater, and music programs. As a season ticketholder with seats to exhibition games forced upon me, I was precluded from seriously considering alternative activities on game nights.

Not only does this fall far short of Fed.R.Civ.P. 56(e)'s requirement that an affidavit in opposition to a motion for summary judgment "set forth specific facts showing that there is a genuine issue for trial," but we consider the purportedly relevant product market so broadly defined as to render that concept all but meaningless as an analytic tool for assessing the anti-competitive effect requisite to a Sherman Act violation.

We agree with the court in American Aloe Corp. v. Aloe Creme Laboratories, Inc., 420 F.2d 1248 (7th Cir.), cert. denied, 398 U.S. 929, 90 S.Ct. 1820, 26 L.Ed.2d 91 (1970) and 400 U.S. 820, 91 S.Ct. 37, 27 L.Ed.2d 47 (1970), reh. denied, 400 U.S. 856, 91 S.Ct. 24, 27 L.Ed.2d 95 (1970), that "before there can be a conclusion as to whether there has been ... a contract in restraint of trade, a determination must be made as to what are the relevant product markets within which to gauge a firm's power or the effect of its activities." In defining the relevant product market, moreover, we are guided by the oft-cited analysis in

Brown Shoe Co. v. United States, 370 U.S. 294, 325, 82 S.Ct. 1502, 1524, 8 L.Ed.2d 510 (1962):

> The outer boundaries of a product market are determined by the reasonable interchangeability of use or the cross-elasticity of demand between the product itself and substitutes for it.

And, the Court in Brown Shoe added that, in determining product line differential, such considerations as the existence of characteristics peculiar to a particular product and product appeal to a distinct class of customers would prove illuminating. Viewed in this light, Coniglio's claim that plays, movies, and musicals are all within the boundaries of the same product market as exhibition football amounts to nothing more than the boundless contention that, by extracting extra dollars from season ticket holders, the Bills leave less in their pockets to spend on any other form of diversion, from a trip to the zoo to a night at the opera. Suffice to say that the extraordinary breadth of the market encompassing such diverse yet assertedly competitive products is far beyond that ever contemplated for a relevant product market.

Nor can Coniglio bootstrap his hollow claim of an anticompetitive effect into a triable issue by relying on the Supreme Court's admonition in Poller v. Columbia Broadcasting System, Inc., 368 U.S. 464, 473, 82 S.Ct. 486, 491, 7 L.Ed.2d 458 (1962), that summary judgment may not be appropriate for complex antitrust litigation "where motive and intent play leading roles, the proof is largely in the hands of alleged conspirators, and hostile witnesses thicken the plot." Unlike Poller, in which the key issue was intent to monopolize, the propriety of summary judgment in this case rests on Coniglio's total failure to demonstrate any adverse effect on competition, actual or potential, an issue perfectly well suited to objective, statistical analysis. In such instances, summary judgment is properly granted to lower the curtain on costly litigation where it is clear beyond cavil that one side simply has no support for its version of alleged facts. See Community of Roquefort v. William Faehndrich, Inc., 303 F.2d 494, 498 (2d Cir.1962).

Coniglio also seeks to avoid the lack of demonstrable, anti-competitive impact of the Bills's ticket sale practice by contending that a deleterious effect on competition is not essential to prove a violation of Section 1 of the Sherman Act. He claims it is sufficient that the tying arrangement merely interfere with the consumer's freedom of choice in deciding whether to purchase the tied product. Although courts have occasionally referred to this as a primary evil of the tying arrangement, see e.g. Associated Press v. Taft–Ingalls Corp., supra, 340 F.2d at 762, it represents no more than the causal determinant of the proscribed restraint on competition in the tied market which ordinarily results from such interference. Associated Press, heavily relied upon by Coniglio, is not to the contrary, for the court was careful to note the existence of United Press International as a competitive wire service. Associated Press v. Taft–Ingalls, Corp., supra, 340 F.2d at 762, 764. See also American Manufacturers Mutual Insurance Co. v. American Broadcasting–Paramount Theatres, supra (adverse effect on competition among television networks for advertising). In sum, therefore, neither the cases marshalled by appellant nor the plain language of Section 1, which speaks specifically of contracts "in restraint of trade or commerce," support his contention that Section 1 can be violated absent a showing of such restraint.

Finally, Coniglio turns to Section 2 of the Sherman Act, 15 U.S.C. § 2, and argues that, in establishing the tying arrangement, Highwood violated that section by unlawfully abusing its monopoly power in the professional football market. Mr. Justice Douglas's opinion for a majority of the Court in United States v. Griffith, 334 U.S. 100, 68 S.Ct. 941, 92 L.Ed. 1236 (1948), sets forth the governing rule:

> The use of monopoly power, however lawfully acquired, to foreclose competition, to gain a competitive advantage, or to destroy a competitor, is unlawful.

334 U.S. at 107, 68 S.Ct. at 945. Accordingly, since we have made plain that Highwood has not used the tying arrangement either to prevent competition or destroy it, its ticket sale practice does not represent an unlawful abuse of its monopoly power. See United States v. Grinnell Corp., 384 U.S. 563, 570–571, 86 S.Ct. 1698, 16 L.Ed.2d 778 (1966); United States v. Aluminum Co. of America, 148 F.2d 416, 429–430 (2d Cir.1945).

As for the remaining defendants, the NFL and its Commissioner, Pete Rozelle, it is readily apparent that if Highwood's tying arrangement is not unlawful, an agreement among the defendants to establish that practice, even if it could be proven, would not be unlawful either.

Notes

1. For another example of alleged ticket tying, see *Diamond v. University of Southern California*, 89 Cal.Rptr. 302 (Ct.App.1970) (school offered hard-to-get Rose Bowl tickets to induce fans to purchase season tickets).

2. Twenty-five years after the Second Circuit decided *Coniglio*, the Bills continue to require season ticketholders to buy tickets to pre-season games and fans continue to complain about the policy. *See* Jack Brown, *Right City, Wrong Plan*, Buff. News, May 10, 1998, at 2B.

3. In a footnote in its opinion in *Coniglio*, the Second Circuit reports the ticket the plaintiff did not want to buy cost $7. *See* 495 F.2d at 1290 n.7. The same seat now sells for $35. Even at this price, Bills tickets remain among the cheapest in the NFL. *See* Rick Maloney, *Buffalo Bills Ticket Prices Rank in NFL's Bottom Tier*, Bus. First–Buff., Sept. 8, 1997, at 10 (noting that the Bills rank 23rd in the 30–team league).

4. During the past 30 years, tickets to sporting events have skyrocketed in price. In 1967, for example, a ticket to the Super Bowl could be had for as little as $8. By 1998, the cost had risen to $325, an increase of more than 4000% (or 129% a year). *See* Craig Barnes, *1967: A Super Oddity*, Fort Lauderdale Sun–Sentinel, Dec. 27, 1998, at 9C. Since 1990, ticket prices generally have increased seven percent a year (at a time when inflation has

hovered around three percent). NBA tickets, for example, rose 25% between 1995 and 1998, while MLB tickets jumped 57% between 1991 and 1998 despite the loss of fans following the 1994–95 players strike. *See further* Luke Cyphers, *New Ballgame for Old Fans*, N.Y. Daily News, May 3, 1998, at 13.

5. Even with its increases, baseball remains the most affordable professional sport. According to Team Marketing Report, a Chicago-based sports industry newsletter, the average cost for a family of four to attend a baseball game in 1998 was $115, including tickets, food, souvenirs, and parking. The same family would have to pay $221 to see an NFL game, $228 for an NHL game, and $214 for an NBA game. *See further A Hit After Strike*, Wash. Post, July 19, 1998, at H1.

6. With three new arenas in its immediate vicinity (Jack Kent Cooke Stadium, the MCI Center, and Camden Yards), Washington, D.C. has the dubious distinction of being the most expensive city in the nation when it comes to buying tickets. Other costly towns include Boston, Chicago, New York, and Philadelphia. *See further* Stephen C. Fehr, *Pricey New Sports Venues Help Make Washington No. 1 for High–Cost Tickets*, Wash. Post, Oct. 31, 1997, at C1.

7. It appears ticket prices will continue to rise for the foreseeable future. Immediately after being eliminated from the 1998 playoffs, for example, the New York Knicks announced the cost of a courtside seat in 1999 would increase by eight percent to $1,350 (a whopping $55,350 per season). *See* Andy Baggott, *Going Out On a Limb*, Wis. St. J., June 2, 1998, at 2D. A short time later, MLB increased the price of World Series games by 100%. *See* Rafael Hermoso, *Series Ticket Prices Double Trouble for Fans*, N.Y. Daily News, Aug. 12, 1998, at 50.

8. Part of the reason for the continuing spiral in prices is the willingness of fans to keep paying. In a recent study of Buffalo Bills season ticketholders, for example, it was discovered price is largely irrelevant (even in times of high unemployment). Instead, the team's recent performance, coupled with its immediate prospects, were found to be the two most important factors when it came time to renew. *See* G. Scott Thomas, *Wins, Not Economy, Sell Tickets*, Bus. First–Buff., July 14, 1997, at 1.

9. Will there come a point when fans refuse to pay more for tickets? Maybe. During the 1997 playoffs, the Miami Heat more than doubled prices during the middle of their series with the New York Knicks but later apologized after being excoriated by both fans and the media. *See further* Dave Lagarde, *Owners Covet Money—Much More Than Fans*, New Orleans Times–Picayune, May 25, 1997, at C3.

Problem 5

In an attempt to boost attendance, a basketball team decided to charge women half price on Sundays. If a male fan sues, claiming the policy is illegal, how is the court likely to rule? *See MacLean v. First Northwest Industries of America, Inc.*, 635 P.2d 683 (Wash.1981).

4. REFUNDS

Tickets normally are sold on a no-refund basis. Nevertheless, disappointed fans sometimes have sought to recover their money.

CASTILLO v. TYSON

N.Y. L.J., Oct. 30, 1998, at 26 (N.Y.Sup.Ct.1998).

RAMOS, Justice.

This nationwide class action involves what was billed as "the biggest fight of all time," the "Sound and the Fury," the rematch bout between defendant Mike Tyson ("Tyson") and Evander Holyfield ("Holyfield") for the heavyweight boxing championship title (the "Bout"). Live and television cable viewers of the fight, now infamously referred to as the "Bite Fight," bring this action claiming that Tyson, the promoter, and the distributors breached a legal duty owed to them when Tyson bit Holyfield during the Bout. They seek a refund of the money they paid for ticket and pay-per-view cable service, alleging that Tyson intentionally caused the Bout to end in his disqualification.

All defendants move to dismiss the complaint pursuant to CPLR § 3211(a)(1) and (7), for failure to state a claim and based upon documentary evidence. They contend that the evidence demonstrates that spectators have no contractual or other right to view "a legitimate heavyweight title fight," and privity between them and the plaintiffs is lacking. Plaintiffs crossmove for an order to compel disclosure of documents before the dismissal motions are decided, and for leave to amend their Amended Complaint "as of right" under CPLR § 3025(a).

The Amended Complaint

On June 28, 1997, after suffering a cut above his eye in the first two rounds, and receiving a warning not to bite his opponent again, Tyson bit Holyfield on the ear and was disqualified, ending the Bout in the third round. The Amended Complaint essentially relies upon the allegation that spectators who paid to watch the Bout "expected to see a legitimate heavyweight title bout fought in accordance with" the rules and regulations of the Nevada Boxing Commission (the "Commission") [Complaint P 35, p.10]. Under the rules and regulations of the Commission, plaintiffs contend a fight is to end either in a knockout (actual or technical) or by a decision of judges after twelve rounds. According to plaintiffs, the Bout ended because Tyson intentionally caused his disqualification which allegedly deprived plaintiffs of what they paid for. Plaintiffs contend that Tyson had devised a scheme where he would enter the ring intending to fight a fair fight, but if a loss appeared likely, then he would intentionally cause his disqualification from the Bout [Amended Complaint PP 58, 59, p. 15]. The alleged scheme was designed not only for Tyson to avoid defeat, but also allegedly to ensure a rematch with Holyfield for another large purse.

Alleging in supplemental papers the existence of a joint venture, plaintiffs contend that Tyson and the organizers of the Bout are liable for Tyson's behavior in the ring. Among them are defendant Mike Tyson Productions, Inc., a company through which Tyson conducts his boxing business (the "Tyson Defendants"); defendants Don King, Don King Productions, Inc. ("DKP"), and Kingvision Pay Per View, Ltd. (collectively referred to as the "King Defendants"), the promoter of the Bout and the distributer of this pay-per-view event; defendant Showtime Networks, Inc. ("Showtime") which held the exclusive contract to telecast the Tyson bout, and its parent and affiliated corporations, defendants Viacom International, Inc., and/or Viacom, Inc., and defendant SET Pay–Per–View (the "Viacom Defendants"). Plaintiffs rely on the respective agreements between these defendants to assert causes of action for breach of express and implied warranty, and unjust enrichment, and as against Tyson only claims for fraud, tortious interference with a contract, wantonness, and negligent misrepresentation.

Discussion

In deciding the instant motions to dismiss, it is well established that this Court must deem the allegations contained in the complaint as true, and construe every inference in favor of the plaintiff (Morone v. Morone, 50 NY2d 481, 484 [1980]; Cohn v. Lionel Corp., 21 NY2d 559, 562 [1968]). However, allegations consisting of bare legal conclusions are not entitled to such consideration, and are inadequate to defeat a dismissal motion (See, City of Albany v. McMorran, 16 AD2d 1021, 1022 [3rd Dept. 1962]). Here, while there is no doubt that Tyson's acts were a horrific display of poor sportsmanship, whether or not spectators of the Bout can maintain this action will depend upon whether or not they can demonstrate the existence of a legally cognizable right to view what plaintiffs characterize as "a legitimate fight." This Court finds that plaintiffs have failed to make such a showing.

Plaintiffs are not a party to any of defendants' agreements, and clearly contractual privity is lacking. "It is ancient law in New York that to succeed on a third-party beneficiary theory, a non-party must be the intended beneficiary of the contract [cite omitted], not an incidental beneficiary to whom no duty is owed." (Suffolk County v. Long Island Lighting Co., 728 F2d 52, 63 [2d Cir 1984]). Only those whom a contract was intended to benefit can claim third-party beneficiary status (See, Port Chester Electrical Construction Corp. v. Atlas, 40 NY2d 652 [1976]). Agreements which govern defendants' involvement in the Bout were submitted by defendants in support of their motions. Included among them was the agreement between Tyson and certain King defendants, dated March 17, 1995, which governed the marketing, licensing and distribution of the Bout on pay-per-view (the "Multi–Fight Agreement"); the Don King Production, Inc., and MGM contract executed on May 24, 1995, as amended November 27, 1995, which provided for the staging and sale of the tickets for the Bout at MGM Grand Hotel in Las Vegas, Nevada (the "MGM Contract"); the DKP and Tyson agreement which granted DKP the exclusive right to promote Tyson's bouts (the

"Tyson Promotional Contract"); and the DKP and Tyson contract which provided that Tyson would be paid $30 million in exchange for his participation in the Bout; and the "Cablevision Agreement between SET and Cablevision System Corp., which provided for the exhibition and distribution of the Bout.

There is no language in any of these contracts which confers on plaintiffs or the class members the right to enforce any obligation to present a particular type of fight. Plaintiffs' reliance upon language in the Agreements referring to defendants' obligation to "distribute," "stage," and "televise" the Bout in order to show the existence of third party status is at best contrived. Words describing the contracting parties' respective obligations pulled randomly from a contract fail to invoke an inference of the contracting parties' intent to benefit a third party. Moreover, both the Multi–Fight Agreement and the MGM Contract contain provisions which expressly negate an intent to confer rights on third parties [Hirth Aff., Ex. C at § 7(*o*) and Ex. D at § 24]. The most powerful indicator of the contracting parties' intention is the language of the contract itself and where a term of a contract expressly bars enforcement by third parties that term is decisive (See, Nepco Forged Products v. Consolidated Edison Co. N.Y., 99 AD2d 508 [2d Dept. 1984]).

Even assuming that there was no express provision precluding third-party beneficiary status, plaintiffs' attempt to allege a right, or an obligation on the part of the defendants to deliver to spectators a particular type of fight is equally lacking. The only contract provision relevant to plaintiffs' claim is the provision of the Multi–Fight Agreement which states that DKP is responsible "for presenting each Event in accordance with the rules, regulations, orders and instructions of any boxing commission...." [Hirth Aff. Ex. C at § 2(I)]. Nothing contained in this provision, however, could be reasonably interpreted to create a right to view a particular type of fight. This Court refuses to read into the provision a nonexistent contract term to impose a duty upon contracting parties.

Although many spectators of the Bout were disappointed by Tyson's behavior in the ring, a court "has no inherent power to right a wrong unless thereby the civil, property, or personal rights of the plaintiff in the action ... are affected. The rights to be affected must be personal as distinguished from the rights in common with the great body of people." (Schieffelin v. Komfort, 212 NY 520, 530 [1914]). The fact is sporting events do end in disqualification of an athlete for having violated the rules of the sport. Particularly in the sport of boxing, "hitting below the belt" and biting are commonly recognized acts which warrant disqualification (Weinstein Aff. Ex. 1, 4, 5). The excitement and thrill for most spectators of sporting events is the anticipation of an unpredictable outcome. Example after example of professional boxers, and other professional athletes, who have been disqualified for rule violations illustrates that judicial notice should be taken of the fact that a spectator can reasonably expect a boxing match to end by disqualification of an athlete (Ecco High Frequency Corp. v. Amtorg Trading Corp., ___ Misc. ___, 81

NYS 2d 610, 617 [Sup Ct NY County 1948] finding that a court may take judicial notice of any fact which is "a matter of common and general knowledge, well established and authoritatively settled, not doubtful or uncertain"; see also, American Broadcasting Companies, Inc. v. Wolf, 76 AD2d 162 [1980]).

For this Court to hold that any of plaintiffs' allegations are sufficient to confer a benefit to which plaintiffs may claim legal entitlement "would not only expose [athletes, promoters, and distributors of sporting events] to countless unforeseeable lawsuits [by unsatisfied spectators], but would also impair the notion of privity of contract." (Suffolk County v. Long Island Lighting, 728 F2d 52, 63 [2nd Cir 1984]; See, Ossining Union Free School District v. Anderson LaRocca Anderson, 73 NY2d 417, 424 [1989]). As ticket holders of a sporting event, plaintiffs and class members are simply licensees who purchased the right to witness the Bout regardless of its eventual outcome (See, Bickett v. Buffalo Bills, Inc., 122 Misc. 2d 880 [Sup. Ct. NY County 1983]; Jacksonville Bulls Football Ltd. v. Blatt, 535 So2d 626, 629 [1988]); Presley v. Nassau, 148 Misc. 2d 125, 130 [Sup. Ct. Nassau County 1990]). That spectators here have no legally cognizable entitlement to a particular kind of fight is further illustrated upon review of their remaining claims.

For instance, plaintiffs' claims for breach of warranty and fraud are both based upon non-actionable "puffery." Either a statement of fact or an affirmation of the quality of the thing sold is required to maintain a fraud or breach of warranty claim (Independent Order of Foresters v. Donaldson, Lufkin & Jenrette, 919 F.Supp. 149, 152 [SD NY 1996]; CBS Inc. v. Ziff–Davis Pub. Co., 75 NY2d 496, 505–06 [1990]; Elghanian v. Harvey, ___ AD2d ___, 671 NYS2d 266 [1st Dept. 1998]). Tyson's and other defendants' statements cited by plaintiffs which predicted Tyson's "sensational victory...."; that he was "going to be champion"; and that he was "confident of his win" are merely predictions and not representations of fact. Not only is the absence of an affirmation fatal to the breach of express or implied warranty claims, warranty actions can not arise from the performance of services (See, R. W. Kern, Inc., et al. v. Circle Industries Corp., 158 AD2d 363 [1st Dept. 1990]). Nor are the predictions of Tyson's former trainer that "Tyson would get himself disqualified" sufficient to plead a fraud claim with the requisite particularity (CPLR § 3016(b)). Merely listing the material elements of fraud without any supporting detail is insufficient to satisfy the pleading requirements of CPLR 3016(b) (Langford v. Cameron, 73 AD2d 1001, 1003 [3rd Dept. 1981]; See also, Barnett v. Madison Square Garden Ctr., Inc., 227 AD2d 178 [1st Dept. 1996]).

The claim of unjust enrichment must fail because, in light of the foregoing findings of the Court, plaintiffs cannot demonstrate that the defendants are in possession of money which rightfully belongs to the plaintiffs (See Indyk v. Habib Bank Ltd., 694 F2d 54 [2nd Cir. 1982]), or that defendants' enrichment was at plaintiffs' expense (Kagan v. K–Tel Entertainment, Inc., 172 AD2d 375 [1st Dept. 1991]). As was found by this Court, plaintiffs have no right to a particular kind of fight. They were mere licensees who had the right to view whatever event transpired regardless of whether it ended in disqualification. Because it is undisputed that plaintiffs had access to view the fight, it cannot be found as a matter of law that they did not receive what they paid for.

Based upon similar reasons, plaintiffs have not stated a claim against Tyson for tortious interference with the contract entered into between plaintiffs and their local cable companies. To plead this claim requires facts showing: (1) the existence of a valid contract; (2) defendant's knowledge of the contract; (3) defendant's intentional inducement of the third party breach or otherwise render[ing the] performance impossible; and (4) damages (Kronos, Inc. v. AVX Corp., 81 NY2d 90, 94 [1993]). It is well settled that in order to succeed in an action alleging tortious interference with a contract, the plaintiffs must properly allege that there was an actual breach of contract (Bancorp v. Fleet/Norstar Financial Group, 87 NY2d 614, 620 [1996] holding that "in order to succeed on a cause of action for inducement of breach of contract a plaintiff obviously must show a breach of contract").

As ticket holders plaintiffs and the class members held only a license arguably which itself is not a contract that could have been subject to a breach (see, Jacksonville Bulls Football, Ltd. v. Blatt, supra, 535 So2d 626, 629 [1988]). Notwithstanding that contention, the local cable companies were obligated to furnish only the proper signal that enabled plaintiffs and the class members to view the Bout. The fact that the plaintiffs had access to view Tyson biting Holyfield's ear demonstrates to this Court that the local cable companies satisfied their obligation.

Moreover, this Court is unconvinced that further discovery would produce facts to bolster the plaintiffs' claims. Examination of the unredacted contract reveals absolutely nothing relevant to this action that was not presented in the redacted copies. There is no indication, other than plaintiffs' conclusory allegations, that other relevant documentary evidence exists. Plaintiffs also fail to explain how additional discovery will lend support to their claims. It is under these circumstances that requests for leave to amend the pleadings, and discovery in lieu of a dismissal of the complaint, must be denied (see, Platt Corp. v. Platt, 20 AD2d 874 [1st Dept. 1964]).

Conclusion

Accordingly, the defendants' motion to dismiss is granted and the Amended Complaint is dismissed with costs and disbursements to defendants, as taxed by the Clerk of the Court.

Notes

1. In addition to poor play, ticket refund actions have been based on a number of other grounds. *See, e.g.*, *Stern v. Cleveland Browns Football Club, Inc.*, 1996 WL 761163 (Ohio Ct.App.1996) (team disclosed it was moving to different city); *Skalbania v. Simmons*, 443 N.E.2d 352 (Ind.Ct.App.1982) (team announced it was folding); *Strauss v. Long Island Sports, Inc.*, 401 N.Y.S.2d 233 (App.Div.1978) (team traded star player).

2. In 1970, President Richard M. Nixon ordered wages and prices frozen to stabilize the economy. As a result, the Oakland Raiders were forced to issue refunds after a court determined the club's decision to raise prices for the 1971 season violated the government's directive. *See Oakland Raiders v. Office of Emergency Preparedness*, 380 F.Supp. 187 (N.D.Cal.1974).

Problem 6

When the players' union called a strike, the owners decided to go forward using rookies, retirees, and amateurs. In response, a group of season ticketholders demanded their money back. If no refunds are given and the case goes to trial, what is the most likely outcome? *See Miami Dolphins, Ltd. v. Genden & Bach, P.A.*, 545 So.2d 294 (Fla.Dist.Ct.App.1989).

5. SCALPERS

Tickets often are hard to get. As a result, many fans turn to "scalpers." The role played by these middlemen has proven highly controversial.

NEW JERSEY ASS'N OF TICKET BROKERS v. TICKETRON

543 A.2d 997 (N.J.Super.Ct.App.Div.),
cert. denied, 550 A.2d 471 (N.J.1988).

GAYNOR, Judge.

In these consolidated cases, plaintiffs challenge the validity and application of N.J.S.A. 56:8–26 et seq., the anti-ticket-scalping law enacted in 1983.

Plaintiffs, New Jersey Association of Ticket Brokers (Ticket), an unincorporated association of ticket brokers operating in New Jersey, and Birn–Mar Tickets, Inc. (Birn–Mar), a New Jersey corporation engaged in the business of ticket brokerage, appeal from the summary judgment dismissing those portions of their complaints attacking the constitutionality of the statute and determining that they and third-party defendants, Michael Birns and Richard Birnback, had violated the statute thereby subjecting them to the statutory penalties. We affirm.

As ticket brokers, plaintiffs individually sell tickets to concerts, sporting events and other entertainments at a premium per ticket, a price in excess of the face value printed on the ticket. The major part of their New Jersey business was the resale of tickets for concerts, Giants' football games and other sporting events staged by the New Jersey Sports & Exposition Authority (NJSEA) at the Meadowlands complex. Assertedly, plaintiffs service a secondary market of those members of the public who are unable to stand in ticket lines because of jobs, school or parental disapproval, or, who do not want tickets months in advance of the event. Tickets for Giants games are obtained from season ticket holders for two or three times the ticket price and concert tickets are purchased from youths who stand in line at premiums of $7 to $25 per ticket. Brokers also allegedly offer expertise in locating prime seat locations.

Statutory control over the resale of tickets commenced with the legislation enacted in 1947 permitting municipalities to enact ordinances regulating this activity. L. 1947, c. 385, codified as N.J.S.A. 40:48–2.18, et seq. Municipalities were authorized to license ticket brokers and to limit the maximum premium upon a resale to $1 plus tax in excess of the original price of the ticket. The enforcement of the ordinance and penalties, not more than $100 for each offense, as well as revocation and suspension of any license, were left to the individual municipalities which had enacted the licensing ordinances. The ineffectiveness of municipal regulation prompted a review by the office of the attorney general in 1982 of various ticket scalping complaints. The abuses thus disclosed induced legislative activity resulting ultimately in the enactment of the legislation under attack in the present litigation.

Under N.J.S.A. 56:8–26, et seq., a ticket agent is a "person who is involved in the business of selling or reselling tickets of admission to places of entertainment who charges a premium in excess of the price, plus taxes, printed on the tickets." N.J.S.A. 56:8–26f. A "place of entertainment" is defined as "any privately or publicly owned or operated entertainment facility within the State of New Jersey such as a theater, stadium, museum, arena, racetrack, or other place where performances, concerts, exhibits, games or contests are held and for which an entry fee is charged." N.J.S.A. 56:8–26d. A "person" is defined as a corporation, company, association, society, firm, partnership or joint stock company as well as an individual. N.J.S.A. 56:8–26c. The statute proscribes the reselling of tickets to a place of entertainment by any person without first having obtained a license from the Division of Consumer Affairs to engage in the business of reselling tickets. N.J.S.A. 56:8–27 and 28; N.J.A.C. 13:45A–20.3(a).

In addition to the payment of an application fee, currently $300, an applicant is required to file a bond in the amount of $10,000, conditioned upon compliance with the statute and regulations, the payment of all damages occasioned to any person by reason of misrepresentation, fraud, deceit or other unlawful act in connection with the licensed business and the promise that the applicant, his agents or employees, will not be guilty of any fraud or extortion. N.J.S.A. 56:8–30.

A further provision requires that each place of entertainment print the price charged on the face of each ticket and include the price in any advertising for the event. N.J.S.A. 56:8–33. The statute limits the premium chargeable on a resale by providing:

> Except for tickets printed prior to the enactment of this act, each ticket shall have endorsed thereon the maximum premium not to exceed 20% of the ticket price or $3.00, whichever is greater, plus lawful taxes, at which the ticket may be resold. No person shall resell, offer to resell, or purchase with the intent to

resell a ticket at any premium in excess of the maximum premium as set forth in this act. [N.J.S.A. 56:8–33]

Plaintiffs maintain that the impact of this law is to compel each person interested in attending a public or private entertainment within the State of New Jersey to stand in line or be eliminated from attendance. According to counsel for Ticket, only two licenses had been issued as of December 7, 1984. Plaintiffs claim there is no point in putting up a bond because they can't make a living by selling tickets within the statutory limit, particularly when they must buy concert tickets from Ticketron offices and pay Ticketron a service fee of $1.25 per ticket.

At the time this action began, Ticketron had a contract with NJSEA designating Ticketron as the exclusive agent of NJSEA for the sale of tickets for events in the Brendan Byrne Arena and Giants Stadium. All concert tickets were initially offered first by Ticketron and subsequently at the box office. The contract with Ticketron expired on July 31, 1985 at which time a five-year contract was awarded by NJSEA to Ticket World USA. Chief among the complaints voiced by plaintiffs was their allegation that the tickets from Ticketron do not afford the best seats and that the Ticketron agents and promoters skim off the very best seating for their own uses and purposes, including resale. An opinion of the attorney general declared that Ticketron (and accordingly its successor Ticket World) as agents of the State were exempt from the operation of the licensing statute.

After the effective date of N.J.S.A. 56:8–26, et seq., Birn–Mar began selling tickets to concerts within New Jersey charging a premium within the statutory limit but coupling that with a consultation fee. On January 7, 1984 it offered two tickets to a concert with a face value of $13.50 for $35 each. The ticket agent represented that $18.50 of the $35 purchase price was a consultation fee and requested the buyer to sign a contract which specified that personal services were performed by the agent in selecting the seat, taking into consideration the patron's weight, sex, age, type of crowd, type of music and other factors.

Again on January 20, 1984, two police officers, seeking tickets to the Van Halen concert at the Meadowlands, were offered tickets by an agent at the Birn–Mar Ticket Box, Bergen Mall, for $18 plus a $17 consultation fee and they were asked to sign what was called a waiver form. These two violations in January 1984 formed the basis for the municipal court complaints which plaintiff Birn–Mar sought to restrain by filing suit. As a result of these problems, Birn–Mar claims that it has closed its New Jersey office.

Plaintiffs jointly claim that resale ticket agents serve a vital social and economic function by catering to the needs of those who are unable to stand in line, by offering an excellent choice of seats and by providing a convenience to the public. Without these services assertedly their customers would be forced to use unlawful scalpers. Further, by maintaining permanent places of business within the State they are giving employment to New Jersey residents, paying state and federal taxes and utilizing public utilities.

Plaintiffs further contend that less confiscatory methods are available to curb the alleged abuses. They also claim that the problem of intimidation and harassment can be dealt with by our criminal laws independently of limiting the resale price or outlawing resales, and additionally urge that the problem of stolen tickets should be dealt with by imposing strict sanctions for theft and resale of stolen tickets. Plaintiffs also point out that they agree to be bound for a refund of the purchase price in the event of a cancellation or postponement of any event. While stating that their average selling price is $30 per ticket, plaintiffs do not deny instances of the sale of tickets for $100 each for extraordinary events or for a front row seat at major concerts. However, Ticket's president, David Emerson, an independent ticket agent, contends that the premiums charged by the agents are not exorbitant.

I.

In asserting a substantive due process violation, although not challenging the licensing or bonding requirements of the legislation, plaintiffs claim that the restrictions imposed on the resale of tickets have virtually forced them out of business. Plaintiffs view the statute as too restrictive in this regard, unrelated to the evil designed to be corrected and confiscatory of their business. As supporting authority for this position, plaintiffs rely upon Tyson and Brother–United Theatre Ticket Offices, Inc. v. Banton, 273 U.S. 418, 47 S.Ct. 426, 71 L.Ed. 718 (1927). Tyson involved the review of a New York statute which prohibited the resale of tickets for theaters or other places of entertainment at a price in excess of $.50 above the price printed on the ticket. The Court concluded that the power to fix prices existed only where the business or the property had become "affected with a public interest," 273 U.S. at 438, 47 S.Ct. at 431, and having found that the resale of amusement tickets did not affect a public interest, held that the statute was in violation of the due process clause of the Fourteenth Amendment. Id. at 439–441, 47 S.Ct. at 431–432.

Plaintiffs' reliance on Tyson is misplaced as the drift away from the public interest standard enunciated in that case has been so great that it can no longer be considered a controlling authority. In Nebbia v. New York, 291 U.S. 502, 54 S.Ct. 505, 78 L.Ed. 940 (1934), the Court, in dealing with the validity of a statute regulating milk prices, found that the concept of "affected with a public interest" was not susceptible of definition. 291 U.S. at 536, 54 S.Ct. at 515. In holding the New York statute fixing $.09 as a price for a quart of milk valid, the Court said that price controls are "unconstitutional only if arbitrary, discriminatory, or demonstrably irrelevant to the policy the Legislature is free to adopt, and hence an unnecessary and unwarranted interference with individual liberty." 291 U.S. at 539, 54 S.Ct. at 517.

The public interest standard of Tyson was deemed discarded by the Court in Olsen v. Nebraska, 313 U.S. 236, 61 S.Ct. 862, 85 L.Ed. 1305

(1941), in upholding a statute regulating fees charged by employment agencies; and also in Ferguson v. Skrupa, 372 U.S. 726, 83 S.Ct. 1028, 10 L.Ed.2d 93 (1963), which held valid a Kansas statute declaring the business of debt adjusting unlawful except insofar as it was practiced by lawyers. Finally, in Gold v. DiCarlo, 235 F.Supp. 817 (S.D.N.Y.1964), aff'd 380 U.S. 520, 85 S.Ct. 1332, 14 L.Ed.2d 266 (1965), the Supreme Court affirmed the decision of a three-judge district court which upheld a New York statute making it unlawful to sell a ticket in excess of $1.50 more than the price printed on the ticket.

The few jurisdictions which have held statutes or ordinances regulating the resale price invalid have done so on the ground that the legislation unreasonably interfered with private business or violated State constitutional provisions. In Kirtley v. State, 227 Ind. 175, 84 N.E.2d 712, 713 (1949), and in Estell v. Birmingham, 51 Ala.App. 462, 286 So.2d 866, 867 (Crim.App.1973), aff'd 291 Ala. 680, 286 So.2d 872 (1973), the Indiana statute and the Birmingham city ordinance precluded the receipt of any profit. The Indiana court stated that it refused to follow the majority and held that the statute interfered with the liberty and property rights of ticket owners. 84 N.E.2d at 715. The Alabama court held that the ordinance was valid under federal constitutional standards, 286 So.2d at 868, but noted that Alabama did not adopt the Nebbia doctrine completely but applied a narrower standard for due process considerations. Id. at 869.

New Jersey has adopted the Nebbia doctrine, embracing its principles to construe not only the federal constitution but parallel provisions of the State Constitution. The New Jersey Constitution (1947), Art. I, par. 1, does not make the constitutionality of governmental price regulation dependent on any public interest determination. See Hutton Park Gardens v. West Orange Town Council, 68 N.J. 543, 560, 350 A.2d 1 (1975). Even prior to the adoption of the 1947 New Jersey Constitution, New Jersey had embraced the principles in Nebbia. State Bd. of Milk Control v. Newark Milk Co., 118 N.J.Eq. 504, 516–519, 179 A.2d 116 (E. & A. 1935) (upholding State regulation of milk prices); Gaine v. Burnett, 122 N.J.L. 39, 43, 4 A.2d 37 (Sup.Ct.1939), aff'd 123 N.J.L. 317, 8 A.2d 604 (E. & A. 1939) (upholding regulation of liquor prices).

Legislative enactments regulating prices are "subject to the same narrow scope of review under principles of substantive due process as are other enactments under the police power: could the legislative body rationally have concluded that the enactment would serve the public interest without arbitrariness or discrimination?" Hutton Park Gardens, 68 N.J. at 563–564, 350 A.2d 1 (citations omitted). We are satisfied that the enactment of the anti-ticket-scalping statute, N.J.S.A. 56:8–26, et seq., by addressing the abuses found to exist in the reselling of tickets, was reasonably related to a proper legislative purpose and promoted the public welfare without discrimination or arbitrariness.

[The remainder of the court's opinion is omitted.]

ANDERSON v. REGENTS OF THE UNIVERSITY OF CALIFORNIA

554 N.W.2d 509 (Wis.Ct.App.),
review denied, 560 N.W.2d 273 (Wis.1996).

GARTZKE, Presiding Judge.

Stanley W. Anderson, et al. appeal from an order dismissing their complaint against the Board of Regents of the University of California (UCLA) for failure to state a claim. Plaintiffs were customers of tour operators and ticket agencies with whom they contracted for tour packages to the 1994 Rose Bowl game held on January 1, 1994, in Pasadena, California. The tours included tickets to the Rose Bowl game. When plaintiffs arrived at Pasadena they learned that tickets were unavailable, and they did not attend the game or they paid more than the $46 face value for tickets.

Plaintiffs allege that UCLA contracted for the plaintiffs' benefit but violated the contract, interfered with contracts the plaintiffs had with tour operators, engaged in a conspiracy, and negligently distributed its Rose Bowl allotment of tickets, to the plaintiffs' damage. We conclude that the complaint fails to state a claim against UCLA and affirm the order dismissing the complaint.

Summary of Facts

The trial court summarized the factual allegations in plaintiffs' second amended complaint as follows:

> The Rose Bowl is sponsored yearly by the Tournament of Roses Association ("Tournament") and features football teams from the Pacific Ten Conference ("PAC–10") collegiate athletic conference and the Big Ten Conference ("The Big Ten") collegiate conference.
>
> In 1994, the PAC–10 was represented by the University of California Los Angeles (UCLA) while the University of Wisconsin represented the Big Ten. UCLA is a public university of the State of California, governed by Cal. Regents.
>
> Participation in the 1994 Rose Bowl [was] controlled by an agreement between the PAC–10, the Big Ten and the Tournament, entitled ["]PAC–10 TOURNAMENT BIG TEN ROSE BOWL AGREEMENT["] ("the Agreement")[,] which was signed by the parties on March 16, 1992. The Agreement contained several provisions governing ticket sales and distribution between the two conferences.
>
> Paragraph 23, entitled ["]Ticket Distribution,["] states in part:
>
> e. Except for mutual complimentary tickets, all game tickets shall be sold at full face value to the persons to whom they are consigned. The price of such tickets shall be included in the determination of Net Income. Notwithstanding the foregoing,

member institutions of the PAC–10 and/or the BIG TEN may establish lower ticket prices for bona fide members of their student bodies; provided, however, that said institution shall account for all such tickets at full face value.

Paragraph 24, entitled [“]Ticket Allocation,[”] states in part:

b. In the event a Conference representative anticipates that it may have unused tickets, it may offer to sell such tickets first to the other Conference, and then to the Tournament.... No other party is obligated to accept such ticket.... The tickets may be offered for sale and sold only at the established prices thereof.

c. The parties agree not to place any excess tickets on general public sale (i.e., other than to its season ticket holders, alumni, faculty, students, and the like) without the prior consent of the [Rose Bowl Management Committee]. The RBMC may, rather than allowing such public sale, either take the tickets on consignment from the offering institution or acquire the tickets itself.

Paragraph 36 of the Agreement provides that the PAC–10, the Big Ten and the Tournament agree to indemnify each other in the event of breach. Paragraph 37 of the Agreement provides that disputes which cannot be resolved by the RBMC shall be resolved by arbitration.

It is the policy of the Tournament to prohibit resale of its tickets by its members to the general public. This policy protects the public from scalpers who sell tickets at inflated prices. The Tournament does not condone the sale of tickets at more than face value; sale to ticket brokers; nor purchase of packages that purport to include tickets to the Rose Bowl game.

UCLA was allotted 40,000 tickets while the University of Wisconsin was allotted 19,000. The full face value of these tickets was $46.00. UCLA “sold” 4,000 of its tickets to an anonymous donor on December 15, 1993, after having refused to transfer part of its ticket allotment to the University of Wisconsin on December 10, 1993. UCLA also sold 1,223 tickets to non-season ticket holders for face value on the condition that they would buy UCLA 1994 football season’s tickets. As a consequence of these transactions, UCLA sold tickets at higher than face value.

As a result of UCLA’s actions, it is alleged that a substantial number of tickets were placed in the hands of scalpers. Accordingly, the plaintiffs allege that they: (1) suffered annoyance, inconvenience, and emotional suffering; (2) were deprived of the value of their tour package by virtue of not seeing the game; and (3) paid excessive prices for their tickets. The plaintiffs seek damages, including punitive damages, based on claims of breach of contract, conspiracy and negligence.

TRIAL COURT'S DECISION

UCLA moved to dismiss the complaint for failure to state a claim. The trial court concluded that California law applies to plaintiffs' claim for breach of contract. Although UCLA is not a named party to the contract, the trial court concluded that it is a party to the Agreement. The court rejected the plaintiffs' claim that they were third-party beneficiaries of the Agreement, and the court therefore held they lack standing to sue for its breach. So far as is material to this appeal, the court held that the plaintiffs' conspiracy claim fails because plaintiffs did not allege or identify the person or persons with whom UCLA conspired. Because the court had already held the plaintiffs lacked standing to sue on the contract, the court concluded they lacked standing to sue for intentional interference with their contract. The court held that the plaintiffs failed to state a claim for negligence because plaintiffs failed to allege that UCLA has a duty to the plaintiffs to make tickets available to their travel agents.

Having found that the complaint fails to state a claim against UCLA, the trial court granted the motion to dismiss.

BREACH OF CONTRACT

A. California Law Governs the Contract Issues

The Agreement provides in part, "This Agreement shall be governed by the laws of the State of California." Under Wisconsin law, the parties to a contract may agree that the law of a particular jurisdiction controls their contractual relations. First Wis. Nat'l Bank v. Nicolaou, 85 Wis.2d 393, 397 n. 1, 270 N.W.2d 582, 584 (Ct.App.1978). We therefore look to California law to determine the contractual relationship, if any, between the parties.

B. UCLA as a Party to the Agreement

Plaintiffs contend that UCLA is a party to the Agreement. UCLA contends this cannot be, since UCLA is not referred to in the Agreement as a party. The Rose Bowl Agreement is between [sic] three named entities: the Big Ten, the PAC–10 and the Tournament.

Under California law, one who is not a party to a contract cannot be sued for its breach. Fruitvale Canning Co. v. Cotton, 115 Cal.App.2d 622, 252 P.2d 953, 955 (1953), overruled on other grounds, Lucas v. Hamm, 56 Cal.2d 583, 15 Cal.Rptr. 821, 825, 364 P.2d 685, 689 (1961).

The Agreement provides that PAC–10 consists of ten western universities, including the University of California, Los Angeles. In § 44(a) of the Agreement, PAC–10 warranted it is authorized to enter the Agreement, and that all required consents and authorizations by all bodies of the PAC–10 member institutions have been obtained and that the PAC–10 is authorized to sign this Agreement on the PAC–10's behalf, subject to final ratification of the signed Agreement by the chief executive officer of each institution of the PAC–10.

Although nothing in the record discloses whether the chief executive officer of UCLA ratified the Agreement, it is beyond dispute that UCLA accepted benefits derived from it. Acceptance of benefits under a contract is the equivalent of a consent to the obligations arising from it. California Civil Code § 1589; Thompson v. Swiryn, 95 Cal.App.2d 619, 213 P.2d 740, 747 (1950). We conclude that UCLA is a party to the Agreement.

C. Plaintiffs as Third–Party Beneficiaries

Plaintiffs contend that the contract provisions governing ticket sales and prohibiting ticket "scalping" primarily benefited prospective ticket holders by limiting the sale price of each ticket to its face value, $46. As prospective ticket purchasers, they contend that they are therefore third-party beneficiaries of the Agreement.

California Civil Code § 1559 provides, "A contract, made expressly for the benefit of a third person, may be enforced by him at any time before the parties thereto rescind it." A third party need not be specifically named as a beneficiary. Marina Tenants Ass'n v. Deauville Marina Dev. Co., 181 Cal.App.3d 122, 226 Cal.Rptr. 321, 324 (1986). "Expressly" in § 1559 means an express manner, in direct or unmistakable terms, explicitly, definitely or directly. City and County of San Francisco v. Western Air Lines, Inc., 204 Cal.App.2d 105, 22 Cal.Rptr. 216, 225 (1962), cert. denied, 371 U.S. 953, 83 S.Ct. 502, 9 L.Ed.2d 502 (1963).

A person not specifically identified in the contract as a beneficiary may recover on it if he or she belongs to a class of persons for whose benefit the contract is made. Marina Tenants, 226 Cal.Rptr. at 324. If its terms necessarily confer a benefit upon a third person which only that person can enjoy, the person is a third-party beneficiary. Id. at 326 (citing Zigas v. Superior Court, 120 Cal.App.3d 827, 174 Cal.Rptr. 806, 810 (Ct.App.1981), cert. denied, 455 U.S. 943, 102 S.Ct. 1438, 71 L.Ed.2d 655 (1982)) ("[The] requirement of HUD approval of rent increases could only benefit the tenants."). The intent to benefit the third person must be evident from reading the contract as a whole in light of the circumstances under which it was entered. Outdoor Servs., Inc. v. Pabagold, Inc., 185 Cal.App.3d 676, 230 Cal.Rptr. 73, 77 (1986).

Reading the contract as a whole, it is unreasonable to conclude that it was intended solely to benefit potential purchasers of tickets. The plaintiffs do not allege that the Agreement itself was made primarily for their benefit, nor can they. The Agreement was entered to govern a sports event played by some 100 students, and to be attended by thousands of fans and watched by millions. It governs which teams may play, the color of the uniforms they may wear, when bands may play and even the type of football which will be used during the game. It incorporates an agreement granting a television network exhibition rights, and it provides for distribution of Rose Bowl revenues. Whatever duties the named parties to the Agreement could possibly have undertaken with regard to plaintiffs relate solely to plaintiffs as potential spectators of the game, and for that the plaintiffs had to have tickets.

Plaintiffs allege that their interests as potential ticket holders advance their interests to those of third-party beneficiaries. They rely on section 23 of the Agreement to support their contention that they, as prospective ticket holders, are primarily benefited by the limitation in the Agreement fixing the sale price of each ticket to its face value, $46. We reject plaintiffs' analysis of section 23.

The first sentence in section 23(e) provides in relevant part, "[A]ll game tickets shall be sold at full face value and shall be accounted for at full face value by the persons to whom they are consigned." This provision does not benefit only the plaintiffs. It imposes both a ceiling and a floor on ticket prices. The intent to impose a floor is shown by an exception to the "full face value" requirement in a later sentence in subparagraph (e). That sentence permits the member institutions to "establish lower ticket prices for bona fide members of their student bodies." The floor on ticket prices does not benefit the plaintiffs.

Relying on Zigas, 174 Cal.Rptr. at 809, plaintiffs assert that, like the tenants in that case, plaintiffs as prospective ticket purchasers are the intended beneficiaries of the ticket contract provisions of the Agreement. In Zigas, the landlord had a contract with Housing and Urban Development (HUD) which governed the landlord's relationship with his tenants. Id. at 807. The Zigas court held that the tenants were third-party beneficiaries of the contract partly because the purpose of the HUD contract was "narrow and specific: to provide moderate rental housing for families with children." Id. at 812.

Unlike the HUD contract construed in Zigas, section 23(e) of the Rose Bowl Agreement does not have a "narrow and specific" purpose which would benefit only plaintiffs. The provision that tickets be sold at full face value confers no benefit upon plaintiffs that only they may enjoy because it also establishes the minimum price for tickets.

Moreover, section 23(e) of the Agreement has a purpose which is unrelated to any possible benefit to the plaintiffs. The provision that tickets be sold at full face value is critical to the provision in the Agreement that if UCLA fails to sell tickets allotted to it, it must make up the difference in the value of unsold tickets in the accounting between the parties to the Agreement. The full face value sales provision is, as the trial court ruled, a ticket accounting mechanism. Whatever benefit plaintiffs as potential ticket purchasers may enjoy as a result of that provision is only incidental. Persons who enjoy only incidental benefits resulting from an agreement between other parties are not third-party beneficiaries of the contract. RESTATEMENT (SECOND) OF CONTRACTS § 315, cmt. a (1981).

Because the plaintiffs are not third-party beneficiaries of the Agreement, the trial court correctly ruled that they lack standing to sue for its breach. We therefore affirm the ruling that the complaint fails to state a claim for breach of contract.

NEGLIGENCE

Plaintiffs assert that when UCLA sold 4,000 Rose Bowl tickets to one person, the reasonable inference is that the person acted as or supplied the tickets to a broker, and that person or the broker therefore had the power to control the market for Rose Bowl tickets and determine the price of the tickets. This, they assert, disrupted the "normal market" for Rose Bowl tickets. For that reason, Wisconsin fans were unable to buy tickets at a reasonable price or were unable to obtain them at all. Plaintiffs were therefore harmed by UCLA's sale of 4,000 tickets to one person, and it was foreseeable that harm would result from that sale to potential ticket buyers. For that reason, plaintiffs assert UCLA is liable to them for its negligence.

When an alleged tort is related to a contract, a duty must exist independently of the performance of the contract for a cause of action in tort to exist. Madison Newspapers, Inc. v. Pinkerton's, Inc., 200 Wis.2d 468, 473, 545 N.W.2d 843, 846 (Ct.App.1996). We ignore the existence of the contract when determining whether the alleged conduct is actionable in tort. Id.

Plaintiffs' negligence theory is consistent with Wisconsin law. The duty of a person alleged to have been negligent under Wisconsin law is stated in A.E. Investment Corp. v. Link Builders, Inc., 62 Wis.2d 479, 483–84, 214 N.W.2d 764, 766 (1974):

> The duty of any person [alleged to have been negligent] is the obligation of due care to refrain from any act which will cause foreseeable harm to others even though the nature of that harm and the identity of the harmed person or harmed interest is unknown at the time of the act. This is the view of the minority in Palsgraf v. Long Island R.R. Co., (1928) 248 N.Y. 339, 162 N.E. 99. . . .
>
> A defendant's duty is established when it can be said that it was foreseeable that his act or omission to act may cause harm to someone. A party is negligent when he commits an act when some harm to someone is foreseeable. Once negligence is established, the defendant is liable for unforeseeable consequences as well as foreseeable ones. In addition, he is liable to unforeseeable plaintiffs.

In this state, a negligent defendant is liable for economic loss. Citizens State Bank v. Timm, Schmidt & Co., 113 Wis.2d 376, 384–85, 335 N.W.2d 361, 365 (1983); A.E. Investment Corp. v. Link Builders, Inc., 62 Wis.2d at 490–91, 214 N.W.2d at 770; Hap's Aerial Enters. v. General Aviation, 173 Wis.2d 459, 460, 496 N.W.2d 680, 681 (Ct.App. 1992).

However, although Wisconsin negligence law makes the tortfeasor totally liable for all foreseeable and unforeseeable consequences of a negligent act, a court may limit or preclude that liability for public policy reasons. Timm, 113 Wis.2d at 386, 335 N.W.2d at 366; Morgan v.

Pennsylvania Gen. Ins. Co., 87 Wis.2d 723, 737, 275 N.W.2d 660, 667 (1979). Ordinarily an appellate court will not decide public policy issues before a full factual resolution of the claims at trial. Coffey v. City of Milwaukee, 74 Wis.2d 526, 542, 247 N.W.2d 132, 140 (1976). But it is not always necessary to have a full trial before deciding the public policy question. Schuster v. Altenberg, 144 Wis.2d 223, 241, 424 N.W.2d 159, 166 (1988); Wilson v. Continental Ins. Co., 87 Wis.2d 310, 324, 274 N.W.2d 679, 686 (1979); Rieck v. Medical Protective Co., 64 Wis.2d 514, 520, 219 N.W.2d 242, 245 (1974).

UCLA contends that under California law, it owed no duty to plaintiffs with respect to their negligence claim. Under California law, "an indispensable factor to liability founded upon negligence is the existence of a duty of care owed by the alleged wrongdoer to the person injured, or to a class of which he is a member." Richards v. Stanley, 43 Cal.2d 60, 271 P.2d 23, 25–26 (1954) (holding defendant who left car unattended and unlocked with the ignition key in the lock had no duty to plaintiffs who suffered injury after thief stole defendant's car and collided with plaintiffs). Because plaintiffs do not dispute the contention in their reply, we assume plaintiffs cannot recover under California law. Madison Teachers, Inc. v. Madison Metro. Sch. Dist., 197 Wis.2d 731, 751, 541 N.W.2d 786, 794 (Ct.App.1995). If plaintiffs cannot recover under Wisconsin law, however, no conflict exists between the laws of the two states. We conclude that for public policy reasons, plaintiffs cannot recover against UCLA for its negligence.

In this state, recovery may be denied against a negligent defendant on grounds of public policy when: (1) the negligence is too remote from the injury; (2) the injury is wholly out of proportion to the culpability of the negligent tortfeasor; (3) in retrospect, it appears highly extraordinary that the negligence should have led to the harm; (4) allowance of recovery would place an unreasonable burden on the negligent tortfeasor; (5) allowance of recovery would likely open the door to fraudulent claims; or (6) allowance of recovery would enter a field having no sensible stopping point. Coffey, 74 Wis.2d at 541, 247 N.W.2d at 140.

Because the demand for Rose Bowl tickets exceeded the number of available tickets, UCLA could not have prevented harm to at least some potential buyers, no matter what it did and no matter what the price at which it sold the tickets and no matter what the sale mechanics. If we were to allow plaintiffs to recover in negligence against UCLA, no rational stopping point would exist.

To allow recovery would place an unreasonable burden on UCLA. Unless bound by statute or contract, a seller may generally rely upon supply and demand to fix the price to allocate a scarce commodity among consumers. For us to allow recovery here would tell sellers that they cannot rely upon supply and demand for that purpose. Plaintiffs do not suggest an alternative method of allocation. We have already held that UCLA had no contractual duty to plaintiffs and no statute has been shown to apply. Perhaps allocation could have been achieved by a lottery, but the impracticability of that method needs no further comment.

Because we conclude that plaintiffs in this case cannot recover under Wisconsin law, and because it is agreed they cannot recover under California law, we conclude that, regardless which state's law applies, plaintiffs cannot recover against UCLA on their negligence claim.

Conspiracy

No difference between the California and Wisconsin law of conspiracy has been brought to our attention. We therefore apply Wisconsin law.

Wisconsin defines a civil conspiracy as " 'a combination of two or more persons by some concerted action to accomplish some unlawful purpose or to accomplish by unlawful means some purpose not in itself unlawful.' " Cranston v. Bluhm, 33 Wis.2d 192, 198, 147 N.W.2d 337, 340 (1967) (quoted source omitted). To state a cause of action for civil conspiracy, the complaint must set forth the formation and operation of the conspiracy, the wrongful act or acts done pursuant to the conspiracy and the resultant damage from such acts. Onderdonk v. Lamb, 79 Wis.2d 241, 247, 255 N.W.2d 507, 510 (1977).

The only allegation in the complaint expressly referring to a conspiracy is that UCLA "engaged in combinations and conspiracies to violate the Rose Bowl Agreement and which were otherwise unlawful in act or purpose."

UCLA cannot conspire with itself. No co-conspirator is named or described in the complaint. The allegation that UCLA put tickets in the hands of scalpers does not establish that UCLA conspired with them. Similarly, the allegation that UCLA sold 4,000 tickets to an individual when it knew or should have known the tickets would be sold at a price greater than face value fails to show that UCLA conspired with that person. The acts of UCLA, the scalpers and the individual buyer are not alleged to have a nexus other than UCLA's sales to them. Thus, no concerted action is alleged. We need not pursue our analysis further.

We conclude the trial court properly dismissed plaintiffs' conspiracy charge against UCLA for failure to state a claim.

Interference With Contract

The parties appear to agree that no choice of law problem exists with regard to plaintiffs' claim that UCLA has interfered with their contractual relations with their tour operators who arranged travel packages for the plaintiffs. Both Wisconsin and California recognize the tort of interference with prospective economic relations. Della Penna v. Toyota Motor Sales, U.S.A. Inc., 11 Cal.4th 376, 45 Cal.Rptr.2d 436, 437, 902 P.2d 740, 741 (1995); Cudd v. Crownhart, 122 Wis.2d 656, 658–59, 364 N.W.2d 158, 160 (Ct.App.1985).

The elements of the tort are: a prospective contractual relationship on behalf of the plaintiff, knowledge by the defendant of the existence of the relationship, intentional acts on the part of the defendant to disrupt the relationship, actual disruption of the relationship, and damages to the plaintiff caused by those acts. Compare Della Penna, 45 Cal.Rptr.2d at 444, 902 P.2d at 748 (citing Buckaloo v. Johnson, 14 Cal.3d 815, 122 Cal.Rptr. 745, 752, 537 P.2d 865, 872 (1975)) with Cudd, 122 Wis.2d at 659–60, 364 N.W.2d at 160, and RESTATEMENT (SECOND) OF TORTS § 766B.

Plaintiffs' theory expressed in their brief is that they had prospective and existing contractual relationships with the tour operators consisting of the plaintiffs' purchases and prospective purchases of tickets as part of travel packages for the Rose Bowl game. The theory continues as follows: UCLA knew of the existence of the demand for tickets by Wisconsin fans and the shortage of those tickets; UCLA "engaged in intentional acts to disrupt the purchase of tickets by Wisconsin fans as part of the travel packages by disrupting the market for tickets"; plaintiffs' relationships with tour operators were disrupted; and damages resulted to the plaintiffs.

However, the closest the complaint comes to alleging an intentional interference by UCLA with a contractual or prospective contractual relationship between the plaintiffs and tour operators is the following:

> The reason that [Rose Bowl] tickets were unavailable to the class was that substantial numbers of tickets were placed in the hands of scalpers who inflated the ticket prices to the extent that the tours were unable to purchase tickets at the price previously represented to the tour operators and thus prevented the operators from providing the tickets to the class as represented.

The complaint alleges that UCLA was "directly responsible for placing the tickets in the hands of scalpers" by [the] described action. Nothing in the complaint, however, alleges that UCLA took those actions for the purpose of interfering with contracts between the plaintiffs and the tour operators.

We conclude the complaint fails to state a claim for interference in plaintiffs' contractual relations with the tour operators.

Conclusion

Because we conclude that the complaint fails to state a claim, we affirm. UCLA has moved for costs and attorney's fees under Rule 809.25(3), Stats., on the grounds that this appeal is frivolous. We deny the motion.

SUNDBY, Judge (dissenting).

University of Wisconsin football fans are among the most dedicated in the country. There was a rumor that when they arrived in Pasadena and were denied admission to the Rose Bowl, there was strong sentiment to storm the "Bastille." We now deny them redress against the culpable party, UCLA. We say that UCLA owed no duty to the University of Wisconsin and Badger fans to live up to its commitment under the agreement between the Big Ten Conference and the PAC–10 Conference.

We say the contract may not be enforced for their benefit. I disagree and dissent.

The "fans" make a good point: If not them, then who? The Big Ten could sue UCLA for breach of the contract. But what would be its damages? The parties damaged would be the fans who lost access to the tickets which should have been allocated to Wisconsin but were allocated by UCLA to others to further ends having nothing to do with the sporting event. For example, UCLA "sold" 4,000 tickets to a deep-pockets donor and 1,233 [sic] tickets to persons on condition that they buy UCLA 1994 season tickets. These shenanigans denied Wisconsin fans an opportunity to purchase tickets or obtain the tickets they believed they had purchased.

When I went into oral argument, I was persuaded by the argument that California's statute required an "express" declaration of intent of the parties to benefit a third person. Clearly, that is incorrect, so we are back to analyzing whether prospective fans and ticket purchasers are third-party beneficiaries of the contract between the two conferences and the management committee. I conclude that they are.

Another issue in this case which we have not reached is whether plaintiffs can maintain a cause of action against UCLA or must first resort to arbitration. This issue was raised at oral argument but has not been briefed. The Big Ten/PAC–10 contract requires arbitration. The law is so well established that a contract which requires arbitration must be honored that a request for additional briefing would be a waste of judicial resources. The cases seem to be unanimous in holding that a third-party beneficiary is subject to the same terms of the contract as the promisee. See, e.g., Mayflower Ins. Co. v. Pellegrino, 212 Cal.App.3d 1326, 261 Cal.Rptr. 224, 226–27 (1989); Harris v. Superior Court, 188 Cal.App.3d 475, 233 Cal.Rptr. 186, 188 (Ct.App.1986); Raffa Assocs., Inc. v. Boca Raton Resort & Club, 616 So.2d 1096, 1097 (Fla.Dist.Ct.App. 1993); Zac Smith & Co. v. Moonspinner Condominium Ass'n, 472 So.2d 1324, 1324–25 (Fla.Dist.Ct.App.1985); District Moving & Storage Co. v. Gardiner & Gardiner, Inc., 63 Md.App. 96, 492 A.2d 319, 322–23 (1985), aff'd, 306 Md. 286, 508 A.2d 487 (1986).

Notes

1. In addition to charging top dollar, ticket scalpers sometimes try to pass off counterfeit tickets as genuine. This, of course, is a crime in every jurisdiction. *See further United States v. Zabare*, 871 F.2d 282 (2d Cir.), *cert. denied*, 493 U.S. 856 (1989); *United States v. Sieger*, 1985 WL 565 (S.D.N.Y. 1985); *United States v. Jones*, 432 F.Supp. 801 (E.D.Pa.1977), *aff'd*, 571 F.2d 154 (3d Cir.), *cert. denied*, 435 U.S. 956 (1978).

2. While ticket scalping is a problem at many sports venues, it is particularly acute at Madison Square Garden, the fabled home of the New York Knicks and the New York Rangers. As a result, Garden officials employ numerous countermeasures, including around-the-clock security, limiting the number of tickets any one individual can purchase, issuing wristbands, requiring buyers to show identification, ousting known ticket scalpers from

lines, hiring undercover agents, and refusing to make tickets available at the box office on the first day of sales. *See* Ward Morehouse III, *MSG Nixes 1st-Day Tix Sales in Anti–Scalping Move*, N.Y. Post, May 8, 1998, at 2.

3. Although scalping most often occurs during the playoffs, every so often a game in the middle of the season becomes hot. In June 1998, for example, the New York Yankees and the New York Mets played each other at Shea Stadium. With the Yankees on a roll and the Mets fighting for a wild card berth, brokers were able to command as much as $600 for $20 seats, notwithstanding a state law forbidding the resale of tickets for more than 10% over their face price. *See Yankees–Mets Subway Series Even Hotter Than Last Year*, Atlanta J. & Const., June 24, 1998, at 5E.

4. Scalpers increasingly are selling their wares over the internet. This has raised a host of difficult jurisdictional questions and promises to become increasingly contentious as more consumers find their way on to the web. *See further People v. Concert Connection, Ltd.*, 629 N.Y.S.2d 254 (App.Div.), *appeal dismissed*, 658 N.E.2d 223 (N.Y.1995), and Amy Joyner & Alisa DeMao, *Scalpers Do Healthy Business Despite Law: Ticket Brokers Openly Reselling Masters Badges at High Profits on Web Sites Without Prosecution*, Augusta (GA) Chron., Apr. 6, 1998, at A6.

5. For a further look at scalping, see, e.g., *United States v. Mount*, 966 F.2d 262 (7th Cir.1992) (length of defendant's sentence was properly based on amount baseball team would have lost if ticket scalping plot had been successful); *Nahra v. Coliseum*, 1993 WL 261582 (Ohio Ct.App.), *appeal dismissed*, 621 N.E.2d 408 (Ohio 1993) (person who warned scalper police were in the area had no basis to complain when charged with obstruction of justice); *Barbet v. Edelstein*, 499 A.2d 1106 (Pa.Super.Ct.1985) (partnership to resell Super Bowl tickets for profit not scalping). *See also* Paul J. Criscuolo, Comment, *Reassessing the Ticket Scalping Dispute: The Application, Effects and Criticisms of Current Anti–Scalping Legislation*, 5 Seton Hall J. Sport L. 189 (1995).

Problem 7

In connection with a planned job transfer, a lawyer has applied for admission to the bar of her new state. The Character & Fitness Committee has recommended her request be denied because she once was convicted of buying scalped tickets (for which she received a suspended sentence). If the attorney appeals the committee's recommendation to the state's supreme court, will she be admitted? *See Florida Bar v. Levin*, 570 So.2d 917 (Fla.1990), *cert. denied*, 501 U.S. 1250 (1991).

C. STADIUMS

Ballparks can be places of unparalleled fun and excitement. They also can be sites of intense strife and turmoil.

1. CONSTRUCTION

Because of their hefty price tag, proposals to build new stadiums often end up being challenged in court. As will be seen, such suits rarely succeed.

COUNCIL OF THE CITY OF NEW YORK v. GIULIANI

679 N.Y.S.2d 14 (App.Div.),
leave to appeal denied, 703 N.E.2d 760 (N.Y.1998).

PER CURIAM.

Over the past few months, Mayor Rudolph W. Giuliani (henceforth "the Mayor") has publicly supported the construction of a new baseball stadium for the New York Yankees in Manhattan. In April of this year, Peter F. Vallone (henceforth "the Speaker"), the Speaker of the Council of the City of New York (henceforth "the Council"), announced an intent to create a voter referendum that would block the Mayor's plan to relocate the Yankees. The proposal, Introductory No. 335 (referred to herein as "Int. 335"), which was designed to be placed on the ballot at the November 3, 1998 general election, would prohibit New York City officials from spending public funds on the construction of a new stadium for the Yankees in Manhattan.

Subsequently, the Mayor stated his intention to create a new Charter Revision Commission (henceforth "the Commission") which would re-examine and possibly amend or replace the City Charter. The Council and the Mayor had put forward proposals for Charter Revision Commissions during the previous winter but had ultimately deferred consideration of the issue. The Mayor's decision to revive the Charter revision idea was admittedly motivated in part by a desire to outmaneuver the Council's referendum plan. Under Municipal Home Rule Law ("MHRL") § 36(5)(e), the placement on the ballot of a validly derived proposal initiated by a Charter Revision Commission will "bump" any other referendum off the ballot, so that the voters can give their full attention to the important task of reviewing the City Charter.

The Commission announced a broad agenda in June 1998, but this agenda was subsequently narrowed to a single topic. Originally, the Commission's stated plan was to consider changes to the Charter provisions relating to land use and economic development, procurement of goods and services, budget efficiency, campaign finance, nonpartisan elections for City officials, and a review of the functions of various City offices, as well as other unspecified issues. Suggested revisions, if any, would be presented to the voters in November.

However, the result of the Commission's first and second public hearings was a decision to defer consideration of all but three issues: campaign finance reform, nonpartisan elections, and a requirement of full-time rather than part-time service for City Council members. This decision was adopted at the Commission's first of five public meetings. After the second public meeting, the Commission further narrowed its agenda to focus solely on campaign finance reform, and accordingly conducted public hearings on this topic. At the end of their review process in August, the Commission voted to approve its campaign finance proposals for submission to the voters of New York City in November.

The Commission also voted to continue studying the other issues for the 1999 general election. Although technically the Commission's term of office would expire, pursuant to MHRL § 36(6)(e), on the day of the election for which it submitted a proposal, the Mayor could reappoint the Commission if its work was not complete.

The instant lawsuit arose because the Council and the Speaker (collectively "plaintiffs") challenge the legitimacy of the process by which the proposals of the Charter Revision Commission were formulated. MHRL § 36(5)(a) mandates that the Commission "review the entire charter," and that if the Commission decides to leave any part of the charter unchanged, "it shall make a report to the public, accompanying its proposals, in which it shall refer specifically to such unchanged part and explain its decision to leave such part unchanged." It is plaintiffs' contention that the Commission neither undertook nor intended to undertake a complete review of the charter; rather, plaintiffs claim, the charter review was a charade whose sole purpose was to put some proposal (whatever it might be) on the ballot to displace Int. 335.

The court agreed and granted plaintiffs an injunction barring defendants from placing the Commission's campaign finance reform proposal on the ballot. Because we find that defendants complied with the requirement of complete review of the charter, as defined by the Court of Appeals in Cruz v. Deierlein, 84 N.Y.2d 890, 620 N.Y.S.2d 791, 644 N.E.2d 1347, we hold that plaintiffs were not entitled to a preliminary injunction. In light of this conclusion, we need not reach the parties' other arguments.

A movant's burden of proof on a motion for a preliminary injunction is particularly high. A preliminary injunction may be issued only where the moving party demonstrates a likelihood of success on the merits, the prospect of irreparable harm if the injunction is not granted, and a balance of equities in the moving party's favor (State of New York v. Fine, 72 N.Y.2d 967, 968–969, 534 N.Y.S.2d 357, 530 N.E.2d 1277). This standard was not met here.

Plaintiffs did not show a likelihood of success on the merits. The sole claim which the court upheld, namely plaintiffs' challenge to the completeness of the Commission's review, is not valid. Our conclusion on this point is controlled by Cruz, supra, in which the Court of Appeals applied MHRL § 36(5)(a) to circumstances much like those presented herein. Just as in New York City today, the Mayor and City Council of Yonkers were engaged in a power struggle in which the Mayor appointed a Charter Revision Commission specifically to preempt the City Council's referendum proposal (which would have curtailed certain mayoral powers) from appearing on the ballot. The Yonkers Commission's report stated that it had examined the entire Charter and decided not to change the balance of the Charter because several topics needed significant further study. As a result, the Yonkers Commission only proposed two amendments to the existing Charter. Its report discussed the history and rationales for those provisions in detail (id. at 892–893, 620 N.Y.S.2d 791, 644 N.E.2d 1347).

The Yonkers City Clerk refused to place the Yonkers Commission's proposals on the ballot, alleging that the Commission had not undertaken a complete review of the Charter. The Court of Appeals, however, found the Yonkers Commission's scope of review to be sufficient (id. at 892, 620 N.Y.S.2d 791, 644 N.E.2d 1347).

The material facts of the instant case are similar to Cruz in many respects. First, in both cases, the Mayor appointed the Commission partly to curtail the City Council's power to place its referendum before the voters. This motivation was implicitly deemed legitimate by the Court of Appeals. Moreover, in Di Prima v. Wagner, 14 A.D.2d 36, 40, 215 N.Y.S.2d 705, affd. 10 N.Y.2d 728, 219 N.Y.S.2d 272, 176 N.E.2d 839, this court upheld the predecessor of MHRL § 36(5)(e), even though that statute raised the real possibility that a politically motivated Mayor might instigate a charter review out of a desire to block local legislation rather than solely out of a "pure" desire to revise the Charter.

The court herein wrongly second-guessed the Commission's assertion that it had conducted a thorough review. It is not a court's place to speculate how much the Commission's action was due to an alleged Mayoral desire to put something on the ballot at all costs, versus the Commission's professed sense that the urgent problem of campaign finance reform required an immediate response even though other Charter sections still remained to be explored. The latter is plausible because a different campaign finance proposal was pending before the City Council. The Commission's report here noted that immediate action was necessary since some candidates for municipal office had already begun fund raising for the 2001 elections. Similarly, in Cruz, the Yonkers Commission focused its review on certain problems because the City Council's proposed Local Laws, if passed, would have codified a different solution to those problems.

Further, under Cruz it is legitimate for the Commission to present only a limited number of amendments and defer the remainder for further study in the hopes that the Commission will be reappointed to continue its work (see, Cruz, supra, at 893, 620 N.Y.S.2d 791, 644 N.E.2d 1347). It also appears that notwithstanding the seemingly strict language of MHRL § 36(5)(a), the Court of Appeals has concluded that a Commission need not enumerate every single section of the Charter in support of its decision to leave such sections unchanged.

The Commission's report herein, which was more than twice the length of the one in Cruz, enumerates various reasons for its conclusion, including: the fact that the Charter had already been extensively overhauled in 1989; concerns voiced at the public hearings that the Commission would need a long time to study many of the proposed issues; and the aforementioned need to implement a new campaign financing scheme in time for municipal candidates to come into compliance therewith. As in Cruz, the report discussed the history and reasoning behind the proposed amendments at length. Additionally, with respect to the other topics that the Commission had initially announced an intent to review, the report detailed the Commission's findings on each issue and buttressed the Commission's conclusion that these topics needed further study.

We also note that plaintiffs failed to demonstrate irreparable injury. Even if Int. 335 did not appear on the ballot, the Mayor could not unilaterally decree that public funds should be spent on a new stadium, absent the City Council's budgetary and land-use powers.

Since we find that the Commission's campaign finance proposal was validly derived, pursuant to MHRL § 36(5)(e), it must take precedence over Int. 335, which will thus not appear on the ballot this November. Accordingly, we dismiss as academic defendants' cross-motion for summary judgment declaring Int. 335 invalid as an illegal exercise of the City Council's powers.

All concur.

KING COUNTY v. TAXPAYERS OF KING COUNTY

949 P.2d 1260 (Wash.1997),
cert. denied, 118 S.Ct. 854 (1998).

TALMADGE, Justice.

This is the third of a series of challenges to state legislation and local implementing ordinances for financing and constructing a new baseball stadium in King County. We are asked in this action to determine if King County's issuance of $336 million in bonds to finance stadium construction is "valid" under RCW 7.25. To determine validity, we must decide if the lease between the Mariners and the public facilities district is an unconstitutional gift of public monies to a private organization; if the taxes authorized by the Legislature to pay for the stadium financing bonds are constitutionally imposed and properly collected; if the state unconstitutionally delegated legislative authority to the public facilities district; and if a proposed local initiative establishing more stringent debt limitations for King County than authorized by statute is applicable to the baseball stadium project.

We hold the bonds issued by King County to finance stadium construction are valid because the use of public funds for a new baseball stadium here is not an unconstitutional gift of public monies to a private organization. Moreover, the taxes imposed to pay for the bonds are constitutionally imposed and properly collected. The state properly delegated authority to the public facilities district. The proposed local initiative is invalid insofar as it attempts to impose additional limitations on local debt not authorized by statute. We therefore affirm the trial court's declaratory judgment validating the $336 million in stadium construction bonds issued by King County.

Issues

1. What is the test for establishing the validity of bonds in a declaratory judgment action under RCW 7.25?

2. Did the lease entered into by the parties here constitute an unconstitutional gift of public funds to a private organization?

3. Were the taxes authorized by the Legislature to pay for the stadium financing bonds constitutionally imposed and handled?

4. Did the Legislature unconstitutionally delegate legislative authority to the District?

5. Can King County establish by ordinance limitations on debt beyond requirements set forth in [the] statute?

FACTS

The Baseball Club of Seattle, L.P. (Mariners), is a Washington limited partnership formed in early 1992 for the express purpose of acquiring the Seattle Mariners Baseball Club to keep it in Seattle. Soon after acquiring the team, the Mariners began meeting with King County officials to modify the Kingdome lease and develop long-term capital plans. In 1994, a King County task force developed a plan for a new home for the Mariners, to be completed by 1999.

The 1995 Legislature considered legislation authorizing the financing of the new Mariners baseball stadium, ultimately enacting a baseball financing program at a special session on October 14, 1995. Laws of 1995, 3rd Sp. Sess., ch. 1 (Stadium Act). The key provision of the Stadium Act permits the "legislative authority" of a county with a population of one million or more to impose a sales and use tax in addition to other taxes under RCW 82.14, not to exceed .017 percent of the selling price in the case of a sales tax, or value of the article used in the case of a use tax. RCW 82.14.0485(1). The Court rejected numerous constitutional challenges to the Stadium Act in CLEAN v. State, 130 Wash.2d 782, 928 P.2d 1054 (1996).

Thereafter, Metropolitan King County Council (Council) on October 25, 1995 enacted Ordinance 12000, creating the Washington State Major League Baseball Stadium Public Facilities District (District), and imposing three special sales and use taxes the Stadium Act authorized, including a .017 percent special stadium sales and use tax, a special stadium sales and use tax on restaurants, bars, and taverns, and a special stadium sales and use tax on car rentals. The special stadium sales and use tax is a credit against the statewide sales and use tax as both RCW 82.14.0485(2) and section 3 of Ordinance 12000 acknowledge. Under the Stadium Act, the revenues from these taxes may be used only to finance the stadium. RCW 84.14.0485(3). The purpose of the District is to construct and operate the new stadium. The Court rejected challenges to Ordinance 12000 in Citizens for More Important Things v. King County, 131 Wash.2d 411, 932 P.2d 135 (1997).

Pursuant to the comprehensive financing mechanism established by the Stadium Act and Ordinance 12000, the District by letter dated January 2, 1997, requested King County to issue bonds in the amount of $336 million, the amount necessary to finance construction of the baseball stadium. The Council passed Ordinance 12593 on January 6,

1997, authorizing the issuance of limited tax general obligation bonds in the requested amount.

Subsequently, on April 2, 1997, the Council passed Ordinance 12686, providing for the issuance and sale of the bonds. The County has already sold the bonds, but the bond sale proceeds are being held in escrow for release or refund, awaiting our decision in this action.

In addition to court challenges to the stadium, baseball stadium opponents have employed other methods to invalidate the stadium funding and construction bonds. On December 4, 1996, opponents filed a proposed initiative petition with the clerk of the Council. The clerk certified the petition as Initiative 16 on December 31, 1996. Section 1 of the initiative provides:

> On or after January 1, 1997, King County shall not issue bonds or otherwise incur debt in an amount in excess of $50,000,000 for construction, remodeling, maintenance, or operation of any building or other facility without first obtaining approval of a majority of voters voting in an election at which the number of voters voting in said election equals at least one-half of the number of voters who are registered to vote at that election; nor shall King County impose or levy any tax to pay any such bond or indebtedness without such voter approval.

Initiative 16 purports retroactively to invalidate Ordinances 12593 and 12686, which, respectively, authorized and issued bonds in an amount in excess of $50 million. Intervenors in this case also filed a referendum petition with the Council clerk on January 7, 1997, proposing that Ordinance 12593 (authorizing issuance of the bonds) be put to a public vote. The Council clerk, based on advice from the King County Prosecuting Attorney's office that Ordinance 12593 was not subject to referendum, did not process the referendum petition.

On January 21, 1997, the County filed a complaint seeking a declaratory judgment under RCW 7.25.020 validating the bonds. Specifically, the County sought a declaration:

> a. confirming the right and authority of King County to issue and sell bonds described in King County Ordinance No. 12593 (the "Bond Ordinance") ... adopted pursuant to the provisions of the [Stadium] Act and Ordinance No. 12000, and that such issuance comports with the requirements of the state constitution, state statutes and is within the County's authority;
>
> b. determining that Initiative 16 is inapplicable to the issuance of the Bonds as authorized by the Bond Ordinance;
>
> c. determining that the Bond Ordinance was lawfully enacted and not subject to referendum.

On February 19, 1997, the trial court heard cross-motions for summary judgment. By memorandum decision dated February 24, 1997, the trial court granted the County's motion for summary judgment and denied the defendants' motion. The trial court entered a declaratory judgment in favor of the County on February 26, 1997, holding the bonds were valid and Initiative 16, if enacted, would "irreconcilably conflict" with state law. On March 26, 1997, after losing their motion for reconsideration, the Taxpayers filed a notice of appeal. We accepted direct review. RAP 4.2(b).

Analysis

The Taxpayers initially contend the bond issue violates Const. art. VIII, §§ 5 and 7. The two sections provide:

> § 5 Credit Not To Be Loaned. The credit of the state shall not, in any manner be given or loaned to, or in aid of, any individual, association, company or corporation.
>
> § 7 Credit Not To Be Loaned. No county, city, town or other municipal corporation shall hereafter give any money, or property, or loan its money, or credit to or in aid of any individual, association, company or corporation, except for the necessary support of the poor and infirm, or become directly or indirectly the owner of any stock in or bonds of any association, company or corporation.

"The 'aid' is in the form of construction at public expense of a new place of business for the [Mariners] to enhance its chance of making money." Brief of Appellants at 9.

At oral argument, counsel for the Taxpayers advanced the view that any benefit to a private organization may be violative of these constitutional provisions. We disagree. As we stated in City of Tacoma v. Taxpayers of Tacoma, 108 Wash.2d 679, 701–02, 743 P.2d 793 (1987), our purpose in that case was to narrow the application of these constitutional provisions to remedy more precisely "the evils the framers sought to prevent." An incidental benefit to a private individual or organization will not invalidate an otherwise valid public transaction. Id. at 705, 743 P.2d 793.

We held in CLEAN the stadium financing plan "does not amount to a gift of state funds nor a lending of the State's credit." CLEAN, 130 Wash.2d at 800, 928 P.2d 1054. We suggested, however, that should the District "enter into an agreement with the Mariners that would permit the ball club to play its games in the stadium for only nominal rent, then the constitutional prohibitions against making a gift of state funds might be implicated." Id. This discussion in CLEAN is essentially the test for an unconstitutional gift of public funds we have articulated in numerous cases.

In deciding whether a public expenditure is a gift under art. VIII, §§ 5 and 7, we have focused on two factors: consideration and donative intent. City of Tacoma v. Taxpayers of Tacoma, 108 Wash.2d 679, 702, 743 P.2d 793 (1987). Thus, to meet the burden of showing violation of the constitutional prohibition against gifts, the Taxpayers must show the lease amounts to "a transfer of property without consideration and with donative intent." General Tel. Co. v. City of Bothell, 105 Wash.2d 579, 588, 716 P.2d 879 (1986).

In assessing consideration, courts do not inquire into the adequacy of consideration, but employ a legal sufficiency test. Adams v. University of Wash., 106 Wash.2d 312, 327, 722 P.2d 74 (1986); Northlake Marine Works, Inc. v. City of Seattle, 70 Wash.App. 491, 857 P.2d 283 (1993). We have been reluctant to engage in an in-depth analysis of the adequacy of consideration because such an analysis interferes unduly with governmental power to contract and would establish a "burdensome precedent" of judicial interference with government decisionmaking. City of Tacoma v. Taxpayers of Tacoma, 108 Wash.2d at 703, 743 P.2d 793.

Legal sufficiency "is concerned not with comparative value but with that which will support a promise." Browning v. Johnson, 70 Wash.2d 145, 147, 422 P.2d 314, amended, 430 P.2d 591 (1967) ("'[A]nything which fulfills the requirements of consideration will support a promise whatever may be the comparative value of the consideration, and of the thing promised.' 1 WILLISTON, CONTRACTS § 115, cited in Puget Mill Co. v. Kerry, 183 Wash. 542, 558, 49 P.2d 57, 64, 100 A.L.R. 1220 (1935)."). The adequacy of the consideration for the lease is a question of law. Nationwide Mut. Fire Ins. Co. v. Watson, 120 Wash.2d 178, 195, 840 P.2d 851 (1992).

The Taxpayers now argue the lease agreement between the District and the Mariners for the use of the new stadium provides for only nominal rent and grossly inadequate consideration, thus implicating the constitutional concern about gifts of state money we mentioned in CLEAN. The Taxpayers argue both donative intent and grossly inadequate return are present here.

A summary review of both the Stadium Act's requirements and the elements of the lease identifies the Mariners' obligations. The Stadium Act required (1) a commitment from the Mariners to play at least 90 percent of its games at the new stadium for the length of the term of the bonds; (2) a contribution of $45 million towards either pre-construction or construction costs of the stadium or associated facilities; and (3) profit-sharing with the District for the term of the bonds of profit earned after accounting for team losses after the effective date of the Act. RCW 82.14.360(4). These provisions all appeared in the lease.

The lease between the Mariners and the District contains the following additional obligations of the Mariners:

- payment of $700,000 in rent per annum
- payment of any construction cost overruns
- payment of any deficiencies on bonds for the parking facility
- maintenance and operation of the ballpark as a "first-class facility" in accordance with a management plan, and with oversight by the District, with enforcement mechanisms to ensure compliance

- making major repairs and capital improvements to the ballpark
- provision of insurance.

Despite the Mariners' obligations under the lease, the Taxpayers call the lease "unconscionable," Brief of Appellants at 24–25, arguing the consideration for the lease in favor of the County is so grossly inadequate the building of the stadium at public expense amounts to an unconstitutional gift. The Taxpayers assert the County will receive nothing in return for its investment; thus, donative intent is present here. This assertion is simply another way of stating their main point: that the lease is so much in favor of the Mariners, it amounts to a gift. In CLEAN, the Court said, "In our judgment, a plain reading of the Stadium Act reveals no intent by the Legislature to donate public funds to the Seattle Mariners." CLEAN, 130 Wash.2d at 799, 928 P.2d 1054. The County and the District, in issuing bonds pursuant to the Stadium Act, have implemented the Stadium Act by obtaining the statutorily required commitments from the Mariners. No donative intent is present here.

The Taxpayers assert the Mariners' obligations under the lease are a "sham and illusory," and "truly do not give the public anything of value." Brief of Appellants at 26. Their arguments do not bear close scrutiny in light of the Mariners' contribution of $45 million to the project, the profit-sharing provision, the 20–year lease obligation, the stadium maintenance requirement, and their obligation to pay insurance.

The Taxpayers say the $45 million will not come out of the pockets of the Mariners, but rather "from revenues of the ballpark owned by the [District]." Brief of Appellants at 27; Clerk's Papers at 104. This argument is without merit. Whether the money comes out of the Mariners' coffers or from income the Mariners would have otherwise received, the Mariners will contribute $45 million.

The Taxpayers claim the profit sharing requirement in the lease is an "illusion," because the Mariners can doctor their books to pump up expenses as offsets to revenues in a way that will never show a profit. Brief of Appellants at 27. The County responds by noting the lease requires the Mariners' payments and expenses "be determined in accordance with generally accepted accounting principles[, GAAP]" Clerk's Papers at 151, and that the County has the right to audit the Mariners' accounting to ensure compliance with GAAP. Moreover, the mere possibility the Mariners may breach its promise in the future on its obligation to share profits with the County does not make this provision of the lease illusory. "An illusory promise is one which according to its terms makes performance optional with the promisor." Mithen v. Board of Trustees of Cent. Wash. State College, 23 Wash.App. 925, 932, 599 P.2d 8 (1979). The Mariners made an enforceable promise to share profits. The promise is not illusory.

The Taxpayers argue "the Club's promise to do business in the new ballpark is illusory because it has escape routes through the lease conditions[.]" Brief of Appellants at 28. The Taxpayers' argument is disingenuous. The cited pages of the lease do not provide "escape" provisions that allow the Mariners to leave of their own volition. They merely set forth certain obligations of the District, which, if not met, would allow the Mariners to terminate the lease. There are no escape routes that make illusory the Mariners' promise to play 90 percent of their games in the new stadium over the term of the lease. The Taxpayers neglect to mention the $700,000 annual rental due from the Mariners.

The Taxpayers contend the Mariners' agreement to be exclusively responsible for operations and maintenance of the ballpark is insignificant because the lease's definition of operations and maintenance does not include replacement or major repair. While the Operations and Maintenance section of the lease does not contain a repair obligation, the Major Maintenance and Capital Improvements section of the lease does. The Mariners agree to perform "all Major Maintenance and Capital Improvements so that the Ballpark is maintained in a manner consistent with [a first-class facility]." Clerk's Papers at 156. "Major Maintenance and Capital Improvements" is defined to include "any work that is reasonably required to be performed ... to repair, restore or replace components of the [Ballpark] necessitated by any damage, destruction, ordinary wear and tear, defects in construction or design, or any other cause, to the condition required for consistency with [a first-class facility]." Clerk's Papers at 156–57. This obligation is substantial, particularly given the very recent history of very substantial public expenditures to repair the Kingdome roof.

Finally, the Taxpayers assert without argument the requirement to maintain insurance is for the benefit of the Mariners. In fact, the insurance the lease requires the Mariners to procure must protect the District "from all claims arising as a result of the ownership, use, management and operation of the [stadium]." Clerk's Papers at 175. The Mariners are required to name the District as an additional insured on its liability policy. Such insurance is obviously not for the Mariners' sole benefit.

At its core, the Taxpayers' argument is the District and the County made a bad deal. While that may or may not be true, "The wisdom of the King County plan is not for the consideration of this court—its constitutionality is." Louthan v. King County, 94 Wash.2d 422, 427, 617 P.2d 977 (1980). The Taxpayers have failed to demonstrate a constitutional infirmity under Const. art. VIII, §§ 5 and 7. The Taxpayers' assertion the Mariners' promises pursuant to the lease are illusory is unsupported. In the absence of donative intent or grossly inadequate return, the Court's review is limited to the legal sufficiency of the consideration for the lease. City of Tacoma v. Taxpayers of Tacoma, 108 Wash.2d at 703, 743 P.2d 793. This lease met the test of legal sufficiency. No violation of art. VIII, §§ 5 or 7 of our constitution is present here.

[The remainder of the court's opinion, as well as the dissent of Justice Sanders, is omitted.]

Notes

1. As these cases demonstrate, courts believe whether a new stadium should be built is a political rather than a judicial question. As a result, it is not surprising that challenges to stadium funding plans nearly always fail. *See further* Emeline C. Acton & Mary Helen Campbell, *Public Funding of Sports Stadiums and Other Recreational Facilities: Can the Deal be "Too Sweet"?*, 27 Stetson L. Rev. 877 (1998).

2. Deep disagreement exists over whether the Yankees need a new stadium and, if so, whether it should be located in the Bronx or Manhattan. In April 1998, several months before the court's ruling in *Giuliani*, the issue became national news when a 500–pound steel beam came loose and crashed 30 feet to the ground. After a thorough inspection, however, city engineers declared the 75–year-old stadium completely safe. *See* Paul Rogers, *Yankee Stadium Back in Business—Damage Repaired, Fans Return*, Northern N.J. Record, Apr. 25, 1998, at A1.

Interestingly, just a few months later, the New York Islanders moved out of their home, the 26–year-old Nassau Veterans Memorial Coliseum, claiming it was unsafe. When engineers hired by Spectacor Management Group, the arena's operator, concluded otherwise, the Islanders were forced to return. *See further* Anthony McCarron, *Judge: Isles Must Play at Coliseum*, N.Y. Daily News, Sept. 30, 1998, at 64.

3. Stadiums are being erected at an astonishing pace. In the 1960s, $500 million was devoted to new sports facilities. In the 1970s, the figure was $1.5 billion, the same as in the 1980s. By contrast, in the 1990s a total of $8 billion will be expended on such construction, with most of the money being spent between 1996 and 1999. *See further* Daniel J. Lathrope, *Federal Tax Policy, Tax Subsidies, and the Financing of Professional Sports Facilities*, 38 S. Tex. L. Rev. 1147 (1997).

4. One reason for the boom in stadium construction is a movement away from multi-purpose facilities. In the 1960s and 1970s, numerous parks were built to house both baseball and football teams, including the Astrodome in Houston (Astros and Oilers), Busch Stadium in St. Louis (Cardinals and Cardinals), Jack Murphy Stadium in San Diego (Padres and Chargers), the Kingdome in Seattle (Mariners and Seahawks), Riverfront Stadium in Cincinnati (Reds and Bengals), Shea Stadium in New York (Mets and Jets), Three Rivers Stadium in Pittsburgh (Pirates and Steelers), and Veterans Stadium in Philadelphia (Phillies and Eagles). In recent years, however, teams in all sports have increasingly demanded their own stadiums for financial, aesthetic, and scheduling reasons. *See further Make Room for Baby: Building the Second Stadium*, Stadium & Arena Financing, July 27, 1998, at 1. *See also City of New York v. New York Jets Football Club, Inc.*, 394 N.Y.S.2d 799 (Sup.Ct.1977) (in clash over game dates, Jets had to defer to Mets as primary tenant).

The demand for single-sport stadiums sometimes leads to absurd results. In 1988, for example, the City of Miami built an arena for the NBA's Heat. In 1993, the NHL's Panthers became co-tenants. By 1995, both teams had become openly critical of the facility's small size and lack of luxury boxes. Yet rather than accept a refurbished arena, each demanded and received a new, publicly-financed building. Today, the Miami Arena is home to a minor-league hockey team and South Florida taxpayers are footing the bill for three stadiums. *See further To Learn Why South Florida is Getting a New Hockey Arena in Sunrise When There's a 9–Year–Old Arena in Miami and a Basketball Arena in the Works, Just Look Toward the Bottom Line*, Fort Lauderdale Sun–Sentinel, July 3, 1997, at 2A.

5. Modern stadiums are enormously expensive to build. In addition to direct expenditures, environmental impact studies must be undertaken, zoning variances obtained, land for approach roads and parking lots acquired, and public transportation routes adjusted. As a result, stadiums typically cost between $150 million and $250 million.

Some projects come with a much higher price tag. In March 1998, the expansion Arizona Diamondbacks christened Bank One Ballpark (more commonly known as the BOB), a $354 million stadium that occupies nine city blocks and boasts a retractable roof, a center field swimming pool, and a restaurant run by rock star Alice Cooper. *See further* Sam Walker, *New Stadiums Wedge in Some Sports: Countless Amenities Generate Revenue to Pay the Players*, Rocky Mtn. News, Apr. 5, 1998, at 2G.

Future stadiums are likely to cost even more as teams compete to have the grandest and most elaborate venues. In April 1998, for example, the Mets proposed that New York City build them a $500 million ballpark to replace aging Shea Stadium. Much of the anticipated cost is due to the fact the club wants the stadium to have both a dome and a removable grass playing field. *See* Richard Sandomir, *Mets Unveil Model Stadium: Its Roof Moves, As Does Grass*, N.Y. Times, Apr. 24, 1998, at A3.

6. Despite the advent of domes, swimming pools, smart seats, and virtual reality game rooms, polls consistently find a sufficient number of restrooms is the single most important amenity as far as women fans are concerned. This has led to new stadiums being designed with twice as many female bathrooms as male bathrooms. *See further* Mark Puls, *No More Stalling: New Stadiums to Have More Bathrooms for Women*, Det. News, Jan. 19, 1997, at A1.

7. Unlike in the past, stadiums now must be built in accordance with federal and state disability laws. For a look at the impact these laws are having on the design and construction of sports facilities, see, e.g., *Paralyzed Veterans of America v. D.C. Arena L.P.*, 117 F.3d 579 (D.C.Cir.1997), *cert. denied*, 118 S.Ct. 1184 (1998); *Independent Living Resources v. Oregon Arena Corp.*, 1 F.Supp.2d 1159 (D.Or.1998); *United States v. Ellerbe Becket, Inc.*, 976 F.Supp. 1262 (D.Minn.1997); *Cortez v. National Basketball Ass'n*, 960 F.Supp. 113 (W.D.Tex.1997).

8. Should public money be spent on stadiums for private teams? After years of defeats, opponents of publicly-funded stadiums believe the tide finally is turning in their favor. In May 1997, for example, voters in Columbus, Ohio, rejected a plan to increase the sales tax by half a percent to build arenas for MLS' Crew and the NHL's Blue Jackets. In November 1997, Pittsburgh residents killed off a similar measure that would have provided stadiums for the Pirates and Steelers. More recently, in May 1998 citizens in

the "Triad" region of North Carolina turned down a one percent tax on prepared food and a 50–cent tax on baseball tickets that would have been used to lure the Twins from Minnesota. *See further* Todd Senkiewicz, Comment, *Stadium and Arena Financing: Who Should Pay?*, 8 Seton Hall J. Sport L. 575 (1998), and Charles Mahtesian, *The Stadium Trap*, Governing Mag., May 1998, at 33.

Problem 8

In exchange for $100,000, a minor league baseball team agreed to have its new stadium honor a local law firm. Because there were so many name partners, the townspeople found it easier to simply say "the ballpark." Upset by this fact, the attorneys sued to have the contract rescinded on the grounds of fraud, impossibility, frustration of purpose, and lack of consideration. How should the court rule on these contentions? *See Pilot Air Freight Corp. v. City of Buffalo*, 1996 WL 107101 (W.D.N.Y.1996).

2. LOCATION

One of the most difficult questions that arises when building a stadium is deciding where to put it. In recent times, this issue often has become a witches' brew of politics, class, and race.

LARAMORE v. ILLINOIS SPORTS FACILITIES AUTHORITY

1996 WL 153672 (N.D.Ill.1996).

ANDERSEN, District Judge.

This lawsuit is brought by residents of areas adjoining the site which was selected for the new Comiskey Park, a new stadium for the Chicago White Sox, Ltd. (the "White Sox") baseball team. Plaintiffs allege that the site was selected, and their neighborhood destroyed, for racially discriminatory reasons. Pending before the court is the motion of defendants the Illinois Sports Facilities Authority (the "Authority"), the City of Chicago (the "City"), and the White Sox for summary judgment. For the reasons stated below, we grant the motion for summary judgment.

BACKGROUND

The Decision to Build a New Comiskey Park

By 1984, the White Sox decided that they would have to move out of old Comiskey Park. The White Sox had sunk millions of dollars into repairing the seventy-year-old facility, and more costly repairs would be needed in the future. Moreover, for obvious economic reasons, the White Sox wanted a stadium that met contemporary standards. The team began exploring a variety of options, including a new stadium in the City, the suburbs or in another state.

In 1985, the City began exploring the possibility of a new multipurpose, domed stadium that would be used by both the White Sox and the Chicago Bears at an old railroad site on Roosevelt Road. The White Sox were interested, but the Bears did not want to share a stadium.

Attempts were made in the legislative session that ended in the summer of 1986 to garner some legislative support for a domed stadium, but the idea never got past the talking stage.

Some time during 1986, the White Sox suggested that the City consider the possibility of building a new stadium near the existing facility. Unlike the Roosevelt Road site, the area around Comiskey Park had all of the necessary infrastructure already in place, which meant a savings of at least $50–60 million. Apparently in response to this suggestion, Rob Mier, the City Commissioner for Economic Development, directed Rodrigo del Canto of the City's Planning Department to examine the possibility of putting a stadium near the existing facility.

Rodrigo del Canto and his assistants assumed that the White Sox would continue to play in the old stadium during the two years it would take to build a new one. Thus, the site where the existing stadium stood could not be used for any portion of the new stadium. They also assumed that the new Comiskey would be the same size as the old Comiskey Park. Based on those assumptions, del Canto and his assistants identified three possible sites—one over the Dan Ryan expressway, one north of old Comiskey Park, and one south of old Comiskey Park. The area north of Comiskey Park is the Armour Square Park neighborhood, which consists of Armour Square Park, a park slightly smaller than Comiskey Park which was surrounded by housing occupied by all white residents. The area south of Comiskey Park is South Armour Square, an all African–American neighborhood. To the west is East Bridgeport, which contains a shopping area in an all-white neighborhood. These three areas are all included in the City's 11th Ward.

Building over the Dan Ryan expressway was extremely costly and, therefore, was the least favored alternative. Building on the northern site would have required using Armour Square Park, which was owned by the Chicago Park District. The southern site required the removal of a number of houses and businesses in South Armour Square. In light of its assumption that the new Comiskey Park would be the same size as the existing facility, del Canto and his assistants concluded that the northern and the southern sites were about equally desirable from a physical and economic point of view. However, the southern site was thought to be more politically feasible. A memorandum drafted to discuss the pros and cons of each site warned that if the northern site was chosen "[n]eighborhood, community and preservation groups will strongly disagree to relocation of public park site." On the other hand, the memo stated that there was no evidence of strong community organizations in South Armour Square and that the residents of that neighborhood had little political support.

The assumption made by the Planning Department that the new stadium would be the same size as the old one turned out to be wrong. In fact, the White Sox wanted a contemporary, first-class stadium that was considerably bigger than old Comiskey Park. A bigger stadium made the northern site much more problematical since the footprint of such a stadium was larger than Armour Square Park. That meant either that: (a) the White Sox would have to play somewhere else for two years so that a portion of the site where the old stadium stood could be used for the new one; or (b) a substantial number of houses north of the Park would have to be eliminated to enable the stadium to be built from Armour Square Park northward. Neither alternative was attractive. The only other place to play during construction—Wrigley Field—could not be used for a variety of reasons. The area north of Armour Square Park was more densely populated than the residential area south of Comiskey Park and had houses with greater market value. The area north of the stadium also was zoned residential, while the area to the south was already zoned for manufacturing uses. Moreover, going north meant taking Armour Square Park, which is Chicago Park District property. In addition, the White Sox and the City already owned land to the south, and they did not own any land to the north. In light of the many difficulties associated with the northern site, the White Sox and Al Johnson, Mayor Harold Washington's adviser on stadium issues, assumed in their discussions that if the new stadium was built in the vicinity of old Comiskey Park, it would be constructed to the south of the existing stadium.

Passage of the Illinois Sports Facilities Act

After the 1986 legislative session ended without any progress being made on a stadium bill, the White Sox announced that they would pursue a site in suburban Addison, Illinois. However, political leaders in DuPage County lost interest in pursuing the Addison deal when voters narrowly rejected the proposed White Sox stadium in a non-binding referendum in November, 1986. Shortly thereafter, White Sox representatives met with Mier and Johnson at City Hall to give the City one last chance to see if something could be done to build a stadium in Illinois before they would be forced to relocate the team—something the White Sox did not want to do. The White Sox proposed a publicly-owned facility financed by rent payments and a new hotel tax, to be located at either Roosevelt Road or 35th and Shields, near old Comiskey. They made it clear, however, that the necessary legislative action had to be taken by the end of the legislative veto session in December or the White Sox would be forced to leave Illinois.

On Thanksgiving or the day after, Mayor Washington met with Johnson and Mier. The Mayor told them that he wanted to keep the White Sox in Chicago, but that he did not want to put local tax money into the project. The Mayor also wanted to keep residential relocation to a minimum. Following the meeting with the Mayor, there was a marathon 12–hour meeting in which representatives of the White Sox and the City negotiated a Memorandum of Understanding ("MOU"), which the Mayor and Jerry Reinsdorf, Chairman of the White Sox, signed on December 1, 1986. The MOU provided that the White Sox and the City administration would approach the Illinois General Assembly and seek authorization and funding for a new stadium to be located in the immediate vicinity of 35th and Shields. It also provided that Chicago

Housing Authority ("CHA") housing, schools and church property would not be condemned in order to construct the new stadium.

There was little discussion before the MOU was signed about the exact stadium site. Early in the meeting, White Sox representatives conceded that the Roosevelt Road site would cost too much to be funded with the proposed hotel tax package. There was no discussion before the MOU was signed as to exactly where the new stadium would be located in the area around 35th and Shields. However, Al Johnson testified in his deposition that he believed everyone at the meeting assumed that the stadium would be located south of old Comiskey. White Sox representatives who gave deposition testimony agreed that they had shared the same assumption. The MOU itself contains some evidence that the City and the White Sox contemplated that the new facility was to be constructed south of the existing stadium inasmuch as all of the kinds of property specifically exempted from condemnation—CHA housing, a school and church property—were located south of the stadium.

In a newspaper article published in the Chicago Tribune on December 7, 1986, Eddie Einhorn, Vice Chairman of the White Sox, was quoted as stating that the new stadium would, in all likelihood, be built just south of the present facility. In the same article, Mayor Washington was quoted as stating that "a couple hundred residents will have to lose their homes under the plan." He was further quoted as stating that "[a]ny displacement is unfortunate, but one must resort to it. A fair offer will be made for their property."

There were three days remaining on the General Assembly's schedule when the MOU was signed. Representatives of the City and the White Sox went to Springfield to persuade the General Assembly to pass the necessary legislation. With the support of Governor Thompson, Mayor Washington and the Democratic leadership of the House and Senate, the Illinois Sports Facilities Act ("the Act") passed at the close of the legislative session and was approved by the Governor on January 20, 1987. 70 ILCS 3205/1 et seq.

The Act created a new unit of local government, the Authority, to issue bonds and to build and operate the new stadium. Section 8(6) of the Act, ILCS ch 85 § 6008(6), directs the Authority to determine the location of the new sports facility. The Act sets forth the boundaries of an area within which the Authority would have the power of eminent domain. The Authority's jurisdiction did not extend to the north of 33rd street, which is the immediate northern edge of Armour Square Park. Moreover, the Act specifically prohibited the Authority from using the eminent domain power to condemn property owned, leased or used by the City, the CHA, the Chicago Board of Education or any church. The Act added Chicago Park District land to the list of property exempt from condemnation, thereby precluding the Authority from condemning Armour Square Park. By so limiting the Authority's condemnation powers, the Act effectively required the Authority to build the new Comiskey Park south of the existing facility.

Preserving Armour Square Park was necessary in order to secure the support of Senator Timothy Degnan, in whose district Comiskey Park was located. In conversations with Tim Wright, one of Mayor Washington's staff members, Degnan and 11th Ward Alderman Huels both emphasized the importance of Armour Square Park to their constituents. Wright did not recall that anyone objected to adding the Park to the list of property that could not be condemned.

The White Sox Raise the Possibility of Moving to Florida

Nothing happened for almost a year after the Act was passed, while the Governor and the Mayor wrangled over appointments to the Authority Board. In October 1987, Jerry Reinsdorf met with the Mayor and Rob Mier to express concern about the continuing delay in starting up the Authority. Reinsdorf told the Mayor that he was pursuing discussions with St. Petersburg, Florida as a back-up option.

Shortly thereafter, the dispute over appointments to the Authority Board was settled. The Governor appointed Tom Reynolds as Chairman of the Authority. Mayor Washington appointed Al Johnson to the Authority Board and also chose Peter Bynoe, an African–American real estate developer, to serve as the Authority's first executive director.

By early 1988, the White Sox had an offer from St. Petersburg to play in its new stadium. That offer put significant pressure on the Authority to move the project ahead. As a result, the Authority proceeded on two fronts, planning for the new stadium, while at the same time hiring an engineering firm (as it was required to do by the 1986 Act) to see if the old stadium could be rehabilitated. Al Johnson believed that it was important to have an engineering study done in order to quiet the objections of citizen groups and others who wanted to save the old ballpark. However, neither he nor Bynoe believed that the White Sox would agree to stay in Illinois to play in a renovated old Comiskey Park which did not meet contemporary stadium design standards. Indeed, the White Sox had always said that they were not interested in a renovated old Comiskey because such a facility would be economically obsolete. On May 6, 1988, the Authority approved schematic drawings prepared by an architectural firm experienced in ballpark design.

The Passage of the Amended Act

The legislation enacted at the end of 1986 authorized the Authority to issue up to $120 million worth of bonds in order to finance the clearance of the site and construction of the new stadium. By the spring of 1988, it became apparent that $120 million would not be enough. At the end of the legislative session, representatives of the Authority, the City and the White Sox returned to Springfield to seek legislation that, among other things, would increase the amount of bonds the Authority was authorized to sell to $150 million.

While the issue was being considered in the Illinois General Assembly, the White Sox continued to negotiate with St. Petersburg, Florida as well. In June, the Florida legislature passed a $30 million appropriation to speed up redesign of the St. Petersburg Suncoast Dome to the White Sox' specifications. The White Sox publicly stated that if the proposed stadium legislation was not enacted by the end of the Illinois legislative session, the White Sox would move to Florida.

Once again, the Mayor, Governor Thompson, and the Democratic leadership in the House and Senate supported the legislation. Nevertheless, there was substantial opposition to public funding of the project, and the bill barely passed at literally the last possible second. Afterwards House Speaker Madigan was quoted in the press as stating that "the governor and I and all the members took risks and passed this bill to keep the White Sox in Chicago."

In addition to authorizing the Authority to sell additional bonds, the amended Act set forth in exact detail the land that the Authority could condemn. Like the earlier version of the Act, the amended Act put CHA property, a school, church and Armour Square Park beyond the reach of the Authority's power of eminent domain. The amended Act also established a 25% minority set-aside program for the contract to build the new stadium and required the Authority to establish an affirmative action program "designed to promote equal employment opportunity which specifies the goals and methods for increasing participation by minorities and women in a representative mix of job classifications required to perform the respective contracts." Finally, the amended Act contained a new provision granting the Authority the power to provide "relocation assistance and compensation for landowners and tenants displaced by any land acquisition of the Authority, including the acquisition of land and construction of replacement housing as the Authority shall determine."

The amended Act set a deadline of September 15, 1988 for the signing of a Management Agreement between the Authority and the White Sox, in which the White Sox would commit to remaining in the new facility for the expected term of the bonds. If no agreement was reached by that point, the Authority's power to levy taxes would be revoked.

The Authority signed a Management Agreement with the White Sox on June 29, 1988. The Management Agreement required the Authority to take title to 80% of the residential property in the area to be condemned and all of certain commercial property by October 15, 1988. If the Authority did not meet that deadline, the Agreement gave the White Sox the option to terminate the Agreement.

The Bess Proposal

In December 1987, an architect named Phillip Bess sent a letter to members of the newly constituted Authority Board suggesting that a ballpark could be designed specifically to be built on Armour Square Park. At that time, the Authority Board did not pursue Bess' suggestion. In August 1988, Bess resurfaced, this time with a scale model of his proposed new stadium. Bess' model was of a small ballpark, without the contemporary features the White Sox considered important to a stadium design. Bess had designed the stadium to fit within Armour Square Park and proposed four multi-level parking facilities.

The Bess proposal was unsatisfactory to the White Sox who, for economic reasons, did not want the kind of ballpark that Bess had designed. Moreover, pursuing the Bess proposal would have put the Authority in a position where it would almost surely lose the White Sox. If the Authority did not have title to most of the property on the southern site by October 15, 1988, the White Sox would have the right to terminate the Management Agreement. If the Management Agreement was terminated, the Authority's ability to impose the necessary taxes would automatically terminate. Under those circumstances, the Authority would literally be required to go back to the drawing board, returning to Springfield, where the General Assembly had previously approved the legislation by the slimmest of margins, for authorization to proceed with an entirely new project. That project would have been dead on arrival because it would have faced the opposition of Senator Degnan and other representatives of the area, who had already made their opposition to the use of Armour Square Park clear.

Bess' plan would also have been vehemently opposed by Walter Netsch, the Chairman of the Chicago Park District Board, and, coincidentally, the husband of State Senator Dawn Clark Netsch. Armour Square Park is an historically important park designed by Frederick Olmstead and noted Chicago architect Daniel Burnham. Netsch greatly regretted the destruction of other parks designed by Burnham when the Dan Ryan expressway was constructed, and he was adamant that Armour Square Park would not be destroyed as well. When Mier asked Netsch if he would consider giving up Armour Square Park, Netsch replied, "no never," expressing his "undying opposition" to such a proposal. The Park District and Netsch had a general policy against giving up or trading Park District land for any purpose.

The Relocation of South Armour Square Residents

The Authority met its October 15, 1988 deadline. By September 15, 1988, the Authority had negotiated settlements with all of the homeowners and tenants who lived in the 175 dwellings that were to be razed to make room for the new stadium, without using the "quick take" authority given to it by Act. The Authority agreed to build new homes for homeowners or pay them fair market value plus a $25,000 bonus. The Authority also agreed to pay relocation costs for tenants and to give a cash settlement to long-term tenants. The Authority spent $10.3 million relocating homeowners and tenants. None of the homeowners or tenants who were relocated by the Authority ever joined in this lawsuit or brought any other action against the Authority, the City, or the White Sox claiming that their rights were in any way abridged. The relocations resulted in approximately 475 African–American residents leaving South Armour Square.

Construction began on the new stadium in May 1989. The first game was played in the new stadium in April 1991.

The Lawsuit

Plaintiffs filed this suit against the Authority, the White Sox, and the City of Chicago alleg[ing] that [their] conduct violates the equal protection clause of the Fourteenth Amendment of the United States Constitution and 42 U.S.C. § 1983. Plaintiffs allege that the defendants engaged in racial discrimination in connection with the decision-making process which led to the destruction of their neighborhood of South Armour Square in order to build the new Comiskey Park.

The plaintiffs are: 1) individual African–American persons who live in Wentworth Gardens, a low-rise development adjacent to the stadium which has federally regulated rents and is operated by the CHA; 2) individual African–American persons who live in T.E. Brown Apartments, a federally regulated eleven-story apartment building adjacent to the stadium; 3) a class of persons who live, or have lived, in Wentworth Gardens or T.E. Brown Apartments since June 29, 1988; and 4) the South Armour Square Neighborhood Coalition, a not-for-profit corporation the members of which are residents of Wentworth Gardens and T.E. Brown Apartments, and the goals of which include the preservation of the South Armour Square neighborhood.

DISCUSSION

In order to establish a violation of the Equal Protection Clause, plaintiffs must demonstrate that they were injured by intentional racial discrimination. Plaintiffs must prove that a discriminatory purpose was "a motivating factor" in the decision to locate the new Comiskey Park to the south of the old ballpark. See Village of Arlington Heights v. Metropolitan Housing Development Corp., 429 U.S. 252, 266 (1977). Although plaintiffs need not demonstrate that race discrimination was the only reason for the decision in question, they must be able to persuade the finder of fact that it was "a motivating factor" in the decision. Id.

Pretext

The first inquiry under Arlington Heights is whether the decision, while race neutral on its face, is an obvious pretext for discrimination. As the Supreme Court observed in Shaw v. Reno, such decisions are rare. 509 U.S. 630 (1993). The inquiry is whether there is any conceivable explanation for such a decision other than a desire to discriminate on the basis of race.

In this case, the decision to place the stadium south of the old ballpark admittedly has had a disparate impact on African–Americans. We can assume that defendants and the General Assembly knew that one consequence of its actions was that a disproportionate burden would fall on the African–American residents of South Armour Square because the stadium would be built south of old Comiskey.

However, the fact that the decisionmakers realize that there is a disparate adverse impact on a particular group, without more, is not probative of discriminatory purpose or intent. The dispositive question is whether plaintiffs have shown that a racially-based discriminatory purpose has, at least in some part, shaped the decision. In this case, defendants offer a race-neutral explanation for the disparate impact. The desire to keep the White Sox in Illinois at the least possible cost is a race-neutral explanation for the decision to build the new Comiskey Park south of the old stadium. Because it already had the infrastructure necessary to serve a major league stadium, the site around the old Comiskey Park was obviously an attractive alternative. Moreover, given the White Sox' desire for a contemporary facility and the difficulty of acquiring Park District land, the southern site was more economically and politically feasible than the northern site.

Neither the General Assembly, nor any of the defendants, had any obligation to ignore the economic and other non-racial concerns that led to the siting decision in order to protect the South Armour Square neighborhood from the adverse effects of a decision to build to the south. For example, when Phillip Bess belatedly proposed fitting a small stadium into Armour Square Park, the Authority was not required to pursue the idea to see whether a workable plan could be devised that would avoid residential relocations in South Armour Square. Instead, the Authority was free to reject the plan on a number of grounds, so long as race was not a factor. The plan was rejected due to the White Sox' desire for a contemporary stadium which would not fit on the site Bess had selected, the need to move quickly in order to avoid losing the Authority's taxing authority which was essential to keeping the White Sox in Illinois, and the Park District's long-standing policy of refusing to give up its land.

In short, the inquiry is not whether something else could have been done which would have had a less disparate impact on African–American residents. The only question is whether the decision to locate the new stadium south of the old one was motivated in part by racial animus against the people living in that area. In this case, there is a race-neutral explanation for the disparate impact of the decision. Therefore, a conceivable explanation exists for the decision other than a desire to discriminate, and plaintiffs have failed to show that the decision is a pretext for racial discrimination. Since the decision passes this hurdle, we proceed to consider whether there is circumstantial evidence which demonstrates a discriminatory purpose or intent.

Historical Pattern of Racial Discrimination

In Arlington Heights, the Supreme Court stated that an historical pattern of racial discrimination could be used to provide circumstantial evidence of discriminatory purpose or intent. The Court explained that "[t]he historical background of the decision is one evidentiary source, particularly if it reveals a series of official actions taken for invidious purposes." Arlington Heights, 429 U.S. at 267. In this case, plaintiffs complain of racial discrimination since 1945 by the City and local governmental agencies which allegedly has resulted in the segregation and isolation of African–American persons in South Armour Square.

This background allegedly includes segregation in public housing and the relocation of the Dan Ryan expressway to create a buffer area to restrain the movement of African–American persons. Plaintiffs argue that the decision to locate the new stadium south of the old one was simply a continuation of previous patterns of discrimination.

Nevertheless, despite years of discovery, plaintiffs have failed to uncover any evidence to support this theory. Whether or not the location of the Dan Ryan was intended to discriminate against African–Americans, the reality of Chicago's political leadership in the late 1980's discredits the claim of a continuing conspiracy. Throughout the period in which the siting decision was made and the legislation was enacted, Chicago had an African–American mayor, first Harold Washington and then Eugene Sawyer. Both Mayor Washington and Mayor Sawyer supported the stadium legislation, believing that the stadium would be located south of old Comiskey and that it would require relocation of a couple hundred African–American residents. Mayor Washington had a significant role in crafting the legislation, taking the steps he believed were necessary to keep the White Sox in Chicago.

Plaintiffs claim that Mayor Washington never really knew for sure where the new stadium would be built. The undisputed facts, however, show that Mayor Washington must have known that the new stadium would be built to the south and that some African–American residents of South Armour Square would be displaced. However, regardless of Mayor Washington's knowledge, many other African–Americans knew and approved of the location of the site. Al Johnson, an African–American who was the Mayor's close aide and later served on the Authority Board, testified that he understood from the beginning that the site would be located south of the old stadium. Mayor Sawyer also supported the stadium with full knowledge of its location. Peter Bynoe, an African–American who was the Authority's first Executive Director, supervised the clearance of the site and the construction of the new stadium. Moreover, eighteen of twenty African–American state legislators voted for the legislation, and seventeen of eighteen African–American aldermen voted for the necessary zoning ordinance. Therefore, the undisputed facts show that many African–Americans played prominent roles throughout the entire process of planning and building the new stadium.

Mr. Bynoe rejected any suggestion that the site selection was racially motivated, stating that he resented any such claim and that he had never been involved "with anything that had that [racial discrimination] as an objective or an ancillary impact." Mr. Bynoe was proud of the fact that the Authority had provided a relocation effort that, in his words, no one had "come close to anywhere else in the world." Al Johnson similarly testified that he believed the Authority had been fair to the people of the South Armour Square neighborhood in selecting the southern site. It defies logic to suggest that all of these prominent African–American political and business leaders actively participated in a racially motivated plot to destroy the South Armour Square neighborhood.

Plaintiffs also argue that historical patterns of discrimination by the Chicago Park District and private citizens in Bridgeport give rise to an inference that the City and the Authority were likely to have acted for a discriminatory purpose. Plaintiffs contend that there was a long-standing pattern of racial discrimination in providing city services, including recreational facilities, to South Armour Square residents, as compared to the white residents of Bridgeport. Plaintiffs also contend that some white residents of Bridgeport harassed African–Americans who attempted to use Armour Square Park and that the Park District tolerated such racism.

In Arlington Heights, the Court noted that some of the opponents of the low-income housing project at issue there "might have been motivated by opposition to minority groups." Arlington Heights, 429 U.S at 269. The Court, however, concluded that proof that private opposition to the project was to some extent racially motivated did not prove that the Village Board had acted because of racial animus. Instead, what was critical was that the Board had applied to the proposed low-income housing project the same policy that it had applied to other requests that did not involve low-income housing.

In this case, the fact that Armour Square Park may have been misused by some racist individuals does not convert a desire to preserve the amenities offered by the park into an improper, racially motivated purpose. Even assuming that some citizen opposition to the destruction of the park was racially motivated, there is no evidence of any improper purpose on the part of any of the decisionmakers. The Park District had a well-known and consistent policy against selling or otherwise allowing park land to be used for other purposes. The Chairman of the Park District Board also had a particular interest in preserving historic parks like Armour Square Park. There is no reason to believe that Senator Degnan—let alone the entire General Assembly—was acting out of a desire to discriminate against African–Americans when he sought to protect Park District property from condemnation by the Authority. Moreover, despite years of discovery, there is not a single piece of evidence that any defendant or legislator ever made any racially-tinged statements about Armour Square Park. Thus, there were a number of legitimate reasons to protect the park.

In sum, given the change in the political realities, plaintiffs simply cannot rely on a past climate of racial discrimination or discrimination by private persons as evidence that the siting decision was racially motivated as well. Indeed, the extensive participation of African–Americans in the process makes it highly likely that the decision to build the new park south of the old stadium was not motivated in any way by an intent to discriminate.

Sequence of Events and Procedural or Substantive Irregularities

The second and third prongs of the Arlington Heights test are sequence of events and procedural or substantive irregularities. Regarding the second factor, sequence of events, the Arlington Heights Court analogized a situation where a particular piece of property was zoned for multi-family uses, but the zoning was changed to single-family after the town heard that a developer was seeking to use the property for a low-income housing development that was likely to have a significant minority population. In such a case, the abrupt change in policy would provide substantial evidence that the decision had been motivated by racial bias. Arlington Heights, 429 U.S. at 267. In Arlington Heights, the Court held that there was no evidence of discriminatory purpose or intent in the Village Board's refusal to rezone property that had always been zoned for single family uses to allow a developer to put in a low income housing development. Id. at 269.

Regarding the third factor, the Arlington Heights Court stated that departures from ordinary procedural or substantive rules might also be probative of discriminatory purpose or intent. Arlington Heights, 429 U.S. at 267. In this case, because the parties rely on the same evidence in analyzing the second and third factors, we will proceed to examine these two prongs of the Arlington Heights test together.

Plaintiffs argue that the record is filled with evidence of departures from normal procedures, all of which suggest that there was a racial motivation for the site selection. Plaintiffs have not provided any evidence, however, to show what "normal" procedures are for a project like Comiskey Park. This is not a situation like Arlington Heights where the zoning board had routine procedures it followed in ruling on requests for zoning changes. Instead, the site selection in this case was the result of a complex political process conducted under intense time pressure. Under those circumstances, there is no "normal" procedure against which to judge the defendants' conduct.

[The remainder of the court's opinion is omitted.]

Notes

1. Ironically, Phillip Bess now is recognized as having been right. One year after new Comiskey Park opened, the Baltimore Orioles' Camden Yards ushered in a wave of "old-time" baseball stadiums that are everything Comiskey Park is not: warm, cozy, fan-friendly, and enormously profitable. As a result, many Chicago White Sox fans today pine for a new-old stadium. *See further* Carol Slezak, *Just Admit It, Jerry: You Need A New Comiskey*, Chi. Sun–Times, Aug. 20, 1997, at 134.

2. For another case raising the same issues (and reaching the same conclusions) as *Laramore*, see *Lake Lucerne Civic Ass'n, Inc. v. Dolphin Stadium Corp.*, 801 F.Supp. 684 (S.D.Fla.1992). *See also* Jon C. Dubin, *From Junkyards to Gentrification: Explicating a Right to Protective Zoning in Low–Income Communities of Color*, 77 Minn. L. Rev. 739 (1993) (pointing out that poor communities often are forced to accept public works shunned by wealthier neighborhoods).

Problem 9

For years, a stadium located in the middle of a quiet residential neighborhood has been used solely by an NFL team. Now, however, a baseball club is about to become a co-tenant. Because of the impact this will have, a local citizens group is demanding strict new noise and pollution limits. Can such regulations be validly enacted? *See Chicago National League Ball Club, Inc. v. Thompson*, 483 N.E.2d 1245 (Ill.1985).

3. OPERATIONS

Like other commercial establishments, all stadiums have "house rules." Given the litigious nature of our society, such rules are increasingly being challenged in court.

ELLIOTT v. UNITED CENTER

126 F.3d 1003 (7th Cir.1997),
cert. denied, 118 S.Ct. 1302 (1998).

WOOD, Circuit Judge.

Millions of spectators have attended games and other events at the United Center, home of the world-famous Chicago Bulls, as well as the Chicago Blackhawks, circuses, ice shows, concerts, and in 1996 the Democratic National Convention. But ever since the United Center opened, replacing the former Chicago Stadium, it has had a policy that prohibits all patrons of the Center from bringing food into the arena. This, according to Thornton Elliott and his co-plaintiffs, has given a "monopoly" on food sales to the Center.

Elliott and his colleagues are licensed peanut vendors who, up until the time the United Center imposed this policy, turned a respectable profit selling peanuts outside the stadium. (For ease of reference, we refer to all plaintiffs collectively as "Elliott" below.) They brought this suit under section 2 of the Sherman Act, 15 U.S.C. § 2, claiming that the United Center's food policy constitutes an illegal attempt to monopolize food sales inside the arena and in the surrounding geographic area. The district court was unpersuaded and dismissed the case under Fed. R.Civ.P. 12(b)(6). We agree. "Food sales within the United Center" does not describe a relevant market that is subject to § 2 strictures, and the allegations fall far short of establishing that the presence of the United Center threatens all other food purveyors in any meaningful geographic area.

According to the complaint, ever since the United Center implemented its food policy in September 1994, patrons are inspected for food when they enter the stadium, and if any is found, it is confiscated by stadium security. If a fan buys a bag of peanuts from Elliott, therefore, she must consume it before she enters the United Center, unless she wants to risk contributing it to the "illegal food" stash collected by the security personnel. Worse yet, if she has a hankering for peanuts during the Bulls game, her desires will go unfulfilled, because the United Center does not offer peanuts for sale in the stadium (except little bags of peanuts for the circus elephants).

This policy has cost Elliott dearly. The complaint (filed on September 22, 1995), alleged that "last year" (i.e. 1994, we assume, although it does not distinguish between the time before and the time after the United Center opened) their sales were over $500,000. Under the new policy, the average sales of peanuts have dropped to approximately one-fifth of sales in previous years. Predictably, some vendors have gone out of business, and the remaining ones are struggling to survive.

The complaint alleged that the relevant market was the one for "food concessions at the United Center." (Complaint, p 21.) Because peanuts are the only food sold directly outside the United Center to United Center patrons, it further alleged that the plaintiffs were the only competitors to the United Center itself in this relevant market. It conceded that the United Center might have had a legitimate business reason to prohibit certain kinds of food, such as cans, bottles, or alcoholic beverages in general, in the interest of maintaining order in the facility, but it claimed that no such reason could be advanced for the blanket food ban.

The complaint points out the United Center's monopoly over the presentation of live National Basketball Association games and live National Hockey League games in the Chicago market, and implicitly argues that the Center is, through the food policy, attempting to extend its monopoly to the alleged food concession market.

The district court, as we noted above, concluded that these allegations were insufficient to state a claim under the Sherman Act. Elliott v. United Center, 1996 WL 400030, at *3 (N.D.Ill. July 15, 1996). In so doing, it followed a recommendation from Magistrate Judge Rebecca R. Pallmeyer to deny the preliminary injunction Elliott had requested, in which she too had concluded that the vendors could not succeed on the merits of their claim. Magistrate Judge Pallmeyer had accepted the plaintiffs' standing to sue, but she found that they had not shown antitrust injury, within the meaning of Brunswick Corp. v. Pueblo Bowl–O–Mat, Inc., 429 U.S. 477, 97 S.Ct. 690, 50 L.Ed.2d 701 (1977), nor had they defined a proper relevant market. The district court agreed, with specific attention to the relevant market finding. Without a relevant market to back it up, virtually all of the remaining antitrust theories collapsed.

The court's order of dismissal also dismissed Elliott's state law claims for interference with business and prospective advantage (raised under the court's supplemental jurisdiction), for two reasons: first, it declined to exercise supplemental jurisdiction since the federal claims had been dismissed so soon, and second, it found that the complaint did not state a claim of intentional tortious interference under Illinois law.

We need go no further in this matter than the market analysis on which both Magistrate Judge Pallmeyer and District Judge James Holderman relied. In order to prevail under § 2 of the Sherman Act, the plaintiffs would need to show "(1) the possession of monopoly power in the relevant market and (2) the willful acquisition or maintenance of that power as distinguished from growth or development as a consequence of a superior product, business acumen, or historic accident." United States v. Grinnell Corp., 384 U.S. 563, 570–71, 86 S.Ct. 1698, 1703–04, 16 L.Ed.2d 778 (1966). Only the relevant market concerns us here. As Judge Easterbrook wrote for this court in Israel Travel Advis. Serv. v. Israel Iden. Tours, 61 F.3d 1250 (7th Cir.1995), "a market is defined to aid in identifying any ability to raise price by curtailing output." Id. at 1252. In what market, then, does the United Center have this kind of power? Elliott replies, the market for food concessions within and around the United Center itself: the fewer the food concessions, the higher the price the United Center can charge for food its patrons consume, and the more consumers will suffer.

But people do not go to the United Center to buy food; they go to watch a basketball game, a hockey game, or some other special event. The United Center can recoup the cost of putting on the event in any of a number of ways. It can charge very high ticket prices, and allow unlimited numbers of food concessions in and around the stadium, or it can charge somewhat lower ticket prices and restrict the number of concessions (thereby earning some of its profits from the food sales). No one argues that the United Center is monopolizing the market for snack food in near west Chicago, because such an argument would be ludicrous on its face.

The United Center is obviously not monopolizing the market for peanuts: it is staying strictly out of the peanut business. True, its ban means that those with a craving for peanuts must satisfy it either before or after the game, but both price and output of peanuts in any geographic area that would be meaningful under the antitrust laws (at least Chicago, we presume) are totally unaffected by the United Center's policies.

The logic of Elliott's argument would mean that exclusive restaurants could no longer require customers to purchase their wines only at the establishment, because the restaurant would be "monopolizing" the sale of wine within its interior. Movie theaters, which traditionally (and notoriously) earn a substantial portion of their revenue from the sales of candies, popcorn, and soda, would be required by the antitrust laws to allow patrons to bring their own food. The fact that there is more than one exclusive restaurant, and more than one movie theater, does not distinguish these examples from the case before us, although we anticipate that Elliott would argue that it does. For Elliott's principal point is that the customer knows that once he is ready to walk through the entry gate, he may not have with him any "outside" food.

The same can be said of any of the establishments we have just mentioned: once inside a restaurant, or a movie theater, the customer is at the mercy of the place he has chosen. The price of the refreshments or the wine is just one part of the price of the evening out. Elliott suggests that the United Center under this theory could also "monopolize" the parking lots around it, which we suppose is true. (It is, in fact, what the

Disney Corporation elected to do when it built Disney World in Orlando, Florida, having learned its lesson about losing economic rents from Disneyland in Anaheim, California. See Molnar, A Tale of 2 Disneys, Seattle Times, May 19, 1991.) He also suggests that the United Center could refuse admittance to any customer not wearing an NBA jersey purchased within the Center; again, perhaps this is theoretically true, although successful businesses normally do not try to shoot themselves in the foot so vigorously.

The serious point here is that the United Center is certainly a popular facility in Chicago. It serves, over the course of a year, millions of customers, and it is undoubtedly a prime spot for vendors of all kinds to ply their wares. But this implies that the relevant market should be expanded to all other comparable places in the Chicago area. Absent collusion, even if each stadium or arena had a policy similar to the United Center's policy, there would be no violation of the antitrust laws. In such an expanded market, furthermore, it is very doubtful that the United Center has any significant market power. And we have explicitly rejected the proposition that a firm can be said to have monopoly power in its own product, absent proof that the product itself has no economic substitutes. See Digital Equip. Corp. v. Uniq Digital Technologies, Inc., 73 F.3d 756, 761 (7th Cir.1996); see also Bendix Corp. v. Balax, Inc., 471 F.2d 149, 160–61 (7th Cir.1972).

We therefore conclude that the district court correctly dismissed Elliott's complaint for failure to state a claim. The judgment below is AFFIRMED.

Notes

1. Although Thornton Elliott lost his antitrust case, some street vendors, relying on the First Amendment, have had success in court. *See, e.g., Lewis v. Colorado Rockies Baseball Club, Ltd.*, 941 P.2d 266 (Colo.1997), and *Kelly v. Buffalo Bills Football Club, Inc.*, 655 N.Y.S.2d 275 (Sup. Ct. 1997), *aff'd*, 673 N.Y.S.2d 347 (App.Div.1998).

2. In addition to street vendors, others who seek access to patrons as they approach stadiums include protesters, panhandlers, and proselytizers. *See, e.g., City of Cleveland v. Bregar*, 667 N.E.2d 42 (Ohio Ct.App.1995), *dismissed*, 661 N.E.2d 755 (Ohio), *cert. denied*, 117 S.Ct. 71 (1996) (fan holding sign that read "FIELD OF GREED" on eve of 1994 baseball strike prosecuted for trespass for refusing to move away from main entrance to Jacobs Field).

3. For an interesting examination of the role lawyers play in formulating stadium policies, see Lisa A. Delpy & Kathleen B. Costello, *Lawyering on the Front Lines: On–Site Legal Counsel for Major Sporting Events*, 6 Marq. Sports L.J. 29 (1995).

Problem 10

During a football game, a fan in the upper deck unfurled a banner which read "Management Bites." Although the sign was not interfering with the game, security guards made her take it down. If she sues, claiming as a taxpayer-financed facility the stadium is a public forum which must accommodate all points of view, what is the most likely outcome? *See* Lawrence A. Israeloff, Note, *The Sports Fan v. The Sports Team Owner: Does a Franchise's Prohibition of Spectators' Banners Violate the First Amendment?*, 24 Colum. J.L. & Soc. Probs. 419 (1991).

4. SAFETY

Not all injuries occur on the field. As the cases that follow make clear, it is sometimes just as dangerous to be in the stands.

TELEGA v. SECURITY BUREAU, INC.

719 A.2d 372 (Pa.Super.Ct.1998).

MONTEMURO, Senior Judge.

Appellants, Mitchell and Karen Telega, appeal from the October 11, 1996 Order of the Allegheny County Court of Common Pleas granting summary judgment in favor of Appellee, Security Bureau, Inc. For the reasons set forth below, we reverse.

Mitchell Telega and his wife, Karen, attended a Pittsburgh Steelers football game at Three Rivers Stadium in Pittsburgh on December 6, 1992. For approximately two years, the Telegas were season ticket holders whose seats were located in Section 41, the pie-shaped end-zone section of the stadium behind the Steelers' goalpost. During the last quarter of the December 6th game, the Steelers' kicker attempted a field goal. The football was catapulted through the uprights of the goalpost, over the stadium net designed to catch it, and into the stands. Mr. Telega, who saw the ball coming his way, stood up in front of his assigned seat, extended his arms, and cleanly fielded the football. When he attempted to sit down, Mr. Telega was thrust from his seat and trampled face first into the cement aisle by aggressive fans who stripped him of the souvenir ball. Mr. Telega suffered numerous injuries from this attack, including facial lacerations, a sprained shoulder and arm resulting in extensive physical therapy, and a broken nose that required surgery.

Prior to this incident, the Telegas and other patrons seated in the end zone section of the stadium lodged complaints with the stadium's Guest Relations Office and security personnel concerning the lack of security and crowd control in their seating area during field goal and extra point attempts. They often complained that the football regularly clears the catch net, lands in the stands, and causes a disturbance among the fans, resulting in a danger to the welfare of the patrons seated in their section. It is undisputed that Appellee, Security Bureau, Inc., was responsible for providing security services at the Stadium during home games.

Appellants filed a complaint asserting a cause of action in negligence against Security Bureau, Inc., Spectacor Management Group, The Stadium Authority of the City of Pittsburgh and Spectacor Management, Inc., alleging that the defendants breached a duty of care owed to Mr. Telega by, inter alia, failing to supervise security guards at the Stadium and failing to regulate crowd control in the end-zone seating area. Security Bureau filed a motion for summary judgment which was granted by Order dated October 11, 1996. Appellants' initial appeal from the grant of summary judgment was quashed by this Court because the October 11th Order was not final as to all of the defendants. On July 22, 1997, upon a praecipe to settle and discontinue, the remaining defendants were removed from the case. Thereafter, Appellants filed this timely appeal challenging the trial court's grant of summary judgment in favor of Security Bureau, Inc.

When reviewing a grant of summary judgment, we must examine the entire record in the light most favorable to the non-moving party, in whose favor we resolve all doubts and reasonable inferences, to determine whether the moving party has established that there is no genuine issue of material fact and that it is entitled to judgment as a matter of law. Kingston Coal Co. v. Felton Mining Co., Inc., 456 Pa.Super. 270, 690 A.2d 284, 287 (Pa.Super.1997). We will not disturb a trial court's grant of summary judgment absent an error of law or an abuse of discretion. Albright v. Abington Memorial Hospital, 548 Pa. 268, 279–80, 696 A.2d 1159, 1165 (1997).

In the instant case, citing to our Supreme Court's decision in Jones v. Three Rivers Management Corp., 483 Pa. 75, 394 A.2d 546 (1978), the trial court determined that because "the risk of injury was obvious, reasonably foreseeable and voluntarily assumed by [Mr. Telega]," (Trial Ct. Op. at 5), Appellee owed him no legal duty. We disagree and find that the trial court's extension of the "no-duty" rule under the circumstances of this case constitutes an error of law warranting reversal.

Jones, supra, is the seminal case discussing the "no-duty" rule in Pennsylvania as it applies to recovery for claims filed against amusement facilities by injured spectators and patrons. This rule, which is related to but distinct from the affirmative defense of assumption of the risk, Berman v. Radnor Rolls, Inc., 374 Pa.Super. 118, 542 A.2d 525, 531 (Pa.Super.1988), recognizes that there are certain inherent risks assumed by spectators or patrons when viewing sporting events or participating in amusements against which the amusement facility has no duty to protect. See, e.g., Bowser v. Hershey Baseball Assoc., 357 Pa.Super. 435, 516 A.2d 61, 63 (Pa.Super.1986) (affirming compulsory nonsuit against plaintiff who was struck in eye by a batted baseball while conducting tryouts; when he agreed to participate on the field during the tryouts, plaintiff voluntarily exposed himself to the risks inherent in baseball such as being hit by a batted ball); Pestalozzi v. Philadelphia Flyers, Ltd., 394 Pa.Super. 420, 576 A.2d 72, 74 (Pa.Super.1990) (following the principles announced in Jones and finding the "no-duty" rule applicable to hockey spectator who was struck by errant hockey puck during the game; being struck by a puck was a common and reasonably foreseeable risk inherent in the game of hockey). Relying on the well-established law governing the liability of amusement facility operators, the Court in Jones concluded that the "no-duty" rule, ordinarily applicable to patrons seated in the stands of the ballpark, should not be extended to a situation where a plaintiff was struck by a batted baseball while standing in an interior walkway of the stadium since the risk of harm in viewing the field from the concourse area could not be characterized as "part of the spectator sport of baseball." Id. at 86–87, 394 A.2d at 552. Although the trial court relies on Jones to support its extension of the "no-duty" rule in the instant matter, we find that the reasoning in Jones compels a different result.

Our courts have long refused to grant recovery for injuries sustained by amusement patrons which were caused by a risk inherent in the activity in question. Id. at 83–84, 394 A.2d at 550. For example, our Supreme Court granted judgment n.o.v. in favor of a defendant-movie theatre where the patron alleged only that his injury was caused by the lighting conditions ordinarily utilized in the exhibition of motion pictures. Beck v. Stanley Co. of America, 355 Pa. 608, 615, 50 A.2d 306, 310 (1947) (noting that there was no evidence indicating that the theater and its aisles were darker than was reasonably necessary or customary). The Court has also denied recovery where a spectator at a stockcar race track was struck by one of the racing vehicles while he was standing in the unprotected "pit" area of the track; the patron admitted that his presence in the pit area was unauthorized and that collisions in this area were common. Shula v. Warren, 395 Pa. 428, 434–35, 150 A.2d 341, 345 (1959)(stating that not only was the appellant unauthorized to be in the pit area, "but he proceeded to the edge of the 'pit' and stood at a point where vehicles with mechanical trouble would customarily leave the track, and it was at this point that he was struck."). The Jones court also discussed Taylor v. Churchill Valley Country Club, 425 Pa. 266, 228 A.2d 768 (1967), where the Court affirmed a directed verdict in favor of the defendant-country club and denied recovery to a golf caddie who was struck by a flying golf ball.

In accordance with the above cases, the Court in Jones defined the "no-duty" rule as it applies to amusement facilities by observing that

> movies must be seen in a darkened room, roller coasters must accelerate and decelerate rapidly and players will bat balls into the grandstand. But even in a "place of amusement" not every risk is reasonably expected. The rationale behind the rule that the standard of reasonable care does not impose a duty to protect from risks associated with baseball naturally limits its application to those injuries incurred as a result of risks any baseball spectator must and will be held to anticipate.

Jones, 483 Pa. at 84–85, 394 A.2d at 551. To illustrate this principle, the Court cited to a California case explaining the difference between the risk of being struck by a batted ball and a flying baseball bat. The California court held that a spectator assumes the risk of being hit with a batted ball because it is a matter of " 'common knowledge' that fly balls are a common, frequent and expected occurrence in this well-known sport, and it is not a matterof 'common knowledge' that flying baseball bats are common, frequent or expected." Id. at 85, 394 A.2d at 551 (citing Goade v. Benevolent and Protective Order of Elks, 213 Cal.App.2d 189, 28 Cal.Rptr. 669 (1963)). Guided by this distinction, our Supreme Court held that the "no-duty" rules apply only to risks which are " 'common, frequent and expected,' ... and in no way affect the duty of theatres, amusement parks and sports facilities to protect patrons from foreseeably dangerous conditions not inherent in the amusement activity." Id. Although an operator of an amusement facility for which admission is charged is not an insurer of his patrons, he will be "liable for injuries to his patrons ... where he fails to use reasonable care in the construction, maintenance, and management of [the facility], having regard to the character of the exhibitions given and the customary conduct of the patrons invited." Id. at 81, 394 A.2d at 549. Thus, it is clear that the central inquiry with respect to whether the "no-duty" rule will apply to a given situation, thereby barring recovery, is whether the injury resulted from a risk which is inherent in the amusement activity.

In the instant matter, Mr. Telega stood up in front of his seat in the end-zone section of the stadium, and caught a football which cleared the goalpost net during a field goal attempt by the Steelers. He was immediately attacked by a group of "displaced" fans who relieved him of the football and thrust him into the aisle, crushing his face into the concrete and causing serious injury. Citing to Jones, supra, the trial court essentially concludes that the risk of being trampled by a group of fans pursuing a souvenir was common to the football game and reasonably foreseeable based on Mr. Telega's experience. We disagree.

The "no-duty" rule applies only when the occurrence which caused the injury is inherent in the activity, i.e., is a common, frequent and expected part of the game or amusement; all other risks which may be present in the amusement facility are governed by the "ordinary" rules of negligence. Jones, 483 Pa. at 85, 394 A.2d at 551. Therefore, the question before this Court is whether a spectator will be held to assume as inherent in the game the risk of being attacked by displaced fans if he catches a soaring football. We believe not.

Although this type of unruly, improper fan conduct may have occurred in Mr. Telega's section of the stadium before, being trampled by displaced fans is not a risk inherent in or so ordinary a part of the spectator sport of football such that it is certain to occur at any and every stadium in the Commonwealth. The trial court's reliance on Mr. Telega's prior knowledge of such "fan upheaval" and his report of this dangerous behavior to management and security personnel is an attempt improperly to shift the focus of the "no-duty" inquiry from the risks inherent in the game of football itself to an examination of other risks which may be present in a particular football stadium. By creating the notion that "if it happened before, it must be customary," the trial court concludes that if a spectator is injured at a football game, and had prior knowledge of the risk of injury, the risk is automatically an inherent part of the spectator sport and recovery is barred. This broad-sweeping extension of the "no-duty" rule inappropriately attributes to Mr. Telega the responsibility to ensure his own safety and protect himself from the behavior of aggressive fans despite the presence of Appellee whose primary obligation it was to regulate crowd control. Indeed, such an interpretation of the "no-duty" rule would permit amusement facility operators to avoid liability for "universally prevalent negligent conditions," Jones, 483 Pa. at 85 n. 6, 394 A.2d at 551 n. 6, and would relieve them of all duty to protect against any risk within the facility. This approach is clearly undesirable and defies the well-established principles of negligence.

The risk involved here is unlike the risk of being struck by an errant puck while a spectator at a hockey game, Pestalozzi, supra, falling down or being bumped by other skaters at a roller skating rink, Berman, supra, or being hit by a batted ball during baseball tryouts, Bowser, supra. Contrary to the instant matter, these cases involve risks that are inherent in the activity itself and are specific to the activity at any appropriate venue. They are, therefore, as a matter of law, risks assumed by the spectators and participants who patronize the amusement facilities. It is not a matter of universal knowledge that an onslaught of displaced fans is a common, frequent or expected occurrence to someone catching a souvenir football. Therefore, it cannot be said that the injuries suffered by Mr. Telega resulted from a risk that any spectator would be held to anticipate and against which an amusement facility has no duty to protect. Certainly this matter would compel a different result had Mr. Telega been injured by the aerial football itself rather than the displaced fans intent on obtaining it.

Pursuant to the established caselaw, an extension of the "no-duty" rule to the kind of risk involved in the instant matter was clearly improper. Therefore, because the trial court committed an error of law in applying the "no-duty" rule and granting summary judgment, we must reverse.

JOYCE, Judge, dissenting.

I respectfully disagree with the majority regarding the application of the "no-duty" rule. The lower court determined that Appellants assumed the risk of personal injury and granted Appellee's motion for summary judgment. Citing to our Supreme Court's decision in Jones v. Three Rivers Management Corp., 483 Pa. 75, 394 A.2d 546 (1978), the lower court reasoned that the "no duty" rule should apply under the circumstances. The majority reversed in an opinion which discusses the historic overview of the application of the "no-duty" rule and concludes that the case at bar is more akin to a spectator being struck by a baseball bat, which does not warrant granting summary judgment, than a spectator being struck by a fly-ball, which would warrant summary judgment. We cannot agree with this conclusion. The no-duty rule applies to situations which are common, frequent and expected. Most importantly, the Courts have found Appellant is required to introduce evidence that the amusement facility in which he was injured deviated in some relevant respect from the established custom in order for the case to go to the jury. Pestalozzi v. Philadelphia Flyers Ltd., 394 Pa.Super. 420, 576 A.2d 72, 74 (Pa.Super.1990). Appellants failed in this respect.

Our review of the record indicated that Appellants had previously attended professional football games at Three Rivers Stadium. (Deposition of William Telega, 4/6/95, at 12). They sat in the same seats for approximately two (2) years and witnessed the fans' upheaval when a football entered the stands after clearing the catch net on many prior occasions. Id. at 12–13. In fact, they had voiced concern over this behavior previously. Id. at 18–19. Specifically, Appellants expressed concern for the welfare of the patrons when such events erupted. Id. at 81. The risk faced in the case at bar was quite common and customary to the football game and reasonably foreseeable based on past experience. Appellants assumed the risk of being injured by displaced fans pursuing a souvenir football. Under these circumstances, I would not disturb the findings of the trial court.

STEWART v. ARA LEISURE SERVICES, INC.

702 So.2d 75 (La.Ct.App.1997).

WALTZER, Judge.

Louie Stewart alleges injury to his knee when, on 21 September 1991, he slipped and fell on a hot dog at the Louisiana Superdome. Stewart and his wife filed suit against ARA Leisure Services, Inc., which operated the food and beverage concessions, and Facility Management of Louisiana, Inc., (Facility Management) which managed Superdome operations. ARA filed a motion for summary judgment in 1996 arguing that, under the facts of the case, it could not be liable under either strict liability or negligence. That motion was heard and denied on 5 September 1996. ARA did not seek supervisory review of that denial.

Subsequently, the case was re-assigned to a different judge. After the reallotment, ARA filed another motion for summary judgment urging the same grounds. On 8 August 1997, the second trial judge denied the motion for summary judgment. ARA here seeks supervisory review of that ruling.

Statement of Facts

It is uncontroverted that Stewart fell near seating section 119, and that the nearest ARA concession booth was adjacent to section 116, over twenty feet away. ARA's contract with Facility Management made ARA responsible for the maintenance of the area within ten feet of its concessions.

Analysis

The Stewarts' negligence claim is based on the assumption that ARA's employees failed to maintain adequately the premises where Stewart fell. In George v. Western Auto Supply Co., Inc., 527 So.2d 428, 429–30 (La.App. 4 Cir.1988), plaintiff sued the property owner, the lessee store and the City for injuries sustained in a slip and fall which occurred on the sidewalk abutting the store. The trial court granted summary judgment in favor of the store. The trial court held that the store's only duty to plaintiff was to refrain from doing anything to the sidewalk which would cause a vice or defect. The court rejected the claim that the store's failure to warn the plaintiff of a hazardous condition on the sidewalk, which was not in the store's custody, did not violate its duty to provide invitees with a safe entrance to and exit from its premises.

The contract between ARA and Facility Management specifically defined ARA's area of responsibility, and the accident clearly occurred outside that area. While the contract set forth the duty ARA owed to Facility Management relative to its maintenance parameters, it could not set forth the duty which ARA owed to Stewart. The Stewarts failed to meet their burden of producing evidence that ARA was responsible for maintenance of the location where Stewart fell.

As to the imposition of strict liability under La. C.C. art. 2317, the Stewarts bear the burden of proving: 1) the thing which caused damages was in the care, custody and control of ARA; 2) the thing had a vice or defect which created an unreasonable risk of harm; and 3) the injuries were caused by a defect. Sistler v. Liberty Mut. Ins. Co., 558 So.2d 1106, 1112 (La.1990).

The Stewarts allege that ARA is strictly liable for a defect in the physical design and layout of the area. ARA's contract provides that Facility Management was solely responsible for the designation of the locations from which ARA operated. ARA had no control over the location of its concession stands.

A "defect" is a flaw or condition of relative permanence inherent in the thing as one of its qualities. Toussant v. Guice, 414 So.2d 850, 852 (La.App. 4 Cir.1982). A temporary condition, such as the hot dog on which Stewart allegedly slipped and fell, does not constitute a defect. Boudreaux v. Farmer, 604 So.2d 641, 652 n. 10 (La.App. 1 Cir.), writs denied, 605 So.2d 1373 and 605 So.2d 1374 (La.1992). Likewise, the assignments of concessions in areas which are arguably too far from the seating area cannot constitute a defect for purposes of strict liability. There is no evidence supporting the Stewarts' claim that the hot dog constituted a defect in the Superdome premises for which ARA was responsible.

The Stewarts argued below that ARA is liable under strict liability because it had "garde" not over the area in which Stewart fell, but rather over the "system of food delivery" in the Superdome. However, the concept of "garde" is intended to limit the imposition of strict liability to things within a party's control, not to expand liability to cover something as far from a concessionaire's control as the dropping of a hot dog by another patron far outside the concessionaire's delineated maintenance area.

Conclusion

We grant ARA's application for supervisory writ, reverse the trial court's ruling denying ARA's motion for summary judgment and grant the motion, dismissing the petition of Louie G. Stewart and Fredna Stewart against ARA at plaintiffs' cost.

GREENBERG v. STERLING DOUBLEDAY ENTERPRISES, L.P.

660 N.Y.S.2d 33 (App.Div.1997).

PER CURIAM.

In an action to recover damages for personal injuries, the plaintiff appeals from (1) an order of the Supreme Court, Westchester County (Cowhey, J.), entered May 7, 1996, which granted the defendant's motion for summary judgment dismissing the complaint and (2) a judgment of the same court entered June 6, 1996, upon the order, dismissing the complaint.

ORDERED that the appeal from the order is dismissed; and it is further,

ORDERED that the judgment is affirmed; and it is further,

ORDERED that the defendant is awarded one bill of costs.

Prior to the commencement of a New York Mets baseball game at Shea Stadium on June 20, 1992, a number of Mets players made themselves available at the edge of the field to sign autographs. A crowd subsequently assembled to take advantage of this opportunity. In an alleged attempt to protect herself from the pushing and shoving of the crowd, the plaintiff propped her left foot up on her seat and placed her right foot on the ground. While in this position, she was purportedly jostled by a member of the crowd, thus causing her left foot to become wedged in the seat and to sustain an injury.

The plaintiff contends that the Supreme Court erred in granting the defendant's motion for summary judgment because issues of fact exist as to whether the defendant breached its duty to take adequate crowd control measures to protect patrons such as herself who were sitting in the area of the stadium where the crowd assembled. We disagree.

When a plaintiff's negligence claim is premised on the theory that her injuries were caused by overcrowding and inadequate crowd control, the plaintiff must establish that "[she] was unable to find a place of safety or that [her] free movement was restricted due to the alleged overcrowding conditions" (Palmieri v. Ringling Bros. & Barnum & Bailey Combined Shows, 237 A.D.2d 589, 655 N.Y.S.2d 646; see, Benanti v. Port Auth. of N.Y. & N.J., 176 A.D.2d 549, 574 N.Y.S.2d 729). The plaintiff has failed to do so here.

Notes

1. Because balls (and other objects) leave the playing field in most sports, suits like *Telega* are common. *See, e.g., Davidoff v. Metropolitan*

Baseball Club, Inc., 463 N.E.2d 1219 (N.Y.1984); *McFatridge v. Harlem Globe Trotters*, 365 P.2d 918 (N.M.1961); *Fisher v. Metropolitan Government of Nashville*, 1997 WL 80025 (Tenn.Ct.App.1997); *Moulas v. PBC Productions Inc.*, 570 N.W.2d 739 (Wis.Ct.App.1997), *aff'd by an equally divided court*, 576 N.W.2d 929 (Wis.1998); *Coronel v. Chicago White Sox, Ltd.*, 595 N.E.2d 45 (Ill.App.Ct.), *appeal denied*, 602 N.E.2d 449 (Ill.1992); *Friedman v. Houston Sports Ass'n*, 731 S.W.2d 572 (Tex.Ct.App.1987); *Valley National Bank v. National Ass'n for Stock Car Auto Racing, Inc.*, 736 P.2d 1186 (Ariz.Ct.App.1987); *Neinstein v. Los Angeles Dodgers, Inc.*, 229 Cal.Rptr. 612 (Ct.App.1986); *Rudnick v. Golden West Broadcasters*, 202 Cal.Rptr. 900 (Ct.App.1984); *Benjamin v. State of New York*, 453 N.Y.S.2d 329 (Ct.Cl. 1982), *aff'd*, 465 N.Y.S.2d 795 (App.Div.1983); *Fish v. Los Angeles Dodgers Baseball Club*, 128 Cal.Rptr. 807 (Ct.App.1976).

Because of the frequency of such suits, several states have given stadium owners immunity from "wayward ball" actions. Shortly after being awarded the Rockies, for example, the Colorado legislature enacted the Baseball Spectator Safety Act of 1993. *See* 13 Colo. Rev. Stat. § 13–21–120 (1997). More recently, in 1998, both Arizona (to protect teams in the "Cactus League") and Utah (to assist the International Hockey League's Grizzlies) passed similar laws. These statutes are largely symbolic, however, because they do not eliminate actions based on negligence. *See further Bill Would Limit Ballparks' Liability for Fans' Injuries*, Dallas Morning News, May 5, 1998, at 12B, and *'Hockey Puck' Bill*, Salt Lake Trib., Mar. 5, 1998, at A6.

2. Like the Stewarts, fans who encounter a dangerous condition within a stadium often sue to recover for their injuries. The outcome of such actions usually turns on whether the defendant had a duty to prevent the harm from occurring. For a representative sampling, see, e.g., *Lako v. Sports Arena, Inc.*, 57 F.3d 1069 (6th Cir.1995); *Higgins v. White Sox Baseball Club, Inc.*, 787 F.2d 1125 (7th Cir.1986); *Slyvester v. Chicago Park District*, 689 N.E.2d 1119 (Ill.1997); *Giambrone v. New York Yankees*, 581 N.Y.S.2d 756 (App.Div.1992); *Boll v. Chicago Park District*, 620 N.E.2d 1082 (Ill.App.Ct. 1991), *appeal denied*, 602 N.E.2d 447 (Ill.1992); *Tuttle v. Miami Dolphins, Ltd.*, 551 So.2d 477 (Fla.Dist.Ct.App.1988), *review denied*, 563 So.2d 635 (Fla.1990).

3. As *Greenberg* makes clear, it is very difficult to win an inadequate crowd control case because there almost always is a place of safety to which an unwilling fan can retreat. In addition, many such suits are dismissed because the plaintiff willingly participated in the shoving and pushing that caused his or her injury. *See further Pallazola v. Town of Foxborough*, 640 N.E.2d 460 (Mass.1994); *Johnson v. Mid–South Sports, Inc.*, 806 P.2d 1107 (Okla.1991); *Vanchieri v. New Jersey Sports and Exposition Authority*, 514 A.2d 1323 (N.J.1986); *Eneman v. Richter*, 577 N.W.2d 386 (Wis.Ct.App. 1998); *Packard v. Rockford Professional Baseball Club*, 613 N.E.2d 321 (Ill.App.Ct.1993), *appeal denied*, 622 N.E.2d 1211 (Ill.1993), *Hering v. New York Yankees*, 560 N.Y.S.2d 455 (App.Div.1990); *Professional Sports, Inc. v. Gillette Security, Inc.*, 766 P.2d 91 (Ariz.Ct.App.1988); *Warner v. Florida Jai Alai, Inc.*, 221 So.2d 777 (Fla.Dist.Ct.App.1969), *writ discharged*, 235 So.2d 294 (Fla.1970); *People v. U.S.T.A. National Tennis Center, Inc.*, 544 N.Y.S.2d 458 (N.Y.C.Crim.Ct.1989).

4. On occasion, the source of a fan's injury is a player. In May 1912, for example, the Detroit Tigers were in New York to face the Hilltoppers (who later gained more fame as the Yankees). After several innings of being heckled, Ty Cobb, the visitors' star center fielder, jumped into the stands and began beating up his antagonist, a man named Claude Lueke. One year earlier, Lueke had lost eight of his fingers in an industrial accident. When another spectator begged the enraged Cobb to stop, pointing out Lueke could not defend himself because of his disability, Cobb screamed, "I don't care if he has no feet!"

Due to the viciousness of the assault, as well as the insensitivity of the remark (which became the subject of much criticism by the local press), AL president Ban Johnson ordered Cobb expelled from baseball for life. Incensed by the harsh penalty, his teammates quickly organized a strike. Fearing that other clubs might join the work stoppage, Johnson relented and let Cobb off with a $50 fine and a 10–day suspension. Buoyed by their victory, several of the protesters later formed the Baseball Players Fraternity, the first union in major league history. For a further look at Cobb's actions, see Jim Van Vliet, *First Players Union Was Conceived After Cobb Went to Fist City*, Sacramento Bee, Aug. 21, 1994, at C8. For other examples of player attacks on fans, see *Manning v. Grimsley*, 643 F.2d 20 (1st Cir.1981); *Simmons v. Baltimore Orioles, Inc.*, 712 F.Supp. 79 (W.D.Va. 1989); *USAA Casualty Ins. Co. v. Schneider*, 620 F.Supp. 246 (E.D.N.Y. 1985); *Ptasznik v. Johnston*, 234 N.W.2d 548 (Mich.Ct.App.1975).

5. Errant equipment, dangerous conditions, boisterous fans, and surly players are not the only causes of spectator injuries: even team mascots, whose antics are supposed to entertain the crowd, have been sued. *See, e.g., Gil de Rebollo v. Miami Heat Ass'ns, Inc.*, 137 F.3d 56 (1st Cir.1998) ("Burnie," mascot of the Miami Heat, accused of psychologically traumatizing plaintiff by trying to get her to dance with him during a time out), and *Lowe v. California League of Professional Baseball*, 65 Cal.Rptr.2d 105 (Ct.App.1997) ("Tremor," mascot of the Cucamonga Quakes, accused of distracting fan and causing him to be hit by foul ball).

6. Because of a sharp increase in the number of injuries caused by drunk or rowdy fans (often referred to as "hooliganism"), many stadiums have been forced to institute strong countermeasures, including beefing up security, cutting off liquor sales at pre-designated times (and placing limits on individual purchases), and providing alcohol-free seating sections (often called "family fun zones"). *See further* Lee Bowman, *Fans Drinking More at Sports Stadiums*, Pitt. Post–Gazette, May 24, 1998, at A16, and Gregg Ebbert, *Where Have the Friendly Fans Gone?*, Allentown Morning Call, Nov. 20, 1997, at B4.

In November 1997, Veterans Stadium, having already taken such steps without success, established the country's first "sports court." Located under the stands and staffed by a regular judge, the court operates during Philadelphia Eagles games and prosecutes fans for such crimes as disorderly conduct and illegal drinking. *See further* Claire Smith, *Fans Who'd Rather Not be in Philadelphia*, N.Y. Times, Nov. 24, 1997, at A1.

7. Although most incidents of hooliganism involve small bands of fans, at times an entire stadium—or even an entire city—is affected. This fre-

quently occurs when a team clinches a long-awaited championship. *See* Kathryn J. McIntyre, *Managing Riot Risk is a Winning Idea*, Bus. Ins., Feb. 2, 1998, at 37, and *More Often Than Not, Winning Cities Lose Out*, St. Petersburg Times, June 22, 1993, at 1A.

8. For a further discussion of spectator injuries, see, e.g., Joshua E. Kastenberg, *A Three Dimensional Model of Stadium Owner Liability in Spectator Injury Cases*, 7 Marq. Sports L.J. 187 (1996); Walter T. Champion, Jr., *"At the Ol' Ball Game" and Beyond: Spectators and the Potential for Liability*, 14 Am. J. Trial Advoc. 495 (1991); Jefferson C. Taylor, Note, *The War on Soccer Hooliganism: The European Convention on Spectator Violence and "Misbehaviour"*, 27 Va. J. Int'l L. 603 (1987); E. Richard Alhadeff, Comment, *Liability for Injuries to Spectators at Automobile Races*, 19 Ala. L. Rev. 396 (1967); Mike McCarthy, *How to Catch a Foul Ball*, Wall St. J., June 12, 1998, at W1; Eugene L. Meyer, *On Monday Night's Injured List: 108 Football Fans*, Wash. Post, Oct. 15, 1997, at A1. *See also Jensen v. City of Pontiac*, 317 N.W.2d 619 (Mich.App.1982) (stadium did not violate Fourth Amendment by requiring fans to undergo visual inspections and surrender "dangerous" items).

Problem 11

Following an exciting win, a group of baseball fans held a tailgate party in the stadium's parking lot. Ninety minutes later, after a substantial amount of alcohol had been consumed, the party broke up. If one of the participants runs over a pedestrian on the way home, can the ballpark be held liable? *See Brandjord v. Hopper*, 688 A.2d 721 (Pa.Super.Ct.), *appeal denied*, 704 A.2d 633 (Pa.1997).

D. BLACKOUTS

Fans unable to attend a game in person normally hope to find it on television. Games often are "blacked out," however, meaning either the league or the network has decided not to make them available in a given area. Because they are extremely unpopular, blackout rules have been the subject of both litigation and legislation.

METROPOLITAN SPORTS FACILITIES COMM'N v. GENERAL MILLS, INC.

470 N.W.2d 118 (Minn.1991).

KEITH, Chief Justice.

The parties dispute the effect the repeal of Minn.Stat. § 473.568 (1978), had on a contract between respondent Metropolitan Sports Facilities Commission and petitioner General Mills that required General Mills to purchase unsold Minnesota Vikings football tickets under specified circumstances. The Commission sought a declaratory judgment and an injunction requiring General Mills to purchase tickets pursuant to the contract. The trial court, holding that the existence of Minn.Stat. § 473.568 (1978), was not a condition precedent to General Mills' performance under the contract, and that the repeal of section 473.568 did not frustrate the purpose of the contract, found the agreement valid and enforceable. A divided court of appeals upheld the trial court's conclusions, rejected General Mills' constitutional arguments, and suggested that General Mills waived any right to terminate the contract by continuing to accept benefits under the contract. Metropolitan Sports Facilities Comm'n v. General Mills, 460 N.W.2d 625 (Minn.App.1990). We affirm.

I

In 1977, the Minnesota Legislature, with the intent of either renovating old Metropolitan Stadium or building a new multi-purpose sports facility, passed the Metropolitan Sports Facilities Act. Act of May 16, 1977, ch. 89, § 1, 1977 Minn.Laws 141, codified at Minn.Stat. § 473.551–595 (1978). The legislation established the Metropolitan Sports Facilities Commission (Commission) to accomplish this goal and to operate the facility, which would be the home of Minnesota's professional football team, the Minnesota Vikings. See generally Minn.Stat. § 473.553 (1990).

The National Football League (NFL) had and still has a blackout rule in its franchise agreement with league teams including the Vikings. The blackout rule prohibits local telecasting of league football games unless the game is 100% sold-out 72 hours before gametime. The Minnesota Legislature, aware of the blackout rule and concerned that the larger seating capacity of a new stadium would result in fewer sellouts and consequently the blackout of more Vikings games, passed a statute that prohibited a tenant of the new sports facility from being a party to an agreement that would blackout the local telecast of a game when at least 90% of the tickets had been sold 72 hours before gametime. Act of May 16, 1977, ch. 89, § 8, 1977 Minn.Laws 141, 147–48, codified at Minn.Stat. § 473.568 (1978).

To accommodate the Vikings, who faced a dilemma due to the conflict between the NFL blackout rule and section 473.568, the 1979 legislature required, as a prerequisite to the issuance of stadium construction bonds, that the Commission enter into one or more agreements with private purchasers who would purchase tickets under specified circumstances to permit the Vikings to comply with the NFL blackout rule and to allow Minnesota residents to watch the telecasts of home Vikings games when at least 90% of the tickets had been sold 72 hours before gametime. Act of May 25, 1979, ch. 203, § 8, 1979 Minn.Laws 375, 381, codified at Minn.Stat. § 473.581, subd. 3(m) (1980). On August 21, 1979, General Mills saved the day for the construction of the Hubert H. Humphrey Metrodome by entering into a ticket-purchase contract that satisfied the requirements of sections 473.568 and 473.581, subdivision 3(m).

The contract provided, in part:

> THEREFORE, in order to satisfy the requirements of Section 473.568 of Minnesota Statutes, 1978, and of Section

473.581, Subdivision 3(m) of the Minnesota Statutes, 1978, as amended, the Commission and the Purchaser agree as follows:

1. This Agreement, and the purchase commitments set forth herein, shall be effective during each of the first twenty years of the operation of the sports facility constructed pursuant to the above statutes. Commencement of operation shall be defined as the date on which the professional football organization which is a major tenant of the facility plays its first home game in the sports facility; provided, however, this Agreement shall not be effective and General Mills shall have no further purchase commitments in the event the [sic] Section 473.568 is finally determined by a court of competent jurisdiction to be unconstitutional and void, or if Section 473.568 is otherwise ineffective except in the case of a repeal thereof based solely upon the continued effectiveness of this Agreement.

2. Purchaser agrees that, if the professional football organization which is a major tenant of the facility cannot comply with the provisions of Minnesota Statutes, 1978, Section 473.568, because of the terms of an agreement under which the professional football league of which the tenant is a member has sold or otherwise transferred all or part of the rights of the league's member organizations in the sponsored telecasting of games of the organization or otherwise, Purchaser will, whenever more than 90% but less than 100% of the tickets of admission for seats at any professional football game to be played in the facility (which tickets were available for purchase by the general public 120 hours or more before the scheduled beginning time of the game either at the sports facility where the game is to be played or at the box office closest to the facility) have been purchased 72 hours or more before the beginning time of the game, purchase or guarantee the purchase of all such tickets which remain unsold as required to permit the telecast to areas within the state which otherwise would not receive the telecast.

In addition to the good will and favorable publicity General Mills enjoyed, the contract granted General Mills one minute of free advertising on the scoreboard during each Vikings home game and convenient access to the Metrodome for its shuttle buses, regardless of whether it was required to purchase tickets.

The Vikings played their first game in the newly-constructed Metrodome in 1982. In 1983 a group of Minnesotans attempted to attract the NFL's Superbowl to the Metrodome. A Superbowl Task Force discovered that the NFL objected to the Metrodome as a potential Superbowl site because Minnesota had the statute on its books that conflicted with the league's blackout rule. As part of the successful effort to bring the Superbowl to Minnesota, the 1984 legislature repealed section 473.568 "based solely upon the continued effectiveness" of any ticket-purchase agreements entered into by the Commission. Act of May 2, 1984, ch. 607, § 2, 1984 Minn.Laws 1446, 1450.

The parties disagreed about the effect of the repeal on the contract but agreed not to determine its validity until General Mills' performance was required. General Mills continued to receive advertising pursuant to the ticket-purchase contract through the 1988–89 football season. When the October 1, 1989, Vikings game did not sell out, the Commission brought this action.

II

A

The court's role in interpreting a contract is to ascertain and give effect to the intention of the parties. Karim v. Werner, 333 N.W.2d 877, 879 (Minn.1983). General Mills and the Commission, freely entering into this contract for the purchase of unsold Vikings tickets, prudently specified the consequences that would attach to the occurrence of several events. The parties anticipated a repeal of section 473.568 in paragraph 1 of the Agreement:

> this Agreement shall not be effective * * * in the event the [sic] Section 473.568 is finally determined by a court of competent jurisdiction to be unconstitutional and void, or if Section 473.568 is otherwise ineffective except in the case of a repeal thereof based solely upon the continued effectiveness of this Agreement.

As anticipated by the parties, the legislature, in fact, repealed section 473.568:

> Minnesota Statutes 1982, section 473.568, is repealed. This repeal is based solely upon the continued effectiveness of the agreement or agreements entered into by the Metropolitan Sports Facilities Commission and the purchaser or purchasers of tickets of admission as provided for by Laws 1979, chapter 203, section 8. Such agreements shall remain in effect throughout their terms and the commission shall have no authority to terminate or modify such agreements.

Act of May 2, 1984, ch. 607, § 2, 1984 Minn.Laws 1446, 1450.

We hold that the trial court correctly determined that the language of the contract is unambiguous. A contract is ambiguous if it is susceptible to more than one interpretation based on its language alone. Lamb Plumbing & Heating Co. v. Kraus–Anderson, Inc., 296 N.W.2d 859, 862 (Minn.1980). When pressed to identify language in the contract that is ambiguous, counsel for General Mills argued that the language is ambiguous because the existence of section 473.568 is fundamental to the contract. The plain language of the contract, however, contemplates a situation in which section 473.568 could be repealed and the agreement would remain in effect. At the time of contracting General Mills and the Commission, resolving several contingencies that could arise during the contract term, agreed that they would remain bound under the contract "in the case of a repeal [of section 473.568] based solely upon the continued effectiveness of this Agreement." This anticipated condition arose, and, according to the provisions of the contract, the parties remain bound under the ticket-purchase contract.

General Mills urges the court to adopt the following interpretation of the contract: section 473.568 would terminate the ticket-purchase contract unless General Mills consented to its continued effectiveness after the repeal. Where a written contract is unambiguous, the court must deduce the parties' intent from the language used. Burnett v. Hopwood, 187 Minn. 7, 14, 244 N.W. 254, 257 (1932); see also Carl Bolander & Sons, Inc. v. United Stockyards Corp., 298 Minn. 428, 433, 215 N.W.2d 473, 476 (1974). A party cannot alter unequivocal language of a contract with speculation of an unexpressed intent of the parties. Kuhlmann v. Educational Publishers, 245 Minn. 171, 176, 71 N.W.2d 889, 893 (1955). General Mills' interpretation finds no support in, and in fact, contradicts the language of the contract. The trial court properly disregarded General Mills' extrinsic evidence advancing its interpretation of the ticket-purchase contract.

B

General Mills contends that the repeal of section 473.568 discharged General Mills' obligations under the contract because the Vikings' inability to comply with the provisions of section 473.568 was a condition precedent to General Mills' obligation to perform. Because section 473.568 was repealed, the argument proceeds, the condition precedent could no longer arise. A condition precedent "is any fact or event, subsequent to the making of a contract, which must exist or occur before a duty of immediate performance arises under the contract." National City Bank v. St. Paul Fire & Marine Ins. Co., 447 N.W.2d 171, 176 (Minn.1989). We agree that the inability of the Vikings to "comply with the provisions of Minnesota Statutes, 1978, Section 473.568" is a condition precedent to General Mills' obligation to perform under the contract. The existence of section 473.568 in current law, however, is not a condition precedent.

The unambiguous language of paragraph 1 of the contract demonstrates that the parties contemplated and provided for a conditional repeal of section 473.568. We presume that the parties intended the clause relating to the repeal of section 473.568 to have effect. See Chergosky v. Crosstown Bell, Inc., 463 N.W.2d 522, 525–26 (Minn.1990). The clause provided that the parties would remain bound "in the case of a repeal [of Section 473.568] based solely upon the continued effectiveness of this Agreement." Paragraph 2 of the contract provides that if the Minnesota Vikings "cannot comply with the provisions of Minnesota Statutes, 1978, Section 473.568" General Mills will purchase tickets according to the terms of the contract. From the plain language of the contract read as a whole, the parties' intent is manifest. The parties referenced the provisions of section 473.568 that existed in 1978, the law in effect at the time of contracting. When the legislature repealed section

473.568 based on the continued effectiveness of ticket-purchase contracts entered into by the Commission, the contract between General Mills and the Commission remained valid. General Mills' obligation to perform still is subject to a condition precedent—the Vikings' inability to comply with the provisions of section 473.568 that existed at the time of contracting. Accordingly, the repeal of section 473.568 does not discharge General Mills from its obligations under the contract.

III

General Mills raises several other claims to support its position that the repeal of section 473.568 discharged its obligations under the ticket-purchase contract. Woven through each of these arguments is a complaint that the legislature acted with the General Mills ticket-purchase contract specifically in mind. General Mills, however, does not contend that the legislature's action constituted special legislation under Minn. Const. art. XII, § 1.

First, General Mills argues that the repealer violates the separation of powers doctrine. General Mills claims that the legislature exercised a judicial function by purporting to determine that General Mills is liable under its contract with the Commission. General Mills argues that the legislature attempted to resolve a disputed claim with the following language in the repealer: "[s]uch agreements shall remain in effect throughout their terms." The legislature certainly could not resolve a contract dispute between the Commission and General Mills. See Sanborn v. Commissioners of Rice County, 9 Minn. 273 (Gil.) 258, 262–63 (1864) (declaring unconstitutional legislation requiring county commissioners to decide claims of Sanborn against a school district). The legislature also could not mandate that the contract remain in effect contrary to the terms of the agreement. The legislature, however, has done neither in this case. No dispute existed between the Commission and General Mills until the legislature acted; the parties then disputed the effect of the legislature's repeal of section 473.568 on the ticket purchase contract, a proper subject for judicial resolution.

General Mills also claims that the repealer violates separation of powers because the legislature instructed the judiciary how to interpret the repealer. The court's function, in construing a statute, is to ascertain and effectuate the intent of the legislature. City of St. Louis Park v. King, 246 Minn. 422, 429, 75 N.W.2d 487, 492–93 (1956). Rather than invading the judicial function, the repeal merely delineates clearly the legislature's intent that the repeal not affect ticket-purchase agreements entered into by the Commission.

Second, General Mills claims that the repeal of section 473.568 violated due process freedom of contract principles. To challenge successfully an interference with the liberty of contract protected by the state and federal due process clauses, one must demonstrate that the action is not rationally related to the achievement of a legitimate governmental purpose. AFSCME Councils 6, 14, 65 and 96 v. Sundquist, 338 N.W.2d 560, 574 (Minn.1983). General Mills argues that the repealer violates due process because the legislature exceeded its constitutional authority by exercising a judicial function. In effect, General Mills is merely clothing its groundless separation of powers claim in this due process claim that also must fail.

In addition, General Mills claims that the legislature forced a contractual position on General Mills. This argument also is without merit. The legislature did not coerce General Mills into entering this contract. These sophisticated parties, presumably with the assistance of experienced and able counsel, exercised their liberty of contract and now are accountable for the product of their negotiations. The legislature did not mandate inclusion of the contract clause providing that the parties would remain bound in the case of a repeal of section 473.568 "based solely on the continued effectiveness of this Agreement." The parties freely negotiated and voluntarily agreed to be bound by the provisions of the ticket-purchase contract.

Finally, General Mills claims that even if the parties agreed to remain obligated in the event of a "repeal [of section 473.568] based solely upon the continued effectiveness of this Agreement," this court cannot give effect to this provision because it attempts to confer a power on the legislature that it otherwise could not constitutionally exercise. General Mills analogizes this case to one in which the parties agreed to submit their claims to the supreme court when the court did not have jurisdiction to hear the case. Cf. State v. Dike, 20 Minn. 363 (Gil.) 314, 317 (1874) (under separation of powers doctrine, court cannot exercise jurisdiction over executive officer even if the officer consents). Here, the parties conferred no power on the legislature. We reiterate that the parties merely anticipated various circumstances that might arise during the term of the contract including possible courses of action the legislature might take. When one of those circumstances materialized, the provisions of the contract, freely agreed to by the parties, afforded the consequences that must follow. The agreement between General Mills and the Commission thus remained in effect after the 1984 repeal of section 473.568.

Affirmed.

SHAW v. DALLAS COWBOYS FOOTBALL CLUB, LTD.

1998 WL 419765 (E.D.Pa.1998).

GAWTHROP, III, District Judge.

Plaintiffs are claiming that defendants have combined, in violation of antitrust laws, to fix, raise, maintain, or stabilize the price for satellite broadcasts of National Football League (NFL) games. They allege that these defendants' conduct caused artificially high and noncompetitive prices for NFL satellite broadcasts. Approximately a dozen NFL games are broadcast each week by free television networks, such as NBC or Fox. In any given week, one may watch on free, non-satellite television a few of these games. Which games one may view on free television depends on the local market; for example, Philadelphia Eagles games are always shown on free, network television to fans in Philadelphia. However—to indulge in a totally hypothetical example—Dallas Cowboys fans in Philadelphia will not be able to watch, in Philadelphia, all of the Dallas Cowboys' games.

In addition, one may purchase from the NFL a weekly satellite television package of all the games broadcast nationwide: NFL Sunday TicketTM. Individuals may subscribe to the Sunday TicketTM program, but they must own a satellite dish antenna and pay an additional fee of $139 per season. Plaintiffs allege that the agreement by the NFL and its members to market the Sunday TicketTM package has restricted the options available to fans for viewing non-network broadcasts of NFL games, thereby reducing competition and artificially raising prices. Defendants have responded by filing this 12(b)(6) motion to dismiss for failure to state a claim under which relief could be granted, claiming (1) that the Sports Broadcasting Act (SBA or the Act) specifically exempts their conduct from antitrust laws, and, (2) that plaintiffs do not adequately allege the joint action necessary for antitrust liability.

DISCUSSION

Section 1 of the Sherman Act states, "every contract, combination ... or conspiracy, in restraint of trade or commerce among the several states, or with foreign nations, is hereby declared to be illegal." 15 U.S.C. § 1. This concededly broad definition has been tempered somewhat by the case law. The Supreme Court has pronounced a "rule of reason," which provides that only agreements which unreasonably restrain trade are illegal, see e.g., Standard Oil v. U.S., 221 U.S. 1, 31 S.Ct. 502, 55 L.Ed. 619 (1911), since to strike all agreements which restrain trade would render business impossible. Under the current state of the law, to make out a Section 1 violation, plaintiffs must prove three elements: a contract, combination, or conspiracy; a restraint of trade; and an effect on interstate commerce. Fuentes v. South Hills Cardiology, 946 F.2d 196, 198 (3d Cir.1991).

Plaintiffs claim that there is an agreement among the defendants to limit the broadcast of professional football games. They allege that this agreement restricts output of televised football games and artificially increases the price for such games. Plaintiffs aver, and defendants do not dispute, that any individual can only see two or three professional football games per week on free, network TV, but that any individual may subscribe to the Sunday TicketTM program for monthly satellite access fees and an additional fee of $139 per season.

I turn now to the first argument by defendants: that their actions are completely exempt from antitrust scrutiny under the Sports Broadcasting Act, 15 U.S.C. § 1291.

I. Antitrust Exemption

The Sports Broadcasting Act was passed in 1961 specifically to reverse United States v. National Football League, 116 F. Supp. 319

(E.D.Pa.1953), a district court ruling that the NFL's sale of a games package to a television network violated § 1 of the Sherman Antitrust Act. See generally, U.S. Football League v. National Football League, 842 F.2d 1335, 1346–47 (2d Cir.1988) (discussing history of agreements between the NFL and the major television networks and history of the SBA). The SBA exempts the sale of certain broadcast rights from the antitrust laws:

> any agreement by or among persons engaging in or conducting the organized professional team sports of football, . . ., by which any league of clubs participating in professional football . . . contests sells or otherwise transfers all or any part of the rights of such league's member clubs in the sponsored telecasting of the games of football, . . . engaged in or conducted by such clubs.

15 U.S.C. § 1291.

The contention between the parties in this case lies in the meaning of the phrase "rights . . . in the sponsored telecasting." Plaintiffs maintain that this phrase pertains only to broadcasts that have formal sponsors, who presumably run commercial advertisements, paying a fee to the station for that privilege, so that it is not necessary and not required that the viewer pay money in order to watch the program. With the broadcast fee being subsidized by the sponsors, therefore, the games are free to the public. Defendants, on the other hand, argue that this phrase exempts from antitrust liability not only their agreements to sell rights to broadcast certain games with formal sponsorship, but also exempts agreements to sell broadcasts of the same games through a non-sponsored medium. They argue that the Sunday TicketTM package is simply a sale of their residual rights in the games which were broadcast on "sponsored telecasts," and, so, the package is a sale of "part of the rights" to the "sponsored telecasts." Their action in selling Sunday TicketTM falls within the SBA, they claim, because they still own a partial right to the games broadcast by the free networks, and Sunday TicketTM is simply a vehicle for selling these retained rights.

The Supreme Court construes exceptions to the antitrust laws narrowly. See, e.g., Union Labor Life Ins. Co. v. Pireno, 458 U.S. 119, 126, 102 S.Ct. 3002, 73 L.Ed.2d 647 (1982). In Pireno, the Court concluded that the Sherman Act stands for Congress's commitment to a free-market system and open competition, and thus any laws that circumvent this goal must be closely examined. Id. The Sports Broadcasting Act is an exception to the general antitrust laws and, so, must be narrowly applied. See Chicago Pro. Sports Ltd. Partnership v. NBA, 961 F.2d 667, 671 (7th Cir.1992), cert. den., 506 U.S. 954, 113 S.Ct. 409, 121 L.Ed.2d 334 (1992) (regarding SBA, "What the industry obtained, the courts enforce; what it did not obtain from the legislature—even if similar to something within that exception—a court should not bestow.").

With these restrictive guidelines in mind, I turn to the task of determining the meaning of the Act. In so doing, I heed the Supreme Court's injunction to "look first to the statutory language and then to the legislative history if the statutory language is unclear." Blum v. Stenson, 465 U.S. 886, 896, 104 S.Ct. 1541, 79 L.Ed.2d 891 (1984); Murphy v. Dalton, 81 F.3d 343, 350 (3d Cir.1996).

WHAT DOES THE TERM "SPONSORED TELECASTING" MEAN?

The question arises as to what is the meaning of the phrase "sponsored telecasting." The term "sponsor" has many definitions, ranging from a legislator proposing a bill, to a godparent presenting a baby for baptism. To the extent that these football games, and their consequent electronic depictions, are all played under the aegis of the NFL, that entity could arguably be called their sponsor. But the more apt definition is "[o]ne that finances a project or an event carried out by another person or group, especially a business enterprise that pays for radio or television programming in return for advertising time." The American Heritage Dictionary of the English Language 17411 (3rd ed.1992). Clearly, that is the sort of sponsorship of which we speak here. Only telecasting which is performed with such a sponsor can meet the meaning of the phrase "rights ... in the sponsored telecasting."

Defendants argue that these broadcasts are nevertheless "sponsored telecasting," since when they were first put on the air, it was in the more traditional corporate-sponsored commercial context, rather than the pre-paid, commercial-free-package context. I, however, look to the broadcast which goes to these particular plaintiffs, not its earlier sponsored incarnation. Were the rule otherwise, the NFL could circumvent the statutory confines, nullify the statutory scheme, simply by always using earlier broadcasts with commercials. I do not believe that to have been Congress's intent; to construe the statute that way would cause the statute to self-destruct—an absurd result.

Since the defendants disagree that this is the plain meaning of the statute, however, it becomes appropriate to look at the record to see what Congress thought it was enacting.

1. Legislative History

There are three pieces of legislative history which, taken together, show that the SBA does not exempt the actions here challenged, that is, the NFL's sale of Sunday TicketTM. First, the SBA was enacted to reverse the decision of Judge Grim, of this court, in which he held that a contract to sell the NFL's pooled-rights to professional football games to CBS violated § 1 of the Sherman Act. U.S. Football League, 842 F.2d at 1347 (citing S.Rep. No. 1087, 87th Cong., 1st Sess. 1, reprinted in 1961 U.S.Code Cong. & Admin. News 3042 and discussing United States v. National Football League, which led to the enactment of the SBA). Thus SBA's legislative context and the specific concern it sought to address was focussed upon but one target: the sale of games to a sponsored television network.

Second, the legislative report on the SBA states that "[t]he exemption provided by Section 1 of H.R. 9096 [the SBA] applies to the sale or transfer of rights in the sponsored telecasting of games." The report then states, "The bill does not apply to closed circuit or subscription television." Telecasting of Professional Sports Contests: Hearing before the Antitrust Committee of the House Committee on the Judiciary on H.R. 8757, 87th Cong. 1st Sess. at 4 (Sept. 13, 1961).

Finally, the NFL itself admitted that the SBA does not exempt the agreement at issue. During its passage through Congress, the House of Representatives heard testimony from then-NFL Commissioner Pete Rozelle concerning the bill: "You understand, do you not, Mr. Rozelle, that this Bill covers only the free telecasting of professional sports contests, and does not cover pay T.V.?" Mr. Rozelle responded under oath, "Absolutely." Id. at 36 (Aug. 28, 1961).

2. *Case Law Precedent*

The issue in this case—whether satellite broadcasting constitutes "sponsored telecasting"—is one of apparent first impression. There seems to be no direct case law; there is but one case that is even obliquely on point, Chicago Pro. Sports Ltd. Partnership v. NBA, 808 F.Supp. 646 (N.D.Ill.1992). There, a television station and the Chicago Bulls, a professional basketball club, brought an antitrust challenge against the NBA for its contract with Turner Network Television (TNT), a cable television network which also broadcast some commercials. The contract contained a clause restricting broadcasts of NBA games by the plaintiff television station on nights when TNT also broadcast the games. Id. at 647. The NBA argued that its agreement with TNT was exempt from antitrust scrutiny because TNT constituted "sponsored telecasting" and thus the agreement fell within the SBA's exemption. Id. at 649. The court held that TNT was more like subscription television than like sponsored telecasting, and so a contract with TNT was not exempt from the Sherman Act under the SBA. Significantly, the court based its decision on three factors: 1) that viewers must pay to receive TNT, 2) that TNT derived its revenue predominantly from subscriptions rather than advertising revenues, and 3) that the legislative history showed that sponsored telecasting was limited to free commercial television. Id. at 649–650. This tends to support the conclusion I have reached in this case.

The Sports Broadcasting Act did not pronounce a broad, sweeping policy, but rather engrafted a narrow, discrete, special-interest exemption upon the normal prohibition on monopolistic behavior. In the SBA, the NFL got what it lobbied for at the time. It cannot now stretch that law to cover other means of broadcast. Accordingly, I find that the defendants' conduct is not exempt from antitrust liability under the SBA.

II. Conspiracy

As to defendants' second argument, that there can be no concerted action because the NFL alone sold NFL Sunday TicketTM, precedent suggests otherwise. In L.A. Mem'l Coliseum Comm'n v. NFL, the court rejected the "single entity" defense of the NFL against a § 1 claim, holding that the NFL alone could still meet the requirement of concerted action. 726 F.2d 1381, 1390 (9th Cir.1984), cert. den., 469 U.S. 990 (1984). Even given that pro-plaintiff precedent, this case goes beyond the one-defendant-created action of the Coliseum case. Plaintiffs do not allege that the NFL acted alone to violate the Sherman Act. Rather, they complain that all the member clubs, through and with the NFL, have conspired to restrain the trade in televised football. Thus, they have adequately pled plural participation.

Finally, defendants claim that the antitrust complaint is too vague and conclusory to hurdle Rule 12(b)(6). In Leatherman v. Tarrant County Narcotics Intell. and Coordination Unit, the Supreme Court held, albeit in another substantive-law context, that Federal Rule of Civil Procedure 8(a) establishes a "liberal system of 'notice pleading'" which "do[es] not require a claimant to set out in detail the facts upon which he bases his claim." 507 U.S. 163, 168, 113 S.Ct. 1160, 122 L.Ed.2d 517 (1993). Greater particularity in pleading is only required for allegations of fraud and mistake. Id. Under Rule 8(a) the plaintiff is not required to specifically describe the full array of facts as to how a conspiracy came about. It is sufficient for the plaintiff to identify "the conspiracy's participants, purpose and motive." Fuentes, 946 F.2d 196, 202 (3d Cir.1991). The plaintiffs here have specifically pled the participants (the NFL and its member clubs), the purpose (to restrict output and so raise prices), and the motive (monetary gain to the defendants). Plaintiffs allege an agreement among the clubs and the NFL; they allege that the agreement unreasonably restricts output of non-network broadcasts of professional football, thus raising the market price to tune into those games. That is enough to state a claim that the agreement is illegal. Hence, the defendants' motion to dismiss must be denied.

Notes

1. For a further look at the Sports Broadcasting Act, see Brett T. Goodman, *The Sports Broadcasting Act: As Anachronistic as the Dumont Network?*, 5 Seton Hall J. Sports L. 469 (1995), and Phillip M. Cox II, *Flag on the Play: The Siphoning Effect on Sports Television*, 47 Fed. Com. L.J. 571 (1995). *See also Colorado High School Activities Ass'n v. National Football League*, 711 F.2d 943 (10th Cir.1983) (construing the Act as it applies to high school football games).

2. Although most owners believe blackouts spur ticket sales, fan advocates argue real-time broadcasting stimulates local interest and ultimately leads to increased sellouts and merchandise sales. *See* Glenn Dickey, *It's Time for NFL to Lift TV Blackouts*, S.F. Chron., Jan. 16, 1998, at C3. Because no reliable studies exist, both claims remain unverified. If you were the general counsel to a league, what advice would you give to the owners concerning blackouts? *See further Unfair to Fans*, Buff. News, Nov. 10, 1996, at 2C (suggesting not having blackouts is a good way to thank fans and build support).

3. In addition to fans, television blackouts have been challenged by a number of other parties, including, most prominently, bars and taverns (who, in an effort to attract patrons, often circumvent blackout rules by illegal means). Courts, however, consistently have rejected such claims. *See, e.g., Cablevision of Michigan, Inc. v. Sports Palace, Inc.*, 27 F.3d 566 (6th Cir.1994); *National Football League v. McBee & Bruno's, Inc.*, 792 F.2d 726 (8th Cir.1986); *WTWV, Inc. v. National Football League*, 678 F.2d 142 (11th Cir.1982); *Joe Hand Promotions v. Burg's Lounge*, 2 F.Supp.2d 710 (E.D.Pa. 1998); *Kingvision Pay Per View, Ltd. v. Williams*, 1 F.Supp.2d 1481 (S.D.Ga. 1998); *Time Warner Cable of New York City v. Taco Rapido Restaurant*, 988 F.Supp. 107 (E.D.N.Y.1997); *National Football League v. Ellicottville Gin Mill, Inc.*, 1995 WL 737935 (W.D.N.Y.1995); *National Football League v. Rondor, Inc.*, 840 F.Supp. 1160 (N.D.Ohio 1993); *Home Box Office v. Carlim, Inc.*, 838 F.Supp. 432 (E.D.Mo.1993); *National Football League v. The Alley, Inc.*, 624 F.Supp. 6 (S.D.Fla.1983); *Hertel v. City of Pontiac*, 470 F.Supp. 603 (E.D.Mich.1979); *Blaich v. National Football League*, 212 F.Supp. 319 (S.D.N.Y.1962).

For a further discussion of the pros and cons of television blackouts, see Alan Fecteau, *NFL Network Blackouts: Old Law Meets New Technology With the Advent of the Satellite Dish*, 5 Marq. Sports L.J. 221 (1995), and Lynne S. Sutphen, Comment, *Sports Bars' Interception of the National Football League's Satellite Signals: Controversy or Compromise?*, 2 Seton Hall J. Sport L. 203 (1992). *See also Off Main Street*, Buff. News, Aug. 25, 1996, at 1B (reporting that as of 1996, the NFL had sued 207 bars and restaurants across the country for illegally showing blacked-out games, with the greatest number of violators—64—being located in western New York).

4. Ironically, the most famous blackout of a sporting event was accidental. On November 17, 1968, a national audience was watching the New York Jets and the Oakland Raiders, perennial AFL rivals, do battle on NBC. With the score tied 29–29 and 1:05 remaining in the game, the Jets lined up for a 26–yard field goal attempt. By this point, due to the unusual number of penalties that had been called, the game had been on for three hours, the maximum time allotted by the network. Thus, an unthinking technician threw a switch and suddenly viewers were watching the children's movie "Heidi." By the time NBC realized what had happened, the Raiders had scored two quick touchdowns to post a stunning 43–32 victory. Besieged by tens of thousands of complaints, NBC president Julian Goodman issued a public apology the next day for what has since become known as "The Heidi Game."

Problem 12

Because the local team spent the better part of each season in last place, its homes games were routinely blacked out. If a group of hearing-impaired fans sue the club, arguing because listening on the radio is not an option for them the blackouts must be lifted, in whose favor will the court rule? *See Stoutenborough v. National Football League, Inc.*, 59 F.3d 580 (6th Cir.), *cert. denied*, 516 U.S. 1028 (1995).

E. COLLECTIBLES

In recent years, the demand for bats, balls, jerseys, caps, and other sports-related souvenirs has skyrocketed. This has led to a sharp jump in prices and a torrent of counterfeit items.

1. COST

Collecting was once the province of kids. Today, however, the field is dominated by adults who treat it as a business and hope to earn substantial returns on their money.

POP GOES THE MARKET: GONE ARE THE BUBBLE–GUM DAYS OF CARD COLLECTING

Scott Munn
The Daily Oklahoman, July 3, 1997, at 25.

Anyone who questions the state of baseball card-collecting needs to go no further than a bunch of 12–year-olds. Give them each five bucks, then watch where most go to buy hours worth of entertainment.

"These days, you can get an average of two packs of cards for that money, but after you open them, the thrill is gone," says Les Springs, who operates The Old Ball Park, an Oklahoma City sports card store. "Usually, kids will go to Blockbuster and rent a Sega game and have a ball for two days."

Once as innocent as the games themselves, card collecting has become a billion-dollar industry dominated by money-waving kids in adult bodies. Because of that, many of today's youngsters have missed the joy of peeling open a 50–cent wax pack, searching for a hero and then trading the other 14 cards with a friend for future considerations.

Ever since 1981, when the market began its explosion from a delightful pastime into a bull market, kids have been slowly replaced as full-time collectors by grown-ups who someday hope to retire on a closet full of cardboard.

Heck, the card hobby is so out of whack, a strip of that horrid bubblegum in every pack is no longer a guarantee. "You don't see many kids at our shop anymore," Springs said. "What we've done is price them right out of the hobby. I don't know if we'll ever get it back to what it was."

Topps was the longtime producer of wax pack baseball cards when, in 1981, it was joined by the Donruss and Fleer brands. The card market remained on even keel until 1987, when people began buying cards by the case and storing them in the extra bedroom closet, hoping to pay for Johnny's education or a Hawaiian retirement vacation.

It has more or less backfired. What was once a single-variety card market is now a counter-top odyssey. There are at least 14 different types of cards available, and that doesn't include the subsets within the sets.

Fifty cents rarely gets a '97 pack of cards, which are sometimes kept inside locked glass cases at discount stores. It may get one card depending on who the guy is—a fan of Bernie Williams can get a Score brand card for 40 cents and have a dime left. Otherwise, it's an average of $2.50 for one pack, a price driven upward by companies' obsession with frills like gloss-coated cards or autographed inserts.

The good old days of gum-stained cards and dull gray backs are indeed extinct. "Interest in cards has fallen off since the early '90s, but you're always going to have the adults interested when they keep reading in magazines what an investment they are," said Topps spokesman Marty Appel. "Everybody seems to be bullish on cards, but we think kids are still interested."

Like Springs, others are skeptical. "I'd like to think the hobby can return to what it used to be, but I don't know if it can," said Tracy Hackler, associate editor of Beckett Baseball Card Monthly, which hobbyists use when referring to card prices. "It grew so much in a short amount of time. Box and pack prices have increased tremendously over the past few years. Companies really need to find a way to get the kids involved again. A kid goes to the store today with his allowance and has trouble buying cards."

People who hoarded cards during the hobby's heyday—1987 through 1992—are getting little return when they show up at hobby shops ready to sell. A dealer might buy a 1987 Donruss set, highlighted by Greg Maddux's $8 rookie card, for $20. An unpopular 1989 Bowman set might get between $5 and $12, then the Ken Griffey Jr. rookie card could end up in a showcase for almost what the entire set was worth.

"I know there are a lot of disheartened people out there," Springs said. "The people who bought all those cards back in the late '80s and early '90s, their options now are limited. They can let them sit in the garage and hope they get out of circulation. Otherwise, if they're hoping to get a big return, it's not going to work right now."

Collecting isn't all in the cards. Sports memorabilia is a new trend that may be a better buy for the money. Space-takers like old sports equipment, pennants, publications and toy-like figurines are becoming popular decor. Many major trade shows have dealers who specialize in those particular items.

Yes, they are pricey. But not everyone has a 1906 Worth baseball stitcher, a ticket sign from the 1946 Fort Worth Cats minor-league baseball team, a Harlem Globetrotters uniform or a brewery advertising poster from the Chicago Fire of the old World Football League.

"I've been seeing the switch to vintage material like that," said Roger Neufeldt, a Norman mail-order dealer who specializes in pre–1975 items. "The glut in the (card) market has turned some collectors off that and into this."

Neufeldt, who drives 50,000 miles a year to hobby shows from coast-to-coast, says, "I don't take a lot of memorabilia with me to shows, but the pennants, programs and publications like magazines and programs are big business now."

Autographs are hot items these days. Signatures of nearly every major superstar are available at many card shops or shows. They usually come with certificates of authenticity. "Everybody who collects cards has Ken Griffey," Springs says, "but not everyone has an autographed Jerry Rice plaque. I think memorabilia is starting to experience the growth that we saw in cards 10 to 15 years ago."

That may mean already high-dollar items could be outlandish by 2012. Neufeldt will be disappointed if his baseball stitcher doesn't sell for $400. He saw a publication by Hall of Famer Frank Chance, printed sometime between 1906 and 1909, sell for $580. Neufeldt says a perfect Babe Ruth signature on a baseball may carry a $6,000 price tag—as opposed to $500 for an imperfect scrawl from the Bambino. Kids? Shoot, there aren't many adults who can afford that.

Notes

1. It is estimated that 5.7 million adults collect sports memorabilia in the United States, and annual retail sales of such merchandise now top $2 billion. *See Bizwatch*, L.A. Daily News, Aug. 30, 1997, at B1. Although many different types of sports mementos are collected, trading cards remain the single most popular item (accounting for nearly half of all sales). *See further* Fred W. Wright Jr., *Is There a Fortune in Those Cards?*, St. Petersburg Times, May 4, 1998, at 9 (Bus.).

2. The most prized trading card is the legendary 1909 Honus Wagner T–206, which has sold for as much as $640,000. Produced by the Piedmont Tobacco Company and distributed in packages of Sweet Caporal cigarettes, the card was discontinued almost immediately because Wagner, who played shortstop for the Pittsburgh Pirates and later was inducted into the Hall of Fame, objected to his likeness being used to promote tobacco to young children (although some historians believe Wagner actually was upset over the fact the company refused to pay him a royalty). *See further* Alexandra Peers, *Honus' Card Fetches Wagnerian Sums*, Pitt. Post–Gazette, Sept. 21, 1996, at A1.

3. In addition to the Wagner card, other items also have commanded princely sums in recent years: $3 million for Mark McGwire's 1998 record-breaking 70th home run ball; $306,000 for the uniform worn by Lou Gehrig during his 1939 farewell speech at Yankee Stadium; $175,000 for a 200–year-old metal golf putter; $126,000 for the first ever home run ball at Yankee Stadium (considered especially valuable because it was hit by Babe Ruth); $84,000 for a Topps No. 1 Andy Pafko baseball card; and $55,000 for the 1966 letter in which boxer Muhammad Ali sought an exemption from the draft on religious grounds. For other examples of high-priced collectibles, see Mike Dodd, *Older Items More Likely to be Big Hit for Collector*, USA Today, Sept. 26, 1996, at 3C.

4. The high price of sports memorabilia has led to an interesting—and controversial—marketing gimmick. In September 1998, Upper Deck cut up a $23,000 Babe Ruth game-used baseball bat and began inserting pieces in a

special set of trading cards. A short time later, the NHL did the same thing to a $25,000 Gordie Howe Detroit Red Wings game-used jersey. *See further* Kevin Allen, *Howe Has His Sweater All Cut Up*, USA Today, Dec. 18, 1998, at 14C. While some people believe "sliver" cards are helping make history affordable, others view them as proof of how low merchandisers will stoop to boost sales. *See, e.g.*, Richard Sandomir, *Sharing History, or Just Ruining It?*, N.Y. Times, Sept. 15, 1998, at D4 (arguing all Ruth's artifacts should be preserved).

5. As pointed out above, people buy sports collectibles for a variety of reasons, including: a) a wish to own a piece of history; b) a belief that the item will turn out to be a good financial investment; c) a hope that it will become a cherished family heirloom; and, d) a need for increased self-esteem and social status. Because of the volatility of the marketplace and the risk of purchasing a forgery, however, there is really only one good reason to ever buy a piece of memorabilia: because its intrinsic beauty appeals to the buyer. Todd Archer, *Souvenirs Good to Keep But Not for Profit*, Cin. Post, June 9, 1997, at 4C.

6. "True" collectibles must be distinguished from "instant" or "manufactured" collectibles, which are created for the express purpose of being sold. While some instant collectibles do appreciate over time, most quickly fall in value and never regain their initial price. *See further* Jim Shulman, *Cashing In On Collectibles*, 20 Target Marketing 96 (Mar. 1997).

7. Because of the willingness of fans to pay for signatures, many athletes now refuse to give free autographs. For example, an eight-year-old fan recently sent Reggie White a card to sign. The Green Bay Packer returned the card—unsigned—with an application to join his fan club for $20. *See Asks for Reggie White's Autograph, Gets Request for $20*, USA Today, Apr. 30, 1998, at 14A (reporting the youngster was devastated by White's actions). Although widely condemned by fans, such practices often are defended by players on the ground they have a right to be compensated for their time and effort, especially given the fact that once he has the autograph, there is nothing to prevent the fan from turning around and selling it.

8. For an interesting case in which a group of collectors alleged a manufacturer's practice of randomly inserting limited edition trading cards into its packages violated the Racketeer Influenced and Corrupt Organizations Act, see *Price v. Pinnacle Brands, Inc.*, 138 F.3d 602 (5th Cir.1998).

Problem 13

A dealer tricked a fan into selling him a quarterback's rookie card for $10 at a time when it was worth $100. Later that year the player won his first Super Bowl and the card's value jumped to $500. If the fan sues the dealer and wins, what damages should the court award? *See* Paul T. Wangerin, *The Strategic Value of Restitutionary Remedies*, 75 Neb. L. Rev. 255 (1996).

2. AUTHENTICITY

In January 1997, the popular comic strip "Peanuts" ran the following two-part series about phony sports collectibles.

PEANUTS

PEANUTS

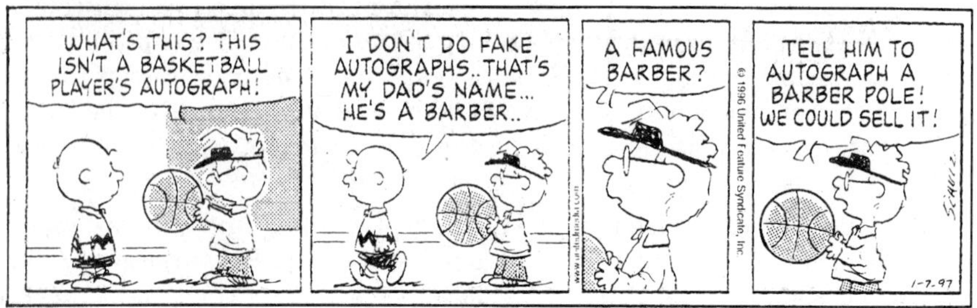

Unfortunately, not everyone is as honest as Charlie Brown. As the reading that follows makes clear, the proliferation of counterfeit sports items has forced drastic countermeasures to be taken.

CAUGHT IN THE ACT OF FORGERY IN CHICAGO: THE FBI BREAKS UP A RING TRAFFICKING IN FAKE SPORTS MEMORABILIA

David Seideman

Sports Illustrated, Oct. 20, 1997, at R8.

Each Monday morning FBI agent Bob Walker trades his uniform—white dress shirt, dark suit and 10–mm Smith & Wesson—for a T-shirt and jeans. For four hours, at an FBI storage facility in Chicago, he becomes the antifan, defacing boxloads of pricey sports memorabilia.

Walker sprays paint over Michael Jordan's signature on a basketball. He uses an industrial-strength solvent to remove Dan Marino's name from a football. He covers Anfernee Hardaway's autograph with indelible ink. For the final touch Walker applies a stamp—FBI OPERATION FOULBALL, FORGERY—that identifies each item as seized contraband.

The FBI is completing the initial phase of Operation Foulball, the first federal crackdown on counterfeit sports memorabilia. This summer, in U.S. district court in Chicago, six men who operated a forgery ring were given sentences of 18 1/2 months in prison to four years of probation for bilking collectors out of as much as $5 million.

Over the past decade sales of sports memorabilia have risen to an estimated $3 billion a year, and fraud has grown exponentially. Agents across the country are engaged in investigations of forgery rings, but so far the case in Chicago has been the most significant. "I do not think any of us expected this was going to be as large as it is," says Mike Bassett, the FBI agent who broke the case.

Bassett's interest was first piqued by a 1994 phone call from a collector who had acquired a game-used, autographed Frank Thomas glove and had been nagged by doubts about its authenticity. Pursuing the tip, Bassett and his partner, Walker, eventually nabbed a Chicago sports-collectibles dealer named Anthony Alyinovich. From 1994 through '96, Alyinovich led a conspiracy to make and sell bogus sports memorabilia: jerseys, bats, balls and photographs bearing the forged autographs of professional athletes. Alyinovich, 31, has admitted that during one five-week period last year he distributed more than 1,700 items of forged memorabilia.

Half the fake memorabilia the FBI has confiscated is allegedly "signed" by Michael Jordan, who rarely gives autographs. When the federal investigation began, agents and prosecutors interviewed a number of stars—including Jordan, Dennis Rodman and Scottie Pippen of the Chicago Bulls; Shawn Kemp, then with the Seattle SuperSonics and now with the Cleveland Cavaliers; and Frank Thomas of the Chicago White Sox—about their signing practices. Each athlete said he hadn't signed the pieces in question and expressed outrage about the forgeries.

Those conversations confirmed the suspicions of assistant U.S. attorneys Joel Bertocchi and David Rosenbloom, who then obtained search warrants and wiretaps that would help them arrest the producers of the fraudulent memorabilia. Bassett and Walker staked out sporting-goods stores around Chicago. They discovered, among other things, a run on size–13 Air Jordan basketball shoes, the ones Jordan himself presumably would use and then autograph. With the help of store owners the agents marked merchandise to enable them to trace the flow of raw material among the counterfeiters. Armed with a search warrant, they then visited Federal Express offices to open packages shipped by the forgery suspects and inspect marked goods that now bore bogus signatures. They resealed the containers and allowed them to be delivered.

Wiretaps and concealed cameras in a Chicago warehouse recorded the forgers' conversations and actions. On the wall of the rented warehouse the counterfeiters posted a chart designating who was responsible for each Bull's signature. Kevin Walsh of Chicago forged the names of six players, and Jon Schwartz of Des Plaines, Ill., signed for the remaining six. Schwartz and Walsh charged Alyinovich fees ranging from $5 per signature on a photograph to $50 for the autograph on a Jordan jersey. The jersey might fetch as much as $1,000 from an unsuspecting fan.

On request, Alyinovich donated forged sports memorabilia to charities that he knew would unwittingly market the material as genuine.

(Buyers at charity events are often willing to pay top dollar.) The conspirators even attempted to con one another.

To create a patina of legitimacy, the forgers issued bogus certificates of authenticity. Stories were concocted to explain the merchandise's origins. Conspirators talked of having paid "hawkers" to obtain signatures outside arenas, hotels and other public places. More often they boasted of contacts who knew someone close to the athletes.

Those convicted—Alyinovich; Barry Carlstrom of Hanover Park, Ill.; Richard Hall of Chicago; Timothy Lee of Sunnyvale, Calif.; Schwartz; James Studley of Rockland, Mass.; and Walsh—were sports groupies and collectors ruled not only by greed but also by passion for the memorabilia they were hawking. The sentencing of Alyinovich has been put off because of his cooperation with the investigation.

Studley pleaded guilty in U.S. district court in Chicago in March and told the judge he understood that he faced a maximum penalty of five years' imprisonment and possible payments of between $250,000 and $600,000, representing restitution to victims. Yet he was preoccupied with retrieving his modestly valued personal collection of pieces signed by Joe DiMaggio, Emmitt Smith and others, seized in the raid. "Can I get those seven items back?" Studley twice begged Rosenbloom outside the courtroom. "Those were real." Eventually Rosenbloom agreed.

Obsessive collectors are easy marks. "When it comes to sports memorabilia, people suspend the skepticism they bring to ordinary affairs of life," Rosenbloom says. "If somebody gave you a $50 check signed by Michael Jordan, you would call the bank. But [if someone charged you] $900 for a jersey, [you'd say] thank you!"

The Feds continue to urge the many honest sports memorabilia dealers to take steps to police their industry. "If one guy [Alyinovich] is responsible for $2.5 million, I wouldn't be surprised if the total fraud is $100 million," speculates Joshua Leland Evans, the Manhattan-based chairman of Leland's Auction House, which specializes in sports memorabilia. Barring the opportunity to see autographs signed in person, collectors ought to buy from reputable dealers. If Dennis Rodman charges $75 for his autograph, buyers should beware of one selling for $14. "If people stopped pumping money into these low-end products, it would help clean up the industry," Walker says.

The first signs of the FBI operation's impact are encouraging. Checking out Chicago-area stores, Rosenbloom and Bertocchi agree that Jordan products are less prevalent than a year earlier. In the FBI storage facility in Chicago, the mountain of bogus memorabilia will keep Bob Walker busy erasing and obliterating signatures for many Mondays to come. The government is donating thousands of basketballs, baseballs, jerseys and caps—all stamped OPERATION FOULBALL—to Chicago's Boys & Girls Clubs and the Cabrini Green Little League, organizations selected by the stars whose signatures were forged. "Through this quality equipment we're giving children an opportunity to chase their dreams," Walker says. It will be poetic justice if one of these children discovers an exceptional talent while wearing a confiscated jersey that was supposed to sell for $600 and dunking an "autographed" $400 basketball.

Notes

1. In large part, unscrupulous dealers are able to flourish because of the public's naivete. *See, e.g., Maldonado v. Collectibles International, Inc.*, 969 F.Supp. 7 (S.D.N.Y.1997) (observing the defendant targeted "unsophisticated consumers with an interest in sports who were looking for a job" in choosing potential customers for its bogus training course). Recognizing this fact, California in 1992 became the first state to enact a "warranty of authenticity" law aimed specifically at sports memorabilia. The statute's provisions are examined in detail in L. Amy Blum & Pamela A. Schockater, *Say It Ain't So, Joe! California Law Requires That Sports Heroes' Signatures be Authentic*, 32 Beverly Hills B.A. J. 55 (Summer/Fall 1997).

2. To deter counterfeiters, Upper Deck, a high-end dealer, authenticates its memorabilia using a process that includes "witnessing the signatures, notarization of an affidavit of authenticity, assigning a number to each product, affixing a numbered hologram to each product and recording the numbers in a data bank." Although these measures make it almost impossible to slip a forgery past Upper Deck, they add considerably to an item's final price. *See further You Want Authenticity? Climb to the Upper Deck*, Newark Star–Ledger, Aug. 20, 1997, at 58, and Tanya Barrientos, *Tips to Make Sure Your Hero's Autograph is Real*, Albany (N.Y.) Times Union, July 26, 1997, at D1.

3. During George Bush's presidency, Topps Inc., the venerable Brooklyn printer, produced 100 special baseball cards showing him in his 1947 Yale University baseball uniform and displaying his career statistics (including a lifetime batting average of .239) on the back. Although all the cards were supposed to be sent to Bush, three later surfaced inside ordinary baseball card packages. The company immediately disputed the authenticity of the "found" cards, but also let it be known if they were genuine they constituted stolen property. Richard Cowen & Paul Dottino, *Bush Baseball Card Surfaces; White House Supposedly Got All 100*, The (N.J.) Record, July 28, 1990, at A3.

4. While most authenticity cases involve fake merchandise, on occasion even genuine goods take on a patina of fraud. *See, e.g., Chicagoland Processing Corp. v. White*, 714 F.Supp. 383 (N.D.Ill.1989) (medallion commemorating first official night game at Wrigley Field held to be authentic even though it was neither the first nor official).

Problem 14

When he spotted a baseball with a rare autograph being sold for $500 at a garage sale, a dealer, knowing that he could easily resell the ball for $10,000, snapped it up. If the ball later turns out to be a fake, will he be able to get his money back? *See Smith v. Zimbalist*, 38 P.2d 170 (Cal.Ct.App. 1934).

Chapter 3

OWNERS

A. OVERVIEW

Being the owner of a sports team can be immensely gratifying and enormously lucrative. It also can be emotionally draining and financially ruinous. As a legal matter, three questions have preoccupied both courts and commentators: 1) what criteria may a league use to evaluate prospective franchisees?; 2) what controls may a league impose on members?; and, 3) what steps may a league take to protect itself from competitors?

B. ADMISSION

Typically, an individual who applies for a sports franchise must be reviewed and voted on by the other owners. Contrary to popular belief, more than a large bank account is needed to win admission. As many a disappointed candidate has discovered, one also has to have the right connections and "play by the rules."

MID-SOUTH GRIZZLIES v. NATIONAL FOOTBALL LEAGUE

720 F.2d 772 (3d Cir.1983),
cert. denied, 467 U.S. 1215 (1984).

GIBBONS, Circuit Judge.

Mid–South Grizzlies, a joint venture, and its members (the Grizzlies) appeal from a summary judgment in favor of the defendants in their suit against the National Football League (NFL), the league members, and League Commissioner Pete Rozelle, seeking damages under Section 4 of the Clayton Act, 15 U.S.C. § 15 (1973). The suit concerns the defendants' refusal to grant the plaintiffs a football franchise. On appeal the Grizzlies contend that the district court erred: (1) in granting summary judgment while the Grizzlies' discovery requests were outstanding; and (2) in granting summary judgment when there were disputed issues of material fact. We affirm.

I.

Background

The NFL is a not-for-profit business league, qualified for exemption from federal income tax under section 501(c)6 of the Internal Revenue Code, 26 U.S.C. § 501(c)(6) (1967). The league has 28 members, each of which is an entity organized for profit, engaged in the business of fielding a professional football team. The NFL was formed by the merger of two predecessor football leagues. That merger took place following the enactment, in 1966, of Pub.L. 89–800, § 6(b)(1), 80 Stat. 1515, which amended Pub.L. 87–331, § 1, 75 Stat. 732 (1961), 15 U.S.C. § 1291. Section 1291, enacted in 1961, granted to certain professional sports leagues a limited exemption from the antitrust laws with respect to the joint sale of television broadcast rights for league games, and the 1966 amendment permitted "a joint agreement by which the members of two or more football leagues combine their operations in expanded single leagues ... if such agreement increases rather than decreases the number of professional football clubs so operating." The 1961 exemption with respect to joint sale of television broadcasting rights, intended to overrule the judgment in United States v. National Football League, 116 F.Supp. 319 (E.D.Pa.1953), does not "otherwise affect the applicability or nonapplicability of the antitrust laws" to any other activities of persons engaged in professional team sports. 15 U.S.C. § 1294. The 1966 exemption does no more than permit the combination of members of two or more leagues into one.

Under the 1974 constitution and by-laws of the NFL each member obliges itself to operate a professional football club which is a member of the league. Each member has a designated "home territory" within which it has "the exclusive right ... to exhibit professional football games played by teams of the League," and "[n]o club in the League shall be permitted to play games within the home territory of any other club unless a home club is a participant." Home territory is defined as a designated city and "the surrounding territory to the extent of 75 miles in every direction from the exterior corporate limits of such city." Constitution and By–Laws, Article IV, Appendix at 1129a, 1138a. (There are special provisions for the New York and San Francisco Metropolitan areas and for Green Bay, Wisconsin.) The addition of a new league member within the home territory of any member requires unanimous consent of the league members. Id. Article 3.1(b). Elsewhere, applicants for membership may be admitted by the affirmative vote of not less than three-fourths or 20 members, whichever is greater. Id. Article 3.3(c). No league member may have a financial interest, direct or indirect, in any other league member. Id. Article 9.1(B)(1).

The combined league began functioning in 1970 with 26 members. Thereafter new home territories were designated for Tampa, Florida, and Seattle, Washington, and member teams with franchises for those home territories began participating in league play in 1976. The uncontradicted affidavit of Commissioner Rozelle establishes that the initiative for establishing those franchises came from the NFL, which negotiated for a stadium location, determined methods of providing the franchise with players, and only then evaluated and selected owners. See, e.g., Rozelle Deposition, Appendix at 1290a, 1431a–1440a.

As authorized by 15 U.S.C. § 1291, the NFL has made a joint sale to three major television networks of the regular season and post-season television rights. Television revenues are divided equally among all members. Receipts from the sale of tickets are shared between the home team, 60%, and the visiting team, 40%. Each home team retains other revenues, derived from its local operations. These include revenue from non-network coverage of pre-season games, and revenue from food and beverage concessions, parking, and sale of team paraphernalia. Such revenue varies both with attendance and depending on the terms of stadium leases. On average, however, more than 70% of each team's revenue is derived from sources other than its operations at the home location. See Defendants' Motion for Summary Judgment, Affidavit of Pete Rozelle, Appendix at 188a.

In 1974 and 1975 the Grizzlies participated in the World Football League from a home team location in Memphis, Tennessee. The members of that league could be found to have been competitors of the members of the NFL in the national market for network television revenue. The World Football League disbanded, however, halfway through the 1975 football season. The NFL had no franchise at Memphis, and a home team designation for that location would not infringe upon the home territory of any NFL member. Upon the demise of the World Football League the Grizzlies applied to the NFL for admission to the league with a designated home territory at Memphis.

At meetings with the NFL Expansion Committee, and with the full NFL membership, the Grizzlies urged that it had in place at Memphis an established, functioning professional football enterprise. The application was rejected. This lawsuit followed.

II.

The Complaint

The Grizzlies' complaint, filed on December 3, 1979, does not charge that the provisions of the NFL's Constitution and By–Laws reserving to its members franchise exclusivity for designated home territories violates the antitrust laws. Indeed, the Grizzlies sought such an exclusive franchise for themselves. Thus this case does not present any issue of possible antitrust violation from the exclusion of potential competitors in the designated exclusive home territories.

Nor do the Grizzlies complain that the NFL's 60–40 home team-visitor revenue sharing arrangement, which is not exempted from antitrust scrutiny by 15 U.S.C. § 1291, caused any injury to their business or property. Indeed, the Grizzlies sought to participate in that arrangement. Moreover, the Grizzlies make no complaint about the operation of the NFL arrangements for joint sale of television rights. They do not charge, for example, that the demise of the World Football League was caused by the NFL's television marketing practices. Nor do they charge that if they had been admitted those practices should have been changed. Rather, as with the 60–40 split of ticket sale revenue, they sought to participate.

Determining what the Grizzlies do not charge as antitrust violations is somewhat easier than determining what is charged. The complaint alleges that Memphis is a highly desirable submarket for major league professional football, that the refusal to consider it as a home territory for a franchise was made pursuant to an agreement or understanding or conspiracy among NFL members, the NFL and the Commissioner, that no valid basis for rejection of the Grizzlies was articulated or formulated by the defendants, and that the rejection amounted to an unreasonable restraint of trade, or a group boycott. One motive for that conspiracy is alleged to have been a desire to punish, intimidate and restrain plaintiffs from participation in major league professional football because they had entered into competition with NFL members by participating in the World Football League. The exclusion, so motivated, and having the effects alleged, is said to be a violation of Section 1 of the Sherman Act, and an attempt to monopolize interstate trade and commerce in professional football in violation of Section 2 of that Act.

III.

The Summary Judgment Record

The defendants moved for summary judgment on March 2, 1981, supporting their motion with affidavits by Commissioner Pete Rozelle and by Daniel M. Rooney, Chairman of the NFL Expansion Committee, to which defendants attached 12 supporting exhibits. At the time of the motion there was outstanding a motion by the Grizzlies to compel answers to certain interrogatories and to compel production of documents. In opposition to the summary judgment motion the Grizzlies filed an extensive brief addressing the merits, and the affidavits of William R. Tathan, I.B. Rowe and Steve Alexander, Esq. The Grizzlies contended that the summary judgment motion should not be considered until the completion of discovery.

On August 13, 1981 the trial court filed a memorandum and order declining to consider the motion for summary judgment until the completion of the Grizzlies' discovery, but restricted the scope of discovery to "matters relating to the NFL's decision not to grant the plaintiffs an NFL franchise at Memphis, Tennessee, and to the NFL's prior practices and standards with respect to the admission of new franchises into the league since the merger of the NFL and the American Football League." 4 App. at 894. The Grizzlies were permitted to depose Mr. Rozelle, Mr. Rooney, and the other members of the NFL Expansion Committee, but solely with respect to the designated subject matter. The order fixed a schedule for renewal of the motion for summary judgment, for filing opposition to it, and for briefing. Id. at 895.

On September 16, 1981 counsel for the Grizzlies wrote to the trial judge asking for clarification of the discovery order. The court was asked if the order was intended

> to focus the parties' attention ... solely upon the issue of whether fair, objective, and articulated standards were applied by the defendants in passing upon plaintiffs' application for membership in the NFL, whether such standards existed at the time, and whether any substantive consideration ... was ever given to plaintiffs' application by the defendants.
>
> If, in fact, it was the Court's intention to focus only on the objective criteria question at this time, and to accept the remaining criteria in the plaintiffs' Complaint as true for the purpose of this motion proceeding, the scope of discovery can be substantially limited without waiving our position, many of the pending discovery requests can be withdrawn, subject to renewal ..., and more specific discovery ... can surely proceed....

Letter of Edward H. Rubenstone, Esq. to Hon. Joseph L. McGlynn, Sept. 16, 1981, 4 App. at 1083–1084. The court replied two days later that "[y]our assumptions concerning the rationale underlying my order dated August 13, 1981 are correct." The court noted the Grizzlies' concession in open court on August 12, 1981 "that under some circumstances, and applying objective, rational and fair decisional criteria, defendants might legitimately, collectively refuse to deal with a potential competitor demanding entry into the professional football market place." The court explained further:

> In an effort to spare all parties the time and expense of what may prove to be unnecessary discovery proceedings, I entered my order of August 13th, which limited discovery "solely to matters relating to the NFL's decision not to grant the plaintiffs an NFL franchise at Memphis, Tennessee, and to the NFL's prior practices and standards with respect to the admission of new franchises into the league since the merger of the NFL and American Football League". If discovery in this discrete area should reveal that the NFL applied objective standards to the plaintiffs' application, there may not be a need to conduct further discovery.

4 App. at 1085. The trial judge also stated his assumption that there was no need to rule on outstanding discovery requests, since counsel's letter stated that he would be able to reach an accord with defense counsel regarding them. He warned, however, that all discovery must be complete by October 31, 1981. Id. at 1086. Further correspondence between the parties and the court took place respecting the issues posed by the NFL's motion for summary judgment, and on December 17, 1981 the trial judge by letter reiterated his intention to consider the NFL motion "because if it is undisputed that the defendants used 'objective, rational and fair decisional criteria' in rejecting plaintiff's application, then that may well be the end of the litigation ball game." 4 App. at 1099.

On December 21, 1981 the defendants filed a renewed motion for summary judgment, relying on the pleadings, depositions, answers to interrogatories, admissions on file, and the Rozelle and Rooney affidavits accompanying their initial motion. 4 App. at 901. The brief in support of the renewed motion is not restricted to the question of whether the decision to reject the Grizzlies' application was based on "objective, rational and fair decisional criteria." Rather it relies on the "undisputed facts" in the record made to date with respect to the nature of the professional football business, and asserts that those facts warrant summary judgment for defendants as a matter of law. Thus the renewed motion put the Grizzlies on notice that the defendants were relying upon the summary judgment record as then comprised, and of the obligation to set forth in affidavits the reasons why additional discovery would be necessary in order to oppose it. Fed.R.Civ.P. 56(f).

On March 10, 1982 the Grizzlies filed a 107 page brief in opposition to the renewed motion for summary judgment. 4 App. at 963 et seq. That brief is not limited to the question whether the Grizzlies' application was rejected on the basis of objective rational and fair decisional criteria. It addresses the full range of issues discussed in the defendants' brief in support of the motion. Although the correspondence between counsel and the court was included in an appendix to the Grizzlies' brief, no affidavit was filed setting forth any reason why additional discovery should be afforded before the court ruled on the motion. Nor was that subject addressed in the brief in opposition to the renewed motion. It surfaced, however, in a Grizzlies' brief in response to defendant's reply brief. Responding to the defendants' contention that the members of the NFL are not competitors, but are engaged in a joint venture in the promotion of an entertainment spectacle, the Grizzlies argued:

> Nevertheless, despite Defendants' heavy reliance on this argument, the "single entity" issue was not the subject of discovery.
>
> Indeed, in order to determine whether there is any merit to Defendants' "single entity" contention, the starting point in discovery would be necessarily an examination of the business and financial records of the individual teams. These records would show what part of each team's revenue is not shared by any other team, what activities generated that revenue, and how the revenue was treated on the team's books. Based on these records, Plaintiffs could prove that the teams are not a "single entity."
>
> In addition, other factors of economic competition between the teams would have to be discovered, along with the views of each team about that economic competition. This would entail (a) a study of the league's operations; (b) an inquiry into the existence of factionalism and voting blocks in league deliberations and at meetings; (c) depositions from representatives of each team; and discovery of a host of other categories of facts

> which need not be listed here. All of this information would be needed before the Court would have an adequate record on which to make a ruling on Defendants' contentions that the separate teams must be viewed as a single entity for antitrust purposes. It suffices to note that depositions were limited by Court Order to the four members of the 1973 NFL "Expansion Committee", and Pete Rozelle, and that the written discovery was confined to the issue of "objective standards". Perhaps it should be noted as well that before the Court entered its August 31, 1981 Order, Plaintiffs had, in fact, filed discovery requests seeking information which would have shed light on Defendants' "single entity" contention, but Defendants objected to all of this discovery. Therefore, the record does not contain evidence for the Court to rule on Defendants' "single entity" contention.

5 App. at 1217–18. This brief made no reference to specific discovery requests addressed to what the Grizzlies characterize as defendants' "single entity" contention. There is no suggestion that there are sources of revenue other than sales of tickets, sales of television rights, and revenues derived from food and beverage concessions, parking, and sales of team paraphernalia. There is no indication that a professional football business located at Memphis, Tennessee would compete with any NFL member for these peripheral sources of revenue. The Grizzlies do not contend that the league members (or the Grizzlies themselves if they were admitted to the league) compete for rather than share in network television and ticket sale revenues.

The trial court addressed the Grizzlies' unfocused contention that there should be additional discovery, noting:

> Plaintiffs have had more than sufficient discovery to fully develop their case. All of the outstanding requests to which defendants have refused to respond are not calculated to lead to relevant evidence necessary to resolving this matter. As a result I find that this case is now ripe for a decision on the merits.

550 F.Supp. at 565.

The Grizzlies contend that this ruling was error, because with additional discovery they could have discovered facts which would suggest the existence of actual or potential competition between their Memphis based team and members of the NFL in some relevant product market.

Where Rule 56(f) affidavits have been filed, setting forth specific reasons why the moving party's affidavits in support of a motion for summary judgment cannot be responded to, and the facts are in the possession of the moving party, we have held that a continuance of the motion for purposes of discovery should be granted almost as a matter of course. Costlow v. United States, 552 F.2d 560, 564 (3d Cir.1977); Ward v. United States, 471 F.2d 667, 671 (3d Cir.1973). But as Judge Friedman so aptly observed:

> It is true that Rule 56(f) also authorizes the court in appropriate cases to refuse to enter summary judgment where the party opposing the motion shows a legitimate basis for his inability to present by affidavit the facts essential to justify his opposition, but to take advantage of this provision he must state by affidavit the reasons for his inability to do so and these reasons must be genuine and convincing to the court rather than merely colorable. It is not enough to rest upon the uncertainty which broods over all human affairs or to pose philosophic doubts regarding the conclusiveness of evidentiary facts. In the world of speculation such doubts have an honored place, but in the daily affairs of mankind and the intensely practical business of litigation they are put aside as conjectural.

Robin Construction Company v. United States, 345 F.2d 610, 614 (3d Cir.1965). Judge Friedman's observations are relevant here in two respects. First, the Grizzlies filed no Rule 56(f) affidavit. Second, treating their response to the defendants' reply brief as if it were such an affidavit, it raises no more than a merely colorable claim that actual or potential competition for revenue other than from ticket sales and sales of television rights could be shown between a professional team based in Memphis and the other members of the NFL.

Considering the already large record compiled prior to its consideration of the summary judgment record, the absence of a Rule 56(f) affidavit, the irrelevance of most of the pending discovery requests, and the conjectural nature of the Grizzlies' contentions as to the possibility of establishment of actual or potential competition in any arguably relevant market, we conclude that the court did not err in considering the motion for summary judgment on the present record.

IV.

The Merits

A. Sherman Act Section 1

Public Law 89–800 establishes as a matter of law that the merger which produced the NFL from two formerly competing leagues did not violate the antitrust laws. Public Law 87–331 establishes as a matter of law that the members may lawfully pool revenues from the sale of television rights. The parties agree that in other respects a rule of reason analysis is appropriate. (In the complaint the Grizzlies alleged that their exclusion was the result of a group boycott, which was a per se violation of Section 1 of the Sherman Act. The per se violation contention is not made in this court.) The Grizzlies, moreover, make no contention that the 60–40 sharing of ticket sale revenue is an unreasonable restraint of trade.

Under a rule of reason analysis a Section 1 violation and a right to recover under Section 4 of the Clayton Act can be established by proof:

> (1) that the defendants contracted, combined, or conspired among each other; (2) that the combination or conspiracy pro-

> duced adverse, anticompetitive effects within relevant product and geographic markets; (3) that the objects of and conduct pursuant to that contract or conspiracy were illegal; and (4) that the plaintiff was injured as a proximate result of that conspiracy.

Fleer Corp. v. Topps Chewing Gum, Inc., 658 F.2d 139, 147 (3d Cir. 1981), cert. denied, 455 U.S. 1019, 102 S.Ct. 1715, 72 L.Ed.2d 137 (1982), quoting Martin B. Glauser Dodge Co. v. Chrysler Corp., 570 F.2d 72, 81 (3d Cir.1977), cert. denied, 436 U.S. 913, 98 S.Ct. 2253, 56 L.Ed.2d 413 (1978). In this case there is no dispute about the requisite concert of action among the defendants. The defendants do deny injury to competition in any relevant market from their rejection of the Grizzlies' application. They urge that any limitations on actual or potential competition in any relevant market were insulated from antitrust scrutiny by the 1961 and 1966 statutes referred to, or, are reasonable as a matter of law. They also urge that as a matter of law there was no competition among league members or between league members and non-members in other markets to which the Grizzlies point.

The Grizzlies identify as the relevant product market major-league professional football, and as the relevant geographic market the United States. The trial court found these markets to be relevant. 550 F.Supp. at 571 n. 33. The court observed as well that "[t]here is no doubt that the NFL currently has a monopoly in the United States in major league football." 550 F.Supp. at 571. The Grizzlies pose as the question on this appeal "whether it can be said as a matter of law that defendants neither acquired nor maintained monopoly power over any relevant market in an unlawful manner." Appellants' Brief at 27.

As to the acquisition of dominant position and monopoly power, the facts are undisputed. Long before the Grizzlies and the World Football League came into existence, Congress authorized the merger of the two major football leagues extant in 1966, and granted to the merged league the power to pool television revenues. That congressional decision conferred on the NFL the market power which it holds in the market for professional football. Congress could not have been unaware that [a] necessary effect of the television revenue sharing scheme which it approved for the NFL would be that all members of that league would be strengthened in their ability to bid for the best available playing and coaching personnel, to the potential disadvantage of new entrants.

In an effort to bolster its "unlawful acquisition of monopoly power" contention, however, the Grizzlies point to certain activities of the NFL and its predecessors which occurred prior to the 1966 legislation authorizing its formation. They point out that in 1961, when the old NFL was seeking legislation which would overrule United States v. National Football League, 116 F.Supp. 319 (E.D.Pa.1953), which prohibited certain television revenue sharing practices, it admitted a new team in Minnesota, the home state of the Senate Majority Leader and Chairman of the Committee which considered the bill; that in 1966, when the old

NFL and AFL leagues were seeking a statutory exemption which would permit their merger, a team was added in New Orleans, the home state of a powerful senator and powerful congressman who supported the legislation. Even the post-merger addition of Seattle and Tampa Bay, according to the Grizzlies, was prompted by a desire to limit the term of proposed legislation prohibiting home teams from blacking out televised games when they were playing. See Pub.L. 93–107, § 1, 87 Stat. 350, repealed by Pub.L. 93–107, § 2, 87 Stat. 351 (1973). If these allegations are true, as we must assume for purposes of a summary judgment motion, they are, perhaps, instructive on the nature of the federal legislative process. For purposes of rule of reason analysis, however, they are irrelevant. It would take a court bolder than this to claim that the congressionally authorized acquisition of market power, even market power amounting to monopoly power, was unlawful under Section 1 of the Sherman Act.

But, the Grizzlies urge, the 1966 statute did not confer the authority to abuse the market power, even though it may have authorized its acquisition. Rather, the merger was approved only "if such agreement increases rather than decreases the number of professional clubs so operating." 15 U.S.C. § 1291. Paraphrasing their argument, it is the Grizzlies' contention that the statute which authorized NFL acquisition of monopoly power in the professional football market required not only that the league members refrain from abusing that power against potential competitors, but that it take affirmative steps to share its market power with others.

This reading of the 1966 legislation is at least plausible. It poses two separate issues. One is the issue of abuse of monopoly power against potential rivals of the NFL in the business of promoting professional football as a spectator spectacle. The other is the issue of admitting others to a share in the NFL's dominant market position. Although the Grizzlies' briefs, both here and in the district court, tend to blur the distinction between those issues, the complaint makes clear that only the second is presented in this case. The only basis on which the Grizzlies seek recovery under Section 4 of the Clayton Act is that they were denied admission to the monopoly, and thus were deprived of a share of the NFL's monopoly power. No claim is made that abuse of NFL market power led to the demise of the World Football League, and no issue is before us concerning activities of the NFL, since that demise, which may have inhibited the development of competition by another football league. The NFL structure as a barrier to entry to the market by another football league is relevant in this case only to the extent that it bears on the obligation to permit entry to the NFL.

There are two possible sources of any NFL obligation to permit entry to its shared market power; the 1966 statute, and the Sherman Act. Each will be considered separately.

The provision in the 1966 statute that "such agreement increases rather than decreases the number of professional football clubs so operating" cannot reasonably be construed as addressing competition, the preservation of which is the object of the Sherman Act. The basic thrust of the 1966 statute is to authorize an arrangement which eliminated competition among the only two viable competitors then in the professional football market. The reference to an increase in the number of professional football teams "so operating" is a reference to professional teams operating under the antitrust exemption for television revenue sharing provided in the 1961 statute. Thus what the 1966 statute suggests is that more home team territories would be added, not to increase competition in professional football, but to permit geographic enlargement of the NFL's market power.

The Grizzlies urge that home team regions derive important economic benefits from the presence of a professional football team, in the form of hotel, restaurant and travel business, stadium employment, and the like. Undoubtedly that is so, and probably such derivative economic benefits were in the minds of those Senators and Congressmen interested in NFL expansion. Those benefits, however, do not result from competition with the NFL or even from competition, other than athletic, among its members. Rather they result from the presence of a franchisee which shares the NFL market power over professional football. Moreover, even if one assumes that Congress intended in the 1966 statute to extend incidental economic benefits on businesses in new home territory areas, it is difficult to see what standing the Grizzlies have to rely on that intent with respect to their claim for league membership. Finally, even if there was a congressional intent to confer economic benefits in some new home territories, nothing in the 1966 statute or its sparse legislative history suggests a basis for concluding that businesses in Memphis, Tennessee, rather than in other metropolitan areas were to receive them.

Since the 1966 statute is not directed at preservation of competition in the market for professional football, and cannot be construed as conferring any economic benefit on the class to which the Grizzlies belong, we conclude that it does not oblige the NFL to permit entry by any particular applicant to the NFL shared market power.

We turn, therefore, to the Sherman Act. As noted above, Sherman Act liability requires an injury to competition. In this case the competition inquiry is a narrow one, because the Grizzlies are not seeking recovery as potential competitors outside the NFL. They identify as the antitrust violation the league's negative vote on their application for membership.

From affidavits, pleadings, and discovery materials which comprise the summary judgment record it could be found, and the trial court assumed, that the Grizzlies met all the qualifications for membership specified in the NFL Constitution and By–Laws. 550 F.Supp. at 568. It is undisputed that in 1974 expansion teams were located at Tampa, Florida, and at Seattle, Washington, raising to 28 the number of league competitors for the 1976 season. It is also undisputed that in deciding on expansion the NFL Expansion Committee considered a socioeconomic study prepared for it by the Stanford Research Institute in December of 1973, which identified fourteen potential locations for new franchises, including Memphis. (The other areas are Mexico City, Birmingham, Alabama, Seattle, Washington, Nassau County, New York, Anaheim, California, Chicago, Illinois, Phoenix, Arizona, Honolulu, Hawaii, Tampa, Florida, the Tidewater area of Virginia, Charlotte–Greensboro, North Carolina, Indianapolis, Indiana, and Orlando, Florida.) The Expansion Committee met with representatives of the Grizzlies, but made a negative recommendation on expansion, as of 1975, beyond 28 teams. The full membership of the league accepted the recommendation of the expansion committee.

The NFL's stated reasons for rejecting the Grizzlies' application included scheduling difficulties created by the presence of an odd number of teams, a long-running collective bargaining dispute with league players, several pending antitrust lawsuits, and league concern over legislation prohibiting television blackouts in home team territories, all of which allegedly made consideration of expansion unpropitious. The Grizzlies contend that there are material issues of disputed fact as to the accuracy of these reasons. They contend that at trial they could prove that the motivation for their rejection was to punish them for having attempted in the past to compete with the NFL in the World Football League, or to reserve the Memphis location for friends of present league team owners.

Assuming, without deciding, that the summary judgment record presents disputed fact issues with respect to the actual motivation of the NFL members, those disputed facts are not material, under Section 1 of the Sherman Act, if the action complained of produced no injury to competition.

As to competition with NFL members in the professional football market, including the market for sale of television rights, the exclusion was patently pro-competitive, since it left the Memphis area, with a large stadium and a significant metropolitan area population, available as a site for another league's franchise, and it left the Grizzlies' organization as a potential competitor in such a league. If there was any injury to competition, actual or potential, therefore, it must have been to intraleague competition.

The NFL defendants' position is that the summary judgment record establishes conclusively the absence of competition, actual or potential, among league members. Rather, they urge, the league is a single entity, a joint venture in the presentation of the professional football spectacle.

For the most part the congressionally authorized arrangements under which the NFL functions eliminate competition among the league members. Indeed it is undisputed that on average more than 70% of each member club's revenue is shared revenue derived from sources other than operations at its home location. The Grizzlies do not challenge the legality of the NFL's revenue sharing arrangements, and seek to participate in them. The Grizzlies emphasize that there nevertheless remains a not insignificant amount of intra-league non-athletic competition. We need not, in order to affirm the summary judgment, accept entirely the NFL's position that there is no intra-league competition. Conceivably within certain geographic submarkets two league members compete with one another for ticket buyers, for local broadcast revenue, and for sale of the concession items like food and beverages and team paraphernalia. Thus rejection of a franchise application in the New York metropolitan area, for example, might require a different antitrust analysis than is suggested by this record. But the Grizzlies were obliged, when faced with the NFL denial of the existence of competition among NFL members and a potential franchisee at Memphis, to show some more than minimal level of potential competition in the product markets in which league members might compete. They made no such showing. The record establishes that the NFL franchise nearest to Memphis is at St. Louis, Mo., over 280 miles away. There is no record evidence that professional football teams located in Memphis and in St. Louis would compete for the same ticket purchasers, for the same local broadcast outlets, in the sale of team paraphernalia, or in any other manner.

The Grizzlies contend on appeal, although they did not so contend in the trial court, that league members compete in what they call the "raw material market" for players and coaching personnel. Entirely apart from the propriety of considering a legal theory not presented in the trial court, there are major defects in this Grizzlies' argument. First, the Grizzlies exclusion from the league in no way restrained them from competing for players by forming a competitive league. Second, they fail to explain how, if their exclusion from the league reduced competition for team personnel, that reduction caused an injury to the Grizzlies' business or property. See Van Dyk Research Corp. v. Xerox Corp., 631 F.2d 251, 255 (3d Cir.1980), cert. denied, 452 U.S. 905, 101 S.Ct. 3029, 69 L.Ed.2d 405 (1981) (Section 4 plaintiff has burden of proving that injury was caused by illegality relied on).

One final Grizzlies' argument in support of their section 1 Sherman Act claim bears mentioning. Relying on the essential facilities doctrine developed in cases such as Silver v. New York Stock Exchange, 373 U.S. 341, 83 S.Ct. 1246, 10 L.Ed.2d 389 (1963), Associated Press v. United States, 326 U.S. 1, 65 S.Ct. 1416, 89 L.Ed. 2013 (1945), and Gamco, Inc. v. Providence Fruit & Produce Bldg., 194 F.2d 484 (1st Cir.), cert. denied, 344 U.S. 817, 73 S.Ct. 11, 97 L.Ed. 636 (1952), they urge that because the NFL is a practical monopoly it had an obligation to admit members on fair, reasonable, and equal terms, absent some procompetitive justification for their exclusion. This Grizzlies argument suffers from the same defect as the others. The essential facilities doctrine is predicated on the assumption that admission of the excluded applicant would result in additional competition, in an economic rather than athletic sense. The Grizzlies have simply failed to show how competition in any arguably relevant market would be improved if they were given a share of the NFL's monopoly power.

Since on the record before us the Grizzlies have shown no actual or potential injury to competition resulting from the rejection of their application for an NFL franchise, they cannot succeed on their section 1 Sherman Act claim.

B. Sherman Act Section 2

The Grizzlies also plead a violation of Section 2 of the Sherman Act. 15 U.S.C. § 2 (1973). That section prohibits attempts to monopolize. In section 2 cases the alleged monopolist is prohibited from acting "in an unreasonably exclusionary manner vis-a-vis rivals or potential rivals. . . ." Byars v. Bluff City News Co., Inc., 609 F.2d 843, 853 (6th Cir.1979). See also Official Airline Guides, Inc. v. FTC, 630 F.2d 920, 926–28 (2d Cir.1980), cert. denied, 450 U.S. 917, 101 S.Ct. 1362, 67 L.Ed.2d 343 (1981) (Federal Trade Commission Act § 5 claim); Mid-Texas Communications v. American Telephone & Telegraph Co., 615 F.2d 1372, 1387 (5th Cir.1980), cert. denied, 449 U.S. 912, 101 S.Ct. 286, 66 L.Ed.2d 140 (1980).

Our analysis of the section 1 Sherman Act claim applies equally to the Grizzlies' section 2 claim. Congress by legislation in 1961 and 1966 authorized the NFL acquisition of the market power which it holds, and the Grizzlies cannot challenge that acquisition. The only action they complain of is their exclusion from the shared monopoly, but they have failed to show that their admission would be contra-competitive in any way. Indeed the Memphis home team market has been left by the NFL for potential competitors. Thus on this record summary judgment on the section 2 Sherman Act claim was also proper.

CONCLUSION

The court did not err in considering the defendants' summary judgment motion on the present record. There are no disputed fact issues material to the legal issues presented. The trial court did not err in applying the Sherman Act. Thus the judgment appealed from will be affirmed.

Notes

1. For admission denial cases in other sports, see, e.g., *Seattle Totems Hockey Club, Inc. v. National Hockey League*, 783 F.2d 1347 (9th Cir.), *cert. denied*, 479 U.S. 932 (1986); *Levin v. National Basketball Ass'n*, 385 F.Supp. 149 (S.D.N.Y.1974); *Morsani v. Major League Baseball*, 663 So.2d 653 (Fla.Dist.Ct.App.1995), *review denied*, 673 So.2d 29 (Fla.1996).

2. As *Mid-South Grizzlies* demonstrates, courts will not order a league to admit a specific person or group to its ranks. Because owners depend heavily on each other for their individual and collective success, courts grant them substantial discretion when making membership decisions. This same rule has been extended to other common enterprises, such as law firms, university faculties, co-op apartments, and fraternal organizations. *See, e.g., Ezold v. Wolf, Block, Schorr and Solis-Cohen*, 983 F.2d 509 (3d Cir.1992), *cert. denied*, 510 U.S. 826 (1993) (woman passed over for partner by law firm); *Jalal v. Columbia University in the City of New York*, 4 F.Supp.2d 224

(S.D.N.Y.1998) (Pakistani professor refused tenure); *Clark v. Hyde Park Building Corp.*, 1985 WL 2498 (N.D.Ill.1985) (African–American couple prevented from buying co-op apartment); *Curran v. Mount Diablo Council of the Boy Scouts of America*, 952 P.2d 218 (Cal.1998) (homosexual man denied opportunity to serve as scout leader).

3. Of all the teams in the WFL, the Grizzlies were without a doubt the strongest. Owned by John Bassett, a successful Toronto businessman with interests in the CFL, WHA, and World Team Tennis, they had originally been slated to play in Toronto as the Northmen. In April 1974, however, the Canadian House of Commons began debating bill C–22, better known as the Canadian Football Act. Designed to protect the CFL from foreign competition, the bill ultimately died in committee. By the time it did, Bassett had decided to move his team to Memphis because the WFL franchise that had been scheduled to play in that city had relocated to Houston. Realizing that "Northmen" would make no sense in Memphis, Bassett rechristened the team the Southmen (a name he would later change to the Grizzlies) and made arrangements to play in the 50,000–seat Liberty Bowl.

During the WFL's inaugural season, the Southmen proved wildly popular (even Elvis Presley came to a game, watching the team beat the Detroit Wheels 34–15 in its home opener on July 10, 1974). On the field, the club compiled a 17–3 record, won the Central Division, but lost to the Florida Blazers in the semi-finals. At the end of the season, Memphis running back J.J. Jennings was named the league's Rookie of the Year and tied for Most Valuable Player honors.

In the off-season, Jim Kiick, Paul Warfield, and Larry Csonka, who had just helped the Miami Dolphins win consecutive Super Bowls, joined the Southmen (the trio were the only bona fide NFL stars to actually jump leagues). In the meantime, the WFL announced that the 1975 season would consist of 18 games and be played in two halves, with the winners of the different halves going on to the playoffs. Once again, the Grizzlies dominated the WFL and easily won the Eastern Division's first half.

The second half of the 1975 season got off to a rocky start for most of the league's teams, and on October 22, 1975, the WFL folded, a victim of inept play, mismanagement, a poor television contract, and fan and media hostility resulting from the discovery that many teams (although not the Grizzlies) had grossly inflated their attendance figures. With nowhere else to turn, Bassett made the decision to sue the NFL. When the United States Supreme Court refused to hear his appeal from the Third Circuit's ruling, the Grizzlies also folded.

Since the demise of the Grizzlies, Memphis has fielded teams in the Arena Football League (Pharaohs), CFL (Mad Dogs), and USFL (Showboats), and has come close to landing an NFL team on several occasions. Finally, in 1997, the Houston Oilers relocated to Memphis and played in the Liberty Bowl as the Tennessee Oilers. In 1998, however, the Oilers relocated to Nashville's Vanderbilt Stadium. For a further look at the history of professional football in Memphis, see Woody Baird, *Memphis' Struggle with NFL Has a History of Two Decades*, Seattle Times, Oct. 12, 1997, at C7.

4. Besides having the right contacts, a prospective owner must be rich. *See further* Michael Santoli, *King of Sports: Why Rupert Murdoch is Paying*

So Much for Premier Athletic Teams, Barron's, Sept. 21, 1998, at 31 (describing Rupert Murdoch's 1997 purchase of the Los Angeles Dodgers for $350 million, and his 1998 purchase of Manchester United, England's best soccer team, for $1 billion, as strategically sound because of their ability to provide programming for his far-flung television empire); Barry Rozner, *Colangelo Says His Type Here to Stay*, Chi. Daily Herald, Mar. 24, 1998, at 1 (Sports) (discussing Arizona Diamondbacks' owner Jerry Colangelo's belief that in the future only the very rich will be able to own teams); Rick Alm, *Billionaires Buying Into the Glamour of Sports*, Dallas Morning News, July 21, 1997, at 2B (reporting that most new owners are billionaires).

Every once in a while a pauper does try to buy a team. In 1996, for example, the NHL failed to properly investigate Dallas businessman John A. Spano. Relying on a background check that cost just $525, the league approved Spano and allowed him to purchase the New York Islanders from John O. Pickett. Within six months, it was discovered that Spano was broke and wanted by the federal authorities for bank and wire fraud. Eventually, Pickett was forced to take back the team, Spano pleaded guilty, and the NHL, deeply embarrassed by the affair, announced it would revise its review process. *See further* Stephen Nidetz, *NHL Bought Background Check for $525*, Chi. Trib., July 26, 1997, at 2 (Sports) (noting the NFL and MLB typically spend between $30,000 and $50,000 to check the backgrounds of potential owners). More recently, in 1998 a group of investors led by Tom Clancy, the best-selling author of high-tech military thrillers, was on the brink of buying the Minnesota Vikings for $201 million. At the last minute, the deal was vetoed by the NFL after it learned (much to its chagrin) that Clancy had only $5 million to invest and planned to borrow the rest of his $60 million capital contribution. *See* Richard Justice, *Clancy's Bid for Vikings Falls Through; NFL Questions Financing*, Wash. Post, May 21, 1998, at E3.

5. For a further look at the admission decisions of sports leagues, see, e.g., Kenneth L. Shropshire, *Diversity, Racism, and Professional Sports Franchise Ownership: Change Must Come From Within*, 67 U. Colo. L. Rev. 47 (1996) (suggesting the reason there are so few African–American owners is due to the "clubbiness" of sports leagues); Christian M. McBurney, Note, *The Legality of Sports Leagues' Restrictive Admissions Practices*, 60 N.Y.U. L. Rev. 925 (1985) (explaining various methods sports leagues use to deter unwanted applicants, such as high expansion fees); *Judge Allows Group to Sue NHL*, Vero Beach (FL) Press J., Sept. 12, 1998, at B5 (reporting on New York State Supreme Court Justice Herman Cahn's decision to allow Lamar Hunt, a disappointed bidder for the expansion Columbus Blue Jackets, to sue both the NHL and the Nationwide Insurance Company of New York for breach of contract and fair dealing); Don Pierson, *Browns Go for Ton of Green—$530 Million*, Chi. Trib., Sept. 9, 1998, at 3N (describing the auction used by the NFL to decide which ownership group would be awarded the expansion Cleveland Browns); Gary Ferman, *Hockey Goes for the Money*, New Miami, Oct. 1, 1993, at 22 (recounting how the NHL in 1992 courted Blockbuster Video's H. Wayne Huizenga and Disney's Michael Eisner to each pay $50 million for an expansion team).

Problem 15

Three years after purchasing his franchise, the owner of a basketball team concluded he had been lied to by league officials as to its value. He therefore refused to pay the balance of the purchase price. Given these facts, does either side have a case against the other? *See Continental Basketball Ass'n, Inc. v. Ellenstein Enterprises, Inc.*, 669 N.E.2d 134 (Ind.1996).

C. CONTROLS

Sports leagues place numerous restrictions on their members. Not surprisingly, these limits have engendered both controversy and litigation.

1. REVENUE

All teams need to maximize income if they are to remain competitive. Because of differences in their home markets, however, some clubs find it easier to do so than others. This, in turn, has led to class warfare between owners.

NATIONAL FOOTBALL LEAGUE PROPERTIES, INC. v. DALLAS COWBOYS FOOTBALL CLUB, LTD.

922 F.Supp. 849 (S.D.N.Y.1996).

SCHEINDLIN, District Judge.

Defendants Dallas Cowboys Football Club, Ltd., Texas Stadium Corporation, and Jerral W. Jones (together, "Defendants") move, pursuant to Fed.R.Civ.P. 12(b)(6), to dismiss this lawsuit for failure to state a claim upon which relief can be granted. For the reasons set forth below, this motion is granted in part and denied in part.

FACTUAL BACKGROUND

The National Football League ("NFL") is an unincorporated association comprised of 30 Member Clubs, including the Defendant Dallas Cowboys Football Club, Ltd. ("Cowboys Partnership"), which owns and operates the football team known as the Dallas Cowboys. Effective October 1, 1982, entities owning 26 of the then 28 Member Clubs entered into a trust agreement (the "Trust Agreement") which created the NFL Trust. The Trust Agreement provided that each Member Club would transfer to the NFL Trust the exclusive right to use its "Club Marks" for commercial purposes (with certain limited exceptions). These "Club Marks" include a team's name, helmet design, uniform design, and identifying slogans. See Schedule G to Trust Agreement, Exhibit D to Affidavit of Richard W. Cass ("Cass Affid."), Attorney for Defendants, at pp 2, 4. The Member Clubs also granted to the NFL Trust the exclusive right to use NFL Marks, such as the NFL Shield Design, and the names "NFL," "American Football Conference," "National Football Conference," and "Super Bowl." See id. at p 6.

As soon as the NFL Trust was created, it entered into a "License Agreement" with Plaintiff NFL Properties, Inc. that provides Plaintiff with "the exclusive right to license the use of the Trust Property on all types of articles of merchandise and in connection with all types of advertising and promotional programs." License Agreement, Exhibit D to Cass Affid., at 3. The Club Marks of the Cowboys Partnership, like the marks of other Member Clubs, are included in the Trust Property exclusively licensed to Plaintiff.

Plaintiff has been active in promoting the NFL and its Member Clubs, and has issued hundreds of licenses for the use of Club Marks. See Complaint at p 18. Plaintiff has also entered into agreements with companies involved in specific product categories—such as soft drinks or charge cards—to be exclusive sponsors of the NFL and its Member Clubs. Sponsors are given the right to use the Club Marks and NFL Marks in advertising, promotion and packaging, to promote themselves as an "Official Sponsor" of the NFL and, in some cases, as an "Official Sponsor" of the Member Clubs. See id. The revenue generated from Plaintiff's sale of licensing and sponsorship rights is shared equally by the Member Clubs, which are the sole shareholders of Plaintiff. See id. at pp 2, 19.

Plaintiff contends that Defendants have embarked upon a wrongful plan and scheme which violates the Trust and License Agreements and infringes upon Plaintiff's rights. Specifically, the Complaint alleges that Defendants have entered into a number of highly-publicized contractual arrangements—with Dr. Pepper, Pepsi, and NIKE—that "impermissibly exploit the Club Marks and the NFL Marks, and thus wrongfully misappropriate revenue that belongs to plaintiff and should be shared among all the Member Clubs." Id. at p 23. The Complaint also alleges that Defendants are negotiating a similar contract with American Express. See id. at p 38. Although all of the contractual arrangements Plaintiff mentions are nominally between the "sponsors" and Defendant Texas Stadium Corporation, Plaintiff claims that Defendants are using Texas Stadium as a "stand in" to help the Cowboys Partnership circumvent its obligations under the Trust and License Agreements. See id. at p 23.

The Complaint further alleges that Defendants misappropriated Club Marks and NFL Marks in solicitation materials they submitted to potential sponsors. In particular, Plaintiff asserts that Defendants used Club Marks—including the Cowboys "Star" logo—and NFL Marks—including the NFL's "Shield" logo—in the solicitation booklet they sent to Dr. Pepper. See id. at p 29. Plaintiff contends that Defendants had no right to use such marks for any purpose. See id. at p 29.

The Complaint contains nine counts. Count I alleges that Defendants' actions violate § 43(a) of the Lanham Act. Counts II and III assert, respectively, that Defendants have acted in concert to cause the Cowboys Partnership to breach express provisions of the Trust and License Agreements and the implied covenant of good faith. Count IV maintains that the Cowboys Partnership has breached its obligations as a settlor of the NFL Trust and as an owner of marks licensed to Plaintiff. Count V alleges that, by engaging in the scheme set forth in the Complaint, the Cowboys Partnership and Defendant Jones have violated fiduciary duties owed to Plaintiff and the other Member Clubs. Count VI asserts that Defendants have been unjustly enriched by their scheme, Count VII that they have misappropriated revenue belonging to Plaintiff, and Count VIII that they have tortiously interfered with contractual rights granted by Plaintiff to its licensees. Finally, Count IX seeks a declaratory judgment establishing that Defendants' actions violate the law, as set forth in Counts I through VIII.

Plaintiff seeks, inter alia, compensatory damages in an amount not yet determined but believed to be in excess of $100 million, treble damages under the Lanham Act, at least $200 million in punitive damages, and a permanent injunction enjoining Defendants from engaging in conduct similar to that alleged in the Complaint. See Complaint at pp I–IV (Prayer for Relief).

Defendants deny that their actions in any way violate either the Trust Agreement or the License Agreement. In support of their argument, Defendants have submitted copies of the contracts Texas Stadium entered into with NIKE, Pepsi, and Dr. Pepper, as well as the contract it eventually entered into with American Express. Defendants maintain that none of these contracts grant sponsors the right to use any Trust Property—namely, either Club Marks or NFL Marks; indeed, they note that the contracts with Pepsi, NIKE and American Express explicitly state that the sponsor is not entitled to use any Club Marks. See Pepsi Contract, Ex. F to Cass Affid., at p 12; NIKE Contract, Ex. G to Cass Affid., at p 3(H)(II); American Express Contract, Ex. H to Cass Affid., at p 8. Defendants argue that all of Plaintiff's claims are based on false assertions that are refuted by the underlying contracts, and that Plaintiff's action should therefore be dismissed.

Analysis

Plaintiff repeatedly alleges in its Complaint that Defendants, through Texas Stadium, have granted sponsors the right to use the mark "Texas Stadium, home of the Dallas Cowboys." See Complaint at pp 31(a), 38, 47–48, 53. Plaintiff also alleges that Defendants have "authoriz[ed] NIKE branded apparel to be worn on the field and on the sidelines during televised NFL games." Id. at p 49. An examination of the contracts at issue reveals that they neither grant the use of the phrase "home of the Dallas Cowboys" nor authorize NIKE apparel to be worn on the Dallas Cowboys' sidelines. Defendants contend that because the contracts do not authorize the alleged misconduct, Plaintiff's entire case must be dismissed.

A. Breach of Contract

Plaintiff's claim for breach of contract withstands Defendants' motion to dismiss for a number of reasons. First, although the contracts do not contain the language discussed above, they do grant other rights which may violate the Trust and License Agreements. The Pepsi contract grants Pepsi the right to use a logo which says "Texas Stadium/Home of America's Favorite Team," which Plaintiff claims is a Club Mark. The logo licensed for use by American Express contains a star which Plaintiff claims is similar to the star that appears on the Dallas Cowboys' helmets. Accepting Plaintiff's allegation that Texas Stadium entered into these contracts as a "stand in" for the Cowboys Partnership, and drawing all inferences in favor of Plaintiff, the use of either of these logos would violate the Trust and License Agreements.

Second, the Complaint alleges that Defendants engaged in conduct which might violate the Trust and License Agreements—namely, a concerted campaign to create the impression that companies such as NIKE and Pepsi were sponsors of the Dallas Cowboys organization.

During a nationally televised game, Defendant Jones, who controls both the Cowboys Partnership and Texas Stadium Corporation, allegedly escorted the CEO of NIKE to the Dallas Cowboys' sideline while both men prominently wore NIKE branded attire. See id. at p 36. The Complaint further alleges that Jones ordered team personnel not to dress in apparel licensed by Plaintiff during this game, so that "[m]illions of television viewers observed no apparel brand other than NIKE" on the Cowboys' sideline. Id. at pp 36(e), 36(g). Hence, despite contractual provisions to the contrary, in practice Defendants may have authorized NIKE apparel to be worn on the Dallas Cowboys' sideline, adjacent to players wearing the Club Marks.

Plaintiff also alleges that, in furtherance of their scheme to mislead the public, the Dallas Cowboys and NIKE jointly issued a press release in which the CEO of NIKE referred to the agreement as one with the "Dallas Cowboys"; and that Defendant Jones announced that the entire Cowboys organization drinks Pepsi, and posed for pictures at a press conference dressed in a "shirt emblazoned with a Cowboys Club Mark and boots emblazoned with a Pepsi logo...." Id. at pp 36(d), 31(c), 31(d). All of the above conduct may constitute an impermissible use of Club Marks (e.g., the name "Dallas Cowboys" and the team's uniforms), since under the Trust and License Agreements the Cowboys Partnership gave Plaintiff the exclusive right to use these marks for commercial purposes. At a minimum, alleging such conduct is sufficient to state a claim for breach of the implied duty of good faith, which constitutes a breach of contract under New York law. See Canstar v. J.A. Jones Constr. Co., 212 A.D.2d 452, 622 N.Y.S.2d 730, 731 (1st Dep't 1995); Fasolino Foods Co. v. Banca Nazionale del Lavoro, 961 F.2d 1052, 1058 (2d Cir.1992).

Finally, the Complaint alleges that Defendants misappropriated Club Marks and NFL Marks in solicitation materials they sent to potential sponsors. Specifically, the Complaint states that Defendants used the Club's "Star" logo and the NFL's "Shield" logo in a solicitation booklet they sent to Dr. Pepper. See Complaint at p 29. Because the

Trust and License Agreements give Plaintiff the exclusive right to use these Marks for commercial purposes, Defendants may have breached these agreements by using these Marks in a solicitation booklet. Defendants' counsel conceded that his clients' use of the Marks in solicitation materials was "[a]bsolutely inappropriate" and "probably violated their obligations...." Transcript of Oral Argument, February 15, 1996, at 11.

B. The Lanham Act

Plaintiff also alleges that Defendants violated § 43(a) of the Lanham Act, 15 U.S.C. § 1125(a), which provides in relevant part:

> (a)(1) Any person who, on or in connection with any goods or services, or any container for goods, uses in commerce any word, term, name, symbol, or device, or any combination thereof, or any false designation of origin, false or misleading description of fact, or false or misleading representation of fact, which—
>
> (A) is likely to cause confusion, or to cause mistake, or to deceive as to the affiliation, connection, or association of such person with another person, or as to the origin, sponsorship, or approval of his or her goods, services, or commercial activities of another person, ... shall be liable in a civil action by any person who believes that he or she is or is likely to be damaged by such act.

Such a claim requires only a valid trademark and a likelihood of confusion on the part of the public. See Nike, Inc. v. Just Did It Enters., 6 F.3d 1225, 1227 (7th Cir.1993).

Plaintiff has the exclusive right to use NFL Marks and Club Marks for commercial purposes. Plaintiff clearly alleges that Defendants have commercially exploited Club Marks and NFL Marks by using them to solicit a sponsorship agreement and by authorizing their use in agreements with Dr. Pepper, Pepsi, [and] NIKE. See Complaint at pp 29, 31, 33. As described above, Plaintiff also alleges that Defendants, through various press conferences and public appearances, have sought to create the impression that a relationship exists between the Cowboys and various sponsor companies. See id. at pp 31(b), 31(c), 31(d), 36. Of course, whether the marks used by Defendants were NFL Marks or Club Marks is a question of fact.

There are decisions of this Court which suggest that an exclusive licensee of the right to distribute goods bearing a certain trademark cannot bring an action under § 43(a) of the Lanham Act against the trademark owner for permitting the use of the trademark in violation of the licensing agreement. See L.G.B. Inc. v. Gitano Group, Inc., 769 F.Supp. 1243, 1249 (S.D.N.Y.1991); Ballet Makers, Inc. v. United States Shoe Corp., 633 F.Supp. 1328, 1335 (S.D.N.Y.1986); Silverstar Enters., Inc. v. Aday, 537 F.Supp. 236, 241 (S.D.N.Y.1982). The reasoning of these cases is that where the trademark owner, who is the source of the goods, authorizes the use of the mark for "genuine" goods, there can be no likelihood of confusion as to the source of the goods and, consequently, the quality of the goods.

Plaintiff's interest in the marks, however, is in authorizing the international corporate sponsorship of goods, not in selling goods. In this context the concepts of genuine goods, quality of goods, and source of goods have little significance. The quality, source, or genuineness of Pepsi or NIKE shoes, for example, are primarily reflected by their respective marks regardless of whether they are sponsored by the Cowboys or the NFL. As neither Plaintiff nor Defendants sell or manufacture goods, it makes little sense to focus on the source of the goods as the courts did in Ballet Makers and the other cited cases. See Mastercard Int'l Inc. v. Sprint Communications Co., 1994 WL 97097 at *4 (S.D.N.Y.), aff'd, 23 F.3d 397 (2d Cir.1994) (rejecting the relevance of the source of goods in the sponsorship context). Rather, in the sponsorship context, the focus should be on the nature of Defendants' activities regarding marks which Plaintiff has the exclusive right to commercially exploit. Plaintiff has pleaded that Defendants have used NFL Marks and Club Marks in a manner which is likely to confuse the public as to Plaintiff's "sponsorship or approval" of Dr. Pepper, Pepsi, and NIKE. See Complaint at pp 47–50. These allegations are sufficient to state a cause of action under the broad language of § 43(a) of the Lanham Act.

C. Other Claims

Plaintiff's other claims arise out of the same set of operative facts as the breach of contract and Lanham Act claims, and are likewise not defeated by the contracts Defendants have submitted. However, Defendants have raised independent objections to several of Plaintiff's common law claims, two of which are convincing.

i. Breach of Implied Covenant of Good Faith

Defendants seek to dismiss Plaintiff's claim for breach of the implied duty of good faith because it is duplicative of Plaintiff's breach of contract claim. "Under New York law, parties to an express contract are bound by an implied duty of good faith, but breach of that duty is merely a breach of the underlying contract." Fasolino Foods, 961 F.2d at 1056. Plaintiff's separate claim for breach of the implied duty of good faith is therefore dismissed as redundant. See Apfel v. Prudential–Bache Sec., 183 A.D.2d 439, 583 N.Y.S.2d 386, 387 (1st Dep't 1992), modified on other grounds and aff'd, 81 N.Y.2d 470, 600 N.Y.S.2d 433, 616 N.E.2d 1095 (1993) ("cause of action alleging a breach of good faith is duplicative of a cause of action alleging breach of contract, since every contract contains an implied covenant of good faith and fair dealing").

ii. Breach of Obligations as Settlor of the NFL Trust Agreement and as Licensor of the Cowboys Club Marks

Defendants contend that Count IV of the Complaint should be dismissed because neither a settlor of a trust nor a licensor is under any duty—beyond that set forth in the underlying trust or licensing agreement—to refrain from taking steps that will reduce the value of the trust property or license. In support of its claim, Plaintiff cites a single case involving a settlor's deliberate interference with a trustee's efforts to fulfill his duties under the trust agreement. See Vandyke v. Webb, 167 A.D. 445, 152 N.Y.S. 508 (1st Dep't 1915). The cause of action recognized in Vandyke is nothing more than a simple breach of the implied duty of good faith. The case does not support Plaintiff's view that a settlor has any duty independent of its obligations under a trust agreement, which include the implied duty of good faith. Count IV is therefore dismissed.

iii. Misappropriation of Property

Defendants assert that the Complaint fails to state a claim for misappropriation of property because it does not adequately identify the property rights allegedly misappropriated. Further, they argue that this claim fails because New York does not recognize a cause of action for the misappropriation of intangible assets. Neither of these arguments has merit. The first fails because the Complaint clearly alleges that Defendants have misappropriated revenue belonging to Plaintiff. See Complaint at p 75. The second is irrelevant because revenue is not an "intangible asset."

Even if the Complaint only alleged that Defendants have misappropriated Club Marks, which are intangible, dismissal would not be warranted. Misappropriation claims that concern intangible rights are generally not recognized. See Ippolito v. Lennon, 150 A.D.2d 300, 542 N.Y.S.2d 3, 6 (1st Dep't 1989). However, in the context of unfair competition, a plaintiff may state a cause of action for the misappropriation of an intangible asset, at least where it is ultimately embodied in a tangible product. See Standard & Poor's Corp. v. Commodity Exchange, 683 F.2d 704, 710 (2d Cir.1982).

iv. Tortious Interference

Defendants contend that the Complaint fails to allege the elements of tortious interference with contract. A plaintiff in such an action must allege that: i) a valid contract existed between plaintiff and a third party; ii) defendant knew of this contract; iii) defendant intentionally induced the third party to breach the contract or otherwise render performance impossible; and iv) plaintiff suffered damages. See Kronos, Inc. v. AVX Corp., 81 N.Y.2d 90, 94, 595 N.Y.S.2d 931, 612 N.E.2d 289 (1993); Enercomp, Inc. v. McCorhill Publishing, Inc., 873 F.2d 536, 541 (2d Cir.1989).

Kronos suggests that a plaintiff can state a claim for tortious interference with contract without actually alleging that the third party breached its contract. However, a plaintiff must at least allege that the defendant's interference made the contract impossible to perform, or that the defendant induced the third party to render performance impossible. See Museum Boutique Intercontinental, Ltd. v. Picasso, 886 F.Supp. 1155, 1163 & n. 19 (S.D.N.Y.1995).

The Complaint meets this requirement. Plaintiff alleges that Defendants' intentional conduct has "interfered with and caused the violation and derogation of contractual rights granted by plaintiff to its licensees and sponsors." Complaint at p 78. Plaintiff has entered into contracts that make companies exclusive sponsors of the NFL and its Member Clubs for specific product categories. Plaintiff alleges that Defendants, by making unilateral arrangements with the direct competitors of these exclusive sponsors, have made it impossible for Plaintiff to honor its contractual obligations. Accordingly, Plaintiff's claim for tortious interference withstands Defendants' motion.

CONCLUSION

For the reasons set forth above, Defendants' motion is granted in part and denied in part.

Notes

1. After further litigation, the NFL and Jones reached a settlement highly favorable to the Cowboys. *See further* J. Scott Hale, *Jerry Jones Versus the NFL: An Opportunity to Apply Logically the Single Entity Defense to the NFL*, 4 Sports Law. J. 1 (1997); William J. Hoffman, Comment, *Dallas' Head Cowboy Emerges Victorious in a Licensing Showdown with the N.F.L.*, 7 Seton Hall J. Sport L. 255 (1997); Richard Alm, *Jerry Jones, NFL Now at Peace*, Dallas Morning News, June 14, 1998, at 1H. A short time later, MLB tried to stop George Steinbrenner from going ahead with his own $95 million footwear contract with Adidas. It backed down, however, after the Yankees sued for antitrust violations. *See further* John Harper, *Yanks' Shoe Firm Deal Okd*, N.Y. Daily News, May 1, 1998, at 110.

2. As the incidents involving Jones and Steinbrenner demonstrate, product licensing has become an important source of revenue for sports clubs. In 1997, for example, the NBA sold $3.1 billion of licensed merchandise, the NFL $3 billion, MLB $1.7 billion, and the NHL $1 billion. As a result, new teams work hard to develop names, logos, and uniforms that will appeal to the public and established teams update their look whenever sales begin to sag (although, as the New York Islanders discovered when they replaced their popular "island" logo with a fisherman in 1995, tinkering with tradition can be a costly mistake).

For a further look at how products are licensed, see, e.g., Julie A. Garcia, Note, *The Future of Sports Merchandise Licensing*, 18 Hastings Comm/Ent L.J. 219 (1995) (describing the licensing programs of the four major professional sports leagues); Valli Herman, *Dressed for Success: Team Wear Becomes High Fashion That's Marketed Beyond Sports Fans*, Dallas Morning News, July 12, 1998, at 20B (relating that in 1997, the New York Yankees, Green Bay Packers, Chicago Bulls, and Detroit Red Wings led their respective leagues in merchandise sales); Tom Linafelt, *Baseball Museum Buoyed by Licensing Revenue*, Denv. Bus. J., May 8, 1998, at 20A (explaining how the Negro Leagues Baseball Museum in Kansas City turned its old logos into a $7.5 million-a-year business); Jeffrey D. Zbar, *Sports Licensee Enters New Game—Ice Cream*, Fort Lauderdale Sun-Sentinel, Mar. 30, 1998, at 12 (Bus.) (describing how a company known as American Scoop is working to become the official ice cream licensee of the sports world); Eric Fisher, *Splashy Logos, Conservative Style Both Score*, Wash. Times, July 28, 1997, at D13 (noting that the sale of minor league baseball merchandise generates

$34 million in annual revenues); Cheryl Jackson, *New Colors Fuel Lucrative Merchandising*, Tampa Trib., Apr. 9, 1997, at 1 (Bus.) (reporting when teams change their logos, sales usually increase by 20%–30%).

3. In recent years, a heated national debate has broken out over the appropriateness of logos that use Native American or Confederate symbols. *See further Harjo v. Pro Football, Inc.*, 30 U.S.P.Q.2d (BNA) 1828 (1994), *appeal dismissed*, 45 U.S.P.Q.2d (BNA) 1789 (1998) (petition to cancel trademark of Washington Redskins denied because beyond Trademark Board's statutory powers); *Munson v. State Superintendent of Public Instruction*, 577 N.W.2d 387 (Wis.Ct.App.1998) (high school did not violate students' civil rights by continuing to use Indian logo and team name); Michelle B. Lee, *Section 2(a) of the Lanham Act as a Restriction on Sports Team Names: Has Political Correctness Gone Too Far?*, 4 Sports Law. J. 65 (1997); Cathryn L. Claussen, *Ethnic Team Names and Logos—Is There a Legal Solution?*, 6 Marq. Sports L.J. 409 (1996); John B. Rhode, Comment, *The Mascot Name Change Controversy: A Lesson in Hypersensitivity*, 5 Marq. Sports L.J. 141 (1994); William Nack, *Look Away, Dixie Land: It's Time for Ole Miss to Acknowledge What the Rebel Flag Truly Stands for and Ban It*, Sports Illustrated, Nov. 3, 1997, at 114. *See also* Jim Bainbridge, *In Missouri, They're Split Over Team's Personality*, Colo. Springs Gazette Telegraph, June 30, 1998, at 6 (Sports) (reporting a new minor league football team was forced to abandon the name "Psychos" after community advocates claimed it was offensive to the mentally ill), and Jim Beseda, *Calgary Team Changes Its Controversial Logo*, Portland Oregonian, Feb. 8, 1995, at E2 (describing the furor caused by an expansion minor league hockey team's decision to call itself the Hitmen and use an assassin-like figure as its mascot).

4. Even more successful than league-wide merchandising pools have been league-wide television packages. Shortly after being elected commissioner in 1960, Pete Rozelle came to believe the NFL's competitive balance was being jeopardized by the ability of teams in major television markets to sell their broadcast rights for much more than teams in small markets (CBS, for example, was paying the New York Giants $175,000 and the Green Bay Packers $35,000). Thus, in 1961 he persuaded Congress to enact the Sports Broadcasting Act, thereby immunizing the sale of league-wide television packages from federal and state antitrust laws. *See* 15 U.S.C. § 1291 (1994). This change has allowed the NFL to reap enormous rewards, including, in 1998, an eight-year deal with CBS, Disney (the parent of ABC and ESPN), and Fox that will pay it $2.2 billion annually. The NBA ($660 million per year), MLB ($340 million per year), and the NHL ($120 million per year) also have benefitted from the Act, although their network deals have been less lucrative due to the greater popularity of football. *See further* Brian Lowry, *Welcome to a Blitz of Sports Coverage*, L.A. Times, Sept. 1, 1998, at F1, and Bill Carter, *Can Football Revive CBS?*, N.Y. Times, Aug. 31, 1998, at C1. *See also* Liz Clarke, *NASCAR is Rethinking Itself: How to Sell Broadcasts is a Top Priority*, Wash. Post, Dec. 16, 1998, at C1 (describing NASCAR's interest in switching from its current practice of having each race track negotiate its own television deal to a single national package negotiated by the association to maximize profits), and Jeff Rusnak, *Super League Pushing Forward*, Fort Lauderdale Sun–Sentinel, Aug. 9, 1998, at 18C

(reporting Europe's top soccer teams are considering forming a "super league" consisting of the continent's best teams because of projections that such an entity could command a television package worth $1.1 billion a year).

5. Although league-wide television packages have been welcomed in the professional ranks, in the early 1980s the College Football Association, a group of universities with exceptionally strong football programs, challenged the NCAA's policy of limiting the number of games that could be shown on national television. The dispute eventually reached the United States Supreme Court, where the NCAA argued its policy was needed to protect weaker schools. In a lengthy opinion by Justice Stevens, the Court ruled the policy violated the federal antitrust laws because it raised prices and reduced output. *See National Collegiate Athletic Ass'n v. Board of Regents of the University of Oklahoma*, 468 U.S. 85 (1984).

6. Even in leagues with pooling arrangements, certain types of income (referred to as "local revenue") are not shared. Money from stadium naming rights, parking, luxury suites, food and beverage concessions, local television and radio contracts, and advertising, for example, typically remain with the home team. *See further* Bill Lubinger et al., *Loges to Hot Dogs: How the Balance Sheet Shapes Up*, Clev. Plain Dealer, May 3, 1998, at 14A (explaining in the NFL such fees can boost a team's earnings by as much as $12 million a year). *See also* Alan J. Ostfield, *Seat License Revenue in the National Football League: Shareable or Not?*, 5 Seton Hall J. Sport L. 599 (1995) (describing the long-running battle among NFL owners over whether teams must share the money they make from permanent seat licenses).

7. The amount of local revenue a team generates depends on many factors, including the size of its home market, its on-field success, the terms of its stadium lease, and other entertainment options available in its community. As a result, wide disparities often exist between clubs in the same league. In the NFL, for example, the Dallas Cowboys, the most valuable team, are worth $413 million, while the Indianapolis Colts, the least valuable team, are worth $227 million. Even larger differences exist in MLB (New York Yankees $362 million versus Montreal Expos $87 million), the NBA (Chicago Bulls $303 million versus Milwaukee Bucks $94 million), and the NHL (New York Rangers $195 million versus Edmonton Oilers $67 million). *See further* Michael K. Ozaninan, *Selective Accounting*, Forbes, Dec. 14, 1998, at 124, and Wilbert M. Leonard, *A Comparative Study of Expenditure, Revenue, and Franchise Value Functions in Professional Sports*, 21 J. Sport Behavior 265 (1998).

Because of the increasing gap between the "haves" and the "have nots," friction among team owners is on the rise, particularly in baseball, and attempts at revenue sharing so far have had only limited success. *See further* Jeffrey A. Rosenthal, *The Football Answer to the Baseball Problem: Can Revenue Sharing Work?*, 5 Seton Hall J. Sport L. 419 (1995) (arguing MLB must adopt revenue sharing if it is to survive as a competitive enterprise); Kevin E. Martens, *Fair or Foul? The Survival of Small–Market Teams in Major League Baseball*, 4 Marq. Sports L.J. 323 (1994) (describing the hardships faced by poorer clubs); Mike Berardino, *A Widening Gap*, Fort Lauderdale Sun–Sentinel, Dec. 14, 1998, at 1D (pointing to the record-setting $105 million contract the Los Angeles Dodgers gave to pitcher Kevin Brown in December 1998 as a prime example of how rich baseball teams have left poor ones behind); Bill Lubinger, *Cleveland's New Ballpark a Financial Home Run*, Austin Am.-Statesman, Apr. 19, 1998, at J1 (noting that teams that play in new stadiums usually earn two to three times more revenue than those in older stadiums).

Problem 16

When a "superstation" approached a highly successful team with an offer to televise its games throughout the country for a hefty fee, the commissioner objected to the deal on the ground that it would violate the league's national cable contract. If the club sues for illegal restraint of trade, how should the court rule? *See Chicago Professional Sports Limited Partnership v. National Basketball Ass'n*, 95 F.3d 593 (7th Cir.1996).

2. CROSS-OWNERSHIP

While most owners find running one sports team to be sufficiently challenging, some do not. As a result, every league has been forced to face the issue of dual proprietorship.

NORTH AMERICAN SOCCER LEAGUE v. NATIONAL FOOTBALL LEAGUE

670 F.2d 1249 (2d Cir.),
cert. denied, 459 U.S. 1074 (1982).

MANSFIELD, Circuit Judge.

The North American Soccer League (NASL) and certain of its member soccer teams (collectively referred to herein as "the NASL") appeal from a judgment of the Southern District of New York, Charles S. Haight, Jr., Judge, dissolving a preliminary injunction and dismissing a complaint seeking a permanent injunction and treble damages for alleged violations of § 1 of the Sherman Act, 15 U.S.C. § 1, by the defendants, the National Football League ("NFL") and certain of its member football clubs (collectively referred to herein as "the NFL"). The NFL cross appeals from the dismissal of its counterclaim, which sought an injunction barring owners of NASL member teams from cross-ownership of NFL teams. Because the conduct complained of by the NASL—an NFL ban on cross-ownership by NFL members of other major professional sports league teams (the "cross-ownership ban")—violates the rule of reason under § 1 of the Sherman Act, we reverse. We affirm the dismissal of the NFL's counterclaim.

The central question in this case is whether an agreement between members of one league of professional sports teams (NFL) to prohibit its members from making or retaining any capital investment in any member of another league of professional sports teams (in this case NASL) violates the antitrust laws. The answer requires an analysis of the facts and application of governing antitrust principles. Most of the facts are not in dispute. The NFL is an unincorporated joint venture consisting of 28 individually owned separate professional football teams, each operated through a distinct corporation or partnership, which is engaged in the business of providing public entertainment in the form of competitive football games between its member teams. It is the only major league professional football association in the United States. Upon becoming a member of the NFL a team owner receives a non-assignable franchise giving him the exclusive right to operate an NFL professional football team in a designated home city and "home territory," and to play football games in that territory against other NFL members according to a schedule and terms arranged by the NFL. See NFL Constitution and By-laws, §§ 3.4, 4.1, 4.2. In a few cities the size of the population and fan interest have led the NFL to grant franchises to two teams on an equal basis in a home territory (e.g., San Francisco Forty Niners and the Oakland Raiders; the New York Giants and the New York Jets).

The success of professional football as a business depends on several factors. The ultimate goal is to attract as many people as possible to pay money to attend games between members and to induce advertisers to sponsor TV broadcasts of such games, which results in box-office receipts from sale of tickets and revenues derived from network advertising, all based on public interest in viewing games. If adequate revenues are received, a team will operate at a profit after payment of expenses, including players' salaries, stadium costs, referees, travel, maintenance and the like. Toward this goal there must be a number of separate football teams, each dispersed in a location having local public fans willing to buy tickets to games or view them on TV; a group of highly skilled players on each team who are reasonably well-matched in playing ability with those of other teams; adequate capital to support the teams' operations; uniform rules of competition governing game play; home territory stadia available for the conduct of the games; referees; and an apparatus for the negotiation and sale of network TV and radio broadcast rights and distribution of broadcast revenues among members.

To perform these functions some sort of an economic joint venture is essential. No single owner could engage in professional football for profit without at least one other competing team. Separate owners for each team are desirable in order to convince the public of the honesty of the competition. Moreover, to succeed in the marketplace by attracting fans the teams must be close in the caliber of their playing ability. As one commentator puts it "there is a great deal of economic interdependence among the clubs comprising a league. They jointly produce a product which no one of them is capable of producing alone. In addition, the success of the overall venture depends upon the financial stability of each club." J. Weistart & C. Lowell, The Law of Sports § 5.11, at 757–58 (1979).

Earlier in this century various professional football leagues existed, outstanding of which were the NFL and AFL (American Football League). In 1970 the AFL merged into the NFL, after receiving Congressional approval to avoid violation of antitrust laws that would otherwise occur. Since then the NFL has assumed full responsibility for national promotion of professional football, granting of team franchises, negotiation of network TV contracts for broadcast rights with respect to its members' games, employment of referees, adoption of game rules, scheduling of season games between members leading up to the league championship game known as the Super Bowl, and many other matters pertaining to the national sport. Although specific team profit figures were not introduced at trial, the record is clear that the NFL and most of its members now generally enjoy financial success. The NFL divides pooled TV receipts equally among members. Pre-season gate receipts from each game are shared on a 50/50 basis between opposing teams, and regular season gate receipts are divided on the basis of 60% for the home team and 40% for the visiting team.

Although NFL members thus participate jointly in many of the operations conducted by it on their behalf, each member is a separately owned, discrete legal entity which does not share its expenses, capital expenditures or profits with other members. Each also derives separate revenues from certain lesser sources, which are not shared with other members, including revenues from local TV and radio, parking and concessions. A member's gate receipts from its home games varies from those of other members, depending on the size of the home city, the popularity of professional football in the area and competition for spectators offered by other entertainment, including professional soccer. As a result, profits vary from team to team. Indeed as recently as 1978, the last year for which we have records, 2 of the 28 NFL teams suffered losses. In 1977 12 teams experienced losses. Thus, in spite of sharing of some revenues, the financial performance of each team, while related to that of the others, does not, because of the variables in revenues and costs as between member teams, necessarily rise or fall with that of the others. The NFL teams are separate economic entities engaged in a joint venture.

The North American Soccer League ("NASL") was founded in 1968 upon the merger of two pre-existing soccer leagues. Like the NFL, the NASL is an unincorporated association of professional soccer teams whose members are separately owned and operated, and are financially independent. Its raison d'etre and the needs of its member teams are essentially the same as those of members of other major professional sports leagues, including the NFL. However, professional soccer is not as mature or lucrative as professional football. Just as was the case with NFL member teams a quarter of a century ago, NASL is struggling to achieve wider popularity and with it greater revenues. Consequently, the risk of investing in an NASL team is considerably greater than that of investing in the NFL.

Soccer was not a widely followed or popular sport when the NASL was founded, and several earlier attempts to put together a professional soccer league failed due to lack of fan interest. The NASL has been the most successful soccer league to date. The district court found that since the NASL was organized "professional soccer has experienced substantial and accelerated growth in fan interest, media following, paid attendance, number of franchises and geographic scope. . . ." 505 F.Supp. 659, 666–67. With this success NASL teams have become increasingly more effective competitors of the NFL teams. The two sports are somewhat similar.

Their seasons substantially overlap. The teams have franchises from their respective leagues in the same locations and frequently use the same stadia. An increasing, although small, percentage of the public are switching their interest as fans and TV viewers from professional football to professional soccer, threatening to reduce revenue which NFL teams derive from gate receipts and TV broadcast rights. Competition between NFL and NASL teams has not only increased on an inter-league basis but also between individual NFL and NASL teams. On the league front both organizations compete for a greater share of finite national and regional TV broadcast and advertising revenues. At the local level NFL teams compete against NASL teams for greater fan support, gate attendance, and local broadcast revenues.

In spite of its success relative to other leagues that have attempted to make soccer a viable competitor, the NASL and its member teams have been, to this point, financially unsuccessful. Last year the teams collectively lost approximately $30 million. Individual NASL franchises have been very unstable; for example, since the trial of this case 8 of the 24 NASL teams have folded. Thus the NASL is the weakest of the major professional sports leagues (the NFL, the NASL, the National Basketball Association, the National Hockey League, and Major League Baseball).

Because of the interdependence of professional sports league members and the unique nature of their business, the market for and availability of capital investment is limited. As the district court found, the economic success of each franchise is dependent on the quality of sports competition throughout the league and the economic strength and stability of other league members. Damage to or losses by any league member can adversely affect the stability, success and operations of other members. Aside from willingness to take the risk of investing in a member of a league in which members have for the most part not demonstrated a record of profits, the potential investor must be reasonably compatible with other members of the league, with a sufficient understanding of the nature of the business and the interdependence of ownership to support not only his newly-acquired team but the sports league of which it is a member. As the district court further noted, these conditions have tended to attract individuals or businesses with distinct characteristics as distinguished from the much larger number of financiers of the type prevailing in most business markets. Although, as the district court observed, the boundaries of this "sports ownership capital and skill" market are not as confined as NASL contends and not limited strictly to present major league sports owners, the sources of sports capital are limited by the foregoing conditions and existing sports league owners constitute a significant source. In short, while capital may be fungible in other businesses, it is not fungible in the business of producing major league professional sports. Regardless of the risk involved in the venture, which may vary greatly from league to league, league members look not merely for money but for a compatible fellow owner, preferably having entrepreneurial sports skill, with whom the other members can operate their joint business enterprise. League members recognize, for example, that if the owner of one team allowed it to deteriorate to the point where it usually lost every game, attendance at games in which that team was playing would fall precipitously, hurting not just that team, but every other team that played it during the season. In view of this business interdependence team owners, through their leagues, are careful about whom they allow to purchase a team in their league and leagues invariably require that the sale of a franchise be approved by a majority of team owners rather than by the selling owner alone.

For these reasons individuals with experience in owning and operating sports teams tend to be the most sought-after potential owners. Indeed, the NFL made clear that it values proven experience in a potential owner. When in 1974 it expanded by 2 teams, 5 of the 8 prospective owners it considered seriously had professional sports team ownership experience; a sixth had experience in non-team sports. The two ownership groups to whom it awarded franchises included individuals with prior professional sports team ownership experience, and the NFL did not award the franchises to the highest bidder, a procedure that would have provided the most immediate financial reward to its owners.

The attractiveness of existing owners of major sports teams as sources of potential capital is further evidenced by the large number of members of major sports leagues who control or own substantial interests in members of other leagues. The record reveals some 110 instances of cross-ownership and some 238 individuals or corporations having a 10% or greater interest in other teams. Over the last 13 years there have been 16 cross-ownerships between NFL and NASL teams. Indeed, since the NASL was organized Lamar Hunt, the owner of the NFL's Kansas City Chiefs, has been involved as an NASL team owner, first of the Dallas Tornado team, then of the Tampa Bay team, and as a promoter of NASL. Since 1975 Elizabeth Robbie, the wife of the NFL's Miami Dolphins owner Joseph Robbie, has been the majority owner of the NASL's Fort Lauderdale franchise. Mr. Robbie has apparently been the actual operator of the soccer team as well as the football team. In the words of the district court, these cross-owners have provided the NASL with an "important element of stability," 465 F.Supp. at 669, which led to professional soccer's becoming a major league sport, and withdrawal of their interests "would have a significantly adverse effect on the NASL," 505 F.Supp. at 668.

In addition to the Hunt and Robbie cross-ownerships Bill Bidwill had a controlling interest in the NFL St. Louis Cardinals and a 3% interest in the NASL California Surf. Earlier cross-ownership by beneficial owners of the NFL Seattle Seahawks of interests in the NASL Seattle Sounders was terminated.

Beginning in the 1950's NFL commissioners had a policy against a team owner maintaining a controlling interest in a team of a competing league, which was first put in writing by the owners themselves in January 1967, at a time when 12 owners of old NFL or AFL teams (the leagues had by then agreed to merge to form the present NFL) were involved in the formation of the predecessors of the NASL. The resolution, which was approved at an owners' meeting, called for the drafting of amendments to the NFL constitution and bylaws prohibiting cross-ownership, but nothing was ever done to comply with it. In 1972 the NFL owners passed another resolution providing that NFL owners were not to acquire operating control of a team in a competing league. The participants agreed that any member holding such a controlling interest would make a "best effort" to dispose of it.

For the next five years the NFL members repeatedly passed the same resolution at meetings, except through inadvertence in 1975. During this period the NASL, which had come close to disbanding in 1968, grew more successful, due in no small part to the efforts of Hunt, who worked tirelessly to promote professional soccer and raise capital for it. NFL owners began to feel competition from the NASL. Leonard Tose, the owner of the Philadelphia Eagles, became one of the most vocal opponents of Hunt's soccer holdings. At approximately the same time the NASL Philadelphia Atoms were leading that league in attendance, and Tose's NFL football team, the Philadelphia Eagles, was losing money. (The Eagles lost money from at least 1969 to 1974, and in 1976 and 1977.) Tose became particularly incensed when Hunt began doing promotional work for the NASL. For example, at one NFL owners' meeting Tose denounced Hunt for allegedly stating in an interview that soccer is the sport of the future. Tose later explained one of the reasons for his concern, stating, "in my view when our truck drivers [fans] have X number of dollars to spend for entertainment in sport, and [sic] any dollar that they spend in another sport could affect what they spend for football." In short, Mr. Tose's business, the NFL Philadelphia Eagles, was suffering from the competition from the NASL Philadelphia Atoms.

Tose was not the only NFL owner upset by competition from a soccer league team. Max Winter, the owner of the NFL's Minnesota Vikings, became concerned about competition from the Minnesota Kicks, an NASL member. As Tose had done, Winter complained about Hunt's NASL soccer team interest at NFL owners' meetings. At his deposition he stated, "I think I said it to the league, in the room, that I object very much that an American Football Conference President [i.e., Hunt] is going to Minneapolis to advance soccer, introduce soccer in my city." Winter discussed Hunt's activities with Tose, stating that he felt that the Kicks "are hurting us, the sports dollar, that they are drawing very well, that we are losing ground as far as media exposure, fan participation. [It g]enerally hurts us."

Finally in 1978 the NFL owners moved to take strong action against Hunt and Robbie. An amendment to the NFL by-laws was proposed that would require both to divest their soccer holdings if they wished to continue to own an NFL team. The proposed amendment, which was to have been voted on at an October 1978 NFL owners' meeting, would also have prevented all majority owners, certain minority owners, officers and directors of NFL teams, and certain relatives of such persons from owning any interest in a team in a "major team sport."

As the district court found, the cross-ownership ban "has a concededly anticompetitive intent and, in its impact on the NASL, will probably have an anticompetitive effect." 505 F.Supp. at 689. The purpose of the ban was to weaken the NASL and its member teams so that they could not compete as effectively against the stronger, more mature, and lucrative NFL teams as they might be able to do with the aid of capital investment by NFL team owners.

On September 28, 1978, the NASL and various of its members commenced this action by serving the NFL with a complaint and an order to show cause why it should not be preliminarily enjoined from adopting the proposed amendment. On February 21, 1979, after hearing oral argument, Judge Haight issued a preliminary injunction prohibiting the enactment of the amendment. The judge found that the NASL would be irreparably injured if the NFL were allowed to adopt the amendment, that there were serious questions going to the merits, and that the balance of the hardships tipped in favor of the NASL. 465 F.Supp. 665. The NFL did not appeal the injunction.

A lengthy trial followed, and on November 17, 1980, Judge Haight issued his decision. 505 F.Supp. 659. Although he found that the purpose and impact of the NFL cross-ownership ban was to suppress competition in interstate commerce on the part of NASL and its members, he denied relief on the ground that in competing against NASL and its members the NFL and its members must be regarded as a "single economic entity," rendering § 1 of the Sherman Act inapplicable for the reason that it is limited to a plurality of actors. Recognizing that individual NFL teams compete with individual NASL teams for the consumer's dollar in their respective localities, the district court nevertheless concluded that this NFL team-member versus NASL team-member competition is subsumed in league versus league competition in the general entertainment market, which he described as "the primary economic competition in professional sports," 505 F.Supp. at 678, stating that in all relevant markets the competition is "between two single economic entities uncomplicated by any relevant competition between the member clubs of a league," id. at 685. Decisions rejecting sports leagues' contentions that they should be treated as "single economic entities" were distinguished on the ground that they involved different types of markets in which the members of a sports league were competing individually against each other (e.g., for players' services, hiring availability and terms, reserve clauses, college drafts, etc.), whereas here the court considered them to act monolithically as one joint enterprise. Supreme Court decisions in non-sports antitrust cases rejecting arguments that business trade restraints were justified on the ground that two or more participants had acted as a joint venture or "single business entity," e.g., Timken Roller

Bearing Co. v. United States, 341 U.S. 593, 71 S.Ct. 971, 95 L.Ed. 1199 (1951), and Perma Life Mufflers, Inc. v. International Parts Corp., 392 U.S. 134, 88 S.Ct. 1981, 20 L.Ed.2d 982 (1968), were distinguished on the ground those combinations, unlike sports leagues, were unnecessary to the successful production and marketing of the product involved, the district judge here stating, "No interdependence or joint action is necessary to make a bearing or a muffler." 505 F.Supp. at 686. Because individual teams acting alone could not produce "Pro Football," Judge Haight reasoned, the combination of those teams through the NFL was justified by its "dominant purpose," the production of the league sport, and was legal under Timken and Perma Life. For the same reason the judge refused to apply the rule of reason as articulated in National Society of Professional Engineers v. United States, 435 U.S. 679, 98 S.Ct. 1355, 55 L.Ed.2d 637 (1978).

Judge Haight further concluded that, while a sports ownership capital market may exist as a submarket of the broad capital funds market, the NASL and its members had failed to prove that the submarket was, as claimed by them, limited to present owners of major sports league teams. He declined to make any finding as to the scope of the submarket and whether the NFL cross-ownership ban foreclosed NASL teams from access to any significant share of it or restrained them from competing against NFL teams in the entertainment market. Instead he chose to rest his decision on the "single economic entity" theory.

NFL's two counterclaims were both rejected as without substance. With respect to the first counterclaim, which sought an injunction prohibiting the NASL and its member teams from engaging in cross-ownership with the NFL on the ground that such activity was analogous to interlocking directorates linking horizontal competitors, the judge ruled that the NFL had not shown any threat of injury from the alleged violation and, assuming that it had proved a threat of injury, an injunction would be mere surplusage because the NFL had the power to end cross-ownership itself.

DISCUSSION

The first issue is whether § 1 of the Sherman Act, which prohibits "[e]very contract, combination in the form of trust or otherwise, or conspiracy, in restraint of trade or commerce among the several States, or with foreign nations" applies to the cross-ownership ban adopted by NFL and its members. The NFL contends, and the district court held, that § 1 does not apply for the reason that the NFL acted as a "single economic entity" and not as a combination or conspiracy within the meaning of that law. We disagree. As the Supreme Court long ago recognized, the Sherman Act by its terms applies to "every" combination or agreement concerning trade, not just certain types. Chicago Board of Trade v. United States, 246 U.S. 231, 238, 38 S.Ct. 242, 244, 62 L.Ed. 683 (1918). The theory that a combination of actors can gain exemption from § 1 of the Sherman Act by acting as a "joint venture" has repeatedly been rejected by the Supreme Court and the Sherman Act has been held applicable to professional sports teams by numerous lesser federal courts. See, e.g., Perma Life Mufflers, Inc. v. International Parts Corp., 392 U.S. 134, 141–42, 88 S.Ct. 1981, 1985–86, 20 L.Ed.2d 982 (1968); Timken Roller Bearing Co. v. United States, 341 U.S. 593, 598, 71 S.Ct. 971, 974, 95 L.Ed. 1199 (1951); Radovich v. National Football League, 352 U.S. 445, 449–52, 77 S.Ct. 390, 392–94, 1 L.Ed.2d 456 (1957); Silver v. New York Stock Exchange, 373 U.S. 341, 83 S.Ct. 1246, 10 L.Ed.2d 389 (1963); Associated Press v. United States, 326 U.S. 1, 65 S.Ct. 1416, 89 L.Ed. 2013 (1945); Linseman v. World Hockey Association, 439 F.Supp. 1315 (D.Conn.1977); Robertson v. National Basketball Association, 389 F.Supp. 867 (S.D.N.Y.1975); Philadelphia World Hockey Club Inc. v. Philadelphia Hockey Club, Inc., 351 F.Supp. 462 (E.D.Pa. 1972); Smith v. Pro Football, Inc., 593 F.2d 1173 (D.C.Cir.1978); Mackey v. NFL, 543 F.2d 606 (8th Cir.1976), cert. denied, 434 U.S. 801, 98 S.Ct. 28, 54 L.Ed.2d 59 (1977); Los Angeles Memorial Coliseum Commission v. NFL ("Coliseum II"), 484 F.Supp. 1274 (C.D.Cal.), rev'd on other grounds, 634 F.2d 1197 (9th Cir.1980); Los Angeles Memorial Coliseum v. NFL ("Coliseum I"), 468 F.Supp. 154, 164 (C.D.Cal.1979); Bowman v. NFL, 402 F.Supp. 754 (D.Minn.1975); Kapp v. NFL, 390 F.Supp. 73 (N.D.Cal.1974), appeal vacated, 586 F.2d 644 (9th Cir.1978), cert. denied, 441 U.S. 907, 99 S.Ct. 1996, 60 L.Ed.2d 375 (1979). Cf. San Francisco Seals Ltd. v. National Hockey League, 379 F.Supp. 966 (C.D.Cal.1974); Levin v. National Basketball Association, 385 F.Supp. 149 (S.D.N.Y. 1974). We are unpersuaded by the efforts of the district judge to distinguish these cases from the present one. Although many involved player relations or playing sites, which affect competition between member teams, at least one raised issues between leagues. In Radovich v. National Football League, supra, the issue was whether an NFL boycott of a player who had previously accepted employment with a competing pro-football league, the All America Conference, violated § 1 of the Sherman Act. The Court held in Radovich that it did, even though that boycott might not, in the words of the district court, "implicate [or] impinge[ ] upon competition between member clubs." 505 F.Supp. at 677.

The characterization of NFL as a single economic entity does not exempt from the Sherman Act an agreement between its members to restrain competition. To tolerate such a loophole would permit league members to escape antitrust responsibility for any restraint entered into by them that would benefit their league or enhance their ability to compete even though the benefit would be outweighed by its anticompetitive effects. Moreover, the restraint might be one adopted more for the protection of individual league members from competition than to help the league. For instance, the cross-ownership ban in the present case is not aimed merely at protecting the NFL as a league or "single economic entity" from competition from the NASL as a league. Its objective also is to shield certain individual NFL member teams as discrete economic entities from competition in their respective home territories on the part of individual NASL teams that are gaining economic strength in those localities, threatening the revenues of such individual teams as the NFL Philadelphia Eagles, owned by Leonard Tose, because of competition by the NASL's Philadelphia team, and the revenues of the NFL Minnesota Vikings because of competition by the successful NASL Minnesota Kicks. The NFL members have combined to protect and restrain not only leagues but individual teams. The sound and more just procedure is to judge the legality of such restraints according to well-recognized standards of our antitrust laws rather than permit their exemption on the ground that since they in some measure strengthen the league competitively as a "single economic entity," the combination's anticompetitive effects must be disregarded.

Even if the NFL were a single firm, that fact would not immunize from § 1 scrutiny the restraint involved here. Vertical agreements between a corporation and its distributors are subject to the rule of reason, Continental TV, Inc. v. GTE Sylvania Inc., 433 U.S. 36, 97 S.Ct. 2549, 53 L.Ed.2d 568 (1977), and we see no reason why an agreement between a corporation and its owners (as the NFL teams owners would be under this assumption) should be treated differently.

Having concluded that § 1 of the Sherman Act is applicable, we next must decide whether the NFL teams' cross-ownership ban violates that statute. The plaintiffs, characterizing the ban as a "group boycott" and "concerted refusal to deal," contend that the conduct is a species of the patently pernicious anticompetitive kind that must be condemned as per se unlawful without further proof. See, e.g., United States v. Socony–Vacuum Oil Co., Inc., 310 U.S. 150, 60 S.Ct. 811, 84 L.Ed. 1129 (1940) (agreements between horizontal competitors to maintain price of their product); United States v. Topco Associates, Inc., 405 U.S. 596, 92 S.Ct. 1126, 31 L.Ed.2d 515 (1972) (allocation of market territories between horizontal competitors); United States v. General Motors Corp., 384 U.S. 127, 86 S.Ct. 1321, 16 L.Ed.2d 415 (1966) (conspiracy between manufacturers and distributors to eliminate price competition by discounters); Klor's, Inc. v. Broadway–Hale Stores, Inc., 359 U.S. 207, 79 S.Ct. 705, 3 L.Ed.2d 741 (1959) (agreement between 10 competing national manufacturers and their distributors not to sell products to petitioner or to sell only at discriminatory prices and unfavorable terms); United States v. Koppers Company, Inc., 652 F.2d 290 (2d Cir.1981) (agreement between competitors to rig bids and allocate market territories). We disagree.

Combinations or agreements are per se violations of the Sherman Act only if they are so "plainly anticompetitive," National Society of Professional Engineers v. United States, 435 U.S. 679, 692, 98 S.Ct. 1355, 1365, 55 L.Ed.2d 637 (1978), and so lacking in any "redeeming virtue," Northern Pac. R. Co. v. United States, 356 U.S. 1, 5, 78 S.Ct. 514, 518, 2 L.Ed.2d 545 (1958), that "because of [their] unquestionably anticompetitive effects," United States v. United States Gypsum Co., 438 U.S. 422, 440, 98 S.Ct. 2864, 2875, 57 L.Ed.2d 854 (1978), "they are conclusively presumed illegal without further examination under the rule of reason generally applied in Sherman Act cases," Broadcast Music,

Inc. v. CBS, 441 U.S. 1, 8, 99 S.Ct. 1551, 1556, 60 L.Ed.2d 1 (1979). Examples are agreements between competitors fixing prices at which they will sell their competing products, limiting their respective marketing areas, or restricting customers to whom their products will be sold or from whom they will be purchased. The cross-ownership ban, though anticompetitive, does not meet these stringent conditions. Although competition exists between NFL members in various respects (e.g., on the playing fields, for players' services and for fans within a home territory where two or more teams are franchised), that competition is not restrained by the cross-ownership ban. Indeed, it is irrelevant to that ban, which is designed to restrain competition by NASL teams against NFL teams, not competition between NFL teams. Bearing in mind the Supreme Court's admonition in Continental TV, Inc. v. GTE Sylvania Inc., 433 U.S. 36, 49–50, 97 S.Ct. 2549, 2557, 53 L.Ed.2d 568 (1977), that "[p]er se rules of illegality are appropriate only when they relate to conduct that is manifestly anticompetitive," we are not prepared, by using "the tyranny of tags and tickets," Cardozo, Mr. Justice Holmes, 44 Harv.L.Rev. 682, 688 (1931), to label league cross-ownership bans automatically unlawful regardless of their effects. As the arguments advanced by the NFL indicate, circumstances could exist that might justify a ban by a weak league as necessary to protect it against serious competitive harm by a cross-owner who threatened to misuse his position in that league to favor a stronger competing league and its members. Under those circumstances a ban "might survive scrutiny under the Rule of Reason even though [it] would be viewed as a violation of the Sherman Act in another context," National Society of Professional Engineers v. United States, supra, 435 U.S. at 686, 98 S.Ct. at 1362.

Because agreements between members of a joint venture can under some circumstances have legitimate purposes as well as anticompetitive effects, they are subject to scrutiny under the rule of reason. Standard Oil Co. v. United States, 221 U.S. 1, 31 S.Ct. 502, 55 L.Ed. 619 (1911); United States v. Addyston Pipe & Steel Co., 85 Fed. 271 (6th Cir.1898). This entails an inquiry into "whether the challenged agreement is one that promotes competition or one that suppresses competition," National Society of Professional Engineers v. United States, supra, 435 U.S. at 691, 98 S.Ct. at 1365, that is, whether the procompetitive effects of this restraint outweigh the anticompetitive effects. As we stated in Eiberger v. Sony Corp. of America, 622 F.2d 1068, 1076 (2d Cir.1980) (quoting Chicago Board of Trade v. United States, 246 U.S. 231, 238, 38 S.Ct. 242, 244, 62 L.Ed. 683 (1918)),

> The true test of legality is whether the restraint imposed is such as merely regulates and perhaps thereby promotes competition or whether it is such as may suppress or even destroy competition. To determine that question the court must ordinarily consider the facts peculiar to the business to which the restraint is applied; its conditions before and after the restraint was imposed; the nature of the restraint and its effect, actual or probable. The history of the restraint, the evil believed to exist,

> the reason for adopting the particular remedy, the purpose or end sought to be attained, are all relevant facts. This is not because good intention will save an otherwise objectionable regulation or the reverse; but because knowledge of intent may help the court to interpret facts and to predict consequences.

Finally, in carrying out a rule of reason analysis, "the existence of [less restrictive] alternatives is obviously of vital concern in evaluating putatively anticompetitive conduct." Berkey Photo, Inc. v. Eastman Kodak Co., 603 F.2d 263, 303 (2d Cir.1979).

In this case, the procompetitive effect claimed by the defendants for the cross-ownership ban is that the ban is necessary for the NFL owners to compete efficiently in the professional sports league market. On the other hand, the voluminous trial record discloses that the NFL's cross-ownership ban would foreclose NASL's teams from continued enjoyment of and access to a significant segment of the market supply of sports capital and skill, thereby restraining at least some NASL teams from competing effectively against NFL teams for fan support and TV revenues. Any resulting restraint would benefit not merely the NFL as a league but those NFL teams that would be otherwise weakened individually and disproportionally (as compared with other NFL teams) by competing NASL teams. This evidence of the defendants' anticompetitive purpose is relevant in judging its potential anticompetitive effect. Eiberger v. Sony Corp. of America, 622 F.2d 1068, 1076 (2d Cir.1980) (quoting Chicago Board of Trade v. United States, 246 U.S. 231, 238, 38 S.Ct. 242, 244, 62 L.Ed. 683 (1918)). Accord, National Society of Professional Engineers v. United States, 435 U.S. 679, 692, 98 S.Ct. 1355, 1365, 55 L.Ed.2d 637 (1978).

NFL argues that there is no such thing as a limited market or submarket for sports capital and skill, only a general market in which "capital is fungible." It further urges that in this much larger market the effect of the cross-ownership ban would be de minimis, working no appreciable anticompetitive restraint on NASL teams, and that their difficulty in attracting capital is attributable to the poor financial outlook of their franchises rather than to the ban. Judge Haight, while noting the weakness of the NASL teams' financial condition and prospects, made no definite finding regarding the existence or scope of a sports capital market other than to state that it was not, as NASL contended, limited to existing or potential major sports team owners, a finding with which we need not disagree. Simultaneously he rejected the NFL's contention as to the scope of the relevant capital market, stating,

> I reject the extremes of both the Guth (NASL) and Caputo (NFL) perceptions. Individuals and corporations alike have identifiable characteristics which incline them toward sports ownership. Findings Nos. 17–18. The absence of such characteristics, in an individual or corporation, effectively removes them from the sports capital market, thereby shrinking the worldwide boundaries envisioned by Caputo. But there is no basis, in logic

> or law, for restricting the boundaries of that submarket, as would Guth, to individuals who are presently controlling owners of a major league team. That narrow perception disregards significant, interchangeable sources of sports capital: individuals who are not presently controlling sports owners; and corporations.

505 F.Supp. at 682.

Since NASL had failed to prove its concept of a narrow sports capital market, the district court declined to make more specific findings other than to indicate that a sports capital market does exist, which is not as small as urged by NASL nor as large as contended by NFL. He concluded that it was unnecessary for him to define the scope of the sports capital market because "if competition does exist in such a submarket, it is, again, competition between two single economic entities," 505 F.Supp. at 684.

Since we have rejected the "single economic theory" in the context of this case, it is necessary to determine whether the record discloses a separate market for sports capital and skill. We are satisfied that it does. As the Supreme Court noted in Brown Shoe Co. v. United States, 370 U.S. 294, 325, 82 S.Ct. 1502, 1524, 8 L.Ed.2d 510 (1962):

> The boundaries of ... a submarket may be determined by examining such practical indicia as industry or public recognition of the submarket as a separate economic entity, the product's peculiar characteristics and uses, unique production facilities, distinct customers, distinct prices, sensitivity to price changes, and specialized vendors.

Because of the economic interdependence of major league team owners and the requirement that any sale be approved by a majority of the league members, an owner may in practice sell his franchise only to a relatively narrow group of eligible purchasers, not to any financier. The potential investor must measure up to a profile having certain characteristics. Moreover, on the supply side of the sports capital market the number of investors willing to purchase an interest in a franchise is sharply limited by the high risk, the need for active involvement in management, the significant exposure to publicity that may turn out to be negative, and the dependence on the drawing power and financial success of the other members of the league. The record thus reveals a market which, while not limited to existing or potential major sports team owners, is relatively limited in scope and is only a small fraction of the total capital funds market. The evidence further reveals that in this sports capital and skill market owners of major professional sports teams constitute a significant portion. Indeed the existence of such a submarket and the importance of the function of existing team owners as sources of capital in that market are implicitly recognized by the defendants' proven intent in adopting the cross-ownership ban. If they believed, as NFL now argues, that all sources of capital were fungible substitutes for investment in NASL sports teams and that the ban would not significantly foreclose the supply of sports capital, they would hardly have gone to the trouble of adopting it. Unless the ban has procompetitive effects outweighing its clear restraint on competition, therefore, it is prohibited by § 1 of the Sherman Act. That law does not require proof of the precise boundaries of the sports capital market or the exact percentage foreclosed; it is sufficient to establish, as was done here, the general outlines of a separate submarket of the capital market and that the foreclosed portion of it was likely to be significant.

NFL argues that the anticompetitive effects of the ban would be outweighed by various procompetitive effects. First it contends that the ban assures it of the undivided loyalty of its team owners in competing effectively against the NASL in the sale of tickets and broadcasting rights, and that cross-ownership might lead NFL cross-owners to soften their demands in favor of their NASL team interests. We do not question the importance of obtaining the loyalty of partners in promoting a common business venture, even if this may have some anticompetitive effect. But in the undisputed circumstances here the enormous financial success of the NFL despite long-existing cross-ownership by some members of NASL teams demonstrates that there is no market necessity or threat of disloyalty by cross-owners which would justify the ban. Moreover, the NFL was required to come forward with proof that any legitimate purposes could not be achieved through less restrictive means. This it has failed to do. The NFL, for instance, has shown no reason why it could not remedy any conflict of interest arising out of NFL–NASL competition for broadcast rights by removing cross-owners from its broadcast rights negotiating committee.

For the same reasons we reject NFL's argument that the ban is necessary to prevent disclosure by NFL cross-owners of confidential information to NASL competitors. No evidence of the type of information characterized as "confidential" is supplied. Nor is there any showing that the NFL could not be protected against unauthorized disclosure by less restrictive means. Indeed, despite the existence of NFL cross-owners for some years there is no evidence that they have abused confidentiality or that the NFL has found it necessary to adopt confidentiality rules or sanctions. Similarly, there is no evidence that cross-ownership has subjected the personnel and resources of NFL cross-owners to conflicting or excessive demands. On the contrary, successful NFL team owners have been involved in ownership and operation of other outside businesses despite their equal potential for demands on the owners' time and resources. Moreover, a ban on cross-ownership would not insure that NFL team owners would devote any greater level of their resources to team operations than they otherwise would.

Although there may be some merit in NFL's contentions that the ban would prevent dilution of the good will it has developed, that it would avoid any disruption of NFL operations because of disputes between its owners or cross-owners, or that it would prevent possible inter-league collusion in violation of the antitrust laws, these procompetitive effects are not substantial and are clearly outweighed by its anticompetitive purpose and effect. Its net effect is substantially to restrain competition, not merely competitors. It therefore violates the rule of reason. See McLain v. Real Estate Board, 444 U.S. 232, 243, 100 S.Ct. 502, 509, 62 L.Ed.2d 441 (1980); Oreck Corp. v. Whirlpool Corp., 579 F.2d 126, 129 n. 4, 132 n. 6 (2d Cir.) (en banc), cert. denied, 439 U.S. 946, 99 S.Ct. 340, 58 L.Ed.2d 338 (1978).

In view of our holding with respect to plaintiffs' claims against NFL, the latter's counterclaim deserves little comment. It amounts to little more than a meritless makeweight. The claim that cross-ownership violates § 1 of the Sherman Act because it is analogous to an interlocking directorate of the type prohibited by § 8 of the Clayton Act, 15 U.S.C. § 19, is wholly unsupported in fact and in law. Absent proof that the leagues are corporate or separate entities with directors, which they are not, § 8 has no application. Moreover, in the absence of evidence that cross-ownership restrains or threatens competition between the two leagues or their member teams, the mere common ownership of some teams and membership of some owners on league committees do not constitute a violation of the antitrust laws. On the contrary, there is evidence of record that cross-ownership, by strengthening some NASL teams, has increased their competition against NFL teams. In any event, as the district court observed, NFL has not offered any evidence that it has suffered or faces a significant threat of injury by reason of cross-ownership, which is essential to the issuance of the injunctive relief requested.

We reverse the order granting judgment [for] the NFL and remand with directions to enter a permanent injunction prohibiting the ban. Because the district court's decision made it unnecessary for it to consider the issue of damages, we remand for consideration of that issue. We affirm the dismissal of NFL's counterclaim requesting an injunction against cross-ownership.

Notes

1. Two years after its victory over the NFL, the NASL disbanded, a victim of poor financial control, breakneck expansion, and numerous management mistakes.

The history of the NASL is one of the most colorful in all of professional sports. The 1966 World Cup final between England and West Germany had been televised live from London by NBC. The game was stirring, with the underdog English ultimately triumphing by a score of 4 to 2. Taking note of the enthusiasm generated by the game, promoters in the United States decided to start a professional soccer league.

From the start, things went badly. Two rival groups—the establishment-backed United Soccer Association and the renegade National Professional Soccer League—fielded teams during 1967. When neither league was able to gain the upper hand, an agreement was reached to combine operations and in 1968 the NASL was born. In its inaugural season, the NASL had 10 teams and played a 32-game schedule. Thereafter, the league made slow but steady progress, and by 1974 had expanded to 15 clubs. Then in 1975, the New

York Cosmos signed the legendary Brazilian soccer star Pelé to a $4.7 million contract, at the time an astounding sum of money. Although his best days were behind him, Pelé gave the NASL instant credibility. When the Cosmos subsequently signed two other foreign superstars—Italy's Giorgio Chinaglia and West Germany's Franz Beckenbauer—the league attained national prominence.

Ironically, the excitement generated by the Cosmos planted the seeds for the NASL's demise. Convinced the time was right for a major push, the league expanded to 24 teams. Unfortunately, many of these new franchises were underfinanced, poorly run, and in weak markets. As a result, within just a few years, the NASL began contracting, ultimately shrinking to nine teams.

In the NASL's final game, played on October 3, 1984, the Chicago Sting defeated the Toronto Blizzard to become the NASL's last champion. Over the next few months, six of the league's teams went out of business. Thus, when the Cosmos announced they would not participate in the 1985 season, it fell to the Blizzard and the Minnesota Strikers (run by Tim Robbie, son of Miami Dolphins owner Joe Robbie) to report the NASL was shutting down.

2. Following the death of the NASL, no further attempts were made to form a professional outdoor soccer league until 1993, when the United States was awarded the 1996 World Cup as a means of jump-starting such an effort. From its inception, MLS has sought to distinguish itself from the NASL. One way it has done so is by operating as a "single entity league," a form of ownership in which each club's proprietor is an investor in the league and all player contracts belong to the central office. MLS believes this organizational structure, which is radically different from the model used by MLB, the NBA, the NFL, and the NHL, will help limit the financial disparities between large and small market clubs, provide economies of scale in purchasing power and cost control, encourage group rather than personal decision making, and avoid antitrust liability.

To date, MLS remains a work in progress. On the one hand, the league has attracted a number of wealthy investors, secured national television contracts with ABC, ESPN, ESPN2, and Univision, and drawn an average of 14,000 fans per game. On the other hand, MLS lost $60 million during its first three years, is expected to lose at least another $50 million in the near future, and has yet to receive more than passing notice from the press. In addition, MLS currently is being sued by its players union, which claims the league is illegally restraining salaries. *See Fraser v. Major League Soccer, L.L.C.*, 7 F.Supp.2d 73 (D.Mass.1998).

Perhaps the most interesting (or disturbing, depending on one's perspective) parallel between MLS and the NASL concerns expansion. Recognizing the NASL's undoing was its rapid growth, MLS began play in 1996 with 10 teams and a 32–game schedule (just like the NASL). MLS teams had been carefully chosen from among 22 applicant groups, and at the time of their introduction it was made clear any future expansion would occur slowly. Nevertheless, in 1998 MLS added two new teams (in Chicago and Miami) and let it be known it hopes to double in size within the next five years. For a further look at MLS and its prospects for success, see Michael Hiestand, *A Family That Plays Together: 3 Owners in Charge of 7 Teams*, USA Today,

Dec. 2, 1998, at 3C (discussing the potentially negative effect of having Philip Anschutz own three MLS teams, Lamar Hunt two, Robert Kraft two, and John Kluge one with an option for a second), and Michael Wilbon, *The Sport Still Can't Get Its Foot in America's Door*, Wash. Post., Oct. 25, 1998, at D10 (explaining why the United States has so far failed to embrace soccer).

3. Besides MLS, a number of other new leagues also are experimenting with so-called "central ownership," an economic theory that dates back to the Pacific Coast Hockey League (which in the 1910s and 1920s was owned by the Patrick family). *See further People v. Mott*, 189 Cal.Rptr. 589 (Ct.App. 1983) (criminal prosecution arising from the sale of investments in the National Sports League, a proposed single entity youth league), and Stefan Fatsis, *New Leagues Go for Central Ownership*, Wall St. J., July 15, 1997, at B1 (listing new leagues that have opted to use a single entity approach).

4. As is explained in Judge Mansfield's opinion, one of the things that upset Leonard Tose was Lamar Hunt's comment that soccer was the future of sports in America. Many other people have used Hunt's line, but with a twist: "Soccer is the future of sports in America, and it always will be." *See, e.g.*, Kevin Hillstrom et al., *The Handy Sports Answer Book* 435 (1998). To a large extent, this remark has proven prophetic. In addition to the problems experienced by the NASL and MLS, numerous indoor professional soccer leagues have perished, with the Continental Indoor Soccer League (December 1997) being the most recent casualty. Nevertheless, in 1998 the National Professional Soccer League expanded to 14 teams and a new league, to be known as the Premier Soccer Alliance, announced it would begin play in 1999 with between 10 and 12 teams. *See further* Jerry Langdon, *NPSL Adds Florida*, Gannett News Serv., May 19, 1998, at ARC.

5. Unlike the NFL, cross-ownership never has been prohibited by MLB, the NBA, or the NHL. As a result, many individuals and companies have engaged in the practice, including Jerry Colangelo (Arizona Diamondbacks and Phoenix Coyotes), Abe Pollin (Washington Capitals and Washington Wizards), Jerry Reinsdorf (Chicago Bulls and Chicago White Sox), Ted Turner (Atlanta Braves, Atlanta Hawks, and Atlanta Thrashers), Cablevision Systems Corporation (New York Knicks and New York Rangers), and Comcast Corporation (Philadelphia Flyers and Philadelphia 76ers). More recently, in February 1999, the owners of the New York Yankees and New Jersey Nets announced they had agreed to merge their teams into a new holding company to be called YankeeNets. *See further* Stephen Nidetz, *Yankees, Nets Plan to Merge*, Chi. Trib., Feb. 26, 1999, at 2 (Sports).

6. In March 1997, the NFL finally gave in on the issue of cross-ownership. By a vote of 24–5–1, it approved a resolution permitting members to control teams in other leagues so long as they are located either in their own territory or in a city without an NFL team. *See* Len Pasquarelli, *Cross-Ownership of Major League Teams OKd*, Atlanta J. & Const., Mar. 12, 1997, at 3C.

The NFL's change of heart can be traced to two developments. First, in 1993, H. Wayne Huizenga, who already owned the Florida Marlins and Florida Panthers, purchased the Miami Dolphins from the family of Joe Robbie. Although the league approved the sale in 1994, it required Huizenga to place the Dolphins' stock in trust for two years and thereafter abide by whatever cross-ownership policy it formulated in the interim. Given the *NASL* precedent, however, it was apparent that Huizenga would be able to make a strong case against the NFL if it forced him to divest either the Dolphins or the Marlins and Panthers. Second, in 1996, Kenneth Behring, the owner of the Seattle Seahawks, threatened, over Commissioner Paul Tagliabue's strong objection, to move his team to Los Angeles. While Paul Allen, the owner of the NBA's Portland Trailblazers, was willing to buy the team from Behring and keep it in Seattle, the cross-ownership rule prevented him from doing so. Thus, by changing its stance, the NFL was able to eliminate two major problems.

7. As should be clear from the foregoing, the NFL's cross-ownership ban will still apply if an owner in one city seeks to take control of a non-NFL sports franchise in another city that either has an NFL team or has been reserved by the league for possible expansion. Assuming this scenario someday becomes the basis of a lawsuit against the NFL, what weight should be given to *NASL*?

Problem 17

A tennis organization prohibits its owners, directors, and officers from sponsoring, advertising, or otherwise participating in tournaments run by its competitors. If one of these persons files suit, claiming the regulation constitutes an impermissible restraint of trade, how is the court likely to rule? *See Volvo North America Corp. v. Men's International Professional Tennis Council*, 857 F.2d 55 (2d Cir.1988).

3. RELOCATION

Because only a limited number of franchises can exist in any given league, cities without teams have little choice but to engage in bidding wars for established clubs. Besides costing taxpayers millions of dollars, such efforts often lead to fervid litigation.

ST. LOUIS CONVENTION & VISITORS COMM'N v. NATIONAL FOOTBALL LEAGUE

154 F.3d 851 (8th Cir.1998).

MURPHY, Circuit Judge.

After St. Louis lost its professional football team to Phoenix in 1988, extensive efforts began to obtain another team and resulted in the successful relocation of the Los Angeles Rams in 1995. Many millions of dollars were spent in order to accomplish the relocation, and the St. Louis Convention and Visitors Center (CVC) sued the National Football League and twenty four of its member teams (collectively the NFL) alleging that these expenditures were made necessary by actions of the NFL in violation of antitrust and tort law. The case was tried before a jury for over four weeks before it ended in a judgment in favor of the NFL. CVC appeals the dismissal of its claim for Sherman Act conspiracy and tortious interference with contract. The NFL cross appeals the refusal of the district court to rule that the league and the member teams do not amount to a single entity for antitrust purposes. We affirm the judgment.

I.

A.

The move of the St. Louis Cardinals football team to Phoenix in 1988 caused the Missouri state legislature, the city of St. Louis and the surrounding county to undertake to find a replacement by the beginning of the 1995 season. The legislature assigned the effort to procure a team to CVC, a body previously created by the Missouri legislature and empowered to promote the convention and tourism business in St. Louis. See Mo. St. Ann. §§ 67.601, 67.607. The initial goal was to obtain one of the two NFL expansion franchises to be established in 1993. In order to attract a team the city resolved to build a convention center in downtown St. Louis called America's Center which would include a new football stadium. The football stadium was called the Trans World Dome, and its $258 million cost was paid from state and local government funds. The stadium lease was assigned to CVC which became its manager and initially subleased the right to present football in the dome to private parties.

Problems associated with control over the lease and the potential ownership group caused St. Louis to be passed over in the NFL's expansion voting. The new franchises were awarded to Jacksonville, Florida and Charlotte, North Carolina. This forced the St. Louis football enthusiasts to adopt another strategy, and they turned their attention toward attracting an existing team. They founded a civic organization called FANS, Inc. (Football at the New Stadium), to assist their efforts. FANS, acting on behalf of CVC, then approached the Los Angeles Rams and began to negotiate a deal for the team to move to St. Louis. As a result a written agreement was eventually signed by CVC and the Rams.

The NFL League Constitution and Bylaws require a favorable vote by three fourths of the team owners to permit relocation, and the proposal for the Rams to move was initially voted down by the owners. It was later approved after the Rams agreed to pay the NFL a $29 million relocation fee. CVC eventually agreed with the Rams to pay $20 million of this fee, despite a clause in their contract allowing CVC to cancel if the fee were to exceed $7.5 million.

The Rams began playing in St. Louis in 1995, and in that year CVC was unable to make some of the payments owed to the team. CVC then brought this suit against the league and twenty four of its member teams. It also made an agreement with the Rams that they would receive half of any recovery obtained in the case in return for forgiveness of the money CVC owed them. The theory CVC presented at trial was that the league's relocation rules and the way they had been applied had created an atmosphere in which teams were unwilling to relocate. It contended that this anti-relocation atmosphere had discouraged interested teams from bidding on the St. Louis lease. The result was a one buyer market which forced the CVC to give more favorable lease terms than it would have in a competitive market.

B.

The league was formed in 1966 by a union of the American Football League and the National Football League, and it functions as the governing body of a joint venture of thirty professional football teams producing "NFL football." The teams are independently owned and managed by different business interests. The league is organized through the League Constitution and Bylaws, an agreement among team members that sets out rules for league management of matters such as game rules, game schedules, team ownership, and location of teams. Most decisions affecting the league are made by vote of team representatives at NFL meetings. When NFL members decided to create two new team franchises for 1993, representatives from various cities made presentations to team owners in order to win a franchise.

St. Louis political leaders and business people were among those who made presentations to the league, and they emphasized the benefits an NFL team could expect from the stadium lease and the city. But there were problems with the St. Louis application for a team. At the time of the expansion decisions the exclusive right to use the Trans World Dome for professional football games was held by St. Louis NFL, Inc., which was controlled by two St. Louis businessmen, Jerry Clinton who owned one third and Jim Orthwein who owned the remaining two thirds. The fact that rights to lease the stadium for football were held by individuals who were unrelated to CVC caused the owners to pass over St. Louis as the site of an expansion team.

CVC's next option was to arrange for an existing team to leave its home city and relocate to St. Louis. Community members formed the civic organization FANS, Inc. in January of 1994, headed by former Senator Thomas Eagleton, to accomplish the task which they were increasingly anxious to complete. Around this time Congressman Richard Gephardt alerted FANS that the Los Angeles Rams were considering relocating from their stadium in Anaheim, California. He had seen a newspaper report that the Rams were discussing a possible move to Baltimore, Maryland. Congressman Gephardt concluded that since Baltimore had been one of St. Louis' main competitors during the expansion process, the city should follow Baltimore's lead and approach the Rams. FANS then contacted John Shaw, the Rams president, and began negotiations on a relocation agreement and stadium lease. During this period, St. Louis was competing with Hartford and Anaheim in addition to Baltimore.

FANS made an initial presentation to the Rams, but talks ended because of problems with Clinton and Orthwein having control over the lease and because FANS had leaked information about the negotiations to the press, including the Rams' list of features it desired in a new stadium (the "wish list"). Discussions resumed only after CVC gained control over the lease, and the Rams told CVC that they would discontinue any business dealings if the CVC approached any other team about moving to St. Louis. CVC never contacted any other team to solicit a bid on the lease. CVC considered it the better course to focus on only one team, and it believed its presentation during the expansion process should have been sufficient to stimulate the interest of other teams.

The Rams and CVC eventually agreed on a lease. The Rams agreed to pay to CVC $25,000 rent per game, plus half of the game day expenses. In return the Rams would receive all of the ticket revenue from Rams games, 75% of the first $6 million in advertising revenue and 90% of the remainder, 100% of the profit from the concessions at Rams games and a portion of the concessions profit from other events. Rams president John Shaw estimated the lease would produce approximately $40 million per season in revenue for the Rams. CVC agreed to a number of other obligations, including promises to pay $28 million to fulfill bond obligations which the Rams owed on Anaheim Stadium, to build a $9.9 million training facility for the team, and to pay the team's moving costs. Once the Rams and CVC reached their agreement, the Rams presented their relocation application to the league owners for approval in March, 1995.

C.

Relocation decisions by the NFL come under Article 4.3 of the league constitution which provides that "[n]o member club shall have the right to transfer its franchise or playing site to a different city, either within or outside its home territory, without prior approval by the affirmative vote of three-fourths of the existing member clubs of the league." While not expressed in the governing documents, the league claims the right to assess a relocation fee on any team seeking to move. At the time CVC was dealing with the Rams, the NFL had levied one previous relocation fee; the Cardinals had been assessed $7.5 million for their move to Phoenix.

After a successful antitrust challenge to an application of Article 4.3 to the relocation of the Oakland Raiders to Los Angeles, see Los Angeles Memorial Coliseum Comm'n v. NFL, 726 F.2d 1381 (9th Cir.1984) (Raiders I), the NFL commissioner had issued procedures for obtaining league approval of any proposed relocation and nine non-exclusive factors (the guidelines) that team owners should consider in deciding how to vote on a move. No guidelines have been promulgated on the imposition or computation of a relocation fee. Under the rules in effect at the time of the Rams move, a NFL team which wanted to move would negotiate a lease and relocation agreement with its new landlord and then apply to the league for permission to relocate. Only the moving team participated in the NFL application process; the new landlord had no direct involvement.

In Raiders I the Ninth Circuit held that Article 4.3 had impermissibly foreclosed competition between stadia seeking NFL tenants and granted exclusive territories to NFL teams. 726 F.2d at 1395. Future applications of the rule could withstand scrutiny, however, if the NFL adopted objective factors for consideration by team owners before voting, as well as clarified procedures including an opportunity for any applicant to make a presentation to the league. Id. at 1397. The NFL commissioner subsequently issued such guidelines. These factors include consideration of the adequacy of the team's current stadium, the extent of demonstrated fan support for the team, and the extent to which the owner has contributed to the need for relocation. CVC complains that the guidelines and the rule have had the effect of discouraging competitive bidding for available stadia, thereby driving up the cost for a locality seeking a team.

Owners voted down the initial application by the Rams because of disagreements between the league and the team on several of the relocation terms, including payment of a relocation fee, sharing of revenues from the sale of "personal seat licenses" (options to purchase tickets), and possible indemnification of the league for television payments it might owe as a consequence of the move. After the initial league vote, and in anticipation of the assessment of a relocation fee, CVC agreed with the Rams it would pay up to $7.5 million of any fee. Either party had the right to void the agreement should the fee exceed that amount.

The Rams and the NFL reentered negotiations, and the NFL commissioner said that the relocation could be approved if the Rams would pay a higher fee. The NFL had "the right to assess whatever fee they thought necessary" since the initial relocation proposal had not satisfied the league guidelines. The Rams then agreed to pay a $29 million relocation fee, to forgo any share in the next two relocation fees levied by the league, to share $17 million in personal seat license revenue with the NFL, and to indemnify the league for up to $12.5 million of any extra expenses arising from the league's television contract. The Rams relocation was approved on April 12, 1995.

The relocation fee was described by the commissioner as reflecting among other things the increased value of the team after the move to St. Louis and the value of that franchise opportunity compared to Anaheim.

The agreement between CVC and the Rams about CVC's obligating itself on any relocation fee was not revealed to the NFL owners during these negotiations, and it does not appear that the owners were informed about it until after the April 12 vote. Following the vote, the Rams and CVC once again entered negotiations, this time on how the charges assessed by the NFL on the Rams would be paid. The parties agreed in June of 1995 that CVC would pay $20 million of the relocation fee and that CVC would be directly liable to the NFL for its payment. CVC did not exercise the agreement's escape clause, and the Rams began playing in St. Louis in 1995. During that year CVC experienced difficulties meeting its financial obligations to the Rams and did not pay approximately $14 million of the amount due. CVC and Rams president Shaw then agreed that CVC would sue the NFL and that the Rams would receive a right to half of any recovery in place of the payments due.

II.

A.

CVC filed this case against the league and twenty four member teams on December 18, 1995, claiming that their actions had violated Sections 1 and 2 of the Sherman Antitrust Act, 15 U.S.C. §§ 1, 2, and that the imposition of the high relocation fee tortiously interfered with CVC's contract with the Rams. CVC's theory was that Article 4.3, the accompanying guidelines, and their application over time functioned as an agreement among the league and the individual teams to restrain relocations, creating an atmosphere which deterred teams from moving and therefore from bidding on the Trans World Dome lease. It contended that the Rams were the only team willing to take the risk of an attempted relocation so they were the only bidder on the lease. As a consequence the Rams were able to obtain very favorable terms from CVC which caused it to lose between $77 and $122 million. CVC requested damages under the Clayton Act which, if established, would be trebled to between $241 and $366 million, and attorney fees. See 15 U.S.C. § 15. The tortious interference claim was based on the theory that the $29 million relocation fee assessed on the Rams was levied through economic duress, since its only choices were to agree to increase its share of the fee from $7.5 million to $20 million or abandon the deal with the Rams. It asserted that the fee made its contract with the Rams substantially more burdensome which constituted tortious interference under Missouri law, as did the use of economic duress.

B.

A number of motions were brought during the pretrial period, including one by the NFL for summary judgment on the Section 1 claim.

The NFL argued that the league and teams form a single economic enterprise incapable of conspiring among themselves. The court denied the motion on the basis of collateral estoppel. The Ninth Circuit had previously ruled against the NFL on the same issue in Raiders I, 726 F.2d at 1387–90 (league not a single economic enterprise because teams have independent value, are separately owned and managed, earn different profits, and compete in various ways). The district court was not persuaded that two subsequent cases dealing with the concept of single economic enterprise required a different result. Copperweld Corp. v. Independence Tube Corp., 467 U.S. 752, 104 S.Ct. 2731, 81 L.Ed.2d 628 (1984) (parent and wholly owned subsidiary cannot conspire with each other under Section 1) and City of Mt. Pleasant v. Associated Elec. Coop., Inc., 838 F.2d 268, 274–76 (8th Cir.1988) (test is whether entities have "pursued interests diverse from those of the cooperative itself"). See White Earth Band of Chippewa Indians v. Alexander, 683 F.2d 1129, 1134 (8th Cir.1982) (change in law required to prevent collateral estoppel).

In a second summary judgment motion the NFL argued for dismissal of all of CVC's claims. The district court granted the motion as to the Missouri antitrust claims on the basis that they were preempted by federal law, citing Partee v. San Diego Chargers Football Co., 34 Cal.3d 378, 194 Cal.Rptr. 367, 668 P.2d 674 (1983) (en banc), and denied it in all other respects. The remaining issues for trial were discussed in some detail in the course of its ruling.

The court's discussion of the Section 1 claim gave direction on several legal points. It indicated that CVC could not succeed on this antitrust claim with a theory that Article 4.3 was per se anticompetitive, but instead would have to show that the alleged anticompetitive effect of the rule outweighed its procompetitive features. The court relied on National Collegiate Athletic Ass'n v. Board of Regents of Univ. of Oklahoma, 468 U.S. 85, 100–103, 104 S.Ct. 2948, 82 L.Ed.2d 70 (1984) (NCAA) (league limits on number of televised games), and Raiders I, 726 F.2d at 1387 (league rule requiring vote to allow a team to relocate). These cases had held that certain rules of sports leagues governing matters such as the number of games to be televised and the division of home territories among professional teams, while perhaps ordinarily per se anticompetitive, were necessary for the existence of the league and should therefore be judged under a rule of reason analysis. CVC would also have to offer proof that the alleged conspiracy to suppress movement of teams in fact caused the absence of competing bids on the Trans World Dome lease before a jury would be permitted to decide whether harm to competition from Article 4.3 and its enforcement outweighed the positive effects on competition. See NCAA, 468 U.S. at 100, 104 S.Ct. 2948; Chicago Board of Trade v. United States, 246 U.S. 231, 238, 38 S.Ct. 242, 62 L.Ed. 683 (1918). This was because CVC's claim was unlike cases alleging damage from a direct application of a regulation, see Raiders I, 726 F.2d at 1384–85 (case arose from owners' vote against relocation under Article 4.3 which required approval for a move). There was nothing in the NFL Constitution and Bylaws or in the deposition evidence to suggest that there was an explicit ban or limit on competitive bidding for leases.

The court also denied summary judgment on CVC's Section 2 and tortious interference claims. It held that CVC could make out a Section 2 monopoly leveraging claim if it could show that the NFL used a monopoly position in the professional football market to gain an advantage in the market for stadia. More evidence was necessary in order to evaluate the NFL's claim that the stadium market was not distinct from the market for professional football. The court determined that there were questions of material fact on the tortious interference claim. These included whether CVC's renegotiation of its lease agreement with the Rams was a necessary consequence of enforcement of Article 4.3 and whether the NFL intended to interfere with that contract. With the case focused on these issues, the parties went to trial.

C.

CVC's case consisted largely of the testimony of various owners, league commissioner Paul Tagliabue, Rams president John Shaw, and several experts. It also presented testimony of individuals involved in the

Rams relocation to St. Louis. FANS leader Senator Eagleton, Congressman Gephardt, and St. Louis County Executive George Westfall all testified about their involvement in the relocation and the interaction with NFL officials. CVC focuses in this appeal on three bodies of evidence.

CVC attempted to show that past applications of Article 4.3 and the related guidelines and the NFL approach to team relocations had created an atmosphere in which teams were afraid to move and that they did not bid on CVC's lease as a result. Several team owners stated in deposition testimony that the purpose of the rules was to ensure stability, and they also testified to differing interpretations of the guidelines and of their relative importance in deciding how to vote. CVC argued that this evidence showed teams could anticipate league disapproval of any moves or use of the rules to extract concessions upon relocating and that teams would therefore not seek out and bid on opportunities to move. Leonard Tose, the former owner of the Philadelphia Eagles, testified that the NFL had sued to stop the Eagles from moving to Phoenix and taken actions which CVC claims necessitated sale of the team. Victor Kiam, the former owner of the New England Patriots, also testified about the attempt to relocate his team, which met with resistance and a forced sale.

CVC claims that the uncertainty about imposition of a relocation fee and its amount was one reason why teams did not seek out relocation opportunities. The league had assessed a relocation fee of $7.5 million on the St. Louis Cardinals when the team moved to Phoenix in the first team relocation after the guidelines were issued. CVC offered evidence on the benefits a predictable formula for calculating the fee would have and pointed out that the NFL has not adopted one.

CVC called Rams president John Shaw in its case in chief. He explained during his testimony that the Rams would obtain a portion of any recovery in this case. Shaw testified about the negotiations between the Rams and CVC and about the Rams' dealings with the NFL during the voting on the relocation proposal. In addition to testifying about the Rams interest in relocating and their negotiations with CVC, he also discussed his own experience with the league and his views about other teams. Shaw testified that based on his experience representing the Rams at league meetings Article 4.3 prevented team movement, that the NFL took an antagonistic approach toward relocations, and that there were high risks of alienating the league or possible penalties in any attempt to move an NFL team. The Rams benefitted in their negotiations with CVC because no other team was bidding as a result of Article 4.3 and its application, and this enabled him to demand a more favorable lease from CVC than he would have been able to get in a competitive environment.

Among the experts called by CVC was Professor John Siegfried, an economics professor at Vanderbilt University who has done research on the economics of sports. Siegfried said that in his opinion the relocation policies had a direct effect on the lease price. He testified that any team which challenged the regulations would be the only bidder on an available lease (in antitrust terms, a "monopsony") and could therefore extract favorable terms from the captive [seller]. In a "freely competitive marketplace with full dissemination of information" he would expect teams to seek out the best lease opportunities and to bid against each other on them. He based his conclusions on "observed market behavior" and the "prospect of earning higher returns at the Trans World Dome."

CVC also used circumstantial evidence to support its argument that the NFL culture caused the lack of bidding on its lease. CVC argued that the purpose of the NFL rules was to deter relocation and that they accomplished that purpose and prevented other teams from bidding on the lease. It claimed that the market would normally produce competition for a lucrative lease, and offered the testimony of Stanley "Bud" Adams, Jr., owner of the Houston Oilers football team, who stated he would have expected high competition for the lease. CVC contends in its brief that from this evidence "a reasonable jury could infer that some external factor was disrupting free competition—and that a set of relocation policies designed and intended to frustrate team movement were the most likely candidate."

D.

The NFL moved for judgment as a matter of law at the close of CVC's case, after four weeks of evidence, and the district court granted the motion as to two of CVC's three remaining claims. The court found that CVC had failed to present evidence that the relocation fee caused a breach in its lease agreement with the Rams, and breach is a necessary element of tortious interference under Missouri law. CVC instead modified its agreement with the Rams to accommodate the size of the fee. The court also found that there had been no evidence that the NFL had intended to interfere with the contract, another required element under state law.

Judgment was granted in the NFL's favor on the Section 2 claim as well, since CVC had not shown that the NFL had a monopoly in the professional football market or that there was a secondary market in NFL stadia. CVC has not appealed the ruling on the Section 2 claim. The court permitted the Section 1 claim to proceed, despite expressing misgivings about CVC's case.

After the NFL had presented two days of evidence and was close to finishing its case, the court convened the charge conference to prepare for submission of the Section 1 claim to the jury. The parties again disagreed about whether CVC could make a submissible case by showing that the NFL's rules and actions must have been what had prevented other teams from bidding on the Trans World Dome lease, as opposed to showing that there had been a connection in fact between the allegedly anticompetitive behavior and the absence of competitive bidding. CVC was asked to explain its Section 1 theory at the conference. Counsel responded that "this application and enforcement of the relocation policies had a very substantial deterrent effect upon anybody but the Rams entering into negotiations with CVC." At this point the NFL moved again for judgment as a matter of law, see Fed.R.Civ.P. 50(a). It argued that without a showing that the NFL's rules and actions had in fact deterred bidding on the St. Louis lease, CVC's claim was in essence a per se attack on Article 4.3 and the guidelines, and the court had already indicated that the rule of reason was the proper method of analysis.

After further briefing and oral argument, the court described the critical question as whether there was evidence tending to show that "the alleged restraint arises out of 'the agreement of the teams to adopt Article 4.3 to empower the commissioner to adopt and promulgate rules in enforcing 4.3 which has resulted in conduct which has precluded teams from coming to bid competitively in St. Louis.' " In other words, in order to go to the jury CVC had to show more than a theoretical connection between the allegedly anticompetitive actions and the events surrounding the Rams move to St. Louis.

Since the court concluded that CVC had presented no evidence to show that the NFL's rule and the guidelines actually had caused league teams other than the Rams to refrain from competitive bidding on the Trans World Dome lease, it granted the Rule 50 motion. CVC had not shown that it had either tried to learn if other teams might be interested in relocating, that there were teams actually interested in moving to St. Louis, or that the failure of the others to bid on the lease was due to the NFL's policies and acts. There was no showing that there had been interested teams who had failed to contact CVC or that at the time CVC was seeking a team there were team owners who had not bid because of past application of league rules or acts of the commissioner to stop relocations. Finally, the court held that CVC had failed to present evidence of antitrust injury. It said there had been no evidence that collusive activity of the league and member teams reduced competitive bidding and that the opinion testimony of CVC's expert on damages lacked foundation in the record and was not consistent with its theory of liability.

III.

CVC's appeal from the judgment focuses on the dismissal of its claim under Section 1 of the Sherman Act and of its claim for tortious interference with contract. It seeks a new trial. CVC argues that its evidence was sufficient to establish a Section 1 violation, contending that it had shown a connection in fact between the NFL rules and actions and the lack of competitive bidding on the lease. It also argues that the tortious interference claim should not have been dismissed because it had established both economic duress and actions which made its agreement with the Rams more burdensome. The NFL responds that CVC did not produce sufficient evidence and no evidence that it sought bids from other teams or that other teams were even in a position to move. The league and teams also suggest that Article 4.3 and the related guidelines could not have affected the number of bidders on the lease because the rules did not become relevant until after the agreement between the Rams and CVC was completed and the Rams made their application to move, in other words well after any bidding period. Finally, the NFL argues that CVC was unable to show there were not independent reasons for the absence of other bids, especially since other owners did not know that the St. Louis lease problems which surfaced during the expansion period had been corrected or that certain acts alleged to have been taken by the commissioner to prevent team relocation had occurred.

The league and teams also cross appeal. They challenge the district court ruling that they were collaterally estopped from arguing that they are a single economic enterprise incapable of conspiracy under Section 1 of the Sherman Act. They contend that the Supreme Court decision in Copperweld Corp., 467 U.S. 752, 104 S.Ct. 2731, and this court's decision in City of Mt. Pleasant, 838 F.2d 268, have changed the law on single economic enterprise since the Ninth Circuit decision in Raiders I. They seek reversal of the collateral estoppel ruling and dismissal of CVC's Section 1 claim on the ground that they amount to a single economic enterprise.

A.

CVC claims that the district court failed to use the correct legal standard for Rule 50, which required it to "(1) resolve direct factual conflicts in favor of the nonmovant, (2) assume as true all facts supporting the nonmovant which the evidence tended to prove, (3) give the nonmovant the benefit of all reasonable inferences, and (4) deny the motion if the evidence so viewed would allow reasonable jurors to differ as to the conclusions that could be drawn." Sip–Top, Inc. v. Ekco Group, Inc., 86 F.3d 827, 830 (8th Cir.1996) (quoting Pumps & Power Co. v. Southern States Indus. Inc., 787 F.2d 1252, 1258 (8th Cir.1986) (cites omitted)). CVC does not believe that the district court viewed the evidence in the light most favorable to it, particularly its evidence on causation. Since it presented enough evidence to survive the earlier motion for summary judgment and introduced more evidence at trial, the Rule 50 motion should have been denied and the case submitted to the jury.

The district court stated the correct legal standard at the time it granted the Rule 50 motion, and our review of the record does not lead to the conclusion that it failed to apply it. See Admiral Theatre Corp. v. Douglas Theatre Co., 585 F.2d 877, 883 (8th Cir.1978). We review the grant of a motion for judgment as a matter of law de novo, using the same standard as the district court. Id. Although CVC claims that the court explicitly declined to consider its evidence of causation, the passages it cites in the district court opinion do not contain any such statement. Rather, the court explained in its opinion that even after weeks of trial it was not clear what legal theory CVC was proceeding with on its Section 1 claim. The court restated its consistent ruling that CVC would not be able to rely solely on the existence of the NFL rules to prove its case. That principle of law was not incorrect, and CVC does not point to any other example to support its argument that the court did not follow the standard.

The court's prior decision on summary judgment did not control the outcome of the Rule 50 motion. The Rule 50 motion was made and considered after the court had had the benefit of over four weeks of trial. It had heard the testimony of many witnesses and received numerous exhibits. There had been the opportunity for extensive legal arguments by the parties. At the time of the summary judgment motion it had been even less clear what CVC's precise legal theory was and what its evidence would be. By the time the district court ruled on the Rule 50 motion, it was able to review all the evidence in light of the legal discussions at the charge conference. It concluded that CVC had not met its burden. Given these facts and the posture of the case, the court was not required to reject the Rule 50 motion because of its earlier order on summary judgment.

B.

CVC contends that its evidence was sufficient to withstand a Rule 50 motion. CVC says that the testimony of John Shaw and Professor Siegfried, together with circumstantial evidence, tended to show that actions by the NFL caused the lack of bidding and the damages it seeks. The NFL replies that none of the evidence shows that the NFL policies, or their implementation, had the actual effect of deterring any team from making a bid on the stadium lease.

Section 1 of the Sherman Antitrust act makes it unlawful to form a conspiracy in restraint of trade. 15 U.S.C. § 1. Restraints which have [a] "pernicious effect on competition and lack of any redeeming virtue" are illegal per se under Section 1 without inquiry into the reasonableness of the restraint or the harm caused. Northern Pac. Rw'y v. United States, 356 U.S. 1, 5, 78 S.Ct. 514, 2 L.Ed.2d 545 (1958); see also Copperweld Corp., 467 U.S. at 768, 104 S.Ct. 2731; United States v. Topco Associates, Inc., 405 U.S. 596, 607–08, 92 S.Ct. 1126, 31 L.Ed.2d 515 (1972). Analysis of whether a restriction's harm to competition outweighs any procompetitive effects is necessary if the anticompetitive impact of a restraint is less clear or the restraint is necessary for a product to exist at all. See Chicago Board of Trade, 246 U.S. at 238, 38 S.Ct. 242; Broadcast Music, Inc. v. Columbia Broadcasting Sys., Inc., 441 U.S. 1, 9–10, 99 S.Ct. 1551, 60 L.Ed.2d 1 (1979). Some trade restrictions by sports leagues have been held to fall into this category. NCAA, 468 U.S. at 94, 104 S.Ct. 2948 (restriction on broadcasts of league games); NBA v. SDC Basketball Club, Inc., 815 F.2d 562, 567–68 (9th Cir.1987) (relocation rules); Sullivan v. NFL, 34 F.3d 1091, 1096 (1st Cir.1994) (prohibition of public ownership of teams). The district court held in this case that the franchise relocation rule and guidelines for evaluation of proposed team moves do not fit the per se category of restraints and should therefore be addressed under a rule of reason analysis. This ruling has not been appealed.

1.

In order to prevail under Section 1, CVC must prove that: (1) there was an agreement among the league and member teams in restraint of trade; (2) it was injured as a direct and proximate result; and (3) its damages are capable of ascertainment and not speculative. Admiral Theatre Corp. v. Douglas Theatre Co., 585 F.2d 877, 883–84 (8th Cir.1978). The first element is established by proof that there was an agreement in restraint of trade and that the challenged action was "part of or pursuant to that agreement." Monsanto v. Spray–Rite Service Corp., 465 U.S. 752, 767, 104 S.Ct. 1464, 79 L.Ed.2d 775 (1984). Other Section 1 challenges to rules of sports leagues have involved situations where the defendants had taken action pursuant to an allegedly anticompetitive rule and the plaintiff attacked the rule itself or the application of the rule. See NCAA, 468 U.S. at 100–101, 104 S.Ct. 2948; Sullivan, 34 F.3d 1091; SDC Basketball Club, 815 F.2d 562. In those cases there was no question that the defendants were acting pursuant to an agreement in restraint of trade, and the issue was whether the agreement was unreasonable. See id. This case is different because CVC has not challenged a vote by team owners or a particular application of the rules, see Raiders I, 726 F.2d at 1385, nor was St. Louis unable to obtain a NFL team. CVC complains instead about market conditions and attributes the conditions existing at the time it was seeking a tenant to an atmosphere created by the rules and the handling of prior relocations.

CVC did not present evidence tending to show that there was even one other team besides the Rams that failed to bid on its lease because of the NFL rules and past applications of them. See Monsanto, 465 U.S. at 764, 104 S.Ct. 1464. In order to prove that Section 1 defendants were acting pursuant to a conspiracy, a plaintiff must present evidence that tends "to exclude the possibility that the alleged coconspirators acted independently," Matsushita Elec. Indus. Co., Ltd. v. Zenith Radio Corp., 475 U.S. at 585, 106 S.Ct. 1348 (quoting Monsanto, 465 U.S. at 764, 104 S.Ct. 1464), because "conduct as consistent with permissible competition as with illegal conspiracy does not, standing alone, support an inference of antitrust conspiracy," The Corner Pocket of Sioux Falls, Inc. v. Video Lottery Technologies, Inc., 123 F.3d 1107, 1109 (8th Cir.1997), cert. denied ___ U.S. ___, 118 S.Ct. 1054, 140 L.Ed.2d 116 (1998) (quoting Matsushita, 475 U.S. 574, 588, 106 S.Ct. 1348 (1986)). See also Monsanto, 465 U.S. at 764, 104 S.Ct. 1464 (1984); Lovett v. General Motors Corp., 998 F.2d 575, 578–79 (8th Cir.1993).

The cited cases involved situations which could amount to a per se violation of the antitrust laws. In a rule of reason case like this one, where there is an issue as to the cause of the lack of competitive bidding, evidence about whether the alleged agreement affected the actions of the other team owners is relevant, as is evidence tending to exclude independent action.

CVC presented no evidence to exclude the possibility that the owners who did not bid on the St. Louis lease were acting for independent business reasons rather than pursuant to the alleged agreement in restraint of trade. Indeed, the evidence at trial was to the contrary. The deposition testimony of the owners reflected their awareness of problems with the St. Louis lease, concern for their existing leases, and loyalty to their communities. These were all independent reasons why teams might not have bid. Moreover, CVC did not present evidence tending to show that all NFL teams would use the same criteria to evaluate a relocation opportunity or automatically attempt to move to the city offering the most lucrative lease. CVC argues that the parties' pretrial stipulation that the league Constitution and Bylaws amounted to an agreement among the NFL and its members was all that was necessary to show the existence of a conspiracy. This evidence did not tend to prove that any team acted pursuant to a conspiracy to prevent bidding on the stadium lease, however. "[A]ntitrust law limits the range of permissible inferences from ambiguous evidence in a § 1 case," and the trial evidence did not support an inference that NFL teams were acting pursuant to the alleged conspiracy when they declined to bid on the Trans World Dome lease. Matsushita, 475 U.S. at 588, 106 S.Ct. 1348.

2.

The district court rested its summary judgment ruling on the issue of causation. In order to satisfy the causation element of a Section 1 case, CVC had to show that the NFL's anticompetitive acts were an actual, material cause of the alleged harm to competition. See National Association of Review Appraisers v. Appraisal Found., 64 F.3d 1130, 1135 (8th Cir.1995); Admiral Theatre Corp. v. Douglas Theatre Co., 585 F.2d 877, 883–84 (8th Cir.1978). Since nothing in the NFL rules expressly prevented competition among teams for leases or stated that only one team could negotiate with a leaseholder at a time, CVC had to show that past suppression of movement and the alleged anti-relocation atmosphere created by previous rule applications effectively prevented all other teams from dealing with the CVC about the St. Louis lease and entering bids on it.

CVC argues that Shaw's testimony was sufficient to prove causation, but his testimony did not tend to prove that the rules deterred any interested owner from bidding in St. Louis or that other owners considered the rules a factor in their lack of interest in the lease. Shaw could not identify a single team that was expressly interested in moving to St. Louis or was prevented from bidding on the lease because of past applications of league relocation rules, and there was no additional evidence that any particular team was able to move at the time CVC was seeking a tenant. In fact, CVC failed to ask any NFL owner whether they were interested in moving to St. Louis at the time it was seeking a team. Shaw was not a disinterested witness, and in the absence of other evidence his testimony was not enough to establish that the rule and its past application had created an anti-relocation atmosphere in the NFL which caused the lack of bidders, especially in light of the fact that Shaw's own team succeeded in moving after negotiating with several cities. See H & B Equipment Co. v. International Harvester Co., 577

F.2d 239, 247 (5th Cir.1978) (plaintiff could not show causation based on corporate officer's testimony alone). Shaw was not a participant in what is alleged to have been a refusal to approach CVC, and his testimony on the motivation of other owners to refrain from bidding could not support a reasonable inference that the rules prevented the competitive bidding which CVC wished to have on the St. Louis stadium.

CVC claims that eight teams had expressed interest in moving since 1991, but the testimony it cites in support contains no indication that any team was interested in moving in 1995, CVC's deadline for a team. It cites the deposition testimony of New Orleans Saints owner Tom Benson who said that teams had expressed interest in St. Louis, but Benson did not identify any teams or the nature of any interest. CVC also does not cite any support elsewhere in the record for Shaw's testimony that the Houston Oilers, Cincinnati Bengals, and New England Patriots could move.

CVC argues that the Tampa Bay Buccaneers were available to move, citing the deposition testimony of a league official. That official stated, however, that the team would have had to pay a penalty on its lease in order to relocate, and CVC does not point to any testimony by team officials indicating they were prepared to move. Senator Eagleton testified, however, that Jerry Clinton had negotiated with the Buccaneers and claimed he could bring them to St. Louis on the same terms as the Rams if an additional $5 million were made available, but Eagleton did not indicate why St. Louis had not attempted to create a competitive bidding situation between the teams.

CVC also claims that the Minnesota Vikings were available, citing testimony by Senator Eagleton, but Eagleton testified that FANS concluded that the Vikings were not interested in St. Louis.

CVC contends that the testimony of its expert, Professor John Siegfried, establishes a causal link between the NFL's actions and the lack of competitive bidding on the lease. A jury may not rest its verdict on an expert's conclusion "without some underlying facts and reasons, or a logical inferential process to support the expert's opinion." Sullivan, 34 F.3d at 1105 (citing Mid–State Fertilizer Co. v. Exchange National Bank, 877 F.2d 1333, 1339 (7th Cir.1989)). Here, there was no evidence on which the jury could have drawn a logical inference from Siegfried's opinion. Siegfried testified that he would have expected to see bidding on the lease, but there was no evidence to support a finding that there were teams that were actually able and desiring to bid, but were prevented from doing it. Moreover, Siegfried rested his conclusions on [an] economic theory that states that in a freely competitive market NFL teams would want to move to the most advantageous lease opportunity, but there was no evidence which tended to show that this was actually the case, especially in light of admissions by CVC witnesses that several team owners would not move because of loyalty to their communities or ownership of their stadia. Siegfried also testified that he had not seen any of the lease agreements involved in the case, any relocation agreement, or any documentation on the lease negotiations. Without evidence tending to show that Siegfried's economic model actually applied to the NFL and the CVC efforts to obtain a team, his testimony is insufficient to create a jury question on the issue of causation. Sip–Top, 86 F.3d at 830 (judgment as a matter of law appropriate where plaintiff only relies on speculation to support theory).

CVC relies also on circumstantial evidence to prove causation. It claims that since the purpose of the rules was to deter team movement and there was a lack of competitive bidding on the Trans World Dome lease, it can be inferred that the rules were the cause of the harm allegedly suffered. See Alexander v. National Farmers Org., 687 F.2d 1173, 1209–10 (8th Cir.1982) ("causal links also may properly be a matter of inference from the circumstances and evidence as a whole."). CVC cites the Alexander case to support its position, but the facts there were significantly different. The plaintiff had produced substantial evidence that its competitor in the dairy distribution business threatened and harassed buyers to stop dealing with it; the defendant's actions were planned at its board meetings and "there was no doubt that the unlawful conspiracy was the material cause" of the plaintiff's injury. Id. The fact that the rules were allegedly intended to discourage relocation does not support the inference that they prevented all other teams besides the Rams from pursuing a possible move to St. Louis. There were many legitimate reasons why owners may not have bid, and without evidence from those who did not bid about why they had not, the circumstantial evidence was insufficient to allow the case to be presented to the jury on causation.

The district court found it particularly significant that CVC had not presented evidence to show that it had sought bids from other teams. See Read v. Medical X–Ray Center, P.C., 110 F.3d 543, 546 (8th Cir.), cert. denied ___ U.S. ___, 118 S.Ct. 299, 139 L.Ed.2d 230 (1997); Admiral Theatre Corp., 585 F.2d at 893–94. Where a plaintiff has otherwise failed to present evidence of causation, he must show that he made "a demand on the defendant to allow the plaintiff to take some action or obtain some benefit, which the defendant's challenged practice is allegedly preventing the plaintiff from taking or obtaining, in order to prove that the practice caused injury in fact." Sullivan v. National Football League, 34 F.3d 1091, 1103 (1st Cir.1994); see also Out Front Productions, Inc. v. Magid, 748 F.2d 166, 169–70 (3d Cir.1984). The record shows no effort by CVC to solicit bids from other NFL teams and CVC did not contact any other NFL team to encourage it to consider the St. Louis opportunity. The negotiations between CVC and the Rams were carried out in secret, and there was undisputed evidence that CVC had made a conscious decision to negotiate with only one team at a time. In fact, the Rams had informed CVC they would back away if there were negotiations with other teams and even suspended talks when CVC leaked information to the press.

CVC claims that the evidence about its presentation to the NFL owners during the expansion process and its publication of the Rams "wish list" during its negotiations was sufficient to show that it had sought interest from other teams. There was undisputed testimony that St. Louis had been passed over for expansion because of problems with its ownership group and lease, and there was no evidence that CVC made owners aware that these problems had been rectified. Publication of the benefits the Rams sought in St. Louis was not the same as informing other owners CVC was seeking additional bidders. CVC "may not recover for losses due to factors other than the [NFL's] anticompetitive violations." National Association of Review Appraisers, 64 F.3d at 1135 (quoting Amerinet Inc. v. Xerox Corp., 972 F.2d 1483, 1494 (8th Cir.1992)). Since CVC failed to present evidence showing that the alleged conspiracy caused it injury, it did not make out the element of causation necessary for a Section 1 claim.

3.

The district court also ruled that CVC failed to present evidence to make out a submissible case of antitrust injury. CVC says that its evidence tended to prove that the NFL's policies caused a reduction in competitive bidding which is an antitrust injury. The NFL replies that the theory of CVC's case was that the very existence of Article 4.3 and the guidelines limited team bidding. It did not show that they operated to make CVC's financial obligations greater than they should have been, [and thus] there was no antitrust injury. The [NFL] also argues that the rules did not result in a reduction in output of the number of games, teams, or stadia which would be necessary to show antitrust injury, citing Chicago Prof'l Sports Ltd. Partnership v. NBA, 95 F.3d 593 (7th Cir.1996).

Antitrust injury is "injury of the type the antitrust laws were intended to prevent and flows from that which makes defendants' acts unlawful." Brunswick Corp. v. Pueblo Bowl–O–Mat, Inc., 429 U.S. 477, 489, 97 S.Ct. 690, 50 L.Ed.2d 701 (1977). CVC failed to offer proof of antitrust injury because it did not present evidence to show that there was a suppression of bidding on the St. Louis lease. There was no evidence at trial that any other willing and able bidder besides the Rams was in the market for a stadium and interested in the St. Louis opportunity at the time CVC was in the market for a tenant. A showing of antitrust injury requires proof that the possibility for the alleged harm to competition actually existed and that competition was diminished by the defendants' actions. "The Sherman Act does not require competitive bidding; it prohibits unreasonable restraints on competition." National Society of Professional Engineers v. United States, 435 U.S. 679, 98 S.Ct. 1355, 55 L.Ed.2d 637 (1978) (organization's ethical rules prohibited competitive bidding). CVC presented no evidence that it was injured by a restraint on competition.

In sum, CVC did not make out a claim under Section 1 of the Sherman Act, and appellees were entitled to judgment as a matter of law. It failed to present sufficient evidence to prove that the lack of expressed interest from other teams in the St. Louis opportunity was caused by Article 4.3 and other acts of a conspiracy consisting of the league and its members, and there was no evidence of antitrust injury.

Because the league and teams are entitled to judgment as a matter of law on the Section 1 claim for the reasons discussed, it is not necessary to reach the issue raised by their cross appeal as to whether they are unable to conspire among themselves because they are a single economic enterprise under Copperweld Corp., 467 U.S. 752, 104 S.Ct. 2731 (1984) and City of Mt. Pleasant, 838 F.2d 268 (8th Cir.1988).

IV.

CVC also claims that the NFL tortiously interfered with its contract with the Rams by charging the $29 million relocation fee after initially voting down the Rams' application to move. CVC argues that it was forced to pay the fee because of economic duress and that the required fee made its obligations to the Rams substantially more burdensome. The NFL responds that CVC failed to establish several of the essential elements of a tortious interference claim under Missouri law. The district court dismissed this claim because of lack of evidence of a breach induced by the NFL's conduct or of any intentional interference.

Missouri law requires a plaintiff alleging tortious interference with a contract to prove "(1) a contract or valid business expectancy; (2) defendant's knowledge of the contract or relationship; (3) a breach induced or caused by defendant's intentional interference; (4) the absence of justification; and (5) damages." Rice v. Hodapp, 919 S.W.2d 240, 245 (Mo.1996) (en banc). CVC presented no evidence that the NFL's imposition of a high relocation fee caused a breach in its contract with the Rams. Despite having the option to terminate its contract with the Rams once it was decided that the fee would exceed $7.5 million, CVC agreed to pay the fee in order to be sure the Rams would play in St. Louis in 1995, the target year it had set. There was also no evidence that the intent behind the NFL's fee was to disrupt the contract between CVC and the Rams. It is not even clear that the team owners knew about the contract at the time the fee was set. CVC contends, however, that the NFL can be liable for tortious interference even without a breach if it caused the performance of the contract to be more burdensome and expensive, citing Restatement (Second) of Torts, § 766A. CVC points to no Missouri authority which has recognized this theory, and a federal court ruling on a point of state law is obligated to follow the law as announced by that state's highest court. Gilstrap v. Amtrak, 998 F.2d 559, 560 (8th Cir.1993); Carman v. Harrison, 362 F.2d 694, 698 (8th Cir.1966). To adopt CVC's theory would be contrary to the Missouri requirement that a plaintiff prove that the defendant induced a breach of contract. Since CVC did not make out the required elements of this state tort, appellees were entitled to a judgment as a matter of law on it.

V.

CVC had ample opportunity to prove the causes of action that are the subject of its appeal, and it took some four weeks to put in its evidence at trial. The many legal issues were briefed and argued by the parties before the district court ruled on them. Since CVC failed to produce sufficient evidence to make out essential elements required under Section 1 of the Sherman Act and under Missouri law on tortious interference, the league and the member teams were entitled to judgment as a matter of law. CVC has not shown on its appeal that it should have a new trial, and the cross appeal is dismissed as moot. Accordingly, we affirm the judgment of the district court.

Notes

1. In addition to league relocation fees, teams that move into an existing franchise's territory are assessed indemnity fees. In 1970, for example, when the AFL and the NFL merged, the New York Jets were required to pay $18 million to the New York Giants while the Oakland Raiders had to give the same amount to the San Francisco 49ers. In 1976, when the ABA was absorbed by the NBA, the New York Nets were obligated to hand over $4 million to the New York Knicks. To raise the money, the team sold its best player, superstar Julius Erving, to the Philadelphia 76ers. In 1982, when the new owner of the Colorado Rockies transferred the franchise to New Jersey, he was compelled to pay $16.5 million to compensate the New York Islanders, New York Rangers, and Philadelphia Flyers. And in 1993, the Los Angeles Kings were given half the $50 million expansion fee paid by the Mighty Ducks of Anaheim.

2. The Rams' move from Anaheim to St. Louis is just one of many franchise shifts that have reshaped the face of professional sports since the end of World War II. Is your favorite team listed below?

MLB
1953: Boston Braves move to Milwaukee
1954: St. Louis Browns move to Baltimore, renamed Orioles
1955: Philadelphia Athletics move to Kansas City
1958: Brooklyn Dodgers move to Los Angeles
New York Giants move to San Francisco
1961: Washington Senators move to Minneapolis, renamed Twins
1966: Los Angeles Angels move to Anaheim, renamed California Angels
Milwaukee Braves move to Atlanta
1968: Kansas City Athletics move to Oakland
1970: Seattle Pilots move to Milwaukee, renamed Brewers
1972: Washington Senators move to Arlington, Texas, renamed Rangers

NBA
1946: Buffalo Bisons move to Tri–Cities (Moline and Rock Island, Illinois, and Davenport, Iowa), renamed Blackhawks
1951: Tri–Cities Blackhawks move to Milwaukee, renamed Hawks
1955: Milwaukee Hawks move to St. Louis
1957: Fort Wayne Pistons move to Detroit
Rochester Royals move to Cincinnati
1960: Minneapolis Lakers move to Los Angeles
1962: Philadelphia Warriors move to San Francisco
1963: Chicago Zephyrs move to Baltimore, renamed Bullets
Syracuse Nationals move to Philadelphia, renamed 76ers
1968: St. Louis Hawks move to Atlanta
1971: San Diego Rockets move to Houston

San Francisco Warriors move to Oakland, renamed Golden State Warriors

1972: Cincinnati Royals move to Kansas City–Omaha, renamed Kings, play games in both cities

1973: Dallas Chaparrals move to San Antonio, renamed Spurs
Baltimore Bullets move to Landover, Maryland, renamed Capital Bullets (later become Washington Bullets)

1975: Kansas City–Omaha Kings stop playing games in Omaha, change name to Kansas City Kings

1977: New York Nets move to New Jersey

1978: Buffalo Braves move to San Diego, renamed Clippers

1979: New Orleans Jazz move to Salt Lake City

1984: San Diego Clippers move to Los Angeles

1985: Kansas City Kings move to Sacramento

1997: Washington Bullets move from Landover, Maryland to Washington, D.C., renamed Wizards

NFL

1946: Cleveland Rams move to Los Angeles

1960: Chicago Cardinals move to St. Louis

1961: Los Angeles Chargers move to San Diego

1963: Dallas Texans move to Kansas City, renamed Chiefs

1976: New York Giants move to New Jersey

1980: Los Angeles Rams move to Anaheim

1982: Oakland Raiders move to Los Angeles

1984: Baltimore Colts move to Indianapolis
New York Jets move to New Jersey

1988: St. Louis Cardinals move to Phoenix

1995: Los Angeles Rams move to St. Louis

1996: Cleveland Browns move to Baltimore, renamed Ravens
Los Angeles Raiders move back to Oakland

1997: Houston Oilers move to Memphis (pending completion of stadium in Nashville)
Washington Redskins move to Raljon, Maryland

1998: Tennessee Oilers move to Nashville, later announce they will call themselves Titans beginning in 1999
New England Patriots agree to move to Hartford

NHL

1974: New England Whalers move from Boston to Springfield, Massachusetts

1975: New England Whalers move from Springfield to Hartford

1976: Kansas City Scouts move to Denver, renamed Colorado Rockies

1980: Atlanta Flames move to Calgary

1982: Colorado Rockies move to New Jersey, renamed Devils

1993: Minnesota North Stars move to Dallas, renamed Stars

1995: Quebec Nordiques move to Denver, renamed Colorado Avalanche

1996: Winnipeg Jets move to Phoenix, renamed Coyotes

1997: Hartford Whalers move to Greensboro, North Carolina (pending completion of arena in Raleigh), renamed Hurricanes
Washington Capitals move from Landover, Maryland to Washington, D.C.

3. Of the many franchise relocations in professional sports, none have come close to inciting the bitterness and hostility caused by Walter O'Malley's decision to move the Brooklyn Dodgers to Los Angeles following the conclusion of the 1957 baseball season.

The Dodgers had been a fixture in Brooklyn since 1884, and as recently as 1955 had won the World Series. Known as the "Bums" because of their often amusing antics on the field, the Dodgers were one of three teams in New York City (the others being the New York Giants and the New York Yankees). Each team had its own following, and partisans spent hours debating whether Duke Snider (Dodgers), Willie Mays (Giants), or Mickey Mantle (Yankees) was the greatest center fielder to ever play the game.

While the Yankees owned a palatial stadium in the Bronx known far and wide as "The House That Ruth Built," the Giants and the Dodgers played in antiquated arenas in, respectively, northern Manhattan (the Polo Grounds) and Crown Heights (Ebbets Field). To improve his team's fortunes, in 1955 O'Malley asked the city's leaders to use their eminent domain power to help him acquire a parcel of land one mile from Ebbets Field, where he hoped to build a state-of-the-art facility. Robert Moses, the man in charge of such decisions, turned O'Malley down, and instead offered to rent him a tract of land in Flushing, a remote area in the borough of Queens that Moses envisioned turning into an urban oasis.

Stymied in New York, O'Malley eventually accepted an offer from politicians in Los Angeles. In return for bringing his team west, the city council gave O'Malley Chavez Ravine, a highly desirable plot of land overlooking downtown. Worried about being the only team on the West Coast, O'Malley suggested to Horace Stoneham, the owner of the Giants, that he move his team to San Francisco. When Stoneham agreed, Brooklyn's fate was sealed.

Forty years later, the borough has yet to either forgive or forget O'Malley's betrayal, and plans regularly surface to place a minor league team on Coney Island, the borough's beach area, and call it the Dodgers. Yet as has been pointed out in a thoughtful book about the affair, see Neil J. Sullivan, *The Dodgers Move West* (1987), O'Malley really had no choice but to leave Brooklyn. Ebbets Field was simply too small and in too congested a neighborhood to be of further use (the Polo Grounds, by contrast, was too large and in too desolate a neighborhood).

Several years after the loss of the Dodgers and the Giants, both Ebbets Field and the Polo Grounds were unceremoniously torn down to make way for low-income housing projects (small plaques now indicate where the two parks once stood). In the meantime, thanks to the efforts of William A. Shea, a prominent attorney, an expansion team was awarded to New York City in 1961. Known as the New York Mets, the team played its first two seasons at the Polo Grounds, decamping in 1964 for a new stadium (named after Shea) built in the exact spot in Flushing which O'Malley had rejected as inadequate.

For a further look at the foregoing events, see Robert M. Jarvis, *When the Lawyers Slept: The Unmaking of the Brooklyn Dodgers*, 74 Cornell L. Rev. 347 (1989).

4. As the court in *CVC* points out, not every team jumps at the idea of relocating. Indeed, there are many reasons why teams decline such offers, including loyalty to their current communities, concern over financial costs, and fear that fans and advertisers in the new city will not be supportive. For an examination of the factors that influence teams, see Daniel S. Mason & Trevor Slack, *Appropriate Opportunism or Bad Business Practice? Stakeholder Theory, Ethics, and the Franchise Relocation Issue*, 7 Marq. Sports

L.J. 399 (1997), and Glen Seredynski et al., *On Team Relocation, League Expansion, and Public Policy: Or, Where Do We Put This Hockey Franchise and Why Would You Care?*, 4 Seton Hall J. Sport L. 663 (1994). *See also Huard v. Shreveport Pirates, Inc.*, 147 F.3d 406 (5th Cir.1998) (describing the numerous problems that befell the CFL's Ottawa Rough Riders after the team relocated to the United States).

5. To a certain extent, of course, CVC's contention that the NFL (like other leagues) disfavors relocations is correct. Not only do franchise shifts alienate fans and invite unwanted attention from lawmakers, they often negatively affect the league's schedule, national television contracts, and expansion plans. *See* W.D. Murray, *NFL Playing Catch–Up After Moves*, Chi. Sun–Times, Sept. 30, 1996, at 49 (describing the effects on the league's television ratings caused the by concurrent relocation of the Browns, Raiders, and Rams). As a result, some commentators have called for legislation allowing leagues to prevent relocations without having to worry about federal and state antitrust laws. *See, e.g.*, Frank P. Scibilia, *Baseball Franchise Stability and Consumer Welfare: An Argument for Reaffirming Baseball's Antitrust Exemption with Regard to its Franchise Relocation Rules*, 6 Seton Hall J. Sport L. 409 (1996), and Katherine C. Leone, Note, *No Team, No Peace: Franchise Free Agency in the National Football League*, 97 Colum. L. Rev. 473 (1997).

6. When the Oakland Raiders announced they intended to relocate to Los Angeles, the City of Oakland sought to block the move through use of its eminent domain power. In *City of Oakland v. Oakland Raiders*, 646 P.2d 835 (Cal.1982) ("Raiders I"), the California Supreme Court held it was theoretically possible for a city to acquire a sports team through condemnation. It therefore reversed the lower courts, which had held that such an action was not legally viable, and remanded the case for further proceedings. Subsequently, in *City of Oakland v. Oakland Raiders*, 220 Cal.Rptr. 153 (Ct.App. 1985) ("Raiders II"), it was decided the City of Oakland could not, consistent with the Commerce Clause of the United States Constitution, prevent the Raiders from moving. No appeal was taken from this decision.

In the interim between *Raiders I* and *Raiders II*, the Baltimore Colts migrated to Indianapolis (moving vans showed up at the team's headquarters in the middle of the night so as to avoid setting off demonstrations by angry fans). Although the City of Baltimore subsequently invoked its eminent domain power to try to force the Colts to return, a federal court ruled the action was moot because the team was no longer within the city's territorial limits. *See Mayor and City Council of Baltimore v. Baltimore Football Club Inc.*, 624 F.Supp. 278 (D.Md.1985).

In time, the Raiders returned to Oakland, the Cleveland Browns resurfaced in Baltimore as the Ravens, and the NFL awarded Cleveland an expansion team (which, like its predecessor, will be called the Browns when it starts play in 1999). Thus, the issue of whether a city, county, or state can use eminent domain to keep a team from moving remains, at least for now, an open question. For a further look at the issue, see Rafael A. Declet, Jr., *We'll Take the Yankees: Assessing the Feasibility of a State Condemnation of Baseball's Greatest Franchise*, 8 Marq. Sports L.J. 53 (1997), and Steven R. Hobson II, Comment, *Preventing Franchise Flight: Could Cleveland Have*

Kept the Browns by Exercising its Eminent Domain Power?, 29 Akron L. Rev. 665 (1996). *See also* Craig A. Sharon & Lloyd H. Mayer, *New Direction for Team Ownership?*, 16 Ent. & Sports Law. 1 (Spr. 1998) (discussing the City of Memphis' highly novel decision to establish a non-profit foundation to own its new AAA expansion baseball team after its AA team moved away).

7. Whenever teams relocate, bills invariably are introduced in Congress to prohibit or restrict such transfers. *See, e.g.*, Professional Football Stabilization Act of 1985, S. 172, 99th Cong. (1985) (Sen. Specter); Professional Sports Community Protection Act of 1985, S. 259, 99th Cong. (1985) (Sen. Eagleton); Professional Sports Team Community Protection Act, S. 287, 99th Cong. (1985) (Sen. Gorton); Sports Community Protection and Stability Act of 1985, S. 298, 99th Cong. (1985) (Sen. DeConcini); Professional Sports Franchise Relocation Act of 1983, H.R. 785, 99th Cong. (1985) (Rep. Dellums); Professional Sports Community Protection Act of 1987, S. 782, 100th Cong. (1987) (Sen. Specter); The Fans Rights Act of 1995, S. 1439, H.R. 2699, 104th Cong. (Sens. Glenn, DeWine, and Gorton and Rep. Stokes); Fan Freedom Act and Community Protection Act of 1996, H.R. 2740, 104th Cong. (1995) (Rep. Hoke); Team Relocation Taxpayer Protection Act of 1996, S. 1529, 104th Cong. (1996) (Sen. DeWine); Professional Sports Franchise Relocation Act of 1996, S. 1625, 104th Cong. (1996) (Sen. Specter); Professional Sports Antitrust Clarification Act of 1996, S. 1696, 104th Cong. (1996) (Sen. Thurmond); Stop Tax–Exempt Arena Debt Issuance Act, S. 1880, 104th Cong. (1996) (Sen. Moynihan); Sports Relocation Reform Act of 1996, H.R. 3805, 104th Cong. (1996) (Rep. Bryant); Professional Sports Franchise Relocation Act of 1998, H.R. 3817, 105th Cong. (1998) (Reps. Meehan and Bryant). To date, none of these measures have been enacted.

For a further look at attempts to stop franchise relocations through government action, see, e.g., Matthew J. Mitten & Bruce W. Burton, *Professional Sports Franchise Relocations From Private Law and Public Law Perspectives: Balancing Marketplace Competition, League Autonomy, and the Need for a Level Playing Field*, 56 Md. L. Rev. 57 (1997); Sanjay J. Mullick, *Browns to Baltimore: Franchise Free Agency and the New Economics of the NFL*, 7 Marq. Sports L.J. 1 (1996); John Wunderli, *Squeeze Play: The Game of Owners, Cities, Leagues, and Congress*, 5 Marq. Sports L.J. 83 (1994); Daniel S. York, Note, *The Professional Sports Community Protection Act: Congress' Best Response to Raiders?*, 38 Hastings L.J. 345 (1987). *See also Florida Panthers Hockey Club, Ltd. v. Miami Sports and Exhibition Authority*, 939 F.Supp. 855 (S.D.Fla.1996), *aff'd mem.*, 116 F.3d 1492 (11th Cir. 1997) (City of Miami could not punish Florida Panthers for deciding to move to suburban Fort Lauderdale by denying team continued use of municipal-owned arena while its new stadium was being built); John K. Harris, Jr., *Fiduciary Duties of Professional Team Sports Franchise Owners*, 2 Seton Hall J. Sport L. 255 (1992) (suggesting professional sports teams should be made subject to public trust laws); Kathleen M. Johnston & Bill Theobald, *We Got It! $50 Million in Incentives Key in Wresting the Athletic Association from Kansas City*, Indianapolis Star, June 1, 1997, at A1 (reporting on the NCAA's much-criticized decision to relocate from Overland Park, Kansas to Indianapolis).

8. One question that has arisen frequently in connection with franchise relocations concerns whether the departing team can take its name and

logo. In *Indianapolis Colts, Inc. v. Metropolitan Baltimore Football Club Limited Partnership*, 34 F.3d 410 (7th Cir.1994), for example, the Seventh Circuit enjoined the defendant, a CFL team that had just moved into Baltimore, from calling itself the Colts due to the likelihood of public confusion. As a result, the new team (which later folded) had to settle for the name "Stallions."

In the course of its opinion, the Seventh Circuit distinguished *Major League Baseball Properties, Inc. v. Sed Non Olet Denarius, Ltd.*, 817 F.Supp. 1103 (S.D.N.Y.1993), *vacated pursuant to settlement*, 859 F.Supp. 80 (S.D.N.Y.1994), a case in which a New York City tavern known as the Brooklyn Dodger Sports Bar and Restaurant was permitted to keep its name over the objection of MLB and the Los Angeles Dodgers. The Seventh Circuit concluded that while there was little risk of the public mistaking a restaurant for a baseball team, there was considerable risk that it would assume the CFL team was the NFL team back from its sojourn to Indiana.

Following the Seventh Circuit's decision, a bill was introduced in Congress that would have forced relocating teams to leave behind their names and logos. *See* Heritage Act of 1996, S. 1598, 104th Cong. (1996) (Sen. Glenn). Although nothing came of this initiative, the NFL did require Art Modell, the owner of the Cleveland Browns, to change his club's name when it moved to Baltimore. As a result, when a new NFL franchise begins playing in Cleveland in 1999, it will be called the Browns and use the same logo and colors as its predecessor. By the same token, when Bud Adams, the owner of the Tennessee Oilers, formerly the Houston Oilers, announced he had decided they would be called the Titans starting in 1999, the NFL "retired" the name Oilers. For a further look at the issue of who owns a departing team's identity, see, e.g., Sean H. Brogan, *Who Are These "Colts?": The Likelihood of Confusion, Consumer Survey Evidence and Trademark Abandonment in Indianapolis Colts, Inc. v. Metropolitan Baltimore Football Club, Ltd.*, 7 Marq. Sports L.J. 39 (1996), and Howard W. Brill, *The Name of the Departed Team: Who Can Use It?*, 15 Whittier L. Rev. 1003 (1994).

9. Closely related to the issue of relocation is realignment. As new clubs are added, and older ones move, it is not uncommon for a league to become geographically unbalanced. Sometimes when this happens, a team agrees to switch conferences or divisions. In 1970, for example, the Baltimore Colts, Cleveland Browns, and Pittsburgh Steelers were each paid $3 million to move from the NFC to the AFC. Likewise, in 1998, the Milwaukee Brewers, an AL member since its founding in 1969, transferred to the NL and the Detroit Tigers shifted from the AL's East Division to the AL's Central Division (thereby allowing the expansion Tampa Bay Devil Rays to be assigned to the Eastern Division). More dramatically, before the start of the 1998–99 season, the NHL redid all its divisions to accommodate its recent expansion.

Typically, however, teams resist realignment. In large part, this is due to a fear that profits will go down if they are forced to give up historic rivalries, placed in different time zones, or thrown into more competitive divisions. In 1992, for example, the Chicago Cubs obtained an injunction prohibiting Commissioner Fay Vincent from switching them to the NL's West Division because the move would have affected the starting times of their television broadcasts. Similarly, in 1997, Acting Commissioner Bud Selig's proposed realignment, which would have affected up to a dozen franchises, was rejected out of hand. The NFL's owners also have been unable to agree on a plan to rationalize their conferences, thereby forcing teams like the Atlanta Falcons (NFC West), Arizona Cardinals (NFC East), Carolina Panthers (NFC West), and Tampa Bay Buccaneers (NFC Central) to continue to play many of their games far from home. *See further* Tracy Ringolsby, *Me-First Mentality Puts Owners Out of Their League*, Rocky Mtn. News, Sept. 18, 1997, at 14C.

Interestingly, the Premier League, England's leading soccer conference, realigns itself annually. After each season, in a process called "relegation," the bottom three teams are replaced by the top three teams in the First Division, England's next best conference. In this way, the Premier League promotes competition and assures fans of top-quality play. *See further* Andrew Cave, *Relegation Costs Sunderland £5m*, (London) Daily Telegraph, July 24, 1997, at 22 (City) (reporting Sunderland's demotion from the Premier League to the First Division cost it five million pounds in reduced television revenues).

Problem 18

Six months ago, the president of a hockey club and the mayor of a city with no professional sports franchises signed a document labelled "Letter of Intent Regarding Construction and Operation of an 18,000 Seat Arena." The introductory paragraph stated: "This letter will serve to express the intention of both parties to seek, in good faith, as soon as practical, the drafting and execution of such documents as may be required to cover all the matters herein expressed and such other matters as may be mutually agreed." Last week, the club notified the city it had decided to remain in its present hometown because its demand for a new, taxpayer-financed stadium finally had been met. If the jilted city sues for breach of contract, will the team be held liable? *See Opdyke Investment Co. v. Norris Grain Co.*, 320 N.W.2d 836 (Mich.1982).

4. FIRE SALES

When faced with dire economic circumstances, some owners resort to selling off their best players at bargain-basement prices. Because of the adverse effect this has on competition, all leagues strongly oppose such moves.

CHARLES O. FINLEY & CO. v. KUHN

569 F.2d 527 (7th Cir.),
cert. denied, 439 U.S. 876 (1978).

SPRECHER, Circuit Judge.

The two important questions raised by this appeal are whether the Commissioner of baseball is contractually authorized to disapprove player assignments which he finds to be "not in the best interests of baseball" where neither moral turpitude nor violation of a Major League Rule is involved, and whether the provision in the Major League Agreement whereby the parties agree to waive recourse to the courts is valid and enforceable.

I

The plaintiff, Charles O. Finley & Co., Inc., an Illinois corporation, is the owner of the Oakland Athletics baseball club, a member of the American League of Professional Baseball Clubs (Oakland). Joe Rudi, Rollie Fingers and Vida Blue were members of the active playing roster of the Oakland baseball club and were contractually bound to play for Oakland through the end of the 1976 baseball season. On or about June 15, 1976, Oakland and Blue entered a contract whereby Blue would play for Oakland through the 1979 season, but Rudi and Fingers had not at that time signed contracts for the period beyond the 1976 season.

If Rudi and Fingers had not signed contracts to play with Oakland by the conclusion of the 1976 season, they would at that time have become free agents eligible thereafter to negotiate with any major league club, subject to certain limitations on their right to do so that were then being negotiated by the major league clubs with the Players Association.

On June 14 and 15, 1976, Oakland negotiated tentative agreements to sell the club's contract rights for the services of Rudi and Fingers to the Boston Red Sox for $2 million and for the services of Blue to the New York Yankees for $1.5 million. The agreements were negotiated shortly before the expiration of baseball's trading deadline at midnight on June 15, after which time Oakland could not have sold the contracts of these players to other clubs without first offering the players to all other American League teams, in inverse order of their standing, at the stipulated waiver price of $20,000.

The defendant Bowie K. Kuhn is the Commissioner of baseball (Commissioner), having held that position since 1969. On June 18, 1976, the Commissioner disapproved the assignments of the contracts of Rudi, Fingers and Blue to the Red Sox and Yankees "as inconsistent with the best interests of baseball, the integrity of the game and the maintenance of public confidence in it." The Commissioner expressed his concern for (1) the debilitation of the Oakland club, (2) the lessening of the competitive balance of professional baseball through the buying of success by the more affluent clubs, and (3) "the present unsettled circumstances of baseball's reserve system."

Thereafter on June 25, 1976, Oakland instituted this suit principally challenging, as beyond the scope of the Commissioner's authority and, in any event, as arbitrary and capricious, the Commissioner's disapproval of the Rudi, Fingers and Blue assignments.

The complaint set forth seven causes of action: (I) that the Commissioner breached his employment contract with Oakland by acting arbitrarily, discriminatorily and unreasonably; (II) that the Commissioner, acting in concert with others, conspired to eliminate Oakland from baseball in violation of federal antitrust laws; (III) that Oakland's constitutional rights of due process and equal protection were violated;

(IV) that Oakland's constitutional rights were violated by the first disapproval of a player assignment where no major league rule was violated; (V) that the defendants (the Commissioner, the National and American Leagues and the Major League Executive Council) induced the breach of Oakland's contracts with Boston and New York; (VI) that the Commissioner did not have the authority to disapprove Oakland's assignments "in the best interests of baseball"; and (VII) that Oakland have specific performance of its contracts of assignment with Boston and New York.

On September 7, 1976, the district court granted the Commissioner's motion for summary judgment as to Counts II, III and IV. Count II was dismissed on the ground that the business of baseball is not subject to the federal antitrust laws. Counts III and IV were dismissed on the ground that Oakland did not allege sufficient nexus between the state and the complained of activity to constitute state action.

A bench trial took place as a result of which judgment on the remaining four counts of the complaint was entered in favor of the Commissioner on March 17, 1977.

On August 29, 1977, the district court granted the Commissioner's counterclaim for a declaratory judgment that the covenant not to sue in the Major League Agreement is valid and enforceable. The court had not relied on that covenant in reaching its two earlier decisions.

Oakland appealed from the judgments of September 7, 1976, March 17, 1977, and August 29, 1977, arguing (1) that the court's failure to issue a finding on the question of procedural fairness constituted error; (2) that the exclusion of evidence of the Commissioner's malice toward the Oakland club constituted error; (3) that other errors were committed during trial; (4) that the antitrust count was not barred by baseball's exemption from federal antitrust law; and (5) that baseball's blanket waiver of recourse to the courts is not enforceable.

II

Basic to the underlying suit brought by Oakland and to this appeal is whether the Commissioner of baseball is vested by contract with the authority to disapprove player assignments which he finds to be "not in the best interests of baseball." In assessing the measure and extent of the Commissioner's power and authority, consideration must be given to the circumstances attending the creation of the office of Commissioner, the language employed by the parties in drafting their contractual understanding, changes and amendments adopted from time to time, and the interpretation given by the parties to their contractual language throughout the period of its existence.

Prior to 1921, professional baseball was governed by a three-man National Commission formed in 1903 which consisted of the presidents of the National and American Leagues and a third member, usually one of the club owners, selected by the presidents of the two leagues. Between 1915 and 1921, a series of events and controversies contributed to a growing dissatisfaction with the National Commission on the part of players, owners and the public, and a demand developed for the establishment of a single, independent Commissioner of baseball.

On September 28, 1920, an indictment issued charging that an effort had been made to "fix" the 1919 World Series by several Chicago White Sox players. Popularly known as the "Black Sox Scandal," this event rocked the game of professional baseball and proved the catalyst that brought about the establishment of a single, neutral Commissioner of baseball.

In November, 1920, the major league club owners unanimously elected federal Judge Kenesaw Mountain Landis as the sole Commissioner of baseball and appointed a committee of owners to draft a charter setting forth the Commissioner's authority. In one of the drafting sessions an attempt was made to place limitations on the Commissioner's authority. Judge Landis responded by refusing to accept the office of Commissioner.

On January 12, 1921, Landis told a meeting of club owners that he had agreed to accept the position upon the clear understanding that the owners had sought "an authority ... outside of your own business, and that a part of that authority would be a control over whatever and whoever had to do with baseball." Thereupon, the owners voted unanimously to reject the proposed limitation upon the Commissioner's authority, they all signed what they called the Major League Agreement, and Judge Landis assumed the position of Commissioner. Oakland has been a signatory to the Major League Agreement continuously since 1960. The agreement, a contract between the constituent clubs of the National and American Leagues, is the basic charter under which major league baseball operates.

The Major League Agreement provides that "[t]he functions of the Commissioner shall be ... to investigate ... any act, transaction or practice ... not in the best interests of the national game of Baseball" and "to determine ... what preventive, remedial or punitive action is appropriate in the premises, and to take such action...." Art. I, Sec. 2(a) and (b).

The Major League Rules, which govern many aspects of the game of baseball, are promulgated by vote of major league club owners. Major League Rule 12(a) provides that "no ... [assignment of players] shall be recognized as valid unless ... approved by the Commissioner."

The Major Leagues and their constituent clubs severally agreed to be bound by the decisions of the Commissioner and by the discipline imposed by him. They further agreed to "waive such right of recourse to the courts as would otherwise have existed in their favor." Major League Agreement, Art. VII, Sec. 2.

Upon Judge Landis' death in 1944, the Major League Agreement was amended in two respects to limit the Commissioner's authority. First, the parties deleted the provision by which they had agreed to waive their right of recourse to the courts to challenge actions of the Commissioner. Second, the parties added the following language to Article I, Section 3:

> No Major League Rule or other joint action of the two Major Leagues, and no action or procedure taken in compliance with any such Major League Rule or joint action of the two Major Leagues shall be considered or construed to be detrimental to Baseball.

The district court found that this addition had the effect of precluding the Commissioner from finding an act that complied with the Major League Rules to be detrimental to the best interests of baseball.

The two 1944 amendments to the Major League Agreement remained in effect during the terms of the next two Commissioners, A. B. "Happy" Chandler and Ford Frick. Upon Frick's retirement in 1964 and in accordance with his recommendation, the parties adopted three amendments to the Major League Agreement: (1) the language added in 1944 preventing the Commissioner from finding any act or practice "taken in compliance" with a Major League Rule to be "detrimental to baseball" was removed; (2) the provision deleted in 1944 waiving any rights of recourse to the courts to challenge a Commissioner's decision was restored; and (3) in places where the language "detrimental to the best interests of the national game of baseball" or "detrimental to baseball" appeared those words were changed to "not in the best interests of the national game of Baseball" or "not in the best interests of Baseball."

The nature of the power lodged in the Commissioner by the Major League Agreement is further exemplified "[i]n the case of conduct by organizations not parties to this Agreement, or by individuals not connected with any of the parties hereto, which is deemed by the Commissioner not to be in the best interests of Baseball" whereupon "the Commissioner may pursue appropriate legal remedies, advocate remedial legislation and take such other steps as he may deem necessary and proper in the interests of the morale of the players and the honor of the game." Art. I, Sec. 4.

The Commissioner has been given broad power in unambiguous language to investigate any act, transaction or practice not in the best interests of baseball, to determine what preventive, remedial or punitive action is appropriate in the premises, and to take that action. He has also been given the express power to approve or disapprove the assignments of players. In regard to nonparties to the agreement, he may take such other steps as he deems necessary and proper in the interests of the morale of the players and the honor of the game. Further, indicative of the nature of the Commissioner's authority is the provision whereby the parties agree to be bound by his decisions and discipline imposed and to waive recourse to the courts.

The Major League Agreement also provides that "[i]n the case of conduct by Major Leagues, Major League Clubs, officers, employees or players which is deemed by the Commissioner not to be in the best interests of Baseball, action by the Commissioner for each offense may include "a reprimand, deprivation of a club of representation at joint meetings, suspension or removal of non-players, temporary or permanent ineligibility of players, and a fine not to exceed $5,000 in the case of a league or club and not to exceed $500 in the case of an individual." Art. I, Sec. 3.

The district court considered the plaintiff's argument that the enumeration in Article I, Section 3 of the sanctions which the Commissioner may impose places a limit on his authority inasmuch as the power to disapprove assignments of players is not included. The court concluded that the enumeration does not purport to be exclusive and provides that the Commissioner may act in one of the listed ways without expressly limiting him to those ways.

The court further concluded that the principles of construction that the specific controls the general, or that the expression of some kinds of authority operates to exclude unexpressed kinds, do not apply since the Commissioner is empowered to determine what preventive, remedial or punitive action is appropriate in a particular case and the listed sanctions are punitive only. In fact, from 1921 until 1964, Article I, Section 3 expressly described the enumerated sanctions as "punitive action."

In view of the broad authority expressly given by the Major League Agreement to the Commissioner, particularly in Section 2 of Article I, we agree with the district court that Section 3 does not purport to limit that authority.

III

Despite the Commissioner's broad authority to prevent any act, transaction or practice not in the best interests of baseball, Oakland has attacked the Commissioner's disapproval of the Rudi–Fingers–Blue transactions on a variety of theories which seem to express a similar thrust in differing language.

The complaint alleged that the "action of Kuhn was arbitrary, capricious, unreasonable, discriminatory, directly contrary to historical precedent, baseball tradition, and prior rulings and actions of the Commissioner." In pre-trial answers to interrogatories, Oakland acknowledged that the Commissioner could set aside a proposed assignment of a player's contract "in an appropriate case of violation of [Major League] Rules or immoral or unethical conduct."

It is clear from reading the findings of fact that the district court determined through the course of the trial that Oakland was contending that the Commissioner could set aside assignments only if the assignments involved a Rules violation or moral turpitude.

In its briefs on appeal, Oakland summarized this branch of its argument by stating that the Commissioner's "disapproval of the assignments ... exceeded [his] authority under the Major League Agreement and Rules; was irrational and unreasonable; and was procedurally unfair." The nub of this diffuse attack seems best expressed in a subsequent heading in the brief that the Commissioner's "abrupt departure from well-established assignment practice and his retroactive application of this change of policy to disapprove [Oakland's] assignments was made without reasonable notice and was therefore procedurally unfair."

The plaintiff has argued that it is a fundamental rule of law that the decisions of the head of a private association must be procedurally fair. Plaintiff then argued that it was "procedurally unfair" for the Commissioner to fail to warn the plaintiff that he would "disapprove large cash assignments of star players even if they complied with the Major League Rules."

In the first place it must be recalled that prior to the assignments involved here drastic changes had commenced to occur in the reserve system and in the creation of free agents. In his opinion disapproving the Rudi, Fingers and Blue assignments, the Commissioner said that "while I am of course aware that there have been cash sales of player contracts in the past, there has been no instance in my judgment which had the potential for harm to our game as do these assignments, particularly in the present unsettled circumstances of baseball's reserve system and in the highly competitive circumstances we find in today's sports and entertainment world."

Absent the radical changes in the reserve system, the Commissioner's action would have postponed Oakland's realization of value for these players. Given those changes, the relative fortunes of all major league clubs became subject to a host of intangible speculations. No one could predict then or now with certainty that Oakland would fare better or worse relative to other clubs through the vagaries of the revised reserve system occurring entirely apart from any action by the Commissioner.

In the second place, baseball cannot be analogized to any other business or even to any other sport or entertainment. Baseball's relation to the federal antitrust laws has been characterized by the Supreme Court as an "exception," an "anomaly" and an "aberration." Baseball's management through a commissioner is equally an exception, anomaly and aberration, as outlined in Part II hereof. In no other sport or business is there quite the same system, created for quite the same reasons and with quite the same underlying policies. Standards such as the best interests of baseball, the interests of the morale of the players and the honor of the game, or "sportsmanship which accepts the umpire's decision without complaint," are not necessarily familiar to courts and obviously require some expertise in their application. While it is true that professional baseball selected as its first Commissioner a federal judge, it intended only him and not the judiciary as a whole to be its umpire and governor.

As we have seen in Part II, the Commissioner was vested with broad authority and that authority was not to be limited in its exercise to situations where Major League Rules or moral turpitude was involved. When professional baseball intended to place limitations upon the Commissioner's powers, it knew how to do so. In fact, it did so during the 20–year period from 1944 to 1964.

The district court found and concluded that the Rudi–Fingers–Blue transactions were not, as Oakland had alleged in its complaint, "directly contrary to historical precedent, baseball tradition, and prior rulings." During his almost 25 years as Commissioner, Judge Landis found many acts, transactions and practices to be detrimental to the best interests of baseball in situations where neither moral turpitude nor a Major League Rule violation was involved, and he disapproved several player assignments.

On numerous occasions since he became Commissioner of baseball in February 1969, Kuhn has exercised broad authority under the best interests clause of the Major League Agreement. Many of the actions taken by him have been in response to acts, transactions or practices that involved neither the violation of a Major League Rule nor any gambling, game-throwing or other conduct associated with moral turpitude. Moreover, on several occasions Commissioner Kuhn has taken broad preventive or remedial action with respect to assignments of player contracts.

On several occasions Charles O. Finley, the principal owner of the plaintiff corporation and the general manager of the Oakland baseball club, has himself espoused that the Commissioner has the authority to exercise broad powers pursuant to the best interests clause, even where there is no violation of the Major League Rules and no moral turpitude is involved.

Twenty-one of the 25 parties to the current Major League Agreement who appeared as witnesses in the district court testified that they intended and they presently understand that the Commissioner of baseball can review and disapprove an assignment of a player contract which he finds to be not in the best interests of baseball, even if the assignment does not violate the Major League Rules and does not involve moral turpitude. Oakland contended that the district court erred in admitting this testimony since parties are bound "only by their objective manifestations and their subjective intent is immaterial." In this bench trial where Oakland was contending that it was not put on notice that transactions alleged to otherwise conform to the Major League Rules might be invalidated, the court could certainly consider what most of the current parties to the agreement believed they were put on notice of when they became signatories.

Oakland relied upon Major League Rule 21, which deals, in Oakland's characterization of it, with "(a) throwing or soliciting the throwing of ball games, (b) bribery by or of players or persons connected with clubs or (c) umpires, (d) betting on ball games, and (e) physical violence and other unsportsmanlike conduct" as indicating the limits of what is "not in the best interests of baseball." However, Rule 21(f) expressly states:

> Nothing herein contained shall be construed as exclusively defining or otherwise limiting acts, transactions, practices or conduct not to be in the best interests of Baseball; and any and all other acts, transactions, practices or conduct not to be in the best interests of Baseball are prohibited, and shall be subject to such penalties including permanent ineligibility, as the facts in the particular case may warrant.

Oakland also took issue with language in the district court's judgment order of March 17, 1977, which relied upon Milwaukee American Ass'n v. Landis, 49 F.2d 298 (N.D.Ill.1931). Oakland contended that the Landis case was distinguishable inasmuch as it involved the violation of a certain rule. In that case Judge Lindley held that the Commissioner "acted clearly within his authority" when he disapproved a player assignment after several assignments of the same player to and from different clubs owned by a single individual. The court said in 49 F.2d at 302:

> Though there is nothing in the rules to prohibit an individual owning control of a Major League club from likewise owning control of Minor League clubs, the intent of the code is such that common ownership is not to be made use of as to give one individual, controlling all of the clubs mentioned, the absolute right, independent of other clubs, to control indefinitely a player acquired and switched about by apparent outright purchases.

We conclude that the evidence fully supports, and we agree with, the district court's finding that "[t]he history of the adoption of the Major League Agreement in 1921 and the operation of baseball for more than 50 years under it, including: the circumstances preceding and precipitating the adoption of the Agreement; the numerous exercises of broad authority under the best interests clause by Judge Landis and ... Commissioner Kuhn; the amendments to the Agreement in 1964 restoring and broadening the authority of the Commissioner; ... and most important the express language of the Agreement itself are all to the effect that the Commissioner has the authority to determine whether any act, transaction or practice is 'not in the best interests of baseball,' and upon such determination, to take whatever preventive or remedial action he deems appropriate, whether or not the act, transaction or practice complies with the Major League Rules or involves moral turpitude." Any other conclusion would involve the courts in not only interpreting often complex rules of baseball to determine if they were violated but also, as noted in the Landis case, the "intent of the [baseball] code," an even more complicated and subjective task.

The Rudi–Fingers–Blue transactions had been negotiated on June 14 and 15, 1976. On June 16, the Commissioner sent a teletype to the Oakland, Boston and New York clubs and to the Players' Association expressing his "concern for possible consequences to the integrity of baseball and public confidence in the game" and setting a hearing for June 17. Present at the hearing were 17 persons representing those notified. At the outset of the hearing the Commissioner stated that he was concerned that the assignments would be harmful to the competitive capacity of Oakland; that they reflected an effort by Boston and New York to purchase star players and "bypass the usual methods of player development and acquisition which have been traditionally used in professional baseball"; and that the question to be resolved was whether the transactions "are consistent with the best interests of baseball's integrity and maintenance of public confidence in the game." He warned that it was possible that he might determine that the assignments not be approved. Mr. Finley and representatives of the Red Sox and Yankees made statements on the record.

No one at the hearing, including Mr. Finley, claimed that the Commissioner lacked the authority to disapprove the assignments, or objected to the holding of the hearing, or to any of the procedures followed at the hearing.

On June 18, the Commissioner concluded that the attempted assignments should be disapproved as not in the best interests of baseball. In his written decision, the Commissioner stated his reasons which we have summarized in Part I. The decision was sent to all parties by teletype.

The Commissioner recognized "that there have been cash sales of player contracts in the past," but concluded that "these transactions were unparalleled in the history of the game" because there was "never anything on this scale or falling at this time of the year, or which threatened so seriously to unbalance the competitive balance of baseball." The district court concluded that the attempted assignments of Rudi, Fingers and Blue "were at a time and under circumstances making them unique in the history of baseball."

We conclude that the evidence fully supports, and we agree with, the district court's finding and conclusion that the Commissioner "acted in good faith, after investigation, consultation and deliberation, in a manner which he determined to be in the best interests of baseball" and that "[w]hether he was right or wrong is beyond the competence and the jurisdiction of this court to decide."

We must then conclude that anyone becoming a signatory to the Major League Agreement was put on ample notice that the action ultimately taken by the Commissioner was not only possible but probable. The action was neither an "abrupt departure" nor a "change of policy" in view of the contemporaneous developments taking place in the reserve system, over which the Commissioner had little or no control, and in any event the broad authority given to the Commissioner by the Major League Agreement placed any party to it on notice that such authority could be used.

Oakland has argued that the district court erred in not finding on the issue of procedural fairness. To the extent that Oakland made this an issue during the course of the trial, the court responded with adequate findings, many of which we have discussed in this Part III.

Finally, Oakland has also argued that the court excluded evidence which tended to show the Commissioner's malice toward Mr. Finley. Finley's own testimony on this subject, as well as the Commissioner's deposition covering the subject, were admitted as part of the record. When counsel for the Commissioner attempted to cross-examine Finley in regard to the same subject, Oakland's counsel objected on the ground of relevancy and the court sustained the objection on the ground that the Commissioner's motivation was not a serious issue in the case. When the Commissioner was being cross-examined the same objection was sustained. However, since the subject had not been covered in direct examination, the court in its discretion could restrict the cross-examination to the scope of the direct; and since the subject of malice and motivation had been covered in Finley's testimony and in the Commissioner's deposition, the court could exclude it as cumulative regardless of its relevancy. The court made an express finding that the Commissioner had not been motivated by malice.

[The remainder of the court's opinion, as well as the concurring opinions of Chief Judge Fairchild and Circuit Judge Tone, are omitted.]

Notes

1. As he feared, Finley ended up getting almost nothing for his stars. Fingers and Rudi, together with Sal Bando, Bert Campaneris, Gene Tenace, and Don Baylor, departed as free agents at the end of the 1976 season, while Blue was eventually dealt to the San Francisco Giants for $390,000 and a handful of prospects. Disgusted by what free agency had wrought, Finley sold the team to the Levi–Strauss Company in 1981 for $12.7 million after failing to convince his fellow owners of the need for a salary cap.

During his 21–year ownership of the Athletics, Finley was one of the game's great innovators. Besides holding such unusual promotions as "Hot Pants Day" and "Bald Man's Day" to increase attendance, he proposed moving the World Series to nighttime to boost fan interest (an idea that succeeded beyond even Finley's expectations), sought to change baseballs from white to orange (and bases from white to multicolor) to make them easier to see on television, pushed for introduction of a "designated hitter" (an idea which was embraced by the AL in 1973 but which continues to be scorned by the NL), suggested speeding up the game by awarding walks after three balls and using a "designated runner," and launched the careers of cookie magnate Debbie Fields (whom he had bake treats for umpiring crews while she was a team employee) and rap star Hammer (whom he hired to be the club's vice president after seeing the 16–year-old dance in the parking lot). For a further look at Finley's life and times, see Tom Friend, *Charles O. Finley—"O" is for Oddball*, N.Y. Times, Dec. 29, 1996, § 6, at 20. *See also Musicians Union, Local No. 6 v. Superior Court of Alameda County*, 447 P.2d 313 (Cal.1968) (describing Finley's bitter battle to keep union musicians out of his stadium).

2. Finley's decision to break up the Athletics was neither novel nor radical. In 1887, for example, Fred K. Stearns, a pharmaceuticals tycoon, began dismantling the Detroit Wolverines after they upended the favored St. Louis Browns in a 15–game playoff. In just 13 months, future Hall of Famers

Dan Brouthers, Hardy Richardson, Jack Rowe, and Deacon White had all been sold and the Wolverines, the best club in baseball, had ceased operations.

In 1914, Connie Mack, the legendary owner of the Philadelphia Athletics, began razing his team after it lost the World Series to the "Miracle" Boston Braves. In the space of less than a year, Mack sold or waived 12 players, including five future Hall of Famers, in exchange for nearly $200,000 (at a time when the entire franchise was worth just $450,000). Surprisingly, Mack later was able to rebuild. But in 1932–35, he again gutted the club by selling nine players for $545,000, including Hall of Famers Al Simmons, Mickey Cochrane, Lefty Grove, and Jimmy Foxx.

Shortly after Finley's decision to strip down the Athletics, the Cincinnati Reds began their own giveaway. In the early 1970s, the "Big Red Machine" won four pennants and two World Championships. But following the 1976 season, the Reds dealt Tony Perez, Will McEnaney, and Gary Nolan and lost Don Gullett to free agency. As a result, the club played listlessly in 1977 and ended up 10 games behind the Dodgers.

In 1992–93, San Diego Padres owner Tom Werner held his own fire sale. To reduce the payroll to $13 million, Werner traded (or declined to re-sign) five of the team's top stars (Fred McGriff, Gary Sheffield, Tony Fernandez, Randy Myers, and Benito Santiago). Shortly after accomplishing his goal, Werner sold the team to software tycoon John Moores for $80 million.

The Padres soon were joined by the Montreal Expos. In April 1995, the franchise many believe would have won the 1994 World Series if it had not been cancelled due to a work stoppage went on a selling frenzy. Within one week, the club let go all-stars Ken Hill, John Wetteland, Marquis Grissom, and Larry Walker. By 1996, every key player from the 1994 squad was gone.

Even more dramatic than the meltdown of the Padres and Expos was the break-up of the Florida Marlins in 1997–98. After winning the World Series in record time for an expansion team, owner H. Wayne Huizenga ordered General Manager Dave Dombrowski to cut the payroll in half. Within seven months, more than a dozen players had been discarded, including such stars as Kevin Brown, Al Leiter, Robb Nen, Moises Alou, Gary Sheffield, Devon White, Bobby Bonilla, and Charles Johnson. When the bloodletting finally came to an end, Huizenga promptly sold the club for $158 million to commodities broker John Henry.

For a further look at the history of baseball fire sales, see, e.g., L. Patrick Auld, *Ownership Control Over Professional Sports Teams' Payrolls: Could Anyone Have Stopped Tom Werner From Dismantling the San Diego Padres?*, 12 U. Miami Ent. & Sports L. Rev. 129 (1994/95); Keith Olbermann, *Bad Breaker–Uppers: The World Champion Marlins' Fire Sale is Nothing New to Baseball*, Sports Illustrated, May 25, 1998, at 86; Mike Berardino, *Cashing Out*, Fort Lauderdale Sun–Sentinel, Mar. 29, 1998, at 8 (Sports).

3. Without question, the most celebrated fire sale in baseball history was conducted by Harry M. Frazee, a theatrical impresario who, in 1916, had purchased the Boston Red Sox. Although the team had won the 1918 World Series and was expected to contend for the 1920 crown, in December 1919

Frazee sold Babe Ruth, his best player, to the New York Yankees for $475,000 in cash and credit to finance a Broadway play entitled "No, No, Nanette." During the next three years, Frazee sent third baseman Joe Dugan and pitchers Herb Pennock, Carl Mays, Waite Hoyt, and George Pipgras to the Yankees to help pay for other shows. Today, many Bostonians are convinced the reason the Red Sox have gone eight decades without winning the World Series is because of Frazee's perfidy, which they refer to as the "Curse of the Bambino." *See further* Dan Shaughnessy, *The Curse of the Bambino* (1990).

4. Probably the most famous fire sale outside of baseball is Peter Pocklington's break-up of the Edmonton Oilers after the team won five championships in six years (1984–90). The dismantling began in 1988, when Pocklington, in financial trouble, sold Wayne Gretzky, Canada's national hero, to the Los Angeles Kings for $15 million. *See* Bob Verdi, *Oilers' Owner Deals Himself Into Infamy*, Chi. Trib., Aug. 22, 1988, at 1 (Sports). Within a few years, Pocklington again was in need of money and finished what he had started by shipping off Mark Messier, Grant Fuhr, Jari Kurri, Paul Coffey, and Esa Tikkanen. *See further* Brent Jang, *The Plight of Peter Pocklington*, Toronto Globe & Mail, July 29, 1998, at A1.

5. The likelihood that future commissioners will block fire sales, or take any other kind of decisive action, is remote. Unlike in the past, when commissioners were independent authority figures chosen for their ability to instill public confidence in their leagues, they now are merely puppets of the men and women who employ them. Indeed, when Bud Selig, himself an owner, was chosen as baseball's new commissioner in July 1998 he observed, "A commissioner is not [a] czar sitting above the law . . . a commissioner has a lot of power, but it must be confined to certain areas." *See* Dan Graziano, *Will Ownership Ties Hinder Selig?*, Palm Beach Post, July 9, 1998, at 2C. For a further look at the decline in the status of sports commissioners, see, e.g., Thomas J. Arkell, *National Hockey League Jurisprudence: Past, Present and Future*, 8 Seton Hall J. Sport L. 135 (1998); Gregor Lentze, *The Legal Concept of Professional Sports Leagues: The Commissioner and an Alternative Approach From a Corporate Perspective*, 6 Marq. Sports L.J. 65 (1995); Craig F. Arcella, Note, *Major League Baseball's Disempowered Commissioner: Judicial Ramifications of the 1994 Restructuring*, 97 Colum. L. Rev. 2420 (1997); Michael J. Willisch, Comment, *Protecting the "Owners" of Baseball: A Governance Structure to Maintain the Integrity of the Game and Guard the Principals' Money Investment*, 88 Nw. U. L. Rev. 1619 (1994).

Problem 19

A new league has been formed whose by-laws are silent with respect to whether trades can be disapproved. If one of its commissioners should someday be taken to court for blocking a deal, will she be able to have the suit dismissed on the ground that she has the "inherent power" to do whatever is necessary to preserve competition? *See Professional Sports, Ltd. v. Virginia Squires Basketball Club Limited Partnership*, 373 F.Supp. 946 (W.D.Tex.1974).

5. TRANSFER OF OWNERSHIP

All leagues worry when owners decide to put their teams up for sale. Thus, just as they have promulgated entry conditions, they also have set exit requirements.

MURRAY v. NATIONAL FOOTBALL LEAGUE

1998 WL 205596 (E.D.Pa.1998).

GILES, District Judge.

Francis Murray ("Murray"), a Pennsylvania resident, and FWM Corporation, a Delaware corporation, the stock of which is wholly owned by Murray, allege that Defendants—the National Football League ("NFL") and its 27 member football clubs and two persons sued in their individual capacities (Paul Tagliabue, as NFL Commissioner, and Neil Austrian, as President of the NFL)—have conspired to restrain trade in the market for the purchase and sale of professional football franchises in violation of the Sherman Antitrust Act, 15 U.S.C. §§ 1 and 2 (West 1985 & Supp.1995). Plaintiffs also assert several state law causes of action against Defendants. Considered herein is Defendants' motion for summary judgment. The court has subject matter jurisdiction pursuant to § 4 of the Clayton Act, 15 U.S.C. § 15, and 28 U.S.C. § 1331. Supplemental jurisdiction over Plaintiffs' state law claims is exercised pursuant to 28 U.S.C. § 1367(a). For the reasons which follow, the court grants Defendants' motion for summary judgment in its entirety.

I. FACTUAL BACKGROUND

In 1986, NEP Partners, L.P. obtained an option to purchase the New England Patriots ("Patriots") football club franchise from then owner William Sullivan. Murray owned one hundred percent (100%) of the stock of N.E.P. Corporation which was the controlling partner of NEP Partners, L.P. In December 1986 NEP borrowed $13.5 million from National Westminster ("NatWest") which was, in turn, loaned to Sullivan.

In October 1988 Murray and [Victor] Kiam formed a limited partnership known as KMS Patriots, L.P. ("KMS Patriots") to acquire the Patriots franchise. (Am. Compl. at p 30.) Through FWM Corporation, Murray became a forty-nine percent (49%) general partner in KMS Patriots. Kiam owned the remaining fifty-one percent (51%) divided between two entities wholly owned by him: VKK Corporation (50.5%), as general partner, and VKK Patriots (.5%), as a limited partner. (Id.)

The Murray–Kiam partnership agreement, approved by the NFL, included a "put" clause that entitled Murray to "put" his 49% interest in the Patriots to Kiam on October 10, 1991, in exchange for a $38 million payment. (Am. Compl. at p 31.) Murray asserts that he intended to use the monies received from the "put" to pay off his creditors and to pursue possible NFL club expansion opportunities in St. Louis, Missouri. (Id.)

Murray held a forty percent (40%) interest in a venture seeking to bring an NFL team to St. Louis. (Id.) Murray further asserts that under the "put" agreement, if Kiam failed to pay the "put" price upon demand, Murray would replace Kiam as the sole general partner of KMS Patriots. (Am. Compl. at p 32.) As controlling partner, Murray asserts that he would have taken steps to relocate the Patriots franchise either to St. Louis or to Hartford, Connecticut. According to him, the "put" agreement was essential to the partnership venture. (Am. Compl. at p 31.)

At the time KMS purchased the Patriots, Murray arranged with NatWest to transform its loan to NEP into a loan to FWM. (Murray Dep. at pp. 383–84.) Murray also pledged FWM's ownership interest in KMS as a security for a number of other loans. Also around this time, Murray asserts that he was negotiating simultaneously with his St. Louis partners to move the Patriots to St. Louis or to apply to the NFL for an expansion team for that city. (Am. Compl. at pp 32–34.) In anticipation of operating a professional football franchise in St. Louis, Murray and his partners allegedly secured a stadium lease, lobbied for and obtained enabling legislation, invested personal funds, and organized operating entities there. A similar plan was allegedly developed for Hartford, Connecticut. (Id.)

Murray and James Orthwein ("Orthwein") were partners in the St. Louis venture. (Am. Compl. at p 35.) In July 1990, Orthwein extended a line of credit to Murray taking, as collateral against the loan, a secured interest in Murray's forty-nine percent interest in the Patriots franchise. Orthwein's secured interest, worth approximately $15.5 million (Plaintiffs' Facts at p 6), became secondary to the secured interest held by NatWest (Am. Compl. at p 37). Murray's continued participation in the St. Louis venture, however, required that he first satisfy the Orthwein and NatWest indebtedness.

On July 8, 1991, Murray notified Kiam that he intended to exercise the "put" on October 10, 1991. (Plaintiffs' Ex. 26.) Murray, Kiam, and the NFL then entered into discussions regarding alternatives to Kiam defaulting on the put, including one suggestion which would have required the NFL to fund the "put" for a temporary period. (Plaintiffs' Ex. 10.)

On September 30, 1991, Murray learned that IBJ Schroder Bank had been given a secured interest in Kiam's interest in the Patriots. The IBJ Schroder loan was a "proceeds loan" which meant that the Schroder Bank had an interest in the proceeds that Kiam would receive from a sale of the Patriots. Murray believed that the loan caused Kiam to violate the League's rules regarding debt limits, and notified the NFL to that effect. (Plaintiffs' Ex. 38) The NFL determined, however, that a "proceeds loan" would not count in a debt limit calculation.

At this juncture, Murray was insisting that he was entitled to $38 million or the controlling interest of the Patriots franchise. Orthwein was insisting that he was entitled to payment on the loan to Murray or foreclosure upon Murray's interest in the Patriots franchise. NatWest was insisting that it was entitled to payment on its loan to Murray and that its right was superior to any execution on assets by Orthwein. Also, at this time, Murray's right to participate in the St. Louis venture was canceled because he failed to repay Orthwein and NatWest.

In early October, Kiam made it clear that he would not pay the $38 million "put" by October 10, 1991. Instead, he requested an extension of time to pay the amount demanded while he disputed Murray's contention that he was entitled under the partnership agreement to become sole owner of the Patriots. (Am. Compl. at p 40.) On October 14, Murray and Kiam signed an agreement providing for an extension of the put payment date to November 12, 1991. (Defendants' Tab 24.) The agreement also provided that two NFL representatives would be appointed to the board of VKK. (Id.)

On October 14, 1991, Orthwein informed the NFL that he intended to foreclose on his secured interest in the Patriots franchise if Kiam failed to perform under the "put" agreement. (Am. Compl. at p 42.) The following day, a meeting was held between Austrian, Kiam, Murray and their counsel. At that meeting, Austrian allegedly affirmed to Murray that the NFL would arbitrate his dispute with Kiam.

Notwithstanding the agreed upon extension to the "put" agreement, on November 4, 1991, Murray sent a letter to Commissioner Tagliabue invoking Article 8.3 of the NFL Constitution and Bylaws which thereby certified the dispute for arbitration. (Article 8.3 provides: "The Commissioner shall have full, complete, and final jurisdiction and authority to arbitrate: (a) Any dispute ... involving two or more holders of an ownership interest in a member club of the League, certified to him by any of the disputants.") Moreover, in that letter Murray asked the NFL promptly to declare in writing that Murray should be designated the general partner of the Patriots. (Plaintiffs' Ex. 35.) Later that same day, NFL counsel Jay Moyer ("Moyer") wrote back to Murray, stating:

> You have long been aware of the arbitration provisions in the NFL's Constitution and Bylaws. In requesting arbitration, you have invoked a process that normally includes notice to the other side, and an opportunity for it to respond; scheduling and holding a hearing at which both sides can present witnesses, or at least legal arguments; reviewing the hearing record; and reaching and formulating a reasoned decision. Compressing the entire arbitration process into this week, as you have requested, would be next to impossible, unless a mutually acceptable truncated procedure can be devised and completed within that time frame.

(Defendants' Tab 26.)

On November 11, 1991, a proposed agreement between Kiam, Murray and NFL negotiators was drafted which included the following: (1) an extension of the put deadline to May 1992; (2) maintenance of the two NFL representatives on the Board of VKK; (3) retention of an investment banker to sell the Patriots; (4) a guarantee by the NFL that, in the event that the team could not be sold for a higher price, the NFL would buy the club for $90 million; and (5) a promise by Kiam to cause the Patriots to vote for St. Louis when the expansion decision was made. (Defendants' Tab 48.) Although Kiam and Murray signed the document, the NFL did not. (Id.) According to Moyer, the NFL did not sign because upon reflection it considered the provision requiring the Patriots to vote for a St. Louis franchise to be an improper condition, one in which the NFL should not be involved. (Moyer Dep. at p. 248.)

On November 12, 1991, NatWest sued Murray, VKK Corporation and Kiam in New York to collect on its loan to Murray, thus placing more pressure on Murray.

Negotiations continued. On November 22, 1991, the NFL negotiators sent an alternative draft agreement to Murray and Kiam which excluded the provision requiring Kiam to support a St. Louis franchise expansion but which did provide that if no buyer could be found who would pay more that $90 million and keep the Patriots in New England, then the NFL would buy the Patriots for $90 million. (Plaintiffs' Ex. 29.) This proposal was to have been presented to the NFL's Finance Committee meeting on December 17, 1991. (Id.)

In a December 10, 1991, letter from Neil Austrian to Kiam, Kiam and Murray were invited to address the December 17, 1991, Finance Committee meeting to discuss the possibility of an NFL buy out. The letter, in part, stated, "Both you and Fran should be prepared to attend with, hopefully, a written plan for the Committee to review and act upon."

It is unclear what resulted from the Finance Committee meeting. There is some indication that the Committee approved the NFL's draft agreement to buy the Patriots. (See Benson Dep. 38–41; February 26, 1992, Boston Globe article Plaintiffs' Ex. 43.) Murray concluded, however, that nothing happened at the meeting and that he does not remember "coming away with anything." (Murray Dep. at p. 162.) In any event, no purchase agreement was ever signed by the NFL.

Following the Finance Committee meeting, Moyer sent a letter to Kiam and Murray stating that arbitration would go forward if Murray still wished as much, and that opening briefs were to be filed not later than January 3, 1992, replies by January 15, 1992, and a hearing would be held at a "subsequent date to be determined." (Defendants' Tab 31.)

By letter of December 26, 1991, Kiam's lawyers objected to the schedule set out by the NFL. Kiam took the position that Murray's arbitration request had been mooted by the November 11, 1991, agreement. By letter of December 30, 1991, Murray's lawyer responded that arbitration was still necessary because the November 11 agreement had never been agreed upon by the NFL. In the letter, Plaintiffs' counsel also highlighted the need for an "expeditious" end to this dispute:

> The parties and the League have known of this issue since October 1988 when the agreements were signed and have worked with them intensely since at least Mr. Murray's letter on July 8, 1991. VKK Corp. and Kiam have known of the request for arbitration for almost two months and have had more than adequate opportunity to prepare any necessary presentation. In light of the parties' long history and familiarity with this issue, the fifteen day time period provided by your December 19 letter for submission of initial memoranda is fair and reasonable. Additionally, resort to the arbitration process will not prevent the parties from continuing to negotiate, if they choose to do so. Any further delay will severely prejudice Mr. Murray and FWM Corporation and will cause them further loss and harm, including with their creditors. The time is long past where FWM Corporation and Mr. Murray can tolerate any further delays without a final resolution. We therefore request that the arbitration proceed as scheduled.

(Defendants' Tab 33.)

On January 3, 1992, Kiam and Murray submitted their opening briefs. Thereafter, several extensions were requested by Kiam, unopposed by Murray's attorney, William Sullivan, and agreed to by the NFL. Joint written requests by Kiam and Murray for extensions were submitted on January 21, January 30, February 7, February 13, February 19, and February 28. (Defendants' Tabs 73–79.) Neither party, however, filed a reply brief. No arbitration hearing date was scheduled.

On March 13, 1992, Murray contends that Orthwein asked him to attend an owners' meeting to persuade Kiam to sell his interest in the Patriots to Orthwein. (Am. Compl. at p 48.) For securing Kiam's agreement, Orthwein allegedly promised Murray that his interests in the Patriots and the St. Louis venture would be preserved. (Id.) Relying on that promise, Murray went to the owners' meeting and secured Kiam's agreement to sell his interest in the Patriots to Orthwein. Murray agreed to pay Kiam $1 million (over three years) in consideration for Kiam's promise. (Am. Compl. at p 49.)

On March 16, 1992, Orthwein purchased NatWest's loan to Murray and assumed control of the NatWest litigation. By reason of that purchase Orthwein then held the first secured interest in Murray's interest in the Patriots. (Am. Compl. at p 50.)

On March 17, 1992, allegedly at Orthwein's suggestion, Murray filed suit against Kiam in the Chancery Court for the State of Delaware seeking an adjudication of his right of control of the Patriots under the "put" agreement, together with injunctive relief. (Am. Compl. at p 51.) On April 27, 1992, the Chancery Court stayed the action believing that the issues raised by Murray were pending in the NatWest litigation. Murray contends that Orthwein refused his request to withdraw the NatWest litigation so that the Chancery Court action could proceed. Instead, Orthwein allegedly demanded Murray's interest in the Patriots pursuant to their loan agreement and threatened to obtain Murray's St. Louis interests as well. (Am. Compl. at p 52.)

On May 11, 1992, Murray and Orthwein settled their dispute by agreeing in writing that Orthwein would succeed to Murray's (49%) interest in the Patriots franchise. (Id.)

In 1993, after Murray no longer had an interest in the Patriots, Murray conceived the idea of persuading Connecticut officials to approve the funding of a new stadium in Hartford that could be the home venue for the Patriots. (Plaintiffs' Facts at p 48.) He discussed this idea with NFL officials and forwarded a series of proposals to Orthwein suggesting that the Patriots move to Hartford. (Id.) Nothing came of this. Murray admits that the events at issue in 1991–1992 were not affected by Murray's Hartford proposal. (Plaintiffs' Facts at p 49.)

In addition, Murray claims that as part of his plan to move the Patriots and/or to win a franchise team in St. Louis, he intended to fund those activities by using Contractually Obligated Income "COI Financing," under which certain revenues normally earned by a team in the course of the presentation of its games would be paid instead to Murray, who theoretically would borrow money secured by the future stream of such revenues. (See Plaintiffs' Facts at pp 50–51.) Murray asserts that any COI prohibition injures competition because that would exclude from the market for ownership and control interests in NFL franchises competitors who seek to use innovative means of financing. (Plaintiffs' Facts at pp 50–51.) There is no expressed NFL policy prohibiting COI financing.

On September 30, 1994, Plaintiffs filed the instant suit. In a Memorandum and Order dated June 26, 1998, this court dismissed Count 1 of the complaint regarding the NFL's relocation policy, and granted individual Defendant Norman Braman's Motion for Summary Judgment, and Individual Defendant James Orthwein's Motion to Dismiss. In that same Order, however, the court declined to grant Defendants' motion to dismiss pertaining to the NFL's financing and arbitration policies, Plaintiffs' § 2 claim, and declined to dismiss Tagliabue and Austrian in their individual capacities. Consequently, pending before the court is Defendants' Motion for Summary Judgment as to NFL's policies regarding arbitration, financing, the claim that the NFL is a monopoly in violation of § 2 of the Sherman Act, and the state law claims.

II. SECTION 1 CLAIMS

The gist of Plaintiffs' remaining claims is that the Defendants conspired in violation of § 1 of the Sherman Antitrust Act, 15 U.S.C. § 1, to restrain trade in the market for the sale and purchase of ownership interests in professional football franchises by adopting and employing anti-competitive policies regarding team financing and dispute resolution.

Section 1 provides in relevant part,

> Every contract, combination in the form of trust or otherwise, or conspiracy, in restraint of trade or commerce among the several States, or within foreign nations, is declared to be illegal.

15 U.S.C. § 1 (West 1973 & Supp.1995).

To defeat a motion for summary judgment in a § 1 case, a plaintiff must present evidence of (1) concerted action by the defendants; (2) that was designed to achieve an unlawful objective; (3) and that produced injury to competition within the relevant product and geographic markets; and (4) injured plaintiff as a proximate result of the concerted actions. Petruzzi's IGA Supermarkets, Inc. v. Darling–Delaware Co., Inc., 998 F.2d 1224, 1229 (3d Cir.1993) (citations omitted).

A. Arbitration

As to the arbitration issue, Defendants argue that Plaintiffs have failed to show evidence for each of the factors required in a § 1 case. Plaintiffs, on the other hand, assert that they have presented sufficient evidence to allow their § 1 claim to go to the jury. Specifically, Plaintiffs assert that the facts show that "Murray was entitled to control of the Patriots, defendants used NFL arbitration policies and procedures to deny him that control, and they did so to prevent Murray from moving the Patriots and challenging the relocation policy." (Plaintiffs' Memo. in Opposition to Defendants' Motion for Summary Judgment "Plaintiffs' Memo." p. 32.)

In addressing the Plaintiffs' challenge of the NFL's arbitration policy, a step by step analysis of the factors required for a § 1 claim is not necessary since the court hereby finds that the "injury to competition" requirement is not met. Accordingly, summary judgment must be granted against Plaintiffs on this issue. See Brunswick Corp. v. Pueblo Bowl–O–Mat, Inc., 429 U.S. 477, 488, 97 S.Ct. 690, 50 L.Ed.2d 701 (1977) (reversing a jury finding for plaintiffs because defendants had not shown anti-competitive effects on the affected industry).

Plaintiffs attempt unsuccessfully to show injury to competition by arguing that arbitration as used by the NFL violates the "essential facilities" doctrine. Satisfaction of the essential facilities doctrine may establish per se liability under § 1. See Hecht v. Pro–Football Inc., 570 F.2d 982, 992–93 (D.C.Cir.1977). Precluding access to a market, without question, will affect competition within the market. Id.

The essential facilities doctrine requires proof of "(1) control of the essential facility by a monopolist; (2) the competitor's inability practically or reasonably to duplicate the essential facility; (3) denial of the use of the facility to a competitor; and (4) the feasibility of providing the facility." See Ideal Dairy Farms, Inc. v. John Labatt, Ltd., 90 F.3d 737, 748 (3d Cir.1996) (citations omitted).

Plaintiffs allege that the NFL and its member teams use the compulsory arbitration policy to restrain trade in the market for the sale of ownership interests in professional football franchises. Furthermore,

Plaintiffs assert that by reason of the compulsory arbitration provision, the NFL effectively denies certain competitors access to the courts to resolve disagreements regarding ownership issues. (Am. Compl. at p 66(b).) Also, Plaintiffs allege that the NFL's failure to hold the requested arbitration hearing and declare Plaintiffs' entitlement was deliberate and designed to prevent Plaintiffs from being named sole owners of the Patriots.

Plaintiffs' evidence and arguments fail to support an essential facilities claim. The evidence shows that they were not denied arbitration by the NFL. While Murray argues that the arbitration was never scheduled for a date certain, he ignores the fact that he failed to comply with an agreed upon prerequisite to the hearing being scheduled and held. Kiam and Murray agreed that each would file reply briefs to the other's opening written salvo, then agreed upon continuances of this mutual obligation while they continued to engage in negotiations to resolve their disputes. Neither filed a reply brief, and they never agreed not to do so. A hearing was never scheduled.

It is undisputed that the following occurred. On November 4, 1991, Murray certified the dispute to the NFL for arbitration and requested an expedited proceeding. In a letter dated November 6, 1991, Kiam informed the NFL that he had defenses to Murray's claims regarding the put agreement. The NFL established a briefing schedule on December 19, 1991, which allowed for initial briefs to be submitted on January 3, 1992, reply submissions by January 15, 1992, and a hearing to be "held at a subsequent date to be determined." (Defendants' Tab 31.) This schedule was deemed "fair and reasonable" by Murray's representative. (Defendants' Tab 33.) Plaintiffs argue that they did not object to the schedule since under the NFL rules the Commissioner acted as the "judge and jury," and they, therefore, did not want to antagonize him. (Plaintiffs' Facts p. 16; Sullivan Dep. at 139–40.)

In early January, Murray and Kiam did submit initial briefs. Thereafter, negotiations continued between Murray, Kiam, their individual creditors and the NFL. Kiam's representative requested numerous extensions in the due date for response submissions. It is undisputed that Plaintiffs' representative did not object to these requests. (Sullivan Dep. at 117–126; Plaintiffs' Tabs 73–79.) It is also undisputed that no response briefs were filed.

Because Plaintiffs failed to perform a triggering task for the arbitration scheduling agreed upon, a rational jury could not find that Plaintiffs were denied arbitration by actions of the NFL as opposed to their own inaction. Thus, because Plaintiffs have failed to present evidence to support their claim that the "essential facilities doctrine" is applicable to this case, they have, therefore, failed to show "injury to competition." As to that claim, summary judgment must be granted.

B. Public Financing

As with Plaintiffs' challenge to the NFL's arbitration policies, their claims against the NFL's restriction on public financing fail at least one prong of the § 1 Sherman Antitrust Act test, and must also be denied.

Plaintiffs bear the burden of showing causation. Defendants' alleged unlawful conduct must be shown to be a material cause of injury to Plaintiffs' business or property. Zenith Radio Corp. v. Hazeltine Research, Inc., 395 U.S. 100, 114 n. 9, 89 S.Ct. 1562, 23 L.Ed.2d 129 (1969).

Plaintiffs argue that the NFL's policy against public financing prevented them from attempting to proceed with a public financing plan. This argument, however, ignores the holding of Out Front Productions, Inc. v. Magid, which holds that a plaintiff who claims that a defendant prevented him from entering into business "must show not only that it had the background, experience, and financial ability to make a viable entrance, but even more important, that it took affirmative actions to pursue the new line of business." 748 F.2d 166, 170 (3d Cir.1984) (citations omitted). Here, Plaintiffs have presented no evidence to support contentions that a public offering would have been viable, and they have presented no evidence to show that they actually developed concrete plans to pursue public ownership or that they took affirmative steps to implement such a plan. Finally, Plaintiffs have not alleged, and have not shown, that they ever sought NFL approval of any public ownership proposal.

Therefore, since no reasonable jury could find that the NFL's public financing policy caused Plaintiffs an antitrust injury, Defendants are entitled to summary judgment on the claim. See id.

III. Violation of § 2 of the Sherman Antitrust Act

Defendants move for summary judgment on Plaintiffs' claim that they have monopolized the market for professional football by adopting anti-competitive policies and by denying Plaintiffs the essential facility of compulsory arbitration. (Am. Compl. at pp 69–73.)

To withstand summary judgment on this claim, Plaintiffs must offer evidence that under § 2 of the Sherman Antitrust Act, 15 U.S.C. § 2, Defendants have (1) possession of monopoly power in the relevant market and (2) the willful acquisition or maintenance of that power in an exclusionary manner. [United States v.] Grinnell Corp., 384 U.S. [563,] at 570–71 [1966]; Fineman v. Armstrong World Indus., Inc., 980 F.2d 171, 197 (3d Cir.1992).

Section 2 sanctions "[e]very person who shall monopolize, or attempt to monopolize, or combine or conspire with any person or persons, to monopolize any part of the trade or commerce among the several States,...." 15 U.S.C. § 2 (West & Supp 1995).

Monopoly power is the power to control prices or to exclude competition. United States v. E.I. du Pont de Nemours & Co., 351 U.S. 377, 76 S.Ct. 994, 100 L.Ed. 1264 (1956). It is the power "to force a purchaser to do something that [the purchaser] would not do in a competitive market." Eastman Kodak Co. v. Image Technical Serv., Inc., 504 U.S. 451, 464, 112 S.Ct. 2072, 119 L.Ed.2d 265 (1992) (citations omitted). The size of a defendant's market share "is a significant determinant of whether the defendant has a dangerous probability of successfully monopolizing the relevant market...." Barr Laboratories, [Inc. v. Abbott Laboratories, 978 F.2d 98, 112 (3d Cir. 1992)].

Central to assessing Plaintiff's monopolization claim is the determination of the relevant product and geographic markets. The burden to define those markets rests with Plaintiffs. Spectrum Sports, Inc. v. McQuillan, 506 U.S. 447, 456, 113 S.Ct. 884, 122 L.Ed.2d 247 (1993). Here, Plaintiffs assert that the relevant product market is the market for the sale and purchase of ownership interests in a professional football franchise. The relevant geographic market has been labeled as the nationwide market for NFL football franchises, generally, and particularly, the metropolitan areas of Boston, Hartford and St. Louis. (Am. Compl. at pp 61–63.)

Plaintiffs allege that the Defendants combined and conspired "to eliminate competitors with access to public financing and other sources of investment capital, including Plaintiffs, from the market for the sale and purchase of ownership interests in NFL professional football franchises, and to create and maintain a monopoly in the ownership of such franchises." (Am. Compl. at p 65.)

Plaintiffs further allege that Defendants have attempted to establish and maintain that monopoly by creating and enforcing policies designed to prevent prospective owners (1) from seeking judicial enforcement of their rights; (2) by selectively enforcing the NFL debt limit rule to the detriment of competitors in the market; (3) by prohibiting the use of public funds and stadium lease revenue to purchase ownership interests in teams; (4) by aiding and abetting certain purchasers to the exclusion of others; and (5) by the NFL making its own offer to purchase a franchise rather than to declare the rights of existing owners. (Am. Compl. at pp 66(a)-(k).) Defendants have allegedly taken these actions to protect present franchise owners from competing with large public or corporate conglomerates, (id. at pp 61), and to protect revenue sharing among the teams derived from expansion franchises and television revenue, (id. at pp 66(k).)

Defendants do not contest that the NFL operates as a monopoly. In fact, the NFL concedes, accepting Plaintiffs' market definition as the market for ownership and control interests in NFL clubs, "the members of the NFL have a 'monopoly' by definition, not as a result of any act by defendants to 'create' or 'maintain' it." (Defendants' Reply Memo. at p. 20.)

As with their § 1 claims, Plaintiffs have failed to offer evidence which supports their contention that the NFL's policies have caused injury to competition by unlawful monopolization. Plaintiffs argue that Defendants used the NFL arbitration policy to exclude all competitors who sought control of the Patriots with any intention of moving the team and that it employed other policies to exclude competitors who attempted to use innovative financing methods such as Contractually Obligated Income ("COI").

Again, since the court has found that the Plaintiffs were not denied arbitration, they cannot prove that the NFL's arbitration policies were used to injure competition. Plaintiffs have not put forth any other alleged examples of the NFL's arbitration policy being used to exclude potential team purchasers. Plaintiffs have merely argued that the NFL might delay arbitration so that justice delayed might become justice denied.

Plaintiffs allegedly developed COI for the proposed St. Louis and Hartford franchises. Plaintiffs admit that they never submitted a definite proposal to the NFL for permission to use this kind of financing for a franchise opportunity. What the NFL would actually have done had Plaintiffs made a proposal to use COI is speculative at best. Consequently, there is no competent evidence to support Plaintiffs' theory that the NFL caused injury to competition because of an alleged bias against innovative financing techniques.

Thus, because Plaintiffs have failed to put forth evidence on injury to competition as required by § 2 of the Sherman Antitrust Act, Count II must be dismissed as a matter of law.

[Similarly, s]ince the court has found no antitrust conspiracy in the actions alleged, there is no basis for the individual liability of Tagliabue and Austrian. Consequently, summary judgment is entered on those claims.

IV. State Law Claims

Defendants also move for summary judgment on Plaintiffs' state law claims for Conspiracy (Count III), Bad Faith Breach of Contract (Count IV), Breach of Fiduciary Duty (Count V), Intentional Interference with Prospective Advantage (Count VI), and Fraud (Count VII). Although the court has granted summary judgment on all of Plaintiffs' remaining federal claims, the court may still maintain jurisdiction pursuant to 28 U.S.C. § 1367(a).

As a threshold matter, Defendants argue that Plaintiffs released Defendants from all past or future liability. Their argument as to this point is that when Murray became an owner of the Patriots in October 1988, he agreed to be bound by the NFL Constitution and By–Laws, which contain a general release clause to the effect that all owners, officers and stockholders of the Patriots agree to release and indemnify the NFL, its employees, and its member teams against all claims for actions which they may have taken or not taken in their official capacities with the NFL. See NFL Constitution and By–Laws § 3.11(c). Defendants argue further that this release clause was agreed upon by Murray in exchange for the valuable consideration of the right to own an NFL member team, and thus should be enforced.

In opposition, Plaintiffs argue four points: that 1) this sort of release cannot protect a party from liability for harm that it has caused intentionally; 2) Defendants have failed to meet their burden of proving the existence of a release which governs the subject matter of the instant lawsuit; 3) the release fails for Defendants' fraud in its inducement; and 4) the alleged release is void for a lack of consideration.

The court agrees that Plaintiffs' state law claims allege intentional torts. Therefore, a general release is not enforceable and Defendants' release must fail. See Farnsworth on Contracts, § 5.2 at 14; 76 C.J.S. Release, § 63 ("intentional torts are outside the scope of a valid release"). The court now examines each state law claim separately.

A. Common Law Conspiracy

Defendants allege that there was a "common law conspiracy" among Defendants to keep the Patriots in New England so that shared television revenues would not be diminished due to the lack of a professional football team in the metropolitan Boston area. Plaintiffs' common law conspiracy claim, however, cannot survive now that summary judgment has been entered on the underlying substantive claims. See Rosen v. Tesoro Petroleum Corp., 399 Pa.Super. 226, 582 A.2d 27, 33 (Pa.Super.Ct.1990) ("[A] claim for civil conspiracy must fail, due to the absence of a valid claim for the underlying tortious acts...."). At the core of the conspiracy claim is that there was a denial of arbitration by the NFL. As that claim goes, so does the civil conspiracy claim. Summary judgment is, therefore, entered on Plaintiffs' common law conspiracy claim.

B. Intentional Interference with Prospective Advantage

Plaintiffs claim that Defendants interfered with their "ability to obtain ownership of an NFL professional football franchise in Boston, Massachusetts; St. Louis, Missouri; and/or Hartford, Connecticut." (Am. Compl. at p 87.) Under Pennsylvania law, to have a valid claim for this tort a plaintiff must prove (1) a purpose or intent to harm plaintiffs by preventing the prospective contractual relationship from occurring and (2) actual damage resulting from the defendant's conduct. See Thompson Coal Co. v. Pike Coal Co., 488 Pa. 198, 412 A.2d 466, 471 (Pa.1979) (citations omitted). Because this court has found that Plaintiffs cannot prove that the NFL caused their alleged injuries, it follows that Plaintiffs cannot maintain a suit for intentional interference with prospective advantage.

C. Breach of Fiduciary Duty and Bad Faith Breach of Contract

Plaintiffs allege that the Defendants by applying their policies on expansion, relocation, public ownership, and arbitration, "breached their good faith contractual obligation to Plaintiffs to adhere to and follow the NFL Constitution, Rules, and Bylaws," (Am. Compl. at p 79), and, further, that Defendants breached their fiduciary duties to Plaintiffs in "failing to adhere to and follow the NFL Constitution, Rules and Bylaws with respect to their treatment of Plaintiffs," (Am. Compl. p 84). Plaintiffs claim that Defendants manifested bad faith through application of the arbitration and relocation policies.

As to the NFL's arbitration policy, the court reiterates its findings that Plaintiffs cannot show as a matter of law that they were denied arbitration.

As to Plaintiffs' claim that the NFL displayed bad faith in refusing to allow them to relocate the Patriots, this cause of action is invalid as a matter of law. It is undisputed that Plaintiffs never had control over the Patriots so they could not relocate the Patriots. Therefore, it is impossible for the NFL to have applied its relocation policies against Plaintiffs in bad faith.

Plaintiffs also allege that Defendants manifested bad faith in ignoring their contractual obligations, that is, by permitting Kiam to violate the NFL debt limits, and by making their own offer to acquire the Patriots rather than permit Plaintiffs to obtain control, and by aiding and abetting Orthwein's acquisition of the team. These arguments also presuppose that Plaintiffs controlled the Patriots. This right of control was to be determined through arbitration. Since Plaintiffs were not denied arbitration, these claims fail.

D. *Fraud*

Plaintiffs allege that "Defendants made misleading representations and statements to Plaintiffs and their representatives regarding the NFL's intention to intervene, arbitrate and resolve the dispute between Plaintiffs and Kiam and VKK...." To prove fraud, a plaintiff must show clear and convincing evidence of "(1) a misrepresentation, (2) a fraudulent utterance thereof, (3) an intention by the maker that the recipient will thereby be induced to act, (3) justifiable reliance by the recipient on a misrepresentation, and (4) damage to the recipient as the proximate result." See e.g., Delahanty v. First Pennsylvania Bank, 318 Pa.Super. 90, 464 A.2d 1243, 1252 (Pa.Super.Ct.1983).

Again, the core of Plaintiffs' fraud claim is that Defendants fraudulently promised to arbitrate the Murray–Kiam dispute. Since Plaintiffs never submitted the reply brief, there was no obligation on the part of the NFL to schedule an arbitration. Hence, there could not have been fraud by the NFL in not scheduling an arbitration hearing. Defendants are, therefore, entitled to summary judgment on this claim.

An appropriate order follows.

ORDER

AND NOW, upon consideration of Defendants' motion for summary judgment and responses thereto, it is hereby ORDERED that the motion is GRANTED. Judgment is hereby entered in favor of Defendants and against Plaintiffs.

Notes

1. Neither the financial difficulties experienced by the Patriots, nor the NFL's offer to take over the team, are without precedent. In 1975, for example, the WFL required each of its members to make a financial contribution to keep the Portland Thunder in business. In that same year, the NHL seized the Pittsburgh Penguins and later found a buyer for the bankrupt club. In 1984, the USFL assumed control of the ailing Chicago Blitz after creditors threatened to shut down the franchise. And in 1998, the

NHL offered to loan the Penguins, who again found themselves in bankruptcy, $18.5 million.

2. In the end, everyone associated with the Patriots made money except Francis Murray: Billy Sullivan Jr. sold the club in 1988 to Victor Kiam for $85 million and then filed suit against the NFL for its refusal to permit stock in the Patriots to be marketed to the public; Victor Kiam, having lost $30 million during his brief (1988–92) tenure as owner, currently has pending a $450 million lawsuit against the league for denying him permission to move to the various cities that had courted him (Baltimore, Jacksonville, and San Antonio); James B. Orthwein, who paid Kiam $100 million for the franchise in 1992, got $168 million when he sold it in 1993; Robert Kraft, the industrialist who purchased the club from Orthwein, got a $375 million offer from the Connecticut legislature in 1998 to relocate to Hartford, the richest such deal in football history; and the NFL, without ever paying a penny, got a wealthy owner in New England (Kraft is a billionaire and Hartford is a mere two hours from Foxboro), returned to St. Louis (via the relocation of the Rams), and now has the opportunity to pit Houston against Los Angeles for the next expansion team, which is expected to sell for approximately $500 million. *See further* Will McDonough, *Would-Be Patriot Owner Murray Loses Out Again*, Boston Globe, May 8, 1998, at D1.

3. As noted above, Billy Sullivan sued the NFL for prohibiting him from solving his financial problems by selling stock in the Patriots to the public (he had planned to offer 49% of the club). Although all four major professional sports leagues have policies that discourage public ownership, the NFL is the only one to ban the practice outright (a special rule, dating back to 1950, exempts the Green Bay Packers and its 110,000 shareholders). After years of litigation, including two trials (the first awarded Sullivan $51 million but was overturned on appeal and the second ended in a hung jury), the NFL settled the case in 1996 for $11.5 million. Of course, Francis Murray made the same claim against the NFL but was unable to show he had taken any concrete steps toward conducting an offering.

In the future, public stock ownership of sports teams is expected to become increasingly common. In November 1996, the Florida Panthers went public and raised $159.2 million, thereby whetting the appetites of many other franchises (including, most notably, the Calgary Flames, Cleveland Indians, Montreal Expos, and Pittsburgh Pirates). A short time later, in February 1997, a bill was introduced in Congress proposing to strip sports leagues that prohibit public ownership of their antitrust exemptions. *See* Give Fans a Chance Act of 1997, H.R. 590, 105th Cong. (1997) (Rep. Blumenauer). Next, in September 1997, MLB passed a rule allowing clubs to sell up to 10% of their voting shares to the public. Finally, in October 1998, the NFL announced plans to sell 600 million certificates to the public secured by the income from its new $17.6 billion television contract. A subsequent downturn in the stock market, however, forced the league to temporarily shelve its plan. For a further look at sports teams and public ownership, see Drew D. Krause, Comment, *The National Football League's Ban on Corporate Ownership: Violating Antitrust to Preserve Traditional Ownership—Implications Arising From William H. Sullivan's Antitrust Suit*, 2 Seton Hall J. Sport L. 175 (1992); *NFL Owners Debate Pros and Cons of Corporate Ownership*, L.A. Times, Aug. 30, 1998, at C3; Steven Kutz & Gregg Wirth, *Catching the Fever: Wall Street is Becoming an Increasingly Ardent Fan of Pro Sports Financing*, Investment Dealers' Dig., Jan. 5, 1998, at 12.

4. Whether privately or to the public, teams are sold for many different reasons, including profit-taking, capital generation, internal disagreements, lack of a suitable successor, death, divorce, and bankruptcy. A number of clubs also have changed hands, or come close to doing so, because of inheritance taxes, including the Chicago Bears, Cincinnati Bengals, Indianapolis Colts, Kansas City Chiefs, Los Angeles Dodgers, Miami Dolphins, and Oakland Athletics. *See further* Sandra Block, *Many Families Forced to Sell Teams*, USA Today, July 25, 1997, at 4B, and W.D. Murray, *Death and Taxes Tough to Handle for Team Owners*, Rocky Mtn. News, June 1, 1997, at 26C. *See also* Myreon S. Hodur, Note, *Ball Four: The IRS Walks the Kansas City Royals*, 19 Hastings Comm. & Ent. L.J. 483 (1997) (describing the innovative approach used by Ewing Kauffman to avoid such taxes).

5. In addition to inheritance taxes, a change in a team's ownership can trigger other tax issues, including, most importantly, the question of how much of the sales price can be allocated to player contracts. Because such contracts are considered intangible assets, and therefore can be amortized rapidly, new owners regularly take highly aggressive positions and, as a result, often end up in court battles with the IRS. *See further P.D.B. Sports, Ltd. v. Commissioner*, 109 T.C. 423 (1997), and Stephen A. Zorn, *"Couldna Done It Without the Players:" Depreciation of Professional Sports Players Contracts Under the Internal Revenue Code*, 4 Seton Hall J. Sport L. 337 (1994).

6. Interestingly, leagues never force owners who commit illegal, immoral, or unethical acts to sell their franchises. When George Steinbrenner pleaded guilty to making unlawful contributions to President Richard Nixon's re-election campaign, for example, he was suspended by MLB for 16 months but allowed to keep the New York Yankees. When Marge Schott uttered racially- and ethnically-offensive remarks, she was twice suspended by MLB but permitted to remain the owner of the Cincinnati Reds (eventually, however, her partners forced her out). When Seattle Seahawks owner Ken Behring was accused of sexual harassment by his longtime secretary (a claim he later paid to have dropped), the NFL took no action against him. When San Francisco 49ers owner Eddie DeBartolo Jr. was indicted for paying $400,000 in bribes to secure a Louisiana riverboat gambling license (a charge to which ultimately he pled guilty), he was granted permission by the NFL to temporarily transfer the team to his sister Denise while he worked out his legal problems. And when Harold Ballard, the owner of the Toronto Maple Leafs, was found guilty on 47 counts of fraud and theft and incarcerated for a year, the NHL allowed him to run the club from a public phone in the visitors' room of the prison. *See further* Dave Caldwell, *Calling the Shots: Owners Can Play By Their Own Rules*, Dallas Morning News, May 26, 1996, at 1B.

7. For a further look at the legal headaches that can arise when an owner seeks to sell his or her franchise, see, e.g., *Giuffre Organization, Ltd. v. Euromotorsport Racing, Inc.*, 141 F.3d 1216 (7th Cir.1998); *National*

Basketball Ass'n v. Minnesota Professional Basketball, Limited Partnership, 56 F.3d 866 (8th Cir.1995); *Professional Hockey Corp. v. World Hockey Ass'n*, 191 Cal.Rptr. 773 (Ct.App.1983).

Problem 20

When an owner placed his team on inactive status due to financial difficulties, the league informed him it planned to seek a buyer for the club and would operate it in the interim. In response, the owner threatened to take legal action. If the dispute ultimately winds up in court, what is the most likely outcome? *See American Indoor Soccer Ass'n v. Capital District Sports & Entertainment, Inc.*, 1993 U.S. Dist. LEXIS 20914 (N.D.Ohio 1993), *aff'd mem.*, 64 F.3d 662 (6th Cir.1995).

D. COMPETITORS

So far, we have examined how leagues deal with internal discord. We now turn to the issue of external competition. As will be seen, this type of conflict has led to even more contentious litigation.

1. RIVAL LEAGUES

Eventually, every successful league breeds a challenger. The law looks with favor on such efforts, believing the public is better served when it has choices.

UNITED STATES FOOTBALL LEAGUE v. NATIONAL FOOTBALL LEAGUE

842 F.2d 1335 (2d Cir.1988).

WINTER, Circuit Judge.

This appeal follows a highly publicized trial and jury verdict of $1.00. The plaintiff is a now-defunct professional football league that began play in this decade; the defendant is a football league founded nearly seventy years ago. The older of the two leagues, the National Football League, is a highly successful entertainment product. So many Americans watched NFL games between 1982 and 1986 that its twenty-eight teams shared $2.1 billion in rights fees from the three major television networks, and perhaps as much as $1 billion in gate receipts. The newer league, the United States Football League, began play in March 1983 with twelve teams and network and cable television contracts with the American Broadcasting Company ("ABC") and the Entertainment and Sports Programming Network ("ESPN"). After three seasons and losses in the neighborhood of $200 million, the USFL played its last game in July 1985. Meanwhile, in October, 1984, blaming its older competitor for its difficulties, the USFL instituted this litigation. Plans to play in the fall of 1986 were abandoned after the jury's verdict that is the principal subject of this appeal.

The USFL and certain of its member clubs brought this suit in the Southern District of New York against the NFL, its commissioner, Alvin

R. "Pete" Rozelle, and twenty-seven of its twenty-eight member clubs. Seeking damages of $1.701 billion and appropriate injunctive relief, the USFL alleged that the NFL violated Sections 1 and 2 of the Sherman Anti–Trust Act, 15 U.S.C. §§ 1 and 2 (1982), and the common law. Forty-eight days of trial before Judge Leisure produced a trial transcript of nearly 7100 pages and thousands of additional pages in exhibits.

After five days of deliberations, the jury found that the NFL had willfully acquired or maintained monopoly power in a market consisting of major-league professional football in the United States. The jury also found that the NFL's unlawful monopolization of professional football had injured the USFL. The jury awarded the USFL only $1.00 in damages, however, an amount that, even when trebled, was no consolation for the USFL.

The jury rejected the remainder of the USFL's claims. It found that the NFL had neither monopolized a relevant television submarket nor attempted to do so; that the NFL did not commit any overt act in furtherance of a conspiracy to monopolize; that the NFL did not engage in a conspiracy in restraint of trade; that the NFL's television contracts were not unreasonable restraints of trade; that the NFL did not control access to the three major television networks; and that the NFL did not interfere either with the USFL's ability to obtain a fall television contract or with its spring television contracts. The USFL's common law claims were also rejected.

Judge Leisure denied the USFL's motions for judgment notwithstanding the verdict on its claims of monopolization of the television submarket, attempted monopolization, unreasonable restraint of trade by means of the network television contracts and essential facilities, and for a new trial on damages on the monopolization of professional football claim, or in the alternative for a new trial. United States Football League v. National Football League, 644 F.Supp. 1040 (S.D.N.Y.1986) ("Opinion No. 16"). The district court also denied the USFL's request for injunctive relief.

On this appeal, the USFL claims that a "litany of erroneous opinions, rulings and instructions" by Judge Leisure resulted in a "verdict of confusion" that "sent one of the most egregious violators in the history of the federal antitrust laws on its way with a pat on the back." USFL Br. at 3–4. Specificially, the USFL contends that the NFL could not legally enter into a pooled-rights agreement with all three networks; that Judge Leisure's jury instructions "destroyed" the effectiveness of the USFL's proof of its television claims and set improperly high standards of liability; that he improperly allowed the NFL to introduce evidence that the USFL was mismanaged; that he excluded other evidence critical to establishing the USFL's claims; and that his incorrect rulings and instructions on damages prevented the USFL from receiving appropriate relief. We affirm.

Summary

We briefly summarize our principal rulings. The jury's finding of illegal monopolization of a market of major-league professional football was based upon evidence of NFL attempts to co-opt USFL owners, an NFL Supplemental Draft of USFL players, an NFL roster increase, and NFL conduct directed at particular USFL franchises. These activities, however, were hardly of sufficient impact to support a large damages verdict or to justify sweeping injunctive relief. For that reason, the USFL candidly admits that "at the heart of this case" are its claims that the NFL, by contracting with the three major networks and by acting coercively toward them, prevented the USFL from acquiring a network television contract indispensable to its survival. The jury expressly rejected the television claims.

The jury was clearly entitled by the evidence to find that the NFL's fall contracts with the three networks were not an anticompetitive barrier to the USFL's bidding against the NFL to acquire a network contract. Moreover, there was ample evidence that the USFL failed because it did not make the painstaking investment and patient efforts that bring credibility, stability and public recognition to a sports league. In particular, there was evidence that the USFL abandoned its original strategy of patiently building up fan loyalty and public recognition by playing in the spring. The original plan to contain costs by adherence to team salary guidelines was discarded from the start. Faced with rising costs and some new team owners impatient for immediate parity with the NFL, the idea of spring play itself was abandoned even though network and cable contracts were available. Plans for a fall season were therefore announced, thereby making 1985 spring play a "lame-duck" season. These actions were taken in the hope of forcing a merger with the NFL through the threat of competition and this litigation. The merger strategy, however, required that USFL franchises move out of large television markets and into likely NFL expansion cities. Because these moves further eroded fan loyalty and reduced the value of USFL games to television, the USFL thereby ended by its own hand any chance of a network contract.

Notwithstanding the jury's evident conclusions that the USFL's product was not appealing largely for reasons of the USFL's own doing and that the networks chose freely not to purchase it, the USFL asks us to grant sweeping injunctive relief that will reward its impatience and self-destructive conduct with a fall network contract. It thus seeks through court decree the success it failed to achieve among football fans. Absent a showing of some unlawful harm to competition, we cannot prevent a network from showing NFL games, in the hope that the network and fans will turn to the USFL. The Sherman Act does not outlaw an industry structure simply because it prevents competitors from achieving immediate parity. This is particularly so in the case of major-league professional football because Congress authorized a merger of the two leagues existing in 1966 and thus created the industry structure in question.

THE TRIAL

1. The Parties' Contentions

The USFL contended at trial that the NFL maintained a monopoly in the market for major league professional football and in a submarket for the network broadcasting rights to such football by the following allegedly predatory tactics:

a. Signing multiyear contracts with the three major television networks;

b. Pressuring the major networks to abstain from televising USFL games in the spring or fall, and successfully preventing any network telecasts of the USFL in the fall, by threatening not to renew NFL contracts or by assigning unattractive NFL games under existing contracts;

c. Establishing contracts with the networks for artificially high rights fees that, because of the so-called "dilution effect" on demand for advertising during NFL games, precluded network broadcasts of the USFL;

d. Seeking to prevent any of the three major networks from signing a contract for the USFL's initial 1983 spring playing season;

e. Rotating the Super Bowl among the three networks and not submitting the Super Bowl, playoff and even regular-season television rights to competitive bidding;

f. Pursuing a strategy outlined in the so-called "Porter Presentation" to "conquer" and bankrupt the USFL, including: co-opting powerful USFL owners, such as Donald Trump and Alfred Taubman, by offering them NFL franchises; encouraging ABC not to continue USFL broadcasts; pressuring ABC by giving it an unattractive schedule for its Monday Night Football program in 1984; targeting important USFL players for signing with the NFL through means such as the NFL's Supplemental Draft and expanded roster; and attempting to bankrupt the weakest USFL teams by driving up USFL player salaries in order to diminish the USFL's size and credibility;

g. Collaborating with the City of Oakland to destroy the Oakland Invaders of the USFL in order to hurt the credibility and image of the Invaders and the entire USFL;

h. Threatening to move an existing NFL franchise or to create a new NFL franchise solely to injure the USFL franchise in Oakland; and

i. Attempting to preclude the USFL's New Jersey Generals from moving to New York City.

The NFL contended that the relevant television submarket included entertainment broadcasting generally and that it had not monopolized either the market for major league professional football or the television submarket because:

a. Its contracts with the three major networks were not exclusionary;

b. The USFL's failure to secure a fall network contract was the result of the independent judgment of each network that the USFL was an inferior product, and of the USFL's self-destructive strategy of forcing a merger with the NFL;

c. It never pressured a network by threatening non-renewal or by assigning a schedule of unattractive games;

d. It never undertook the strategy outlined in the Porter Presentation;

e. It never sought to injure the USFL's Oakland franchise or to preclude the New Jersey Generals from playing in New York City; and

f. The losses suffered by the USFL were due to its own mismanagement.

2. *The History of Major–League Professional Football*

The NFL is an unincorporated association presently consisting of twenty-eight independent, for-profit football clubs. It was founded in 1920 in a Canton, Ohio Hupmobile showroom under the name American Professional Football Association. In 1922, it changed its name to the National Football League. The original teams were the Akron Pros, the Canton Bulldogs, the Cleveland Indians, the Dayton Triangles, the Decatur Staleys, the Hammond Pros, the Massillon Tigers, the Muncie Flyers, the Rock Island Independents and the Rochester Jeffersons, although Massillon and Muncie never played any games. By 1926, the NFL had grown to twenty-two franchises. By 1931, it had shrunk back to ten. The first championship game was not played until 1933. The first NFL draft of college players took place in 1935. All NFL teams played the same number of games for the first time in 1936. As late as 1952, NFL teams encountered bankruptcy. Indeed, NFL Commissioner Rozelle once testified that "41 franchises failed in the first 41 years of the League's existence." Transcript of Proceedings at 55, United States v. National Football League, No. 12808 (E.D.Pa. July 27, 1961).

A competing league, the All–America Football Conference ("AAFC"), was organized in 1945 and operated for four seasons with teams in Brooklyn, Buffalo, Chicago, Cleveland, Los Angeles, Miami, New York and San Francisco. American Football League v. National Football League, 205 F.Supp. 60, 65 (D.Md.1962) ("AFL v. NFL"), aff'd, 323 F.2d 124 (4th Cir.1963). Baltimore replaced Miami in 1947, and after the 1948 season, the Brooklyn team merged with the New York team. Id. The AAFC ceased operations in 1949 when the Baltimore, Cleveland and San Francisco teams were absorbed by the NFL, raising the number of its teams to thirteen. Id. Shortly thereafter, that number was reduced to twelve, where it remained until 1960. Id. The NFL's twelve teams were the Baltimore Colts, Chicago Bears, Chicago (later St. Louis) Cardinals, Cleveland Browns, Detroit Lions, Green Bay Packers, Los Angeles Rams, New York Giants, Philadelphia Eagles, Pittsburgh Steelers, San Francisco Forty–Niners and Washington Redskins. Id. at 62. The Dallas Cowboys, Minnesota Vikings, Atlanta Falcons and New Orleans Saints were added as expansion teams in 1960, 1961, 1966 and 1967, respectively. Joint Pretrial Order at 14, p 28.

The American Football League ("AFL") was founded in late 1959 by Lamar Hunt, a scion of a Texas oil family, and began play in the fall of 1960. The demand for professional football was then sufficiently great to enable the AFL to obtain a contract with ABC for the years 1960–63. The new league was fueled in part by the NFL's cautious approach toward expansion; many of the AFL's original owners had unsuccessfully sought NFL franchises, and the majority of the AFL teams were located in cities without an NFL team. See generally AFL v. NFL, 205 F.Supp. at 66–75. The original eight teams were the Boston Patriots, Buffalo Bills, Dallas Texans, Denver Broncos, Houston Oilers, Los Angeles (San Diego after the 1960 season) Chargers, New York Titans, and Oakland Raiders. Id. at 62. The Miami Dolphins joined the AFL in 1966, the Cincinnati Bengals in 1968. Joint Pretrial Order at 14, p 28. The AFL brought an unsuccessful antitrust suit against the NFL in 1962. See AFL v. NFL, 323 F.2d 124 (4th Cir.1963), aff'g 205 F.Supp. 60.

In 1966, the NFL and the AFL agreed to merge, largely because the competition for players had sharply increased salaries. Congress exempted this merger from the antitrust laws by legislation discussed infra. The merger became fully effective when a twenty-six-team NFL began play in 1970 with two conferences, the National Football Conference and American Football Conference. The NFL reached its present size of twenty-eight teams when expansion teams began play in Seattle and Tampa in 1976.

In 1974, the World Football League ("WFL") was founded. The WFL lasted for one-and-one-half seasons before disbanding. Its teams were underfinanced and played in mostly smaller markets. The WFL never obtained a television contract with a major network, although its games were televised by a syndicated network. At least one of the league's teams tried unsuccessfully to enter the NFL through litigation. See Mid–South Grizzlies v. National Football League, 720 F.2d 772 (3d Cir.1983) (rejecting antitrust claim by WFL team denied admission to NFL).

The USFL was founded in May 1982 by David Dixon as a league that would play spring football. The league began play in March 1983 with teams in Birmingham, Boston, Chicago, Denver, Los Angeles, Michigan, New Jersey, Oakland, Philadelphia, Phoenix, Tampa and Washington. In part because of the location of its teams in major television markets, the USFL was able to obtain multimillion dollar network and cable television contracts with ABC and ESPN. Nevertheless, for reasons explored in detail infra, the USFL demonstrated little stability. Over its three seasons of spring football (one of which was a "lame-duck" season commenced after an announced decision to shift to fall play), the USFL clubs played in twenty-two cities and had thirty-nine principal owners. None of the majority owners of an original USFL team was a majority owner by 1986 when a planned fall schedule was aborted by the $1.00 verdict.

3. *The NFL's Television Contracts*

The growth of the NFL was closely related to the growth of television. Beginning in 1951, the Dumont network televised five regular season games (twelve by 1954), as well as the championship game each year. In the mid–1950's, the Columbia Broadcasting System ("CBS") began broadcasting certain NFL regular season games for $1.8 million per year, and the National Broadcasting Company ("NBC") acquired the right to televise the NFL championship game. The broadcast rights to games were controlled by individual teams during the 1950's, however.

In 1961, the NFL teams agreed to sell their collective television rights as a single package and to share broadcast revenues equally among all franchises. This decision was in response to arguments by Commissioner Rozelle that the league's competitive balance on the field would eventually be destroyed if teams in major television markets continued to sell their broadcast rights individually. In the long run, he believed, great differentials in television revenues among teams would lead to a competitive imbalance that would diminish the overall attractiveness of the NFL's product. See Transcript of Proceedings at 67–68, United States v. National Football League, No. 12808 (E.D.Pa. July 27, 1961) (testimony of Commissioner Rozelle); see also United States Football League v. National Football League, 634 F.Supp. 1155, 1161 & n. 2 (S.D.N.Y.1986) ("Opinion No. 2"). Rozelle's arguments were bolstered by the policy of the recently organized AFL to pool television rights and revenues in its first broadcast contract with ABC.

Before the NFL could enter a pooled-rights television contract, however, it had to overcome several legal obstacles. An earlier attempt by the NFL to control the sale of television rights by its teams had been deemed a violation of Section 1 of the Sherman Act in United States v. National Football League, 116 F.Supp. 319 (E.D.Pa.1953). In that case, the government sought to enjoin the enforcement of Article X of the NFL's by-laws, which regulated the broadcast of distant games into the home territories of other teams. Applying Rule-of-Reason analysis, Judge Grim held that the restriction on the broadcast of outside games when home teams were playing away was an impermissible restraint of trade. Id. at 327. The Final Judgment provided that:

> The defendants are jointly and severally . . . enjoined . . . from directly or indirectly entering into . . . any contract, agreement or understanding with the league defendant or any member club of the league defendant, . . . having the purpose or effect of restricting the areas within which broadcasts or telecasts of games . . . may be made.

United States v. National Football League, No. 12808, Final Judgment § V (E.D.Pa. Dec. 28, 1953), quoted in Opinion No. 2, 634 F.Supp. at 1159.

In 1961, the NFL brought a pooled-rights agreement with CBS before Judge Grim for a determination as to whether the agreement violated the 1953 Final Judgment. This contract provided that CBS would have the "right to determine, entirely within its own discretion ... which games shall be televised and where such games be televised." United States v. National Football League, 196 F.Supp. 445, 447 (E.D.Pa.1961). Judge Grim held that CBS's authority to determine when and where games would be broadcast violated Section V of the Final Judgment. Id. A subsequent motion by the NFL for a modification or suspension of the Final Judgment was denied. Judge Grim accordingly enjoined the execution and performance of the pooled-rights contract between the NFL and CBS, and further enjoined the NFL from entering into "any other contract and agreement having similar purpose or effect." United States v. National Football League, No. 12808 (E.D.Pa. July 28, 1961) (order construing 1953 Final Judgment).

Specifically intending to alter Judge Grim's order, see S.Rep. No. 1087, 87th Cong., 1st Sess. 1, reprinted in 1961 U.S.Code Cong. & Admin.News 3042, 3042, Congress enacted the Sports Broadcasting Act of 1961, which exempted from the antitrust laws pooled-rights agreements entered into by professional sports leagues. Pub.L. No. 87–331, § 1, 1961 U.S.Code Cong. & Admin.News 822, 75 Stat. 732 (codified as amended at 15 U.S.C. § 1291) (Supp. IV 1986). In order to protect college games from competition with pro football telecasts, the exemption did not apply to the broadcast of professional football games on Friday nights and Saturdays during the college football season. Id. § 2 (codified as amended at 15 U.S.C. § 1293 (1982)).

The first NFL pooled-rights contract was with CBS. For the 1962 and 1963 seasons, CBS was the only network permitted to bid for this contract because it had individual rights contracts running through 1963 with nine teams. The NFL received $4,650,000 per season from CBS during these two seasons. For the 1964–65 NFL contract, CBS outbid NBC and ABC with an offer of $14,100,000 per season. In 1964, the AFL, which had had a contract with ABC, entered into a five-year, $36 million contract with NBC.

In 1966, Congress amended the Sports Broadcasting Act specifically to confer antitrust immunity on the NFL–AFL merger. Pub.L. No. 89–800, § 6(b)(1), 80 Stat. 1515 (codified as amended at 15 U.S.C. § 1291). At the same time, the restriction on Friday night and Saturday telecasts was expanded to include protection for high school football. Id. § 6(b)(3). In passing this legislation, Congress was plainly informed that, upon consolidation of the two leagues, the NFL would have broadcast contracts with at least two networks. Professional Football League Merger: Hearings on S. 3817 Before Antitrust Subcomm. (Subcomm. No. 5) of the House Comm. on the Judiciary, 89th Cong., 2d Sess. 64, 66, 119 (1966).

In 1970, the NFL entered into a contract with ABC to televise a game nationally on Monday nights. Since then, all three major television networks have broadcast NFL games, and the NFL's annual revenues from television have increased by more than 800 percent. The NFL teams received approximately $186 million for the 1970–73 seasons; $268 million for the 1974–77 seasons; $646 million for the 1978–81 seasons; and $2.1 billion over the five-year period 1982–86.

The ABC, CBS and NBC contracts from 1970 onward have given each network rights of first negotiation and first refusal to decide whether to continue its NFL contract for subsequent years. The NFL's 1982–86 contracts were nonexclusive and did not forbid a network from televising another football league's games at any time when it was not broadcasting NFL games. NBC was thus legally free to televise to a particular city another league's games on Sunday afternoons directly opposite NFL games on CBS when there was no NFL game scheduled for NBC to be televised to that city. CBS had a similar option. ABC was legally free to televise another league's games all afternoon each Sunday. All three networks were legally free to telecast another league's games in prime time. Because the NFL was forbidden by its network contracts to televise games on cable, cable television contracts were open to a competing league, although such contracts are less lucrative than network contracts. When the NFL's network contracts expired in 1981 and 1986, the networks were free to contract with a competing league's games for all time slots.

The NFL's three-network "tie-up" was a central issue at trial. The USFL claimed that the NFL intentionally set out to tie up the three networks as a means of excluding competitors. In support of its theory, the USFL introduced a memorandum from NFL general counsel Jay Moyer written during the NFL's 1973 network contract negotiations stating that "an open network may well be an open invitation to formation of a new league." Commissioner Rozelle testified, however, that in 1970, before contacting ABC and signing the Monday night football contract with it, he unsuccessfully approached CBS and NBC, both of which already televised NFL games, about their interest in prime-time football. The USFL also emphasized at trial a June 1984 CBS business study suggesting that the fall broadcast of USFL games on Sundays would reduce the network's advertising revenues from NFL games by $49 million to $53 million over three years. This "dilution effect," the USFL argued, created a $50 million barrier to entry by a new league.

The USFL also sought to show that the NFL had placed unlawful pressure on the networks to prevent the broadcast of USFL games. Much of this evidence consisted of statements by USFL representatives and hearsay and speculation by third parties. Officials from the three networks and one cable network testified that the NFL had not exerted any pressure on them regarding the broadcast of USFL games. Several network officials did testify, however, that they feared that televising the USFL in the fall might jeopardize their NFL relationships—a fear somewhat at odds with the USFL claim that the NFL needed three network contracts to produce the "dilution effect." Executives from all three major networks also testified that by 1986, after the USFL had left several large television markets and was encountering financial and other difficulties, the USFL was not an attractive entertainment product.

4. "Conquering the USFL": Predatory Tactics

The USFL also sought to prove monopolization by the NFL through predatory tactics unrelated to television. It thus introduced a memorandum prepared by NFL labor negotiator Jack Donlan entitled "Spending the USFL Dollar," which urged NFL owners to bid for USFL players to drive up USFL costs. The USFL's proof of predatory behavior, however, consisted primarily of allegations concerning the recommendations of the so-called "Porter Presentation," and of the so-called Oakland and New York "conspiracies."

The Porter Presentation was a two-and-one-half hour presentation, entitled USFL v. NFL, by Harvard Business School Professor Michael Porter to sixty-five NFL executives attending a multiday seminar on labor negotiations. Porter's presentation, which was not previewed by anyone in the NFL, set out a strategy for the NFL to "conquer the USFL."

The USFL claimed that the NFL implemented a recommendation of the Porter Presentation by attempting to "co-opt" USFL owners with promises of an NFL franchise. Donald Trump, owner of the USFL's New Jersey Generals, testified that he was offered an NFL franchise by Commissioner Rozelle in exchange for his blocking the USFL's proposed move to the fall and his preventing the league from filing the instant action. Rozelle denied that he made such an offer to Trump. In addition, hearsay testimony by Al Davis, owner of the NFL's Los Angeles Raiders, a team not sued by the USFL, indicated an attempt to co-opt Alfred Taubman of the Michigan Panthers. Taubman, however, denied that he was offered an NFL team.

The USFL also claimed that the NFL followed Professor Porter's recommendation to "dissuade" ABC from continuing its USFL contract. Supporting evidence consisted largely of hearsay introduced to show the state of mind of the networks. The declarants denied making any such statements. Jim Spence of ABC did testify, however, that the NFL informed him that the NFL owners were "not enamored" with the network's USFL contract. Nevertheless, ABC subsequently offered the USFL a four-year, $175 million contract for spring football beginning in 1986. The USFL also claimed that the NFL used a method recommended by Porter to pressure ABC by offering it unattractive Monday night games that would and did earn low ratings in 1984. In response, NFL officials testified that the 1984 Monday Night Football schedule was settled before the Porter Presentation, that "weak" teams such as Buffalo and Cincinnati appeared on that schedule fewer times than in prior years, and that any change in ABC's ratings was due to economic conditions that affected the entire sports television marketplace.

Finally, the USFL claimed that the NFL followed Porter's recommendations for competing for players. This evidence consisted of the NFL's decision to conduct a supplemental draft of players still under USFL contract in March 1984, an increase in NFL roster size from forty-five to forty-nine, conversations between the Dallas Cowboys and USFL star Herschel Walker, and NFL salary offers to relatively unknown USFL players such as Todd Fowler.

The USFL also contended that the NFL and the City of Oakland conspired to destroy the USFL's Oakland Invaders in return for an NFL promise that Oakland would receive an NFL team. This so-called "Oakland conspiracy" was based on the testimony of Al Davis that he "sensed" that the NFL wanted to "destroy" the Invaders and on Commissioner Rozelle's public statement that Oakland, having lost the Raiders, would be considered for an NFL expansion franchise.

The "New York conspiracy" involved a claim that the NFL and the NFL's New York Jets conspired to mislead New York City and State officials into believing that the Jets were willing to return from New Jersey to New York. The purpose of this conspiracy was to block the USFL's New Jersey team from moving to a new domed stadium in New York. Proof of this conspiracy consisted of testimony by Senator Alphonse D'Amato and Vincent Tese, Chairman and Chief Executive Officer of the New York State Urban Development Corporation, that Leon Hess, owner of the Jets, had promised to return his team to New York. In addition, Al Davis testified that there was an "understanding" reached at a 1983 NFL owners' meeting to keep a USFL team out of New York. Other participants in this meeting denied any such understanding or agreement.

5. *Damages*

The USFL's evidence of damages consisted of the testimony of economist Nina Cornell, who sought to estimate the league's losses by two methods. Method A was based on the assumption that the gate and television revenues of an unhindered USFL could be estimated by using the gate receipts and television revenues of the old AFL. Dr. Cornell estimated the USFL's damages under this method at $565 million. Method B was based on the June 1984 CBS business study examining the fall broadcast of USFL games. She estimated the USFL's damages under this method at $301 million.

Dr. Cornell's damage calculations rested on several other assumptions. First, of course, she assumed that illegal NFL conduct was the cause of the USFL's failure to obtain a network contract. Second, Dr. Cornell assumed that the NFL could lawfully contract with only one network. Third, her calculations attributed the USFL's damages entirely to illegal NFL conduct and not at all to the USFL's own mismanagement.

Finally, she assumed that there would be no increased player costs to the USFL resulting from the shift to fall play and that salaries would remain stable from 1986 to 1992. Tension existed between her assumption of stable salaries and her projections of large increases in USFL revenues as a result of playing in the fall during the 1986 to 1992 seasons. Player salaries had already increased dramatically because of the two leagues' competition for players, even when they were playing in different seasons. No reason was given to expect a stabilization of wages when the leagues would play in the same season and the USFL would have substantially greater revenues to compete for players. Moreover, a cornerstone of the USFL's television claim was that a network contract was essential so that it could compete for quality players, a position that is hardly consistent with stability in player salaries.

6. Management of the USFL

The USFL was conceived and organized in 1981 to play in the spring rather than the fall. Its founders believed that public demand for football was not satisfied by the NFL's and the colleges' fall seasons; that cable television, which could not televise NFL games under the existing NFL-network contracts, would offer unique opportunities for television revenues and exposure; that a spring football league would face limited competition; that there was a sufficient supply of football players for two leagues; and that a spring league could draft college players and put them on the field even before the NFL draft.

The USFL's founders placed a high priority on the fans' perception of the quality of play. They intended to use major stadiums and to hire well-known coaches. At the same time, they wanted the league to control costs. For its first season, therefore, the USFL established budget guidelines for player salaries of between $1.3 and $1.5 million per team.

The USFL's founders did not seek to obtain a television contract for fall play. Before fielding a team, however, the USFL received bids for a spring television contract from ABC and NBC and from two cable networks, ESPN and the Turner Broadcasting System. The league entered a four-year contract with ABC, and a two-year contract with ESPN. The ABC agreement provided for ABC to pay the USFL $18 million for the 1983 and 1984 seasons, with options exercisable by ABC at $14 million for 1985 and at $18 million for 1986. ESPN contracted to televise USFL games for two years at rights fees of $4 million for 1983 and $7 million for 1984. The USFL began with eight of its twelve teams in the nation's top ten television markets. The ABC contract required the USFL to field teams in the three largest television markets (New York, Los Angeles and Chicago) and in at least four of the five other top-ten television markets in which teams were originally located (Philadelphia, Boston, Detroit, San Francisco/Oakland and Washington).

The USFL's first year of play, 1983, was a mixed success. The league received extensive media exposure when it signed Heisman Trophy winner Herschel Walker to a three-year, $3,250,000 contract. The Nielsen television rating for the first week of games was 14.2, a figure comparable to NFL ratings. As the season went on, however, the USFL's television ratings declined; average television ratings for the year were 6.23 on ABC and 3.28 on ESPN. Average attendance for the year was approximately 25,000. Nevertheless, these figures were consistent with the league's and networks' preseason projections.

On the financial side, the picture was not as bright. The USFL lost a total of almost $40 million, or an average of $3.3 million per team. The league had projected losses of only about $2 million per year for each team over the first three years. The unanticipated financial losses were chiefly the result of the failure to stay within the original salary guidelines. Indeed, in a November 1983 letter to other owners, Tad Taube of the Oakland team warned that: "If we are not successful in establishing player [salary] caps I can guarantee you that there will not be a USFL within three years, irrespective of improved revenue [from] television.... We have sighted the enemy and they are us!"

The USFL's second year was marked by change. Four teams shifted locations. For example, the owner of the Chicago franchise exchanged that franchise for the Phoenix franchise, taking his winning Chicago coach and players while the original Phoenix team moved to Chicago under a new owner. The league, over the objection of some owners, expanded from twelve teams to eighteen. Five of the original owners left the league. Some of the new owners, notably Donald Trump of the New Jersey Generals, believed that the USFL ought to play in the fall. Thereafter, the issue of when to play became divisive, and several owners came to believe that Trump was trying to bring about a merger with the NFL that would include only some USFL teams.

The NFL introduced extensive evidence designed to prove that the USFL followed Trump's merger strategy, and that this strategy ultimately caused the USFL's downfall. The merger strategy, the NFL argued, involved escalating financial competition for players as a means of putting pressure on NFL expenses, playing in the fall to impair NFL television revenues, shifting USFL franchises out of cities where NFL teams played into cities thought to be logical expansion (through merger) cities for the NFL, and, finally, bringing the antitrust litigation now before us.

Throughout the second half of 1983 and early 1984, several USFL owners escalated spending on player salaries. USFL teams, for example, signed established NFL players such as running back Joe Cribbs and defensive back Gary Barbaro. Trump, in particular, signed a number of players who were still under contract with the NFL to future contracts, including superstar Lawrence Taylor of the New York Giants. USFL owners also signed many top players coming out of college, for example, wide receiver Anthony Carter and quarterback Jim Kelly. The USFL's spending on players greatly outpaced its revenues. The owner of the Los Angeles team, for example, committed the team to $13.1 million in salaries and bonuses for just one season. He even entered into a multiyear, $40 million contract with just one player, Steve Young of Brigham Young University.

By the end of the 1984 season, USFL franchises in two of the top three television markets, Chicago and Los Angeles, had failed, and only four of the original owners remained in the league. The league was not a failure as entertainment, however. Despite a decline in the USFL's television ratings to 5.7 on ABC and 2.8 on ESPN, ABC exercised its option to carry the USFL in the spring of 1985 at $14 million and offered a new contract worth $175 million for four years in the spring beginning in 1986. ESPN offered a contract worth $70 million over three years.

Nevertheless, during an August 1984 owners' meeting, the USFL decided to move to the fall in 1986. This decision was made despite: (i) ABC's warning that such a move would breach its contract for the spring of 1985 and 1986; (ii) the contrary recommendations of a management consulting firm, McKinsey & Company, which the USFL had retained for $600,000 to consider the advisability of a fall season; and (iii) the contrary recommendations of the USFL's directors of operations and marketing.

Moreover, Eddie Einhorn, a USFL owner who was to represent the USFL in negotiations to secure a network contract for the fall, warned that moving from large television markets to "merger" cities too quickly might preclude the securing of a network contract. Nevertheless, in the ensuing months, the USFL withdrew from Chicago, Detroit, Philadelphia, Pittsburgh and Washington, D.C.—each a large television market with an NFL team—and moved into Baltimore (which had lost its NFL team in 1984) and Orlando (which had no NFL team). Through mergers, the USFL bolstered franchises in Oakland (which had lost the NFL Raiders to Los Angeles) and Phoenix (which had been discussed as a possible NFL expansion city). The decision to move to the fall damaged the USFL's relations with ABC and ESPN. The former withheld a significant portion of the USFL's rights fees for the 1985 season, while the latter demanded a renegotiation of its proposed 1985–87 USFL contract.

In October 1984, the instant litigation was begun. The USFL's 1985 "lame-duck" spring season appears to have been affected adversely by the now publicly announced move to the fall. The league's television ratings declined to 4.1 on ABC and 2.0 on ESPN. By the end of the season, several owners had withdrawn financial support for their teams, and a number of clubs were no longer meeting their payrolls and other bills. The USFL scheduled eight teams for its fall 1986 season, which was ultimately cancelled after the verdict in this case. Only one team (New Jersey), was in a top-ten television market. One other team (Tampa Bay), was in a top-twenty market. Three teams were located in Florida (Jacksonville, Orlando and Tampa Bay) but only one was west of the Mississippi River (Phoenix). In three years, USFL teams had left fourteen of the twenty-two cities in which they had played.

7. *The Verdict*

The jury found the NFL liable on the USFL's claim of actual monopolization, concluding that the older league had willfully acquired or maintained monopoly power in a market consisting of major league professional football in the United States (Question No. 4). The jury also found that the NFL's unlawful monopolization had caused injury to the USFL (Question No. 5). In ruling on the NFL's motion for judgment notwithstanding the verdict with respect to these findings, the district court held that sufficient evidence existed that the NFL had engaged in predatory conduct. This evidence related to: (1) NFL efforts to co-opt USFL owners and potential owners; (2) the NFL Supplemental Draft of USFL players; (3) the NFL's move to a forty-nine-man roster; and (4) the NFL's activity directed at specific USFL franchises such as the Oakland Invaders. Opinion No. 16, 644 F.Supp. at 1058.

The USFL was unsuccessful on its remaining claims. The jury found that none of the defendants had violated Section 2 by attempting to monopolize a relevant market (Question No. 7), or by conspiring to monopolize (Question Nos. 12–14). In addition, the jury found that even though "one or more defendants [had] participate[d] in a contract, combination or conspiracy to exclude competition within major league professional football" (Question No. 20), that combination was not an unreasonable restraint of trade in violation of Section 1 (Question No. 21). The fatal blow, however, was the complete rejection of the USFL's television claims. The jury found that the NFL had not willfully acquired or maintained a monopoly in a relevant television submarket (Question No. 4). It further found that the NFL's contracts with all three television networks for the right to broadcast the league's regular season and championship games through the 1986–87 season were not an unreasonable restraint of trade violative of Section 1 (Question No. 24). Finally, the jury rejected the USFL's "essential facilities" claim, specifically finding that "defendants [did not] have the ability to deny actual or potential competitors access to a national broadcast television contract" (Question No. 33), although it also found that such a contract was "essential to the ability of a major league professional football league to compete successfully in the United States" (Question No. 31) and "that potential competitors of the NFL, cannot as a practical matter, duplicate the benefits of a network contract" (Question No. 32).

Discussion

On appeal, the USFL raises a host of claims with respect to the NFL's liability, the district court's evidentiary rulings, damages charge, and denial of injunctive relief.

1. *Liability*

a. *The Sports Broadcasting Act*

The USFL contends that the Sports Broadcasting Act of 1961 limits the antitrust exemption for pooled-rights contracts to a single contract with one network. Therefore, it argues, the NFL's multiple contractual arrangements with three networks violates the injunction in United States v. National Football League, 116 F.Supp. 319 (E.D.Pa.1953), a decision claimed by the USFL collaterally to estop the NFL from denying that its arrangements with the networks violate Section 1 of the Sherman Act.

The Sports Broadcasting Act states that:

> The antitrust laws ... shall not apply to all joint agreement by or among persons engaging in or conducting the organized professional team sport [ ] of football, ... by which any league of clubs participating in professional football ... contests sells or otherwise transfers all or any part of the rights of such league's member clubs in the sponsored telecasting of the game [ ] of football....

15 U.S.C. § 1291. This statutory language thus neither states nor implies that the exemption limits the NFL to a contract with only one network. Moreover, the legislation does contain express limitations on the exemption designed to protect college football from televised competition with the NFL, which suggests by implication that no other limitations exist.

Faced with statutory language unambiguously hostile to its claims, the USFL resorts to alleged ambiguities in the legislative history. Upon examination, however, the legislative history offers no reason to depart from the statutory language. For example, NFL Commissioner Rozelle stated during the congressional hearings on the Act that if all the networks were tied up by the NFL, a competing league "would ... possibly be at a major disadvantage" and that the bill was designed to allow the NFL to televise on one network. Telecasting of Professional Sports Contests: Hearings on H.R. 8757 Before the Antitrust Subcomm. (Subcomm. No. 5) of the House Comm. on the Judiciary, 87th Cong., 1st Sess. 35 (1961). These remarks were made, however, during a colloquy in which Rozelle twice stated explicitly that the proposed legislation would allow the NFL to utilize all three networks. Moreover, he predicted that, although the NFL had a present intention to use only one network, in twenty years a "single network may no longer be desirable, and it may become much better for the public and the league to use more than one network." Id. Rozelle's testimony thus provides little comfort to the USFL.

More tellingly, the USFL also relies upon the following passage in the House Report accompanying the 1961 legislation:

> Some concern has been expressed that the language of this section might be considered to give an absolute exemption from the antitrust laws for any kind of television arrangements entered into by a league, and particularly an arrangement which might involve several networks and might thus exclude a competing league from all television coverage. This is not the intent of H.R. 9096 which is designed to permit the sale of television rights by a league and its member clubs to a single network. The committee does not intend that an exemption from the antitrust laws should be made available to a league or its members where the intent or effect of a joint agreement is to exclude a competing league or its members from the sale of any of their television rights.

H.R.Rep. No. 1178, 87th Cong., 1st Sess. 4 (1961). This language was apparently included at the suggestion of AFL Commissioner Joe Foss, who testified that the proposed legislation should guard against agreements with networks that unreasonably excluded competing leagues. See Opinion No. 2, 634 F.Supp. at 1162.

We believe the USFL exaggerates the import of that statement in the House Report. The report says no more than that multiple pooled-rights agreements may be the subject of a monopolization or unreasonable restraint of trade claim by a competing league. Precisely such claims were submitted to the jury in this case and rejected by it.

The Senate Report does not expressly address the issue of multiple network contracts, other than to conclude ambiguously that the public interest would be served "with minimal sacrifice of antitrust principles by exempting joint agreements under which a league sells or transfers pooled television rights of its members to a purchaser." S.Rep. No. 1087, 87th Cong., 1st Sess., reprinted in 1961 U.S.Code Cong. & Admin.News 3042, 3044.

In any event, the passage of the 1966 NFL–AFL merger statute provides conclusive evidence that Congress did not intend the 1961 Act to prohibit NFL contracts with more than one network. When considering this legislation, Congress was explicitly informed that the merged league would continue to broadcast its games on "at least 2 networks," and no concern whatsoever was expressed in Congress that such conduct was either undesirable or would go beyond the scope of the 1961 Act's exemption. Moreover, while permitting the merger, Congress added a further limitation to the exemption to protect high school games from televised competition with the NFL. The lack of a "one network" limitation in the 1966 merger bill thus dooms the USFL's claims. Accordingly, we hold that the mere existence of the NFL contracts with the three networks does not violate the antitrust laws. Having made this determination, we need not consider whether the decree in United States v. National Football League has any collateral-estoppel effect.

b. The "Dilution Effect"

The USFL does not argue that there was insufficient evidence to support the jury's rejection of its claim that the NFL prevented it from obtaining a network contract. The failure to make this argument is understandable in light of the swift dismissal such a claim would encounter. However, the USFL does the next-best thing by attacking the district court's instructions regarding "intent and effect" and "legitimate business purpose," both discussed immediately infra, on grounds that these instructions led the jury to ignore an "unchallenged showing of anticompetitive effect" and "textbook example of an anticompetitive practice." Moreover, the USFL continues to seek broad injunctive relief concerning the NFL's television contracts on the ground that such relief is necessary to bring competition to the industry. Because these claims are based on the so-called "dilution effect" of the NFL's contracts with the three networks, a separate discussion of the concept of a "dilution effect" and its role in the professional football industry is necessary.

The term "dilution effect" comes from a CBS business study ordered by Neil Pilson, CBS Sports' President, and completed in June 1984. CBS conducted the study because it was apprehensive over ABC's signing a USFL fall contract and desired the leverage a second league would afford it in its negotiations with the NFL. The study estimated the economic impact on CBS of the televising of USFL games in the fall under various scenarios. One scenario posited only ABC televising USFL games on Sundays. The scenarios most pertinent to the present discussion posited CBS and either NBC or ABC televising USFL games. Under these scenarios, CBS would televise both USFL and NFL games on Sundays. The final scenario posited USFL games being televised by NBC and ABC on fall Sundays. No study was made of CBS being the only network with a USFL contract because CBS was not interested in such an arrangement.

As explained by Pilson, the value of a USFL fall contract to CBS was determined (in simplified fashion) as follows. From the estimated gross advertising revenues would be subtracted estimates of: (i) expenses related to production; (ii) losses in revenues that would otherwise have been earned by programs preempted by USFL games, or "preemptive impact"; (iii) decreases in advertising revenues from NFL games resulting from the addition of USFL games, or "dilution effect"; and (iv) rights fees to the USFL. Pilson testified that when these estimates were made in June 1984, the resultant calculation, CBS's profit, was negative. The USFL argues that, but for the "dilution effect" of $50 million, the sum would have been sufficiently positive to make a USFL contract attractive. The USFL assumes that the "dilution effect" was experienced equally by all three networks and thus concludes that the effect of NFL's network contracts was to exclude all competition.

The district court instructed the jury to analyze the NFL's television contracts in light of the CBS study. Specifically, the jury was told to consider "[t]he high NFL rights fees charged to the networks, which plaintiffs allege triggered a dilution effect that makes it economically infeasible for any network to offer a satisfactory television contract to any professional football league other than the NFL." The jury rejected the USFL's claims as to the "dilution effect" in finding that the NFL had not monopolized a television submarket, that the NFL television contracts were not an unreasonable restraint, and that the NFL did not have the power to exclude a competing league from obtaining a network contract. There was ample evidence to support these conclusions.

First, the USFL concedes, as it must, that the "dilution effect" is nonexistent when the NFL network contracts expire and negotiations over new contracts are under way. Whatever exclusionary effect exists is only for the term of the three NFL network contracts, and all leagues are free to compete on the basis of the quality of their product upon the expiration of these contracts.

The district court's instructions directed the jury to consider the length of these contracts, then five years, in determining whether they were reasonable. Its verdict, therefore, is dispositive because the duration of the contracts was hardly unreasonable as a matter of law.

Second, there was no evidence that the result of the calculations described above would be the same for ABC as for CBS. ABC's contract was largely confined to televising a single NFL game in prime time on a weekday night. Its Sundays were free of football, and it would not encounter the scheduling problems faced by CBS in televising both NFL and USFL games on Sunday afternoons. ABC was thus free to schedule games so as to maximize revenue. Moreover, whatever "dilution effect" ABC's prime-time games might suffer was not necessarily identical to that faced by CBS. The jury might easily conclude, absent evidence to the contrary, that the "dilution effect" on CBS from back-to-back NFL–USFL telecasts on Sunday afternoons would be greater than on ABC, which would not broadcast NFL games on Sunday. And there was no evidence to the contrary. The USFL, which bore the burden of proof on this issue, called two witnesses from ABC in a position to testify about the "dilution effect" on ABC. Neither witness was questioned about the "dilution effect." Both did testify, however, that the USFL's exodus from major television markets and its other difficulties greatly diminished the value of USFL telecasts by 1985 and 1986.

Third, the conduct of the NFL and the networks indicates that neither believed their contracts to be exclusionary. Notwithstanding the early opinion of the NFL's Moyer about a network without a contract being an "open invitation to a new league," the NFL's actual conduct displayed no marked desire to lock up all three networks. Prime-time weekday telecasts were offered to NBC and CBS, both of whom already had NFL contracts, before ABC was approached. It was the testimony of both the ABC executives and CBS's Pilson, elicited by counsel for the USFL, that Rozelle routinely used the threat of leaving them without an NFL contract in order to extract from them the largest possible rights fees. If the "dilution effect" theory of exclusion were correct, the NFL could not credibly threaten to leave one network without a contract. If the theory were correct, moreover, the last network to sign with the NFL would have a bargaining advantage because its agreement would be essential to the NFL's monopoly, much as the owner of the last lot in a tract of land needed for a construction project can demand the highest price. In the NFL-network negotiations, the opposite was the case, and the last network to sign was at a bargaining disadvantage. Thus, in 1982, the NFL first signed agreements with ABC and NBC and then approached CBS. According to Pilson, CBS regarded itself as being in a very disadvantageous bargaining position. As a result, CBS paid $736 million for the new contract, an increase of more than 100% over its previous contract. On the basis of this evidence, therefore, the jury would have been hard-pressed to conclude that the NFL needed a contract with CBS to freeze out a competing league, a circumstance that would have precluded a credible threat to leave CBS without a contract and the resultant hefty increase in rights fees.

Fourth, even if the "dilution effect" theory were alive and well in 1986, the jury could have found that that "effect" was not a cause of the USFL's failure to get a network contract in that year. The CBS study was made in 1984 and was based on estimates of revenues that were plainly excessive given the circumstances of 1986. Immediately after the study was completed, the Supreme Court decided National Collegiate Athletic Association v. Board of Regents, 468 U.S. 85, 104 S.Ct. 2948, 82 L.Ed.2d 70 (1984), invalidating the NCAA's exclusive control over the televising of college football games. This decision had the effect of multiplying greatly the number of college games telecast and of reducing advertising revenue generally for football games. An ABC witness also testified there was a proliferation of sporting events on network and cable television after the fall of 1984 that also reduced the advertising fees that could be charged for professional football. In addition, there were the problems of the USFL itself. The league had failed to establish fan loyalty in most places because of repeated franchise moves. Most importantly, the USFL had abandoned most major television markets, thereby rendering telecasts of its games much less valuable than had been estimated by the earlier CBS study. Finally, the disagreements among the USFL owners, the financial condition of some of the franchises, and the "lame-duck" spring season of 1985 further lessened the value of USFL telecasts in 1986. In fact, Pilson himself testified that by 1986 the events described above had rendered the "dilution effect" irrelevant to CBS's decision not to televise the USFL. In light of this evidence, the jury was free to conclude that the revenues to be expected from USFL telecasts were so low that no network would purchase them even if there were no "dilution effect."

c. *"Intent and Effect" Charge*

We now consider the district court's instruction regarding liability on the USFL's television-related claims. The USFL contends that it should not have been required to show that the intent and effect of the NFL's television contracts with the major networks were exclusionary (rather than simply intent or effect) in order to prove a Section 2 claim. In addition, the USFL contends that the district court erred with respect to the Section 1 television instruction because it applied the intent-and-effect standard to the Rule-of-Reason claims. We reject both contentions.

The Supreme Court has repeatedly defined monopolization as the "willful acquisition or maintenance" of monopoly power. E.g., Aspen Skiing Co. v. Aspen Highlands Skiing Corp., 472 U.S. 585, 596 n. 19, 105 S.Ct. 2847, 2854 n. 19, 86 L.Ed.2d 467 (1985); United States v. Grinnell Corp., 384 U.S. 563, 570–71, 86 S.Ct. 1698, 1703–04, 16 L.Ed.2d 778 (1966); Berkey Photo, Inc. v. Eastman Kodak Co., 603 F.2d 263, 274 (2d Cir.1979), cert. denied, 444 U.S. 1093, 100 S.Ct. 1061, 62 L.Ed.2d 783 (1980). The willfulness element certainly requires proof of intent. See Aspen Skiing, 472 U.S. at 602 n. 28, 105 S.Ct. at 2858 n. 28 (quoting

United States v. Aluminum Co. of Am., 148 F.2d 416, 432 (2d Cir.1945) ("Alcoa") ("In order to fall within § 2, the monopolist must have ... the intent to monopolize.")). Proof of effect is required by definition alone to satisfy the "acquisition or maintenance" requirement.

A requirement that both intent and effect be proven is necessary to enable a trier of fact to make the critical distinction between conduct that defeats a competitor because of efficiency and consumer satisfaction, and conduct that "not only (1) tends to impair the opportunities of rivals, but also (2) either does not further competition on the merits or does so in an unnecessarily restrictive way." Aspen Skiing, 472 U.S. at 605 n. 32, 105 S.Ct. at 2859 n. 32 (quoting 3 P. Areeda & D. Turner, Antitrust Law 78 (1978)). Hopes and dreams alone cannot support a Section 2 claim of monopolization. Berkey Photo, 603 F.2d at 273–75. If they did, the nationwide advertisement "Ford wants to be your car company" would constitute an open-and-shut Section 2 case. Success alone is not enough or the antitrust laws would have their greatest impact on the most efficient entrepreneurs and would injure rather than protect consumers.

Proof of intent and effect is also of evidentiary value. Distinguishing between efficient and predatory conduct is extremely difficult because it is frequently the case that "[c]ompetitive and exclusionary conduct look alike." Easterbrook, On Identifying Exclusionary Conduct, 61 Notre Dame L.Rev. 972, 972 (1986). Evidence of intent and effect helps the trier of fact to evaluate the actual effect of challenged business practices in light of the intent of those who resort to such practices.

The present case is in fact a useful example of the intent-and-effect approach to determining whether certain practices are predatory. As the preceding discussion of the "dilution effect" indicates, the jury's conclusion that the NFL's three network contracts were not exclusionary was supported by evidence that a quality league could either have overcome the "dilution effect" or have acquired a contract when the NFL's contracts expired. The conduct of the NFL itself and the networks showed their disbelief in any exclusionary effect by the NFL's threatening to leave a network without NFL games and the networks' taking the threat seriously. The evidence also supported the conclusion that when the NFL locked up the third network, CBS, in the 1982 negotiations, it did so to obtain $736 million in rights fees, not to exclude competitors.

Judge Leisure's instructions to the jury with respect to the Section 1 Rule-of-Reason claim stated that intent was not determinative as to whether a practice was an unreasonable restraint of trade:

> Examining the combination's purpose may assist you in determining the effects of the agreement on competition. The mere fact that the defendants had a good motive or sound purpose for entering into an agreement, however, does not in and of itself prevent you from finding that the agreement was an unreasonable restraint of trade.

> On the other hand, the mere fact that defendants entered into an agreement with the intent of excluding competition, is not enough to establish a Section [1] violation. Even if you find that defendants' intent was evil or unlawful, you still must find evidence of anticompetitive effect before you can find a particular restraint of trade is unreasonable.

We disagree with the USFL that proof of either anticompetitive intent or effect is sufficient in a Rule-of-Reason case under Section 1. Unlike a per se price-fixing case, a Rule-of-Reason case requires the fact finder to balance the procompetitive and anticompetitive effects of any restraint. See, e.g., National Soc'y of Professional Eng'rs v. United States, 435 U.S. 679, 691 & n. 17, 98 S.Ct. 1355, 1365 & n. 17, 55 L.Ed.2d 637 (1978). Except for Oreck Corp. v. Whirlpool Corp., 579 F.2d 126, 133 (2d Cir.) (in banc), cert. denied, 439 U.S. 946, 99 S.Ct. 340, 58 L.Ed.2d 338 (1978), the cases cited by the USFL are per se price-fixing cases. We have previously stated, however, that we "doubt" that the purpose-or-effect requirement stated in Oreck "is a disjunctive rule," and that "it is difficult to conceive of a viable private action for damages under section 1 if some unreasonable restraint of trade has not been effected." Borger v. Yamaha Int'l Corp., 625 F.2d 390, 397 & n. 4 (2d Cir.1980). Other courts agree, see, e.g., Cascade Cabinet Co. v. Western Cabinet & Millwork, Inc., 710 F.2d 1366, 1372–73 (9th Cir.1983); Davis–Watkins Co. v. Service Merchandise, 686 F.2d 1190, 1202–03 (6th Cir. 1982); H & B Equip. Co. v. International Harvester Co., 577 F.2d 239, 246 (5th Cir.1978), and we now hold, for reasons stated in our discussion of the Section 2 claim, that an anticompetitive effect must be shown to make out a Section 1 Rule-of-Reason violation.

d. Legitimate Business Opportunities and Profit–Maximization Charge

The USFL further argues that the district court erroneously charged the jury that the NFL's three network contracts were lawful if motivated by any "legitimate" purpose, including profit maximization.

This charge was consistent with settled precedent. "[A] firm with lawful monopoly power has no general duty to help its competitors, whether by holding a price umbrella over their heads or by otherwise pulling its competitive punches." Olympia Equip. Leasing Co. v. Western Union Tel. Co., 797 F.2d 370, 375 (7th Cir.1986), cert. denied, 480 U.S. 934, 107 S.Ct. 1574, 94 L.Ed.2d 765 (1987); see Ball Memorial Hosp., Inc. v. Mutual Hosp. Ins., Inc., 784 F.2d 1325, 1338 (7th Cir.1986); Berkey Photo, 603 F.2d at 274, 276, 287. A monopolist may not, of course, use its market power, whether obtained lawfully or not, to prevent or impede competition in the relevant market. See Aspen Skiing, 472 U.S. at 605, 105 S.Ct. at 2859; Berkey Photo, 603 F.2d at 274.

The USFL challenges this charge on the ground that setting prices at a profit-maximizing level is an anticompetitive act. We disagree. Prices not based on superior efficiency do not injure competitors, see Matsushita Elec. Indus. Co. v. Zenith Radio Corp., 475 U.S. 574, 582–83,

106 S.Ct. 1348, 1354, 89 L.Ed.2d 538 (1986), but rather invite competitive entry. As we stated in Berkey Photo:

> Setting a high price may be a use of monopoly power, but it is not in itself anticompetitive. Indeed, although a monopolist may be expected to charge a somewhat higher price than would prevail in a competitive market, there is probably no better way for it to guarantee that its dominance will be challenged than by greedily extracting the highest price it can.

603 F.2d at 294. The USFL responds to this argument by falling back on its claim that professional football is not a typical market because of the "dilution effect," an argument rejected by the jury and discussed supra.

e. Television Submarket Definition

Regarding the relevant television submarket, the district court instructed the jury, first, to determine who were the potential purchasers of television broadcast rights for professional football in the fall. The jury was then, second, to determine from the perspective of those buyers what other products, if any, were reasonably interchangeable with broadcast rights to professional football. The USFL claims in particular that, in instructing the jury to determine who were potential purchasers, the district court erred by stating that:

> If you find that a professional football league would reasonably consider selling its broadcast rights to cable television companies or to individual television stations, then all those buyers must be included in the relevant submarket.

We do not agree with the USFL that this charge was error because it emphasized the view of potential buyers in determining the relevant submarket. See United States v. E.I. du Pont de Nemours & Co., 351 U.S. 377, 404, 76 S.Ct. 994, 1012, 100 L.Ed. 1264 (1956); see also United States v. Waste Management, Inc., 743 F.2d 976, 979–80 (2d Cir.1984) (defining relevant market by first determining potential buyers and then determining what products were reasonably interchangeable from buyers' perspectives); JBL Enters., Inc. v. Jhirmack Enters., Inc., 698 F.2d 1011, 1016–17 (9th Cir.), cert. denied, 464 U.S. 829, 104 S.Ct. 106, 78 L.Ed.2d 109 (1983). The fact that a cable contract might be less desirable, even much less desirable, to a league than a network contract is not relevant to determining the product submarket.

In any event, the USFL never objected to the relevant submarket instruction, and the objection was thus waived under Fed.R.Civ.P. 51. Contrary to its claim on appeal, the USFL did not "distinctly" object to this instruction, but merely proposed changes in language in the draft charge. These suggestions did not constitute a general objection to the entire charge. Indeed, the district judge expressly stated his understanding that the parties had objected only "to the extent [of] proposed changes in the charge". This was apparently the understanding of the USFL as well because the league raised a "general objection" to the intent-and-effect charge.

f. The Supplemental "Unambiguous Evidence" Charge

[This portion of the court's opinion is omitted.]

g. Consumer–Satisfaction Charge

The district judge also charged that in considering whether the NFL had engaged in anticompetitive conduct, the jury might "consider ... whether in a freely competitive market there would be any dissatisfaction with the present choices on the part of the buyers" or "whether or not the choices of those who purchased the rights to show or televise football have been restricted."

This instruction was correct. An inquiry into consumer preference is obviously relevant to a determination of whether a monopolist has engaged in predatory conduct. See Aspen Skiing, 472 U.S. at 605, 105 S.Ct. at 2858. Given the USFL's vigorously pressed claim that the NFL coerced the networks not to televise USFL games, it was entirely proper to allow the jury to consider whether the networks eschewed USFL fall contracts because of NFL coercion or because they were satisfied with the NFL's product.

h. Essential–Facilities Charge

Finally, the USFL contends that it was held to an improperly high standard of proof on its "essential-facilities" claim. We set out the pertinent charge:

> Plaintiffs allege that defendants violated Sections [1] and [2] of the Sherman Act by conspiring to and in fact denying plaintiffs access to a satisfactory national broadcast television contract for future seasons, with any one of the three networks. The legal basis for this particular claim by plaintiffs is that a network contract is an essential facility which the USFL or any other professional football league needs in order to compete in major league professional football.
>
> You should only consider this claim if you have already found, pursuant to my earlier instructions, that defendants possess monopoly power in a relevant market or submarket. If you have not found that defendants possess monopoly power, you must return a verdict in defendants' favor on this claim.
>
> In order to prove their essential "facilities" claim, plaintiffs must prove all of the following elements by a preponderance of the evidence:
>
> First: That a national broadcast television contract with at least one of the three networks, CBS, NBC or ABC is essential to the ability of a professional football league to compete successfully in the United States;
>
> Second[:] [T]hat potential competitors of the NFL cannot as a practical matter, duplicate the benefits of a network contract;
>
> Third: That the defendants control access to each of the three networks, that is, the defendants themselves have the

ability by their actions to deny actual or potential competitors, such as the USFL, access to national broadcast television—access to a national broadcast television contract;

Fourth: That the defendants through their actions have exercised their ability to deny actual or potential competitors access to a national broadcast television contract by denying the USFL such access;

Fifth: That a national broadcast television contract between one or more of the networks and a professional football league other than the NFL would not interfere with any of the defendants' lawful dealings with those networks.

The USFL argues first that this charge erred in failing to distinguish between a network television contract in the spring and one in the fall. The charge did, however, address the USFL's denial of "access to a satisfactory national broadcast contract for future seasons". The jury was well aware of the USFL's claim that a spring contract was unsatisfactory as an "inferior facility" or "minor league." It thus either rejected that characterization of spring football or rejected the USFL's claim that the NFL could deny the USFL access to a network in the fall. The spring-fall issue was thus before the jury.

The USFL next claims that it was error for the district court to require a showing of monopoly power in a relevant submarket or market before considering the essential-facilities claim. We fail to see why the USFL challenges this instruction because the jury did find monopoly power in a relevant market and therefore did consider the essential-facilities claim. Had the challenged instruction been omitted, the verdict would have been exactly the same.

Finally, the USFL claims that the district court erred by instructing the jury that one element of an essential-facilities claim is that an antitrust defendant "control access" to the facility. In the USFL's view, this element requires a showing only of "defendants' contribution to the prevention of plaintiffs' access to the facility." The requirement that the defendant control access to the facility is established in the caselaw, see, e.g., MCI Communications Corp. v. AT & T Co., 708 F.2d 1081, 1132 (to establish liability under the essential facilities doctrine, plaintiff must prove defendant's "control of the essential facility"), modified on other grounds, 1983–2 Trade Cas. (CCH) p 65,520 (7th Cir.), cert. denied, 464 U.S. 891, 104 S.Ct. 234, 78 L.Ed.2d 226 (1983), and is necessary because an essential-facilities claim must be brought against the party that can provide access to the facility.

2. *The District Court's Evidentiary Rulings*

a. The USFL's Merger Strategy

The USFL vigorously contends that the NFL's introduction of evidence of its merger strategy enabled the NFL to present an impermissible in pari delicto or unclean-hands defense under the guise of damage causation. This claim is frivolous.

It is true that a plaintiff's own anticompetitive conduct generally cannot be raised as a defense to liability in an antitrust action. See Perma Life Mufflers, Inc. v. International Parts Corp., 392 U.S. 134, 139, 88 S.Ct. 1981, 1984, 20 L.Ed.2d 982 (1968) (rejecting in pari delicto defense that plaintiff's participation in challenged scheme barred recovery); Kiefer–Stewart Co. v. Joseph E. Seagram & Sons, Inc., 340 U.S. 211, 214, 71 S.Ct. 259, 261, 95 L.Ed. 219 (1951) (rejecting unclean-hands defense based on plaintiff's involvement in unrelated conduct). The defense may be available, however, when the plaintiff was present at the creation and had a complete and continuing involvement in the monopolization scheme. See Perma Life, 392 U.S. at 140, 88 S.Ct. at 1985; P. Areeda & D. Turner, Antitrust Law p 348c (1978).

Whatever its force or content, the in pari delicto defense was never interposed by the NFL, and the evidence in question was quite properly admitted as relevant to causation and damages. Stretching dictum in Perma Life beyond recognition, the USFL misreads that decision to proscribe the introduction of evidence that might "prejudice the jury improperly into evaluating 'the relative moral worth of the parties.'" USFL Reply Br. at 14 (quoting Perma Life, 392 U.S. at 139, 88 S.Ct. at 1984). Neither Perma Life nor Kiefer–Stewart suggests that otherwise readily admissible evidence must be excluded because it might also be relevant to an in pari delicto or unclean-hands defense. In fact, Perma Life explicitly states that such evidence "can of course be taken into consideration in computing damages." 392 U.S. at 140, 88 S.Ct. at 1985; see also First Beverages, Inc. v. Royal Crown Cola Co., 612 F.2d 1164, 1175 (9th Cir.) (plaintiff's anticompetitive conduct could be introduced "to disprove part or all of the claimed damages"), cert. denied, 447 U.S. 924, 100 S.Ct. 3016, 65 L.Ed.2d 1116 (1980); Pearl Brewing Co. v. Jos. Schlitz Brewing Co., 415 F.Supp. 1122, 1131 (S.D.Tex.1976) ("evidence introduced by defendant of such conduct, if any, by a plaintiff which heretofore was labeled as 'in pari delicto' now is appropriate when it provides rebuttal to that plaintiff's allegations of causation of injury by defendant and resulting damages therefrom"). Such evidence also can be used for purposes of impeachment. See Memorex Corp. v. IBM Corp., 555 F.2d 1379, 1384 n. 8 (9th Cir.1977).

As with any evidence, therefore, the district judge had broad discretion to determine whether the probative value of the evidence of a merger strategy was "substantially outweighed by the danger of unfair prejudice, confusion of the issues, or misleading the jury." Fed.R.Evid. 403. His decision that evidence of business decisions made by the USFL pursuant to the merger strategy was highly relevant to the issues of causation and damages and not outweighed by any prejudicial effect was clearly correct. This evidence was highly probative on the central issue of whether the USFL's alleged injury and damages, particularly with regard to its failure to obtain a fall network contract, were caused by the NFL's anticompetitive conduct or by the USFL's own deliberate business judgments. See, e.g., Costner v. Blount Nat'l Bank, 578 F.2d 1192, 1195 (6th Cir.1978); Heatransfer Corp. v. Volkswagenwerk, A.G., 553 F.2d

964, 983 (5th Cir.1977), cert. denied, 434 U.S. 1087, 98 S.Ct. 1282, 55 L.Ed.2d 792 (1978); Borger v. Yamaha Int'l Corp., 625 F.2d at 399.

For example, Eddie Einhorn, the USFL owner who was to represent the USFL in negotiations with the networks for a fall contract, warned his fellow owners at a meeting in August 1984:

> We're starting to look for merger cities. Let's be honest about it. We're getting out of certain cities because we don't—they're getting taken in by the other League, and we're looking for merger cities. We've got to get it on the table tomorrow or this afternoon and start looking at this damn thing. I have the television; I got other problems.
>
> You can't get out of all the cities ahead of time because then you got no TV markets left. It's one of these chicken and egg deals. It's great to get out of them if we're absorbed; but if you're going to exist and need someone else to pay us television money, we can't get out of every city we've got here and just move into cities that aren't in the NFL or we're not going to have any product.

It quite simply defies logic for the USFL to assert on the one hand that it was denied a network contract indispensable to its survival because of the NFL's anticompetitive acts and to argue on the other for exclusion of evidence that the owners of USFL franchises knowingly lessened the value of their product to television. Courts do not exclude evidence of a victim's suicide in a murder trial.

To take another example, USFL Commissioner Usher testified that the USFL suffered a "tumbling" of teams and abandoned its spring season because NFL "pressure" caused ABC to withhold broadcast rights payments and to reject any proposal to televise the USFL. He further stated that the USFL sought competition between, rather than a merger of, the leagues, and that NFL pressure forced the USFL to move its teams from highly-rated television markets into low-rated non-NFL markets. Given that testimony, Judge Leisure would have erred had he not concluded that:

> certain of Usher's answers ... put in issue the fact of the merger motive ... [t]hus ... put[ting] in issue plaintiffs' theory that the cause of the moves to the [non-NFL] cities was NFL conduct. In addition, Usher has put in evidence the state of mind of the USFL owners who, he claims, moved the teams because of NFL competitive pressures.
>
> The proffered trial exhibits ... suggest that the reason the USFL decided to move those teams was to position the league for a merger. Certainly, if Usher claims that the basis for the USFL owners' decisions for [moving] the teams was by reason of NFL conduct, the NFL should be entitled to show that there is evidence that suggests that the USFL owners had a different motive.

Moreover, it was clearly proper for the NFL to use evidence of this strategy for impeachment purposes. See Memorex, 555 F.2d at 1384 n. 8. Although the USFL's desire to exclude this evidence is understandable, its own claims made it inevitable that the merger strategy and its resultant effect on the USFL's value as a television product would become an issue at trial. Indeed, the door was ajar to such evidence as early as the USFL's counsel's opening statement, in which he outlined the USFL's television claims. See United States v. Bari, 750 F.2d 1169, 1180 (2d Cir.1984) (door may be opened through counsel's opening statement), cert. denied, 472 U.S. 1019, 105 S.Ct. 3482, 87 L.Ed.2d 617 (1985).

Judge Leisure correctly circumscribed the uses to which the evidence of a merger strategy was put and gave a limiting instruction to the jury four times. In part, that limiting instruction stated that "the nature of plaintiffs' conduct must have no bearing on your evaluation of whether the defendants did anything in violation of the antitrust laws." We have on "numerous occasions" found that such "an instruction was sufficient to enable the jury to limit its consideration of the evidence to the purpose for which it was offered." United States v. Siegel, 717 F.2d 9, 18 (2d Cir.1983).

Finally, we reject the USFL's claim that particular items of evidence of its merger strategy were inadmissible on other grounds. It was hardly an abuse of discretion to admit USFL owner Myles Tannenbaum's view of the three ways to make money in professional football, namely "tickets, television and triple damages," to show that plaintiffs, after failing in the marketplace, sought to compel a merger through the threat of antitrust litigation. See Argus v. Eastman Kodak Co., 801 F.2d 38, 43 (2d Cir.1986) (relying on evidence that plaintiff had been "searching for the means of entering the antitrust fray"), cert. denied, 479 U.S. 1088, 107 S.Ct. 1295, 94 L.Ed.2d 151 (1987). With respect to the McKinsey & Company report advising against a shift to fall play, Judge Leisure limited its use to showing that advice paid for by, and given to, the USFL owners was not followed. The report was not admitted for the truth of the statements contained therein. See Siegel, 717 F.2d at 18.

b. Prior NFL Antitrust Judgments

In his Opinion No. 3, Judge Leisure excluded from evidence prior court decisions that found the NFL to have violated Section 1 of the Sherman Act. 634 F.Supp. at 1171–75. The USFL contends on appeal that this ruling was error, and that the NFL used this ruling as a "shield" to present a "good monopolist" defense.

Prior antitrust violations and the history of competition in a market may, in appropriate cases, be admissible to establish market power and intent to monopolize. See, e.g., United States v. Grinnell Corp., 384 U.S. at 576, 86 S.Ct. at 1706; Lorain Journal Co. v. United States, 342 U.S. 143, 152–53, 72 S.Ct. 181, 186, 96 L.Ed. 162 (1951). Such evidence also may be admissible to establish the intent, motive and method of a conspiracy under Section 1. See Continental Ore Co. v. Union Carbide &

Carbon Corp., 370 U.S. 690, 710, 82 S.Ct. 1404, 1416, 8 L.Ed.2d 777 (1962). In order for the NFL's prior antitrust judgments to be admissible, however, the USFL bore the burden of demonstrating that the conduct underlying those prior judgments had a direct, logical relationship to the conduct at issue in this case. See Buckhead Theatre Co. v. Atlanta Enters., Inc., 327 F.2d 365, 368–69 (5th Cir.) (evidence of prior antitrust judgment irrelevant unless plaintiff introduced evidence that practices complained of in prior case "had an injurious effect upon the plaintiff"), cert. denied, 379 U.S. 888, 85 S.Ct. 158, 13 L.Ed.2d 92 (1964); Bray v. Safeway Stores, Inc., 392 F.Supp. 851, 866 (prior antitrust judgment admitted where underlying conduct was same as that alleged in main case) (citing FTC v. Cement Inst., 333 U.S. 683, 705, 68 S.Ct. 793, 805, 92 L.Ed. 1010 (1948)), vacated per settlement, 403 F.Supp. 412 (N.D.Cal.1975).

Judge Leisure found that the USFL never made such a showing, and, although we do not fully embrace his reasoning, we agree that the prior judgments should not have been admitted as evidence of a long-standing conspiracy somehow casting light on current alleged illegalities. Two of the decisions in question, Smith v. Pro Football, Inc., 593 F.2d 1173 (D.C.Cir.1978) (invalidating rules for NFL player draft); Mackey v. National Football League, 543 F.2d 606 (8th Cir.1976) (invalidating "Rozelle Rule" for compensation of free agents), are not consistent with our decision in Wood v. National Basketball Ass'n, 809 F.2d 954 (2d Cir.1987). The three others, Los Angeles Memorial Coliseum Comm'n v. National Football League, 726 F.2d 1381 (9th Cir.) (invalidating NFL Rule 4.3 limiting franchise relocation), cert. denied, 469 U.S. 990, 105 S.Ct. 397, 83 L.Ed.2d 331 (1984), later opinion, 791 F.2d 1356 (9th Cir.1986), cert. denied, ___ U.S. ___, 108 S.Ct. 92, 98 L.Ed.2d 53 (1987); North Am. Soccer League v. National Football League, 670 F.2d 1249 (2d Cir.) (invalidating rule forbidding franchise owners from owning other professional sports teams), cert. denied, 459 U.S. 1074, 103 S.Ct. 499, 74 L.Ed.2d 639 (1982), and United States v. National Football League, 116 F.Supp. 319 (E.D.Pa.1953) (invalidating rules limiting broadcast of games into home territories of other teams), involve difficult antitrust questions that were (and, in circuits other than the place of decision, may still be) fair game for litigation. Accordingly, these cases are at best marginally probative of an ongoing intent to exclude competitors.

Judge Leisure excluded the latter three judgments on the ground that they involved intraleague restraints, whereas the instant litigation involves interleague competition. Although we hesitate to adopt a rule that anticompetitive restraints among competitors can never reveal monopolistic intent toward would-be entrants, we do note that sports leagues raise numerous difficult antitrust questions involving horizontal restraints and group boycotts. The very concept of a league involving separate business entities (teams) requires concerted behavior among them and the exclusion of outsiders. Even the drawing up of a schedule requires that horizontal competitors (teams) conform to jointly made decisions and necessarily excludes others. See R. Bork, The Antitrust

Paradox 332 (1978). Moreover, the antitrust law governing horizontal arrangements among competitors and group boycotts has been fluid. With regard to arrangements among competitors, compare United States v. Socony–Vacuum Oil Co., 310 U.S. 150, 223, 60 S.Ct. 811, 844, 84 L.Ed. 1129 (1940) ("[u]nder the Sherman Act a combination formed for the purpose and with the effect of raising, depressing, fixing, pegging, or stabilizing the price of a commodity in interstate or foreign commerce is illegal per se"), with Broadcast Music, Inc. v. CBS, Inc., 441 U.S. 1, 23, 99 S.Ct. 1551, 1564, 60 L.Ed.2d 1 (1979) ("[n]ot all arrangements among actual or potential competitors that have an impact on price are per se violations of the Sherman Act or even unreasonable restraints"). With regard to group boycotts, compare Klor's Inc. v. Broadway–Hale Stores, Inc., 359 U.S. 207, 212, 79 S.Ct. 705, 709, 3 L.Ed.2d 741 (1959) ("[g]roup boycotts, or concerted refusals by traders to deal with other traders, have long been held to be in the forbidden [per se] category"), with Jefferson Parish Hospital District No. 2 v. Hyde, 466 U.S. 2, 30–31, 104 S.Ct. 1551, 1567–68, 80 L.Ed.2d 2 (1984) (exclusion of physician from hospital staff privileges not violation of antitrust laws "[w]ithout a showing of actual adverse effect on competition" in product market), and Northwest Wholesale Stationers, Inc. v. Pacific Stationery & Printing Co., 472 U.S. 284, 296, 105 S.Ct. 2613, 2620, 86 L.Ed.2d 202 (1985) (group boycott was not per se illegal absent proof that buying cooperative possessed market power).

Accordingly, we are wary of allowing a trier of fact to draw inferences of intent from the outcome of prior lawsuits in an area so fraught with uncertainty and doubt. Our wariness in this regard is enhanced by the fact that the lawsuits most pertinent to the instant action—involving claims by another league or a team in another league—were in fact won by the NFL. American Football League v. National Football League, 323 F.2d 124 (4th Cir.1963); Mid–South Grizzlies v. National Football League, 720 F.2d 772 (3d Cir.1983). The district court thus acted within its discretion in excluding evidence of prior antitrust judgments against the NFL on the grounds that their prejudicial value outweighed their probative value under Fed.R.Evid. 403. See International Shoe Mach. Corp. v. United Shoe Mach. Corp., 315 F.2d 449, 459 (1st Cir.) ("Whether admitted purely as 'background' evidence or not, evidence of a judicial determination of prior illegal conduct on the part of the defendant cannot help but have a great emotive impact on a jury."), cert. denied, 375 U.S. 820, 84 S.Ct. 56, 11 L.Ed.2d 54 (1963); see also Bohack Corp. v. Iowa Beef Processors, Inc., 715 F.2d 703, 709 (2d Cir.1983) (appellate court reluctant to overturn trial court decision under Rule 403 unless arbitrary or irrational).

We next consider several related evidentiary issues. The USFL claims that a statement by Commissioner Rozelle that the NFL was "in bed with" the City of Oakland should have been admitted. This statement, made during testimony before the Senate Judiciary Committee on a bill that would have given the NFL greater control over franchise relocation, indicated that the NFL had cooperated closely with the City of Oakland during the course of litigation seeking to keep the NFL Raiders in that city. The USFL hoped to use this statement to demonstrate the existence of a conspiracy between the NFL and the City of Oakland to destroy the USFL Invaders in order to bring about the return of the Raiders to Oakland. Judge Leisure again acted within his discretion in ruling that Rozelle's statement did not tend to prove such a conspiracy and that the statement's probative value was thus outweighed by its prejudicial effect because of the need for foundation testimony regarding the Raiders' litigation against the NFL. For similar reasons, exclusion of excerpts from minutes of the Oakland–Alameda County Coliseum Board of Directors was proper.

Judge Leisure was also well within his discretion in excluding Al Davis's testimony about what Davis called the NFL's "habitual disregard" of antitrust advice. This evidence would have put before the jury the precise evidence of prior antitrust judgments previously and correctly deemed inadmissible. Moreover, Judge Leisure correctly found that this testimony was not admissible "habit" evidence under Fed.R.Evid. 406, because testimony as to "three or four episodes over a 20–year period" was hardly sufficient to "conclude that a pattern of behavior exists with respect to the conduct at issue here." See G.M. Brod & Co. v. U.S. Home Corp., 759 F.2d 1526, 1533 (11th Cir.1985) (error to admit collateral evidence of routine practice that falls short of "adequacy of sampling and uniformity of response" required by Rule 406). Finally, Judge Leisure properly prevented the USFL from attempting to impeach Commissioner Rozelle through an affidavit of Lamar Hunt, an NFL owner who also owned a professional soccer team. This testimony was hearsay and, if allowed, would have resulted in a "mini-trial about the NASL case [or] about the position Hunt took in that litigation." See Bari, 750 F.2d at 1178–79 (no abuse of discretion in refusing to permit cross-examination of witness that would lead to "mini-trial").

c. *Legislative Process Evidence*

The USFL claims that the district court erroneously excluded evidence relating to the activities of the NFL in Congress. This evidence included (1) the NFL's lobbying activities in connection with the 1961 Sports Broadcasting Act and the 1966 NFL–AFL merger legislation, (2) Congress's motives in enacting this legislation, and (3) Senator Alphonse D'Amato's knowledge of the NFL's use of "pressure" tactics in its congressional lobbying.

Legislative lobbying efforts cannot of course be the basis of antitrust liability. See Eastern R.R. Presidents Conference v. Noerr Motor Freight, Inc., 365 U.S. 127, 135–36, 81 S.Ct. 523, 528, 5 L.Ed.2d 464 (1961); United Mine Workers of Am. v. Pennington, 381 U.S. 657, 669–72, 85 S.Ct. 1585, 1593–94, 14 L.Ed.2d 626 (1965). Evidence of such lobbying may be admitted, however, "if it tends reasonably to show the purpose and character of the particular transactions under scrutiny," Pennington, 381 U.S. at 670 n. 3, 85 S.Ct. at 1593 n. 3 (quoting FTC v. Cement

Inst., 333 U.S. at 705, 68 S.Ct. at 805), and that evidence is more probative than prejudicial. Id.

We address first the exclusion of evidence about the Sports Broadcasting Act and the 1966 merger legislation. The USFL objects to the exclusion of a House Committee Report on the Sports Broadcasting Act, which stated that Congress expected professional sports leagues to institute competitive bidding for their television rights as soon as existing contracts expired. See H.R.Rep. No. 1178, 87th Cong., 1st Sess. (1961). The USFL sought to demonstrate by this report that the NFL had misled Congress by promising to put NFL telecasts (especially of the championship game) up for competitive bidding. Judge Leisure properly ruled that the interpretation of legislative history was not an issue of fact for the jury, see Stissi v. Interstate & Ocean Transp. Co., 765 F.2d 370, 374 (2d Cir.1985), and that such evidence was otherwise excludable under Fed.R.Evid. 403 as overly prejudicial and confusing.

As to the NFL–AFL merger legislation, the USFL sought to introduce evidence that it was approved in part because the NFL had promised two powerful Louisiana lawmakers that a franchise would be awarded to New Orleans. The district court's refusal to admit such evidence was not an abuse of discretion. We also reject the USFL claim with regard to the exclusion of allegedly "doctored" minutes of NFL League meetings. In a pre-trial ruling, Judge Leisure correctly found that these minutes, which were submitted to Congress in connection with the merger legislation, had not been doctored, and that plaintiffs' claim was just a "diversionary tactic."

Finally, we address the district court's exclusion of Senator D'Amato's testimony about the NFL's use of "pressure" tactics in Congress. These tactics allegedly included threats to certain members of the House and Senate to remove franchises from their states and promises to others to move franchises to their states. The USFL argued that these lobbying activities fell within the "sham" exception to Noerr–Pennington. We agree, however, with Judge Leisure that efforts to persuade government officials simply by appealing to their political interests have Noerr–Pennington protection. See Noerr, 365 U.S. at 142–44, 81 S.Ct. at 532–33; Mid–South Grizzlies, 720 F.2d at 784; Bustop Shelters, Inc. v. Convenience & Safety Corp., 521 F.Supp. 989, 995 (S.D.N.Y.1981).

Evidence of lobbying may, as we have already stated, nevertheless be admitted as purpose or character evidence. See Pennington, 381 U.S. at 670–71 n. 3, 85 S.Ct. at 1593 n. 3. Judge Leisure thus allowed Senator D'Amato to testify about the Senator's own experience with the NFL's lobbying after formation of the USFL in 1982, but forbade any reference to prior lawsuits or to particular legislation. Senator D'Amato was also not permitted to testify concerning double-hearsay statements made by NFL officials to other members of Congress. Even if these statements could survive a hearsay objection, however, they were properly excluded on two other grounds. First, the testimonial privilege that members of Congress enjoy under the Speech or Debate Clause of the Constitution, art. I, § 6, cannot be waived by another member (in this case, Senator D'Amato). As Judge Leisure stated, the underlying purpose of the Speech or Debate Clause, which is to "protect the integrity of the legislative process by insuring the independence of individual legislators," United States v. Brewster, 408 U.S. 501, 507, 92 S.Ct. 2531, 2535, 33 L.Ed.2d 507 (1972), would be "ill-served" if such waivers were permitted. Second, this testimony was properly excluded under Fed. R.Evid. 403 because of its potentially prejudicial impact on the jury.

Finally, with regard to all of the excluded evidence relating to the legislative process, we tend to share the view of the Third Circuit that, "[i]f these allegations are true, ... they are, perhaps, instructive on the nature of the federal legislative process. For purposes of [the Sherman Act], however, they are irrelevant." Mid–South Grizzlies, 720 F.2d at 784.

d. Examination of Damages Experts

The USFL further claims that Judge Leisure erred by not permitting the cross-examination of Dr. Bruce Owen, the NFL's damages expert, about testimony he gave in unrelated cases. In the cases in question, Buffalo Broadcasting Co. v. American Society of Composers, Authors & Publishers, 546 F.Supp. 274, 293 n. 42 (S.D.N.Y.1982) (rejecting testimony of defendant's expert Owen, in part because he had testified as government economist that ASCAP was anticompetitive cartel), rev'd, 744 F.2d 917 (2d Cir.1984), cert. denied, 469 U.S. 1211, 105 S.Ct. 1181, 84 L.Ed.2d 329 (1985), and Southern Pacific Communications Co. v. AT & T Co., 556 F.Supp. 825, 913 (D.D.C.1982) (rejecting testimony of plaintiff's expert Owen, in part because of role as government economist favoring AT & T break-up), aff'd, 740 F.2d 980, 740 F.2d 1011 (D.C.Cir.1984), cert. denied, 470 U.S. 1005, 105 S.Ct. 1359, 84 L.Ed.2d 380 (1985), Dr. Owen's testimony was rejected by the district court but vindicated on appeal. See Buffalo Broadcasting, 744 F.2d at 931–33 & n. 12; Southern Pacific, 740 F.2d at 1000–02. It was well within Judge Leisure's discretion to avoid a confusing and certainly complex digression into two earlier trials and appeals. See Bari, 750 F.2d at 1178–79. We note that such a digression is not required by Walker v. Firestone Tire & Rubber Co., 412 F.2d 60, 63–64 (2d Cir.1969), in which the expert in question had given extremely contradictory testimony regarding his qualifications in an earlier unrelated trial. Probing into the qualifications of an expert is a far cry from probing into differing judicial reactions to Owen's prior testimony in totally unrelated cases.

Moreover, the record does not support the USFL claim that the district court allowed the NFL to challenge the USFL's damages case unfairly. Fed.R.Evid. 104(a) permits voir dire of an expert witness, where, as here, an expert's testimony involved two industries, professional football and television, and various complex economic models and assumptions. The district court also properly allowed the NFL to question Dr. Cornell about the effect of injunctive relief on the USFL's damages, namely "what effect, if any, ... a cessation of illegal conduct by defendants would have on plaintiffs' future." This cross-examination did no more than probe Dr. Cornell's direct testimony that future damages were appropriate because the USFL would suffer damage "as long as the particular behavior complained about ... continues."

e. Miscellaneous Evidentiary Claims

We briefly address the USFL's remaining evidentiary claims. The record contradicts the USFL's claim that it was not permitted to examine New York Jets' owner Leon Hess about his alleged conflict of interest as an NFL owner and ABC director and about statements made by Senator D'Amato and Vincent Tese. The district court also acted within its discretion when it excluded a letter to Hess from Mayor Edward Koch regarding the return of the Jets to New York City, even though Hess's reply was admitted. The Koch letter was excluded on the grounds that it was both hearsay and unduly prejudicial under Rule 403. The doctrine of completeness, Fed.R.Evid. 106, does not compel admission of otherwise inadmissible hearsay evidence. See United States v. Terry, 702 F.2d 299, 314 (2d Cir.), cert. denied, 461 U.S. 931, 103 S.Ct. 2095, 77 L.Ed.2d 304 (1983).

Judge Leisure also properly excluded a 1982 letter from the Senate Judiciary Committee to Roone Arledge of ABC regarding sportscaster Howard Cosell's testimony on legislation concerning sports franchise relocation. The USFL claimed that Arledge, at Rozelle's request, had sought to reschedule Cosell's testimony in order to increase the likelihood that the bill would be voted out of committee before Congress adjourned. However, the USFL failed to establish a sufficient foundation for the admission of this letter under the public record exception of Fed.R.Evid. 803(8).

In addition, the USFL claims that an exchange of letters in 1970 between then ABC President Leonard Goldenstein and the president of an earlier United States Football League, which never fielded any teams, was improperly excluded from evidence. In his reply, Goldenstein had stated that ABC was not interested in televising another league because it had just signed an NFL contract for Monday Night Football. The USFL hoped to show by this evidence that the NFL's television contracts prevented the networks from broadcasting another league. Judge Leisure, however, acted within his discretion in concluding that the NFL would be unduly prejudiced under Fed.R.Evid. 403 by the admission of these letters and that a proper foundation for this hearsay evidence had not been established pursuant to Fed.R.Evid. 803(6). On the other hand, he did admit evidence relating to the WFL's futile attempts to obtain television contracts after Rozelle had testified that he told CBS officials of his "surprise" that Robert Wussler, president of CBS Sports, had attended a meeting with the WFL.

The district court also excluded testimony by Ed Garvey, former head of the NFL Players Association, regarding ABC's unwillingness, without NFL approval, to consider broadcasting touch football games during the halftime of NFL games. Such testimony was clearly irrelevant and misleading with respect to any alleged television conduct by the NFL because it had nothing to do with the USFL or NFL control over the networks. Instead it concerned the production only of NFL games.

Finally, we consider the USFL's attempt to impeach Tex Schramm of the Dallas Cowboys by showing that his testimony that the unionization of the USFL was never discussed at NFL meetings was false. First, no foundation was laid to introduce handwritten notes of an NFL official allegedly reflecting the comments of an NFL players union official at an NFL meeting. Second, these notes were, as Judge Leisure found, being offered for their truth, not simply for the fact that the statements were made, and were properly excluded as multiple hearsay under Fed.R.Evid. 805.

3. *The District Court's Damages Instructions*

The USFL contends that it received an award of only $1.00 because of incorrect jury instructions regarding damages. Again, we disagree. Specifically, the USFL challenges the instructions with respect to an antitrust plaintiff's burden of proving the amount of damages and with respect to nominal damages.

a. The $1.00 Award

The jury was given the following nominal damages instruction:

> Just because you have found the fact of some damage resulting from a given unlawful act, that does not mean that you are required to award a dollar amount of damages resulting from that act. You may find, for example, that you are unable to compute the monetary damages resulting from the wrongful act, except by engaging in speculation or guessing, or you find that you cannot separate out the amount of the losses caused by the wrongful act from the amount caused by other factors, including perfectly lawful competitive acts and including business decisions made by the plaintiffs or the plaintiffs' own mismanagement. Or you may find that plaintiffs failed to prove an amount of damages. You may decline to award damages under such circumstances, or you may award a nominal amount, say $1.

The jury's $1.00 award was consistent with this instruction. The NFL offered much evidence of self-destructive USFL decisions, and the jury's nominal award suggests that it credited this proof, as it was free to do. Moreover, it is now clear that Dr. Cornell's testimony was based on a number of assumptions entailing legal premises that were incorrect or factual conclusions that were rejected by the jury. In awarding only nominal damages, the jury might reasonably have concluded that the USFL had failed to prove any damages.

b. Nominal Damages in Antitrust Cases

We also reject the USFL's claim that the award of nominal damages in antitrust cases is somehow "suspect." Other courts routinely approve the award of such damages, see, e.g., Rosebrough Monument Co. v. Memorial Park Cemetery Ass'n, 666 F.2d 1130, 1147 (8th Cir.1981), cert.

denied, 457 U.S. 1111, 102 S.Ct. 2915, 73 L.Ed.2d 1321 (1982), and the USFL cites no authority holding that nominal damages are impermissible in an antitrust case. It is true that we questioned the award of nominal damages in dictum, Herman Schwabe, Inc. v. United Shoe Mach. Corp., 297 F.2d 906, 909 n. 4 (2d Cir.) ("possibility of awarding nominal damages under § 4 of the Clayton Act ... seems dubious in light of the language of the statute and the Supreme Court opinions"), cert. denied, 369 U.S. 865, 82 S.Ct. 1031, 8 L.Ed.2d 85 (1962). However, our observations were made in the context of a directed verdict based on the plaintiff's failure to prove damages. The USFL's reliance upon Schwabe is, as the district court noted, "remarkably ironic" because the rationale of Schwabe would deny the USFL any damages at all. Opinion No. 16, 644 F.Supp. at 1053.

c. Proof of Antitrust Injury and Damages

We next consider whether the district court properly instructed the jury with respect to an antitrust plaintiff's burden of proving the amount of damages. To recover treble damages under Section 4 of the Clayton Act, 15 U.S.C. § 15 (1982), an antitrust plaintiff must prove that its injury was, in fact, caused by the defendant's violation of the antitrust laws. Argus, 801 F.2d at 41; MCI Communications, 708 F.2d at 1161.

Judge Leisure instructed the jury as follows with respect to injury causation:

> [P]laintiffs do not have to prove that the unlawful activity that the defendants allegedly engaged in was the sole cause of their injuries. Plaintiffs meet their burden if they show that the defendants' unlawful acts substantially contributed to their injuries, even though other facts may have contributed significantly. An antitrust plaintiff is not required to show that the defendants' acts were a greater cause of the injury than other factors. Plaintiffs need only show that their injury to some degree resulted from defendants' violation.

The USFL understandably does not challenge this instruction, which was consistent with established precedent. See Zenith Radio Corp. v. Hazeltine Research, Inc., 395 U.S. 100, 114 n. 9, 89 S.Ct. 1562, 1572 n. 9, 23 L.Ed.2d 129 (1969); Litton Sys., Inc. v. AT & T Co., 700 F.2d 785, 823 n. 49 (2d Cir.1983), cert. denied, 464 U.S. 1073, 104 S.Ct. 984, 79 L.Ed.2d 220 (1984). Rather, the USFL challenges Judge Leisure's instruction that the jury could award no damages or one dollar in damages if they found that they could not "separate out the amount of losses caused by [NFL misconduct] from the amount caused by other factors, including perfectly lawful competitive acts and including business decisions made by the [USFL] or the [USFL's] own mismanagement."

The USFL claims that this instruction was incorrect because the NFL should have borne the burden of separating out the amount of USFL losses caused by the NFL's wrongful acts from the amount caused by other factors such as the USFL's unsuccessful merger strategy. It is true that once proof of injury causation has been established, courts have allowed antitrust plaintiffs considerable latitude in proving the amount of damages. Proof of amount of damages thus need not conform to a particular theory or model, see Locklin v. Day–Glo Color Corp., 429 F.2d 873, 880 (7th Cir.1970) (citing Continental Ore Co. v. Union Carbide & Carbon Corp., 370 U.S. 690, 82 S.Ct. 1404, 8 L.Ed.2d 777 (1962)), cert. denied, 400 U.S. 1020, 91 S.Ct. 582, 27 L.Ed.2d 632 (1971), and exact proof of the amount of damages is not required. See J. Truett Payne Co. v. Chrysler Motors Corp., 451 U.S. 557, 566, 101 S.Ct. 1923, 1929, 68 L.Ed.2d 442 (1981) (acceptance of "degree of uncertainty" in measure of antitrust damages is necessary because of difficulty of ascertaining "what plaintiff's situation would have been in the absence of the defendant's antitrust violation"). An antitrust plaintiff must thus provide only sufficient evidence to support a "just and reasonable estimate" of damages. Bigelow v. RKO Radio Pictures, Inc., 327 U.S. 251, 264, 66 S.Ct. 574, 579, 90 L.Ed. 652 (1946); see also Story Parchment Co. v. Paterson Parchment Paper Co., 282 U.S. 555, 563, 51 S.Ct. 248, 250, 75 L.Ed. 544 (1931) (proof of antitrust damages sufficient "if the evidence show[s] the extent of the damages as a matter of just and reasonable inference, although the result be only approximate").

Whatever latitude is afforded antitrust plaintiffs as to proof of damages, however, is limited by the requirement that the damages awarded must be traced to some degree to unlawful acts. MCI Communications, 708 F.2d at 1161. That latitude is thus circumscribed by the need for proof of causation. The Supreme Court emphasized this in Bigelow by relaxing the standard for proving amount of damages only after "proof of defendant['s] wrongful acts and their tendency to injure plaintiff['s] business, and from the evidence of the decline in prices, profits and values, not shown to be attributable to other causes." 327 U.S. at 264, 66 S.Ct. at 579.

A plaintiff's proof of amount of damages thus must provide the jury with a reasonable basis upon which to estimate the amount of its losses caused by other factors, such as management problems, a general recession or lawful factors.

4. The District Court's Denial of Injunctive Relief

Finally, the USFL claims that the district court should have granted sweeping injunctive relief under Section 16 of the Clayton Act, 15 U.S.C. § 26 (1982). In particular, the USFL requested membership in the NFL, separation of the NFL into two leagues, each league being limited to one network, or a prohibition on the NFL from broadcasting its games in more than one afternoon time slot on Sunday. Judge Leisure held that the requested relief was unrelated to the monopolization of the market for major-league professional football verdict and not justified by the record as a whole.

The USFL contends that the jury's monopolization verdict compelled the district court to "pry open to competition [the] market that has been closed by defendants' illegal restraints." USFL Br. at 70 (quoting Zenith Radio, 395 U.S. at 133, 89 S.Ct. at 1582).

However, this argument simply glosses over the critical fact that the jury did not find the NFL liable on any of the USFL's television-related claims. With regard to the findings implied by the monopolization verdict that the NFL engaged in predatory conduct through attempts to co-opt USFL owners, creation of a Supplemental Draft, or expansion in roster size, Judge Leisure denied relief on the ground that the USFL provided no evidence that such conduct was likely to continue or recur. The USFL has not asked us to overturn that denial of relief.

Instead, the USFL seeks sweeping injunctive relief on the ground that the NFL's single league structure, in conjunction with television contracts with the three networks, creates an impenetrable barrier to entry by a competing league into the market of professional football. No matter what the jury found, however, such relief would not have been appropriate. First, Congress has authorized the NFL's single-league structure and its joint economic operations. Second, at the time the district court denied the relief, the NFL's contracts with the networks had expired. There was thus no "tie-up" of the three networks and no barrier to entry created by the "dilution effect." There was only free competition between the NFL's product and the USFL's product. Of course, the district court also properly rejected this claim in view of the jury's outright rejection of all of the USFL's television-related claims.

What the USFL seeks is essentially a judicial restructuring of major-league professional football to allow it to enter. Because of the explicit congressional authorization in 1966 for the NFL–AFL merger and single-league operation, the USFL does not attack the league structure directly. Instead, the USFL asks us to prevent networks from broadcasting, and fans from watching, NFL games in the hope that they will turn to the USFL. Absent a showing of an unlawful barrier to entry, however, new sports leagues must be prepared to make the investment of time, effort and money that develops interest and fan loyalty and results in an attractive product for the media. The jury in the present case obviously found that patient development of a loyal following among fans and an adherence to an original plan that offered long-run gains were lacking in the USFL. Instead, the USFL quickly changed to a strategy of competition with the NFL in the fall, hoping thereby to force a merger of a few USFL teams into the NFL. That led to a movement of USFL teams out of large television markets and a resultant reduction in value of USFL games to television. As USFL owner and negotiator Einhorn predicted, abandoning major television markets precluded the possibility of obtaining a network contract. The USFL hoped, however, that if a merger did not occur, a jury verdict in the instant litigation followed by a decree effectively forcing a network to televise its product would save the day. Instead, the jury found that the failure of the USFL was not the result of the NFL's television contracts but of its own decision to seek entry into the NFL on the cheap.

Conclusion

For the foregoing reasons, we affirm the jury's verdict and the judgments entered thereon. We thus need not consider the NFL's conditional cross-appeal.

Notes

1. The USFL did not walk away a complete loser from its battle with the NFL. Because the jury found the NFL guilty of some illegal behavior, the USFL was awarded $5.5 million in attorneys' fees and $62,000 in costs. *See United States Football League v. National Football League*, 704 F.Supp. 474 (S.D.N.Y.), *aff'd*, 887 F.2d 408 (2d Cir.1989), *cert. denied*, 493 U.S. 1071 (1990). For a further look at the USFL's tumultuous history, see Jim Byrne, *The $1 League: The Rise and Fall of the USFL* (1987).

2. The USFL was the third test in three decades for the NFL (the earlier two being the AFL in the 1960s and the WFL in the 1970s). It now appears, however, that the NFL is about to face its most formidable challenger. As explained earlier in this chapter, in January 1998 the NFL signed a blockbuster television deal with ABC, CBS, ESPN, and Fox, thereby leaving NBC and TBS without professional football for the next eight years. In response, the two networks announced they were looking into forming their own league. *See further* Jim Allen, *A Second Pro Football Team for Chicago? I Love It, Daley Says*, Chi. Daily Herald, May 29, 1998, at 3 (Sports), and Richard Sandomir, *Turner, NBC, Left Out of N.F.L., Plan League*, N.Y. Times, May 28, 1998, at C4. *See also* Leonard Shapiro, *Football League at the Start: An Expensive Idea Often Tried*, Wash. Post, Mar. 17, 1998, at E1 (detailed explanation of the many obstacles that must be overcome to start a professional football league).

3. In addition to the NFL, each of the other three major professional sports have experienced internecine warfare. Between 1913 and 1915, for example, MLB fought a short but fierce battle with the upstart Federal League (an encounter which ended when MLB agreed to pay its feisty rival $600,000 to disband, a step which set in motion the litigation that ultimately led to Justice Holmes' 1922 decision placing baseball beyond the reach of the federal antitrust laws). In the 1950s, MLB was confronted first by the Pacific Coast League (a threat which was squelched when, as explained earlier in this chapter, the Brooklyn Dodgers and New York Giants relocated to California) and then by the Continental League (which collapsed after its chief goal—obtaining an NL expansion team for New York City—was achieved with the addition of the New York Mets in 1962). More recently, in October 1987, plans for a third baseball league, to be called the United Baseball League, were moving forward when the stock market's sudden crash caused investors to get cold feet. For a further look at the history of rival professional baseball leagues, see Andrew Zimbalist, *Baseball Economics and Antitrust Immunity*, 4 Seton Hall J. Sport L. 287 (1994).

The NBA's first encounter with a rival came in 1967, when the ABA began play with 10 teams. Known for its colorful athletes (such as Julius "Dr. J" Erving, one of the first slam dunk specialists, and Connie Hawkins, who had been blacklisted by the NBA for his part in a college basketball gambling scandal), uniforms (such as the Miami Floridans' hot orange and magenta), names (such as the Baltimore Hustlers, a moniker that raised so many eyebrows it was quickly changed to the Claws), and ball (a riot of red, white, and blue that had been suggested by George Mikan, the league's first commissioner, because of how it would look on television), the ABA lasted nine years and introduced such dubious innovations as the three-point field goal and scantily-clad "ball girls." In 1976, the NBA made peace with its rival and absorbed four of its teams (the Denver Nuggets, Indiana Pacers, New York Nets, and San Antonio Spurs). The wackiness of the ABA, which often was described as "The Lively League," is vividly recalled in Terry Pluto, *Loose Balls: The Short, Wild Life of the American Basketball Association* (1990).

The NBA's second encounter with a rival occurred in 1996. Convinced there finally was sufficient demand for professional women's basketball, the NBA made plans to introduce a summer league, which it dubbed the Women's National Basketball Association, in June 1997. But a rival known as the American Basketball League beat the NBA to the punch by launching a fall-winter league several months ahead of the WNBA. Despite its head-start, larger salaries, and superior players, however, the ABL proved no match for the better-financed and better-run WNBA. As the ABL struggled to make ends meet in second-rate stadiums with crowds that averaged just over 4,000, the WNBA was drawing close to 11,000 fans per game in NBA arenas. And while the ABL had to pay little-watched networks to air its games, the WNBA struck lucrative deals with NBC, ESPN, and Lifetime and became a merchandising juggernaut. Faced with these overwhelming obstacles, the ABL was forced to declare bankruptcy in December 1998. *See further* Selena Roberts, *Love's Labor is Lost as A.B.L. Goes Dark*, N.Y. Times, Dec. 23, 1998, at C19, and Richard Sandomir, *Millions of Dollars Too Short, With No Network at the Door*, N.Y. Times, Dec. 23, 1998, at C21.

The NHL's turn to face a rival arrived in 1972, when a group of California entrepreneurs led by Santa Ana attorney Gary Davidson announced formation of a 12–team league they called the WHA. Although initially dismissed by the NHL, the WHA proved a determined competitor, helped in large part by successful player raids that netted such superstars as Bobby Hull, Gerry Cheevers, J.C. Tremblay, Bernie Parent, and Derek Sanderson. Finally, in 1979, after years of both leagues being bled dry by escalating player salaries, a truce was declared: in return for ceasing operations, four of the WHA's teams (the Edmonton Oilers, Hartford Whalers, Quebec Nordiques, and Winnipeg Jets) were allowed to join the NHL. For a further description of the WHA, see Scott A. Surgent, *The Complete Historical and Statistical Reference to the World Hockey Association, 1972–1979* (1995).

4. One of the most obvious issues whenever a rival league is formed concerns its right to hire away players. After years of bitter litigation, the following answer has emerged: teams can only prevent athletes from jumping to another league while they are subject to a bona fide contract. *See further Cincinnati Bengals v. Bergey*, 453 F.Supp. 129, 139 n. 1 (S.D.Ohio 1974) (collecting cases).

5. Unlike professional sports, where rival leagues always have fought each other tooth-and-nail, college football conferences for years worked together to ensure there would not be a true national champion. Although seemingly counter-intuitive, the arrangement allowed numerous teams to play for (and then claim) a mythical championship while permitting bowl game organizers to each call their particular contest the national championship game. Even after a College Bowl Alliance was formed to ensure the

regular emergence of an undisputed champion, the lack of a playoff system left the status quo intact.

Concerned by the ability of the bowl organizers to perennially shut out schools lacking name recognition or large legions of fans willing to travel to distant bowl sites, Congress in 1997 held hearings to determine whether any antitrust laws were being broken. In response, the Bowl Alliance agreed the champions of the Western Athletic Conference and Conference USA would receive one or both of the two at-large bids if they finished among the top six teams in the national media and coaches polls. Mollified by this promise (the hearings originally had been called for by senators from the home states of these conferences), Congress dropped its inquiry.

In 1998, the Bowl Alliance, now renamed the Bowl Championship Series (BCS) to reflect the addition of the Big Ten and Pacific 10 conferences (whose champions previously had been contractually committed to playing each other in the Rose Bowl), adopted a new method of determining match-ups. Rather than relying solely on voter polls, the BCS utilizes a complicated formula based on both subjective and objective factors (including, most importantly, strength of schedule). Nevertheless, in its first year the new plan nearly failed to produce a championship game until, on the last weekend of the regular season, the underdog University of Miami Hurricanes stunned the previously unbeaten UCLA Bruins and the Texas A & M University Aggies did likewise to the Kansas State University Wildcats. As a result of the imperfections in the BCS ranking system, it is possible Congress may someday decide to take another look at the bowls. For a further description of the evolution of the BCS, see, e.g., Steve Wieberg & Jack Carey, *Focusing on a National Title: Intent is to End Controversy*, USA Today, Aug. 6, 1998, at 1C, and Jim Short, *In Search of a True No. 1*, Riverside (CA) Press–Enterprise, June 10, 1998, at C1. *See also* Cynthia G. Farbman, *Forced to be a Fan: An Analysis and History of the IRS's Proposed Regulations Regarding Corporate Sponsorship*, 2 Sports Law. J. 53 (1995) (discussing an earlier attempt to regulate the bowls by taxing the income received from corporate sponsors).

6. In the parlance of antitrust law, anything which an aspirant needs to compete successfully is an "essential facility" and therefore cannot be illegally withheld (or interfered with) by competitors. In the world of sports, there are at least four types of essential facilities: wealthy owners, talented players, lucrative national television contracts, and suitable stadiums. Recall, however, the plaintiffs' unsuccessful argument in *Murray* that NFL arbitration also was an essential facility because without it access to professional football was impossible.

Both *NASL* and *USFL* are examples of traditional essential facilities litigation. In the former, of course, the NASL claimed its ability to attract wealthy investors was being impeded by the NFL's cross-ownership ban. In the latter, the USFL insisted its failure to secure quality players and a fall television contract were due to the NFL's decision to expand its rosters, conduct a supplemental draft, and seek exclusivity from the networks.

In contrast to lawsuits over owners, players, and television contracts, which typically are fought at the national level, lawsuits concerning stadium access occur locally in those cities which possess only one professional-quality arena. Thus, for example, in *Shayne v. National Hockey League*, 504 F.Supp. 1023 (E.D.N.Y.1980), the plaintiff accused the NHL of placing an expansion team (the New York Islanders) on Long Island in 1972 solely to thwart his plan to move a WHA franchise into the Nassau County Veterans Memorial Coliseum, which at the time was nearing completion and looking for an anchor tenant. Finding no causal connection between the league's actions and the plaintiff's injury, the court granted summary judgment in favor of the NHL. Similarly, in *Scallen v. Minnesota Vikings Football Club, Inc.*, 574 F.Supp. 278 (D.Minn.1983), the prospective owner of the Minneapolis–St. Paul USFL franchise sued the Minnesota Vikings after he failed to obtain a lease from the Metrodome, the area's sole major league stadium. Once again, no causal connection could be demonstrated by the plaintiff and the suit was dismissed. For other cases of this sort, see, e.g., *Fishman v. Wirtz*, 807 F.2d 520 (7th Cir.1986) (access to Chicago Stadium), and *Hecht v. Pro–Football, Inc.*, 570 F.2d 982 (D.C.Cir.1977), *cert. denied*, 436 U.S. 956 (1978) (access to Robert F. Kennedy Stadium).

For a further look at the theoretical underpinnings of the essential facilities doctrine, see, e.g., James R. Ratner, *Should There Be An Essential Facility Doctrine?*, 21 U.C. Davis L. Rev. 327 (1988), and Daniel E. Troy, Note, *Unclogging the Bottleneck: A New Essential Facility Doctrine*, 83 Colum. L. Rev. 441 (1983). *See also Brenner v. World Boxing Council*, 1981 WL 2015 (S.D.N.Y.1981) (promoter blacklisted by boxing association allowed to argue access to contenders is an essential facility).

7. Despite their differences, the AFL, Federal League, Continental League, ABA, and WHA all had one thing in common: they grew out of failed attempts by their organizers to secure franchises in their sport's established league.

Historically, sports leagues have resisted expansion out of a fear of diluting the quality of their product and a reluctance to share profits with newcomers. By the same token, when they have undertaken expansion (usually to create a bigger "footprint" so as to be able to obtain a more handsome national television contract), successful applicants have had to pay large admission fees to "compensate" existing teams. For a further look at expansion in professional sports, see, e.g., *First Northwest Industries of America, Inc. v. Commissioner*, 649 F.2d 707 (9th Cir.1981) (dispute over tax treatment to be accorded to expansion fees collected when NBA created three new clubs); Thomas A. Piraino, Jr., *The Antitrust Rationale for the Expansion of Professional Sports Leagues*, 57 Ohio St. L.J. 1677 (1996) (arguing more must be done to spur expansion); Mike Eisenbath, *Angelos Suggests Cutting Some Teams*, St. Louis Post–Dispatch, Apr. 29, 1998, at D1 (discussing Baltimore Orioles owner Peter Angelos' view that MLB should eliminate some teams so as to make the rest stronger).

8. While sports leagues disdain expansion in their primary markets, they are quite willing to enter secondary markets. Thus, for example, in 1991 the NFL created the World League of American Football (subsequently renamed the NFL Europe League) to generate interest overseas, in 1997 it agreed to subsidize the CFL in return for a piece of the latter's profits and greater access to its players, and in 1999 it secured an option to buy up to 49% of the Arena Football League. *See further* Paul R. Genender, Note, *A*

Transcontinental Alley–Oop: Antitrust Ramifications of Potential National Basketball Association Expansion Into Europe, 4 Duke J. Comp. & Int'l L. 291 (1994); Jeff Jensen, *Faced With Maturing Businesses But No Letup in Competition, Pro Leagues Are Acting More Like Brand Marketers, Determined to Reach Consumers at the Grass–Roots Level and Overseas*, Advertising Age, Apr. 14, 1997, at 20; Richard Alm, *NFL Hopes Name Makes World of Difference*, Dallas Morning News, Mar. 31, 1998, at 7B; Mike Spence, *With Eye on Growth, NHL Goes to the Games: League Eager to Get Worldwide Exposure for Sport*, Colo. Springs Gazette, Jan. 18, 1998, at SP8; Howard Schneider, *NFL to Give $3 Million, Expertise to CFL*, Wash. Post, Apr. 10, 1997, at E9; Ross Atkin, *Mexico in the Super Bowl? Hmm . . . US Leagues Promote Their Games Overseas—For Love and Money*, Christian Sci. Monitor, Jan. 22, 1997, at 1.

Problem 21

To gain credibility, a start-up league challenged its older rival to a championship game. When the latter refused, the new league suggested holding joint playoffs. Once again, its idea was rejected. Given these facts, have any antitrust violations been committed? *See Eleven Line, Inc. v. North Texas State Soccer Ass'n, Inc.*, 1998 WL 574893 (N.D.Tex.1998).

2. FREE RIDERS

Besides direct competition, successful leagues often are confronted by companies trying to cash in on their success. Not surprisingly, they have taken a very hard line against such interlopers.

NATIONAL BASKETBALL ASS'N v. MOTOROLA, INC.

105 F.3d 841 (2d Cir.1997).

WINTER, Circuit Judge.

Motorola, Inc. and Sports Team Analysis and Tracking Systems ("STATS") appeal from a permanent injunction entered by Judge Preska.

The injunction concerns a handheld pager sold by Motorola and marketed under the name "SportsTrax," which displays updated information of professional basketball games in progress. The injunction prohibits appellants, absent authorization from the National Basketball Association and NBA Properties, Inc. (collectively the "NBA"), from transmitting scores or other data about NBA games in progress via the pagers, STATS's site on America On–Line's computer dial-up service, or "any equivalent means."

The crux of the dispute concerns the extent to which a state law "hot-news" misappropriation claim based on International News Service v. Associated Press, 248 U.S. 215, 39 S.Ct. 68, 63 L.Ed. 211 (1918) ("INS"), survives preemption by the federal Copyright Act and whether the NBA's claim fits within the surviving INS-type claims. We hold that a narrow "hot-news" exception does survive preemption. However, we also hold that appellants' transmission of "real-time" NBA game scores and information tabulated from television and radio broadcasts of games in progress does not constitute a misappropriation of "hot news" that is the property of the NBA.

The NBA cross-appeals from the dismissal of its Lanham Act claim. We hold that any misstatements by Motorola in advertising its pager were not material and affirm.

I. Background

The facts are largely undisputed. Motorola manufactures and markets the SportsTrax paging device while STATS supplies the game information that is transmitted to the pagers. The product became available to the public in January 1996, at a retail price of about $200. SportsTrax's pager has an inch-and-a-half by inch-and-a-half screen and operates in four basic modes: "current," "statistics," "final scores" and "demonstration." It is the "current" mode that gives rise to the present dispute. In that mode, SportsTrax displays the following information on NBA games in progress: (i) the teams playing; (ii) score changes; (iii) the team in possession of the ball; (iv) whether the team is in the free-throw bonus; (v) the quarter of the game; and (vi) time remaining in the quarter. The information is updated every two to three minutes, with more frequent updates near the end of the first half and the end of the game. There is a lag of approximately two or three minutes between events in the game itself and when the information appears on the pager screen.

The other three SportsTrax modes involve information that is far less contemporaneous than that provided in the "current" mode. In the "statistics" mode, the SportsTrax pager displays a variety of player and team statistics, such as field goal shooting percentages and top scorers. However, these are calculated only at half-time and when the game is over. In the "final scores" mode, the unit displays final scores from the previous day's games. In the "demonstration" mode, the unit merely simulates information shown during a hypothetical NBA game. The core issue in the instant matter is the dissemination of continuously-updated real-time NBA game information in the "current" mode. Because we conclude that the dissemination of such real-time information is lawful, the other modes need no further description or discussion.

SportsTrax's operation relies on a "data feed" supplied by STATS reporters who watch the games on television or listen to them on the radio. The reporters key into a personal computer changes in the score and other information such as successful and missed shots, fouls, and clock updates. The information is relayed by modem to STATS's host computer, which compiles, analyzes, and formats the data for retransmission. The information is then sent to a common carrier, which then sends it via satellite to various local FM radio networks that in turn emit the signal received by the individual SportsTrax pagers.

Although the NBA's complaint concerned only the SportsTrax device, the NBA offered evidence at trial concerning STATS's America On–

Line ("AOL") site. Starting in January, 1996, users who accessed STATS's AOL site, typically via a modem attached to a home computer, were provided with slightly more comprehensive and detailed real-time game information than is displayed on a SportsTrax pager. On the AOL site, game scores are updated every 15 seconds to a minute, and the player and team statistics are updated each minute. The district court's original decision and judgment, National Basketball Ass'n v. Sports Team Analysis and Tracking Sys. Inc., 931 F.Supp. 1124 (S.D.N.Y.1996), did not address the AOL site, because "NBA's complaint and the evidence proffered at trial were devoted largely to SportsTrax." National Basketball Ass'n v. Sports Team Analysis and Tracking Sys. Inc., 939 F.Supp. 1071, 1074 n. 1 (S.D.N.Y.1996). Upon motion by the NBA, however, the district court amended its decision and judgment and enjoined use of the real-time game information on STATS's AOL site. Id. at 1075 n. 1. Because the record on appeal, the briefs of the parties, and oral argument primarily addressed the SportsTrax device, we similarly focus on that product. However, we regard the legal issues as identical with respect to both products, and our holding applies equally to SportsTrax and STATS's AOL site.

The NBA's complaint asserted six claims for relief: (i) state law unfair competition by misappropriation; (ii) false advertising under Section 43(a) of the Lanham Act, 15 U.S.C. § 1125(a); (iii) false representation of origin under Section 43(a) of the Lanham Act; (iv) state and common law unfair competition by false advertising and false designation of origin; (v) federal copyright infringement; and (vi) unlawful interception of communications under the Communications Act of 1934, 47 U.S.C. § 605. Motorola counterclaimed, alleging that the NBA unlawfully interfered with Motorola's contractual relations with four individual NBA teams that had agreed to sponsor and advertise SportsTrax.

The district court dismissed all of the NBA's claims except the first—misappropriation under New York law. The court also dismissed Motorola's counterclaim. Finding Motorola and STATS liable for misappropriation, Judge Preska entered the permanent injunction, reserved the calculation of damages for subsequent proceedings, and stayed execution of the injunction pending appeal. Motorola and STATS appeal from the injunction, while NBA cross-appeals from the district court's dismissal of its Lanham Act false-advertising claim. The issues before us, therefore, are the state law misappropriation and Lanham Act claims.

II. The State Law Misappropriation Claim

A. *Summary of Ruling*

Because our disposition of the state law misappropriation claim rests in large part on preemption by the Copyright Act, our discussion necessarily goes beyond the elements of a misappropriation claim under New York law, and a summary of our ruling here will perhaps render that discussion—or at least the need for it—more understandable.

The issues before us are ones that have arisen in various forms over the course of this century as technology has steadily increased the speed and quantity of information transmission. Today, individuals at home, at work, or elsewhere, can use a computer, pager, or other device to obtain highly selective kinds of information virtually at will. International News Service v. Associated Press, 248 U.S. 215, 39 S.Ct. 68, 63 L.Ed. 211 (1918) ("INS") was one of the first cases to address the issues raised by these technological advances, although the technology involved in that case was primitive by contemporary standards. INS involved two wire services, the Associated Press ("AP") and International News Service ("INS"), that transmitted newsstories by wire to member newspapers. Id. INS would lift factual stories from AP bulletins and send them by wire to INS papers. Id. at 231, 39 S.Ct. at 69–70. INS would also take factual stories from east coast AP papers and wire them to INS papers on the west coast that had yet to publish because of time differentials. Id. at 238, 39 S.Ct. at 72. The Supreme Court held that INS's conduct was a common-law misappropriation of AP's property. Id. at 242, 39 S.Ct. at 73–74.

With the advance of technology, radio stations began "live" broadcasts of events such as baseball games and operas, and various entrepreneurs began to use the transmissions of others in one way or another for their own profit. In response, New York courts created a body of misappropriation law, loosely based on INS, that sought to apply ethical standards to the use by one party of another's transmissions of events.

Federal copyright law played little active role in this area until 1976. Before then, it appears to have been the general understanding—there being no caselaw of consequence—that live events such as baseball games were not copyrightable. Moreover, doubt existed even as to whether a recorded broadcast or videotape of such an event was copyrightable. In 1976, however, Congress passed legislation expressly affording copyright protection to simultaneously-recorded broadcasts of live performances such as sports events. See 17 U.S.C. § 101. Such protection was not extended to the underlying events.

The 1976 amendments also contained provisions preempting state law claims that enforced rights "equivalent" to exclusive copyright protections when the work to which the state claim was being applied fell within the area of copyright protection. See 17 U.S.C. § 301. Based on legislative history of the 1976 amendments, it is generally agreed that a "hot-news" INS-like claim survives preemption. H.R. No. 94–1476 at 132 (1976), reprinted in 1976 U.S.C.C.A.N. 5659, 5748. However, much of New York misappropriation law after INS goes well beyond "hot-news" claims and is preempted.

We hold that the surviving "hot-news" INS-like claim is limited to cases where: (i) a plaintiff generates or gathers information at a cost; (ii) the information is time-sensitive; (iii) a defendant's use of the information constitutes free riding on the plaintiff's efforts; (iv) the defendant is in direct competition with a product or service offered by the plaintiffs; and (v) the ability of other parties to free-ride on the efforts of the plaintiff or others would so reduce the incentive to produce the product or service that its existence or quality would be substantially threatened. We conclude that SportsTrax does not meet that test.

B. *Copyrights in Events or Broadcasts of Events*

The NBA asserted copyright infringement claims with regard both to the underlying games and to their broadcasts. The district court dismissed these claims, and the NBA does not appeal from their dismissal. Nevertheless, discussion of the infringement claims is necessary to provide the framework for analyzing the viability of the NBA's state law misappropriation claim in light of the Copyright Act's preemptive effect.

1. *Infringement of a Copyright in the Underlying Games*

In our view, the underlying basketball games do not fall within the subject matter of federal copyright protection because they do not constitute "original works of authorship" under 17 U.S.C. § 102(a). Section 102(a) lists eight categories of "works of authorship" covered by the act, including such categories as "literary works," "musical works," and "dramatic works." The list does not include athletic events, and, although the list is concededly non-exclusive, such events are neither similar nor analogous to any of the listed categories.

Sports events are not "authored" in any common sense of the word. There is, of course, at least at the professional level, considerable preparation for a game. However, the preparation is as much an expression of hope or faith as a determination of what will actually happen. Unlike movies, plays, television programs, or operas, athletic events are competitive and have no underlying script. Preparation may even cause mistakes to succeed, like the broken play in football that gains yardage because the opposition could not expect it. Athletic events may also result in wholly unanticipated occurrences, the most notable recent event being in a championship baseball game in which interference with a fly ball caused an umpire to signal erroneously a home run.

What "authorship" there is in a sports event, moreover, must be open to copying by competitors if fans are to be attracted. If the inventor of the T-formation in football had been able to copyright it, the sport might have come to an end instead of prospering. Even where athletic preparation most resembles authorship—figure skating, gymnastics, and, some would uncharitably say, professional wrestling—a performer who conceives and executes a particularly graceful and difficult—or, in the case of wrestling, seemingly painful—acrobatic feat cannot copyright it without impairing the underlying competition in the future. A claim of being the only athlete to perform a feat doesn't mean much if no one else is allowed to try.

For many of these reasons, Nimmer on Copyright concludes that the "[f]ar more reasonable" position is that athletic events are not copyrightable. 1 M. Nimmer & D. Nimmer, Nimmer on Copyright § 2.09[F] at 2–170.1 (1996). Nimmer notes that, among other problems, the number of joint copyright owners would arguably include the league, the teams, the athletes, umpires, stadium workers and even fans, who all contribute to the "work."

Concededly, caselaw is scarce on the issue of whether organized events themselves are copyrightable, but what there is indicates that they are not. See Production Contractors, Inc. v. WGN Continental Broadcasting Co., 622 F.Supp. 1500 (N.D.Ill.1985) (Christmas parade is not a work of authorship entitled to copyright protection). In claiming a copyright in the underlying games, the NBA relied in part on a footnote in Baltimore Orioles, Inc. v. Major League Baseball Players Assn., 805 F.2d 663, 669 n. 7 (7th Cir.1986), cert. denied, 480 U.S. 941, 107 S.Ct. 1593, 94 L.Ed.2d 782 (1987), which stated that the "[p]layers' performances" contain the "modest creativity required for copyright ability." However, the court went on to state, "Moreover, even if the [p]layers' performances were not sufficiently creative, the [p]layers agree that the cameramen and director contribute creative labor to the telecasts." Id. This last sentence indicates that the court was considering the copyright ability of telecasts—not the underlying games, which obviously can be played without cameras.

We believe that the lack of caselaw is attributable to a general understanding that athletic events were, and are, uncopyrightable. Indeed, prior to 1976, there was even doubt that broadcasts describing or depicting such events, which have a far stronger case for copyrightability than the events themselves, were entitled to copyright protection. Indeed, as described in the next subsection of this opinion, Congress found it necessary to extend such protection to recorded broadcasts of live events. The fact that Congress did not extend such protection to the events themselves confirms our view that the district court correctly held that appellants were not infringing a copyright in the NBA games.

2. *Infringement of a Copyright in the Broadcasts of NBA Games*

As noted, recorded broadcasts of NBA games—as opposed to the games themselves—are now entitled to copyright protection. The Copyright Act was amended in 1976 specifically to insure that simultaneously-recorded transmissions of live performances and sporting events would meet the Act's requirement that the original work of authorship be "fixed in any tangible medium of expression." 17 U.S.C. § 102(a). Accordingly, Section 101 of the Act, containing definitions, was amended to read:

> A work consisting of sounds, images, or both, that are being transmitted, is "fixed" for purposes of this title if a fixation of the work is being made simultaneously with its transmission.

17 U.S.C. § 101. Congress specifically had sporting events in mind:

> [T]he bill seeks to resolve, through the definition of "fixation" in section 101, the status of live broadcasts—sports, news coverage, live performances of music, etc.—that are reaching the public in unfixed form but that are simultaneously being recorded.

H.R. No. 94–1476 at 52, reprinted in 1976 U.S.C.C.A.N. at 5665.

The House Report also makes clear that it is the broadcast, not the underlying game, that is the subject of copyright protection. In explaining how game broadcasts meet the Act's requirement that the subject matter be an "original work[ ] of authorship," 17 U.S.C. § 102(a), the House Report stated:

> When a football game is being covered by four television cameras, with a director guiding the activities of the four cameramen and choosing which of their electronic images are sent out to the public and in what order, there is little doubt that what the cameramen and the director are doing constitutes "authorship."

H.R. No. 94–1476 at 52, reprinted in 1976 U.S.C.C.A.N. at 5665.

Although the broadcasts are protected under copyright law, the district court correctly held that Motorola and STATS did not infringe NBA's copyright because they reproduced only facts from the broadcasts, not the expression or description of the game that constitutes the broadcast. The "fact/expression dichotomy" is a bedrock principle of copyright law that "limits severely the scope of protection in fact-based works." Feist Publications, Inc. v. Rural Tel. Service Co., 499 U.S. 340, 350, 111 S.Ct. 1282, 1290, 113 L.Ed.2d 358 (1991). " 'No author may copyright facts or ideas. The copyright is limited to those aspects of the work—termed 'expression'—that display the stamp of the author's originality.' " Id. (quoting Harper & Row, Publishers, Inc. v. Nation Enter., 471 U.S. 539, 547, 105 S.Ct. 2218, 2224, 85 L.Ed.2d 588 (1985)).

We agree with the district court that the "[d]efendants provide purely factual information which any patron of an NBA game could acquire from the arena without any involvement from the director, cameramen, or others who contribute to the originality of a broadcast." 939 F.Supp. at 1094. Because the SportsTrax device and AOL site reproduce only factual information culled from the broadcasts and none of the copyrightable expression of the games, appellants did not infringe the copyright of the broadcasts.

C. *The State Law Misappropriation Claim*

The district court's injunction was based on its conclusion that, under New York law, defendants had unlawfully misappropriated the NBA's property rights in its games. The district court reached this conclusion by holding: (i) that the NBA's misappropriation claim relating to the underlying games was not preempted by Section 301 of the Copyright Act; and (ii) that, under New York common law, defendants had engaged in unlawful misappropriation. Id. at 1094–1107. We disagree.

1. *Preemption Under the Copyright Act*

a) *Summary*

When Congress amended the Copyright Act in 1976, it provided for the preemption of state law claims that are interrelated with copyright claims in certain ways. Under 17 U.S.C. § 301, a state law claim is preempted when: (i) the state law claim seeks to vindicate "legal or equitable rights that are equivalent" to one of the bundle of exclusive rights already protected by copyright law under 17 U.S.C. § 106—styled the "general scope requirement"; and (ii) the particular work to which the state law claim is being applied falls within the type of works protected by the Copyright Act under Sections 102 and 103—styled the "subject matter requirement."

The district court concluded that the NBA's misappropriation claim was not preempted because, with respect to the underlying games, as opposed to the broadcasts, the subject matter requirement was not met. 939 F.Supp. at 1097. The court dubbed as "partial preemption" its separate analysis of misappropriation claims relating to the underlying games and misappropriation claims relating to broadcasts of those games. Id. at 1098, n. 24. The district court then relied on a series of older New York misappropriation cases involving radio broadcasts that considerably broadened INS. We hold that where the challenged copying or misappropriation relates in part to the copyrighted broadcasts of the games, the subject matter requirement is met as to both the broadcasts and the games. We therefore reject the partial preemption doctrine and its anomalous consequence that "it is possible for a plaintiff to assert claims both for infringement of its copyright in a broadcast and misappropriation of its rights in the underlying event." Id. We do find that a properly-narrowed INS "hot-news" misappropriation claim survives preemption because it fails the general scope requirement, but that the broader theory of the radio broadcast cases relied upon by the district court were preempted when Congress extended copyright protection to simultaneously-recorded broadcasts.

b) "Partial Preemption" and the Subject Matter Requirement

The subject matter requirement is met when the work of authorship being copied or misappropriated "fall[s] within the ambit of copyright protection." Harper & Row, Publishers, Inc. v. Nation Enter., 723 F.2d 195, 200 (1983), rev'd on other grounds, 471 U.S. 539, 105 S.Ct. 2218, 85 L.Ed.2d 588 (1985). We believe that the subject matter requirement is met in the instant matter and that the concept of "partial preemption" is not consistent with Section 301 of the Copyright Act. Although game broadcasts are copyrightable while the underlying games are not, the Copyright Act should not be read to distinguish between the two when analyzing the preemption of a misappropriation claim based on copying or taking from the copyrightable work. We believe that:

> [O]nce a performance is reduced to tangible form, there is no distinction between the performance and the recording of the performance for the purposes of preemption under § 301(a). Thus, if a baseball game were not broadcast or were telecast without being recorded, the Players' performances similarly would not be fixed in tangible form and their rights of publicity would not be subject to preemption. By virtue of being video-

> taped, however, the Players' performances are fixed in tangible form, and any rights of publicity in their performances that are equivalent to the rights contained in the copyright of the telecast are preempted.

Baltimore Orioles, 805 F.2d at 675 (citation omitted).

Copyrightable material often contains uncopyrightable elements within it, but Section 301 preemption bars state law misappropriation claims with respect to uncopyrightable as well as copyrightable elements. In Harper & Row, for example, we held that state law claims based on the copying of excerpts from President Ford's memoirs were preempted even with respect to information that was purely factual and not copyrightable. We stated:

> [T]he [Copyright] Act clearly embraces "works of authorship," including "literary works," as within its subject matter. The fact that portions of the Ford memoirs may consist of uncopyrightable material ... does not take the work as a whole outside the subject matter protected by the Act. Were this not so, states would be free to expand the perimeters of copyright protection to their own liking, on the theory that preemption would be no bar to state protection of material not meeting federal statutory standards.

723 F.2d at 200 (citation omitted). The legislative history supports this understanding of Section 301(a)'s subject matter requirement. The House Report stated:

> As long as a work fits within one of the general subject matter categories of sections 102 and 103, the bill prevents the States from protecting it even if it fails to achieve Federal statutory copyright because it is too minimal or lacking in originality to qualify, or because it has fallen into the public domain.

H.R. No. 94–1476 at 131, reprinted in 1976 U.S.C.C.A.N. at 5747. See also Baltimore Orioles, 805 F.2d at 676 (citing excerpts of House Report 94–1476).

Adoption of a partial preemption doctrine—preemption of claims based on misappropriation of broadcasts but no preemption of claims based on misappropriation of underlying facts—would expand significantly the reach of state law claims and render the preemption intended by Congress unworkable. It is often difficult or impossible to separate the fixed copyrightable work from the underlying uncopyrightable events or facts. Moreover, Congress, in extending copyright protection only to the broadcasts and not to the underlying events, intended that the latter be in the public domain. Partial preemption turns that intent on its head by allowing state law to vest exclusive rights in material that Congress intended to be in the public domain and to make unlawful conduct that Congress intended to allow. This concern was recently expressed in ProCD, Inc. v. Zeidenberg, 86 F.3d 1447 (7th Cir.1996), a case in which the defendants reproduced non-copyrightable facts (telephone listings) from plaintiffs' copyrighted software. In discussing preemption under Section 301(a), Judge Easterbrook held that the subject matter requirement was met and noted:

> ProCD's software and data are "fixed in a tangible medium of expression", and the district judge held that they are "within the subject matter of copyright". The latter conclusion is plainly right for the copyrighted application program, and the judge thought that the data likewise are "within the subject matter of copyright" even if, after Feist, they are not sufficiently original to be copyrighted. [ProCD, Inc. v. Zeidenberg,] 908 F.Supp. [640] at 656–57 [(W.D.Wis.1996)]. Baltimore Orioles, Inc. v. Major League Baseball Players Ass'n, 805 F.2d 663, 676 (7th Cir.1986), supports that conclusion, with which commentators agree.... One function of § 301(a) is to prevent states from giving special protection to works of authorship that Congress has decided should be in the public domain, which it can accomplish only if "subject matter of copyright" includes all works of a type covered by sections 102 and 103, even if federal law does not afford protection to them.

ProCD, 86 F.3d at 1453 (citation omitted). We agree with Judge Easterbrook and reject the separate analysis of the underlying games and broadcasts of those games for purposes of preemption.

c) The General Scope Requirement

Under the general scope requirement, Section 301 "preempts only those state law rights that 'may be abridged by an act which, in and of itself, would infringe one of the exclusive rights' provided by federal copyright law." Computer Assoc. Int'l, Inc. v. Altai, Inc., 982 F.2d 693, 716 (2d Cir.1992) (quoting Harper & Row, 723 F.2d at 200). However, certain forms of commercial misappropriation otherwise within the general scope requirement will survive preemption if an "extra-element" test is met. As stated in Altai:

> But if an "extra element" is "required instead of or in addition to the acts of reproduction, performance, distribution or display, in order to constitute a state-created cause of action, then the right does not lie 'within the general scope of copyright,' and there is no preemption."

Id. (quoting 1 Nimmer on Copyright § 1.01[B] at 1–15).

ProCD was in part an application of the extra-element test. Having held the misappropriation claims to be preempted, Judge Easterbrook went on to hold that the plaintiffs could bring a state law contract claim. The court held that the defendants were bound by the software's shrinkwrap licenses as a matter of contract law and that the private contract rights were not preempted because they were not equivalent to the exclusive rights granted by copyright law. In other words, the contract right claims were not preempted because the general scope requirement was not met. ProCD, 86 F.3d at 1455.

We turn, therefore, to the question of the extent to which a "hot-news" misappropriation claim based on INS involves extra elements and is not the equivalent of exclusive rights under a copyright. Courts are generally agreed that some form of such a claim survives preemption. Financial Information, Inc. v. Moody's Investors Service, Inc., 808 F.2d 204, 208 (2d Cir.1986), cert. denied, 484 U.S. 820, 108 S.Ct. 79, 98 L.Ed.2d 42 (1987) ("FII"). This conclusion is based in part on the legislative history of the 1976 amendments. The House Report stated:

> "Misappropriation" is not necessarily synonymous with copyright infringement, and thus a cause of action labeled as "misappropriation" is not preempted if it is in fact based neither on a right within the general scope of copyright as specified by section 106 nor on a right equivalent thereto. For example, state law should have the flexibility to afford a remedy (under traditional principles of equity) against a consistent pattern of unauthorized appropriation by a competitor of the facts (i.e., not the literary expression) constituting "hot" news, whether in the traditional mold of International News Service v. Associated Press, 248 U.S. 215 [39 S.Ct. 68, 63 L.Ed. 211] (1918), or in the newer form of data updates from scientific, business, or financial data bases.

H.R. No. 94–1476 at 132, reprinted in 1976 U.S.C.C.A.N. at 5748 (footnote omitted), see also FII, 808 F.2d at 209 (" 'misappropriation' of 'hot' news, under International News Service, [is] a branch of the unfair competition doctrine not preempted by the Copyright Act according to the House Report" (citation omitted)). The crucial question, therefore, is the breadth of the "hot-news" claim that survives preemption.

In INS, the plaintiff AP and defendant INS were "wire services" that sold news items to client newspapers. AP brought suit to prevent INS from selling facts and information lifted from AP sources to INS-affiliated newspapers. One method by which INS was able to use AP's news was to lift facts from AP news bulletins. INS, 248 U.S. at 231, 39 S.Ct. at 69–70. Another method was to sell facts taken from just-published east coast AP newspapers to west coast INS newspapers whose editions had yet to appear. Id. at 238, 39 S.Ct. at 72. The Supreme Court held (prior to Erie R. Co. v. Tompkins, 304 U.S. 64, 58 S.Ct. 817, 82 L.Ed. 1188 (1938)), that INS's use of AP's information was unlawful under federal common law. It characterized INS's conduct as amount[ing] to an unauthorized interference with the normal operation of complainant's legitimate business precisely at the point where the profit is to be reaped, in order to divert a material portion of the profit from those who have earned it to those who have not; with special advantage to defendant in the competition because of the fact that it is not burdened with any part of the expense of gathering the news. INS, 248 U.S. at 240, 39 S.Ct. at 72–73.

The theory of the New York misappropriation cases relied upon by the district court is considerably broader than that of INS. For example, the district court quoted at length from Metropolitan Opera Ass'n v. Wagner–Nichols Recorder Corp., 199 Misc. 786, 101 N.Y.S.2d 483 (N.Y.Sup.Ct.1950), aff'd, 279 A.D. 632, 107 N.Y.S.2d 795 (1st Dep't 1951). Metropolitan Opera described New York misappropriation law as standing for the "broader principle that property rights of commercial value are to be and will be protected from any form of commercial immorality"; that misappropriation law developed "to deal with business malpractices offensive to the ethics of [ ] society"; and that the doctrine is "broad and flexible." 939 F.Supp. at 1098–1110 (quoting Metropolitan Opera, 101 N.Y.S.2d at 492, 488–89).

However, we believe that Metropolitan Opera's broad misappropriation doctrine based on amorphous concepts such as "commercial immorality" or society's "ethics" is preempted. Such concepts are virtually synonymous for wrongful copying and are in no meaningful fashion distinguishable from infringement of a copyright. The broad misappropriation doctrine relied upon by the district court is, therefore, the equivalent of exclusive rights in copyright law.

Indeed, we said as much in FII. That decision involved the copying of financial information by a rival financial reporting service and specifically repudiated the broad misappropriation doctrine of Metropolitan Opera. We explained:

> We are not persuaded by FII's argument that misappropriation is not "equivalent" to the exclusive rights provided by the Copyright Act.... Nor do we believe that a possible exception to the general rule of preemption in the misappropriation area—for claims involving "any form of commercial immorality," ... quoting Metropolitan Opera Ass'n v. Wagner–Nichols Recorder Corp., 199 Misc. 786, 101 N.Y.S.2d 483, ...—should be applied here. We believe that no such exception exists and reject its use here. Whether or not reproduction of another's work is "immoral" depends on whether such use of the work is wrongful. If, for example, the work is in the public domain, then its use would not be wrongful. Likewise, if, as here, the work is unprotected by federal law because of lack of originality, then its use is neither unfair nor unjustified.

FII, 808 F.2d at 208. In fact, FII only begrudgingly concedes that even narrow "hot news" INS-type claims survive preemption. Id. at 209.

Moreover, Computer Associates Intern., Inc. v. Altai Inc. indicated that the "extra element" test should not be applied so as to allow state claims to survive preemption easily. 982 F.2d at 717. "An action will not be saved from preemption by elements such as awareness or intent, which alter 'the action's scope but not its nature'.... Following this 'extra element' test, we have held that unfair competition and misappropriation claims grounded solely in the copying of a plaintiff's protected expression are preempted by section 301." Id. (citation omitted).

In light of cases such as FII and Altai that emphasize the narrowness of state misappropriation claims that survive preemption, most of the broadcast cases relied upon by the NBA are simply not good law. Those cases were decided at a time when simultaneously-recorded broadcasts were not protected under the Copyright Act and when the state law claims they fashioned were not subject to federal preemption. For example, Metropolitan Opera, 101 N.Y.S.2d 483, involved the unauthorized copying, marketing, and sale of opera radio broadcasts. As another example, in Mutual Broadcasting System v. Muzak Corp., 177 Misc. 489, 30 N.Y.S.2d 419 (Sup.Ct.1941), the defendant simultaneously retransmitted the plaintiff's baseball radio broadcasts onto telephone lines. As discussed above, the 1976 amendments to the Copyright Act were specifically designed to afford copyright protection to simultaneously-recorded broadcasts, and Metropolitan Opera and Muzak could today be brought as copyright infringement cases. Moreover, we believe that they would have to be brought as copyright cases because the amendments affording broadcasts copyright protection also preempted the state law misappropriation claims under which they were decided.

Our conclusion, therefore, is that only a narrow "hot-news" misappropriation claim survives preemption for actions concerning material within the realm of copyright. See also 1 McCarthy on Trademarks and Unfair Competition (4th ed. 1996), § 10:69, at 10–134 (discussing National Exhibition Co. v. Fass, 133 N.Y.S.2d 379 (Sup.Ct.1954), Muzak, 30 N.Y.S.2d 419, and other cases relied upon by NBA that pre-date the 1976 amendment to the Copyright Act and concluding that after the amendment, "state misappropriation law would be unnecessary and would be preempted: protection is solely under federal copyright").

In our view, the elements central to an INS claim are: (i) the plaintiff generates or collects information at some cost or expense, see FII, 808 F.2d at 206; INS, 248 U.S. at 240, 39 S.Ct. at 72–73; (ii) the value of the information is highly time-sensitive, see FII, 808 F.2d at 209; INS, 248 U.S. at 231, 39 S.Ct. at 69–70; Restatement (Third) Unfair Competition, § 38 cmt. c.; (iii) the defendant's use of the information constitutes free-riding on the plaintiff's costly efforts to generate or collect it, see FII, 808 F.2d at 207; INS, 248 U.S. at 239–40, 39 S.Ct. at 72–73; Restatement § 38 at cmt. c.; McCarthy, § 10:73 at 10–139; (iv) the defendant's use of the information is in direct competition with a product or service offered by the plaintiff, FII, 808 F.2d at 209, INS, 248 U.S. at 240, 39 S.Ct. at 72–73; (v) the ability of other parties to free-ride on the efforts of the plaintiff would so reduce the incentive to produce the product or service that its existence or quality would be substantially threatened, FII, 808 F.2d at 209; Restatement, § 38 at cmt. c.; INS, 248 U.S. at 241, 39 S.Ct. at 73 ("[INS's conduct] would render [AP's] publication profitless, or so little profitable as in effect to cut off the service by rendering the cost prohibitive in comparison with the return.") Some authorities have labeled this element as requiring direct competition between the defendant and the plaintiff in a primary market.

INS is not about ethics; it is about the protection of property rights in time-sensitive information so that the information will be made available to the public by profit seeking entrepreneurs. If services like AP were not assured of property rights in the news they pay to collect, they would cease to collect it. The ability of their competitors to appropriate their product at only nominal cost and thereby to disseminate a competing product at a lower price would destroy the incentive to collect news in the first place. The newspaper-reading public would suffer because no one would have an incentive to collect "hot news."

We therefore find the extra elements—those in addition to the elements of copyright infringement—that allow a "hot news" claim to survive preemption are: (i) the time-sensitive value of factual information, (ii) the free-riding by a defendant, and (iii) the threat to the very existence of the product or service provided by the plaintiff.

2. *The Legality of SportsTrax*

We conclude that Motorola and STATS have not engaged in unlawful misappropriation under the "hot-news" test set out above. To be sure, some of the elements of a "hot-news" INS claim are met. The information transmitted to SportsTrax is not precisely contemporaneous, but it is nevertheless time-sensitive. Also, the NBA does provide, or will shortly do so, information like that available through SportsTrax. It now offers a service called "Gamestats" that provides official play-by-play game sheets and half-time and final box scores within each arena. It also provides such information to the media in each arena. In the future, the NBA plans to enhance Gamestats so that it will be networked between the various arenas and will support a pager product analogous to SportsTrax. SportsTrax will of course directly compete with an enhanced Gamestats.

However, there are critical elements missing in the NBA's attempt to assert a "hot-news" INS-type claim. As framed by the NBA, their claim compresses and confuses three different informational products. The first product is generating the information by playing the games; the second product is transmitting live, full descriptions of those games; and the third product is collecting and retransmitting strictly factual information about the games. The first and second products are the NBA's primary business: producing basketball games for live attendance and licensing copyrighted broadcasts of those games. The collection and retransmission of strictly factual material about the games is a different product: e.g., box-scores in newspapers, summaries of statistics on television sports news, and real-time facts to be transmitted to pagers. In our view, the NBA has failed to show any competitive effect whatsoever from SportsTrax on the first and second products and a lack of any free-riding by SportsTrax on the third.

With regard to the NBA's primary products—producing basketball games with live attendance and licensing copyrighted broadcasts of those games—there is no evidence that anyone regards SportsTrax or the AOL site as a substitute for attending NBA games or watching them on television. In fact, Motorola markets SportsTrax as being designed "for those times when you cannot be at the arena, watch the game on TV, or listen to the radio . . ."

The NBA argues that the pager market is also relevant to a "hot-news" INS-type claim and that SportsTrax's future competition with Gamestats satisfies any missing element. We agree that there is a separate market for the real-time transmission of factual information to pagers or similar devices, such as STATS's AOL site. However, we disagree that SportsTrax is in any sense free-riding off Gamestats.

An indispensable element of an INS "hot-news" claim is free riding by a defendant on a plaintiff's product, enabling the defendant to produce a directly competitive product for less money because it has lower costs. SportsTrax is not such a product. The use of pagers to transmit real-time information about NBA games requires: (i) the collecting of facts about the games; (ii) the transmission of these facts on a network; (iii) the assembling of them by the particular service; and (iv) the transmission of them to pagers or an on-line computer site. Appellants are in no way free-riding on Gamestats. Motorola and STATS expend their own resources to collect purely factual information generated in NBA games to transmit to SportsTrax pagers. They have their own network and assemble and transmit data themselves.

To be sure, if appellants in the future were to collect facts from an enhanced Gamestats pager to retransmit them to SportsTrax pagers, that would constitute free-riding and might well cause Gamestats to be unprofitable because it had to bear costs to collect facts that SportsTrax did not. If the appropriation of facts from one pager to another pager service were allowed, transmission of current information on NBA games to pagers or similar devices would be substantially deterred because any potential transmitter would know that the first entrant would quickly encounter a lower cost competitor free-riding on the originator's transmissions.

It may well be that the NBA's product, when enhanced, will actually have a competitive edge because its Gamestats system will apparently be used for a number of in-stadium services as well as the pager market, resulting in a certain amount of cost sharing. Gamestats might also have a temporal advantage in collecting and transmitting official statistics. Whether this is so does not affect our disposition of this matter, although it does demonstrate the gulf between this case and INS, where the free-riding created the danger of no wire service being viable.

However, that is not the case in the instant matter. SportsTrax and Gamestats are each bearing their own costs of collecting factual information on NBA games, and, if one produces a product that is cheaper or otherwise superior to the other, that producer will prevail in the marketplace. This is obviously not the situation against which INS was intended to prevent: the potential lack of any such product or service because of the anticipation of free-riding.

For the foregoing reasons, the NBA has not shown any damage to any of its products based on free-riding by Motorola and STATS, and the

NBA's misappropriation claim based on New York law is preempted. In view of our disposition of this matter, we need not address appellants' First Amendment and laches defenses.

III. The NBA'S Cross-Appeal

The NBA cross-appeals from the district court's dismissal of its false advertising claim under Section 43(a) of the Lanham Act, 15 U.S.C. § 1125(a). This claim was based on a January 1996 Motorola press release stating that SportsTrax provides "updated game information direct from each arena" which "originate[s] from the press table in each arena" and on a statement appearing on the spine of the retail box and on the retail display stand that SportsTrax provides "game updates from the arena."

NBA argues that because STATS reporters collect their information from television and radio broadcasts, the information is not "direct from each arena" or even "from the arena." Motorola responds that the statement about information coming from the press table was an isolated remark occurring only in that press release. It also claims that the assertion that the game updates come "from the arena" is not literally false, presumably because the factual information does originate in the arena.

To establish a false advertising claim under Section 43(a), the plaintiff must demonstrate that the statement in the challenged advertisement is false. "Falsity may be established by proving that (1) the advertising is literally false as a factual matter, or (2) although the advertisement is literally true, it is likely to deceive or confuse customers." Lipton v. Nature Co., 71 F.3d 464, 474 (2d Cir.1995). However, in addition to proving falsity, the plaintiff must also show that the defendants "misrepresented an 'inherent quality or characteristic'" of the product. National Assoc. of Pharmaceutical Mfrs. v. Ayerst Lab., 850 F.2d 904, 917 (2d Cir.1988) (quoting Vidal Sassoon, Inc. v. Bristol–Myers Co., 661 F.2d 272, 278 (2d Cir.1981)). This requirement is essentially one of materiality, a term explicitly used in other circuits. See American Tel. & Tel. Co. v. Winback and Conserve Program, Inc., 42 F.3d 1421, 1428 n. 9 (3d Cir.1994) (plaintiff alleging false advertising must prove "that the deception is material in that it is likely to influence purchasing decisions") (citations and internal quotation marks omitted), cert. denied, ___ U.S. ___, 115 S.Ct. 1838, 131 L.Ed.2d 757 (1995); ALPO Petfoods, Inc. v. Ralston Purina Co., 913 F.2d 958, 964 (D.C.Cir.1990) (false or misleading ads must be "material in their effects on buying decisions"); Taquino v. Teledyne Monarch Rubber, 893 F.2d 1488, 1500 (5th Cir. 1990) (deception must be "material, in that it is likely to influence the purchasing decision"); see also 3 McCarthy on Trademarks § 27:35 at 27–54 (there must be "some showing that the defendant's misrepresentation was 'material' in the sense that it would have some effect on consumers' purchasing decisions.").

The district court found, "[a]fter viewing the complained-of statements in this action in their context," that "[t]he statements as to the particular origin of game updates constitute nothing more than minutiae about SportsTrax." 939 F.Supp. at 1110. We agree with the district court that the statements in question are not material in the present factual context. The inaccuracy in the statements would not influence consumers at the present time, whose interest in obtaining updated game scores on pagers is served only by SportsTrax. Whether the data is taken from broadcasts instead of being observed first-hand is, therefore, simply irrelevant. However, we note that if the NBA were in the future to market a rival pager with a direct datafeed from the arenas—perhaps with quicker updates than SportsTrax and official statistics—then Motorola's statements regarding source might well be materially misleading. On the present facts, however, the complained-of statements are not material and do not misrepresent an inherent quality or characteristic of the product.

IV. Conclusion

We vacate the injunction entered by the district court and order that the NBA's claim for misappropriation be dismissed. We affirm the district court's dismissal of the NBA's claim for false advertising under Section 43(a) of the Lanham Act.

Notes

1. *Motorola* was authored by Circuit Judge Ralph K. Winter, who also wrote *USFL*. As both opinions make clear, Judge Winter, a former Yale Law School professor and early backer of the law-and-economics movement, is ardently pro-competition. For a further look at his views, see, e.g., Ralph K. Winter, *On "Protecting the Ordinary Investor,"* 63 Wash. L. Rev. 881 (1988).

2. Unfortunately, *Motorola* raises more questions than it answers. For example, may a web site on the internet provide up-to-the-minute scores accompanied by live action pictures? Likewise, may a television or radio station give detailed contemporaneous accounts of fights being broadcast over pay-per-view? Yet another issue left open by the opinion is the impact of the First Amendment. For a further examination of these matters, see Holly M. Burch, *A Sports Explosion: Intellectual Property Rights in Professional Athletic Franchises*, 5 Sports Law. J. 29 (1998); Paul M. Enright, Comment, *"Sportstrax: They Love This Game!"—A Comment on the NBA v. Motorola*, 7 Seton Hall J. Sport L. 449 (1997); Claudia Werner, Note, *NBA v. Motorola & Stats, Inc.: Real-Time Basketball Scores—News or Property?*, 7 DePaul-LCA J. Art & Ent. L. 288 (1997).

3. A very different set of factors come into play when a defendant attempts to use, without permission, a league's or team's name, logo, colors, or wardrobe. In such cases, the courts typically have found trademark infringement and issued an injunction. *See, e.g., San Francisco Arts & Athletics, Inc. v. United States Olympic Committee*, 483 U.S. 522 (1987) (defendant enjoined from calling its athletic competition the "Gay Olympic Games"); *Boston Athletic Ass'n v. Sullivan*, 867 F.2d 22 (1st Cir.1989) (defendant enjoined from using Boston Marathon's logo on its t-shirts); *Dallas Cowboys Cheerleaders, Inc. v. Pussycat Cinema, Ltd.*, 604 F.2d 200 (2d Cir.1979) (defendant enjoined from using team's cheerleading costume to promote the pornographic film "Debbie Does Dallas"); *Boston Professional*

Hockey Ass'n, Inc. v. Dallas Cap & Emblem Mfg., Inc., 510 F.2d 1004 (5th Cir.), *cert. denied*, 423 U.S. 868 (1975) (defendant enjoined from reproducing NHL's insignia on its clothing); *Board of Trustees of the University of Arkansas v. Professional Therapy Services, Inc.*, 873 F.Supp. 1280 (W.D.Ark. 1995) (defendant enjoined from using school's nickname and logo for its medical clinic); *Chicago Blackhawk Hockey Team v. Madsen*, 1991 WL 18411 (N.D.Ill.1991) (defendant enjoined from using the cipher "HAWK" to promote his team hotline); *National Football League Properties, Inc. v. New Jersey Giants*, 637 F.Supp. 507 (D.N.J.1986) (defendant enjoined from manufacturing products bearing words "New Jersey Giants" to describe New York football team); *United States Olympic Committee v. International Federation of Bodybuilders*, 219 U.S.P.Q. (BNA) 353 (D.D.C.1982) (defendant enjoined from using Olympic rings and colors to publicize its Mr. and Ms. Olympia contests); *Augusta National, Inc. v. Northwestern Mutual Life Insurance Co.*, 193 U.S.P.Q. 210 (S.D.Ga.1976) (defendant enjoined from using "Masters" in name of its golf tournament); *Israelite House of David v. Murphy*, 6 F.Supp. 914 (S.D.N.Y.1934) (defendant enjoined from imitating baseball team known for its "Jewish" style of dress). For a case in which infringement was *not* found, see *WCVB-TV v. Boston Athletic Ass'n*, 926 F.2d 42 (1st Cir.1991).

4. Although most sports infringement cases involve a latecomer taking advantage of an originator (known as "forward confusion"), occasionally the opposite occurs (referred to as "reverse confusion"). *See, e.g., Dream Team Collectibles, Inc. v. NBA Properties, Inc.*, 958 F.Supp. 1401 (E.D.Mo.1997) (dispute over use of the name "Dream Team"), and *Harlem Wizards Entertainment Basketball, Inc. v. NBA Properties, Inc.*, 952 F.Supp. 1084 (D.N.J.1997) (dispute over use of the name "Wizards").

5. The subject of free riding in sports has produced a substantial body of commentary, including Andrew D. Baharlias, *... Yes, I Think the Yankees Might Sue If We Named Our Popcorn 'Yankees Toffee Crunch'. A Comprehensive Look at Trademark Infringement Defenses in the Context of the Professional and Collegiate Sports Industry*, 8 Seton Hall J. Sport L. 99 (1998); Anne M. Wall, *Sports Marketing and the Law: Protecting Proprietary Interests in Sports Entertainment Events*, 7 Marq. Sports L.J. 77 (1996); Ted Curtis & Joel H. Stempler, *So What Do We Name the Team? Trademark Infringement, the Lanham Act and Sports Franchises*, 19 Colum.-VLA J.L. & Arts 23 (1994/95). *See also United States Golf Ass'n v. St. Andrews Systems, Data–Max, Inc.*, 749 F.2d 1028 (3d Cir.1984) (amateur golf association could not prevent computer company from using its formula for calculating golfers' handicap), and *Jaguar Cars, Ltd. v. National Football League*, 886 F.Supp. 335 (S.D.N.Y.1995) (describing the dispute between the manufacturer of Jaguar automobiles and the Jacksonville Jaguars that eventually was settled by having the team switch from the carmaker's "leaping jaguar" logo to a snarling jaguar's head).

Problem 22

When a new league was formed, it decided its ball would be red, white, and blue rather than the orange used by its competitors. Will the league be able to trademark its ball? *See American Basketball Ass'n v. AMF Voit, Inc.*, 358 F.Supp. 981 (S.D.N.Y.), *aff'd mem.*, 487 F.2d 1393 (2d Cir.1973), *cert. denied*, 416 U.S. 986 (1974).

Chapter 4

Players

A. OVERVIEW

Because competition at any level involves both risks and rewards, athletes sometimes have turned to the courts for protection. As a result, four key issues have emerged: 1) who is eligible to play?; 2) when does a right to compensation arise?; 3) what constitutes acceptable working conditions?; and, 4) how should inappropriate off-field behavior be handled?

B. ELIGIBILITY

Going out for the team is a time-honored tradition. For some players, however, the quest to make the squad ends even before it begins.

KNAPP v. NORTHWESTERN UNIVERSITY

101 F.3d 473 (7th Cir.1996),
cert. denied, 117 S.Ct. 2454 (1997).

EVANS, Circuit Judge.

Nicholas Knapp wants to play NCAA basketball for Northwestern University—so badly that he is willing to face an increased risk of death to do so. Knapp is a competent, intelligent adult capable of assessing whether playing intercollegiate basketball is worth the risk to his heart and possible death, and to him the risk is acceptable. Usually, competent, intelligent adults are allowed to make such decisions. This is especially true when, as here, the individual's family approves of the decision and the individual and his parents are willing to sign liability waivers regarding the worst-case scenario should it occur.

Northwestern, however, refuses to allow Knapp to play on or even practice with its men's basketball team. Knapp, currently a sophomore at Northwestern, has the basketball skills to play at the intercollegiate level, but he has never taken the court for his team. Although Northwestern does not restrict him from playing pick-up basketball games, using recreational facilities on campus, or exerting himself physically on his own, the university disqualified Knapp from playing on its intercollegiate basketball team.

The issue in this case boils down to whether the school—because of § 504 of the Rehabilitation Act of 1973, as amended, 29 U.S.C. § 794—will be forced to let Knapp don a purple uniform and take the floor as a member of Northwestern's basketball team.

Prior to his senior year of high school Knapp was rated among the best basketball players in Illinois. He was recruited by numerous universities, including Northwestern. At the end of Knapp's junior year at Peoria's Woodruff High School, Northwestern orally offered him an athletic scholarship to play basketball. Knapp orally accepted the offer.

A few weeks into his senior year, Knapp suffered sudden cardiac death—meaning his heart stopped—during a pick-up basketball game. Paramedics used cardiopulmonary resuscitation, defibrillation (i.e., electric shocks), and injections of drugs to bring Knapp back to life. A few weeks later, doctors implanted an internal cardioverter-defibrillator in Knapp's abdomen. The device detects heart arrhythmia and delivers a shock to convert the abnormal heart rhythm back to normal. In other words, if Knapp's heart stops again the device is supposed to restart it.

On the day following his sudden cardiac death, Northwestern informed Knapp and his family that whatever the ultimate medical decision, Northwestern would honor its commitment for a scholarship. Seven weeks after his collapse Knapp signed a national letter of intent to attend Northwestern.

Knapp did not play basketball during his senior year in high school, but he was always a superb student, and in June 1995 he graduated as the valedictorian of his class. In September 1995 he enrolled as a Northwestern student.

On November 7, 1995, Dr. Howard Sweeney, Northwestern's head team physician, declared Knapp ineligible to participate on Northwestern's men's basketball team for the 1995–96 school year. Dr. Sweeney based his decision on Knapp's medical records in which several treating physicians recommended that Knapp not play competitive basketball, the report of team physician Dr. Mark Gardner following a physical examination of Knapp, published guidelines and recommendations following two national medical conferences known as the Bethesda Conferences regarding eligibility of athletes with cardiovascular abnormalities, and recommendations of physicians with whom Dr. Gardner and Dr. Sweeney consulted. After the basketball season ended, Northwestern and the Big Ten declared Knapp permanently medically ineligible to play basketball. Northwestern's athletic director, Rick Taylor, later confirmed that Northwestern will never voluntarily let Knapp play intercollegiate basketball as a Wildcat.

As a result, Knapp has never practiced with the Northwestern team nor played in a college game. His scholarship nevertheless continues and he attends practices (though he is not allowed to do anything but watch, apparently). He also receives other benefits afforded to athletes (such as tutoring, counseling, and training table), in addition to the full range of academic and nonacademic offerings the university provides to all students.

On the same day Dr. Sweeney declared him ineligible, Knapp filed a complaint in federal district court asserting that Northwestern's actions violated the Rehabilitation Act. The suit sought declaratory relief, preliminary and permanent injunctive relief, and compensatory damages. Knapp's undisputed goal is to force Northwestern to allow him to play varsity basketball.

In May 1996 Northwestern filed a motion for summary judgment, and Knapp thereafter requested a permanent injunction. The district court held a hearing on September 6, 1996, solely to determine whether Knapp presently is medically eligible to play intercollegiate basketball. Presented with conflicting evidence, the district court found Knapp medically eligible and Northwestern in violation of the Rehabilitation Act. After subsequent hearings on the issue of reasonable accommodation, the district court denied Northwestern's motion for summary judgment and entered a permanent injunction prohibiting Northwestern from excluding Knapp from playing on its basketball team for any reason related to his cardiac condition.

The district court's decision was based on the affidavit of Knapp and the testimony and affidavits of two experts presented by Northwestern and three experts presented by Knapp. All the experts agreed Knapp had suffered sudden cardiac death due to ventricular fibrillation; even with the internal defibrillator, playing intercollegiate basketball places Knapp at a higher risk for suffering another event of sudden cardiac death compared to other male college basketball players; the internal defibrillator has never been tested under the conditions of intercollegiate basketball; and no person currently plays or has ever played college or professional basketball after suffering sudden cardiac death and having a defibrillator implanted. Northwestern's experts, cardiologists who participated in at least one of the Bethesda conferences, testified that playing intercollegiate basketball significantly and unacceptably increases Knapp's risk of death. At least one of Northwestern's experts stated that individuals with internal defibrillators should not play intercollegiate basketball. Knapp's expert cardiologists, one of whom, Dr. Lawrence Rink, is Knapp's treating cardiologist and an Indiana University basketball team physician, testified that although Knapp is at an increased risk for sudden cardiac death, that risk, especially with the internal defibrillator in place, is insubstantial or at least acceptable.

After tasting defeat in the district court, Northwestern filed an emergency notice of appeal on September 27, 1996. It also sought a stay of enforcement of the injunction. We expedited the proceedings, granted the stay pending this decision, and heard oral arguments on November

7, 1996, ironically one year to the day after Dr. Sweeney first declared that Knapp could not play basketball for Northwestern.

We review the district court's grant of a permanent injunction for abuse of discretion. United States v. Kaun, 827 F.2d 1144, 1148 (7th Cir.1987). Factual determinations are reviewed under a clearly erroneous standard and legal conclusions are given de novo review. A factual or legal error may be sufficient to establish an abuse of discretion. Id. Interpretation of the Rehabilitation Act presents legal questions calling for de novo review.

The Rehabilitation Act, which is the sole basis for Knapp's claim, ensures that

> [n]o otherwise qualified individual with a disability in the United States, as defined in section 7(8) [29 USCS § 706(8)], shall, solely by reason of her or his disability, be excluded from the participation in, be denied the benefits of, or be subjected to discrimination under any program or activity receiving Federal financial assistance....

29 U.S.C. § 794(a). To prevail on his claim for discrimination under the Act, Knapp must prove that: (1) he is disabled as defined by the Act; (2) he is otherwise qualified for the position sought; (3) he has been excluded from the position solely because of his disability; and (4) the position exists as part of a program or activity receiving federal financial assistance. Byrne v. Board of Educ., School of West Allis–West Milwaukee, 979 F.2d 560, 563 (7th Cir.1992). Northwestern does not dispute that it receives federal financial assistance and that it has excluded Knapp from its intercollegiate basketball program solely because of his cardiac condition, so our focus is on whether Knapp is an "otherwise qualified individual with a disability."

To show that he is disabled under the terms of the Act, Knapp must prove that he

> (i) has a physical ... impairment which substantially limits one or more of [his] major life activities, (ii) has a record of such an impairment, or (iii) is regarded as having such an impairment.

29 U.S.C. § 706(8)(B). Knapp satisfies the first element of part (i) of this definition. A cardiovascular problem constitutes a physical impairment under § 706(8)(B). 34 C.F.R. § 104.3(j)(2)(i)(A); 45 C.F.R. § 84.3(j)(2)(i)(A). Northwestern does not dispute this fact, but it instead zeros in on the second element of the disability definition: whether playing intercollegiate basketball is part of a major life activity and, if so, whether its diagnosis of Knapp's cardiac condition substantially limits Knapp in that activity.

In determining whether a particular individual has a disability as defined in the Rehabilitation Act, the regulations promulgated by the Department of Health and Human Services with the oversight and approval of Congress are of significant assistance. School Bd. of Nassau County, Fla. v. Arline, 480 U.S. 273, 279, 107 S.Ct. 1123, 1126, 94

L.Ed.2d 307 (1987); Byrne, 979 F.2d at 563. Those regulations define "major life activities" as basic functions of life "such as caring for one's self, performing manual tasks, walking, seeing, hearing, speaking, breathing, learning, and working." 34 C.F.R. § 104.3(j)(2)(ii); 45 C.F.R. § 84.3(j)(2)(ii). Regulations regarding equal employment opportunities under the Americans with Disabilities Act, 42 U.S.C. § 12101 et seq., adopt the same term and definition and an interpretive note provides a bit more guidance: " 'Major life activities' are those basic activities that the average person in the general population can perform with little or no difficulty." 29 C.F.R. pt. 1630, app. § 1630.2.

The regulations promulgated pursuant to the Rehabilitation Act do not define "substantial limitation," and this is not an oversight. In commentary following the regulations, both the Department of Education and the Department of Health and Human Services acknowledge "the lack of any definition in the proposed regulation of the phrase 'substantially limits.' The Department does not believe that a definition of this term is possible at this time." 34 C.F.R. pt. 104, app. A, subpt. A(3); 45 C.F.R. pt. 84, app. A, subpt. A(3). "The court must ask 'whether the particular impairment constitutes for the particular person a significant barrier to [a major life activity].' " Byrne, 979 F.2d at 565 (quoting Forrisi v. Bowen, 794 F.2d 931, 933 (4th Cir.1986)).

This case is difficult because it does not fit neatly under the Rehabilitation Act. The "disability" Knapp claims is the basis for discrimination against him is not a continuing one like blindness or deafness. At any given moment in time when Knapp's heart is functioning properly his disability does not affect him. He is truly disabled only when his heart stops, which may or may not happen to him again. The disability regarding which Northwestern allegedly discriminates, therefore, actually is the greater risk of harm for Knapp than the risk faced by other male college basketball players. In addition, other impairments usually do not have as severe a result as is possible in this case. A person who is deaf, for instance, will not suddenly die on the basketball court because of that disability. Here, Knapp's disability is all or nothing. Finally, because Knapp's disability affects one of the most central organs of the body, his disability to some extent affects all major life activities—if his heart stops, he will not breathe, see, speak, walk, learn, or work. Once again it is all or nothing—either his heart is functioning and no major life activities are limited at that moment, or it has stopped and the most major life activity of all—living—has been affected.

In any event, the parties here have framed their arguments as involving solely the major life activity of learning. Knapp contends that playing an intercollegiate sport is an integral part of his major life activity of learning and that his education will be substantially limited if he cannot play on the team. He states that he does not believe he can obtain confidence, dedication, leadership, perseverance, discipline, and teamwork in any better way. The district court agreed with him, determining that for Knapp, playing on the Northwestern basketball team was part of the major life activity of learning and that he was substantially limited from such learning by the university.

In their arguments, the parties have separated "substantially limited" and "major life activities" into two independent criteria. We do not believe that such a complete separation should be made, at least in regard to learning and working. A comment on this point by the Sixth Circuit is insightful:

> The court in [citation omitted] treated "substantially limiting" and "major life activity" as distinct statutory qualifications. [Citation omitted.] However, at least with respect to the major life activity of "working", they constitute an inseparable whole.
>
> An impairment that affects only a narrow range of jobs can be regarded either as not reaching a major life activity or as not substantially limiting one.

Jasany v. United States Postal Service, 755 F.2d 1244, 1249 n. 3 (6th Cir.1985). We think this same interrelationship applies regarding learning. If playing NCAA basketball reaches a major life activity, then it is likely that deprivation of that activity would, for the individual basketball player, be a substantial limitation. Likewise, if playing intercollegiate basketball does not reach the status of major life activity, then it is most likely that deprivation will not be a substantial limitation.

We do not think that the definition of "major life activity" can be as particularized as Knapp wants it to be. Playing intercollegiate basketball obviously is not in and of itself a major life activity, as it is not a basic function of life on the same level as walking, breathing, and speaking. Not everyone gets to go to college, let alone play intercollegiate sports. We acknowledge that intercollegiate sports can be an important part of the college learning experience for both athletes and many cheering students—especially at a Big Ten school. Knapp has indicated that such is the case for him. But not every student thinks so. Numerous college students graduate each year having neither participated in nor attended an intercollegiate sporting event. Their sheepskins are no less valuable because of the lack of intercollegiate sports in their lives. Not playing intercollegiate sports does not mean they have not learned. Playing or enjoying intercollegiate sports therefore cannot be held out as a necessary part of learning for all students.

A few cases, none of them binding on us, have considered school team sports a major life activity in and of themselves. See Pahulu v. University of Kansas, 897 F.Supp. 1387 (D.Kan.1995) (intercollegiate football may be a major life activity); see also Sandison v. Michigan High School Athletic Ass'n, Inc., 863 F.Supp. 483, 489 (E.D.Mich.1994) (participation on the cross-country and track teams an important and integral part of education and a major life activity), rev'd on other grounds, 64 F.3d 1026 (6th Cir.1995). In other cases involving school athletics, whether they constituted part of the major life activity of learning is not even discussed. See Grube v. Bethlehem Area Sch. Dist.,

550 F.Supp. 418 (E.D.Pa.1982) (disability assumed, so major life activity not discussed); see also Wright v. Columbia Univ., 520 F.Supp. 789 (E.D.Pa.1981) (parties did not dispute that player was disabled).

Because intercollegiate athletics may be one part of the major life activity of learning for certain students, the parties here have framed the analysis of what constitutes a major life activity into a choice between a subjective test or an objective test—whether we look at what constitutes learning for Nick Knapp or what constitutes learning in general for the average person. The Rehabilitation Act and the regulations promulgated under it give little guidance regarding whether the determination of what constitutes a major life activity turns on an objective or subjective standard. And while we have previously said that whether a person is disabled is "an individualized inquiry, best suited to a case-by-case determination," we have also indicated that "the definition of 'major life activity' in the regulations 'cannot be interpreted to include working at the specific job of one's choice,' " Byrne, 979 F.2d at 565. Other courts have been across the board on whether the test is objective or subjective. Compare Pahulu, 897 F.Supp. at 1393 ("for Pahulu, intercollegiate football may be a major life activity, i.e., learning"), and Sandison, 863 F.Supp. at 489 (participation on high school teams is "as to them a major life activity"), with Welsh v. City of Tulsa, Okla., 977 F.2d 1415, 1417 (10th Cir.1992) (major life activity of working does not necessarily mean working at the job of one's choice).

We decline to define the major life activity of learning in such a way that the Act applies whenever someone wants to play intercollegiate athletics. A "major life activity," as defined in the regulations, is a basic function of life "such as caring for one's self, performing manual tasks, walking, seeing, hearing, speaking, breathing, learning, and working." 34 C.F.R. § 104.3(j)(2)(ii); 45 C.F.R. § 84.3(j)(2)(ii). These are basic functions, not more specific ones such as being an astronaut, working as a firefighter, driving a race car, or learning by playing Big Ten basketball.

However, major life activities are defined in a more individualized manner during the "substantial limitation" analysis, where, according to Byrne, 979 F.2d at 565, we look at whether the particular impairment constitutes a significant barrier for the particular person. What impairment will significantly impede learning for a person obtaining her third doctorate is not the same as one which would affect the average tenth grader's ability to learn. But any narrowing of what constitutes learning for a particular individual occurs within reasonable limits—coverage of the Rehabilitation Act is not open-ended or based on every dream or desire that a person may have. Not every impairment that affects an individual's major life activities is a substantially limiting impairment. The key obviously is the extent to which the impairment restricts the major life activity. Roth v. Lutheran General Hospital, 57 F.3d 1446, 1454 (7th Cir.1995). For that individual, "[t]he impairment must limit [learning] generally." Byrne, 979 F.2d at 565. Just as "[i]t is well established that an inability to perform a particular job for a particular employer is not sufficient to establish a handicap [in regard to working]," the inability to engage in a particular activity for a particular university is not sufficient to establish a disability in regard to education. Id.; see Heilweil v. Mt. Sinai Hosp., 32 F.3d 718 (2d Cir.1994) (no disability because asthmatic condition did not substantially limit breathing or working except while in one room of building), cert. denied, 513 U.S. 1147, 115 S.Ct. 1095, 130 L.Ed.2d 1063 (1995); Welsh, 977 F.2d at 1419 (sincere desire to become a firefighter does not mean inability to become one due to sensory deprivation in fingers substantially limits ability to work); Daley v. Koch, 892 F.2d 212, 215 (2d Cir.1989) (being declared unsuitable for particular position of police officer not substantial limitation of major life activity). An impairment that interferes with an individual's ability to perform a particular function, but does not significantly decrease that individual's ability to obtain a satisfactory education otherwise, does not substantially limit the major life activity of learning. Welsh, 977 F.2d at 1418.

Because learning through playing intercollegiate basketball is only one part of the education available to Knapp at Northwestern, even under a subjective standard, Knapp's ability to learn is not substantially limited. Knapp's scholarship continues, allowing him access to all academic and—except for intercollegiate basketball—all nonacademic services and activities available to other Northwestern students, in addition to all other services available to scholarship athletes. Although perhaps not as great a learning experience as actually playing, it is even possible that Knapp may "learn" through the basketball team in a role other than as a player. Knapp is an intelligent student and athlete, and the inability to play intercollegiate basketball at Northwestern forecloses only a small portion of his collegiate opportunities. Like the firefighter in Welsh, who did not show that his education and training limited him to being a firefighter, Welsh, 977 F.2d at 1419, Knapp has not shown that his education and training limit him to do nothing but play basketball. The fact that Knapp's goal of playing intercollegiate basketball is frustrated does not substantially limit his education. The Rehabilitation Act does not guarantee an individual the exact educational experience that he may desire, just a fair one. Consequently, we hold that Knapp as a matter of law is not disabled within the meaning of the Rehabilitation Act.

Even if we were inclined to find Knapp disabled under the Rehabilitation Act, he would still come up short because we also hold as a matter of law that he is not, under the statute, "otherwise qualified" to play intercollegiate basketball at Northwestern. A qualified disabled person, with respect to postsecondary education services, is a "person who meets the academic and technical standards requisite to admission or participation in the [school's] education program or activity." 34 C.F.R. § 104.3(k)(3); 45 C.F.R. § 84.3(k)(3). An explanatory note to the regulations states that the term "technical standards" means "all nonacademic admissions criteria that are essential to participation in the program in question." 34 C.F.R. pt. 104, app. A, subpt. A(5); 45 C.F.R. pt. 84, app. A, subpt. A(5).

Section 794 does not compel educational institutions to disregard the disabilities of disabled persons. Southeastern Community College v. Davis, 442 U.S. 397, 405, 99 S.Ct. 2361, 2366, 60 L.Ed.2d 980 (1979). It requires only that an "otherwise qualified" disabled person not be excluded from participation in a federally funded program solely because of the disability. Id. In other words, although a disability is not a permissible ground for assuming an inability to function in a particular context, the disability is not thrown out when considering if the person is qualified for the position sought. Id. at 405–06, 99 S.Ct. at 2366–67. "An otherwise qualified person is one who is able to meet all of a program's requirements in spite of his handicap," id. at 406, 99 S.Ct. at 2367, with reasonable accommodation, see Arline, 480 U.S. at 287–88 n. 17, 107 S.Ct. at 1131 n. 17 ("when a handicapped person is not able to perform the essential functions of the job, the court must also consider whether any reasonable accommodation by the employer would enable the handicapped person to perform those functions").

Legitimate physical qualifications may in fact be essential to participation in particular programs. Southeastern, 442 U.S. at 407, 99 S.Ct. at 2367.

Paragraph (k) of § 84.3 defines the term "qualified handicapped person." Throughout the regulation, this term is used instead of the statutory term "otherwise qualified handicapped person." The Department believes that the omission of the word "otherwise" is necessary in order to comport with the intent of the statute because, read literally, "otherwise" qualified handicapped persons include persons who are qualified except for their handicap, rather than in spite of their handicap.

Under such a literal reading, a blind person possessing all the qualifications for driving a bus except sight could be said to be "otherwise qualified" for the job of driving. Clearly, such a result was not intended by Congress. In all other respects, the terms "qualified" and "otherwise qualified" are intended to be interchangeable.

A significant risk of personal physical injury can disqualify a person from a position if the risk cannot be eliminated. Chiari v. City of League City, 920 F.2d 311, 317 (5th Cir.1991). But more than merely an elevated risk of injury is required before disqualification is appropriate. Mantolete v. Bolger, 767 F.2d 1416, 1424 (9th Cir.1985). Any physical qualification based on risk of future injury must be examined with special care if the Rehabilitation Act is not to be circumvented, since almost all disabled individuals are at a greater risk of injury. Bentivegna v. United States Dept. of Labor, 694 F.2d 619, 622 (9th Cir.1982).

In Mantolete, the Ninth Circuit addressed the standard to apply in determining if an individual is otherwise physically qualified to perform an activity when the possibility of future injury exists:

> [I]n some cases, a job requirement that screens out qualified handicapped individuals on the basis of possible future injury is necessary. However, we hold that in order to exclude such individuals, there must be a showing of a reasonable probability of substantial harm. Such a determination cannot be based merely on an employer's subjective evaluation or, except in cases of a most apparent nature, merely on medical reports. The question is whether, in light of the individual's work history and medical history, employment of that individual would pose a reasonable probability of substantial harm....
>
> In applying this standard, an employer must gather all relevant information regarding the applicant's work history and medical history, and independently assess both the probability and severity of potential injury. This involves, of course, a case-by-case analysis of the applicant and the particular job.

767 F.2d at 1422; see Chiari, 920 F.2d at 317 (disabled person not qualified for job if there is genuine substantial risk that worker could be injured or could injure others and employer cannot modify job to eliminate risk). We agree this is the appropriate standard. We now turn, however, to who should make such an assessment.

In this case, the severity of the potential injury is as high as it could be—death. In regard to the probability of injury, Dr. John H. McAnulty, one of Knapp's experts, testified at the injunction hearing that the annual risk of death to Knapp as a result of his cardiac condition under a worst-case scenario is 2.4 percent and that playing intercollegiate basketball would elevate this annual risk to 2.93 percent, or 1 in 34. In other words, if 34 Nick Knapps played basketball for a year, chances are one would die. Dr. Brian Olshansky, another expert for Knapp, put Knapp's risk of death for the 1996–97 basketball season at no greater than 1 in 100. These estimates took into account Knapp's internal defibrillator, apparently the only "accommodation" possible for Knapp's condition. Although the doctors indicated that these numbers were merely estimates, all agreed that the risk to Knapp is higher than to the average male collegiate basketball player. Knapp's experts believed it was an acceptable level of risk.

Northwestern's experts agreed with the school's team doctors that Knapp's participation in competitive Big Ten basketball presented an unacceptable level of risk. According to Dr. Barry J. Maron, one of Northwestern's experts, based on a 10–year study, the risk of nontraumatic death for the average male college basketball player is 1 in 28,818. Dr. Maron further testified that participation in intercollegiate basketball significantly increases Knapp's risk of death, although he believed the precise risk could not be quantified. Dr. Douglas J. Zipes agreed. According to both Drs. Zipes and Maron, the most important fact in assessing Knapp's current risk of sudden cardiac death while playing intercollegiate basketball is the fact that his previous sudden cardiac death was induced by playing basketball.

Knapp's and Northwestern's experts disagreed on the effect of the passage of time on the likelihood that Knapp would suffer another sudden cardiac death. Almost all experts agreed that the internal defibrillator had never been tested under conditions like an intercollegiate basketball game or practice and that it was unclear whether the device would actually work under the stress and physical conditions of a high-intensity sport. Dr. Olshansky, though, indicated that biweekly "interrogations" of the defibrillator would minimize the risk of its failure. Knapp has had his defibrillator checked on a regular basis and has had no problems with it.

The district court judge in this case believed that in the face of conflicting opinion evidence regarding risk, and the fact that no scientific data existed to quantify that risk, the decision on whether Knapp should play falls in the lap of the court:

> We have nothing more exotic here than highly qualified experts, in agreement on all the basic scientific principles and differing only in their medical judgment on the final question.... All possess the education, training and experience required to become experts and none disputes the expertise of the others. The range of disagreement is extremely narrow, confined only to the dimensions of the risk of recurrence and the effect of the passage of time on that risk.... [M]y task is to consider all the opinions and determine which are most persuasive. It is what the trial of disputes such as this will sometimes require. It might have been better to have left the choice to a panel of physicians, but Congress left it with the courts and the random assignment of this case has left it here with me....
>
> I again find the opinions of Drs. McAnulty, Rink and Olshansky to be persuasive and I find that the risk to Nicholas Knapp of a repeat episode is not substantial.

We disagree with the district court's legal determination that such decisions are to be made by the courts and believe instead that medical determinations of this sort are best left to team doctors and universities as long as they are made with reason and rationality and with full regard to possible and reasonable accommodations. In cases such as ours, where Northwestern has examined both Knapp and his medical records, has considered his medical history and the relation between his prior sudden cardiac death and the possibility of future occurrences, has considered the severity of the potential injury, and has rationally and reasonably reviewed consensus medical opinions or recommendations in the pertinent field—regardless whether conflicting medical opinions exist—the university has the right to determine that an individual is not otherwise medically qualified to play without violating the Rehabilitation Act. The place of the court in such cases is to make sure that the decision-maker has reasonably considered and relied upon sufficient evidence specific to the individual and the potential injury, not to determine on its own which evidence it believes is more persuasive.

Other courts have held the same. In Pahulu, for instance, an intercollegiate football player presented testimony of three specialists in an attempt to show that his risk of permanent neurological injury was no greater than any other player's and that the University of Kansas declared him physically ineligible based on misconceptions. The Kansas district court nevertheless found that "the conclusion of the KU physicians, although conservative, is reasonable and rational ... and is supported by substantial competent evidence for which the court is unwilling to substitute its judgment." Pahulu, 897 F.Supp. at 1394. We reject those cases intimating that a school's rational decision has no weight. See Poole v. South Plainfield Bd. of Educ., 490 F.Supp. 948, 954 (D.N.J.1980) (school board incorrectly "insisted nonetheless in imposing its own rational decision over the rational decision of the Pooles").

In Arline, where a school teacher with tuberculosis was fired and thereafter sued her employer under the Rehabilitation Act, the Supreme Court stated that an "otherwise qualified" inquiry must be individualized and should include

> " ... facts, based on reasonable medical judgments given the state of medical knowledge, about (a) the nature of the risk ..., (b) the duration of the risk ..., [and] (c) the severity of the risk...."
>
> In making these findings, the courts normally should defer to the reasonable medical judgments of public health officials.

Arline, 480 U.S. at 287–88, 107 S.Ct. at 1130–31. The Court, however, refrained from addressing the deferential weight of the medical judgments of private physicians on which the employer relied. Id. Although the Bethesda Conferences were not convened by public health officials and such guidelines should not substitute for individualized assessment of an athlete's particular physical condition, the consensus recommendations of several physicians in a certain field do carry weight and support the Northwestern team doctors' individualized assessment of Knapp.

We do not believe that, in cases where medical experts disagree in their assessment of the extent of a real risk of serious harm or death, Congress intended that the courts—neutral arbiters but generally less skilled in medicine than the experts involved—should make the final medical decision. Instead, in the midst of conflicting expert testimony regarding the degree of serious risk of harm or death, the court's place is to ensure that the exclusion or disqualification of an individual was individualized, reasonably made, and based upon competent medical evidence. So long as these factors exist, it will be the rare case regarding participation in athletics where a court may substitute its judgment for that of the school's team physicians.

In this case, the district court found that if

> as a matter of law and fact, all that is required, as Pahulu [cite omitted] holds, is that Northwestern make a rational decision that Knapp's risk is substantial based on reasonable evidence to

which courts must defer, then I find Northwestern has done this.

Because we hold today as a matter of law that a court must allow Northwestern to make its own determinations of substantial risk and severity of injury if they are based on reliable evidence, the district court's order forcing Northwestern to let Knapp play must be reversed.

We note further that the district court did not distinguish between the reasonableness of Northwestern's decision to exclude Knapp back in the 1995–96 season and the reasonableness of its decision to bar him from playing this year and the next two. Knapp contends that no proper finding of reasonableness appears in the record because the district court stated that the issue to be addressed was Knapp's condition this fall rather than the rectitude or irrectitude of Northwestern's actions. Dr. Sweeney's and Dr. Gardner's bases for deeming Knapp ineligible in 1995–96 do appear in the record, however, and both testified regarding the present season that, based upon their prior information and the newer testimony of Drs. Rink, Olshansky, McAnulty, Maron, and Zipes, they still believed Knapp remains at a substantial risk of death by playing intercollegiate basketball.

In closing, we wish to make clear that we are not saying Northwestern's decision necessarily is the right decision. We say only that it is not an illegal one under the Rehabilitation Act. On the same facts, another team physician at another university, reviewing the same medical history, physical evaluation, and medical recommendations, might reasonably decide that Knapp met the physical qualifications for playing on an intercollegiate basketball team. Simply put, all universities need not evaluate risk the same way. What we say in this case is that if substantial evidence supports the decision-maker—here Northwestern—that decision must be respected.

Section 794 prohibits authorities from deciding without significant medical support that certain activities are too risky for a disabled person. Decisions of this sort cannot rest on paternalistic concerns. Knapp, who is an adult, is not in need of paternalistic decisions regarding his health, and his parents—more entitled to be paternalistic toward him than Northwestern—approve of his decision. See Wright at 794 (Columbia's decision not to allow student with sight in only one eye to play football "contrary to the express wishes of his parents who, together with their son, have reached a rational decision concerning the risk involved"). In regard to cases involving risk of future injury, a school's perception of the threat of such injury cannot be based on unfounded fears or stereotypes; it must be based on objective evidence. Chiari, 920 F.2d at 317. But here, where Northwestern acted rationally and reasonably rather than paternalistically, no Rehabilitation Act violation has occurred. The Rehabilitation Act "is carefully structured to replace ... reflexive actions to actual or perceived handicaps with actions based on reasoned and medically sound judgments...." Arline, 480 U.S. at 284–85, 107 S.Ct. at 1129.

For these reasons, the district court's grant of the permanent injunction and denial of Northwestern's motion for summary judgment are reversed and the case is remanded with instructions to enter summary judgment in favor of Northwestern.

KLECZEK v. RHODE ISLAND INTERSCHOLASTIC LEAGUE, INC.

768 F.Supp. 951 (D.R.I.1991).

LAGUEUX, District Judge.

Plaintiffs Edward Kleczek and Alyce Kleczek brought this action on behalf of their son Brian, a South Kingstown High School student who desires to play on that school's girls' field hockey team. Defendants are the Rhode Island Interscholastic League, Inc. ("RIIL"), which is a private nonprofit organization, and various officials associated with South Kingstown High School, including the Superintendent of Schools, the Principal, and the School Committee and its individual members.

Presently before the Court is plaintiffs' motion for preliminary injunction. Plaintiffs seek an order enjoining defendants from preventing or interfering with Brian's participation in interscholastic field hockey. Plaintiffs also seek an order enjoining defendants from obstructing the South Kingstown High School field hockey team's participation in interscholastic competition because of the fact that Brian is male. For the reasons set forth below, plaintiffs' motion for a preliminary injunction must be denied.

I. Background

In August of 1990, at the beginning of his sophomore year, Brian Kleczek tried out for the South Kingstown High School girls' field hockey team. Based upon his skills, the team coach determined that Brian was best qualified to compete on the junior varsity squad. The coach did not have to cut any players to make room for Brian. The total number of players interested in competing did not exceed the maximum number that the coach indicated would be the roster limit. In short, any student interested and committed made the team; ability only determined placement on either the varsity or junior varsity team. Of course, if many more students had tried out for the team, the coach would have had to exclude some to keep a manageable number.

Brian became interested in playing on the team because his older sister had played varsity field hockey for South Kingstown High and also because he had himself played the sport in physical education class at the high school. Because South Kingstown High School does not field a boys' field hockey team, nor do any such teams exist in Rhode Island, Brian decided to try-out for the girls' team. South Kingstown High School does field three fall teams that allow male participation: football, cross-country, and soccer.

Brian's parents supported his decision to try-out for the team. On August 27, 1990, they wrote to the athletic director at the high school requesting his permission to allow Brian to play. The principal of the high school, defendant Eric Wertheimer, then requested the RIIL to allow Brian to compete. The RIIL refused, pointing to Article 25, Section 1 of its Rules and Regulations which limits competition in field hockey to only girls. Prompted by the Kleczeks, Mr. Wertheimer then requested the RIIL to waive the application of Article 25, Section 1 in Brian's case. A committee of the RIIL conducted a hearing on the requested waiver and heard testimony from several witnesses. It thereafter concluded, by a unanimous vote, that no waiver should be permitted and that Brian should not be allowed to join the team. The RIIL notified Mr. Wertheimer of its decision on September 26, 1990. As a result, Brian spent last fall on the sidelines, serving as a manager for the team and occasionally joining in team practices.

Plaintiffs filed this suit on February 21, 1991. They alleged that the actions of the defendants violate Brian's rights under Title IX (20 U.S.C. § 1681), the federal equal protection clause (U.S. Const. amend. XIV), Section 16–38–1.1 of the General Laws of Rhode Island, and Article I, Section 2 of the Rhode Island Constitution. A hearing was held on plaintiffs' motion for a preliminary injunction on May 20, 1991. The matter is now in order for decision.

II. Discussion

The First Circuit has recently reaffirmed the well-settled standard that governs a district court's determination of a motion for preliminary injunction. The four-part test requires careful consideration of the following factors: (1) The likelihood of success on the merits; (2) The potential for irreparable injury; (3) A balancing of the relevant equities (most importantly, the hardship to the nonmovant if the restrainer issues as contrasted with the hardship to the movant if interim relief is withheld); and (4) The effect on the public interest of a grant or denial of the restrainer. Narragansett Indian Tribe v. Guilbert, 934 F.2d 4, 5 (1st Cir.1991). Application of this standard to the facts of this case mandates denial of plaintiffs' motion for a preliminary injunction. Denial of the motion is necessary primarily because plaintiffs have failed to demonstrate a likelihood of success on the merits. In addition, consideration of the other three factors supports the denial of injunctive relief.

A. Probability of Success

It is "critical" for a party seeking a preliminary injunction to demonstrate a probability of success on the merits. Narragansett Indian Tribe, 934 F.2d at 6. Of course, a party need not prove its claims at the preliminary injunction stage, only that it is likely to be able to prove its claims later. Plaintiffs have not done this. Indeed, at this point, the chances of plaintiffs actually succeeding on the merits appear quite slim. See id. (noting that conclusions as to probability of success are only statements of "probable outcomes"). The Court reaches this conclusion because plaintiffs have failed to demonstrate the existence of federal funding which makes Title IX applicable. Furthermore, even if Title IX is assumed to apply, plaintiffs have not shown that it is likely that they would succeed under the plain meaning of the applicable regulations. In addition, plaintiffs have not shown that they are likely to succeed on their claim under the federal equal protection clause. Because success on both federal claims appears unlikely, the Court would have the discretion to refuse to exercise jurisdiction over the pendent state claims.

1. Title IX

Title IX prohibits sex discrimination in any "program or activity receiving Federal financial assistance." 20 U.S.C. § 1681. Both the RIIL and the South Kingstown athletic program are programs or activities within the prospective reach of Title IX. See 20 U.S.C. § 1687. However, because neither appears to receive federal financial assistance, they remain outside of Title IX's grasp.

The funding issue was explored carefully by counsel at the hearing held on this motion. David D. Gainey, the Chairman of the RIIL's Principal's Committee on Athletics, testified that the league receives no federal funds. Indeed, he also testified that the league does not even receive state funds. Instead, the league is funded entirely from dues collected from member schools, revenues collected from state championship events, and corporate sponsorship of some of those championships.

In addition, defendant Arthur Campbell, the Superintendent of Schools for South Kingstown, testified about the school system's receipt of federal funds. On examination by plaintiffs' counsel, Mr. Campbell stated that the school system receives federal funds and also pays membership dues to RIIL. However, when examined in more detail by RIIL's attorney, Mr. Campbell testified that the school system only receives "restrictive" federal funds, which are to be used for specific designated purposes such as vocational education programs, math and science training, reading programs, and so on. He also testified that no federal funds are used to support any school activity, including athletics.

On this evidence, plaintiffs are very unlikely to prevail on their Title IX claim. Proving that South Kingstown High School receives some federal money and that it in turn expends some money for membership in the RIIL is legally insufficient for Title IX purposes. The First Circuit has clearly held that Title IX adopts a "programmatic approach rather than an institutional approach to combating sex discrimination in education." Rice v. President and Fellows of Harvard College, 663 F.2d 336, 339 n. 1 (1st Cir.1981) (citing Othen v. Ann Arbor School Bd., 507 F.Supp. 1376, 1380–83 (E.D.Mich.1981), aff'd, 699 F.2d 309 (6th Cir. 1983)), cert. denied, 456 U.S. 928, 102 S.Ct. 1976, 72 L.Ed.2d 444 (1982). See also North Haven Bd. of Educ. v. Bell, 456 U.S. 512, 537, 102 S.Ct. 1912, 1926, 72 L.Ed.2d 299 (1982) (noting the "program-specific focus" of Section 1681 of Title IX).

Thus, in order to even have a chance of succeeding on their Title IX claim, plaintiffs must demonstrate that the RIIL and the South Kingstown athletic program are recipients of federal funds. Because the prospect of that happening appears remote, the Court must hold that plaintiffs have failed to demonstrate a likelihood of success on the merits of their Title IX claim. See Yellow Springs Exempted Village School Dist. Bd. of Educ. v. Ohio High School Athletic Ass'n, 647 F.2d 651, 656 (6th Cir.1981); Lantz by Lantz v. Ambach, 620 F.Supp. 663, 665 (S.D.N.Y. 1985).

Even if Title IX eventually proves to be applicable, the Court believes that plaintiffs have not shown a likelihood of succeeding under the regulations promulgated under the authority of Title IX. The applicable regulation provides in pertinent part:

> (a) General. No person shall, on the basis of sex, be excluded from participation in, be denied the benefits of, be treated differently from another person or otherwise be discriminated against in any interscholastic, intercollegiate, club or intramural athletics offered by a recipient, and no recipient shall provide any such athletics separately on such basis.
>
> (b) Separate teams. Notwithstanding the requirements of paragraph (a) of this section, a recipient may operate or sponsor separate teams for members of each sex where selection for such teams is based upon competitive skill or the activity involved is a contact sport. However, where a recipient operates or sponsors a team in a particular sport for members of one sex but operates or sponsors no such team for members of the other sex, and athletic opportunities for members of that sex have previously been limited, members of the excluded sex must be allowed to try-out for the team offered unless the sport involved is a contact sport. For the purposes of this part, contact sports include boxing, wrestling, rugby, ice hockey, football, basketball and other sports the purpose or major activity of which involves bodily contact.

45 C.F.R. § 86.41.

Under the obvious plain meaning of the regulation, Brian need not be provided the opportunity to play on the girls' field hockey team because athletic opportunities at South Kingstown High School have not previously been limited for members of his sex. Indeed, the evidence introduced at the hearing on this motion clearly establishes that only the female sex has had limited athletic opportunities at the high school.

Of course, Gomes v. Rhode Island Interscholastic League, 469 F.Supp. 659 (D.R.I.), vacated, 604 F.2d 733 (1st Cir.1979), held that to read the regulation to refer to "overall" athletic opportunities for one sex would give rise to serious questions about the regulation's constitutionality. Id. at 664. To avoid inviting such questions, Gomes construed the regulation to refer to the opportunities of members of one sex to participate in a particular sport. Thus, under the Gomes construction of the regulation, "A separate and exclusive female team may be established only when males previously had, and presumably continue to have, adequate athletic opportunities to participate in that sport." Id. at 665.

Plaintiffs here simply can not point to Gomes to support their contention that they are likely to succeed on the merits of their Title IX claim. For one thing, other courts have called into question the necessity of Gomes's construction of the regulation, which disregarded the plain language of the regulation and substituted new language to avoid a feared constitutional problem. See, e.g., Mularadelis v. Haldane Cent. School Bd., 74 A.D.2d 248, 427 N.Y.S.2d 458, 463–64 (1980). Indeed, since the date of the Gomes decision, other courts have ruled that it is constitutionally permissible to enforce the plain meaning of the regulations.

Furthermore, the subsequent history of the Gomes decision must be considered. The District Court granted injunctive relief on May 1, 1979. Seven days later, the First Circuit stayed the injunction. It did so because it believed "the district court's order would disrupt the sports season" and because it believed that the RIIL, which was the defendant in the action, had demonstrated a "probability of success on the merits." See Gomes v. Rhode Island Interscholastic League, 604 F.2d 733, 735 (1st Cir.1979). Despite the First Circuit's expedited handling of the appeal, "the League's volleyball season had been played and Gomes was about to graduate" from high school by the time oral argument was heard on June 8, 1990. Id. The Court, therefore, dismissed the appeal as moot and remanded the case for dismissal of Gomes's complaint. Certainly, this subsequent history casts a shadow over the precedential value of the District Court's decision in Gomes.

Furthermore, even if a Gomes-like construction of the phrase "and athletic opportunities for members of that sex have previously been limited" was appropriate, another clause of the same regulation will probably prohibit plaintiffs from succeeding under Title IX. Section 86.41(b) provides that "members of the excluded sex must be allowed to try-out for that team unless the sport involved is a contact sport." The regulation then lists several examples of contact sports such as football, rugby, and basketball "the purpose or major activity of which involves bodily contact." 45 C.F.R. § 86.41(b).

Plaintiffs argue that field hockey is a "non contact" sport, and therefore contend that the "unless" clause of Section 86.41(b) does not preclude Brian's inclusion on the team. However, the evidence presented to the Court indicates that field hockey is in reality an "incidental contact" sport, more akin to basketball than volleyball or tennis.

For example, Ms. Victoria Tefft, the South Kingstown field hockey coach, testified that the rules do not allow body contact between players ("checking") and that penalties are imposed for violations. Nevertheless, she conceded that players often do come into contact with each other, especially when the officiating is poor. Furthermore, she testified that novice players frequently violate a basic tenet of the game when moving the ball by placing their bodies between the ball and an opponent. In addition to body contact, Ms. Tefft testified that players "frequently" get hit by both the ball and an opposing player's stick, and wear shin guards and mouth guards to protect against serious injury.

Ms. Elizabeth Marquis, field hockey coach at Pilgrim High School, testified that several types of contact are inherent in a field hockey game including the ball hitting players' shins, lifted balls and lifted sticks that hit other parts of the body, and head-on collisions.

Field hockey obviously involves a great deal of incidental contact. The Title IX regulations do not require teams to offer try-outs to members of an excluded sex when a contact sport is involved. See Lantz by Lantz, 620 F.Supp. at 665 (applying this principle in the context of football). Although the purpose of field hockey is not to make bodily contact, such contact is inevitable in a sport that combines running, sticks, a hard ball, and a wide-open playing field.

In sum, plaintiffs have not shown that they are likely to succeed on the merits of their Title IX claim for three reasons: (1) the programs and activities of the defendants in question do not receive federal funds; (2) the overall athletic opportunities for males at South Kingstown High School have not been limited; and (3) the evidence indicates that field hockey is not a "non-contact" sport.

2. *Equal Protection Clause*

Plaintiffs have also failed to demonstrate a probability of success on the merits of their equal protection claim. In order to uphold a statutory classification based on gender, the defendants here would have the burden of showing that "the classification serves 'important governmental objectives and that the discriminatory means employed' are 'substantially related to the achievement of those objectives.' " Mississippi Univ. for Women v. Hogan, 458 U.S. 718, 724, 102 S.Ct. 3331, 3336, 73 L.Ed.2d 1090 (1982). Defendants will most likely prevail under that standard. Indeed, in Clark v. Arizona Interscholastic Ass'n, 695 F.2d 1126, 1131 (9th Cir.1982), cert. denied, 464 U.S. 818, 104 S.Ct. 79, 78 L.Ed.2d 90 (1983), the Ninth Circuit held that the policy of an interscholastic league similar to the RIIL of precluding boys from playing on a girls' volleyball team did not violate the equal protection clause. The Court determined that there was "clearly a substantial relationship between the exclusion of males from the team and the goal of redressing past discrimination and providing equal opportunities for women." Id.

It is beyond question that redressing the disparate athletic opportunities available to males and females is an important governmental interest. See Mularadelis, 427 N.Y.S.2d at 464; see also Hoover v. Meiklejohn, 430 F.Supp. 164, 170 (D.Colo.1977) (noting that because the athletic opportunity for females has historically been limited, "the encouragement of female involvement in sports is a legitimate objective"). Excluding males from female teams is substantially related to achieving that objective. See Clark, 695 F.2d at 1131; Hoover, 430 F.Supp. at 170. But see Attorney General v. Massachusetts Interscholastic Athletic Ass'n, 378 Mass. 342, 393 N.E.2d 284 (1979) (holding that such a classification could not pass muster under the strict scrutiny required by the Massachusetts Equal Rights Amendment). For these reasons, plaintiffs have not demonstrated that they are likely to prevail on their claim under the equal protection clause.

3. State Claims

The Court need not inquire into whether plaintiffs have shown a likelihood of success on their state claims under Section 16–38–1.1 of the Rhode Island General Laws, which prohibits sex discrimination in the public schools, and Article I, Section 2 of the Rhode Island Constitution, which prohibits sex discrimination by the state, its agents or anyone doing business with the state.

If plaintiffs' federal claims indeed prove to be without merit, then there no longer will be an independent basis of federal subject matter jurisdiction in this suit. In that situation, this Court would have the discretion to refuse to exercise pendent jurisdiction over the state claims. Jones v. State of Rhode Island, 724 F.Supp. 25, 34 (D.R.I.1989).

B. The Other Factors

Plaintiffs' failure to establish the likelihood of their success on the merits is alone sufficient to permit this Court to deny their motion for a preliminary injunction. However, a review of the three other factors involved in the preliminary injunction standard also counsel denial of plaintiffs' motion. First, Brian, who is about to start his junior year, will not suffer irreparable injury if the motion is denied. This case should be reached on its merits well before his high school eligibility expires. Second, a balancing of the equities of the situation weighs in the defendants' favor. Withholding injunctive relief simply means that Brian must wait until this case is resolved on its merits. Granting injunctive relief would interject a substantial degree of uncertainty and disruption into the efforts of school officials to field a team and the efforts of the RIIL to organize and run a uniform league. Because plaintiffs' chances of ultimate success on the merits appear so meagre at this point, the wiser course is to avoid imposing such hardship on the defendants in the first instance. Finally, allowing injunctive relief would not only affect the parties to this action, but all those associated with interscholastic field hockey in Rhode Island. Certainly, consideration of their interest in well-settled rules favors denial of plaintiffs' motion.

III. Conclusion

In sum, an analysis of the four-part standard for passing on a motion for preliminary injunction requires this Court to deny plaintiffs' motion. Most importantly, plaintiffs have not shown a likelihood of success on the merits. In addition, the three other factors favor not granting interim injunctive relief. Therefore, plaintiffs' motion for preliminary injunction is hereby denied.

GRIMSON v. IMMIGRATION AND NATURALIZATION SERVICE

934 F.Supp. 965 (N.D.Ill.1996).

GETTLEMAN, District Judge.

This case, much like the National Hockey League playoffs and the Energizer Bunny, just keeps going and going and going. Plaintiff Allan Stuart Grimson, a citizen of Canada, has filed a complaint for declaratory and injunctive relief pursuant to 28 U.S.C. §§ 2201, 1361, seeking to overturn defendant Immigration and Naturalization Service's ("INS") denial of his visa petition. Both parties have moved for summary judgment pursuant to Fed.R.Civ.P. 56. For the reasons set forth below, plaintiff's motion is granted, defendant's cross-motion is denied, and the decision of the INS is reversed.

Procedural History

This is the third time that this case has reached this district court. Plaintiff is a professional hockey player. He has played in the "professional leagues" since the 1982–83 season when he began playing for the Regina, Saskatchewan team in the now defunct World Hockey League. He has been playing in the NHL since the 1989 season. He is currently a member of the Detroit Red Wings, one of the better teams in the league.

Plaintiff initially filed a visa petition with defendant INS on January 20, 1993, seeking classification as a priority worker of extraordinary ability pursuant to 8 U.S.C. § 1153(b)(1)(A). The petition was denied by the Director of the INS Northern Service Center on the ground that plaintiff had failed to demonstrate that he was a player of extraordinary ability as defined by the INS. Plaintiff appealed to the Administrative Appeals Unit ("AAU"), contending that he had achieved sustained national and international acclaim as a professional hockey player, and that the Northern Service Center had recently classified four other hockey players of comparable ability as aliens of extraordinary ability.

The AAU affirmed the denial of plaintiff's petition, holding that, "while the record indicates that the petitioner had played several seasons with an NHL team, it has not been established that the petitioner has achieved the sustained national or international acclaim required for classification as an alien with extraordinary ability, that he is one of the small percentage who have risen to the very top of his field of endeavor, or that his entry into the United States would substantially benefit prospectively the United States."

Plaintiff then filed an action in this court pursuant to 28 U.S.C. §§ 2201 and 1361 for declaratory and injunctive relief with respect to the INS's denial of his visa petition. Judge Kocoras, to whom that case was assigned, remanded it back to the INS for further evidentiary proceedings, concluding that remand would allow plaintiff to take into consideration the INS's statutory interpretation of extraordinary ability when submitting further documentary evidence. Of particular note is Judge Kocoras's conclusion rejecting the INS's argument that it need not compare plaintiff's petition to those of other hockey players who had been granted visas, concluding that such position "not only lacked merit but borders on the specious." Judge Kocoras concluded that how the INS treated others in the field, particularly those alleged to possess no greater skill than petitioner, was highly irrelevant under the statutory scheme.

Plaintiff's petition was again denied by the Director of the Northern Service Center, which denial was again affirmed by the AAU. Plaintiff then filed the present action seeking declaratory and injunctive relief. On March 23, 1995, this court issued a memorandum opinion and order again remanding the case to the INS for further evidentiary proceedings. This court specifically directed plaintiff to submit and defendant to consider evidence regarding the necessity of a player with plaintiff's style of play and abilities, and evidence comparing his skill, salary level and other abilities to those of comparable players in the NHL, players who fulfill the same role for their respective teams. In addition, the court directed defendant to consider plaintiff's argument that a sustained career in the NHL demonstrates extraordinary ability.

Consistent with this court's instruction, on remand plaintiff submitted evidence of his current salary and contract with the Detroit Red Wings, a table from the Hockey News showing the 1996 players' salaries, newspaper and magazine articles about plaintiff, and an affidavit from Darren Pang, former renown NHL goal tender and current television broadcaster and NHL analyst for ESPN. Pang is a recognized expert on NHL hockey. Pang's affidavit lists all the "enforcers" in the league and their current salaries. It also sets forth the necessity for an enforcer, and indicates that most teams carry two such players on their rosters.

Finally, Pang's affidavit indicates that plaintiff is currently the third rated and third highest paid enforcer in the NHL (the other two being paid more because of their goal scoring ability), and that plaintiff was rated the fifth best enforcer in 1993 when he filed his original petition.

DISCUSSION

As in plaintiff's previous case, this case turns on the interpretation of "extraordinary ability" as used in the priority worker category under 8 U.S.C. § 1153(b)(1)(A)(i), which provides:

> (b) Preference allocation for employment-based immigrants
>
> Aliens subject to the worldwide level specified in section 1151(d) of this title for employment-based immigrants in a fiscal year shall be allotted visas as follows:
>
> (1) Priority workers
>
> Visas shall first be made available in a number not to exceed 28.6 percent of such worldwide level, plus any visas not required for the classes specified in paragraphs (4) and (5), to qualified immigrants who are aliens described in any of the following subparagraphs (A) through (C):

(A) Aliens with extraordinary ability

An alien is described in this subparagraph if—(i) the alien has extraordinary ability in the sciences, arts, education, business, or athletics which has been demonstrated by sustained national or international acclaim and whose achievements have been recognized in the field through extensive documentation.

The statute itself does not define extraordinary ability; however, the regulations promulgated by the INS define the term as "a level of expertise indicating that the individual is one of that small percentage who has risen to the very top of the field of endeavor." 8 C.F.R. § 204.5(h)(2). A petition for relief under this section must be accompanied by evidence that the alien has "sustained national or international acclaim and that his or her achievements have been recognized in the field of expertise." 8 C.F.R. § 204.5(h)(3). The regulations set forth various types of evidence that may be submitted to meet this evidentiary burden, including the documentation of memberships and associations which require outstanding achievements, major media publications relating to the alien's work in the field at issue, and evidence that the alien has commanded a large salary in relation to others in the field. 8 C.F.R. § 204.5(h)(3)(i-ix).

On remand from this court, the Director again completely rejected all plaintiff's evidence and denied his petition. First, relying on In the Matter of Katigbak, 14 I & N Decisions 45 (1971); Matter of Wing's Tea House, 16 I & N Decisions 158 (1977), and 8 CFR 103.2(b)(12) (which became effective in 1994, after plaintiff filed his petition), the Director determined that evidence relating to plaintiff's career after January 12, 1993 (the day plaintiff filed [his] petition) would not be considered because it could not establish eligibility at the time of filing the petition.

Next, the Director rejected plaintiff's argument that a sustained career in professional hockey and four years in the NHL should be considered as evidence of extraordinary ability. The Director determined that plaintiff had failed to present evidence that four years in the NHL as an enforcer qualified as a sustained career. The Director then rejected those portions of Pang's affidavit in which he attested that plaintiff's $300,000 salary in 1993 ranked him among the highest paid enforcers, and that plaintiff was considered among the top five enforcers in the league at that time. The basis for rejecting this evidence was that the affidavit contained no backup information for what the Director determined to be conclusory statements. The affidavit, however, indicates Mr. Pang's background and extensive knowledge of the NHL. He clearly states that he is familiar with plaintiff and the other enforcers in the league, and gives a basis for his opinions. He further states that if called to testify, he would testify that in his opinion in 1993 plaintiff was one of the top five enforcers in the league, and was so considered among his peers.

It is apparent to this court that at the heart of defendant's refusal to grant plaintiff a visa (as it has to other comparable NHL players) is its distaste for the role he plays on a hockey team. As stated in the Director's decision, "the service has never argued that the role of enforcer is not prevalent in the NHL. The necessity of such a role appears to be debatable. The service does argue that the sport itself has never condoned the kind of activity that petitioner is known for, as evidenced by the number of penalty minutes he is charged." The decision further states, "[A]t the time the petition was filed, the petitioner's main claim to fame was that he held the record for the most penalty minutes in a game. The amount of penalties the petitioner amasses is indicative of the amount of fighting he does but quantity does not equate to extraordinary ability." Despite this language, however, the only evidence presented to the Director was that plaintiff was the fifth best enforcer in the league at the time he filed his petition. The decision to simply ignore this evidence was an abuse of discretion.

Moreover, it is apparent from the above quoted language that the Director simply rejects the notion that an enforcer can have extraordinary ability limited to the role that he plays on a hockey team. Indeed, as set forth in defendant's memorandum in support of his cross-motion for summary judgment, defendant's position remains that because plaintiff engages in conduct which is "disfavored," his abilities cannot properly be considered as a factor supportive of his claim to be an athlete of extraordinary ability. This court disagrees. The only evidence that was presented to the Director indicates that the role of an enforcer is necessary to the success of an NHL hockey team. The fact that a player is penalized for fighting does not mean that it is not both a necessary and accepted element of the game. Indeed, if it was not a necessary and accepted element of the game, the league would simply ban fighting altogether. Moreover, plaintiff presented evidence that his role as an enforcer entails much more than fighting. Pang's affidavit indicates that the role of an enforcer is to fight when necessary, but also to protect the team stars from being roughed up by the opposing team. An enforcer also serves as a deterrent to fighting, depending upon the reputation of the team's enforcer.

The fact remains that plaintiff has presented evidence sufficient to demonstrate that he is currently among the top three players in the world at what he does, and in 1993, when he filed his petition, he was among the top five players in the world. It goes without saying that there are countless players attempting to replace him every day. Yet, in 1993 he was, and remains today, among the best in the world. He has reached the very top of his field of endeavor. There is virtually no evidence in the record (let alone substantial evidence) to support defendant's finding that plaintiff is not among the best in the world, or that he is not an athlete of extraordinary ability.

The court concludes that the decision to reject plaintiff's role and unquestioned ability as an enforcer was without rational explanation, and that there was not substantial evidence for the factual finding that plaintiff is not at the top of his field of endeavor. Accordingly, plaintiff's motion for summary judgment is granted, defendant's cross-motion is denied, and defendant is ordered to issue plaintiff the visa he seeks.

Notes

1. Besides disability, gender, and nationality, attempts have been made to disqualify players on a number of other grounds. *See, e.g.*, *Pottgen v. Missouri State High School Activities Ass'n*, 103 F.3d 720 (8th Cir.1997) (too old); *Langston v. ACT*, 890 F.2d 380 (11th Cir.1989) (academic cheating); *Behagen v. Amateur Basketball Ass'n of the United States*, 884 F.2d 524 (10th Cir.1989), *cert. denied*, 495 U.S. 918 (1990) (loss of amateur status); *Ponce v. Basketball Federation of the Commonwealth of Puerto Rico*, 760 F.2d 375 (1st Cir.1985) (residency); *Deesen v. Professional Golfers' Ass'n of America*, 358 F.2d 165 (9th Cir.), *cert. denied*, 385 U.S. 846 (1966) (lack of past success); *Linseman v. World Hockey Ass'n*, 439 F.Supp. 1315 (D.Conn. 1977) (too young); *Ali v. Division of State Athletic Comm'n*, 308 F.Supp. 11 (S.D.N.Y.1969) (criminal record); *Kirby v. Michigan High School Athletic Ass'n*, 585 N.W.2d 290 (Mich.1998) (weight); *Calandra v. State College Area School District*, 512 A.2d 809 (Pa.Commw.Ct.1986) (religion).

2. In addition to Nicholas Knapp, a number of other athletes have been ruled ineligible because of physical or mental disabilities. *See, e.g.*, *Washington v. Illman*, 1997 WL 138827 (2d Cir.1997) (power lifter—limited range of motion); *Neeld v. National Hockey League*, 594 F.2d 1297 (9th Cir.1979) (hockey player—blind in one eye); *Bowers v. National Collegiate Athletic Ass'n*, 9 F.Supp.2d 460 (D.N.J.1998) (football player—perception problems); *Tatum v. National Collegiate Athletic Ass'n*, 992 F.Supp. 1114 (E.D.Mo.1998) (basketball player—exam phobia); *Ganden v. National Collegiate Athletic Ass'n*, 1996 WL 680000 (N.D.Ill.1996) (swimmer—decoding impairment). For a further discussion, see Mark R. Freitas, *Applying the Rehabilitation Act and the Americans With Disabilities Act to Student-Athletes*, 5 Sports Law. J. 139 (1998); Adam A. Milani, *Can I Play?: The Dilemma of the Disabled Athlete in Interscholastic Sports*, 49 Ala. L. Rev. 817 (1998); Matthew J. Mitten, *Disability Issues in Sport: Enhanced Risk of Harm to One's Self as a Justification for Exclusion from Athletics*, 8 Marq. Sports L.J. 189 (1998).

3. As the court in *Kleczek* explains, in 1972 Congress passed Title IX to ensure male and female athletes would have an equal chance to play. Since its enactment, the law has proven extraordinarily successful, so much so that men are beginning to claim discrimination. *See further Kelley v. Board of Trustees of the University of Illinois*, 832 F.Supp. 237 (C.D.Ill.1993), *aff'd*, 35 F.3d 265 (7th Cir.1994), *cert. denied*, 513 U.S. 1128 (1995) (university did not act illegally when it cut men's swimming team to pay for women's swimming team), and Jim Donaldson, *Proportionality Makes Title IX Compliance Irrational*, Fort Worth Star-Telegram, Oct. 9, 1998, at 2 (Sports) (decrying the loss of athletic opportunities for men). For a further discussion of the statute and its effects, see, e.g., *Boucher v. Syracuse University*, 1998 WL 167296 (N.D.N.Y.1998); Brian L. Porto, *Completing the Revolution: Title IX as Catalyst for an Alternative Model of College Sports*, 8 Seton Hall J. Sport L. 351 (1998); John C. Weistart, *Setting a Course for College Athletics: Can Gender Equity Find a Place in Commercialized College Sports?*, 3 Duke J. Gender L. & Pol'y 191 (1996); Note, *Cheering on Women and Girls in*

Sports: Using Title IX to Fight Gender Role Oppression, 110 Harv. L. Rev. 1627 (1997). *See also National Collegiate Athletic Ass'n v. Smith*, 119 S.Ct. 924 (1999) (finding that the statute does not apply to the NCAA).

4. For athletes like Allan Grimson, immigration requirements are a continuing source of aggravation. In addition, many leagues (particularly in Europe) limit the number of foreign players a team may carry on its roster. For a further look at how restrictions on aliens affect sports, see, e.g., Martin J. Greenberg & James T. Gray, *Citizenship Based Quota Systems in Athletics*, 6 Marq. Sports L.J. 337 (1996), and Thomas R. Dominczyk, Comment, *The New Melting Pot: As American Attitudes Toward Foreigners Continue to Decline, Athletes are Welcomed with Open Arms*, 8 Seton Hall J. Sport L. 165 (1998).

5. Over the years, the NCAA has promulgated numerous regulations regarding eligibility. For the most part, these directives seek to ensure student athletes are academically qualified when they enter college, make sufficient progress in their studies, and graduate on time. In March 1999, however, a federal judge in Philadelphia struck down its requirement (known as Proposition 16) that entering freshmen score at least 820 on the SAT. *See Cureton v. National Collegiate Athletic Ass'n*, 1999 WL 118667 (E.D.Pa.1999). The NCAA immediately announced it would appeal the decision. *See further* David Barron, *NCAA Seeks Stay of Ruling on SAT*, Hous. Chron., Mar. 11, 1999, at 1 (Sports).

6. No sporting event has generated more eligibility disputes than the Olympics. In 1994, following a highly-publicized lawsuit involving the disqualification of runner Butch Reynolds, see *Reynolds v. International Amateur Athletic Fed'n*, 23 F.3d 1110 (6th Cir.), *cert. denied*, 513 U.S. 962 (1994), the International Olympic Committee established its own "sports court" to ensure future disputes would be handled in a uniform and orderly manner. Formally known as the International Court of Arbitration for Sport and headquartered in Lausanne, Switzerland, the tribunal currently is the exclusive dispute resolution mechanism for roughly half the world's sports federations. For a further discussion of the ICAS, see Nancy K. Raber, *Dispute Resolution in Olympic Sport: The Court of Arbitration for Sport*, 8 Seton Hall J. Sport L. 75 (1998), and Melissa R. Bitting, Comment, *Mandatory, Binding Arbitration for Olympic Athletes: Is the Process Better or Worse for "Job Security"?*, 25 Fla. St. U. L. Rev. 655 (1998). For a more general look at the legal issues surrounding the Olympics, see Sara Lee Keller–Smith & Sherri A. Affrunti, *Going for the Gold: The Representation of Olympic Athletes*, 3 Vill. Sports & Ent. L.J. 443 (1996), and Ronald T. Rowan, *Legal Issues and the Olympics*, 3 Vill. Sports & Ent. L.J. 395 (1996).

7. Despite the passage of nearly three decades, *Denver Rockets v. All–Pro Management, Inc.*, 325 F.Supp. 1049 (C.D.Cal.), *stayed*, 1971 WL 3015 (9th Cir.), *reinstated*, 401 U.S. 1204 (1971), remains one of the more notable cases on the subject of eligibility. Spencer Haywood was a talented basketball player who, shortly after entering college, left to join the ABA's Denver Nuggets. Following a contract dispute, Haywood jumped to the NBA's Seattle SuperSonics. Haywood's new contract was voided, however, because of an NBA rule prohibiting teams from employing anyone whose college class had not yet graduated (the ABA had no such ban). Haywood sued, claiming

the policy violated federal antitrust laws. Although recognizing the league was motivated by good intentions, the courts sided with Haywood. As a result, the number of underclassmen and high school students turning pro increases with each passing year. *See further* Scott R. Rosner, *Must Kobe Come Out and Play? An Analysis of the Legality of Preventing High School Athletes and College Underclassmen From Entering Professional Sports Drafts*, 8 Seton Hall J. Sport L. 539 (1998).

Problem 23

Following male-to-female sex reassignment surgery, a player sought to enter a women's tennis tournament. Her application was denied, however, when the organizers learned of the operation. If she sues, how should the court rule? *See Richards v. United States Tennis Ass'n*, 400 N.Y.S.2d 267 (Sup.Ct.1977).

C. COMPENSATION

Most of us participate in sports for fun and exercise. Highly-talented athletes, however, expect to be remunerated for their efforts.

1. INDIVIDUAL BARGAINING

Most players do not belong to unions. Instead, they negotiate directly with management regarding the terms of their contracts.

GONZALEZ v. DON KING PRODUCTIONS, INC.

17 F.Supp.2d 313 (S.D.N.Y.1998).

POLLACK, Senior District Judge.

Plaintiff Miguel Angel Gonzalez ("Gonzalez") brought claims for fraud, tortious interference with contract, and a declaratory judgment against defendants Don King Productions, Inc. ("DKP"), Don King, Dana Jamison and Hector Elizalde. DKP counterclaimed for breach of contract and injunctive relief. These claims are not before the court today and are preserved for future adjudication.

Gonzalez moves pursuant to FRCP Rule 56 for an order voiding the contract between himself and promoter Don King. For the purposes of this motion, Gonzalez's sole contention is that the contract lacks an essential term regarding compensation and represents an unenforceable agreement to agree. For the reasons below, Gonzalez's motion for summary judgment is denied.

Omission of Essential Terms

When parties fail to state an essential term clearly or omit such a term, courts attempt to ascertain the intent of the parties and enforce the contract. Striking down a contract as "indefinite and in essence meaningless 'is at best a last resort.' " 166 Mamaroneck Avenue Corp. v. 151 East Post Road Corp., 78 N.Y.2d 88, 91, 575 N.E.2d 104, 106, 571 N.Y.S.2d 686, 688 (1991) (citing Heyman Cohen & Sons v. Lurie Woolen

Co., 232 N.Y. 112, 114, 133 N.E. 370 (1921)). The court must find that the contract is so indefinite that it "[reaches] the point where construction becomes futile." Don King Productions v. Douglas, 742 F.Supp. 741, 762 (S.D.N.Y.1990) (citing Cohen & Sons, 232 N.Y. at 114, 133 N.E. 370, and other New York cases).

BACKGROUND

Plaintiff Gonzalez, a citizen of Mexico, is a highly ranked professional boxer. Defendant Don King is the chief executive officer and sole owner of DKP. Defendants Jamison and Elizalde are employees of DKP.

This action involves two contracts. The first contract, dated February 15, 1996, is an exclusive Promotional Agreement ("Promotional Agreement") between Gonzalez and DKP. The second contract, dated January 15, 1998, is an agreement ("Bout Agreement") for a boxing match with Julio Cesar Chavez held on March 7, 1998 ("Chavez Match"). The Bout Agreement incorporates some of the terms of the Promotional Agreement.

The Bout Agreement provides for a purse of $750,000 for the Chavez Match. DKP paid this purse, and it is not disputed in this motion.

Paragraph 11 of the Bout Agreement is the focus of the dispute here. It gives DKP the option to promote four of Gonzalez's matches following the Chavez Match. The relevant portions of Paragraph 11 provide as follows:

> FIGHTER hereby grants PROMOTER FOUR (4) separate and distinct options to promote FIGHTER in his next FOUR (4) fights following the BOUT hereunder [the Chavez Match] without any intervening bouts....
>
> In the event FIGHTER loses or draws the BOUT, or any option Bout, FIGHTER'S purse for each bout subsequent to such loss or draw shall be negotiated between PROMOTER and FIGHTER but shall not be less than AS PER PROMOTIONAL AGREEMENT unless a different sum is mutually agreed upon. The foregoing options as well as all other terms set forth in this Agreement are valid and enforceable regardless of the outcome of any bout provided for hereunder, i.e., win, lose or draw.

The language, "AS PER PROMOTIONAL AGREEMENT," is manually typed into a blank space on the agreement.

The Promotional Agreement states the following:

> 4(b) Subsequently, when and if you have won your first fight and all of the subsequent fights protected by this Contract, your prize money for each fight shall be negotiated and agreed upon by the parties of this Contract, but shall not be less than ($75,000.00) unless the parties of this Contract agree otherwise....
>
> 4(d) In the event that you loose [sic] your first fight ... your prize money for each subsequent fight in which you are

> defeated, shall be negotiated and agreed upon between the parties of this contract, but shall be no less than ($25,000.00) unless the parties of this Contract agree otherwise.

Thus, Gonzalez and DKP apparently agreed that if Gonzalez won the Chavez Match, he would receive at least $75,000 for the next fight, unless the parties agreed otherwise. If Gonzalez lost the Chavez Match, he would receive at least $25,000 in subsequent matches, unless the parties agreed otherwise. However, neither the Promotional Agreement nor the Bout Agreement explicitly states the purse for subsequent matches in the event of a draw in the Chavez Match.

The Chavez Match ended in a draw. The parties now dispute whether the purse for subsequent matches can be determined with sufficient certainty to enforce the contract.

DISCUSSION

Gonzalez contends that the omission of a purse for fights following a draw renders the contract so indefinite that it constitutes an unenforceable agreement to agree. Cobble Hill Nursing Home, Inc. v. Henry & Warren Corp., 74 N.Y.2d 475, 548 N.Y.S.2d 920, 548 N.E.2d 203 (1989) sets forth New York law on indefinite price terms. In Cobble Hill, the New York Court of Appeals stated that an agreement must be "reasonably certain in its material terms" in order to be enforced. Id. at 482, 548 N.Y.S.2d 920, 548 N.E.2d 203. However, " ... a price term may be sufficiently definite if the amount can be determined objectively without the need for new expressions by the parties; a method for reducing uncertainty to certainty might, for example, be found within the agreement or ascertained by reference to an extrinsic event, commercial practice or trade usage." Id. at 483, 548 N.Y.S.2d 920, 548 N.E.2d 203.

Here, the Bout Agreement states that purses for fights following a loss or a draw are to be determined from the Promotional Agreement. Notably, the Bout Agreement groups losses and draws together, stating that the purse for fights following either "a loss or a draw" shall not be less than as provided for in the Promotional Agreement. It also states that the agreement is enforceable regardless of whether the fight ends in a win, loss or draw. The Promotional Agreement does not explicitly provide a price term for fights following a draw. However, it states that purses for fights following a loss "shall be negotiated and agreed upon ..., but shall be no less than ($25,000) unless the parties to this contract agree otherwise." The provision for fights following a win is similar, but provides for a minimum purse of $75,000.

Although the contract is poorly drafted, it is sufficiently definite to survive a motion for summary judgment. The Promotional Agreement contains explicit price terms from which the minimum purse for fights following a draw might be inferred, so the "shall be negotiated" language is not fatal to the contract. Similarly, the Bout Agreement's statement that the purse shall be as per the Promotional Agreement "unless a different sum is mutually agreed upon" does not destroy the contract. When read in context, this provision could be interpreted as setting a default purse of $25,000 if the parties cannot agree. See Don King Productions v. Douglas, 742 F.Supp. 741, 763, n. 21 (S.D.N.Y.1990) (stating that similar contract provisions could be construed as setting a default price).

Objective evidence presented at trial may shed light on the intended meaning of the disputed provisions. See Heyman v. Commerce and Industry Insurance Co., 524 F.2d 1317, 1320 (2d Cir.1975) (holding that "[t]he parties have a right to present oral testimony or other extrinsic evidence at trial to aid in interpreting a contract whose provisions are not wholly unambiguous"); Davis v. Chevy Chase Financial Limited, 667 F.2d 160, 170 (D.C.Cir.1981) ("We cannot agree that the opaque language of [the contested provision] is so clear that the introduction of relevant parol and other evidence would not aid in the process of construction. At base, the question is one of the intent of the parties; where that intent is unclear, as here, summary judgment is an inappropriate tool for dispute resolution."). Extrinsic evidence of a contract's meaning is admissible if it "does not vary or contradict the written terms of the contract, but merely aids in their interpretation." Heyman, 524 F.2d at 1320, n. 2. For example, DKP could show at trial that the parties had treated losses and draws the same in the past, or that the typical industry practice is to provide the same purse for losses and draws. See Lowell v. Twin Disc, Inc., 527 F.2d 767, 770 (2d Cir.1975) (stating that "the court may and should look to the prior negotiations to determine what was intended"); Eskimo Pie Corp. v. Whitelawn Dairies, Inc., 284 F.Supp. 987 (S.D.N.Y.1968) (allowing extrinsic evidence on the meaning of the word "non-exclusive"). Once a factfinder has heard all the evidence, it may be able to ascertain the parties' intent regarding the missing term.

Resolving all ambiguities and inferences against Gonzalez, the Court cannot conclude that the contract is nothing more than an agreement to agree. Such an interpretation would tend to render the contract's express price terms meaningless and therefore should be avoided if possible. See Galli v. Metz, 973 F.2d 145, 149 (2d Cir.1992) ("Under New York law an interpretation of a contract that has 'the effect of rendering at least one clause superfluous or meaningless ... will be avoided if possible.' ") (internal citation omitted). See generally RESTATEMENT (SECOND) CONTRACTS § 203 (1979) (stating that "an interpretation which gives a reasonable, lawful, and effective meaning to all the terms is preferred to an interpretation which leaves a part unreasonable ... or of no effect" and noting that "specific terms and exact terms are given greater weight than general language").

The proper interpretation of the contract presents material factual issues that cannot be resolved as a matter of law. Accordingly, Gonzalez's motion for summary judgment is denied.

CONARD v. UNIVERSITY OF WASHINGTON

834 P.2d 17 (Wash.1992),
cert. denied, 510 U.S. 827 (1993).

DOLLIVER, Justice.

In February 1983, petitioners Kevin Conard and Vincent Fudzie (plaintiffs) were recruited by the University of Washington (UW) to play football. Both plaintiffs signed national letters of intent and received offers of athletic financial assistance for three consecutive quarters commencing the first day of class of the fall quarter of the 1983 academic year. After signing letters of intent, student athletes who transfer to another university lose 2 years of athletic eligibility.

Each offer of financial assistance covered tuition, compulsory fees, room and board, and course-related books, and each had the following provision regarding renewal:

> This assistance will be considered for renewal during subsequent periods of attendance as long as you are a student in good standing, maintain normal progress toward graduation and are in compliance with all eligibility requirements of this institution, the Pacific–10, and the NCAA [National Collegiate Athletic Association].

The offers also stated the assistance "may be gradated or terminated only in accordance with the legislation of the NCAA, principal details of which appear on the attached sheet." The following NCAA rules were attached and signed by Conard, Fudzie, and their guardians:

> 2. Financial aid shall not be revoked or altered during any period for which it has been granted except that the University may revoke aid in whole or in part if the student:
>
> a. is rendered ineligible for intercollegiate competition; or
>
> b. fraudulently misrepresents any information on the application for admission, letter-of-intent or tender; or
>
> c. engages in serious misconduct warranting substantial disciplinary penalty; or
>
> d. voluntarily withdraws from a sport for personal reasons.
>
> Any such gradation or cancellation of aid is permissible only if such action is taken for proper cause by the regular disciplinary or scholarship awards authorities of the institution and the student-athlete has had an opportunity for a hearing. Under (d) above, such gradation or cancellation of aid may not occur prior to the conclusion of the academic term....
>
> 4. After completion of the above stated period of this award, upon the recommendation of the Head Coach, the Director of Athletics, and the Faculty Representative, the Committee on Financial Aid will consider granting renewal of the

> assistance, providing you (1) meet the academic requirements of the National Collegiate Athletic Association, the Pacific–10/Nor Pac Conference and the University, and (2) are a student in good standing in every respect as determined by the rules, regulations and administrative decisions of the University, the Pacific–10/Nor Pac Conference and the National Collegiate Athletic Association.

The Department of Intercollegiate Athletics (DIA) makes recommendations regarding the renewal and nonrenewal of athletic scholarships. The DIA policies and procedure manual provides:

> If a coach wishes to withdraw a recommendation for financial aid at anytime, justification within the rules of the Conference and the Associations (AIAW/NCAA) must be fully established. Each student-athlete is entitled to due process and if the student-athlete requests an appeal as well as a hearing, one will be provided.

The opportunity for a hearing is also set forth in section 3–4–(g) of the NCAA constitution.

> In the latter event [a decision of nonrenewal], the institution also shall inform the student-athlete that if he or she believes the grant has not been renewed for questionable reasons, the student-athlete may request, and shall have the opportunity for, a hearing before the institutional agency making the financial award. The institution shall have established reasonable procedures for the prompt hearing of such a request.

Both plaintiffs allege they understood their scholarships were for 4 or 5 years depending on whether they were asked not to play or "redshirt" their freshman years. Both stated it is "commonly understood" that such scholarships are to last at least 4 years and neither had heard of an athlete whose scholarship had been "revoked".

Eric S. Godfrey is the Assistant Vice President for Student Affairs, the Director of Financial Aid, and the Chairman of UW's Athletic Financial Aid Committee which hears appeals from athletes whose awards are not renewed. Godfrey stated that "the commitment on the part of the University, in compliance with the NCAA regulations, is if the student meets these conditions, the aid will be renewed for the next academic period." Both Godfrey and Don James, the head coach of the UW football team, stated that in order for the committee not to renew a student's athletic financial aid there needed to be a finding of serious misconduct.

However, serious misconduct is not defined by any UW, NCAA, or Pac–10 rule or regulation contained in the record. James testified there are no written guidelines as to what constitutes serious misconduct, and it is up to the discretion of the coach and the "financial aid people" on a case-by-case basis to determine whether certain acts constituted serious misconduct. Godfrey stated whether conduct constituted serious misconduct is evaluated generally in light of UW's student conduct code and specifically by the team rules promulgated by James.

The team rules are outlined by James for the players at the beginning of every season and represent broad guidelines governing general conduct, conduct in the dressing room, conduct at practice, and conduct dealing with the press, procedures regarding injuries, and a prohibition on gambling. The rules begin with the following statement:

> The following general rules are for your benefit. Since it is impossible to cover every point or eventuality in a statement of team policy such as this, you are expected to conduct yourself at all times in a manner that will reflect credit upon you, your teammates, the football program, and the University of Washington.

In the fall 1983, plaintiffs matriculated at UW and joined the football team playing on the fifth string. There were a series of incidents involving the plaintiffs, individually and together, between that time and December 1985 when James removed them from the team and told them he would not recommend the renewal of their scholarships. The fact that the incidents, themselves, took place is not disputed, although particular aspects of the events are in dispute.

First, in November 1983, UW police notified James that Conard had been arrested for using a stolen student food credit card. James alleges that neither player denied using the card, and Fudzie states that he knew about it. James alleges he warned both players that "subsequent actions by them might result in . . . a loss of their athletic scholarships." No formal disciplinary proceedings were brought by UW.

Next, in 1984 there were several incidents involving plaintiffs. In one incident UW police informed James that Fudzie had punched out some windows in a residence hall. Fudzie admitted the damage and paid restitution. On a separate occasion, it was reported that Fudzie entered a student's room and assaulted a student. In another incident, Fudzie and Conard were reported to have entered a student's room and threatened the student with bodily harm. James alleges he counseled both players as to these incidents and again warned them that if such behavior continued, they could lose their scholarships.

Also in 1984, plaintiffs attempted to extort money from a female student by blackmailing her with photographs taken while she was engaged in sexual acts with another student. As a result of the incident, plaintiffs spent a weekend in jail on charges of extortion, but no further action was taken. James again counseled the players and warned them that unless they stayed out of trouble he would not recommend the renewal of their scholarships.

In 1985, James counseled Conard for his lack of respect for and unacceptable behavior towards service and equipment personnel. Conard was also counseled for his failure to report an injury to the trainers pursuant to the team rules. Both conversations resulted in a further warning to Conard as to the probability of the nonrenewal of his scholarship.

Finally, in December 1985, the UW football team traveled to Anaheim, California to participate in the Freedom Bowl. On the morning of December 22, plaintiffs did not report for practice with the rest of the team. Plaintiffs were later found to have spent the night in jail at the Santa Ana Police Department as the result of an altercation at a restaurant the previous evening. The police report conflicts with the account of the events given by plaintiffs. The police report states that plaintiffs were asked to leave and then escorted out of the restaurant by police for violating the establishment's dress code; while leaving, they challenged the police officers to a fight; and when the police attempted to arrest plaintiffs after they left the restaurant and were driving away, they resisted arrest. Fudzie stated that the restaurant had a policy of racial exclusion, that the officers assaulted Fudzie and Conard, who are African–Americans, and that two of the officers involved in the incident have resigned from the police force due to the incident. James states that as far as he was concerned, given the previous warnings to the plaintiffs, they should have just walked away from the incident; it was irrelevant why they were asked to leave. After the incident, James informed plaintiffs they would not play in the Freedom Bowl, they were off the team, and he would not recommend their scholarships be renewed for the next year.

On June 24, 1986, the Athletic Financial Aid Committee convened to review recommendations for renewal and nonrenewal forwarded to them by the DIA. On July 1, 1986, in accordance with the NCAA constitution, Godfrey informed each plaintiff by letter that his athletic financial aid was not being renewed for the 1986–87 academic year. Also in accordance with the NCAA constitution, the letters informed them they could request a hearing before the Athletic Financial Aid Committee to appeal the decision of nonrenewal.

Conard did not request a hearing. As a result of low scholarship, he was dropped from UW and was scholastically ineligible to return to UW after spring quarter 1986. Conard did not petition for reinstatement and transferred to San Diego State University.

By letter dated September 3, 1986, Fudzie requested a hearing which was held on September 22, 1986. The record contains a transcript of the informal hearing. Godfrey presided over the hearing in which Fudzie gave his version of the events and challenged the information the DIA had received verbally from James. The committee members were allowed to question Fudzie, who was not represented by counsel. Fudzie was then excused. After deliberation, the committee recommended Godfrey request James provide a written statement regarding his recommendation of nonrenewal. James submitted a written statement and documents evidencing the team rules and Fudzie's past misconduct. These documents were provided to the committee members, and based upon all the evidence, they determined unanimously that the decision of nonrenewal was reasonable and appropriate. Fudzie was notified of the decision and given a copy of the materials submitted by James.

Although Fudzie lost his athletic scholarship, he received financial aid in the amount of $10,118 for the 1986–87 academic year. While Fudzie was not awarded any aid for the following year because his aid application was not received until after the deadline, he remained at UW and received a Bachelor of Arts degree in accounting on June 11, 1988.

In December 1988, plaintiffs brought suit against UW for breach of contract and against James, his wife, and UW for interference with contractual relations. The trial court granted summary judgment in favor of UW and dismissed the suit in its entirety; the plaintiffs appealed. The Court of Appeals affirmed on the breach of contract and interference of contractual relations claims, but held, sua sponte, that plaintiffs had a constitutionally protected claim of entitlement to the renewal of their scholarships. See Conard v. University of Wash., 62 Wash.App. 664, 671, 814 P.2d 1242 (1991). The Court of Appeals affirmed the dismissal of Conard's complaint because he had not requested a hearing and because he was scholastically ineligible to return for the 1986–87 academic year. Conard, 62 Wash.App. at 669, 814 P.2d 1242. The Court of Appeals reversed the dismissal of Fudzie's complaint against UW and remanded the case for an adversarial hearing because it held the informal hearing afforded Fudzie was constitutionally inadequate. Conard, 62 Wash.App. at 674, 814 P.2d 1242.

Plaintiffs petitioned for review of the dismissal of their breach of contract claim against UW for not renewing their football scholarships, for finding no violation of Conard's due process rights, and for not providing monetary damages for the violation of Fudzie's due process rights. UW seeks review of the Court of Appeals' decision finding a violation of Fudzie's due process rights and remanding for a new hearing. This court granted review "solely to determine if the University's termination of petitioners' athletic scholarships violated their due process rights and, if so, what remedy is appropriate."

Initially, we note the Court of Appeals raised the due process issue sua sponte. We presume the Court of Appeals in its discretion found the issue "should be considered to properly decide [the] case", pursuant to RAP 12.1(b), even though it was not raised in the complaint or the briefs on review. RAP 12.1(b) provides that an appellate court "may notify the parties and give them an opportunity to present written argument on the issue raised by the court." While not mandated, this procedure usually proves to be helpful in the decisionmaking and review process at both appellate levels.

Our grant of review is limited in this case to whether UW's nonrenewal of the plaintiffs' athletic scholarships violated due process under the federal constitution. Plaintiffs assert violations of due process under the federal and state constitutions in their petition for review. We will not consider the state claim, however, because the Court of Appeals' holding was limited to a federal due process violation, and the plaintiffs do not set forth the requisite analysis under State v. Gunwall, 106 Wash.2d 54, 720 P.2d 808 (1986) properly to raise an independent state constitutional challenge. See Petition for Review, at 10. See, e.g., Rozner v. Bellevue, 116 Wash.2d 342, 351–52, 804 P.2d 24 (1991). Our review also does not include the contract portion of this case which was determined on summary judgment in favor of UW.

The scope of the Fourteenth Amendment's procedural protection of property interests is not coextensive with contract rights. See Perry v. Sindermann, 408 U.S. 593, 599–601, 92 S.Ct. 2694, 2698–2699, 33 L.Ed.2d 570 (1972); Board of Regents v. Roth, 408 U.S. 564, 576–78, 92 S.Ct. 2701, 2708–09, 33 L.Ed.2d 548 (1972). The terms of a contract may be the source of a property interest, see Roth, 408 U.S. at 566 n. 1, 92 S.Ct. at 2703 n. 1, but protected property interests include all benefits to which there is a "legitimate claim of entitlement". Roth, 408 U.S. at 577, 92 S.Ct. at 2709. Such a claim is "more than an abstract need or desire for" and "more than a unilateral expectation of" the benefit. Roth, 408 U.S. at 577, 92 S.Ct. at 2709. Property interests are created by "state law—rules or understandings that secure certain benefits and that support claims of entitlement to those benefits." Roth, 408 U.S. at 577, 92 S.Ct. at 2709.

A person's interest in a benefit is a "property" interest for due process purposes if there are such rules or mutually explicit understandings that support his claim of entitlement to the benefit and that he may invoke at a hearing. Perry, 408 U.S. at 601, 92 S.Ct. at 2699.

Protected interests also may be created if there are statutes or other rules which contain " 'substantive predicates' " or " 'particularized standards or criteria ...' " to guide the discretion of decision makers and which contain " 'explicitly mandatory language,' i.e., specific directives to the decisionmaker that if the regulations' substantive predicates are present, a particular outcome must follow ..." (Citations omitted.) Kentucky Dep't of Corrections v. Thompson, 490 U.S. 454, 462–63, 109 S.Ct. 1904, 1910, 104 L.Ed.2d 506 (1989). Although Thompson involved a liberty interest, the above test has been applied in various contexts to determine if protected property interests have been created. See Specter v. Garrett, 971 F.2d 936, 955 (3d Cir.1992); Abdullah v. Gunter, 949 F.2d 1032 (8th Cir.1991); Wallace v. Robinson, 940 F.2d 243 (7th Cir.1991); Jacobs, Visconsi & Jacobs Co. v. Lawrence, Kan., 927 F.2d 1111 (10th Cir.1991); Tarpeh–Doe v. United States, 904 F.2d 719 (D.C.Cir.1990); see also Allen v. Beverly Hills, 911 F.2d 367, 370 (9th Cir.1990); Loehr v. Ventura Cy. Comm'ty College Dist., 743 F.2d 1310, 1315 (9th Cir.1984); Goodisman v. Lytle, 724 F.2d 818, 820–21 (9th Cir.1984); Parks v. Watson, 716 F.2d 646, 657 (9th Cir.1983); Jacobson v. Hannifin, 627 F.2d 177, 180 (9th Cir.1980).

Unless a legitimate claim of entitlement to the renewal of plaintiffs' scholarships was created by the terms of the contract, by a mutually explicit understanding, or by substantive procedural restrictions on the part of the decision maker, plaintiffs have no constitutional due process protections.

(1) CONTRACT

The offers of athletic financial aid to plaintiffs were clear and unambiguous in offering aid for "three consecutive quarters". "If you enroll, you will receive this assistance for three consecutive quarters ..." Both the trial court and Court of Appeals held there was no genuine issue of material fact that the duration of the athletic financial aid contracts between plaintiffs and UW was for only three consecutive quarters. See Conard, 62 Wash.App. at 670, 814 P.2d 1242.

While review of the due process issue raises the question whether the terms of the contract created a protected property interest, the terms of the contract, as found by the Court of Appeals, control this case. Consequently, the duration of the financial aid awards of 1 academic year precludes the contracts from creating a protected property interest for 4 years.

The contract terms also do not create a legitimate claim of entitlement to the renewal of the scholarships. The offers provided only that "[t]his assistance will be considered for renewal during subsequent periods ..." The NCAA rules, attached to the offers, similarly provided only for consideration of renewal.

> After completion of the above stated period of this award, upon the recommendation of the Head Coach, the Director of Athletics, and the Faculty Representative, the Committee on Financial Aid will consider granting renewal of the assistance ...

Thus, the duration of the contracts is for only 1 academic year, and terms are not sufficiently definite to establish a legitimate claim of entitlement to the renewal of plaintiffs' athletic scholarships.

(2) MUTUALLY EXPLICIT UNDERSTANDINGS

The plaintiffs allege they had a claim of entitlement to the renewal of their scholarships as long as they complied with the rules of the UW, the NCAA, and the Pac–10. See Petition for Review, at 14. Plaintiffs assert they relied upon the language of their contracts and the common understanding, based upon the surrounding circumstances and the conduct of the parties, that the aid would be renewed if certain conditions were met. The issue is whether this record supports a "mutually explicit understanding" creating a protected property interest in the renewal of the scholarships.

Plaintiffs assert there was a "common understanding" that scholarships were for a minimum of 4 years. Plaintiffs do not cite to any specific persons who made assurances to them regarding a right to renewal. Godfrey did state that "the commitment on the part of the University, in compliance with the NCAA regulations, is if the student meets these conditions, the aid will be renewed for the next academic period."

Significantly however, nothing in the record indicates Godfrey told this to the plaintiffs, and neither plaintiff asserts he relied upon this or similar statements when accepting the offers.

Both plaintiffs allege they did not know of any student whose aid was not renewed who was in compliance with those conditions. This assertion, however, is insufficient to create a common law of renewal. [P]laintiffs point to no written UW rule or policy which supports their entitlement. In fact, the language in the offers and the NCAA regulations do not accord with this statement. The offers state that if the student athlete meets certain conditions, "[t]his assistance will be considered for renewal during subsequent periods of attendance ..." The NCAA regulations provide an opportunity for a hearing if the student athlete feels the aid was not renewed "for questionable reasons".

[T]he language of the offers and the NCAA regulations are not sufficiently certain to support a mutually explicit understanding creating a protected property interest. [T]he fact that scholarships are, in fact, normally renewed does not create a "common law" of renewal, absent other consistent and supportive UW policies or rules. As argued by UW, the usual renewal of scholarships only reflects the rarity of this level of misconduct. While the statement by Godfrey, if specifically relied on by the plaintiffs, may have been sufficient to create an issue of material fact as to whether there was a mutually explicit understanding, neither plaintiff makes such an allegation.

Moreover, plaintiffs have not established they actually met the conditions of the offers. Plaintiffs assert that "a valid finding of misconduct was never made against either Conard or Fudzie." Petition for Review, at 13. This assertion is made because plaintiffs were apparently exonerated of any misconduct in the restaurant incident at the Freedom Bowl in 1985, and no formal disciplinary proceedings were brought against them as to the alleged prior misconduct. Petition for Review, at 5.

However, the language of the offers and the NCAA constitution do not require a finding of misconduct in order not to renew the scholarships. Such a finding is required only if the aid is altered or terminated during the period for which it was awarded. The language of the offers makes clear that serious misconduct is only required to be shown if UW seeks to gradate or terminate aid "during any period for which it has been granted ..." Here, UW did not alter or terminate plaintiffs' aid during the period for which it was granted, and no finding of serious misconduct need be made. The Court of Appeals agreed and held:

> Likewise, since there was no revocation of aid during the contract period, it is unnecessary to determine if Fudzie was guilty of serious misconduct supporting such a revocation.

Conard, 62 Wash.App. at 670–71, 814 P.2d 1242. Nonetheless, both Godfrey and James testified that in order for the committee not to renew a student's athletic financial aid there needed to be a finding of serious misconduct. Such a finding was made by James and the committee based on plaintiffs' cumulative pattern of misconduct. Even if such a finding were required in making the decision not to renew, however, the record does not establish a mutually explicit understanding that plaintiffs' cumulative pattern of misconduct would not constitute serious misconduct.

Serious misconduct is not defined in any UW or NCAA rule or policy. James testified the determination whether acts constitute serious misconduct is a discretionary decision made on a case-by-case basis. Godfrey stated that whether acts constitute serious misconduct is left to the discretion of the committee and evaluated in light of the broad guidelines found in UW's student conduct code and the team rules promulgated by James.

The broad guidelines set forth in the team rules are not sufficiently specific to create a mutually explicit understanding as to what acts would violate their terms, and plaintiffs have presented no language from the UW student conduct code which would create such an understanding. Therefore, even if there was a mutually explicit understanding that the plaintiffs' scholarships could not be renewed absent a finding of serious misconduct, these broad guidelines are not sufficiently definite to establish a mutually explicit understanding that plaintiffs' cumulative pattern of misconduct would not constitute such serious misconduct.

(3) Procedural Requirements

Lastly, procedural guaranties may create protected property interests when they contain " 'substantive predicates' " to guide the discretion of decision makers and "specific directives to the decisionmaker that if the regulations' substantive predicates are present, a particular outcome must follow ..." Kentucky Dep't of Corrections v. Thompson, 490 U.S. 454, 462–63, 109 S.Ct. 1904, 1910, 104 L.Ed.2d 506 (1989).

In this case, the NCAA constitution and the DIA policies and procedure manual provide for a hearing and due process respectively. However, there are no articulable standards nor explicitly mandatory language in the contracts, the NCAA constitution, or the DIA manual. The contracts provide that the aid will be considered for renewal if certain conditions are met. As in Thompson, the contracts do not state that aid must be renewed if the conditions are met or that aid must not be renewed if they are not met. The NCAA constitution states that there will be an opportunity for a hearing if the student athlete believes the aid was not renewed for "questionable reasons". This language does not provide an articulable standard and does not mandate a particular outcome. Lastly, the DIA manual states:

> If a coach wishes to withdraw a recommendation for financial aid at anytime, justification within the rules of the Conference and the Associations (AIAW/NCAA) must be fully established.

The record does not indicate and plaintiffs do not point to any other applicable NCAA or AIAW rules other than those already addressed. The discretion of the decision makers in this case is not sufficiently limited to create a protected property interest. Therefore, even though the DIA manual speaks to due process, such a procedural guaranty cannot create a protected property interest in a vacuum. There must be some substantive standard and explicitly mandatory language to give the hearing substance.

We hold, on the record in this case, that plaintiffs do not have a protected property interest in the renewal of their athletic scholarships. We decline to address whether plaintiffs have a protected liberty interest because plaintiffs failed to assign error to and adequately brief this issue. See John Doe v. Puget Sound Blood Ctr., 117 Wash.2d 772, 785, 819 P.2d 370 (1991). Because plaintiffs do not have a protected interest in the renewal of their scholarships, we need not address whether the hearing provided by UW was constitutionally adequate, or what the appropriate remedy would be if a violation had occurred.

The Court of Appeals' decision holding plaintiffs had a protected property interest in the renewal of their scholarships and remanding Fudzie's case for a rehearing is reversed. The Court of Appeals' decision is affirmed in all other respects.

Notes

1. As *Gonzalez* makes clear, athletes are subject to the same contract principles that govern other workers. *See further Boston Celtics Limited Partnership v. Shaw*, 908 F.2d 1041 (1st Cir.1990) (anticipatory repudiation); *Hennigan v. Chargers Football Co.*, 431 F.2d 308 (5th Cir.1970) (renewal option); *Childs v. Meadowlands Basketball Associates*, 954 F.Supp. 994 (D.N.J.1997) (misrepresentation); *Central Sports Army Club v. Arena Associates, Inc.*, 952 F.Supp. 181 (S.D.N.Y.1997) (tortious interference); *Professional Hockey Club Central Sports Club of the Army v. Detroit Red Wings, Inc.*, 787 F.Supp. 706 (E.D.Mich.1992) (duress); *Rivers v. New York Jets*, 460 F.Supp. 1233 (E.D.Mo.1978) (restraint of trade); *Sample v. Gotham Football Club, Inc.*, 59 F.R.D. 160 (S.D.N.Y.1973) (unequal bargaining power); *Minnesota Muskies, Inc. v. Hudson*, 294 F.Supp. 979 (M.D.N.C.1969) (unclean hands); *National Football League Management Council v. Superior Court of Alameda County*, 188 Cal.Rptr. 337 (Ct.App.1983) (interpretation); *Kirst v. Silna*, 163 Cal.Rptr. 230 (Ct.App.1980) (third-party beneficiary); *McGrew v. Kraft Patriots, Inc.*, 1995 WL 810346 (Mass.Super.Ct.1995) (reformation); *Morris v. New York Football Giants, Inc.*, 575 N.Y.S.2d 1013 (Sup.Ct.1991) (arbitration clause).

2. Student athletes like those in *Conard* receive no compensation for their efforts apart from their scholarships. They also are subject to strict limits on the amounts they can earn from outside jobs and are not eligible for workers' compensation if they are injured. As a result, many observers accuse both the NCAA and its member universities of systematically exploiting players, particularly in revenue-producing sports such as basketball and football. For a further discussion of this much-debated issue, see, e.g., Eric J. Sobocinski, *College Athletes: What is Fair Compensation?*, 7 Marq. Sports L.J. 257 (1996); Stephen L. Ukeiley, *No Salary, No Union, No Collective Bargaining: Scholarship Athletes Are an Employer's Dream Come True*, 6 Seton Hall J. Sport L. 167 (1996); Michael P. Acain, Comment, *Revenue*

Sharing: A Simple Cure for the Exploitation of College Athletes, 18 Loy. L.A. Ent. L.J. 307 (1998); Mark R. Whitmore, Note, *Denying Scholarship Athletes Worker's Compensation: Do Courts Punt Away a Statutory Right?*, 76 Iowa L. Rev. 763 (1991).

3. Many professional athletes supplement their incomes by endorsing products. In 1998, for example, Chicago Bulls superstar Michael Jordan earned a whopping $45 million from deals with companies such as Nike, Gatorade, Rayovac, Hanes, and WorldCom/MCI; golfer Tiger Woods took in $25 million (Nike, American Express, Titleist, Rolex, Wheaties); Detroit Pistons forward Grant Hill reaped $17 million (Fila, McDonald's, Sprite, Kellogg's, GMC); Los Angeles Lakers center Shaquille O'Neal collected $10 million (Reebok, Pepsi, Taco Bell, WB Sport); and NASCAR driver Jeff Gordon received $8.3 million (Pepsi, Ray–Ban, Unilever). *See further* Peter Spiegel, *Heir Gordon*, Forbes, Dec. 14, 1998, at 189.

4. Because of the public's unflagging interest in athletes, numerous goods are sold bearing their names and likenesses. Not surprisingly, this has led to frequent litigation over the extent to which players can control the use of their identities. *See, e.g., Allison v. Vintage Sports Plaques*, 136 F.3d 1443 (11th Cir.1998) (Clifford Allison); *Cardtoons, L.C. v. Major League Baseball Players Ass'n*, 95 F.3d 959 (10th Cir.1996) (current and retired MLB players); *Abdul-Jabbar v. General Motors Corp.*, 85 F.3d 407 (9th Cir.1996) (Kareem Abdul–Jabbar); *In re Major League Baseball Players Alumni Ass'n*, 996 F.2d 1236 (Fed.Cir.1993) (retired MLB players); *Pirone v. MacMillan, Inc.*, 894 F.2d 579 (2d Cir.1990) (Babe Ruth); *Baltimore Orioles, Inc. v. Major League Baseball Players Ass'n*, 805 F.2d 663 (7th Cir.1986), *cert. denied*, 480 U.S. 941 (1987) (MLB players); *Cepeda v. Swift & Co.*, 415 F.2d 1205 (8th Cir.1969) (Orlando Cepeda); *MJ & Partners Restaurant Limited Partnership v. Zadikoff*, 10 F.Supp.2d 922 (N.D.Ill.1998) (Michael Jordan); *Score Board, Inc. v. Upper Deck Co.*, 959 F.Supp. 234 (D.N.J.1997) (Ken Griffey, Jr.); *Hillerich & Bradsby Co. v. Christian Brothers, Inc.*, 943 F.Supp. 1136 (D.Minn.1996) (Mark Messier); *Coscarart v. Major League Baseball*, 1996 WL 400988 (N.D.Cal.1996) (retired MLB players); *Aikman v. AAA Sports Inc.*, 1992 WL 204397 (S.D.N.Y.1992) (NFL quarterbacks); *Ali v. Playgirl, Inc.*, 447 F.Supp. 723 (S.D.N.Y.1978) (Muhammad Ali); *Spahn v. Julian Messner, Inc.*, 233 N.E.2d 840 (N.Y.1967), *appeal dismissed*, 393 U.S. 1046 (1969) (Warren Spahn); *Montana v. San Jose Mercury News, Inc.*, 40 Cal.Rptr.2d 639 (Ct.App.1995) (Joe Montana); *Namath v. Sports Illustrated*, 371 N.Y.S.2d 10 (App.Div.1975), *aff'd*, 352 N.E.2d 584 (N.Y.1976) (Joe Namath); *Shamsky v. Garan, Inc.*, 632 N.Y.S.2d 930 (Sup.Ct.1995) (1969 New York Mets). *See also* Scott Newman, *Players Want Real Cash from Fantasy Leagues*, Fort Worth Star–Telegram, Aug. 25, 1998, at 2 (Sports) (reporting NFL players want to charge rotisserie league operators up to $1 million for using their names).

5. A number of athletes have ended their careers broke (or nearly so) because of unsound investments, inadequate insurance, greedy relatives, extravagant spending, substance abuse, bad tax planning, marital difficulties, or legal problems. In 1998, for example, Olympic gymnast Dominique Moceanu sued her parents after discovering they had spent all her money; former New York Giants linebacker Lawrence Taylor filed for bankruptcy due to an expensive drug habit; and banned boxer Mike Tyson, hounded by

tax problems and unable to make a living outside the ring, begged authorities to give him back his license. *See further* Glenn Dickey, *Athletes Are Thrown for a Loss*, S.F. Chron., Feb. 12, 1998, at D2 (reporting on the money woes of Kareem Abdul–Jabbar, Bjorn Borg, and Jack Clark); Sean Horgan, *Fame Offers No Protection Against Financial Missteps*, Indianapolis Star, Jan. 18, 1998, at E1 (recounting the problems of Tony Gwynn, Harmon Killebrew, Willie Mays, Brooks Robinson, Bryan Trottier, Johnny Unitas, and Danny White); Bob Glauber, *Life After Football*, Newsday, Jan. 12, 1997, at B6 (discussing the difficulties faced in retirement by Mark Duper, E.J. Junior, and Ickey Woods).

To protect themselves from such hardships, prudent athletes retain qualified experts. For a look at the different strategies that can be used to safeguard a player's wealth, see, e.g., John K. Harris, Jr., *Essentials of Estate Planning for the Professional Athlete*, 11 U. Miami Ent. & Sports L. Rev. 159 (1993); Bret M. Kanis, Comment, *The Utility of Personal Service Corporations for Athletes*, 22 Pepp. L. Rev. 629 (1995); Mark Calvey, *Sports Stars Need Help Playing the Numbers Game*, S.F. Bus. Times, Sept. 4, 1998, at 18; Mark L. Silow, *Intricacies of Tax Planning for Professional Athletes*, Legal Intelligencer, Feb. 24, 1998, at 7. *See also* Marc Yassinger, *An Updated Consideration of a Taxing Problem: The Harmonization of State and Local Tax Laws Affecting Nonresident Professional Athletes*, 19 Hastings Comm/Ent L.J. 751 (1997).

Problem 24

When its rival folded, a football league, concerned about the impact a sudden influx of new players might have on its competitive balance, froze all hiring for the remainder of the season. If one of the affected athletes sues, claiming the policy impermissibly interferes with his right to make a living, how should the court rule? *See Bowman v. National Football League*, 402 F.Supp. 754 (D.Minn.1975).

2. COLLECTIVE BARGAINING

Athletes in professional team sports have formed unions to represent their interests. As the following cases explain, such organizations operate within a complex framework adopted by Congress, administered by the National Labor Relations Board, and added to by the courts.

SILVERMAN v. MAJOR LEAGUE BASEBALL PLAYER RELATIONS COMMITTEE

67 F.3d 1054 (2d Cir.1995).

WINTER, Circuit Judge.

This is an appeal by the Major League Baseball Player Relations Committee, Inc. ("PRC") and the constituent member clubs of Major League Baseball ("Clubs") from a temporary injunction issued by Judge Sotomayor pursuant to section 10(j) of the National Labor Relations Act ("NLRA"), 29 U.S.C. § 160(j). The PRC is the collective bargaining representative for the twenty-eight Clubs. The Major League Baseball

Players Association is a union that is the exclusive bargaining representative for the forty-man rosters of each major league club. The injunction is based on the district court's conclusion that appellants violated NLRA §§ 8(a)(1) and (5), 29 U.S.C. §§ 158(a)(1) and (5), by unilaterally implementing terms and conditions of employment that differed from those in the last collective agreement. It orders the PRC and the Clubs to: (i) abide by the terms of an expired collective agreement, (ii) rescind any actions taken that are inconsistent with that agreement and (iii) bargain in good faith with the Players Association. See Silverman v. Major League Baseball Player Relations Comm., Inc., 880 F.Supp. 246, 261 (S.D.N.Y.1995). The injunction is to remain in effect until either (i) the expired agreement is replaced by a new collective bargaining agreement, (ii) the National Labor Relations Board ("NLRB") renders a final disposition of the matters pending before it in the related administrative case, or (iii) the district court finds, upon petition of either of the parties, that an impasse has occurred. See id. We affirm.

Background

On January 1, 1990, the most recent collective agreement ("Basic Agreement") between appellants and the Players Association became effective. It contained provisions implementing a combination of free agency and a reserve system—that is, a compromise between free competitive bidding for a player's services and an individual club's exclusive rights to those services.

Free agency, in its purest form, is a status in which the rights to a player's athletic services are not owned by a club and may be shopped around by the player in a quest for the most attractive bid. However, for more than a century, Major League Baseball has had a reserve system that to one degree or another affords individual clubs exclusive property rights to the athletic services of certain players. Before the players were organized and a collective bargaining relationship was established, the standard players contract with a club reserved to the club exclusive rights to a player's services and provided for an annual right of renewal of the contract by the club in question. The Clubs interpreted the contract as allowing the club in question to renew all of an individual player's contract, including the right of renewal provision. So interpreted, this provision—known generally as the "reserve clause"—bound a player to one club in perpetuity until traded or released. After the Clubs recognized the Players Association and entered into a collective agreement with it, an arbitrator held in a grievance proceeding that the reserve clause allowed a renewal for only one year rather than a succession of years. See National & American League Professional Baseball Clubs v. Major League Baseball Players Ass'n, 66 Lab.Arb. (BNA) 101 (1976) (Seitz, Arb.). Since then, appellants and the Players Association have struggled to accommodate their conflicting interests in the free agency and reserve issues, and a variety of compromises have from time to time been reached. However, relations have been acrimonious, and several strikes and lockouts have occurred. This appeal itself arises out of a strike that terminated the 1994 season before the playoffs and World Series.

Article XX of the Basic Agreement that became effective in 1990 contains a series of provisions that govern free agency and reserve rights. Players with six or more years of major league service are free agents and may seek competing bids in an effort to obtain the best contract, which may of course give exclusive rights to the club for a stipulated number of years. See Silverman, 880 F.Supp. at 250. Free agency is guaranteed by an anti-collusion provision, Article XX(F), which prohibits the Clubs from acting in concert with each other with respect to the exercise of rights under Article XX. See id. Article XX(F) thus prevents the Clubs from agreeing either to refuse to bid for the services of free agents or to offer only low bids to them. Article XX(F) also prohibits players from acting in concert with regard to Article XX rights. See id.

Players with less than six years of service remain under reserve to their individual clubs, although a club may reserve a player only once. Although a minimum annual salary is provided, players with less than three years of major league service must negotiate with their clubs to determine their salary for the coming season. Article XX allows certain reserved players—generally those with more than three but less than six years of service—to demand salary arbitration. See id. at 251. Salary arbitration is a mechanism for determining the individual salaries for that group of reserved players if they cannot arrive at an agreement with their clubs. The player and the club each present the arbitrator with a suggested salary figure for a new one-year contract. The arbitrator then inserts either the player's or the club's figure into a blank uniform contract that the parties have already signed. See id. Article VI(F)(12) provides the following with regard to the criteria to be used, and the evidence to be heard, by the arbitrator:

> (12) Criteria. (a) The Criteria will be the quality of the Player's contribution to his Club during the past season (including but not limited to his overall performance, special qualities of leadership and public appeal), the length and consistency of his career contribution, the record of the Player's past compensation, comparative baseball salaries . . ., the existence of any physical or mental defects on the part of the Player, and the recent performance record of the Club including but not limited to its League standing and attendance as an indication of public acceptance (subject to the exclusion stated in subparagraph (b)(i) below). Any evidence may be submitted which is relevant to the above criteria, and the arbitrator shall assign such weight to the evidence as shall to him appear appropriate under the circumstances. The arbitrator shall, except for a Player with five or more years of Major League service, give particular attention, for comparative salary purposes, to the contracts of Players with Major League service not exceeding one annual service group above the Player's annual service group. This

shall not limit the ability of a Player or his representative, because of special accomplishment, to argue the equal relevance of salaries of Players without regard to service, and the arbitrator shall give whatever weight to such argument as he deems appropriate.

(b) Evidence of the following shall not be admissible:

(i) The financial position of the Player and the Club;

(ii) Press comments, testimonials or similar material bearing on the performance of either the Player or the Club, except that recognized annual Player awards for playing excellence shall not be excluded;

(iii) Offers made by either Player or Club prior to arbitration;

(iv) The cost to the parties of their representatives, attorneys, etc.;

(v) Salaries in other sports or occupations.

The Basic Agreement expired on December 31, 1993, pursuant to the PRC's notice of termination. Although negotiations for a successor agreement did not get underway until March 1994, the PRC and the Players Association continued to observe the terms of the expired Basic Agreement. Prior to the commencement of negotiations, the Clubs and the Players Association had completed individual salary arbitration hearings and had entered into individual player contracts for the 1994 baseball season, which began in April 1994. See Silverman, 880 F.Supp. at 251.

Negotiations for a new collective bargaining agreement continued unsuccessfully. The PRC offered its first formal economic proposal to the Players Association at a meeting on June 14, 1994. It included a "salary cap," a mechanism that establishes a ceiling on the total player salaries paid by each club. The ceiling may allow some flexibility, depending on the details. Generally, the aggregate salaries of each team are determined by an agreed upon formula and must remain above a minimum percentage of industry revenues, also determined by an agreed upon formula, but below a maximum percentage of those revenues. See Wood v. National Basketball Ass'n, 809 F.2d 954, 957 (2d Cir.1987). The PRC proposal also eliminated the salary arbitration system and substituted restricted free agency rights for those reserved players previously eligible for salary arbitration. As an alternative to the PRC's proposed salary cap, the Players Association suggested a revenue sharing and luxury "tax" plan that would impose a tax on high-paying clubs. Subsequent proposals reflected disagreement over appropriate tax rates and payroll thresholds above which clubs would be subject to the tax. See Silverman, 880 F.2d at 251–52.

The players struck on August 12, and the 1994 baseball season never resumed. On December 22, 1994, the PRC declared an impasse in negotiations and stated that it intended unilaterally to impose a salary cap and to implement other changes in the terms and conditions of employment, including the elimination of salary arbitration. See Silverman, 880 F.2d at 252. The Players Association responded with a unilateral ban on players signing individual contracts with the Clubs.

Thereafter, cross-charges of unfair labor practices were filed with the National Labor Relations Board ("NLRB") by the Players Association and the Clubs. The Players Association alleged that the Clubs had engaged in unfair labor practices by unilaterally implementing the salary cap and other terms because the parties were not at an impasse.

On February 3, 1995, counsel for the PRC notified the NLRB General Counsel that the PRC would revoke the implementation of unilateral changes and restore the status quo ante. The General Counsel indicated that the Players Association charges would be dismissed as a result. Counsel for the PRC informed the General Counsel, however, that the PRC did not believe itself obligated to maintain provisions of the Basic Agreement that involved non-mandatory subjects of bargaining. He mentioned salary arbitration in that regard and also suggested that the Clubs might decide to bargain exclusively through the PRC. The NLRB General Counsel declined to offer an advisory opinion on these matters.

Three days later, by memorandum dated February 6, counsel for the PRC notified the Clubs that, until a new collective bargaining agreement was ratified or until further notice, individual clubs had no authority to negotiate contracts with individual players because the PRC was now the Clubs' exclusive bargaining representative. This amounted to an agreement among the Clubs not to hire free agents and thus was a departure from the anti-collusion provision, Article XX(F) of the Basic Agreement. It also amounted to an elimination of salary arbitration, because salary arbitration is a method of arriving at a wage for an individual player contract with a club.

The Players Association thereupon filed a new unfair labor practice charge, and the General Counsel issued a complaint alleging, inter alia, that the Clubs and the PRC had violated Sections 8(a)(1) and (5) of the NLRA by unilaterally eliminating, before an impasse had been reached, competitive bidding for the services of free agents, the anti-collusion provision, and salary arbitration for certain reserved players. The NLRB found that these matters were related to wages, hours, and other terms and conditions of employment and were therefore mandatory subjects for collective bargaining. It then authorized its General Counsel to seek an injunction under NLRA § 10(j). On March 27, the NLRB Regional Director filed a petition seeking a temporary injunction restraining the alleged unfair labor practices.

The district court agreed that the NLRB had reasonable cause to conclude that free agency and salary arbitration were mandatory subjects of bargaining and that the Clubs' unilateral actions constituted an unfair labor practice. The district court also concluded that injunctive relief was warranted. This appeal followed. We denied a stay on April 4.

DISCUSSION

The NLRB is authorized under Section 10(j) of the NLRA to petition for temporary injunctive relief from a district court to enjoin ongoing unfair labor practices. 29 U.S.C. § 160(j). If the court has reasonable cause to believe that an unfair labor practice has occurred and that injunctive relief would be just and proper, it should grant appropriate relief. Kaynard v. MMIC, Inc., 734 F.2d 950, 953 (2d Cir.1984). The court need not make a final determination that the conduct in question is an unfair labor practice. Kaynard v. Mego Corp., 633 F.2d 1026, 1033 (2d Cir.1980). It need find only reasonable cause to support such a conclusion. See id.; MMIC, 734 F.2d at 953. Appropriate deference must be shown to the judgment of the NLRB, and a district court should decline to grant relief only if convinced that the NLRB's legal or factual theories are fatally flawed. See Mego, 633 F.2d at 1031, 1033; Kaynard v. Palby Lingerie, Inc., 625 F.2d 1047, 1051 (2d Cir.1980). In reviewing a district court's grant of injunctive relief pursuant to Section 10(j), a court of appeals must also accord deference to the district court's decision, at least with regard to those aspects that are traditionally left to the district court's discretion. Mego, 633 F.2d at 1030.

We turn now to the merits of the regional director's petition. The petition invokes basic principles of labor law. Section 8(d) of the NLRA mandates that employers and unions bargain in good faith over "wages, hours, and other terms and conditions of employment." 29 U.S.C. § 158(d). These are so-called mandatory subjects of bargaining. Under caselaw, the parties may propose and bargain over, but may not insist upon, permissive subjects of bargaining. NLRB v. Wooster Div. of Borg-Warner Corp., 356 U.S. 342, 349, 78 S.Ct. 718, 723, 2 L.Ed.2d 823 (1958). When a collective agreement expires, an employer may not alter terms and conditions of employment involving mandatory subjects until it has bargained to an impasse over new terms. NLRB v. Katz, 369 U.S. 736, 741–43, 82 S.Ct. 1107, 1110–11, 8 L.Ed.2d 230 (1962). Thereafter, it may implement the new terms. Generally, when an agreement expires, an employer need not bargain to an impasse over terms and conditions involving permissive subjects but may alter them upon expiration. Allied Chem. & Alkali Workers v. Pittsburgh Plate Glass Co., 404 U.S. 157, 187–88, 92 S.Ct. 383, 402, 30 L.Ed.2d 341 (1971).

Many of the usual issues that arise in impasse cases are not disputed in the instant matter. The parties agree that the PRC, in directing the Clubs to decline to bargain individually with free agents, unilaterally departed from much of Article XX, which provides for a limited form of free agency and forbids collusive behavior by the Clubs in negotiating with free agents. It is also undisputed that the PRC unilaterally departed from the Basic Agreement's provisions with regard to salary arbitration. The PRC does not claim that it had bargained to an impasse over the free agency, the anti-collusion, or the salary arbitration provisions. Finally, it is also agreed that, if those provisions involved mandatory subjects of bargaining, their unilateral abrogation before impasse was a refusal to bargain in good faith.

The PRC and the Clubs argue that the anti-collusion and free agency provisions of the Basic Agreement do not involve mandatory subjects of bargaining and are therefore not subject to the Katz rule that unilateral implementation of new terms is an unfair labor practice unless the employer has bargained to an impasse over these new terms. See Silverman, 880 F.Supp. at 254. The PRC and the Clubs contend that an injunction compelling them to maintain the free agency and anti-collusion provisions undermines their right as a multi-employer group to bargain collectively through an exclusive representative. If so, they would be permissive subjects of bargaining. See Borg–Warner, 356 U.S. at 349, 78 S.Ct. at 722–23. With regard to salary arbitration, the PRC and the Clubs argue that it is the equivalent of interest arbitration—arbitration of the terms of a new collective agreement—and thus not a mandatory subject of bargaining. See International Bhd. of Elec. Workers (Collier Elec. Co.), 296 N.L.R.B. 1095, 1098, 1989 WL 224423 (1989).

We are unpersuaded that an injunction compelling the PRC and the Clubs to observe the anti-collusion and free agency provisions of the Basic Agreement infringes on their right as a multi-employer group to bargain through an exclusive representative.

Free agency and the ban on collusion are one part of a complex method—agreed upon in collective bargaining—by which each major league player's salary is determined under the Basic Agreement. They are analogous to the use of seniority, hours of work, merit increases, or piece work to determine salaries in an industrial context. The PRC and the Clubs describe free agency and the ban on collusion as provisions undermining their right to select a joint bargaining representative because those provisions entail individual contracts with clubs. However, the argument ignores the fact that free agency is simply a collectively bargained method of determining individual salaries for one group of players. The anti-collusion provision is not designed to prevent the PRC from representing the Clubs. Rather, that provision guarantees that free agency will be a reality when permitted by the Basic Agreement. The injunction thus does not in any way prevent the PRC from bargaining as the Clubs' exclusive representative with the Players Association over the elimination of free agency in its entirety or for a modified version of the same, and thereafter from implementing any proposals incorporated into a collective bargaining agreement.

The question, therefore, is whether the free agency, anti-collusion, and reserve issues are—or there is reasonable cause to believe they are—otherwise mandatory subjects of bargaining. Section 8(d) of the NLRA defines the duty to bargain as "the obligation ... to meet ... and confer in good faith with respect to wages, hours, and other terms and conditions of employment...."

In Wood v. Nat'l Basketball Ass'n, 809 F.2d 954 (2d Cir.1987), we noted that free agency and reserve issues are "at the center of collective bargaining in much of the professional sports industry," id. at 961, and that "it is precisely because of [free agency's] direct relationship to wages and conditions of employment that [it is] so controversial and so much the focus of bargaining in professional sports." Id. at 962.

Wood noted that collective bargaining between professional athletes and leagues raises "numerous problems with little or no precedent in standard industrial relations." Id. at 961. Such is the case with a free agency and reserve system. For the most part, unionized employees in the industrial sector may leave one employer for another without restriction. The employee may have no bargaining rights with regard to the terms of hire by the new employer, which may be set by a collective agreement, but is nevertheless generally free to go from one unionized job to another.

The professional sports industry has a very different history and very different economic imperatives. Most professional sports leagues have always had some form of what has become known as the reserve system. See Flood v. Kuhn, 407 U.S. 258, 259 n. 1, 92 S.Ct. 2099, 2100 n. 1, 32 L.Ed.2d 728 (1972) (baseball); Robertson v. National Basketball Ass'n, 556 F.2d 682, 686 n. 6 (2d Cir.1977) (basketball); Mackey v. National Football League, 543 F.2d 606, 610 (8th Cir.1976) (football), cert. dismissed, 434 U.S. 801, 98 S.Ct. 28, 54 L.Ed.2d 59 (1977); McCourt v. California Sports, Inc., 600 F.2d 1193, 1194 (6th Cir.1979) (hockey). As noted, this is a system by which the right to a player's services becomes the property of a particular club with limited freedom for the player to seek employment with another club. The reserve system in one form or another has been used in major league baseball for over a century. Until the arbitration decision in 1976, the reserve system prevented players from offering their athletic services to competing teams. A player's services were thus the property of a single team until he was traded or released.

In enforcing a complete reserve system, Major League Baseball was exercising monopsony power—a buyer's monopoly. However, there are many reasons, apart from maximizing the transfer of revenues from players to clubs, why reserve systems exist within professional sports. Fans might not be interested in games between teams that had entirely new lineups for every contest. Moreover, high quality play may require that individuals practice and play with the same teammates for at least some period of time. Teams may also want to recoup what they regard as training costs invested in players while they gained experience. In antitrust litigation, the leagues perennially argue that some form of reserve system is necessary for competitive balance. See Mackey, 543 F.2d at 611. Indeed, even in a system of complete free agency, one would expect to see many long-term agreements binding individual players to particular clubs.

There are also reasons, apart from maximizing the transfer of revenues to players, why a union of professional athletes would seek free agency. It is very difficult to set individual salaries in professional sports through collective bargaining. Although unions of professional athletes may bargain for uniform benefits and minimum salaries, they do not usually follow their industrial counterparts and seek relatively fixed salaries by job description, seniority, or other formulae. Players often play positions requiring very different skills. Moreover, the level of performance and value to a team in attracting fans differs radically among players, with star athletes or popular players being far more valuable than sub-par or nondescript players. Usually, therefore, players unions seek some form of free agency as a relatively simple method of setting individual salaries.

Most importantly, however, both the leagues and the players unions view free agency and reserve issues as questions of what share of revenues go to the clubs or to the players. The more restrictive the reserve system is, the greater the clubs' share. The greater the role of free agency, the greater the players' share.

To hold that there is no reasonable cause for the NLRB to conclude that free agency and reserve issues are mandatory subjects of bargaining would be virtually to ignore the history and economic imperatives of collective bargaining in professional sports. A mix of free agency and reserve clauses combined with other provisions is the universal method by which leagues and players unions set individual salaries in professional sports. Free agency for veteran players may thus be combined with a reserve system, as in baseball, or a rookie draft, as in basketball, see Wood, 809 F.2d at 957, for newer players. A salary cap may or may not be included. See id. To hold that any of these items, or others that make up the mix in a particular sport, is merely a permissive subject of bargaining would ignore the reality of collective bargaining in sports.

Indeed, free agency is in many ways nothing but the flip side of the reserve system. A full reserve system does not eliminate individual bargaining between teams and players. It simply limits that bargaining to one team. If free agency were a permissive subject of collective bargaining, then so would be the reserve system.

With regard to salary arbitration, we will assume, but not decide, that if it is a form of interest arbitration, it may be unilaterally eliminated. See George Koch & Sons, Inc., 306 N.L.R.B. 834, 839, 1992 WL 64220 (1992) (interest arbitration permissive subject of bargaining). Interest arbitration is a method by which an employer and union reach new agreements by sending disputed issues to an arbitrator rather than settling them through collective bargaining and economic force. See New York Typographical Union No. 6 v. Printers League, 919 F.2d 3, 3 n. 2 (2d Cir.1990). The salary arbitration provisions of the Basic Agreement are a method by which salaries for some players who are not eligible for free agency—those with three to six years of major league service—are set. The Basic Agreement sets forth criteria by which the arbitrator is to reach a decision. These criteria include the player's performance in the prior year, the length and consistency of career contribution, physical or mental defects, recent performance of the team on the field and at the gate, and salaries of certain comparable players. The Basic Agreement also forbids the arbitrator from considering certain facts that might otherwise be relevant. Finally, the Basic Agreement requires that the arbitrator pick either the club's suggested salary or the player's.

We decline to analogize Article VI(F) of the Basic Agreement to interest arbitration. Salary arbitration provides limited discretion to the arbitrator to set salaries for designated players who are not eligible for free agency. The discretion afforded the arbitrator is arguably less than the discretion afforded arbitrators in grievance arbitration involving disputes arising under an existing collective agreement, which is beyond question a mandatory subject of bargaining. In grievance arbitration, an arbitrator may permissibly imply a term even though the term has no explicit support in the text of the collective agreement. See United Steelworkers of America v. Warrior & Gulf Navigation Co., 363 U.S. 574, 581–82, 80 S.Ct. 1347, 1352–53, 4 L.Ed.2d 1409 (1960) ("The labor arbitrator's source of law is not confined to the express provisions of the contract, as the industrial common law—the practices of the industry and the shop—is equally a part of the collective bargaining agreement although not expressed in it."); see also Holly Sugar Corp. v. Distillery, Rectifying, Wine & Allied Workers Int'l Union, 412 F.2d 899, 903 (9th Cir.1969). Similarly, a term may be implied from past practices even though somewhat inconsistent with the agreement. See International Chem. Workers Union, Local No. 728 v. Imco Container Co., 78 L.R.R.M. (BNA) 2014, 1971 WL 800 (S.D.Ind.1971). We thus decline to analogize salary arbitration to interest arbitration, and, therefore, we hold that there is reasonable cause to believe that it is a mandatory subject of bargaining.

With regard to whether the granting of relief was "just and proper," 29 U.S.C. § 160(j), we review the district court's determination only for abuse of discretion. Mego, 633 F.2d at 1030; Palby Lingerie, 625 F.2d at 1051. We see no such abuse in the present matter. Given the short careers of professional athletes and the deterioration of physical abilities through aging, the irreparable harm requirement has been met. The unilateral elimination of free agency and salary arbitration followed by just three days a promise to restore the status quo. The PRC decided to settle the original unfair labor practice charges while embarking on a course of action based on a fallacious view of the duty to bargain. We see no reason to relieve it of the consequences of that course.

We therefore affirm.

BROWN v. PRO FOOTBALL, INC.

518 U.S. 231 (1996).

Justice BREYER delivered the opinion of the Court.

The question in this case arises at the intersection of the Nation's labor and antitrust laws. A group of professional football players brought this antitrust suit against football club owners. The club owners had bargained with the players' union over a wage issue until they reached impasse. The owners then had agreed among themselves (but not with the union) to implement the terms of their own last best bargaining offer. The question before us is whether federal labor laws shield such an agreement from antitrust attack. We believe that they do. This Court has previously found in the labor laws an implicit antitrust exemption that applies where needed to make the collective-bargaining process work. Like the Court of Appeals, we conclude that this need makes the exemption applicable in this case.

I

We can state the relevant facts briefly. In 1987, a collective-bargaining agreement between the National Football League (NFL), a group of football clubs, and the NFL Players Association, a labor union, expired. The NFL and the Players Association began to negotiate a new contract. In March 1989, during the negotiations, the NFL adopted Resolution G–2, a plan that would permit each club to establish a "developmental squad" of up to six rookie or "first-year" players who, as free agents, had failed to secure a position on a regular player roster. See App. 42. Squad members would play in practice games and sometimes in regular games as substitutes for injured players. Resolution G–2 provided that the club owners would pay all squad members the same weekly salary.

The next month, April, the NFL presented the developmental squad plan to the Players Association. The NFL proposed a squad player salary of $1,000 per week. The Players Association disagreed. It insisted that the club owners give developmental squad players benefits and protections similar to those provided regular players, and that they leave individual squad members free to negotiate their own salaries.

Two months later, in June, negotiations on the issue of developmental squad salaries reached an impasse. The NFL then unilaterally implemented the developmental squad program by distributing to the clubs a uniform contract that embodied the terms of Resolution G–2 and the $1,000 proposed weekly salary. The League advised club owners that paying developmental squad players more or less than $1,000 per week would result in disciplinary action, including the loss of draft choices.

In May 1990, 235 developmental squad players brought this antitrust suit against the League and its member clubs. The players claimed that their employers' agreement to pay them a $1,000 weekly salary violated the Sherman Act. See 15 U.S.C. § 1 (forbidding agreements in restraint of trade). The Federal District Court denied the employers' claim of exemption from the antitrust laws; it permitted the case to reach the jury; and it subsequently entered judgment on a jury treble-damage award that exceeded $30 million. The NFL and its member clubs appealed.

The Court of Appeals (by a split 2–to–1 vote) reversed. The majority interpreted the labor laws as "waiv[ing] antitrust liability for restraints on competition imposed through the collective-bargaining process, so long as such restraints operate primarily in a labor market characterized by collective bargaining." 50 F.3d 1041, 1056 (C.A.D.C.1995). The Court held, consequently, that the club owners were immune from antitrust liability. We granted certiorari to review that determination. Although we do not interpret the exemption as broadly as did the Appeals Court, we nonetheless find the exemption applicable, and we affirm that Court's immunity conclusion.

II

The immunity before us rests upon what this Court has called the "nonstatutory" labor exemption from the antitrust laws. Connell Constr. Co. v. Plumbers, 421 U.S. 616, 622, 95 S.Ct. 1830, 1835, 44 L.Ed.2d 418 (1975); see also Meat Cutters v. Jewel Tea Co., 381 U.S. 676, 85 S.Ct. 1596, 14 L.Ed.2d 640 (1965); Mine Workers v. Pennington, 381 U.S. 657, 85 S.Ct. 1585, 14 L.Ed.2d 626 (1965). The Court has implied this exemption from federal labor statutes, which set forth a national labor policy favoring free and private collective bargaining, see 29 U.S.C. § 151; Teamsters v. Oliver, 358 U.S. 283, 295, 79 S.Ct. 297, 304, 3 L.Ed.2d 312 (1959); which require good-faith bargaining over wages, hours and working conditions, see 29 U.S.C. §§ 158(a)(5), 158(d); NLRB v. Borg–Warner Corp., 356 U.S. 342, 348–349, 78 S.Ct. 718, 722–723, 2 L.Ed.2d 823 (1958); and which delegate related rulemaking and interpretive authority to the National Labor Relations Board, see 29 U.S.C. § 153; San Diego Building Trades Council v. Garmon, 359 U.S. 236, 242–245, 79 S.Ct. 773, 778–780, 3 L.Ed.2d 775 (1959).

This implicit exemption reflects both history and logic. As a matter of history, Congress intended the labor statutes (from which the Court has implied the exemption) in part to adopt the views of dissenting justices in Duplex Printing Press Co. v. Deering, 254 U.S. 443, 41 S.Ct. 172, 65 L.Ed. 349 (1921), which justices had urged the Court to interpret broadly a different explicit "statutory" labor exemption that Congress earlier (in 1914) had written directly into the antitrust laws. Id., at 483–488, 41 S.Ct., at 182–184 (Brandeis, J., joined by Holmes and Clarke, JJ., dissenting) (interpreting § 20 of the Clayton Act, 38 Stat. 738, 29 U.S.C. § 52); see also United States v. Hutcheson, 312 U.S. 219, 230–236, 61 S.Ct. 463, 465–468, 85 L.Ed. 788 (1941) (discussing congressional reaction to Duplex). In the 1930's, when it subsequently enacted the labor statutes, Congress, as in 1914, hoped to prevent judicial use of antitrust law to resolve labor disputes—a kind of dispute normally inappropriate for antitrust law resolution. See Jewel Tea, supra, at 700–709, 85 S.Ct., at 1607–1614 (opinion of Goldberg, J.); Marine Cooks v. Panama S.S. Co., 362 U.S. 365, 370, n. 7, 80 S.Ct. 779, 783, n. 7, 4 L.Ed.2d 797 (1960); A. Cox, Law and the National Labor Policy 3–8 (1960); cf. Duplex, supra, at 485, 41 S.Ct., at 183 (Brandeis, J., dissenting) (explicit "statutory" labor exemption reflected view that "Congress, not the judges, was the body which should declare what public policy in regard to the industrial struggle demands"). The implicit ("nonstatutory") exemption interprets the labor statutes in accordance with this intent, namely, as limiting an antitrust court's authority to determine, in the area of industrial conflict, what is or is not a "reasonable" practice. It thereby substitutes legislative and administrative labor-related determinations for judicial antitrust-related determinations as to the appropriate legal limits of industrial conflict. See Jewel Tea, supra, at 709–710, 85 S.Ct., at 1614–1615.

As a matter of logic, it would be difficult, if not impossible, to require groups of employers and employees to bargain together, but at the same time to forbid them to make among themselves or with each other any of the competition-restricting agreements potentially necessary to make the process work or its results mutually acceptable. Thus, the implicit exemption recognizes that, to give effect to federal labor laws and policies and to allow meaningful collective bargaining to take place, some restraints on competition imposed through the bargaining process must be shielded from antitrust sanctions. See Connell, supra, at 622, 95 S.Ct., at 1835 (federal labor law's "goals" could "never" be achieved if ordinary anticompetitive effects of collective bargaining were held to violate the antitrust laws); Jewel Tea, supra, at 711, 85 S.Ct., at 1615 (national labor law scheme would be "virtually destroyed" by the routine imposition of antitrust penalties upon parties engaged in collective bargaining); Pennington, supra, at 665, 85 S.Ct., at 1590–1591 (implicit exemption necessary to harmonize Sherman Act with "national policy . . . of promoting 'the peaceful settlement of industrial disputes by subjecting labor-management controversies to the mediatory influence of negotiation' ") (quoting Fibreboard Paper Products Corp. v. NLRB, 379 U.S. 203, 211, 85 S.Ct. 398, 403, 13 L.Ed.2d 233 (1964)).

The petitioners and their supporters concede, as they must, the legal existence of the exemption we have described. They also concede that, where its application is necessary to make the statutorily authorized collective-bargaining process work as Congress intended, the exemption must apply both to employers and to employees. Accord Volkswagenwerk Aktiengesellschaft v. Federal Maritime Comm'n, 390 U.S. 261, 287, n. 5, 88 S.Ct. 929, 943, n. 5, 19 L.Ed.2d 1090 (1968) (Harlan, J., concurring); Jewel Tea, supra, at 729–732, 735, 85 S.Ct., at 1624–1626 (opinion of Goldberg, J.); Brief for AFL–CIO as Amicus Curiae in Associated Gen. Contractors of Cal., Inc. v. Carpenters, O.T.1981, No. 81–334, pp. 16–17; see also P. Areeda & H. Hovenkamp, Antitrust Law p 229'd (1995 Supp.) (collecting recent circuit court cases); cf. H.A. Artists & Associates, Inc. v. Actors' Equity Assn., 451 U.S. 704, 717, n. 20, 101 S.Ct. 2102, 2110, n. 20, 68 L.Ed.2d 558 (1981) (explicit "statutory" exemption applies only to "bona fide labor organization[s]"). Nor does the dissent take issue with these basic principles. Consequently, the question before us is one of determining the exemption's scope: Does it apply to an agreement among several employers bargaining together to implement after impasse the terms of their last best good-faith wage offer? We assume that such conduct, as practiced in this case, is unobjectionable as a matter of labor law and policy. On that assumption, we conclude that the exemption applies.

Labor law itself regulates directly, and considerably, the kind of behavior here at issue—the postimpasse imposition of a proposed employment term concerning a mandatory subject of bargaining. Both the Board and the courts have held that, after impasse, labor law permits employers unilaterally to implement changes in preexisting conditions, but only insofar as the new terms meet carefully circumscribed conditions. For example, the new terms must be "reasonably comprehended" within the employer's preimpasse proposals (typically the last rejected proposals), lest by imposing more or less favorable terms, the employer unfairly undermined the union's status. Storer Communications, Inc., 294 N.L.R.B. 1056, 1090 (1989); Taft Broadcasting Co., 163 N.L.R.B. 475, 478 (1967), enf'd, 395 F.2d 622 (C.A.D.C.1968); see also NLRB v. Katz, 369 U.S. 736, 745, and n. 12, 82 S.Ct. 1107, 1112–1113, and n. 12, 8 L.Ed.2d 230 (1962). The collective-bargaining proceeding itself must be free of any unfair labor practice, such as an employer's failure to have bargained in good faith. See Akron Novelty Mfg. Co., 224 N.L.R.B. 998, 1002 (1976) (where employer has not bargained in good faith, it may not implement a term of employment); 1 P. Hardin, The Developing Labor Law 697 (3d ed.1992) (same). These regulations reflect the fact that impasse and an accompanying implementation of proposals constitute an integral part of the bargaining process. See Bonanno Linen Serv., Inc., 243 N.L.R.B. 1093, 1094 (1979) (describing use of impasse as a bargaining tactic), enf'd, 630 F.2d 25 (C.A.1 1980), aff'd, 454 U.S. 404, 102 S.Ct. 720, 70 L.Ed.2d 656 (1982); Colorado–Ute Elec. Assn., 295 N.L.R.B. 607, 609 (1989), enf. denied on other grounds, 939 F.2d 1392 (C.A.10 1991), cert. denied, 504 U.S. 955, 112 S.Ct. 2300, 119 L.Ed.2d 223 (1992).

Although the caselaw we have cited focuses upon bargaining by a single employer, no one here has argued that labor law does, or should, treat multiemployer bargaining differently in this respect. Indeed, Board and court decisions suggest that the joint implementation of proposed terms after impasse is a familiar practice in the context of multiemployer bargaining. See, e.g., El Cerrito Mill & Lumber Co., 316 N.L.R.B. 1005 (1995); Paramount Liquor Co., 307 N.L.R.B. 676, 686 (1992); NKS Distributors, Inc., 304 N.L.R.B. 338, 340–341 (1991), rev'd, 50 F.3d 18 (C.A.9 1995); Sage Development Co., 301 N.L.R.B. 1173, 1175 (1991); Walker Constr. Co., 297 N.L.R.B. 746, 748 (1990), enf'd, 928 F.2d 695 (C.A.5 1991); Food Employers Council, Inc., 293 N.L.R.B. 333, 334, 345–346 (1989); Tile, Terrazzo & Marble Contractors Assn., 287 N.L.R.B. 769, 772 (1987), enf'd, 935 F.2d 1249 (C.A.11 1991), cert. denied, 502 U.S. 1031, 112 S.Ct. 871, 116 L.Ed.2d 776 (1992); Salinas Valley Ford Sales, Inc., 279 N.L.R.B. 679, 686, 690 (1986); Carlsen Porsche Audi, Inc., 266 N.L.R.B. 141, 152–153 (1983); Typographic Service Co., 238 N.L.R.B. 1565 (1978); United Fire Proof Warehouse Co. v. NLRB, 356 F.2d 494, 498–499 (C.A.7 1966); Cuyamaca Meats, Inc. v. Butchers' and Food Employers' Pension Trust Fund, 638 F.Supp. 885, 887 (S.D.Cal. 1986), aff'd, 827 F.2d 491 (C.A.9 1987), cert. denied, 485 U.S. 1008, 108 S.Ct. 1474, 99 L.Ed.2d 703 (1988). We proceed on that assumption.

Multiemployer bargaining itself is a well-established, important, pervasive method of collective bargaining, offering advantages to both management and labor. See Appendix (multiemployer bargaining accounts for more than 40% of major collective-bargaining agreements, and is used in such industries as construction, transportation, retail trade, clothing manufacture, and real estate, as well as professional sports); NLRB v. Truck Drivers, 353 U.S. 87, 95, 77 S.Ct. 643, 647, 1 L.Ed.2d 676 (1957) (Buffalo Linen) (Congress saw multiemployer bargaining as "a vital factor in the effectuation of the national policy of promoting labor peace through strengthened collective bargaining"); Charles D. Bonanno Linen Service, Inc. v. NLRB, 454 U.S. 404, 409, n. 3, 102 S.Ct. 720, 723, n. 3, 70 L.Ed.2d 656 (1982) (Bonanno Linen) (multiemployer bargaining benefits both management and labor, by saving bargaining resources, by encouraging development of industry-wide worker benefits programs that smaller employers could not otherwise afford, and by inhibiting employer competition at the workers' expense); Brief for Respondent NLRB in Bonanno Linen, O.T.1981, No. 80–931, p. 10, n. 7 (same); General Subcommittee on Labor, House Committee on Education and Labor, Multiemployer Association Bargaining and its Impact on the Collective Bargaining Process, 88th Cong., 2d Sess. 10–19, 32–33 (Comm. Print 1964) (same); see also C. Bonnett, Employers' Associations in the United States: A Study of Typical Associations (1922) (history). The upshot is that the practice at issue here plays a significant role in a collective-bargaining process that itself comprises an important part of the Nation's industrial relations system.

In these circumstances, to subject the practice to antitrust law is to require antitrust courts to answer a host of important practical questions about how collective bargaining over wages, hours and working conditions is to proceed—the very result that the implicit labor exemption seeks to avoid. And it is to place in jeopardy some of the potentially beneficial labor-related effects that multiemployer bargaining can achieve. That is because unlike labor law, which sometimes welcomes anticompetitive agreements conducive to industrial harmony, antitrust law forbids all agreements among competitors (such as competing employers) that unreasonably lessen competition among or between them in virtually any respect whatsoever. See, e.g., Paramount Famous Lasky Corp. v. United States, 282 U.S. 30, 51 S.Ct. 42, 75 L.Ed. 145 (1930) (agreement to insert arbitration provisions in motion picture licensing contracts). Antitrust law also sometimes permits judges or juries to premise antitrust liability upon little more than uniform behavior among competitors, preceded by conversations implying that later uniformity might prove desirable, see, e.g., United States v. General Motors Corp., 384 U.S. 127, 142–143, 86 S.Ct. 1321, 1329, 16 L.Ed.2d 415 (1966); United States v. Foley, 598 F.2d 1323, 1331–1332 (C.A.4 1979), cert. denied, 444 U.S. 1043, 100 S.Ct. 727, 728, 62 L.Ed.2d 728 (1980), or accompanied by other conduct that in context suggests that each competitor failed to make an independent decision, see, e.g., American Tobacco Co. v. United States, 328 U.S. 781, 809–810, 66 S.Ct. 1125, 1138–1139, 90 L.Ed. 1575 (1946); United States v. Masonite Corp., 316 U.S. 265, 275, 62 S.Ct. 1070, 1076, 86 L.Ed. 1461 (1942); Interstate Circuit, Inc. v. United States, 306 U.S. 208, 226–227, 59 S.Ct. 467, 474–475, 83 L.Ed. 610 (1939). See generally 6 P. Areeda, Antitrust Law pp 1416–1427

(1986); Turner, The Definition of Agreement Under the Sherman Act: Conscious Parallelism and Refusals to Deal, 75 Harv. L.Rev. 655 (1962).

If the antitrust laws apply, what are employers to do once impasse is reached? If all impose terms similar to their last joint offer, they invite an antitrust action premised upon identical behavior (along with prior or accompanying conversations) as tending to show a common understanding or agreement. If any, or all, of them individually impose terms that differ significantly from that offer, they invite an unfair labor practice charge. Indeed, how can employers safely discuss their offers together even before a bargaining impasse occurs? A preimpasse discussion about, say, the practical advantages or disadvantages of a particular proposal, invites a later antitrust claim that they agreed to limit the kinds of action each would later take should an impasse occur. The same is true of postimpasse discussions aimed at renewed negotiations with the union. Nor would adherence to the terms of an expired collective-bargaining agreement eliminate a potentially plausible antitrust claim charging that they had "conspired" or tacitly "agreed" to do so, particularly if maintaining the status quo were not in the immediate economic self-interest of some. Cf. Interstate Circuit, supra, at 222–223, 59 S.Ct., at 472–473; 6 Areeda, supra, at p 1425. All this is to say that to permit antitrust liability here threatens to introduce instability and uncertainty into the collective-bargaining process, for antitrust law often forbids or discourages the kinds of joint discussions and behavior that the collective-bargaining process invites or requires.

We do not see any obvious answer to this problem. We recognize, as the Government suggests, that, in principle, antitrust courts might themselves try to evaluate particular kinds of employer understandings, finding them "reasonable" (hence lawful) where justified by collective-bargaining necessity. But any such evaluation means a web of detailed rules spun by many different nonexpert antitrust judges and juries, not a set of labor rules enforced by a single expert administrative body, namely the Labor Board. The labor laws give the Board, not antitrust courts, primary responsibility for policing the collective-bargaining process. And one of their objectives was to take from antitrust courts the authority to determine, through application of the antitrust laws, what is socially or economically desirable collective-bargaining policy. See Jewel Tea, 381 U.S., at 716–719, 85 S.Ct., at 1617–1619 (opinion of Goldberg, J.).

[The remainder of the Court's opinion is omitted.]

Justice STEVENS, dissenting.

The basic premise underlying the Sherman Act is the assumption that free competition among business entities will produce the best price levels. National Soc. of Professional Engineers v. United States, 435 U.S. 679, 695, 98 S.Ct. 1355, 1367, 55 L.Ed.2d 637 (1978). Collusion among competitors, it is believed, may produce prices that harm consumers. United States v. Socony–Vacuum Oil Co., 310 U.S. 150, 226, n. 59, 60 S.Ct. 811, 846, n. 59, 84 L.Ed. 1129 (1940). Similarly, the Court has held, a market-wide agreement among employers setting wages at levels that would not prevail in a free market may violate the Sherman Act. Anderson v. Shipowners Assn. of Pacific Coast, 272 U.S. 359, 47 S.Ct. 125, 71 L.Ed. 298 (1926).

The jury's verdict in this case has determined that the market-wide agreement among these employers fixed the salaries of the replacement players at a dramatically lower level than would obtain in a free market. While the special characteristics of this industry may provide a justification for the agreement under the rule of reason, see National Collegiate Athletic Assn. v. Board of Regents of Univ. of Okla., 468 U.S. 85, 100–104, 104 S.Ct. 2948, 2960–2962, 82 L.Ed.2d 70 (1984), at this stage of the proceeding our analysis of the exemption issue must accept the premise that the agreement is unlawful unless it is exempt.

The basic premise underlying our national labor policy is that unregulated competition among employees and applicants for employment produces wage levels that are lower than they should be. Whether or not the premise is true in fact, it is surely the basis for the statutes that encourage and protect the collective-bargaining process, including the express statutory exemptions from the antitrust laws that Congress enacted in order to protect union activities. Those statutes were enacted to enable collective action by union members to achieve wage levels that are higher than would be available in a free market. See Trainmen v. Chicago R. & I.R. Co., 353 U.S. 30, 40, 77 S.Ct. 635, 640, 1 L.Ed.2d 622 (1957).

The statutory labor exemption protects the right of workers to act collectively to seek better wages, but does not "exempt concerted action or agreements between unions and nonlabor parties." Connell Constr. Co. v. Plumbers, 421 U.S. 616, 621–622, 95 S.Ct. 1830, 1834–1835, 44 L.Ed.2d 418 (1975). It is the judicially crafted, nonstatutory labor exemption that serves to accommodate the conflicting policies of the antitrust and labor statutes in the context of action between employers and unions. Ibid.

The limited judicial exemption complements its statutory counterpart by ensuring that unions which engage in collective bargaining to enhance employees' wages may enjoy the benefits of the resulting agreements. The purpose of the labor laws would be frustrated if it were illegal for employers to enter into industry-wide agreements providing supra-competitive wages for employees. For that reason, we have explained that "a proper accommodation between the congressional policy favoring collective bargaining under the NLRA and the congressional policy favoring free competition in business markets requires that some union-employer agreements be accorded a limited nonstatutory exemption from antitrust sanctions." Id., at 622, 95 S.Ct., at 1835.

Consistent with basic labor law policies, I agree with the Court that the judicially crafted labor exemption must also cover some collective action that employers take in response to a collective bargaining agent's demands for higher wages. Immunizing such action from antitrust scrutiny may facilitate collective bargaining over labor demands. So, too, may immunizing concerted employer action designed to maintain the integrity of the multi-employer bargaining unit, such as lockouts that are imposed in response to "a union strike tactic which threatens the destruction of the employers' interest in bargaining on a group basis." NLRB v. Truck Drivers, 353 U.S. 87, 93, 77 S.Ct. 643, 646, 1 L.Ed.2d 676 (1957).

In my view, however, neither the policies underlying the two separate statutory schemes, nor the narrower focus on the purpose of the nonstatutory exemption, provides a justification for exempting from antitrust scrutiny collective action initiated by employers to depress wages below the level that would be produced in a free market. Nor do those policies support a rule that would allow employers to suppress wages by implementing noncompetitive agreements among themselves on matters that have not previously been the subject of either an agreement with labor or even a demand by labor for inclusion in the bargaining process. That, however, is what is at stake in this litigation.

[The remainder of Justice Stevens' dissent is omitted.]

Notes

1. Since their emergence in the 1960s, players unions have compiled a mixed record. On the plus side, they have secured better pay for their members. By 1998, for example, average salaries in the four major professional sports leagues stood at $2.6 million (NBA), $1.38 million (MLB), $1.1 million (NHL), and $910,000 (NFL). *See* Jeffrey Denberg, *Stern Sends Letter to NBA Players*, Atlanta J. & Const., Dec. 18, 1998, at H8. On the negative side, they frequently have turned out to be weak, corrupt, or incompetent. For a further look at their successes and failures, see, e.g., *National Football League Players Ass'n v. Pro–Football, Inc.*, 79 F.3d 1215 (D.C.Cir.1996); *Morio v. North American Soccer League*, 632 F.2d 217 (2d Cir.1980); *Forbes v. Eagleson*, 19 F.Supp.2d 352 (E.D.Pa.1998); *Sharpe v. National Football League Players Ass'n*, 941 F.Supp. 8 (D.D.C.1996); *Cincinnati Bengals, Inc. v. Thompson*, 553 F.Supp. 1011 (S.D.Ohio 1983). *See also* Darryl Hale, *Step Up to the Scale: Wages and Unions in the Sports Industry*, 5 Marq. Sports L.J. 123 (1994).

2. In addition to United States law, bi-national leagues, such as MLB, the NBA, and the NHL, also are subject to Canadian law. This fact occasionally has led to friction because of differences in the labor policies of the two countries. *See further* J. Jordan Lippner, Note, *Replacement Players for the Toronto Blue Jays?: Striking the Appropriate Balance Between Replacement Worker Law in Ontario, Canada and the United States*, 18 Fordham Int'l L.J. 2026 (1995).

3. No group of owners has been accused more often of acting in bad faith during labor negotiations than those in baseball. *See generally* Roger I. Abrams, *Legal Bases: Baseball and the Law* (1998). Part of the reason for this is that until recently, MLB enjoyed a special exemption from the federal antitrust laws because of Justice Holmes' ruling that baseball games did not constitute interstate commerce. *See Federal Baseball Club of Baltimore v. National League of Professional Baseball Clubs*, 259 U.S. 200 (1922). Al-

though recognizing the decision was wrong (and therefore refusing to extend its rationale to other sports), the Supreme Court twice reaffirmed it on the grounds of stare decisis. *See Toolson v. New York Yankees, Inc.*, 346 U.S. 356 (1953), and *Flood v. Kuhn*, 407 U.S. 258 (1972). Recently, however, the decision was partially abrogated by the Curt Flood Act of 1998 (to be codified at 15 U.S.C. § 27a). The statute strips baseball of its antitrust immunity in all labor matters, but does not affect such aspects of the game as relocation, league expansion, and the minor leagues. *See further* Thomas C. Picher, *Baseball Antitrust's Exemption Repealed: An Analysis of the Effect on Salary Cap and Salary Taxation Provisions*, 7 Seton Hall J. Sport L. 5 (1997), and Joshua Hamilton, Comment, *Congress in Relief: The Economic Importance of Revoking Baseball's Antitrust Exemption*, 38 Santa Clara L. Rev. 1223 (1998).

4. Although many matters are discussed whenever a union and a group of owners sit down to bargain, the key issue invariably turns out to be money. On the one hand, the union wants to obtain the highest possible salaries for its members. On the other hand, the owners want to keep their payrolls as low as possible. The 1998 NBA lockout provides a good case study of these clashing agendas.

The NBA annually generates revenues of $2 billion. Thus, when the union and owners began meeting in April 1998, the challenge was to find a way to distribute this enormous sum. The union sought minimum salaries of $300,000, maximum salaries of $10–$15 million (depending on years of service, with higher salaries allowed upon payment by the team of a so-called "luxury tax"), a guaranteed 56% of league revenues, and an exception permitting clubs over the salary cap to re-sign "middle class" players for $2.6 million. The owners responded by offering minimum salaries of $275,000, maximum salaries of $8.75–$12.25 million (depending on years of service, with no luxury tax option), a guaranteed 53% of league revenues, and a "middle class" exception of $1 million. *See Key Issues Separating the League and the Union*, N.Y. Times, Dec. 30, 1998, at C21. With neither side willing to compromise, the NBA was forced to delay the start of its 1998–99 season. Finally, however, in January 1999, with the season about to be cancelled, the players gave in and accepted the owners' proposals. *See further* Mark Starr & Allison Samuels, *Taking It Hard to the NBA Hoop*, Newsweek, Jan. 18, 1999, at 48.

5. During negotiations, both sides possess powerful weapons. For its part, the union can call a strike and shut down the league, as occurred in MLB in 1981 and 1994 and the NFL in 1982 and 1987. For their part, the owners can lock out the players, as happened in the NHL in 1994 and the NBA in 1998. In addition, the owners can hire replacement workers, as was done in the NFL in 1987 and MLB in 1995. For a further discussion of collective bargaining in professional sports, see, e.g., C. Peter Goplerud III, *Collective Bargaining in the National Football League: A Historical and Comparative Analysis*, 4 Vill. Sports & Ent. L.J. 13 (1997); Michael Tannenbaum, *A Comprehensive Analysis of Recent Antitrust and Labor Litigation Affecting the NBA and NFL*, 3 Sports Law. J. 205 (1996); Jonathan C. Tyras, Comment, *Players Versus Owners: Collective Bargaining and Antitrust After Brown v. Pro Football, Inc.*, 1 U. Pa. J. Lab. & Employment L. 297 (1998).

6. Besides players and owners, work stoppages involving athletes affect the financial well-being of businesses that depend upon games for customers (such as hotels, bars, restaurants, and stadium vendors). During the NBA's lockout, for example, it was estimated Chicago's economy lost $10 million for each cancelled Bulls game. *See* Terrence E. Armour, *Out of Sight, Out of Mind*, Chi. Trib., Dec. 6, 1998, at 1 (Sports). For a further look at the widespread impact of strikes and lockouts, see Howard Beck, *Left Feeling Empty: NBA Lockout is Trouble for Many People Besides Players and Owners*, L.A. Daily News, Nov. 4, 1998, at S1; *Baseball Strike Expected to Have Impact on Economy*, Tulsa World, Aug. 8, 1994, at S3; Stephen Heffner, *Jai Alai Players' Strike Costly*, Providence J.-Bull., May 12, 1988, at 3A.

7. When the union and owners do reach an understanding, it is memorialized in a collective bargaining agreement (CBA). This document sets forth, usually in minute detail, the rights and obligations of the parties. Thus, the typical CBA covers such topics as player movement (e.g., drafts, trades, waivers, and free agency), payroll limits (e.g., salary caps and luxury taxes), and working conditions (e.g., fines, suspensions, grievances, and appeals). *See further Smith v. Houston Oilers, Inc.*, 87 F.3d 717 (5th Cir.), *cert. denied*, 117 S.Ct. 510 (1996) (termination pay); *Bidwill v. Garvey*, 943 F.2d 498 (4th Cir.1991), *cert. denied*, 502 U.S. 1099 (1992) (pension contributions); *Wood v. National Basketball Ass'n*, 809 F.2d 954 (2d Cir.1987) (draft); *White v. National Football League*, 972 F.Supp. 1230 (D.Minn.1997) (signing bonus); *Bridgeman v. National Basketball Ass'n*, 838 F.Supp. 172 (D.N.J. 1993) (salary cap); *Tampa Bay Area NFL Football, Inc. v. Jarvis*, 668 So.2d 217 (Fla.Dist.Ct.App.1996) (workers' compensation benefits).

8. Because of the comprehensive nature of modern CBAs, individual players and teams need only reach agreement on a few basic terms. *See, e.g.*, Joseph M. Weiler, *Legal Analysis of the NHL Player's Contract*, 3 Marq. Sports L.J. 59 (1992). Once this is accomplished, the completed contract must be submitted to the league for a determination that it complies with the CBA. This is more demanding than it sounds. In December 1998, for example, MLB announced it would take disciplinary action after it was revealed the Toronto Blue Jays had withheld parts of Roger Clemens' 1996 deal from review. *See* Murray Chass, *Baseball to Fine Beeston Over Clemens's Contract*, N.Y. Times, Dec. 25, 1998, at C18. Similarly, in July 1996, the Miami Heat's agreement with Juwan Howard was voided because it was found to violate the NBA's salary cap. *See* Mark Asher, *NBA Rejects Heat's Contract with Howard*, Wash. Post, Aug. 1, 1996, at D1. For a further look at the approval process, see *National Hockey League Players' Ass'n v. Bettman*, 1994 WL 738835 (S.D.N.Y.1994).

Problem 25

Believing his team had violated the league's collective bargaining agreement, a linebacker lodged a grievance with the union. It in turn referred the matter to an attorney. When the arbitrator subsequently ruled in favor of the club, the player filed a legal malpractice action. If the lawyer argues he has no liability because his client was the union, how should the court rule? *See Peterson v. Kennedy*, 771 F.2d 1244 (9th Cir.1985), *cert. denied*, 475 U.S. 1122 (1986).

D. WORKING CONDITIONS

Like other employees, athletes are subject to a variety of government- and employer-mandated rules. As one might expect, these requirements have sometimes led to litigation.

1. EQUIPMENT

Every sport has developed regulations regarding the type of equipment competitors can use. Yet no matter how carefully they are written, such standards always leave room for disagreement.

MERCURY BAY BOATING CLUB INC. v. SAN DIEGO YACHT CLUB

557 N.E.2d 87 (N.Y.1990).

ALEXANDER, Judge.

On September 7 and 9, 1988, in the waters off San Diego, California, Mercury Bay Boating Club Inc.'s challenger vessel, the New Zealand, a monohull-keel yacht, was defeated two races to none by San Diego Yacht Club's defending twin-hulled catamaran, the Stars and Stripes, in the 27th America's Cup match. Contending that San Diego's defense of the Cup by sailing an inherently faster multihull catamaran against a larger, but slower monohull yacht was unsportsmanlike, antithetical to the concept of "friendly competition between foreign countries" and a "gross mismatch" in violation of the America's Cup Deed of Gift and San Diego's obligations as trustee, Mercury Bay obtained a judgment in New York Supreme Court disqualifying San Diego's catamaran, declaring the New Zealand to be the winner of the two races and directing that San Diego transfer the America's Cup to Mercury Bay.

A divided Appellate Division reversed, 150 A.D.2d 82, 545 N.Y.S.2d 693, declared the Stars and Stripes to be an eligible vessel and the winner of the two races, and therefore that San Diego was the rightful holder of the America's Cup. We agree that the Stars and Stripes was an eligible vessel under the terms of the Deed of Gift and that San Diego breached no fiduciary duty in racing a catamaran against Mercury Bay's challenging yacht. Accordingly, we affirm.

I

The America's Cup, a silver cup trophy, is the corpus of a charitable trust created in the 19th century under the laws of New York. So called because it was won by the yacht America in a race around the Isle of Wight in 1851, the America's Cup was donated by its six owners to the New York Yacht Club in 1857. The Cup was twice returned to George Schuyler, the sole surviving donor, when questions arose as to the terms of the trust in which the Cup was to be held. Schuyler executed the present Deed of Gift in 1887, donating the Cup to the New York Yacht Club, to be held in trust "upon the condition that it shall be preserved as a perpetual Challenge Cup for the friendly competition between foreign countries''.

Pursuant to the Deed of Gift, the holder of the Cup is its sole trustee and is to be succeeded by a competitor who successfully challenges the trustee in a race for the Cup. Unless otherwise agreed by the parties, the terms of the challenge are specified in the deed. The relevant provisions of the deed provide:

> "This Cup is donated upon the condition that it shall be preserved as a perpetual Challenge Cup for friendly competition between foreign countries.
>
> "Any organized Yacht Club of a foreign country * * * shall always be entitled to the right of sailing a match for this Cup, with a yacht or vessel propelled by sails only and constructed in the country to which the Challenging Club belongs, against any one yacht or vessel constructed in the country of the Club holding the Cup.
>
> "The competing yachts or vessels, if of one mast, shall be not less than forty-four feet nor more than ninety feet on the load water-line; if of more than one mast they shall be not less than eighty feet nor more than one hundred and fifteen feet on the load water-line.
>
> "The Challenging Club shall give ten months' notice, in writing, naming the days for the proposed races * * * Accompanying the ten months' notice of challenge there must be sent the name of the owner and a certificate of the name, rig, and following dimensions of the challenging vessel, namely, length on load water-line; beam at load water-line and extreme beam; and draught of water, which dimensions shall not be exceeded; and a custom-house registry of the vessel must also be sent as soon as possible. Centre-board or sliding keel vessels shall always be allowed to compete in any race for the Cup, and no restriction nor limitation whatever shall be placed upon the use of such centre-board or sliding keel, nor shall the centre-board or sliding keel be considered a part of the vessel for any purposes of measurement.
>
> "The Club challenging for the Cup and the Club holding the same may, by mutual consent, make any arrangement satisfactory to both as to the dates, courses, number of trials, rules and sailing regulations, and any and all other conditions of the match, in which case the ten months' notice may be waived.
>
> "In case the parties cannot mutually agree upon the terms of a match, then three races shall be sailed, and the winner of two of such races shall be entitled to the Cup. All such races shall be on ocean courses * * * [These ocean courses] shall be selected by the Club holding the Cup; and these races shall be sailed subject to its rules and sailing regulations so far as the

same do not conflict with the provisions of this deed of gift, but without any time allowances whatever. The challenged Club shall not be required to name its representative vessel until at a time agreed upon for the start, but the vessel when named must compete in all the races, and each of such races must be completed within seven hours."

Although the defending club, as holder of the Cup, is its trustee, it is nevertheless required to compete with challengers for the Cup. Nothing in the deed limits the design of the defending club's vessel other than the length on water-line limits applicable to all competing vessels, nor are the competing vessels expressly limited to monohulls. Moreover, there is no requirement that the defending vessel have the same number of hulls as the challenging vessel, or even that the competing vessels be substantially similar.

Prior to 1988, the America's Cup competitions generally were conducted under the mutual consent provisions of the deed, with the contestants agreeing upon the date, time and length of the races and, beginning in 1930, even upon the choice of vessels to be raced. Although multihull vessels were in use at the time the deed was executed in 1887 and during all the ensuing years, none ever competed for the America's Cup prior to the match at issue here. Between 1930 and 1937, the agreed-upon vessels were large ocean-going vessels known as J-boats, which subsequently became too expensive to build and maintain. Consequently, the yachting community lost interest in the America's Cup competition and the New York Yacht Club, which had successfully defended the Cup 16 times before 1937, received no challenges for a 20–year period thereafter. Attempting to revive interest in the competition, in 1956 the New York Yacht Club obtained a court order amending the Deed of Gift to reduce the minimum load water-line length to its present 44 feet and to eliminate the requirement that the challenging vessel sail to the match "on its own bottom", a requirement that had disadvantaged foreign challengers. These amendments allowed the competition to be conducted in yachts of the international 12–meter class, which measure 44 feet on the load waterline. Thereafter, in response to the increased interest in the competition by many challengers and with the consent of those challengers, the New York Yacht Club instituted an elimination series, conducted in these 12–meter yachts, in which the winner of the series was entitled to sail a match against the defender of the Cup.

The America's Cup races were conducted in these elimination series at 3–to–4–year intervals for a period of 30 years, with the New York Yacht Club retaining the Cup until 1983 when it lost to the Royal Perth Yacht Club of Australia. Three years later, 13 yacht clubs representing six nations competed to determine which would challenge Royal Perth for the Cup. In the finals, Stars & Stripes '87 of the San Diego Yacht Club defeated Royal Perth's defender Kookaburra III four races to none.

San Diego planned to defend the Cup in 1990 or 1991 in a 12–meter yacht, adhering to the traditional multiple challenger format. In 1987, as yacht clubs all over the world prepared to compete in that event, Mercury Bay issued a notice of challenge to San Diego, which for the first time in 30 years, deviated from the multiple challenger format as well as the tradition of holding the races in 3–to–4–year intervals. Mercury Bay demanded a match in less than a year and disclosed that it would race a yacht measuring 90 feet on the load water-line, the maximum length permitted in the deed and a size yacht that had not been built in 50 years. As most foreign yacht clubs were already preparing for a race of 12–meter yachts, they would have been unable to compete on the terms demanded by Mercury Bay; indeed, of the 19 bids received by San Diego, Mercury Bay's was the only challenge which deviated from the traditional format. To justify its unorthodox challenge, Mercury Bay advised San Diego that it sought to compete in a vessel larger than those of recent matches because such a yacht, by "utilizing technology outside any class or rating rule would be most likely to offer real opportunity of innovative design to the benefit of yachting at large".

San Diego announced that the terms of the challenge were unacceptable under the Deed of Gift and notified other challengers that the next match would be held in 1990 or 1991 in 12–meter yachts. Mercury Bay commenced an action in New York Supreme Court seeking a declaration of the validity of its challenge, and a preliminary injunction prohibiting San Diego from considering any other challenges until Mercury Bay's challenge was decided.

In its capacity as trustee of the America's Cup, San Diego commenced an action pursuant to EPTL 8–1.1(c)(1), seeking interpretation or amendment of the Deed of Gift to authorize a continuation of the traditional 12–meter yacht elimination series format employed by both the New York Yacht Club and the Royal Perth Yacht Club, the only two prior trustees. The Attorney–General of the State of New York, which represents the beneficiaries of charitable trusts under EPTL 8–1.1(f), supported San Diego's position in both actions.

Supreme Court rejected San Diego's application to interpret or amend the Deed of Gift and granted Mercury Bay's motion for a preliminary injunction, declaring the notice of challenge valid. The court held that San Diego's options were to "accept the challenge, forfeit the Cup, or negotiate agreeable terms with the challenger".

Although the parties thereafter made several proposals in an attempt to negotiate agreeable terms, they were unsuccessful, and San Diego proceeded with preparations for its defense of the Cup. In late January 1988, San Diego announced its decision to race in a catamaran whose dimensions, although smaller than Mercury Bay's monohull yacht, fell within the limitations expressed in the Deed of Gift.

Mercury Bay moved to hold San Diego in contempt of Supreme Court's prior order validating Mercury Bay's challenge, arguing that the use of a catamaran, a type of vessel never before raced in an America's

Cup match, would deny it the "match" to which it was entitled under the deed because the catamaran is, by design, inherently faster than a monohull vessel. According to Mercury Bay, the deed required the defending club to race a vessel which was "like or similar" to the challenging vessel. Supreme Court denied the motion and directed the parties to reserve their protests until after completion of the America's Cup races. As indicated, the match was held on September 7 and 9, 1988 and San Diego defeated Mercury Bay two races to none.

San Diego had little time to celebrate before it found itself back in court. Mercury Bay moved to have the results of the race set aside, have itself declared the winner and for an order directing that the Cup be awarded to it. Concluding that the deed implicitly required the America's Cup race to be held only between vessels which were "somewhat evenly matched" and that San Diego's use of a catamaran constituted an attempt to "retain the Cup at all costs so that it could host a competition on its own terms" which violated the spirit of the deed, Supreme Court disqualified San Diego's catamaran, declared Mercury Bay the winner of the two races and directed San Diego to transfer the America's Cup to Mercury Bay.

In reversing Supreme Court, the Appellate Division concluded that the Deed of Gift unambiguously permitted matches between "yacht[s] or vessel[s]" meeting the length specifications articulated within the deed, that San Diego's catamaran was an eligible vessel, and therefore that San Diego is the rightful holder of the America's Cup. Mercury Bay appeals by leave of the Appellate Division.

II

Mercury Bay asks us to set aside the results of the 1988 America's Cup match because, in its view, San Diego's defense of the Cup in a catamaran violated the spirit of the Deed of Gift as exemplified both by its terms and various items of extrinsic evidence. It argues that the donors of the Cup never intended to permit such a catamaran defense because a race between a catamaran and a monohull yacht is an inherently unfair "mismatch" which the monohull yacht has no chance of winning. Instead, Mercury Bay contends that the donors intended to restrict the defender's choice of vessel to the type selected by the challenger and to require further that the particular vessel used afford the challenger a chance of winning the match. Mercury Bay also argues that by sailing a catamaran to defend the Cup, San Diego breached its fiduciary duties as trustee under the Deed of Gift.

Although these arguments are clothed in the legal rubric of interpreting the "intent" of the drafters of the trust instrument and determining the fiduciary duties owed by the trustee, the gravamen of Mercury Bay's complaint is that such a race between a multihull catamaran and a monohull yacht is inherently "unfair", whether or not the donors intended to permit it. The measure of "fairness" in this regard, according to Mercury Bay and the dissenters, are standards of sportsmanship as determined by reference to practices which are presently the custom in sporting activities generally and yacht racing in particular.

The question of whether particular conduct is "sporting" or "fair" in the context of a particular sporting event, however, is wholly distinct from the question of whether it is legal. Questions of sportsmanship and fairness with respect to sporting contests depend largely upon the rules of the particular sport and the expertise of those knowledgeable in that sport; they are not questions suitable for judicial resolution (see, e.g., Crouch v. National Assn. For Stock Car Auto Racing, 2 Cir., 845 F.2d 397, 403; Finley & Co. v. Kuhn, 7 Cir., 569 F.2d 527, 539). As sporting activities evolve in light of changing preferences and technologies, it would be most inappropriate and counterproductive for the courts to attempt to fix the rules and standards of competition of any particular sport. To do so would likely result in many sporting contests being decided, not in the arena of the sport, but in the courts.

Moreover, the Deed of Gift governing the conduct of the America's Cup competitions contemplates that such issues of fairness and sportsmanship be resolved by members of the yachting community rather than by the courts. The deed provides that where the defending and the challenging yacht clubs have not agreed upon the terms of the match, it is to be conducted as specified in the deed and pursuant to the rules and regulations of the defending club, so long as they do not conflict with the deed. As the deed broadly defines the vessels eligible to compete in the match, it is these rules and regulations which the donors intended to govern disputes relating to racing protocol such as the fairness of the vessels to be used in a particular match.

The Deed of Gift provides: "In case the parties cannot mutually agree upon the terms of a match, then three races shall be sailed, and the winner of two of such races shall be entitled to the Cup. All such races shall be on ocean courses * * * [These ocean courses] shall be selected by the Club holding the Cup; and these races shall be sailed subject to its rules and regulations so far as the same do not conflict with the provisions of this deed of gift, but without any time allowances whatever". In light of this plain language, and the undisputed fact that the applicable rules of the San Diego Yacht Club provide that an IYRU jury was to resolve protests arising out of the match, the fact that amici curiae argue that the courts should resolve the question of the propriety of San Diego's defense (see, dissenting opn, at 277–278, at 863–864 of 557 N.Y.S.2d, at 99–100 of 557 N.E.2d) is simply irrelevant.

This court may properly determine only the legal issues with which it is presented.

In this case, the dispute over the eligibility of the chosen vessels should have been governed and determined by the rules of yacht racing promulgated by the International Yacht Racing Union (IYRU) and followed by the defending San Diego Yacht Club. Pursuant to these rules, an international jury referees the match and decides all protests jointly submitted to it by the parties. The international jury established to resolve all disputes arising out of the 1988 America's Cup match was composed of five members, all IYRU-certified racing Judges of vast experience and international repute, from countries other than the United States and New Zealand. Despite Mercury Bay's repeated claims of the unfairness of San Diego's catamaran defense and notwithstanding San Diego's request that a protest be submitted to the international jury, Mercury Bay deliberately chose to keep the issue from these yachting experts, who were of course, best suited to resolve it. Having thus chosen to seek relief in a judicial forum, Mercury Bay is limited to a resolution of only the legal issues presented.

A

The legal issue we must determine is whether the donors of the America's Cup, as the settlors of the trust in which it is held, intended to exclude catamarans or otherwise restrict the defender's choice of vessel by the vessel selected by the challenger. Long-settled rules of construction preclude an attempt to divine a settlor's intention by looking first to extrinsic evidence (New York Life Ins. & Trust Co. v. Hoyt, 161 N.Y. 1, 8–10, 55 N.E. 299). Rather, the trust instrument is to be construed as written and the settlor's intention determined solely from the unambiguous language of the instrument itself (Central Union Trust Co. v. Trimble, 255 N.Y. 88, 93, 174 N.E. 72; Loch Sheldrake Assocs. v. Evans, 306 N.Y. 297, 304, 118 N.E.2d 444; Gross v. Cizauskas, 53 A.D.2d 969, 970, 385 N.Y.S.2d 832). It is only where the court determines the words of the trust instrument to be ambiguous that it may properly resort to extrinsic evidence (New York Life Ins. & Trust Co. v. Hoyt, supra; Gross v. Cizauskas, 53 A.D.2d, at 970, 385 N.Y.S.2d 832, supra; 2A Scott, Trusts § 164.1, at 253–254 [Fratcher 4th ed.]). The rationale underlying this basic rule of construction is that the words used in the instrument itself are the best evidence of the intention of the drafter of the document. Therefore, we must examine the plain language of the Deed of Gift at issue here.

Contrary to Mercury Bay's contentions, nowhere in the Deed of Gift have the donors expressed an intention to prohibit the use of multihull vessels or to require the defender of the Cup to race a vessel of the same type as the vessel to be used by the challenger. In fact, the unambiguous language of the deed is to the contrary. The deed accords a foreign yacht club "the right of sailing a match for [the America's] Cup, with a yacht or vessel propelled by sails only and constructed in the country to which the Challenging Club belongs, against any one yacht or vessel constructed in the country of the Club holding the Cup".

Given its plain and natural meaning, the phrase "any one yacht or vessel" requires the defender to defend in a single vessel of any type. If, as the dissenters argue, the term "any" was intended to mean "one", in the sense of limiting the defender to a defense in a single vessel (dissenting opn., at 286, at 868 of 557 N.Y.S.2d, at 104 of 557 N.E.2d), the term would be redundant, since the very next word in the phrase so limits the defense to "one" vessel. By limiting the defense to a single vessel, the deed ensures a "match" which will be a one-on-one competition. In this match, however, the deed expressly permits a defense by any type of yacht or vessel, and restricts the actual vessels to be used only by the length on load water-line restrictions applicable to all "competing vessels", the latter phrase again making clear the donors' intention to leave both the defender's and the challenger's choice of vessel otherwise unrestricted.

Notwithstanding the broad language of the deed, Mercury Bay argues that the donors could not have intended to permit a catamaran defense because the dimensions which the deed requires the challenger to disclose are relevant to monohull but not multihull vessels. This argument misapprehends the role of the dimensions in the competitions contemplated by the deed. Because the deed allows a challenge to be mounted upon 10 months' notice, the defender of the Cup is allowed only this short time to construct a defending vessel although the challenger has had unlimited time to mount a challenge and thus may have taken years designing and constructing its challenging vessel. By requiring the challenger to disclose certain dimensions with its 10–month notice, the deed provides the defender with notice of the vessel it will be facing and thus removes the competitive advantage which would otherwise inure to the challenger. For the same reason, the deed does not require the defender to disclose any details about its vessel until the start of the race. Thus, the challenger's disclosed dimensions, which may not be exceeded, limit only the challenging vessel, and do not restrict the defending vessel. So understood, the question of whether the dimensions themselves relate to multihull vessels is simply not relevant to the issue of whether the deed precludes a catamaran defense.

In this case, we are not presented with the issue to which Mercury Bay's arguments are relevant—whether the required dimensions preclude the use of a catamaran by a challenger because the dimensions specified do not relate to multihull vessels and therefore do not provide the defender with the disclosure mandated by the deed. While we have no occasion to address this question, we note that the applicability of the required dimensions to multihull vessels is hotly contested by the parties before us, both of whom have submitted expert evidence supporting their respective positions.

We also reject Mercury Bay's contention that the phrase "friendly competition between foreign countries" connotes a requirement that the defender race a vessel which is of the same type or even substantially similar to the challenging vessel described in the 10–month notice. Neither the words themselves nor their position in the deed warrant that construction. Although the stated purpose of the Deed of Gift is to foster "the friendly competition between foreign countries", that general phrase does not delineate any of the specific requirements of the matches to be held. Moreover, while each match is a competition, the deed permits the competitors to both construct and race the fastest vessels possible so long as they fall within the broad criteria of the deed. Thus the defender does not become a competitor only when "the first warning gun of the race goes off" (dissenting opn., at 279, at 864 of 557 N.Y.S.2d, at 100 of 557 N.E.2d); the deed makes clear that the design and construction of the yachts as well as the races, are part of the competition contemplated. Mercury Bay's suggestion, argued explicitly below and implicit here, that the vessels must be evenly matched is belied by its own assertion that the deed permits a match between a 44–foot monohull and a 90–foot monohull—two vessels which, although within the load water-line length restrictions in the deed and of the same type, cannot be said to be "evenly matched" given the much greater speed potential of the larger boat. Indeed, such a requirement that the vessels be "evenly matched" is antithetical to the consent provisions of the deed. There is no point in permitting a defender to give or withhold its consent on the terms of the matches if by simply making a challenge, the challenger could force the defender to accede to its terms. As the Appellate Division majority noted, the donors, who chose to be specific about other aspects of the match, including the load water-line lengths of the competing vessels, could have easily included an express requirement that the vessels be evenly matched but did not do so.

In our view, the phrase "friendly competition between foreign countries" more aptly refers to the spirit of cooperation underlying the competitions contemplated by the deed. The matches were to be between yacht clubs of different countries, and the deed contemplated that they would cooperate as to the details of the matches to be held. It was in this spirit of cooperation that the competitors had, since 1958, agreed to race in 44–foot yachts. Indeed, it was Mercury Bay, not San Diego, that departed the agreed-upon conditions of the previous 30 years. San Diego responded to Mercury Bay's competitive strategy by availing itself of the competitive opportunity afforded by the broad specifications in the deed.

Accordingly, we conclude that the unambiguous language of the Deed of Gift, permitting the defending club to defend the Cup in "any one yacht or vessel" within the specified range of load water-line length, does not require the defender to race a vessel of the same type or "evenly matched" to that of the challenger and does not preclude the defender's use of a catamaran. Because the deed provisions on these issues are unambiguous, we may not look beyond the four corners of the deed in ascertaining the donors' intent and therefore may not consider any extrinsic evidence on the meaning of these provisions. Consequently, we reject the analysis of the dissent, which repeatedly resorts to extrinsic evidence to support its construction of the terms of the deed (dissenting opn., at 281–283, 285–286, 287–288, at 865–867, 868–869, 870 of 557 N.Y.S.2d, at 101–103, 104–105, 106 of 557 N.E.2d). Indeed because the plain language of the Deed of Gift is unambiguous, such resort to extrinsic evidence to impute a different meaning to the terms expressed is improper (Central Union Trust Co. v. Trimble, 255 N.Y., at 93, 174 N.E. 72, supra).

B

We also reject Mercury Bay's contention that notwithstanding the plain language of the Deed of Gift, San Diego breached its fiduciary duty as the trustee of the America's Cup. We have described a fiduciary's duty as requiring "[n]ot honesty alone, but the punctilio of an honor the most sensitive" (Meinhard v. Salmon, 249 N.Y. 458, 464, 164 N.E. 545; see also, 2A Scott, Trusts § 170, at 311 [Fratcher 4th ed.]; Restatement [Second] of Trusts § 170). This strict standard is the usual and appropriate measure of a trustee's fiduciary obligations because the trustee must administer the trust for the benefit of the beneficiaries and cannot compete with the beneficiaries for the benefits of the trust corpus (2A Scott, Trusts § 170 [Fratcher 4th ed.]; Restatement [Second] of Trusts § 170). Thus, the trustee owes the beneficiary an undivided duty of loyalty and cannot, for example, take the economic benefit of a trust (see, e.g., Matter of Scarborough Props. Corp., 25 N.Y.2d 553, 558, 307 N.Y.S.2d 641, 255 N.E.2d 761).

Unlike the trusts in which this strict rule of undivided loyalty was developed, the America's Cup trust promotes a sporting competition in which the donors clearly intended that the trustee compete on equal terms with the trust beneficiaries. Indeed, the trustee of the America's Cup is obligated to use its best efforts to defend its right to hold the Cup and thus to defeat the beneficiaries in the contemplated competition. It is thus inappropriate and inconsistent with the competitive trust purpose to impose upon the trustee of a sporting trust such as this one the strict standard of behavior which governs the conduct of trustees who are obligated not to compete with the trust beneficiaries.

To be sure, the trustee of the America's Cup is obligated to act in good faith and in the spirit of friendly competition by reasonably attempting to reach an accord on the terms of the matches to be held. Where that is not possible, however, the specific terms of the deed govern and the trustee must use its best efforts to compete for the Cup within the specified terms. As we have discussed, by racing a vessel which met the load water-line specifications in the Deed of Gift and which was constructed in its country, San Diego fully complied with the terms and spirit of the trust instrument. The deed placed no other restraints on the defending club's efforts to win the competition, even though the defending club was also designated the trustee. Thus there can be no argument that the trustee was obligated to construe the deed in a way contrary to its plain language. We conclude that in the context of this sporting trust, San Diego fulfilled its fiduciary obligations by reasonably trying to come to an agreement on the terms for Mercury Bay's proposed match, and failing that, by faithfully adhering to the challenge provisions in the deed.

We reject Mercury Bay's contention that San Diego was required to race a vessel of the same type as its challenging vessel because it was only in that way that San Diego could administer the trust so as to give Mercury Bay, a trust beneficiary, a "fair" competition. This amounts simply to an argument that San Diego's conduct was "unsportsmanlike" and "unfair", issues which, as we have discussed, the Deed of Gift appropriately leaves to yachting experts.

We conclude therefore that in racing a catamaran, San Diego complied with the terms of the Deed of Gift and did not violate any fiduciary obligation owed under those terms or in the administration of the trust. Any question as to sportsmanship and fairness, such as the propriety of races between monohull and multihull vessels, are questions which the trust instrument appropriately leaves to the expertise of persons actively involved in yacht racing; they are not questions suitable for judicial resolution.

Accordingly, the order of the Appellate Division should be affirmed, with costs.

[The concurring opinion of Chief Judge Wachtler and the dissenting opinion of Judge Hancock are omitted.]

MARTIN v. PGA TOUR, INC.

994 F.Supp. 1242 (D.Or.1998).

COFFIN, United States Magistrate Judge.

This case presents profound questions regarding the application of the Americans with Disabilities Act (ADA). Does the ADA apply to athletic events or sports organizations? If so, are the most elite events and organizations, such as those at the professional level, somehow exempt from coverage? If the ADA is applicable, may a rule of competition be modified to accommodate a disabled competitor, or are the rules untouchable because any alteration of any rule would fundamentally alter the nature of the competitions?

Casey Martin is a disabled professional golfer. He can do everything well in the game of golf except walk to and from his shots. Because of a congenital deformity, his right leg is severely atrophied and weakened. He is placed at significant risk of fracturing his tibia by the simple act of walking, because of the increasing loss of bone stock and weakening of this bone that has occurred over the lifetime of this disorder. According to the medical testimony, walking also places Martin at significant risk of hemorrhaging as well, and creates an increased chance of developing deep venous thrombosis (blood clots).

The condition plaintiff suffers from causes him severe pain and discomfort. The slightest touching of his right leg at or below the knee is extremely painful. Beyond this, the condition causes him pain while playing golf, pain while carrying on daily activities and pain even while he is at rest.

A video of plaintiff's condition introduced into evidence at the trial, provides compelling evidence of the nature and extent of his disability: The right leg appears to be about half the size of plaintiff's left leg. When plaintiff removes his double set of support stockings and stands upright, the leg immediately discolors and swells in size because the circulatory condition with which he is afflicted prevents the blood from flowing through his veins back to the heart. Instead, gravity, combined with "incompetent" valves which fail to close properly, pulls the blood back down his leg. The leg becomes engorged in blood because the arteries pump blood to his leg but the veins fail to circulate blood back to the heart. To relieve this situation, plaintiff must lie down and elevate the leg.

A double set of support or compression stockings provides plaintiff with enough venous pressure to allow him to remain upright for periods of time. As he has gotten older (he is now 25 years of age), his leg has steadily worsened because of his disability. Whereas he used to be able to walk a golf course (albeit with difficulty), he can no longer do so. As noted, he is at substantial risk of serious physical harm by the mere act of walking.

Dr. Donald Jones, plaintiff's treating physician, counsels that it is medically necessary for Casey Martin to be permitted a cart if he is to play the game of golf. As he summarized plaintiff's condition:

> [T]he medical records reflect a 25–year-old male with a rare congenital vascular malformation of the right lower extremity which has led to, number one, chronic pain secondary to vascular engorgement and progressive loss of bone stock, pain so severe that he has at least considered to explore the use of time contingent narcotics; number two, a documented sleep disorder secondary to chronic pain which leads, according to Dr. Holmes, to an exhaustion syndrome; number three, the need to wear two compression stockings at all times; number four, it has resulted in marked muscular atrophy and weakness in his right calf; number five, it has affected his knee through multiple intra-articular bleeds, causing abnormalities which are painful; and number six, and most important from the orthopedic aspect, it has resulted in a weakened tibia which is at risk for fracture and potential limb loss and/or serious post-fracture complications.

Transcript at pp. 99–100.

Defendant PGA Tour does not contest that plaintiff has a disability within the meaning of the ADA, nor does it contest that his disability prevents him from walking the course during a round of golf. However, prior to this trial, defendant did not review plaintiff's medical records nor view the videotaped presentation of his condition. The PGA's position in this case has been twofold:

> First, it asserts that the ADA does not apply to its professional golf tournaments; and
>
> Second, the PGA asserts that the requirement of walking is a substantive rule of its competition and that a waiver of the rule would, accordingly, result in a fundamental alteration of its competitions, which the ADA does not require.

The first defense raised by the PGA—that the ADA is inapplicable to its tournaments—has been extensively discussed in this court's order dated January 30, 1998 (#69), wherein I found that the PGA Tour was not exempt, as a "private club," from ADA coverage and also found that its tournaments were conducted at places—i.e., golf courses—that were specifically included within the definition of places of "public accommodation" subject to the ADA.

The second defense encompasses the concept that the ADA does not require a covered entity to work a fundamental alteration of the nature of its business or programs in order to accommodate the disabled, nor need the entity accommodate if to do so would result in an undue hardship to the entity.

A few examples suffice to illustrate this point: Suppose a bookstore normally does not stock books in braille. A blind customer demands the accommodation of a supply of such books. The bookstore need not comply with the request, as such an accommodation would fundamentally alter the nature of its business. See 28 C.F.R. Ch. 1 Pt. 36, App. B at p. 632 (July 1, 1997 edition). Or, to use another example cited by the PGA, a day care center normally does not provide individualized care (i.e., one attendant for each child) to its customers. A disabled child, in need of individualized attention, requests such an accommodation. The day care center need not comply because such would fundamentally alter the nature of the service the center provides.

There are few reported cases wherein the ADA has been applied to sports programs:

The Sixth Circuit Court of Appeals applied the ADA to the Michigan High School Athletic Association on two separate occasions regarding eligibility requirements. In McPherson v. MHSAA, 119 F.3d 453 (6th Cir.1997) the court considered whether the MHSAA's eight semester rule—which provided that any student who has completed eight semesters of high school is ineligible for interscholastic sports competition—violated the ADA when applied to a student with a learning disability which prevented him from completing high school in eight semesters. The court initially noted that the simple fact that the MHSAA labeled the rule necessary did not make it so, but that the court had an independent responsibility to determine whether the rule is in fact necessary. Id. at 461. The court determined the rule—[which was intended] to limit the level of athletic experience and range of skills of the players in order to create a more even playing field for the competitors, to limit the size and physical maturity of high school athletes for the safety of all participants, and to afford the players who observe the rule a fair opportunity to compete for playing time—was necessary. The court then found that requiring the MHSAA to waive the rule would work a fundamental alteration in its sports programs and would impose an immense financial and administrative burden on the MHSAA by forcing it to make "near impossible determinations" about a particular student's physical and athletic maturity.

Two years prior the court similarly found that waiver of an age regulation in high school sports fundamentally altered the program. See

Sandison v. MHSAA, 64 F.3d 1026 (6th Cir.1995). The court noted, as it did in McPherson, that individually determining whether each older student possessed an unfair competitive advantage was not a reasonable accommodation. Id. at 1037.

The Eighth Circuit was confronted with a similar age eligibility rule of the Missouri State High School Athletic Association. See Pottgen v. MSHSAA, 40 F.3d 926 (8th Cir.1994). In Pottgen the court found that the age requirement was essential to the high school athletic program and that an individualized inquiry into the necessity of the requirement in the plaintiff's case was inappropriate. Id. at 930.

The District Court for the District of New Jersey found that complete abandonment of the "core course" requirement would fundamentally alter the nature of NCAA athletic programs. Bowers v. National Collegiate Athletic Assoc., 974 F.Supp. 459 (D.N.J.1997). The Bowers court found the "core course" requirement essential because it was reasonably necessary to accomplish the purpose of the NCAA program. However, the court also noted that the rule authorized waiver of the requirement on a case-by-case basis for individualized consideration and as such was adequate to reasonably accommodate students with learning disabilities. Id. at 467.

From this rather limited background of athletic ADA case law, the PGA asserts that the court should focus on whether an athletic rule is "substantive"—i.e., a rule which defines who is eligible to compete or a rule which governs how the game is played. If it is, according to the PGA's argument, the rule cannot be modified without working a fundamental alteration of the competition, and the ADA consequently does not require any modification to accommodate the disabled.

I note, however, that even in those cases most heavily relied upon by the PGA the courts examined the purpose of each of the rules in question to determine if the requested modification was reasonable.

In Sandison and McPherson, the eligibility requirements imposed were closely fitted with the purpose of high school athletics—to allow students of the same age group to compete against each other. The learning-disabled plaintiffs who had passed beyond the age or semester limits while still remaining in high school could not compete without fundamentally altering the nature of the services at issue. That the plaintiffs in those cases may have been less skilled athletes than their peers missed the point. High school athletics are for youths of a certain age group (14–18). Eliminating the curriculum or age-eligibility requirements for high school athletes clearly changes the fundamental nature of such competition.

Similarly, in Bowers, the issue was the "core course" requirement for student-athletes at the collegiate level. An athlete had to be a qualified student to compete. A complete waiver of the academic requirement would obviously alter the fundamental nature of the program, and, as noted, individual assessments and exemptions were permitted.

That is not to say that athletic associations have unfettered discretion to set eligibility requirements as they see fit. May a high school athletic association expressly define eligibility requirements so as to exclude the learning or other disabled? If it did, would the courts simply be left to conclude that any change in such a rule would fundamentally alter the rules of competition and by virtue of such be unreasonable? For example, may a high school league promulgate a rule prohibiting competitors from using corrective lenses to assist their vision at athletic events—and be immune from ADA scrutiny because an accommodation to the sight-impaired would fundamentally alter a rule of competition?

Essentially, then, the PGA Tour's contention that it alone may set the rules of competition, and that any modification of any of its rules (which may be necessary to accommodate the disabled) fundamentally alters the nature of PGA tournaments, is simply another version of its argument that the PGA Tour is exempt from the provisions of the ADA. It is not. The court has the independent duty to inquire into the purpose of the rule at issue, and to ascertain whether there can be a reasonable modification made to accommodate plaintiff without frustrating the purpose of the rule, and without altering the fundamental nature of PGA Tour competition.

Although the PGA Tour is a professional sports organization and professional sports enjoy a much higher profile and display of skills than collegiate or other lower levels of competitive sports, the analysis of the issues does not change from one level to the next. High school athletic associations have just as much interest in the equal application of their rules and the integrity of their games as do professionals. Put differently, if it is unreasonable to accommodate Casey Martin's disability with a cart at the PGA Tour level because of its rules of competition, it is equally unreasonable to so accommodate a similarly disabled golfer at the high school level if the same rules were applicable.

It is also worth noting that the ADA does not distinguish between sports organizations and other entities when it comes to applying the ADA to a specific situation. Businesses and schools have rules governing their operations which are of equal importance (in their sphere) as the rules of sporting events. Conversely, the disabled have just as much interest in being free from discrimination in the athletic world as they do in other aspects of everyday life. The key questions are the same: does the ADA apply, and may a reasonable modification be made to accommodate a disabled individual?

An example from a prior case filing (see Civil Number 93–6068–TC) illustrates the tension that exists between the disabled seeking equal access and an entity that must modify its rules or practices to accommodate: A man afflicted with cerebral palsy books an international flight on a commercial airline from Oregon to Germany. The first leg of the flight takes the disabled individual from Eugene, Oregon to Chicago, Illinois, where he changes planes for the next leg of the trip. The captain of the airlines for the international leg, however, decides that the individual's condition (which hasn't changed since the first flight) renders him unfit to travel safely, and so he orders him off the plane. This unfortunate person's journey is interrupted solely because of his disability, and he is relegated to languish in a hotel room (away from his home and away from his destination) until a captain can be found who is willing to admit him as a passenger.

The rule at stake in the above example is the age-old rule that the captain is in charge of the ship. This rule has an obvious and important substantive purpose. Nonetheless, are the disabled not entitled to travel to their destinations with the same degree of reliance on their arrangements as the able-bodied? Put differently, doesn't the ADA (or its counterpart, the Rehabilitation Act) require the airlines to modify the rule to provide a reasonable accommodation—i.e., a flight there and back without interruption by an uncomfortable captain—under the specific circumstances of his case, even though such might modify a substantive rule of its operation?

It is with these concepts in mind that I approach Casey Martin's request for an accommodation.

First, I set forth (and perhaps restate to some extent), a general overview of the ADA. As I reject (without detailed elaboration) plaintiff's claims that he is a PGA Tour employee and that the Nike Tour is a "course or examination" under the Act, I will discuss only his remaining claim, i.e., the "public accommodation claim" under Title III of the Act.

Title III of the ADA provides:

> No individual shall be discriminated against on the basis of disability in the full and equal enjoyment of the goods, services, facilities, privileges, advantages, or accommodations of any place of public accommodation....
>
> [D]iscrimination includes failure to make reasonable modifications in policies, practices, or procedures, when such modifications are necessary to afford such goods, services, facilities, privileges, advantages, or accommodations to individuals with disabilities, unless the entity can demonstrate that making such modifications would fundamentally alter the nature of the good, service, facility, privilege, advantage, or accommodation being offered or would result in an undue burden....
>
> [D]iscrimination also includes the imposition or application of eligibility criteria that screen out or tend to screen out an individual with a disability or any class of individuals with disabilities from fully and equally enjoying any goods, services, facilities, privileges, advantages or accommodations, unless such criteria can be shown to be necessary for the provision of the goods, services, facilities, privileges, advantages, or accommodations being offered.

42 U.S.C. §§ 12182(a), 12182(b)(2)(A)(i) and (ii).

The ADA was enacted by Congress in 1990 "to provide a clear and comprehensive national mandate for the elimination of discrimination against individuals with disabilities." Congress found that "individuals with disabilities continually encounter various forms of discrimination, including ... failure to make modifications to existing facilities and practices...." Congress intended to protect disabled persons not just from intentional discrimination but also from "thoughtlessness," "indifference," and "benign neglect." See Crowder v. Kitagawa, 81 F.3d 1480, 1483–1484 (9th Cir.1996).

The ADA defines disability with respect to an individual as:

> (A) a physical or mental impairment that substantially limits one or more of the major life activities of such individual;
>
> (B) a record of such impairment; or
>
> (C) being regarded as having such an impairment.

42 U.S.C. § 12102(2). The phrase physical or mental impairment means:

> (i) Any physiological disorder or condition, cosmetic disfigurement, or anatomical loss affecting one or more of the following body systems: neurological; musculoskeletal; special sense organs; respiratory, including speech organs; cardiovascular; reproductive; digestive; genitourinary; hemic and lymphatic; skin; and endocrine; or
>
> (ii) Any mental or psychological disorder such as mental retardation, organic brain syndrome, emotional or mental illness, and specific learning disabilities.

28 C.F.R. § 36.104(1). The phrase major life activity means:

> functions such as caring for oneself, performing manual tasks, walking, seeing, hearing, speaking, breathing, learning, and working.

28 C.F.R. § 36.104(2). The following factors should be considered in determining whether an individual is substantially limited in a major life activity:

> 1. the nature and severity of the impairment;
>
> 2. the duration or expected duration of the impairment; and
>
> 3. the permanent or long term impact, or the expected permanent or long term impact of or resulting from the impairment.

29 C.F.R. § 1630.2(j)(2).

Temporary, non-chronic impairments of short duration, with little or no long term or permanent impact, are usually not disabilities. Such impairments may include, but are not limited to, broken limbs, sprained joints, concussions, etc. Sanders v. Arneson Products, 91 F.3d 1351, 1354 (9th Cir.1996). Temporary injury with minimal residual effects cannot be the basis for a sustainable claim under the ADA. Id.

Plaintiff has the burden of demonstrating that he is disabled and has done so. Plaintiff also has the burden of proving that a modification was requested and that the requested modification is reasonable. "Plaintiff meets this burden by introducing evidence that the requested modification is reasonable in the general sense, that is, in the general run of the cases." Johnson v. Gambrinus Co., 116 F.3d 1052, 1059 (5th Cir. 1997). With respect to this element, the use of a cart is certainly not unreasonable in the game of golf. As noted hereafter, the Rules of Golf do not require walking, and even the PGA Tour permits cart use at two of the four types of tournaments it stages. While the PGA Tour permits cart use at those two events, it imposes no handicap system or stroke penalties on those who opt for carts as opposed to those who elect to walk. This is certainly compelling evidence that even the PGA Tour does not consider walking to be a significant contributor to the skill of shotmaking. In addition, the NCAA and PAC 10 athletic conference permit the use of carts as an accommodation to disabled collegiate golfers. Under the Johnson analysis such evidence meets plaintiff's burden of demonstrating that a cart is a reasonable modification to accommodate his disability in the game of golf in the general sense, that is in the general run of cases.

The PGA Tour stages the PGA Tour, senior PGA Tour, the Nike Tour, and the Qualifying School Tournament. The Senior Tour is for PGA Tour golfers of 50+ years in age. The Qualifying School Tournament screens those who are competing for entry into the PGA Tour and Nike Tour. The PGA Tour admits the most skilled golfers; the Nike Tour admits those at the next highest level. The PGA Tour allows cart use on the Senior PGA Tour and in the two preliminary rounds of the Qualifying School Tournament.

Defendant then must make the requested modification unless it meets its burden of proving that the requested modification would fundamentally alter the nature of its public accommodation. "The type of evidence that satisfies this burden focuses on the specifics of the plaintiff's or defendant's circumstances and not on the general nature of the accommodation." Id. Defendant argues that an individualized inquiry into the necessity of the walking rule in Casey Martin's case is not appropriate. See, e.g., Pottgen, 40 F.3d at 930–31. However, Johnson suggests otherwise. An individualized assessment finds support in the Ninth Circuit as well. See Crowder, 81 F.3d at 1486 ("the determination of what constitutes reasonable modification is highly fact-specific, requiring case-by-case inquiry"). See also Stillwell v. Kansas City, Missouri Bd. of Police Commissioners, 872 F.Supp. 682, 687 (W.D.Mo.1995) (individualized assessment necessary to determine if plaintiff can meet the purpose of defendant's rule). Thus, the ultimate question in this case is whether allowing plaintiff, given his individual circumstances, the requested modification would fundamentally alter PGA and Nike Tour golf competitions.

THE RULES OF GOLF

The general "Rules of Golf" are promulgated by the United States Golf Association (USGA) and the Royal and Ancient Golf Club of St. Andrews, Scotland (R & A).

Rule 1–1 provides as follows:

> The Game of Golf consists in playing a ball from the teeing ground into the hole by a stroke or successive strokes in accordance with the rules.

Nothing in the Rules of Golf requires or defines walking as part of the game. In its reported Decisions on the Rules of Golf regarding the Rules of Golf, the USGA has expressed that it is permissible to ride a cart in golf unless such is prohibited by the local rules defining the conditions of competition for particular events. In Appendix I to the Rules of Golf we find:

Transportation

> If it is desired to require players to walk in a competition, the following condition is suggested:
>
> Players shall walk at all times during a stipulated round.

The PGA Tour promulgates a pamphlet entitled "Conditions of Competition and Local Rules" which govern PGA Tour and Nike Tour tournaments. The preamble to this document provides, in pertinent part, as follows:

> The Rules of the United States Golf Association govern play, as modified by the PGA Tour.

One of those modifications appears in Section A—Conditions of Competition:

> p 6 Transportation—Appendix I
>
> Players shall walk at all times during a stipulated round unless permitted to ride by the PGA Tour Rules Committee.

No written policy has been cited by either party which governs the Rules Committee in its exercise of discretion regarding a waiver of the walking requirement. On the occasions when the walking rule has been waived, it has been waived for all competitors (e.g., to shuttle players from the 9th green to the 10th tee where considerable distance is involved). No waiver has ever been granted for individualized circumstances (such as disability).

Prior to requesting use of a cart as an accommodation for his disability, plaintiff explored the possibility of various artificial aids to walking. I allow Dr. Jones to describe what those were, and why they won't work:

> By August 1996 at the age of 24, Casey reported to me that he was having tremendous difficulty with ambulation. He was having great difficulty walking 18 holes of golf. He was not only having trouble with the golf, but was also now having signifi-

cant discomfort with the requirements of daily living. At this point I immobilized his leg in a removable brace and started a physical therapy program. Neither was beneficial.

By now Casey was becoming extremely frustrated, so I decided to accompany him during a number of rounds during the summer of 1996.

Q. You are talking about rounds of golf?

A. Rounds of golf.

Q. Okay.

A. In hopes that I could observe some characteristics of his gait that would allow me to provide him with some form of stabilizing device. During this time, we tried in-shoe orthosis; that is, shoe inserts, which were of minimal benefit.

Q. What were they intended to do?

A. They will stabilize the hindfoot, and there's a biomechanical region whereas if you stabilize the hindfoot, the tibia doesn't rotate with the gait and will hopefully decrease the pain.

Q. The right leg is slightly longer also?

A. Yes.

Q. Okay. And that right leg being longer, is due to this condition?

A. Yes.

Q. Okay. All right. What was next?

A. We also placed him into ankle-foot orthosis. Now, that's a plastic brace that extended from the toes to the mid-calf and is for the purpose of stabilizing his hindfoot and, also, protecting his tibia. Casey found that it was virtually impossible to golf in this device because it limited his hindfoot motion as well as the fact that it caused considerable discomfort over his calf which is very sensitive. It was during this time that I became increasingly concerned about the well being of Casey's lower extremity. I can recall playing two rounds of Golf with Casey where he was unable to finish the 18 holes while walking. I also recall this summer one round of golf where we used a golf cart. The ground was moderately wet and unstable. We could not park as close to the tee box or to the green as we normally would. As a result, Casey had to stop his round at about the 14th hole because he was having difficulty just getting to the tee box and green.

Transcript at pp. 88–90.

Thus, Casey Martin cannot walk the course, and only a cart will permit him to compete on the Nike Tour. As with the disabled airline passenger, he finds himself in conflict with a substantive rule of operation.

According to the PGA Tour, the purpose of the walking rule is to inject the element of fatigue into the skill of shot-making. I accept that assertion and expressly find from the evidence produced at trial that such is a cognizable purpose of the rule from the standpoint of the ADA.

The question thus is—may the walking rule be modified to accommodate Casey Martin without fundamentally altering the nature of the game being played at the PGA Tour's tournaments?

In answering the question, as noted previously, I reject the defendant's contention that the plaintiff's individual circumstances are irrelevant to the inquiry. See Johnson, Crowder, Stillwell, cited supra p. 1249.

Furthermore, the fatigue factor injected into the game of golf by walking the course cannot be deemed significant under normal circumstances. Dr. Gary Klug, a professor in physiology at the University of Oregon, and an expert on the physiological basis for fatigue, calculates that approximately 500 calories are expended in walking a course of golf (approximately 5 miles of walking in a 5 hour time period). He describes the energy expenditure as follows: "nutritionally it's less than a Big Mac." He further notes that these calories are expended over a 5 hour period, and that the golfers have numerous intervals of rest and opportunities for refreshment (or calorie replacement).

While the PGA Tour cited Ken Venturi's memorable 1964 U.S. Open win in which he overcame severe and near-fatal exhaustion as he finished the course in high heat and humidity, Dr. Klug indicates that Mr. Venturi's fatigue was induced by heat exhaustion and fluid loss—not walking. According to Dr. Klug, tests have disclosed that fatigue from exercise—as measured by oxygen consumption—is not significantly influenced by heat or humidity. Rather, dehydration is the critical factor in such situations. Many spectators at the 1964 U.S. Open had to be treated for exhaustion as well, and they were not walking.

Furthermore, fatigue at lower intensity exercise is primarily a psychological phenomenon, according to Dr. Klug. Stress and motivation are the key ingredients here. Place an individual in the middle of the Los Angeles freeway at rush hour, and he will get fatigued in a hurry without moving a muscle. If someone pedals a bicycle for 30 minutes and says "I've had it," but is promised $1,000 if he goes another 5 minutes, his fatigue may well disappear.

Every individual differs in psychological fatigue components, but walking has little to do with such components. If anything, from the evidence introduced at trial, most PGA Tour golfers appear to prefer walking as a way of dealing with the psychological factors of fatigue. When given the option of cart-riding or walking—such as at the Senior PGA Tour or PGA Tour Qualifying Tournament—the vast majority have opted to walk. Why would this be if walking truly fatigued them so that they hit worse shots than if they ride? As the saying goes, "the proof of the pudding is in the eating."

And then we come to Casey Martin's unique circumstances. If the majority of able-bodied elect to walk in "carts optional" tournaments, how can anyone perceive that plaintiff has a competitive advantage by using a cart given his condition?

The fatigue plaintiff endures just from coping with his disability is undeniably greater than the fatigue injected into tournament play on the able-bodied by the requirement that they walk from shot to shot. Walking at a slow pace—to the able-bodied—is a natural act, of little more difficulty than breathing. It is how we were designed to move from place to place.

Walking for Casey Martin is a different story.

In the first place, he does walk while on the course—even with a cart, he must move from cart to shot and back to the cart. In essence, he still must walk approximately 25% of the course. On a course roughly five miles in length, Martin will walk 1 1/4 miles.

The plaintiff is in significant pain when he walks, and even when he is getting in and out of the cart. With each step, he is at a risk of fracturing his tibia and hemorrhaging. The other golfers have to endure the psychological stress of competition as part of their fatigue; Martin has the same stress plus the added stress of pain and risk of serious injury. As he put it, he would gladly trade the cart for a good leg. To perceive that the cart puts him—with his condition—at a competitive advantage is a gross distortion of reality.

As plaintiff easily endures greater fatigue even with a cart than his able-bodied competitors do by walking, it does not fundamentally alter the nature of the PGA Tour's game to accommodate him with a cart.

It lends emphasis to the point that the walking rule may be modified without fundamentally altering the PGA's game to consider several other PGA rules in a hypothetical context.

Rule 6–4 of the Rules of Golf specifies:

Caddie

The player may have only one caddie at any one time, under penalty of disqualification.

Rule 8 provides:

Advice; Indicating Line of Play Definitions

"Advice" is any counsel or suggestion which could influence a player in determining his play, the choice of a club or the method of making a stroke.

Information on the Rules or on matters of public information, such as the position of hazards or the flagstick on the putting green, is not advice.

The "line of play" is the direction which the player wishes his ball to take after a stroke, plus a reasonable distance on either side of the intended direction. The line of play extends

> vertically upwards from the ground, but does not extend beyond the hole.
>
> And Rule 8–1 states:
>
> Advice
>
> During a stipulated round, a player shall not give advice to anyone in the competition except his partner. A player may ask for advice during a stipulated round from only his partner or either of their caddies.

May these be modified to accommodate a disabled golfer—e.g., a blind golfer?

Interestingly, the USGA promulgates a pamphlet entitled A Modification of the Rules of Golf for Golfers with Disabilities. The Preface to the Pamphlet reads:

> This publication contains permissible modifications to the Rules of Golf for use by disabled golfers. This is not intended to be a revision of the Rules of Golf as they apply to able-bodied players. As is the case for the Rules of Golf themselves, these modifications, along with the philosophy expressed herein, have been agreed upon by the United States Golf Association and the Royal and Ancient Golf Club of St. Andrews, Scotland.
>
> Under the category of Blind Golfers, the pamphlet provides:
>
> Definition of "Coach"
>
> The status of the coach and the duties which he may perform should be defined clearly. Without such clarification, it would be difficult, for example, to determine how a blind golfer must proceed if his ball were to strike his or another player's coach after a stroke. Therefore, the following definition is recommended:
>
> Coach
>
> A "coach" is one who assists a blind golfer in addressing the ball and with the alignment prior to the stroke. A coach has the same status under the rules as a caddie.
>
> Note: A player may ask for and receive advice from his coach.
>
> And the Caddie and Advice rules are modified as follows:
>
> Rule 6–4 (Caddie)
>
> There is nothing in the rules which would prohibit the coach of a blind golfer from functioning as his caddie. For a variety of reasons, however, a coach may not be able to perform the duties of a caddie. Therefore, it is permissible for a blind golfer to have both a coach and a caddie. In such circumstances, however, the coach may not carry or handle the player's clubs except in helping the player take his stance or as permitted by analogy to Decision 6–4/4.5. Otherwise, the player would be subject to disqualification for having more than one caddie.

> Rule 8–1 (Advice)
>
> In view of the Definition of "Coach," it is recommended that Rule 8–1 be modified as follows:
>
> 8–1. Advice
>
> During a stipulated round, a player shall not give advice to anyone in the competition except his partner. A player may ask for advice during a stipulated round from only his partner, either of their caddies or, if applicable, their coaches.

Judy Bell, a former president of the USGA, testified that the Golfers with Disabilities pamphlet was not meant for the PGA Tour, but only for recreational golfers. While that may be, it begs the question of how the PGA Tour would handle the request of a blind pro golfer to have a coach in addition to a caddie. At oral argument, the attorney for the Tour was asked whether Rules 6–4 and 8–1 could be modified without fundamentally altering the nature of the PGA's competition. To quote from the colloquy:

> THE COURT: How about the caddie and the coach for the blind golfer, as the pamphlet describes?
>
> MR. MALEDON: Your Honor, my answer would be the same. As long as it does not fundamentally alter the nature of the competition, there's not a problem with it. But again, Your Honor, you'd have [to] know the facts. You'd have to look at the purpose for the rule. And I submit to you, Your Honor, that engaging in those kinds of analogies do not advance the ball in terms of what we are talking about here.
>
> THE COURT: If I look at whether the purpose of the walking rule is to enhance competition by injecting fatigue into the equation, do I look at what Mr. Martin's disability does to him specifically insofar as inducing fatigue?
>
> MR. MALEDON: No, Your Honor. Absolutely not.

The paradox presented in the PGA Tour's position is readily apparent. A modification of the "one caddie only" rule to accommodate a blind golfer by providing him with a coach does not become the "reasonable" thing to do unless the PGA first conducts an individualized assessment of the golfer's disability—i.e., the PGA Tour must first recognize that he is blind, and then consider whether providing him a coach under his circumstances would give him a competitive advantage over the other golfers who aren't blind and thus don't need a coach. Yet in Casey Martin's situation, the PGA Tour adamantly refuses to assess the requested modification in light of the specifics of his disability. Inconsistently, it insists in this case that any modification of any of its rules would fundamentally alter the nature of its competition.

The rules, as demonstrated, are not so sacrosanct. The requested accommodation of a cart is eminently reasonable in light of Casey Martin's disability.

Notes

1. The most famous equipment dispute in recent times occurred in July 1983 at Yankee Stadium. With the New York Yankees leading the Kansas City Royals 4–3 in the top of the ninth, future Hall of Famer George Brett hit a two-out, two-run home run. After a protest by Yankees manager Billy Martin, however, home plate umpire Tim McClelland nullified the home run and called Brett out because his bat had too much pine tar on it. In response, the Royals filed a complaint with AL President Lee MacPhail, who ruled the bat legal. When the game was resumed three weeks later, the Royals won 5–4. *See further* Jared T. Finkelstein, Comment, *In re Brett: The Sticky Problem of Statutory Construction*, 52 Fordham L. Rev. 430 (1983).

2. Sometimes, players use patently illegal equipment—such as corked bats, doctored balls, and oversized pads—to gain an unfair advantage. For a look at the various techniques employed by dishonest athletes, see, e.g., *Collins v. State of New York*, 617 N.Y.S.2d 1010 (Ct.Cl.1994), *aff'd*, 637 N.Y.S.2d 714 (App.Div.1996) (padding removed from boxing gloves to make them more lethal); *Cheating in Other Sports?*, Boston Globe, Apr. 17, 1998, at C7 (detailing incidents in baseball, bobsledding, boxing, fencing, golf, hockey, and running); Chris Cobbs, *Belle Broke First Rule of Cheating: Don't Get Caught*, Phoenix Gazette, July 20, 1994, at D1 (suggesting equipment tampering occurs in all sports).

3. Athletes are not the only ones affected by equipment rules. Over the years, numerous lawsuits have been filed by manufacturers of non-sanctioned products. In August 1998, for example, Easton Sports, Inc. brought a $267 million action against the NCAA to prevent its inventory from being rendered obsolete by rule changes requiring aluminum bats to be less powerful. *See* Ed Guzman, *Coming Changes to Aluminum Bats Alarm a Maker*, N.Y. Times, Aug. 8, 1998, at B16. For other such disputes, see *Gilder v. PGA Tour, Inc.*, 936 F.2d 417 (9th Cir.1991) (golf clubs); *M & H Tire Co. v. Hoosier Racing Tire Corp.*, 733 F.2d 973 (1st Cir.1984) (racing tires); *Gunter Harz Sports v. U.S. Tennis Ass'n, Inc.*, 665 F.2d 222 (8th Cir.1981) (tennis rackets); *Weight-Rite Golf Corp. v. U.S. Golf Ass'n*, 766 F.Supp. 1104 (M.D.Fla.1991), *aff'd mem.*, 953 F.2d 651 (11th Cir.1992) (golf shoes); *Eureka Urethane, Inc. v. PBA, Inc.*, 746 F.Supp. 915 (E.D.Mo.1990), *aff'd*, 935 F.2d 990 (8th Cir.1991) (bowling balls).

Problem 26

A group of orthodox Jewish basketball players sought permission to keep their yarmulkes on during games. When their request was turned down, they filed a religious discrimination lawsuit against the league. How should the court rule? *See Menora v. Illinois High School Ass'n*, 683 F.2d 1030 (7th Cir.1982), *cert. denied*, 459 U.S. 1156 (1983).

2. INJURIES

While certain injuries are an unavoidable part of the game, others occur only when an opposing player engages in conduct not sanctioned by the rules.

McKICHAN v. ST. LOUIS HOCKEY CLUB, L.P.

967 S.W.2d 209 (Mo.Ct.App.1998).

GRIMM, Presiding Judge.

In this personal injury case, plaintiff, a professional hockey goaltender, was injured during a game. He sued the opposing player (defendant player) who charged into him. In addition, he sued the defendant player's "owner," defendant herein.

Defendant player filed a counterclaim. About three weeks before trial, plaintiff and defendant player dismissed their claims against each other with prejudice. The case proceeded against defendant under a vicarious liability theory and a jury awarded plaintiff $175,000.

Both parties appeal. Defendant raises six points; its second point controls. In that point, defendant alleges the trial court erred in finding it vicariously liable for defendant player's acts because the conduct at issue was a risk inherent in professional hockey and one assumed by plaintiff. We agree and reverse. Plaintiff's cross-appeal claiming the trial court erred in granting defendant's motion for directed verdict on his punitive damages claim is denied as moot.

Background

In 1988, plaintiff signed a contract with the Vancouver Canucks, a professional National Hockey League team. The team assigned him to its professional "minor league" International Hockey League (IHL) team, the Milwaukee Admirals.

On December 15, 1990, the Milwaukee Admirals played the Peoria Rivermen in a regulation IHL game in Peoria, Illinois. The Peoria Rivermen is an IHL team affiliated with defendant.

IHL hockey is played on an ice rink measuring at least 200 feet by 85 feet with goals on opposing ends of the ice. The rink is surrounded by a wall made partially of clear plexiglass, customarily referred to as the "boards."

The rink is divided in two by a center line. On each side of the center line is a line called the "blue line." The blue lines are parallel to the center line and have to be at least 60 feet from the boards behind the goals. A game consists of three twenty-minute periods.

In the second period, an incident took place between plaintiff and defendant player. Plaintiff was penalized as a result of that incident.

During the third period, plaintiff and defendant player were both playing and "on the ice." A videotape of the incident discloses that defendant player was skating near center ice and plaintiff was positioned in front of his goal. The hockey puck was shot in the general direction of plaintiff's goal by defendant player's teammate. However, it traveled over the goal and the boards and out of play. As the puck was traveling, plaintiff skated several yards to the side of the goal.

A linesman blew his whistle stopping play. About this time, plaintiff began turning his body toward the boards and moved closer to them. As plaintiff was moving away from the goal, defendant player was skating from the near blue line toward plaintiff.

Defendant player continued skating toward plaintiff after a second whistle. Holding his stick, defendant player partially extended both arms and hit plaintiff with his body and the stick, knocking plaintiff into the boards. Plaintiff fell to the ice and was knocked unconscious. Defendant player received a "match penalty" from the referee and was suspended for a period of games by the IHL.

DISCUSSION

Defendant's second point alleges the trial court erred in denying its motion for judgment notwithstanding the verdict. It contends that the "contact at issue, a check between opposing players, is a risk inherent in professional hockey and one assumed by professional hockey players."

The case was tried under Illinois contact sports law as it has been applied to amateur sports. To the extent that this law is relevant, the practical significance of which forum's law applies is minimal if any because Missouri has essentially adopted the Illinois standard.

In amateur contact sports, both Illinois and Missouri courts have held that ordinary negligence is insufficient to state a claim for an injury caused by a co-participant. See, e.g. Pfister v. Shusta, 167 Ill.2d 417, 212 Ill.Dec. 668, 669, 657 N.E.2d 1013, 1014 (1995); Ross v. Clouser, 637 S.W.2d 11, 14 (Mo.banc 1982). Rather, in amateur contact sports, liability must be predicated on "willful and wanton or intentional misconduct." Pfister, 212 Ill.Dec. at 669, 657 N.E.2d at 1014.

In Pfister, the plaintiff and the defendant were engaged in a spontaneous can kicking game in the hall of a college dormitory. During the game, the plaintiff allegedly pushed the defendant and the defendant responded by pushing the plaintiff. As a result, the plaintiff was injured when his left hand and forearm went through a glass door of a fire extinguisher case. Id. at 670, 657 N.E.2d at 1015. The Illinois Supreme Court adopted the "willful and wanton" requirement first created by an Illinois appellate court in Nabozny v. Barnhill, 31 Ill.App.3d 212, 334 N.E.2d 258 (1975).

Nabozny involved a high school soccer game. The plaintiff, a goalie, went down on his left knee, received a pass, and pulled the ball to his chest. The defendant, an opposing player, was running toward the ball and continued to run toward the plaintiff after he gained possession of the ball. The defendant kicked the plaintiff's head causing injuries. Id. 334 N.E.2d at 259–60.

The Nabozny court held that the ordinary care standard did not apply in this amateur contact sport. Instead, it adopted a new rule "in order to control a new field of personal injury litigation." Id. at 261. It held that a participant would be liable for injuries if the participant's conduct was either "deliberate, wilful or with a reckless disregard for the safety of the other player." Id. at 261

Missouri essentially adopted the Nabozny rule in Ross. Ross, 637 S.W.2d at 13–14. Ross involved a slow pitch church league softball game. There, the defendant base runner was injured after colliding with the plaintiff, an opposing third baseman. Id. at 13. The trial court submitted the case to the jury on a negligence theory. In reversing and remanding, the supreme court stated "a cause of action for personal injuries incurred during athletic competition must be predicated on recklessness, not mere negligence...." Id. at 13–14. This heightened standard has been accepted by many jurisdictions and applied to both formal and informal amateur contact sports. See Pfister, 212 Ill.Dec. at 670–671, 657 N.E.2d at 1015–1016.

Under these decisions involving amateur contact sports, ordinary negligence principles are inapplicable. Thus, these courts have implicitly found that conduct which might be "unreasonable" in everyday society is not actionable because it occurs on the athletic field. In contact sports, physical contact and injuries among participants [are] inherent and unwarranted judicial intervention might inhibit the game's vigor. See Pfister, 212 Ill.Dec. at 673, 657 N.E.2d at 1018; Ross, 637 S.W.2d at 14.

All of the above cases discuss the contact sports law in the context of amateur sports. Neither parties' briefs, nor our own research, disclose any Illinois or Missouri case applying the contact sports law to professional sports. In fact, the parties have referred us to only two cases discussing participant liability in professional athletics, Averill v. Luttrell, 44 Tenn.App. 56, 311 S.W.2d 812 (1957) and Hackbart v. Cincinnati Bengals, Inc., 601 F.2d 516 (10th Cir.1979).

Averill involves minor league professional baseball players. There, the plaintiff was at bat when the pitcher threw three inside pitches and a fourth pitch which hit the plaintiff. The plaintiff threw his bat in the direction of the pitcher's mound. As that happened, the catcher, "without any warning whatsoever, stepped up behind [the plaintiff] and struck him a hard blow on the side or back of the head with his fist." Id. 311 S.W.2d at 814. The plaintiff sued both the catcher and his baseball club and obtained a judgment against both defendants.

Only the baseball club appealed. The Averill court reversed the judgment. The opinion does not discuss the standard of care owed by one professional player to another. Rather, it held that the club was not liable for the wilful acts of the catcher when he stepped outside of the club's business and committed an act wholly independent and foreign to the scope of his employment. Id.

The other case is Hackbart. In that case, the plaintiff, a professional football player, placed one knee on the ground after his team intercepted a pass and watched the play. An opposing player hit the back of the plaintiff's head with his right forearm, causing both players to fall to the ground. Hackbart, 601 F.2d at 519. Later, the plaintiff sued the opposing player and his team for a neck injury. The trial court entered judgment for the defendants and the plaintiff appealed. On appeal, the Hackbart court reversed and remanded. Id. at 527. It held that "recklessness is the appropriate standard." Id. at 524.

In addition to considering whether the contact sports exception is applicable to the facts before us, the doctrines of assumption of risk and consent also must be considered. In general, a voluntary participant in any lawful sport assumes all risks that reasonably inhere to the sport insofar as they are obvious and usually incident to the game. See Pfister, 212 Ill.Dec. at 673, 657 N.E.2d at 1018. Under contact sports analysis as applied to amateur sports, participants in team sports assume greater risks of injury than nonparticipants or participants in non-contact sports. Id. at 672, 657 N.E.2d at 1017.

In practice, the concepts of duty, assumption of risk, and consent must be analyzed on a case-by-case basis. Whether one player's conduct causing injury to another is actionable hinges upon the facts of an individual case. Ross, 637 S.W.2d at 14. Relevant factors include the specific game involved, the ages and physical attributes of the participants, their respective skills at the game and their knowledge of its rules and customs, their status as amateurs or professionals, the type of risks which inhere to the game and those which are outside the realm of reasonable anticipation, the presence or absence of protective uniforms or equipment, the degree of zest with which the game is being played, and other factors. Id.

We apply these concepts and factors to the case before us. The specific game was a professional hockey game, not an amateur game. It was not a pickup, school, or college game.

Rough play is commonplace in professional hockey. Anyone who has attended a professional hockey game or seen one on television recognizes the violent nature of the sport. In order to gain possession of the puck or to slow down the progress of opponents, players frequently hit each other with body checks. They trip opposing players, slash at them with their hockey sticks, and fight on a regular basis, often long after the referee blows the whistle. Players regularly commit contact beyond that which is permitted by the rules, and, we are confident, do it intentionally. They wear pads, helmets and other protective equipment because of the rough nature of the sport.

Professional hockey is played at a high skill level with well conditioned athletes, who are financially compensated for their participation. They are professional players with knowledge of its rules and customs, including the violence of the sport. In part, the game is played with great intensity because its players can reap substantial financial rewards. We also recognize that the professional leagues have internal mechanisms for penalizing players and teams for violating league rules and for compensating persons who are injured.

In summary, we find that the specific conduct at issue in this case, a severe body check, is a part of professional hockey. This body check, even several seconds after the whistle and in violation of several rules of the game, was not outside the realm of reasonable anticipation. For better or for worse, it is "part of the game" of professional hockey. As such, we hold as a matter of law that the specific conduct which occurred here is not actionable.

STATE v. FLOYD

466 N.W.2d 919 (Iowa Ct.App.1990).

SCHLEGEL, Presiding Judge.

Defendant William Maurice Floyd appeals his convictions following a jury trial. Defendant was found guilty of two counts of assault without intent to inflict serious injury but causing bodily injury, a serious misdemeanor, violating Iowa Code section 708.2(2). We affirm and remand.

The incidents resulting in this prosecution occurred during the evening of August 15, 1988. Defendant had been participating in a four-on-four basketball game for the Council Bluffs YMCA recreational summer league championship. By all accounts, the half-court game was rough, though not necessarily dirty, and tempers were as hot as the action on the court. Play was very physical, and the fouls were hard; there was considerable "hacking" and a lot of shoving for rebounds. Each team was aggressive and sought to intimidate its opponent with deed and word.

The opposing team had not lost a game during the regular season and had beaten defendant's team twice. During the first half of play, passions were aroused when a member of defendant's team, Andre Brown, struck Scott Rogers, a member of the opposing team, in the face as Rogers attempted to inbound the basketball. Brown was ejected from the game but remained in the gymnasium to watch the game. The game score remained fairly even until the second half of play, when defendant's team pulled ahead by eight to ten points.

With three to five minutes left to play in the game and with his team lagging behind on the scoreboard, Rogers was aggressively guarding John Floyd, defendant's cousin. John Floyd was dribbling the basketball beyond the free-throw line when Rogers fouled him in an attempt to steal the ball. The foul was a "reach-in" type that caught John Floyd either in the face or on the arm. The referee stopped play to report Rogers' foul to the scorer. The ensuing events developed quickly.

With play still stopped, Rogers and John Floyd exchanged words. The evidence conflicts as to precisely what was said. It appears John Floyd told Rogers to stop fouling. According to John Floyd, who is black, Rogers, who is white, used a racial slur in response. John Floyd shoved Rogers, and the referee called a technical foul on John Floyd. As Rogers stepped back and raised his unclenched hands, John Floyd hit Rogers in the face with a fist, knocking Rogers to the floor. Michael Kenealy, Rogers' teammate, had attempted to intervene, but failed and pushed John Floyd away from the downed Rogers. Two or three members of defendant's team then attacked Kenealy, hitting him from behind in the head and ribs.

As these incidents unfolded, Gregg Barrier and John McHale (Rogers' teammates) and defendant and the ejected player, Brown, were on the sidelines. They were not involved in the play immediately prior to [the] happenings described above. Although the order of defendant's actions is not entirely clear, it is clear that defendant left his team's bench area after play had been stopped and punches had been thrown. Defendant then assaulted McHale and Gregg Barrier on the sidelines and Duane Barrier on the basketball court.

McHale, who was simply standing on the sidelines when disturbances began to occur on the court, suffered the worst from blows by defendant. Defendant hit McHale and knocked him to the floor. McHale suffered a concussion, severe hemorrhaging, and loss of brain tissue. He spent the next two days in intensive care. He has permanently lost the sense of smell, has some amnesia, and is at risk of epileptic seizures.

Leaving McHale unconscious on the floor and bleeding profusely, defendant attacked Gregg Barrier and Duane Barrier. Like McHale, Gregg Barrier was on the sidelines, but was returning from a water fountain. Gregg Barrier was able to cover up against defendant's punches to the back of his head and shoulders, and defendant did not seriously injure him.

Duane Barrier had been in the game when play had been halted. As Duane Barrier watched the incidents on the court, defendant approached and punched him in the side of the head. When Duane Barrier turned to see what had hit him, defendant hit him squarely on the nose. Duane Barrier suffered a severely deviated septum and required reconstructive surgery.

The record includes descriptions of various attacks by different members of defendant's team. These cowardly antics seem primarily to have involved John Floyd and Andre Brown. The disturbance lasted a few minutes and even spread to the YMCA staff offices, where members of defendant's team beat Rogers as he attempted to call an ambulance for McHale.

The State filed two charges of willful injury, see Iowa Code § 708.4 (1989) (class "C" felony), against defendant. He was convicted by a jury on two counts of the lesser included offense of assault causing bodily injury, see Iowa Code §§ 708.1(1), 708.2(2) (1989) (serious misdemeanor). The trial court sentenced defendant to serve the maximum sentence of one year, see Iowa Code § 903.1(1)(b) (1989), for each conviction, and to serve these terms consecutively, see Iowa Code § 901.8 (1989). Defendant appeals, arguing he falls within the assault exception for voluntary participants in sporting events, see Iowa Code § 708.1 (1989) (last unnumbered paragraph). He further appeals, arguing that the trial court abused its discretion in sentencing him to consecutive maximum terms.

This is a case of first impression in this State, and one of a handful of reported criminal prosecutions for sports-related violence in North America. In People v. Freer, 86 Misc.2d 280, 281–84, 381 N.Y.S.2d 976, 977–79 (Dist.Ct.1976), an amateur football player was convicted of third degree assault. After a tackle and pileup, the defendant got up on one knee and punched the supine complainant in the eye. A similar prosecution against a professional hockey player in Minnesota ended in a mistrial. State v. Forbes, No. 63280 (Minn. 4th Dist. Aug. 12, 1975).

Section 708.1(1) defines an "assault" as occurring when, without justification, a person carries out

> [a]ny act which is intended to cause pain or injury to, or which is intended to result in physical contact which will be insulting or offensive to another, coupled with apparent ability to execute the act.

The last, unnumbered paragraph of section 708.1, however, provides

> that where the person doing any of the above enumerated acts, and such other person, are voluntary participants in a sport, social or other activity, not in itself criminal, and such act is a reasonably foreseeable incident of such sport or activity, and does not create an unreasonable risk of serious injury or breach of peace, the act shall not be an assault.

We are bound to give statutes reasonable interpretations based on what the legislature has said, Iowa R.App.P. 14(f)(13), and we seek only a common sense understanding of circumstances to which this statute may apply. If there is an ambiguity in the statute, we resort to statutory construction. Metier v. Cooper Transport Co., Inc., 378 N.W.2d 907, 912 (Iowa 1985). We may consider the language used in the statute, the objects sought to be accomplished, the evils and mischief sought to be remedied, and place a reasonable construction on the statute which will best effectuate its purpose rather than defeat it. Id. We must examine both the language used and the purpose for which the legislation was enacted and consider all parts together without giving undue importance to one single or isolated portion. Id. The commentators have argued that the legislature intended "to accommodate the assault law to reality, in that many acts which our society considers to be quite acceptable, and even desirable, are technically assaults by whatever rational definition that term may be given." J. Yeager & R. Carlson, Iowa Practice: Criminal Law and Procedure § 176 (1979).

We do not attempt an empirical definition of when persons are "voluntary participants in a sport." It is unnecessary for us to engage in such an exercise in this case. We have no doubt that defendant and his victims had been participants. Given that play had officially ceased, that an altercation had broken out, and that defendant and some of his victims had been on the sidelines and not engaged in play activities, it is clear that defendant and his victims were not, at that time, "voluntary participants in a sport." There simply is no nexus between defendant's acts and playing the game of basketball.

As discussed in Note, Sports Violence as Criminal Assault: Development of the Doctrine by Canadian Courts, 1986 Duke L.J. 1030, the Canadian courts have generally recognized that incidents that occur after cessation of play, as after a whistle blown for the express purpose of so signaling, are not part of the game. Id. at 1048–50 (citing Re Duchesneau, [1979] 7 C.R.3d 70, 83 (Que. Youth Trib.1978)). The Canadian courts have also recognized that such a bright-line rule, which is attractive because of its ease of application, cannot be blindly used without some evaluation of the circumstances. Id. (citing Regina v. Leyte, 13 C.C.C.2d 458, 459 (Ont.Prov.Ct.1973)).

We reject defendant's suggestion that he is protected from prosecution for acts committed by him while he is on a playing surface until the final buzzer, gun, whistle, goal, or out. In carving out this exception, the legislature clearly contemplated a person who commits acts during the course of play, and the exception seeks to protect those whose acts otherwise subject to prosecution are committed in furtherance of the object of the sport. In addition, we recognize that there are difficult questions of to how much violence a "voluntary participant" consents, but because of our ruling, we need not address this issue.

We further reject defendant's contentions that our construction of the exception to the assault statute will either ruin competitive sporting or flood the courts with these cases. On the contrary, our decision does not mandate that all, or for that matter any, cases like this be prosecuted, and it certainly does not attempt to place in jeopardy all who commit acts otherwise subject to prosecution when play is supposed to have ceased. We are confident that in closer cases the inquiry necessarily will shift, and the reasonable foreseeability of the incident and the so-called "consent" defense will separate the cases with merit from those without. As ever, we must rely on sound prosecutorial discretion or await legislative action.

Several law review commentators have urged prosecutors to use criminal sanctions to curb the perceived rise in sports violence. See Comment, Controlling Sports Violence: Too Late for the Carrots—Bring on the Big Stick, 74 Iowa L.Rev. 681, 682–83, 701, 705–08 (1989); see also Note, Sports Violence as Criminal Assault: Development of the Doctrine by Canadian Courts, 1986 Duke L.J. 1030, 1033, 1038–48; Comment, It's Not How You Play the Game, It's Whether You Win or Lose: The Need for Criminal Sanctions to Curb Violence in Professional Sports, 12 Hamline L.Rev. 71, 88 (1988); Comment, Consent in Criminal Law: Violence in Sports, 75 Mich.L.Rev. 148, 174 (1976). The paucity of sports violence cases could well be construed as showing that [the] statutory exception and prosecutorial discretion combination serves as an adequate filter of sports-related cases.

Had we concluded that defendant and his victims were sports participants when these events occurred, we are not disposed toward finding that defendant's acts were "reasonably foreseeable incident[s]" of basketball. We need not go into detail in deciding what, if any, contact is "incident" to basketball. We are aware that in the heat of play in basketball one might, depending on the circumstances, expect a certain amount of pushing and shoving for position, the occasional elbow, and a fair number of open-handed slaps. It strains the imagination and contorts the concept of foreseeability beyond recognition to assert that the brutal assaults carried out by defendant in this case could have been "reasonably foreseeable incident[s]." When they walk onto the court or stand on the sidelines, average reasonable basketball players are unprotected and unprepared for suddenly being set upon from the side or rear with a flurry of punches to the head. Moreover, that violence in fact occurs during a sporting event such as basketball, as defendant notes at length, and perhaps occurs more often when participants already are in physical contact with each other, does not necessarily make it a reasonably foreseeable incident. The legislature recognized this in enacting this exception, and a jury of defendant's peers agreed.

While there may be a continuum, or sliding scale, grounded in the circumstances under which voluntary participants engage in sport (e.g., professional or amateur) which governs the type of incidents in which an individual volunteers (i.e., consents) to participate, it seems clear that such distinctions have no application here because of the stoppage of play. See Note, Sports Violence as Criminal Assault: Development of the Doctrine by Canadian Courts, 1986 Duke L.J. 1030, 1053 (citing Regina v. St. Croix, 47 C.C.C.2d 122 (Ont.Co.Ct.1979), and Re Duchesneau, [1979] 7 C.R.3d 70, 84 (Que.Youth Trib.1978)).

Even had we found defendant's acts reasonably foreseeable incidents to participants in basketball games, we conclude that they may "create an unreasonable risk of serious injury or breach of peace." The legislature wisely saw that there is a limit to the level of violence which we, as a society, will, or perhaps should, tolerate in the pursuit of sport. Defendant's acts reached and surpassed that level.

The law review commentators are unanimous in their disapprobation of sports-related violence and the effect it has on society. See Note, Sports Violence as Criminal Assault: Development of the Doctrine by Canadian Courts, 1986 Duke L.J. 1030, 1030–31, 1054; Comment, It's Not How You Play the Game, It's Whether You Win or Lose: The Need for Criminal Sanctions to Curb Violence in Professional Sports, 12 Hamline L.Rev. 71, 88–89 (1988); Comment, Controlling Sports Violence: Too Late for the Carrots—Bring on the Big Stick, 74 Iowa L.Rev. 681, 683–90 (1989); Comment, Consent in Criminal Law: Violence in Sports, 75 Mich.L.Rev. 148, 174 (1976).

We noted above our belief that an average reasonable basketball player is unprotected and unprepared for fist fights, and we think this is particularly so under the circumstances described above. The legislature obviously did not intend to protect a basketball player who, regardless of his status as "participant," launches random attacks from the sidelines on other players. At least for the game of basketball, such acts "create an unreasonable risk of serious injury or breach of peace." The facts—

the permanent injuries sustained by two of defendant's victims—and the manner in which these injuries were inflicted support our assessment.

We hold that Iowa Code section 708.1(1) does apply to defendant William Floyd. We further hold that the exception stated in the last, unnumbered paragraph of section 708.1 is not applicable to defendant. Defendant was therefore properly tried for assault under section 708.1.

[The remainder of the court's opinion, addressing various procedural issues, is omitted.]

Notes

1. Suits like *McKichan* can be found in nearly all sports. For a representative sampling, see *De Sole v. United States*, 947 F.2d 1169 (4th Cir.1991) (yacht racing); *Jaworski v. Kiernan*, 696 A.2d 332 (Conn.1997) (soccer); *Crawn v. Campo*, 643 A.2d 600 (N.J.1994) (softball); *Knight v. Jewett*, 834 P.2d 696 (Cal.1992) (touch football); *Thompson v. McNeill*, 559 N.E.2d 705 (Ohio 1990) (golf); *Turcotte v. Fell*, 502 N.E.2d 964 (N.Y.1986) (horse racing); *Connell v. Payne*, 814 S.W.2d 486 (Tex.Ct.App.1991) (polo); *Hanson v. Kynast*, 526 N.E.2d 327 (Ohio Ct.App.1987) (lacrosse). *See also* Ray Yasser, *In the Heat of Competition: Tort Liability of One Participant to Another; Why Can't Participants be Required to be Reasonable?*, 5 Seton Hall J. Sport L. 253 (1995); Barbara Svoranos, Comment, *Fighting? It's All in a Day's Work on the Ice: Determining the Appropriate Standard of a Hockey Player's Liability to Another Player*, 7 Seton Hall J. Sport L. 487 (1997); Brendon D. Miller, Note, *Hoke v. Cullinan: Recklessness as the Standard for Recreational Sports Injuries*, 23 N. Ky. L. Rev. 409 (1996).

2. In addition to *Floyd*, several other criminal prosecutions have been brought against players for their on-field behavior. *See, e.g., State v. Shelley*, 929 P.2d 489 (Wash.Ct.App.1997); *Regina v. Ciccarelli*, 54 C.C.C.3d 121 (Ontario Dist.Ct.1989); *Regina v. Green*, 16 D.L.R.3d 137 (Ontario Prov.Ct. 1970); *Regina v. Maki*, 14 D.L.R.3d 104 (Ontario Prov.Ct.1970). Nevertheless, such actions remain the exception rather than the rule. For a useful look at the pros and cons of using the criminal law to discipline athletes, see Linda S. Calvert Hanson & Craig Dernis, *Revisiting Excessive Violence in the Professional Sports Arena: Changes in the Past Twenty Years?*, 6 Seton Hall J. Sports L. 127 (1996); Daniel R. Karon, *Winning Isn't Everything, It's the Only Thing. Violence in Professional Sports: The Need for Federal Regulation and Criminal Sanctions*, 25 Ind. L. Rev. 147 (1991); Wayne R. Cohen, Comment, *The Relationship Between Criminal Liability and Sports: A Jurisprudential Investigation*, 7 U. Miami Ent. & Sports L. Rev. 311 (1990).

3. While most injuries are accidental, some athletes are known for playing dirty: baseball's John McGraw and Ty Cobb, basketball's Bill Laimbeer and John Stockton, football's Conrad Dobler and Kevin Gogan, and hockey's Dave Schultz and Billy Smith, for example, all excelled at the cheap or late hit. Nevertheless, when the issue comes up, the first name mentioned almost always is Oakland Raiders safety Jack "The Assassin" Tatum.

Tatum made his mark in August 1978 in a game against New England. During a pass route, he administered a "crackdown" on Patriots wideout Darryl Stingley. The blow snapped Stingley's spinal cord and left him permanently paralyzed below the waist. Despite the severity of the injury, Tatum refused to apologize for his actions. Instead, he wrote a book entitled *They Call Me Assassin* (1979) in which he boasted: "I never make a tackle just to bring someone down. I want to punish the man I'm going after. I like to believe my best hits border on felonious assault." For a further look at dirty players, see, e.g., Michael Silver, *Dirty Dogs*, Sports Illustrated, Oct. 26, 1998, at 46; Kevin B. Blackistone, *For Most of Sports' Cheap–Shot Artists, It's Hit or Sit*, Dallas Morning News, Dec. 8, 1993, at 2B; *Brat, Lip, Bambino Lead Team of Dirtiest, Nastiest Players*, Sacramento Bee, July 2, 1990, at D2.

4. Besides unchecked aggressiveness, fellow participants pose other dangers. In November 1991, for example, Los Angeles Lakers forward Magic Johnson was found to be HIV-positive. When he subsequently attempted a comeback in 1992, resistance on the part of some players caused him to abandon the effort after only a short time. A second attempt in 1996 ended the same way. *See further* Anthony DiMaggio, Comment, *Suffering in Silence: Should They Be Cheered or Feared? (Mandatory HIV Testing of Athletes as a Health and Safety Issue)*, 8 Seton Hall J. Sport L. 663 (1998).

In January 1994, skater Tonya Harding had Nancy Kerrigan, her main rival, beaten with a tire iron so Harding would be assured of qualifying for the Winter Olympics. When the plot came to light, Harding received a lifetime ban from the United States Figure Skating Association, was stripped of her 1994 national championship, and pled guilty to one count of hindering prosecution (for which she received three years probation and a $110,000 fine). *See further* Thomas A. Mayes, Comment, *Tonya Harding's Case: Contractual Due Process, the Amateur Athlete, and the American Ideal of Fair Play*, 3 UCLA Ent. L. Rev. 109 (1995).

5. Tonya Harding's vicious plan to injure Nancy Kerrigan is just one instance of athletes being deliberately harmed. In September 1972, for example, 11 members of the Israeli national team were executed by the Palestinian terrorist organization "Black September" while participating in the Summer Olympics at Munich, West Germany. *See further Ladany v. William Morrow & Co.*, 465 F.Supp. 870 (S.D.N.Y.1978). In January 1991, a Houston homemaker named Wanda Holloway was arrested for trying to hire a hit man to kill Verna Heath, the mother of her daughter's leading rival for the high school cheerleading squad, in the hope Amber Heath would be so grief-stricken she would drop out of the competition. *See further State v. Holloway*, 886 S.W.2d 482 (Tex.Ct.App.1994), *cert. denied*, 516 U.S. 922 (1995). In April 1993, tennis champion Monica Seles was knifed in the back by a deranged man at a tournament in Hamburg, Germany. The attack left her sidelined for 27 months with both physical and emotional problems. *See further Chronology of the Seles Attack*, USA Today, June 6, 1995, at 13C. And in July 1994, Colombian soccer player Andres Escobar was murdered for having scored a goal against his own team at the 1994 World Cup. *See further* Pamela Mercer, *Colombian Who Made World Cup Error is Killed*, N.Y. Times, July 3, 1994, § 1, at 2. For other such incidents, see Bob Ryan, *Fanfare Could be Dangerous*, Boston Globe, Feb. 28, 1997, at E1.

6. In addition to targeted attacks, athletes must be wary of random fan violence. In October 1995, for example, the Seattle Mariners were forced off the field after patrons began flinging batteries, coins, and other objects on to

the field during a playoff game at Yankee Stadium. Similarly, in December 1995, 15 spectators were arrested and 175 were ejected for hurling snowballs during a contest between the San Diego Chargers and the New York Giants at the Meadowlands. And in August 1996, the Los Angeles Dodgers had to forfeit a game against the St. Louis Cardinals after hundreds of baseballs were thrown from the stands. *See further Camera Cops—Put the Snowball Down: You're Being Watched by the Pros*, Austin Am.-Statesman, July 10, 1997, at C1 (describing the increasing use of security cameras to maintain order at ballparks). *See also People v. O'Grady*, 667 N.Y.S.2d 895 (N.Y.C. Crim.Ct.1997) (criminal action against protester who ran onto field during 1996 World Series).

7. Some athletes are injured as a result of defective equipment. *See, e.g., Traub v. Cornell University*, 1998 WL 187401 (N.D.N.Y.1998) (basketball court—overly-rigid rim); *Owen v. R.J.S. Safety Equipment, Inc.*, 591 N.E.2d 1184 (N.Y.1992) (race track—improper barriers); *Maddox v. City of New York*, 487 N.E.2d 553 (N.Y.1985) (baseball field—faulty drainage system); *Classen v. Izquierdo*, 520 N.Y.S.2d 999 (Sup.Ct.1987) (boxing ring—inadequate medical facilities). For a further discussion, see Shea Sullivan, *Football Helmet Products Liability: A Survey of Cases and a Call for Reform*, 3 Sports Law. J. 233 (1996).

8. Artificial playing surfaces are another source of injuries. *See, e.g., Houston Oilers, Inc. v. Harris County*, 960 F.Supp. 1202 (S.D.Tex.1997) (game cancelled after referees found field at Houston Astrodome to be in dangerous condition); *Heldman v. Uniroyal, Inc.*, 371 N.E.2d 557 (Ohio Ct.App.1977) (professional tennis player could not recover for knee injury suffered while competing on defendant's "Roll-a-Way" flooring); Steve Rock, *Snag Carpet—Vet's Surface Strikes Fear in Hearts, Knees*, K.C. Star, Sept. 27, 1998, at 1 (Sports) (discussing the many problems with the synthetic turf at Philadelphia's Veterans Stadium, universally considered the NFL's worst playing surface). For a further discussion, see Brian J. Duff, Comment, *Game Plan for a Successful Products Liability Action Against Manufacturers of Artificial Turf*, 5 Seton Hall J. Sport L. 223 (1995).

9. Players also are vulnerable to weather-related injuries. In *McAleer v. Smith*, 860 F.Supp. 924 (D.R.I.1994), for example, a boat participating in the 1984 Cutty Sark International Tall Ships Race sank when a sudden storm arose. Of the 28 people aboard, only nine survived. Similarly, in *Maussner v. Atlantic City Country Club, Inc.*, 691 A.2d 826 (N.J.Super.Ct.App.Div.1997), a golfer was hit by lightning as he attempted to leave the fairway. For additional examples of such injuries, see, e.g., Michael Flynn, *Lightning: A Double Hit for Golf Course Operators*, 6 Marq. Sports L.J. 133 (1995); Marlys Duran, *Detectors Warn of Lightning at Recreation Sites: High–Tech Equipment Starting to Take Place of Human Eyes, Ears at Golf Courses, Pools*, Rocky Mtn. News, June 28, 1998, at 35A; Mike Hendricks, *When Sports Becomes Life and Death*, K.C. Star, Apr. 3, 1998, at C1.

10. Human athletes are not the only competitors who suffer injuries. Each year, a shocking number of animals are maimed or killed in sporting events. *See, e.g., Dalton v. Delta Air Lines, Inc.*, 1974 U.S. Dist. LEXIS 6117 (S.D.Fla.1974) (greyhound racing); *Commonwealth v. Turner*, 14 N.E. 130 (Mass.1887) (fox hunting); *State v. Cleve*, 949 P.2d 672 (N.M.Ct.App.1997)

(deer hunting); *State v. Ham*, 691 P.2d 239 (Wash.Ct.App.1984) (gamecock fighting); Ivor Herbert, *Let This be Final Blow to Brutal Jockeys*, London (Sunday) Mail, Aug. 23, 1998, at 80 (horse racing); Todd Wilkinson, *Rodeos Sweep American West, But Raise Concern of Cruelty*, Christian Sci. Monitor, Apr. 30, 1997, at 1 (steer and calf roping). *See also* William Nack & Lester Munson, *Blood Money*, Sports Illustrated, Nov. 16, 1992, at 18 (discussing the notorious practice of killing race horses for insurance purposes).

11. For a further discussion of sports injuries, see, e.g., Stanley L. Grazis, *Liability of Participant in Team Athletic Competition for Injury to or Death of Another Participant*, 55 A.L.R.5th 529 (1998); Andrew Rhim, Comment, *The Special Relationship Between Student–Athletes and Colleges: An Analysis of a Heightened Duty of Care for the Injuries of Student–Athletes*, 7 Marq. Sports L.J. 329 (1996); Greg Garber, *With Millions of Dollars Hanging in the Balance, the Playing Field Now Includes Athletes and Teams that are ... Covered Against a Loss*, Hartford Courant, Aug. 11, 1998, at C1. *See also SEG Sports Corp. v. State Athletic Comm'n*, 952 F.Supp. 202 (S.D.N.Y.1997), and *Ohio State Boxing Comm'n v. Adore, Ltd.*, 673 N.E.2d 1016 (Ohio Ct.App.1996), both of which describe competitions that put a premium on causing injury.

Problem 27

A workers' compensation statute prohibits recovery of an award whenever an "injury has been solely occasioned by an employee's wilful intention to bring about the injury or death of himself or another." Given this language, can boxers collect benefits? *See Estate of Gross v. Three Rivers Inn, Inc.*, 667 N.Y.S.2d 71 (App.Div.1997), *rev'd*, 1998 WL 806436 (N.Y. 1998).

3. HOSTILE ENVIRONMENT

Athletes today increasingly complain of being forced to perform in antagonistic surroundings. The following cases provide a look at two such claims.

YOST v. UNIVERSITY OF MARYLAND

1993 WL 524757 (D.Md.1993).

HARGROVE, District Judge.

In this 42 U.S.C. § 1983 and § 1985 suit against the University of Maryland Board of Regents and several employees of the University, Plaintiff alleges violations of her rights under the First Amendment, state constitutional violations, and related state tort and contract claims. Presently the court has before it Defendants' partial Motion to Dismiss for lack of jurisdiction over plaintiff's claims for injunctive relief, the Eleventh Amendment bar to suits for damages against state agencies, and for failure to state a cause of action under 42 U.S.C. § 1985(3). The court has reviewed the memoranda and for the reasons that follow, will grant Defendants' partial Motion to Dismiss. The court will dismiss Plaintiff's complaint in its entirety as to Defendants Board of Regents ("the University"), Dr. William Kirwan ("Kirwan"), and Andrew Geiger ("Geiger"); and plaintiff's claims of conspiracy and for injunctive relief as to defendants Margaret M. Meharg ("Meharg") and Dr. Susan Tyler ("Tyler"). No hearing is deemed necessary. Local Rule 105(6) (D.Md. 1992).

FACTS

Plaintiff, VICKI LEE YOST ("YOST") is a resident of the State of Maryland and a homosexual. From 1988 to 1992 Yost was a field hockey player at the University of Maryland. These four seasons from 1988 to 1992 consist of her entire period of College athletic eligibility. Yost has not yet earned a degree, but is not presently a student at the University of Maryland and is no longer eligible to serve the university as an athlete.

Defendant Board of Regents is the governing board of the University of Maryland and is sued in its official supervisory capacity. Defendant Dr. William Kirwan is the President of the University of Maryland and is sued in his official supervisory capacity. Defendant Andrew Geiger is the Athletic Director of the University of Maryland and is sued in his official supervisory capacity.

Plaintiff Yost seeks an order enjoining these three defendants from further violating the rights of female homosexual athletes at the University of Maryland and requiring them to prepare a plan to end the alleged discrimination.

Defendant Dr. Susan Tyler is the Assistant Athletic Director of the University of Maryland and is sued in her official and individual capacities. Defendant Margaret M. Meharg is the Head Coach for the Women's Field Hockey team for the University of Maryland and is sued in her individual and official capacities. Plaintiff Yost seeks compensatory and punitive damages against these two defendants for conspiracy to violate her rights and an order enjoining them from further violating her federal and state law rights.

Yost alleges that during the time that she was a National Collegiate Athletic Association ("NCAA") athlete for the University of Maryland defendants Meharg and Tyler agreed to project for the Women's Athletic Department an image of heterosexuality. Yost further alleges that it was their goal to suppress any athletic student conduct, speech, appearance, assembly, and association in conflict with that image.

In February 1990, in response to questioning by defendant Meharg, Yost admitted that she was "gay", and was informed by Meharg that her sexual orientation was not acceptable to the University of Maryland, and in particular to defendant Tyler. At this time Meharg made numerous derogatory and stereotypical remarks about Yost's sexual orientation and ordered her to conceal it from the field hockey team, the Athletic Department, and members of the public who might directly or indirectly associate Yost with the University of Maryland. In addition Meharg ordered Yost not to "be seen" with her girlfriend, accept rides to or from practice or class from her, or visit with her on the College Park campus for any reason. Defendant Meharg then threatened Yost that in the event that she did not comply with these orders Meharg would deny Yost the benefit of her scholarship and her place on the team. At this point Yost requested a written release from Meharg to enable her to play for another University's field hockey team. Meharg denied her request.

Throughout the remainder of Yost's two remaining seasons of eligibility Meharg summoned Yost to her office several times to reinforce her demand that Yost conceal her sexual orientation. During these meetings Meharg reaffirmed her prohibitions against Yost inviting friends that Meharg perceived to be homosexual to games, joining the Lesbian Speakers Bureau, joining the Gay and Lesbian Student Union, and visiting homosexual establishments if she wished to retain her position on the team and her Athletic Scholarship. Meharg met any resistance to this policy with extreme hostility and increased pressure.

DISCUSSION

Yost alleges that her field hockey coach, and other University employee defendants, conspired to restrict her freedom of speech and association in violation of the First Amendment as a condition of scholarship and playing time. Yost asserts that the purpose of defendants in restricting her rights was to suppress any public exhibition of any lesbian athlete's sexual orientation in order to project and preserve a false image of heterosexuality among University of Maryland female athletes.

I. 42 U.S.C. § 1985(3) Conspiracy

In its Motion to Dismiss and supporting memoranda the University argues that the complaint fails to state a cause of action for conspiracy under 42 U.S.C. § 1985(3) because the statute does not apply to intra-corporate conspiracy, and plaintiff must be a member of a protected class in order to assert a claim under § 1985(3). The court will dismiss the claim of conspiracy on the second ground.

Section 1985(3) derives its significance from the Civil Rights Act of 1871, also known as the Ku Klux Klan Act. See Harrison v. KVAT Food Management, Inc., 766 F.2d 155, 156–157 (4th Cir.1985). This act was passed in response to the widespread violence and acts of terror directed at blacks and their republican supporters in the post-reconstruction era south. The failure or inability of local southern government to control the Klan was viewed as a "conspiracy to establish democratic hegemony in the south". Id.; See Cong.Globe, 42nd. Cong. 1st Sess. 245–436 (1871).

Although this statute was originally interpreted to afford a remedy to blacks whose civil rights were violated, its language has been applied to private conspiracies to deprive others of civil rights. Griffin v. Breckenridge, 403 U.S. 88, 102 (1971). However, courts construe the statute very narrowly to allow recovery only in situations parallel to the "political terrorism" encountered by blacks which prompted its enactment. Harrison, supra, 766 F.2d at 157. The purpose of the conspiracy must be the deprivation of equal rights under law based on "some racial, or perhaps otherwise class-based, invidiously discriminatory animus behind the conspirators' action." Griffin, supra, 403 U.S. at 102. The Griffin court expanded the interpretation of the statute, but expressly reserved the question of whether conspiracy motivated by invidiously discriminatory animus other than racial bias would be actionable under § 1985(3). Id. at 102, n. 9.

Since Griffin, many federal courts have faced the question of whether or not non-racial discrimination can be the basis for a conspiracy claim under § 1985(3). In some of these decisions, the right to bring an action under § 1985(3) has been extended to non-racially discriminatory conspiracies. However, it is "a close question whether § 1985 was intended to reach any class-based animus other than animus against Negroes and those who championed their cause." United Brotherhood of Carpenters, etc. v. Scott, 463 U.S. 825, 836 (1983). In recognition of the statute's legislative history, the Scott court found disconcerting the argument that § 1985(3) might provide a remedy for every concerted effort by one political group to nullify the influence or do injury to a competing group through the interference with their freedom of speech. Id.

Plaintiff Yost argues that her status as a homosexual athlete and the animus of the University of Maryland and its employees toward her status motivated the discriminatory actions of her coach. However, consistent with the narrow approach of the statute, courts have consistently held that "homosexuals are not a class within the meaning of § 1985(3)." DeSantis v. Pacific Telephone & Telegraph Co., Inc., 608 F.2d 327, 333 (9th Cir.1979). Therefore, plaintiff's claims of conspiracy under § 1985(3) must fail.

II. Injunctive Relief

In its Motion to Dismiss and supporting memoranda the University also argues that the complaint fails to establish jurisdiction for injunctive relief because Yost has completed her four years of NCAA eligibility and fails to allege how she will be harmed in the future by the University's alleged discriminatory treatment of female homosexual athletes. The court will dismiss the claims for injunctive relief because plaintiff has failed to state a live case or controversy as required by Article III.

In order to rescue her claims for injunctive relief, Yost argues that she has standing to request injunctive relief based on future harm which might affect other University of Maryland lesbian athletes. However, in the absence of the certification of Yost's case as a class action, this argument cannot survive the Article III requirement that the plaintiff have a legally cognizable interest in the result of this claim. Yost acknowledges in her Opposition Memorandum that ordinarily one must assert only her own legal interests and cannot rest a claim to relief on the legal rights or interest of third parties. Yost also recognizes that it is the policy of the court to consider only controversies between the parties before it in order to avoid pronouncements on unsettled questions of law where the third parties whose rights are being violated may be the best advocates of their own positions. However she argues that her case fits into the exceptions to the rule.

Each of the exceptions Yost uncovers require that plaintiff have "first-party" standing under Article III before attempting to assert the rights of others not before the court. Therefore they do not apply to the case sub judice. Plaintiff admits that her exception applies only "where a plaintiff asserting third party standing has suffered concrete, redressable injury (that is, where plaintiff has Article III standing)", before "the courts will examine additional factors in determining whether plaintiff may assert the rights of others". Plaintiff's Opp.Mem. at p. 8. In this case Yost has not proven that she has standing to assert claims for injunctive relief. Therefore she cannot attempt to circumvent the need for a case or controversy between herself and the University by invoking jus tertii.

Based on her inability to first establish her own right to injunctive relief under Article III, Yost has not met the requirement for third-party standing. Therefore her entire claim for injunctive relief must fail.

COX v. NATIONAL FOOTBALL LEAGUE

29 F.Supp.2d 463 (N.D.Ill.1998).

PLUNKETT, Judge.

Plaintiff Bryan Cox ("Cox") has sued his employer, the National Football League ("the NFL") and its Commissioner, Paul Tagliabue ("Tagliabue"), for retaliatory employment discrimination under 42 U.S.C. § 2000e et seq. ("Title VII"). The defendants have moved for summary judgment and have moved to strike certain exhibits accompanying plaintiff's response to their summary judgment motion and those portions of the response that refer to such exhibits. For the reasons set forth below, the Court grants in part and denies in part defendants' motion to strike and grants defendants' motion for summary judgment.

I. Facts

The following facts are undisputed. Plaintiff Cox is a professional football player who has played for, and has been employed by, the Miami Dolphins and the Chicago Bears, two member teams of the NFL. (Defs.' Stmt. Mat'l Facts ("Defs.' 12M Stmt.") p 2.) Defendant NFL is a business 'enterprise that operates a professional football league. (Id. p 1.) Tagliabue is an employee of the NFL and serves as its Commissioner. (Id.)

In July 1994, Cox filed a Title VII race discrimination lawsuit against the NFL and Tagliabue. (Id. p 44.) Cox sought an injunction to order defendants to institute policies that would prevent players from being subjected to the kind of racial epithets by fans that he was subjected to while entering Rich Stadium in Buffalo, New York for a game on September 23, 1993. (Pl.'s 12N Stmt. Mat'l Facts Requiring Denial Defs.' Mot. Summ. J. ("Pl.'s 12N Stmt.") pp 1–4.)

Within days after he filed the lawsuit, the NFL ordered Cox to participate in the NFL drug abuse program. (Id. p 10.) He was required to undergo drug tests on August 1 and 16, 1994. (Id. p 11.) Dr. Trop, who evaluated Cox for possible substance abuse, noted that Cox engaged in heavy drinking in December 1993, but that there was no evidence to support active substance abuse. (Pl.'s Ex. 9, Dr. Trop Letter of 8/26/94.) After September 12, 1994, the NFL did not require Cox to provide urine samples. (Id. p 13.) The team physician, Dr. St. Mary, advised Cox to abstain from alcohol during the 1994 season. (Id. p 12.) On January 17, 1995, Dr. Brown, the NFL's Medical Advisor, advised Cox that the NFL had adopted a new drug abuse program and that the new program required him to report his whereabouts during the off-season. (Id. p 14.)

In addition, shortly after Cox filed the lawsuit, the NFL Director of Communications released a statement which provided that the NFL has "implemented new security measures for the 1994 season to address [Bryan Cox's] concerns and to supplement previous procedure.... The steps were taken in part because of the incident last season involving Bryan Cox which highlighted the issue of racial harassment of players and coaches by fans." (Defs.' 12M Stmt. p 46.) Cox stipulated to the dismissal of the case without prejudice in February 1995. (Id. p 49.)

The NFL maintains disciplinary policies and distributes a memorandum describing the policies annually with a "Message from the Commissioner." (Defs.' 12M Stmt. pp 4–5.) In a section entitled "Offense Against Game Official," the 1996 disciplinary memorandum, which Cox received, provides that "[p]layers, coaches, and other club personnel must maintain proper respect for game officials at all times" and that "[n]on-physical abuse of officials, including extreme profanity and other abusive language, is ... prohibited." (Id. p 6.) In a section entitled "Sportsmanship," the memorandum provides that: "every NFL game is broadcast on radio and television," "[t]he League and its participants are severely criticized whenever obscene or profane language or obscene gestures are carried or shown on the air," and "[s]erious incidents of this kind will warrant disciplinary action by the League." (Id. p 7.) Further, the memorandum warns that "[r]epeat violations may entail higher fines, ejection and/or suspension" and that "[i]f appropriate, violations committed in prior seasons will be considered when the level of discipline is established." (Id. p 8.)

On October 6, 1996, during a game between the Chicago Bears and Green Bay Packers and after a Packers touchdown, Cox threw his helmet to the ground under the goal post and three officials called a penalty on Cox for unsportsmanlike conduct. (Id. p 11.) During the extra point attempt, Cox verbally abused game official Billy Smith by repeatedly shouting obscenities at him in a loud voice, calling him a "motherfucker," and then telling him to "suck my dick." (Id. p 12.) Cox made obscene gestures toward Smith by "giving him the finger" several times while standing two to three feet from him. (Id. p 13.) Cox's berating of Smith was broadcast live, his display of obscene gestures toward Smith was broadcast on replay by FOX television, and all of his conduct was visible to fans in Soldier Field. (Id. p 14.)

Commissioner Tagliabue met with key NFL officials to review the incident and Jerry Seeman, Director of Officiating, Gene Washington, Director of Football Development, and Peter Hadhazy, Director of Football Operations, recommended suspension without pay due to Cox's repugnant treatment of a game official. (Id. pp 19–24.) Tagliabue determined that Cox's conduct represented "a unique set of circumstances" due to Cox's unusual and disturbing loss of control of his emotions, his unprovoked abuse of a game official, his continuing pattern of abuse toward officials as well as fans, and the NFL's past unsuccessful attempts to deter similar misconduct by Cox. (Id. pp 25–27.) Prior to October 1996, Cox had been disciplined for using profanity and making obscene gestures toward officials and fans. (Id. pp 32–39.) Based on the "totality of those circumstances," Tagliabue determined that Cox should be fined in an amount equal to his paycheck for one game, which was approximately $87,000.00. (Id. p 28.)

On January 23, 1997, Cox filed a charge of discrimination with the Equal Employment Opportunity Commission ("EEOC") stating that defendants had retaliated against him in violation of Title VII. (Id. p 51.) He received a right-to-sue letter from the EEOC on February 26, 1997. (Pl.'s Ex. 5, Compl., Ex. A.) Cox filed the Complaint against the defendants in the instant action on May 21, 1997. (Pl.'s Ex. 5, Compl.)

II. Motion to Strike Certain Exhibits and Portions of Response Brief

Defendants have moved to strike plaintiff's exhibits 2–4, 6, 8–12, 14, 20–22, and 24, plaintiff's video exhibit, and the portions of Cox's brief that refer to such exhibits.

First, defendants move to strike Exhibits 2–4, 6, and 8–12, which are documents and correspondence exchanged between defendants and Cox, because none of these documents are supported by an affidavit from a person verifying their origin, truth, or accuracy. Plaintiff has since filed an affidavit by Michael Baird, Cox's attorney, verifying that such exhibits are true and accurate copies. (See Pl.'s Resp. Defs.' Mot. Strike, Ex. D, Baird Aff.) Thus, the Court denies defendants' motion to strike Exhibits 2–4, 6, and 8–12.

Second, defendants move to strike Exhibit 14, which is a compilation of raw data of fines imposed by the NFL by the National Football League Players Association ("NFLPA") during the years 1994 to 1997, because Cox has failed to properly authenticate the exhibit and has failed to indicate what the statistical summaries are supposed to represent or illustrate. Since the filing of defendants' motion to strike, Cox has provided the affidavit of Tim English, staff counsel to NFLPA, which properly authenticates the compilation as a business record. (See Pl.'s Resp. Defs.' Mot. Strike, Ex. F, English Aff.) Defendants' argument that plaintiff has failed to indicate what the statistical summaries are supposed to represent or illustrate goes more toward the appropriate weight the Court should give the evidence, which the Court discusses below, and not whether the evidence is admissible. Thus, defendants' motion to strike Exhibit 14 is denied.

Third, defendants move to strike Exhibits 20–22 and 24, which are various excerpts from books, magazine articles, and newspapers, because such exhibits are not properly authenticated and, even if they could be properly authenticated, they would still be inadmissible hearsay.

Exhibit 22 is an article from Sports Illustrated titled "How Zebras Get Their Stripes" and Exhibit 24 is an article from USA Today titled "Remember When Profanity Meant Something?" Because these exhibits are excerpts from a newspaper and a periodical, they are self-authenticating and, thus, require no affidavit for authentication. Fed.R.Evid. 902(6). But are they inadmissible hearsay? Cox relies on the Sports Illustrated article for author Rick Lipsey's recounting of a story by NFL referee Norm Schachter about an altercation with Dick Butkus of the Chicago Bears in 1972. (See Pl.'s 12N Stmt. p 37.) Exhibit 22 clearly constitutes inadmissible hearsay. Cox relies on Exhibit 24, however, to show that defendants were aware of the contents of the USA Today article, which stated that the "supply of genuinely offensive language has dwindled to nothing" and that profanity serves as a "safety valve," prior to their decision to fine Cox. Therefore, because the statements in Exhibit 24 are being offered to establish the then existing state of mind, i.e., motive, of the defendants, such statements are an exception to the hearsay rule. The Court thus grants defendants' motion to strike Exhibit 22 and denies the motion as to Exhibit 24.

Exhibit 20 contains excerpts from a book titled "Sunday Zebras" by Art Holst and Exhibit 21 contains excerpts from a book titled "Impartial Judgment" by Jim Tunney and Glenn Dickey. With regard to Exhibits 20 and 21, Cox failed to submit any pleading, deposition, answer to interrogatories, admissions on file, or affidavit to authenticate these exhibits. These unsworn excerpts from books inappropriately put before the Court material outside the proper scope of Rules 56(c) and 56(e). Moreover, even if Exhibits 20 and 21 were properly authenticated, they are not admissible. Cox offers Exhibit 20 and 21 to attack the defendants' position that the type of profanity used together with the obscene gestures displayed by Cox toward official Billy Smith on October 6, 1996 were unprecedented. Although Cox relies on Exhibit 20 to describe an altercation between former NFL referee Art Holst and a player, Dick Modzelewski, such altercation involved no verbal profanity or obscene gestures. (See Pl.'s 12N Stmt. p 33.) Therefore, Exhibit 20 is inadmissible based on relevance. Next, Cox relies on Exhibit 21 to establish that former NFL official Jim Tunney understands when players occasionally explode and to describe that Coach George Halas once called him an SOB during a game. Again, the fact that Tunney understands why players occasionally explode and the fact that Halas once called an official an SOB is immaterial to the Court's determination of whether defendants had a real, legitimate interest in protecting game officials from a player's ongoing pattern of verbal abuse involving profanity and obscenity. Therefore, the Court grants defendants' motion to strike Exhibits 20 and 21.

Fourth, the defendants move to strike the video exhibit submitted with Plaintiff's 12N Statement. The video exhibit contains: (1) excerpts from the NFL film titled "Tough Guys," (2) footage of Herman Moore making physical contact with an official, (3) excerpts regarding Cox on two ESPN shows, (4) footage of Curtis Conway making intentional physical contact with an official and throwing his helmet broadcast on FOX Television, and (5) real-time footage of the play at issue on October 6, 1996 broadcast on FOX Television.

In the Memorandum in Support of Defendants' Motion to Strike, however, defendants limit their argument to the inadmissibility of video excerpts from the NFL film titled "Tough Guys" cited in paragraphs 38 through 42 of Plaintiff's 12N Statement. Thus, the Court limits its review accordingly.

First, defendants argue that excerpts from "Tough Guys" have not been properly authenticated. The Court agrees because Cox failed to submit any pleading, deposition, answer to interrogatories, admission on file, or affidavit to authenticate these video excerpts. These unsworn video excerpts inappropriately put before the Court material not contemplated by Rules 56(c) and 56(e).

Second, defendants argue that even if such excerpts could be properly authenticated, the statements contained in these excerpts are inadmissible hearsay. The statements include: (1) former NFL player Deacon Jones describing former Chicago Bear Dick Butkus' meanness; (2) a commentator describing the playing style and attitude of former Chicago Bear defensive linesman Ed O'Bradovich and former Pittsburgh middle linebacker Jack Lambert; (3) a quote from an interview with O'Bradovich with many "bleeps" to cover his use of profanity; (4) a scene showing Lambert calling an official an "asshole"; and (5) a scene showing an altercation between former New York Giants linebacker Lawrence Taylor and an official with many of Taylor's words "bleeped" out. Cox argues that these excerpts are admissible under Fed.R.Evid. 801(d)(2)(D) as an admission of an agent of a party. The unanswered question is: an admission as to what? Surely Cox cannot be offering these statements as an admission that profanity or rage exists in the NFL because defendants do not even contend that NFL players have never used profanity or lost their temper during a game. As discussed below, the NFL merely contends that it has a legitimate interest in fining a player who has demonstrated an ongoing pattern of verbal abuse of officials in an amount that will deter such a player from further abuse. The statements contained in the excerpts from "Tough Guys" do not provide an admission to the contrary. Therefore, defendants' motion to strike is granted only as to the excerpts from the film "Tough Guys" contained in the video exhibit submitted with Plaintiff's 12N Statement.

In sum, the Court grants defendants' motion to strike with regard to Exhibits 20–22 and excerpts from "Tough Guys" included in plaintiff's video exhibit. The Court denies defendants' motion to strike with regard to Exhibits 2–4, 6, 8–12, 14, and 24.

III. Motion for Summary Judgment

First, defendants move for summary judgment as to defendant Tagliabue on the grounds that Title VII does not impose liability on individuals. The Court and plaintiff agree. In Williams v. Banning, the Seventh Circuit held that a supervisor sued in his individual capacity is not an "employer" as defined by Title VII. 72 F.3d 552, 553 (7th Cir.1995). Under Title VII, "[t]he term 'employer' is a statutory expression of traditional respondeat superior liability." Geier v. Medtronic, Inc., 99 F.3d 238, 244 (7th Cir.1996). "[A]n employer is liable for a supervisory employee's [discriminatory conduct] ... if the supervisor's acts fell within the scope of his authority or were foreseeable, and the employer failed to take appropriate remedial action." Banning, 72 F.3d at 555. Because Cox has sued Tagliabue in his individual capacity and Tagliabue is merely a supervisor, he is not subject to Title VII liability. In addition, because the alleged retaliation, e.g., fining Cox the equivalent of one game check, occurred in the scope of Tagliabue's authority, a remedy is available against the NFL in this action. The Court thus grants defendants' motion for summary judgment as to Tagliabue.

Next, defendants move for summary judgment on Cox's Title VII retaliation claim. "The retaliation provision of Title VII forbids an employer to 'discriminate against any individual ... because he has made a charge ... or participated in any manner in an investigation, proceeding, or hearing under' Title VII." Eiland v. Trinity Hosp., 150 F.3d 747, 753 (7th Cir.1998). To establish a prima facie case of retaliation, "a plaintiff must show that: (1) he engaged in statutorily protected expression; (2) he suffered an adverse action by the employer; and (3) there is a causal link between the protected expression and the adverse action." Johnson v. City of Fort Wayne, Ind., 91 F.3d 922, 938–39 (7th Cir.1996).

Cox has established the first prong of the prima facie case. It is undisputed that Cox engaged in statutorily protected expression when he filed a Title VII race discrimination suit against defendants on July 26, 1994 in the United States District Court for the Southern District of New York. (Defs.' 12(M) Stmt. p 44.)

With regard to the second prong, the record shows two potential adverse employment actions: (1) the NFL ordered him to participate in a drug abuse program and (2) the NFL fined Cox one game check for unsportsmanlike conduct. The Court addresses each in turn.

First, the Court is convinced that Cox is prohibited from obtaining relief on claims regarding the NFL's ordering of drug testing and abstinence from alcohol because such activity occurred outside of the 300–day window. In Illinois, a complainant must file a complaint within 300 days of the occurrence of the event that forms the basis of the Title

VII claim. 42 U.S.C. § 2000e–5(e); Koelsch v. Beltone Elecs. Corp., 46 F.3d 705, 707 (7th Cir.1995).

Cox filed his EEOC complaint alleging retaliation on January 23, 1997. (Defs.' 12M Stmt. p 51.) The 300–day window thus precludes relief based on events that occurred prior to March 29, 1996. Because the NFL ordered Cox to undergo drug testing from August 1 to September 12, 1994 and ordered him to abstain from alcohol during the 1994 season, such claims are obviously time-barred. (See Pl.'s 12(N) Stmt. pp 11–14.) Moreover, the Court finds that the continuing violation doctrine, a doctrine which the plaintiff does not mention in his response brief, is plainly inapplicable.

Further, the NFL's requiring Cox to report to the Regional Staff to keep the staff informed of his location during the off-season (in the event that the NFL needed to conduct a drug test) does not amount to an adverse employment action. "The alleged adverse employment actions ... must be material." Rabinovitz v. Pena, 89 F.3d 482, 488 (7th Cir.1996). The Seventh Circuit has held that "a materially adverse change in the terms and conditions of employment must be more disruptive than a mere inconvenience or an alteration of job responsibilities." Crady v. Liberty Nat'l Bank & Trust Co. of Ind., 993 F.2d 132, 136 (7th Cir.1993). "A materially adverse change might be indicated by a termination of employment, a demotion evidenced by a decrease in wage or salary, a less distinguished title, a material loss of benefits, significantly diminished material responsibilities, or other indices that might be unique to a particular situation." Id.

The NFL's requiring Cox to report as to his whereabouts in the off-season did not decrease Cox's salary, diminish his responsibilities, or result in a material loss of benefits. At best, such requirement constituted an inconvenience and, thus, it fails to rise to the level of a material adverse change in the terms and conditions of Cox's employment with the NFL.

Second, Cox argues that the NFL's fine of $87,500.00, or one of Cox's game checks, was an adverse employment action. Because the fine resulted in a significant decrease in Cox's salary, the Court finds that it constitutes an adverse employment action. Thus, Cox has established the second prong of the prima facie case with regard to the $87,500.00 fine.

With regard to the third prong, however, Cox has failed to establish a causal link between his Title VII race discrimination suit and the NFL's fining him $87,500.00. "In order to demonstrate a 'causal link,' the plaintiff must demonstrate that the employer would not have taken the adverse action 'but for' the protected expression." Johnson v. University of Wisc.-Eau Claire, 70 F.3d 469, 479 (7th Cir.1995) (quoting Klein v. Trustees of Ind. Univ., 766 F.2d 275, 280 (7th Cir.1985)). "Generally, a plaintiff may establish such a link through evidence that the discharge took place on the heels of protected activity." Dey v. Colt Const. & Dev. Co., 28 F.3d 1446, 1458 (7th Cir.1994). "As the temporal distance between ... [the] protected expression and the adverse action increase[s], it is less likely that there is a causal link between the two events." McKenzie v. Illinois Dep't of Transp., 92 F.3d 473, 485 (7th Cir.1996). Further, any "substantial time lapse between the events is counter-evidence of any causal connection." Johnson, 70 F.3d at 480.

Cox filed his Title VII discrimination suit against defendants in July 1994 and the NFL imposed the $87,500.00 fine in October 1996. The Seventh Circuit has held that much shorter time lapses fail to establish a causal link. See, e.g., Hughes v. Derwinski, 967 F.2d 1168, 1174 (7th Cir.1992) (holding that a four-month time lapse between protected conduct and adverse action does not raise an inference of retaliation); Juarez v. Ameritech Mobile Communications, Inc., 957 F.2d 317, 321 (7th Cir.1992) (holding that nearly six-month time lapse is too long). Further, in this case, the two-year time lapse is substantial and thus serves as counter-evidence of a causal connection. See, e.g., Johnson, 70 F.3d at 480 (stating that a twenty-month lapse between protected expression and adverse employment action was counter-evidence of any causal connection).

Moreover, regardless of the time lapse, Cox has failed to demonstrate that the NFL would not have fined him $87,500.00 but for his filing a discrimination case against defendants in 1994. It is undisputed that during a game between the Chicago Bears and Green Bay Packers on October 6, 1996, after a Packers touchdown, Cox threw his helmet to the ground under the goal post and that three officials called a penalty on Cox for unsportsmanlike conduct. (Compare Defs.' 12M Stmt. p 11 with Pl.'s Resp. Defs.' 12M Stmt. p 11.) It is also undisputed that during the extra point attempt, Cox verbally abused game official Billy Smith by repeatedly shouting obscenities at him in a loud voice, calling him a "motherfucker," and then telling him to "suck my dick." (Compare Defs.' 12M Stmt. p 12 with Pl.'s Resp. Defs.' 12M Stmt. p 12.) Cox admits making obscene gestures toward Smith by "giving him the finger" several times while standing two to three feet from him. (Compare Defs.' 12M Stmt. p 13 with Pl.'s Resp. Defs.' 12M Stmt. p 13.) It is undisputed that Cox's berating of Smith was broadcast live, his display of obscene gestures toward Smith was broadcast on replay by FOX television, and all of his conduct was visible to fans in Soldier Field. (Compare Defs.' 12M Stmt. p 14 with Pl.'s Resp. Defs.' 12M Stmt. p 12.) Further, it is undisputed that the NFL's 1996 Game–Related Discipline Rules provide that "[n]on-physical abuse of officials, including extreme profanity and other [abusive] language is prohibited" and players "should be aware that disciplinary action will result from ... abuse of game officials or fans ... and public obscenity." (Defs.' Ex. L, NFL's Letter to Cox of 10/10/96 at 2.) Cox admits that "[i]t was appropriate for the League to fine plaintiff for his conduct in the October 6, 1996 game." (Compare Defs.' 12M Stmt. p 15 with Pl.'s Resp. Defs.' 12M Stmt. p 15.) With regard to the amount of the fine, Cox admits that Commissioner Tagliabue met with key NFL officials to review the incident and that Jerry Seeman, Director of Officiating, Gene Washington, Director of Football Development, and Peter Hadhazy, Director of Football Operations, recommended suspension without pay due to Cox's repugnant treatment of a game official. (Compare Defs.' 12M Stmt. pp 19–24 with Pl.'s Resp. Defs.' 12M Stmt. pp 19–24.) Further, it is undisputed that Tagliabue determined that Cox's conduct represented "a unique set of circumstances" due to Cox's unusual and disturbing loss of control of his emotions, his unprovoked abuse of a game official, his continuing pattern of abuse toward officials as well as fans, and the NFL's past unsuccessful attempts to deter similar misconduct by Cox. (Compare Defs.' 12M Stmt. pp 25–27 with Pl.'s Resp. Defs.' 12M Stmt. pp 25–27.) Cox does not dispute that prior to October 1996, he had been fined for verbally abusing officials and for use of obscene gestures and that the 1996 discipline memorandum provides: "Repeat violations may entail higher fines, ejection, and/or suspension." (Compare Defs.' 12M Stmt. pp 8, 32 with Pl.'s Resp. Defs.' 12M Stmt. pp 8, 32.) Finally, Cox admits that based on the "totality of those circumstances," Tagliabue determined that Cox should be fined in an amount equal to his paycheck for one game, which was approximately $87,000.00. (Compare Defs.' 12M Stmt. p 28 with Pl.'s Resp. Defs.' 12M Stmt. p 28.)

Having admitted he displayed the behavior as outlined above and that it was appropriate for the NFL to fine him, Cox limits his argument to this: the punishment did not fit the crime. This argument, however, does little to establish "but for" causation and is merely an attempt to establish that the NFL's reasons for the punishment were a pretext for its alleged retaliatory motive. Indeed, Cox in his Brief in Response to the Defendants' Motion for Summary Judgment fails to explain how "but for" causation exists in this case and merely skips to a "pretext" argument. Thus, Cox has failed to meet his burden of establishing the third element of the prima facie case.

Even if Cox could establish a prima facie case of retaliation, the Court would still grant the NFL's motion for summary judgment. If a prima facie case is established, "the employer must offer a legitimate, nondiscriminatory reason for its actions. The burden then shifts back to the plaintiff to demonstrate that the employer's proffered explanation is merely a pretext for retaliation." Pafford v. Herman, 148 F.3d 658, 670 (1998). The plaintiff can meet this ultimate burden of persuasion "by showing that a discriminatory reason more likely motivated the employer or that the employer's proffered reason is unworthy of credence." Perfetti v. First Nat'l Bank of Chicago, 950 F.2d 449, 450–51 (7th Cir.1991). "It is not enough for the plaintiff to show that a reason given for a job action is not just, or fair, or sensible." Pignato v. American Trans Air, Inc., 14 F.3d 342, 349 (7th Cir.1994).

As discussed above, the NFL has stated legitimate, nondiscriminatory reasons for fining Cox the equivalent of one game check. While Cox appears to argue that the NFL's proffered reasons are unworthy of credence, he fails to meet his ultimate burden of persuasion in establishing that the NFL's proffered reasons are a pretext for retaliation.

First, Cox's factual statement that the NFL has never imposed a fine against a professional football player or coach for verbally abusing a game official that did not also include physical contact is not supported by plaintiff's Exhibit 14. (See Pl.'s 12N Stmt. p 25; Pl.'s Ex. 14.) Exhibit 14 is a collection of raw data of NFL fines imposed on players from 1994 to 1997 only and, thus, it is not a complete historical summary. Moreover, the record is devoid of any explanation of the types of violations, which are far from self-explanatory. For instance, in 1995, the data shows that the NFL fined four players for "Contact with Game Official" and one player for "Fight—Game Official Injured." However, in 1996 and 1997, the data shows the NFL fined players on nine occasions for "Actions Against Officials." It is unclear from the raw data whether the 1996–97 violations for "Actions Against Officials" merely involved verbal profanity against a game official since, unlike the 1995 violations, there is no mention of contact with an official. Moreover, several fines, including Cox's $87,500 fine, are merely described as "Multiple Violations" or "Multiple." Therefore, because the raw data is limited to four years and because the record lacks a competent explanation of the meaning of the raw data, Cox's statement that no player or coach has ever been fined by the NFL for verbally abusing an official is not supported by the record. Thus, Cox's averment cannot be deemed to controvert the Defendants' Rule 12M Statement.

Second, Cox argues that although defendants describe his use of profanity as detrimental to the League, the NFL uses such conduct to promote the NFL's "tough guy" image. Cox's reliance on the NFL film "Tough Guys" to prove pretext is misplaced. As discussed above, the film is inadmissible as an admission of a party opponent because the film admits nothing regarding the NFL's policy and practice of fining NFL players for continued use of profanity and obscene gestures toward officials. Further, Cox's use of profanity was but one of many reasons for imposing the $87,500.00 fine. According to Tagliabue, the NFL fined Cox $87,500.00 because of a unique set of factors: Cox's unusual and disturbing loss of control of his emotions, the unprovoked nature of his abuse of a game official, his continuing pattern of abuse toward officials as well as fans, and the NFL's past unsuccessful attempts to deter similar misconduct by Cox. Thus, any argument that merely suggests that profanity, in and of itself, is not a valid reason for imposing the $87,500.00 fine does not refute the many other reasons for the NFL's actions.

Third, Cox argues that the defendants' concern about the fans' reaction to profanity and obscenity is a mere pretext for retaliation. Cox opines that defendants' failure to maintain any record of these sorts of complaints means their concern is phony. The record belies this argument because records show that the NFL fined at least two players in 1996 for making obscene gestures and even Cox himself was fined in 1993 for verbally abusing officials with profanity. Further, Cox does not dispute that the NFL has repeatedly communicated to players its policy prohibiting extreme profanity and abusive behavior toward officials. Thus, this argument fails to raise a genuine issue of material fact regarding whether the defendants' proffered reasons were a pretext for retaliation.

Fourth, Cox points to alleged inequities between the fines imposed by the NFL on players for making physical contact with an official and his fine for verbally abusing an official to establish that the NFL's reasons for fining him are a pretext for retaliation. While Cox received an $87,500.00 fine for multiple violations for verbally abusing an official, Oakland Raiders offensive linemen Steve Wisniewski received a $20,000.00 fine for making intentional physical contact with an official on October 17, 1996. In addition, on November 2, 1996, Curtis Conway was fined $10,000.00 for making intentional physical contact with an official and slamming his helmet on the ground. Cox's argument, however, ignores the fact that his own conduct, albeit verbal and not physical, was part of a continuing pattern of abuse toward officials. Cox does not argue, and the record does not show, that Wisniewski or Conway had been fined previously for multiple incidents of abusing an official. In contrast to Wisniewski and Conway, Cox had been fined in December 1993 for misconduct involving five different incidents of abusing an official by use of profanity and obscenity. (Defs.' 12M Stmt. p 32; Cox Dep. Ex. E, NFL's Letter of 12/14/93.) In addition, Cox had been fined for using profanity and obscenity toward fans. (Defs.' 12M Stmt. p 32; Cox Dep. Ex. E, NFL's Letter of 12/14/93; Cox Dep. Ex. I, NFL's Letter of 12/20/95; Cox Dep. Ex. I, NFL's Letter of 9/26/96.) Moreover, the 1996 discipline memorandum provides that "[r]epeat violations may entail higher fines, ejection, and/or suspension." (Compare Defs.' 12M Stmt. pp 8, 32 with Pl.'s Resp. Defs.' 12M Stmt. pp 8, 32.) Therefore, this argument does not raise a genuine issue as to any material fact regarding whether defendants' interest in protecting game officials from an ongoing pattern of abuse by its players is phony. (Compare Defs.' 12M Stmt. pp 8, 32 with Pl.'s Resp. Defs.' 12M Stmt. pp 8, 32.)

In sum, Cox has failed to establish a prima facie case of retaliation and has failed to meet his ultimate burden of persuading the Court that the NFL's proffered reasons for fining him $87,500.00 were a pretext for retaliation. The Court thus grants defendants' motion for summary judgment.

Notes

1. Despite such roles models as Olympic diver Greg Louganis, tennis champion Martina Navratilova, golfer Muffin Spencer–Devlin, and figure skater Rudy Galindo, homosexual athletes like Vicki Yost continue to find themselves ostracized and ridiculed by coaches, teammates, opponents, and fans. As a result, many choose to either hide their sexual orientation or forego competitive sports completely. For a further look at the hardships faced by gay competitors, see, e.g., Susan K. Cahn, *Coming on Strong: Gender and Sexuality in Twentieth–Century Women's Sport* (1994); Michael A. Messner, *Power at Play: Sports and the Problem of Masculinity* (1992); Darrell Fry, *Fear Still Harms Outside Closet*, St. Petersburg Times, Dec. 16, 1998, at 1C; Scott Boeck, *Oberlin AD: Gay Student–Athletes "Terrified,"*

USA Today, Aug. 28, 1998, at 10C; George Diaz, *Gay Athletes Fight Silent War: Many Want to Go Public, But They Fear Losing Support of Public, Teammates*, Orlando Sentinel, Mar. 30, 1997, at D6.

2. At one time, African-Americans were excluded from many leagues. Today, however, they constitute 79% of the NBA, 66% of the NFL, and 17% of MLB. *See* James P. Pinkerton, *When Sports, Race and Politics Collide*, Memphis Comm. Appeal, Apr. 21, 1998, at A9. Nevertheless, racism in sports is pervasive, seemingly intractable, and often fanned by promoters and the media to boost sales. For a further examination of the subject from various viewpoints, see, e.g., *Williams v. Eaton*, 468 F.2d 1079 (10th Cir.1972); *Hodges v. National Basketball Ass'n*, 1998 WL 26183 (N.D.Ill.1998); *Hysaw v. Washburn University of Topeka*, 690 F.Supp. 940 (D.Kan.1987); Jack F. Williams & Jack A. Chambliss, *Title VII and the Reserve Clause: A Statistical Analysis of Salary Discrimination in Major League Baseball*, 52 U. Miami L. Rev. 461 (1998); Phoebe W. Williams, *Performing in a Racially Hostile Environment*, 6 Marq. Sports L.J. 287 (1996); Timothy Davis, *The Myth of the Superspade: The Persistence of Racism in College Athletics*, 22 Fordham Urb. L.J. 615 (1995); Allison Samuels, *Race, Respect and the NBA*, Newsweek, Dec. 21, 1998, at 55.

3. Sexual orientation and race are not the only grounds on which hostile environment claims have been based. In March 1996, for example, Denver Nuggets guard Mahmoud Abdul–Rauf was indefinitely suspended by the NBA when he refused, for religious reasons, to stand during the national anthem. After one game and the loss of $30,000 in pay, however, Abdul–Rauf agreed to stand in silent prayer during the song. *See further* Kelly B. Koenig, *Mahmoud Abdul–Rauf's Suspension for Refusing to Stand for the National Anthem: A "Free Throw" for the NBA and Denver Nuggets, or a "Slam Dunk" Violation of Abdul–Rauf's Title VII Rights?*, 76 Wash. U. L.Q. 377 (1998). For other types of hostile work environment claims, see, e.g., *Caldwell v. American Basketball Ass'n, Inc.*, 66 F.3d 523 (2d Cir.1995), *cert. denied*, 518 U.S. 1033 (1996) (union activities), and *Klemencic v. Ohio State University*, 10 F.Supp.2d 911 (S.D.Ohio 1998) (sexual harassment).

4. As *Cox* demonstrates, many hostile environment claims arise following the imposition of discipline. For a look at punishment in team sports, see, e.g., *Brant v. United States Polo Ass'n*, 631 F.Supp. 71 (S.D.Fla.1986), and Jan Stiglitz, *Player Discipline in Team Sports*, 5 Marq. Sports L.J. 167 (1995). For a look at punishment in individual sports, see, e.g., *Blalock v. Ladies Professional Golf Ass'n*, 359 F.Supp. 1260 (N.D.Ga.1973), and *Lindemann v. American Horse Shows Ass'n, Inc.*, 624 N.Y.S.2d 723 (Sup.Ct.1994).

Problem 28

Worried about its potential liability, a football team posted the following memorandum at its training facility: "To ensure the comfort and safety of all employees and guests, no pornographic material of any kind shall be kept, read, or displayed on the premises (including the locker room)." If one of the players sues the club, claiming his First Amendment rights are being violated, how should the court rule? *See Robinson v. Jacksonville Shipyards, Inc.*, 760 F.Supp. 1486 (M.D.Fla.1991).

4. DRUGS

In recent years, numerous steps have been taken to curb drug abuse by athletes. Predictably, these efforts have led to a spate of lawsuits.

VERNONIA SCHOOL DISTRICT 47J v. ACTON

515 U.S. 646 (1995).

Justice SCALIA delivered the opinion of the Court.

The Student Athlete Drug Policy adopted by School District 47J in the town of Vernonia, Oregon, authorizes random urinalysis drug testing of students who participate in the District's school athletics programs. We granted certiorari to decide whether this violates the Fourth and Fourteenth Amendments to the United States Constitution.

I

A

Petitioner Vernonia School District 47J (District) operates one high school and three grade schools in the logging community of Vernonia, Oregon. As elsewhere in small-town America, school sports play a prominent role in the town's life, and student athletes are admired in their schools and in the community.

Drugs had not been a major problem in Vernonia schools. In the mid-to-late 1980's, however, teachers and administrators observed a sharp increase in drug use. Students began to speak out about their attraction to the drug culture, and to boast that there was nothing the school could do about it. Along with more drugs came more disciplinary problems. Between 1988 and 1989 the number of disciplinary referrals in Vernonia schools rose to more than twice the number reported in the early 1980's, and several students were suspended. Students became increasingly rude during class; outbursts of profane language became common.

Not only were student athletes included among the drug users but, as the District Court found, athletes were the leaders of the drug culture. 796 F.Supp. 1354, 1357 (D.Ore.1992). This caused the District's administrators particular concern, since drug use increases the risk of sports-related injury. Expert testimony at the trial confirmed the deleterious effects of drugs on motivation, memory, judgment, reaction, coordination, and performance. The high school football and wrestling coach witnessed a severe sternum injury suffered by a wrestler, and various omissions of safety procedures and misexecutions by football players, all attributable in his belief to the effects of drug use.

Initially, the District responded to the drug problem by offering special classes, speakers, and presentations designed to deter drug use. It even brought in a specially trained dog to detect drugs, but the drug problem persisted. According to the District Court:

> "[T]he administration was at its wits end and ... a large segment of the student body, particularly those involved in interscholastic athletics, was in a state of rebellion. Disciplinary problems had reached 'epidemic proportions.' The coincidence of an almost three-fold increase in classroom disruptions and disciplinary reports along with the staff's direct observations of students using drugs or glamorizing drug and alcohol use led the administration to the inescapable conclusion that the rebellion was being fueled by alcohol and drug abuse as well as the student's misperceptions about the drug culture."

Ibid.

At that point, District officials began considering a drug-testing program. They held a parent "input night" to discuss the proposed Student Athlete Drug Policy (Policy), and the parents in attendance gave their unanimous approval. The school board approved the Policy for implementation in the fall of 1989. Its expressed purpose is to prevent student athletes from using drugs, to protect their health and safety, and to provide drug users with assistance programs.

B

The Policy applies to all students participating in interscholastic athletics. Students wishing to play sports must sign a form consenting to the testing and must obtain the written consent of their parents. Athletes are tested at the beginning of the season for their sport. In addition, once each week of the season the names of the athletes are placed in a "pool" from which a student, with the supervision of two adults, blindly draws the names of 10% of the athletes for random testing. Those selected are notified and tested that same day, if possible.

The student to be tested completes a specimen control form which bears an assigned number. Prescription medications that the student is taking must be identified by providing a copy of the prescription or a doctor's authorization. The student then enters an empty locker room accompanied by an adult monitor of the same sex. Each boy selected produces a sample at a urinal, remaining fully clothed with his back to the monitor, who stands approximately 12 to 15 feet behind the student. Monitors may (though do not always) watch the student while he produces the sample, and they listen for normal sounds of urination. Girls produce samples in an enclosed bathroom stall, so that they can be heard but not observed. After the sample is produced, it is given to the monitor, who checks it for temperature and tampering and then transfers it to a vial.

The samples are sent to an independent laboratory, which routinely tests them for amphetamines, cocaine, and marijuana. Other drugs, such as LSD, may be screened at the request of the District, but the identity of a particular student does not determine which drugs will be tested. The laboratory's procedures are 99.94% accurate. The District follows strict procedures regarding the chain of custody and access to test results. The laboratory does not know the identity of the students whose samples it tests. It is authorized to mail written test reports only to the superintendent and to provide test results to District personnel by telephone only after the requesting official recites a code confirming his authority. Only the superintendent, principals, vice-principals, and athletic directors have access to test results, and the results are not kept for more than one year.

If a sample tests positive, a second test is administered as soon as possible to confirm the result. If the second test is negative, no further action is taken. If the second test is positive, the athlete's parents are notified, and the school principal convenes a meeting with the student and his parents, at which the student is given the option of (1) participating for six weeks in an assistance program that includes weekly urinalysis, or (2) suffering suspension from athletics for the remainder of the current season and the next athletic season. The student is then retested prior to the start of the next athletic season for which he or she is eligible. The Policy states that a second offense results in automatic imposition of option (2); a third offense in suspension for the remainder of the current season and the next two athletic seasons.

C

In the fall of 1991, respondent James Acton, then a seventh-grader, signed up to play football at one of the District's grade schools. He was denied participation, however, because he and his parents refused to sign the testing consent forms. The Actons filed suit, seeking declaratory and injunctive relief from enforcement of the Policy on the grounds that it violated the Fourth and Fourteenth Amendments to the United States Constitution and Article I, § 9, of the Oregon Constitution. After a bench trial, the District Court entered an order denying the claims on the merits and dismissing the action. 796 F.Supp. at 1355. The United States Court of Appeals for the Ninth Circuit reversed, holding that the Policy violated both the Fourth and Fourteenth Amendments and Article I, § 9, of the Oregon Constitution. 23 F.3d 1514 (1994). We granted certiorari. 513 U.S. 1013, 115 S.Ct. 571, 130 L.Ed.2d 488 (1994).

II

The Fourth Amendment to the United States Constitution provides that the Federal Government shall not violate "[t]he right of the people to be secure in their persons, houses, papers, and effects, against unreasonable searches and seizures...." We have held that the Fourteenth Amendment extends this constitutional guarantee to searches and seizures by state officers, Elkins v. United States, 364 U.S. 206, 213, 80 S.Ct. 1437, 1441–1442, 4 L.Ed.2d 1669 (1960), including public school officials, New Jersey v. T.L.O., 469 U.S. 325, 336–337, 105 S.Ct. 733, 740, 83 L.Ed.2d 720 (1985). In Skinner v. Railway Labor Executives' Assn., 489 U.S. 602, 617, 109 S.Ct. 1402, 1413, 103 L.Ed.2d 639 (1989), we held that state-compelled collection and testing of urine, such as that required by the Student Athlete Drug Policy, constitutes a "search" subject to the demands of the Fourth Amendment. See also Treasury

Employees v. Von Raab, 489 U.S. 656, 665, 109 S.Ct. 1384, 1390, 103 L.Ed.2d 685 (1989).

As the text of the Fourth Amendment indicates, the ultimate measure of the constitutionality of a governmental search is "reasonableness." At least in a case such as this, where there was no clear practice, either approving or disapproving the type of search at issue, at the time the constitutional provision was enacted, whether a particular search meets the reasonableness standard " 'is judged by balancing its intrusion on the individual's Fourth Amendment interests against its promotion of legitimate governmental interests.' " Skinner, supra, at 619, 109 S.Ct. at 1414 (quoting Delaware v. Prouse, 440 U.S. 648, 654, 99 S.Ct. 1391, 1396, 59 L.Ed.2d 660 (1979)). Where a search is undertaken by law enforcement officials to discover evidence of criminal wrongdoing, this Court has said that reasonableness generally requires the obtaining of a judicial warrant, Skinner, supra, at 619, 109 S.Ct. at 1414. Warrants cannot be issued, of course, without the showing of probable cause required by the Warrant Clause. But a warrant is not required to establish the reasonableness of all government searches; and when a warrant is not required (and the Warrant Clause therefore not applicable), probable cause is not invariably required either. A search unsupported by probable cause can be constitutional, we have said, "when special needs, beyond the normal need for law enforcement, make the warrant and probable-cause requirement impracticable." Griffin v. Wisconsin, 483 U.S. 868, 873, 107 S.Ct. 3164, 3168, 97 L.Ed.2d 709 (1987) (internal quotation marks omitted).

We have found such "special needs" to exist in the public-school context. There, the warrant requirement "would unduly interfere with the maintenance of the swift and informal disciplinary procedures [that are] needed," and "strict adherence to the requirement that searches be based upon probable cause" would undercut "the substantial need of teachers and administrators for freedom to maintain order in the schools." T.L.O., supra, 469 U.S. at 340, 341, 105 S.Ct. at 742. The school search we approved in T.L.O., while not based on probable cause, was based on individualized suspicion of wrongdoing. As we explicitly acknowledged, however, " 'the Fourth Amendment imposes no irreducible requirement of such suspicion,' " id. at 342, n. 8, 105 S.Ct. at 743, n. 8 (quoting United States v. Martinez–Fuerte, 428 U.S. 543, 560–561, 96 S.Ct. 3074, 3084, 49 L.Ed.2d 1116 (1976)). We have upheld suspicionless searches and seizures to conduct drug testing of railroad personnel involved in train accidents, see Skinner, supra; to conduct random drug testing of federal customs officers who carry arms or are involved in drug interdiction, see Von Raab, supra; and to maintain automobile checkpoints looking for illegal immigrants and contraband, Martinez–Fuerte, supra, and drunk drivers, Michigan Dept. of State Police v. Sitz, 496 U.S. 444, 110 S.Ct. 2481, 110 L.Ed.2d 412 (1990).

III

The first factor to be considered is the nature of the privacy interest upon which the search here at issue intrudes. The Fourth Amendment does not protect all subjective expectations of privacy, but only those that society recognizes as "legitimate." T.L.O., 469 U.S. at 338, 105 S.Ct. at 741. What expectations are legitimate varies, of course, with context, id. at 337, 105 S.Ct. at 740, depending, for example, upon whether the individual asserting the privacy interest is at home, at work, in a car, or in a public park. In addition, the legitimacy of certain privacy expectations vis-a-vis the State may depend upon the individual's legal relationship with the State. For example, in Griffin, supra, we held that, although a "probationer's home, like anyone else's, is protected by the Fourth Amendmen[t]," the supervisory relationship between probationer and State justifies "a degree of impingement upon [a probationer's] privacy that would not be constitutional if applied to the public at large." 483 U.S. at 873, 875, 107 S.Ct. at 3168, 3169. Central, in our view, to the present case is the fact that the subjects of the Policy are (1) children, who (2) have been committed to the temporary custody of the State as schoolmaster.

Traditionally at common law, and still today, unemancipated minors lack some of the most fundamental rights of self-determination—including even the right of liberty in its narrow sense, i.e., the right to come and go at will. They are subject, even as to their physical freedom, to the control of their parents or guardians. See 59 Am.Jur.2d § 10 (1987). When parents place minor children in private schools for their education, the teachers and administrators of those schools stand in loco parentis over the children entrusted to them. In fact, the tutor or schoolmaster is the very prototype of that status. As Blackstone describes it, a parent "may ... delegate part of his parental authority, during his life, to the tutor or schoolmaster of his child; who is then in loco parentis, and has such a portion of the power of the parent committed to his charge, viz. that of restraint and correction, as may be necessary to answer the purposes for which he is employed." 1 W. Blackstone, Commentaries on the Laws of England 441 (1769).

Fourth Amendment rights, no less than First and Fourteenth Amendment rights, are different in public schools than elsewhere; the "reasonableness" inquiry cannot disregard the schools' custodial and tutelary responsibility for children. For their own good and that of their classmates, public school children are routinely required to submit to various physical examinations, and to be vaccinated against various diseases. According to the American Academy of Pediatrics, most public schools "provide vision and hearing screening and dental and dermatological checks.... Others also mandate scoliosis screening at appropriate grade levels." Committee on School Health, American Academy of Pediatrics, School Health: A Guide for Health Professionals 2 (1987). In the 1991–1992 school year, all 50 States required public-school students to be vaccinated against diphtheria, measles, rubella, and polio. U.S. Dept. of Health & Human Services, Public Health Service, Centers for Disease Control, State Immunization Requirements 1991–1992, p. 1. Particularly with regard to medical examinations and procedures, therefore, "students within the school environment have a lesser expectation of privacy than members of the population generally." T.L.O., 469 U.S. at 348, 105 S.Ct. at 746 (Powell, J., concurring).

Legitimate privacy expectations are even less with regard to student athletes. School sports are not for the bashful. They require "suiting up" before each practice or event, and showering and changing afterwards. Public school locker rooms, the usual sites for these activities, are not notable for the privacy they afford. The locker rooms in Vernonia are typical: no individual dressing rooms are provided; shower heads are lined up along a wall, unseparated by any sort of partition or curtain; not even all the toilet stalls have doors. As the United States Court of Appeals for the Seventh Circuit has noted, there is "an element of 'communal undress' inherent in athletic participation," Schaill by Kross v. Tippecanoe County School Corp., 864 F.2d 1309, 1318 (1988).

There is an additional respect in which school athletes have a reduced expectation of privacy. By choosing to "go out for the team," they voluntarily subject themselves to a degree of regulation even higher than that imposed on students generally. In Vernonia's public schools, they must submit to a preseason physical exam (James testified that his included the giving of a urine sample, App. 17), they must acquire adequate insurance coverage or sign an insurance waiver, maintain a minimum grade point average, and comply with any "rules of conduct, dress, training hours and related matters as may be established for each sport by the head coach and athletic director with the principal's approval." Record, Exh. 2, p. 30, p 8. Somewhat like adults who choose to participate in a "closely regulated industry," students who voluntarily participate in school athletics have reason to expect intrusions upon normal rights and privileges, including privacy. See Skinner, 489 U.S. at 627, 109 S.Ct. at 1418–1419; United States v. Biswell, 406 U.S. 311, 316, 92 S.Ct. 1593, 1596, 32 L.Ed.2d 87 (1972).

IV

Having considered the scope of the legitimate expectation of privacy at issue here, we turn next to the character of the intrusion that is complained of. We recognized in Skinner that collecting the samples for urinalysis intrudes upon "an excretory function traditionally shielded by great privacy." Skinner, 489 U.S. at 626, 109 S.Ct. at 1418. We noted, however, that the degree of intrusion depends upon the manner in which production of the urine sample is monitored. Ibid. Under the District's Policy, male students produce samples at a urinal along a wall. They remain fully clothed and are only observed from behind, if at all. Female students produce samples in an enclosed stall, with a female monitor standing outside listening only for sounds of tampering. These conditions are nearly identical to those typically encountered in public restrooms, which men, women, and especially school children use daily. Under such conditions, the privacy interests compromised by the process of obtaining the urine sample are in our view negligible.

The other privacy-invasive aspect of urinalysis is, of course, the information it discloses concerning the state of the subject's body, and the materials he has ingested. In this regard it is significant that the tests at issue here look only for drugs, and not for whether the student is, for example, epileptic, pregnant, or diabetic. See Skinner, supra, at 617, 109 S.Ct. at 1413. Moreover, the drugs for which the samples are screened are standard, and do not vary according to the identity of the student. And finally, the results of the tests are disclosed only to a limited class of school personnel who have a need to know; and they are not turned over to law enforcement authorities or used for any internal disciplinary function. 796 F.Supp. at 1364; see also 23 F.3d at 1521.

Respondents argue, however, that the District's Policy is in fact more intrusive than this suggests, because it requires the students, if they are to avoid sanctions for a falsely positive test, to identify in advance prescription medications they are taking. We agree that this raises some cause for concern. In Von Raab, we flagged as one of the salutary features of the Customs Service drug-testing program the fact that employees were not required to disclose medical information unless they tested positive, and, even then, the information was supplied to a licensed physician rather than to the Government employer. See Von Raab, 489 U.S. at 672–673, n. 2, 109 S.Ct. at 1394–1395, n. 2. On the other hand, we have never indicated that requiring advance disclosure of medications is per se unreasonable. Indeed, in Skinner we held that it was not "a significant invasion of privacy." Skinner, 489 U.S. at 626, n. 7, 109 S.Ct. at 1418, n. 7. It can be argued that, in Skinner, the disclosure went only to the medical personnel taking the sample, and the Government personnel analyzing it, see id. at 609, 109 S.Ct. at 1408–1409, but see id. at 610, 109 S.Ct. at 1409 (railroad personnel responsible for forwarding the sample, and presumably accompanying information, to the Government's testing lab); and that disclosure to teachers and coaches—to persons who personally know the student—is a greater invasion of privacy. Assuming for the sake of argument that both those propositions are true, we do not believe they establish a difference that respondents are entitled to rely on here.

The General Authorization Form that respondents refused to sign, which refusal was the basis for James's exclusion from the sports program, said only (in relevant part): "I ... authorize the Vernonia School District to conduct a test on a urine specimen which I provide to test for drugs and/or alcohol use. I also authorize the release of information concerning the results of such a test to the Vernonia School District and to the parents and/or guardians of the student." App. 10–11. While the practice of the District seems to have been to have a school official take medication information from the student at the time of the test, see App. 29, 42, that practice is not set forth in, or required by, the Policy, which says simply: "Student athletes who ... are or have been taking prescription medication must provide verification (either by a copy of the prescription or by doctor's authorization) prior to being tested." App. 8. It may well be that, if and when James was selected for random testing at a time that he was taking medication, the School District would have permitted him to provide the requested information in a confidential manner—for example, in a sealed envelope delivered to the testing lab. Nothing in the Policy contradicts that, and when respondents choose, in effect, to challenge the Policy on its face, we will not assume the worst. Accordingly, we reach the same conclusion as in Skinner: that the invasion of privacy was not significant.

V

Finally, we turn to consider the nature and immediacy of the governmental concern at issue here, and the efficacy of this means for meeting it. In both Skinner and Von Raab, we characterized the government interest motivating the search as "compelling." Skinner, supra, 489 U.S. at 628, 109 S.Ct. at 1419 (interest in preventing railway accidents); Von Raab, supra, 489 U.S. at 670, 109 S.Ct. at 1393 (interest in insuring fitness of customs officials to interdict drugs and handle firearms). Relying on these cases, the District Court held that because the District's program also called for drug testing in the absence of individualized suspicion, the District "must demonstrate a 'compelling need' for the program." 796 F.Supp. at 1363. The Court of Appeals appears to have agreed with this view. See 23 F.3d at 1526. It is a mistake, however, to think that the phrase "compelling state interest," in the Fourth Amendment context, describes a fixed, minimum quantum of governmental concern, so that one can dispose of a case by answering in isolation the question: Is there a compelling state interest here? Rather, the phrase describes an interest which appears important enough to justify the particular search at hand, in light of other factors which show the search to be relatively intrusive upon a genuine expectation of privacy. Whether that relatively high degree of government concern is necessary in this case or not, we think it is met.

That the nature of the concern is important—indeed, perhaps compelling—can hardly be doubted. Deterring drug use by our Nation's schoolchildren is at least as important as enhancing efficient enforcement of the Nation's laws against the importation of drugs, which was the governmental concern in Von Raab, supra, 489 U.S. at 668, 109 S.Ct. at 1392, or deterring drug use by engineers and trainmen, which was the governmental concern in Skinner, supra, at 628, 109 S.Ct. at 1419. School years are the time when the physical, psychological, and addictive effects of drugs are most severe. "Maturing nervous systems are more critically impaired by intoxicants than mature ones are; childhood losses in learning are lifelong and profound"; "children grow chemically dependent more quickly than adults, and their record of recovery is depressingly poor." Hawley, The Bumpy Road to Drug–Free Schools, 72 Phi Delta Kappan 310, 314 (1990). See also Estroff, Schwartz, & Hoffmann, Adolescent Cocaine Abuse: Addictive Potential, Behavioral and Psychiatric Effects, 28 Clinical Pediatrics 550 (Dec. 1989); Kandel, Davies, Karus, & Yamaguchi, The Consequences in Young Adulthood of Adolescent Drug Involvement, 43 Arch. Gen. Psychiatry 746 (Aug. 1986). And, of course, the effects of a drug-infested school are visited not just upon the users, but upon the entire student body and faculty, as the educational process is disrupted. In the present case, moreover, the necessity for the

State to act is magnified by the fact that this evil is being visited not just upon individuals at large, but upon children for whom it has undertaken a special responsibility of care and direction. Finally, it must not be lost sight of that this program is directed more narrowly to drug use by school athletes, where the risk of immediate physical harm to the drug user or those with whom he is playing his sport is particularly high. Apart from psychological effects, which include impairment of judgment, slow reaction time, and a lessening of the perception of pain, the particular drugs screened by the District's Policy have been demonstrated to pose substantial physical risks to athletes. Amphetamines produce an "artificially induced heart rate increase, [p]eripheral vasoconstriction, [b]lood pressure increase, and [m]asking of the normal fatigue response," making them a "very dangerous drug when used during exercise of any type." Hawkins, Drugs and Other Ingesta: Effects on Athletic Performance, in H. Appenzeller, Managing Sports and Risk Management Strategies 90, 90–91 (1993). Marijuana causes "[i]rregular blood pressure responses during changes in body position," "[r]eduction in the oxygen-carrying capacity of the blood," and "[i]nhibition of the normal sweating responses resulting in increased body temperature." Id. at 94. Cocaine produces "[v]asoconstriction[,] [e]levated blood pressure," and "[p]ossible coronary artery spasms and myocardial infarction." Ibid.

As for the immediacy of the District's concerns: We are not inclined to question—indeed, we could not possibly find clearly erroneous—the District Court's conclusion that "a large segment of the student body, particularly those involved in interscholastic athletics, was in a state of rebellion," that "[d]isciplinary actions had reached 'epidemic proportions,' " and that "the rebellion was being fueled by alcohol and drug abuse as well as by the student's misperceptions about the drug culture." 796 F.Supp. at 1357. That is an immediate crisis of greater proportions than existed in Skinner, where we upheld the Government's drug testing program based on findings of drug use by railroad employees nationwide, without proof that a problem existed on the particular railroads whose employees were subject to the test. See Skinner, 489 U.S. at 607, 109 S.Ct. at 1407–1408. And of much greater proportions than existed in Von Raab, where there was no documented history of drug use by any customs officials. See Von Raab, 489 U.S. at 673, 109 S.Ct. at 1395; id. at 683, 109 S.Ct. at 1400 (Scalia, J., dissenting).

As to the efficacy of this means for addressing the problem: It seems to us self-evident that a drug problem largely fueled by the "role model" effect of athletes' drug use, and of particular danger to athletes, is effectively addressed by making sure that athletes do not use drugs. Respondents argue that a "less intrusive means to the same end" was available, namely, "drug testing on suspicion of drug use." Brief for Respondents 45–46. We have repeatedly refused to declare that only the "least intrusive" search practicable can be reasonable under the Fourth Amendment. Skinner, supra, at 629, n. 9, 109 S.Ct. at 1420, n. 9 (collecting cases). Respondents' alternative entails substantial difficulties—if it is indeed practicable at all. It may be impracticable, for one thing, simply because the parents who are willing to accept random drug testing for athletes are not willing to accept accusatory drug testing for all students, which transforms the process into a badge of shame. Respondents' proposal brings the risk that teachers will impose testing arbitrarily upon troublesome but not drug-likely students. It generates the expense of defending lawsuits that charge such arbitrary imposition, or that simply demand greater process before accusatory drug testing is imposed. And not least of all, it adds to the ever-expanding diversionary duties of schoolteachers the new function of spotting and bringing to account drug abuse, a task for which they are ill-prepared, and which is not readily compatible with their vocation. In many respects, we think, testing based on "suspicion" of drug use would not be better, but worse.

VI

Taking into account all the factors we have considered above—the decreased expectation of privacy, the relative unobtrusiveness of the search, and the severity of the need met by the search—we conclude Vernonia's Policy is reasonable and hence constitutional.

We caution against the assumption that suspicionless drug testing will readily pass constitutional muster in other contexts. The most significant element in this case is the first we discussed: that the Policy was undertaken in furtherance of the government's responsibilities, under a public school system, as guardian and tutor of children entrusted to its care. Just as when the government conducts a search in its capacity as employer (a warrantless search of an absent employee's desk to obtain an urgently needed file, for example), the relevant question is whether that intrusion upon privacy is one that a reasonable employer might engage in, see O'Connor v. Ortega, 480 U.S. 709, 107 S.Ct. 1492, 94 L.Ed.2d 714 (1987); so also when the government acts as guardian and tutor the relevant question is whether the search is one that a reasonable guardian and tutor might undertake. Given the findings of need made by the District Court, we conclude that in the present case it is.

We may note that the primary guardians of Vernonia's schoolchildren appear to agree. The record shows no objection to this districtwide program by any parents other than the couple before us here—even though, as we have described, a public meeting was held to obtain parents' views. We find insufficient basis to contradict the judgment of Vernonia's parents, its school board, and the District Court, as to what was reasonably in the interest of these children under the circumstances.

The Ninth Circuit held that Vernonia's Policy not only violated the Fourth Amendment, but also, by reason of that violation, contravened Article I, § 9 of the Oregon Constitution. Our conclusion that the former holding was in error means that the latter holding rested on a flawed premise. We therefore vacate the judgment, and remand the case to the Court of Appeals for further proceedings consistent with this opinion.

[The concurring opinion of Justice Ginsburg is omitted.]

Justice O'CONNOR, with whom Justice STEVENS and Justice SOUTER join, dissenting.

The population of our Nation's public schools, grades 7 through 12, numbers around 18 million. See U.S. Dept. of Education, National Center for Education Statistics, Digest of Education Statistics 58 (1994) (Table 43). By the reasoning of today's decision, the millions of these students who participate in interscholastic sports, an overwhelming majority of whom have given school officials no reason whatsoever to suspect they use drugs at school, are open to an intrusive bodily search.

In justifying this result, the Court dispenses with a requirement of individualized suspicion on considered policy grounds. First, it explains that precisely because every student athlete is being tested, there is no concern that school officials might act arbitrarily in choosing who to test. Second, a broad-based search regime, the Court reasons, dilutes the accusatory nature of the search. In making these policy arguments, of course, the Court sidesteps powerful, countervailing privacy concerns. Blanket searches, because they can involve "thousands or millions" of searches, "pos[e] a greater threat to liberty" than do suspicion-based ones, which "affec[t] one person at a time," Illinois v. Krull, 480 U.S. 340, 365, 107 S.Ct. 1160, 1175, 94 L.Ed.2d 364 (1987) (O'Connor, J., dissenting). Searches based on individualized suspicion also afford potential targets considerable control over whether they will, in fact, be searched because a person can avoid such a search by not acting in an objectively suspicious way. And given that the surest way to avoid acting suspiciously is to avoid the underlying wrongdoing, the costs of such a regime, one would think, are minimal.

But whether a blanket search is "better" than a regime based on individualized suspicion is not a debate in which we should engage. In my view, it is not open to judges or government officials to decide on policy grounds which is better and which is worse. For most of our constitutional history, mass, suspicionless searches have been generally considered per se unreasonable within the meaning of the Fourth Amendment. And we have allowed exceptions in recent years only where it has been clear that a suspicion-based regime would be ineffectual. Because that is not the case here, I dissent.

[The remainder of Justice O'Connor's dissent is omitted.]

SCHULZ v. UNITED STATES BOXING ASS'N

105 F.3d 127 (3d Cir.1997).

POLLAK, District Judge (sitting by designation).

This case involves a court's authority to order a private organization that sponsors prizefights to strip a champion of his title.

Defendant Francois Botha defeated plaintiff Axel Schulz in a fight for the International Boxing Federation (IBF) heavyweight championship. Botha then tested positive for use of steroids. After a hearing, the

IBF declined to disqualify Botha, allowing him to retain his IBF crown. Schulz sued and the district court issued a preliminary injunction mandating that the IBF disqualify Botha. Botha, the IBF, and the IBF's parent United States Boxing Association (USBA) now appeal the grant of the preliminary injunction.

I. BACKGROUND

Three major bodies regulate and promote the sport of professional boxing: the World Boxing Association, the World Boxing Council, and the International Boxing Federation with its parent United States Boxing Association. Each of these organizations classifies boxers by weight class, ranks the boxers within each class, and, for a participation fee, sponsors—or "sanctions"—both championship and non-championship bouts. The IBF was formed to provide a mechanism through which the United States Boxing Association, a national organization, could crown world champions. According to its literature, the IBF was organized "by representatives of various athletic commissions and other interested persons for the purpose of obtaining greater efficiency and uniformity in the supervision of professional boxing and to encourage and assist professional boxing." App. 274.

The IBF has promulgated a set of rules and regulations governing IBF-sanctioned bouts. Rule 20, entitled "Anti-doping," requires boxers to provide a urine specimen after each fight to be tested for, among other substances, anabolic steroids and pain killers. This rule adds that "[s]hould that specimen prove positive, disciplinary action will follow." App. 284. In addition, Rule 26, entitled "Penalties," provides as follows:

> Should anyone be found in violation of the rules and regulations of the IBF or USBA by any Committees impaneled by the President, they may be subject to fine, forfeiture of monies, vacation of title or any other discipline directed by the Committee and approved by the President for the good of the organization.

App. 291.

On December 9, 1995, Francois Botha of South Africa fought Axel Schulz of Germany in Stuttgart for the vacant IBF heavyweight championship. Before the bout, each fighter paid the IBF more than $45,000 in "sanctioning fees" and other fees. Each boxer's representative also signed a document entitled "Rules for IBF/USBA & Intercontinental Championship Bouts" ("Bout Rules"). The Bout Rules were also signed by Robert W. Lee, president of the IBF/USBA, and by a representative of the local boxing commission, the German Boxing Federation. The Bout Rules begin by stating that "[t]he Championship fight will be governed by the rules and regulations of the IBF/USBA and local Boxing Commission. . . ." App. 83. The Bout Rules then set out four pages of detailed requirements. The last of these is entitled "AntiDoping" and reads as follows:

> Each boxer is required to take a urinalysis immediately following the bout. Said specimen must be taken with a Ringside Physician and Commission Inspector on hand. The specimens should be taken in a plastic container and properly marked by the physician and boxer. It should be divided into two parts for each boxer, with bottles [sic] #1 being submitted to the laboratory. Should either boxer's specimen be positive for drugs, etc., all parties will be notified and another test made at a laboratory selected by the boxer and the local Commission. Should that specimen prove positive, disqualification and disciplinary action will follow.
>
> Specimens will be tested for the following drugs: [here appears a list that includes anabolic steroids and pain killers.]

App. 87.

An identical "Anti-doping" rule appears in an IBF/USBA document titled "Ring Officials Guide and Medical Seminar Outline." This Guide's introduction states that "[t]he major purpose of this Ring Officials Guide is to establish criteria to be followed in all IBF/USBA boxing matches so that uniformity in actions, responsibilities, duties and total performance of ring officials can be attained. . . ." App. 65.

In the Stuttgart fight, Botha defeated Schulz in a split decision to win the IBF heavyweight championship. Each fighter then gave a urine specimen. Botha's specimen was sent to a German laboratory, where it tested positive for anabolic steroids. In accord with the anti-doping Bout Rule, Botha was then allowed to choose where the sample would be tested a second time; his choice, the UCLA Olympic Analytical Laboratory, also found anabolic steroids in his urine. During this period, Botha vigorously denied using steroids.

The German Boxing Federation—the local boxing commission that signed the Bout Rules—recommended on February 15, 1996 that the IBF disqualify Botha and that Schulz be designated IBF world champion. The Federation also barred all the boxers, promoters, referees, and trainers whom it licensed from taking part in Botha's bouts for two years.

On Saturday, February 24, 1996, upwards of two months after the Stuttgart bout, the IBF held a hearing in Elizabeth, New Jersey, to determine what action would be taken as a result of the positive steroid tests. The hearing was conducted by the IBF's Executive Committee and its subcommittee, the Championship Committee; the Championship Committee was to make a recommendation to the Executive Committee, which had final authority. All persons having an interest in the outcome of the Botha/Schulz bout were notified of the hearing and given an opportunity to be heard. The committees heard testimony from Botha, from his attorney and two of his doctors, and from representatives of Schulz, the German Boxing Federation, and Michael Moorer.

Moorer was at the time a former IBF and World Boxing Association heavyweight champion. In September 1995, Moorer had sued the IBF in federal court in New Jersey over the IBF's rankings, seeking to block the Botha/Schulz bout because, he argued, he was entitled to fight next for the title. A settlement agreement signed later that month provided that Moorer would dismiss his action in return for a guarantee that he would, within 180 days of the Botha/Schulz bout, fight the winner for the IBF title. At the IBF's February 24, 1996 hearing, Moorer's counsel reminded the IBF of its agreement with Moorer.

Botha's testimony at the hearing was a surprise: he admitted for the first time that he had taken the drug found in his urine. He argued, however, that he had not known that what he took was a steroid. Botha stated that he had injured his arm in 1988 and his South African doctor had given him two prescriptions for the pain and swelling. In March 1995, after Botha had moved to California, his South African doctor had sent him a third medication for his continuing arm stiffness, which was the steroid (Deca Durabolin) that turned up in his urine. (There is a good deal of controversy about the steroids' possible impact on Botha's capacity as a fighter, but the controversy does not appear to bear upon the issue before this court, namely the appropriateness of the district court's preliminary injunction.)

After hearing all the testimony, the IBF Championship and Executive Committees recessed to deliberate. When they returned, IBF President Robert W. Lee announced the IBF's decision:

> We will not vacate the title of Francois Botha. There are mitigating circumstances which cause us to feel that we should not vacate the title of Francois Botha.
>
> However, what we will do is we will fine Francois Botha in the amount of $50,000 for having taken these substances into his system that were in violation of our rules.
>
> Secondly, we will order a rematch between Francois Botha and Axel Schulz to take place within 180 days of today or not later than August 24, 1996.
>
> Thirty days prior to that fight taking place Francois Botha must give a urinalysis to show that he no longer has these substances in his system.
>
> The winner between Francois Botha and Axel Schulz will be obliged to fight Michael Moorer within 120 days of the date that they fight....

App. 210–11. This announcement triggered vehement protests in the hearing room, but, after some wrangling, the hearing was adjourned with the IBF's decision unchanged.

At the hearing, the IBF did not explain the "mitigating circumstances" that led it to decline to disqualify Botha. After this suit was initiated, IBF President Lee stated in a "certification" submitted to the district court that the mitigating circumstances were: (1) that the steroid was prescribed by a doctor for a 1988 injury; (2) that Botha admitted taking the medication but denied knowing that it was a steroid; (3) that

Botha exhibited none of the typical signs of prolonged steroid use; (4) that the Executive Committee believed the steroid use did not appear to have affected the outcome of the fight; (5) that Botha had ceased taking the medication; and (6) that the championship should, in the Committee's view, be decided in the ring rather than on the sidelines. App. 298.

Over the weekend [following its decision], however, the members of the IBF Executive Committee conferred over the phone. On Monday, February 26, the Executive Committee issued an amended ruling in writing, stating that its members had not previously given sufficient consideration to the IBF's commitment to Moorer. The amended ruling preserved the $50,000 fine against Botha but restructured the scheduled fights: Moorer would challenge Botha for the title before June 9, 1996, with Schulz to fight the winner of this bout within 120 days.

Schulz, together with his promoters Cedric Kushner Promotions and Der Firmer Sauerland Promotion, and his manager Wilfried Sauerland, brought suit in the District of New Jersey, naming the USBA and IBF as defendants, with Botha and Moorer joined as necessary defendants because their rights were affected. Moorer filed a counterclaim and crossclaim seeking specific performance of his settlement agreement with the IBF. The district court had jurisdiction pursuant to 28 U.S.C. § 1332.

After a hearing, the district court found that Schulz and his co-plaintiffs had met the criteria for preliminary injunctive relief. On March 29, 1996, the court accordingly ordered that (1) the USBA and IBF "amend their decision of February 26, 1996 so as to disqualify Francois Botha"; (2) Moorer and Schulz "proceed to a bout prior to June 9, 1996 as set forth in the September 19, 1995 settlement agreement" between Moorer and the USBA and IBF; (3) the USBA and IBF "determine the consequences of the order with respect to the ratings of the various boxers in conjunction with the IBF rules"; and (4) plaintiffs post a $100,000 bond.

The IBF/USBA and Botha separately appeal the issuance of the preliminary injunction, which Schulz and Moorer seek to have upheld. This court has jurisdiction pursuant to 28 U.S.C. § 1292. A motions panel of this court denied the IBF's motion for a stay and Botha's motion for an expedited appeal.

On June 22, 1996, Moorer and Schulz fought the bout mandated by the preliminary injunction. Moorer won, regaining the IBF championship belt. On November 9, 1996 (some ten days after the argument of this appeal), Moorer fought Botha, successfully defending his title with a twelfth-round TKO.

II. Analysis

A.

Without discussing specific precedents, the district court summarized the law governing this case as follows:

> We are dealing here with a private association, albeit one in which the public has a substantial interest. Under New Jersey law a private association has the right to adopt, administer and interpret its internal regulations and is granted substantial deference when judicial review is sought. When, however, an association departs from its own prescribed procedures, or where its actions are in total violation of its own rules and regulations, a court will intervene to protect the property rights and other substantial interests of those who are subject to its rules.
>
> The critical question is whether the IBF violated its rules when it failed to disqualify Botha for his drug use.

App. 533–34.

After reviewing the Bout Rules and the IBF rules and regulations, the district court concluded:

> It is abundantly clear to me that IBF and USBA have established a policy that has been made crystal clear to the boxers who fight under their aegis that no boxer is to take the drugs proscribed in the rules, and that if a boxer does take such drugs he will be disqualified regardless of what other disciplines may be imposed. The broad general language which appears in Rule 26 cannot trump the unmistakably clear language of the Bout Rules which the IBF and the boxers sign and the Ring Officials Guide which IBF and USBA promulgate. It is hard to imagine how the two organizations can adopt any other policy if they were to retain the confidence of the public and the fighting profession.

App. 536–37. On this basis, the district court concluded that Schulz had a high likelihood of succeeding on the merits.

B.

With the opinion of the district court as predicate, we proceed to examine whether the court had the authority to set aside the IBF's decision not to disqualify Botha. As the court properly observed, the courts of New Jersey (and like courts in other jurisdictions) will ordinarily defer to the internal decisions of private organizations. Indeed, "[c]ourts have been understandably reluctant to interfere with the internal affairs of [private] associations and their reluctance has ordinarily promoted the health of society." Falcone v. Middlesex County Medical Society, 34 N.J. 582, 170 A.2d 791, 796 (1961).

We must therefore ascertain, first, whether Schulz had "an interest sufficient to warrant judicial action," and—if the answer to the first question is in the affirmative—second, whether "that interest [was] subjected to an unjustifiable interference" by the IBF. In considering the first prong, we observe that Schulz's status in the boxing community, as well as his public reputation, were clearly affected by the IBF's decision not to disqualify Botha. In addition, although Schulz would not have become the champion on Botha's disqualification [because, under the IBF's rules, a challenger cannot become champion based on another challenger's being ruled ineligible], he had an economic interest in being declared the winner of his bout with Botha. We therefore conclude that Schulz had an interest in the IBF's decision sufficient to warrant judicial action.

In determining whether Schulz's interest was "subjected to an unjustifiable interference" by the IBF, we must inquire whether the IBF's refusal to disqualify Botha violated either public policy or fundamental fairness. If the refusal offended either of these principles, then judicial intervention was warranted.

We turn first to public policy. Public policy on its own can justify judicial protection of a plaintiff's interests. In determining New Jersey public policy, we turn to the enactments of the state legislature as an authoritative source.

The New Jersey legislature has declared, as "the public policy of [the] State,"

> that it is in the best interest of the public ... that boxing ... should be subject to an effective and efficient system of strict control and regulation in order to ... [p]romote the public confidence and trust in the regulatory process and the conduct of boxing....

N.J.Stat. § 5:2A–2. Moreover, the regulations of the state Department of Law and Public Safety implementing this statute also evince a purpose to instill public confidence in the sport. The Department's 1995 proposal for readoption of its regulations noted that "[t]he rules in this chapter have helped New Jersey be recognized as a leader in the area of boxing regulation" and observed that a primary purpose of the rules was "furthering the trust and confidence of the public." 27 N.J.R. 2096 (June 5, 1995).

Both the legislative and executive branches of the New Jersey state government have, therefore, made it clear that they consider it to be the public policy of the state to inspire the "trust and confidence" of the citizenry in boxing. The public's confidence that the outcome of a prizefight is fair rests squarely on the assumption that the result was not improperly influenced—by illicit equipment, by gifts, or by the involvement of managers convicted of crimes of moral turpitude.

The regulations of the state Department of Law and Public Safety also make clear that "the public confidence and trust" in boxing are promoted by banning the use of substances that can affect a boxer's performance. See N.J.Admin.Code tit. 13:46 § 12.3(a) (1995). The regulations provide that "[t]he use of any drug ... by a boxer either before or during a match, shall result in the immediate disqualification of the boxer from the match and indefinite suspension from boxing." Id.

This express statement of public policy by New Jersey's political branches is mirrored in the Bout Rules that the IBF drafted and required the pugilists to sign before the Stuttgart fight. Given the strength of New Jersey's public policy, we concur in the district court's observation that the IBF could not have established a less demanding protocol. Of course, the bout took place not in New Jersey but in Germany; however, to the extent we have any information regarding the policy of the fight venue, we observe that the German Boxing Federation not only recommended that Botha be disqualified for his steroid use, but banned all persons whom it licenses from participating in Botha's bouts for two years.

New Jersey has adopted an express policy of promoting the public trust and confidence in boxing, and has specifically mandated disqualification of boxers who use drugs. The IBF itself has adopted, and reaffirmed shortly before the contest at issue here, an identical rule mandating disqualification for drug use. The public's trust and confidence in boxing is undermined if one of the sport's major sanctioning bodies flouts its own rule which comports with the state's public policy. We conclude, at this preliminary stage, that the IBF's failure to disqualify Botha likely violated New Jersey's public policy. Because we decide this case on the basis of public policy, we need not reach the question whether the IBF's decision not to disqualify Botha was a violation of "fundamental fairness."

[The remainder of the court's opinion is omitted.]

Notes

1. How comfortable are you with the result in *Acton*? Would your feelings change if, instead of athletes, the school district had targeted those involved in the yearbook, student government, or honor society? For a further look at the decision and its implications, see, e.g., Joseph S. Dressner, *Guilty Until Proven Innocent: Random Urinalysis Drug Testing Upheld in Vernonia School District 47J v. Acton*, 4 Sports Law. J. 115 (1997); Carla E. Laszewski, Note, *Gone to Pot: Student Athletes' Fourth Amendment Rights After Vernonia School District 47J v. Acton*, 40 St. Louis U. L.J. 575 (1996); Samantha Osheroff, Note, *Drug Testing of Student Athletes in Vernonia School District v. Acton: Orwell's 1984 Becomes Vernonia's Reality in 1995*, 16 Loy. L.A. Ent. L.J. 513 (1995).

2. Although *Acton* concerns high school athletes, the use of illegal drugs occurs at every level of competition. As a result, testing is now commonplace throughout sports. *See, e.g., Department of Recreation and Sports of Puerto Rico v. World Boxing Ass'n*, 942 F.2d 84 (1st Cir.1991); *Holmes v. National Football League*, 939 F.Supp. 517 (N.D.Tex.1996); *Shoemaker v. Handel*, 619 F.Supp. 1089 (D.N.J.1985), *aff'd*, 795 F.2d 1136 (3d Cir.), *cert. denied*, 479 U.S. 986 (1986). For an interesting article questioning the wisdom of these efforts, see Dante Marrazzo, *Athletes and Drug Testing: Why Do We Care if Athletes Inhale?*, 8 Marq. Sports L.J. 75 (1997).

3. Alcoholism is another problem that has affected some athletes. In April 1997, for example, golfer John Daly was forced to withdraw from the Masters tournament after falling off the wagon. *See Agent Says Daly Was Aware of Relapse*, Albany (N.Y.) Times Union, Apr. 2, 1997, at C2. Similarly,

in February 1998, Houston Rockets forward Charles Barkley admitted during a television interview he had a drinking problem that was hurting his game. *See Barkley Admits Drinking Problem*, Fort Lauderdale Sun–Sentinel, Feb. 16, 1998, at 3C. For a further look at athletes and alcohol, see Glenn Dickey, *Hoist a Few? Fine, But Keep Your Nose Clean*, S.F. Chron., Feb. 6, 1986, at 67 (discussing the battles waged by such notable figures as Billy Martin, Mickey Mantle, Don Newcombe, and Jim Thorpe).

4. Axel Schulz is not the only athlete to claim ignorance when accused of using an improper substance. In December 1998, for example, the International Tennis Federation decided not to ban Czech tennis player Petr Korda, who had tested positive for steroids while playing at Wimbledon, because he had been "unaware that he had taken or been administered the banned substance." *See further ITF Might Believe Korda, But Others Aren't So Sure*, Orange County (CA) Reg., Dec. 24, 1998, at D5. In January 1999, the ITF's decision was appealed to the International Court of Arbitration for Sport, and a final ruling is not expected until late 1999. *See further* Josh Young, *Korda's Exoneration Shows Leadership Void*, Wash. Times, Feb. 13, 1999, at D6.

While the truth may never be known about either Schulz or Korda, the facts surrounding another group of athletes finally have emerged. Between 1968 and 1988, the small nation of East Germany dominated the Olympics, winning more than 300 medals (principally in swimming and track and field). Although steroids were widely suspected, the allegation remained unproved. After the fall of the Berlin Wall in 1989, however, historians began looking into the issue; in 1998, various East German officials finally broke down and admitted what they had done. They also revealed that of the up to 10,000 athletes who were given banned substances, nearly all were told they were getting vitamins. *See further* David Walsh, *The Victims of Injustice*, London (Sunday) Times, Dec. 13, 1998, at 18.

5. To prevent the use of steroids and other performance-enhancing drugs, athletes now undergo regular screening for such products. This has led to numerous challenges by individuals disputing positive test results. *See, e.g., Foschi v. United States Swimming, Inc.*, 916 F.Supp. 232 (E.D.N.Y. 1996); *Walton-Floyd v. United States Olympic Committee*, 965 S.W.2d 35 (Tex.Ct.App.1998); *Brennan v. Board of Trustees for University of Louisiana Systems*, 691 So.2d 324 (La.Ct.App.1997); Steven Downes, *Drug Charges Haunt Slaney*, Sunday (London) Times, Nov. 29, 1998, at 19; Barbara Huebner, *Pippig Will Appeal on Failed Drug Test*, Boston Globe, Oct. 8, 1998, at E1; Ira Berkow, *FINA's Testing is Marred, Too*, N.Y. Times, Aug. 9, 1998, at 31. In response to such complaints, the International Olympic Committee in August 1998 called for creation of a special agency to coordinate sports drug testing throughout the world. *See further IOC Proposes Anti–Drug Agency*, Fort Lauderdale Sun–Sentinel, Aug. 21, 1998, at 13C.

6. Screening also has set off a heated debate as to which substances should be prohibited. During the 1998 baseball season, for example, home run slugger Mark McGwire admitted taking androstenedione, a drug legal in baseball but banned in other sports. The revelation led to a protracted discussion of its safety and efficacy, cast a temporary shadow over McGwire's accomplishments, and caused MLB to study the issue. *See further Baseball*

Takes Look at Andro, But Ban is Far from Done Deal, Austin Am.-Statesman, Oct. 30, 1998, at C4, and Chuck Landon, *Andro: Is It Good or Bad?*, Charleston Daily Mail, Oct. 14, 1998, at 1B. For similar controversies involving other products, see, e.g., Amanda J. Gruber & Harrison G. Pope, Jr., *Ephedrine Abuse Among 36 Female Weightlifters*, 7 Am. J. Addictions 256 (1998) (discussing ephedrine, a central nervous system stimulant); Neil Wilson, *Cyclists Given Baby Milk for a Head Start*, London Daily Mail, Sept. 19, 1998, at 73 (discussing colostrum, an ingredient found in baby milk); Paul Swiech, *Muscle Up: Creatine Delivers Short–Term Results But Some Wonder About Long–Term Effects*, Bloomington (IL) Pantagraph, July 6, 1998 (discussing creatine, a synthetic protein).

7. Besides illegal and performance-enhancing drugs, many athletes become addicted to painkillers. In May 1996, for example, Green Bay Packers quarterback Brett Favre revealed he was hooked on Vicodin, a powerful prescription opioid, and spent 45 days in a drug rehabilitation center. *See further Favre Reveals Painkiller Problem*, Des Moines Reg., May 15, 1996, at 1 (Sports). Similar admissions have been made by a number of players. *See, e.g., Bayless v. Philadelphia National League Club*, 472 F.Supp. 625 (E.D.Pa.1979), *aff'd mem.*, 615 F.2d 37 (2d Cir.1980) (minor league baseball pitcher Patrick Bayless); Rob Draper, *Redmond Suffering for Painkiller Abuse*, London (Sunday) Mail, July 26, 1998, at 86 (distance runner Derek Redmond); Gary D'Amato & Tom Silverstein, *Ex-Substance Abusers Advise Favre*, Seattle Post–Intelligencer, May 21, 1996, at D6 (Dallas Cowboys linebacker Thomas "Hollywood" Henderson and Green Bay Packers kicker Chester Marcol). For a further look at the use of painkillers in sports, see, e.g., Jarrett Bell, *Subculture of Pain: Blame Egos, Pride, Even Love of the Game*, Seattle Times, May 26, 1996, at D3; Tom Witosky, *In Arenaball, Pain is Price of Any Gain*, Des Moines Reg., May 23, 1996, at 1 (Sports); Kevin Sherrington, *Painful Memories: After Glory Ends, NFL Alumni Often Left With Scars, Addictions*, Dallas Morning News, Oct. 1, 1995, at 28B. *See also* Rob Draper, *Ronaldo in World; Brazil Doctor Comes Clean on Painkillers as Nation Ponders a Hero's Plight*, London (Sunday) Mail, July 19, 1998, at 96 (discussing how Brazilian soccer player Ronaldo nearly died from the painkiller lignocaine, which had been prescribed by team doctors in the hopes it would allow him to play in the 1998 World Cup final).

8. It is not only human athletes who are affected by drugs. Both performance-enhancing and performance-hindering substances have been given to race horses and dogs by dishonest owners, jockeys, trainers, grooms, and veterinarians. *See, e.g., State v. Brumage*, 435 N.W.2d 337 (Iowa 1989); *Goodman v. Superior Court in and for the County of Maricopa*, 665 P.2d 83 (Ariz.1983); *Simmons v. Division of Pari–Mutuel Wagering*, 412 So.2d 357 (Fla.1982); *Commonwealth v. Nelson*, 346 N.E.2d 839 (Mass.1976); *Plante v. Department of Business and Professional Regulation*, 716 So.2d 790 (Fla. Dist.Ct.App.1998); *Kline v. Illinois Racing Board*, 469 N.E.2d 667 (Ill.App. Ct.1984). *See also* Luke P. Iovine, III & John E. Keefe, Jr., *Horse Drugging—The New Jersey Trainer Absolute Insurer Rule: Burning Down the House to Roast the Pig*, 1 Seton Hall J. Sport L. 61 (1991), and Ray Kerrison, *Got Milk? Some Horses Do; State's Cutbacks Leave NYRA With No Money for Testing*, N.Y. Post, June 28, 1998, at 82.

9. While no proof exists that athletes abuse drugs more often than other members of the population, the public is firmly convinced they do. In September 1998, for example, former Olympic gold medalist Florence Griffith–Joyner died at her home in Mission Video, California, at the age of 38. Despite never having tested positive for drugs, her death immediately was attributed to them. Even after the coroner announced she had died from positional asphyxiation during an epileptic seizure, suspicion continued to surround Joyner. *See further* John Jeansonne, *An Athlete Suddenly Dies, or a Record is Broken ... And the Question Is: Drugs?*, Newsday, Oct. 4, 1998, at C15. *See also* Alison R. Jones & John T. Pichot, *Stimulant Use in Sports*, 7 Am. J. Addictions 243 (1998).

Problem 29

Feeling pressure to win at any cost, a kicker began taking a variety of drugs. By the time his football career came to an end, he had developed a serious habit. As a result, he lost numerous jobs, was arrested several times, had two marriages fail, and attempted suicide. Given these facts, can the player make out a cause of action against either his former teams or the league? *See Sweeney v. Bert Bell NFL Player Retirement Plan*, 961 F.Supp. 1381 (S.D.Cal.1997), *aff'd in part, reversed in part, and remanded*, 156 F.3d 1238 (9th Cir.1998).

E. OFF–FIELD BEHAVIOR

Athletes sometimes get into trouble while away from their jobs. Unlike ordinary citizens, however, their scrapes with the law often wind up on the front page.

COLSTON v. GREEN

1998 WL 128890 (Fla.Dist.Ct.App.1998).

BARFIELD, Chief Judge.

The mother [Karen E. Colston] challenges those portions of a final order in a paternity proceeding relating to child support and reimbursement of medical bills incurred in connection with the birth of the child. We affirm in part, reverse in part, and remand for further proceedings.

The mother currently works as an office manager and is pursuing a master's degree in business administration. The father [Willie A. Green] is a 31–year-old professional football player who in March 1997 signed a four-year contract with the Denver Broncos Football Club (Denver) that provides for increasing yearly salaries and a $900,000 signing bonus (paid in three installments in 1997 and a final installment in 1998). The father testified that the signing bonus was used to avoid the National Football League's "salary cap." The parties do not dispute that under the contract, Denver has agreed to pay him a total of $925,000 in 1997, $900,000 in 1998, $1,225,000 in 1999, and $1,350,000 in 2000.

The child was born in June 1993. In September 1993, the mother initiated the paternity action against the father, who was playing for the

Detroit Lions at the time. On April 14, 1994, the trial court entered an order finding him to be the child's father and ordered him to pay $1,500 per month temporary child support "until further order of Court." In October 1994, he filed a petition for modification, alleging that after entry of the original order, he had been released by Detroit and had been signed by the Tampa Bay Buccaneers at a "substantially reduced salary," that he had recently been released by Tampa, and that he "does not anticipate having any earned income for approximately two years while he completes his undergraduate education so that he can become gainfully employed." After a hearing on December 14, 1994, the trial court entered an order on December 19, 1994, in which it imputed an income of $1,500 per month to the father, ordered him to pay child support arrearages, reduced his temporary child support obligation to $400 per month effective November 1994, and ordered him to provide the mother's attorney with any future contract with a professional football team, noting that it would "consider modification of child support upon Defendant receiving compensation from the NFL for playing professional football."

On June 19, 1995, the mother filed a motion for contempt and for reinstatement of the original temporary child support award. She asserted that the December 19, 1994, modification order reducing the father's temporary child support obligation "was based on the testimony of the Defendant that he was unemployed and had no prospects of returning to his previous employment, where he earned in excess of $250,000 per year, with a National Football League Team" and that "he anticipated obtaining employment as a Recreation Director in Athens, Georgia for which he expected to be compensated at the rate of $1,500.00 per month." She asserted that at the time the father gave this testimony, "he had in fact previously signed a contract with the Carolina Panthers of the National Football League," that she had later discovered this fact from newspaper articles, and that "[i]n furtherance of his clear intent to mislead the Court, the Defendant GREEN has, as of this date, failed to provide counsel with a copy of the aforereferenced contract with the Carolina Panthers." She sought an order reinstating the original temporary child support order retroactive to November 1994, finding the father in contempt and sentencing him to incarceration, and requiring him to pay her attorney fees and costs.

The father's response to the motion admitted that he had signed a contract with the Carolina Panthers "subsequent to the last hearing" which provides for a salary of $100,000 or $250,000, depending upon whether he makes the club's roster during the 1995 regular season, but asserted that no modification of child support was presently justified because "[u]ntil such time as the regular season begins, Defendant's sole compensation is in the amount of $200 per week, during training camp and in the amount of $600 per week during pre-season (the month of August)." Attached to the response was the father's contract with the Carolina Panthers, which was signed on December 15, 1994, and which indicated that he would be paid $100,000 in 1995 (increasing to $250,000 if he is a member of the club's active or inactive roster during the 1995 season) and $400,000 in 1996, plus pre-season and post-season travel expenses, bonuses for various contingencies, and a $20,000 signing bonus to be paid in two installments, on the date of signing and on January 15, 1995.

On July 26, 1995, the trial court entered an order in which it reserved ruling on the mother's motion, but ordered the father to pay $4,251 in temporary attorney fees and costs, to continue paying $400 per month in temporary child support, and to direct his employer to send $1,200 per week to his attorney's trust account, to be retained in trust "until further order of this Court."

On September 27, 1995, the trial court adopted an agreement signed by the parties as superseding all prior support orders. Under the consent order, they would share joint custody of the child, the monthly financial support would be at the discretion of the parents "according to the needs of the child," and final resolution of the matter "will commence upon the relocation of [the mother and the child] by [the father], to the Atlanta, Georgia area."

In December 1995, the mother filed a motion for relief from the stipulated consent order, alleging that she had been induced into the agreement through the father's fraudulent representations. She also filed a motion for an emergency hearing on child support, contempt and attorney's fees, which requested an order finding the father in contempt for not having his employer send $1,200 per week to his attorney's trust account and ordering him to direct his employer to forward to his attorney any further monies due him, to pay $2,000 per month child support plus health care, dental care, and day care, to reimburse her "for all the medical and dental expenses incurred on behalf of the parties' minor child, including those related to the birth of said child," and to pay her attorney fees and costs.

The father responded that he had paid more than $3,000 for the support of his child since the September 1995 agreement was signed, that the mother had voluntarily vacated his residence in Atlanta, that no emergency existed, that neither he nor his attorney would be available for a hearing in December 1995, and that "no prejudice will accrue to Plaintiff in continuing this hearing to a time when Defendant and his counsel are available for hearing."

On December 21, 1995, the court entered an order continuing the hearing on the emergency motion and ordering the father to pay $1,000 per month temporary child support, to pay $2,000 in temporary attorney fees, and to pay his own attorney's firm $15,000 "to be held in trust by the aforesaid firm for the purpose of the firm paying, on behalf of the Defendant, the aforesaid child support and attorney's fees in accordance with this Order."

The hearing on the mother's pending motions was held on May 29, 1997. Each party presented a financial affidavit and various child support guidelines worksheets. The mother testified that she had $4,160 in outstanding medical bills as a result of the child's birth. She admitted that the father had given her money to pay the medical insurance premium for the child, but stated that when she told him that the premium had been misquoted by $60, he would not give her the extra $60, and because she did not have $60 to pay the extra amount of the premium, the baby was not covered by her health insurance. She admitted that she never told the father that if he did not send her the extra $60 he would be responsible for the child's birth expenses. The parties agreed that the child support guidelines require $1,437 per month child support for the first $10,000 per month of the parents' combined net income plus five percent of any combined income over $10,000, and that if the trial judge deviates more than five percent from that amount, he must give written reasons for the deviation.

At the end of the hearing, the judge ruled on the visitation schedule, then addressed the child support issues:

> ... Well, we've got a lot of difficulties with the moneys as to what something is or isn't. Is it a bonus or is it nonrecurring income, it's not going to happen again. So I'm going to make my best efforts.
>
> I'm going to set the child support in the amount of $1,500 starting June 1st for the child. I'm going to order that $300 of that monies be placed into a trust account for the benefit of the child with its primary purpose being to secure future child support payments and hopefully, if things work out for the benefit of the child, after he turns 18.
>
> I'm going to further order that Mr. Green place $20,000 into that trust account and start it. And in consideration of him doing that, I'm going to deny the request for any retroactive child support. I will not determine the effect of the agreement or whether I should go back to 1993 on child support....

The final order, entered on June 11, 1997, "nunc pro tunc May 29, 1997," determined that the father's $900,000 signing bonus was "nonrecurring income" under the guidelines "and accordingly should not be used in computing the amount of child support due," that the amount of child support owed by the father "pursuant to the Child Support Guidelines, is $1,500 per month," and that "the present need of the child while in the custody of his mother, Karen Elaine Colston, is $1,200 per month." It then stated:

> The Plaintiff has claimed in excess of $76,000 in child support arrearages based upon computing child support pursuant to an application of the Child Support Guidelines to all of the Defendant's earnings since the birth of the child (including Defendant's signing bonus). The Court having considered the agreement entered into by the parties on September 19, 1995, and this Court's order adopting the same, and having considered a reasonable sum of child support arrearage for which the Defendant shall be responsible, the Court determined that said sum

> should be in the amount of $20,000 that should be placed in trust for the child's future support needs inasmuch as all of the child's prior support needs have been made from child support paid by the Defendant to the Plaintiff.

Finding that the father presently earns "substantial sums of money as a football player," but that his future earning capacity is "unknown," the court ordered the $20,000 child support arrearage and $300 of the monthly $1500 child support payment to be deposited into a trust account with Merrill Lynch "which shall not be subject to any withdrawal [except for administration expenses] without further order of the court." It also denied the mother's claim for reimbursement of $4,160.72 in outstanding medical bills incurred in connection with the birth of the child.

On appeal, the mother asserts that the trial court abused its discretion in the following ways: 1) by failing to follow the child support guidelines, section 61.30, Florida Statutes (1995); 2) by determining that the father's professional football "signing bonus" was nonrecurring income, in light of subsection 61.30(2)(a)2; 3) by failing to consider the father's contract salary for 1998, 1999, and 2000, without bonus income; 4) by ordering a portion of the child support monies to be placed in trust for the minor child; 5) by entering a final judgment which is at variance with the court's ruling; 6) by failing to award sufficient retroactive child support; and 7) by failing to order the father to reimburse her for medical bills incurred in connection with the birth of the child. She seeks reversal of the final order and remand for clarification of the order and for reconsideration of retroactive and future child support.

We find that the trial court did not abuse its discretion by denying the mother's claim for reimbursement of medical expenses relating to the birth of the child, based upon the evidence presented at the hearing that the father gave her money to pay for coverage of the child through her group health insurance. The denial of this claim is therefore affirmed.

However, we find that the trial court failed to comply with subsection 61.30(2)(a), Florida Statutes (1995), when it refused to consider the father's signing bonus in calculating his gross income for the purpose of determining the minimum guideline child support need under subsection 61.30(6), and that this failure to comply with the statute affected all further calculations. The lack of clarity in the trial court's order, which does not explain how the court arrived at either the father's "guideline" $1,500 per month child support obligation or the $20,000 arrearages figure, and which does not appear to rule on the mother's December 1995 motion for relief from the September 27, 1995, consent order, requires reversal of portions of the order relating to child support. The trial court's rulings relating to the father's signing bonus, the determination of the "guideline" support obligation of the father, the amount of child support arrearages, and the placing of child support monies in a trust are reversed. The case is remanded to the trial court for further consideration of these and other issues.

BRZONKALA v. VIRGINIA POLYTECHNIC INSTITUTE AND STATE UNIVERSITY

132 F.3d 949 (4th Cir.1997), *aff'd in part and rev'd in part*, 169 F.3D 820 (4th Cir.1999) (en banc).

MOTZ, Circuit Judge.

This case arises from the gang rape of a freshman at the Virginia Polytechnic Institute by two members of the college football team, and the school's decision to impose only a nominal punishment on the rapists. The victim alleges that these rapes were motivated by her assailants' discriminatory animus toward women and sues them pursuant to the Violence Against Women Act of 1994. She asserts that the university knew of the brutal attacks she received and yet failed to take any meaningful action to punish her offenders or protect her, but instead permitted a sexually hostile environment to flourish; she sues the university under Title IX of the Education Amendments of 1972. The district court dismissed the case in its entirety. The court held that the complaint failed to state a claim under Title IX and that Congress lacked constitutional authority to enact the Violence Against Women Act. Because we believe that the complaint states a claim under Title IX and that the Commerce Clause provides Congress with authority to enact the Violence Against Women Act, we reverse and remand for further proceedings.

I.

Christy Brzonkala entered Virginia Polytechnic Institute ("Virginia Tech") as a freshman in the fall of 1994. On the evening of September 21, 1994, Brzonkala and another female student met two men who Brzonkala knew only by their first names and their status as members of the Virginia Tech football team. Within thirty minutes of first meeting Brzonkala, these two men, later identified as Antonio Morrison and James Crawford, raped her.

Brzonkala and her friend met Morrison and Crawford on the third floor of the dormitory where Brzonkala lived. All four students talked for approximately fifteen minutes in a student dormitory room. Brzonkala's friend and Crawford then left the room.

Morrison immediately asked Brzonkala if she would have sexual intercourse with him. She twice told Morrison "no," but Morrison was not deterred. As Brzonkala got up to leave the room Morrison grabbed her, and threw her, face-up, on a bed. He pushed her down by the shoulders and disrobed her. Morrison turned off the lights, used his arms to pin down her elbows and pressed his knees against her legs. Brzonkala struggled and attempted to push Morrison off, but to no avail. Without using a condom, Morrison forcibly raped her.

Before Brzonkala could recover, Crawford came into the room and exchanged places with Morrison. Crawford also raped Brzonkala by holding down her arms and using his knees to pin her legs open. He, too, used no condom. When Crawford was finished, Morrison raped her for a third time, again holding her down and again without a condom.

When Morrison had finished with Brzonkala, he warned her "You better not have any fucking diseases." In the months following the rape, Morrison announced publicly in the dormitory's dining room that he "like[d] to get girls drunk and fuck the shit out of them."

Following the assault Brzonkala's behavior changed radically. She became depressed and avoided contact with her classmates and residents of her dormitory. She changed her appearance and cut off her long hair. She ceased attending classes and eventually attempted suicide. She sought assistance from a Virginia Tech psychiatrist, who treated her and prescribed anti-depressant medication. Neither the psychiatrist nor any other Virginia Tech employee or official made more than a cursory inquiry into the cause of Brzonkala's distress. She later sought and received a retroactive withdrawal from Virginia Tech for the 1994–95 academic year because of the trauma.

Approximately a month after Morrison and Crawford assaulted Brzonkala, she confided in her roommate that she had been raped, but could not bring herself to discuss the details. It was not until February 1995, however, that Brzonkala was able to identify Morrison and Crawford as the two men who had raped her. Two months later, she filed a complaint against them under Virginia Tech's Sexual Assault Policy, which was published in the Virginia Tech "University Policies for Student Life 1994–1995." These policies had been formally released for dissemination to students on July 1, 1994, but had not been widely distributed to students. After Brzonkala filed her complaint under the Sexual Assault Policy she learned that another male student athlete was overheard advising Crawford that he should have "killed the bitch."

Brzonkala did not pursue criminal charges against Morrison or Crawford, believing that criminal prosecution was impossible because she had not preserved any physical evidence of the rape. Virginia Tech did not report the rapes to the police, and did not urge Brzonkala to reconsider her decision not to do so. Rape of a female student by a male student is the only violent felony that Virginia Tech authorities do not automatically report to the university or town police.

Virginia Tech held a hearing in May 1995 on Brzonkala's complaint against Morrison and Crawford. At the beginning of the hearing, which was taped and lasted three hours, the presiding college official announced that the charges were being brought under the school's Abusive Conduct Policy, which included sexual assault. A number of persons, including Brzonkala, Morrison, and Crawford testified. Morrison admitted that, despite the fact that Brzonkala had twice told him "no," he had sexual intercourse with her in the dormitory on September 21. Crawford, who denied that he had sexual contact with Brzonkala (a denial corroborated by his suitemate, Cornell Brown), confirmed that Morrison had engaged in sexual intercourse with Brzonkala.

The Virginia Tech judicial committee found insufficient evidence to take action against Crawford, but found Morrison guilty of sexual assault. The university immediately suspended Morrison for two semesters (one school year), and informed Brzonkala of the sanction. Morrison appealed this sanction to Cathryn T. Goree, Virginia Tech's Dean of Students. Morrison claimed that the college denied him his due process rights and imposed an unduly harsh and arbitrary sanction. Dean Goree reviewed Morrison's appeal letter, the file, and tapes of the three-hour hearing. She rejected Morrison's appeal and upheld the sanction of full suspension for the Fall 1995 and Spring 1996 semesters. Dean Goree informed Brzonkala of this decision in a letter dated May 22, 1995. According to Virginia Tech's published rules, the decision of Dean Goree as the appeals officer on this matter was final.

In the first week of July 1995, however, Dean Goree and another Virginia Tech official, Donna Lisker, personally called on Brzonkala at her home in Fairfax, Virginia, a four-hour drive from Virginia Tech. These officials advised Brzonkala that Morrison had hired an attorney who had threatened to sue the school on due process grounds, and that Virginia Tech thought there might be merit to Morrison's "ex post facto" challenge that he was charged under a Sexual Assault Policy that was not yet spelled out in the Student Handbook. Dean Goree and Ms. Lisker told Brzonkala that Virginia Tech was unwilling to defend the school's decision to suspend Morrison for a year in court, and a rehearing under the Abusive Conduct Policy that pre-dated the Sexual Assault Policy was required. To induce Brzonkala to participate in a second hearing, Dean Goree and Ms. Lisker assured her that they believed her story, and that the second hearing was a mere technicality to cure the school's error in bringing the first complaint under the Sexual Assault Policy.

The Virginia Tech judicial committee scheduled the second hearing for late July. This hearing turned out to be much more than a mere formality, however. The second hearing lasted seven hours, more than twice as long as the first hearing. Brzonkala was required to engage her own legal counsel at her own expense. Moreover, the university belatedly informed her that student testimony given at the first hearing would not be admissible at the second hearing and that if she wanted the second judicial committee to consider this testimony she would have to submit affidavits or produce the witnesses. Because she received insufficient notice, it was impossible for Brzonkala to obtain the necessary affidavits or live testimony from her student witnesses. In contrast, the school provided Morrison with advance notice so that he had ample time to procure the sworn affidavits or live testimony of his student witnesses. Virginia Tech exacerbated this difficulty by refusing Brzonkala or her attorney access to the tape recordings of the first hearing, while granting Morrison and his attorney complete and early access to those tapes. Finally, Virginia Tech officials prevented Brzonkala from mentioning

Crawford in her testimony because charges against him had been dismissed; as a result she had to present a truncated and unnatural version of the facts.

Nevertheless, after the second hearing, the university judicial committee found that Morrison had violated the Abusive Conduct Policy, and re-imposed the same sanction: an immediate two semester suspension. On August 4, 1995, the college again informed Brzonkala, in writing, that Morrison had been found guilty and been suspended for a year.

Morrison again appealed. He argued due process violations, the existence of new information, and the asserted harshness and arbitrariness of the sanction imposed on him as grounds for reversal of the judicial committee's decision. Senior Vice–President and Provost Peggy Meszaros overturned Morrison's sanction on appeal. She found "that there was sufficient evidence to support the decision that [Morrison] violated the University's Abusive Conduct Policy and that no due process violation occurred in the handling of [Morrison's] case." However, the Provost concluded that the sanction imposed on Morrison—immediate suspension for one school year—was "excessive when compared with other cases where there has been a finding of violation of the Abusive Conduct Policy." Provost Meszaros did not elaborate on the "other cases" to which she was referring. Instead of an immediate one year suspension, the Provost imposed "deferred suspension until [Morrison's] graduation from Virginia Tech." In addition, Morrison was "required to attend a one-hour educational session with Rene Rios, EO/AA Compliance Officer regarding acceptable standards under University Student Policy."

Provost Meszaros informed Morrison of the decision to set aside his sanction by letter on August 21, 1995. Although Brzonkala had been informed in writing of the result at every other juncture in the disciplinary proceedings, Virginia Tech did not notify her that it had set aside Morrison's suspension or that he would be returning to campus in the Fall. Instead, on August 22, 1995, Brzonkala learned from an article in The Washington Post that the university had lifted Morrison's suspension and that he would return in the Fall 1995 semester. In fact, Morrison did return to Virginia Tech in the Fall of 1995—on a full athletic scholarship.

Upon learning that the university had set aside Morrison's suspension and was permitting him to return in the Fall, Brzonkala canceled her own plans to return to Virginia Tech. She feared for her safety because of previous threats and Virginia Tech's treatment of Morrison. She felt that Virginia Tech's actions signaled to Morrison, as well as the student body as a whole, that the school either did not believe her or did not view Morrison's conduct as improper. She was also humiliated by the procedural biases of the second hearing and by the decision to set aside the sanction against Morrison. Brzonkala attended no university or college during the Fall 1995 term.

On November 30, 1995, Brzonkala was shocked to learn from another newspaper article that the second Virginia Tech judicial committee did not find Morrison guilty of sexual assault, but rather of the reduced charge of "using abusive language." Despite the fact that the school had accused and convicted Morrison of sexual assault at the initial hearing, despite Morrison's testimony at that hearing that he had had sexual intercourse with Brzonkala after she twice told him "no," and despite the fact that Dean Goree and Donna Lisker had unambiguously stated that the second hearing would also address the "sexual assault" charge against Morrison, the administrators altered the charge. The university never notified either Brzonkala or her attorney about the change, leaving her to learn about it months after the fact from a newspaper article.

Brzonkala believes and so alleges that the procedural irregularities in, as well as the ultimate outcome of, the second hearing were the result of the involvement of Head Football Coach Frank Beamer, as part of a coordinated university plan to allow Morrison to play football in 1995.

On December 27, 1995, Brzonkala initially filed suit against Morrison, Crawford, and Virginia Tech; on March 1, 1996, she amended her complaint. She alleged inter alia that Virginia Tech, in its handling of her rape claims and failure to punish the rapists in any meaningful manner, violated Title IX of the Education Amendments of 1972, 20 U.S.C. §§ 1681–1688 (1994). She also alleged that Morrison and Crawford brutally gang raped her because of gender animus in violation of Title III of the Violence Against Women Act of 1994, 42 U.S.C. § 13981 (1994) ("VAWA"). The United States intervened to defend the constitutionality of VAWA.

On May 7, 1996 the district court dismissed the Title IX claims against Virginia Tech for failure to state a claim upon which relief could be granted. See Brzonkala v. Virginia Polytechnic & State Univ., 935 F.Supp. 772 (W.D.Va.1996) ("Brzonkala I"). On July 26, 1996 the court dismissed Brzonkala's VAWA claims against Morrison and Crawford, holding that although she had stated a cause of action under VAWA, enactment of the statute exceeded Congressional authority and was thus unconstitutional. See Brzonkala v. Virginia Polytechnic & State Univ., 935 F.Supp. 779 (W.D.Va.1996) ("Brzonkala II").

II.

Title IX of the Education Amendments of 1972 provides in relevant part:

> No person in the United States shall, on the basis of sex, be excluded from participation in, be denied the benefits of, or be subjected to discrimination under any education program or activity receiving Federal financial assistance....

20 U.S.C. § 1681(a).

Virginia Tech concedes that it is an "education program ... receiving Federal financial assistance." Hence, we need only determine whether Brzonkala has stated a claim that she was "subjected to discrimination" by Virginia Tech "on the basis of sex." 20 U.S.C. § 1681(a). The district court recognized that Brzonkala pled a Title IX claim on the basis of two distinct legal theories: a hostile environment theory, that Virginia Tech responded inadequately to a sexually hostile environment; and a disparate treatment theory, that Virginia Tech discriminated against Brzonkala because of her sex in its disciplinary proceedings. The district court rejected both, holding that her complaint failed to state a Title IX claim on which relief could be granted under either theory. See Brzonkala I, 935 F.Supp. at 775–78. We now consider whether Brzonkala stated a claim under either of these theories.

A.

We begin with the hostile environment claim. To assess Brzonkala's Title IX hostile environment assertions we must address two issues: (1) what legal standard to apply to a hostile environment claim under Title IX and (2) whether Brzonkala's complaint satisfies that standard.

1.

Title IX unquestionably prohibits federally supported educational institutions from practicing "discrimination" "on the basis of sex." 20 U.S.C. § 1681(a) (1994). Because of Title IX's "short historical parentage," Doe v. Claiborne County, Tenn., 103 F.3d 495, 514 (6th Cir.1996), we have not previously faced a hostile environment claim under Title IX. Therefore, in determining whether an educational institution's handling of a known sexually hostile environment is actionable "discrimination" under Title IX, we must look to the extensive jurisprudence developed in the Title VII context.

Virginia Tech argues that this was error, relying solely upon Rowinsky v. Bryan Indep. Sch. Dist., 80 F.3d 1006 (5th Cir.), cert. denied, 117 S.Ct. 165, 136 L.Ed.2d 108 (1996). Rowinsky dealt with a hostile environment claim by two female students against a school district for its response to sexual harassment by certain male students. A divided panel of the Fifth Circuit defined the question presented as "whether the recipient of federal education funds can be found liable for sex discrimination when the perpetrator is a party other than the grant recipient or its agents." Id. at 1010. In answering this question, the court determined that the language and legislative history of Title IX indicated that the statute "applies only to the practices of the recipients themselves," not third parties. Id. at 1013. The Rowinsky court reasoned that Title VII principles were inapplicable because "[i]n an employment context, the actions of a co-worker sometimes may be imputed to an employer through a theory of respondeat superior," but a school may not be held responsible for the harassment of one student by another. Id. at 1011 n. 11. Accordingly, the Fifth Circuit held that "[i]n the case of [Title IX] peer sexual harassment, a plaintiff must demonstrate that the school district responded to sexual harassment claims differently based on sex. Thus, a school district might violate Title IX if it treated sexual harassment of boys more seriously than sexual harassment of girls. . . . " Id. at 1016.

We have no trouble agreeing with the Fifth Circuit that Title IX "applies only to the practices of the recipients themselves." Id. at 1013. However, in this respect Title IX is no different from Title VII—the Rowinsky majority's failure to recognize this results in a deeply flawed analysis. In framing the question in terms of liability for the acts of third parties, Rowinsky misstates what a plaintiff, under either Title VII or Title IX, hopes to prove in a hostile environment claim. Under Title VII, a plaintiff cannot recover because a fellow employee sexually harassed the plaintiff, but only because an employer could have, but failed to, adequately remedy known harassment. As we recently noted, "an employer is liable for a sexually hostile work environment created by . . . [an] employee only if the employer knew or should have known of the illegal conduct and failed to take prompt and adequate remedial action." Andrade v. Mayfair Management, Inc., 88 F.3d 258, 261 (4th Cir.1996). Consequently, a defendant employer is held responsible under Title VII for the employer's own actions, its inadequate and tardy response, not the actions of fellow employees.

Similarly, in a Title IX hostile environment action a plaintiff is not seeking to hold the school responsible for the acts of third parties (in this case fellow students). Rather, the plaintiff is seeking to hold the school responsible for its own actions, i.e. that the school "knew or should have known of the illegal conduct and failed to take prompt and adequate remedial action." Andrade, 88 F.3d at 261. Brzonkala is not attempting to hold Virginia Tech responsible for the acts of Morrison and Crawford per se; instead she is challenging Virginia Tech's handling of the hostile environment once she notified college officials of the rapes. Therefore, the entire focus of Rowinsky's analysis as to whether a school may be held responsible for the acts of third parties under Title IX misses the point. Brzonkala does not seek to make Virginia Tech liable for the acts of third parties. She seeks only to hold the school liable for its own discriminatory actions in failing to remedy a known hostile environment.

A defendant educational institution, like a defendant employer, is, of course, liable for its own discriminatory actions: even the Rowinsky majority acknowledges this. Rowinsky, 80 F.3d at 1012 (Title IX "prohibits discriminatory acts" by educational institutions receiving federal financial assistance). Responsibility for discriminatory acts includes liability for failure to remedy a known sexually hostile environment. Accordingly, the district court was correct in applying Title VII principles to define the contours of Brzonkala's hostile environment claim. We now turn to that application.

2.

Under Title VII "to prevail on a 'hostile work environment' sexual harassment claim, an employee must prove: (1) that he [or she] was harassed 'because of' his [or her] 'sex'; (2) that the harassment was unwelcome; (3) that the harassment was sufficiently severe or pervasive to create an abusive working environment; and (4) that some basis exists for imputing liability to the employer." Wrightson v. Pizza Hut of America, Inc., 99 F.3d 138, 142 (4th Cir.1996). Similarly, under Title IX a plaintiff asserting a hostile environment claim must show: "1) that she [or he] belongs to a protected group; 2) that she [or he] was subject to unwelcome sexual harassment; 3) that the harassment was based on sex; 4) that the harassment was sufficiently severe or pervasive so as to alter the conditions of her [or his] education and create an abusive educational environment; and 5) that some basis for institutional liability has been established." Kinman v. Omaha Public Sch. Dist., 94 F.3d 463, 467–68 (8th Cir.1996); Seamons v. Snow, 84 F.3d 1226, 1232 (10th Cir.1996) (same); Brown v. Hot, Sexy & Safer Prods., Inc., 68 F.3d 525, 540 (1st Cir.1995), cert. denied, 516 U.S. 1159, 116 S.Ct. 1044, 134 L.Ed.2d 191 (1996) (same); Nicole M. v. Martinez Unified Sch. Dist., 964 F.Supp. 1369, 1376 (N.D.Cal.1997) (same); see also Doe, 103 F.3d at 515 (holding that the elements of a "hostile environment claim under Title VII equally apply under Title IX"); Oona, R.S. v. McCaffrey, 122 F.3d 1207, 1210 (9th Cir.1997) (applying Title VII standards to Title IX hostile environment claim); Murray v. New York Univ. College of Dentistry, 57 F.3d 243, 248–51 (2d Cir.1995) (same); Collier v. William Penn Sch. Dist., 956 F.Supp. 1209, 1213–14 (E.D.Pa.1997) (same); Pinkney v. Robinson, 913 F.Supp. 25, 32 (D.D.C.1996) (same); Bosley v. Kearney R–1 School Dist., 904 F.Supp. 1006, 1021–22 (W.D.Mo.1995) (same); Kadiki v. Virginia Commonwealth Univ., 892 F.Supp. 746, 749–50 (E.D.Va.1995) (same); Ward v. Johns Hopkins Univ., 861 F.Supp. 367, 374 (D.Md.1994) (same).

Virginia Tech concedes that Brzonkala has properly alleged the first three elements—that she was a member of a protected class, that she was subject to unwelcome harassment, and that this harassment was based on her sex. Virginia Tech contends, however, that Brzonkala has not alleged that she was subjected to a sufficiently abusive environment, or established that Virginia Tech may be held liable for that environment. Accordingly, we address these two elements.

a.

A Title IX plaintiff must allege sexual harassment "sufficiently severe or pervasive so as to alter the conditions of her education and create an abusive educational environment." Kinman, 94 F.3d at 468. Virginia Tech argues that because Brzonkala did not return to school she experienced no hostile environment. The district court agreed, holding that:

> [T]he hostile environment that Brzonkala alleged never occurred. Brzonkala left [Virginia Tech] due to her concern of possible future reprisal in reaction to her pressing charges. She did not allege that this future reprisal actually occurred. Second, Brzonkala did not perceive that the environment was in fact abusive, but only that it might become abusive in the future.

Brzonkala I, 935 F.Supp. at 778.

Brzonkala pled that she was violently gang raped, and rape "is 'not only pervasive harassment but also criminal conduct of the most serious nature' that is 'plainly sufficient to state a claim for "hostile environment" sexual harassment.'" Gary v. Long, 59 F.3d 1391, 1397 (D.C.Cir.), cert. denied, 516 U.S. 1011, 116 S.Ct. 569, 133 L.Ed.2d 493 (1995) (quoting Meritor [Sav. Bank v. Vinson], 477 U.S. [57], at 67, 106 S.Ct. [2399], at 2405–06 [(1986)]); cf. Brock v. United States, 64 F.3d 1421, 1423 (9th Cir.1995) ("Just as every murder is also a battery, every rape committed in the employment setting is also discrimination based on the employee's sex."); Baskerville v. Culligan Int'l Co., 50 F.3d 428, 430 (7th Cir.1995) (citing Meritor and recognizing sexual assault as an extreme example of sexual harassment); Karen Mellencamp Davis, Note, Reading, Writing, and Sexual Harassment: Finding a Constitutional Remedy When Schools Fail to Address Peer Abuse, 69 Ind. L.J. 1123, 1124 (1994) ("Rape and molestation provide drastic examples of the types of sexual harassment students inflict on their peers.").

Moreover, "even a single incident of sexual assault sufficiently alters the conditions of the victim's employment and clearly creates an abusive work environment for purposes of Title VII liability." Tomka v. Seiler Corp., 66 F.3d 1295, 1305 (2d Cir.1995) (citing Meritor, 477 U.S. at 67, 106 S.Ct. at 2405–06); see also King v. Board of Regents, 898 F.2d 533, 537 (7th Cir.1990) (acknowledging that "a single act [of discrimination] can be enough" to state a hostile environment claim under Title VII).

Thus, the district court failed to recognize that the rapes themselves created a hostile environment, and that Virginia Tech was aware of this environment and never properly remedied it. Indeed, the university Provost's rationale for overturning Morrison's immediate suspension for one school year—that this punishment was "excessive when compared with other cases"—itself evidences an environment hostile to complaints of sexual harassment and a refusal to effectively remedy this hostile environment. Given the seriousness of the harassment acts, the total inadequacy of Virginia Tech's redress, and Brzonkala's reasonable fear of unchecked retaliation including possible violence, Brzonkala did not have to return to the campus the next year and personally experience a continued hostile environment. Brzonkala "should not be punished for a hostile environment so severe that she was forced out entirely by loss of her legal claim against those responsible for the situation." Patricia H. v. Berkeley Unified Sch. Dist., 830 F.Supp. 1288, 1298 (N.D.Cal.1993); see also Carrero v. New York City Housing Auth., 890 F.2d 569, 578 (2d Cir.1989) ("A female employee need not subject herself to an extended period of demeaning and degrading provocation before being entitled to seek the remedies provided under Title VII.").

b.

The remaining issue is whether "some basis for institutional liability has been established." Seamons, 84 F.3d at 1232. "[A]n employer is liable for a sexually hostile work environment created by ... [an] employee only if the employer knew or should have known of the illegal conduct and failed to take prompt and adequate remedial action." Andrade, 88 F.3d at 261. We must determine whether Brzonkala has alleged facts sufficient to support an inference that Virginia Tech "knew or should have known of the illegal conduct and failed to take prompt and adequate remedial action." Virginia Tech certainly knew about the rapes once Brzonkala informed the school and initiated disciplinary proceedings against Morrison and Crawford. The question, therefore, is whether Virginia Tech took prompt and adequate remedial action once it was on notice of the rapes. See Paroline v. Unisys Corp., 879 F.2d 100, 106 (4th Cir.1989), vacated in part on other grounds, 900 F.2d 27 (4th Cir.1990) (en banc). This inquiry is necessarily fact-based, and whether a response is "prompt and adequate" will depend on the specific allegations (and ultimately evidence) in each case. Id. at 106–07.

Brzonkala alleges that after she was brutally raped three times she ceased attending classes, attempted suicide, and sought the aid of the school psychiatrist. Despite Virginia Tech's awareness of these developments no university official, including the psychiatrist, ever made more than a cursory inquiry into the cause of her distress. Furthermore, she alleges that when she directly reported the rapes to Virginia Tech authorities, the college neither provided a fair hearing nor meted out appropriate punishment. During the first hearing her attacker essentially admitted that he raped her after she twice told him no. The first hearing resulted in a finding that Morrison had committed sexual assault, and his suspension for one school year. This result was upheld by an appeals officer, and under Virginia Tech's published rules that decision was final and not subject to change.

Nevertheless, Virginia Tech voided the first hearing and reopened the case against her admitted rapist, assertedly in violation of its own rules and on the basis of a specious legal argument. The second hearing was procedurally biased against Brzonkala in numerous ways, and unbeknownst to her, Morrison was only charged with the lesser offense of using abusive language. Still, Morrison was again found guilty, and suspended for the next school year. On appeal a senior college official determined that there was sufficient evidence that Morrison had violated the University's Abusive Conduct Policy, and that Morrison's due process argument was meritless. Nonetheless, the appeals officer decided that suspending Brzonkala's rapist for a school year was "excessive when compared with other cases." The university then overturned that suspension and permitted her attacker to return to school with a full athletic scholarship.

Virginia Tech took this action without notifying Brzonkala, although she had been informed of the university's actions in the case at every previous juncture. This decision caused her to fear for her safety and to withdraw from college altogether. As punishment for his admitted rape Morrison received a "deferred suspension until [his] graduation from Virginia Tech" and "a one-hour educational session."

In short, Brzonkala alleges that Virginia Tech permitted, indeed fostered, an environment in which male student athletes could gang rape a female student without any significant punishment to the male attackers, nor any real assistance to the female victim. She alleges a legion of procedural irregularities in the hearing process, Virginia Tech's disregard for its own rules of finality, and its eventual decision to impose virtually no penalty for an admitted rape. These facts, if proven, would allow a jury to find that Virginia Tech's response to Brzonkala's gang rape was neither prompt nor adequate.

Virginia Tech argues that because it did levy some punishment against Morrison, its response was adequate. A defendant need not "make the most effective response possible" to sexual harassment. See Spicer v. Virginia Dept. of Corrections, 66 F.3d 705, 710 (4th Cir.1995) (en banc). This does not mean, however, that any remedy, no matter how delayed or weak, will be adequate. Rather, we have consistently held under Title VII that a defendant employer is "liable for sexual harassment committed by its employees if no adequate remedial action is taken." Id. Similar reasoning applies in the Title IX context. In light of the seriousness of Brzonkala's allegations, the long and winding disciplinary process, and the proverbial slap on the wrist as punishment, we cannot conclude at this preliminary stage that Virginia Tech's remedy was either prompt or adequate.

For all of these reasons, Brzonkala has alleged sufficient facts to state a Title IX hostile environment claim against Virginia Tech.

B.

Brzonkala also alleges a Title IX disparate treatment claim, i.e., that Virginia Tech discriminated against her on the basis of sex during the disciplinary proceedings against Morrison and Crawford. In analyzing Brzonkala's claim, Title VII again "provide[s] a persuasive body of standards to which we may look in shaping the contours of a private right of action under Title IX." [Preston v. Virginia ex rel. New River Community College, 31 F.3d 203, 207 (4th Cir.1994).]

Proof of discriminatory intent is necessary to state a disparate treatment claim under Title VII. International Bhd. of Teamsters v. United States, 431 U.S. 324, 335 n. 15, 97 S.Ct. 1843, 1854 n. 15, 52 L.Ed.2d 396 (1977). Absent some indication in the statute or regulations, Title IX similarly requires proof of discriminatory intent to state a disparate treatment claim. As such, we must examine Brzonkala's complaint to see if she has alleged sufficient facts to infer such intent. See Yusuf v. Vassar College, 35 F.3d 709, 715 (2d Cir.1994).

In this case Brzonkala has alleged a flawed proceeding and made a conclusory assertion that Virginia Tech discriminated in favor of male football players. But she has not alleged any discriminatory statements or treatment by Virginia Tech, or any systematic mistreatment of women or rape victims.

Nevertheless, Brzonkala maintains that she has made sufficient allegations of Virginia Tech's discriminatory intent. First, she argues that Virginia Tech's policy of not automatically reporting rapes to the police shows a discriminatory intent. Brzonkala does not allege, however, that the university discouraged or hindered her (or other rape victims) from filing charges, or that the university generally treats rape less seriously in its own disciplinary proceedings. Nor does she state facts to support an inference that the university created its nonreporting policy to discriminate against rape victims. Without an allegation that Virginia Tech itself fails to punish rapists, or impedes criminal investigations, or separate facts to establish that the policy was a result of gender bias, the university has not discriminated against rape victims, because these victims can always pursue criminal charges themselves. In fact, because of the intensely personal nature of the crime, as well as the present day difficulties inherent in pursuing rape charges, a victim of rape may not always want to press charges or involve the police. See Brzonkala I, 935 F.Supp. at 777.

Next, Brzonkala relies upon allegations that her access to evidence, like that of the plaintiff in Yusuf, was hampered, as the factual basis for a finding of discriminatory intent. It is true that in Yusuf the plaintiff alleged numerous procedural difficulties. Yusuf, 35 F.3d at 712–13. But, in Yusuf the plaintiff also asserted that "males accused of sexual harassment at Vassar are 'historically and systematically' and 'invariably found guilty, regardless of the evidence, or lack thereof.' " Id. at 716. This sort of systematic discrimination, on top of the procedural irregularities, sufficed to state a claim of disparate treatment. Here we have nothing but "allegations of a procedurally or otherwise flawed proceeding that has led to an adverse and erroneous outcome combined with a conclusory allegation of gender discrimination." Id. at 715. These allegations are "not sufficient to survive a motion to dismiss." Id.; cf. Houck v. Virginia Polytechnic Inst. & State Univ., 10 F.3d 204, 206–07 (4th Cir.1993) ("[I]n the Title VII context, isolated incidents or random comparisons demonstrating disparities in treatment may be insufficient to draw a prima facie inference of discrimination without additional evidence that the alleged phenomenon of inequality also exists with respect to the entire relevant group of employees."); Cook v. CSX Transp. Corp., 988 F.2d 507, 511–13 (4th Cir.1993) (same).

Finally, Brzonkala contends that the woefully inadequate punishment meted out against Morrison is in and of itself proof of sex discrimination. Again, without more, this does not prove intentional gender discrimination against Brzonkala. In sum, the district court correctly dismissed Brzonkala's Title IX claim of disparate treatment.

III.

We now turn to the question of whether the district court erred in dismissing Brzonkala's claim that Morrison and Crawford violated Title III of the Violence Against Women Act of 1994 ("VAWA"). See 42 U.S.C. § 13981 (1994). The district court held that Brzonkala alleged a valid

VAWA claim, but that VAWA was beyond congressional authority, and thus unconstitutional. See Brzonkala II, 935 F.Supp. at 801. We agree with the district court that Brzonkala stated a claim under VAWA. We conclude, however, that Congress acted within its authority in enacting VAWA and hold that the district court erred in ruling the statute unconstitutional.

[The remainder of the court's discussion concerning the constitutionality of the VAWA is omitted.]

LUTTIG, Circuit Judge, dissenting.

Fully aware of the importance of the matter before us today, I would unhesitatingly affirm the judgment below on the essential reasoning set forth by the district court. Brzonkala v. Virginia Polytechnic & State University, 935 F.Supp. 779 (W.D.Va.1996). Judge Kiser's lengthy opinion is an excellent legal analysis of the constitutionality of the Violence Against Women Act under Article I, § 8, cl. 3 of the Constitution. That analysis is thorough, scholarly, and, most important, abidingly faithful to the Supreme Court's decision in United States v. Lopez, 514 U.S. 549, 115 S.Ct. 1624, 131 L.Ed.2d 626 (1995). The district court's analysis describes in detail the Supreme Court's new analytical framework for addressing Commerce Clause challenges, and meticulously and dispassionately applies the principles and reasoning from Lopez in addressing the challenge to the legislation at issue in this case.

[The remainder of Judge Luttig's dissent is omitted.]

Notes

1. Like Willie Green, a number of athletes have been involved in paternity and child support suits. *See, e.g., Finley v. Scott*, 707 So.2d 1112 (Fla.1998); *Johnson v. Superior Court of Los Angeles County*, 77 Cal.Rptr.2d 624 (Ct.App.1998); *Niagara County Department of Social Services v. C.B.*, 651 N.Y.S.2d 785 (App.Div.1996); *W.S. v. X.Y.*, 676 A.2d 179 (N.J.App.Div. 1996); *Jackson v. Presley*, 586 So.2d 213 (Ala.Ct.Civ.App.1991); *Dunbar v. Tart*, 430 So.2d 530 (Fla.Dist.Ct.App.1983); *Hinkle v. Hinkle*, 685 A.2d 175 (Pa.Super.Ct.1996); *Gastineau v. Gastineau*, 573 N.Y.S.2d 819 (Sup.Ct.1991). *See also* Grant Wahl & L. Jon Wertheim, *Paternity Ward: Fathering Out-of-Wedlock Kids Has Become Commonplace Among Athletes, Many of Whom Seem Oblivious to the Legal, Financial and Emotional Consequences*, Sports Illustrated, May 4, 1998, at 62 (listing the following players as among those who have had out-of-wedlock children: Kenny Anderson, Larry Bird, Oscar De La Hoya, Patrick Ewing, Steve Garvey, Juan Gonzalez, Juwan Howard, Allen Iverson, Shawn Kemp, Jason Kidd, Stephon Marbury, Dave Meggett, Mark Messier, Hakeem Olajuwon, Jim Palmer, Gary Payton, Scottie Pippen, Andre Rison, Alonzo Spellman, Latrell Sprewell, Gary Sheffield, Roscoe Tanner, and Isiah Thomas).

2. In March 1998, Christy Brzonkala and Kathy Redmond (who was raped by a University of Nebraska football player) organized the National Coalition Against Violent Athletes. *See further* Margo Harakas, *Fame & Violence*, Fort Lauderdale Sun–Sentinel, May 13, 1998, at 1E. Their decision to do so was spurred in part by Jeffrey Benedict's *Public Heroes, Private*

Felons: Athletes and Crimes Against Women (1997). According to Benedict, approximately 100 official criminal complaints of physical or sexual assault were filed against male college athletes in both 1995 and 1996. Moreover, while they make up just three percent of the male student population, Benedict found athletes are involved in 19% of the sexual assaults and 37% of the domestic violence incidents on campuses.

For a further look at athletes and sexual abuse, see, e.g., *Barber v. Cincinnati Bengals, Inc.*, 95 F.3d 1156 (9th Cir.1996) (rape); *Ankers v. Rodman*, 995 F.Supp. 1329 (D.Utah 1997) (battery); *Tyson v. Trigg*, 883 F.Supp. 1213 (S.D.Ind.1994), *aff'd*, 50 F.3d 436 (7th Cir.1995), *cert. denied*, 516 U.S. 1041 (1996) (rape); *Doe v. Johnson*, 817 F.Supp. 1382 (W.D.Mich. 1993) (HIV transmission); *In re Quinn*, 517 N.W.2d 895 (Minn.1994) (rape); *Rollins v. Baker*, 683 So.2d 1138 (Fla.Dist.Ct.App.1996) (domestic violence); *Timpson v. Transamerica Insurance Co.*, 669 N.E.2d 1092 (Mass.Ct.App.), *review denied*, 674 N.E.2d 246 (Mass.1996) (sexual harassment); Timothy Davis & Tonya Parker, *Student-Athlete Sexual Violence Against Women: Defining the Limits of Institutional Responsibility*, 55 Wash. & Lee L. Rev. 55 (1998); Anna L. Jefferson, *The NFL and Domestic Violence: The Commissioner's Power to Punish Domestic Abusers*, 7 Seton Hall J. Sports L. 353 (1997); Note, *Out of Bounds: Professional Sports Leagues and Domestic Violence*, 109 Harv. L. Rev. 1048 (1996). For an interesting article that argues male athletes often are set upon by women seeking money, fame, or both, see *Athletes and Sexual Misconduct: Do They Create the Scandals or Do the Scandalous Find Them?*, Jet, May 11, 1998, at 52.

3. Crimes by athletes are not limited to rape and sexual assault. In their book *Pros and Cons: Criminals Who Play in the NFL* (1998), for example, Jeffrey Benedict and Don Yaeger relate that of the 509 players in the NFL during the 1996–97 season who lived in states offering access to police records, 21% had arrest records on such charges as homicide, kidnapping, armed robbery, drug trafficking, illegal gun possession, and drunk driving. They also point out that due to restrictive public access laws, the sealing of juvenile criminal records, and the transient nature of professional athletes, their findings are likely to be significantly understated.

4. More often than not, teams and the public are willing to overlook an athlete's transgressions. *See further* Dave Joseph, *Brutes and Junkies, That's Entertainment*, Fort Lauderdale Sun–Sentinel, Nov. 2, 1998, at 1D (pointing out that Mike Tyson, Latrell Sprewell, Magic Johnson, Steve Howe, and Lawrence Phillips, among others, were forgiven time and again); George Diaz, *Violence of Athletes Should be Scorned*, Orlando Sentinel, Mar. 27, 1998, at C1 (making similar observations about Wilfredo Cordero, Barry Bonds, John Daly, Scottie Pippen, Robert Parish, Jose Canseco, Warren Moon, Darryl Strawberry, and O.J. Simpson); Paul Woody, *It's the Desire to Win, Not Dollars, That is Corrupting American Sports*, Richmond Times Dispatch, Dec. 7, 1997, at D4 (discussing the special treatment accorded Charles Barkley, Michael Jordan, Shaquille O'Neal, Michael Westbrook, and Dexter Manley).

5. To be fair, it should be pointed out athletes sometimes find their fame works against them. *See further* Sam Stanton, *The Violent Athlete*, Sacramento Bee, Nov. 30, 1997, at C1, and Joe Hawk, *Visibility Can Make*

Athletes Victims as Well as Perpetrators, Las Vegas Rev.-J., Jan. 5, 1997, at 1C. As a result, one writer has proposed trying athletes accused of crimes in "high profile" courts specially designed to ensure they receive a fair trial. *See* Laurie N. Robinson, Comment, *Professional Athletes—Held to a Higher Standard and Above the Law: A Comment on High-Profile Criminal Defendants and the Need for States to Establish High-Profile Courts*, 73 Ind. L.J. 1313 (1998). If you were a state legislator, would you be inclined to vote for such a proposal?

6. For a further look at the off-field behavior of athletes, see, e.g., *Davis v. Six Sixteen, Inc.*, 122 F.3d 1060 (4th Cir.1997) (nightclub altercation); *Williams v. City of Dallas*, 178 F.R.D. 103 (N.D.Tex.1998) (false rape report); *United States v. Rose*, 1990 U.S. Dist. LEXIS 8629 (S.D.Ohio 1990) (tax evasion); *Morris v. State*, 487 So.2d 291 (Fla.1986) (cocaine trafficking); *Caldwell v. Griffin Spalding County Board of Education*, 503 S.E.2d 43 (Ga.Ct.App.1998) (rookie hazing); *Mellanby v. Chapple*, 1995 Ont. C. J. LEXIS 1540 (Ont.Ct.Just. 1995) (barroom fight). *See also* Gil B. Fried, *Illegal Moves Off-the-Field: University Liability for Illegal Acts of Student-Athletes*, 7 Seton Hall J. Sport L. 69 (1997) (suggesting strategies for dealing with violent players); Clarence J. Rowe, *Aggression and Violence in Sports*, 28 Psych. Annals 265 (1998) (analyzing the link between on-field aggression and off-field violence); Rick Dorsey, *Robinson's Mishap Pulls Falcons Down*, Augusta (GA.) Chron. Feb. 1, 1999, at 2 (Sports) (suggesting the poor performance of the Atlanta Falcons in Super Bowl XXXIII was due to the distractions generated by free safety Eugene Robinson's arrest hours before the game for trying to pick up a prostitute); Margie Mason, *Is Champions for Christ, the Sports Ministry that Caters to Jacksonville Jaguars and Other Athletes, a Marketing Tool or Merely Misunderstood?*, Fla. Times-Union, Aug. 9, 1998, at A1 (reviewing concerns raised about ministries that target athletes); Rick Reilly, *Need an Excuse? Take It From the Pros*, Sports Illustrated, Mar. 16, 1998, at 134 (pointing out many players refuse to accept responsibility for their actions); Maryann Hudson, *From Box Scores to the Police Blotter*, L.A. Times, Dec. 27, 1995, at A1 (noting in 1995, 345 American and Canadian sports figures were implicated in 252 incidents involving the criminal justice system).

Problem 30

When he was sued for having transmitted genital herpes to a casual acquaintance, a famous basketball player sought to introduce the following evidence about her: 1) she was employed as a nude dancer; 2) she had an active sex life both before and after their affair; and, 3) she had undergone breast augmentation surgery. If the plaintiff objects to the admission of this information on the grounds it is both irrelevant and highly prejudicial, how should the court rule? *See Judd v. Rodman*, 105 F.3d 1339 (11th Cir.), *petition for rehearing en banc denied*, 114 F.3d 1204 (11th Cir.1997).

Chapter 5

AGENTS

A. OVERVIEW

Many athletes find it helpful to retain an agent. In addition to negotiating contracts, they perform a variety of other services: overseeing money management and investment decisions; providing insurance, tax, and estate planning advice; and soliciting endorsement deals. In the legal arena, three questions surround agents: 1) what duties do they owe to their clients?; 2) when are they entitled to be paid?; and, 3) should they be regulated?

B. DUTIES

Agents are supposed to act in the best interests of their clients. Not surprisingly, however, players sometimes feel cheated by their agents. As the following cases demonstrate, courts require substantial proof before they will make such a finding.

DETROIT LIONS, INC. v. ARGOVITZ

580 F.Supp. 542 (E.D.Mich.1984),
aff'd in part and remanded, 767 F.2d 919 (6th Cir.1985).

DeMASCIO, District Judge.

The plot for this Saturday afternoon serial began when Billy Sims, having signed a contract with the Houston Gamblers on July 1, 1983, signed a second contract with the Detroit Lions on December 16, 1983. On December 18, 1983, the Detroit Lions, Inc. (Lions) and Billy R. Sims filed a complaint in the Oakland County Circuit Court seeking a judicial determination that the July 1, 1983, contract between Sims and the Houston Gamblers, Inc. (Gamblers) is invalid because the defendant Jerry Argovitz (Argovitz) breached his fiduciary duty when negotiating the Gamblers' contract and because the contract was otherwise tainted by fraud and misrepresentation. Defendants promptly removed the action to this court based on our diversity of citizenship jurisdiction.

For the reasons that follow, we have concluded that Argovitz's breach of his fiduciary duty during negotiations for the Gamblers' contract was so pronounced, so egregious, that to deny recision would be unconscionable.

Sometime in February or March 1983, Argovitz told Sims that he had applied for a Houston franchise in the newly formed United States Football League (USFL). In May 1983, Sims attended a press conference in Houston at which Argovitz announced that his application for a franchise had been approved. The evidence persuades us that Sims did not know the extent of Argovitz's interest in the Gamblers. He did not know the amount of Argovitz's original investment, or that Argovitz was obligated for 29 percent of a $1.5 million letter of credit, or that Argovitz was the president of the Gamblers' Corporation at an annual salary of $275,000 and 5 percent of the yearly cash flow. The defendants could not justifiably expect Sims to comprehend the ramifications of Argovitz's interest in the Gamblers or the manner in which that interest would create an untenable conflict of interest, a conflict that would inevitably breach Argovitz's fiduciary duty to Sims. Argovitz knew, or should have known, that he could not act as Sims' agent under any circumstances when dealing with the Gamblers. Even the USFL Constitution itself prohibits a holder of any interest in a member club from acting "as the contracting agent or representative for any player."

Pending the approval of his application for a USFL franchise in Houston, Argovitz continued his negotiations with the Lions on behalf of Sims. On April 5, 1983, Argovitz offered Sims' services to the Lions for $6 million over a four-year period. The offer included a demand for a $1 million interest-free loan to be repaid over 10 years, and for skill and injury guarantees for three years. The Lions quickly responded with a counter offer on April 7, 1983, in the face amount of $1.5 million over a five-year period with additional incentives not relevant here. The negotiating process was working. The Lions were trying to determine what Argovitz really believed the market value for Sims really was. On May 3, 1983, with his Gamblers franchise assured, Argovitz significantly reduced his offer to the Lions. He now offered Sims to the Lions for $3 million over a four-year period, one-half of the amount of his April 5, 1983, offer. Argovitz's May 3rd offer included a demand for $50,000 to permit Sims to purchase an annuity. Argovitz also dropped his previous demand for skill guarantees. The May 10, 1983 offer submitted by the Lions brought the parties much closer.

On May 30, 1983, Argovitz asked for $3.5 million over a five-year period. This offer included an interest-free loan and injury protection insurance but made no demand for skill guarantees. The May 30 offer now requested $400,000 to allow Sims to purchase an annuity. On June 1, 1983, Argovitz and the Lions were only $500,000 apart. We find that the negotiations between the Lions and Argovitz were progressing normally, not laterally as Argovitz represented to Sims. The Lions were not "dragging their feet." Throughout the entire month of June 1983, Mr. Frederick Nash, the Lions' skilled negotiator and a fastidious lawyer, was involved in investigating the possibility of providing an attractive annuity for Sims and at the same time doing his best to avoid the granting of either skill or injury guarantees. The evidence establishes that on June 22, 1983, the Lions and Argovitz were very close to reaching an agreement on the value of Sims' services.

Apparently, in the midst of his negotiations with the Lions and with his Gamblers franchise in hand, Argovitz decided that he would seek an offer from the Gamblers. Mr. Bernard Lerner, one of Argovitz's partners in the Gamblers agreed to negotiate a contract with Sims. Since Lerner admitted that he had no knowledge whatsoever about football, we must infer that Argovitz at the very least told Lerner the amount of money required to sign Sims and further pressed upon Lerner the Gamblers' absolute need to obtain Sims' services. In the Gamblers' organization, only Argovitz knew the value of Sims' services and how critical it was for the Gamblers to obtain Sims. In Argovitz's words, Sims would make the Gamblers' franchise.

On June 29, 1983, at Lerner's behest, Sims and his wife went to Houston to negotiate with a team that was partially owned by his own agent. When Sims arrived in Houston, he believed that the Lions organization was not negotiating in good faith; that it was not really interested in his services. His ego was bruised and his emotional outlook toward the Lions was visible to [Gene] Burrough [Argovitz's partner] and Argovitz. Clearly, virtually all the information that Sims had up to that date came from Argovitz. Sims and the Gamblers did not discuss a future contract on the night of June 29th. The negotiations began on the morning of June 30, 1983, and ended that afternoon. At the morning meeting, Lerner offered Sims a $3.5 million five-year contract, which included three years of skill and injury guarantees. The offer included a $500,000 loan at an interest rate of 1 percent over prime. It was from this loan that Argovitz planned to receive the $100,000 balance of his fee for acting as an agent in negotiating a contract with his own team. Burrough testified that Sims would have accepted that offer on the spot because he was finally receiving the guarantee that he had been requesting from the Lions, guarantees that Argovitz dropped without too much quarrel. Argovitz and Burrough took Sims and his wife into another room to discuss the offer. Argovitz did tell Sims that he thought the Lions would match the Gamblers financial package and asked Sims whether he (Argovitz) should telephone the Lions. But, it is clear from the evidence that neither Sims nor Burrough believed that the Lions would match the offer. We find that Sims told Argovitz not to call the Lions for purely emotional reasons. As we have noted, Sims believed that the Lions' organization was not that interested in him and his pride was wounded. Burrough clearly admitted that he was aware of the emotional basis for Sims' decision not to have Argovitz phone the Lions, and we must conclude from the extremely close relationship between Argovitz and Sims that Argovitz knew it as well. When Sims went back to Lerner's office, he agreed to become a Gambler on the terms offered. At that moment, Argovitz irreparably breached his fiduciary duty. As agent for Sims he had the duty to telephone the Lions, receive its final offer, and present the terms of both offers to Sims. Then and only then could it be said that Sims made an intelligent and knowing decision to accept the Gamblers' offer.

During these negotiations at the Gamblers' office, Mr. Nash of the Lions telephoned Argovitz, but even though Argovitz was at his office, he declined to accept the telephone call. Argovitz tried to return Nash's call after Sims had accepted the Gamblers' offer, but it was after 5 p.m. and Nash had left for the July 4th weekend. When he declined to accept Mr. Nash's call, Argovitz's breach of his fiduciary duty became even more pronounced. Following Nash's example, Argovitz left for his weekend trip, leaving his principal to sign the contracts with the Gamblers the next day, July 1, 1983. The defendants, in their supplemental trial brief, assert that neither Argovitz nor Burrough can be held responsible for following Sims' instruction not to contact the Lions on June 30, 1983. Although it is generally true that an agent is not liable for losses occurring as a result of following his principal's instructions, the rule of law is not applicable when the agent has placed himself in a position adverse to that of his principal.

During the evening of June 30, 1983, Burrough struggled with the fact that they had not presented the Gamblers' offer to the Lions. He knew, as does the court, that Argovitz now had the wedge that he needed to bring finality to the Lions' negotiations. Burrough was acutely aware of the fact that Sims' actions were emotionally motivated and realized that the responsibility for Sims' future rested with him. We view with some disdain the fact that Argovitz had, in effect, delegated his entire fiduciary responsibility on the eve of his principal's most important career decision. On July 1, 1983, it was Lerner who gave lip service to Argovitz's conspicuous conflict of interest. It was Lerner, not Argovitz, who advised Sims that Argovitz's position with the Gamblers presented a conflict of interest and that Sims could, if he wished, obtain an attorney or another agent. Argovitz, upon whom Sims had relied for the past four years, was not even there. Burrough, conscious of Sims' emotional responses, never advised Sims to wait until he had talked with the Lions before making a final decision. Argovitz's conflict of interest and self dealing put him in the position where he would not even use the wedge he now had to negotiate with the Lions, a wedge that is the dream of every agent. Two expert witnesses testified that an agent should telephone a team that he has been negotiating with once he has an offer in hand. Mr. Woolf, plaintiff's expert, testified that an offer from another team is probably the most important factor in negotiations. Mr. Lustig, defendant's expert, believed that it was prudent for him to telephone the Buffalo Bills and inform that organization of the Gamblers' offer to Jim Kelly, despite the fact that he believed the Bills had already made its best offer to his principal. The evidence here convinces us that Argovitz's negotiations with the Lions were ongoing and it had not made its final offer. Argovitz did not follow the common practice described by both expert witnesses. He did not do this because he knew that the Lions would not leave Sims without a contract and he further knew that if he made that type of call Sims would be lost to the Gamblers, a team he owned.

On November 12, 1983, when Sims was in Houston for the Lions game with the Houston Oilers, Argovitz asked Sims to come to his home and sign certain papers. He represented to Sims that certain papers of his contract had been mistakenly overlooked and now needed to be signed. Included among those papers he asked Sims to sign was a waiver of any claim that Sims might have against Argovitz for his blatant breach of his fiduciary duty brought on by his glaring conflict of interest. Sims did not receive independent advice with regard to the wisdom of signing such a waiver. Despite having sold his agency business in September, Argovitz did not even tell Sims' new agent of his intention to have Sims sign a waiver. Nevertheless, Sims, an unsophisticated young man, signed the waiver. This is another example of the questionable conduct on the part of Argovitz who still had business management obligations to Sims. In spite of his fiduciary relationship he had Sims sign a waiver without advising him to obtain independent counseling.

Argovitz's negotiations with Lustig, Jim Kelly's agent, illustrates the difficulties that develop when an agent negotiates a contract where his personal interests conflict with those of his principal. Lustig, an independent agent, ignored Argovitz's admonishment not to "shop" the Gamblers' offer to Kelly. Lustig called the NFL team that he had been negotiating with because it was the "prudent" thing to do. The Gamblers agreed to pay Kelly, an untested rookie quarterback $3.2 million for five years. His compensation was $60,000 less than Sims', a former Heisman Trophy winner and a proven star in the NFL. Lustig also obtained a number of favorable clauses from Argovitz; the most impressive one being that Kelly was assured of being one of the three top paid quarterbacks in the USFL if he performed as well as expected. If Argovitz had been free from conflicting interests he would have demanded similar benefits for Sims. Argovitz claimed that the nondisclosure clause in Kelly's contract prevented him from mentioning the Kelly contract to Sims. We view this contention as frivolous. Requesting these benefits for Sims did not require disclosure of Kelly's contract. Moreover, Argovitz's failure to obtain personal guarantees for Sims without adequately warning Sims about the risks and uncertainties of a new league constituted a clear breach of his fiduciary duty.

The parties submitted a great deal of evidence and argued a number of peripheral issues. Although most of the issues were not determinative factors in our decision, they do demonstrate that Argovitz had a history of fulfilling his fiduciary duties in an irresponsible manner. One cannot help but wonder whether Argovitz took his fiduciary duty seriously. For example, after investing approximately $76,000 of Sims' money, Argovitz, with or without the prior knowledge of his principal, received a finder's fee. Despite the fact that Sims paid Argovitz a 2 percent fee, Argovitz accepted $3800 from a person with whom he invested Sims' money. In March 1983, Argovitz had all of his veteran players, including Sims, sign a new agency contract with less favorable payment terms for the players even though they already had an ongoing agency agreement with him. He did this after he sold his entire agency business to Career Sports. Finally, Argovitz was prepared to take the remainder of his 5 percent agency fee for negotiating Sims' contract with the Gamblers from monies the Gamblers loaned to Sims at an interest rate of 1 percent over prime. It mattered little to Argovitz that Sims would have to pay interest on the $100,000 that Argovitz was ready to accept. While these practices by Argovitz are troublesome, we do not find them decisive in examining Argovitz's conduct while negotiating the Gamblers' contract on June 30 and July 1, 1983. We find this circumstantial evidence useful only insofar as it has aided the court in understanding the manner in which these parties conducted business.

We are mindful that Sims was less than forthright when testifying before the court. However, we agree with plaintiff's counsel that the facts as presented through the testimony of other witnesses are so unappealing that we can disregard Sims' testimony entirely. We remain persuaded that on balance, Argovitz's breach of his fiduciary duty was so egregious that a court of equity cannot permit him to benefit by his own wrongful breach. We conclude that Argovitz's conduct in negotiating Sims' contract with the Gamblers rendered it invalid.

Conclusions of Law

1. This court's jurisdiction is based on diversity of citizenship and, therefore, Michigan's conflict of laws rules apply. Klaxon Co. v. Stentor Electric Mfg. Co., 313 U.S. 487, 496, 61 S.Ct. 1020, 1021, 85 L.Ed. 1477 (1941).

2. The Michigan courts would apply the law of Texas because all of the contracts giving rise to a claim of fraud or breach of fiduciary duty occurred in Texas. Rubin v. Gallagher, 294 Mich. 124, 292 N.W. 584 (1940); Hardy v. Monsanto Enviro–Chem Systems, Inc., 414 Mich. 29, 84–85, 323 N.W.2d 270 (1982) (Moody, Jr., J., dissenting in part); Wells v. 10–X Manufacturing Co., 609 F.2d 248, 253 (6th Cir.1979). Moreover the parties have stipulated to the application of Texas law.

3. The relationship between a principal and agent is fiduciary in nature, and as such imposes a duty of loyalty, good faith, and fair and honest dealing on the agent. Anderson v. Griffith, 501 S.W.2d 695, 700 (Tex.Civ.App.1973).

4. A fiduciary relationship arises not only from a formal principal-agent relationship, but also from informal relationships of trust and confidence. Thigpen v. Locke, 363 S.W.2d 247, 253 (Tex.1962); Adickes v. Andreoli, 600 S.W.2d 939, 945–46 (Tex.Civ.App.1980).

5. In light of the express agency agreement, and the relationship between Sims and Argovitz, Argovitz clearly owed Sims the fiduciary duties of an agent at all times relevant to this lawsuit.

6. An agent's duty of loyalty requires that he not have a personal stake that conflicts with the principal's interest in a transaction in which

he represents his principal. Burleson v. Earnest, 153 S.W.2d 869 (Tex. Civ.App.1941).

7. A fiduciary violates the prohibition against self-dealing not only by dealing with himself on his principal's behalf, but also by dealing on his principal's behalf with a third party in which he has an interest, such as a partnership in which he is a member. Daniel v. Henderson, 183 S.W.2d 242 (Tex.Civ.App.1944), aff'd sub nom., Southern Trust & Mortgage Co. v. Daniel, 143 Tex. 321, 184 S.W.2d 465 (1944).

8. Where an agent has an interest adverse to that of his principal in a transaction in which he purports to act on behalf of his principal, the transaction is voidable by the principal unless the agent disclosed all material facts within the agent's knowledge that might affect the principal's judgment. Burleson v. Earnest, 153 S.W.2d at 874–75.

9. The mere fact that the contract is fair to the principal does not deny the principal the right to rescind the contract when it was negotiated by an agent in violation of the prohibition against self-dealing. As stated in Burleson:

> The question, therefore, does not relate to the mala fides of the agent nor to whether or not a greater sum might have been procured for the property, nor even to whether or not the vendor received full value therefor. The self-interest of the agent is considered a vice which renders the transaction voidable at the election of the principal without looking into the matter further than to ascertain that the interest of the agent exists.

10. Once it has been shown that an agent had an interest in a transaction involving his principal antagonistic to the principal's interest, fraud on the part of the agent is presumed. The burden of proof then rests upon the agent to show that his principal had full knowledge, not only of the fact that the agent was interested, but also of every material fact known to the agent which might affect the principal and that having such knowledge, the principal freely consented to the transaction.

11. It is not sufficient for the agent merely to inform the principal that he has an interest that conflicts with the principal's interest. Rather, he must inform the principal "of all facts that come to his knowledge that are or may be material or which might affect his principal's rights or interests or influence the action he takes." Anderson v. Griffith, 501 S.W.2d 695, 700 (Tex.Civ.App.1973).

12. Argovitz clearly had a personal interest in signing Sims with the Gamblers that was adverse to Sims' interest—he had an ownership interest in the Gamblers and thus would profit if the Gamblers were profitable, and would incur substantial personal liabilities should the Gamblers not be financially successful. Since this showing has been made, fraud on Argovitz's part is presumed, and the Gamblers' contract must be rescinded unless Argovitz has shown by a preponderance of the

evidence that he informed Sims of every material fact that might have influenced Sims' decision whether or not to sign the Gamblers' contract.

13. We conclude that Argovitz has failed to show by a preponderance of the evidence either: 1) that he informed Sims of the following facts, or 2) that these facts would not have influenced Sims' decision whether to sign the Gamblers' contract:

a. The relative values of the Gamblers' contract and the Lions' offer that Argovitz knew could be obtained.

b. That there [were] significant financial differences between the USFL and the NFL not only in terms of the relative financial stability of the Leagues, but also in terms of the fringe benefits available to Sims.

c. Argovitz's 29 percent ownership in the Gamblers; Argovitz's $275,000 annual salary with the Gamblers; Argovitz's five percent interest in the cash flow of the Gamblers.

d. That both Argovitz and Burrough failed to even attempt to obtain for Sims valuable contract clauses which they had given to Kelly on behalf of the Gamblers.

e. That Sims had great leverage, and Argovitz was not encouraging a bidding war that could have advantageous results for Sims.

14. Under Texas law, a nonbinding prior act cannot be ratified, and the right to seek recision cannot be waived, unless the party against whom these defenses are asserted had full knowledge of all material facts at the time the acts of ratification or waiver are alleged to have occurred.

15. At no time prior to December 1, 1983, was Sims aware of the material nondisclosures outlined above; accordingly, the defenses of ratification and waiver must be rejected.

16. Defendants' asserted defenses of estoppel and laches are also without merit.

17. As a court sitting in equity, we conclude that recision is the appropriate remedy. We are dismayed by Argovitz's egregious conduct. The careless fashion in which Argovitz went about ascertaining the highest price for Sims' service convinces us of the wisdom of the maxim: no man can faithfully serve two masters whose interests are in conflict.

Judgment will be entered for the plaintiffs rescinding the Gamblers' contract with Sims.

BIAS v. ADVANTAGE INTERNATIONAL, INC.

905 F.2d 1558 (D.C.Cir.),
cert. denied, 498 U.S. 958 (1990).

SENTELLE, Circuit Judge.

This case arises out of the tragic death from cocaine intoxication of University of Maryland basketball star Leonard K. Bias ("Bias"). James

Bias, as Personal Representative of the Estate of Leonard K. Bias, deceased ("the Estate"), appeals an order of the District Court for the District of Columbia which granted summary judgment to defendants Advantage International, Inc. ("Advantage") and A. Lee Fentress on the Estate's claims arising out of a representation agreement between Bias and Advantage. Advantage and Fentress (collectively "the defendants") cross-appeal the District Court's grant of summary judgment to the Estate on the defendants' counterclaims, but the defendants represent that they will not press their appeal of the District Court's order with respect to the counterclaims if this Court affirms the District Court's summary judgment to the defendants with respect to the Estate's claims. For the reasons which follow, we affirm the order of the District Court granting to the defendants summary judgment with respect to the Estate's claims and we do not address the District Court's order with respect to the defendants' counterclaims.

BACKGROUND

On April 7, 1986, after the close of his college basketball career, Bias entered into a representation agreement with Advantage whereby Advantage agreed to advise and represent Bias in his affairs. Fentress was the particular Advantage representative servicing the Bias account. On June 17 of that year Bias was picked by the Boston Celtics in the first round of the National Basketball Association draft. On the morning of June 19, 1986, Bias died of cocaine intoxication. The Estate sued Advantage and Fentress for two separate injuries allegedly arising out of the representation arrangement between Bias and the defendants. The Estate also sued Fidelity Security Life Insurance Company and Reebok International, Ltd. The District Court awarded summary judgment to Fidelity and Reebok and the Estate does not appeal the District Court's orders with respect to those two defendants.

First, the Estate alleges that, prior to Bias's death, Bias and his parents directed Fentress to obtain a one-million dollar life insurance policy on Bias's life, that Fentress represented to Bias and Bias's parents that he had secured such a policy, and that in reliance on Fentress's assurances, Bias's parents did not independently seek to buy an insurance policy on Bias's life. Although the defendants did obtain increased disability coverage for Bias, in a one-million dollar disability insurance policy with an accidental death rider, they did not secure any life insurance coverage for Bias prior to his death.

Second, on June 18, 1986, the day after he was drafted by the Boston Celtics, Bias, through and with Fentress, entered into negotiations with Reebok International, Ltd. ("Reebok") concerning a potential endorsement contract. The Estate alleges that after several hours of negotiations Fentress requested that Bias and his father leave so that Fentress could continue negotiating with Reebok representatives in private. The Estate alleges that Fentress then began negotiating a proposed package deal with Reebok on behalf of not just Bias, but also other players represented by Advantage. The Estate contends that

Fentress breached a duty to Bias by negotiating on behalf of other players, and that because Fentress opened up these broader negotiations he was unable to complete the negotiations for Bias on June 18. The Estate claims that as a result of Fentress's actions, on June 19, when Bias died, Bias had no contract with Reebok. The Estate alleges that the contract that Bias would have obtained would have provided for an unconditional lump sum payment which Bias would have received up front.

The District Court awarded the defendants summary judgment on both of these claims. With respect to the first claim, the District Court held, in effect, that the Estate did not suffer any damage from the defendants' alleged failure to obtain life insurance for Bias because, even if the defendants had tried to obtain a one-million dollar policy on Bias's life, they would not have been able to do so. The District Court based this conclusion on the facts, about which it found no genuine issue, that Bias was a cocaine user and that no insurer in 1986 would have issued a one-million dollar life insurance policy, or "jumbo" policy, to a cocaine user unless the applicant made a misrepresentation regarding the applicant's use of drugs, thereby rendering the insurance policy void.

With respect to the Estate's second claim, the District Court concluded that the defendants could not be held liable for failing to produce a finished endorsement contract with Reebok before Bias's death because the defendants had no independent reason to expedite the signing of the endorsement contract to the extent argued by the Estate, and because the defendants could not have obtained a signed contract before Bias's death even if they had tried to do so.

The Estate appeals both of the District Court's conclusions, arguing that there is a genuine issue as to Bias's insurability and regarding the defendants' failure to sign a Reebok contract on Bias's behalf prior to Bias's death.

The Insurance Issue

The District Court's determination that there was no genuine issue involving Bias's insurability rests on two subsidiary conclusions. First, the District Court concluded that there was no genuine issue as to the fact that Bias was a drug user. Second, the District Court held that there was no dispute about the fact that as a drug user, Bias could not have obtained a jumbo life insurance policy. We can only affirm the District Court's award of summary judgment to the defendants on the insurance issue if both of these conclusions were correct.

A. Bias's Prior Drug Use

The defendants in this case offered the eyewitness testimony of two former teammates of Bias, Terry Long and David Gregg, in order to show that Bias was a cocaine user during the period prior to his death. Long and Gregg both described numerous occasions when they saw Bias ingest cocaine, and Long testified that he was introduced to cocaine by Bias and that Bias sometimes supplied others with cocaine.

Although on appeal the Estate attempts to discredit the testimony of Long and Gregg, the Estate did not seek to impeach the testimony of these witnesses before the District Court, and the Estate made no effort to depose these witnesses. Instead, the Estate offered affidavits from each of Bias's parents stating that Bias was not a drug user; the deposition testimony of Bias's basketball coach, Charles "Lefty" Driesell, who testified that he knew Bias well for four years and never knew Bias to be a user of drugs at any time prior to his death; and the results of several drug tests administered to Bias during the four years prior to his death which may have shown that, on the occasions when the tests were administered, there were no traces in Bias's system of the drugs for which he was tested.

Because the Estate's generalized evidence that Bias was not a drug user did not contradict the more specific testimony of teammates who knew Bias well and had seen him use cocaine on particular occasions, the District Court determined that there was no genuine issue as to the fact that Bias was a drug user. We agree.

There is no question that the defendants satisfied their initial burden on the issue of Bias's drug use. The testimony of Long and Gregg clearly tends to show that Bias was a cocaine user. We also agree with the District Court that the Estate did not rebut the defendants' showing. The testimony of Bias's parents to the effect that they knew Bias well and did not know him to be a drug user does not rebut the Long and Gregg testimony about Bias's drug use on particular occasions. The District Court properly held that rebuttal testimony either must come from persons familiar with the particular events to which the defendants' witnesses testified or must otherwise cast more than metaphysical doubt on the credibility of that testimony. Bias's parents and coach did not have personal knowledge of Bias's activities at the sorts of parties and gatherings about which Long and Gregg testified. The drug test results offered by the Estate may show that Bias had no cocaine in his system on the dates when the tests were administered, but, as the District Court correctly noted, these tests speak only to Bias's abstention during the periods preceding the tests. The tests do not rebut the Long and Gregg testimony that on a number of occasions Bias ingested cocaine in their presence.

The Estate could have deposed Long and Gregg, or otherwise attempted to impeach their testimony. The Estate also could have offered the testimony of other friends or teammates of Bias who were present at some of the gatherings described by Long and Gregg, who went out with Bias frequently, or who were otherwise familiar with his social habits. The Estate did none of these things. The Estate is not entitled to reach the jury merely on the supposition that the jury might not believe the defendants' witnesses. We thus agree with the District Court that there was no genuine issue of fact concerning Bias's status as a cocaine user.

B. The Availability of a Jumbo Policy in Light of Bias's Prior Drug Use

The defendants submitted affidavits from several experts who testified that in their expert opinions no insurer in 1986 would have issued a jumbo policy without inquiring, at some point in the application process, about the applicant's prior drug use. Dr. Francis Achampong, an Associate Professor of Business Law and Insurance and an occasional consultant for the insurance industry, asserted that life insurance companies will always and as a routine matter ask an applicant whether the applicant has ever used cocaine before issuing a term life policy of this size to that applicant. Joint Appendix ("J.A.") 61. Dr. Achampong testified that insurers inquire about prior drug use at some stage of the application process, generally either in the initial application, during the medical examination, during the follow-up character investigation, or at some other stage. J.A. 466. Dr. Achampong further concluded that an affirmative answer to this question renders an applicant uninsurable because, "[a]s a matter of standard underwriting procedure, insurance companies do not issue term life insurance policies, let alone $1 million term policies, to applicants they know have recently used cocaine." J.A. 61. Bernard R. Wolfe, a licensed insurance agent experienced in evaluating the insurance needs of professional athletes, offered essentially the same opinion that insurance companies do not issue substantial term life insurance policies without first investigating an applicant's prior drug use and that insurance companies do not issue substantial term life insurance policies to applicants who use cocaine. J.A. 79.

The Estate responded with expert testimony of its own showing that in 1986 some companies did not inquire about an applicant's prior drug use at the application stage and that other companies at that time did not inquire about an applicant's prior drug use at the medical examination stage of the application process. The Estate did not offer any testimony showing that a company existed at that time which would not have inquired about an applicant's prior drug use at some stage in the process. Moreover, the Estate did not offer any testimony tending to show that even if an applicant did admit to being a cocaine user, a company existed in 1986 which would have issued a jumbo policy to that applicant. The District Court thus concluded that the Estate had failed to rebut the defendants' showing that as a cocaine user Bias would have been unable to obtain a jumbo policy. The District Court recognized that Bias might have been able to obtain a policy by lying about his prior drug use, but rightly concluded that such a knowing and material misrepresentation in response to a direct question would have rendered void any policy which Bias thereby obtained. See D.C.Code Ann. § 35–414 (1988).

We agree with the District Court. The defendants offered evidence that every insurance company inquires about the prior drug use of an applicant for a jumbo policy at some point in the application process. The Estate's evidence that some insurance companies existed in 1986 which did not inquire about prior drug use at certain particular stages in the application process does not undermine the defendant's claim that at some point in the process every insurance company did inquire about drug use, particularly where a jumbo policy was involved. The Estate failed to name a single particular company or provide other evidence that a single company existed which would have issued a jumbo policy in 1986 without inquiring about the applicant's drug use. Because the Estate has failed to do more than show that there is "some metaphysical doubt as to the material facts," the District Court properly concluded that there was no genuine issue of material fact as to the insurability of a drug user.

The Reebok Contract

We find no merit in the Estate's claim based on the Reebok contract negotiations. Neither the language of the representation agreement between Bias and Advantage nor any other evidence could support a finding that the defendants breached any duty to Bias by failing to push to obtain a signed contract on June 18, 1986.

Even if the defendants were under some duty to try to sign a contract for Bias as quickly as possible, the Estate has offered no evidence to rebut the defendants' showing that the contract could not possibly have been signed prior to Bias's death, irrespective of the defendants' actions. The defendants offered testimony from Reebok officials that the language of any agreement between Reebok and Bias would have had to be reviewed by the Reebok legal department before Reebok would have signed the agreement. J.A. 144. The Estate did not counter the defendants' evidence that an endorsement contract cannot be negotiated, drafted, and signed in a single day. In fact, the Estate's own expert testified that a contract between Bias and Reebok could not feasibly have been signed on June 18, 1986. J.A. 125. The Estate must do more than merely argue that the feasibility of obtaining a signed endorsement contract in a single day is a question for the jury; it must offer some basis for its claim that a jury could reasonably conclude that the contract could have been drafted and signed on June 18. Because the Estate failed to do this, we affirm the District Court's award of summary judgment to the defendants on this claim.

Conclusion

In order to withstand a summary judgment motion once the moving party has made a prima facie showing to support its claims, the nonmoving party must come forward with specific facts showing that there is a genuine issue for trial. Fed.R.Civ.P. 56(e). The Estate has failed to come forward with such facts in this case, relying instead on bare arguments and allegations or on evidence which does not actually create a genuine issue for trial. For this reason, we affirm the District Court's award of summary judgment to the defendants in this case.

MANDICH v. WATTERS

970 F.2d 462 (8th Cir.1992).

LOKEN, Circuit Judge.

Retired professional hockey player Daniel G. Mandich appeals the district court's summary judgment dismissing Mandich's suit against his former agent, William W. Watters. Mandich sued Watters for secretly negotiating an illegal side agreement with the Minnesota North Stars that deprived Mandich of post-retirement salaries under his 1985 player's contract. The district court held that this claim was collaterally estopped by a National Hockey League (NHL) arbitrator's resolution of Mandich's prior contract claim against the North Stars. We affirm.

I.

Mandich severely injured his right knee during a North Stars game in January 1984. He signed a new one-year contract in August 1984, while attempting to rehabilitate the knee. He played in a few games near the end of the 1984–85 season and hoped to resume his hockey career in the fall of 1985.

In negotiating Mandich's contract for the 1985–86 season, Watters and North Stars General Manager Lou Nanne knew that Mandich would retire that fall if his knee injury proved disabling, and that Mandich would collect $175,000 in NHL disability insurance benefits if he retired before playing twenty post-injury NHL games. However, the NHL Standard Player's Contract provided that a player "disabled ... by reason of an injury sustained during the course of his employment as a hockey player ... shall be entitled to receive his remaining salary due in accordance with the terms of this contract." Therefore, when Mandich and the North Stars signed a two-year contract on May 15, 1985, calling for a salary of $105,000 in the first year and $120,000 in the second (the "1985 Contract"), Watters and Nanne made an oral side agreement—if Mandich retired early enough to receive the disability benefits, the North Stars would have no further salary obligation under the 1985 Contract.

The 1985 Contract was on the Standard Player's Contract form, as required by the collective bargaining agreement between the NHL and the NHL Players Association. Paragraph 21 of that form provided, "this Agreement contains the entire agreement between the Parties and there are no oral or written inducements, promises or agreements except as provided herein." Nevertheless, Watters and Nanne later testified that side agreements were a common NHL practice. Watters also testified that the 1985 Contract was a good deal for Mandich, because he would get $175,000 if his injury forced him to retire before playing twenty games, and he would have a two-year contract at attractive salaries if he was able to resume his career.

In the fall of 1985, Mandich participated in training camp, played sparingly in several early season games, and then was sent to a minor league team where his knee could be rigorously tested. Unfortunately, the knee performed poorly. On November 19, after team doctors told him his injury was disabling, Mandich went to Nanne's office to announce his decision to retire. Nanne asked Mandich to sign a "Letter of Agreement" memorializing the side agreement. Mandich objected, claiming Watters had never told him of such an arrangement. Nanne telephoned Watters, who told Mandich over a speakerphone that this was indeed part of his contract. Mandich reluctantly signed the letter agreement but then filed a grievance to recover his full 1985 Contract salaries.

Mandich's grievance was submitted to NHL President John Ziegler for binding arbitration, as required by the collective bargaining agreement and paragraph 19 of the 1985 Contract. After receiving documentary evidence and conducting a hearing, Ziegler issued his eight page written decision. Without deciding whether the side agreement was binding and enforceable, Ziegler ruled in favor of the North Stars, concluding that the parties had agreed "the 1985 contract would not be effective if Mandich was physically unable to perform"; that Mandich was physically unable to perform "by reason of a career-ending injury occurring in January of 1984" for which he received $175,000 in disability benefits; that the 1985 Contract "never came into effect" because "[t]here was a total failure of consideration on the player's part as well as a breach of an essential condition, viz., failure to report in good physical condition"; and that the collective bargaining agreement did not require full pay out of the post-injury 1985 Contract.

Mandich then petitioned a Minnesota state court to vacate the arbitration award, arguing that Ziegler was not impartial and had exceeded his powers. See Minn.Stat. § 572.19, Subd. 1(2), (3). The state trial court upheld the award. It concluded that the oral agreement between Watters and Nanne was valid, an issue that Ziegler had avoided, and that Ziegler was not biased. It also upheld Ziegler's interpretation of the 1985 Contract:

> The arbitrator concluded that the presence of petitioner's injury precluded him from fulfilling his obligations under the terms of the agreement. Again, this court cannot conclude that the arbitrator exceeded his authority in finding the terms of the agreement as he did or applying those terms to the undisputed facts before him.

In its conclusion, the court also commented, "Were this court free to explore the relative merits of the parties' positions in a de novo fashion, the application of basic principles of contract law would likely leave the petitioner in a much different position."

On appeal, the Minnesota Court of Appeals affirmed, upholding the side agreement and summarily rejecting Mandich's argument that Ziegler was biased. A dissent harshly criticized Ziegler's contract analysis as "wholly illegitimate" and concluded that Ziegler had exceeded his authority as an arbitrator. Mandich v. North Star Partnership, 450 N.W.2d 173 (Minn.Ct.App.1990). The Minnesota Supreme Court declined further review.

Mandich then commenced this suit, seeking to recover the unpaid salaries provided in the 1985 Contract on the ground that Watters breached his duty as agent by negotiating an illegal and unauthorized side agreement. Watters, a resident of Canada, removed. Mandich then filed an amended complaint which pleaded a violation of the National Labor Relations Act. However, Mandich has argued no issue of federal law on appeal, and both parties have treated this as a diversity case in which Minnesota law governs.

The district court granted Watters's motion for summary judgment, concluding that the arbitrator's determination that the 1985 Contract never came into effect is binding on Mandich and precludes his claim for salaries provided in that contract. On appeal, Mandich concedes that his claim against Watters depends upon the enforceability of the 1985 Contract and contends that the district court erred in applying collateral estoppel to resolve this issue against him.

II.

Federal courts must "give the same preclusive effect to state court judgments that those judgments would be given in the courts of the State from which the judgments emerged." Kremer v. Chemical Constr. Corp., 456 U.S. 461, 466, 102 S.Ct. 1883, 1889, 72 L.Ed.2d 262 (1982). In Minnesota, collateral estoppel precludes a party from relitigating a legal or factual issue that was actually litigated in a prior proceeding and was essential to the judgment rendered. See Hauser v. Mealey, 263 N.W.2d 803, 806 (Minn.1978). The party invoking collateral estoppel must show: "(1) the issue was identical to one in a prior adjudication; (2) there was a final judgment on the merits; (3) the estopped party was a party or in privity with a party to the prior adjudication; and (4) the estopped party was given a full and fair opportunity to be heard on the adjudicated issue." Kaiser v. Northern States Power Co., 353 N.W.2d 899, 902 (Minn.1984).

It is now settled in Minnesota that an arbitration award is a prior adjudication for collateral estoppel purposes. See Aufderhar v. Data Dispatch, Inc., 452 N.W.2d 648, 651 (Minn.1990). However, no reported Minnesota case has discussed how to apply to arbitration awards the complex rules that define the collateral estoppel effect of judicial determinations. Equating the arbitrator's award with a lower court's judgment, Mandich launches a novel two-pronged attack on the district court's collateral estoppel analysis. Although arbitrator Ziegler squarely decided the crucial question against him, Mandich argues, that decision may not be given collateral estoppel effect, first, because the Minnesota trial court affirmed on multiple grounds no one of which was "essential to the judgment," and second, because the Minnesota Court of Appeals affirmed on an alternative ground, the validity of the Watters/Nanne side agreement.

The fatal flaw in these arguments is their initial premise, that an arbitration award is like a trial court decision for collateral estoppel purposes. Mandich is invoking principles derived from the nature of appellate review of trial court decisions. See Restatement (Second) of Judgments § 27, comments i, o. The general rule is that, "if a judgment is appealed, collateral estoppel only works as to those issues specifically passed upon by the appellate court." Hicks v. Quaker Oats Co., 662 F.2d 1158, 1168 (5th Cir.1981); see Dow Chemical v. U.S. Environmental Protection Agency, 832 F.2d 319, 323 (5th Cir.1987). The rule is based upon the fact that "a 'full and fair opportunity to litigate' includes the right to appeal an adverse decision." Gray v. Lacke, 885 F.2d 399, 406 (7th Cir.1989), cert. denied, 494 U.S. 1029, 110 S.Ct. 1476, 108 L.Ed.2d 613 (1990).

Mandich's attempt to apply this rule to the state court decisions upholding Ziegler's award overlooks the limited scope of judicial review of an arbitrator's decision. Minnesota law favors arbitration awards and by statute severely limits the grounds upon which a reviewing court may vacate an award. "[A]n arbitrator, in the absence of any agreement limiting his authority, is the final judge of both law and fact." State v. Minnesota Teamsters Local No. 320, 316 N.W.2d 542, 544 (Minn.1982). The reviewing court does not review the merits of the arbitrator's decision; indeed, "the fact that the relief was such that it could not or would not be granted by a court of law or equity is not ground for vacating or refusing to confirm the award." Minn.Stat. § 572.19, Subd. 1.

Thus, Mandich's arguments that Ziegler's failure-of-consideration determination does not deserve preclusive effect because the Minnesota trial court affirmed upon multiple grounds, and because the Court of Appeals affirmed on an alternative ground, must fail. Mandich's right to appeal Ziegler's award did not include the right to have the arbitrator's interpretation of the 1985 Contract reviewed on the merits, either by the trial court or the Court of Appeals. The state courts' lengthy discussion of the merits of Ziegler's decision was in response to Mandich's argument that Ziegler was partial because "no rational basis exists for [his] determination." 450 N.W.2d at 177. Applying this "rational basis" standard while reserving judgment as to its propriety, the district court declined to vacate the award, and the Court of Appeals affirmed. This was not the equivalent of full-fledged appellate review on the merits. "[O]nce arbitrability is established, the role of the judiciary does not encompass a reexamination of the merits of the case." Ramsey County v. AFSCME, 309 N.W.2d 785, 790 (Minn.1981).

In these circumstances, we agree with the district court that the only relevant question is whether the failure-of-consideration issue was squarely addressed by the arbitrator and was essential to his decision. It clearly was. Although Ziegler's opinion perhaps suggests a predisposition toward upholding the side agreement, he expressly declined to do so. The sole ground for his award was that the 1985 Contract never came into existence. That award was upheld upon judicial review. If arbitration awards are to be given meaningful collateral estoppel effect, as the Minnesota Supreme Court has declared, then relitigation of Ziegler's core determination that the 1985 Contract is unenforceable must be precluded.

Mandich also argues that he was denied a "full and fair opportunity" to litigate Ziegler's failure-of-consideration theory because neither party briefed it nor argued it at the arbitration hearing. The Minnesota courts have found that a party to a prior arbitration was denied a "full and fair opportunity" to litigate an issue when he had "no meaningful participation" in the proceeding, Houlihan v. Fimon, 454 N.W.2d 633, 637 (Minn.Ct.App.1990), or the decision was based "on only part of the pertinent facts and parties." Johnson v. Consolidated Freightways, Inc., 420 N.W.2d 608, 614 (Minn.1988). These exceptions obviously do not apply here. Mandich invoked arbitration seeking to enforce the salary provisions of the 1985 Contract. His claim obviously put at issue the existence and enforceability of that contract. The North Stars' theory at the hearing was that Mandich failed to live up to his bargain because he was physically unable to play hockey during the contract term. Ziegler's failure-of-consideration analysis relied on the evidence submitted by both parties. We reject the contention, for which Mandich cites no authority, that the issue was not fairly litigated because Ziegler relied upon an interpretation of the contract that was not specifically urged by either party to the arbitration.

Finally, Mandich argues that giving Ziegler's award preclusive effect "would work an injustice on the party against whom estoppel is urged." Johnson, 420 N.W.2d at 614. However, we find no such injustice in this case. Mandich agreed to the binding arbitration he now seeks to avoid in the very contract whose salary provisions he would enforce against Watters. Mandich was represented by counsel at the arbitration proceeding, the arbitrator ruled squarely against him on the question here at issue, and two reviewing courts declined to vacate that award. In these circumstances, we think the governing principle was stated by the Minnesota Supreme Court in Aufderhar, 452 N.W.2d at 652–53:

> Because it is clear Aufderhar was afforded "a full and fair opportunity to be heard" on the damage issue, we perceive no reason to deny the application of estoppel to prevent relitigation of that issue. To the contrary, to permit it here is entirely consistent with the public policy underlying this court's traditional encouragement of alternative forms of dispute resolution, as well as policies designed to promote judicial efficiency.

For the above reasons, the judgment of the district court is affirmed.

Notes

1. On first blush, it may appear that judges make it too easy for agents to avoid liability. Players often have unrealistic expectations, however, and are quick to blame their agents when the marketplace fails to provide them with what they think is fair compensation. In addition, many athletes who are happy with a deal when it is first struck later become disgruntled when others receive more lucrative contracts. Nevertheless, as *Argovitz* shows,

courts will not hesitate to punish agents who engage in clearly unconscionable activities. *See also Jones v. Childers*, 18 F.3d 899 (11th Cir.1994) (agent held liable to professional athletes for knowingly recommending unsuitable tax shelters).

2. *Bias* and *Mandich*, on the other hand, are good examples of agents being blamed just because things did not work out as hoped. As both courts recognized, the agents did the best they could under difficult circumstances. This is easier to see in *Bias*, of course, where the player's drug habit was the cause of the losses suffered by his family. But even in *Mandich*, it is hard to fault the agent. Operating as he was in an atmosphere in which side deals, although "illegal," were common, he got the best contract he could for a client whose health was in serious doubt.

3. Until very recently, players preferred to handle their own business affairs (although New York Yankees slugger Babe Ruth had a financial adviser as early as 1924 and Chicago Bears legend Red Grange used a theatrical promoter to negotiate a barnstorming contract in 1925). It generally is acknowledged that the first true sports agent was Bob Woolf, who began his career in 1965 by representing Boston Red Sox pitcher Earl Wilson. For a further look at Woolf's career, see Tom Long, *Bob Woolf, 65; Lawyer Pioneered Financial Management of Athletes*, Boston Globe, Dec. 1, 1993, at 59.

4. One of the best-known stories about the early days of sports agency involves Green Bay Packers All–Pro center Jim Ringo. When Ringo's agent called on Packers coach Vince Lombardi to begin negotiating a contract for the 1964 season, he was asked to wait. A few minutes later, Lombardi returned and announced, "You've come to the wrong place. Mr. Ringo is no longer employed by the Packers. He now works for the Philadelphia Eagles."

Many modern day coaches and general managers share Lombardi's disdain for agents. Nevertheless, even Utah Jazz forward Karl Malone, who for years had represented himself, announced after the 1998 NBA finals he would retain an agent to negotiate his next contract. *See* Loren Jorgensen, *Malone Hires Manley as Agent*, Salt Lake City Deseret News, July 14, 1998, at D1. For a further discussion of the impact of agents on sports, see Stephen W. Zucker, *Sports Negotiations: The Art of the Contract*, 7 DePaul U. J. Art & Ent. L. 194 (1997); Daniel M. Faber, *The Evolution of Techniques for Negotiation of Sports Employment Contracts in the Era of the Agent*, 10 U. Miami Ent. & Sports L. Rev. 165 (1993); Marc Katz, *Agents Changed Face of NFL Player Deals*, Dayton Daily News, June 15, 1994, at 5D.

5. Ironically, it is not just coaches and general managers who despise agents—even players often view them with contempt, going so far as to call them parasites and leeches. *See further Faigin v. Kelly*, 978 F.Supp. 420 (D.N.H.1997) (quarterback sued after labeling his former agent "untrustworthy"), *Henderson v. Times Mirror Co.*, 669 F.Supp. 356 (D.Colo.1987), *aff'd*, 876 F.2d 108 (10th Cir.1989) (coach sued after describing agent as a "sleaze bag" who "slimed up from the bayou"); *Woy v. Turner*, 573 F.Supp. 35 (N.D.Ga.1983) (owner sued after claiming agent's unethical negotiating tactics contributed to the death of his team's general manager); *Ryan v. Infinity Broadcasting of Pennsylvania*, 33 Phila. 297 (Pa.Ct.C.P.1997)

(sportscasters sued after asserting sports agent, son of a famous football coach, was using improper means to get his father's players to switch to his agency). *See also* Edward V. King, Jr., *Practical Advice for Agents: How to Avoid Being Sued*, 4 Marq. Sports L.J. 89 (1993); Craig Neff, *Den of Vipers*, Sports Illustrated, Oct. 19, 1987, at 76; Buster Olney, *Agents' Negotiating Tactics Criticized*, N.Y. Times, Dec. 16, 1998, at C26.

6. Notwithstanding the feelings of those inside sports, agents have succeeded in captivating the public. In 1996, for example, Tom Cruise played a sports agent with a conscience in the Oscar-winning movie "Jerry Maguire." Besides being a box office smash, the movie made the phrase "Show me the money!" a staple of conversation. A short time later, Robert Wuhl began starring in the HBO series "Arli$$," a comedy about a fictional sports agent named Arliss Michaels. Many real-life agents—including Leigh Steinberg, David Falk, and Drew Rosenhaus—also have become media darlings. *See* Dan Markowitz, *Sports Agents as Stars in Their Own Right*, N.Y. Times, Nov. 30, 1997, § 14 (WC), at 1, and Larry Lebowitz, *Power Players: They're the Million–Dollar Super Agents Emerging from Behind the Million–Dollar Players*, Fort Lauderdale Sun–Sentinel, Dec. 18, 1996, at 1E.

7. Although many people dream of becoming sports agents, breaking into the field is very difficult. *See further* Plott Brice, *How to Succeed in Sports Agency: Learn the World of Business First*, Atlanta J. & Const., Dec. 12, 1996, at 3C, and Don Pierson, *Vainisi Sitting on Other Side of Fence; Former Bears GM Waits to be Drafted as Player Agent*, Chi. Trib., June 16, 1996, at 9C. African–Americans have found it particularly tough, in large part because many athletes believe white agents are treated with more respect. *See further* Kenneth L. Shropshire, *Sports Agents, Role Models and Race–Consciousness*, 6 Marq. Sports L.J. 267 (1996), and Marc J. Spears, *Black Agents Seek Bigger Share*, Hous. Chron., July 12, 1998, at 5 (Sports).

Problem 31

While representing a star cornerback, an agent recommended a specific company to prepare his tax returns. This turned out to be poor advice, however, and the player ended up having to pay substantial penalties and interest to the IRS. If he sues the agent to recover these sums, how is the court likely to rule? *See Zinn v. Parrish*, 644 F.2d 360 (7th Cir.1981).

C. FEES

Agents earn commissions based on the amounts they are able to negotiate for their clients. As will be seen, this rather simple arrangement has led to innumerable disputes.

1. SUITS AGAINST PLAYERS

Despite (or perhaps because of) the enormous amounts earned by their clients, agents often find they must sue to get their bills paid.

ROSENTHAL v. JORDAN

783 S.W.2d 452 (Mo.Ct.App.1990).

GAERTNER, Judge.

Plaintiff appeals from an adverse judgment entered on a jury verdict for defendant in her breach of contract claim. We reverse and remand.

Plaintiff is the widow of Morris Rosenthal, an attorney who died on July 6, 1978. By virtue of Letters of Refusal issued by the Probate Court of the City of St. Louis on September 1, 1978, she became the successor in interest to Mr. Rosenthal's rights to an agent's commission under the contract which is the subject matter of this action. Defendant, Shelby Jordan, is a professional football player. Some years prior to the events in issue, defendant retained Mr. Rosenthal in connection with a contract dispute with the Houston Oilers Football Club. That matter was settled amicably. Defendant played with the New England Patriots Football Club during the 1974–1975 season. For reasons not disclosed in the evidence he did not play in 1976. Defendant testified that he approached the Patriots coach, Chuck Fairbanks, about returning to the team in 1977. Fairbanks offered him four one-year contracts at specified salaries on a "take it or leave it basis." On June 3, 1977, defendant wrote two letters, one to Mr. Rosenthal and one to the Patriots, stating that he wished to have Mr. Rosenthal represent him on future contract negotiations. On June 26, 1977, defendant and Mr. Rosenthal executed the contract at issue in this case. Drafted by Mr. Rosenthal, the contract provides as follows:

> I, the undersigned, Shelby Jordan, hereby employ Morris M. Rosenthal, as Attorney to represent me in negotiations and agreements for a Contract and/or multiple year contracts for my services as a professional football player with the New England Patriots Football Club, Inc., and/or any National Football League teams to whom I may be, or may become eligible to offer my services and enter into contracts with, under the NFL collective bargaining agreement and in accordance with the Constitution, By–Laws, Rules, and Regulations of the League and of the Club, as provided for and contained in the Player Contract for the National Football League.
>
> In consideration of services rendered and to be rendered to me as my representative in connection with agreements and negotiations for contracts, as herein above mentioned, I hereby agree to pay to Morris M. Rosenthal, as compensation for any and all contracts negotiated by him, as follows: Ten percent (10%) of the total amount of the base compensation paid to me by the Club each football season during the term of any contract and Ten percent (10%) of the total amount of any and all bonus agreements earned, due and paid to me by the Club during the term of any contract.

> Payment of compensation to Morris M. Rosenthal will be made as follows: Payment of the base contract compensation shall be paid by me in weekly installments, commencing with the first and ending with the last regularly scheduled league game played by the Club under such season. Payment of the compensation for any and all bonus amounts earned shall be due and payable by me immediately upon receipt of same. As additional compensation for his services, I agree to pay to Morris M. Rosenthal, ten percent (10%) of the total amount of each proportionate share paid to me as a member of a Club that participates in any conference play-off games, championship games or super bowl game during the term of any contract, including Pro Bowl as designated in Article XXIX, § 1.

On July 7, 1977, defendant signed four one-year NFL Standard Player Contracts with the Patriots. Under each contract defendant was employed as a "skilled football player" from April 1 of the first year to April 1 of the next year. The contracts were not "guaranteed" but were terminable at will by the football club. Defendant was to receive an annual salary payable in equal weekly installments over the regular season. If at anytime for any reason, other than injury, he was cut from the team or discharged, no further compensation would be paid.

Defendant played football pursuant to the 1977–1978 contract which provided for an annual salary of $36,000. Pursuant to defendant's authorization ten percent of this amount was paid directly to Mr. Rosenthal by the Patriots in weekly installments during the regular football season. Defendant also played during the 1978 season pursuant to the 1978–1979 contract which provided for a salary of $42,000. No payment of any agent's commission was paid during that year as Mr. Rosenthal had died on July 6, 1978.

The 1979–1980 contract, which called for a salary of $48,000, and the 1980–1981 contract with a salary of $54,000, were both superseded by contracts negotiated in 1979 by defendant and his wife without representation. These new contracts provided for salaries of $65,000 and $75,000 respectively.

On April 1, 1980, plaintiff filed this action alleging that three player contracts signed by defendant on July 7, 1977, for the 1977–1978, 1978–1979, and 1979–1980 seasons had been negotiated by Mr. Rosenthal and that he had thereby fully performed his obligations under the agency contract before his death. The petition further alleged that defendant had refused to make or authorize any payment since the death of Mr. Rosenthal and prayed for damages in the sum of $17,500. Defendant answered by general denial and the allegation of ten affirmative defenses. Prior to trial, the court below sustained plaintiff's motion to strike certain affirmative defenses, including the allegation that Mr. Rosenthal failed to perform his obligation under the agency contract.

On appeal plaintiff argues that it was error for the trial court to permit the introduction of evidence regarding Mr. Rosenthal's failure to perform the contract, to refuse her proffered instruction predicated upon MAI 26.02, submitting as the sole issue for jury determination defendant's breach of the contract and the giving of an instruction, MAI 26.06, submitting the dual issues of Mr. Rosenthal's performance and defendant's breach. In effect, plaintiff's argument is that the pre-trial order striking the affirmative defense allegations constituted a final determination of any issue regarding Mr. Rosenthal's performance of his contractual obligation and relieved her of any burden of proof with regard thereto. We disagree. Pleading and proof of performance or tender of performance is essential to recovery on an express contract. Miran Investment Co. v. Medical West Building Corp., 414 S.W.2d 297, 302 (Mo.1967). Thus, failure of performance is not an affirmative defense which contemplates additional facts not included in allegations necessary to support a plaintiff's case and which, if proven, allow a defendant to avoid legal responsibility, even though plaintiff's allegations are also established by the evidence. Parker v. Pine, 617 S.W.2d 536, 542 (Mo.App.1981). Defendant's denial of plaintiff's allegation that Mr. Rosenthal fully performed his obligations under the agency contract controverts an issue essential to plaintiff's right of recovery. The fact that the affirmative defense allegations of failure of performance were stricken is of no consequence.

Plaintiff offered into evidence, as admissions, defendant's deposition testimony that Mr. Rosenthal negotiated the player contracts on his behalf and as his representative pursuant to the agency contract. Defendant's trial testimony, somewhat corroborated by the testimony of Chuck Fairbanks, was that no negotiations took place. Rather, the transaction was merely the acceptance of the earlier "take it or leave it" offer made to defendant before the agency contract was executed. This dispute supports the trial court's instruction, MAI 26.06, requiring the jury to find that Mr. Rosenthal performed his obligations and defendant failed to do so as a predicate to a verdict in favor of plaintiff.

Thus, a crucial issue is what Mr. Rosenthal was required to do in order to satisfy his contractual obligations. On this point plaintiff introduced evidence showing Mr. Rosenthal represented defendant in the negotiations leading to the four player contracts signed on July 7, 1977. She maintains this fulfilled all he agreed to do to be entitled to receive ten percent of the compensation paid to defendant pursuant to these contracts. Defendant not only disputed Mr. Rosenthal's involvement in securing the four contracts, but also insists Mr. Rosenthal was obligated to continue to represent him throughout the term of the four contracts. Over plaintiff's strenuous and repeated objections defendant was permitted to testify that he expected Mr. Rosenthal to be his lawyer for four years, not only to represent him in negotiations for football contracts but also in negotiating endorsement agreements, assisting in financial and tax planning, and advising on investments. Plaintiff unsuccessfully sought to exclude the testimony of defendant's "expert witness," Larron Jackson, a former professional football player whose qualifications as an expert were based upon his serving as a player representative for the

NFL Player's Association during the player's strike in 1974 and in assisting his teammates in resolving contract problems and grievances with management. He was allowed to testify that the relationship between professional football players and their agents or attorneys was "ongoing" and that they "performed duties or have discussions with you or become involved with the NFL for reasons other than negotiating contracts."

The language of the agency contract signed by Mr. Rosenthal and defendant on June 26, 1977, imposes upon Mr. Rosenthal no duty to perform anything beyond representing defendant in negotiating contracts for his services as a professional football player with the New England Patriots or any other National Football League team. The conclusion is inescapable that the introduction of the evidence regarding defendant's subjective expectations and Jackson's opinion regarding the relationship between agents and other professional football players was an impermissible effort to vary the terms of a written contract by parol evidence.

In overruling plaintiff's objections to this testimony regarding defendant's subjective intent and the relationship of other players and agents, the trial court repeatedly expressed the view that the primary issue was the intention of the parties and that whether the contract was "ambiguous or not, I think the parol evidence can come in as to the intention of the parties." On the contrary, the well-established principles are set forth in Edgewater Health Care, Inc. v. Health Systems Management, Inc., 752 S.W.2d 860, 865 (Mo.App.1988):

> The cardinal rule in the interpretation of a contract is to ascertain the intention of the parties and to give effect to that intention. Where there is no ambiguity in the contract the intention of the parties is to be gathered from it and it alone, and it becomes the duty of the court and not the jury to state its clear meaning. Kalen v. Steele, 341 S.W.2d 343, 346 (Mo.App. 1960). Of course, whether the terms of an agreement are ambiguous is a question of law. If it is determined that an ambiguity exists, it is then for the trier of fact to resolve the ambiguity. Mal Spinrad of St. Louis, Inc. v. Karman, Inc., 690 S.W.2d 460, 464 (Mo.App.1985). An ambiguity is said to exist in a written instrument 'only when it is reasonably susceptible of different constructions' Kalen, 341 S.W.2d at 346–47. In determining whether vel non an ambiguity exists, the whole instrument must be considered.

Defendant attempts to justify the admission of the parol evidence by arguing the trial court ruled that the contract contained "some ambiguousities," even though the court found it unnecessary to expand on that "because of [its] view that the intention of the parties is relevant." Apparently in an effort to clarify this statement by the trial court, defendant points to his own testimony that he considered the language of the second paragraph of the agency contract, that Mr. Rosenthal was to be compensated for "services rendered and to be rendered to me as my representative in connection with agreements and negotiations for contracts," to include negotiations for contracts involving product endorsements. This argument overlooks the modifying phrase in the second paragraph which limits the contracts to those "herein above mentioned," i.e. to contracts with the New England Patriots and other NFL teams. Moreover, even if we were to accept defendant's argument, it would not justify the admission of evidence regarding contractual obligations imposed upon Mr. Rosenthal to render services as a financial planner, an investment advisor and a tax consultant. The language of the contract is not reasonably susceptible to an interpretation imposing any duty upon Mr. Rosenthal beyond representation of defendant in the negotiation of player contracts with NFL football teams.

Since defendant's evidence created a disputed issue regarding whether or not Mr. Rosenthal had furnished such representation in connection with the four player contracts, the jury was properly instructed to determine the issue of his performance. However, under the evidence admitted the decision of the jury could well have been based upon Mr. Rosenthal's failure to render services relating to endorsements, taxes, investments or financial planning. The admission of the evidence of defendant's subjective expectations and of the relationship of other players and their agents was prejudicially erroneous.

Because of this error we are required to reverse the judgment and remand the case for a new trial. On retrial it should be noted that plaintiff's contention that the services to be rendered by Mr. Rosenthal were completed upon the execution of the four player contracts in July, 1977, thus entitling him to ten percent of the amount of each contract, is not supported by the evidence or by the language of the agency contract. He was entitled to ten percent of the compensation paid to defendant "during the term of any contract" which he negotiated as defendant's representative. Although there is evidence from which a jury might find Mr. Rosenthal rendered services in connection with the four one-year contracts, there is no evidence the defendant was paid compensation pursuant to such contracts, except for the 1977–78 season, for which Mr. Rosenthal was paid his ten percent, and for the 1978–79 season, for which he was not. The original contracts for the years 1979–80 and 1980–81 were superseded by later contracts negotiated solely by defendant and his wife. Nothing in the agency contract furnishes Mr. Rosenthal any entitlement to a commission on compensation paid to defendant under contracts which Mr. Rosenthal did not negotiate.

Accordingly, the judgment is reversed and the cause is remanded for a new trial.

LUSTIG PRO SPORTS ENTERPRISES, INC. v. KELLY

1992 WL 369289 (Ohio Ct.App.1992),
appeal dismissed, 612 N.E.2d 1244 (Ohio 1993).

SWEENEY, Presiding Judge.

Defendants-appellants, James Edward Kelly, et al., timely appeal the trial court's judgment entered in favor of appellee, Lustig Pro Sports Enterprises, Inc. (hereinafter "LPS"), in the amount of $71,400 on their complaint alleging that appellant James Kelly owed appellee three percent commissions for the 1989–90 and 1990–91 seasons under a negotiations contract entered into between appellants and appellee. For the reasons set forth below, we affirm the judgment of the trial court.

The pertinent testimony adduced at the bench trial is as follows. Gregory J. Lustig, a principal of Lustig Pro Sports (LPS), testified that Jim Kelly entered into a negotiation contract with LPS on March 14, 1983, under which LPS was to receive three percent of any salary and bonuses to be earned by Jim Kelly as a result of a player contract to be negotiated by LPS. At that time, Jim Kelly also entered into a financial services contract with a separate but related company known as Consultants Development Group (hereinafter "CDG"). Under the financial services contract, CDG was to receive annually two percent of the player's gross income for the year or ten thousand dollars, whichever was less, for financial services to be rendered to Jim Kelly in the form of money management, investment advising, and tax planning.

In 1983, LPS negotiated a five-year contract between Jim Kelly and the Houston Gamblers of the USFL for a total compensation package of $3,150,000.00. The contract called for [a] $1 million signing bonus and an annual salary starting at $275,000 and extending to $650,000 the fifth year. The Houston Gamblers could not fund the signing bonus up front and, thus, paid Mr. Kelly two hundred thousand dollars in cash, guaranteed a bank loan taken by Mr. Kelly for five hundred thousand dollars, and agreed to pay Mr. Kelly annual installments of one hundred sixty thousand dollars to offset the loan repayments. In 1986, after Mr. Kelly had received all but the last two annual installment payments, the Houston Gamblers and the entire USFL folded. LPS then negotiated a five-year contract for the years 1986 to 1990 for Mr. Kelly with the Buffalo Bills of the NFL.

During these years, the financial services contract was also in effect between CDG and Mr. Kelly. In 1984, CDG and Mr. Kelly mutually agreed that instead of compensating CDG at the contract rate of the lesser of two percent or ten thousand dollars, Mr. Kelly would be billed at a flat rate of ten thousand dollars per year. In 1986, the contract was orally modified again. CDG agreed to continue to provide financial services to Mr. Kelly only if he would agree to change the compensation to a flat two percent of his gross annual income. Mr. Lustig testified that the modification was necessary in that the type of services they were getting into in dealing with the NFL far exceeded the scope of the contract and that other players were being charged two percent for financial services. Mr. Kelly agreed to modify the fee to a flat two percent of his gross annual income.

For the years 1986, 1987 and 1988, Mr. Kelly paid the combined flat five percent, under the negotiation contract and financial services contract, without protest. In 1988, Mr. Kelly terminated the contracts with LPS and CDG. Under the terms of the negotiation contract, LPS was entitled to receive payment of its three percent commission on Mr. Kelly's compensation for the 1989–90 and 1990–91 seasons, which amounted to eighty-one thousand dollars in commissions. It is undisputed that Mr. Kelly has refused to pay the amounts owed for 1989 and 1990. This refusal to pay the amounts owed resulted in the filing of the appellee's complaint in this case.

Daniel Kelly, president of Jim Kelly Enterprises and Jim's younger brother, testified as a defense to payment under the negotiation contract that Jim Kelly was entitled to a set-off of sums paid in excess of the amount owed. Dan Kelly testified that from 1983 to 1988, a total of $328,635 in commissions was paid, a sum which exceeded three percent of Jim Kelly's income for those years by $118,875.00. Dan Kelly testified that the excess sums represented over-billings by LPS. However, on cross-examination, it was revealed that Mr. Kelly did not figure into that alleged overpayment that an additional two percent of that total amount of commissions paid represented sums paid under the financial services agreement.

Based upon the above, the trial court granted judgment in favor of appellee on its complaint in the amount of $71,400.00. Appellants now timely appeal, raising four assignments of error for our review.

Assignment of Error I

THE TRIAL COURT ERRED IN AWARDING APPELLEE ANY SUM, IN LIGHT OF THE UNDISPUTED EVIDENCE THAT APPELLANT HAD FULLY COMPENSATED APPELLEE FOR ITS SERVICES.

Assignment of Error II

THE TRIAL COURT ERRED IN CONSIDERING OR FINDING A MODIFICATION OF THE FINANCIAL SERVICES AGREEMENT.

In Assignments of Error I and II, appellants argue that the trial court's judgment was not supported by sufficient evidence. Specifically, appellants contend that (1) insufficient evidence existed to support that the financial services contract was orally modified to a flat commission rate of two percent of Mr. Kelly's gross annual income and (2) the evidence demonstrated that the amount owed in commissions for the 1989–90 and 1990–91 seasons was offset by overpayments made to LPS during prior years. These arguments are without merit.

Judgments supported by some competent, credible evidence going to all the essential elements of the case will not be reversed by a reviewing court as being against the manifest weight of the evidence. C.E. Morris Co. v. Foley Construction Co. (1978), 54 Ohio St.2d 279. We will make every reasonable presumption in favor of the trial court's judgments. Seasons Coal Co. v. Cleveland (1984), 10 Ohio St.3d 77. Furthermore, the weight to be given the evidence and witness credibility are primarily for the factfinder. Shore Shirley & Co. v. Kelly (1988), 40 Ohio App.3d 10.

In the present case, we find that the testimony of Greg Lustig that appellants orally agreed to a modification of the financial services contract in 1986 to a flat two percent commission provided the trial court with sufficient evidence to conclude that an oral modification of the contract took place. Consistent with that agreement, the evidence demonstrates that from 1986 to 1988, appellants were charged and willingly paid the flat two percent commission under the financial services contract. Thus, sufficient evidence exists to support performance by the parties of the oral modification.

Furthermore, we find that appellants failed to provide sufficient evidence of overpayments to support their defense that they were entitled to a set-off of the amounts owed appellee for the 1989–90 and 1990–91 seasons. On cross-examination, Dan Kelly admitted that what he considered overpayments of commission to appellee were possible commissions owed under the financial services contract with CDG. Therefore, the trial court did not err in concluding that appellants failed to prove that they were overcharged and, thus, entitled to a set-off of amounts owed to appellee under the negotiation contract.

Assignments of Error I and II are overruled.

ASSIGNMENT OF ERROR III

THE TRIAL COURT ERRED IN FAILING TO FIND THAT APPELLEE'S CONDUCT MATERIALLY BREACHED THE COMMISSION AGREEMENT THEREBY RELIEVING APPELLANTS OF THEIR OBLIGATIONS THEREUNDER.

Appellants argue that the trial court, in concluding that appellee was not entitled to a commission on Mr. Kelly's bonus payments for the years 1984–85 and 1985–86, should have made a further finding that appellee materially breached the negotiation contract by receiving commissions for those years. Based on this material breach, appellants contend they had a right to rescind the contract. This argument is not well taken.

An appellate court need not consider a question not presented, considered or decided by a lower court. Hungler v. Cincinnati (1986), 25 Ohio St.3d 338. Appellants did not seek the remedy of rescission for appellee's alleged breach of contract at the trial court level and, therefore, are barred from raising it for the first time on this appeal.

Assignment of Error III is not well taken and is overruled.

Assignment of Error IV

THE TRIAL COURT ERRED IN PROCEEDING WITH TRIAL AFTER A PARTY PLAINTIFF AND KEY TRIAL WITNESS FOR APPELLANTS WAS SPIRITED OUT OF COURT TO DEPRIVE APPELLANT OF THE OPPORTUNITY TO EXAMINE HIM.

Appellants argue that the trial court erred in failing to continue the trial until appellants could secure a witness, Arnold Faigin, former principal of LPS. This argument is not well taken.

Appellants did not make a motion for continuance of the trial and, therefore, cannot now raise said error for the first time on appeal. Hungler, supra.

Accordingly, Assignment of Error IV is not well taken and is overruled.

Judgment affirmed.

Notes

1. For other cases in which agents have sued players to collect their fees, see, e.g., *Pro Tect Management Corp. v. Worley*, 1990 WL 170358 (S.D.N.Y.1990); *Total Economic Athletic Management of America, Inc. v. Pickens*, 898 S.W.2d 98 (Mo.Ct.App.1995); *Allen v. McCall*, 521 So.2d 182 (Fla.Dist.Ct.App.1988); *Walters v. Harmon*, 516 N.Y.S.2d 874 (Sup.Ct.1987).

2. Athletes who believe they have been cheated by their agents (or fear they might be) sometimes turn to family members to represent them. Perhaps the best-known example is Philadelphia Flyers center Eric Lindros, whose agent always has been his dad Carl. Using a relative, however, is no guarantee one will avoid legal battles over money. Tennis superstar Steffi Graf almost went to jail (and eventually paid a hefty fine) after it was discovered her father Peter had failed to pay taxes on her winnings.

Problem 32

A star goalie retained an agent to help him negotiate a new contract. Although the general manager made a generous proposal, the agent convinced the player to jump to a new league that was offering more money. Six months later, it folded and the athlete returned to his old team for much less money than originally offered. If he files an action for fraud and asks that a constructive trust be imposed on the agent's fee, how should the court rule? *See Brown v. Woolf*, 554 F.Supp. 1206 (S.D.Ind.1983).

2. SUITS AGAINST OTHER AGENTS

When they are not busy chasing after their clients, agents spend much of their time fending off competitors.

SPEAKERS OF SPORT, INC. v. PROSERV, INC.

1998 WL 473469 (N.D.Ill.1998).

MAROVICH, District Judge.

Plaintiff Speakers of Sport, Inc. ("Speakers") filed this action against Defendant ProServ, Inc. ("ProServ") alleging unfair competition, tortious interference with prospective business advantage, and a violation of the Illinois Consumer Fraud Act, 815 ILCS § 505 et seq., arising out of Speakers' representation of Ivan Rodriguez ("Rodriguez"), a Major League Baseball player. ProServ now moves for summary judgment. For the reasons set forth below, this Court grants ProServ's motion.

BACKGROUND

Unless otherwise noted, the following facts are undisputed. Speakers is an Illinois corporation engaged in the business of representing professional baseball players in connection with their contractual relations with Major League Baseball teams. ProServ is a Washington, D.C. corporation in the business of representing a broader spectrum of professional athletes. Given the potential overlap of their businesses, it is not surprising that Speakers and ProServ will occasionally compete for representation of the same athlete. The object of their mutual affection in this case is Ivan Rodriguez ("Rodriguez").

Rodriguez is a Major League Baseball player with the Texas Rangers. He has played for the Rangers since 1991 and is considered "the American League's best defensive catcher." ESPN.SportsZone (visited Aug. 5, 1998) <http://www.ESPN.SportsZone.com/mlb/profiles/bio/4680.html>. When Rodriguez came into the League, he was represented by Scott Boras ("Boras"). Then, in July 1991, Rodriguez signed the first of several year-long, terminable at-will agreements designating Speakers as his agent. Speakers served as Rodriguez's agent until February 1995.

At some point in late 1994, Rodriguez and his wife became dissatisfied with the service provided by Speakers. In particular, the Rodriguezes were concerned that Speakers devoted too much time and attention to other athletes and not enough to Rodriguez. The Rodriguezes began thinking about switching agents and met with Boras—Rodriguez's original agent—and Mike Powers ("Powers") from ProServ. Powers apparently talked to Rodriguez about ProServ and invited him and his wife to come to Washington, D.C. to meet with other representatives from ProServ.

In mid-February 1995, Rodriguez and his wife took Powers up on his invitation and went to the D.C. area to meet with several executives and staff personnel from ProServ. During these meetings, ProServ discussed the services that it could provide for Rodriguez and referenced the fact that ProServ had its own marketing department that would "actively seek endorsement opportunities." (Dell Aff. at p 7.) Speakers insists that during these meetings, ProServ "promised" Rodriguez that he could obtain two to four million dollars in endorsements a year if he signed with ProServ. ProServ acknowledges that it may have referenced its successful marketing efforts on behalf of its other clients, e.g., Nancy Kerrigan, although ProServ denies that it ever suggested to Rodriguez that he should or could expect to obtain comparable endorsement opportunities—much less two to four million dollars worth of opportunities.

(Id. at p 8.) Nevertheless, the fact remains that Rodriguez left these meetings with the distinct impression that he could earn between two and four million dollars in endorsements if he signed with ProServ. (Rodriguez Dep. at 23.)

On February 24, 1995, Rodriguez signed a letter—drafted by ProServ—terminating his contract with Speakers. This letter was subsequently faxed to Speakers by someone at ProServ. Several days later, on February 27, 1995, Rodriguez signed a contract with ProServ and a player designation form identifying ProServ as his new agent. Rodriguez explained that he switched from Speakers to ProServ because they would "treat [him] better and they were going to get [him] contracts of baseball and they were going to get [him] two to four million marketing." (Id.) English is not Rodriguez's native language.

Shortly before signing with ProServ, Speakers claims that it discussed Rodriguez's endorsement potential with him. Speakers contends that its representatives told Rodriguez, on several occasions, that they believed it would be "impossible" for ProServ to produce endorsements in the amount of two to four million dollars. In fact, Speakers' Chairman and part owner, James Bonner ("Bonner"), telephoned Rodriguez and told him that he did not believe that ProServ could possibly obtain that level of endorsements for him. Bonner also gave Rodriguez several other reasons why he did not believe that it was in Rodriguez's "best interest" to switch to ProServ, including the fact that ProServ had limited experience representing baseball players and was "experiencing financial difficulties." (Speakers 12(N) Statement at p 56.) Bonner went so far as to send a letter to the President of ProServ. (This letter was carbon copied to Rodriguez, although it is unclear whether he actually read it.) [The letter] stat[ed] that in his view, ProServ's "comments may have made [Rodriguez] feel good; but are nothing more than pure fantasy and gross exaggeration. However, we are willing to be proven wrong." (Speakers Ex. A–2.) Apparently, so was Rodriguez, because he ignored Speakers' warnings and told them that if it was possible for ProServ to get "millions of dollars" in endorsements for Nancy Kerrigan—allegedly $30 million—he believed it would be possible for ProServ to secure four million dollars for him. (Cuza Aff. at p 14.)

Needless to say, Rodriguez did not earn two to four million dollars in endorsements in 1995. Moreover, in February 1996, Rodriguez lost his arbitration with the Texas Rangers which was handled by ProServ. Shortly thereafter, Rodriguez fired ProServ as his agent. Although Rodriguez met with representatives from Speakers about the possibility of resuming their relationship in the spring of 1996, he ultimately decided to hire Jeff Moorad—a different agent altogether.

In October 1997, Speakers filed a three-count Complaint alleging that ProServ's representations to Rodriguez about his endorsement opportunities were "false" and constituted tortious interference with prospective business advantage. Speakers maintains that these alleged misrepresentations caused it to lose Rodriguez as a client and the yearly fees that his business would have generated. More specifically, Speakers points to the $42 million, five-year contract Rodriguez recently received from the Rangers as an example of how it was damaged. Unfortunately for both parties, Jeff Moorad was the only agent who received fees from this contract. Further proof that timing is everything.

DISCUSSION

Tortious Interference

Under Illinois law, to prevail on a claim of tortious interference with prospective economic advantage, a plaintiff must prove: (1) his reasonable expectation of entering into (or continuing) a valid business relationship; (2) the defendant's knowledge of the plaintiff's expectancy; (3) purposeful interference by the defendant that prevents the plaintiff's legitimate expectancy from ripening into a valid business relationship; and (4) damages to the plaintiff resulting from such interference. Dowd & Dowd, Ltd. v. Gleason, 181 Ill.2d 460, 484, 230 Ill.Dec. 229, 693 N.E.2d 358, 370 (Ill.1998) (citations omitted).

The thrust of Speakers' claim in this case is that ProServ purposefully interfered in its relationship with Rodriguez by making representations to him about his endorsement potential which it knew to be false. ProServ responds with a plethora of arguments. Most significantly, ProServ argues that: (1) Speakers cannot establish that it had a reasonable business expectancy of continuing to represent Rodriguez after February 24, 1995; and (2) ProServ is protected against this action by the privilege of competition so long as its actions were not solely motivated by spite or ill will.

A. *Speakers' Reasonable Business Expectation*

Initially, ProServ argues that "[a]s a matter of law, Speakers had no business expectancy in representing [Rodriguez] after the earlier of his date of termination of the contract (February 24, 1995) or the expiration date (June 21, 1995)." (ProServ Mem. at 9.) ProServ also points out that Speakers cannot claim any damages under a tortious interference with prospective economic advantage theory for the period covered by the June 1994 contract because a contract actually existed—thus, requiring a claim for tortious interference with contract. In essence, ProServ's legal argument would seem to foreclose Speakers from ever bringing a tortious interference claim under these circumstances. This Court does not agree.

Illinois courts have recognized that "the gravamen of the charge [of tortious interference with prospective economic advantage] is interference with an existing relationship, and the absence of a binding contract does not bar recovery." Dowd & Dowd, 181 Ill.2d at 484, 230 Ill.Dec. 229, 693 N.E.2d at 370 (citing Anderson v. Anchor Organization for Health Maintenance, 274 Ill.App.3d 1001, 1013, 211 Ill.Dec. 213, 654 N.E.2d 675, 685 (1st Dist.1995)). With this in mind, actions for interference with at-will contracts have been classified as actions for tortious interference with prospective economic advantage. See Fellhauer v. City of Geneva,

142 Ill.2d 495, 510, 154 Ill.Dec. 649, 568 N.E.2d 870, 877 (Ill.1991); Anderson, 274 Ill.App.3d at 1013, 211 Ill.Dec. 213, 654 N.E.2d at 685. This Court can discern no legal barrier preventing Speakers from recovering for an alleged interference with its existing relationship with Rodriguez—as evidenced by its year-long, terminable at-will agreement.

Next, ProServ goes to great lengths to argue that Rodriguez was unhappy with Speakers and was already looking for a new agent before being approached by ProServ. ProServ also maintains that Speakers could not have reasonably expected to remain as Rodriguez's agent given his history of "flip-flopping" between agents. Not surprisingly, Speakers responds by citing to evidence that Rodriguez felt good about his relationship with Speakers and that it was only ProServ's "false promise" which caused him to switch agents. Happy or not, it should be noted that Rodriguez had been with Speakers for the past two-and-a-half years despite his fickle relationship with previous agents. After a careful review of the record, the Court finds this to be a disputed issue of material fact sufficient to preclude summary judgment on the question of Speakers' reasonable expectancy of continuing its relationship with Rodriguez.

B. Privilege of Competition

Neither party disputes that there are some "purposeful or intentional interferences" with economic advantage that are not actionable. "[O]ne may not simply sue any competitor who lures away customers." Downers Grove Volkswagen, Inc. v. Wigglesworth Imports, Inc., 190 Ill.App.3d 524, 528, 137 Ill.Dec. 409, 546 N.E.2d 33, 36 (2d Dist.1989). Thus, in Illinois there is a "privilege of competition" that "allows one to divert business from one's competitors generally as well as one's particular competitors provided one's intent is, at least in part, to further one's business and is not solely motivated by spite or ill will." Soderlund Brothers, Inc. v. Carrier Corp., 278 Ill.App.3d 606, 615, 215 Ill.Dec. 251, 663 N.E.2d 1,8 (1st Dist.1995); see Restatement (Second) of Torts § 768 (1979). However, if the acts of competition include "wrongful conduct" such as "fraud, deceit, intimidation, or deliberate disparagement," they are not protected by the privilege. Id.

Speakers maintains that ProServ's "false promise" to Rodriguez either constituted fraud or was in furtherance of a "scheme or device to accomplish fraud." (Speakers Mem. at 10.) Alternatively, Speakers argues that even if ProServ's "promise" to Rodriguez did not constitute fraud, it was still "improper conduct" and therefore actionable under a tortious interference theory of liability. The Court does not agree and believes that Speakers has interpreted the privilege of competition far too narrowly.

If the Court views the facts in the light most favorable to Speakers, as it must, then it would appear that ProServ represented—intentionally or not—to Rodriguez that he could expect to earn between two and four million dollars in endorsements. Speakers insists that "[n]o reasonable agent could honestly suggest, let alone promise, that Mr. Rodriguez could obtain endorsements in the amounts suggested by ProServ." (Speakers Mem. at 10–11.) Yet, apart from the declarations of various Speakers' executives detailing their "experience in the business," Speakers has offered this Court no independent evidence to suggest that ProServ's expectations for Rodriguez were "impossible" or "unreasonable." Nor has Speakers provided this Court with any "realistic" estimation of what Rodriguez could expect to earn in endorsements. Thus, the Court finds itself in a situation comparable to the one that probably faced Rodriguez—one agent says one thing while another says something else. Still, there is simply no evidence before the Court to suggest that the estimates offered by ProServ were "impossible" or "unreasonable."

Even if this information had been made available to the Court, it would not resolve the dispute over whether the numbers given to Rodriguez were "false" or somehow constituted "fraud." It is not as if ProServ assured a lucrative endorsement deal to a minor league utility infielder with no chance at the majors. Both parties agree that Rodriguez was and is an extremely talented baseball player—talented enough to be paid over eight million dollars a year. Just because Rodriguez did not earn two to four million dollars in endorsements in 1995 does not necessarily make ProServ's estimates unreasonable when they were given, much less "false" or "fraudulent." To this end, Illinois law is "well settled" that representations of "future income" are not actionable as fraud because they do not constitute statements of fact. See Dougherty v. Zimbler, 922 F.Supp. 110, 114 (N.D.Ill.1996); see also Soderlund Brothers, 278 Ill.App.3d at 619, 215 Ill.Dec. 251, 663 N.E.2d at 10–11 ("Matters of fact are distinguishable from expressions of opinion, and the latter cannot form the basis of an action of fraud.").

When viewed in the light most favorable to Speakers, what ProServ offered Rodriguez was an opinion or an estimate of what its marketing department could do for him, not a guarantee or a promise. Speakers had several opportunities to persuade Rodriguez that ProServ's estimate was impossible and unrealistic, but Rodriguez obviously did not agree. Maybe Rodriguez believed that the estimate was accurate or maybe he just liked the fact that ProServ had more confidence in his marketability than Speakers did. In any event, ProServ's erroneous prediction of Rodriguez's endorsement opportunities for 1995 did not rise to the level of fraud or even "improper conduct." See Sohaey v. Van Cura, 240 Ill.App.3d 266, 291, 180 Ill.Dec. 359, 607 N.E.2d 253, 272 (2d Dist.1992) ("Statements relative to future or contingent events, expectations, or probabilities are generally regarded as mere expressions of opinion or conjectures."); West v. Western Cas. and Sur. Co., 846 F.2d 387, 393 (7th Cir.1988) (same).

More importantly, the record clearly demonstrates that ProServ's statements to Rodriguez were not made with malice to deliberately hinder Speakers' business. Nor were they calculated to disparage Speakers in any way. Unlike the cases cited by Speakers, this case does not involve any allegations that ProServ acted in bad faith or engaged in improper conduct designed to harm Speakers. See, e.g., Downers Grove

Volkswagen, 190 Ill.App.3d at 528, 137 Ill.Dec. 409, 546 N.E.2d at 36 (improper conduct where defendant printed information about a competitor with reckless disregard for the truth); Dowd & Dowd, 181 Ill.2d at 484, 230 Ill.Dec. 229, 693 N.E.2d at 370 (departing members of law firm breached fiduciary duties to the firm and improperly solicited business from firm's major client before departing); Soderlund Brothers, 278 Ill.App.3d at 620, 215 Ill.Dec. 251, 663 N.E.2d at 11 (improper conduct where defendant made seven false statements about its competitor). There is simply no evidence in the record to suggest that ProServ's conduct was even partially, much less "solely," motivated by spite or ill will toward Speakers. Accordingly, the Court finds that ProServ's conduct was in furtherance of its business and is protected by the privilege of competition.

Speakers' Remaining Claims

Speakers has asserted separate claims against ProServ for unfair competition and violating the Illinois Consumer Fraud Act. Because this Court has already concluded that ProServ's alleged representation to Rodriguez was merely an estimate or an opinion—and therefore not actionable as fraud—it cannot form the basis for a claim under the Illinois Consumer Fraud Act or the common law of unfair competition. See, e.g., Borcherding v. Anderson Remodeling Co., Inc., 253 Ill.App.3d 655, 661, 191 Ill.Dec. 699, 624 N.E.2d 887, 892 (2d Dist.1993) (opinion or "puffing" are not actionable under the Consumer Fraud Act); Totz v. Continental DuPage Acura, 236 Ill.App.3d 891, 904, 177 Ill.Dec. 202, 602 N.E.2d 1374, 1383 (2d Dist.1992) (same); Sohaey, 240 Ill.App.3d at 291, 180 Ill.Dec. 359, 607 N.E.2d at 272 (same); Zenith Electronics Corp. v. Exzec, Inc., 1997 WL 798907, at *14 (N.D.Ill.Dec.24, 1997) (common law of unfair competition falls under the rubric of tortious interference with economic advantage and requires similar elements of proof); Wilson v. Electro Marine Sys., Inc., 915 F.2d 1110, 1118 (7th Cir.1990) (applying New York law) (legal theory of unfair competition is "elusive" and has been limited to activity which "so 'shock[s] judicial sensibilities' or violates 'standards of commercial morality' that it cannot be tolerated"); Lynch Ford, Inc. v. Ford Motor Co., Inc., 957 F.Supp. 142, 146 (N.D.Ill. 1997) (adopting 7th Circuit definition from Wilson).

CONCLUSION

For the foregoing reasons, the Court grants ProServ's motion for summary judgment.

Notes

1. For a further look at client tampering by agents, see *Gregory v. Rosenhaus*, 1996 U.S. Dist. LEXIS 21321 (N.D.Miss.1996).

2. Besides competitors, agents are sometimes hauled into court by "runners," persons who agree to use their influence to steer a particular athlete to them in return for a kickback. In July 1998, for example, Thomas Cronin sued agent Joe Cubas over pitcher Orlando Hernandez's $6.6 million contract with the New York Yankees. According to the complaint, Cubas

promised to give Cronin one-third of his commission in exchange for Cronin's help in convincing Hernandez to retain Cubas. *See further* Mary Hladky, *Stranded on the Sidelines: Man Sues Sports Agent of Cuban Defector for Share of Commission*, Broward Daily Bus. Rev., July 23, 1998, at A1.

Problem 33

Because she was overwhelmed with work, an agent asked a former associate to handle an upcoming negotiation in return for part of her fee. Shortly after signing his new contract, the athlete was arrested for murder and the team terminated his employment. If the agent is unable to collect her commission as a result of these developments, will she still have to pay her ex-employee for his work? *See Andrews v. Merriweather*, 1991 WL 38689 (N.D.Ill.1991).

D. REGULATION

Most sports agents are both competent and ethical. Nevertheless, the profession does have its share of bad apples, as the following cases make clear.

UNITED STATES v. WALTERS

997 F.2d 1219 (7th Cir.1993).

EASTERBROOK, Circuit Judge.

Norby Walters, who represents entertainers, tried to move into the sports business. He signed 58 college football players to contracts while they were still playing. Walters offered cars and money to those who would agree to use him as their representative in dealing with professional teams. Sports agents receive a percentage of the players' income, so Walters would profit only to the extent he could negotiate contracts for his clients. The athletes' pro prospects depended on successful completion of their collegiate careers. To the NCAA, however, a student who signs a contract with an agent is a professional, ineligible to play on collegiate teams. To avoid jeopardizing his clients' careers, Walters dated the contracts after the end of their eligibility and locked them in a safe. He promised to lie to the universities in response to any inquiries. Walters inquired of sports lawyers at Shea & Gould whether this plan of operation would be lawful. The firm rendered an opinion that it would violate the NCAA's rules but not any statute.

Having recruited players willing to fool their universities and the NCAA, Walters discovered that they were equally willing to play false with him. Only 2 of the 58 players fulfilled their end of the bargain; the other 56 kept the cars and money, then signed with other agents. They relied on the fact that the contracts were locked away and dated in the future, and that Walters' business depended on continued secrecy, so he could not very well sue to enforce their promises. When the 56 would neither accept him as their representative nor return the payments, Walters resorted to threats. One player, Maurice Douglass, was told that his legs would be broken before the pro draft unless he repaid Walters' firm. A 75–page indictment charged Walters and his partner Lloyd Bloom with conspiracy, RICO violations (the predicate felony was extortion), and mail fraud. The fraud: causing the universities to pay scholarship funds to athletes who had become ineligible as a result of the agency contracts. The mail: each university required its athletes to verify their eligibility to play, then sent copies by mail to conferences such as the Big Ten.

After a month-long trial and a week of deliberations, the jury convicted Walters and Bloom. We reversed, holding that the district judge had erred in declining to instruct the jury that reliance on Shea & Gould's advice could prevent the formation of intent to defraud the universities. 913 F.2d 388, 391–92 (1990). Any dispute about the adequacy of Walters' disclosure to his lawyers and the bona fides of his reliance was for the jury, we concluded. Because Bloom declined to waive his own attorney-client privilege, we held that the defendants must be retried separately. Id. at 392–93. On remand, Walters asked the district court to dismiss the indictment, arguing that the evidence presented at trial is insufficient to support the convictions. After the judge denied this motion, 775 F.Supp. 1173 (N.D.Ill.1991), Walters agreed to enter a conditional Alford plea: he would plead guilty to mail fraud, conceding that the record of the first trial supplies a factual basis for a conviction while reserving his right to contest the sufficiency of that evidence. In return, the prosecutor agreed to dismiss the RICO and conspiracy charges and to return to Walters all property that had been forfeited as a result of his RICO conviction. Thus a case that began with a focus on extortion has become a straight mail fraud prosecution and may undergo yet another transformation. The prosecutor believes that Walters hampered the investigation preceding his indictment. See In re Feldberg, 862 F.2d 622 (7th Cir.1988) (describing some of the investigation). The plea agreement reserves the prosecutor's right to charge Walters with perjury and obstruction of justice if we should reverse the conviction for mail fraud.

"Whoever, having devised ... any scheme or artifice to defraud, or for obtaining money or property by means of false or fraudulent pretenses, representations, or promises ... places in any post office or authorized depository for mail matter, any matter or thing whatever to be sent or delivered by the Postal Service ... or knowingly causes [such matter or thing] to be delivered by mail" commits the crime of mail fraud. 18 U.S.C. § 1341. Norby Walters did not mail anything or cause anyone else to do so (the universities were going to collect and mail the forms no matter what Walters did), but the Supreme Court has expanded the statute beyond its literal terms, holding that a mailing by a third party suffices if it is "incident to an essential part of the scheme," Pereira v. United States, 347 U.S. 1, 8, 74 S.Ct. 358, 363, 98 L.Ed. 435 (1954). While stating that such mailings can turn ordinary fraud into mail fraud, the Court has cautioned that the statute "does not purport to reach all frauds, but only those limited instances in which the use of the mails is a part of the execution of the fraud." Kann v. United States, 323 U.S. 88, 95, 65 S.Ct. 148, 151, 89 L.Ed. 88 (1944). Everything thus turns on matters of degree. Did the schemers foresee that the mails would be used? Did the mailing advance the success of the scheme? Which parts of a scheme are "essential"? Such questions lack obviously right answers, so it is no surprise that each side to this case can cite several of our decisions in support. Compare United States v. McClain, 934 F.2d 822, 835 (7th Cir.1991), and United States v. Kwiat, 817 F.2d 440, 443–44 (7th Cir.1987), among cases reversing convictions because use of the mails was too remote or unforeseeable, with Messinger v. United States, 872 F.2d 217 (7th Cir.1989), among many cases holding that particular uses of the mails were vital to the scheme and foreseeable.

"The relevant question ... is whether the mailing is part of the execution of the scheme as conceived by the perpetrator at the time." Schmuck v. United States, 489 U.S. 705, 715, 109 S.Ct. 1443, 1450, 103 L.Ed.2d 734 (1989). Did the evidence establish that Walters conceived a scheme in which mailings played a role? We think not—indeed, that no reasonable juror could give an affirmative answer to this question. Walters hatched a scheme to make money by taking a percentage of athletes' pro contracts. To get clients he signed students while college eligibility remained, thus avoiding competition from ethical agents. To obtain big pro contracts for these clients he needed to keep the deals secret, so the athletes could finish their collegiate careers. Thus deceit was an ingredient of the plan. We may assume that Walters knew that the universities would ask athletes to verify that they were eligible to compete as amateurs. But what role do the mails play? The plan succeeds so long as the athletes conceal their contracts from their schools (and remain loyal to Walters). Forms verifying eligibility do not help the plan succeed; instead they create a risk that it will be discovered if a student should tell the truth. Cf. United States v. Maze, 414 U.S. 395, 94 S.Ct. 645, 38 L.Ed.2d 603 (1974). And it is the forms, not their mailing to the Big Ten, that pose the risk. For all Walters cared, the forms could sit forever in cartons. Movement to someplace else was irrelevant. In Schmuck, where the fraud was selling cars with rolled-back odometers, the mailing was essential to obtain a new and apparently "clean" certificate of title; no certificates of title, no marketable cars, no hope for success. Even so, the Court divided five to four on the question whether the mailing was sufficiently integral to the scheme. A college's mailing to its conference has less to do with the plot's success than the mailings that transferred title in Schmuck.

To this the United States responds that the mailings were essential because, if a college had neglected to send the athletes' forms to the conference, the NCAA would have barred that college's team from competing. Lack of competition would spoil the athletes' pro prospects. Thus the use of the mails was integral to the profits Walters hoped to reap, even though Walters would have been delighted had the colleges neither asked any questions of the athletes nor put the answers in the mail. Let us take this as sufficient under Schmuck (although we have our doubts). The question remains whether Walters caused the universities to use the mails. A person "knowingly causes" the use of the mails when he "acts with the knowledge that the use of the mails will follow in the ordinary course of business, or where such use can reasonably be foreseen." United States v. Kuzniar, 881 F.2d 466, 472 (7th Cir.1989), quoting Pereira, 347 U.S. at 8–9, 74 S.Ct. at 363. The paradigm is insurance fraud. Perkins tells his auto insurer that his car has been stolen, when in fact it has been sold. The local employee mails the claim to the home office, which mails a check to Perkins. Such mailings in the ordinary course of business are foreseeable. E.g., United States v. Richman, 944 F.2d 323 (7th Cir.1991). Similarly, a judge who takes a bribe derived from the litigant's bail money causes the use of the mails when the ordinary course is to refund the bond by mail. E.g., United States v. Murphy, 768 F.2d 1518, 1529–30 (7th Cir.1985). The prosecutor contends that the same approach covers Walters.

No evidence demonstrates that Walters actually knew that the colleges would mail the athletes' forms. The record is barely sufficient to establish that Walters knew of the forms' existence; it is silent about Walters' knowledge of the forms' disposition. The only evidence implying that Walters knew that the colleges had students fill out forms is an ambiguous reference to "these forms" in the testimony of Robert Perryman. Nothing in the record suggests that Perryman, a student athlete, knew what his university did with the forms, let alone that Perryman passed this information to Walters. So the prosecutor is reduced to the argument that mailings could "reasonably be foreseen." Yet why should this be so? Universities frequently collect information that is stashed in file drawers. Perhaps the NCAA just wants answers available for inspection in the event a question arises, or the university wants the information for its own purposes (to show that it did not know about any improprieties that later come to light). What was it about these forms that should have led a reasonable person to foresee their mailing? Recall that Walters was trying to break into the sports business. Counsel specializing in sports law told him that his plan would not violate any statute.

These lawyers were unaware of the forms (or, if they knew about the forms, were unaware that they would be mailed). The prosecutor contends that Walters neglected to tell his lawyers about the eligibility forms, spoiling their opinion; yet why would Walters have to brief an expert in sports law if mailings were foreseeable even to a novice?

In the end, the prosecutor insists that the large size and interstate nature of the NCAA demonstrate that something would be dropped into the mails. To put this only slightly differently, the prosecutor submits that all frauds involving big organizations necessarily are mail frauds, because big organizations habitually mail things. No evidence put before the jury supports such a claim, and it is hardly appropriate for judicial notice in a criminal case. Moreover, adopting this perspective would contradict the assurance of Kann, 323 U.S. at 95, 65 S.Ct. at 151, and many later cases that most frauds are covered by state law rather than § 1341. That statute has been expanded considerably by judicial interpretation, but it does not make a federal crime of every deceit. The prosecutor must prove that the use of the mails was foreseeable, rather than calling on judicial intuition to repair a rickety case.

There is a deeper problem with the theory of this prosecution. The United States tells us that the universities lost their scholarship money. Money is property; this aspect of the prosecution does not encounter a problem under McNally v. United States, 483 U.S. 350, 107 S.Ct. 2875, 97 L.Ed.2d 292 (1987). Walters emphasizes that the universities put his 58 athletes on scholarship long before he met them and did not pay a penny more than they planned to do. But a jury could conclude that had Walters' clients told the truth, the colleges would have stopped their scholarships, thus saving money. So we must assume that the universities lost property by reason of Walters' deeds. Still, they were not out of pocket to Walters; he planned to profit by taking a percentage of the players' professional incomes, not of their scholarships. Section 1341 condemns "any scheme or artifice to defraud, or for obtaining money or property." If the universities were the victims, how did he "obtain" their property?, Walters asks.

According to the United States, neither an actual nor a potential transfer of property from the victim to the defendant is essential. It is enough that the victim lose; what (if anything) the schemer hopes to gain plays no role in the definition of the offense. We asked the prosecutor at oral argument whether on this rationale practical jokes violate § 1341. A mails B an invitation to a surprise party for their mutual friend C. B drives his car to the place named in the invitation. But there is no party; the address is a vacant lot; B is the butt of a joke. The invitation came by post; the cost of gasoline means that B is out of pocket. The prosecutor said that this indeed violates § 1341, but that his office pledges to use prosecutorial discretion wisely. Many people will find this position unnerving (what if the prosecutor's policy changes, or A is politically unpopular and the prosecutor is looking for a way to nail him?). Others, who obey the law out of a sense of civic obligation rather than the fear of sanctions, will alter their conduct no matter what policy the prosecutor follows. Either way, the idea that practical jokes are federal felonies would make a joke of the Supreme Court's assurance that § 1341 does not cover the waterfront of deceit.

Practical jokes rarely come to the attention of federal prosecutors, but large organizations are more successful in gaining the attention of public officials. In this case the mail fraud statute has been invoked to shore up the rules of an influential private association. Consider a parallel: an association of manufacturers of plumbing fixtures adopts a rule providing that its members will not sell "seconds" (that is, blemished articles) to the public. The association proclaims that this rule protects consumers from shoddy goods. To remain in good standing, a member must report its sales monthly. These reports flow in by mail. One member begins to sell "seconds" but reports that it is not doing so.

These sales take business away from other members of the association, who lose profits as a result. So we have mail, misrepresentation, and the loss of property, but the liar does not get any of the property the other firms lose. Has anyone committed a federal crime? The answer is yes—but the statute is the Sherman Act, 15 U.S.C. § 1, and the perpetrators are the firms that adopted the "no seconds" rule. United States v. Trenton Potteries Co., 273 U.S. 392, 47 S.Ct. 377, 71 L.Ed. 700 (1927). The trade association we have described is a cartel, which the firm selling "seconds" was undermining. Cheaters depress the price, causing the monopolist to lose money. Typically they go to great lengths to disguise their activities, the better to increase their own sales and avoid retaliation. The prosecutor's position in our case would make criminals of the cheaters, would use § 1341 to shore up cartels.

Fanciful? Not at all. Many scholars understand the NCAA as a cartel, having power in the market for athletes. E.g., Arthur A. Fleisher III, Brian L. Goff & Robert D. Tollison, The National Collegiate Athletic Association: A Study in Cartel Behavior (1992); Joseph P. Bauer, Antitrust and Sports: Must Competition on the Field Displace Competition in the Marketplace?, 60 Tenn.L.Rev. 263 (1993); Roger D. Blair & Jeffrey L. Harrison, Cooperative Buying, Monopsony Power, and Antitrust Policy, 86 Nw.U.L.Rev. 331 (1992); Lee Goldman, Sports and Antitrust: Should College Students be Paid to Play?, 65 Notre Dame L.Rev. 206 (1990); Richard B. McKenzie & E. Thomas Sullivan, Does the NCAA Exploit College Athletes? An Economic and Legal Reinterpretation, 32 Antitrust Bull. 373 (1987); Stephen F. Ross, Monopoly Sports Leagues, 73 Minn. L.Rev. 643 (1989). See also NCAA v. University of Oklahoma, 468 U.S. 85, 104 S.Ct. 2948, 82 L.Ed.2d 70 (1984) (holding that the NCAA's arrangements for the telecasting of college football violated the Sherman Act); Banks v. NCAA, 977 F.2d 1081 (7th Cir.1992) (showing disagreement among members of this court whether the NCAA's restrictions on athletes violate the Sherman Act). The NCAA depresses athletes' income—restricting payments to the value of tuition, room, and board, while receiving services of substantially greater worth. The NCAA treats this as desirable preservation of amateur sports; a more jaundiced eye would see it as the use of monopsony power to obtain athletes' services for less than the competitive market price. Walters then is cast in the role of a cheater, increasing the payments to the student athletes. Like other cheaters, Walters found it convenient to hide his activities. If, as the prosecutor believes, his repertory included extortion, he has used methods that the law denies to persons fighting cartels, but for the moment we are concerned only with the deceit that caused the universities to pay stipends to "professional" athletes. For current purposes it matters not whether the NCAA actually monopsonizes the market for players; the point of this discussion is that the prosecutor's theory makes criminals of those who consciously cheat on the rules of a private organization, even if that organization is a cartel. We pursue this point because any theory that makes criminals of cheaters raises a red flag.

Cheaters are not self-conscious champions of the public weal. They are in it for profit, as rapacious and mendacious as those who hope to collect monopoly rents. Maybe more; often members of cartels believe that monopoly serves the public interest, and they take their stand on the platform of business ethics, e.g., National Society of Professional Engineers v. United States, 435 U.S. 679, 98 S.Ct. 1355, 55 L.Ed.2d 637 (1978), while cheaters' glasses have been washed with cynical acid. Only Adam Smith's invisible hand turns their self-seeking activities to public benefit. It is cause for regret if prosecutors, assuming that persons with low regard for honesty must be villains, use the criminal laws to suppress the competitive process that undermines cartels. Of course federal laws have been used to enforce cartels before; the Federal Maritime Commission is a cartel-enforcement device. Inconsistent federal laws also occur; the United States both subsidizes tobacco growers and discourages people from smoking. So if the United States simultaneously forbids cartels and forbids undermining cartels by cheating, we shall shrug our shoulders and enforce both laws, condemning practical jokes along the way. But what is it about § 1341 that labels as a crime all deceit that inflicts any loss on anyone? Firms often try to fool their competitors, surprising them with new products that enrich their treasuries at their rivals' expense. Is this mail fraud because large organizations inevitably use the mail? "[A]ny scheme or artifice to defraud, or for obtaining money or property by means of false or fraudulent pretenses, representations, or promises" reads like a description of schemes to get money or property by fraud rather than methods of doing business that incidentally cause losses.

None of the Supreme Court's mail fraud cases deals with a scheme in which the defendant neither obtained nor tried to obtain the victim's property. It has, however, addressed the question whether 18 U.S.C. § 371, which prohibits conspiracies to defraud the United States, criminalizes plans that cause incidental loss to the Treasury. Tanner v. United States, 483 U.S. 107, 130, 107 S.Ct. 2739, 2752, 97 L.Ed.2d 90 (1987), holds that § 371 applies only when the United States is a "target" of the fraud; schemes that cause indirect losses do not violate that statute. McNally tells us that § 371 covers a broader range of frauds than does § 1341, see 483 U.S. at 358–59 n.8, 107 S.Ct. at 2881, n.8, and it follows that business plans causing incidental losses are not mail fraud. We have been unable to find any appellate cases squarely resolving the question whether the victim's loss must be an objective of the scheme rather than a byproduct of it, perhaps because prosecutions of the kind this case represents are so rare. According to the prosecutor, however, there have been such cases, and in this circuit. The United States contends that we have already held that a scheme producing an incidental loss violates § 1341. A representative sample of the cases the prosecutor cites shows that we have held no such thing.

For example, United States v. Ashman, 979 F.2d 469, 477–83 (7th Cir.1992), affirms convictions for fraud in a matched-order scheme on the floor of the Chicago Board of Trade. Customers sent orders for execution "at the market." Traders paired some of these orders off the market at times chosen to divert profits to themselves. This deprived the customers of the benefits provided by an open-outcry auction; more important, it moved money directly from customers' accounts to the traders' accounts. The transfers were the objective of the scheme. Nothing comparable took place here; no money moved from the universities to Walters. There is, however, some parallel in Ashman: we held that trades executed after the market was limit-up or limit-down could not support mail fraud convictions. Id. at 479. Once the market had moved the limit for the day, customers received the same price no matter when or with whom they traded. A customer willing to trade at a known price is like a university willing to give a scholarship to a known athlete. A customer who loses the honesty of the traders, but no money, has not been defrauded of property; a university that loses the benefits of amateurism likewise has been deprived only of an intangible right, which per McNally does not support a conviction.

The United States recasts this argument by contending that the universities lost (and Walters gained) the "right to control" who received the scholarships. This is an intangible rights theory once removed—weaker even than the position rejected in Toulabi v. United States, 875 F.2d 122 (7th Cir.1989), and United States v. Holzer, 840 F.2d 1343 (7th Cir.1988), because Walters was not the universities' fiduciary. Borre v. United States, 940 F.2d 215 (7th Cir.1991), did not purport to overrule Toulabi and Holzer, and is at all events a case in which the fraud (a) transferred property from victim to perpetrator, and (b) was committed by a group of schemers that includes the victim's fiduciary.

United States v. Richman sustained mail fraud convictions arising out of a lawyer's attempt to bribe the claims adjuster for an insurance company. Retained to represent the victim of an accident, the lawyer offered the adjuster 5% of any settlement. Here was a fraud aimed at obtaining money from the insurer—a settlement was the objective rather than a byproduct of the scheme. The lawyer defended by contending that, because his client really had been injured, the insurer would have paid anyway. 944 F.2d at 330. This was highly implausible; why was the lawyer willing to bribe the adjuster? The scheme was designed to increase the settlement, or to induce the insurer to pay even if its insured was not negligent. At all events, we observed, the statute prohibits schemes that are designed to bilk other persons out of money or other property; the lawyer's scheme had this objective even though the deceit might have been unnecessary. 944 F.2d at 330–31. Walters lacked any similar design to separate the universities from their money. Then there is United States v. Jones, 938 F.2d 737 (7th Cir.1991). The Joneses impersonated loan brokers. In exchange for $4,000 paid up front, they promised to procure large loans for their clients. Although they accepted almost $10 million in fees, they never found funding for a single client. Next they dispersed the money in an effort to prevent the assessment and collection of taxes on the booty. Our holding that the scam violated both § 371 and § 1343 (wire fraud) by preventing the

United States from taking its cut of the proceeds does not support a conclusion that any deceit that incidentally causes a loss to someone also violates federal law.

Many of our cases ask whether a particular scheme deprived a victim of property. E.g., Lombardo v. United States, 865 F.2d 155, 159–60 (7th Cir.1989). They do so not with an emphasis on "deprive" but with an emphasis on "property"—which, until the enactment of 18 U.S.C. § 1346 after Walters' conduct, was essential to avoid the "intangible rights" doctrine that McNally jettisoned. No one doubted that the schemes were designed to enrich the perpetrators at the victims' expense; the only difficulty was the proper characterization of the deprivation. Not until today have we dealt with a scheme in which the defendants' profits were to come from legitimate transactions in the market, rather than at the expense of the victims. Both the "scheme or artifice to defraud" clause and the "obtaining money or property" clause of § 1343 contemplate a transfer of some kind. Accordingly, following both the language of § 1341 and the implication of Tanner, we hold that only a scheme to obtain money or other property from the victim by fraud violates § 1341. A deprivation is a necessary but not a sufficient condition of mail fraud. Losses that occur as byproducts of a deceitful scheme do not satisfy the statutory requirement.

Anticipating that we might come to this conclusion, the prosecutor contends that Walters is nonetheless guilty as an aider and abettor. If Walters did not defraud the universities, the argument goes, then the athletes did. Walters put them up to it and so is guilty under 18 U.S.C. § 2, the argument concludes. But the indictment charged a scheme by Walters to defraud; it did not depict Walters as an aide de camp in the students' scheme. The jury received a boilerplate § 2 instruction; this theory was not argued to the jury, or for that matter to the district court either before or after the remand. Independent problems dog this recasting of the scheme—not least the difficulty of believing that the students hatched a plot to employ fraud to receive scholarships that the universities had awarded them long before Walters arrived on the scene, and the lack of evidence that the students knew about or could foresee any mailings. Walters is by all accounts a nasty and untrustworthy fellow, but the prosecutor did not prove that his efforts to circumvent the NCAA's rules amounted to mail fraud.

REVERSED.

COLLINS v. NATIONAL BASKETBALL PLAYERS ASS'N

850 F.Supp. 1468 (D.Colo.1991),
aff'd, 976 F.2d 740 (10th Cir.1992).

MATSCH, District Judge.

Defendants, National Basketball Players Association (NBPA), the exclusive bargaining representative for all of the players in the National

Basketball Association (NBA), and Charles Grantham (Grantham), Co–Chairman of the Committee on Agent Registration and Regulation of the NBPA (collectively NBPA, Defendants), moved for summary judgment on all claims of Plaintiff Thomas P. Collins (Collins, Plaintiff). Collins challenges the legality of the NBPA Regulations Governing Player Agents (Regulations) and the operation of Article XXXI of the NBPA's collective bargaining agreement with the NBA (NBPA–NBA Agreement) which forbids NBA teams from negotiating with agents who are not certified by the NBPA. Collins alleges that these restrictions are a "group boycott" and per se violation of Sections 1 and 2 of the Sherman Act. 15 U.S.C. §§ 1 & 2. Collins also claims that defendants tortiously interfered with his contracts and intentionally interfered with his prospective business advantage.

The NBPA is a labor organization within the meaning of § 2 of the National Labor Relations Act (NLRA), 29 U.S.C. § 152. For more than thirty years the NBA has recognized the NBPA as the exclusive bargaining representative for all professional basketball players employed by each of the NBA member teams, pursuant to § 9 of the NLRA, 29 U.S.C. § 159. As the exclusive bargaining representative for all of the professional basketball players employed by the twenty-seven NBA member teams, the NBPA has the exclusive authority to negotiate individualized salaries and conditions of employment on behalf of each player. The NBA and the NBPA have entered into collective bargaining agreements for the past twenty years. Grantham Decl. p 3. Like other unions, the NBPA negotiates minimum salaries, pension benefits, health insurance, and a grievance-arbitration procedure. The NBPA also negotiates issues unique to professional sports including a minimum individual player salary and a maximum amount any member team can pay to the aggregate of its players, the college draft, the ability of players to move from team to team, players' playoff compensation, travel accommodations, playing conditions, medical treatment and licensing rights. Id. p 4.

Like other sports and entertainment unions, the NBPA believes that the collective good of the entire represented group is maximized when individualized salary negotiations occur within a framework that permits players to exert leverage based on their unique skills and personal contributions. Id. p 5. The NBPA therefore has authorized the players or their individually selected agents to negotiate individual compensation packages. Id. This delegation of representational authority to individual players and their agents has always been limited solely to the authority to negotiate individual compensation packages, and to enforce them through the grievance-arbitration procedure established by the NBPA–NBA Agreement. Id. p 6; NBPA–NBA Agreement at 2, 139–154.

Player agents were unregulated by the NBPA before 1986. By the mid–1980s, a substantial number of players had complained to the officers of the NBPA about agent abuses. Id. p 7. Specifically, players complained that the agents imposed high and non-uniform fees for negotiation services, insisted on the execution of open-ended powers of attorney giving the agents broad powers over players' professional and financial decisions, failed to keep players apprised of the status of negotiations with NBA teams, failed to submit itemized bills for fees and services, and, in some cases, had conflicts of interest arising out of representing coaches and/or general managers of NBA teams as well as players. Id. Many players believed they were bound by contract not to dismiss their agents regardless of dissatisfaction with their services and fees, because the agents had insisted on the execution of long-term agreements. Id. Some agents offered money and other inducements to players, their families and coaches to obtain player clients. Id.

In response to these abuses, the NBPA established the Regulations, a comprehensive system of agent certification and regulation, to insure that players would receive agent services that meet minimum standards of quality at uniform rates. First, the Regulations provide that a player agent may not conduct individual contract negotiations unless he signs the "Standard Player Agent Contract" promulgated by the Committee. The "Standard Player Agent Contract" limits player agent fees by prohibiting any fee or commission on any contract which entitles the player to the minimum salary and by limiting agent fees on all contracts.

Second, the Regulations contain a "code of conduct" which specifically prohibits an agent from providing or offering money or anything of value to a player, a member of a player's family or a player's high school or college coach for the purpose of inducing the player to use that agent's services. Id. p 11. The code also prohibits agents from engaging in conduct that constitutes an actual or apparent conflict of interest (such as serving as an agent for a player while also representing an NBA team, general manager or head coach), engaging in any unlawful conduct involving dishonesty, fraud, deceit, misrepresentation, or engaging in any other conduct that reflects adversely on his fitness to serve in a fiduciary capacity as a player agent or jeopardizes the effective representation of NBA players. Id.; see Regulations, Section 3B.

Third, the Regulations restrict the representation of players to individuals who are certified player agents, and set up a program for the certification of agents who are then bound by the Regulations' fee restrictions and code of conduct. Prospective player agents must file the "Applications for Certification as an NBPA Player Agent" with the Committee. The Committee is authorized to conduct any informal investigation that it deems appropriate to determine whether to issue certification and may deny certification to any applicant:

> (1) Upon ... determining that the applicant has made false or misleading statements of a material nature in the Application; (2) Upon ... determining that the applicant has ever misappropriated funds, or engaged in other specific fraud, which would render him unfit to serve in a fiduciary capacity on behalf of players; (3) Upon ... determining that the applicant has engaged in any other conduct that significantly impacts adversely on his credibility, integrity or competence to serve in a fiduciary capacity on behalf of players; or (4) Upon ... deter-

> mining that the applicant is unwilling to swear or affirm that he will comply with these Regulations and any amendments thereto and that he will abide by the fee structure contained in the standard form player-agent contract incorporated into these Regulations.

Regulations, Section 2C.

Any prospective agent whose application for certification is denied may appeal that denial by filing a timely demand for arbitration. Regulations, Section 2D. The arbitration procedure incorporates by reference the Voluntary Labor Arbitration Rules of the American Arbitration Association, and includes the right to be represented by counsel, to cross-examine the Committee's witnesses, to present testimonial and documentary evidence and to receive a transcript. Grantham Decl. p 13, Regulations, Section 2D, Section 6E & F. The arbitrator is empowered to order certification if he determines, based on the evidence, that the Committee did not meet its burden of establishing a basis for denying certification. The arbitrator's decision is final and binding on all parties and is not subject to judicial review. The NBPA's selected arbitrator, George Nicolau, is experienced and highly qualified in handling labor relations in the sports industry. He is currently the chairman of the arbitration panel for the Major League Baseball and Major League Baseball Players Association and the contract arbitrator for the Major Indoor Soccer League and Major Indoor Soccer League Players Association. The NBPA player representatives of each NBA team approved the Regulations which became effective on March 7, 1986. Regulations, Section 4C.

After unilaterally promulgating the Regulations, the NBPA obtained, in arms length collective bargaining, the NBA's agreement to prohibit all member teams from negotiating individual player salary contracts with any agent who was not certified by the NBPA. Grantham, Decl. pp 15, 17. Article XXXI of the NBPA–NBA Agreement provides:

> Section 1. The NBA shall not approve any Player Contract between a player and a Team unless such player: (i) is represented in the negotiations with respect to such Player Contract by an agent or representative duly certified by the [NBPA] in accordance with the [NBA's] Agent Regulation Program and authorized to represent him; or (ii) acts on his own behalf in negotiating such Player Contract.
>
> Section 2. The NBA shall impose a fine of $1,000 upon any Team that negotiates a Player Contract with an agent or representative not certified by the [NBPA] in accordance with the [NBPA's] Agent Regulation Program, if at the time of such negotiations, such Team either (a) knows that such agent or representative has not been so certified or (b) fails to make reasonable inquiry of the NBA as to whether such agent or representative has been so certified.

Collins was an agent for several NBA players from 1974 until 1986. Collins applied for and received certification in 1986 soon after the Regulations took effect. In late 1986 or early 1987, he voluntarily ceased functioning as a player agent because of a lawsuit filed against him by a former NBA player client, Kareem Abdul–Jabbar, the former center of the Los Angeles Lakers, but retained his certification. Collins said he would not resume agent activities until he was exonerated of all charges in the pending lawsuit. In that case, Abdul–Jabbar, together with Ain Jeem, Inc. a corporation Abdul–Jabbar had established, alleged that Collins had committed numerous serious breaches of the fiduciary duty he owed as an agent to Abdul–Jabbar. Id. p 20. The alleged breaches included mishandling of Abdul–Jabbar's federal and state income tax returns which caused Abdul–Jabbar to pay approximately $300,000 in interest charges and late penalties; improvidently investing Abdul–Jabbar's money; mismanaging Abdul–Jabbar's assets; and transferring funds from Abdul–Jabbar's accounts without permission to the accounts of other players who were also Collins' clients. Id. In 1988, Collins' certification was revoked because he failed to pay agent dues and failed to attend at least one agent seminar as required by the Regulations. Grantham Decl. p 21.

Collins and Abdul–Jabbar settled the Ain Jeem lawsuit on November 7, 1989 and on February 15, 1990, Collins submitted an application to be recertified as a player agent. His application noted that there was still pending against him another lawsuit filed by another NBA player, Lucius Allen, and that eight of his former player clients—Jabbar, Alex English, Lucius Allen, Rickey Sobers, Terry Cummings, Ralph Sampson, Rudy Hackett and Brad Davis—had discharged him by the end of 1986. Grantham Decl. pp 23, 24; Application, Collins Affidavit, Exhibit 4.

The Committee commenced an informal investigation into Collins' application, requested from him all pleadings in the Allen lawsuit against him, the Ain Jeem settlement agreement, and certain discovery documents from the Ain Jeem suit. Grantham Decl. p 25. Collins replied that the Allen complaint had been inactive for three years (it was eventually dismissed) and that the Ain Jeem settlement was confidential. He provided the Committee with a redacted version that included only the confidentiality agreement and the following language: "As this dispute has been resolved without a trial, plaintiffs acknowledge that there has been no finding that defendants engaged in misrepresentation, misappropriation, conversion, breach of fiduciary duty or negligence." Id. The Committee received no further portion of the Ain Jeem settlement agreement or information regarding its terms from Abdul–Jabbar or his counsel. Id.

The Committee believed that its fiduciary duty to the players, who were prospective clients of Collins, required it to continue investigating the allegations against Collins to determine whether Collins had breached fiduciary responsibilities to Abdul–Jabbar or other NBPA members. Collins insisted that the quoted language of the settlement agreement and resulting dismissal of the Ain Jeem lawsuit, with prejudice, cleared him of all charges of breach of fiduciary responsibilities. He claimed, simultaneously with the settlement, Abdul–Jabbar had paid off a $300,000 bank loan that Collins had incurred. Id. p 27. Abdul–Jabbar's counsel denied Collins' claim that Abdul–Jabbar had repaid a $300,000 bank loan that Collins had incurred, and provided the Committee with non-confidential discovery material from the Ain Jeem case relevant to the allegations that Collins breached his fiduciary duties as Abdul–Jabbar's agent. Id. p 31. On July 6, 1990, the Committee sent Collins a letter referring to that discovery material which listed questions concerning each of the allegations raised in that case. Collins responded by denying any wrongdoing and responding to the allegations. On September 6, the Committee granted Collins "interim certification" which allowed him to represent Terry Cummings while the Committee continued its investigation.

The Committee then conducted an informal investigatory hearing with both Collins and Abdul–Jabbar present to examine the conflicting information submitted by the two men. Id. p 36. Although Collins could have had legal counsel present, the hearing took place on November 15, 1990, without counsel appearing for either Abdul–Jabbar or Collins. Id. pp 35, 36. By letter dated December 14, 1990, the Committee issued its decision denying Collins certification as a player agent. The letter explained that based on the allegations against him by Abdul–Jabbar and the information gathered by the Committee, the Committee concluded that Collins was unfit to serve in a fiduciary capacity on behalf of NBA players and that he made false or misleading statements to the Committee concerning a relevant subject in connection with the investigation into his application. Specifically, the Committee found: (1) Collins violated fiduciary duties to his former client Kareem Abdul–Jabbar and Ain Jeem, Inc. in his preparation and filing of federal and state tax returns, causing penalties and interest in excess of $300,000 to be imposed on Mr. Abdul–Jabbar and the corporation. (2) In handling the financial and business affairs of Mr. Abdul–Jabbar and other players, Collins acknowledged commingling funds from one account to another without authorization and resulting in losses of over $200,000 to Mr. Abdul–Jabbar. (3) Collins ignored requests by Mr. Abdul–Jabbar to invest money in safe investments, and invested in speculative ventures, many of which produced negative investment results. (4) In December 1985, Collins converted a corporate indebtedness of approximately $290,000 into a personal obligation of Mr. Abdul–Jabbar's without his approval. He also caused Mr. Abdul–Jabbar to execute loan documents relating to several investments making him jointly and severally liable for repaying loans. (5) Collins told the Committee that he had not filed his own Federal income taxes for the four year period 1986 through 1989 (even though he admitted earning over $300,000 in 1986). (6) Collins falsely represented to the Committee that Mr. Abdul–Jabbar paid $300,000 of Collins indebtedness to the Bank of California in connection with settling a lawsuit filed by Mr. Abdul–Jabbar and Ain–Jeem against Collins. Id. p 36; Collins Affidavit, Exhibit 20. The Committee had taken ten months to deny Collins' application—eight months longer than the NBPA's self established deadline.

The Committee informed Collins that under the Regulations he had a right to challenge the denial through final and binding arbitration. Soon after, Collins' counsel wrote to the Committee objecting that the November 15 hearing failed to provide Collins with appropriate process and that the failure to certify Collins violated the Sherman Act. The Committee responded that Collins could bring the case to arbitration at which the Committee would be obligated to establish through credible evidence that "Mr. Collins has engaged in conduct which would justify not recertifying him." Grantham Decl. p 40. Collins did not demand arbitration. After the 30 day period for invoking arbitration under the Regulations had lapsed, Grantham informed Collins, by letter dated February 4, 1991 he no longer would be permitted to engage in any activities relating to salary negotiations on behalf of any NBA player. After waiving the right to challenge the NBPA action by arbitration, Collins brought this action challenging the Regulations, Article XXXI of the NBPA–NBA Agreement and their application to him.

Collins claims that the actions of the NBPA violate the Sherman Act and cannot be justified under labor exemptions. He claims the Defendants' actions create a group boycott against him and constitute a per se violation of the Sherman Act by restraining him from representing individual basketball players in salary negotiations with their teams. In effect, Collins contests the union's monopolization of the representation of basketball players in their negotiations with NBA teams. He further alleges that the NBPA has waived any right to assert a labor exemption because it did not regulate Collins until 1986. Finally, Plaintiff alleges tortious interference with contracts and interference with prospective business advantage.

The NBPA Regulations and Article XXXI of the NBPA–NBA Agreement are exempt from antitrust law. Collins claims that the limitation of the market for the representation of basketball players is an antitrust violation. Although the Regulations do limit agents' representational ability, the identified "market" for the representation of NBA basketball players in salary negotiations is explicitly precluded by the federal labor laws. Were that market not exempt from the Sherman Act, then all collective bargaining by labor unions would be a violation of the antitrust laws, because in all collective bargaining other potential bargaining agents are entirely excluded from the relevant market. As the exclusive representative for all of the NBA players, the NBPA is legally entitled to forbid any other person or organization from negotiating for its members. Its right to exclude all others is central to the federal labor policy embodied in the NLRA. NLRB v. Allis–Chalmers Mfg. Co., 388 U.S. 175, 180, 87 S.Ct. 2001, 2006, 18 L.Ed.2d 1123 (1967). Indeed, the NLRA specifically empowers the exclusive bargaining representative to "monopolize" the representation of all employees in the bargaining unit. Section 9 provides:

> Representatives designated or selected for the purposes of collective bargaining by the majority of the employees in a unit appropriate for such purposes shall be the exclusive representatives of all the employees in such unit for the purposes of collective bargaining in respect to rates of pay, wages, hours of employment, or other conditions of employment....

29 U.S.C. § 159(a). Under the NLRA the employer—the NBA member team—may not bargain with any agent other than one designated by the union and must bargain with the agent chosen by the union. General Electric Co. v. NLRB, 412 F.2d 512, 517 (2d Cir.1969); Emporium Capwell Co. v. Western Addition Community Organization, 420 U.S. 50, 63–69, 95 S.Ct. 977, 985–88, 43 L.Ed.2d 12 (1975) (Union may forbid employees or any other agent chosen by individual employees, from bargaining separately with the employer over any issue). A union may delegate some of its exclusive representational authority on terms that serve union purposes, as the NBPA has done here. The decision whether, to what extent and to whom to delegate that authority lies solely with the union. Morio v. North American Soccer League, 501 F.Supp. 633, 640 (S.D.N.Y.1980), aff'd, 632 F.2d 217 (2d Cir.1980).

Collins argues that the Regulations establish a group boycott against him and are therefore a per se antitrust violation. He cites Connell Const. Co., Inc. v. Plumbers and Steamfitters Local Union No. 100, 421 U.S. 616, 95 S.Ct. 1830, 44 L.Ed.2d 418 (1975) as support. The case is inapposite. In Connell, the union imposed a group boycott against its competition by forcing a general contractor to agree to subcontract all of its work only to firms that employed union members. The Court held that the union's indiscriminate exclusion of non-union subcontractors from a portion of the market violated the antitrust laws. Unlike the Connell agreement, the Regulations do not establish a "group boycott" against Collins. A group boycott is a concerted refusal by traders to deal with other traders. Klor's, Inc. v. Broadway–Hale Stores, Inc., 359 U.S. 207, 212, 79 S.Ct. 705, 709, 3 L.Ed.2d 741 (1959). Collins does not trade or compete with the NBPA, the NBA or the NBA member teams. His trade is dependent upon the professional basketball teams and players but he has no protected interest under the law. He is neither a competitor nor an employer.

The only market the Regulations affect is the market for the representation of players in their salary negotiations with the NBA member teams. The number and identity of the teams and of the players is unchanged by the Regulations. Competition among the teams for players is not affected by the Regulations. No competitor of the union or of any member team is excluded by the Regulations.

Collins asserts that the NBPA cannot properly negotiate all of the player salaries without agents because negotiating the salaries of all of the players on an NBA team within the minimum salary and the team cap is an inherent conflict of interest and invalid. This situation is not qualitatively different from the common circumstances of a trade union representing employees with different pay scales in negotiating with their employer. Although the exact limits are more clearly defined in this case than in most industry bargaining situations, the available funds are always limited by economic forces. "The complete satisfaction of all who are represented is hardly to be expected." Ford Motor Co. v. Huffman, 345 U.S. 330, 338, 73 S.Ct. 681, 686, 97 L.Ed. 1048 (1953). Union leadership must always choose among competing interests of the union's members. See Humphrey v. Moore, 375 U.S. 335, 350, 84 S.Ct. 363, 372, 11 L.Ed.2d 370 (1964) (no breach of fair representation to take position contrary to some of the interests of some of those union represents).

The statutory labor exemptions to the Sherman Act apply both to the NBPA's promulgation of the Regulations that govern agent certification and to the decision to include Article XXXI in the NBPA–NBA Agreement which precludes non-certified agents from representing players in individual salary negotiations making them immune from antitrust review. Section 1 of the Sherman Act prohibits "[e]very contract, combination ... or conspiracy, in restraint of trade," and Section 2 prohibits monopolies or conspiracies to monopolize trade. 15 U.S.C. §§ 1 & 2.

If the Sherman Act were strictly applied, the formation of a labor union as an exclusive bargaining representative would be proscribed. But the labor laws were enacted to allow workers to speak with one voice and to exert leverage over their employers. Congress enacted Sections 6 and 20 of the Clayton Act to exempt traditional labor activity from the antitrust laws. Section 6 states, in pertinent part:

> The labor of a human being is not a commodity or article of commerce. Nothing contained in the antitrust laws shall be construed to forbid the existence and operation of labor ... organizations, instituted for the purposes of mutual help ... or to forbid or restrain individual members of such organizations from lawfully carrying out the legitimate objects thereof; nor shall such organizations, or the members thereof, be held or construed to be illegal combinations or conspiracies in restraint of trade, under the antitrust laws.

15 U.S.C. § 17. Section 20 forbids federal court injunctions in any case involving a dispute concerning terms and conditions of employment and exempts specific union activities from the operation of antitrust laws. 29 U.S.C. § 52.

Union activity is further protected from antitrust scrutiny in the Norris–LaGuardia Act which restricts the power of federal courts to issue any injunction in a case growing out of a labor dispute, and forbids the issuance of any injunction "contrary to the public policy of the United States." 29 U.S.C. §§ 101 & 102. The term "labor dispute" includes any controversy concerning terms or conditions of employment regardless of whether the disputants stand in the proximate relation of employer and employee. 29 U.S.C. § 113(c). The Act declares that public policy approves of the efforts of workers to organize, designate representatives of their own choosing, and engage in concerted activities for collective bargaining or other mutual aid or protection. The NLRA expressly accords workers the right to organize, to bargain collectively through an exclusive representative and to engage in concerted actions, and forbids employers to interfere with those rights. 29 U.S.C. §§ 157, 158, 159, 163.

United States v. Hutcheson, 312 U.S. 219, 61 S.Ct. 463, 85 L.Ed. 788 (1941), declared that the Sherman, Clayton and Norris–LaGuardia Acts must be harmonized when determining whether labor union activities violate antitrust legislation. "Conduct which [the labor laws] permit is not to be declared a violation of federal law." Allen Bradley, Co. v. Local Union No. 3, IBEW, 325 U.S. 797, 806, 65 S.Ct. 1533, 1538, 89 L.Ed. 1939 (1945). The Hutcheson Court held that labor unions acting in their self interest and not in combination with non labor groups are exempt from Sherman Act liability. In Hutcheson, a union struck, picketed and boycotted its employer in support of the union's claimed right to perform work given by the employer to a rival union. The Court noted that the union's activities were protected by § 20 of the Clayton Act and held that they did not violate the Sherman Act.

So long as a union acts in its self-interest and does not combine with non-labor groups, the licit and the illicit under Section 20 [of the Clayton Act] are not to be distinguished by any judgment regarding the wisdom or unwisdom, the rightness or wrongness, the selfishness or unselfishness of the end of which the particular union activities are the means. Hutcheson, 312 U.S. at 232, 61 S.Ct. at 466.

The labor exemption is denied, and antitrust laws are applied to union agreements with one or more employers, when those agreements deny rival employers access to the market or expressly control wages for the purpose of destroying those rivals; that is, when unions "aid and abet businessmen who are violating the [Clayton] Act." P. Areeda and D. Turner, 2 Antitrust Law: An Analysis of Antitrust Principles and Their Application p 229e, at 202 (1978), Allen Bradley, 325 U.S. at 807, 65 S.Ct. at 1538. In Allen Bradley the Court held that a union had violated the Sherman Act when it combined with manufacturers and contractors to erect a sheltered local business market in order to "bar all other businessmen from [the market] and to charge the public prices above a competitive level." The labor exemption was denied because the union had not acted alone to further its own goals but had combined with businessmen who had complete power to eliminate all competition among themselves and prevent competition from other firms. Areeda and Turner, 2 Antitrust Law p 229e, at 203.

Under Hutcheson and Allen Bradley Co., a union's activities are entitled to the statutory labor exemption whenever they are covered by the Clayton and Norris–LaGuardia Acts, and thereby in the union's legitimate self interest and not undertaken in combination with an employer, business or non labor group to restrain competition or control prices in the employer's or business group's product market. Hutcheson,

312 U.S. at 232, 61 S.Ct. at 466. A union meeting this test is immune from liability under the antitrust laws even if its actions impose restraints on competition in the relevant product market.

Both the Regulations and Article XXXI are within the statutory exemption from antitrust regulation. When promulgating the Regulations and when negotiating Article XXXI, the NBPA acted in its own interest, independently of any employers and without denying access to rival employers. The number and identity of the employers remains unchanged regardless of the Regulations or Article XXXI. A union's actions are in its "self-interest" if they bear a reasonable relationship to a legitimate union interest. Adams, Ray & Rosenberg v. William Morris Agency, Inc., 411 F.Supp. 403 (C.D.Cal.1976). The NBPA regulatory program fulfills legitimate union purposes and was the result of legitimate concerns: it protects the player wage scale by eliminating percentage fees where the agent does not achieve a result better than the collectively bargained minimum; it keeps agent fees generally to a reasonable and uniform level, prevents unlawful kickbacks, bribes, and fiduciary violations and protects the NBPA's interest in assuring that its role in representing professional basketball players is properly carried out. Although Collins claims any benefit is in the player's self interest, not the union's, it is impossible to separate the two—the union is composed of its members and exists solely to serve the players. When the players benefit, the union benefits as well.

The second prong of the test is also met. Collins incorrectly claims that when enacting the Regulations, the NBPA combined with a non labor group and thus fails to earn a statutory exemption. The most analogous case is H.A. Artists & Associates v. Actors' Equity Assn., 451 U.S. 704, 101 S.Ct. 2102, 68 L.Ed.2d 558 (1981), in which the Supreme Court upheld similar regulations against an antitrust challenge. In H.A. Artists, theatrical agents who represented members of Actors Equity Association for purposes of procuring employment and negotiating individual salaries above the collectively bargained minimum, challenged that union's licensing system, which regulated the agents and required union members to employ only union-licensed agents. The Equity regulations, like the NBPA regulations at issue here, permitted only those agents who were licensed by the union to represent union members in individual salary negotiations with employers. The Equity regulations protected and sought to maximize wages by requiring agents to renounce any commission on any portion of a contract under which an actor or actress received no more than the collectively bargained minimum wages, and by limiting commissions in other respects. The Equity regulations also allowed actors to terminate their representation contracts with agents, and required agents to honor their fiduciary obligations. The Equity regulations were a response to historical abuses by agents, and were designed to secure better services from agents at lower rates.

The Court held that the Actors' Equity regulations met the Hutcheson–Allen Bradley Co. test for the statutory labor exemption. First, the

Regulations were designed to promote the union's legitimate self-interest. Id. at 720–21, 101 S.Ct. at 2112. Second, there was no combination with either a non-labor group or a non-party to a labor dispute. The Court held there was no combination between the union and the employers—the theatrical producers—to create or maintain the regulation system. Rather, the union unilaterally developed the regulatory system in response to agent abuses and to benefit union members. Id. at 707, 101 S.Ct. at 2105. The Court concluded that although some agents agreed to the regulations, there was no combination with a non-labor group or persons who were not party to a labor dispute. The agents themselves were a labor group because they had an "economic interrelationship" with the union and its members "affecting legitimate union interests." That is, "the[y] represented[ed] ... union members in the sale of their labor ... [a function] that in most nonentertainment industries is performed exclusively by unions." Id. at 721, 101 S.Ct. at 2112. Thus, any dispute between the agents and the union regarding the representation of union workers was a "labor dispute"—which was outside of the purview of the antitrust laws. Id. at 721, 101 S.Ct. at 2112.

The NBPA Regulations similarly meet the second part of the Hutcheson–Allen Bradley Co. test. The NBPA did not combine with a non-labor group or a non-party to a labor dispute when promulgating the Regulations or negotiating Article XXXI. The NBPA unilaterally developed its Regulations in response to agent abuses and to benefit its members. It did not develop them in collusion with the employer group or to assist the employer group effort to restrain competition or control the employer group's product market.

Like the Equity agents, the player agents are a labor group. Although basketball players, unlike actors, can and do obtain employment without an agent, most players employ agents to negotiate their salaries and can fall victim to unscrupulous agent behavior. The player agents have a clear economic interrelationship with the players they represent; their remuneration is directly dependent on the relationship set up with the player and the salary obtained for him. Because they represent persons in the negotiation of terms of employment, the agents are clearly parties to a labor dispute within the meaning of the NLRA, 29 U.S.C. § 113(c). As such, they would meet the second prong of the test regardless of whether there is a combination with a non labor group.

Article XXXI of the NBPA–NBA Agreement also meets the second prong and is entitled to the statutory exemption. Article XXXI was obtained in arms length collective bargaining at the urging of the NBPA after it unilaterally promulgated the Regulations. It was not agreed to at the behest of or in combination with the NBA, the employer group. Regardless of Article XXXI, pursuant to § 9 of the NLRA, the NBA member teams may not negotiate salaries with anyone other than the NBPA without NBPA approval. It therefore follows that Article XXXI of the NBPA–NBA Agreement does little more than memorialize in explicit terms what the NBA member teams' legal duty would be under the NLRA: to deal only with the NBPA or agents specified by the NBPA.

The provision adds no new requirements to the NBA and thus creates no problem for the statutory exemption of the Regulations.

Article XXXI of the NBPA–NBA Agreement presents none of the concerns contained in the cases in which employer-union activities have been found to fall outside of the statutory exemption. Unlike Allen Bradley, the union activity is not designed to help employers control competition and prices. In fact, Article XXXI which requires teams to negotiate only with NBPA certified agents has no effect on the market for teams' services or on the market relating to any team. There is no combination with employer interests. With respect to the teams, the situation after the agreement is identical to the situation before it. The union serves its legitimate goals of protecting its representational function and the employer group's market is unchanged.

The agreement is similarly unlike the union-employer agreements in United Mine Workers of America v. Pennington, 381 U.S. 657, 85 S.Ct. 1585, 14 L.Ed.2d 626 (1965), and Connell Const. Co., Inc. v. Plumbers and Steamfitters Local Union No. 100, 421 U.S. 616, 95 S.Ct. 1830, 44 L.Ed.2d 418 (1975). In Pennington the Court held that a union forfeits its antitrust exemption when it agrees with a group of employers to impose a wage scale on other bargaining units and thus conspires to curtail competition. 381 U.S. at 665–666, 85 S.Ct. at 1591. In Pennington the union-employer agreement fell outside of NLRA protection because the union and the employees could not, consistent with federal labor policy, bargain about wages, hours and working conditions of other bargaining units or the whole industry. Id. at 666, 85 S.Ct. at 1591. There is neither an employer conspiracy nor any effect on the employers' competitive position in the sports-entertainment market as a result of the NBPA–NBA Agreement. The union's regulation of its authorized representatives in the salary-bargaining process is protected by the NLRA.

In Connell, the union obtained an agreement from a general contractor whose workers the union did not represent, that the general contractor would subcontract work only to subcontractors who employed the union's members. In so doing, the union imposed a direct restraint on the market in which subcontractors could compete. 421 U.S. at 625–26, 95 S.Ct. at 1836–37. The Court held the agreement with the general contractor by which this restraint was imposed was not entitled to protection under the NLRA, because the union did not represent the general contractor's employees and had no right under the NLRA to bargain with their employer. Id. at 626, 95 S.Ct. at 1837. In this case, there is no restraint on the employers' market and there is NLRA protection for the union activity. Accordingly, both the Regulations and Article XXXI of the Agreement are immune from antitrust scrutiny under the statutory labor exemption.

Even if Article XXXI of the Agreement were not entitled to the statutory exemption, it would be immune from antitrust review under the nonstatutory exemption to the antitrust laws. The Supreme Court has determined that when a union-employer agreement falls within the protection of the national labor policy, a proper accommodation between the policy favoring collective bargaining under the NLRA and the congressional policy favoring free competition in business markets requires that some agreements be accorded a limited nonstatutory labor exemption from antitrust sanctions. Connell, 421 U.S. at 622, 95 S.Ct. at 1835; Meat Cutters v. Jewel Tea Co., 381 U.S. 676, 85 S.Ct. 1596, 14 L.Ed.2d 640 (1965). Unlike the statutory exemption which immunizes activities that are expressly described in the Clayton and Norris-LaGuardia Acts, the nonstatutory exemption immunizes labor arrangements that are the ordinary implication of activities contemplated by the federal labor laws. Areeda and Turner, 2 Antitrust Law p 229a, at 192. When the agreement is reached through bona fide, arms-length bargaining between the union and the employers, and the terms of the agreement are not the product of an initiative by the employer group but were sought by the union in an effort to serve the legitimate interests of its members, it is free from antitrust scrutiny. Jewel Tea, 381 U.S. at 688–89, 85 S.Ct. at 1601; Connell, 421 U.S. at 622, 95 S.Ct. at 1835 (nonstatutory exemption denied because direct restraints on market imposed by union outside of federally protected collective bargaining relationship).

In Jewel Tea, the butchers' union sought from the Jewel grocery store chain a provision—which it had already obtained from a multiemployer grocery association encompassing most other grocers in the area—restricting meat sales to limited weekday and Saturday hours. Jewel ultimately capitulated, agreeing to include the meat sale hours restriction in its contract with the union. The effect of the collective bargaining agreements was to limit competition among grocers. They were contractually committed not to sell meat after 6 P.M. or on Sunday. Because the union sought the marketing restriction to serve its members' concern of limiting working hours, an issue well within the terms and conditions of employment over which they were entitled to negotiate, the Court held that the union's efforts to obtain the restriction "through bona-fide, arm's length bargaining in pursuit of their own labor union policies, falls within the protection of the national labor policy and is therefore exempt from the Sherman Act." Id. at 689–90, 85 S.Ct. at 1601–02. The Court recognized that the agreements affected competition among employers but held that the NLRA allowed the union to negotiate those issues.

The nonstatutory exemption similarly immunizes the Regulations from Sherman Act scrutiny. The Regulations were unilaterally developed in response to player complaints and to further NBPA labor policies. The NBPA–NBA Agreement, including Article XXXI, was agreed to in arms-length collective bargaining. The provision was not sought "at the behest of or in combination with" any employer or other non labor group as forbidden by Jewel Tea. There is no economic benefit to the NBPA or the NBA member teams as a result of this provision and there is no effect on the employer's product or service market as a result of the provision.

Collins argues that even if the Regulations and Article XXXI would be entitled to the labor exemption to the antitrust laws, the NBPA has waived the right to invoke the exemption by failing to regulate agents until 1986. He further claims that the NBPA is estopped from refusing to certify him because he relied on the fact that he would be certified. This argument is frivolous. A representative body must be able to protect its members' interests whenever there is a risk of their being compromised, regardless of when that risk arises. When the NBPA learned of agent abuses it was not foreclosed from taking corrective action. Indeed, in its fiduciary role to its members, it was required to act in their best interest, which includes eliminating abusive forces. If the NBPA were precluded from acting then unions would be unable to change any of their policies and would be saddled by the practices and policies in place at the day of inception. Simply stating this proposition demonstrates its lack of merit.

Equally ludicrous is Collins' estoppel argument. Collins asserts that because he earned his living by representing NBPA members, he was entitled to rely on his assumption that he would continue in that function indefinitely. Accordingly, he contends that the NBPA is estopped from applying the Regulations to deny him certification. Collins had no assurances that the NBPA would not impose regulations or eliminate player agents entirely. The lack of regulation in the past was not an implied promise that there would be no regulation in the future. There were no promises, express or implied, by the NBPA that Collins had a tenured position as an agent.

Collins argues that the Committee's use of Abdul–Jabbar's allegations against him is improper. He argues first, that the Committee incorrectly accepted the allegations as true and second, even if they were true, that the allegations cannot be used in determining whether to certify him because they were unrelated to his work as a negotiator but related only to his work as an investment manager. The Committee's use of the allegations in deciding not to recertify Collins was certainly justified. By not appealing the Committee decision as directed by the Regulations, Collins forfeited the right to challenge the Committee's decision, the facts or the process. The court expresses no opinion as to the accuracy of those allegations, but because they were not challenged, the Committee was entitled to treat them as true when deciding whether to certify Collins. The Committee's findings gave the Committee ample reason to deny certification under Section 2C of the Regulations. Contrary to Collins' suggestion, it is perfectly appropriate for the NBPA to question the integrity of those who will act as the agents and fiduciaries of its members in those areas which fall under union supervision.

Collins' argument that the claims of breach of fiduciary duty are unrelated to his appropriateness as a negotiating agent is flawed. The Regulations specifically give the Committee the power to deny certification to anyone who makes false or misleading statements to the Committee, who misappropriates funds, who acts in a way that impacts his credibility or who is unfit to serve as a fiduciary. It is beyond question that the Committee found Collins unfit under each of these criteria. Although Collins claims his alleged fiduciary violations are unrelated to his negotiating skills, he is wrong. The NBPA has the right to restrict delegation of bargaining authority to honest people.

Collins charges Defendants tortiously interfered with his contracts and intentionally interfered with his prospective business advantage. These claims are really no more than another challenge of the NBPA's right to exercise its representational monopoly. Neither of these state tort law claims states a proper cause of action. Colorado law provides that an interference with a contract or prospective business relation is tortious if, and only if, the interference is improper—i.e., unjustified or not privileged. See, e.g., Trimble v. City and County of Denver, 697 P.2d 716, 726 (Colo.1985) (en banc); Restatement (Second) of Torts § 766 (1979). When determining whether a party has acted improperly, the court must consider the nature of the actor's conduct, his motive, the interests of the person with whom the actor interferes, the interests sought to be advanced by the actor, the social interests in protecting the freedom of action of the actor and the contractual interests of the other, the proximity or remoteness of the actor's conduct to the interference and the relations between the parties. Trimble, 697 P.2d at 726; Restatement (Second) of Torts § 767 (1979). The NBPA's actions were justified and privileged under the Regulations. The NBPA's implementation of the Regulations, and their denial of Collins' certification application were to protect players from agent abuses. Because Collins chose not to challenge the Committee's findings, this court must accept them as true for purposes of this motion. Had Collins challenged the findings in arbitration, the method prescribed by the Regulations themselves, then he might have been able to have had some of the findings reversed. As it stands, all must be considered correct. If any one of the findings is true, the Committee was empowered to deny Collins certification under Section 2C of the Regulations. Such action was proper and justified. The Committee has a fiduciary obligation to the players. Certification of Collins would have breached that duty. The NBPA's conduct is by definition privileged. Therefore, Collins has no claim for tortious interference with contracts or prospective business relationship.

Upon the foregoing, it is

ORDERED that Defendants' motion for summary judgment is GRANTED and all of Plaintiff's claims are dismissed. Judgment will enter for the Defendants, with costs to be awarded.

Notes

1. In response to NCAA rule violations like those at issue in *Walters*, more than two dozen states now have laws which make it illegal for agents to recruit college players (and in some instances also make it a crime to accept such representation). In addition, the National Conference of Commissioners on Uniform State Laws is expected to complete work on its Uniform Athlete Agents Act by mid–1999. For a further description of these efforts, see, e.g., Rob Remis, *The Art of Being a Sports Agent in More Than*

One State: Analysis of Registration and Reporting Requirements and Developments of a Model Strategy, 8 Seton Hall J. Sport L. 419 (1998); Thomas J. Arkell, *Agent Interference with College Athletics: What Agents Can and Cannot Do and What Institutions Should Do in Response*, 4 Sports Law. J. 147 (1997); Todd L. Erdman, *The Long Awaited Quadruple Play: Proposed Amendments to Four Major Areas of the Alabama Athlete Agents Regulatory Act of 1997*, 8 DePaul U. J. Art & Ent. L. 191 (1997); Linda S. Calvert Hanson, *The Florida Legislature Revisits the Regulation and Liability of Sports Agents and Student Athletes*, 25 Stetson L. Rev. 1067 (1996); James Malone & Daren Lipinsky, Comment, *The Game Behind the Games: Unscrupulous Agents in College Athletics and California's Miller–Ayala Act*, 17 Loy. L.A. Ent. L.J. 413 (1997); Ricardo J. Bascuas, Note, *Cheaters, Not Criminals: Antitrust Invalidation of Statutes Outlawing Sports Agent Recruitment of Student Athletes*, 105 Yale L.J. 1603 (1996); Curtis D. Rypma, Note, *Sports Agents Representing Athletes: The Need for Comprehensive State Legislation*, 24 Val. U. L. Rev. 481 (1990).

2. As is explained in *Collins*, sports agents who wish to represent NBA players must obtain certification from the players union. Similar programs exist in the other major professional sports. Nevertheless, things appear to have gotten worse rather than better: only a handful of agents have been decertified, the number of players filing complaints against their agents is increasing, and when the NFL Players Association (NFLPA) asked agents it had approved to take an open-book exam on the league's collective bargaining agreement (the starting point for all contract negotiations), half declined to do so and 40% of those who completed the test failed. *See further* Mike Freeman, *Protecting Players From Their Agents; Misconduct Leaves N.F.L. Union Fearful of Incompetence and Greed*, N.Y. Times, July 26, 1998, § 8, at 1. *See also* Michael Silver & Don Yeager, *Leap of Faith*, Sports Illustrated, Aug. 24, 1998, at 34 (describing the numerous mistakes made by Greg Feste, an NFL-certified agent, during a multi-million dollar contract negotiation).

For a further look at the unions and their agent certification programs, see, e.g., Ethan Lock, *The Regulatory Scheme for Player Representatives in the National Football League: The Real Power of Jerry Maguire*, 35 Am. Bus. L.J. 319 (1998); Jamie P.A. Shulman, *The NHL Joins In: An Update on Sports Agent Regulation in Professional Team Sports*, 4 Sports Law. J. 181 (1997); Gary P. Konn, *Sports Agents Representing Professional Athletes: Being Certified Means Never Having to Say You're Qualified*, 6 Ent. & Sports Law. 1 (Winter 1988).

3. In October 1998, the NFLPA suspended Jeff Nalley for two years after finding him guilty of buying Curtis Enis $1,000 worth of clothing while he was still a member of the Penn State football team, thereby causing Enis to be suspended from the Citrus Bowl. It also fined Nalley $15,000, payable if and when he resumes representing players. The penalty is the harshest ever levied by the NFLPA. *See further Ex–Agent for Enis Banned for 2 Years*, N.Y. Times, Oct. 23, 1998, at C27. If you had been advising the NFLPA, what penalty would you have recommended for Nalley?

4. In addition to the rules of the various player associations, agents who also are lawyers are subject to their state's attorneys' ethics code. *See, e.g., Cuyahoga County Bar Ass'n v. Glenn*, 649 N.E.2d 1213 (Ohio 1995)

(lawyer suspended for one year, and required to make full restitution as condition of reinstatement, for improperly retaining percentage of proceeds paid by Chicago Bears following renegotiation of player's employment contract). This has created a disincentive for agents to become lawyers and has led some attorney-agents to complain that they are being unfairly held to a higher standard. These issues are explored at length in Walter T. Champion, Jr., *Attorneys Qua Sports Agents: An Ethical Conundrum*, 7 Marq. Sports L.J. 349 (1997); Richard M. Nichols, *Agent, Lawyer, Agent/Lawyer ... Who Can Best Represent Student Athletes?*, 14 Ent. & Sports Law. 1 (Fall 1996); Sara L. Keller–Smith & Sherri A. Affrunti, *Going for the Gold: The Representation of Olympic Athletes*, 3 Vill. Sports & Ent. L.J. 443 (1996); Daniel L. Shneidman, *Selected Issues of Client Representation by "Sports" Lawyers Under the Model Rules of Professional Conduct*, 4 Marq. Sports L.J. 129 (1993); Paul T. Dee, *Ethical Aspects of Representing Professional Athletes*, 3 Marq. Sports L.J. 111 (1992); Robert E. Fraley & F. Russell Harwell, *The Sports Lawyer's Duty to Avoid Differing Interests: A Practical Guide to Responsible Representation*, 11 Hastings Comm/Ent L.J. 165 (1989); Jamie E. Brown, Comment, *The Battle the Fans Never See: Conflicts of Interest for Sports Lawyers*, 7 Geo. J. Legal Ethics 813 (1994).

5. Although Congress has shown no interest in the idea, the suggestion that a national law is needed to regulate sports agents is an oft-made one. For a look at the pros and cons of such legislation, see, e.g., Alec Powers, *The Need to Regulate Sports Agents*, 4 Seton Hall J. Sport L. 253 (1994), and David L. Dunn, Note, *Regulation of Sports Agents: Since at First It Hasn't Succeeded, Try Federal Legislation*, 39 Hastings L.J. 1031 (1988).

6. Are there too many rules governing the conduct of agents? At least one commentator has suggested this may be the case. *See* Jan Stiglitz, *A Modest Proposal: Agent Deregulation*, 7 Marq. Sports L.J. 361 (1997).

Problem 34

California state law requires sports agents to register with the Commissioner of Labor, but exempts full-time attorneys "when acting as legal counsel." If a lawyer who represents athletes fails to register and is prosecuted as a result, will he be able to beat the charges by arguing he was always "acting as legal counsel"? *See Wright v. Bonds*, 1997 WL 377111 (9th Cir.1997).

Chapter 6

COACHES

A. OVERVIEW

Even the most talented players are unlikely to succeed unless they have the proper guidance. As a result, every team devotes substantial effort to finding and keeping the best coaches. From a legal perspective, four questions have arisen with great frequency: 1) what procedures must be followed in hiring a coach?; 2) what rules must be observed in firing a coach?; 3) what obligations does a coach have to his or her players?; and, 4) what acts fall within the scope of a coach's employment?

B. HIRING DECISIONS

As a general matter, a club may select whomever it wishes to be its coach. In making this choice, however, it may not engage in unlawful discrimination.

LEE v. WISE COUNTY SCHOOL BOARD

133 F.3d 915 (4th Cir.1998)

PER CURIAM.

David Edward Lee, Jr., appeals the district court's grant of summary judgment in favor of the Wise County School Board on his claim of religious discrimination in violation of Title VII. Lee maintains that the school board declined to rehire him as a basketball coach on account of his religion. The district court held that Lee failed to establish a prima facie case of religious discrimination and that Lee's poor performance as a coach provided a legitimate nondiscriminatory reason for its decision not to rehire him. We hold that the school board has provided an adequate reason for its failure to rehire and that Lee has failed to create a triable dispute over whether that reason is pretextual. Accordingly, we affirm the district court.

I.

Lee was head coach of the men's basketball team since 1979 at Powell Valley High School, located in Big Stone Gap, Virginia. He also taught English and coached tennis at Powell Valley. Lee attended a Methodist church and had been actively involved in religious affairs such as the Fellowship of Christian Athletes.

From the 1990–91 school year through the 1994–95 school year, the men's basketball team never posted a winning season. During 1994 and 1995, parents and members of the community voiced complaints to Bruce Robinette, a member of the Wise County School Board, and David Dowdy, principal at Powell Valley, about Lee's inadequate job performance as head basketball coach. According to Robinette, the criticisms increased over the course of the 1994–95 school year, and he eventually advised the parents to bring their concerns to the attention of the full school board.

During a school board meeting held on June 28, 1995, a delegation of parents appeared to register their complaints about Lee. To allow the parents to air their concerns privately, the board went into executive session. The parents complained that Lee was not devoting enough time or attention to the basketball program due to other pursuits such as work for a company named Amway and his own painting business. The parents also observed that the basketball team was unable to attend a camp in North Carolina because Lee had failed to submit a timely application. Every school board member stated that the board did not discuss Lee's religious affiliation, convictions, or activities at this meeting. The board did not take any action at that time.

Following the meeting, the Superintendent of the Wise County School System, Dr. Jim Graham, met with Dowdy to investigate the basis of the parents' complaints. Dowdy had not attended the June 28 school board meeting. Dowdy told Graham that he believed Lee was distracted from coaching by a number of things and had lost the desire to coach. Dowdy and Graham discussed a wide range of topics, including the fact that some parents had previously asked Dowdy about Lee's religious activities. According to Dowdy, he and Graham never discussed Lee's religion or his religious beliefs "in a derogatory or negative fashion."

During the next board meeting, held on July 13, 1995, the board again considered the renewal of Lee's contract as a basketball coach. The board discussed the complaints about Lee's neglect of the basketball program. Although the board never formally voted on Lee's contract, it reached a general consensus that Lee would not be rehired as a basketball coach. The board members did not discuss Lee's religious affiliation, convictions, practices, or activities at this meeting.

After the July meeting, Dr. Graham met with principal Dowdy and advised him of the board's consensus. In Wise County, to renew coaching contracts, a principal submits a slate of coaches to the division superintendent who reviews these recommendations and forwards a list to the school board. For the 1995–96 school year, Dowdy did not recommend Lee as the men's basketball coach. Instead, he recommended Jimmy Mitchell, another Powell Valley employee, who eventually was hired as the interim head coach for that year.

Lee filed a charge with the Equal Employment Opportunity Commission and later brought this complaint. In his complaint, Lee alleged, inter alia, that the school board discriminated against him on the basis of his religion by failing to rehire him as the head basketball coach. The district court granted the school board's motion for summary judgment. Lee now appeals.

II.

Title VII prohibits employment discrimination on the basis of religion. 42 U.S.C. § 2000e–2(a). Absent direct evidence of discrimination, a plaintiff must first demonstrate a prima facie case of discrimination. McDonnell Douglas Corp. v. Green, 411 U.S. 792, 802 (1973); Chalmers v. Tulon Co. of Richmond, 101 F.3d 1012, 1017 (4th Cir.1996), cert. denied, 118 S.Ct. 58 (1997). Once a party has made a prima facie case, the employer must provide a legitimate nondiscriminatory justification for its action. Texas Dep't of Community Affairs v. Burdine, 450 U.S. 248, 253 (1981); Chalmers, 101 F.3d at 1017–18. If the employer advances such a justification, the plaintiff then must prove that this justification is a mere pretext for an actual discriminatory motive. St. Mary's Honor Ctr. v. Hicks, 509 U.S. 502, 507–08 (1993); Chalmers, 101 F.3d at 1018.

Lee challenges the district court's holding that he did not establish a prima facie case of religious discrimination. To uphold summary judgment in this case, we need not resolve that question. Assuming that Lee has demonstrated a prima facie case, the school board advanced a legitimate nondiscriminatory justification for its decision not to rehire him—Lee was spending too much time on outside activities and was not sufficiently dedicated to the Powell Valley basketball program. Lee has failed to create a genuine issue over whether this justification was pretextual. The school board, therefore, is entitled to summary judgment.

The school board offered ample evidence to demonstrate Lee's lack of commitment as a basketball coach. Board members relied on complaints about Lee's outside activities such as his Amway distributorship and painting business as proof of his neglect. Some board members also cited the specific complaint that the basketball team was unable to attend a camp because Lee had failed to submit a timely application. Thus, the school board has advanced a legitimate nondiscriminatory reason for its decision not to rehire Lee as the head basketball coach.

Lee has failed to create any dispute over whether this reason was merely pretextual. Lee makes much of board member Charles Mutter's affidavit. Mutter apparently overheard a comment during the June 1995 board meeting that Lee was very religious and may have baptized someone in his swimming pool. We believe, however, that Lee overstates the impact of this isolated remark. In the same affidavit, Mutter specified that this comment was "not directed at the board." In fact, Mutter was the only board member who mentioned overhearing such a comment. Mutter also averred that the board never discussed Lee's religion. Mutter's reference to this random remark does not show, or even suggest, that the reason for the board's decision was pretextual.

Lee maintains that, after the June 1995 board meeting, Superintendent Graham and Principal Dowdy discussed the various complaints about Lee, including concerns that parents had expressed to Dowdy about some of Lee's religious practices. Lee draws the inference that his religion must have factored into the decision because Graham and Dowdy were aware of these earlier comments. Lee, however, overlooks one critical fact. Parents do not make the day-to-day decisions for a school district. Merely because Dowdy and Graham might have been aware of scattered parental comments, we cannot assume that the parents' concerns affected the decision not to rehire Lee. Dowdy and Graham both denied that religion ever factored into the decision not to renew Lee's contract. Every school board member denied that they ever discussed Lee's religion during the June and July meetings. Thus, Dowdy's and Graham's mere awareness of parents' comments about Lee's religion does not suggest any pretext.

III.

The school board provided ample evidence that Lee was diverted by other pursuits and had not devoted sufficient attention to his coaching duties. Lee's contentions that religion motivated the high school's coaching change are nothing more than speculations. Accordingly, we affirm the judgment of the district court.

STANLEY v. UNIVERSITY OF SOUTHERN CALIFORNIA

13 F.3d 1313 (9th Cir.1994).

ALARCON, Circuit Judge.

Marianne Stanley, former head coach of the women's basketball team at the University of Southern California (USC), appeals from an order denying her motion for a preliminary injunction against USC and Michael Garrett, the athletic director for USC (collectively USC).

Coach Stanley contends that the district court abused its discretion in denying a preliminary injunction on the ground that she failed to present sufficient evidence of sex discrimination or retaliation to carry her burden of establishing a clear likelihood of success on the merits. Coach Stanley also claims that the court misapprehended the nature of the preliminary injunction relief she sought. In addition, she argues that the district court clearly erred in finding that USC would suffer significant hardship if the preliminary injunction issued. Coach Stanley further asserts that she was denied a full and fair opportunity to present testimonial evidence at the preliminary injunction hearing and to demonstrate that USC's purported justification for paying a higher salary to George Raveling, head coach of the men's basketball team at USC, was a pretext for sex discrimination and retaliation. We affirm because we conclude that the district court did not abuse its discretion in denying the motion for a preliminary injunction. We also hold that the district court did not deny Coach Stanley a full and fair opportunity to present evidence of sex discrimination, retaliation, and pretext.

I. Pertinent Facts

Coach Stanley signed a four-year contract with USC on July 30, 1989, to serve as the head coach of the women's basketball team. The expiration date of Coach Stanley's employment contract was June 30, 1993. Coach Stanley's employment contract provided for an annual base salary of $60,000 with a $6,000 housing allowance.

Sometime in April of 1993, Coach Stanley and Michael Garrett began negotiations on a new contract. The evidence is in dispute as to the statements made by the parties. Coach Stanley alleges in her declarations that she told Garrett that she "was entitled to be paid equally with the Head Men's Basketball Coach, George Raveling[,] and that [she] was seeking a contract equal to the one that USC had paid the Head Men's Basketball Coach" based on her outstanding record and the success of the women's basketball program at USC. She also requested a higher salary for the assistant coaches of the women's basketball team. According to Coach Stanley, Garrett verbally agreed that she should be paid what Coach Raveling was earning, but he asserted that USC did not have the money at that time. He indicated that "he would get back [to her] with an offer of a multi-year contract ... that would be satisfactory." Garrett alleges in his affidavit, filed in opposition to the issuance of the preliminary injunction, that Coach Stanley told him that "she wanted a contract that was identical to that between USC and Coach Raveling."

On April 27, 1993, Garrett sent a memorandum which set forth an offer of a three-year contract with the following terms:

> 1993–94 Raising your salary to $80,000 with a $6,000 housing allowance.
>
> 1994–95 Salary of $90,000 with a $6,000 housing allowance.
>
> 1995–96 Salary of $100,000 with a $6,000 housing allowance.
>
> Presently, Barbara Thaxton's base salary is $37,000 which I intend to increase to $50,000. It is not my policy to pay associate or assistant coaches housing allowances. Therefore that consideration is not addressed in this offer.

The memorandum concluded with the following words: "I believe this offer is fair, and I need you to respond within the next couple of days so we can conclude this matter. Thank you." According to Garrett, Coach Stanley said the offer was "an insult."

Coach Stanley alleged that, after receiving this offer, she informed Garrett that she "wanted a multi-year contract but his salary figures were too low." Coach Stanley also alleged that she told Garrett she "was to make the same salary as was paid to the Head Men's Basketball Coach at USC." Garrett asserted that Coach Stanley demanded a "three-year contract which would pay her a total compensation at the annual rate of $96,000 for the first 18 months and then increase her total compensation to the same level as Raveling for the last 18 months." He rejected her counter offer.

Coach Stanley alleged that Garrett stated to her that he thought his proposal was fair and he would "not spend a lot of time negotiating a contract." According to Coach Stanley, Garrett's attitude toward her changed and he became "hostile." Garrett told her that she would not be paid the same as Coach Raveling and that she should be satisfied with being the second highest paid women's basketball coach in the PAC–10 Conference.

After this discussion, Coach Stanley retained attorney Timothy Stoner to negotiate the terms of the new contract. Coach Stanley alleged that Garrett rejected her offer "to negotiate a contract that would allow me to gradually work my way to the contract salary and benefits level that USC had provided to George Raveling." Coach Stanley alleged further that Garrett refused to "negotiate in good faith." He withdrew the multi-year contact offer he had previously made to her. Coach Stanley also alleged that Garrett told her attorney that he would offer a one-year contract at a $90,000 salary, plus a $6,000 housing allowance.

Garrett alleges that Stoner proposed a three-year contract with compensation starting at $88,000 in the first year, $97,000 in the second year, and $112,000 in the third year. According to Garrett's affidavit, Coach Stanley also made certain "unprecedented demands, such as: free room and board for her daughter who is anticipated to attend USC as an undergraduate student; radio and television shows where Stanley and the women's team would be spotlighted; and monetary payments tied to conference championships, wins in NCAA play-off games, and coach of the year honors." Garrett indicated that these "incentives" were unacceptable to USC.

On June 21, 1993, Garrett transmitted a written offer of a one-year contract to Mr. Stoner. The offer contains the following terms with reference to salary:

> In consideration of the performance of her duties and responsibilities as Head Women's Basketball Coach, USC shall pay to Stanley an annual salary of $96,000, commencing as of the effective date of this Agreement and payable in equal monthly installments. Stanley shall also be eligible to participate in all of the USC employee benefits as set forth from time to time in the USC Staff Handbook.

Coach Stanley alleges that she contacted Garrett sometime thereafter, "to remind him of the promise he and the University made to me for a multi-year contract that would fairly compensate me for my services and efforts...." Garrett told her that she had until the end of that business day to accept the one-year contract at $96,000 or USC would begin to look at other candidates for her position.

Garrett alleged that he received a telephone call from Coach Stanley on July 13, 1993, in which she "renewed her demand for the three-year contract on the economic terms previously proposed by her counsel." Garrett reiterated that a one-year contract at $96,000 was USC's final offer. Garrett told Coach Stanley that her final decision to reject or accept the offer had to be communicated to him by the end of the day.

Garrett alleged that Coach Stanley did not accept the offer. The following day, Coach Stanley sent a memorandum requesting additional time to consider the offer because she was too distressed to make a decision. Garrett sent a memorandum to Coach Stanley on July 15, 1993, in which he stated, inter alia:

> My job as athletic director is to look out for the best interests of our women's basketball program as a whole, and that is what I have been trying to do all along. The best interests of the program are not served by indefinitely extending the discussions between you and the University, which have already dragged on for weeks. That is why I told you on Tuesday that I needed a final answer that day. Since I did not hear from you, as it now stands the University has no offers on the table. If you want to make any proposals, I am willing to listen. Meanwhile, for the protection of the program, I must, and am, actively looking at other candidates. I am sorry that you feel distressed by this situation. As I have said, I have to do what is best for our women's basketball program. Finally, I was not aware that you were in Phoenix on official University business. Your contract with the University expired at the end of June, and I must ask you not to perform any services for the University unless and until we enter into a new contract. I will arrange for you to be compensated on a daily basis for the time you have expended thus far in July on University business....

Coach Stanley did not reply to Garrett's July 15, 1993 memorandum. Instead, on August 3, 1993, her present attorney, Robert L. Bell, sent a letter via facsimile to USC's Acting General Counsel in which he indicated that he had been retained to represent Coach Stanley. Bell stated he desired "to discuss an amicable resolution of the legal dispute between [his] client and the University of Southern California." Bell stated that if he did not receive a reply by August 4, 1993, he would "seek recourse in court." On August 4, 1993, USC's Acting General Counsel sent a letter to Bell via facsimile in which he stated that "[w]e are not adverse to considering carefully a proposal from you for an 'informal resolution.' "

II. PROCEDURAL BACKGROUND

On August 5, 1993, Coach Stanley filed this action in the Superior Court for the County of Los Angeles. She also applied ex parte for a temporary restraining order (TRO) to require USC to install her as head coach of the women's basketball team.

The complaint sets forth various federal and state sex discrimination claims, including violations of the Equal Pay Act (EPA), 29 U.S.C. § 206(d)(1) (1988), Title IX, 20 U.S.C. § 1681(a) (1988), the California Fair Employment and Housing Act (FEHA), Cal. Gov't Code § 12921 (West Supp.1993), and the California Constitution, Cal. Const. art. 1, § 8 (West 1983). The complaint also alleges common law causes of action including wrongful discharge in violation of California's public policy, breach of an implied-in-fact employment contract, intentional infliction of emotional distress, and conspiracy. As relief for this alleged conduct, Coach Stanley seeks a declaratory judgment that USC's conduct constituted sex discrimination, a permanent injunction restraining the defendants from discrimination and retaliation, an order "requiring immediate installation of [p]laintiff to the position of Head Coach of Women's Basketball at the USC," three million dollars in compensatory damages, and five million dollars in punitive damages.

On August 6, 1993, the Los Angeles Superior Court issued an oral order granting Coach Stanley's ex parte application for a TRO, pending a hearing on her motion for a preliminary injunction. The TRO ordered USC to pay Coach Stanley an annual salary of $96,000 for her services as head basketball coach of the women's team, and all benefits under the 1989 contract were to remain in effect. The record shows that, on June 30, 1993, the date that her four-year employment contract expired, Coach Stanley's salary was $62,000 per year with a $6,000 housing allowance.

On the same day that the TRO was issued, USC removed the action to the District Court for the Central District of California. On August 11, 1993, the district court ordered that the hearing on Coach Stanley's motion for a preliminary injunction be held on August 26, 1993, and that the TRO issued by the state court be extended and remain in effect until that date.

Coach Stanley and Garrett submitted their declarations prior to the August 26, 1993, hearing. At the hearing, Coach Stanley submitted the declaration of her physician, Dr. Elizabeth Monterio, regarding Coach Stanley's emotional state. Coach Stanley also made offers of proof as to the testimony of various witnesses. The court accepted the proffered testimony as true for purposes of ruling on the motion for preliminary injunction. These witnesses included one of the captains of the women's basketball team, two assistant coaches, and Timothy Stoner, Coach Stanley's former counsel.

Pursuant to Coach Stanley's request, the district court reviewed Coach Raveling's employment contract in camera. Later that day, the district court denied the motion for a preliminary injunction.

III. Discussion

The gravamen of Coach Stanley's multiple claims against USC is her contention that she is entitled to pay equal to that provided to Coach Raveling for his services as head coach of the men's basketball team because the position of head coach of the women's team "require[s] equal skill, effort, and responsibility, and [is performed] under similar working conditions." Appellant's Opening Brief at 34. She asserts that USC discriminated against her because of her sex by rejecting her request. She also maintains that USC retaliated against her because of her request for equal pay for herself and her assistant coaches. According to Coach Stanley, USC retaliated by withdrawing the offer of a three-year contract and instead presenting her with a new offer of a one-year contract at less pay than that received by Coach Raveling.

We begin our analysis mindful of the fact that we are reviewing the denial of a preliminary injunction. There has been no trial in this matter. Because the hearing on the preliminary injunction occurred 21 days after the action was filed in state court, discovery had not been completed. Our prediction of the probability of success on the merits is based on the limited offer of proof that was possible under the circumstances. We obviously cannot now evaluate the persuasive impact of the evidence that the parties may bring forth at trial.

A. Standard of Review.

We review the denial of a motion for preliminary injunction for abuse of discretion. Chalk v. United States Dist. Court, 840 F.2d 701, 704 (9th Cir.1988).

Coach Stanley argues that she did not seek a mandatory preliminary injunction. She asserts that she was "not seeking to be instated by USC, she was seeking to continue her employment with USC." Appellant's Opening Brief at 28. Coach Stanley maintains that she requested a prohibitory preliminary injunction and that the district court erred in applying the test for a mandatory preliminary injunction.

A prohibitory injunction preserves the status quo. Johnson v. Kay, 860 F.2d 529, 541 (2d Cir.1988). A mandatory injunction " 'goes well beyond simply maintaining the status quo pendente lite [and] is particularly disfavored.' " Anderson v. United States, 612 F.2d 1112, 1114 (9th Cir.1979) (quoting Martinez v. Mathews, 544 F.2d 1233, 1243 (5th Cir.1976)). When a mandatory preliminary injunction is requested, the district court should deny such relief " 'unless the facts and law clearly favor the moving party.' " Id. Our first task is to determine whether Coach Stanley requested a prohibitory injunction or a mandatory injunction.

Coach Stanley's four-year contract terminated on June 30, 1993. She was informed by Garrett on July 15, 1993, that her employment contract had expired and that she should not perform any services for the university until both parties entered into a new contract. On August 6,

1993, the date this action was filed in state court, Coach Stanley was no longer a USC employee.

Accordingly, an injunction compelling USC to install Coach Stanley as the head coach of the women's basketball team and to pay her $28,000 a year more than she received when her employment contract expired would not have maintained the status quo. Instead, it would have forced USC to hire a person at a substantially higher rate of pay than she had received prior to the expiration of her employment contract on June 30, 1993. The district court did not err in concluding that Coach Stanley was seeking a mandatory injunction, and that her request was subject to a higher degree of scrutiny because such relief is particularly disfavored under the law of this circuit. Anderson, 612 F.2d at 1114.

B. There Has Been No Clear Showing of a Probability of Success on the Merits of Coach Stanley's Claim for Injunctive Relief.

In light of our determination that Coach Stanley requested a mandatory preliminary injunction, we must consider whether the law and the facts clearly favor granting such relief. To obtain a preliminary injunction, Coach Stanley was required to demonstrate that her remedy at law was inadequate. Beacon Theatres, Inc. v. Westover, 359 U.S. 500, 506–07 & n. 8, 79 S.Ct. 948, 954–55 & n. 8, 3 L.Ed.2d 988 (1959) ("The basis of injunctive relief in the federal courts has always been irreparable harm and inadequacy of legal remedies.") (footnote omitted).

In her motion for a preliminary injunction filed in the state court, Coach Stanley requested an order "enjoining the defendants from forcing plaintiff to enter into an unfair and sex discriminatory contract and interfering with plaintiff (sic) continued performance as head coach of women's basketball until such time as the Court may enter a final determination on the merits of this action." As described above, the state court granted a temporary restraining order installing Coach Stanley to the position of head coach of the women's basketball team, at a higher annual salary, 37 days after her four-year contract had expired. On August 6, 1993, this matter was removed to the district court, before the state court could rule on the motion for a preliminary injunction.

The district court ordered USC and Garrett to file their opposition to Coach Stanley's motion for a preliminary injunction on August 18, 1993. On August 24, 1993, Coach Stanley filed her reply. In her reply, Coach Stanley states:

> Thus, Plaintiff, in her motion for TRO, and in this hearing for a preliminary injunction, is simply seeking to maintain the status quo between the parties at the firm and final salary offered by Defendants and to restrain Defendants from wrongfully locking out Plaintiff from the performance of her duties as Head Women's Basketball Coach simply because she is engaged in protected activities, i.e., seeking equal pay and benefits as are provided to the Head Men's Basketball Coach at U.S.C.

Plaintiff's Reply to Defendants' Opposition to Plaintiff's Motion For Preliminary Injunction at 11.

To the extent that Coach Stanley is seeking money damages and back pay for the loss of her job, her remedy at law is adequate. Cf. Anderson v. United States, 612 F.2d at 1115 (mandatory injunction is inappropriate where retroactive promotion and back pay are available if the employee succeeds on the merits). The district court, however, construed the motion for a preliminary injunction as including a request that future discrimination or retaliation based on the fact that she is a woman be enjoined. We do so as well for purposes of resolving the present appeal.

1. Merits of Coach Stanley's Claim of Denial of Equal Pay for Equal Work.

The district court concluded that Coach Stanley had failed to demonstrate that there is a likelihood that she would prevail on the merits of her claim of a denial of equal pay for equal work because she failed to present facts clearly showing that USC was guilty of sex discrimination in its negotiations for a new employment contract. The thrust of Coach Stanley's argument in this appeal is that she is entitled, as a matter of law, "to make the same salary as was paid to the Head Men's Basketball Coach at USC." Appellant's Opening Brief at 9. None of the authorities she has cited supports this theory.

In her reply brief, Coach Stanley asserts that she has "never said or argued in any of her submissions that the compensation of the men's and women's basketball coaches at USC or elsewhere must be identical." Appellant's Reply Brief at 2. Coach Stanley accuses USC of mischaracterizing her position. This argument ignores her insistence to Garrett that she was entitled to the "same salary" received by Coach Raveling. The denotation of the word "same" is "identical." Webster's Third New International Dictionary 2007.

In her reply brief, Coach Stanley asserts that she merely seeks equal pay for equal work. In Hein v. Oregon College of Education, 718 F.2d 910 (9th Cir.1983), we stated that to recover under the Equal Pay Act of 1963, 29 U.S.C. § 206(d)(1) (1988), "a plaintiff must prove that an employer is paying different wages to employees of the opposite sex for equal work." Hein, 718 F.2d at 913. We concluded that the jobs need not be identical, but they must be "substantially equal." Id. (internal quotation and citation omitted).

The EPA prohibits discrimination in wages "between employees on the basis of sex ... for equal work, on jobs the performance of which requires equal skill, effort, and responsibility, and which are performed under similar working conditions." 29 U.S.C. § 206(d)(1) (1988). Each of these components must be substantially equal to state a claim. Forsberg v. Pacific Northwest Bell Tel., 840 F.2d 1409, 1414 (9th Cir.1988).

Coach Stanley has not offered proof to contradict the evidence proffered by USC that demonstrates the differences in the responsibilities of the persons who serve as head coaches of the women's and men's basketball teams. Coach Raveling's responsibilities as head coach of the men's basketball team require substantial public relations and promotional activities to generate revenue for USC. These efforts resulted in revenue that is 90 times greater than the revenue generated by the women's basketball team. Coach Raveling was required to conduct twelve outside speaking engagements per year, to be accessible to the media for interviews, and to participate in certain activities designed to produce donations and endorsements for the USC Athletic Department in general. Coach Stanley's position as head coach did not require her to engage in the same intense level of promotional and revenue-raising activities. This quantitative dissimilarity in responsibilities justifies a different level of pay for the head coach of the women's basketball team. See Horner v. Mary Inst., 613 F.2d 706, 713–14 (8th Cir.1980) (evidence that male physical education teacher had a different job from a female physical education teacher because he was responsible for curriculum precluded finding that jobs were substantially similar; court may consider whether job requires more experience, training, and ability to determine whether jobs require substantially equal skill under EPA).

The evidence presented by USC also showed that Coach Raveling had substantially different qualifications and experience related to his public relations and revenue-generation skills than Coach Stanley. Coach Raveling received educational training in marketing, and worked in that field for nine years. Coach Raveling has been employed by USC three years longer than Coach Stanley. He has been a college basketball coach for 31 years, while Coach Stanley has had 17 years experience as a basketball coach. Coach Raveling had served as a member of the NCAA Subcommittee on Recruiting. Coach Raveling also is the respected author of two bestselling novels. He has performed as an actor in a feature movie, and has appeared on national television to discuss recruiting of student athletes. Coach Stanley does not have the same degree of experience in these varied activities. Employers may reward professional experience and education without violating the EPA. Soto v. Adams Elevator Equip. Co., 941 F.2d 543, 548 & n. 7 (7th Cir.1991).

Coach Raveling's national television appearances and motion picture presence, as well as his reputation as an author, make him a desirable public relations representative for USC. An employer may consider the marketplace value of the skills of a particular individual when determining his or her salary. Horner, 613 F.2d at 714. Unequal wages that reflect market conditions of supply and demand are not prohibited by the EPA. EEOC v. Madison Community Unit Sch. Dist. No. 12, 818 F.2d 577, 580 (7th Cir.1987).

The record also demonstrates that the USC men's basketball team generated greater attendance, more media interest, larger donations, and produced substantially more revenue than the women's basketball team.

The total average attendance per women's team game during Coach Stanley's tenure was 751 as compared to 4,035 for the men's team during the same period. The average sales of season ticket passes to faculty and staff for women's games were 13, while the average sales for men's games were 130. Alumni and other fans, on average, purchased 71 passes for women's home games as compared to over 1,200 season passes for men's home games during the same period. A season pass to the men's home games was more than double the price of a season pass to women's home games.

The same disparity exists with respect to media interest in the men's and women's basketball teams. Television and radio stations paid USC to broadcast the men's basketball games; all of the home games and many games off campus were broadcast on network or cable stations. All of the games were broadcast on commercial radio. Approximately three of the women's basketball games were broadcast on cable stations as part of a contract package that also covered several other sports.

Donations and endowments were likewise greater for the men's basketball team, totalling $66,916 during the time period of Coach Stanley's contract, as compared to $4,288 for the women's basketball team.

The same was true for revenue production. While the women's basketball team produced a total revenue of $50,262 during Coach Stanley's four years, the men's team generated $4,725,784 during the same time period.

As a result, USC placed greater pressure on Coach Raveling to promote his team and to win. The responsibility to produce a large amount of revenue is evidence of a substantial difference in responsibility. See Jacobs v. College of William and Mary, 517 F.Supp. 791, 797 (E.D.Va.1980) (duty to produce revenue demonstrates that coaching jobs are not substantially equal), aff'd without opinion, 661 F.2d 922 (4th Cir.), cert. denied, 454 U.S. 1033, 102 S.Ct. 572, 70 L.Ed.2d 477 (1981).

Coach Stanley did not offer evidence to rebut USC's justification for paying Coach Raveling a higher salary. Instead, she alleged that the women's team generates revenue, and that she is under a great deal of pressure to win. Coach Stanley also alleged that, as head coach, she had won four national women's basketball championships, but that Coach Raveling had won none. In addition, while head coach at USC, Coach Stanley was named PAC–10 Coach-of-the-Year in 1993 and the women's basketball team played in the last three NCAA Tournaments and advanced to the NCAA Sweet Sixteen in 1993 and the NCAA Elite [Eight] in 1992. She also described numerous speaking engagements in which she had participated.

Coach Stanley argues that Jacobs is distinguishable because, in that matter, the head basketball coach of the women's team was not required to produce any revenue. Jacobs, 517 F.Supp. at 798. Coach Stanley appears to suggest that a difference in the amount of revenue generated by the men's and women's teams should be ignored by the court in comparing the respective coaching positions. We disagree.

We agree with the district court in Jacobs that revenue generation is an important factor that may be considered in justifying greater pay. We are also of the view that the relative amount of revenue generated should be considered in determining whether responsibilities and working conditions are substantially equal. The fact that the men's basketball team at USC generates 90 times the revenue than that produced by the women's team adequately demonstrates that Coach Raveling was under greater pressure to win and to promote his team than Coach Stanley was subject to as head coach of the women's team.

Coach Stanley's reliance on Burkey v. Marshall County Board of Education, 513 F.Supp. 1084 (N.D.W.Va.1981), and EEOC v. Madison Community Unit School District No. 12, 818 F.2d 577 (7th Cir.1987) to support her claim of sex discrimination is misplaced. In Burkey, the women coaches were "uniformly paid one-half (1/2) of the salary which male coaches of comparable or identical boys' junior high school sports were paid." Burkey, 513 F.Supp. at 1088. Here, however, Coach Stanley has not shown that her responsibilities were identical.

In Madison, the Seventh Circuit held that the plaintiff established a prima facie EPA claim because "male and female coaches alike testified that the skill, effort, and responsibility required were the same and the working conditions [were] also the same—not merely similar, which is all the Act requires." Madison, 818 F.2d at 583. In the instant matter, the uncontradicted evidence shows that Coach Raveling's responsibilities, as head coach of the men's basketball team, differed substantially from the duties imposed upon Coach Stanley.

Coach Stanley contends that the failure to allocate funds in the promotion of the women's basketball team demonstrated gender discrimination. She appears to argue that USC's failure to pay her a salary equal to that of Coach Raveling was the result of USC's "failure to market and promote the women's basketball team." The only evidence Coach Stanley presented in support of this argument is that USC failed to provide the women's team with a poster containing the schedule of games, but had done so for the men's team. This single bit of evidence does not demonstrate that Coach Stanley was denied equal pay for equal work. Instead, it demonstrates, at best, a business decision to allocate USC resources to the team that generates the most revenue.

The district court also was "unconvinced" by Coach Stanley's claim that USC's disparate promotion of men's and women's basketball teams had "caused the enormous differences in spectator interest and revenue production." The court rejected Coach Stanley's assertion that the differences were due to societal discrimination and that this was evidence of a prima facie case under the EPA. The court reasoned that societal discrimination in preferring to witness men's sports in greater numbers cannot be attributed to USC. We agree. Cf. Madison, 818 F.2d at 580–82 (EPA does not prohibit wages that reflect market conditions of supply and demand, which may depress wages in jobs held mainly by women).

At this preliminary stage of these proceedings, the record does not support a finding that gender was the reason that USC paid a higher salary to Coach Raveling as head coach of the men's basketball team than it offered Coach Stanley as head coach of the women's basketball team. Garrett's affidavit supports the district court's conclusion that the head coach position of the men's team was not substantially equal to the head coach position of the women's team. The record shows that there were significant differences between Coach Stanley's and Coach Raveling's public relations skills, credentials, experience, and qualifications; there also were substantial differences between their responsibilities and working conditions. The district court's finding that the head coach positions were not substantially equal is not a "clear error of judgment." Martin v. International Olympic Comm., 740 F.2d 670, 679 (9th Cir. 1984).

2. *Merits of Coach Stanley's Claim of Retaliation.*

The district court also rejected Coach Stanley's claim that USC terminated her contract or failed to renew her contract in retaliation for her involvement in protected activities. Rather, the court found that her contract had expired and she refused to accept any of the renewal options that USC offered. This finding is not clearly erroneous. Although Coach Stanley contends that she accepted the multi-year contract and continued only to negotiate the terms of the compensation, the district court found this assertion to be "contrary to the weight of the evidence which clearly suggests that Ms. Stanley failed to accept USC's three-year contract because she was dissatisfied with the proposed compensation." The record supports this finding. Coach Stanley rejected the three-year contract offered by USC. She made a counter offer which USC did not accept. The disagreement on the amount of pay precipitated an impasse in the negotiations.

Coach Stanley's argument that Garrett retaliated against her because she demanded equal pay does not square with the evidence she has produced. After she demanded the same pay that Coach Raveling receives, she was offered a multi-year contract at a substantially higher salary than she had received under her original employment agreement. This offer remained open until June 7, 1993. The offer was rejected by Coach Stanley.

Contrary to Coach Stanley's contention, the offer of a one-year contract at an increase of $28,000 in total compensation does not clearly demonstrate retaliation. Rather, it tends to show that USC wanted to retain her services, at a substantial increase in salary. The fact that she was offered a one-year contract after her four-year contract expired does not demonstrate discrimination or retaliation. The record shows Coach Raveling was offered a one-year renewal contract after his initial five-year contract expired.

We express no opinion as to whether Coach Stanley ultimately will establish a prima facie case of sex discrimination or retaliation at trial. We hold only that Coach Stanley has failed to demonstrate that the law and the facts clearly favor her position. See Anderson v. United States, 612 F.2d 1112, 1114 (9th Cir.1979).

C. There Has Been No Showing of a Nexus Between Hardship and the Conduct of USC.

The district court found that Coach Stanley presented sufficient facts from which it could be inferred that she suffered emotional distress, loss of business opportunity, and injury to her reputation following the expiration of her four-year employment contract and the failure of negotiations for a new contract. The court was "persuaded that Coach Stanley [had] sustained her burden to demonstrate a threat of imminent irreparable harm if preliminary injunctive relief [was] denied." Neither party challenges this finding.

The district court also concluded, however, that Coach Stanley failed to demonstrate that the facts clearly show that USC discriminated or retaliated against her on the basis of her gender. As discussed above, Coach Stanley failed to demonstrate that the facts developed in the record and the law clearly favored the issuance of a mandatory preliminary injunction. She has failed to show that the injury she suffered was caused by the alleged wrongful conduct of USC.

D. The District Court's Finding that the Balance of Hardships Do Not Tip Sharply in Coach Stanley's Favor is Not Clearly Erroneous.

Coach Stanley challenges the district court's finding that the balance of hardships did not tip sharply in her favor. She argues that USC presented no evidence to demonstrate any hardship.

Although the district court found that the balance of hardships was "tipped to some degree in [Coach] Stanley's favor[,]" it found that USC would suffer some prejudice if the injunction was granted. Garrett's affidavit and supporting exhibits demonstrate that a preliminary injunction would cause USC hardship. This evidence establishes that Garrett wanted to conclude contract negotiations before the June 30, 1993 expiration of Coach Stanley's contract because

> [t]he summer months are critical for recruiting of student athletes. In addition, it is essential that the head coach be in place by the time the students arrive for the Fall term, which at USC generally is the Monday before Labor Day. This is because the coach is responsible for providing general supervision of and counselling to the student athletes in their academic and personal lives. In addition, practices commence soon after the Fall term begins in preparation for pre-season games.

The district court drew a logical inference of hardship from this evidence. The district court reasoned that issuing the injunction would force USC into a unilateral contract which would provide Coach Stanley with a significant pay increase, but would not require any commitment by Coach Stanley to remain at USC as the head coach of women's basketball. If Coach Stanley were reinstated to the position pursuant to a preliminary injunction, her compensation would be $96,000, a sum she rejected when it was offered to her previously. Accordingly, USC would have a head coach who was dissatisfied with the terms of her employment. Her state of mind, and the impermanence of her position, would likely affect the ability of the school to recruit athletes concerned about the quality and identity of the coaching staff for the next four years. The court concluded that if USC was not permitted to seek out "a replacement of Coach Stanley prior to commencement of the Fall semester, USC will suffer a serious hardship."

The record supports the district court's finding that USC would suffer some hardship if the preliminary injunction issued. In light of the evidence of the impact on the women's basketball program if USC were forced to hire an employee, pendente lite, who claims the school discriminates on the basis of sex, we conclude that the district court did not clearly err in finding that the balance of hardships did not tip sharply in Coach Stanley's favor.

E. The District Court's Finding that the Public's Interest Was Not Served by Granting the Preliminary Injunction Is Not Clearly Erroneous.

Coach Stanley argues that the strong public interest in preventing intentional sex discrimination and discriminatory employment practices weighs in favor of granting the preliminary injunction. We agree with the district court that "[t]his argument would be quite persuasive had [Coach] Stanley come forward with some evidence that her termination was the result of sex discrimination and that she was reasonably likely to prevail on the merits of her discrimination claim."

Coach Stanley failed to present evidence that she would probably prevail on her claims of sex discrimination and retaliation. The evidence also does not establish that the balance of hardships tipped sharply in her favor. Consequently, the district court did not err in concluding that the public's interest in preventing sex discrimination and discriminatory employment practices did not clearly favor granting a mandatory preliminary injunction.

F. Procedural Challenges to the Preliminary Injunction Hearing.

[This portion of the court's opinion, finding that the hearing had not violated the plaintiff's procedural rights, is omitted.]

IV. Conclusion

The district court did not abuse its discretion in denying a mandatory preliminary injunction. Coach Stanley did not meet her burden of demonstrating the irreducible minimum for obtaining a preliminary injunction: "that there is a fair chance of success on the merits." Martin v. International Olympic Comm., 740 F.2d at 675. Because mandatory preliminary injunctions are disfavored in this circuit, we are compelled to review the record to determine whether the facts and the law clearly favor Coach Stanley. Anderson, 612 F.2d at 1114. The evidence offered at the hearing on the motion for a preliminary injunction demonstrated that Coach Stanley sought pay from USC equal to Coach Raveling's income from that university, notwithstanding significant differences in job pressure, the level of responsibility, and in marketing and revenue-producing qualifications and performance. A difference in pay that takes such factors into consideration does not prove gender bias or violate the Equal Pay Act. The unfortunate impasse that occurred during the negotiations for the renewal of the employment contract of an outstanding basketball coach followed the offer of a very substantial increase in salary—not sex discrimination or retaliation. Because Coach Stanley failed to demonstrate that the law and the facts clearly favor her position, the judgment is AFFIRMED.

Notes

1. As *Lee* demonstrates, courts will not permit bad coaches to hide behind unsubstantiated claims of discrimination. Nevertheless, prejudice often plays a role in hiring. In 1992, for example, James Jackson, an African–American who had been turned down for numerous coaching jobs in the World League of American Football, filed a lawsuit against the NFL (the WLAF's parent). Although Jackson had a strong case, his action fizzled after the NFL was dismissed as a defendant. *See Jackson v. National Football League*, 1994 WL 282105 (S.D.N.Y.1994). In January 1998, the possibility of filing a similar lawsuit was discussed privately by several of the NFL's African–American assistant coaches. The idea was not pursued, however, out of fear that anyone participating as a plaintiff would do irreparable harm to his future. *See further* Mike Freeman, *Black Coaches Are Angry with NFL Over Hiring*, N.Y. Times, Jan. 20, 1998, at C2.

2. Besides racial prejudice, African–Americans face a second hurdle: most teams prefer to hire candidates who possess head coaching experience. As a result, having any sort of a record, even a losing one, is preferable to having no record at all. *See further* Jerry Magee, *It's Time to Play Musical Chairs, Coaches Edition*, San Diego Union–Trib., Jan. 5, 1997, at C2.

3. As in other close-knit professions, nepotism sometimes occurs in coaching. While such hiring normally consists of fathers giving jobs to their sons, instances of brothers employing brothers also can be found. For a further look at the subject, see Scott MacKay, *Like Father, Like Son? Nepotism Rule Could Block Harrick From Hiring His Son*, Providence (R.I.) J.-Bull., June 26, 1998, at 1A.

4. In response to cases like *Stanley*, the EEOC in October 1997 issued guidelines to help clarify how the Equal Pay Act is to be applied to coaches. Under the new standards, males and females are to be compared on the basis of their duties and not their sports. *See further* Carol Slezak, *No Excuses Left for Coaches' Pay Gap*, Chi. Sun–Times, Nov. 12, 1997, at 140 (noting that female coaches typically earn 37% less than their males counterparts), and Mark Asher, *EEOC Gives Guidelines on Pay for Coaches*, Wash. Post., Nov. 5, 1997, at C1 (explaining schools now will have to provide a reason other than gender for salary differences).

5. In recent years, the incomes of many coaches have risen dramatically. As a result, it is becoming increasingly common to find coaches earning in excess of $1 million a year, and some, like Rick Pitino (Boston Celtics—$7 million) and Pat Riley (Miami Heat—$3 million), are paid considerably more.

See further Peter Spiegel, *Cashing In*, Forbes, Dec. 15, 1997, at 176 (professional sports), and Steve Wilstein, *Coaches Line the Road to Riches*, Bergen (N.J.) Record, Jan. 1, 1997, at S5 (college sports). Moreover, successful coaches—such as Bills Parcells, Jim Leyland, and Mike Holmgren—often are the subject of intense bidding wars. *See further Eckles v. Sharman*, 548 F.2d 905 (10th Cir.1977) (dispute between the Utah Stars and the Los Angeles Lakers over Bill Sharman after he won the 1971 ABA championship), and Mark A. Conrad, *Mike Keenan's Power Play—A Slap Shot Against the Rangers and a Slap on the Wrist by the NHL*, 5 Seton Hall J. Sport L. 637 (1995) (dispute between the New York Rangers and the St. Louis Blues over Mike Keenan after he won the 1994 Stanley Cup).

6. While attention normally is focused on the earnings of head coaches, in January 1998 the spotlight temporarily shifted to entry-level coaches. Agreeing with a lower court, a federal appeals panel struck down an NCAA rule restricting the salaries of such assistants to $16,000 per year. *See Law v. National Collegiate Athletic Ass'n*, 134 F.3d 1010 (10th Cir.), *cert. denied*, 119 S.Ct. 65 (1998). In March 1999, the NCAA agreed to settle the case by paying $54.5 million. *See further Coaches NCAA Settle on $54.5 Million*, Atlanta J. & Const., Mar. 10, 1999, at 2D.

Problem 35

To increase interest in the minority community, a basketball team hired an African–American to replace one of its white assistant coaches. If the former employee sues the team for racial discrimination, how should the court rule? *See Scholz v. RDV Sports, Inc.*, 710 So.2d 618 (Fla.Dist.Ct.App.), *review denied*, 718 So.2d 170 (Fla.1998).

C. FIRING DECISIONS

As the preceding materials have shown, teams are expected to follow the law when hiring their coaching staffs. Predictably, this same rule applies to termination decisions.

DELI v. UNIVERSITY OF MINNESOTA

511 N.W.2d 46 (Minn.Ct.App.1994).

FLEMING, Judge.

Relators Katalin Deli and Gabor Deli were discharged from their employment at the respondent University of Minnesota by Chris Voelz, Director of the Women's Inter-collegiate Athletics. Their separate grievances contesting Voelz's decision were consolidated, and a hearing was held before a three-person panel appointed by the University's Academic Staff Advisory Committee.

In letters to University President Nils Hasselmo, the panel concluded that Gabor Deli's termination should be upheld, but that just cause for Katalin Deli's termination did not exist. The panel recommended that Katalin Deli be reinstated.

President Hasselmo recused himself from review of the panel's recommendations, and appointed Elton A. Kuderer, Chairman of the

Board of Regents, to issue final decisions in the matters. Following his review of the record, Regent Kuderer concluded that just cause existed for both dismissals.

Katalin and Gabor Deli have filed separate petitions for certiorari, which have been consolidated by this court. They question whether "just cause" existed for their dismissals and whether the procedures which were followed were fair. We affirm the University's decisions.

FACTS

Husband and wife Gabor and Katalin Deli emigrated to the United States from Hungary in 1971. In 1973, Katalin Deli became the head women's gymnastics coach at the University. Gabor Deli was hired in 1976 as an assistant gymnastics coach.

On July 1, 1990, Katalin Deli's contract was renewed for a three-year term. The contract specifically stated Katalin Deli's employment was governed by University rules and regulations "as fully described in that certain policy manual entitled University of Minnesota Academic Professional and Administrative Staff Policies and Procedures, * * * (the 'Manual')."

The contract further provided that it could be terminated by the University "in accordance with the policies and procedures contained in the Manual." The Manual, in turn, provided that an employee could be dismissed for "just cause." While the Manual did not specifically define just cause, it was defined by Katalin Deli's contract as including but not limited to various violations of NCAA rules or

> e. Failure by Deli to perform the duties assigned under the terms of this Agreement.

Katalin Deli's duties under the contract included "[p]ositively representing the University and the University's athletic programs in private and public forums" and "[s]uch other duties as may be assigned by the Director."

Gabor Deli had a year-to-year appointment with the University. Gabor Deli's appointment was also governed by the Manual. Under its terms, he could be terminated for just cause prior to the expiration date of his appointment. As already noted, the Manual did not define "just cause." Absent just cause, Gabor Deli was entitled to written notice of nonrenewal prior to the end date of his appointment and, based on his years of service, 12–months pay.

In March 1992, Voelz learned of an incident in which a videotape containing sexually explicit scenes of the Delis had been distributed and viewed by several student athletes. Voelz began an informal investigation of the incident; over the next few months, she interviewed student athletes and the Delis. Voelz found that the video had been made by Gabor Deli without his wife's knowledge. Voelz concluded that just cause existed to discharge both of the Delis from their employment.

Before the prehearing conference on the Delis' grievances, the University submitted a list of potential witnesses and copies of its proposed exhibits, which included the notes of Voelz's investigation. At the prehearing conference, the panel requested additional documentation, including

> 4) Reports, letters, etc. involving disciplinary action taken by the University of Minnesota over the past four years involving coaches in both men's and women's athletic programs. (Provided anonymously)
>
> 5) A list of persons in the Academic Professional employment category fired for "just cause" at the University of Minnesota over the past five years.

The panel reminded the parties that it "is only empowered to make a decision on whether there was just cause for the dismissals and whether University policies and procedures were followed." The panel further clarified that it would follow the University of Minnesota Academic Professional and Administrative Personnel Rules of Procedure for Grievance Appeals, July 1987 ("Rules").

Issues

I. Were the procedures which were followed fair and unprejudicial?

II. Did the University provide clear and convincing evidence that Gabor and Katalin Deli were terminated for "just cause?"

Analysis

Our standard of review in certiorari proceedings is limited. We may only question whether jurisdiction was proper, whether the proceedings were regular and fair, and whether the decisions below were arbitrary, oppressive, unreasonable, fraudulent, made under an incorrect theory of law, or without any evidence to support it. Dietz v. Dodge County, 487 N.W.2d 237, 239 (Minn.1992).

I.

The Delis argue that they were prejudiced by Voelz's failure to follow the proper procedure prior to terminating them. The Manual specifically states that an appointing authority must report to and seek the approval of the vice president of academic affairs prior to terminating a staff member for just cause. It further states that "[n]o one is authorized to orally change the policies and procedures set forth in this booklet." Voelz failed to obtain the approval of the senior vice president; rather, she reported the results of her investigation to President Hasselmo and obtained his approval prior to terminating the Delis.

Generally, an agency's decision which is made upon unlawful procedure mandates reversal only if a party's substantial rights have been prejudiced. See Northern Messenger, Inc. v. Airport Couriers, Inc., 359 N.W.2d 302, 305 (Minn.App.1984). The Delis claim that they were prejudiced by Voelz's actions in not seeking the approval of the senior vice president. As Katalin Deli notes in her brief, the most telling statement is that made by Regent Kuderer when he acknowledges that "while it is possible, it is highly unlikely that the [senior vice president] would at any time disagree with the recommendations sanctioned by the President." She insists that had the senior vice president been consulted, he might have arrived at a different decision than Voelz or President Hasselmo. The Delis further argue that, by virtue of his regular approval of termination decisions, the senior vice president was in a position to evaluate their cases as compared to others and decide whether dismissal was the appropriate disposition.

According to the University, the procedure set out in the Manual was established before 1989, when department heads and the athletic directors reported to the senior vice president for academic affairs. In 1989, President Hasselmo directed that the men's and women's athletic directors report directly to him. Thus, President Hasselmo was Voelz's immediate supervisor; the senior vice president had no supervisory control over her. The University, however, fails to explain why the Manual, which was issued in 1990 and revised in 1991, was not amended to reflect this change.

The University further argues that extensive settlement discussions took place between it and the Delis prior to their termination. Since any such settlement would have to be approved by President Hasselmo, it was crucial that he be advised of Voelz's investigation and decisions. Again, this does not explain why Voelz did not seek the senior vice president's approval prior to terminating the Delis.

While we do not condone Voelz's disregard of the proper procedures, we conclude, as did the panel and Regent Kuderer, that her failure to obtain the approval of the senior vice president did not affect the eventual outcome of this case and did not prejudice the Delis. Under the Manual, Voelz could have obtained a "written variance" from the senior vice president to allow her to consult with President Hasselmo. There is nothing to suggest that this approval would have been withheld or otherwise denied, particularly given the fact that Voelz's direct supervisor was not the senior vice president, but President Hasselmo. Under these circumstances, we do not believe the Delis were substantially prejudiced by President Hasselmo's involvement in the decision to terminate them.

The Delis further challenge a number of the procedures followed during the grievance proceedings. They argue that the grievance proceeding was unfair and rendered them unable to effectively challenge the University's decisions to terminate them.

Due process requirements are met in a case such as this when a terminated teacher or employee is given (1) clear and actual notice of the reasons for termination in sufficient detail to enable [the terminated teacher] to present evidence relating to them; (2) notice of both the names of those who have made allegations against the teacher and the specific nature and factual basis for the charges; (3) a reasonable time and opportunity to present testimony in his or her own defense; and (4) a hearing before an impartial board or tribunal. King v. University of Minn., 774 F.2d 224, 228 (8th Cir.1985) (quoting Brouillette v. Board of Directors of Merged Area IX, 519 F.2d 126, 128 (8th Cir.1975)), cert. denied, 475 U.S. 1095, 106 S.Ct. 1491, 89 L.Ed.2d 893 (1986).

The Delis first insist that the University failed to comply with Minn.Stat. § 181.933, subd. 1 (1990) (upon request by terminated employee, employer must inform employee in writing of "truthful reason for the termination"). The Delis further insist that the grievance procedures followed in this case failed to comply with the notice requirements established in King, 774 F.2d at 228.

In response to the Delis' requests for a more complete statement of the charges against them, the University submitted Voelz's termination letters. Prior to the prehearing conference, the University also submitted a list of potential witnesses and copies of its exhibits, which included notes of Voelz's interviews with the student athletes during her investigation. From these documents, the Delis could ascertain the specific nature and factual bases for the charges against them. See Mueller v. Regents of Univ. of Minn., 855 F.2d 555, 559 (8th Cir.1988) (notice letter need not restate details of charges and identity of accusers if such information is ascertainable from other documents and information which has already been provided).

The Delis argue that they were prevented from conducting either formal or informal discovery prior to the hearing. As already noted, the parties exchanged lists of potential witnesses and copies of proposed exhibits prior to the hearing. Given the fact that the panel was limited to addressing whether just cause existed for the University's decisions and whether the proper procedures were followed, additional discovery was not crucial or necessary to the Delis' case. See Surf & Sand Nursing Home v. Department of Human Servs., 422 N.W.2d 513, 520 (Minn.App. 1988) (even where discovery is allowed, agency may decide not to allow it because no material or relevant information could be obtained from the discovery sought), pet. for rev. denied (Minn. June 23, 1988).

The Delis argue that they were hampered by their lack of subpoena power and were unable to compel witnesses to testify. The Delis have failed, however, to identify any witness whom they wished to call but who was unavailable or unwilling to testify. Indeed, the University issued a memo to its staff encouraging those with evidence relevant to the grievance proceedings to testify. In addition, a memo from President Hasselmo reassured staff that those who testified should do so truthfully and without fear of reprisal.

The panel refused to allow the Delis to make their own tape recording of the proceedings. They insist that this was important, because it would have given them an opportunity to review previous testimony and because portions of the testimony are missing from the transcript. There were, however, many individuals present at the hearings taking notes. If any missing testimony was crucial to their cases, the Delis could have prepared a statement under Minn.R.Civ.App.P. 110.03 or 110.04. While the record of the hearings in this case is not perfect, it is extensive, voluminous, and sufficient for our review.

The Delis argue that they were prejudiced when the panel allowed the University to call several rebuttal witnesses who were not included in its original list of potential witnesses. Those witnesses included several women's coaches and a consultant. Because these witnesses were called for the sole purpose of rebutting the Delis' attack of Voelz's management style, they were not relevant to the issues decided by the panel.

The Delis argue the panel improperly rejected computerized hearsay newspaper data, which showed the treatment afforded various coaches when they were subject to charges similar or identical to those involving the Delis. In particular, this data showed that several members of the coaching staff within the men's department had not been terminated or suspended after having violated NCAA rules.

The information sought to be admitted by the Delis is very similar to that contained in documents the University gave to the panel following the prehearing conference. The documents contain records of any disciplinary action over the previous four years taken against coaches in the men's and women's athletic programs, and a list of other persons in the Delis' employment category fired for "just cause" over the previous five years. The panel properly rejected the offered computerized newspaper data as cumulative and repetitive.

Gabor Deli argues he was barred from making appropriate inquiries into the backgrounds of the panel members so that he might challenge them for bias. While he could have challenged the membership of the panel under the Rules, however, he did not do so. In any event, there is no evidence suggesting any panel member was biased.

Gabor Deli argues he was prejudiced during the grievance hearing by the surprise injection of sexually oriented hearsay testimony by Voelz. Gabor Deli, however, did not object to Voelz's testimony during the hearing. In addition, her testimony regarding inappropriate conduct on his part did not affect the outcome of the proceeding; it was not cited by Voelz as a reason for her decision to terminate Gabor Deli, or by the panel or Regent Kuderer as a basis for their decisions upholding Voelz's termination decision.

During the grievance proceeding, the Delis learned that the panel was being advised by an attorney who has represented the University for more than 20 years. The Delis argue that this attorney may have rendered partial advice to the panel because of his financial interest in continuing to represent the University.

Apparently, the panel requested outside counsel to advise it on difficult legal issues that might arise. The record shows that the panel consulted with this attorney on a number of legal issues, including the drafting of a confidentiality agreement. It does not appear that the panel consulted with him regarding the ultimate issue in this case, whether just cause existed to terminate the Delis.

The panel rejected the Delis' attempt to name President Hasselmo as a respondent. The Delis claim that his testimony would have shown that a different employment standard was used in dismissing them than was used with other coaches. In addition, they insist that President Hasselmo played a major role in Voelz's decision to terminate the Delis. However, the Delis never actually requested that President Hasselmo appear as a witness. In addition, the evidence the panel requested fails to support the Delis' assertion that a different standard has been applied to other coaches.

II.

Under the Rules, the University had the burden of proving just cause by clear and convincing evidence. In order to prove a claim by clear and convincing evidence, a party's evidence should be unequivocal and uncontradicted, and intrinsically probable and credible. Kavanagh v. The Golden Rule, 226 Minn. 510, 516–17, 33 N.W.2d 697, 700 (1948).

Minnesota courts have not adopted a standard definition of "just cause." The jury instruction guide offers the following definition of termination for good cause:

> A termination is for good cause if the [employee] breached the standards of job performance established and uniformly applied by the [employer].

4 Minnesota Practice, CIVJIG 663 (Supp.1993). By its terms, this definition of just cause contemplates that an employer treat employees uniformly when applying job standards. Id. Further, under this definition, the termination of an employee for any cause not affecting job performance or otherwise relating to job duties might be considered arbitrary and unreasonable. See Ekstedt v. Village of New Hope, 292 Minn. 152, 162–63, 193 N.W.2d 821, 827–28 (1972) (quoting State ex rel. Hart v. Common Council, 53 Minn. 238, 244, 55 N.W. 118, 120 (1893)).

With respect to the termination of Gabor Deli, the panel concluded only one of Voelz's reasons constituted just cause for his dismissal:

> Item #1—You used University equipment to make videotapes of you and your wife engaged in sexual activity and distributed it to University of Minnesota women's gymnastics student-athletes on two separate occasions. The panel only heard direct testimony related to the second incident. Although use of University equipment violates University policy, this in itself is not grounds for dismissal. The use of the term "distributed" may be incorrect; while Mr. Deli did not consciously distribute the videotape, he allowed it to be discovered by not taking steps to erase it or copy it onto another tape or otherwise prevent it from becoming available to others. Even though the other three items were not sufficient for termination, this

> incident alone would constitute just cause for dismissal. The panel assumes the point of view that coaches and teachers must accept tremendous guidance responsibilities for their students and such irresponsible behavior cannot be tolerated.

In sustaining the panel's decision, Regent Kuderer found that the videotapings were done "intentionally" by Gabor Deli, that the tapings were done on a segment of tapes of gymnastics meets or events which "Gabor Deli knew would be reviewed by the student athletes," and that Gabor Deli gave the videotapes to the students.

The evidence involving the making and distribution of the videotapes is largely undisputed: Gabor Deli admitted that he made the tapes without his wife's knowledge and that the only precaution he took to insure no one else would view the sex scenes was to leave blank spaces after the recorded gymnastics events. He further admitted that he gave the tapes to student athletes to review the gymnastics events.

We believe that this evidence establishes just cause for Gabor Deli's dismissal. Whether intended or not, such serious indiscretions by a person in Gabor Deli's position may be grounds for dismissal. A coach occupies a public position as an ambassador or representative for the University, and the University has a right to expect certain conduct of such persons. Conduct like that exhibited here only served to taint the University's reputation, and rendered Gabor Deli ineffective as its representative.

Perhaps more important, however, was Gabor Deli's role as a teacher of young people. As the panel noted, coaches "must accept tremendous guidance responsibilities for their students and such irresponsible behavior cannot be tolerated." Thus, we conclude that the University proved just cause to terminate Gabor Deli by clear and convincing evidence.

With respect to Katalin Deli's grievance, the panel addressed three of the reasons for Voelz's decision, which the University identified as "significant." The panel concluded that none constituted just cause for termination:

> Item #2—In May 1991 Ms. Deli transported a transfer student athlete to the Olympic Academy in violation of NCAA rules. When an accident occurred in route to the Academy, Ms. Deli, in the presence of other team members, instructed the transfer student to lie about her identity. The panel accepts that Ms. Deli probably told the student to lie and while Panel members do not condone this type of behavior, it in itself does not constitute just cause for termination.
>
> Item #6—Ms. Deli instructed team members in 1990–91 to tell Chris Voelz, Athletic Director, they were travelling to the Academy for practice only three times per week, when in fact they were travelling more often. The testimony the Panel heard indicates there was great variability in the off-campus travel

> arrangements among the various coaches and teams. The women's athletic department was aware the van was being checked out every day and could have investigated this issue at any time. This seemed to be both a safety issue and an authority issue. There was an indication of insubordination; however there are other more appropriate options for handling this behavior and it does not constitute just cause for termination.
>
> Item #9—Ms. Deli failed to have a spotter in the gym at all times pursuant to Ms. Voelz'[s] directions. As with the previous two charges, this seemed to be an issue of insubordination, yet there were also issues of safety that concern the Panel. Again, this was not sufficient for termination.

While Regent Kuderer made findings substantially similar to those made by the panel, he concluded that these three incidents constituted just cause for Katalin Deli's dismissal. In his attached memorandum, he explained:

> Collegiate athletics are supposed to teach student athletes to play by the rules. The conduct of Katalin Deli in directing her students to lie to the Director and to law enforcement people is contrary to the rules and moral values of our society. Such an example is counterproductive, contrary, and just plain wrong. The University has a right to demand high ethical and moral standards and it is apparent from the facts brought forth before the Grievance Panel that Katalin Deli has not met those standards. Katalin Deli was in a position to build character in the student athletes by her example. Lying to authorities and violating the rules are not examples of character building and should not be part of intercollegiate athletics. Her dismissal for cause was justified.

As with the evidence pertaining to the videotapes, the evidence involving these three incidents is relatively undisputed. The issue appears to be one not only of dishonesty, but also of insubordination. Both may be grounds for termination. See, e.g., Mair v. Southern Minn. Broadcasting Co., 226 Minn. 137, 138–39, 32 N.W.2d 177, 178 (1948) (employee must obey reasonable orders that are not inconsistent with his employment contract); Cherveny v. 10,000 Auto Parts, 353 N.W.2d 685, 688 (Minn.App.1984) (employee's dishonesty in investigation by employer constitutes misconduct sufficient to disqualify employee from receiving unemployment benefits).

Again, we believe that this evidence establishes just cause for Katalin Deli's dismissal by clear and convincing evidence. While the panel obviously did not agree that Katalin Deli's conduct was serious enough to warrant dismissal, Voelz's decision was based on her belief that she could no longer trust or work with Katalin Deli. Voelz, who had been Katalin Deli's supervisor since 1988, should be given some discretion in determining whether Katalin Deli's conduct was serious enough to warrant dismissal or whether Voelz could continue to work with Katalin Deli to correct that conduct.

Finally, both of the Delis argue that the University's decisions are arbitrary and unreasonable because it treated them differently than it treated other coaches for similar violations of NCAA rules. The panel and Regent Kuderer, however, essentially agreed with the Delis that the alleged NCAA violations were of minor significance and did not constitute just cause for their terminations. The Delis do not argue that the University retained other coaches after conduct similar to making and distributing sexually explicit videotapes to students, as was the case with Gabor Deli. Neither do the Delis argue that the University retained other coaches after they refused to follow the athletic director's orders, or lied to the athletic director and instructed students to lie, as was the case with Katalin Deli. Indeed, as the panel concluded, the Delis' charges of discrimination were not supported by either the testimony adduced at the hearings or by the documentation provided to the panel.

Decision

The University's decisions terminating Katalin and Gabor Deli for just cause are affirmed.

MADDOX v. UNIVERSITY OF TENNESSEE

62 F.3d 843 (6th Cir.1995).

BROWN, Circuit Judge.

The plaintiff-appellant, Robert Maddox, a former assistant football coach at the University of Tennessee, brought suit against the school, its Board of Trustees, and its athletic director, Doug Dickey (collectively "UT"), under § 504 of the Rehabilitation Act of 1973, as amended, 29 U.S.C. § 701, et seq., and the Americans with Disabilities Act of 1990 ("ADA"), 42 U.S.C. § 12101, et seq., alleging discriminatory discharge on the basis of his disability, alcoholism. The district court granted UT's motion for summary judgment, concluding that Maddox was not terminated solely by reason of, or because of, his handicap, but rather, because of a well-publicized incident in which Maddox was arrested for driving under the influence of alcohol. Maddox appealed. We AFFIRM.

I. Facts

On February 17, 1992, Doug Dickey, acting as UT's athletic director, extended to Maddox an offer of employment as an assistant football coach. The position did not carry tenure and was terminable at will in accordance with the policies of the Personnel Manual. As part of the hiring process, Maddox completed an application. On the line after "Describe any health problems or physical limitations, which ... would limit your ability to perform the duties of the position for which you are applying," Maddox wrote "None." In response to the question "have you ever been arrested for a criminal offense of any kind?" Maddox replied "No." These responses were not accurate. According to what Maddox alleges in this lawsuit, he suffers from the disability of alcoholism. Also, Maddox was arrested three times before 1992, once for possession of a controlled substance, and twice for driving a motor vehicle under the influence of alcohol. As to the first answer, Maddox claims that it is in fact correct because "it has never affected my coaching ability . . . I never drank on the job." As to the second question, Maddox claims that another university employee, Bill Higdon, advised him not to include the information concerning his prior arrests on the application.

On May 26, 1992, after Maddox began working at UT, a Knoxville police officer arrested Maddox and charged him with driving under the influence of alcohol and public intoxication. According to newspaper reports, the accuracy of which is not contested, Maddox backed his car across a major public road at a high rate of speed, almost striking another vehicle. When stopped by the officer, Maddox was combative, his pants were unzipped, and he refused to take a breathalyzer. He also lied to the arresting officer, stating that he was unemployed. This incident was highly publicized, and UT was obviously embarrassed by the public exposure surrounding the event.

Maddox entered an alcohol rehabilitation program at a UT hospital after his arrest. UT first placed Maddox on paid administrative leave. In June 1992, however, Dickey and then Head Coach Johnny Majors determined that the allegations were accurate and jointly issued a letter notifying Maddox that his employment was being terminated. They testified that termination was necessary because of: 1) the criminal acts and misconduct of Maddox; 2) the bad publicity surrounding the arrest; and 3) the fact that Maddox was no longer qualified, in their minds, for the responsibilities associated with being an assistant coach. (In addition to the "coaching" responsibilities on the field, Coach Majors described other essential job functions of an assistant coach as: 1) the recruitment of high school football players, 2) serving as a positive role model for athletes on the university's football team, 3) counseling players on various issues, including the use and abuse of alcohol and drugs, and 4) promoting a positive image as a representative of not only the football program but the university as well.)

Both Dickey and Majors deny that they were aware that Maddox was an alcoholic or that Maddox's alcoholism played any part in the decision to discharge him. Nevertheless, Maddox brought this action alleging that the termination was discriminatory on the basis of his alcoholism in violation of his rights under the Rehabilitation Act and the ADA. UT responded by filing a motion for summary judgment which the district court granted. The court recognized that, under both statutes, a plaintiff must show that he was fired by reason of his disability. In the court's view, summary judgment was appropriate because Maddox could not establish the existence of a genuine issue of material fact with respect to whether he had been fired by reason of his status as an alcoholic rather than by reason of his criminal misconduct. Maddox now appeals.

II. Analysis

Maddox Was Not Terminated Because of His Disability

Maddox raises a number of issues on appeal which he contends show that the district court erred in granting summary judgment to the defendants. Maddox first alleges that the district court erred in analyzing his claim under the Rehabilitation Act. Section 504 of the Act provides, "[n]o otherwise qualified individual with a disability ... shall, solely by reason of her or his disability, be excluded from the participation in, be denied the benefits of, or be subject to discrimination under any program or activity receiving Federal financial assistance." 29 U.S.C. § 794(a).

The ADA parallels the protection of the Rehabilitation Act, prohibiting employers from discriminating "against a qualified individual with a disability because of the disability of such individual in regard to ... discharge of employees." 42 U.S.C. § 12112(a). The district court held that its reasoning with respect to the Rehabilitation Act claim applied with equal force to the ADA claim. We agree and will therefore review the respective claims accordingly.

Thus, in order to establish a violation of the Rehabilitation Act, a plaintiff must show: (1) The plaintiff is a "handicapped person" under the Act; (2) The plaintiff is "otherwise qualified" for participation in the program; (3) The plaintiff is being excluded from participation in, being denied the benefits of, or being subjected to discrimination under the program solely by reason of his handicap; and (4) The relevant program or activity is receiving Federal financial assistance. Doherty v. Southern College of Optometry, 862 F.2d 570, 573 (6th Cir.1988), cert. denied, 493 U.S. 810, 110 S.Ct. 53, 107 L.Ed.2d 22 (1989).

It is not disputed in this case that UT constitutes a program receiving Federal financial assistance under the Act. Likewise, we assume, without deciding, that alcoholics may be "individuals with a disability" for purposes of the Act. See Tinch v. Walters, 765 F.2d 599, 603 (6th Cir.1985); Fuller v. Frank, 916 F.2d 558, 560 (9th Cir.1990). Thus, our analysis focuses on whether Maddox is "otherwise qualified" under the Act and whether he was discharged "solely by reason of" his disability. The burden of making these showings rests with Maddox. Chandler v. City of Dallas, 2 F.3d 1385, 1390 (5th Cir.1993), cert. denied, 511 U.S. 1011, 114 S.Ct. 1386, 128 L.Ed.2d 61 (1994).

In support of its motion for summary judgment, UT contended that both factors weighed in its favor. First, Dickey and Majors contended that they did not even know that Maddox was considered an alcoholic in making both the decision to hire and fire him. Moreover, they contended that Maddox was discharged, not because he was an alcoholic, but because of his criminal conduct and behavior and the significant amount of bad publicity surrounding him and the school. UT alternatively contended that Maddox is nevertheless not "otherwise qualified" to continue in the position of assistant football coach.

The district court granted UT's motion for summary judgment, specifically holding that UT did not discharge Maddox solely by reason of his disability. The court found it beyond dispute that Maddox's discharge resulted from his misconduct rather than his disability of alcoholism. The court noted,

> It cannot be denied in this case, Mr. Maddox was charged with ... [driving while under the influence and public intoxication] which would not be considered socially acceptable by any objective standard. The affidavit testimony of Mr. Dickey and Mr. Majors is clear on the point that it was this specific conduct, not any condition to which it might be related, which provoked the termination of Mr. Maddox's employment.

As a result, the court found it unnecessary to decide the alternative ground of whether Maddox was "otherwise qualified."

Maddox contends that the district court erred in distinguishing between discharge for misconduct and discharge solely by reason of his disability of alcoholism. Maddox claims that he has difficulty operating a motor vehicle while under the influence of alcohol and therefore he characterizes drunk driving as a causally connected manifestation of the disability of alcoholism. Thus, Maddox contends that because alcoholism caused the incident upon which UT claims to have based its decision to discharge him, UT in essence discharged him because of his disability of alcoholism. In support, Maddox relies on Teahan v. Metro–North Commuter R.R. Co., 951 F.2d 511, 516–17 (2d Cir.1991), cert. denied, 506 U.S. 815, 113 S.Ct. 54, 121 L.Ed.2d 24 (1992), in which the Second Circuit held that a Rehabilitation Act plaintiff can show that he was fired "solely by reason of" his disability, or at least create a genuine issue of material fact, if he can show that he was fired for conduct that is "causally related" to his disability.

In Teahan, the defendant company discharged the plaintiff because of his excessive absenteeism. The plaintiff responded by claiming that his absenteeism was caused by his alcoholism and therefore protected under the Rehabilitation Act. The district court disagreed and granted summary judgment for the employer because, the court found, Teahan was fired for his absenteeism and not because of his alcoholism. The Second Circuit reversed the district court's grant of summary judgment on appeal, however, rejecting the court's distinction between misconduct (absenteeism), and the disabling condition of alcoholism. The court presumed that Teahan's absenteeism resulted from his alcoholism and held that one's disability should not be distinguished from its consequences in determining whether he was fired "solely by reason" of his disability. Id. Thus, Maddox argues that, in the instant case, when UT acted on the basis of the conduct allegedly caused by the alcoholism, it was the same as if UT acted on the basis of alcoholism itself.

We disagree and hold that the district court correctly focused on the distinction between discharging someone for unacceptable misconduct and discharging someone because of the disability. As the district court noted, to hold otherwise, an employer would be forced to accommodate all behavior of an alcoholic which could in any way be related to the alcoholic's use of intoxicating beverages; behavior that would be intolerable if engaged in by a sober employee or, for that matter, an intoxicated but non-alcoholic employee.

Despite Teahan, a number of cases have considered the issue of misconduct as distinct from the status of the disability. In Taub v. Frank, 957 F.2d 8 (1st Cir.1992), the plaintiff Taub, a heroin addict, brought suit against his former employer, the United States Postal Service, alleging discriminatory discharge under the Rehabilitation Act. The Post Office discharged Taub after he was arrested for possession of heroin for distribution. The district court granted the Post Office's motion for summary judgment and Taub appealed. The First Circuit affirmed and held that Taub could not prevail on his Rehabilitation Act claim because his discharge resulted from his misconduct, possession of heroin for distribution, rather than his disability of heroin addiction. The court reasoned that addiction-related criminal conduct is simply too attenuated to extend the Act's protection to Taub.

The conduct/disability distinction was also recognized by the Fourth Circuit in Little v. F.B.I., 1 F.3d 255 (4th Cir.1993). In Little, the F.B.I. discharged the plaintiff, known by his supervisors to be an alcoholic, after an incident in which he was intoxicated on duty. The district court granted summary judgment in favor of the F.B.I. on the basis that the plaintiff was no longer "otherwise qualified" to serve as an F.B.I. agent. The Fourth Circuit affirmed, noting as an additional basis that the plaintiff's employment was not terminated because of his handicap. Id. at 259. The court noted, "based on no less authority than common sense, it is clear that an employer subject to the ... [Rehabilitation] Act must be permitted to terminate its employees on account of egregious misconduct, irrespective of whether the employee is handicapped." Id.; see also Landefeld v. Marion Gen. Hosp., Inc., 994 F.2d 1178, 1183 (6th Cir.1993) (Nelson, J., concurring) ("The plaintiff was clearly suspended because of his intolerable conduct, and not solely because of his mental condition.").

Moreover, language within the respective statutes makes clear that such a distinction is warranted. Section 706(8)(C) of the Rehabilitation Act states:

> "[I]ndividuals with a disability" does not include any individual who is an alcoholic whose current use of alcohol prevents such individual from performing the duties of the job in question or whose employment, by reason of such current alcohol abuse, would constitute a direct threat to property or the safety of others.

29 U.S.C. § 706(8)(C)(v). Likewise, the ADA specifically provides that an employer may hold an alcoholic employee to the same performance and behavior standards to which the employer holds other employees "even if any unsatisfactory performance is related to the alcoholism of such employee." 42 U.S.C. § 12114(c)(4). These provisions clearly contem-

plate distinguishing the issue of misconduct from one's status as an alcoholic.

At bottom, we conclude that the analysis of the district court is more in keeping with the purposes and limitations of the respective Acts, and therefore, we decline to adopt the Second Circuit's reasoning in Teahan. Employers subject to the Rehabilitation Act and ADA must be permitted to take appropriate action with respect to an employee on account of egregious or criminal conduct, regardless of whether the employee is disabled. In the instant case, for example, while alcoholism might compel Maddox to drink, it did not compel him to operate a motor vehicle or engage in the other inappropriate conduct reported. Likewise, suppose an alcoholic becomes intoxicated and sexually assaults a coworker? We believe that it strains logic to conclude that such action could be protected under the Rehabilitation Act or the ADA merely because the actor has been diagnosed as an alcoholic and claims that such action was caused by his disability.

Pretext

Maddox alternatively contends that even if UT has successfully disclaimed reliance on his disability in making the employment decision, the district court nevertheless erred in determining that Maddox had produced no evidence that the reasons articulated by UT were a pretext for discrimination. A Rehabilitation Act plaintiff may demonstrate pretext by showing that the asserted reasons had no basis in fact, the reasons did not in fact motivate the discharge, or, if they were factors in the decision, they were jointly insufficient to motivate the discharge. Chappell v. GTE Products Corp., 803 F.2d 261, 266 (6th Cir.1986), cert. denied, 480 U.S. 919, 107 S.Ct. 1375, 94 L.Ed.2d 690 (1987).

Maddox first alleges that Dickey and Majors knew that Maddox was an alcoholic. Setting aside for a moment the legal significance of this statement, it is not supported factually in the record. Dickey and Majors, the district court found, had no knowledge of Maddox's previous criminal history prior to the DUI arrest involved here. In fact, Dickey states that if he had known of the prior arrests, he would not have hired him. More importantly, however, assuming that Dickey and Majors did know of Maddox's alcoholism, as we must do on a summary judgment motion, that knowledge does not translate into evidence that alcoholism was the basis for the termination. To the contrary, the university stated that the criminal conduct and the bad publicity surrounding it formed the basis of the termination, which we conclude is sufficient to motivate the discharge.

Maddox also claims that he knew of other coaches in the football program who drank alcohol in public and who were arrested for DUI but who were not discharged. This point is also irrelevant. Whether Maddox had such knowledge is immaterial. There is no evidence in the record establishing that Majors or Dickey had knowledge of the public intoxication of any other coach, or failed to reprimand or terminate any coach who they knew to have engaged in such behavior.

Maddox finally contends that UT's conclusion that he is no longer qualified to be an assistant coach at UT is without merit. Maddox claims that his misconduct did not affect his "coaching" responsibilities because an assistant coach's duties are limited to the practice and playing fields, and do not comprise of serving as a counselor or mentor to the players or serving as a representative of the school. Maddox relies on the fact that none of these functions were explained to him in his formal job description.

We first note that this allegation seems more appropriate for determining whether he was "otherwise qualified" rather than whether he was discharged because of his disability. Nevertheless, Maddox's position is simply unrealistic. It is obvious that as a member of the football coaching staff, Maddox would be representing not only the team but also the university. As in the instant case, UT received full media coverage because of this "embarrassing" incident. The school falls out of favor with the public, and the reputation of the football program suffers. Likewise, to argue that football coaches today, with all the emphasis on the misuse of drugs and alcohol by athletes, are not "role models" and "mentors" simply ignores reality.

The district court's grant of summary judgment in favor of the defendants is AFFIRMED.

Notes

1. Unfortunately, the Delis and Robert Maddox are not the only coaches to have exercised poor judgment:

> In April 1995, Dennis Erickson, newly installed as the head coach of the Seattle Seahawks, was arrested for driving with a blood alcohol level twice the legal limit. To avoid prosecution, Erickson agreed to enter a two-year alcohol abuse counseling program. *See further* Adam Shefter, *Incident with Erickson Adds to Seattle's Woes*, Rocky Mtn. News, May 7, 1995, at 6B.
>
> In May 1995, Atlanta Braves manager Bobby Cox was arrested for striking his wife during a domestic dispute. Pamela Cox subsequently revealed she had covered up similar incidents in the past to protect her husband from embarrassing media exposure. *See further Atlanta Baseball Manager Charged in Wife Beating*, S.F. Examiner, May 8, 1995, at A2.
>
> In August 1997, Dallas Cowboys head coach Barry Switzer was stopped at the Dallas–Fort Worth airport when he tried to board an airplane with a loaded (and unlicensed) .38–caliber revolver. Switzer, who later claimed he had forgotten he had the gun on him, was fined a record $75,000 by team owner Jerry Jones and pled guilty to a weapons misdemeanor. *See further* Mike Cochran, *Switzer Pleads Guilty to Gun Charge*, Baton Rouge Advocate, Dec. 3, 1997, at 8D.
>
> In May 1998, coaches Pat Riley and Jeff van Gundy were rebuked by NBA Commissioner David Stern for their behavior during a fight between the Miami Heat and New York Knicks.

Similar incidents had marred the clubs' 1997 playoff series. *See further Riley, van Gundy Get Stern Lecture on Brawling*, Sacramento Bee, May 20, 1998, at E6.

In July 1998, Bruno Roussel, coach of Festina, the top-ranked team in the Tour de France, was suspended by the International Cycling Union. According to published reports, Roussel was alleged to have procured performance-enhancing drugs for his riders. *See further* Samuel Abt, *Coach of Team in Tour Suspended Over Drug Questions*, N.Y. Times, July 17, 1998, at C18.

In December 1998, Sadaharu Oh, Japan's all-time home run leader and current manager of the Daiei Hawks of the Pacific League, came under a cloud of suspicion during an investigation into cheating. Oh could be permanently banned from Japanese baseball for failing to prevent the scandal, which allegedly involved Daiei employees stealing signs from opposing catchers by watching strategically-placed television monitors. *See further Sign–Stealing Scam Involves Oh*, N.Y. Times, Dec. 4, 1998, at C29.

2. The negative publicity coaches receive is not always warranted. In *In re Disciplinary Action Against Peterson*, 584 N.W.2d 773 (Minn.1998), for example, the Minnesota Supreme Court publicly reprimanded and placed on probation a lawyer named Lori C. Peterson for her attempt to blackmail Minnesota Vikings head coach Dennis Green.

In 1992, Green and a woman with whom he had had an affair entered into an agreement under which Green paid the woman and promised not to discuss the relationship. In 1996, the woman, wrongly believing Green had violated the arrangement, retained Peterson to sue Green. After the case was dismissed, the trial judge fined Peterson $10,000 for first threatening Green with public exposure if he did not settle and then filing a complaint that contained inflammatory and irrelevant allegations and sought exorbitant damages. The judge's decision triggered an investigation by the State Bar's Office of Lawyers Professional Responsibility and eventually led to the Minnesota Supreme Court's order. *See further* James Walsh, *Supreme Court Reprimands Lawyer Lori Peterson*, Minneapolis Star Trib., Oct. 16, 1998, at 3B.

3. It is not unusual for the firing of a coach to result in both expensive litigation and bad press. In April 1998, for example, the NCAA was forced to issue an apology and pay $2.5 million to settle a lawsuit brought by Fresno State basketball coach Jerry Tarkanian. In his complaint, Tarkanian had accused the NCAA of engaging in a 26–year campaign to run him out of college coaching. *See* John Nadel, *NCAA Settles with Tarkanian for $2.5 Million*, Springfield (IL) St. J.-Reg., Apr. 3, 1998, at 20. Similarly, in September 1998, Notre Dame was ordered to pay $566,000 for discharging Joseph Moore, an assistant football coach, in violation of the Age Discrimination in Employment Act. *See further Moore v. University of Notre Dame*, 22 F.Supp.2d 896 (N.D.Ind.1998).

4. Although firing remains the ultimate sanction, teams need not go that far to register their displeasure with a coach's performance. Other options include: reduction in pay, suspension, public reprimand, loss of

perquisites, and decreased autonomy. For a further discussion, see Michael S. Selvaggi, *The College v. The Coach*, 3 Seton Hall J. Sport L. 221 (1993).

5. Sometimes, of course, coaches get fired even though they have done nothing wrong. Teams that want to send a message, appease critics, or signal a change in direction frequently do so by firing their coaches. Immediately after the NFL's 1998 regular season ended, for example, five different clubs took this step. *See further* Mike Freeman, *With Season Over, Purge Claims 5 N.F.L. Coaches*, N.Y. Times, Dec. 29, 1998, at C21. As a result, coaches are rarely surprised when their tenures turn out to be short-lived. *See further* Martin J. Greenberg, *College Coaching Contracts: A Practical Perspective*, 1 Marq. Sports L.J. 207 (1991), and Dan Cook, *NBA Coach's Future? It's in the Stars*, San Antonio Express–News, Feb. 21, 1997, at 1C.

6. In addition to having to placate management and fans, coaches also must stay on the good side of the team's star player. The New York Rangers fired Roger Neilson, for example, at the insistence of Mark Messier. Likewise, the Orlando Magic dumped Brian Hill in response to Penny Hardaway's complaints and the Buffalo Sabres cast out Ted Nolan to mollify Dominik Hasek. *See further* Alan Greenberg, *Players Call the Shots, Not Coaches*, Hartford Courant, Mar. 2, 1997, at E8.

Problem 36

Immediately before a tough game, a basketball coach told his team to "go out and play like a bunch of n-----s." When the university president learned of the incident, he fired the coach on the spot. If he sues, claiming the dismissal violates both the First Amendment and academic freedom, how should the court rule? *See Dambrot v. Central Michigan University*, 55 F.3d 1177 (6th Cir.1995).

D. OBLIGATIONS TO PLAYERS

In recent years, an increasing number of players have sued their coaches. Such actions normally are grounded on one of four theories: broken promise, improper training methods, inadequate supervision, or sexual abuse.

1. BROKEN PROMISE

To succeed on this type of claim, a player must show he or she reasonably relied on a coach's promise and, as a result, suffered a legal detriment. As the following incident demonstrates, such cases pose enormous burden of proof problems for plaintiffs.

FORTAY v. UNIVERSITY OF MIAMI

1994 WL 62319 (D.N.J.1994).

WOLIN, District Judge.

In August of 1993, Plaintiff Bryan Fortay ("Fortay") instituted this well-publicized civil proceeding against the University of Miami and the other named defendants. Fortay's twenty-five count complaint contains myriad claims sounding in tort, contract and civil rights. Certain defendants have responded to Fortay's complaint with motions to dismiss for lack of personal jurisdiction or improper venue, or in the alternative, to transfer the action to the Southern District of Florida. Under Federal Rule of Civil Procedure 12, the moving defendants also request dismissal of certain or all counts of Fortay's complaint for failure to state a claim, and, should any counts survive 12(b)(6) scrutiny, an order for a more definite statement. The moving defendants and Fortay have briefed the issues extensively. The Court heard oral argument on February 14, 1994, having previously advised the parties that it would hear argument only on the issues of jurisdiction and venue.

Given that questions of jurisdiction and venue require fact intensive analysis, the Court eschews a lengthy summary of the facts in favor of a detailed parsing below of Fortay's complaint and the affidavits submitted on these motions. In short, Fortay's complaint recounts a story about a promising young high school quarterback, who is recruited and signed to a football scholarship at the University of Miami, which perennially fields one of the top collegiate football teams in the country. Promised the starting quarterback job, Fortay views his college opportunity as a stepping stone to the National Football League ("NFL"). Ultimately, the university and its coaching staff renege on their promises and pass over Fortay for the starting position. Meanwhile, Fortay becomes unwittingly ensnared and implicated in the schemes of his guidance counselor who has been defrauding the federal government of financial aid money. The university denies wrongdoing and throws Fortay to prosecutorial wolves. Fortay avoids indictment by entering a pre-trial diversion program and cooperating with the government. By this time, Fortay has left Miami and transferred to Rutgers University in New Jersey, losing a year of football eligibility in the process.

The fact that Fortay's story has transmogrified into a twenty-five count civil action not only reflects the antagonistic elements of modern college sports—amateur student athletes lured to perform in a circus of big money gate receipts, television, and endorsements—but suggests, as Fortay's claims seek a toehold in the world of contract and tort law, that the tension is such that it may no longer be wished away. There is too much at stake—so much money that a sea of green washes away the vestigial illusion that major college sports are not simply a farm system for the professional leagues.

The Court offers this observation not to cast judgment on the status of modern college athletics, but merely to suggest some explanation why the complaints of the disgruntled student-athlete have finally reached the courthouse doors.

Discussion

The moving defendants ask the Court to dismiss Fortay's complaint for lack of personal jurisdiction or improper venue, pursuant to Rule 12(b)(1) or 12(b)(3), respectively, of the Federal Rules of Civil Procedure. Alternatively, they request that the action be transferred to the Southern District of Florida (1) under 28 U.S.C. § 1406 because venue is improper, or (2) under 28 U.S.C. § 1404 in the interests of justice and convenience.

In considering these motions, the Court keeps in mind the three relevant burdens of proof. Where defendant raises a proper jurisdictional defense, the plaintiff bears the burden of demonstrating jurisdictional facts via sworn affidavits or other competent evidence. Time Share Vacation Club v. Atlantic Resorts, Ltd., 735 F.2d 61, 63 (3d Cir.1984). Where venue is challenged as improper, the burden is on the plaintiff to present facts sufficient to rebut the defense. Banque de la Mediterranee–France, S.A. v. Thergen, Inc., 780 F.Supp. 92, 94 (D.R.I.1992). Where transfer of venue is sought pursuant to 28 U.S.C. § 1404, the moving party carries the burden of establishing that transfer is warranted and generally must submit "adequate data of record" to facilitate the court's analysis. Ricoh Co. v. Honeywell, Inc., 817 F.Supp. 473, 480 (D.N.J. 1993).

Accordingly, the parties have submitted affidavits, exhibits and certifications in support of their respective positions on jurisdiction and venue. Without further delay, the Court turns to these materials and to the complaint to ascertain those facts relevant to the pending motions.

A. The Parties

1. Plaintiff

Plaintiff Bryan Fortay is a citizen of the State of New Jersey, residing in East Brunswick, New Jersey. (Fortay Affidavit ("BF Affidavit") p 2) In February, 1989, Fortay, the starting quarterback at East Brunswick High School, and consensus high school All–American, chose to accept a scholarship from the University of Miami to study and to play football. (BF Affidavit pp 22; Complaint p I–1) Fortay was enrolled as [a] student-athlete at the university from the fall of 1989 until August 1991, when he transferred to Rutgers University in New Jersey ("Rutgers"), where he currently attends college. (Complaint p 1; BF Affidavit p 2)

2. Defendants

Defendant University of Miami ("UM"), located in Coral Gables, Florida, is a private university with a faculty of approximately 1700 and with an enrollment in excess of 13,700 students, including undergraduate, graduate, law and medical students. (Complaint pp 2–3)

Defendant Edward T. Foote, II ("Foote") is a citizen and resident of the State of Florida, Dade County. (Foote Affidavit p 4) Foote is the President of UM. (Id. p 5; Complaint p 4)

Defendant Sam Jankovich ("Jankovich") is a citizen of the State of Washington, who resides in Florida during the winter months and in Idaho for the remainder of the year. (Jankovich Affidavit p 4) He was the Athletic Director at UM during the academic years 1989–90 and 1990–91. (Complaint p 5)

Defendant Anna Price ("Price") is a citizen and resident of the State of Florida, Dade County. (Price Affidavit p 4) She is the Assistant Athletic Director for Academic Support at UM. (Id. p 5; Complaint p 6)

Defendant Dave Scott ("Scott") is a citizen and resident of the State of Florida, Dade County. (Scott Affidavit p 4) He is the Assistant Director for Operations at UM. (Id. p 5; Complaint p 7)

Defendant Doug Johnson ("D. Johnson") is a citizen and resident of the State of Florida, Dade County. (D. Johnson Affidavit (Sept. 13, 1993) p 4) He is the Associate Athletic Director for Internal Operations and Compliance at UM. (Id. p 5; Complaint p 8)

Defendant Tony Russell ("Russell") was the Assistant Director of the Academics Athletic Department at UM during the academic years 1989–90 and 1990–91.

Defendant Dennis Erickson ("Coach Erickson") is the Head Football Coach at UM. (Coach Erickson Affidavit p 1; Complaint p 10) Since being hired to this position in 1989, Coach Erickson has been a permanent resident of Miami, Florida. (Coach Erickson Affidavit p 2)

B. Statement of Facts

The Court endeavors to set forth the facts of this case which are relevant to the pending motions. The following is gleaned mostly from Fortay's complaint and the affidavits in opposition to defendants' motions. However, the Court will note where defendants have rebutted Fortay's allegations via affidavit.

1. Recruitment and Signing by UM

In the spring of 1988, Fortay's junior year of high school, most of the major college football teams began to initiate recruiting contacts with Fortay through letters, brochures and occasional telephone calls to his home in East Brunswick, New Jersey. (BF Affidavit pp 3–4) UM's first correspondence arrived at the Fortay home in April, 1988. (Id. p 5)

Over the course of 1988, Fortay would receive numerous letters from UM personnel touting UM's (1) elite football program and its penchant for developing NFL-quality quarterbacks (id., Exhibits A, D, H–J), (2) academic requirements for scholarship athletes (id., Exhibits B–C), (3) health and training facilities (id., Exhibits E, G), and (4) academic and vocational resources (id., Exhibit F).

During the first weekend of December, 1988, Fortay visited UM to meet the staff and view the school. (BF Affidavit p 14) On or about December 20, 1988, Fortay made a verbal commitment to attend UM, which the UM football staff acknowledged by mailgram and letter. (Id. p 18, Exhibits K–L; Peter Fortay Affidavit ("PF Affidavit") p 13)

Prior to making the verbal commitment, Fortay received visits at home in New Jersey (1) on two occasions by Dave Campo ("Campo"), defensive backfield coach for UM's football team, and (2) on one occasion, collectively, by Campo, Jimmy Johnson ("Coach Johnson"), UM's head football coach, Gary Stevens ("Stevens"), and Art Kehoe ("Kehoe"). (BF Affidavit pp 13, 15; PF Affidavit pp 10–11; Kehoe Affidavit pp 3–4; Campo Affidavit pp 3–5) During the group visit to the Fortay home, certain promises were made to Fortay, the extent and subject of which are in dispute.

According to the Fortays, during this meeting with Coach Johnson and the others, Fortay was told that if he made a verbal commitment to Miami, recruitment of other quarterbacks in his class would cease. (BF Affidavit p 16; PF Affidavit p 11) According to Stevens, Campo and Kehoe, none of the UM personnel guaranteed Fortay the starting quarterback position and a career in the NFL, but merely promised a scholarship, the opportunity to compete for the starting job early in his career and the chance to travel with the team. (Campo Affidavit p 5; Kehoe Affidavit pp 4–5; Stevens Affidavit (Jan. 5, 1994) p 3)

On February 8, 1989, Fortay and his father, Peter Fortay, met with Stevens at East Brunswick High School in New Jersey and signed a Letter of Intent formalizing Fortay's decision to enroll at UM in exchange for an athletic scholarship. (BF Affidavit p 22; PF Affidavit, Exhibits GG, HH)

Never adopted by the NCAA, but utilized by an organization of NCAA schools entitled the Collegiate Commissioners Association, the Letter of Intent was designed to regulate the intense competition amongst member schools for high school recruits. When, after a designated date, a member school signs a recruit to a Letter of Intent, the other schools must cease efforts to recruit that athlete. (Complaint p XII:4–8) As for the recruit, the Letter of Intent is binding as long as a valid recommendation or award of financial aid is presented to the recruit at the time of signing. Once signed, the recruit is subject to the terms of the Letter of Intent, which operate to limit the recruit's athletic eligibility subsequent to a transfer to another school. (PF Affidavit, Exhibit GG)

Fortay made the formal commitment to UM based on the belief that he would be the starting quarterback at UM and the team would be built around him. (BF Affidavit pp 16, 18–19, 21)

After signing the Letter of Intent, Fortay received at home more phone calls and letters from UM personnel with information regarding work-out schedules, housing, enrollment, class schedules and religious worship. (BF Affidavit p 23, Exhibits Q–M)

2. The Coaching Change

In February 1989, just after Fortay had signed the Letter of Intent, Coach Johnson announced that he was leaving UM for the head coaching job with the NFL's Dallas Cowboys. (BF Affidavit p 24) Following Coach Johnson's announcement, Fortay received, at home, letters from Coach Johnson and defendant Jankovich and nearly daily phone calls from defendant Scott, designed mostly to reassure Fortay about his decision to enroll at UM and to apprise him of the status of the coaching staff. (BF Affidavit pp 25–27, Exhibits R–S; PF Affidavit pp 17).

Prior to March 8, 1988, UM announced the hiring of Coach Erickson to replace Coach Johnson at the helm of the UM football program. (BF Affidavit p 29; PF Affidavit p 20) Following UM's announcement, Coach Erickson contacted Fortay by phone and by letter to assure him that the commitments, goals and play system of Coach Johnson's regime would not be changed. (BF Affidavit pp 29–30)

Unhappy with this change in circumstances, Fortay and his father travelled to Miami to procure a release from the Letter of Intent. (BF Affidavit p 31; PF Affidavit p 21) They met with Coach Erickson, who informed Fortay that he would be the starter for at least two years in a system better suited for entry into the NFL. (BF Affidavit p 32; PF Affidavit pp 22, 26, 27) Despite Erickson's assurances, Peter Fortay met with defendant Jankovich to request a release from the Letter of Intent. Jankovich assured Fortay's father about Coach Erickson and his son's future. (PF Affidavit p 25) UM refused to release Fortay from the Letter of Intent. (PF Affidavit p 29)

In April 1989, Fortay decided to honor the Letter of Intent rather than to enroll elsewhere and lose two years of eligibility. (PF Affidavit p 29) Fortay matriculated in the fall of 1989.

3. *Fortay at UM: A Football Dream Gone Bust*

During his first collegiate season, Fortay was "red-shirted," meaning that he was not on the active roster, but would be able to practice and learn the offense without losing a year of eligibility. However, Fortay lost his red-shirt status, and a year of eligibility, after UM's starting quarterback suffered an injury and Fortay played in two regular season games. (BF Affidavit pp 33–34) Contrary to Erickson's assurances, he received no more playing time that season beyond his appearances in the two games. (Id. p 35)

During spring practices in 1990, Fortay was competing with Gino Torretta for the back-up position. Apparently, the competition for the spot was intense. Fortay became dissatisfied after sensing that Coach Erickson favored Torretta. Fueled by his son's concerns, Peter Fortay flew to Miami to discuss the situation with Coach Erickson, who again made assurances as to Fortay's future. (BF Affidavit pp 37–40; PF Affidavit pp 30–34, 35). Subsequently, to save Fortay's eligibility, Coach Erickson red-shirted Fortay for the 1990 season. (BF Affidavit p 41)

Ultimately, Torretta was named UM's starting quarterback for the 1991 season, despite the fact that Fortay outperformed Torretta in spring and fall practices. (BF Affidavit pp 42–44) Five days later, Fortay packed his bags and transferred to Rutgers, losing a year of eligibility in the process under NCAA regulations. (BF Affidavit p 47)

4. *Fortay at UM: The Pell Grant Scandal*

Fortay first met defendant Russell in the spring of 1988, when Fortay travelled to Miami to visit UM. (BF Affidavit p 48) After matriculating at UM, Fortay was assigned to Russell, who was to provide Fortay guidance and assistance. In the fall of 1989, Russell asked Fortay if he had applied for a Pell Grant, a form of federal financial aid. Fortay had not so applied, and Russell advised him that he was eligible for the aid based upon his athletic and scholarship status. (BF Affidavit pp 49–51)

Subsequently, Russell assisted Fortay in filling out a Pell Grant application. Fortay gave him $75 dollars, which Russell had said was the required processing fee. A few months later, Fortay received a check from UM. Fortay and Russell went through the same procedure the following fall. (BF Affidavit pp 53–57)

In 1991, Russell came under investigation by the federal government for illegally obtaining the financial aid. Subsequently, Fortay and other UM students and football players were implicated in the scheme. In July 1991, Coach Erickson and defendant D. Johnson convened a team meeting to discuss the Pell Grant scandal and assure those involved that UM would resolve the issues. (BF Affidavit pp 58–59) Later that summer, D. Johnson approached Fortay at summer camp and asked him to talk to investigators about the scandal. Fortay complied and was interrogated by FBI agents without counsel and without any representative of UM present. (Id. pp 61–64)

Having returned to New Jersey to attend Rutgers, Fortay was threatened with prosecution for his involvement in the scandal. Eventually, he avoided prosecution by entering a pre-trial diversion program under which he was required to meet monthly with a probation officer and make restitution for the monies illicitly received. (BF Affidavit pp 65–67)

C. The Complaint

Based on the foregoing allegations and averments, Fortay filed a twenty-five count complaint in search of actual, compensatory and punitive damages for the broken promises of stardom at UM and in the NFL and the injury, embarrassment and humiliation suffered as a result of the Pell Grant scandal. While finding Fortay's complaint exasperatingly cumbersome and unartful, the Court will attempt to outline the document and Fortay's legal claims and theories.

In Count One, Fortay asserts UM and the individual defendants negligently misrepresented that he would become UM's starting quarterback, luring him to sign with and enroll at UM.

Count Two alleges that defendant Russell fraudulently misrepresented that Fortay would be eligible for a Pell Grant, and that UM negligently allowed Fortay to meet with federal investigators, without any legal representation, to discuss the Pell Grant scandal.

Count Three alleges that UM and the individual defendants negligently breached a supervisory duty to Fortay by failing to prevent, and accept responsibility for, the Pell Grant scandal.

Count Four contains a request for punitive damages and alleges that defendants, having negligently "lured and courted" Fortay into believing that UM football would lead him to stardom in the NFL, "wantonly and willfully" disregarded Fortay's quarterbacking skills in selecting Torretta for the starting quarterback position in 1991.

Count Five also contains a request for punitive damages and alleges that defendants recklessly allowed Fortay to come under the guidance of Russell, thus exposing Fortay to federal prosecution in the Pell Grant scandal.

Counts Six through Eight allege that prior to December 21, 1988, UM and Fortay entered into a contract under which Fortay would attend UM. Fortay asserts that UM, its athletic department and staff, and the individual defendants breached their contractual duties to plaintiff by violating federal and NCAA regulations and failing to provide Fortay the promised education and athletic training.

Based upon the alleged contract, Count Nine asserts that defendants breached the implied covenant of good faith and fair dealing by failing to supervise Fortay's athletic career and education and by exposing him to the Pell Grant scandal.

Count Ten charges UM with negligent supervision of Russell. This count also includes assertions that UM discriminated against Fortay and intentionally breached its contractual obligations by not elevating him permanently to the starting quarterback position.

In Count Eleven, Fortay seeks to recover from defendants attorney fees and costs incurred as a result of the Pell Grant scandal.

Count Twelve appears to restate Fortay's breach of contract claims and contains a request for damages resulting from the emotional distress, embarrassment and humiliation Fortay has allegedly suffered as a result of defendants' conduct.

Count Thirteen alleges that defendants breached their fiduciary duty to Fortay.

Count Fourteen alleges that defendants intentionally, recklessly and negligently inflicted upon Fortay severe emotional distress through their allegedly outrageous conduct.

Count Fifteen alleges that UM breached its duty to supervise and care for student-athletes, both on and off the field, by allowing Russell to perpetrate his fraud.

On a theory of vicarious liability, Count Sixteen alleges that UM's athletic department and staff breached their duty to supervise Fortay.

Count Seventeen alleges that Russell's actions were reasonably foreseeable, that defendants failed to take measures to prevent Russell's fraud, and, as a result, that defendants are vicariously liable for Russell's actions.

Count Eighteen alleges that Foote, as President of UM, negligently supervised UM's coaches and staff.

Count Nineteen alleges that Fortay and UM entered into an employment agreement under which UM breached its obligations.

Counts Twenty and Twenty–One allege that defendants negligently breached the duties owed to Fortay under the Letter of Intent.

Count Twenty–Two alleges that UM violated NCAA regulations governing a member institution's responsibility for the conduct of its coaching staff.

Count Twenty–Three alleges that UM violated NCAA regulations by disregarding Russell's fraudulent schemes.

Count Twenty–Four alleges that defendants failed to advise Fortay of his constitutional right to counsel prior to his questioning by federal agents.

Count Twenty–Five alleges that UM deprived Fortay of his civil rights under 42 U.S.C. section 1983.

D. Transfer of Venue Under 28 U.S.C. § 1404(a)

Defendants seek a transfer of venue from this Court to the Southern District of Florida under 28 U.S.C. § 1404(a), which provides:

> For the convenience of parties and witnesses, in the interest of justice, a district court may transfer any civil action to any other district or division where it might have been brought.

Fortay does not dispute that this action originally could have been brought in the Southern District of Florida.

The decision whether to transfer an action rests in the sound discretion of the trial court "appraising the practical inconvenience posed to the litigants and to the court should a particular action be litigated in one forum or another." Lony v. E.I. DuPont de Nemours & Co., 886 F.2d 628, 632 (3d Cir.1989); Plum Tree, Inc. v. Stockment, 488 F.2d 754, 756 (3d Cir.1973). In making its determination, the Court will consider certain factors enunciated by the Supreme Court in Gulf Oil Corp. v. Gilbert, 330 U.S. 501, 508–09, 67 S.Ct. 839, 843 (1947). These factors (the "Gulf Oil factors") fall into two groups: those relating to the convenience of the litigants and those affecting the public interest in the fair and efficient administration of justice.

Fortay's Choice of Forum

In weighing the Gulf Oil factors, this Court must generally defer to plaintiff's choice of forum unless the balance is tipped strongly in favor of transfer. See Gulf Oil, 330 U.S. at 508, 67 S.Ct. at 843; Shutte v. Armco Steel Corp., 431 F.2d 22, 24 (3d Cir.1970), cert. denied, 401 U.S. 910, 91 S.Ct. 871 (1971). However, plaintiff's choice of forum is accorded no special consideration when the nucleus of operative facts is outside the forum state. Ricoh Co., 817 F.Supp. at 481. In other words, "the preferred forum is that which is the center of gravity of the accused activity." S.C. Johnson & Son v. Gillette Co., 571 F.Supp. 1185, 1188 (N.D.Ill.1983).

While endeavoring below to determine whether the balance of Gulf Oil factors favors transfer, the Court is satisfied that the center of gravity for the majority of defendants' alleged wrongdoings is not New

Jersey. Notwithstanding certain representations and promises made by the UM football staff to Fortay in New Jersey via letter and personal visits, the balance of the alleged wrongdoings occurred in Florida, including: (1) additional promises and representations about Fortay's career by Coach Erickson and others, (2) the performance and breaches of the alleged contracts, (3) the various torts stemming from the denial of the starting quarterback job, and (4) the entire Pell Grant scandal.

According to the Court's conservative calculations, at least fifteen of the twenty-five counts allege wrongdoing that occurred entirely outside of New Jersey. Given the nature and extent of alleged activity outside the forum state, the Court will not accord any greater significance to Fortay's choice of forum in relation to the other Gulf Oil factors.

Access to Proof and Witness Convenience

In addressing these two Gulf Oil factors, the Court must "scrutinize the substance of the dispute between the parties to evaluate what proof is required, and determine whether the pieces of the evidence cited by the parties are critical, or even relevant" to Fortay's claims or defendants' potential defenses. Van Cauwenberghe v. Biard, 486 U.S. 517, 528, 108 S.Ct. 1945, 1952 (1988).

While Fortay's rambling complaint makes characterization of his claims difficult, the task is not impossible. The Court recognizes that the various claims arise from (1) certain defendants' promises and representations during the recruiting process, (2) the alleged breach of those promises, and the commission of various torts during Fortay's enrollment at UM, and (3) the entire Pell Grant scandal.

Certain of the defendants assert that most, if not all of the evidence pertinent to the entire action is located in Miami. Documents concerning the Pell Grant scandal are located in the files of UM and the United States Attorney's office in Florida. UM files also hold documents relating to the operation of UM's football program and recruiting practices. (Josefsberg Affidavit p 5) Beyond the correspondence received by Fortay from UM, which has been submitted on the pending motions, Fortay cites to no other potentially relevant documentary evidence which is located in New Jersey.

Moving defendants also argue that beside Fortay and his father, most of the key witnesses in the action reside in Florida, including the named defendants Foote, Price, Scott, D. Johnson, Russell and Coach Erickson. (Josefsberg Affidavit p 4) On the Pell Grant claims, moving defendants expect to call two employees of the federal government who handled the government's investigation: Deborah Diller of the Federal Bureau of Investigation and Martin Goldberg, Assistant United States Attorney. Both reside in Florida. (Id.) On Fortay's claims involving recruiting and unfulfilled expectations, Stevens, Campo and Kehoe have attested to certain relevant facts and would likely be called as non-party witnesses. (Stevens Affidavit (Oct. 27, 1993) p 2; Stevens Affidavit (Jan. 5, 1994) p 3; Campo Affidavit pp 4–5; Kehoe Affidavit pp 3–5)

Defendants also identify a plethora of other potential non-party witnesses residing in Florida, including former students involved in the Pell Grant scandal, UM Athletic Department staff, UM financial aid officers, other coaches and players from the UM football teams during the years 1989–1991 and other former and current UM athletes. (Price Affidavit p 9; D. Johnson Affidavit (Sept. 13, 1993) p 9)

In contrast to moving defendants, Fortay has offered no affidavits or certifications identifying potential witnesses from New Jersey whom he might call in support of his claims. While nonmoving parties do not bear the burden of persuasion on a motion to transfer, courts generally require some factual offering to facilitate the balancing of convenience of witnesses. Ricoh, 817 F.Supp. at 884, 885 n. 25. Fortay's counsel attempts to certify that defense counsel might depose members of the Rutgers football staff. (Shebell Certification p 2) The Court considers irrelevant such soothsaying with respect to defendants' intentions and case preparation.

In conjunction with witness convenience, the Court must also consider witness availability. The Third Circuit has recognized the burden that confronts litigating parties and a trial court when key non-party witnesses are not willing to testify and are beyond the reach of the court's compulsory process. Lacey v. Cessna Aircraft Co., 932 F.2d 170, 183 (3d Cir.1991). As detailed above, moving defendants have identified a large number of non-party witnesses, some of whom are no longer—or never were—under UM's control, and some of whom are beyond the subpoena power of this court and have expressed an unwillingness to travel to New Jersey to testify. (Harley Affidavit pp 2–3, 5; Stevens Affidavit (Oct. 27, 1993) pp 2–3, 5; Josefsberg Affidavit p 4; Price Affidavit p 9; D. Johnson Affidavit (Sept. 13, 1993) p 9)

Based upon the parties' submissions, the Court finds that the access to proof and witness convenience factors here favor adjudication in Florida rather than New Jersey. The majority of potentially relevant proof—documentary evidence and deposition and trial testimony of party and non-party witnesses—is to be found in Florida. As to witness convenience, the Court finds that Fortay has failed to identify any other New Jersey witnesses besides Bryan and Peter Fortay. A transfer here would not effect a simple shift of inconvenience from defendants to Fortay. Given the number of party and non-party witnesses in Florida, Fortay has provided the Court no basis to conclude that the convenience of witnesses favors the retention of this action in New Jersey.

Obstacles to a Fair Trial

The issue of fair trial is raised by none of the parties in a comparison of the New Jersey and Southern Florida venues. Fortay, however, argues that should the action be transferred, the Court should select the Northern, rather than Southern, District of Florida, citing a potential for favoritism in Southern Florida where allegedly there exists great interest in UM football and a certain loathing of Fortay in the aftermath of his departure from UM.

The Court views this request with skepticism. A district court in the Northern District of Florida may exercise jurisdiction over all defendants here. Beyond this fact, the district would have no other relation to the parties and the events associated with this lawsuit, making it an unwelcome candidate for venue consideration under the rubric of convenience and justice.

Moreover, the Court finds Fortay's concern about bias inadequately supported by the record, which includes one article about Fortay from the Miami Herald. In authorizing a transfer from the Northern District of New York to the Middle District of Florida, the district court in Aquatic Amusement [Assocs., Ltd. v. Walt Disney World Co., 734 F. Supp. 54 (N.D.N.Y. 1990)] rejected a similar argument based upon the submission of two magazine articles, offered by plaintiff as evidence that Florida jurors would favor defendant Disney in the Florida forum. 734 F.Supp. at 59.

While UM football may generally be revered in Southern Florida, this Court rejects the notion that an impartial jury could not be selected from this populous and diverse region of Florida. The Court will not engage in such gross speculation. It serves little purpose and, for sake of argument, cuts both ways. There might be many potential jurors in Southern Florida whose view of UM has been negatively colored by the Pell Grant scandal, the attendant publicity and the allegations that the local university has sacrificed its own students to avoid incrimination.

To the extent that the prospect of a fair trial may be questioned in any forum—whether it be New Jersey or Florida—the Court is satisfied that the bias of any potential jurors can be handled adequately by this Court or a district court in Southern Florida. See In re Wyoming Tight Sands Antitrust Cases, 723 F.Supp. 561, 563 (D.Kan.1988) (concluding that bias of jurors due to news accounts can be addressed and avoided through voir dire).

State and Local Interests and the Burden of Jury Duty

Under Gulf Oil, the Court must also be aware of the local interests implicated by this lawsuit in the respective districts or, more specifically, in the communities in which they sit. Ricoh, 817 F.Supp. at 486. Along these same lines, the burden of jury duty should not be "imposed upon the people of a community which has no relation to the litigation." Ferens v. John Deere Co., 494 U.S. 516, 529–30, 110 S.Ct. 1274, 1282–83 (1990).

Fortay argues that New Jersey has a significant interest in protecting its blue chip high school athletes and their families from the unrelenting avarice and duplicity of universities and their athletic departments, whose recruiting antics often betray a motivation to generate dollars, rather than to cultivate a productive and educated individual. Such predatory practices seem more prevalent with each recruiting season. The Court recognizes New Jersey's concern to be valid and would agree that the burden of jury duty for New Jersey citizens would not be particularly onerous given that certain of Fortay's claims arise out of conduct and activities occurring in New Jersey.

However, with respect to Fortay's claims, the citizens of Florida possess an interest significantly more profound. A major private university in their community not only may have been engaging in unsavory recruiting practices, but may also have wrongfully facilitated and denied knowledge of the criminal activities of its staff and students. Given the gravity of Fortay's allegations and the community's relationship with UM, citizens of Florida should bear the burden of jury duty. Surely, Florida's interest in the alleged criminalizing of Florida students by a local university is of a significantly greater magnitude than New Jersey's interest in protecting its high school athletes from rogue recruiters and from their own naivete.

Choice of Law Considerations

An action generally should be tried in a district familiar with the law governing the case. Gulf Oil, 330 U.S. at 508, 67 S.Ct. at 843. The Court iterates that choice of law is merely one factor to be considered and in certain circumstances may be accorded little weight. See Viacom Int'l, Inc. v. Melvin Simon Productions, Inc., 774 F.Supp. 858, 868 (S.D.N.Y. 1991) (according factor little weight where operative facts had no connection to forum state); Sandvik [Inc. v. Continental Ins. Co.], 724 F.Supp. [303], at 311 & n. 16 [(D.N.J.1989)] (leaving choice of law in contract action to transferee court where place of contracting had not been settled on transfer motion).

The Court gives no weight to the law that may apply to Fortay's claims, especially in view of the balance of factors currently favoring venue in Florida. Conceivably, New Jersey law might apply to any valid claims based upon contracts entered into in New Jersey. However, the operative facts of the Pell Grant scandal have little connection to New Jersey and, in all likelihood, the tort claims arising from [the] scandal would require application of Florida law. Generally speaking, this Court has as little experience with Florida law as a court in the Southern District of Florida has with New Jersey law.

In any event, this Court would not even undertake a choice of law analysis until after requiring Fortay to redraft his complaint. Therefore, the Court will leave the choice of law question to the transferee court, which must then apply the applicable choice of law rules in New Jersey under Van Dusen v. Barrack, 376 U.S. 612, 639, 84 S.Ct. 805, 821 (1964).

CONCLUSION

Based on the foregoing, the Court finds that the Gulf Oil factors favor litigating this action in the Southern District of Florida rather than in the District of New Jersey. Therefore, the Court will grant moving defendants' motion to transfer the entire action, as to all defendants, to the Southern District of Florida. The Court will leave the pending motions under Federal Rule of Procedure 12 for resolution by the transferee court.

Notes

1. Following the entry of Judge Wolin's transfer order, Fortay and the University of Miami engaged in extensive discovery. On the eve of trial, however, the parties entered into a confidential settlement. As a result, the question of whether a binding promise had been made was never resolved. *See further* Craig Barnes, *UM, Fortay Settle Lawsuit*, Fort Lauderdale Sun–Sentinel, June 25, 1996, at 2C. In the meantime, Fortay, having played briefly in the World League of American Football and the Arena Football League, enrolled in law school at Temple University.

2. In your opinion, did either Coach Johnson or Coach Erickson make a legally binding promise to Fortay, or were their statements mere puffing? *See further* James K. Ornstein, Comment, *Broken Promises and Broken Dreams: Should We Hold College Athletic Programs Accountable for Breaching Representations Made in Recruiting Student–Athletes?*, 6 Seton Hall J. Sport L. 641 (1996). *See also Lesser v. Neosho County Community College*, 741 F.Supp. 854 (D.Kan.1990) (claim against baseball coach for concealing draconian nature of team rules during recruitment).

3. Sometimes, instead of doing too little for a player, a coach tries to do too much. In February 1998, University of Connecticut senior Nykesha Sales was two points shy of becoming her school's all-time women's basketball scoring champion when an injury ended her college career. Huskies coach Geno Auriemma then devised a plan whereby Sales was allowed to make an uncontested lay-up in a game against Villanova University. When word of the gesture got out, a fierce debate erupted over the shot's propriety. *See further* Greg Garber & Lori Riley, *The Upshot: A Record–Breaking Basket Touches a National Nerve*, Hartford Courant, Feb. 26, 1998, at A1 (listing other coaches who have helped players achieve milestones).

Problem 37

To recruit a star prospect, a college basketball coach assured him he would get the extra academic help he needed. No such assistance was provided, however, and the player flunked out of school. Given these facts, has there been a breach of contract? *See Ross v. Creighton University*, 957 F.2d 410 (7th Cir.1992).

2. IMPROPER TRAINING METHODS

To succeed on this type of claim, a player must demonstrate his or her coach utilized improper methods of instruction or motivation. For a variety of reasons, these suits usually fail.

RUTLEDGE v. ARIZONA BOARD OF REGENTS

711 P.2d 1207 (Ariz.Ct.App.1985).

OGG, Judge.

This appeal arises from the alleged assault of former Arizona State University (A.S.U.) football player Kevin Rutledge (Rutledge) by former head football coach Frank Kush (Kush). Rutledge filed suit against Kush, A.S.U., the Arizona Board of Regents (Board), and various other A.S.U. officials.

Facts

We begin by setting forth a brief summary of the facts giving rise to the lawsuit. Rutledge was a member of the 1978 A.S.U. football team. He was a sophomore, having been on the varsity team the previous year as a freshman. Prior to the start of the 1978 season, Rutledge was considered the team's starting punter and was also a back-up defensive back. Apparently Kush was not satisfied with Rutledge's performance during pre-season camp, resulting in Kush ordering that Rutledge was not to suit-up for the first game of the 1978 season. Kush asserted at trial that the reason he did not have Rutledge suit-up for the first game was that he hoped that Rutledge would become irritated and thus motivate himself to concentrate and perform better.

Rutledge asserted that the reason he did not suit-up was that he was to be "red-shirted" during the 1978 season, due to the physical effects of a January, 1978 automobile accident. When a player is "red-shirted", he does not participate in his team's scheduled games during the year. If he is physically able, however, he may still continue to practice with the team. By "red-shirting" for a year a player retains his eligibility to play varsity ball his fifth year in college, if he has not yet graduated at that time. Kush denied that he knew of Rutledge's alleged injuries or that Rutledge was to be red-shirted because of his alleged injuries.

Rutledge did suit-up and punt in the next six games, including the October 28th game at the University of Washington. A.S.U. played an exceptionally poor game against Washington and Rutledge was no exception. Rutledge testified that, after a third consecutive poor punt late in the game, Kush approached Rutledge while he was standing on the sidelines, grabbed the face mask of Rutledge's helmet, pulled it sideways so that Rutledge was facing Kush, began shaking the face mask and calling Rutledge various obscenities, and finally delivered an uppercut punch to Rutledge's face. Rutledge testified that he suffered a split lip as a result of the punch. Kush denied having punched Rutledge and testified that he could not recall if he had grabbed Rutledge's face mask.

Rutledge asserted that after the Washington game, Kush and assistant coach William Maskill did everything they could to force Rutledge to leave A.S.U. and forfeit his scholarship. Rutledge did in fact leave A.S.U., transferring to the University of Nevada at Las Vegas prior to the 1979 football season. Rutledge maintained at trial that he was forced to leave A.S.U. as a result of "constant physical and mental abuse" from both Kush and Maskill. Kush denied pressuring Rutledge into leaving the team.

Rutledge filed a complaint in Maricopa County Superior Court on October 22, 1979. Named as defendants in the lawsuit were: (1) the Board of Regents; (2) A.S.U.; (3) Frank Kush; (4) William Maskill; (5) Gary Horton; and (6) Fred Miller. On January 11, 1980, the complaint was amended to join as defendants in the action Frances Kush, Mary Helen Maskill, Jean Miller, John Schwada, Jane Doe Schwada, George Hamm and Jane Doe Hamm.

Rutledge's first amended complaint contained an allegation (Count V) that various defendants had violated 42 U.S.C. §§ 1983 and 1985(2). On May 30, 1980, the trial court granted defendants' motion to dismiss Count V. Rutledge subsequently filed his second amended complaint, setting forth nine claims for relief.

Count I of the second amended complaint alleged that Kush had assaulted and battered Rutledge during the October 28, 1978 football game against Washington. Count II alleged that Kush and Maskill intentionally interfered with Rutledge's contractual and advantageous business and educational relationship with A.S.U. Count III accused both Kush and Maskill of conspiracy to interfere with Rutledge's contractual and advantageous business and educational relationship with A.S.U. Count IV alleged that Kush misrepresented the availability of football scholarships during the 1977–1978 school year. Count V set forth a claim for defamation against Kush. Count VI alleged that Kush and Maskill were liable for intentional infliction of emotional distress.

Count VII was based upon respondeat superior and was asserted against A.S.U., the Board of Regents, Miller, Hamm and Schwada for the actions of Kush and Maskill. Count VIII alleged that the Board of Regents breached its contract with Rutledge by allowing Kush and Maskill to coerce Rutledge into leaving A.S.U., thereby forfeiting his scholarship. Count IX was asserted against the Board of Regents, Miller, Schwada and Hamm for negligent supervision of Kush. Rutledge sought compensatory and punitive damages under all counts except Counts VII (respondeat superior), VIII (breach of contract), and IX (negligent supervision), in which he sought only compensatory damages.

Prior to trial, Counts III (conspiracy to breach contract) and VI (intentional infliction of emotional distress) against Kush and Maskill were dismissed following motions for summary judgment. Additionally, the Board of Regents was granted summary judgment on Count IX (negligent supervision). Defendants Miller were dismissed from the lawsuit on December 9, 1980. Rutledge has not appealed from these judgments.

Thus, following pretrial rulings, the following issues remained for trial: 1. As to Kush: (a) Assault and battery; (b) Intentional interference with contractual relations; (c) Defamation; (d) Misrepresentation. 2. As to Maskill: Intentional interference with contractual relations. 3. As to the Board of Regents: (a) Breach of contract; (b) Liability under respondeat superior for the actions of Kush and Maskill. 4. As to Hamm (as to whom Rutledge acknowledges in his reply brief that his claims have not been preserved on appeal) and Schwada: Negligent supervision of Kush.

Trial commenced on January 26, 1981. On February 12, 1981, the trial court ordered that the trial be bifurcated. The court ordered that the claims of assault and battery, defamation and misrepresentation against Kush and the Board of Regents be tried first. The remaining issues of intentional interference with contract, breach of contract and negligent supervision were ordered tried after the jury returned a verdict on the first three claims. The trial court ordered that the jury would be permitted to consider all evidence presented in the first phase of the trial during their deliberations in the second phase of the trial.

On March 17, 1981, the trial court granted Kush's motion for a directed verdict on the defamation claim (Count V). On March 20, 1981, the jury returned verdicts in favor of Kush and the Board of Regents on the remaining claims of assault and battery and misrepresentation. Phase two of the trial resulted in jury verdicts in favor of all defendants on all remaining claims. Rutledge's subsequent motion for a new trial was denied. Pursuant to A.R.S. § 12–341.01(A), the trial court awarded the Board of Regents $20,000.00 in attorneys' fees.

Rutledge raises several issues for our review. We discuss each issue as set forth below.

BIFURCATION

As previously noted, the trial court ordered that the claims of assault and battery, defamation and misrepresentation be tried prior to the claims of intentional interference with contract, breach of contract and negligent supervision. See Rule 42(b), Arizona Rules of Civil Procedure. The trial court's rationale for bifurcating trial of Rutledge's claims was set forth in a minute entry as follows:

> IT IS ORDERED that evidence of alleged mistreatment of other football players is admissible against the Defendant Kush on the Plaintiff's cause of action for interference with contractual relationship to prove that the Defendant Kush's coaching methods may have resulted in breaches of contract and that the Defendant Kush knew or should have known that such behavior would result in Plaintiff abandoning his scholarship and on the issue of punitive damages for interference with contractual relationship. It is not admissible under any other theory in connection with any claims for assault, defamation or misrepresentation or punitive damages relating to such theories. LaFrentz v. Gallagher, 105 Ariz. 255, 462 P.2d 804 (1969). A limiting instruction to the effect that the jury could consider the evidence on the contract issue but not on the assault issue would be ineffective. The trial will, therefore, be bifurcated.

Rutledge presents three arguments which he asserts constitute grounds for reversible error as a result of the trial court's bifurcation order. First, Rutledge maintains that the trial court erred in holding that Kush's alleged abuse of other A.S.U. football players was not admissible against Kush on the claims of assault and battery, defamation or misrepresentation. Specifically, Rutledge asserts that, while the trial court properly concluded that prior assaultive acts of Kush were not admissible to prove that Kush assaulted Rutledge, see LaFrentz v. Gallagher, 105 Ariz. 255, 462 P.2d 804 (1969), the court erred in holding that the prior acts were not admissible on the issue of punitive damages flowing from the alleged assault and battery. Rutledge takes the position that the prior assaultive acts were admissible to establish his claim of malice, a prerequisite to the jury's awarding punitive damages. We disagree, finding the LaFrentz v. Gallagher case on point and dispositive.

Rutledge's proferred evidence of prior abusive conduct by Kush pertained to other players and not to Rutledge himself. Thus, it appears that this evidence would be of little if any probative value in showing malice toward Rutledge. Moreover, none of the proffered evidence pertained to Kush's alleged abuse of other players contemporaneous to his alleged assault of Rutledge. Thus, the evidence would not arguably relate to Kush's state of mind at the time of his alleged assault of Rutledge. See Furrh v. Rothschild, 118 Ariz. 251, 575 P.2d 1277 (App.1978); Forquer v. Pinal County, 22 Ariz.App. 266, 526 P.2d 1064 (App.1974). Thus, we conclude that the trial court did not err in precluding Rutledge's proffered evidence of prior assaultive conduct pertaining to the issue of malice on Rutledge's punitive damages claim on the assault and battery claim.

Rutledge next argues that the trial court should have given a limiting instruction, rather than bifurcating the trial. Rutledge maintains that bifurcation led to distortion, disjunction and confusion of the evidence constituting reversible error.

The trial court is given broad discretion under Rule 42(b), Arizona Rules of Civil Procedure, in determining whether claims should be tried separately so as to avoid prejudice. Morley v. Superior Court, 131 Ariz. 85, 638 P.2d 1331 (1981); Anderson Aviation Sales Co., Inc. v. Perez, 19 Ariz. App. 422, 508 P.2d 87 (1973). The trial court specifically found that a limiting instruction would be ineffective. In view of the fact that the proffered evidence consisted of allegations of assaultive actions on other players, we do not find an abuse of discretion. Clearly the trial court did not err in its conclusion that the jury would have difficulty divorcing the alleged prior assaultive acts from the issue of whether Kush assaulted Rutledge in the case at bar.

Rutledge's last argument pertaining to bifurcation is that, by allowing the same jury to sit in the second phase of the trial, after it had rendered a verdict against him in the first phase, he was denied the right to a fair trial before an impartial jury during phase two of the trial. Contrary to Rutledge's assertions, there is no constitutional problem in separately trying different claims to the same jury.

Jury Instructions

A. *Qualified Privilege*

Rutledge asserts that the trial court improperly instructed the jury concerning Kush's and Maskill's qualified privilege to interfere with Rutledge's contract (scholarship) with A.S.U. The trial court instructed the jury as follows:

> In certain situations, an employee may have a qualified privilege to cause a breach of his employer's contract with a third person. In order to assert such a privilege, the employee must prove that his acts were taken in good faith belief that they were for

> the interests of his employer, and that he did not employ wrongful means to cause a breach of his employer's contract.

Rutledge maintains that the instruction is an incorrect statement of the law in Arizona in that it does not address "the quality of the interest of the employer which is being served." Specifically, Rutledge asserts that the instruction must specify that the employer's interests being served must be "lawful". Rutledge submitted a proposed instruction which specified that the employee's act must be for the "best lawful interest of his employer." The trial court deleted the words "best lawful" and instructed the jury as noted above.

Rutledge relies on the case of Ong Hing v. Arizona Harness Raceway, Inc., 10 Ariz.App. 380, 459 P.2d 107 (1969), to support his assertion. In Ong Hing, we addressed the issue of personal liability of corporate directors for inducing a breach of the corporation's contract with a third party:

> . . . [T]he acts of such directors should be privileged provided that the acts complained of were in good faith and the director believed that his acts were for the best lawful interests of the corporation.

10 Ariz.App. at 388, 459 P.2d at 115. Thus, the instruction submitted by Rutledge was a correct statement of the law regarding qualified privilege in Arizona. However, a party is not entitled to its own instructions simply because it is a correct statement of the law. Hallmark v. Allied Products Corp., 132 Ariz. 434, 646 P.2d 319 (App.1982); Sequoia Mfg. Co. v. Halec Const. Co., 117 Ariz. 11, 570 P.2d 782 (App.1977). It is not error to refuse to give requested instructions where the concepts contained therein are adequately conveyed through given instructions. Hallmark v. Allied Products, supra. We conclude that instructions given adequately set forth the qualified privilege defense.

The jury was advised that an employee may not employ "wrongful means" to cause the breach of his employer's contract. Another instruction provided the jury with guidelines for determining whether the employee's conduct was wrongful and read as follows:

> In determining whether an actor's conduct in intentionally interfering with the contract or a business expectancy of another is wrongful you may consider the following factors: (a) The nature of the actor's conduct, (b) The actor's motive. In this respect a good faith belief that the acts were in the interests of the employer means that the employee had an intent to benefit the employer by his actions and did not act purely from the pursuit of personal goals or solely for his personal gain; (c) The interests of the other with which the actor's conduct interferes; (d) The interests sought to be advanced by the actor; (e) The social interests in protecting the freedom of action of the actor and contractual interests of the other; (f) The proximity or remoteness of the actor's conduct to the interference; (g) The relations between the parties.

Clearly, the instructions given by the trial court were sufficiently broad to allow counsel to argue that the interests of the employer to be advanced had to be "lawful". See Porterie v. Peters, 111 Ariz. 452, 532 P.2d 514 (1975); Hallmark v. Allied Products, supra; Sequois Mfg., supra.

B. Limiting Instruction Pertaining to Prior Bad Acts

Rutledge argues that the trial court erred by instructing the jury during phase two of the trial as follows:

> Evidence of the defendant Kush's treatment of other players who allegedly left the team as a result of such treatment is admissible against the defendant Kush on the issue of whether he knew or should have known that his treatment of Kevin Rutledge would cause Kevin Rutledge to leave the team. It is also admissible against the defendant Schwada on the issue of whether he knew or should have known that such treatment would cause players to leave the team. It is not admissible against any other defendant or for any other purpose. Evidence of the defendant Kush's treatment of any player, whether he left the team or not, is admissible on the claim against defendant Schwada for negligent supervision. It is not admissible against any other defendant or for any other purpose.

Rutledge takes the position that evidence of all of Kush's alleged abuses of football players shows that Kush's actions in forcing Rutledge to forego his scholarship at A.S.U. were intentional. We find Rutledge's position on this issue to be confusing. Clearly, if players were mistreated by Kush but did not leave the team, such conduct would not tend to prove that Kush intended to coerce Rutledge into leaving the team. In fact, the opposite is true. If Kush did mistreat other players and they did not leave the team, the inference is that Kush's alleged mistreatment of Rutledge was not intended to coerce him into leaving but to increase his performance. In those instances in which players did in fact leave the team as a result of Kush's alleged mistreatment, relevancy is established. This is precisely how the jury was instructed by the trial court. We find no error.

Rutledge's assertion that Kush's alleged mistreatment of other players was admissible during phase two on the issue of punitive damages is moot in light of the fact that the jury failed to find that Rutledge was entitled to an award of actual damages. LaFrentz v. Gallagher, supra.

CONCLUSION

This was a long, bitter and hard-fought trial. The record indicates that the trial court did an admirable job of controlling the proceedings and ensuring that all parties obtained a fair trial. Based upon our resolution of the issues raised on appeal, the judgment of the trial court is affirmed.

The Board of Regents has requested an award of its attorneys' fees incurred on appeal. Pursuant to Rule 21(c)(1), Arizona Rules of Civil Appellate Procedure, and A.R.S. § 12–341.01(A), we award the Board its attorneys' fees, the amount of which will be determined upon the filing of the Board's statement of costs.

Notes

1. Nine years after filing his lawsuit, Kevin Rutledge's final appeal was turned down. *See Rutledge v. Arizona Board of Regents*, 859 F.2d 732 (9th Cir.1988). Today, he is an insurance salesman in Tucson, Arizona. Meanwhile, Frank Kush, who lost his job as a result of the scandal, went on to coach in the NFL, CFL, and USFL and was later elected to the College Football Hall of Fame. In 1996, Arizona State University named its football field in his honor. *See further* Chris Dufresne, *The New Camp Kush*, L.A. Times, Nov. 14, 1996, at C1.

2. Besides Frank Kush, a number of other coaches have had fiery relations with their players, including, most notably, Vince Lombardi (Green Bay Packers), Billy Martin (New York Yankees), Bobby Knight (Indiana University), Woody Hayes (Ohio State University), Mike Ditka (Chicago Bears), and Bill Parcels (New York Giants). Of course, not all coaches are hotheads: both Phil Jackson (Chicago Bulls) and Joe Torre (New York Yankees)—two of the most successful field generals of the 1990s—have shown a special knack for keeping cool under pressure.

For a further look at coaches and their individual temperaments, see Mike Vaccaro, *Storm Warnings: Violence Casts Cloud Over Athletes, Coaches*, K.C. Star, Dec. 7, 1997, at C4. *See also Bauer v. Murphy*, 530 N.W.2d 1 (Wis.Ct.App.), *review denied*, 537 N.W.2d 570 (Wis.1995) (coach who called player a "disgrace" in front of entire team because of alleged affair did not commit actionable libel); *Iacco v. Bohannon*, 245 N.W.2d 791 (Mich.Ct.App. 1976) (coach who insulted player to motivate him not liable for defamation); *Robitaille v. Vancouver Hockey Club Ltd.*, 124 D.L.R.3d 228 (B.C.Ct.App. 1981) (team responsible for coach who refused to give injured player sufficient time to heal); Michael Mayo, *Yatil's New Route? It's Down and Out*, Fort Lauderdale Sun–Sentinel, Aug. 21, 1998, at 1C (suggesting Miami Dolphins coach Jimmy Johnson publicly baited player into returning too early and thereby reinjuring himself).

3. While still rare, instances of players assaulting coaches are increasing. In December 1997, for example, Latrell Sprewell of the Golden State Warriors choked and threatened his coach, P.J. Carlesimo, during a practice session. Despite Sprewell's attempt to portray himself as a victim of racial discrimination, the NBA suspended him for one year, the Warriors terminated his contract, Converse dropped him as its spokesman, and the NBA players union refused to support him. *See further* Mark Starr & Allison Samuels, *Hoop Nightmare*, Newsweek, Dec. 15, 1997, at 26. Although an arbitrator shortened Sprewell's suspension to 68 games, a federal judge later threw out his civil rights lawsuit against the NBA and the Warriors. *See further* Selena Roberts, *Sprewell's Suit Against N.B.A. Is Tossed Out*, N.Y. Times, July 31, 1998, at C19.

More recently, in December 1998, the Carolina Panthers suspended linebacker Kevin Greene for one game after he attacked assistant coach Kevin Steele on national television. Unlike Sprewell, Greene quickly apologized for his actions and accepted his punishment. *See further* Bill Plaschke, *Is It About Race? Kevin Greene vs. Latrell Sprewell*, L.A. Times, Dec. 17, 1998, at D1.

4. In an attempt to curb violent conduct between coaches and players, the International Tennis Federation in December 1998 issued a coaches' code of ethics. The Federation hopes the new code, which permits both players and coaches to report unacceptable behavior, will become a standard part of coaches' education programs. *See further A Code of Ethics for Both Tours*, N.Y. Times, Dec. 23, 1998, at C22.

Problem 38

During a pre-season drill conducted under a blazing sun, a football player died from heat exhaustion. His estate subsequently filed a wrongful death suit. If the coach moves to dismiss on the ground such drills are necessary to get the team in shape, how should the court rule? *See Roventini v. Pasadena Independent School District*, 183 F.R.D. 500 (S.D.Tex.1998).

3. INADEQUATE SUPERVISION

To succeed on this type of claim, a player must prove he or she was exposed to a heightened risk of injury due to a coach's negligence. As will be seen, these sorts of lawsuits often come down to a question of what was reasonably foreseeable.

LAICHE v. KOHEN

621 So.2d 1162 (La.Ct.App.1993).

PER CURIAM.

This appeal is from a May 29, 1992, judgment of the Twenty–Third Judicial District Court granting defendants Lance Kohen, David Duplessis and their professional liability insurer, Horace Mann Insurance Company, summary judgment. For the following reasons, we affirm.

On September 7, 1989, St. Amant Elementary School and Galvez Elementary School played a scrimmage football game. S.J. Laiche, Jr. (hereinafter S.J.), a 110 pound, eighth grader, playing on the St. Amant team, sustained a fractured leg during the course of the game. S.J. was injured as he approached the Galvez end-zone and was struck by two Galvez tacklers. The football which S.J. was carrying "began to bobble" and became lodged underneath his right leg. Then a third St. Amant player, also an eighth grader, but who weighed approximately 270 pounds, fell across S.J.'s legs. S.J.'s right leg was fractured during the incident. No penalty was called against any of the players.

On March 29, 1990, Stanley J. Laiche, Sr. and Charlene Laiche, individually and on behalf of their minor son, S.J., filed suit against Lance Kohen (coach of the St. Amant team), David Duplessis (coach of the Galvez team), Ascension Parish School Board, and Horace Mann Insurance Company.

Plaintiffs alleged, in relevant part, that the coaches were liable for S.J.'s injuries due to their:

> a) allowing and/or requiring smaller elementary school students to scrimmage with disproportionately larger elementary school students without regard to consideration of height and weight differences among the players....
>
> c) failing to protect smaller players from injuries caused by much larger players.

Additionally, plaintiffs alleged that the Ascension Parish School Board was liable for S.J.'s injuries due to its:

> a) failing to develop, adopt and/or implement a system or procedure to prevent extremely large elementary school players from practicing and/or otherwise participating in scrimmage with relatively smaller players, particularly at grammar school levels;
>
> b) failing to develop, adopt, and/or implement a system or procedure to require that participants in football scrimmages be selected on the basis of similar height and weight classifications.

On May 21, 1990, defendants, Lance Kohen, David Duplessis, and Horace Mann Insurance Company, filed an answer setting forth, inter alia, the following affirmative defense:

> The risk encountered by [S.J.] is not a risk which falls into the ambit of the duty upon Coaches Kohan (sic) and Duplessis in their positions as elementary school football coaches.

On February 5, 1991, the defendant coaches and their insurer moved for summary judgment alleging, in relevant part:

> 1
>
> Coaches Duplessis and Kohen had no duty to prevent [S.J.], an eighth grade football player, from getting hurt in a regular, supervised, refereed interschool football game when the tackle which hurt him was neither unexpected nor unsportsmanlike and is an inherit (sic) part of the game well known to S.J. and his parents.
>
> 2
>
> The two coaches had no authority to develop, adopt and/or implement a system or procedure to prohibit a larger players (sic) from playing against relatively smaller players.

Both coaches also filed sworn affidavits, stating that they did not have the authority "to adopt, develop and/or implement a system or procedure prohibiting larger players from playing against relative (sic) smaller players."

The district court heard the motion and granted the same without assigning written reasons. Plaintiffs' suit against the Ascension Parish School Board was not disturbed by the district court.

Plaintiffs have appealed, assigning error to the district court's finding that, as a matter of law, the coaches owed no duty to S.J.

A motion for summary judgment shall be rendered forthwith if the pleadings, depositions, answers to interrogatories, and admissions on file, together with the affidavits, if any, show that there is no genuine issue as to material fact, and that [the] mover is entitled to judgment as a matter of law. La.Code Civ.P. art. 966.

In the case sub judice, there are no genuine issues as to the material facts. If the coaches were without a legal duty to protect against the "particular risk involved," here the risk of injury from playing in a football game with players of different weights, then defendants were indeed entitled to summary judgment.

A duty has been defined as "an obligation, to which the law will give recognition and effect, to conform to a particular standard of conduct toward another." Prosser and Keeton on the Law of Torts 356 (5th ed. 1984). The imposition of a legal duty depends on a case-by-case analysis. Gresham v. Davenport, 537 So.2d 1144 (La.1989); Harvey v. Ouachita Parish School Board, 545 So.2d 1241, 1244 (La.App. 2d Cir.1989).

Indeed, a determination of whether or not the coaches had the duty plaintiffs allege they did necessitates that we bear in mind the particular facts of the case sub judice and be certain of the applicability of other decisions in the jurisprudence in light of those facts, before we look to those decisions for guidance. We are not called upon to decide whether or not the coaches herein had any duty to allow S.J. to access medical treatment. Thus, we need not be concerned with decisions finding coaches to have breached duties owed to their players after they denied injured or sick players medical treatment. See Jarreau v. Orleans Parish School Board, 600 So.2d 1389 (La.App. 4th Cir.), writ denied, 605 So.2d 1363 (La.), writ denied, 605 So.2d 1378 (La.1992), and Mogabgab v. Orleans Parish School Board, 239 So.2d 456 (La.App. 4th Cir.), writ refused, 256 La. 1152, 241 So.2d 253 (La.1970).

Also inapplicable is the Second Circuit's decision in Pitre v. Louisiana Tech University, 596 So.2d 1324 (La.App. 2d Cir.1991), on rehearing, (Lindsay, Sexton, J.J., dissenting), writ denied, 604 So.2d 998 (La.1992), upon which plaintiffs rely. Pitre, 596 So.2d at 1324, decided whether or not a university owed a duty to one of its resident students injured in a sledding accident on its campus. The Second Circuit held that "Tech had a duty to protect or warn against this unreasonably dangerous activity." Pitre, 596 So.2d at 1324, 1333. The Second Circuit's holding was based on facts neither present nor analogous to those herein.

We note that Pitre, 596 So.2d at 1324, recognized a duty on the part of a university and not individual coaches or teachers. Moreover, the duty recognized in Pitre, 596 So.2d at 1324, was one to protect or warn against an unreasonably dangerous activity—sledding down a snow covered hill, atop a trash can lid, on one's back, head first into a parking lot containing cement encased light posts. The football game S.J. was injured in is hardly analogous to the activity causing injury in Pitre, 596 So.2d at 1324.

Defendants rely on the Louisiana Supreme Court's seminal tort law decision, Murray v. Ramada Inns, Inc., 521 So.2d 1123 (La.1988). Murray, 521 So.2d at 1123, is well known for its abolition of the doctrine of assumption of the risk. The Louisiana Supreme Court held that it would no longer bar plaintiffs from recovery "on the ground that [the plaintiff] knew of the unreasonable risk created by the defendant's conduct and voluntarily chose to encounter that risk." The Court noted that this kind of plaintiff conduct had been labeled "implied secondary" assumption of the risk. Murray, 521 So.2d at 1123, 1129. However, the Louisiana Supreme Court was careful to add the caveat:

> Nor does our decision today mean that the result reached in the sports spectator or amusement park cases (common law's 'implied primary' assumption of risk cases) was incorrect. However, rather than relying on the fiction that the plaintiffs in such cases implicitly consented to their injuries, the sounder reasoning is that the defendants were not liable because they did not breach any duty owed to the plaintiffs.

Murray, 521 So.2d at 1123, 1134. Continuing its reservation, the Court stated:

> Again, this is not to say that a duty is owed or breached in all situations that involve injury. We have held, for example, that the duty which a landowner owes to persons entering his property is governed by a standard of reasonableness, and that a potentially dangerous condition that should be obvious to all comers is not, in all instances, unreasonably dangerous. See, e.g., Shelton v. Aetna Casualty & Surety Co., 334 So.2d 406, 410–11 (La.1976). However, the key to a finding of no liability in such cases is not the plaintiff's subjective awareness of the risk, but the determination that the defendant did not act unreasonably vis-a-vis the plaintiff, or injure the plaintiff through the instrumentality of an unreasonably dangerous thing in his custody.

Murray, 521 So.2d at 1123, 1136. Additionally, Justice Cole, assigning additional reasons for the Court's decision, felt that it was important to explain:

> There is no suggestion a defendant will be liable in those instances where there is no duty to protect against the risk of injury sustained by the plaintiff.

Murray, 521 So.2d at 1123, 1137.

After a thorough review of the pleadings, depositions and affidavits before us, in light of the pertinent jurisprudence, we are unable to find a basis for imposing upon the coaches herein a duty to their players to protect against the risk of injury from playing a football game with players of different weights. We do not base our decision today upon any "subjective awareness of the risk" on the part of S.J. Rather, we base our decision on the fact that the coaches herein "did not act unreasonably vis-a-vis [S.J.], or injure [S.J.] through the instrumentality of an unreasonably dangerous thing in [their] custody." Murray, 521 So.2d at 1123, 1136. The coaches herein had "no duty to protect against the risk of injury sustained by [S.J.]." Murray, 521 So.2d at 1123, 1137. Therefore, the district court's granting defendants summary judgment was correct; and we will not disturb the same.

For the foregoing reasons, the district court's May 29, 1992, judgment granting defendants' motion for summary judgment is affirmed at plaintiffs' costs.

Note

For a further look at a coach's duty to properly supervise his or her players, see Anthony S. McCaskey & Kenneth W. Biedzynski, *A Guide to the Legal Liability of Coaches for a Sports Participant's Injuries*, 6 Seton Hall J. Sport L. 7 (1996). *See also Stineman v. Fontbonne College*, 664 F.2d 1082 (8th Cir.1981) (softball player could recover for coach's imprudent response to her injury); *Palmer v. Mount Vernon Township High School District 201*, 662 N.E.2d 1260 (Ill.1996) (school district not liable for coach's failure to tell basketball player to wear safety equipment); *Benitez v. New York City Board of Education*, 541 N.E.2d 29 (N.Y.1989) (school board could be sued for ignoring high school coach's warning that placing team in more competitive football division would lead to increased injuries); *Westhead v. Fagel*, 611 A.2d 758 (Pa.Super.Ct.1992) (defamation action brought by college basketball coach accused of contributing to athlete's death through poor supervision dismissed for lack of jurisdiction).

Problem 39

Called away to answer the phone, a high school volleyball coach told his team to set up the court. When the net was halfway in position, one of the players suddenly tried to jump over it. The coach returned just in time to see him land head first and break his back. If the athlete sues, claiming improper supervision, how should the court rule? *See Barretto v. City of New York*, 655 N.Y.S.2d 484 (App.Div.), *appeal denied*, 684 N.E.2d 281 (N.Y. 1997).

4. SEXUAL ABUSE

To succeed on this type of claim, a player must show that a coach requested or engaged in improper sexual conduct. As the following case indicates, athletes who plead this cause of action often run into statute of limitations problems.

NOLDE v. FRANKIE

964 P.2d 477 (Ariz.1998).

McGREGOR, Justice.

The plaintiffs appeal the trial court's order granting summary judgment in favor of the defendants on grounds that the statute of limitations bars this action. Because the trial court erred in its application of the law, we reverse and remand for the trial court to determine whether an issue of material fact exists as to whether defendant Frankie induced plaintiffs to delay filing their action, and whether their delay was reasonable.

I.

Each of the three plaintiffs in this action alleges she became sexually involved with defendant Bruce Frankie while she was still a minor. Frankie was, at all relevant times, a teacher and athletic coach at Washington High School (the school), and coached each of the plaintiffs. The school operates within the defendant Glendale Union High School District (the district).

Plaintiff Kathleen Andersen attended the school from 1972 through 1976. Frankie began a sexual relationship with her when she was a 17–year-old senior. The relationship continued until she was 19 years of age.

Plaintiff Mary Ella Nolde attended the school from 1981 through 1985. During her freshman year, when Nolde was 14 years old, Frankie initiated a sexual relationship with her. Frankie discontinued the relationship with Nolde during the early part of her senior year, in 1984.

Frankie began a sexual relationship with plaintiff Mya Johnson in 1983, when Johnson was 14 years old. This relationship continued through Johnson's graduation from the school in 1987 and thereafter for four more years.

Each of the plaintiffs came from a broken family and initially considered Frankie a father-figure. Frankie devoted personal attention to the girls and made them feel special and loved. Before they became sexually involved with Frankie, each of them developed a strong emotional attachment to him. Even after the sexual relationship began, each desired to please Frankie and to maintain her emotional relationship with him.

During his sexual abuse of Nolde and Johnson, Frankie instructed them never to disclose the sexual nature of his relationships with them. He warned them that he would lose his job and family if anyone were to learn of the relationships. Although none of the plaintiffs personally experienced physical abuse at the hands of Frankie, they all perceived him as intimidating and as prone to using violence against anyone who crossed him. They all asserted that Frankie made them feel special and loved and that they saw themselves as being at fault for allowing a sexual relationship to occur. In addition, the plaintiffs believed that

Frankie emotionally and psychologically dominated them during and after their relationships with him.

During the years following their sexual relationships with Frankie, the plaintiffs experienced various effects of the abuse, including depression, dysfunctional personal relationships, and physical illness. In July 1993, Nolde and Johnson, ages 25 and 24 respectively, filed a complaint against Frankie and the district. The complaint alleged claims for intentional infliction of emotional distress, outrage, invasion of privacy, assault, battery, and breach of fiduciary duty. Andersen joined the action as a plaintiff in February 1994, at age 36.

The defendants moved for summary judgment on grounds that the statute of limitations bars the action. In response, the plaintiffs asserted three arguments. First, they argued that their causes of action did not accrue until they knew or should have known of the causal connection between their injuries and Frankie's conduct. They contended that an issue of material fact exists as to when the causes of action accrued based on this "delayed discovery." Second, they argued that expert testimony established that they suffer from post-traumatic stress disorder, which prevented them from bringing a timely action. Third, they argued that because of Frankie's conduct toward them, equity precluded the defendants from asserting the statute of limitations defense.

After holding that Arizona law does not provide any basis for equitable tolling of the statute of limitations and that the plaintiffs were not under any disability that would toll the statute, the trial court granted the defendants' motions. The court of appeals affirmed and the plaintiffs filed a petition for review to this court. We granted review and have jurisdiction pursuant to Arizona Constitution, article VI, section 5.

II.

Under most circumstances, we would affirm the trial court's judgment because the limitations statute would bar plaintiffs' action as a matter of law. See Garza v. Fernandez, 74 Ariz. 312, 316, 248 P.2d 869, 871 (1952) (court will affirm summary judgment if no material issue of fact exists and moving party is entitled to judgment as a matter of law). The statute of limitations period for a personal injury action is two years, commencing on the date the action accrues. A.R.S. § 12–542.1 (1992). Because a cause of action that arises during a plaintiff's minority does not accrue until the plaintiff reaches eighteen years of age, A.R.S. § 12–502.A. (1992), the plaintiffs had two years from the date they reached majority to bring their respective causes of action. As plaintiffs admit, they did not file their action within the two-year time period.

The statute of limitations serves an important purpose. The statute protects defendants and the courts from litigation of stale claims in which "plaintiffs have slept on their rights and evidence may have been lost or witnesses' memories faded." Brooks v. Southern Pac. Co., 105 Ariz. 442, 444, 466 P.2d 736, 738 (1970). The policy underlying the limitations statute "is sound and necessary for the orderly administration of justice." Id.

However, a defendant may not use the statute of limitations as a shield for inequity. See Hosogai v. Kadota, 145 Ariz. 227, 231, 700 P.2d 1327, 1331 (1985); Waugh v. Lennard, 69 Ariz. 214, 221, 211 P.2d 806, 810 (1949). Hence, notwithstanding the important policy served by the limitations statute, Arizona courts have recognized equitable exceptions to the application of the statute when necessary to prevent injustice. Hosogai, 145 Ariz. at 231, 700 P.2d at 1331.

One such exception applies when a defendant induces a plaintiff to forbear filing suit. In Certainteed Corporation v. United Pacific Insurance Company, 158 Ariz. 273, 762 P.2d 560 (App.1988), for instance, the court estopped a defendant insurer from raising the limitations defense because the insurer had induced its claimant to delay filing suit. The insurer repeatedly delayed in responding to a legitimate insurance claim filed by the claimant, and represented that the claimant need not initiate litigation for the insurer to settle the claim. 158 Ariz. at 278, 762 P.2d at 565.

The Certainteed court held that "[a]n estoppel with respect to a contractual limitation period will exist if an insurer by its conduct induces its insured to forego litigation, by leading him to reason and believe a settlement or adjustment of his claim will be effected without the necessity of bringing suit." Id. at 277, 762 P.2d at 564.

Thus, in determining whether a defendant is estopped from asserting the limitations defense based on inducement to forbear filing suit, a trial court must determine: (1) whether the defendant engaged in affirmative conduct intended to cause the plaintiff's forbearance; (2) whether the defendant's conduct actually caused the plaintiff's failure to file a timely action; (3) whether the defendant's conduct reasonably could be expected to induce forbearance; and (4) whether the plaintiff brought the action within a reasonable time after termination of the objectionable conduct. Ordinarily, each of these inquiries will involve questions of fact, and therefore will be resolved by the factfinder. In some cases, however, a court appropriately may conclude as a matter of law that no reasonable jury could find for the plaintiff on one or more of these inquiries. See Orme Sch. v. Reeves, 166 Ariz. 301, 309, 802 P.2d 1000, 1008 (1990) (stating that summary judgment is appropriate if facts submitted in support of a claim or defense "have so little probative value, given the quantum of evidence required, that reasonable people could not agree with the conclusion advanced by the proponent of the claim or defense").

From the record before us, we cannot ascertain whether the trial judge considered the plaintiffs' argument that the doctrine of estoppel by inducement should apply to prevent defendants from urging the statute of limitations. It appears, however, that the judge did not measure the plaintiffs' allegations against the standard defined above. For that reason, we remand this action to permit the trial judge to determine whether Frankie's affirmative conduct actually and reasonably induced the plaintiffs to delay filing suit, and whether their delay was reasonable.

The trial court may find that summary judgment is appropriate as to one or more of the plaintiffs. If not, the trier of fact must resolve these factual issues.

III.

The plaintiffs next argue that an issue of fact exists as to whether each of the plaintiffs was of unsound mind for purposes of A.R.S. § 12–502.A, and thus, whether that disability tolled the statute of limitations. A person of unsound mind is one who "is unable to manage his affairs or to understand his legal rights or liabilities." Allen v. Powell's Int'l, Inc., 21 Ariz.App. 269, 270, 518 P.2d 588, 589 (1974). We recently affirmed this two-pronged definition of unsound mind in Doe v. Roe, 191 Ariz. 313, 955 P.2d 951 (1998), and Florez v. Sargeant, 185 Ariz. 521, 917 P.2d 250 (1996).

A.

To justify tolling a limitations statute because a person lacks ability to manage his daily affairs, we require "hard evidence that a person is simply incapable of carrying on the day-to-day affairs of human existence." Florez v. Sargeant, 185 Ariz. 521, 526, 917 P.2d 250, 255 (1996). Such evidence provides "empirical facts easily verifiable and more difficult to fabricate than a narrow claim of inability to bring the action." Id. This court's decisions in Doe and Florez illustrate the showing needed to toll the statute on this basis.

One of the plaintiffs in Florez submitted expert affidavits stating that he suffered from post-traumatic stress disorder, depression, sexual identity problems, and other problems; the other plaintiff's expert affidavit stated that she suffered from post-traumatic stress disorder. Id. at 523–24, 917 P.2d at 252–53. The expert affidavits opined that because of these psychological problems, the plaintiffs were of unsound mind for purposes of section 12–502.A. Id. at 527, 917 P.2d at 256. Notwithstanding these conclusory assertions, we held that the defendants were entitled to summary judgment. The undisputed evidence demonstrated that the plaintiffs were able to maintain employment, to handle financial affairs, to manage their daily affairs, and to take care of themselves. Id. at 526, 917 P.2d at 255. "[S]imply attaching the post-traumatic stress disorder label to a person's symptoms is insufficient to satisfy the Allen definition of unsound mind." Id. at 525, 917 P.2d at 254.

By contrast, the plaintiff in Doe presented evidence that, as a result of her mental problems, she was unable to manage her daily affairs:

> The record contains evidence from which one could conclude that for a considerable period of time Plaintiff was unable to function in day-to-day affairs. She experienced suicidal ideation, was in denial of the abuse she suffered, and required psychological and psychiatric therapy and treatment as well as institutionalization for her mental condition; because she was unable to function at work, she had to quit her job and was unable to seek other employment. Because of her denial and inability to articu-

> late or discuss the abusive acts, a jury could find that Plaintiff, unlike the Florez plaintiffs, was disabled and thus unable to seek or address the issues with legal counsel for approximately two years. Also, unlike the Florez plaintiffs, Plaintiff was not ready to talk about it; nor was she ready to deal with it. Unlike the affidavit in Florez, the affidavits in this case present facts, not mere conclusory opinions of post-traumatic stress disorder or unsound mind.

191 Ariz. at 327, 955 P.2d at 965.

The plaintiffs in the instant case, like those in Florez, failed to present evidence sufficient to create an issue of material fact as to whether they were unable to manage their daily affairs for purposes of meeting Allen's unsound mind definition. As a matter of law, the plaintiffs did not meet the daily affairs prong of Allen.

B.

The plaintiffs likewise did not present evidence sufficient to raise an issue of fact as to whether they failed to bring suit within the limitations period because they were unable to understand their legal rights and liabilities. In Doe, we considered the interaction between the limitations statute and the delayed discovery of a cause of action attributable to alleged repressed memory of severe sexual abuse. 191 Ariz. at 315, 955 P.2d at 953. We concluded that the plaintiff's evidence, which indicated that she had repressed memories of her sexual abuse and had denied that such abuse had taken place, provided a basis for concluding that she was unable to understand and assert her legal rights at the time her cause of action accrued. Id. at 329, 955 P.2d at 967.

The plaintiffs here made no comparable showing. None of the plaintiffs allege that they ever were in denial that the sexual abuse occurred. Neither do they claim that they repressed memories of the abuse. To the contrary, the plaintiffs admit that they were aware at all times that Frankie had abused them sexually. The personal and expert affidavits submitted by plaintiffs, stating that they were unable to understand their legal rights arising out of their sexual relationships with Frankie, provide mere conclusory statements that are not sufficient to withstand a motion for summary judgment. See Pace v. Sagebrush Sales Co., 114 Ariz. 271, 275, 560 P.2d 789, 793 (1977); Rule 56(e), Ariz. R. Civ. P.

Because the plaintiffs failed to raise an issue of material fact as to either prong of the Allen definition of unsound mind, A.R.S. § 12–502.A does not apply to toll the statute of limitations.

IV.

The plaintiffs also argue that their causes of action did not accrue until they discovered the causal connection between their psychological injuries and Frankie's sexual abuse of them, and that an issue of fact exists as to whether the plaintiffs filed this action within two years of their discovering the cause of their injuries.

Under Arizona's discovery rule, a cause of action based on sexual abuse accrues when the plaintiff becomes aware of the "what" and the "who" elements of the claim, see Doe, 191 Ariz. at 323, 955 P.2d at 961, i.e., the conduct constituting the sexual abuse and the identity of the abuser. If a plaintiff possesses at least "a minimum requisite of knowledge sufficient to identify that a wrong occurred and caused injury," then the cause of action accrues. Id.

These plaintiffs admittedly have been aware at all times that they were sexually abused and that Frankie was the abuser. The plaintiffs knew, or should have known, by the time they reached majority, that Frankie's sexual conduct toward them as minors caused personal injury, even if they did not know the extent of such injuries. Therefore, the discovery rule did not delay accrual of their causes of action, even if they were not aware of the existence or extent of resulting psychological injury.

V.

For the foregoing reasons, we vacate the opinion of the Court of Appeals, reverse the trial court's judgment in favor of the defendants, and remand for further proceedings.

Notes

1. For other cases involving coaches having (or seeking) sex with their players, see, e.g., *Doe v. Rains County Independent School District*, 76 F.3d 666 (5th Cir.1996); *Butler v. USA Volleyball*, 673 N.E.2d 1063 (Ill.App.Ct. 1996), *appeal denied*, 679 N.E.2d 378 (Ill.1997); *People v. Rossi*, 585 N.Y.S.2d 816 (App.Div.), *appeal denied*, 602 N.E.2d 242 (N.Y.1992). *See also* John T. Wolohan, *Sexual Harassment of Student Athletes and the Law: A Review of the Rights Afforded Students*, 5 Seton Hall J. Sport L. 339 (1995), and Mike Fish, *Some Male Coaches Pay Too Much Attention*, Atlanta J. & Const., Sept. 23, 1998, at D1.

2. The problem of sexual abuse by coaches is not limited to the United States. In 1996, for example, a University of Winnipeg study found that 22% of Canadian Olympic competitors had experienced sexual encounters with authority figures. In 1997, revered Canadian junior hockey coach Graham James was sentenced to three-and-a-half years in prison after Sheldon Kennedy, one of James' former players, detailed 300 instances of abuse. And in 1998, former Irish Olympic swimming coach Derry O'Rourke was sentenced to 12 years in jail for sexually abusing 11 teenage girls between 1976 and 1992; Paul Ssali, the coach of the She Kobs, Uganda's women's national soccer team, was forced to resign after being accused by his players of being a sexual predator; and the Corel Women's Tennis Association announced it was looking into allegations a top European coach had sex with at least six of his trainees while they were in their teens. *See further* Ethan J. Skolnick, *Skaters Share Nightmare of Coaches in Control*, Palm Beach Post, June 21, 1998, at 1C, and Jay Baltezore, *Sex Suits Unveil Dirty Secret of Olympic Training Groups*, Salt Lake Trib., Nov. 4, 1997, at A1.

Problem 40

To protect its underage citizens, a state enacted a law making it a felony for anyone to use a position of authority to gain sexual favors from a minor. If a high school coach is charged with violating the statute, will he be able to have the indictment quashed on the grounds the legislation is unreasonable, arbitrary, and beyond the police power? *See Scadden v. State*, 732 P.2d 1036 (Wyo.1987).

E. SCOPE OF EMPLOYMENT

Not everything a coach does falls within the scope of his or her employment. Accordingly, courts sometimes must draw a line between a coach's professional and private acts.

SMITH v. GARDNER

998 F.Supp. 708 (S.D.Miss.1998).

LEE, Chief Judge.

This cause is before the court on the motion of defendant Board of Regents of San Jacinto College District (the College) for summary judgment pursuant to Rule 56 of the Federal Rules of Civil Procedure. Plaintiff Larry W. Smith has responded in opposition to the motion and the court, having considered the memoranda of authorities, together with attachments, submitted by the parties, concludes that the motion is well taken and should be granted.

In the early morning hours of March 17, 1996, plaintiff was involved in a two-car automobile accident with defendant Gardner in downtown Meridian. Plaintiff filed this action against Gardner and the College, as his employer, seeking to recover damages for injuries alleged to have been sustained in that accident, which plaintiff claims was caused by negligence on the part of defendant Gardner who, at the time of the accident, was employed as an assistant baseball coach by the College and was in Meridian with the team for baseball games that were scheduled to be played on March 16 and March 17, 1996. Plaintiff sued the College on the theory that it is vicariously liable for Gardner's alleged negligence. The College, however, seeks summary judgment contending that as a matter of law, it cannot be found liable for Gardner's acts since, as shown by the undisputed facts of record, Gardner was not acting within the course and scope of his employment with the College at the time of the accident.

Both parties apparently recognize that the facts pertinent to the "course and scope of employment" issue are essentially undisputed. What they dispute is the conclusion to be drawn from those facts. The court has considered the facts in light of the applicable law and concludes that, as a matter of law, the College is entitled to summary judgment.

On March 14, 1996, the College's baseball team, consisting of twenty-two players, head coach Chris Rupp, assistant coach Gardner and student assistant D.J. Wilson, left Houston, Texas bound for Mississippi, where the team was to play a series of games. The team traveled in three school-owned vans, which were driven by Rupp, Gardner and Wilson. After playing games on the Mississippi Gulf Coast on March 15, the team traveled to Meridian for a March 16 doubleheader with Meridian Community College. Following the games on March 16, the team checked into the Best Western in Meridian, ate dinner at a local restaurant, and returned to the hotel for the night. Around midnight, following the team's 11:00 p.m. curfew, Gardner decided to go out and buy some beer. Without advising anyone he was leaving, he took one of the school vans to a nearby gas station and bought a six-pack of beer. He then returned to the hotel where, over the next couple of hours, he drank approximately half of the six-pack. Around 3:00 a.m., Gardner decided to go out and buy some Skoal. So, he again left the hotel in the school van without telling anyone he was leaving and went back to the store for Skoal. After making the purchase, Gardner, rather than returning to the hotel, decided to check out the sights in downtown Meridian. At 3:22 a.m., while driving around downtown, he was involved in the accident that is the subject of this litigation.

When police officers arrived on the scene, an intoxilizer was administered to Gardner, which revealed that he had a blood alcohol level of .132, in excess of the legal limit of .10. Gardner was taken to the police station, and Coach Rupp was contacted and advised of what had occurred. Rupp went to the station and posted bail for Gardner with money that had been wired by Gardner's mother, and the two then returned to the hotel, where they loaded the team and equipment into the remaining vans to travel to Meridian Community College for another game.

As the court has observed, plaintiff in this case seeks to place liability for the accident on the College on the basis of respondeat superior, or vicarious liability. "Under Mississippi law, an employer is liable for the tortious conduct of his employees if that employee was acting within the scope of his employment." Tichenor v. Roman Catholic Church of the Archdiocese of New Orleans, 32 F.3d 953, 959 (5th Cir.1994). The test for determining whether an employee's tortious act is within the scope of his employment is "whether [the act] was done in the course of and as a means to the accomplishment of the purposes of his employment and therefore in furtherance of the master's business," Odier v. Sumrall, 353 So.2d 1370, 1372 (Miss.1978), or whether the employee was instead "engaged in affairs of his own or ... pursuing some purpose unrelated to his master's business, acting as much outside the scope of his employment as he would be were his working day ended, or his task completed," Seedkem South, Inc. v. Lee, 391 So.2d 990, 995 (Miss.1980). See also Tichenor, 32 F.3d at 959 (quoting Seedkem South); Thatcher v. Brennan, 657 F.Supp. 6, 8–9 (S.D.Miss.1986); Odier, 353 So.2d at 1372 (employer not liable if "at the time of the act the servant had abandoned his employment and was about some purpose of his own not incidental to the employment"). The Mississippi Supreme Court elaborated on this test in Seedkem, stating:

> The general rule is that if an employee who is delegated to perform certain work for his employer steps or turns aside from his master's work or business to serve some purpose of his own, not connected with the employer's business, or, as it is often expressed, deviates or departs from his work to accomplish some purpose of his own not connected with his employment—goes on a "frolic of his own"—the relation of master and servant is thereby temporarily suspended, and the master is not liable for his acts during the period of such suspension, he is then acting upon his own volition, obeying his own will, not as a servant, but as an independent person, even though he intends to and does return to his employer's business after he has accomplished the purpose of his detour from duty.

Seedkem, 391 So.2d at 995 (quoting 35 Am.Jur., p. 989, Master and Servant, par. 555).

In support of its motion for summary judgment in the case at bar, the College argues that while Gardner was obviously an employee of the College on March 17, 1996, he was not acting within the scope of his employment at the time of the accident but rather was on a personal errand which constituted a distinct deviation from the responsibilities of his employment.

In his response to defendant's motion, plaintiff argues, inter alia, that the "whole trip was part of Gardner's employment" since the trip, which was for the College's benefit, required Gardner to be far from home for an extended period of time. Plaintiff states that the College derived certain benefits from having a baseball team and sending it on a trip such as the trip to Meridian, including student recruitment and promotion of the College.

Clearly, though, the law does not support the proposition that because Gardner was required to be out-of-town on a school-sponsored trip, then any and all acts he might undertake while out-of-town would necessarily occur within the scope of his employment, regardless of their relationship to the duties and purposes of his employment.

Plaintiff next points out that the College had to know that given the nature of the trip and the distance from home, the coaches' duties would extend beyond merely coaching baseball, and further knew that the coaches would have to use the school vans for purposes other than strictly going to and from the ball park. Observing further that the College did not specifically undertake to limit the coaches' use of the school vans on out-of-town trips and thus implicitly granted them discretion on how to use the vans, plaintiff concludes that this discretion might reasonably be found to include such errands as picking up some Skoal at a local store and then driving a short distance down the road. The fact is, after returning with the team from eating and retiring to his own hotel room for the night, Gardner was "acting as much outside the scope of his employment as he would be were his working day ended, or his task completed." Seedkem South, Inc. v. Lee, 391 So.2d 990, 995 (Miss.1980). And in thereafter drinking enough beer to become legally intoxicated and then driving around sightseeing in downtown Meridian in the middle of the night while his co-workers and team members in his charge were fast asleep back at the hotel, Gardner was not in any sense about any conceivable business of the College; he was doing nothing toward the accomplishment of any purpose of his employment nor was he performing any act which might reasonably be considered incidental to his employment. Rather, he was obviously a frolicking employee, "engaged in affairs of his own." Cf. Breland & Whitten v. Breland, 243 Miss. 620, 139 So.2d 365 (1962) (worker's compensation case holding that attorney who fell in tub while showering in hotel room where staying while out of town to investigate case for firm was not acting in course and scope of employment, for his activity was purely personal and disconnected from employment). Consequently, the College is not liable for Gardner's alleged negligence relating to the accident with plaintiff.

Plaintiff argues that Gardner's trip to obtain some Skoal was "merely incidental to his employment" because "[i]t is a well known fact that all baseball teams use quite a bit of dip and/or chewing tobacco," so that "[p]rocurement of this tobacco product is an accepted part of baseball and would be incidental to Gardner's employment as a baseball coach." Defendants appropriately term this argument "intriguing" in light of NCAA rules banning the use of tobacco products at any sports practice or game, including baseball. But even apart from that, plaintiff did not just drop by the store to pick up some Skoal for the team. Rather, after drinking half a six-pack of beer alone in his hotel room in the middle of the night, he went out to buy Skoal for himself, and then went riding around town. Nothing about this trip was incidental to his employment. Having reached this conclusion, the court does not address the College's contention that it can have no liability for Gardner's acts since such acts constituted not only a clear violation of College policy against alcohol consumption but also a violation of the criminal laws of the State of Mississippi relative to driving while intoxicated.

Accordingly, it is ordered that the College's motion for summary judgment is granted.

BOLTON v. TULANE UNIVERSITY OF LOUISIANA

692 So.2d 1113 (La.Ct.App.),
writ denied, 701 So.2d 982 (La.1997).

PLOTKIN, Judge.

This consolidated appeal involves four separate rulings on motions for summary judgment contained in a single trial court judgment, all of which turn on a determination of whether plaintiff Mae Ola Bolton was in the course and scope of her employment as an assistant women's basketball coach at defendant Tulane University at the time she was injured in a car accident. For the reasons which follow, we reverse the trial court judgments and grant summary judgment in favor of defendants Tulane University, Hartford Insurance Co., Elizabeth Yopp, State Farm Insurance Co., and Allstate Indemnity Co., dismissing them from the suit.

Consolidated with the above judgment for purposes of this appeal is a summary judgment in the same case dismissing defendant National Car Rental Systems, Inc. (hereinafter referred to as "National"), owner and alleged insurer of the car in which Ms. Bolton was riding at the time of the accident. That judgment is based on the trial court's finding that National had no insurance liability for the accident in question under the contract governing the relationship between the parties. Because we find that genuine issues of material fact exist, we reverse the summary judgment in favor of National. The case is remanded to the trial court for further proceedings on the issue of National's liability to Ms. Bolton.

FACTS AND PROCEDURAL HISTORY

The facts of the instant case are undisputed. Plaintiff Ola Mae Bolton was hired by Candy Harvey, Tulane's head women's basketball coach, as an assistant coach effective in August of 1993. Among Ms. Bolton's most important job duties were responsibilities related to the recruitment of new players for the team, responsibilities she shared with the other assistant coach, Elizabeth Yopp, who had been working for Ms. Harvey for some two years prior to the time Ms. Bolton was hired. Both Ms. Bolton and Ms. Yopp received a set monthly salary. As a part of their recruiting activities, they were required to travel, including some late night travel and some overnight travel during which they had to stay in hotels. When travelling on a recruitment trip, the assistant coaches typically drove vehicles rented on a Tulane account, or paid for with a Tulane credit card. All expenses of these recruitment trips were paid by Tulane.

During official National College Athletic Association ("NCAA") "quiet periods," a prospective basketball team member could travel to a university for an "official visit," paid for by the university. Although Tulane often paid for prospective players to fly to New Orleans for an "official visit," at other times—especially when the student lived close to New Orleans or lived in an area which was not easily accessible by air—the assistant coaches personally drove from New Orleans to the student's home and brought the student back to Tulane for the official visit. At the end of the visit, the assistant coaches personally drove the student back to her home. These types of trips were considered typical recruitment trips which were paid for by Tulane.

The women's basketball team coaches arranged such an official visit for Yvette Porter, a high school senior basketball player from Louisville, Mississippi, for a weekend during a "quiet period" on November 6–7, 1993. Because Ms. Porter lived in an area not easily accessible by air, the decision was made for the assistant coaches to provide automobile transportation for Ms. Porter, as described above. Prior to the weekend, the coaches agreed that Ms. Bolton would drive to Jackson, Mississippi, to retrieve Ms. Porter after she played in a softball game for her high school on Saturday, November 6. Ms. Yopp was to make the four-hour trip to return Ms. Porter to her home in Louisville, Mississippi, on Sunday, November 7. In anticipation of the trip, Ms. Bolton rented an automobile from National.

Ms. Bolton successfully completed her part of the agreement, driving to Jackson, Mississippi, and bringing Ms. Porter back to Tulane on the morning of Saturday, November 6. Ms. Porter stayed in New Orleans overnight, engaging in various activities with team members and the coaches, and visiting with Tulane professors. During the entire weekend, one of the coaches transported Ms. Porter to activities in the automobile rented from National. Near the end of her stay in New Orleans, Ms. Porter attended a practice session of the Tulane women's basketball team as an observer. Thereafter, she was treated to dinner at Copeland's restaurant on St. Charles Avenue with a couple of the team members and all three coaches.

The dinner at Copeland's lasted longer than the coaches had anticipated, not ending until approximately 9 p.m. Nevertheless, Ms. Porter had to be returned to her home in Louisville, Mississippi, prior to 8 a.m. on the morning of Monday, November 8, pursuant to an NCAA rule. As Ms. Yopp prepared for the return trip to Louisville, Mississippi, Ms. Bolton "volunteered" to accompany her on the trip in order to help with the driving because of the lateness of the hour. Neither Ms. Yopp nor Ms. Harvey asked her to make the trip, but they were very pleased when she decided to do so.

The trip from New Orleans to Louisville, Mississippi, was apparently uneventful. The assistant coaches took turns driving, and Ms. Porter was successfully delivered to her home prior to the deadline. However, during the trip back to New Orleans from Louisville, Mississippi, sometime after midnight, while Ms. Yopp was driving the automobile, an accident occurred on Highway 15 south of Louisville, Mississippi. Ms. Yopp apparently fell asleep at the wheel; Ms. Bolton was allegedly already sleeping at the time. The car went down a ravine; Ms. Bolton sustained severe injuries, including a broken neck.

Tulane paid workers' compensation benefits to Ms. Bolton for some period of time after the accident; additionally, Tulane paid many of Ms. Bolton's medical expenses. Thereafter, Ms. Bolton filed a tort action against the following defendants: Ms. Yopp, driver of the automobile; Tulane, Ms. Yopp's employer; Hartford, Tulane's insurer (hereinafter collectively referred to as "Tulane"); State Farm, Ms. Yopp's personal automobile liability insurer (hereinafter referred to as "State Farm"); National, owner of the automobile and insurer under a contract; and Allstate Indemnity Co., Ms. Bolton's uninsured motorist (UM) insurer (hereinafter referred to as "Allstate"). All of the defendants responded by filing motions for summary judgment.

The motion for summary judgment filed by Tulane was premised on the argument that Ms. Bolton's exclusive remedy against Tulane is workers' compensation under the provisions of LSA–R.S. 23:1032 because Ms. Bolton was negligently injured by a co-employee while in the course and scope of her employment. Because the workers' compensation tort immunity defense is not personal to the employer, State Farm and Allstate premised their motions for summary judgment on the same argument, as described in greater detail below. Ms. Bolton filed a cross motion for summary judgment, claiming that she was not in the course and scope of her employment at the time of the accident.

The trial court granted Ms. Bolton's motion for summary judgment, finding that she was not in the course and scope of her employment with Tulane at the time of the accident. Based on the same finding, the trial court denied the motions for summary judgment filed by Tulane, State Farm, and Allstate. Tulane, State Farm, and Allstate appeal the summary judgment in favor of Ms. Bolton on the course and scope issue. State Farm also appeals the denial of its motion for summary judgment. Tulane and Allstate filed applications for supervisory writs in this court seeking review of the judgments denying their motions for summary judgment on the course and scope issue; the applications for supervisory writs were converted to appeals and consolidated with this appeal.

The motion for summary judgment filed by National was premised on provisions of the rental agreement signed by Ms. Bolton. The trial court granted the motion for summary judgment filed by National based on the language of the contract between the parties. Ms. Bolton appealed the judgment granting the motion for summary judgment in favor of National.

MOTIONS FOR SUMMARY JUDGMENT BASED ON COURSE AND SCOPE ISSUE

As indicated above, four of the trial court's rulings on review in this appeal turn on a determination of whether Ms. Bolton was within the course and scope of her employment with Tulane at the time of the accident. If she was within the course and scope of her employment, then Tulane, State Farm, and Allstate are all entitled to summary judgment because Ms. Bolton's exclusive remedy is workers' compensation. The trial court found that Ms. Bolton was not within the course and scope of her employment and therefore granted a summary judgment on this issue in Ms. Bolton's favor. Because the parties agree on the facts relative to this issue, no genuine issues of material fact exist. Thus, this court is required to review those facts de novo in the light of the applicable law and determine whether any of the parties are entitled to judgment as a matter of law.

We note first that the trial court's granting of the motion for summary judgment on the course and scope issue in Ms. Bolton's favor was improper because it constituted a partial summary judgment which decided only one of several issues Ms. Bolton would be required to prove at trial in order to recover from any of the defendants. The Louisiana Supreme Court in the recent case of Norlander v. Illinois National

Insurance Co., 96–1627 (La.10/4/96), 680 So.2d 1166, held that the granting of a motion for summary judgment finding only that an employee was not within the course and scope of his employment "was an improper use of summary judgment that promoted piecemeal appeals." Id. at 1167. Thus, the granting of the motion for summary judgment in Ms. Bolton's favor is improper for that reason, as well as for the other reasons discussed below.

Unlike the granting of a motion for summary judgment finding that an employee was not within the course and scope of his employment, which is improper as described above, the granting of a motion for summary judgment finding that an employee was within the course and scope of his employment is a proper use of a motion for summary judgment. In Norlander, 680 So.2d at 1167, the Louisiana Supreme Court specifically stated that "[a] motion for summary judgment was proper for the defendant's alleged employer to seek dismissal from the action based on defendant's being outside the course and scope of employment." Although the alleged employee in the instant case is the plaintiff rather than the defendant, the same principle applies. Granting a motion for summary judgment on the course and scope issue in favor of Tulane, State Farm, and Allstate in the instant case would be proper because it would result in the dismissal of those defendants from the suit, which does not promote piecemeal appeals. Thus, we will analyze whether Tulane, State Farm, and Allstate are entitled to judgment as a matter of law because Ms. Bolton was within the course and scope of her employment at the time of the accident giving rise to the instant suit.

A. Applicable law

Ms. Bolton claims that Mississippi law should be applied in the instant case because the accident happened in Mississippi. Under Mississippi law, Ms. Bolton claims, she would be entitled under the circumstances of this case to choose either to seek a tort recovery against Tulane or to seek workers' compensation benefits, regardless of whether she was in the course and scope of her employment at the time of the accident.

In the instant case, the record reveals both that Ms. Bolton's employment was principally localized in Louisiana and that she was working under a contract of hire made in Louisiana. Thus, Louisiana's workers' compensation scheme applies to this suit.

B. Course and scope of Ms. Bolton's employment with Tulane under Louisiana law

The extent of an employer's liability for paying workers' compensation benefits to an injured employee is controlled by LSA–R.S. 23:1031(A), which provides as follows:

> If an employee not otherwise eliminated from the benefits of this Chapter receives personal injury by accident arising out of and in the course of his employment, his employer shall pay

compensation in the amounts, on the conditions, and to the person or persons hereinafter designated.

The exclusivity of these provisions is established by LSA–R.S. 23:1032, which provides, in pertinent part, as follows:

> The rights and remedies herein granted to an employee or his dependent on account of an injury, or compensable sickness or disease for which he is entitled to compensation under this Chapter, shall be exclusive of all other rights and remedies of such employee.

Under the jurisprudence interpreting the above articles, an employee's exclusive remedy against his employer for an injury occurring within the course and scope of his employment is workers' compensation benefits. Tucker v. Northeast Louisiana Tree Service, 27,768 (La.App.2d Cir. 12/6/95), 665 So.2d 672, 676, writs denied, 96–0063, 0100 (La.3/8/96), 669 So.2d 404.

Generally, a party to a lawsuit seeking to prove that an employee was within the course and scope of his employment must prove two elements: (1) that the injury suffered by the employee arose out of the employment ("the arising-out-of requirement"), and (2) that the employee suffered the injury during the course of his employment ("the during-course-of requirement"). See Kennedy v. Martin Gas Transportation Co., 96–100 (La.App. 3d Cir. 8/21/96), 680 So.2d 1195, 1196. An employer who seeks to avail itself of the tort immunity of the workers' compensation statutes bears the burden of proving entitlement to the immunity—i.e. that the worker was within the course and scope of his employment at the time of his injury. Tucker, 665 So.2d at 677.

The Louisiana Supreme Court discussed the requirements of LSA–R.S. 23:1032 in Guillory v. Interstate Gas Station, 94–1767 (La.3/30/95), 653 So.2d 1152 as follows:

> The terms "arising out of" and "in the course of" constitute a dual requirement. The former suggests an inquiry into the character or origin of the risk while the latter brings into focus the time and place relationship between the risk and the employment. The two requirements cannot, however, be considered in isolation from each other. A strong showing ... with reference to the arise-out-of requirement may compensate for a relatively weak showing on the during-course-of requirement, or vice versa. As a corollary it follows that whenever the showing with respect to both requirements is relatively weak a denial of compensation is indicated.

Id. at 1154.

Some of the factors to be weighed in determining course and scope of employment include the following: (1) "the time, place and purpose of the act in relation to the service of the employer," (2) "the relationship between the employee's act and the employer's business," (3) "the reasonable expectation of the employer that the employee would perform the act." Reed v. House of Decor, Inc., 468 So.2d 1159, 1161 (La.1985); Michaleski, 472 So.2d at 21.

The exclusive workers' compensation remedy has been applied in cases where an accident occurred during a trip taken by an employee "in the interest of his employer's business," under circumstances indicating that the employer's consent to the travel may be fairly implied. Jepsen v. B–Con Construction Co., 475 So.2d 112, 115–16 (La.App. 2d Cir.1985), citing Thomas v. RPM Corporation, 449 So.2d 18 (La.App. 1st Cir.), writ denied, 450 So.2d 965 (La.1984); Reynolds v. Be–Neat Tank Cleaning Corp., 425 So.2d 881 (La.App. 4th Cir.1983). When an accident occurs while "the employee is on a mission contemplated by employer and employee for which he is to be compensated," the employee is considered to be within the course and scope of his employment. Michaleski v. Western Preferred Casualty Co., 472 So.2d 18, 21 (La.1985).

1. Arising-out-of requirement

A determination of whether an accident arises out of the employment requires that a court consider only the following questions: 1) Was the employee then engaged about his employer's business and not merely pursuing his own business or pleasure; and (2) did the necessities of that employer's business reasonably require that the employee be at the place of the accident at the time the accident occurred? Meaux [v. Cormier], 554 So.2d [285,] at 287 [(La.Ct.App.1989)], quoting Kern v. Southport Mill, 174 La. 432, 141 So. 19 (La.1932). See also Yates [v. Naylor Industrial Services, Inc.], 569 So.2d [616,] at 620 [(La.Ct.App. 1990), writ denied, 572 So. 2d 92 (La.1991)].

Applying the above principles to the instant case, we find that the risk which caused the accident which resulted in Ms. Bolton's injuries unquestionably arose out of her employment duties. Ms. Bolton's boss, Ms. Harvey, was present when Ms. Bolton decided to accompany Ms. Yopp on the trip to return Ms. Porter to her home. Ms. Harvey testified concerning her reaction to the idea as follows: "I said that I thought that was a very good idea and that actually I was very pleased that that was what was taking place." Harvey deposition, p. 39. Ms. Harvey admitted that the offer was not a requirement of the job and that she did not order Ms. Bolton to accompany Ms. Yopp on the return trip, although it did fall "within the ramifications of her job." Id. at 40.

Ms. Harvey testified that she was pleased with the idea for a couple of reasons, both of which were beneficial to Tulane. The first reason was that Ms. Yopp needed company on the return trip because she was leaving so late at night and having two drivers taking turns would be safer. Id. at 69. The second reason was grounded in the fact that having an additional person to engage the recruit in conversation would make the trip more enjoyable for the recruit. Id. Ms. Bolton was especially suited to make Ms. Porter feel more comfortable, Ms. Harvey said, because she was well-known in the area where Ms. Porter lived and had a prior relationship with Ms. Porter's coach and because she had been present when Ms. Harvey made the home visit with Ms. Porter. Id. at 70.

Ms. Harvey also said that Ms. Bolton's being involved in additional recruiting was a "favorable thing" for her to do. Id. at 67. Getting Ms. Porter back home safely was the "official business" of Tulane, she said. Id. at 71. Ms. Harvey stated several times that she felt that Ms. Bolton was engaged in the responsibilities of her employment with Tulane when she offered to accompany Ms. Yopp on the trip to return Ms. Porter to her home. From this testimony, we can easily conclude that the trip was taken in the interest of Tulane's business with the consent of Ms. Bolton's supervisor, Ms. Harvey.

The only reason the two assistant coaches were riding in the automobile after midnight when the accident happened was the NCAA's requirement that Ms. Porter be returned to her home prior to 8 a.m. that morning. In the absence of the demands of her employment, Ms. Bolton would not have been at the site of the accident. The circumstances of this case definitely meet the requirements established by Meaux because of the following findings: (1) Ms. Porter was engaged in [her] employer's business, not merely pursuing her own business or pleasure, and (2) the necessities of Tulane's business reasonably required Ms. Bolton to be at the place of the accident when the accident occurred. See Meaux, 554 So.2d at 287.

2. *During-course-of requirement*

Generally, an employee who sustains injury while actively engaged in the performance of his duties during working hours, either "on the employer's premises or at other places where employment activities take the employee" is considered to have occurred during the course of his employment. Mundy v. Department of Health & Human Resources, 593 So.2d 346, 349 (La.1992); Tucker, 665 So.2d at 677. Workers' compensation coverage has also been extended to include "accidents at places where employment duties are performed off the employer's premises." Mundy, 593 So.2d at 349; Tucker, 665 So.2d at 677. The principal criteria to consider to determine the during-course-of employment issue are time, place, and employment activity. Mundy, 593 So.2d at 349; Tucker, 665 So.2d at 677. Moreover, an accident is considered to have occurred during the course of an injured employee's employment when "it happens during the time of employment and at a place contemplated by one's employment." Yates, 569 So.2d at 620; Meaux, 554 So.2d at 288.

Applying the above principles to the instant case, we find that the accident which caused Ms. Bolton's injuries unquestionably occurred during the time of Ms. Bolton's employment at a place contemplated by her employment. Yates, 569 So.2d at 620. Ms. Bolton was paid a set amount of money for her services to Tulane; Ms. Bolton's boss, Ms. Harvey, testified by deposition that Ms. Bolton's workings hours varied depending on various circumstances. According to Ms. Harvey, Ms. Bolton was required to be actively engaged in recruiting new players for the team; she was paid for her recruitment activities. Thus, we can conclude that Ms. Bolton's injuries occurred during her working hours, despite the fact the accident occurred after midnight on a Monday morning.

Additionally, the accident occurred at a place other than the employer's premises where employment activities took the employee. See Mundy, 593 So.2d at 349. The accident also occurred during a trip taken by an employee "in the interest of his employer's business" under circumstances indicating that the employer's consent to the travel may be fairly implied. Jepsen, 475 So.2d at 115–16.

3. Totality of the circumstances

The relationship between the arising-out-of requirement and the during-course-of requirement for determining whether a given accident falls under the exclusivity provisions of workers' compensation remedy has been described as follows:

> [T]he two elements should not be understood as entirely separate requirements to be rigidly and independently exacted. Rather, they should be understood simply as closely intertwined issues that may usefully illuminate the common sense practical question of whether the employee's injury bears some significant relationship to the employer's business operation.

Yates, 569 So.2d at 620. Thus, the determination is based on a consideration of the "totality of the circumstances." Jepsen, 475 So.2d at 112.

A consideration of the totality of the circumstances in the instant case in light of the above legal principles easily convinces us that Ms. Bolton was within the course and scope of her employment with Tulane at the time of the accident which caused her injuries. All of these factors taken together show that Ms. Bolton was on a "mission contemplated by employer and employee," for which Ms. Bolton was compensated. Michaleski, 472 So.2d at 21. Certainly, the trip had a "significant relationship" to Tulane's business. Yates, 569 So.2d at 620.

Ms. Bolton has sought to avoid the exclusivity of the workers' compensation remedy by arguing that she was motivated to offer to go on the return trip by her "good Christian upbringing," not by her job responsibilities. However, even if we assume that Ms. Bolton was motivated by her own character to volunteer for the return trip, that fact does not foreclose a finding that Ms. Bolton was in the course and scope of her employment with Tulane at the time of the accident because "[a]n employee's personal mission and his employer's business are not necessarily mutually exclusive." Jepsen, 475 So.2d at 116.

Accordingly, the motion for summary judgment filed by Ms. Bolton's employer, Tulane, and her co-employee who caused her injuries while she was in the course and scope of her employment, Ms. Yopp, is granted. Ms. Bolton's sole remedy against Tulane, Hartford, and Ms. Yopp is under the provisions of the workers' compensation statutes. LSA–R.S. 23:1035.1(1); LSA–R.S. 23:1032. Tulane, Hartford, and Ms. Yopp are hereby dismissed from the case.

C. Liability of State Farm and Allstate

As indicated above, the motions for summary judgment filed by State Farm and Allstate were also based on the course and scope of employment issue. State Farm was sued in its capacity as Ms. Yopp's liability insurer, while Allstate was sued in its capacity as Ms. Bolton's UM insurer. In her brief in opposition to State Farm's appeal and in oral argument, Ms. Bolton admitted that the insurers are not liable for her accident if she was within the course and scope of her employment with Tulane at the time of the accident. We agree.

It is well settled in Louisiana law, that the tort immunity defense under the workers' compensation statute is not personal to the employer, but may be invoked by an insurer sued under the direct action statute. Dauzat v. State Farm Insurance Co., 473 So.2d 920 (La.App. 3d Cir.[1985]; ; Lee v. Allstate Insurance Co., 467 So.2d 44, 47 (La.App. 4th Cir.1985), writ denied, 472 So.2d 593 (La.1985); Green v. Turner, 437 So.2d 956, 959 (La.App. 2d Cir.1983); Carlisle [v. State Through DOTD], 400 So.2d 284 [(La.App.3d Cir.), writ denied 404 So.2d 1256 (La.1981)].

Because the tort immunity defense is a general defense, it may be invoked by the tortfeasor's liability insurer. Dauzat, 473 So.2d 920; Green, 437 So.2d 956; Carlisle, 400 So.2d 284. Because Ms. Yopp, who is insured by State Farm, is not liable to Ms. Bolton because of the tort immunity defense, neither is her liability insurance company. See Carlisle, 400 So.2d at 287. By the same token, Ms. Bolton's UM insurer is not liable because there is no underlying uninsured or underinsured person who is liable to pay Ms. Bolton. Id. Accordingly, motions for summary judgment are also granted in favor of State Farm and Allstate, who are hereby dismissed from the case.

LANGUAGE OF NATIONAL CONTRACT

The trial court's granting of the motion for summary judgment in favor of National was apparently based on the trial court's acceptance of National's reading of the contracts between the two parties. Typically, interpretation of contract provisions is a matter of law which may properly be decided on a motion for summary judgment. However, because of a unique factual situation involved in the instant case, we find that summary judgment was improvidently granted because of remaining genuine issues of material fact.

A conflict exists in the instant case concerning which of two contractual agreements governs National's relationship with Tulane as renter of the automobile and thus National's insurance obligation to Ms. Bolton. At the time Ms. Bolton rented the automobile from National, she signed a standard rental agreement which provided only $10,000 in liability and UM insurance. However, National had entered an "exclusive agreement" with the NCAA, of which Tulane is an affiliate, which was admittedly in effect at the time of the accident in question. The $100,000 liability and UM insurance coverage provided by that exclusive agreement was ten times greater than the liability coverage provided by the standard rental agreement. National claims that the standard rental contract applies to this accident, while Ms. Bolton claims the exclusive agreement applies. The trial court granted National's motion for summary judgment on this issue, finding that National "did not afford liability coverage or protection for the claims set forth in this litigation." The trial court failed to determine which contract controls.

National's argument that the standard rental contract, rather than the exclusive agreement controls is premised on language in the exclusive agreement under the heading "Insurance," which provided for the greater insurance coverage only "when the rate at the time of rental is a SimCom rate pursuant to this Agreement." Language in the section of the exclusive agreement under the heading "Promotional Rate Discount" stated that the standard rental agreement applied for "rental transactions utilizing these promotional rate discounts."

In support of its motion for summary judgment, National filed an affidavit from its employee Ginny Olsby, who stated that she investigated the accident which resulted in Ms. Bolton's injuries and determined that Ms. Bolton rented the automobile at a promotional rate discount, not at SimCom rates. However, no corroborating evidence of the rate or other documents were submitted.

We find that the evidence presented by National was insufficient to meet National's burden of proving that all genuine issues of material fact had been resolved. National did not present any proof of the rate actually paid by Tulane for the automobile, nor did it present any proof of the SimCom rates or the promotional rate discounts in effect at the time. Because National's motion for summary judgment was not properly supported by competent evidence, the trial court improperly granted the motion for summary judgment in National's favor.

National claimed in oral argument that its affidavit should be accepted as sufficient to resolve all genuine issues of material fact because Ms. Bolton failed to present any countervailing affidavits or other evidence in opposition to its motion for summary judgment. However, until the party seeking summary judgment has met its burden of proof, the party opposing the motion has no responsibility for presenting countervailing evidence. The burden of proof remains on the mover under the new law. National did not meet its burden of proof. It is not entitled to summary judgment.

Because of our finding on this issue, we pretermit the other issues raised by Ms. Bolton in this portion of the appeal. The trial court judgment granting the motion for summary judgment in favor of National is hereby reversed.

Conclusion

For the above and foregoing reasons, the following trial court judgments are reversed: (1) the judgment granting summary judgment in favor of Ms. Bolton; (2) the judgments denying summary judgment in favor of Tulane, State Farm, and Allstate; and (3) the judgment granting summary judgment in favor of National. Additionally, summary judgment is granted in favor of Tulane, Hartford, Ms. Yopp, State Farm, and Allstate; those defendants are hereby dismissed from the suit. The case is remanded for further proceedings on National's liability to Ms. Bolton consistent with this opinion.

Note

To protect both students and their families, every athletic conference has established rules which limit the number of contacts a school may have with a recruit, as well as their nature, timing, and duration. *See further Thomas v. Pearl*, 998 F.2d 447 (7th Cir.1993), *cert. denied*, 510 U.S. 1043 (1994), and *Brentwood Academy v. Tennessee Secondary Schools Athletic Ass'n*, 13 F. Supp. 2d 670 (M.D.Tenn.1998). *See also* Ray Yasser, *A Comprehensive Blueprint for the Reform of Intercollegiate Athletics*, 3 Marq. Sports L.J. 123 (1993).

Problem 41

During a midnight bedcheck, a team's star quarterback and its coach resumed a longstanding argument. This time, however, the quarrel escalated and the two came to blows. In the ensuing brawl, the player sustained grievous injuries from which he eventually died. If the decedent's parents sue the university, claiming the coach's attack was within the scope of his employment, how is the court likely to rule? *See Copeland v. Samford University*, 686 So.2d 190 (Ala.1996).

Chapter 7

DOCTORS

A. OVERVIEW

Sooner or later, all competitors suffer injuries. When they do, medical experts are called in to help them recover. This has forced the legal system to confront three questions: 1) what constitutes malpractice?; 2) can a physician's negligence be attributed to a third party?; and, 3) when will a trainer be held liable for a player's injuries?

B. MALPRACTICE

Athletes who claim to be victims of incompetent treatment face a heavy burden of proof. To prevail, they must show the applicable standard of care was not met.

1. THEORIES

Malpractice suits typically are based on one (or more) of the following four causes of action: failure to properly diagnose, failure to properly treat, failure to properly inform, or failure to keep a confidence.

CAPONE v. DONOVAN

480 A.2d 1249 (Pa.Super.Ct.1984).

WIEAND, Judge.

If a plaintiff's football injury has been misdiagnosed and mistreated successively by several physicians so as to result in a permanent injury, does settlement with one physician bar an action against the other physicians? The trial court held that a second action was barred and entered summary judgment in favor of the physicians. We reverse.

Gerard Capone, Jr., sustained a broken arm during football scrimmage at Bucknell University on September 13, 1977. He was treated the same day by Doctors J. Arnold Donovan, Jr., and M.J. Stackowski, who took x-rays and applied a long-arm cast. During succeeding weeks, while he continued to be treated by Doctors Donovan and Stackowski, Capone's arm failed to heal properly. On October 7, 1977, Capone went to see Dr. Anthony J. Persico, a physician who practiced in the vicinity of Capone's home in New Jersey. Persico took additional x-rays and applied a splint wrapped in an ace bandage. Capone saw Dr. Persico three or four times but discomfort resulted from the continued failure of the arm to heal. Finally, when in July, 1978 the arm still had not healed, Capone visited Dr. Francis P. Milone. Milone performed surgery to correct the injury. He told Capone that, because of the nature of the fracture, surgery should have been performed immediately after the injury was sustained.

Capone and his parents commenced an action in the courts of New Jersey to recover damages attributable to Dr. Persico's failure to make a correct diagnosis and render proper treatment. That case was settled for the sum of $25,000. A release was executed as follows:

> KNOW ALL MEN BY THESE PRESENTS:
>
> That the Releasor, for and in consideration of the sum of Twenty–Five Thousand and no/100 ($25,000.00) Dollars lawful Money of the United States of America, to the Releasor in hand paid by ANTHONY J. PERSICO, M.D. hereinafter designated as the Releasee, the receipt whereof is hereby acknowledged, has remised, released and forever discharged, and by these Presents does remise, release and forever discharge the said Releasee of and from all debts, obligations, reckonings, promises, covenants, agreements, contracts, endorsements, bonds, specialties, controversies, suits, actions, causes of actions, trespasses, variances, judgments, extents, executions, damages, claims or demands, in law or in equity, which against the said Releasee, the Releasor ever had, now has or hereafter can, shall, or may have, for, upon or by reason of any matter, cause or thing whatsoever, from the beginning of the world to the day of the date of these Presents.
>
> More particularly from any and all claims arising out of a lawsuit instituted in the Superior Court of New Jersey, Law Division, Bergen County, Docket No. L–63505–78MM.

Capone and his parents also commenced the instant malpractice action against Doctors Donovan and Stackowski in which the trial court entered summary judgment in favor of the physicians. In an appeal from that judgment, Capone argues that the physicians were not joint tortfeasors and that, in any event, the trial court erred in entering summary judgment.

If the tortious conduct of two or more persons causes a single harm which cannot be apportioned, the actors are joint tortfeasors even though they may have acted independently. Restatement (Second) of Torts § 879 (1977). See: Pratt v. Stein, 298 Pa.Super. 92, 150, 444 A.2d 674, 704–705 (1982); Voyles v. Corwin, 295 Pa.Super. 126, 130, 441 A.2d 381, 383 (1982); Lasprogata v. Qualls, 263 Pa.Super. 174, 179 n. 4, 397

A.2d 803, 805 n. 4 (1979). If two or more causes combine to produce a single harm which is incapable of being divided on a logical, reasonable, or practical basis, and each cause is a substantial factor in bringing about the harm, an arbitrary apportionment should not be made. Restatement (Second) of Torts § 433A Comment i (1977); Prosser, Law of Torts § 47, p. 330 (1941). Whether harm is capable of apportionment is a question of law for the court. Voyles v. Corwin, supra; Lasprogata v. Qualls, supra at 181, 397 A.2d at 806; Restatement (Second) of Torts § 434(1)(b) (1977). Most personal injuries are by their very nature incapable of division. Restatement (Second) of Torts § 433A, Comment i (1977). In the instant case, the harm allegedly caused to appellants-plaintiffs by the failure of three physicians to diagnose and/or treat properly the broken arm sustained by Gerard Capone, Jr., was incapable of division among the physicians on a "logical, reasonable, or practical basis."

It is appellants' contention that Doctors Donovan, Stackowski and Persico misinterpreted x-rays and, therefore, failed to diagnose Capone's injury as a Monteggia fracture of the arm. As a consequence, they failed to treat the injury properly and thus caused a permanent, partial loss of motion of the elbow. In addition to a diminished future earning capacity, it is alleged, the failure to treat the injury properly caused unnecessary pain and suffering to Capone and a loss of services to his parents. Appellants did not allege that Dr. Persico, who treated Capone after Doctors Donovan and Stackowski, had aggravated an existing condition. They contended, rather, that Persico had failed to correct a deteriorating condition of the elbow and that the alleged malpractice of all treating physicians combined to produce a permanent injury.

Under these circumstances, Capone's permanent injury was not susceptible of a logical apportionment among the treating physicians; any attempt to do so would necessarily result in an arbitrary division. The duty of care owed by each physician was the same; the alleged negligence of each was the same; and the harm caused as a result of their combined negligence was single and indivisible. The physicians, therefore, were joint tortfeasors. See: Pratt v. Stein, supra; Wade v. S.J. Groves & Sons Co., 283 Pa.Super. 464, 473–474, 424 A.2d 902, 906–907 (1981).

It does not follow that the release given to Dr. Persico effected a release of Doctors Donovan and Stackowski. By statute it is provided in Pennsylvania that,

> A release by the injured person of one joint tort-feasor, whether before or after judgment, does not discharge the other tort-feasors unless the release so provides, but reduces the claim against the other tort-feasors in the amount of the consideration paid for the release or in any amount or proportion by which the release provides that the total claim shall be reduced if greater than the consideration paid.

42 Pa.C.S. § 8326.

The law is clear, therefore, that the release executed by plaintiffs to Dr. Persico was ineffective to release Doctors Donovan and Stackowski unless the release so provided. See: Sochanski v. Sears, Roebuck Co., 689 F.2d 45, 48 n. 2 (3d Cir.1982); Brown v. Pittsburgh, 409 Pa. 357, 362, 186 A.2d 399, 402 (1962). Cf. Lasprogata v. Qualls, supra. The release executed upon settlement of the New Jersey action against Dr. Persico purported to release Dr. Persico alone. Such a release did not effect a release of Doctors Donovan and Stackowski. The only effect of the release was to require a reduction in any verdict recovered against them by the sum of $25,000 already paid in settlement of the New Jersey action against Dr. Persico. See: Sochanski v. Sears, Roebuck Co., supra; Pilosky v. Dougherty, 179 F.Supp. 148, 150 (E.D.Pa.1959); Daugherty v. Hershberger, 386 Pa. 367, 126 A.2d 730 (1956).

The plaintiffs are entitled to only one satisfaction for the harm which they have sustained. See: Brown v. Pittsburgh, supra; Hilbert v. Roth, 395 Pa. 270, 149 A.2d 648 (1959); Lasprogata v. Qualls, supra. Whether the sum of $25,000 recovered from Dr. Persico represented recovery in full will be an issue of fact for the jury. The present state of the record does not permit a court to determine as a matter of law that plaintiffs have already recovered in full for the harm caused by the alleged mistreatment of the football injury sustained by Gerard Capone, Jr. [In addition,] Capone may have a separate claim against the appellee physicians for unnecessary pain, if any, caused by a failure to treat the arm properly before treatment by Dr. Persico began.

Reversed and remanded for further proceedings.

MORELAND v. LOWDERMILK

709 F.Supp. 722 (W.D.La.1989).

STAGG, Chief Judge.

This case is about a fine, young, female, equine athlete whose untimely demise is sought to be laid at the door of her attending veterinarian. Her owners seek monetary damages based on her potential earnings on the race track and as a brood mare of a future generation of purse winners. After many years of hearing and deciding cases involving sick people and their doctors, this is this court's first veterinary malpractice case. It is brought by Mike and Jane Moreland, who raised Sandhill Diamond from a colt and, as a two- and three-year-old filly, moved her from track to track on the racing circuit.

Named as defendants are the three veterinarians who allegedly treated Sandhill Diamond, D.M. Lowdermilk, D.M. Cooley and R.A. Burgess and their liability insurer, Associated Indemnity Corp. The defendants have asserted a counterclaim seeking to recover monies owed for veterinary services provided. A bench trial was held on February 23–24, 1989. After hearing six live witnesses, reading the depositions and exhibits filed in evidence and reviewing my trial notes, I conclude (1) that the plaintiffs have not carried their burden of proving that Dr.

Lowdermilk's services were the cause of the loss of Sandhill Diamond and (2) that the plaintiffs owe for the services rendered by him.

FINDINGS OF FACT

Vagabond Nell gave birth to Sandhill Diamond on April 6, 1983, on the plaintiffs' farm in Imperial, Nebraska. Sandhill Diamond entered the racing circuit in 1985. Her trainer was Linda Davidson, Jane Moreland's sister. Though not of a particularly strong pedigree, Sandhill Diamond, over her racing career, earned a racing index of 4.9 which placed her in the top 10 per cent of thoroughbred winners in the country. At the time of her untimely death on October 13, 1986, Sandhill Diamond was the leading Nebraska filly and had career race winnings in excess of $100,-000.

Late in the afternoon on Sunday, October 5, 1986, Sandhill Diamond ran what was to be her last race at Louisiana Downs in Bossier City, Louisiana. In that race she finished third or, more commonly, "showed." According to Linda Davidson, the horse drank only five gulps of water after the race. Davidson also testified that on October 5, the mare did not eat her evening feed and she was unsure whether the horse had eaten any hay.

According to Davidson, Sandhill Diamond ate neither feed nor hay on October 6. Davidson advised Dr. Lowdermilk on that date that she had a mare who had not eaten her night feed. Dr. Lowdermilk responded that it was probably due to post-race stress.

Davidson became concerned on October 7 because she believed the horse still had neither eaten nor drunk anything. Her belief that Sandhill Diamond had not drunk water was based on a periodic check of the water bucket in the horse's stall. Davidson admitted that she was not with the horse around the clock. According to Davidson, however, no one else would be allowed in that stall. It was not disputed, however, that others had access to the area and could have added water to the bucket without Davidson's knowledge. On the other hand, Dr. Lowdermilk was under the impression that the horse had been drinking some. He also testified that he understood the mare was drinking two to three gallons of water per day after October 7.

The court is unpersuaded, either by the testimony of Dr. Lowdermilk or Linda Davidson, regarding the amount of the horse's water intake. The evidence on this point is inconclusive as neither Dr. Lowdermilk nor Davidson spent enough time with the mare to testify convincingly regarding how much water she drank. Though either Dr. Lowdermilk or another doctor from his office checked on the horse two to three times a day, beginning on October 7, the visits were normally brief. Davidson spent several hours around the stall but admitted that she would go elsewhere on the race track and, from noon to 6:00 P.M., would not be at the track.

Dr. Lowdermilk examined the horse on October 7, 1986, and strongly suspected that Sandhill Diamond suffered from thromboembolic colic.

"Colic" refers to any abdominal pain. "Thromboembolic colic" is the type of abdominal disease that is reserved to situations where there is a vascular compromise to the bowel. "Thrombi" are organized clots attached to the walls of the blood vessels, such as the cranial mesenteric artery. These thrombi become dislodged, function as emboli, and block other blood vessels that include arterial supply to certain segments of the bowel.

The damage resulting from thromboembolic colic is due primarily to migrating strongylus vulgaris larvae—more commonly referred to as blood worms. As this parasite goes through its migration stages, it usually nests in the cranial mesenteric artery that supplies blood to the large intestines and the cecum. Though these larvae initially locate in the cranial mesenteric artery, they migrate in to the wall of that artery and eventually make it back to the bowel. They then penetrate into the lumen of the bowel, where they mature as adults and begin producing eggs that pass with the feces. The life cycle from the time of infestation of larvae until the time they become mature adults producing eggs is approximately six months. Some of the eggs emerge in the feces and into the grass. It is through grazing in an infested area that horses normally ingest the parasite.

On October 7, Sandhill Diamond's vital signs appeared normal, but her gut sounds were slightly weak. A fecal exam performed on that day was positive for blood worms. Dr. Lowdermilk gave the horse Banamine and d-Panthenol. Banamine is a nonsteroidal anti-inflammatory drug that was given for pain. D–Panthenol is an intestinal stimulant. This was given because Sandhill Diamond had not passed feces since the race. In addition to Banamine and d-Panthenol, Dr. Lowdermilk gave the horse an analgesic for pain. Also on October 7, Dr. Lowdermilk gave Sandhill Diamond one gallon of mineral oil through a nasogastric tube. Electrolytes were administered intravenously.

On October 8, Dr. Lowdermilk administered the same drugs that he had given on October 7 but did so in the morning, afternoon and evening. A blood sample was taken for a complete blood count (hereinafter "CBC"). The CBC contained a reading for the packed cell volume which is an indication of whether the horse is dehydrated. Once again, mineral oil was given through the nasogastric tube, and other fluids were given intravenously. Though Sandhill Diamond, as she had on the 7th, showed signs of discomfort, her vital signs and CBC were normal.

On October 9, Dr. Lowdermilk repeated the medication—but only once during the day. The mare showed signs of improvement as oil came through. The horse also passed, for the first time since October 5, a few fecal balls. According to the testimony of Dr. Alicia Bertone, an expert in equine veterinary medicine, this was a positive indication that intestinal movement had begun again. Even Davidson testified that the horse seemed to improve on the 9th.

On October 10, Dr. Lowdermilk administered the same medications that he had on the three previous days. Sandhill Diamond had, on that day, a swollen knee and a small puncture. Dr. Lowdermilk treated the swollen knee by giving the horse some antibiotics and Naquasone. Naquasone is a steroid diuretic and an anti-inflammatory drug used in the treatment of trauma and swellings. It will also draw fluid from abnormal compartments in the body. Sandhill Diamond passed more manure on the 10th and showed minimal signs of improvement. Her gut sounds were better, though still not quite normal.

Sandhill Diamond's condition began to decline rapidly on October 11. She developed a fever and, for the first time, showed clinical signs of dehydration. Dr. Lowdermilk administered an antibiotic in an effort to reduce the temperature. Bute, Banamine and d-Panthenol were also administered on that morning. By evening, the horse showed signs of shock.

In an effort to treat the shock, Dr. Lowdermilk gave the horse SoluDelta Cortef with electrolytes. The morning medication was repeated and a gallon of mineral oil was given between 8:00 and 10:00 P.M. Dr. Lowdermilk advised Davidson that the horse "was not going to make it," and that she had basically two choices: euthanasia or watch the horse suffer and die. Distraught with these alternatives, Davidson insisted there must be another choice. Dr. Lowdermilk then said that he would give the horse a rectal exam, and, if Sandhill Diamond was not torn inside, he would administer more antibiotics and hope for the best. The exam was conducted and additional antibiotics were given.

Both Dr. Lowdermilk and Davidson left the horse at about 10:00 P.M. Davidson returned at 11:00 P.M. She telephoned Dr. Lowdermilk and told him that Sandhill Diamond's legs were cold and that the mare was in pain. Dr. Lowdermilk stated that he would come out to the race track and put the horse to sleep. Dissatisfied with this response, Davidson telephoned her sister and brother-in-law. The Morelands advised her to try to find someone else, whereupon Davidson contacted Dr. R.J. Wolfe.

Dr. Wolfe arrived at the race track at 1:30 A.M. on October 12. According to Dr. Wolfe, the mare was clinically in shock. The horse's gut sounds were depressed and abnormal. He believed that the filly was colicked and probably had peritonitis. Peritonitis is the infection or inflammation of the peritoneum, the surface that lines the entire abdominal area covering all of the intestinal tract. When heavily colonized by bacteria, the peritoneum turns into a body cavity that is akin to a very large abscess.

Dr. Wolfe ran two diagnostic tests—a hemotocrit and a total protein count—both of which indicated the horse was dehydrated. Dr. Wolfe administered fluid therapy of 20 liters and gave the horse Banamine, Dyprone, Gentocin, which is an antibiotic, and Heparin, an anticoagulant. The Dyprone was given to lower the horse's temperature, stabilize gut motility and reduce pain.

Dr. Wolfe felt the mare needed to get to a hospital and a veterinarian who specialized in abdominal surgery. Toward this end, the mare was transferred to Dr. Robert D. Lewis in Elgin, Texas. Sandhill Diamond arrived at Dr. Lewis' clinic around noon on October 12. At that time, the mare had blue mucus membranes, a clinical indication of shock, and an abnormal heart rate. Dr. Lewis performed an abdominocentesis, or more commonly referred to as an abdominal tap, which documented an ongoing and extensive septic peritonitis. An intravenous catheter was installed in the mare and four gallons of intravenous saline were administered at a high rate to try to get the horse's blood pressure back up. A Foley's catheter was placed in the mare's abdominal cavity to drain the peritoneal fluids. Later, prior to surgery, an additional ten gallons of fluids were administered.

Dr. Lewis telephoned the Morelands and advised them that Sandhill Diamond's symptoms were strongly suggestive of thromboembolic colic, to which the peritonitis was secondary. He stated that the peritonitis was grave enough to kill the horse. He felt that he could not provide more conclusive information without performing an exploratory laparotomy. Dr. Lewis advised the Morelands that Sandhill Diamond, in his opinion, was a poor candidate for surgery. Because the Morelands did not want to leave any stones unturned, the surgery was requested and performed.

The exploratory surgery revealed rampant peritonitis which resulted from a classic case of a thromboembolic disease. Dr. Lewis also found evidence of gangrene which affected areas throughout the entire large colon. The most affected region in the large colon was the pelvic flexure area which is the most distal extremity of the loop of the large colon that is the farthest from the main arterial supply. This area was gangrenous and near the point of rupture.

On page 45 of his deposition, Dr. Lewis described the bowel as normally pink and healthy looking: "Then you will have a black spot, and you have these all over splotched, and it's kind of like a Dalmation (sic) dog appearance to the colon." Dr. Lewis examined the horse's cranial mesenteric artery which he found to be abnormally large for a three-year-old mare. Since the strongylus vulgaris larvae migrate through this artery, Dr. Lewis concluded that the enlarged artery was consistent with his diagnosis of thromboembolic colic. Between 60 and 70 per cent of the large colon was removed in the operation.

Sandhill Diamond died about 1:00 P.M. on October 13. Dr. Lewis's opinion was that the horse died due to overwhelming septic shock that resulted in cardiac failure. Septic shock, according to Dr. Lewis, is an abnormal exposure of the circulatory system to bacteria and their toxins. The shock results in hemoconcentration, and a drop in blood pressure due to the effect of the toxins on the vascular system.

The septic shock, in Dr. Lewis's opinion, was triggered originally by a thromboembolic episode, or shower of emboli, that was due to significant cranial mesenteric artery disease. The artery disease was caused by the migration of strongylus vulgaris larvae—bloodworms burrowing into artery walls creating thrombi. These thrombi become dislodged most commonly during transport or an athletic event. Regarding whether the mare's chances would have been improved had Dr. Lewis received her earlier, he testified: "I don't know if I could have—this mare had enough disease that if I had gotten her earlier in the case, I got a strong suspicion the outcome inevitably may have been the same because she had a severe case of it, but I don't know that, you know."

ANALYSIS OF LAW AND FACTS

Plaintiffs contend that Dr. Lowdermilk's treatment of Sandhill Diamond, as a specialist in equine veterinary practice, fell below the accepted standard of care due to the following errors:

> 1. Failing to maintain at least normal fluids in the horse which Dr. Lowdermilk had diagnosed as having thromboembolic colic;
>
> 2. Failing to administer fluids through the insertion of a nasogastric tube;
>
> 3. Failing to administer anticoagulants and antibiotics upon diagnosis of thromboembolic colic;
>
> 4. Failing to administer antibiotics which had been balanced against gram negative and gram positive organisms;
>
> 5. Administering an antibiotic on October 10 that had not been balanced against gram negative and gram positive organisms;
>
> 6. Failing to repeatedly run various tests, including a complete blood count, packed cell volume, total protein, rectal exams and an abdominal tap; and
>
> 7. Administering Naquasone, a diuretic, to a dehydrated horse.

Under Louisiana law, which this court sitting in diversity is Erie-bound to follow, standards governing medical malpractice actions control in veterinary malpractice cases. Ladnier v. Norwood, 781 F.2d 490, 492 (5th Cir.1986); Carter v. Louisiana State University, 520 So.2d 383, 387 (La.1988). The locality standard of care is inapplicable to a veterinary specialist. Id. Under La.Rev.Stat.Ann. § 9:2794 (West Supp.1989), a plaintiff in a malpractice action bears a three-part burden:

> 1. [W]here the defendant practices in a particular specialty and where the alleged acts of medical negligence raise issues peculiar to the particular medical specialty involved, then the plaintiff has the burden of proving the degree of care ordinarily practiced by [veterinarians] ... within the involved medical specialty.
>
> 2. That the defendant either lacked this degree of knowledge or skill or failed to use reasonable care and diligence, along with his best judgment in the application of that skill, and

> 3. That as a proximate result of this lack of knowledge or skill or the failure to exercise this degree of care the plaintiff suffered injuries that would not otherwise have been incurred.

Injury alone does not raise a presumption of negligence. Id. at § 9:2794.C. As this court held in Sewell v. United States, 629 F.Supp. 448, 454–55 (W.D.La.1986):

> In determining whether the plaintiff has met his burden of proof, the court relies upon the testimony and opinion of medical experts. [Citations omitted.] This expert testimony must be tempered by the knowledge that Louisiana law does not hold the physician to a standard of perfection.

See also Garrett v. United States, 667 F.Supp. 1147, 1150–51 (W.D.La. 1987).

This court concludes that the plaintiffs have not come forward with sufficient evidence to sustain their burden of proof with respect to any of the elements required by La.Rev.Stat.Ann. § 9:2794.

The Degree of Care Ordinarily Practiced by Equine Veterinary Specialists Versus Alleged Breaches

In an effort to establish the applicable standard of care, plaintiffs offered the testimony of Dr. J. Eugene Schneider. Dr. Schneider is an associate professor at the Department of Surgery and Medicine at Kansas State University. The issues of whether plaintiffs established the applicable standard of care and whether Dr. Lowdermilk breached that standard are so intertwined that the court will address them together.

If one listened only to the testimony of Dr. Schneider, it would appear that there is but a singular way to treat a horse diagnosed as having colic or suspected of having thromboembolic colic. Fortunately, this court had the benefit of not only Dr. Schneider's testimony but that of Drs. Lewis, Bertone and Lowdermilk. The sum total of this testimony, as will be discussed more fully hereinafter, satisfies the court that there is significant latitude recognized as acceptable in the specialty of equine veterinary medicine when treating colic and, in particular, thromboembolic colic.

According to Dr. Schneider, the equine veterinarian treating for thromboembolic colic should first determine whether the horse is dehydrated. This may be done by what is known as the skin turgor test, which involves pinching the skin in the neck area and observing skin reaction. Monitoring water intake and urinary outflow is another method to determine dehydration. Diagnostic tests, including packed cell volume and total protein tests, are also recognized means. Dr. Schneider testified that the total protein test is probably the most accurate method. Dr. Bertone testified, however, that the most accurate determinator of dehydration is to ascertain the horse's body weight and then observe how much fluid loss occurs. Dr. Bertone also placed great weight on clinical signs such as those as would be obtained from the skin turgor test.

Dr. Lowdermilk performed the skin turgor test and obtained the packed cell volume count. The skin turgor test was done repeatedly, according to Dr. Lowdermilk. Based on these tests, he did not believe Sandhill Diamond was dehydrated between October 7 and 10.

After determining whether the horse is dehydrated, Dr. Schneider would administer fluids. Dr. Schneider testified that Dr. Lowdermilk breached the accepted standard of care by not administering fluids beginning on the 7th. Dr. Schneider's opinion, however, is flawed because it is based on the assumption that Sandhill Diamond did not drink anything after the race on October 5. As indicated, the testimony concerning how much fluids the horse drank is inconclusive. Accordingly, an opinion as to whether the horse was dehydrated, based on water intake, is equally inconclusive.

According to Dr. Lowdermilk—and there is no testimony to the contrary—there were no clinical signs of dehydration on October 7, 8, 9 or 10. This is supported by the skin turgor tests and the packed cell volume test. Dr. Bertone testified that the level of dehydration that would be necessary to have an adverse effect on the intestinal tract would have shown up from the skin turgor test. If this level of dehydration had been present, the horse would also have shown an elevated heart rate, sweating, anxiety and poor coloration. According to Dr. Bertone, a horse can be up to 4 per cent dehydrated and not show any clinical signs of dehydration. In order for a horse to suffer intestinally from dehydration, it would have to be 10 per cent dehydrated. Studies as to how long it would take for a horse to be 10 per cent dehydrated with no water intake are inconclusive. One study showed that 10 per cent dehydration, with zero intake, could occur as early as two days while another study showed it would take seven days.

In addition to determining if the horse is dehydrated and then administering fluids, Dr. Schneider testified that the following should be done: (1) administer antibiotics in all cases from day one; (2) conduct a variety of diagnostic tests, including complete blood count, packed cell volume, total protein, rectal exams and an abdominal tap; and (3) administer anticoagulants.

With regard to the use of antibiotics, Dr. Lowdermilk testified that he did not deem them necessary as the mare's vital signs were normal on October 7–8, and the horse seemed to improve on October 9–10. Dr. Bertone expressly disagreed with Dr. Schneider's statement that antibiotics should be given in every case. She felt that there was no reason to give antibiotics unless there was a clinical indication of their necessity. Dr. Lewis testified that antibiotics would be used only if there was an indication that the horse's abdominal cavity had been exposed to bacteria. He referred to such instances as "profound cases."

Dr. Schneider's testimony that Dr. Lowdermilk should have repeatedly run various tests met with considerable disagreement. Dr. Bertone testified that whether to conduct the tests discussed by Dr. Schneider depended entirely on clinical symptoms displayed by the horse. Given the symptoms related by Dr. Lowdermilk, Dr. Bertone felt that no additional diagnostic testing was warranted. Dr. Bertone also cited a survey that questioned numerous veterinarians about how many diagnostic tests they used in colic cases. The results of this survey showed that only 10 per cent of the veterinarians questioned performed blood work or an abdominal tap. Dr. Bertone further testified that she would not perform an abdominal tap if the horse's vital signs were normal or if the horse appeared to be improving. Dr. Bertone expressed the same opinion about the necessity of an analysis of blood gases.

With regard to the necessity of rectal exams, Dr. Lewis testified that the general trend with practitioners in the field is that this is an undesirable test. Dr. Lewis found no fault with this trend. Rectal exams involve a certain amount of risk. Dr. Lewis testified that rectal rupture in a horse can easily occur during the course of a rectal exam. Rectal exams, according to Dr. Lewis, are less likely to be done in a stall environment. He testified that he rarely performs this test unless the horse is confined to a stanchion. Dr. Lewis cited two examples of the hazards of conducting a rectal exam without a stanchion—in one of these cases, he suffered a shattered arm and, in the other, the mare dropped and broke his partner's arm.

Based on the cumulative testimony of Drs. Schneider, Bertone and Lewis, the court agrees with Dr. Lowdermilk that there is not a cookbook formula for treating thromboembolic colic. It is also noteworthy that Dr. Schneider's opinion was based not only upon the inconclusive assumption that Sandhill Diamond was dehydrated on the 7th, but also upon the assumption that an affirmative diagnosis of thromboembolic colic had been made by Dr. Lowdermilk. On this point, Dr. Lowdermilk testified at trial that he "strongly suspected" and "felt relatively sure" that the horse suffered thromboembolic colic. The clinical signs, however, indicated, if anything, a mild case. Dr. Bertone testified that the clinical signs on October 7 would not have caused her to treat for thromboembolic colic. She further testified that a conclusive diagnosis could only be made after an exploratory laparotomy or necropsy—an examination of the body after death.

Two conclusions can be drawn from the testimony of Drs. Schneider, Bertone and Lewis: (1) experts in equine veterinary medicine disagree on the proper treatment for thromboembolic colic; and (2) the same experts disagree on how Sandhill Diamond should have been treated. The effect of these conclusions is that plaintiffs have failed first to sustain their burden of proving the degree of care ordinarily practiced by equine veterinary specialists and, second, that Dr. Lowdermilk either lacked this degree of knowledge or skill or failed to use reasonable care and diligence.

The findings of fact outlining treatment given by Dr. Lowdermilk indicate a pattern of treatment consistent with a strong suspicion of thromboembolic colic. This conclusion is drawn from the testimony of both Drs. Bertone and Lewis. Dr. Bertone expressly examined each type of treatment given by Dr. Lowdermilk and found no error. Dr. Lewis testified that Dr. Lowdermilk administered "routine-type medication that is used for treating colics." Dr. Lewis continued: "As far as any drugs he [Dr. Lowdermilk] had administered which contributed to the demise of the horse, I would say no."

To summarize, Dr. Schneider's testimony, when considered with that of Drs. Bertone, Lewis and Lowdermilk, does not convince the court that his recommended method of treatment evidences the degree of care ordinarily practiced by equine veterinary specialists treating colic or "a strong suspicion" of thromboembolic colic. Even assuming, arguendo, that Dr. Schneider's method controlled, his opinion that Dr. Lowdermilk breached the standard is based upon two assumptions which this court rejects. The first erroneous assumption is that Sandhill Diamond was dehydrated. This assumption has not been supported by adequate proof. The second assumption is that Dr. Lowdermilk conclusively diagnosed Sandhill Diamond as having thromboembolic colic on October 7. As already indicated, this was not the case. The court finds that the treatment given by Dr. Lowdermilk is consistent with the treatment that either Dr. Bertone or Dr. Lewis would have given in a race track environment. The court believes that the standard of care described by Drs. Bertone and Lewis is a more accurate representation of the degree of care ordinarily practiced by equine veterinary specialists. Accordingly, plaintiffs have failed to sustain the first two elements of their burden of proof required by La.Rev.Stat.Ann. § 9:2794.

Proximate Cause Versus the Inevitable Downfall

As set forth in the findings of fact, it was Dr. Lewis' opinion that Sandhill Diamond died due to an overwhelming septic shock that resulted in cardiac failure. The septic shock was triggered by a thromboembolic episode that was due to significant cranial mesenteric artery disease. This disease was caused by the inordinate concentration of strongylus vulgaris larvae which had not been treated for nine months. Dr. Lewis' examination of the cranial mesenteric artery revealed that it was abnormally large for a three-year-old mare. This finding was consistent with his conclusion that the horse had a severe case of thromboembolic colic which originated from the migration of bloodworms. Since Dr. Lewis was the only veterinarian who observed first-hand the condition of Sandhill Diamond's intestines, the court accords his testimony as to the cause of death considerable weight.

Due to the extent of the infestation of parasites and the resulting disease, Dr. Lewis expressed serious doubt as to whether any treatment between October 7 and 11 could have saved Sandhill Diamond. On this point, he testified:

> But if one assumes that this shower of thrombi all occurred as the result of the race on Sunday and all these clots dropped at one time, then I doubt that—I doubt that medical therapy was going to get this mare over her problem.

* * *

> On this particular case ... obviously this mare had grave secondary complications but she also had a grave condition.
>
> Had I gotten this [mare] earlier, I don't know if it would have affected the outcome really because of the degree of disease she had. That's the point I was trying to make.
>
> * * *
>
> [T]his mare had enough disease that if I had gotten her earlier in the case, I got a strong suspicion that the outcome inevitably may have been the same because she had a severe case of it, but I don't know that, you know.

Lewis Deposition at 55, 77, 110.

Similarly, Dr. Bertone testified that the thromboembolic episode that occurred on October 10 or 11 could not have been prevented by prior treatment. This opinion was based on two facts: (1) the extent of the infestation of strongylus vulgaris larvae found by Dr. Lewis; and (2) the location of the infected areas of the large colon. More specifically, there were gangrenous portions of the large colon that could not be surgically removed and would ultimately result in the horse's death.

Dr. Bertone also testified that the death was not preventable by Dr. Lowdermilk because the episode can occur at any time, without notice, in a horse that has this migrating parasite. With respect to the suddenness that the disease may cause death, Dr. Lewis testified:

> Some of these horses can be normal one day, sick the next, and literally dead within 48 hours if it's a severe enough case.
>
> * * *
>
> Some of these cases, as I said, will really sneak up on you. They are very insidious, and they can really fool you.
>
> * * *
>
> [In] any abdominal disease case things can happen fast once they get to a point.... A mare can—a brood mare can twist a large colon and be dead in two hours, if you are talking about generic abdominal disease. But things can happen remarkably fast in the abdomen of a horse.

Lewis Deposition at 80, 116–17.

All of the veterinarians who testified, including Dr. Schneider, stated that the soundest manner to prevent the infestation of parasites and virtually eliminate the possibility of any colic is to have the horse "wormed" every 60 days. Sandhill Diamond had not been wormed in over nine months at the time of her death. Even Dr. Schneider admitted that this failure properly to worm the horse would have contributed to the migration of bloodworms that resulted in the thromboembolic colic. According to Dr. Bertone, nothing could have saved Sandhill Diamond except a proper worming program.

A worming treatment costs approximately $10. Davidson testified that she doesn't worm a horse while it is on the race track circuit. The reason given by Davidson is that she would have to stop training the horse for a day. Also, she was under the impression that the drugs would remain in the system for approximately a week and would show up in the tests performed after each race, causing "problems." Dr. Lewis testified, however, that good trainers of race horses will worm every 60 days.

Based upon the foregoing, this court concludes that the precipitating cause of Sandhill Diamond's death was overwhelming septic shock that was triggered by a thromboembolic episode. The episode was made possible by severe cranial mesenteric artery disease that resulted from the migration of strongylus vulgaris larvae. The sole cause of the migration of this parasite was failure to maintain a proper worming program—not the actions or inactions of Dr. Lowdermilk. Accordingly, even if the court were to find—which it clearly does not—that Dr. Lowdermilk breached the accepted professional standard of care, then the court would nonetheless deny plaintiffs recovery because neither the treatment given by Dr. Lowdermilk nor any additional treatment would have prevented the thromboembolic episode and septic shock that resulted in Sandhill Diamond's death.

The Counterclaim

At the end of October 1986, the Morelands were sent a statement of charges for services provided by Dr. Lowdermilk or his partner between September 1 and October 11. In response to a complaint by Mrs. Moreland regarding an itemization of charges, Dr. Lowdermilk mailed a letter to her on November 12, 1986, setting forth with some detail services rendered. In January of 1987, the Morelands were sent a past-due notice showing a balance of $863. Demand letters were sent to the Morelands on August 24, 1987 and September 15, 1987. Mrs. Moreland admitted receiving these bills and demand letters but stated that she did not pay the bills because she felt that Dr. Lowdermilk did not render proper medical services.

It is undisputed that the services were rendered. The court has concluded that these services were adequate and within the accepted standard of care for equine veterinary medicine. Accordingly, pursuant to La.Rev.Stat.Ann. § 9:2781.A, the Morelands are liable for the past-due balance, plus reasonable attorney's fees for collection of the claim. The attorney's fee award shall be limited solely to the prosecution of the counterclaim and shall not include services rendered in defense of plaintiffs' complaint. The parties are encouraged to agree on a reasonable amount of attorney's fees while reserving the right to contest the award on appeal. If counsel are unable to agree on an amount, counsel for the counterclaimant shall file a motion for attorney's fees with supporting affidavits and documentation. The motion will be handled in the court's regular motion practice.

Counsel for Dr. Lowdermilk is instructed to submit, within ten (10) days of today's date, a proposed judgment that has been approved as to form and content by counsel for the plaintiffs. The judgment shall reflect the court's ruling not only on the counterclaim but also on the main demand.

KRUEGER v. SAN FRANCISCO FORTY NINERS

234 Cal.Rptr. 579 (Ct.App.1987).

NEWSOM, Associate Justice.

On August 19, 1980, appellant filed a complaint for damages and declaratory relief against respondent San Francisco 49'ers and other defendants not involved in this appeal. After a series of demurrers and amendments to the pleadings, the case proceeded to court trial on the sole cause of action for fraudulent concealment of medical information. The trial court found in favor of respondent and this appeal followed.

Appellant began playing professional football with the San Francisco 49'ers (hereafter respondent or the 49'ers) in 1958. He was a defensive lineman for the 49'ers until retiring in 1973, missing only parts of two seasons due to injuries. During his career, however, appellant played despite suffering numerous injuries. He broke his arm and the ring finger on each hand, cracked or broke his nose "innumerable times," suffered multiple dislocations of the fingers and thumbs on both hands, incurred a "blow-out" fracture of the right ocular orbit, developed an eye infection or "pterygium" caused by a foreign substance becoming lodged in the eye, sprained his right knee, and developed hypertension, among other maladies.

The injuries and damages to appellant's left knee are the focus of the present suit. While in college in 1955, appellant had surgery on his left knee to repair a torn meniscus. Then, in October of 1963, he ruptured the medial collateral ligament in his left knee. Dr. Lloyd Taylor, a physician who treated 49'ers' players, performed an operation on the knee which, appellant was told, effectuated a "good repair." Thereafter, appellant engaged in rehabilitative therapy with the team trainer and was given a knee brace which he later wore while playing until he removed it in 1967.

Dr. Taylor noted in his report of the operation that the anterior cruciate ligament—the function of which is to prevent the tibia from shifting forward on the femur—"appeared to be absent" from appellant's left knee. Such an injury can produce instability in the knee, particularly if combined with other injuries. According to appellant, he was not told that his left knee evidently lacked the anterior cruciate ligament.

In the spring of 1964, appellant began experiencing pain and considerable swelling in his left knee. He again received treatment from physicians retained by the 49'ers, specifically Dr. Taylor and Dr. Lloyd Milburn, which consisted of aspiration of bloody fluid from the knee by means of a syringe and contemporaneous injection of novocain and cortisone, a steroid compound. Appellant testified that he received approximately 50 such "Kepplemann" treatments during 1964, and an average of 14 to 20 per year from 1964 to 1973. Dr. Milburn could not recall administering Kepplemann treatments with such frequency, and testified that his records indicated only seven such treatments. Appellant also testified that he was never advised by the 49'ers medical staff of the dangers associated with steroid injections in the knee, such as possible rupturing of tendons, weakening of joints and cartilage, and destruction of capillaries and blood vessels. He also offered expert medical testimony that the adverse effects of steroids were known at that time. The same medical expert also testified that the number of steroid injections appellant claimed to have undergone would have been inappropriate and quite "unusual."

Appellant's left knee continued to plague him during his football career, and in 1971 he underwent another operation performed by Dr. Taylor to remove "loose bodies" in the knee resulting from chronic chondromalacia patella—thinning and loss of cartilage on the undersurface of the kneecap, a condition fully consistent with known adverse reaction to prolonged steroid use. X-rays taken between 1964 and 1971 revealed "degenerative post-traumatic changes" in appellant's left knee joint. Appellant testified—without contradiction—that he was not told of either of these afflictions by the 49'ers medical staff.

[Charles] Krueger also testified that he suffered a "hit" on the outside of the knee during a game in 1970. He felt a piece of the knee break off. Notwithstanding the obvious severity of the injury, appellant was given Empirin codeine and directed to return to the game. For the remainder of the season, he could feel a "considerable piece of substance" dislodged on the outside of his left knee joint; nevertheless, he played the remaining five games of the season. At no time did the team doctors ever advise him that he risked permanent injury by continuing to play without surgery. Krueger testified unequivocally that, had he been advised not to play, he would have followed that advice.

Dr. Milburn could not recall either specifically discussing appellant's x-rays with him or advising him about the chronic condition from which he was suffering. He testified generally—without specific reference to Krueger's case—that it was his custom, and that of Dr. Taylor, to be "honest and thorough" with athletes.

Appellant retired from football following the 1973 season. In April of 1974, he entered St. Mary's Hospital for a rhinoplasty and complete physical examination which, however, did not include either x-raying or testing of his knees. Neither Dr. Milburn, who had arranged the physical, nor any other orthopedist examined him at that time.

Not until 1978 was appellant treated again for his injured knee. At that time, he received a Kepplemann treatment from Dr. Milburn, and x-rays were taken of both legs. According to appellant it was not until this visit to Dr. Milburn in 1978 that he was shown x-rays of his knees and advised for the first time that he suffered from chronic and permanent disability in the knee.

Defendant was referred to Dr. Taylor, who subsequently performed on him a tibial osteotomy, which is a shaving of planes from the leg bone followed by regrafting of the tendons and ligaments to the bone. The operation did nothing to alleviate appellant's severe discomfort, and in fact, he thereafter developed calcification in the knee and suffered greater pain than had been the case before the surgery. He presently suffers from traumatic arthritis and a crippling degenerative process in the left knee. He cannot stand up for prolonged periods, and cannot run. He is also unable to walk on stairs without severe pain. His condition is degenerative and irreversible.

On this appeal Krueger argues error in the trial court's finding that he failed to prove all of the elements of fraudulent concealment. Pivotally, the court found that appellant would have continued to play football even if he had been advised of the nature and extent of his injuries—a finding which negated the element of proximate cause.

In reviewing the trial court's findings, we are bound by the substantial evidence rule, with all presumptions and inferences to be drawn in favor of the judgment. (Gray v. Fox (1984) 151 Cal.App.3d 482, 487, 198 Cal.Rptr. 720; Doctor v. Lakeridge Const. Co. (1967) 252 Cal.App.2d 715, 718, 60 Cal.Rptr. 824.) "[T]he power of an appellate court begins and ends with the determination as to whether there is any substantial evidence, contradicted or uncontradicted, which will support the finding of fact." (Green Trees Enterprises, Inc. v. Palm Springs Alpine Estates, Inc. (1967) 66 Cal.2d 782, 784, 59 Cal.Rptr. 141, 427 P.2d 805.) "Factual matters are viewed most favorably to the prevailing party (Nestle v. City of Santa Monica (1972) 6 Cal.3d 920 [101 Cal.Rptr. 568, 496 P.2d 480]) and conflicts are decided in favor of the respondent. (Cecka v. Beckman & Co. (1972) 28 Cal.App.3d 5 [104 Cal.Rptr. 374].)" (12319 Corp. v. Business License Com. (1982) 137 Cal.App.3d 54, 64, 186 Cal.Rptr. 726.)

Appellant's action was for fraud or deceit. Specifically, the claim is based upon Civil Code sections 1709 and 1710. Section 1709 provides that "[o]ne who willfully deceives another with intent to induce him to alter his position to his injury or risk, is liable for any damage which he thereby suffers." Section 1710, subdivision (3) defines deceit as "[t]he suppression of a fact, by one who is bound to disclose it or who gives information of other facts which are likely to mislead for want of communication of that fact...."

The elements of a cause of action for fraud or deceit are as follows: a misrepresentation or suppression of a material fact; knowledge of any falsity; intent to induce reliance; actual and justifiable reliance; and resulting damages. (Muraoka v. Budget Rent-A-Car, Inc. (1984) 160 Cal.App.3d 107, 119, 206 Cal.Rptr. 476; Hilliard v. A.H. Robins Co. (1983) 148 Cal.App.3d 374, 414–415, 196 Cal.Rptr. 117; Nelson v. Gaunt (1981) 125 Cal.App.3d 623, 635, 178 Cal.Rptr. 167.) " 'Deceit may be negative as well as affirmative; it may consist in suppression of that which it is one's duty to disclose, as well as in the declaration of that which is false.' (Gillespie v. Ormsby [1954], 126 Cal.App.2d 513, 527 [272 P.2d 949].)" (Stevens v. Marco (1956) 147 Cal.App.2d 357, 379, 305 P.2d 669.) Under section 1710, the intentional concealment of a material fact is actionable fraud only if there is a fiduciary relationship giving rise to a duty to disclose it. (Moe v. Transamerica Title Ins. Co. (1971) 21 Cal.App.3d 289, 306, 98 Cal.Rptr. 547; Nece v. Bennett (1963) 212 Cal.App.2d 494, 496, 28 Cal.Rptr. 117; Stevens v. Marco, supra, 147 Cal.App.2d at p. 378, 305 P.2d 669.) The relationship between physician and patient is fiduciary in nature and creates a duty to disclose. (Nelson v. Gaunt, supra, 125 Cal.App.3d 623, 635, 178 Cal.Rptr. 167; Bowman v. McPheeters (1947) 77 Cal.App.2d 795, 176 P.2d 745.)

Respondent submits that the record fails to substantiate appellant's claim that material medical information was concealed from him. We disagree. Appellant testified unequivocally that the team's physicians never disclosed to him the adverse effects of steroid injections, or the true nature and extent of the damage to his left knee, particularly the dangers associated with the prolonged violent traumatic impact inherent in professional football. Nor, he testified, was he informed that x-rays taken of his legs revealed the severely degenerated condition of his left knee.

The evidence offered by respondent never directly contradicted appellant's testimony. Thus, Dr. Milburn was able to recall only that he customarily discussed and reviewed player's injuries with them, sometimes using anatomical models. Dr. Milburn was "sure" that appellant was aware of "the type of injury that he had," and testified he had neither concealed information from appellant nor advised anyone else to do so. The testimony of other physicians and orthopedic consultants who treated appellant was consistent with Dr. Milburn's.

If the case were simply one of conflicting evidence, we would, of course, affirm the judgment. As to the crucial issue of full disclosure, however, we find the evidence uncontradicted; as will appear, the requisite disclosure was never made. That the team physicians withheld no material information from Krueger is not, in our view, the proper focus of inquiry. The critical question is whether full disclosure of his medical condition was ever made to Krueger.

In Cobbs v. Grant (1972) 8 Cal.3d 229, 104 Cal.Rptr. 505, 502 P.2d 1, our high court announced the "informed consent doctrine," which requires "as an integral part of the physician's overall obligation to the patient ... a duty of reasonable disclosure of the available choices with respect to proposed therapy and of the dangers inherently and potentially involved in each." (Id., at p. 243, 104 Cal.Rptr. 505, 502 P.2d 1; see also Truman v. Thomas (1980) 27 Cal.3d 285, 291, 165 Cal.Rptr. 308, 611 P.2d 902.) The physician must disclose to the patient all information necessary to make a knowledgeable decision about proposed treatment. (Cobbs v. Grant, supra, 8 Cal.3d at p. 242, 104 Cal.Rptr. 505, 502 P.2d 1; Moore v. Preventive Medicine Medical Group, Inc. (1986) 178 Cal.App.3d

728, 738, 223 Cal.Rptr. 859.) The duty to disclose is imposed so that patients might meaningfully exercise their right to make decisions affecting their own bodies. (Truman v. Thomas, supra, 27 Cal.3d at p. 292, 165 Cal.Rptr. 308, 611 P.2d 902.) Hence, even if the patient rejects a recommended procedure, the duty to disclose is nonetheless recognized. (Ibid; see also Moore v. Preventive Medicine Medical Group, Inc., supra, 178 Cal.App.3d at p. 737, 223 Cal.Rptr. 859.)

In our opinion, the duty of full disclosure within the context of a doctor-patient relationship defines the test for concealment or suppression of facts under Civil Code section 1710, subdivision (3). The failure to make such disclosure constitutes not only negligence, but—where the requisite intent is shown—fraud or concealment as well. A physician cannot avoid responsibility for failure to make full disclosure by simply claiming that information was not withheld.

The testimony that, following his knee surgery in 1963, Krueger was not advised of the adverse effects of steroid injections, or of the risks associated with the continued pursuit of his profession, was uncontradicted. That is, while respondent produced testimony that the physicians treating appellant told him of the general nature of his injury, and did not conceal certain information from him, there is no evidence that appellant was ever informed of the continuing risks associated with his injuries. Hence, the requisite disclosure was never made.

The element of intent also must be established in all fraudulent concealment cases. (Doctor v. Lakeridge Const. Co., supra, 252 Cal. App.2d 715, 718, 60 Cal.Rptr. 824.) While actual "intent to deceive" need not be shown, a plaintiff must establish that at the time information was concealed defendant had the intent to induce plaintiff to adopt or abandon a course of action (Peskin v. Squires (1957) 156 Cal.App.2d 240, 243, 319 P.2d 405)—in the present case, to induce him to continue playing football despite his injuries.

Dr. Milburn testified that he neither minimized nor concealed appellant's medical condition for the purpose of prolonging the latter's career. Nor, he testified, did he tell any of the other treating physicians to do so. Likewise, he testified, the 49'ers never advised him to suppress information regarding the condition of appellant's knee. Such testimony was corroborated by that of other involved medical personnel.

Nevertheless, we think the record unequivocally demonstrates that, in its desire to keep appellant on the playing field, respondent consciously failed to make full, meaningful disclosure to him respecting the magnitude of the risk he took in continuing to play a violent contact sport with a profoundly damaged left knee. The uncontradicted record shows that Krueger was in acute pain from 1963 on, that he was regularly anesthetized between and during games, and endured repeated, questionable steroid treatments administered by the team physician. X-rays had been taken which fully depicted the extent of his degenerative condition, but he was never so informed. In 1970, part of his knee broke away and yet he was still not given an honest assessment of the seriousness of his condition. Respondent's claim of no concealment cannot be substituted for the professional warnings to which Krueger was at this point so clearly entitled. And it is in this palpable failure to disclose, viewed in the light of the 49'ers compelling obvious interest in prolonging appellant's career, that we find the intent requisite for a finding of fraudulent concealment.

Respecting the element of reliance, appellant's testimony was that he accepted and acted upon the medical advice of the physicians as provided by respondent. No contradictory evidence appears. " '[P]atients are generally persons unlearned in the medical sciences, . . .' " and consequently are entitled to rely upon physicians for full disclosure of material medical information. (Truman v. Thomas, supra, 27 Cal.3d 285, 291, 165 Cal.Rptr. 308, 611 P.2d 902.) Reliance is thus established.

Respondent contends that appellant was or should have been cognizant of the seriousness and permanent nature of the injury to his left knee, but we find no credible evidence supportive of this claim. Certainly, appellant knew that his injury was serious. He was entitled, however, to rely upon respondent's physicians for medical treatment and advice without consulting outside sources or undertaking independent investigation. (Stevens v. Marco, supra, 147 Cal.App.2d 357, 378–379, 305 P.2d 669; Hayter v. Fulmor (1949) 92 Cal.App.2d 392, 400, 206 P.2d 1101.)

Turning to the issues of proximate cause and damages, we note the trial court's finding that appellant's desire to continue playing was so intense that he would have continued even had he been informed of the magnitude of the risk involved. This finding seems to us mere conjecture. Appellant demonstrated throughout his football career a courageous—some might say foolhardy—willingness to endure pain and injuries for the sake of his team and employer, but no credible evidence suggests that he ever assessed and accepted the prospect of permanent disability. On the contrary, he testified that he would have retired had respondent's physicians recommended that course of action, and no contrary evidence was offered by respondent.

Accordingly, we conclude there is no substantial evidence to support the judgment entered by the trial court; and conversely, that appellant established all the elements of a fraudulent concealment case based upon nondisclosure of material medical information.

The judgment is reversed and the cause is remanded to the trial court, judgment to be entered in favor of appellant, with damages as established by the evidence upon retrial limited to that single issue. Costs to appellant.

POWELL v. VOY

1994 WL 621970 (N.D.Cal.1994).

HENDERSON, Chief Judge.

Background

Plaintiff John Powell is a world class discus thrower and a former member of four U.S. Olympic teams. He has lived in Santa Clara County since 1971. Powell was a member of The Athletic Congress ("TAC"), a national organization which regulates amateur track and field athletes in the United States. TAC is officially sponsored and authorized by the U.S. Olympic Committee ("USOC"). Defendant Dr. Robert Voy was the Chief Medical Officer and Director of Sports Medicine for the USOC. Dr. Voy resides in Nevada.

Dr. Voy wrote a book entitled "Drugs, Sport and Politics" ("the book"), which was published in September of 1990. In the book, Dr. Voy detailed events that occurred in the TAC Outdoor National Championships, held in San Jose in June, 1987. Dr. Voy was present at the meet in his official USOC capacity to supervise and conduct the testing of athletes for prohibited substances, such as steroids. Powell participated in and won the discus competition, and after the competition he reported to Dr. Voy, to give a urine specimen for testing. Powell's specimen tested positive for steroids, as did a second sample. Such a violation would ordinarily result in taking away the competitor's title and a possible suspension from competition. However, at a hearing held for Powell, a technical error in the coding of the bottle containing the sample, as well as in the chain of custody, indicated a breach in USOC protocol and resulted in Powell not being punished. In his book, Dr. Voy writes that Powell "was found positive for the anabolic androgenic steroid nandrolone" and went on to suggest that Powell should not have been let off. Dr. Voy gave an interview on a 1992 television program aired by Arts and Entertainment Network and entitled "More Than Just A Game," in which he repeated that plaintiff had taken drugs and was excused because of a technicality.

Powell filed this action against Dr. Voy, alleging libel, slander, invasion of privacy, intentional and negligent infliction of emotional distress, and breach of fiduciary duty. In February of 1993, this Court heard defendant Voy's Motion to Dismiss pursuant to Fed.R.Civ.P. 12(b)(2) for lack of personal jurisdiction. This Court denied the motion and referred the case to arbitration. Arbitration was unsuccessful and plaintiff has requested a trial de novo from the arbitration award which was filed on October 17, 1994. Before the Court is defendant's motion for partial summary judgment.

Discussion

I. Statute of Limitations on Book Claims

Plaintiff asserts seven separate causes of action based on defendant Voy's statements in the book and the television show: 1) breach of fiduciary duty; 2) intentional infliction of emotional distress; 3) negligent infliction of emotional distress; 4) negligence in releasing confidential medical information; 5) libel; 6) invasion of privacy; and 7) slander (television show only). Defendant argues that under California Civil Code § 3425.3, plaintiff may bring only one suit for publication of the book, and any claims based on statements in the book are barred by the statute of limitations.

Section 3425.3, also known as the Uniform Single Publication Act, provides:

> No person shall have more than one cause of action for damages for libel or slander or invasion of privacy or any other tort founded upon any single publication or exhibition or utterance, such as any one issue of a newspaper or book or magazine or any one presentation to an audience or any one broadcast over radio or television or any one exhibition of a motion picture. Recovery in any action shall include all damages for any such tort suffered by the plaintiff in all jurisdictions.

Cal.Civ.Code § 3425.3. Defendant seems to read this statute as allowing only one type of cause of action for a public statement. However, this statutory language is merely intended to prevent plaintiffs from bringing a separate cause of action for each copy or instance of the allegedly tortious statement. See Fleury v. Harper & Row, Publishers, Inc., 698 F.2d 1022, 1026 (1983) (Uniform Single Publication Act adopted in order to abrogate common law rule that each copy of a book gives rise to separate cause of action and endless tolling of statute).

Defendant next argues that these claims are barred by the applicable statute of limitations. California Code of Civil Procedure § 340(3) sets out a one year statute of limitations for, among others, libel, slander, and all "injury to ... one caused by the wrongful act or neglect of another." Cal.Civ.Code § 340(3). This statute of limitations applies to all plaintiff's causes of action: counts one, three and four involving negligence or breach of duty (see Rodibaugh v. Caterpillar Tractor Co., 225 Cal.App.2d 570, 572 (1st Dist.1964) (§ 340.3 applies to all personal injury torts)); count two, intentional infliction of emotional distress (see Murphy v. Allstate Ins. Co., 83 Cal.App.3d 38, 50 (4th Dist.1978)); counts five and seven, libel and slander; and count six, invasion of privacy (see Cain v. State Farm Mutual Auto. Ins. Co., 62 Cal.App.3d 310, 313 (1st Dist.1976)).

Plaintiff's cause of action based on the book accrued upon the first general distribution of the book to the public. See McGuiness v. Motor Trend Magazine, 129 Cal.App.3d 59, 61 (2d Dist.1982); Belli v. Roberts Brothers Furs, 240 Cal.App.2d 284 (1966). The limitations period begins to run even if the plaintiff was unaware of the publication. Johnson v. Harcourt, Brace, Jovanovich, Inc., 43 Cal.App.3d 880 (2d Dist.1974); see also McGuiness, 129 Cal.App.3d at 62 (no tolling of statute if there was no active concealment of defamatory statement).

In this case, the parties agree that the first publication of the book was in September, 1990. (Defendant's Motion p. 5; Plaintiff's Opposition, p. 10). This suit was not filed until October 14, 1992. Therefore plaintiff's fifth cause of action for libel is dismissed because it is barred by the statute of limitations. Moreover, the portion of plaintiff's claims in causes of action one through five based on publication of the book Drugs, Sport and Politics is also barred by the statute of limitations and is dismissed.

However, each of plaintiff's causes of action one through six rests in part on defendant's statements in the June 1992 television interview (as does all of count seven for slander). Defendant's statements on television can be the basis of a separate cause of action. Schneider v. United Airlines, Inc. 208 Cal.App.3d 71, 77 (1989); Kanarek v. Bugliosi, 108 Cal.App.3d 327, 332–33 (1980) (with separate publications on different occasions, "the publication reaches a new group and the repetition justifies a new cause of action." Id. at 33.). Thus plaintiff's count seven, and counts one through six insofar as they are premised on defendant's television statements, are not barred by the statute of limitations.

II. No Doctor–Patient Relationship

Defendant contends that there never was a physician-patient relationship between plaintiff and defendant, and therefore moves that the court dismiss plaintiff's first and fourth causes of action, respectively breach of doctor-patient and fiduciary relationship and negligent performance of duties as a physician. The material facts surrounding the relationship are undisputed. Defendant was employed as "Chief Medical Officer" for the USOC, and as such was responsible for supervising drug testing of athletes that took place at the 1987 TAC championships. (Plaintiff's Exh. G; First Amended Complaint p 14.) Defendant rendered no medical care to plaintiff other than functioning as a urine testing supervisor. (See Voy Depo.) The parties also agree that determination of duty is a question of law, Weirum v. RKO General, Inc. 15 Cal.3d 40, 46 (1975), and that generally "all persons are required to use ordinary care to prevent others from being injured as a result of their conduct." Cal.Civ.Code § 1714; Rowland v. Christian, 69 Cal.2d 108, 112 (1968).

Defendant cites a line of cases in which no doctor-patient relationship was found. Foremost among these is Keene v. Wiggins 69 Cal. App.3d 308 (1977). In Keene, a doctor was hired by an insurance company to examine the plaintiff and rate the injury. The plaintiff filed a medical malpractice suit, charging that he had relied on the negligently prepared report. The court of appeals held that "where a physician neither offers or [sic] intends to treat, care for or otherwise benefit the person examined, ... the doctor is not liable to the person being examined for negligence in making that report. His duty to observe a professional standard of care in the preparation of that report runs only to the carrier and to the employer requesting it." Id. at 313. The analogy here is at least partially apt; defendant was employed by USOC not to treat the plaintiff, but to supervise drug testing. Defendant's duty to use a professional standard of care ran to USOC, not to plaintiff.

Clearly the defendant and plaintiff were not in a traditional doctor-patient relationship. Plaintiff's fourth cause of action, negligence, cannot withstand this motion insofar as it alleges that defendant should have met the standard of care of a treating physician. Similarly, plaintiff's first cause of action, "Breach of Fiduciary Duty," cannot be premised upon a physician-patient relationship.

Plaintiff, however, also tries to allege breach of a fiduciary duty. California law recognizes that an individual is entitled to have his medical history kept private. See, e.g., Cutter v. Brownbridge, 183 Cal.App.3d 836, 842 (1986). Plaintiff contends not that defendant breached or should be held to a high standard of medical skill, but that he divulged confidential information which he gained only by virtue of his status as supervisor of the testing. Although the plaintiff's argument has intuitive appeal, plaintiff has cited no authority that supports finding a fiduciary relationship, beyond reciting the facts of the case.

Plaintiff does invoke the duty test enunciated in Rowland v. Christian, 69 Cal.2d 108, 113 (1968), which considers factors such as the moral blame attached to defendant's conduct and the foreseeability of harm to the plaintiff. However, this test determines only whether the defendant has a duty at all to the plaintiff, not whether the relationship is a fiduciary one. Thus this Court is unwilling to recognize a fiduciary relationship between plaintiff and defendant as a matter of law.

CONCLUSION

Defendant's motion for partial summary judgment is GRANTED to the following extent:

1) Cause of action five is hereby DISMISSED;

2) Causes of action one and four are hereby DISMISSED;

3) Causes of action two, three, and six are hereby DISMISSED insofar as they rely upon statements in the book.

Notes

1. As *Capone* and *Moreland* demonstrate, doctors are expected to provide competent medical care. The fact that a given diagnosis or course of treatment turns out to be unsuccessful, however, is not in and of itself proof of malpractice. *See further Mires v. Evans*, 1986 WL 8117 (E.D.Pa.1986), and *Durocher v. Rochester Equine Clinic*, 629 A.2d 827 (N.H.1993).

2. Physicians sometimes jump to the wrong conclusion. During the 1989 season, for example, Dr. William Cahan was watching a New York Mets–Los Angeles Dodgers game on television when he became convinced baseball commissioner A. Bartlett Giamatti's swollen fingers were a mark of lung disease. After passing an urgent message on to Giamatti, Cahan watched a videotape and realized the hands belonged to a man sitting behind Giamatti. Ironically, Giamatti died of a heart attack one day after receiving Cahan's warning. *See Mistaken Warning*, USA Today, Sept. 6, 1989, at 2C.

3. Doctors who treat athletes often find themselves on the cutting edge of medicine and some, such as Frank Jobe, an orthopedic surgeon whose revolutionary reconstruction of pitcher Tommy John's left arm in 1974 permanently changed the nature of sports medicine, achieve both fame and fortune. Nevertheless, they face a much greater risk of malpractice lawsuits than their more conservative colleagues. As a result, many observers believe that the definition of medical malpractice needs to be completely rethought in the context of competitive sports. *See further* James H. Davis, *"Fixing" the Standard of Care: Motivated Athletes and Medical Malpractice*, 12 Am. J.

Trial Advoc. 215 (1988). *See also* Frank Litsky, *Doctors Hope Experimental Drug Will Aid Paralyzed Gymnast*, N.Y. Times, July 24, 1998, at C22 (describing the numerous difficulties encountered by Dr. Vincent Leone when he sought permission to use the experimental drug GM–1 on Sang Lan, a 17–year-old Chinese gymnast who sustained a severe spinal injury after landing on her head during the 1998 Goodwill Games).

4. Like Charles Krueger, many athletes believe team doctors are more interested in getting them back on the field than getting them back to good health. Although not free from doubt, a substantial body of circumstantial evidence supports these claims. *See further Gambrell v. Kansas City Chiefs Football Club, Inc.*, 562 S.W.2d 163 (Mo.Ct.App.1978); Sigmund J. Solares, *Preventing Medical Malpractice of Team Physicians in Professional Sports: A Call for the Players Union to Hire the Team Physicians in Professional Sports*, 4 Sports Law. J. 235 (1997); Stewart E. Niles Jr. & Roderick K. West, *In Whose Interest? The Return of the Injured Athlete to Competition*, 25 Brief 8 (Spr. 1996); Matthew J. Mitten, *Team Physicians and Competitive Athletes: Allocating Legal Responsibility for Athletic Injuries*, 55 U. Pitt. L. Rev. 129 (1993); Jennifer L. Woodlief, *The Trouble with Charlie: Fraudulent Concealment of Medical Information in Professional Football*, 9 Ent. & Sports Law. 3 (Spr. 1991); Scott Polsky, Comment, *Winning Medicine: Professional Sports Team Doctors' Conflicts of Interest*, 14 J. Contemp. Health L. & Pol'y 503 (1998). *See also* Rob Huizenga, *"You're Okay, It's Just a Bruise"—A Doctor's Sideline Secrets About Pro Football's Most Outrageous Team* (1994).

5. To be fair, there are instances when an injured player refuses to follow a doctor's advice. This appears to have occurred with San Francisco 49ers running back Jerry Rice, who came back too early from torn ligaments and immediately re-injured his knee. *See further* Sabin Russell, *Rice's Injury Puts Spotlight on Team Doctors: Pressure to Win Conflicts with Players' Need to Heal*, S.F. Chron., Dec. 18, 1997, at A1. *See also Barbay v. National Collegiate Athletic Ass'n*, 1987 WL 5619 (E.D.La.1987) (refusal of college football player to heed medical opinion regarding dangers of using steroids to heal knee injury).

In addition, athletes sometimes hide their medical conditions so as to strengthen their bargaining positions. *See, e.g., Islanders, Lindros Settle*, Bergen (N.J.) Record, Jan. 16, 1998, at S4 (noting Brett Lindros, who was forced to retire after just two seasons in the NHL, had gone to great lengths to hide his health problems prior to being picked by the New York Islanders in the first round of the 1994 draft). For a further look at the Lindros affair, see *Boston Mutual Insurance Co. v. New York Islanders Hockey Club, L.P.*, 165 F.3d 93 (1st Cir.1999).

6. As *Powell* indicates, athletes become very upset when doctors disparage them. By the same token, doctors take great offense when their skills are questioned. For an interesting case in which a team physician sued after being called incompetent by a sportswriter, see *Hunter v. Hartman*, 545 N.W.2d 699 (Minn.Ct.App.1996).

7. Although most people equate being a team doctor with glamour and fun, such jobs actually pay poorly, produce tremendous stress, involve erratic hours, and pose a certain amount of risk. *See, e.g., Loupe v. State Farm Fire & Casualty Co.*, 685 So.2d 186 (La.Ct.App.1996) (Southern University foot-

ball team physician injured when player ran over him). For a further look at the sacrifices and rewards of being a team doctor, see Mark Waller, *Soccer Doc Role Calls for 110 Per Cent Commitment*, Fin. Pulse, Mar. 8, 1998, at 32, and Adrian Dater, *Being a Dentist for Colorado Avalanche No Laughing Matter*, Denver Post, Mar. 16, 1997, at D9. *See also* Christopher McEvoy, *Pro Team Docs Think Marketing*, Sporting Goods Bus., Nov. 10, 1997, at 18 (describing the role the Association of Professional Team Physicians is beginning to play in evaluating and endorsing medical products).

Problem 42

Pursuant to the rules of the state wagering board, a veterinarian entered a race track's stalls and began drawing blood to check for illegal drugs. While attending one of the horses, the needle inexplicably shattered. Because post time was just a few hours away and he still had two dozen samples to collect, he did not stay with the filly but instead told a groom to obtain help. By the time this could be done, one of the fragments had migrated to the animal's lungs, thereby ending her promising racing career. If the veterinarian is sued for malpractice, will he be able to avoid liability by arguing he acted appropriately? *See Restrepo v. State*, 550 N.Y.S.2d 536 (Ct.Cl.1989), *aff'd*, 580 N.Y.S.2d 874 (App.Div.1992).

2. DEFENSES

Doctors who are sued for malpractice have a variety of defenses available to them, including: lack of a doctor-patient relationship, workers' compensation, time bar, and, in certain instances, statutory immunity.

MURPHY v. BLUM

554 N.Y.S.2d 640 (App.Div.1990).

PER CURIAM.

In an action, inter alia, to recover damages for medical malpractice, the plaintiffs appeal from so much of an order of the Supreme Court, Nassau County (Levitt, J.), entered February 1, 1989, as dismissed the complaint pursuant to CPLR 3211(a)(7) for failure to state a cause of action.

ORDERED that the order is affirmed insofar as appealed from, with one bill of costs to the respondents appearing separately and filing separate briefs.

The plaintiff Donald Murphy, while employed as a referee for the third-party defendant, the National Basketball Association (hereinafter the NBA), was required by the NBA to undergo a yearly physical examination to ensure that he would be able to withstand the rigors of his job. The 1978 examination was performed by the defendant, Dr. Richard Blum. Dr. Blum also analyzed the results of an exercise stress test performed upon the plaintiff by Dr. Kenneth Rubin. Dr. Rubin advised Dr. Blum that Murphy's test was "abnormal with respect to ST segment changes". Dr. Blum orally apprised the Supervisor of NBA

Officials, Norm Drucker, of his findings. He also sent the NBA a letter stating his findings. Drucker advised Murphy that "[i]t was not what they would call a good stress test for you from your standpoint". Drucker thereafter forwarded the results of the examinations to Murphy's personal physician. During the ensuing season, Murphy suffered cardiac arrest and could no longer maintain his position as an NBA referee.

A doctor engaged only for the purpose of examining a person for workers' compensation or similar purposes is under a common-law duty to use reasonable care and his best judgment when conducting the examination (see, Twitchell v. MacKay, 78 A.D.2d 125, 434 N.Y.S.2d 516). Such a doctor, however, only assumes the duties associated with the functions undertaken (see, Ferguson v. Wolkin, 131 Misc.2d 304, 499 N.Y.S.2d 356). No duty exists concerning treatment or the giving of expert opinions if the doctor was retained solely to examine the plaintiff (Ferguson v. Wolkin, supra, at 306, 499 N.Y.S.2d 356). Since Dr. Blum was retained by the NBA solely for the purpose of advising it whether Murphy would be physically capable of performing his duties as a referee and not to treat or advise the plaintiff, no physician-patient relationship existed in this case (see, Mrachek v. Sunshine Biscuit, Inc., 308 N.Y. 116, 123 N.E.2d 801). Therefore, the court correctly dismissed the plaintiffs' action for failure to state a cause of action (see, CPLR 3211[a][7]).

HENDY v. LOSSE

819 P.2d 1 (Cal.1991).

BAXTER, Justice.

Review was granted in this matter to determine the effect, if any, of a 1982 amendment of Labor Code section 3602, on the right of a person who suffers an industrial injury to sue a coemployee physician whose treatment allegedly aggravated the injury. The Court of Appeal held that while section 3602, as amended, no longer permits actions against a physician employer under the "dual capacity" doctrine, a coemployee action may be maintained under section 3601.

We disagree. While the Court of Appeal was correct in its conclusion that section 3601 alone governs the right of an employee to seek damages for industrial injuries caused by a coemployee, the immunity granted coemployees by section 3601 bars this medical malpractice action against Gary Losse, M.D., because he was acting within the scope of his employment when the conduct complained of occurred.

I

Background

Insofar as they are relevant to plaintiff's cause of action against defendant Losse for medical malpractice and thus to the issue before the court, the allegations of the verified complaint reflect the following:

> Plaintiff John Hendy suffered injury to his right knee on August 11, 1986, while playing in a football game as an employee of the San Diego Chargers Football Company (Club). He was treated for that injury by defendant Losse, who was employed as a Club physician. As a condition of his continued receipt of salary and medical care at the expense of his employer, plaintiff was required to consult the Club physician.
>
> Defendant Losse examined plaintiff pursuant to his employment by the Club, and advised plaintiff to continue playing football. From May 11, 1987, and continuing to September 1987, defendant Losse negligently diagnosed and/or treated plaintiff and advised plaintiff to continue playing football. On or about May 28, 1987, plaintiff suffered another injury to his right knee during a training session. He again consulted Dr. Losse, and defendant Losse again advised plaintiff to continue playing football. Dr. Losse lacked the knowledge and skill necessary to properly diagnose and treat plaintiff's condition or, although aware of the condition, advised plaintiff to continue to play football, with the result that plaintiff suffered irreparable and permanent injury to his right knee. On or about September 8, 1987, when he consulted a physician who was not employed by the Club, plaintiff discovered that the cause of his injuries was defendant's failure to properly diagnose and treat his condition.

The complaint stated five causes of action, only the fourth and fifth of which, plaintiff John Hendy's claim against Dr. Losse for medical malpractice and plaintiff Wanda Hendy's loss of consortium claim against Dr. Losse, are in dispute here.

The first three counts stated causes of action against the Club for negligent hiring and against both the Club and Dr. Losse for intentional misrepresentation and negligent misrepresentation. These three counts were removed to federal court and were remanded to state court only after the court of appeal had filed its opinion. The trial court sustained the Club's demurrer to the fifth count and the Court of Appeal affirmed the judgment for the Club. Plaintiffs' answer did not raise any issues in addition to those set forth in the petition for review.

The Club is not a party to the proceedings in this court. Our references to "defendant" are to Dr. Losse. Because Wanda Hendy's loss of consortium claim is dependent upon John Hendy's right to sue defendant and will not be discussed separately, our references to "plaintiff" are to John Hendy.

Defendant demurred to the cause of action for medical malpractice on the ground that plaintiff's exclusive remedy for his employment-related injury was within the workers' compensation system. In support of the demurrer defendant asked that the court take judicial notice, pursuant to Code of Civil Procedure section 430.30 and Evidence Code section 452, of both the National Football League employment contract and the collective bargaining agreement between the league's management council and the National Football League Players Association, both of which governed plaintiff's employment.

The collective bargaining agreement included a provision outlining the players' right to medical care and treatment, and made the cost of medical services to be rendered by Club physicians the responsibility of the Club. The contract between plaintiff and the Club provided that plaintiff would receive "such medical and hospital care during the term of this contract as the Club physician may deem necessary...." The contract between defendant and the Club is not part of the record.

Plaintiff opposed the demurrer on two grounds—(1) defendant was acting in a dual capacity when he diagnosed and treated plaintiff, and (2) the action was permitted under subdivision (b)(2) of section 3602, which permits an action at law against an employer for damages proximately caused by aggravation of a work-related injury if the "injury is aggravated by the employer's fraudulent concealment of the existence of the injury and its connection with the employment...."

The trial court sustained the demurrer without leave to amend, ruling that a 1982 amendment of section 3602 made workers' compensation plaintiff's exclusive remedy even if a dual capacity situation existed, and that the complaint failed to state facts to establish concealment of either the injury or its relation to plaintiff's employment. The Court of Appeal held that because section 3602 applies only to lawsuits against employers, its limitation on use of the dual capacity doctrine applied only to actions against employers and had no impact on an injured employee's right to sue a coemployee.

II

Development of the Dual Capacity Doctrine

Section 3600 establishes the conditions under which an employer's liability for compensation established by the Workers' Compensation Act is in lieu of any other liability of the employer to the employee for an injury suffered on the job. Section 3602 provides in turn, with exceptions not relevant here, that when compensation is payable under section 3600, the right to recover compensation is "the sole and exclusive remedy of the employee or his or her dependents against the employer...." A parallel, but not identical, exclusive remedy provision, section 3601, prohibits actions against coemployees for injuries they cause when acting within the scope of their employment.

A judicially recognized exception to the exclusive remedy restriction on actions against employers—the "dual capacity doctrine"—has been understood to also permit an action for damages against a coemployee physician if the injury to the plaintiff employee was caused or aggravated by the defendant. This case arises because the Legislature has imposed limits on the dual capacity doctrine by amendment of section 3602.

A. *Dual Capacity of Employers*

The dual capacity doctrine posits that an employer may have or assume a relationship with an employee other than that of employer-employee, and that when an employee seeks damages for injuries arising out of the secondary relationship the employee's claim is not subject to the exclusive remedy provisions of the Workers' Compensation Act. The doctrine was first enunciated in Duprey v. Shane (1952) 39 Cal.2d 781, 249 P.2d 8, which, like this case, involved a medical malpractice claim.

At the time Duprey was decided, section 3601 governed actions against employers by injured employees. It then provided: "Where the conditions of compensation exist, the right to recover such compensation pursuant to the provisions of this division is, except as provided in section 3706, the exclusive remedy against the employer for the injury or death."

Plaintiff Duprey was employed as a practical nurse by defendants who were partners engaged in the practice of chiropractic medicine. The plaintiff was injured on the job. She was treated by one of her employers and by a fellow employee, also a chiropractor, who was another defendant. The treatment aggravated her injuries. She applied for and received compensation from the Industrial Accident Commission (IAC) for the original injury and resulting disability, and then sued Dr. Shane, her employer, and Dr. Harrison, her coemployee, for malpractice in causing the subsequent injury. After a jury trial, the plaintiff was awarded damages for that injury.

On appeal from the judgment, the defendants claimed, inter alia, that the IAC had exclusive jurisdiction over the plaintiff's claim, relying on section 3601 for that proposition. The Court of Appeal, whose opinion this court adopted, disagreed and affirmed the judgment for the plaintiff.

The court reasoned: " '[W]hen the employing doctor elected to treat the industrial injury, the doctor assumed the same responsibilities that any doctor would have assumed had he been called in on the case.... [S]uch third party doctor can be sued for malpractice resulting in an aggravation of an industrial injury, or a new injury. It follows that the employer-doctor may be sued for malpractice when he elects to treat the industrial injury.' " (Duprey v. Shane, supra, 39 Cal.2d 781, 789, 249 P.2d 8, bracketed deletions from Court of Appeal opinion omitted.) In further explanation, the court noted the right of an injured employee to sue a doctor provided by the employer's insurer for malpractice, and concluded that the employee did not lose that right if an employer who was a doctor treated the injury. " 'In such event, the employer-doctor is a 'person other than the employer' within the meaning of section 3852 of the Labor Code.... In treating the injury Dr. Shane did not do so because of the employer-employee relationship, but did so as an attending doctor, and his relationship to [plaintiff] was that of doctor and patient.' " (39 Cal.2d at p. 793, 249 P.2d 8, bracketed deletions from Court of Appeal opinion omitted.)

Use of the phrase "dual capacity" to describe this secondary relationship between the chiropractor/employer and patient/employee in Duprey v. Shane, supra, 39 Cal.2d 781, 249 P.2d 8, and analogous relationships in later cases apparently stems from the defendants' argument in Duprey that the result would recognize a "dual legal personality," a disfavored concept. Rejecting that argument, this court held: " 'It is true that the law is opposed to the creation of a dual personality, where to do so is unrealistic and purely legalistic. But where, as here, it is perfectly apparent that the person involved ... bore towards his employee two relationships—that of employer and that of a doctor—there should be no hesitancy in recognizing this fact as a fact. Such a conclusion, in this case, is in precise accord with the facts and is realistic and not legalistic. We conclude, therefore, that an employee injured in an industrial accident may sue the attending physician for malpractice if the original injury is aggravated as a result of the doctor's negligence, and that such right exists whether the attending doctor is the insurance doctor or the employer.' " (Duprey v. Shane, supra, 39 Cal.2d at p. 793, 249 P.2d 8.)

B. Dual Capacity and Coemployees

The Duprey decision also permitted the plaintiff to pursue her action against her coemployee, Dr. Harrison. The court did not identify any existing bar to that suit or explain the necessity for its analogy of that action to the action against the employer. We said only that Harrison was also subject to suit because " 'it is hard to see how Dr. Harrison is in any different position than the insurance company doctor would have been had he been called in to treat [plaintiff].' " (Duprey v. Shane, supra, 39 Cal.2d at pp. 794–795, 249 P.2d 8, bracketed deletions from Court of Appeal opinion omitted.)

There was no statutory limitation on actions against coemployees at the time Duprey was decided. Section 3852 had provided since its enactment in 1937 (Stats.1937, ch. 90, p. 273) that an employee's claim for workers' compensation did not affect his or her right of action "against any person other than the employer." Suits against coemployees were permitted.

In 1959, following Duprey, section 3601 was amended to include coemployees. Prior to that year, workers' compensation had been the exclusive remedy only as against an employer for the injury or death of an employee.

"Prior to 1959 when section 3601 was amended, there was no doubt that the common law right of an employee to sue a coemployee for injuries negligently inflicted while on the job [citation], was preserved in this jurisdiction by section 3852. Baugh v. Rogers (1944) 24 Cal.2d 200, 214 [148 P.2d 633] held that 'Our workmen's compensation laws were not designed to relieve one other than the employer from any liability imposed by statute or common law.' [Citation.] At that time and until 1959, section 3601 merely stated: 'Where the conditions of compensation exist, the right to recover such compensation ... is ... the exclusive remedy against the employer for the injury or death.' (Stats.1937, ch. 90, p. 269.)" (Saala v. McFarland (1965) 63 Cal.2d 124, 127, 45 Cal.Rptr. 144, 403 P.2d 400.)

As amended in 1959, section 3601 made workers' compensation the "exclusive remedy for injury or death of an employee against the employer or against any other employee of the employer acting within the scope of his or her employment...." (Stats.1959, ch. 1189, § 1, p. 3275.) The immunity granted coemployees was more limited than that extended to employers, however. Workers' compensation was the exclusive remedy only if the employee was "acting within the scope of his or her employment.... " (Ibid.)

This court considered the impact of the 1959 amendment in Saala v. McFarland, supra, 63 Cal.2d 124, 45 Cal.Rptr. 144, 403 P.2d 400. There, the plaintiff employee suffered a compensable injury when she was struck by an automobile driven by a coemployee on a parking lot maintained by the employer. She sued the coemployee, who claimed that the immunity from suit granted coemployees by the 1959 amendment of section 3601 was coextensive with that granted employers by sections 3600 and 3601. This court rejected the argument:

> [W]e cannot agree with defendant's contention that the Legislature intended to exempt from the common law liability retained in section 3852 all employee actions causing harm to coemployees to the identical extent that the common employer is exempted from civil liability because of its provision for workmen's compensation....
>
> The presumption that an overall change is intended where a statute is amended following a judicial decision [citation] is given its full effect if section 3601 as amended is construed to change the law stated in those cases and exempt from civil liability only a coemployee's actions within the scope of employment, rather than those "arising out of and in the course of the employment."

Saala v. McFarland, supra, 63 Cal.2d 124, 128, 45 Cal.Rptr. 144, 403 P.2d 400.

The limitation of coemployee immunity to acts within the scope of employment reflects apparent legislative recognition that, because coemployees do not have financial obligations imposed on them under the workers' compensation law comparable to those imposed on an employer, granting the same broad immunity was not justified. Employers are granted immunity from suit in most cases because, regardless of fault, they are obligated to provide benefits to an injured employee. (S.G. Borello & Sons, Inc. v. Department of Industrial Relations (1989) 48 Cal.3d 341, 354, 256 Cal.Rptr. 543, 769 P.2d 399; Pacific Gas & Elec. Co. v. Ind. Acc. Com. (1961) 56 Cal.2d 219, 233, 14 Cal.Rptr. 548, 363 P.2d 596.) An employee is liable only for tortious conduct. There is no reason to grant employees the same broad immunity from suit that employers enjoy.

The 1959 amendment therefore granted a limited immunity to employees. That immunity protects employees from damage actions by coemployees, but only if the defendant was acting within the scope of employment when his conduct injured the plaintiff. This court's earlier recognition of coemployee liability in Duprey v. Shane, supra, 39 Cal.2d 781, 249 P.2d 8, was consistent with the limitation created by the 1959 amendment of section 3601. However, courts which relied on that decision and the "dual capacity" doctrine thereafter as a basis for permitting actions against coemployees did not recognize, as this court did in Saala v. McFarland, supra, 63 Cal.2d 124, 45 Cal.Rptr. 144, 403 P.2d 400, that coemployees were not exempted from suit when the workers' compensation system was created, and that section 3601 establishes an immunity from suit for coemployees which is distinct from that granted employers by section 3602.

Thus, in Hoffman v. Rogers (1972) 22 Cal.App.3d 655, 99 Cal.Rptr. 455, a malpractice action was permitted against a coemployee physician who allegedly aggravated an industrial injury. In Hoffman, as in the present case, the services for which the physician was employed included treatment of industrial injuries. Relying on the statement in Duprey v. Shane, supra, 39 Cal.2d 781, 794, 249 P.2d 8, that the principles underlying our conclusion that the employer could be held liable were equally applicable to the coemployee physician, the Court of Appeal held that the 1959 amendment of section 3601 did not affect the "dual legal personality" rule enunciated in Duprey. (22 Cal.App.3d at p. 662, 99 Cal.Rptr. 455.)

III

Legislative Restriction of Dual Capacity

Prior to the 1982 amendment, section 3602 stated only: "In all cases where the conditions of compensation do not concur, the liability of the employer is the same as if this division had not been enacted." (Stats. 1937, ch. 90, p. 269.)

In 1982, the Legislature amended sections 3601 and 3602. Since that amendment, section 3601 has applied only to coemployees. Section 3602 has governed civil liability of employers. As amended, section 3602 provides in pertinent part:

> (a) Where the conditions of compensation set forth in Section 3600 concur, the right to recover such compensation is, except as specifically provided in this section and Sections 3706 and 4558, the sole and exclusive remedy of the employee or his or her dependents against the employer, and the fact that either the employee or the employer also occupied another or dual capacity prior to, or at the time of, the employee's industrial injury shall not permit the employee or his or her dependents to bring an action at law for damages against the employer.

Defendant argues that this amendment reflects a legislative intent to abrogate the dual capacity doctrine as to coemployees as well as employers. As a result, he claims, coemployees are entitled to the same protection against suit that employers now enjoy, and may not be held liable on a dual capacity theory.

Failing to recognize the significance of section 3601, defendant argues that the language of section 3602, as amended, and the legislative history of the 1982 amendment, reflect an intent to abolish the dual capacity doctrine altogether—as to both employers and coemployees—except as expressly provided in section 3602.

Plaintiff argues in response that the 1982 amendment does not affect application of the doctrine in malpractice actions against employer-physicians in medical malpractice cases involving aggravation of industrial injury, and has no effect whatsoever on actions against coemployees. He also argues that, regardless of the impact of the 1982 amendment on actions against employers, the legislative history of the 1982 amendments reflects no consideration of the dual capacity rule as applied to coemployees. Therefore, he reasons, the Legislature cannot be deemed to have intended that the restrictions imposed in section 3602 be extended to actions governed by section 3601.

Plaintiff's view has been accepted by one commentator. Professor Larson states in his treatise: "The dual capacity doctrine was legislatively abolished in 1982 as to the employer as a third-party defendant, but apparently not as to the co-employee doctor." (2A Larson, The Law of Workmen's Compensation (4th ed. 1990) § 72.61(b), p. 228.47, fn. 65.1.)

The legislative history of the 1982 amendment of section 3602 (Stats.1982, ch. 922, § 6, p. 3367), also suggests that the Legislature did not intend that the restriction of the dual capacity doctrine inserted into section 3602 be incorporated into section 3601. The Legislative Counsel's Digest of Assembly Bill No. 684 (1981–1982 Reg.Sess.), which amended section 3602, referred only to actions against employers, stating: "This bill would provide that the right to workers' compensation is the sole and exclusive remedy of the employee against the employer, and the fact that either party occupied another or dual capacity shall not permit the employee to bring an action at law for damages against the employer."

Defendant relies on the same legislative history, but none of that history includes any reference to actions against coemployees or suggests that the Legislature intended any change in the existing ban on actions against coemployees who were acting within the scope of their employment. One item on which defendant relies, a report of the conference committee on the bill amending section 3602, states that "the bill contains strict limitations on the 'dual capacity' doctrine," but the report does not support a conclusion that the Legislature had in mind any change in the dual capacity doctrine as it applies to coemployees. To the contrary, the report explains that the "provisions are necessary so that California employers are not held liable for the payment of both worker's compensation benefits and tort liability awards for a substantial number of work-related injuries." (Report by Conference Committee on Assembly Bill 684, pp. 2–3.) Like the Legislative Counsel's digest, this report refers only to the impact of the dual capacity doctrine on employers. For that reason, and because coemployees are not subject to the potential for dual liability, and employers do not face that danger for acts committed by employees which are outside the scope of their employment, this report does not support a conclusion that the Legislature intended the amendment of section 3602 to affect the liability of coemployees.

We agree with plaintiff, therefore, that the legislative history of the 1982 amendment of section 3602 does not suggest that the Legislature intended to expand the immunity of coemployees when it amended section 3602. The legislative history reflects no consideration of, or intent to alter, the liability of coemployees.

While coemployees are not protected by the exclusive remedy provisions of section 3602, however, they do enjoy the immunity created by section 3601. That section expressly immunizes coemployees for acts within the scope of employment. Because the judicially recognized dual capacity doctrine did not and could not create an exception to the statutory immunity granted coemployees in 1959, the amendment of section 3601 in 1982 to restrict or preclude application of that doctrine to coemployees was unnecessary. Therefore, while we agree with plaintiff that the 1982 amendment of section 3602 (to restrict the dual capacity doctrine theretofore applied to employers) does not affect the liability of coemployees, it does not follow that this suit may be prosecuted.

In the 1982 amendments to the workers' compensation law the Legislature made a less extensive, but equally significant, amendment to the coemployee immunity provision of section 3601. That amendment supports, indeed compels, a conclusion that a coemployee physician enjoys immunity from suit for malpractice under the 1959 amendment of section 3601 if the coemployee physician was acting within the scope of employment when the injury was caused.

Prior to the 1982 amendments, section 3601 already included the exclusive remedy language that was added to section 3602 in 1982. As amended in 1959 (Stats.1959, ch. 1189, § 1, pp. 3275–3276) and by subsequent nonsubstantive amendments, subdivision (a) of section 3601 provided:

> (a) Where the conditions of compensation exist, the right to recover such compensation, pursuant to the provisions of this division is, except as provided in Section 3706, the exclusive remedy for injury or death of an employee against the employer or against any other employee of the employer acting within the scope of his employment, except that an employee, or his dependents in the event of his death, shall, in addition to the right to compensation against the employer, have a right to bring an action at law for damages against the other employee, as if this division did not apply, in the following cases:
>
> (1) When the injury or death is proximately caused by the willful and unprovoked physical act of aggression of such other employee.
>
> (2) When the injury or death is proximately caused by the intoxication of such other employee.

In the 1982 amendment of section 3601, however, the Legislature added an express restriction on nonstatutory exceptions to the exclusive remedy rule applicable to coemployees.

As amended to apply only to coemployees, section 3601, subdivision (a), now states: "Where the conditions of compensation set forth in Section 3600 concur, the right to recover such compensation, pursuant to the provisions of this division is, except as specifically provided in this section, the exclusive remedy for injury or death of an employee against any other employee of the employer acting within the scope of his or her employment. . . ." Those statutory exceptions encompass only injury caused by wilful and unprovoked physical aggression of a coemployee and those caused by a coemployee's intoxication. And, consistent with the legislative purpose of preventing dual liability for employers, subdivision (b) of section 3601 provides that the employer may not be held liable for a damage award against a coemployee when suit is brought under one of the exceptions.

The 1982 amendment of section 3601 confirms therefore the legislative intent that there be no judicially created exceptions to the immunity that has been granted to coemployees.

Plaintiff argues that a malpractice action should be permitted against a coemployee physician even if the physician was providing treatment pursuant to his employment obligations because a physician's duties as a professional are separate from the employment relationship. The statute is clear, however. If one employee is acting within the scope of employment at the time the employee injures another employee, workers' compensation is the injured employee's exclusive remedy against the coemployee. The rule proposed by plaintiff cannot be reconciled with the statutory language.

The Court of Appeal disagreed with the trial court's ruling on the impact of the 1982 amendment of section 3602, because it believed that the failure of the Legislature to amend section 3601 in the same way that section 3602 had been amended in 1982 had to be understood as reflecting only an intent to restrict application of the dual capacity doctrine to employers. The Court of Appeal failed to recognize, however, that section 3601 already created an immunity which is absolute if a coemployee defendant was acting within the scope of employment when the plaintiff suffered the industrial injury.

The Legislature has made it clear that if a coemployee was acting within the scope of his or her employment, the only exceptions to the immunity created by section 3601 are those created by statute. Therefore, while we agree with the conclusion of the Court of Appeal that the amendment of section 3602 has no impact on section 3601, that court erred in permitting this medical malpractice action to proceed without regard to whether the defendant was acting within the scope of his employment.

IV

SCOPE OF EMPLOYMENT

Since section 3601 governs this action, the dispositive question is whether defendant was acting within the scope of his employment when he negligently treated and/or diagnosed plaintiff's injury.

Saala v. McFarland, supra, 63 Cal.2d 124, 45 Cal.Rptr. 144, 403 P.2d 400, is instructive in defining the "scope of employment" limitation of section 3601. " 'Conduct is within the scope of employment only if the servant is actuated to some extent by an intent to serve his master.' [Citations.]" (63 Cal.2d at p. 129, 45 Cal.Rptr. 144, 403 P.2d 400.) Approaching the question from another perspective, a coemployee's conduct is within the scope of his or her employment if it could be imputed to the employer under the doctrine of respondeat superior. If the coemployee was not "engaged in any active service for the employer," the coemployee was not acting within the scope of employment. (Id. at p. 130, 45 Cal.Rptr. 144, 403 P.2d 400.)

We explained in Saala v. McFarland, supra, that this test implements the purpose of the exclusive remedy rule which protects employers. Adopting the reasoning of the referee we stated there:

> [T]he purpose of section 3601 is to make workmen's compensation the exclusive remedy of an injured workman against his employer. That purpose would be defeated if a right of action existed against a fellow employee acting in the scope of his employment in such a way that the fellow employee's negligence could be imputed to the employer. For that reason workmen's compensation was also made the exclusive remedy against a fellow workman "acting within the scope of his employment." The words "acting within the scope of his employment" should be construed in the light of the purpose of the section, so as not to extend the immunity beyond respondeat superior situations.

63 Cal.2d at p. 130, 45 Cal.Rptr. 144, 403 P.2d 400.

The statutory immunity established by section 3601 applies here. The allegations of the complaint and the employment contract, of which judicial notice has been taken, compel a conclusion that defendant was acting within the scope of his employment when he diagnosed and treated plaintiff. The Club was obligated to provide treatment for injuries related to plaintiff's employment, and defendant was under an obligation arising out of his employment relationship with the Club to provide that treatment. Unlike the situation of the defendants in Duprey v. Shane, supra, 39 Cal.2d 781, 249 P.2d 8, defendant did not step out of his coemployee role when he treated plaintiff. He did exactly what he was employed to do.

The conditions necessary to invoke the immunity granted by section 3601 are present here since both the original injury and the alleged aggravation arose out of and in the course of plaintiff's employment and "at the time of the injury, [plaintiff was] performing service growing out of and incidental to his ... employment and [was] acting within the course of his ... employment." In addition "the injury [was] proximately caused by the employment...." (§ 3600, subd. (a)(2) & (3).) Since the conditions of section 3600 were met, and defendant was acting within the scope of his employment when he diagnosed and/or treated plaintiff, section 3601, by its express terms, makes workers' compensation plaintiff's exclusive remedy. His action against defendant is statutorily barred.

If a coemployee provides medical services other than those contemplated by the employee's employment and in so doing is not acting for the employer, he or she no longer enjoys the "immunity" from suit which section 3601 creates for acts which are within the scope of employment. In Hoffman v. Rogers, supra, 22 Cal.App.3d 655, 99 Cal. Rptr. 455, for example, the coemployee physician provided postsurgical treatment to the plaintiff. In so doing, he engaged in a course of care and treatment beyond the preliminary diagnosis and referral which were the duties incidental to his employment. (Id. at p. 659, 99 Cal.Rptr. 455.) In those circumstances, the coemployee may have assumed the "dual capacity" of a treating physician. Although analyzed by the court under the dual capacity doctrine, that doctrine was not necessary to the result since the exclusive remedy rule of section 3601 limited actions against coemployees only if the injury was caused by an act within the scope of the defendant coemployee's employment.

By contrast, in Wickham v. North American Rockwell Corp. (1970) 8 Cal.App.3d 467, 87 Cal.Rptr. 563, workers' compensation benefits were held to be the injured employee's exclusive remedy for negligent diagnosis by a company physician. There, because the conditions of employment were dangerous to employees' health, a staff of physicians was employed for the purpose of examining, diagnosing, and treating employee ailments. The Court of Appeal agreed with the trial court which had sustained without leave to amend defendant's demurrer to a complaint alleging that one of those coemployee physicians had negligently failed to diagnose a progressive lung disease. The court reasoned that the medical services were provided because the employment posed an inherent health hazard, and the physical examinations provided by the employer were contemplated by the work. The complaint alleged that the coemployee physician was acting within the scope of his employment. Therefore, the court could not conclude, "as the court did in Duprey, that when defendant [physician] examined plaintiff he did so in some capacity and relationship other than that which he ordinarily enjoyed, namely, that of a fellow employee." (Id. at p. 474, 87 Cal.Rptr. 563.) Again, although the court failed to consider the limits of the immunity granted by section 3601, the result was consistent with those limits.

Here, too, defendant is not alleged to have any relationship to plaintiff other than a coemployee whose role was to provide medical care for injuries that are inherent in the nature of plaintiff's employment.

The express language of section 3601 makes workers' compensation plaintiff's sole remedy in these circumstances.

V

Leave to Amend

The trial court in this case failed to note the omission of any allegations suggesting that defendant was acting outside the scope of his employment when he negligently diagnosed the nature of plaintiff's industrial injury. The court believed that Hoffman v. Rogers, supra, 22 Cal.App.3d 655, 99 Cal.Rptr. 455, was factually on point, although defendant had argued that the complaint alleged only conduct within the scope of his employment duties. The court nonetheless sustained defendant's demurrer without leave to amend in the belief that the 1982 amendment of section 3602 made workers' compensation plaintiff's exclusive remedy even though a dual capacity situation had existed when defendant diagnosed and treated plaintiff.

Plaintiff suggests that if granted leave to amend he would allege that defendant was an independent contractor. While plaintiff's allegation that defendant Losse was an employee was made on information and belief he did not suggest to the trial court that a factual basis for amendment of the complaint to allege that defendant Losse was an independent contractor existed, and he has not demonstrated to this court either that the allegation that Losse was an employee was the result of inadvertence or mistake, or that he has since discovered a factual basis for alleging that Losse was an independent contractor. (Blank v. Kirwan (1985) 39 Cal.3d 311, 318, 216 Cal.Rptr. 718, 703 P.2d 58.)

In these circumstances, although the allegation that defendant was an employee was made on information and belief, leave to amend need not be granted.

VI

Disposition

The judgment of the Court of Appeal is reversed.

LOWERY v. JUVENAL

559 S.W.2d 119 (Tex.Ct.Civ.App.1977).

REYNOLDS, Justice.

A take nothing judgment was rendered in this personal injury suit when the affirmative defense of limitation was established as a matter of law and no issue of its inapplicability was raised. Affirmed.

During the 1971–72 school term, Gregory J. Lowery was a senior student attending Texas Tech University and a scholarship-member of its basketball team. In a 1971 pre-season practice, Lowery received an injury to his left ankle and, during a game in the forepart of 1972, he sustained a muscle pull in his left groin. These injuries were treated by

Dr. Wallace Hess, the designated team physician, and by Jim Juvenal, the team trainer. Neither the doctor nor the trainer treated Lowery's injuries after the end of the basketball season in March of 1972.

On 3 February 1976, Lowery filed this suit, naming as defendants Juvenal, Gerald Myers, the head basketball coach, Dr. Hess, and Texas Tech University. Denominating his suit as one "to recover for personal injuries and damages," Lowery recited the receipt of the two injuries, for which no defendant was assigned any responsibility, and related the treatment he said he received from Dr. Hess and Juvenal. Alleged are the development of new bone formations in the pelvic area and in the left ankle and chronic tendinitis. Lowery sought damages "as a result of the negligent acts" and the "negligent conduct" of the defendants without particularizing how any act or conduct constituted negligence.

Answering without excepting to the generality of the petition, each defendant interposed affirmatively the two-year statute of limitation as a bar to Lowery's alleged cause of action. Deposition of all individual parties to the action confirmed that the last treatment Lowery received from any defendant was in 1972, almost four years before this suit was filed.

Juvenal, Coach Myers and Dr. Hess then moved for summary judgment, and the university urged its affirmative defense, on the ground that the pleadings and the depositions showed that Lowery's cause of action was, as a matter of law, barred by the two-year statute of limitation. Lowery offered no controverting evidence.

The trial court, considering the pleadings and the summary judgment proof to establish that limitation had run, rendered judgment that Lowery take nothing. Lowery has appealed.

On appeal, Lowery asserts, and we accept, that this suit is "for personal injuries received as a result of the negligent treatment provided him by the Defendants during the 1971–72 basketball season at Texas Tech University." Lowery concedes that Vernon's Ann.Civ.St. art. 5526 mandates that an action for personal injury "shall be commenced and prosecuted within two years after the cause of action shall have accrued, and not afterward." Within the meaning of the statute, the cause of action accrues, and limitation begins to run, when facts exist which authorize the claimant to seek judicial relief. Williams v. Pure Oil Co., 124 Tex. 341, 78 S.W.2d 929, 931 (1935).

It is undisputed that the treatment Lowery received from any defendant was administered more than two years before Lowery filed this suit to recover damages for negligent treatment. Thus, the judgment rendered was warranted upon the establishment of the affirmative defense of limitation as a matter of law both by Lowery's own pleadings, Smith v. Coffee's Shop for Boys & Men, Inc., 536 S.W.2d 83, 85 (Tex.Civ.App.Amarillo 1976, no writ), and by the summary judgment proof, Siegel v. McGavock Drilling Company, 530 S.W.2d 894, 896 (Tex.Civ.App.Amarillo 1975, writ ref'd n. r. e.), unless, for some applicable reason, the two-year statute of limitation did not start running until after Lowery was treated and less than two years before he filed this suit.

In attempting to escape the established defense of limitation, Lowery does not mention, either in his brief or in his deposition, any treatment which he considers negligent and which was either concealed at the time it was given or he did not discover until after it was administered. Rather, he contends that the running of limitation was postponed until his action for negligent treatment accrued less than two years before he filed this suit for the pleaded reason that:

> At all times material herein, each Defendant fraudulently concealed and conspired together to fraudulently conceal the extent and seriousness of the injuries suffered by the Plaintiff such that, despite acting as an ordinary and prudent person would act, he was unable to discover the extent of his injuries until the winter of 1974.

Noticeably absent from the pleading is any suggestion, much less an allegation, raising the issue that defendants fraudulently concealed any negligent treatment or the issue that Lowery later discovered that he had received negligent treatment. Thus, Lowery has no pleading negating the applicability of the two-year statute of limitation to his asserted cause of action for negligent treatment. Of course, one may recover only in the right in which he sues and upon the facts pleaded as the basis of that right, and he cannot recover through a right not asserted. Starr v. Ferguson, 140 Tex. 80, 166 S.W.2d 130, 132 (1942).

To prevail, the defendants were required to establish that their defense met Lowery's case as pleaded. Torres v. Western Casualty and Surety Company, 457 S.W.2d 50, 52 (Tex.1970). They have done so.

SOREY v. KELLETT

849 F.2d 960 (5th Cir.1988).

THORNBERRY, Circuit Judge.

This is an appeal from the district court's pretrial order denying a claim of qualified immunity to causes of action based on Mississippi law. We hold that this court has jurisdiction of the appeal, and we reverse.

I.

Eric Sorey played football under an athletic scholarship at the University of Southern Mississippi (USM). One day in early August 1986, Sorey collapsed on the football practice field. He was taken to the training room complaining of nausea and severe stomach cramps. His condition did not improve, and two hours later he was taken to the USM clinic. Sorey remained at the clinic for four or five hours, during which time he was examined by the team physician, Dr. Boyd Kellett. When Sorey failed to improve, a fellow student took him to Methodist Hospital, but he died on the way.

Eric Sorey's mother, Elnora Sorey, filed this action in district court alleging claims under 42 U.S.C. § 1983 and state tort and contract law. She named as defendants USM; the members of Mississippi's Board of Trustees of the State Institutions of Higher Learning; USM's head football coach, Jim Carmody; USM's athletic trainer, Earnest Harrington; and Dr. Kellett. The basis for Sorey's federal and state claims included alleged negligence by Harrington and Kellett, violation of a nondelegable duty to take care of football players by Coach Carmody, and failure to provide sufficient funds to hire competent employees by the Board of Trustees.

All defendants were named in their official capacities, and the noninstitutional defendants were also named in their individual capacities. The district court eventually dismissed the federal claims against all defendants, and the state claims against all defendants except Carmody, Harrington, and Kellett in their individual capacities. The district court denied motions by Carmody, Harrington, and Kellett to dismiss or for summary judgment on the basis of qualified immunity. Those defendants brought this immediate appeal of the court's order.

II.

Under 28 U.S.C. § 1291, the courts of appeals have jurisdiction over "final decisions" of the district courts. Ordinarily, this section precludes review of a district court's pretrial orders until appeal from the final judgment. In Cohen v. Beneficial Industrial Loan Corp., 337 U.S. 541, 69 S.Ct. 1221, 1225–26, 93 L.Ed. 1528 (1949), however, the Supreme Court held that some district court decisions belong to "that small class which finally determine claims of right separable from, and collateral to, rights asserted in the action, too important to be denied review and too independent of the cause itself to require that appellate consideration be deferred until the whole case is adjudicated." Under this "collateral order doctrine," some decisions that otherwise would be interlocutory may be appealed as final decisions under § 1291.

The Court has held that a final pretrial order denying a claim of qualified immunity under federal law is a final decision appealable under the collateral order doctrine. Mitchell v. Forsyth, 472 U.S. 511, 105 S.Ct. 2806, 86 L.Ed.2d 411 (1985). The Court noted that an essential characteristic of an issue appealable under the collateral order doctrine is that "unless it can be reviewed before [the proceedings terminate], it can never be reviewed at all." 105 S.Ct. at 2815 (quoting Stack v. Boyle, 342 U.S. 1, 72 S.Ct. 1, 7, 96 L.Ed. 3 (1951)). For example, the Court had previously held that a denial of absolute immunity was appealable, Nixon v. Fitzgerald, 457 U.S. 731, 102 S.Ct. 2690, 73 L.Ed.2d 349 (1982), because "the essence of absolute immunity is its possessor's entitlement not to have to answer for his conduct in a civil damages action." Mitchell, 105 S.Ct. at 2815. Qualified immunity, the Court held, shared that characteristic of absolute immunity. The consequences with which the Court was concerned when it recognized qualified immunity were "not limited to liability for money damages; they also include[d] 'the general costs of subjecting officials to the risks of trial—distraction of officials from their governmental duties, inhibition of discretionary action, and deterrence of able people from public service.' " Id. (quoting Harlow v. Fitzgerald, 457 U.S. 800, 102 S.Ct. 2727, 2737, 73 L.Ed.2d 396 (1982)). Qualified immunity, as a result, "is an immunity from suit rather than a mere defense to liability; and like an absolute immunity, it is effectively lost if a case is erroneously permitted to go to trial." Id., 105 S.Ct. at 2816.

The present case, however, is different from Mitchell because the asserted defense here is one of qualified immunity under state law. This circuit has not previously addressed whether state officials have an immediate right to appeal a denial of qualified immunity when the immunity is claimed solely under state law. From Mitchell's framework of analysis, however, it is clear that our decision must turn on whether the state's doctrine of qualified immunity, like the federal doctrine, provides a true immunity from suit and not a simple defense to liability. The Sixth Circuit reached the same conclusion when it confronted this issue. In Marrical v. Detroit News, Inc., 805 F.2d 169 (6th Cir.1986) (per curiam), the court said:

> [T]he right to an interlocutory appeal from the denial of a claim of absolute or qualified immunity under state law can only exist where the state has extended an underlying substantive right to the defendant official to be free from the burdens of litigation arising from acts taken in the course of his duties.

Id. at 172.

Initially, we must address Sorey's argument that, under Erie Railroad Co. v. Tompkins, 304 U.S. 64, 58 S.Ct. 817, 82 L.Ed. 1188 (1938), we must dismiss the appeal because the Mississippi rules of procedure do not allow an appeal as a matter of right from a decision in state court denying a claim of qualified immunity. Appealability under 28 U.S.C. § 1291, however, is clearly a matter of federal law; state procedural law is not directly controlling. Budinich v. Becton Dickinson & Co., 486 U.S. 196, 108 S.Ct. 1717, 100 L.Ed.2d 178 (1988) (holding in a diversity case that federal law determines appealability under the collateral order doctrine). As a result, Mississippi's procedural rules are relevant only for what they reveal about the state's view on the substantive issue of whether qualified immunity is an immunity from suit or merely a defense to liability.

Mississippi courts have not directly considered whether the state's doctrine of qualified immunity provides an immunity from suit or a defense to liability. The courts have expressed generalized concerns of protecting official decision makers from liability. In State ex rel. Brazeale v. Lewis, 498 So.2d 321, 322 (Miss.1986), for example, the court wrote: "The basis for extending sovereign immunity [sic] to government officials lies in the inherent need to promote efficient and timely decision-making without lying in fear of liability for miscalculation or error in those actions." Also, in Davis v. Little, 362 So.2d 642, 644 (Miss.1978), the court noted that "the purpose of the immunity is to protect the official in his decision-making role." But those cases did not present the issue of whether qualified immunity was a defense to liability or an immunity from suit. More telling, therefore, is Mississippi's rule that a successful defense of qualified immunity entitles an official to dismissal before trial. See, e.g., Lewis (affirming the trial court's grant of a motion to dismiss before trial on the basis of qualified immunity); White v. City of Tupelo, 462 So.2d 707 (Miss.1984) (same). In addition, although there is no appeal as a matter of right to the Mississippi Supreme Court when a claim of qualified immunity is denied, the court has accepted interlocutory appeals of such denials through a certification procedure similar to 28 U.S.C. § 1292(b). See, e.g., Region VII, Mental Health–Mental Retardation Center v. Isaac, 523 So.2d 1013, 1015 (Miss.1988).

When the Sixth Circuit considered this question as presented under Michigan law, it refused to allow immediate appeal from a denial of Michigan qualified immunity because it found "no reason to believe that the Michigan Supreme Court ... intended to afford state officers immunity from suit as well as from liability." Marrical, 805 F.2d at 173. In Marrical, however, the court specifically found that Michigan courts were aware of the "longstanding" distinction drawn between immunity from suit and immunity from liability. Despite that awareness, the Michigan courts had repeatedly described qualified immunity only as an immunity from liability. Id. Furthermore, the court in Marrical was "offered no cases in which a Michigan court has granted summary judgment or dismissal before trial in order to protect against the burdens of litigation." Id. at 174. Neither assertion is true of Mississippi, and we therefore think that the Marrical result cannot be directly applied here.

We are persuaded that the Mississippi courts would recognize that the social costs of litigation against public officials—"the expenses of litigation, the diversion of official energy from pressing public issues, and the deterrence of able citizens from acceptance of public office," Harlow, 102 S.Ct. at 2736—suggest that qualified immunity should be an immunity from suit, not merely a defense to liability. As a result, a denial of Mississippi qualified immunity, like a denial of federal qualified immunity, is properly appealable under the collateral order doctrine.

III.

In Mississippi, public officials sued in their individual capacities have a limited, qualified immunity that extends to "discretionary," not to "ministerial" acts. Davis v. Little, 362 So.2d 642, 643 (Miss.1978). A discretionary act is one requiring "personal deliberation, decision and judgment." Id. (quoting W. Prosser, Law of Torts § 132 (4th ed. 1971)). A ministerial act, by contrast, is one "positively imposed by law and its performance required at a time and in a manner or upon conditions which are specifically designated, the duty to perform under the conditions specified not being dependent upon the officer's judgment or discretion." Poyner v. Gilmore, 171 Miss. 859, 864, 158 So. 922, 923 (1935).

The district court in this case interpreted Mississippi law to mean that discretionary decisions are "policy decisions," and that officials engaging in policy decisions are entitled to immunity because "[j]udges and jurors are in no better position to evaluate the reasonableness of policy determinations than are those officials who were charged with making them." Pruett v. City of Rosedale, 421 So.2d 1046, 1052 (Miss. 1982) (en banc). As a result, the district court held that Kellett, Harrington, and Carmody, defendants in this case, were not entitled to public official immunity because, when Sorey was injured, they "were not acting to further any public health goal but were simply administering medical care."

Since the district court's decision, however, the Mississippi Supreme Court has decided another case with very similar facts. In Marshall v. Chawla, 520 So.2d 1374 (Miss.1988), surviving heirs sued a doctor at a state hospital for negligence that led to the death of the patient. The doctor asserted that he was protected by "the qualified immunity given to public officials acting in a discretionary capacity within the scope of their duties." Id. at 1375. The court first cited its earlier decision in Hudson v. Rausa, 462 So.2d 689 (Miss.1984), which had granted immunity to a physician employed by the State Board of Health and charged with carrying out a program to prevent the spread of tuberculosis. Hudson had rejected a narrow view of discretionary actions, and had held that "the discretion given to the defendants applied not only to their decisions with reference to instituting a program of control, but also to the treatment administered in carrying out such policies." Id. at 695. As a result, Hudson had sustained the defendants' immunity defense. In attempting to distinguish Hudson, the plaintiffs in Marshall argued that the doctor in Marshall was not a "health department official implementing a health policy enacted for the good of the people of the state as a whole, ... [but] simply a physician employed by the state hospital to treat the general public...." 520 So.2d at 1376. The court, however, rejected that position, and held that Hudson "came very close to saying that 'all' medical decisions would be immunized from suit if they occurred in the context of a state institution...." Id. at 1375–76. The court then said:

> [I]n the case of medical doctors in public service, special circumstances are present which make a broader grant of immunity sound policy.... [Vulnerability to liability for negligence] might very well deter doctors from entering government service in the first place. The protection of qualified immunity no doubt serves as a powerful incentive to many doctors to serve in state eleemosynary institutions and this in turn, makes medical care available to many who [might] not be able to afford medical care in private facilities.... Following Hudson, we reaffirm the immunity enjoyed by physicians on the staff of state eleemosynary institutions.

Id. at 1377.

We think that Marshall mandates a finding that defendant Kellett, the team physician, and defendant Harrington, the team trainer, were performing discretionary functions in administering medical treatment to Sorey. We can find no distinction between the kind of decisions that Harrington and Kellett are alleged to have made concerning Sorey's medical care and those that the defendant doctor in Marshall made. Although it may seem harsh to accord such broad immunity from liability to state employees engaged in medical care, Marshall makes it clear that Mississippi has struck such a balance between the needs of injured persons and the state's interest in unfettered decision making by public employees.

[The remainder of the court's opinion, finding that Coach Carmody also was entitled to qualified immunity, is omitted.]

Notes

1. For an interesting case in which immunity was granted to a doctor whose recommendation resulted in an applicant being denied a boxing license, see *Colome v. State Athletic Comm'n of California*, 55 Cal.Rptr.2d 300 (Ct.App.1996).

2. In addition to the defenses outlined above, doctors also sometimes argue contributory negligence. *See, e.g., Pascal v. Carter*, 647 A.2d 231 (Pa.Super.Ct.1994) (radiologist who had misread football player's X-ray could not use fact player had delayed getting medical care to reduce his liability).

3. While malpractice actions are both difficult and time-consuming, the possibility of securing a large recovery has led some athletes to pursue such suits. In October 1985, for example, Citadel linebacker Marc Buoniconti (son of former Miami Dolphins linebacker Nick Buoniconti) was permanently paralyzed while making a tackle against East Tennessee State University. He subsequently sued The Citadel and its doctor for allowing him to play hurt and for providing him with an ill-conceived brace that made him more vulnerable to injury. Although the school settled on the eve of trial for $800,000, team physician E.K. Wallace Jr. insisted on going forward. After five weeks of testimony, a Charleston jury found he was not responsible for the tragedy.

In December 1991, the estate of Loyola Marymount University basketball player Hank Gathers dropped its suit against cardiologist Dr. Vernon Hattori in exchange for $1 million (the limit of his malpractice insurance policy). Gathers, who had been cleared to play despite having an abnormal heart rhythm, collapsed during the conference championship game. Several months later, Gathers' family reached a $1.6 million settlement with the university.

In June 1995, a jury awarded former left wing Glen Seabrooke $5.5 million after finding Philadelphia Flyers doctor John Gregg liable for improperly ordering physical therapy following a November 1988 injury. As a result of the treatment, Seabrooke permanently lost the use of his left arm and was forced to retire.

Four months after Seabrooke's record-setting verdict, former Boston Red Sox second baseman Marty Barrett obtained a $1.7 million judgment against team doctor Arthur Pappas. When Barrett tore up his right knee during a June 1989 game against the Toronto Blue Jays, Pappas failed to recommend surgery and instead suggested physical therapy. At least some observers believe Pappas did so because, as a part-owner of the franchise, he was trying to save money.

For a further look at these and other incidents, see, e.g., Cathy J. Jones, *College Athletes: Illness or Injury and the Decision to Return to Play*, 40 Buff. L. Rev. 113 (1992); Craig A. Issacs, Comment, *Conflicts of Interest for Team Physicians: A Retrospective in Light of Gathers v. Loyola Marymount University*, 2 Alb. L.J. Sci. & Tech. 147 (1992); G. Larry Sandefer, *College Athletic Injuries: Does the Buoniconti Case Create a Duty of an Athlete Not to Play?*, 63 Fla. B.J. 34 (Feb. 1989); Joseph Nocera, *Bitter Medicine*, Sports Illustrated, Nov. 6, 1995, at 74.

Problem 43

During a particularly hard-fought contest, a halfback suffered a career-ending injury. He later decided to sue his former team's physicians for failing to provide proper care. Although their practice is 900 miles from where the player lives, he plans to argue because they accompany the club on its once-a-year trip to his city, personal jurisdiction exists in his state. If they object, how will the court rule? *See Sherwin v. Indianapolis Colts, Inc.*, 752 F.Supp. 1172 (N.D.N.Y.1990).

C. VICARIOUS LIABILITY

Injured athletes sometimes attempt to hold a third party liable for a physician's malpractice. Doing so is quite difficult, however, because doctors typically work as independent contractors.

ROSENSWEIG v. STATE

158 N.E.2d 229 (N.Y.1959).

FULD, Judge.

Knocked out by Roger Donoghue in the eighth round of a bout held in Madison Square Garden on August 29, 1951, following two very hard blows to the head, George Flores died several days later of a cerebral hemorrhage and cerebral edema. This suit for wrongful death followed, it being alleged by his administrator that the State of New York was negligent in licensing and permitting Flores to fight when it knew, or should have known, that he was not in proper physical condition to engage in the fight. Flores had participated in two earlier fights, one on July 24, the other on August 14 (also against Donoghue), and each had come to an end when Flores suffered a technical knockout. The claim of negligence is based on the hypothesis that death was not the result of the blows received in his last fight, but rather the aggravation of a brain injury previously suffered, which should have been detected by the doctors, assertedly employees of the State, who found him physically fit to fight.

Flores had been examined before and after each of the fights by physicians selected, the record indicates, by the corporation promoting the matches from a panel set up by the Medical Advisory Board of the New York State Athletic Commission. The doctor who examined him after the conclusion of the first fight, on July 24, found him 'O.K.' Dr. Bockner, who was at the second fight, examined him twice, several hours apart, before the match got under way and described his 'physical condition [as] perfect.'

Then, after the fight had been stopped, the doctor again examined him twice—in the ring immediately after the knockout and, the second time, a half hour later, in his dressing room. Observing that Flores had suffered no cuts, no bruises and no concussion and that his heart, his system and reflexes were all 'perfectly normal,' Dr. Bockner expressed the opinion that he 'left the ring in good shape and * * * could continue to fight.' When application was made for Flores to take part in a match to be held on August 29, an electroencephalogram (EEG) was ordered as a precautionary measure and Flores was considered 'suspended' until the results of the encephalogram became known. One was taken and it revealed no abnormality and was interpreted as 'normal' and 'generally good'; although it did indicate a 'slowing anteriorly', that was not significant, it was said, because no earlier tracing was available for comparison.

The physician present at the last fight was Dr. Nardiello. Aware of Flores' earlier technical knockouts, the doctor testified that he not only 'spen[t] a lot of time with him,' subjecting him to a thorough physical examination shortly before the bout began, but that he also studied the reports of the other doctors and the electroencephalogram taken some days before. Based on all this, it was Dr. Nardiello's opinion that Flores was 'in excellent condition.' Indeed, it was his view—as well as of Donoghue, Flores' opponent—that he met his death as a result of injury sustained during the fight itself; the blow, a devastating one, was a left hook to the head, a 'hard * * * solid punch,' 'with [Donoghue's] full weight behind it,' 'perfectly timed and perfectly thrown.'

Flores went into a coma some hours after the fight. A brain operation was performed which was unsuccessful in saving his life. The surgeon who performed the operation, Dr. Daniels, testified that he observed 'no scar tissue' and 'no evidence' of any 'injury pre-existing the injury' received in the ring during the August 29th bout, but he voiced an opinion, in answer to a hypothetical question, that Flores may have sustained a concussion before that date. Dr. Helpern, the medical examiner who performed the autopsy, stated that he found no indications of any prior injury.

On the other hand, Dr. Somberg testified that, based on his examination of the medical record, it was his opinion that Flores had received injuries in the earlier contests and that death was caused 'by the damage that he took' in those fights, 'plus the damage in the third fight, plus the damage of his head striking the canvas.' Dr. Somberg also asserted that it was better medical practice that a boxer severely beaten about the head should not fight again for six weeks or two months.

The Court of Claims awarded the claimant $80,000; it was its view that the doctors who examined Flores were servants of the State and that they were negligent in not discovering that he had suffered a brain injury before his last fight. Upon appeal, the judgment was reversed and the claim dismissed. Although it expressed a 'serious doubt' as to whether the doctors were employees of the State, the Appellate Division found it unnecessary to decide that question, holding that, even assuming the existence of an employer-employee relationship, the claimant failed to establish either negligence or causation.

Our approach is different. We choose to place our decision on the ground not decided by the Appellate Division and, accordingly, we do not pass upon the issue of negligence. Study of the problem persuades us that the doctors were not employees of the State and, consequently, even if they were careless, their negligence could not in any event be imputed to the State.

Although this State has wisely waived its sovereign immunity against suit generally (Court of Claims Act, § 8) and, perhaps, 'more completely than any other American jurisdiction' (Herzog, Liability of the State of New York for 'Purely Governmental' Functions, 10 Syracuse L.Rev. 30), it is essential, at the very least, that the person for whose negligent conduct the State is sought to be charged be engaged in its service. The doctors who examined Flores were, quite obviously, not employees of the State, but it is suggested on behalf of the claimant that an intention on the part of the State to assume liability for the acts of these doctors is to be found in the legislation relating to boxing. Analysis of the statute, however, as well as its history, demonstrates the contrary.

'The common law of New York,' it has been noted, 'placed no bar on the holding or conduct of [boxing] matches.' Zwirn v. Galento, 288 N.Y. 428, 432–433, 43 N.E.2d 474, 477. However, for many decades the penal laws of this State contained a complete prohibition of prize fighting (L.1856, ch. 98; Penal Code [L.1881, ch. 676], § 458; now Penal Law, Consol.Laws, c. 40, § 1710). Its reintroduction dates from 1911, when the Legislature passed a law permitting boxing exhibitions to be resumed under stringent regulations, subject to the supervision of a newly created State Athletic Commission, and provided that the contests were to be excepted from the ban of the penal laws (L.1911, ch. 779). The objectives of this legislation were well described by Justice Seabury, as he then was, a few years after its enactment in Fitzsimmons v. New York State Athletic Comm., 15 Misc.2d 831, 833, 146 N.Y.S. 117, 120, affirmed 162 App.Div. 904, 147 N.Y.S. 1111:

> Confronted with the question as to whether it should prohibit prize fighting or sparring altogether, or leave such contests unaffected by legislation, the lawmaking body of this state has

> adopted a middle course, and has legalized boxing when conducted under State control. Two main purposes have prompted such legislation: First, the desire to prevent as far as possible certain brutal and degrading features which have in the past sometimes attended such contests, and, second, to promote and protect such contests when conducted within the legitimate limits of a sport. To achieve those purposes the state has created the Athletic Commission and authorized that Commission to prescribe stringent rules governing the conditions under which such contests can be held. * * * Reading [the] two statutes together, it is apparent that the vocation of prize fighting or sparring is an occupation subject to governmental control.

Further elaboration occurred with the enactment in 1920 of the so-called Walker Boxing Law which, continuing the State Athletic Commission, has remained on the books without any fundamental changes to the present time (L.1920, ch. 912, as amended by L.1948, ch. 754; L.1952, ch. 666, McK.Unconsol.Laws, § 9101 et seq.). The statute, exceedingly broad in its coverage, provides for rigid supervision of the premises in which the matches or exhibitions are held, of all who participate in the exhibitions in any capacity and of the methods of conducting the matches. The primary means employed to effect enforcement is a system of licensing, with exclusion of the unlicensed and power to penalize the licensed for violations or infringements. The standards imposed by the statute, it is provided, may be implemented by regulations promulgated by the commission, a power, we note, which has been frequently exercised.

The statute itself reflects a high concern for the physical fitness of the fighters scheduled to engage in the matches. Such fitness will, of course, enhance the competitive character of the contest and it may fairly be assumed that the Legislature was at least as concerned with the physical welfare of the contestants themselves. Accordingly, the statute, as it read in 1951 when the fight took place, prescribed that 'All boxers must be examined by a physician designated by the commission before entering the ring' (§ 23, as amended by L.1948, ch. 754, § 5 [now § 25]), that a physician must be 'in attendance at every boxing * * * match' (§ 13, as amended by L.1948, ch. 754, § 3 [now § 26]) and that a report of physical examinations must be filed by the corporation promoting the match 'not later than twenty-four hours after the termination of a contest' (Laws 1920, c. 912, § 24; § 23, as amended by L.1948, ch. 754, § 5 [now § 25]). The doctors so employed are selected from a list of 'qualified physicians' recommended to the commission 'from time to time' by its Medical Advisory Board, a body consisting of nine members appointed by the Governor (§ 12–a, as added by L.1948, ch. 754, § 2 [now § 4]; § 13, as amended by L.1948, ch. 754, § 3 [now § 26]). The board also recommends to the commission the fees for such physicians which are to be paid by the promoting corporation. (Ibid.). In addition, the board 'from time to time' is to submit to the commission for approval 'such additional regulations and standards of examination as in their judgment will safeguard the physical welfare of professional boxers * * * licensed by the commission' (§ 12–a, subd. 2, as added by L.1948, ch. 754 [now § 4, subd. 2]).

Turning more directly to the action before us, the only negligence charged or found is that of the doctors who conducted the examination of Flores. But, on the plainest principles of construction, the State has carefully avoided making these physicians its own servants or employees. It is true that the State established the panel—which now consists of some 60 doctors, half of whom are in the New York City area—but this is only the customary exercise of the police power in the regulation of a permitted subject. All persons require a license to practice medicine in this State, and the establishment of a limited number of such doctors to perform a specialized service is no more than similar selection for other subjects of specialization, such as psychiatry.

To be sure, the corporation promoting the contest was required to employ for this purpose a physician included on the panel. This, without more, is a phenomenon of everyday occurrence. No one would seriously suggest that every person to whom the State has issued a license to practice his profession or trade thereby becomes an employee or agent of the State. Nor is such a relationship created by virtue of the fact that the State may also prescribe the amount of the fee to be charged; regulation, no matter how close or stringent, is not thereby transmuted into government operation. Indeed, where the employment is made mandatory, it is not uncommon to prescribe the fee in order to prevent gouging. It is a familiar experience to many that only specially licensed tow trucks are permitted to come to the assistance of motorists on certain highways and that the towing fee is prescribed. By so doing, the authorities do not make themselves responsible for the manner in which the service is performed.

There is nothing in the Walker Boxing Law or in the Rules of the State Athletic Commission which suggests that the examining doctors, paid by the promoting corporation, are servants of the State or, in performing their duties, are subject to control or supervision by the commission. The plain fact of the matter is that, however stringent the requirements, the scheme embodied in the statute is solely a regulatory measure. Every such regulatory statute presupposes public purposes. The Legislature evidently considered that the reduction in the risk of permanent injury to fighters constituted such a purpose, and that was its right. There is no indication, however, that there was any design to transfer such risks to the State. By providing a safeguard through the requirement of a physical examination, the State did not undertake to insure that it would always be effective. It is difficult to conceive that the Legislature, in enacting the statute, ever considered the possibility that these doctors could be deemed servants of the State for whose negligence it would be held responsible. Precisely similar requirements are imposed for referees and judges whose fees are likewise prescribed by the commission (§§ 1, 7; Rules of Commission, former rule 41 [N.Y.Off.Comp. of

Codes, Rules & Regulations, Vol. 2, p. 1220], now rule F, § 11 [N.Y.Off. Comp. of Codes, Rules & Regulations, 8th Off.Supp., p. 540]), and yet it could hardly be claimed that the State would be answerable in damages if, for instance, a referee negligently failed to terminate a bout. The State adopted a parallel scheme when it created the State Harness Racing Commission (Pari–Mutuel Revenue Law [L.1940, ch. 254, as amended], art. II, § 35 et seq., particularly §§ 41, 41–a, added by L.1953, ch. 391, § 8, McK.Unconsol.Laws, §§ 7561 et seq., 7593 et seq., 7599, 7599–a) and, if the claimant's position were here upheld, all racing officials who are licensed and have their compensation fixed by that commission would, by a parity of reasoning, become servants of the State. Such an enlargement of public employment should be made consciously if it is intended. Regulation is ordinarily regarded as a means of avoiding governmental operation, rather than a subtle embodiment of it. See, e.g., Lavitt v. United States, D.C., 87 F.Supp. 149, affirmed 2 Cir., 177 F.2d 627.

In other words, although the State has by these measures sought to make a dangerous sport less dangerous and, indeed, may have retained a limited power of supervision over the physical examinations provided for, that does not mean that the Legislature constituted the examining doctor a servant or employee of the State so as to render it liable for his negligent act. It is probable that, even in a purely private context, persons situated as are these doctors would be held to be 'independent contractors,' for whose independent negligent acts the party requesting the performance of the service would not be responsible. Cf. Broderick v. Cauldwell–Wingate Co., 301 N.Y. 182, 187, 93 N.E.2d 629, 631, and Moore v. Charles T. Wills, Inc., 250 N.Y. 426, 428–429, 165 N.E. 835, 836 [general contractor not liable for independent negligent act of subcontractor]. However that may be, we reject the novel thesis that a person may be a 'constructive' state agent. Agency cannot be thrust upon the State against its will and only the Legislature can authorize persons to perform services for the State as its servants, and this the Legislature carefully refrained from doing in the case of these doctors. Although we have come upon no decision by a New York court in which the contention urged by the claimant has been advanced, an argument not too unlike it was considered and rejected in a case arising under the Federal Tort Claims Act, 28 U.S.C.A. §§ 1346, 2671 et seq. See Lavitt v. United States, D.C., 87 F.Supp. 149, 150–151, affirmed 2 Cir., 177 F.2d 627, 630, supra.

In the view which we have taken, we do not reach the question of the State's responsibility if the doctors had been in its employ (see Herzog, op. cit., 10 Syracuse L.Rev. 30, 36–38). We rest our decision solely on the ground that, since the physicians who examined Flores were not employees or agents of the State, no suit may be maintained against it for their alleged negligence.

The judgment appealed from should be affirmed, without costs.

[The dissenting opinion of Judge Dye is omitted.]

CHUY v. PHILADELPHIA EAGLES FOOTBALL CLUB

595 F.2d 1265 (3d Cir.1979) (en banc).

ROSENN, Circuit Judge.

This appeal presents several interesting questions growing out of the employment by the Philadelphia Eagles Football Club ("the Eagles") of a former professional player, Don Chuy ("Chuy"). The unexpected and unfortunate termination of Chuy's employment evoked charges by him that the Eagles had not played the game according to the rules when Chuy blew the whistle terminating his football career. Chuy ultimately reduced those charges to an antitrust and diversity action in the United States District Court for the Eastern District of Pennsylvania.

I. Background

Chuy joined the Eagles in 1969, having been traded from the Los Angeles Rams, another professional football club with which he had played for a half dozen years. On June 16, 1969, he met with the Eagles general manager, Palmer "Pete" Retzlaff, in Philadelphia, Pennsylvania, to negotiate a contract with the Eagles for the 1969, 1970, and 1971 football seasons. The parties concluded their negotiations by executing three National Football League (NFL) standard form player contracts on June 16, 1969, covering the 1969, 1970, and 1971 football seasons respectively at a salary of $30,000 for each season, with a $15,000 advance for the 1969 season.

The contracts each contained a standard NFL injury-benefit provision entitling a player injured in the performance of his service to his salary "for the term of his contract." Chuy sustained a serious injury to his shoulder during his first season in a game between the Eagles and the New York Giants in November, 1969. Sidelined for the remainder of the season, Chuy had to be hospitalized for most of December, 1969. During the hospitalization, his diagnosis revealed a pulmonary embolism, a blood clot in his lung, which marked the end of his professional athletic career. Following the advice of his physician, Chuy decided to retire from professional football and notified the Eagles of his intention. At the same time, Chuy requested that the Eagles pay him for the remaining two years of what he asserted was a three-year contract.

The Eagles requested that Chuy submit to a physical examination which Dr. Dick D. Harrell conducted in March, 1970. After extensive tests, Dr. Harrell concluded that Chuy suffered from an abnormal cell condition, presumably stress polycythemia, which may have predisposed him to the formation of dangerous blood clots. He therefore recommended to the Eagles that Chuy should "not be allowed to participate further in contact sports." Shortly after receiving Dr. Harrell's recommendation, General Manager Retzlaff informed Hugh Brown, a sports columnist for the Philadelphia Bulletin, that Chuy had been advised to quit football because of his blood clot condition. Brown thereupon telephoned Dr. James Nixon, the Eagles' team physician, for further information on Chuy's medical status.

On April 9, 1970, Hugh Brown's by-lined column in the Philadelphia Bulletin carried an account of Chuy's premature retirement. The column opened with the following:

> It's a jaw-breaker ... Polycythemia Vera ... and the question before the house is how Don Chuy, the Eagles' squatty guard, got hit with the jaw-breaker.
>
> "One of the consequences of Polycythemia Vera," said Dr. James Nixon, the Eagles' physician, "is that the blood cells get in each other's way. It's a definite threat to form embolisms, or emboli."

The remainder of the column quoted Retzlaff, Dr. Nixon, and Chuy's attorney concerning Chuy's medical condition and his effort to obtain compensation for the additional two years of his putative three-year contract. The Associated Press wire service picked up the story and articles appeared the next day in newspapers throughout the country, including the Los Angeles Times. The articles reported that Chuy had been "advised to give up football and professional wrestling because of a blood condition" and that, according to Dr. James Nixon, the Eagles' physician, "Chuy is suffering from polycythemia vera. Nixon said it is considered a threat to form blood clots."

After reading the Los Angeles Times article, Chuy testified that he panicked and immediately called his personal physician, Dr. John W. Perry. Dr. Perry informed Chuy that polycythemia vera was a fatal disease but that, from his records, Chuy did not have that disease. Dr. Perry added that he would run a series of tests to confirm his diagnosis. Chuy testified that he became apprehensive, despite Dr. Perry's assurances, broke down emotionally, and, frightened by the prospect of imminent death, refused to submit to any tests. Chuy stated that for the next several months, he could not cope with daily routines and he avoided people. He returned to Dr. Perry, who gave him numerous tests which disproved the presence of polycythemia vera. Nonetheless, Chuy testified that he continued to be apprehensive about death and that marital difficulties also developed.

Chuy eventually brought suit against the Eagles and the National Football League, alleging antitrust violations, breach of contract, intentional infliction of emotional distress and defamation. The district court dismissed the antitrust claim, 407 F.Supp. 717 (E.D.Pa.1976), and the dismissal has not been appealed. The court submitted the remaining claims to the jury by special interrogatories, and the jury returned a verdict for the plaintiff. On the basis of the jury's findings, the district court molded a damages award for breach of contract in the amount of $45,000, which reflected $60,000 salary due for the 1970 and 1971 seasons, less a $15,000 debt Chuy owed the Eagles. The jury also awarded Chuy $10,000 compensatory damages for the intentional infliction of emotional distress claim and punitive damages in the sum of

$60,590.96. On the defamation claim, the jury found in its answer to the special interrogatories that Dr. Nixon's statements tended to injure Chuy's reputation, but that the columnist, Hugh Brown, did not understand that the publication of the doctor's statements would harm Chuy's reputation. The district court thereupon entered judgment against Chuy on his defamation claim.

After the entry of judgment against the Eagles in the aggregate sum of $115,590.96, both parties filed post-trial motions seeking either judgment notwithstanding the verdict (judgment n. o. v.) or a new trial. The Eagles addressed their motions to the contract and intentional infliction of emotional distress claims. Chuy's motion sought a new trial on the defamation claim. The district court denied all post-trial motions and both parties have appealed. We affirm.

The Eagles' appeal and Chuy's cross-appeal were initially heard by a panel of this court. The court ordered the judgment of the original panel to be vacated and the case reheard by the court in banc.

II. Breach of Contract

[This portion of the court's opinion, holding that the Eagles were obligated to pay Chuy for 1970 and 1971, is omitted.]

III. Intentional Infliction of Emotional Distress

Plaintiff's recovery of damages for emotional distress, stemming from having read Dr. Nixon's statement that Chuy was suffering from polycythemia vera, was predicated upon the principle enunciated in section 46 of the Restatement (Second) of Torts (1965). That section provides:

> One who by extreme and outrageous conduct intentionally or recklessly causes severe emotional distress to another is subject to liability for such emotional distress, and if bodily harm to the other results from it, for such bodily harm.

Thus, there are four elements to the action under § 46: (1) the conduct must be extreme and outrageous; (2) the conduct must be intentional or reckless; (3) it must cause emotional distress; and (4) the distress must be severe. Although the Pennsylvania Supreme Court has not as yet specifically adopted in its entirety the Restatement's formulation and comments, Pennsylvania courts have signalled their acceptance of this evolving tort. Papieves v. Lawrence, 437 Pa. 373, 263 A.2d 118 (1970); Forster v. Manchester, 410 Pa. 192, 189 A.2d 147 (1963); Jones v. Nissenbaum, Rudolph & Seidner, 244 Pa.Super. 377, 368 A.2d 770 (1976). In light of the extant case law, we believe that the black letter rule of § 46 of the Restatement, along with the interpretive comments, may be applied as the basis in Pennsylvania law for the tort of intentional infliction of emotional distress.

The Eagles argue that the district court should not have submitted to the jury the question whether Dr. Nixon's statements constituted "extreme and outrageous conduct"; that the court gave improper instructions concerning the intent necessary for the tort and that there was insufficient evidence for the jury to find the requisite intent; that Chuy's allegedly exaggerated and unreasonable reaction to Dr. Nixon's remarks precludes the Eagles' liability; and that the Eagles cannot be vicariously liable even if Dr. Nixon intentionally or recklessly caused Chuy severe emotional distress.

The Eagles contend first that the trial judge erred in submitting to the jury the issue whether Dr. Nixon's statements constituted "extreme and outrageous conduct." They assert that an actor's conduct must be examined as a matter of law by the court in limine. Comment h to § 46, upon which the Eagles rely, divides the functions of the court and jury in a conventional manner. The court must determine, as a matter of law, whether there is sufficient evidence for reasonable persons to find extreme or outrageous conduct. If the plaintiff has satisfied this threshold evidentiary requirement, the jury must find the facts and make its own characterization. The district court followed precisely the Restatement's procedure.

In applying the legal standard for sufficiency of the evidence to support a finding of extreme and outrageous conduct, the district court correctly ruled that if Dr. Nixon advised sportswriter Brown that Chuy suffered from polycythemia vera, knowing that Chuy did not have the disease, such conduct could reasonably be regarded as extreme and outrageous. According to comment d of the Restatement, it has not been sufficient for a finding of liability that "the defendant has acted with an intent which is tortious or even criminal, or that he has intended to inflict emotional distress, or even that his conduct has been characterized by 'malice.' "

We recognize that Dr. Nixon testified that he never told Brown of a positive diagnosis of polycythemia vera and that he only suggested that Chuy may have suffered from polycythemia, a non-fatal blood condition. The jury, however, believed Brown's recollection of the phone conversation with Dr. Nixon. We are bound to accept the jury's finding.

Accepting as we must at this stage Chuy's version of the events, we have a statement to the press by a physician assumed to know the facts that a person is suffering from a potentially fatal disease, even though the physician was aware that the person was not stricken with that condition. This, of course, constituted intolerable professional conduct. Disseminating the falsehood through the national press compounded the harm. Surely Dr. Nixon's statements, as understood by the jury, went beyond the "mere insults, indignities ... or annoyances" which people are prepared to withstand.

The Eagles next contend that the district court erred in charging the jury on intent and recklessness. Section 46 does not recognize liability for mere negligent infliction of emotional distress. See Conway v. Spitz, 407 F.Supp. 536 (E.D.Pa.1975). However, reckless conduct causing emotional distress renders an actor as liable as if he had acted intentionally. See comment i to § 46. To facilitate the jury's answer to the interrogatories, the trial judge gave instructions on the elements of the tort of infliction of emotional distress. With respect to requisite intent, he stated that the plaintiff could prevail only if the jury found (a) that Dr. Nixon's statement was intentional and (b) that the natural and probable consequences of making the statement were that it would become known to Chuy and that such awareness would cause him emotional distress.

As we understand the Eagles' argument, unless Dr. Nixon was aware that his comments were substantially certain to cause Chuy severe emotional distress, his remarks cannot be found to be "reckless." We are persuaded, however, that if Dr. Nixon's statements were intentional, he need not have been aware of the natural and probable consequences of his words. It is enough that Chuy's distress was substantially certain to follow Dr. Nixon's rash statements. Intentionally to propagate a falsehood, the natural and probable consequences of which will be to cause the plaintiff emotional distress, is equivalent, in the language of the Restatement's comment i, to the "deliberate disregard of a high degree of probability that the emotional distress will follow." Thus, the district court's instruction comported with the Restatement's requirements for recklessness.

Having been properly charged, the jury reasonably could have found that the requirements of section 46 as to intent had been met. The testimony given by Brown sufficiently supported a finding that Dr. Nixon's remarks were reckless.

Beyond the characterization of Dr. Nixon's statement as reckless and outrageous, the Eagles assert that Chuy's reaction to the statement was exaggerated and unreasonable. The Eagles point to evidence that Chuy, after reading the statement attributed to Dr. Nixon in the local newspaper, refused to undergo tests which he had been advised would disprove the presence of polycythemia vera. Nor did Chuy attempt to communicate with Dr. Nixon or Dr. Harrell to verify the newspaper account of his illness. Instead, Chuy became depressed and despondent, delaying tests for a period of six months. The Eagles assert that Chuy's failure to secure prompt medical verification of his putative illness was unjustified, precluding liability for the infliction of emotional distress.

Comment j to § 46 requires that a plaintiff prove that he suffered severe distress that is not unreasonable, exaggerated, or unjustified. The same comment further notes that severe distress may encompass mental anguish, fright, horror, grief, worry, and other emotional disturbances. The extent of the severity is to be measured by whether any "reasonable man could be expected to endure it." Restatement (Second) of Torts, § 46, comment j. The jury in this case was asked to determine whether the "natural and probable" impact of Dr. Nixon's statements rendered the statements beyond the bounds of decency and it responded affirmatively. Thus, implicit in the jury's affirmative answer is its determination that a person of ordinary sensibility could not have withstood the distress without severe mental anguish and that Chuy did not feign his mental anxiety.

None of the cases cited by the Eagles requires as an element of the cause of action that the victim of infliction of emotional distress seek to alleviate that distress by immediate medical treatment or verification. The district court instructed the jury that if they found that Chuy unreasonably failed to minimize his injuries, they could accordingly reduce his damage award. We believe these instructions correctly distinguished between the severity of distress as an element of liability and the failure of the victim reasonably to mitigate damages. The jury therefore was properly instructed on the significance of Chuy's reluctance to undergo extensive medical testing after sustaining emotional distress.

Even assuming, arguendo, that Dr. Nixon committed a tort, the Eagles contend they should not have been held vicariously liable as a master responsible for the torts of a servant. Under Pennsylvania law, a master-servant relationship is established if the employer had the power to control and direct the conduct of the employee. A master is liable for the torts of his servant if the latter's tortious conduct was within the scope of his employment, i.e., conduct performed to further the business of the employer and not for the servant's personal purposes. Norton v. Railway Express Agency, Inc., 412 F.2d 112, 114 (3d Cir.1969); Mauk v. Wright, 367 F.Supp. 961, 965–66 (M.D.Pa.1973). The existence of a master-servant relationship and conduct without the scope of employment are factual issues for the jury. Norton, supra; Anzenberger v. Nickols, 413 Pa. 543, 198 A.2d 309 (1964).

The jury in this case specifically found that the Eagles had the right to control and actually did control the substance of Dr. Nixon's statements to the press concerning the physical condition of the team's players. Although the Eagles may be correct that Dr. Nixon performed his surgical duties as an independent contractor immune from team control, the jury was properly instructed to focus only on Dr. Nixon's role as press spokesman about players' medical status. There was ample evidence that in this limited function, Dr. Nixon was subject to control by team officials. Moreover, the frequency of Dr. Nixon's performance of this role established that he did it within the scope of his employment.

We conclude that the district court properly rendered a verdict against the Eagles, holding them vicariously responsible for Dr. Nixon's tortious statement to Brown. In so doing, we reject any suggestion by the Eagles that the master, to be held liable for this tort, must either participate in it or exhibit scienter.

IV. Punitive Damages

The district court instructed the jury that it could award punitive damages as a penalty to the defendant and as a deterrent to others who might be likeminded, if the jury concluded that such damages were appropriate. The Eagles advance several grounds for rejecting the jury's award of punitive damages in this case. First, they contend that punitive damages cannot be awarded for a § 46 tort because the liability-producing conduct must be extreme and outrageous by definition. Enhancing a verdict with punitive damages would in their view be a form of double punishment for an offense which is compensable at all only because of its outrageous nature. Eckenrode v. Life of America Insurance Co., 470 F.2d 1, 5 (7th Cir.1972) (punitive damages denied because "the outrageous quality of the defendant's conduct forms the basis of the action" and compensatory damages sufficiently punitive). Second, the Eagles argue that punitive damages were improperly imposed upon the principal for the torts of its agent. Third, the Eagles contend that the jury was improperly instructed on the measurement of punitive damages and that the amount levied was excessive in comparison with the compensatory award.

Pennsylvania courts recognize the standards governing punitive damages set forth in § 908 of the Restatement of Torts (1939). Medvecz v. Choi, 569 F.2d 1221, 1226 (3d Cir. 1977). See Chambers v. Montgomery, 411 Pa. 339, 344, 192 A.2d 355, 358 (1963); Hughes v. Babcock, 349 Pa. 475, 480–81, 37 A.2d 551, 554 (1944).

Punitive damages, as defined by section 908(1) of the Torts Restatement, are damages other than compensatory or nominal, "awarded against a person to punish him for his outrageous conduct." We see no inconsistency in awarding punitive damages by the same legal standard used in determining liability for compensatory damages. The purposes of the two forms of damages are quite distinct under Pennsylvania law. This court, in applying Pennsylvania law, recently enunciated the purposes of punitive damages in tort actions:

> The question in medical malpractice cases, as in tort actions generally, is whether there has been sufficiently aggravated conduct contrary to the plaintiffs' interests, involving bad motive or reckless indifference, to justify the special sanction of punitive damages. That sanction serves the dual function of penalizing past conduct constituting an aggravated violation of another's interests, and of deterring such behavior in the future.

Medvecz v. Choi, supra at 1227. See also Thomas v. American Cystoscope Makers, Inc., 414 F.Supp. 255, 263 (E.D.Pa.1976). This being so, predicating compensatory damages upon a finding of outrageous conduct does not preclude a separate assessment of punitive damages to punish past and deter future tortious conduct.

The Eagles argue that, as a general rule, punitive damages should not be assessed against a principal who does not participate in or approve the tortious conduct of his agent. The rationale suggested is that damages designed to punish wrongdoers, rather than make victims whole, should be assessed only against parties personally responsible for tortious conduct. The Eagles assert that, on the facts of this case, they were innocent of wrongdoing in regard to Dr. Nixon's statements. In the absence of managerial participation in or approval of Dr. Nixon's statements, the Eagles claim that punitive damages in the nature of a penalty were inappropriate.

The Eagles rely on § 909 of the Restatement of Torts, adopted as § 217C of the Restatement (Second) of Agency (1958), which circumscribes the scope of an employer's or principal's liability for punitive damages. Although no Pennsylvania cases have been cited which apply this provision, we do not write on a clean slate. In Skeels v. Universal C. I. T. Credit Corp., 335 F.2d 846 (3d Cir.1964), this court, in a diversity action, considered whether Pennsylvania adhered to the rule of § 909 of the Restatement of Torts limiting an employer's exposure to punitive damages for the torts of his employee. Judge Hastie, in reviewing the state court precedents, concluded that Pennsylvania followed the "less restrictive" rule enunciated in Lake Shore & Michigan Southern Railway v. Rosenzweig, 113 Pa. 519, 544, 6 A. 545, 553 (1886), that a corporation is liable for exemplary damages for the acts of its servant, acting within the scope of his authority. Skeels v. Universal C. I. T. Credit Corp., supra at 852. Accord, Philadelphia Traction Co. v. Orbann, 119 Pa. 37, 12 A. 816 (1888); Gerlach v. Pittsburgh Railways, 94 Pa.Super. 121 (1928).

Judge Hastie recognized the potential harshness of this rule and concluded for the court that "the conduct of the agent who inflicts the injury complained of must be rather clearly outrageous to justify the vicarious imposition of exemplary damages upon the principal." 335 F.2d at 852. We are persuaded to follow Judge Hastie's analysis in reviewing the record in this case.

We note that the Eagles did not request, and so were not refused, an instruction delineating a narrow compass for the award of punitive damages against an employer for the intentional torts of his employee. The Eagles requested, pursuant to Fed.R.Civ.P. 51, an instruction on punitive damages which did not mention a special standard for vicarious liability. Rather, the instruction would have required the jury to find that the act of making the statements was done with a bad motive or reckless indifference to others.

The instruction did not request the jury to determine whether the Eagles' management participated in or approved the reckless acts. The district court informed the parties that it would cover the defendant's request for a charge on punitive damages in its instructions. The actual instruction to the jury accurately reflected Pennsylvania law stated above. The jury was instructed to award in its discretion punitive damages as a penalty and deterrent for "dereliction and malice."

In deciding that Dr. Nixon's statements were extreme and outrageous, the jury found a basis for the underlying cause of action, as well as a punitive award. In light of this court's prior construction of Pennsylvania law in Skeels v. Universal C.I.T. Credit Corp., supra, punitive damages could properly have been assessed against either Dr. Nixon or the Eagles.

In sum, we believe that Pennsylvania courts would adopt a standard of vicarious liability for punitive damages which would encompass the conduct of Dr. Nixon found by the jury to be outrageous. The award of such damages is properly left to the jury as factfinder. The jury in this case made such an award on the basis of instructions consistent with those proposed by the defendants and in accord with governing Pennsylvania law.

V. DEFAMATION

[This portion of the court's opinion, finding that Chuy was not defamed by Dr. Nixon's statements, is omitted.]

The judgment of the district court will be affirmed. The parties to bear their own costs.

[The dissenting opinions of Circuit Judge Van Dusen and Aldisert, which deal respectively with the defamation claim and the appropriateness of having granted rehearing en banc, are omitted.]

Note

As *Chuy* dramatically shows, doctors often possess extremely sensitive information about athletes. How such information should be handled remains a much-disputed issue. During the 1997 baseball season, for example, New York Mets psychiatrist Dr. Allan Lans told manager Bobby Valentine he was concerned pitcher Pete Harnisch, whom he was treating for depression, might be suicidal. When the manager later let this information slip to the media, Harnisch became enraged. Nevertheless, most medical ethicists stood behind Lans, arguing his decision to speak with Valentine constituted a "reasonable precaution." *See further* Steve Hirsch, *Ballclubs, Psychiatrists Walk Fine Line*, Bergen (N.J.) Record, Sept. 5, 1997, at S1.

Similarly, in October 1998, Mike Tyson petitioned the Nevada boxing commission for reinstatement of his license, which he had lost 16 months earlier for biting Evander Holyfield's ears during their championship bout. Concerned about the fighter's mental health, the commissioners ordered him to undergo psychiatric testing. Tyson did so, but then balked at submitting the results because the commission planned to make them public pursuant to the state's open records law. Eventually, however, Tyson gave in after the courts sided with the commission. *See further* Phyllis Coleman & Robert M. Jarvis, *This Time, Mike Tyson Got the Raw Deal*, Clev. Plain Dealer, Oct. 20, 1998, at 9B.

More recently, in December 1998, former New York Yankees center fielder Joe DiMaggio ordered his doctor to stop issuing reports about his hospitalization for lung cancer. The physician, Dr. Earl Barron, had been providing daily updates about the 84–year-old superstar's condition, including his level of sedation and the amount of fluid in his lungs, leading to such cliched headlines as "Last of the ninth, two out." *See further* Harvey Araton, *Score One for Decorum: DiMaggio Draws Curtain*, N.Y. Times, Dec. 14, 1998, at D2.

Problem 44

Assume a doctor can prove the following: (a) he receives an annual retainer from the club, (b) he is obligated to attend all regular season games (although he may send a substitute with the team's permission), (c) he may not perform any medical procedure without the club's prior express approval, and, (d) he is required to give pre-season physicals at a hospital designated by the team. Based on these facts, should he be treated as an employee or an independent contractor if he is sued for malpractice? *See Bryant v. Fox*, 515 N.E.2d 775 (Ill.Ct.App.1987).

D. TRAINERS

Trainers play a critical role in maintaining the health and well-being of an athlete. Besides designing and overseeing strength and conditioning programs, dispensing nutrition and diet advice, and conducting physical therapy sessions, they often are the first persons to reach an injured player on the field, assess his or her condition, and take measures to prevent further harm. Yet because trainers are not doctors, courts have struggled over when to impose liability on them.

GILLESPIE v. SOUTHERN UTAH STATE COLLEGE

669 P.2d 861 (Utah 1983).

DURHAM, Justice.

This is an action to recover damages for personal injuries to the plaintiff Rickey Gillespie and for emotional injuries to, and loss of educational and employment opportunities by, the plaintiff Ghislaine Gillespie, Rickey's wife. At the conclusion of the plaintiffs' case, the trial court dismissed Ghislaine's cause of action. In addition, after the entry of the jury's special verdict finding that the defendant Southern Utah State College (hereafter "College") was not negligent, the trial court also dismissed Rickey's cause of action. We affirm.

Rickey was attending the College on a basketball scholarship for the 1977–78 school year. On January 4, 1978, Rickey sprained his ankle in a practice scrimmage. The basketball coach turned the treatment of Rickey's injury over to David Slack, a student trainer for the College. The treatment applied by Mr. Slack consisted of spraying the ankle with a tape adherent, applying a pre-wrap to prevent the tape from coming into contact with the skin, and then taping it.

After taping the ankle, Mr. Slack instructed Rickey to immerse his ankle in a bucket of ice water for ten to fifteen minutes, then to remove it and walk on it for three to five minutes, and to repeat this cycle two to three more times. Rickey followed this procedure for the remainder of the practice scrimmage and then continued it for two hours at home. Later that evening, Mr. Slack brought a bag of ice to Rickey's apartment, helped Rickey into bed, elevated his foot, and put the bag of ice on his ankle. The ice lasted approximately two hours.

On January 5, 1978, the morning after the injury, Mr. Slack made arrangements for Rickey to see the third-party defendant Dr. Scott L. Brown that afternoon. Dr. Brown noted in passing that due to the swelling the tape was difficult to remove. Dr. Brown took an x-ray of Rickey's ankle which revealed that it was not fractured, only sprained. Upon inquiry regarding the treatment that Mr. Slack had prescribed for

Rickey's ankle, Mr. Slack replied that he had been "icing" it. Dr. Brown assumed that "icing" meant applying ice packs. Dr. Brown instructed Rickey and Mr. Slack to continue wrapping and "icing" Rickey's ankle for a period not to exceed 72 hours from the time of injury and prescribed codeine for pain.

After leaving Dr. Brown's office, Rickey and Mr. Slack went to the training room where Rickey's ankle was retaped with a pressure bandage to allow for swelling and the ice water immersion treatments were continued. That evening, Mr. Slack brought a bag of ice to Rickey's apartment and told Rickey to continue the ice water immersion treatments. There was testimony indicating that Rickey slept that night with his ankle submerged in a bucket of ice water.

On the evening of January 6, 1978, two days after the injury, Rickey sat on the bench and periodically immersed his foot in ice water during the first and second halves of the basketball game. After the game, he continued the ice water immersion treatments at home. On the evening of January 7, 1978, Rickey again periodically immersed his foot in ice water during the first and second halves of the basketball game. Rickey did not recall any treatment after the game. On January 8, 1978, Rickey may have used the ice treatments during the day.

Late in the afternoon on January 9, 1978, the basketball coach and/or Mr. Slack started Rickey on warm whirlpool treatments. That evening, Mr. Slack visited Rickey at his home and found him using the ice water immersion treatment because Rickey said that it made his foot feel better. Mr. Slack immediately called Dr. Brown, who instructed Mr. Slack to stop the ice water treatment, to wrap Rickey's foot with Atomic Balm, which created heat, and to have Rickey sleep with his foot elevated.

On the morning of January 10, 1978, six days after the injury, Rickey visited Dr. Brown, who sent Rickey to the Valley View Hospital to be admitted and treated for the injury to his foot. Rickey was diagnosed as suffering from thrombo phlebitis and as having apparent frostbite of the fourth and fifth toes along with smaller areas on the bottom of his foot and heel. On January 23, 1978, Rickey was discharged from the Valley View Hospital for further treatments at a hospital nearer to his home in Milwaukee, Wisconsin. Dr. Rydlewicz, who treated Rickey in Milwaukee, rated Rickey's right lower extremity as being ninety percent disabled due to amputation of a gangrenous toe, removal of some tissue and muscle of the right foot, and osteomyelitis of the right foot. During his testimony at trial, Dr. Rydlewicz also expressed his concern as to whether Rickey's foot could be saved because of the osteomyelitis, and said that a below the knee amputation may be necessary at some future time.

On March 2, 1979, Rickey and Ghislaine filed suit against the College claiming that the basketball coach and Mr. Slack were negligent in their treatment of Rickey's injury. On August 14, 1979, the College filed a third-party complaint against Dr. Brown. At trial, at the conclusion of the plaintiffs' case, the trial court dismissed Ghislaine's cause of action. The jury subsequently returned a special verdict in which it found that: (1) Rickey was 100% negligent and such negligence was the proximate cause of his injuries, and (2) the College and Dr. Brown were not negligent. Based on the jury's special verdict, the trial court also dismissed Rickey's cause of action.

On appeal, Rickey claims that the jury verdict should be set aside because the jury's finding of no negligence by the College was contrary to the evidence and an abuse of the jury's deliberative process. Rickey also claims that the trial court erred in the instruction that it gave to the jury regarding the standard of care for an athletic trainer. Ghislaine claims that the trial court erred in dismissing her cause of action.

Rickey contends that the jury's verdict that the College was not negligent is contrary to the uncontroverted evidence and therefore should be set aside. Rickey claims that the evidence is uncontroverted that Mr. Slack's taping of Rickey's ankle on January 4, 1978, which did not allow for swelling, was negligent. If the evidence were uncontroverted, Rickey's assertion would merit consideration. However, the evidence was not uncontroverted. While some of the physicians and trainers that testified at trial stated that Mr. Slack's tight taping of Rickey's ankle might, in conjunction with the ice immersion treatments and the failure to elevate the ankle, have contributed to Rickey's injuries, there was other testimony to the contrary. Although Dr. Brown agreed with the above general statements by the other physicians and trainers, he testified on redirect examination that Mr. Slack's tight taping did not play any part in Rickey's injury.

The testimony of the other physicians and trainers was based on hypothetical questions. They did not personally examine the tightness of the taping of Rickey's ankle. Dr. Brown, on the other hand, personally examined and removed the taping. We acknowledge the personal tragedy suffered by the plaintiffs, but we are constrained to recognize that the jury was free to find Dr. Brown's testimony more credible and base its findings thereon. Thus, viewing the evidence in a light most favorable to the jury's verdict, we will not upset the jury's verdict because the evidence does not so clearly preponderate in Rickey's favor that reasonable persons could not differ on the outcome of the case.

Rickey also claims that the trial court erred in the instruction that it gave to the jury regarding the standard of care required of an athletic trainer. The instruction given is virtually identical to that contained in J. Crockett, Jury Instruction Forms for Utah No. 50.3, at 130–31 (1957) (captioned "Limitation Upon Duty Owed By Physician to Patient"). Rickey's argument is that the instruction was improper because: (1) Mr. Slack is not a physician nor a professional, and (2) by providing treatment to an injury that would have healed by itself if left alone, Mr. Slack became a "guarantor" of good results. These arguments are without merit. Even if the giving of the instruction was error, it was harmless in this case because it held Mr. Slack to the higher standard of care that governs physicians and surgeons rather than the lower standard that may be applicable to laymen or athletic trainers. Furthermore, the second argument cannot prevail because it would mean that anyone, including physicians and surgeons, who treated an ordinary sprained ankle or another injury that would heal by itself if left unattended would be "strictly" liable without fault for any adverse consequences resulting from the treatment. No authority has been cited, nor has our research revealed any, that supports such an extension of tort law. Thus, the trial court did not err in giving the instruction regarding an athletic trainer's standard of care.

On appeal, Ghislaine claims that the trial court erred in dismissing her cause of action. The trial court did so at the conclusion of the plaintiffs' evidence on the ground that Utah does not recognize a cause of action for loss of consortium. See, e.g., Ellis v. Hathaway, 27 Utah 2d 143, 493 P.2d 985 (1972); Corbridge v. M. Morrin & Son, Inc., 19 Utah 2d 409, 432 P.2d 41 (1967). Ghislaine contends that her cause of action is for an independent tort and not for loss of consortium. Even if this contention is correct, the jury's finding of no negligence by the College would have barred her recovery on a cause of action based on negligence. Therefore, we do not address the merits of Ghislaine's claim of error because, even if error, the trial court's dismissal of her cause was harmless.

PINSON v. STATE

1995 WL 739820 (Tenn.Ct.App.1995).

FARMER, Judge.

The Appellant, State of Tennessee, appeals a final order of the Tennessee Claims Commission, finding Appellant negligent and awarding Appellee, Michael Ray Pinson (Pinson), judgment for $300,000 for injuries sustained by Pinson while playing football for the University of Tennessee at Martin (UTM).

In 1983, Pinson received a football scholarship to UTM. Pinson decided not to play football that year, and did not enroll at UTM. In August 1984, Pinson enrolled at UTM and reported to football camp for practice. He passed his physical examination and began participating in practice. On August 25, 1984, Pinson suffered a blow to the head during a football practice. He walked to the sidelines, said that he had been "kicked in the head," and collapsed unconscious.

During the time that Pinson was unconscious, the UTM athletic trainer, James Richard Lyon (Lyon), examined Pinson. Lyon's personal notes from the day of Pinson's injury show that Lyon found palsy on the left side of Pinson's face, no control of the left side of his body, unequal pupils and no response to pain, sound or movement. These notes also show that Pinson remained unconscious for a period of ten minutes.

After his examination of Pinson, Lyon summoned an ambulance which transported Pinson to the Volunteer General Hospital in Martin,

Tennessee. Lyon did not personally accompany Pinson to the hospital but had a student trainer accompany Pinson. Lyon did not give the trainer any instructions about the information that the trainer should give the emergency room doctor. Hospital records show that the trainer informed an emergency room nurse that Pinson lost consciousness for about two minutes. Although Lyon visited the emergency room shortly after Pinson arrived, Lyon did not speak to a doctor about the neurological signs he had observed on the practice field.

At Volunteer General, Pinson's head was X-rayed and found to be normal. No CT scan was ever done. Pinson was assigned to Dr. O. K. Smith for follow-up care and was admitted to the hospital for observation. Although all neurological checks were normal, hospital records show that Pinson complained of headaches to the hospital staff. Pinson complained that one of these headaches was so severe that it made him sick to his stomach.

On August 26, 1984, Dr. Smith telephoned Lyon and told him that Pinson should not participate in football practice for a week and that, if any further trouble arose, Pinson should return to Dr. Smith or another physician. On that same day, Dr. Smith released Pinson to Lyon, and Lyon transported Pinson from the hospital to UTM.

When Lyon picked up Pinson, he complained to Lyon of a headache. Lyon did not record this headache in the UTM records. On August 27, 1984, Pinson complained of a headache and was given Empirin #4 by Lyon. On August 28, 1984, Pinson told Lyon that he had a headache, but that it was milder than the one he had on the previous day. Lyon's notes of August 30, 1984, which refer to Pinson, contain the statement "Headache!".

On September 3, 1984, Lyon contacted Dr. Ira Porter, the UTM team physician. Lyon told Dr. Porter that Pinson was asymptomatic for a concussion on September 3. Lyon did not tell Dr. Porter about Pinson's headaches on the 26th, 27th, 28th, or 30th. Relying on Lyon's report of Pinson's condition, Dr. Porter concurred with Dr. Smith's prior advice that Pinson could return to practice if there were no further problems.

On September 3, 1984, Pinson returned to practice. He participated in practice, traveled as a member of the team and played in at least two games. Testimony from Pinson's mother, roommate and girlfriend indicated that Pinson suffered headaches and complained of dizziness, nausea and blurred vision throughout this three week period from September 3 to September 24. Lyon did not report any of these symptoms to Dr. Porter. On September 24, Pinson walked to the sideline during a practice, stated that he had been "kicked in the head" and collapsed unconscious.

Pinson was eventually taken to Jackson–Madison County General Hospital where he underwent brain surgery. Surgeons there found that Pinson had sustained a chronic subdural hematoma of three to four weeks duration of several hundred cubic centimeters and an acute subdural hematoma of approximately 25–30 cubic centimeters and a shift of mid-line structures of almost 1.5 centimeters. Pinson remained in a coma for several weeks and was transferred to the Lamar Unit of Baptist Hospital in Memphis for intensive rehabilitative treatment. As a result of his injuries, Pinson suffered severe and permanent neurological damage.

Pinson brought an action for negligence against Appellant before the Tennessee Claims Commission. A trial upon the merits was held before Claims Commissioner Martha B. Brasfield.

At the time of trial, Pinson was a hemiparetic. He had no use of his left arm and very little use of his left leg. He had a shunt to relieve fluid build-up in his brain. He also suffered from severe cognitive problems and frequent seizures. These maladies rendered him unable to hold a job. Additionally, Pinson and his mother had incurred approximately $200,000 in medical bills due to his injury.

The expert testimony of Dr. Howard L. Ravenscraft and Dr. Carol Dooley indicated that if any one of the physicians at Volunteer General Hospital had been informed of the neurological symptoms that Pinson exhibited on August 25, 1984 (i.e., palsy on the left side of the face, no control of left side of the body, and the fact that Pinson was hit on the football field, then walked to the sidelines and collapsed unconscious) they would have likely ordered a CT scan in addition to the x-rays and other treatment Pinson received. It is undisputed that a CT scan on August 25, 1984, would have helped to reveal the original subdural hematoma.

Three medical experts, Dr. Ravenscraft, Dr. Dooley and Dr. Harry Friedman, testified that Pinson's actions immediately following the blow to his head would have been highly relevant information in Pinson's treatment. The fact that, prior to falling unconscious, Pinson had walked to the sideline and announced that he had been hit in the head indicated that he had experienced a "lucid interval". A lucid interval occurs when there is a neurological sequence that follows the pattern of (1) trauma, (2) consciousness, and (3) loss of consciousness. A lucid interval is usually a sign of a serious head injury.

Expert testimony also revealed that the length of time Pinson was unconscious could have also been important information for the treating physician. Dr. Ravenscraft and Dr. Dooley both testified that a doctor, upon being informed of a five to ten minute loss of consciousness, would have been more likely to schedule a CT scan. Dr. Smith testified that if he had been informed of Pinson's lucid interval and ten minute loss of consciousness, he likely would have ordered a CT scan.

Dr. Friedman, Dr. Ravenscraft and Dr. Dooley testified that if the chronic subdural hematoma had existed from three to four weeks prior to September 24, 1984 it would have caused significant headaches. They further testified that if the chronic subdural hematoma had been properly diagnosed prior to September 24, 1984, Pinson still would have undergone corrective brain surgery, but would have very likely led a normal life.

Commissioner Brasfield found that Lyon had a duty (1) to report Pinson's neurological signs which he observed on August 25, 1984 to a medical doctor, and (2) to report Pinson's subsequent headaches to a medical doctor as Dr. Smith had instructed. She found Lyon negligent (1) in not reporting his observations of Pinson's condition on August 25, 1984, to the emergency room physicians, and (2) in not reporting Pinson's complaints of headaches to Dr. Smith or Dr. Porter, following Pinson's first injury.

Commissioner Brasfield ruled that Lyon's negligence was the proximate cause of Pinson's injuries since Lyon's negligence caused Pinson's chronic subdural hematoma not to be properly diagnosed.

Commissioner Brasfield awarded damages to Pinson in the amount of $1,500,000. She took notice of the fact that other individuals had been sued in the Circuit Court of Weakley County for their negligence in the treatment of Pinson. Commissioner Brasfield found that Appellant was liable for thirty percent (30%) of Pinson's damages, or $450,000. She did not apportion any fault to Pinson. Pursuant to T.C.A. § 9–8–307(e) [which caps damages against the state in tort actions], she found that Pinson was entitled to a judgment against Appellant in the amount of $300,000.

Appellant presents the following issues for review:

> I. Did the Claims Commission err in finding that the UT athletic trainer had a duty to initiate a transfer of medical information to Claimant's physicians?
>
> II. Did the Claims Commission err in finding that the UT athletic trainer breached his duty to report head injury symptoms if such duty existed?
>
> III. Did the Claims Commission err in finding that any breach of duty by the UT athletic trainer was the proximate cause of Claimant's injuries?

Under the law in this state, no claim for negligence can succeed in the absence of any one of the following elements: (1) a duty of care owed by the defendant to the plaintiff; (2) conduct falling below the applicable standard of care amounting to a breach of that duty; (3) an injury or loss; (4) causation in fact; and (5) proximate, or legal cause. Haynes v. Hamilton County, 883 S.W.2d 606, 611 (Tenn.1994); Perez v. McConkey, 872 S.W.2d 897, 905 (Tenn.1994); Bradshaw v. Daniel, 854 S.W.2d 865, 869 (Tenn.1993); McClenahan v. Cooley, 806 S.W.2d 767, 774 (Tenn. 1991).

This Court's review of the Claims Commission's decision that the required elements of negligence exist, in this case, must be de novo with a presumption of correctness unless the preponderance of the evidence is to the contrary. T.R.A.P. 13(d); Union Carbide Corp. v. Huddleston, 854 S.W.2d 87, 91 (Tenn.1993); Beare v. State, 814 S.W.2d 715, 717 (Tenn. 1991). It is the Appellant's burden to establish that a preponderance of the evidence is contrary to the Commissioner's findings. Beare, 814 S.W.2d at 717.

First, Appellant argues that Pinson's negligence claim must fail because UTM athletic trainer Lyon had no affirmative duty to inform Pinson's doctors about the neurological signs exhibited by Pinson directly after his first injury. Appellant argues that Lyon had a duty to report these signs only if requested to do so by a physician.

Lyon testified that the standard of care of an athletic trainer was only to accurately report to a physician information which the physician requested, including any observed physical symptoms. Lyon further testified that it was the trainer's duty to follow the physician's orders in treating an athlete. Appellant argues that the record is devoid of any evidence that an athletic trainer has a duty to seek out and volunteer information to a physician or guess what information a physician might need for purposes of evaluating or treating an injured athlete. Appellant further points out that there is no statutory duty that would require a trainer to volunteer information to an athlete's doctor.

As support for its argument, Appellant cites T.C.A. § 63–24–101(1), a statute dealing with the certification of athletic trainers with the Board of Medical Examiners. T.C.A. § 63–24–101(1) provides in pertinent part:

> "Athletic Trainer" means a person with specific qualifications as set forth in this chapter, who is employed by and works with an athletic team and who, upon the advice and consent of his team physician, carries out the practice of prevention or physical rehabilitation, or both, of injuries incurred by participating athletes at his educational institution.... In carrying out these functions, the athletic trainer is authorized to use whatever physical modalities as are deemed necessary by a team physician.

T.C.A. § 63–24–101(1) (1990). T.C.A. § 63–24–101 was amended in 1993, and T.C.A. § 63–24–101(2) now states:

> "Athletic trainer" means a person with specific qualifications as set forth in this chapter, who, upon the advice, consent and oral or written prescriptions of a physician, carries out the practice of prevention, recognition, evaluation, management, disposition, treatment, or rehabilitation of athletic injuries, and, in carrying out these functions the athletic trainer is authorized to use physical modalities, such as heat, light, sound, cold, electricity, or mechanical devices related to prevention, recognition, evaluation, management, disposition, rehabilitation, and treatment.

While we do not believe either of these statutes was intended by the legislature to define the duty of an athletic trainer, we do believe they are illustrative in determining the role of a trainer in an athletic program.

To begin our analysis, we note that the trial court typically has the exclusive responsibility to determine whether the law will recognize a duty imposed on the defendant for the plaintiff's benefit. Roberts v. Robertson County Bd. of Educ., 692 S.W.2d 863, 869 (Tenn.App.1985); Dill v. Gamble Asphalt Materials, 594 S.W.2d 719, 721 (Tenn.App.1979). Here, the Claims Commissioner held that Lyon had a duty (1) to report Pinson's neurological signs which he observed on August 25, 1984 to a medical doctor, and (2) to report Pinson's subsequent headaches to a medical doctor as Dr. Smith had instructed.

Upon reviewing the record, we believe that a duty arose from the fact that, as a college athlete, Pinson enjoyed a "special relationship" with UTM. Kleinknecht v. Gettysburg College, 989 F.2d 1360, 1372 (3d Cir. 1993). Accordingly, we hold that UTM and its employee, Lyon, had a duty to exercise reasonable care under the circumstances. See Doe v. Linder Const. Co., Inc., 845 S.W.2d 173, 196 (Tenn.1992). Here, Pinson was not engaged in his own private affairs at UTM at the time of his injury. Id. Instead, he was participating in a scheduled athletic practice for an intercollegiate team sponsored by UTM under the supervision of UTM employees.

Whether UTM breached its duty turns upon whether UTM and Lyon exercised the appropriate standard of care in their treatment of Pinson. We believe that the evidence preponderates toward the Claims Commissioner's finding that Lyon did not exercise the appropriate standard of care in his treatment of Pinson. In Tennessee, the applicable standard of care may be established by the defendant's own admissions. Tutton v. Patterson, 714 S.W.2d 268, 270 (Tenn.1986).

Applying the standard of care for an athletic trainer offered by Lyon himself at trial, we find that Lyon breached his duty when, contrary to the instructions of Dr. Smith, Lyon failed to report Pinson's headaches to a physician before allowing Pinson to return to practice. It is undisputed that Dr. Smith instructed Lyon that Pinson was not to return to contact for one week and to report if any further trouble arose. Dr. Smith further instructed Lyon to report any signs of a head injury, including headaches, to Dr. Smith or to another physician.

It is further undisputed that on September 3, Lyon telephoned Dr. Porter, and discussed Pinson's condition. During that telephone conversation, Porter asked Lyon "if [Pinson] was having headaches, visual problems, visual disturbances, vomiting, drowsiness, weakness." Lyon told Dr. Porter that Pinson was asymptomatic for a head injury on September 3.

Appellant contends that Lyon did not breach any duty owed to Pinson because Pinson was asymptomatic for a concussion on September 3. Appellant argues that Lyon did not have a duty to disclose any information about Pinson's previous complaints on August 26th, 27th, 28th or 30th to Dr. Porter because Dr. Porter inquired only as to Pinson's condition on September 3.

We are unpersuaded by Appellant's argument. On August 26, Dr. Smith instructed Lyon to report any further signs of head injury, including headaches, to a physician. Evidence presented at trial showed that Pinson suffered headaches from August 26 until the date of his second injury on September 24. Lyon's testimony and notes from this time period indicate that Lyon was aware of these headaches. On September 3, Dr. Porter asked Lyon if Pinson was experiencing any signs of head injury. Despite overwhelming evidence that Pinson was experiencing headaches and that Lyon knew about them, Lyon responded that Pinson was not exhibiting any signs of a serious head injury. It flies in the face of reason for Lyon, as a certified athletic trainer, to suggest that he had no duty to report Pinson's prior headaches to Dr. Porter on September 3, particularly when he had been instructed by Dr. Smith to inform a doctor of any further symptoms of a head injury.

Appellant contends that Lyon told Dr. Porter that Pinson had a headache on August 27, and that Dr. Porter authorized Lyon to give Pinson Empirin #4 on that date. Appellant further contends that Dr. Porter spoke with Pinson at a football practice on August 30. Dr. Porter denied that he ever had any such conversations with Lyon about Pinson. As such, there was a sharp conflict in the testimony of the witnesses as to whether Lyon had actually informed Dr. Porter of Pinson's headaches. The Claims Commissioner found that Lyon had never contacted Dr. Porter.

Whether Lyon reported Pinson's headache to Dr. Porter prior to September 3 was a question of fact before the trial court. Where issues in a case turn upon the truthfulness of witnesses, the trier of fact in a non jury case has the opportunity to observe the witnesses and their manner and demeanor while testifying and is in a far better position than this Court to decide those issues. State ex rel. Balsinger v. Town of Madisonville, 222 Tenn. 272, 435 S.W.2d 803 (1968); Town of Alamo v. Forcum–James Co., 205 Tenn. 478, 327 S.W.2d 47 (1959); Leek v. Powell, 884 S.W.2d 118 (Tenn.App.1994). The weight, faith and credit to be given to any witness' testimony lies in the first instance with the trier of fact and the credibility accorded will be given great weight by the appellate court. Id. We do not find that the evidence preponderates against the Commissioner's finding.

Because we have held that Lyon had a duty to convey requested information to a physician, we believe it unnecessary to decide whether Lyon had a duty to convey his unsolicited observations of Pinson's condition to the emergency room staff immediately after Pinson's first injury.

Appellant, as its final issue, argues that UTM's and Lyon's conduct was not the proximate cause of Pinson's injuries. In Tennessee, a three-pronged test is applied to determine proximate cause:

> (1) the tortfeasor's conduct must have been a "substantial factor" in bringing about the harm being complained of; and (2) there is no rule or policy that should relieve the wrongdoer from

> liability because of the manner in which the negligence has resulted in the harm; and (3) the harm giving rise to the action could have reasonably been foreseen or anticipated by a person of ordinary intelligence and prudence.

Boling v. Tennessee State Bank, 890 S.W.2d 32, 36 (Tenn.1994) (quoting McClenahan v. Cooley, 806 S.W.2d 767, 775 (Tenn.1991)).

The court in Lindsey v. Miami Development Corp., 689 S.W.2d 856, 861 (Tenn.1985) cited Dean Prosser with approval stating:

> The plaintiff must introduce evidence which affords a reasonable basis for the conclusion that it is more likely than not that the conduct of the defendant was a cause in fact of the result. A mere possibility of such causation is not enough; and when the matter remains one of pure speculation or conjecture or the probabilities are at best evenly balanced, it becomes the duty of the court to direct a verdict for the defendant....
>
> The plaintiff is not, however, required to prove the case beyond a reasonable doubt. The plaintiff need not negative entirely the possibility that the defendant's conduct was not a cause and it is enough to introduce evidence from which reasonable persons may conclude that it is more probable that the event was caused by the defendant than that it was not....

Lindsey, 689 S.W.2d at 861–62 (quoting Prosser & Keeton, Torts, § 41, p. 269 (5th ed. 1984)).

In the instant case, Dr. Joseph R. Rowland, a neurosurgeon, testified that on September 24, 1984 he treated Pinson for a chronic subdural and an acute subdural hematoma. Dr. Rowland testified that the chronic hematoma was of three to four weeks duration and that the acute subdural hematoma was of one to five hours duration. Dr. Rowland testified that the acute clot was caused by direct trauma to the brain or by bleeding from the membrane of the chronic subdural hematoma.

It is impossible and unnecessary to determine from the record whether Pinson's permanent neurological injuries stemmed from damage to his brain from the acute or chronic subdural hematoma. The Claims Commissioner found that Pinson's first injury would have been properly diagnosed and treated if Lyon had reported the neurological symptoms exhibited by Pinson from August 26 to September 24. Dr. Dooley testified that if Lyon had reported Pinson's headaches, Pinson would have been subjected to a neurological consult and a CT scan. It is undisputed that this CT scan would have helped reveal Pinson's injured brain. If Pinson's injury had been properly diagnosed prior to September 24, 1984, it is undisputed that Pinson would likely have had little or no permanent neurological deficit.

It is clear from the record that Pinson's chronic subdural hematoma made the occurrence of an acute subdural hematoma much more probable. Dr. Dooley testified that the state of Pinson's brain due to the chronic subdural hematoma between September 3 and September 24 was "extremely swollen and very fragile." Dr. Dooley explained that a trivial amount of trauma could have caused the acute subdural hematoma to develop. Thus, regardless of whether Pinson's permanent injuries were caused by the chronic or acute subdural, it is clear that Lyon's conduct contributed significantly to Pinson's overall injury.

Accordingly, we hold that Lyon's negligence in not reporting Pinson's headaches to a physician, after having been instructed to do so, was more likely than not a substantial factor in the misdiagnosis of Pinson's head injury. We further believe that Pinson's permanent injuries could have reasonably been foreseen or anticipated by a person of ordinary intelligence and prudence. It seems extremely foreseeable that withholding requested information from a team physician could result in permanent injury to a football player who had collapsed unconscious the previous week. Finally, we are unaware of any public policy that would require us to hold a university unaccountable when the negligence of its employee results in severe injuries to an athlete. Therefore, we hold that Lyon's negligence in not reporting Pinson's headaches was a proximate cause of Pinson's permanent injuries.

In summation, we find that UTM and its employee, Lyon, had a duty to exercise reasonable care under the circumstances in respect to Pinson. We further find that UTM breached this duty when Lyon failed to exercise the appropriate standard of care of an athletic trainer. Finally, we find that UTM's breach of duty is a proximate cause of Pinson's permanent injuries.

The judgment of the Claims Commission is affirmed. Costs are taxed to Appellant, for which execution may issue if necessary.

SEARLES v. TRUSTEES OF ST. JOSEPH'S COLLEGE

695 A.2d 1206 (Me.1997).

LIPEZ, Justice.

Paul Searles appeals from the summary judgment entered for the defendants in the Superior Court (Franklin County, Marden, J.). Searles alleged that while playing basketball for St. Joseph's College the negligence of the defendants caused him permanent injuries and that they breached a contract to pay the medical expenses related to his injuries. Because we conclude that genuine issues of material fact exist on Searles's negligence claims, we vacate the judgment in part.

Paul Searles entered St. Joseph's College as a freshman in 1988, having been awarded an athletic scholarship. Searles alleges that while playing basketball he began experiencing pain in his knees during the fall semester of 1988. In January 1989 Searles was diagnosed with patellar tendinitis. He continued to play basketball for the remainder of the school year, and he returned to play for the 1989–1990 season. He stopped playing in 1990 and had surgery on his knees in 1990 and again in 1991.

In 1994 Searles filed the present action against St. Joseph's College, Rick Simonds, the school's basketball coach, and Peter Wheeler, the athletic trainer, alleging that "[d]espite medical advice and information suggesting that the Plaintiff should not be playing basketball, Defendant Simonds insisted that Paul Searles play. [As a] result, Paul Searles's knees became permanently impaired." Searles sought damages for his injuries and reimbursement for related medical expenses, alleging the existence of an oral contract requiring the school to pay his medical bills. Searles also alleged intentional infliction of emotional distress and sought punitive damages. The court granted the defendants' motion for a summary judgment on all counts of Searles's complaint. Searles does not challenge the judgment on Counts III and IV, but he contends on appeal that the court erred by granting a summary judgment on the negligence and contract counts of his complaint.

Searles's amended complaint has seven counts: breach of contract (Count I); negligence by Simonds and the liability of St. Joseph's on the basis of respondeat superior (Counts II and V); intentional infliction of emotional distress (Count III); punitive damages (Count IV); negligence by Wheeler and the responsibility of St. Joseph's on the basis of respondeat superior (Counts VI and VII).

The Negligence Claim Against Wheeler

The court concluded that Searles had presented "no evidence of a standard of care required of athletic trainers." As an athletic trainer, Wheeler has the duty to conform to the standard of care required of an ordinary careful trainer. Williams v. Inverness Corp., 664 A.2d 1244, 1246 (Me.1995).

Athletic trainers are licensed by the State, 32 M.R.S.A. §§ 14351–14362 (Supp.1996). 32 M.R.S.A. § 14354 (Supp.1996) provides:

> 1. Athletic training. When providing athletic training to an athlete without referral from a doctor of medicine, osteopathy, podiatry, or dentistry, the athletic trainer is subject to the following requirements:
>
> A. An athletic trainer may not make a medical diagnosis. The athletic trainer shall refer to a licensed doctor of medicine, osteopathy, podiatry or dentistry an athlete whose physical condition, either at the initial evaluation or during subsequent treatment, the athletic trainer determines to be beyond the scope of the practice of the athletic trainer.
>
> B. If there is no improvement in an athlete who has sustained an athletic injury within 15 days of initiation of treatment, the athletic trainer shall refer the athlete to a licensed doctor of medicine, osteopathy, podiatry or dentistry or a licensed physical therapist.
>
> C. If an athletic injury requires treatment for more than 45 days, the athletic trainer shall consult with, or refer the athlete to, a licensed doctor of medicine, surgery, osteopathy,

podiatry or dentistry, or a licensed physical therapist. The athletic trainer shall document the action taken.

Establishing the standard of care for these licensed professionals in their treatment of athletes ordinarily requires expert testimony. Forbes v. Osteopathic Hosp. of Maine, Inc., 552 A.2d 16, 17 (Me.1988) ("ordinarily, a plaintiff can discharge his burden of proof for a claim of negligent medical care only by expert medical testimony establishing the appropriate standard of medical care...."). See also Seven Tree Manor, Inc. v. Kallberg, 688 A.2d 916 (professional engineer); Jim Mitchell and Jed Davis, P.A., v. Jackson, 627 A.2d 1014, 1017 (Me.1993) (attorneys). We have long recognized that expert testimony may not be necessary "where the negligence and harmful results are sufficiently obvious as to lie within common knowledge...." Cyr v. Giesen, 150 Me. 248, 252, 108 A.2d 316, 318 (1954). Unlike the standard of reasonable care for the health and safety of student athletes applicable to a basketball coach, which can be ascertained by a lay jury, the standard of care applicable to an athletic trainer who treats physical injuries or who must make judgments about the severity of a physical condition does not ordinarily lend itself to common knowledge. See, e.g., Gillespie v. Southern Utah State College, 669 P.2d 861, 864 (Utah 1983).

The gravamen of Searles's allegations against Wheeler, set forth in Counts VI and VII of his complaint, involves more than a claim that Wheeler negligently conducted a course of treatment of Searles's injuries that contributed to a worsening of his condition, or that he failed to appreciate the seriousness of Searles's condition. Searles claims that Wheeler "failed to advise Coach Simonds that Paul Searles should not be playing basketball and the condition of Paul Searles's knees was such that continued play before complete healing will likely cause permanent injury." The deposition of Wheeler demonstrates an awareness of the acuteness of Searles's knee problems. Simonds states in his deposition that he was never advised by Wheeler that Searles could be permanently impaired by continued play, and he does not recall the trainer suggesting that Searles should not play. He also asserts that the trainer decided whether an injured player could play basketball, not the coach. To the extent that Searles's claim of negligence against Wheeler involves a failure by Wheeler to communicate to Simonds the nature and extent of Searles's knee problems, or a failure by Wheeler to advise Searles that he should not play basketball in light of Wheeler's knowledge of Searles's medical condition, Searles did not have to provide expert testimony about the standard of care applicable to an athletic trainer. Jurors could apply their common knowledge in determining whether such failures, if they occurred, constituted a breach by Wheeler of his duty to exercise reasonable care for the health and safety of Searles.

In deciding that a summary judgment was improperly granted on the negligence counts of Searles's complaint, we do not address the merits of Searles's contentions. Nor are we asked to decide whether Searles was himself responsible for his own injuries. It is for a jury to determine what responsibility, if any, Searles bears for the injuries he suffered while playing basketball.

[The remainder of the court's opinion, dealing with the claims against the other defendants, is omitted.]

Note

For a further look at the qualifications and duties of trainers, see Sheila W. Foard, *Trainer's Occupation Changes Over Years*, Albuquerque J., Aug. 2, 1998, at C9, and Bill Benner, *Highly Skilled Trainers are Vital at All Levels of Competition*, Indianapolis Star, Oct. 17, 1997, at D1. *See also Rooney v. Tyson*, 697 N.E.2d 571 (N.Y.1998) (suit to determine enforceability of oral contract providing trainer would be employed by boxer for "as long as he fought professionally").

Problem 45

A state law makes it a crime for anyone except a duly-licensed physician to practice medicine, which is defined as including "making diagnoses." If a trainer gives a diagnosis, can he be held liable for damages in a civil suit? *See Orr v. Brigham Young Univ.*, 960 F.Supp. 1522 (D.Utah 1994), *aff'd*, 108 F.3d 1388 (10th Cir.1997).

Chapter 8

REFEREES

A. OVERVIEW

Regardless of whether they are called referees, umpires, linesmen, or judges, all officials perform the same role: ensuring fair play. From a legal standpoint, these individuals present four questions: 1) when can they be denied work?; 2) are their mistakes legally actionable?; 3) what job risks do they assume?; and, 4) do they have any duty to protect players and spectators?

B. QUALIFICATIONS

All leagues have established their own standards for hiring and retaining referees. Not surprisingly, the application of these yardsticks occasionally has given rise to claims of illegal discrimination.

POSTEMA v. NATIONAL LEAGUE OF PROFESSIONAL BASEBALL CLUBS

799 F.Supp. 1475 (S.D.N.Y.1992),
approved as modified, 998 F.2d 60 (2d Cir.1993).

PATTERSON, District Judge.

This is an action for damages and injunctive relief alleging employment discrimination in violation of: (1) Title VII of the Civil Rights Act of 1964, as amended by the Civil Rights Act of 1991, 42 U.S.C. § 2000e–2(a)(1); (2) New York's Human Rights Law, N.Y.Exec.L. § 296; and (3) the common law of restraint of trade.

Defendant American League of Professional Baseball Clubs ("American League") moves: (a) pursuant to Rule 56 of the Federal Rules of Civil Procedure for summary judgment on Plaintiff's Title VII claim; (b) pursuant to Rule 12(b)(6) of the Federal Rules of Civil Procedure for dismissal of Plaintiff's Human Rights Law claim; and (c) pursuant to Rules 12(b)(1) and 12(b)(6) of the Federal Rules of Civil Procedure for dismissal of Plaintiff's common law restraint of trade claim.

Defendants National League of Professional Baseball Clubs ("National League"), Triple–A Alliance of Professional Baseball Clubs ("Triple–A"), and the Baseball Office for Umpire Development ("BOUD") join in parts (b) and (c) of the American League's motion.

For the reasons set forth below, the motions are granted in part and denied in part.

BACKGROUND

I. The Parties

Plaintiff Pamela Postema, a California resident, is a former professional baseball umpire.

Defendant National League is an unincorporated association of professional baseball clubs that constitute the National League, one of the two major leagues of professional baseball. The National League has its principal place of business and headquarters in New York City.

Defendant American League is an unincorporated association of professional baseball clubs that constitute the American League, the other major league of professional baseball. The American League also has its principal place of business and headquarters in New York City.

Defendant Triple–A is an unincorporated association of minor league professional baseball clubs that constitute and operate the Triple–A Alliance minor league. Triple–A consists of AAA-rated baseball clubs that were formerly members of two separate AAA minor leagues, the American Association and the International League. Triple–A has its principal place of business and headquarters in Grove City, Ohio.

Triple–A and the other minor leagues of professional baseball are members of the National Association of Professional Baseball Leagues (the "National Association"), an unincorporated association of minor leagues in the United States. The National Association, which is not a party to this action, has its principal place of business in New York City. The National League, American League, and the National Association are all subject to the common oversight and direction of the Commissioner of Baseball.

Defendant BOUD is an unincorporated affiliate of the other Defendants and of the National Association. Its principal place of business and headquarters is in St. Petersburg, Florida. BOUD is vested with responsibility for finding, evaluating, overseeing, training, developing, and supervising umpires for professional baseball games played by members of the National Association.

II. Events Underlying This Lawsuit

After graduating from umpiring school with the rank of 17th in a class of 130 students, Plaintiff began work in 1977 as a professional baseball umpire in the Gulf Coast League, a rookie league. At that time, she was the fourth woman ever to umpire a professional baseball game. Plaintiff worked in the Gulf Coast League during 1977 and 1978. In 1979, she was promoted to the Class A Florida State League, where she umpired during the 1979 and 1980 seasons. In 1981, Plaintiff was promoted to the AA Texas League, and she umpired there in 1981 and 1982. She was the first woman to ever umpire a professional baseball game above the Class A level.

In 1983, Plaintiff was promoted to the AAA Pacific Coast League, where she umpired from 1983 to 1986. In 1987, her contract was acquired by Triple–A, and she umpired in that league from 1987 until her discharge in 1989.

Plaintiff alleges that during her employment as a Triple–A umpire, Defendants conferred on her significant duties and responsibilities, including the following:

- In 1987, Plaintiff was the home plate umpire for the Hall of Fame exhibition game between the New York Yankees and the Atlanta Braves.
- In 1988, Plaintiff was selected to umpire the Venezuela All Star game.
- In 1988 and 1989, Plaintiff was the chief of her umpiring crew, with ultimate responsibility for its umpiring calls and performance.
- In 1988 and 1989, Plaintiff was appointed to umpire major league spring training games.
- In 1989, Plaintiff was the home plate umpire for the first Triple–A Minor League All Star Game.
- In 1989, Plaintiff was asked by Triple–A to become a supervisor for umpires in the minor league system.
- From 1987 to 1989, Plaintiff received high praise from qualified and experienced baseball people, including Chuck Tanner, Tom Trebelhorn, Hal Lanier, and Roger Craig, all current or former managers of major league teams.

Notwithstanding these responsibilities and honors, Plaintiff alleges that throughout her career as a minor league umpire she was subjected to continual, repeated, and offensive acts of sexual harassment and gender discrimination. Such acts included the following:

- On numerous occasions, players and managers addressed her with a four-letter word beginning with the letter "c" that refers to female genitalia.
- Players and managers repeatedly told Plaintiff that her proper role was cooking, cleaning, keeping house, or some other form of "women's work," rather than umpiring.
- Bob Knepper, a pitcher with the Houston Astros, told the press that although Plaintiff was a good umpire, to have her as a major league umpire would be an affront to God and contrary to the teachings of the Bible.

• During arguments with players and managers, Plaintiff was spat upon and was subjected to verbal and physical abuse to a greater degree than male umpires.

• In 1987, the manager of the Nashville Hounds kissed Plaintiff on the lips when he handed her his lineup card.

• At a major league spring training game in 1988, Chuck Tanner, then the manager of the Pittsburgh Pirates, asked Plaintiff if she would like a kiss when he gave her his lineup card.

• Although Plaintiff was well known throughout baseball as an excellent ball and strike umpire, she was directed and required by Ed Vargo, the Supervisor of Umpiring for the National League, to change her stance and technique to resemble those used by him during his career. No such requirement was placed on male umpires.

Plaintiff continually took action against such conduct through warnings, ejections, and reports. Although the existence of such conduct was well known throughout baseball, no one in a position of authority, including Defendants, took action to correct, stop, or prevent such conduct.

Plaintiff alleges that at the time she began her service with Triple–A, she was fully qualified to be a major league umpire, and she had repeatedly made known to Defendants her desire for employment in the major leagues. While she was not promoted to or hired by the National League or American League, male umpires having inferior experience, qualifications, and abilities were repeatedly and frequently promoted and hired by the National and American Leagues.

Plaintiff alleges that in 1988 and 1989, "events came to a head" in her effort to become a major league umpire. Specifically, in July 1987, Dick Butler, then Special Assistant to the President of the American League and the former supervisor of umpires for the American League, told Newsday that for Plaintiff to become a major league umpire:

> She realizes that she has to be better than the fellow next to her. She's got to be better because of the fact that she's a girl. I'm not saying it's fair, but it exists and she's not going to change it.

These comments were widely reported in the media, including in the Los Angeles Times. Defendants neither issued any statements contradicting, retracting, or correcting Butler's statements, took any remedial or disciplinary action with respect to Butler, nor otherwise said or did anything to communicate that Butler had not stated the true position of professional baseball, including Defendants.

In 1988, Bob Knepper made the above referenced remarks which resulted in national press coverage and widespread public controversy.

On May 14, 1989, Larry Napp, Assistant Supervisor of Umpires for the American League, told the Richmond Times–Dispatch that Plaintiff would never become a major league umpire. He stated:

> She's a nice person, and she knows the rules. But the thing is, she's got to do the job twice as good as the guy, if he's a good one, to get the job.

Defendants neither issued any statements contradicting, retracting, or correcting Napp's statements, took any remedial or disciplinary action with respect to Napp, nor otherwise said or did anything to communicate that Napp had not stated the true position of professional baseball, including Defendants.

During the 1989 season, Ed Vargo required Plaintiff to adopt the above mentioned changes in her umpiring technique.

Plaintiff alleges that during the 1989 season, Defendants either ignored or criticized her. She and her partner were the only two of the nine minor league umpires invited to 1989 spring training who were not given the opportunity to fill in for ill or vacationing major league umpires, an opportunity which was given to male umpires with inferior abilities, experience, and qualifications. At the end of the 1989 season, Plaintiff received an unfairly negative written performance evaluation which alleged that she had a "bad attitude." Prior to 1989, Plaintiff had never received a written performance evaluation.

On November 6, 1989, Triple–A discharged and unconditionally released Plaintiff from her employment as an umpire. The reason for Plaintiff's discharge was that the National League and American League were not interested in considering her for employment as a major league umpire. Plaintiff alleges that the sole reason for her discharge, for her inability to obtain a job in the major leagues, and for the Defendants' other discriminatory conduct was Defendants' malicious, wanton, willful, knowing, and intentional discrimination on the basis of gender.

Plaintiff requests the following relief: actual damages, punitive or exemplary damages, interest on all damages, an award of costs and attorney's fees, an order requiring Defendants to employ Plaintiff as an umpire in the major league, and an injunction preventing Defendants from engaging in the unlawful conduct complained of herein.

Discussion

I. Title VII Claims

Plaintiff asserts essentially two separate Title VII claims against the American League: a claim for failure to hire or promote, and a claim for wrongful termination.

The American League maintains that it is entitled to summary judgment with respect to Plaintiff's claim for failure to hire or promote because: (1) any claim Plaintiff has arising from the American League's most recent umpire hiring is time-barred, and (2) Plaintiff cannot establish a prima facie case of discrimination in promotion or hiring where no one, either male or female, was hired for or promoted to the position sought.

Plaintiff admits that since 1988, the American League has had only one opening for and has hired only one umpire; former minor league umpire Jim Joyce was hired in April 1989. American League 3(g) Stmt. pp 3–4. Plaintiff further admits that she did not file a charge of employment discrimination with the EEOC until April 4, 1990, more than 300 days after Joyce was hired. American League 3(g) Stmt. p 5. Accordingly, any claim Plaintiff might have arising from the Joyce hiring is time-barred, and the American League is entitled to summary judgment.

The American League maintains that it is also entitled to summary judgment on Plaintiff's claims which accrued during the 300 days prior to her EEOC filing and which are therefore timely. The American League argues that because it did not hire or promote any umpires during that period, the absence of a vacancy for the position sought prevents Plaintiff from establishing her requisite prima facie case of employment discrimination.

In McDonnell Douglas Corp. v. Green, 411 U.S. 792, 93 S.Ct. 1817, 36 L.Ed.2d 668 (1973), the Supreme Court ruled that an individual Title VII plaintiff must carry the initial burden of proof by establishing a prima facie case of discrimination. On the specific facts there involved, the Court found that the burden was met by showing that a qualified applicant, who was a member of a protected group, had unsuccessfully sought a job for which there was a vacancy and for which the employer continued thereafter to seek applicants with similar qualifications. Id. at 802, 93 S.Ct. at 1824. The American League argues that because there was no vacancy in the position sought by Plaintiff, she is unable to satisfy the McDonnell Douglas test, and she therefore cannot establish a prima facie case.

McDonnell Douglas does not, however, outline the only possible way a Title VII plaintiff can establish a prima facie case. Indeed, in International Brotherhood of Teamsters v. United States, 431 U.S. 324, 358, 97 S.Ct. 1843, 1866, 52 L.Ed.2d 396 (1977), the Court noted:

> The importance of McDonnell Douglas lies, not in its specification of the discrete elements of proof there required, but in its recognition that any Title VII plaintiff must carry the initial burden of offering evidence adequate to create an inference that an employment decision was based on discriminatory criterion illegal under the [Civil Rights] Act [of 1964].

Thus, Plaintiff's inability to satisfy the McDonnell Douglas test does not bar her Title VII complaint, so long as she may establish a prima facie case by some other method.

Plaintiff relies on Trans World Airlines, Inc. v. Thurston, 469 U.S. 111, 105 S.Ct. 613, 83 L.Ed.2d 523 (1985), and argues that McDonnell Douglas is irrelevant because she can establish her prima facie case by direct evidence. Specifically, she intends to offer the statements of American League officials Larry Napp and Dick Butler which suggested that Plaintiff would have to outperform male umpires to obtain a position in the major leagues.

In Thurston, the plaintiffs challenged a policy whereby vacant positions were created for airline pilots under age 60 who were forced to stop flying, but not for pilots forced into retirement at age 60. The defendant raised the absence of vacancies as a defense, but the Court refused to shield the defendant from liability where the existence of vacancies was due solely to the effect of the discriminatory policy under attack. Id. at 121, 105 S.Ct. at 621. The Court noted that because there was direct evidence of discrimination, namely the facially discriminatory policy at issue, the plaintiffs need not satisfy the McDonnell Douglas test:

> The McDonnell Douglas test is inapplicable where the plaintiff presents direct evidence of discrimination. The shifting burdens of proof set forth in McDonnell Douglas are designed to assure that the "plaintiff [has] his day in court despite the unavailability of direct evidence."

Id. at 121, 105 S.Ct. at 621–22.

Plaintiff's reliance on Thurston is, however, misplaced. Thurston does not stand for a general proposition that a plaintiff may sue for discrimination in hiring or promotion where there was no vacancy in the position sought and no person, either within or without the protected group, was hired. Thurston did not hold, and Plaintiff has not cited any case which holds, that a plaintiff may sue under Title VII for discriminatory hiring or promotion where there was no vacancy in the position sought. As the Supreme Court has explained, "[I]t is a [Title VII] plaintiff's task to demonstrate that similarly situated employees were not treated equally." Texas Dep't of Community Affairs v. Burdine, 450 U.S. 248, 258, 101 S.Ct. 1089, 1096, 67 L.Ed.2d 207 (1981). The essence of a Title VII plaintiff's prima facie case must be differential treatment of similarly situated employees. Martin v. Citibank, N.A., 762 F.2d 212, 216 (2d Cir.1985). Here, where the American League did not hire or promote any umpires during the relevant time period, either male or female, Plaintiff cannot show that she was treated any differently than male applicants, and her complaint does not make out a prima facie case of discrimination in hiring or promotion.

Accordingly, the American League is also entitled to summary judgment on Plaintiff's hiring and promotion claim arising from events which occurred within 300 days of the filing of her EEOC charge.

The American League argues that it is entitled to summary judgment on Plaintiff's termination claim because when it expressed a lack of interest in hiring Plaintiff in October 1989, it treated her no differently than it treated male umpires. Martin J. Springstead, the American League's Supervisor of Umpires, states that in October 1989, Edwin L. Lawrence, the Executive Director of BOUD, submitted to him the names of a number of umpires employed by Triple–A, including Plaintiff's, and inquired whether the American League had a current interest in hiring any of these umpires. Mr. Springstead asserts that he advised Lawrence that the American League had no interest in hiring any of the umpires because it had no vacancies in its umpiring staff. Affidavit of Martin J. Springstead, sworn to on February 27, 1992, pp 8–9.

Plaintiff's Local Rule 3(g) Statement and an affidavit submitted by Plaintiff's counsel pursuant to Rule 56(f) suggest that in the American League's communications with BOUD in October 1989, the American League did more than simply tell BOUD that it had no umpire vacancies at that time. Rather, Plaintiff raises the possibility that the submission of her name was intended to give the American League an opportunity to express whether it ever intended to hire Plaintiff. See Pl. 3(g) Stmt. pp 1–5. Furthermore, Plaintiff implies that the American League either understood that its expressed lack of interest in Plaintiff would cause her termination by Triple–A, or otherwise intended to encourage Triple–A to terminate Plaintiff. Pl. 3(g) Stmt. pp 5–8. Plaintiff requests that she be given an opportunity to conduct discovery to explore, inter alia, the content and nature of the October 1989 communications between the American League and BOUD. Affidavit of Daniel R. Shulman, sworn to on March 26, 1992, p 2.

The American League was not Plaintiff's employer at the time of her termination. Nevertheless, if Plaintiff shows such involvement by the American League in her termination by Triple–A, then she will allege a violation of Title VII against the American League. "It is clear from the language of the statute that Congress intended that the rights and obligations it created under Title VII would extend beyond the immediate employer-employee relationship." United States v. Yonkers, 592 F.Supp. 570, 590 (S.D.N.Y.1984). Where a third-party takes discriminatory action that causes an employer to terminate an employee, that third-party may be held liable under Title VII. Sibley Memorial Hospital v. Wilson, 488 F.2d 1338, 1341 (D.C.Cir.1973) (covered employer may not discriminatorily interfere with an individual's employment opportunities with another individual).

Accordingly, Plaintiff will have an opportunity to conduct discovery to determine whether the American League was involved in her termination. The American League's motion for summary judgment on Plaintiff's termination claim is therefore denied without prejudice to its renewal after discovery has been completed.

II. Claims Under New York Human Rights Law

New York's Human Rights Law contains an election of remedies provision which states:

> Any person claiming to be aggrieved by an unlawful discriminatory practice shall have a cause of action in any court of appropriate jurisdiction for damages and such other remedies as may be appropriate, unless such person had filed a complaint hereunder with any local commission on human rights, ...

> provided that, where the division has dismissed such complaint for administrative convenience, such person shall maintain all rights to bring suit as if no complaint had been filed.

N.Y.Exec.L. § 297(9). Plaintiff filed charges of discrimination with the EEOC against the American League and the National League, and the EEOC in turn referred Plaintiff's complaints to the New York State Division of Human Rights ("SDHR"). Shulman Aff., Exhs. A–B. Plaintiff also filed an EEOC charge against BOUD, and the EEOC filed the charge with the St. Petersburg Human Relations Department ("St. Petersburg HRD"), a local commission on human rights. BOUD 3(g) Stmt. pp 1–2.

Defendants maintain that because Plaintiff filed complaints with local commissions on human rights, the election of remedies provision divests this Court of subject matter jurisdiction. Plaintiff notes that she did not file any complaints with the SDHR or the St. Petersburg HRD. Rather, the EEOC referred her complaints to those local commissions. Therefore, because she made no meaningful election of remedies, she argues that her claims should not be barred by § 287(9).

In Scott v. Carter–Wallace, Inc., 147 A.D.2d 33, 541 N.Y.S.2d 780 (1st Dep't 1989), appeal dismissed, 75 N.Y.2d 764, 551 N.Y.S.2d 903, 551 N.E.2d 104 (1989), the court noted that a jurisdictional anomaly results when a plaintiff attempts to sue under both Title VII and the Human Rights Law. Title VII requires the plaintiff first to file with a state or local anti-discrimination commission. The election of remedies provision of the Human Rights Law, however, provides that such a filing bars later suit in a judicial forum. Id. 541 N.Y.S.2d at 782. Despite this anomaly, the court specifically rejected the argument that the plaintiff himself, and not the EEOC, must file with the state or local commission to constitute a valid election of remedies under § 297(9). Id. at 782–3. Accord Promisel v. First American Artificial Flowers, Inc., 943 F.2d 251, 257 (2d Cir.1991) (under New York law, EEOC's automatic referral of a discrimination complaint to the SDHR "is deemed to exercise plaintiff's option for an administrative forum," and bars plaintiff from pursuing the claim in a judicial forum), cert. denied, 502 U.S. 1060, 112 S.Ct. 939, 117 L.Ed.2d 110 (1992); Cholewa v. New York News Inc., No. 89 Civ. 4929, 1991 WL 198731, 1991 U.S.Dist. LEXIS 13253 (S.D.N.Y. Sept. 23, 1991).

Accordingly, Plaintiff's argument that she did not elect an administrative remedy is rejected.

Plaintiff maintains that regardless of whether she elected an administrative remedy, her Human Rights Law claims against the American League and National League should not be barred because those claims fall within § 297(9)'s express exception for dismissals for administrative convenience. In support thereof, she attaches copies of the SDHR's May 1, 1992 "Administrative Convenience Dismissal" of her American League and National League complaints. Affidavit of Gregory Merz, sworn to on April 6, 1992, Exhs. A–B.

Defendant notes that the SDHR sent Plaintiff letters dated May 22, 1990 acknowledging its receipt from the EEOC of Plaintiff's complaints against the National League and American League. Those letters advised Plaintiff that her complaints would be kept on file by the SDHR until the EEOC reported the results of its investigation. After notification of the EEOC's determination, Plaintiff was required to notify the SDHR whether: (1) having received an unfavorable EEOC determination, she wished to provide newly discovered information to the SDHR; or (2) having received a favorable EEOC determination, she wished to proceed to a public hearing before the SDHR. If Plaintiff failed to notify the SDHR of her intentions within the 30–day period, her complaints would be administratively closed. Shulman Aff., Exhs. A–B.

Plaintiff received the EEOC's unfavorable determination of her complaints on October 21, 1991. Complaint p 1. Defendants assert, and Plaintiff does not deny, that Plaintiff did not contact the SDHR until March 23, 1992, long after the 30–day period expired. By letter of that date, Plaintiff's attorneys wrote to the SDHR requesting dismissals for administrative convenience to permit the instant lawsuit. American League Reply Mem. at 13–14. Thus, Defendants argue that the Court should find the SDHR's administrative convenience dismissals void because (1) the dismissals were obtained solely to allow the instant litigation, and (2) the SDHR reopened Plaintiff's cases that were, or should have been, administratively closed merely to effect dismissals for administrative convenience.

In Drummer v. DCI Contracting Corp., 772 F.Supp. 821 (S.D.N.Y. 1991), the court rejected the defendant's argument that a dismissal for administrative convenience obtained by the plaintiff solely to permit it to pursue judicial relief was arbitrary and therefore void. The court determined that the applicable New York regulation specifically endorses dismissal for administrative convenience where such dismissal is obtained solely to permit the plaintiff to pursue a judicial action. Id. at 830. Accord Realmuto v. Yellow Freight Systems, Inc., 712 F.Supp. 287, 290–91 (E.D.N.Y.1989) (administrative convenience dismissal was proper where plaintiff requested dismissal so that he could bring judicial action).

As for Defendants' argument that the SDHR's opening of a closed complaint simply to effect a dismissal for administrative convenience is arbitrary, Defendants cite no regulation, statute, or case law in support of their position. The applicable regulation provides that the SDHR has "unreviewable discretion" to dismiss a complaint for administrative convenience prior to a public hearing. 9 NYCRR § 465(d)(2)(vi)(1). Thus, the State has mandated that courts defer to the SDHR's determinations in this area.

Accordingly, the Court has jurisdiction over Plaintiff's Human Rights Law claims against Triple–A, the American League and the National League. Because Plaintiff has not shown that her complaint filed with the St. Petersburg HRD was dismissed for administrative convenience, the EEOC's filing of that complaint bars the prosecution of Plaintiff's Human Rights Law claim against BOUD.

III. Restraint of Trade Claims

Defendants move to dismiss Plaintiff's state law restraint of trade claims for lack of subject matter jurisdiction and for failure to state a claim, arguing that the claims are preempted by baseball's exemption to antitrust law. Plaintiff responds that her claims are not preempted because the baseball exemption is not so broad as to immunize baseball from claims arising from its relationship with its umpires.

The Supreme Court created the so-called "baseball exemption" in Federal Baseball Club, Inc. v. National League of Professional Baseball Clubs, 259 U.S. 200, 42 S.Ct. 465, 66 L.Ed. 898 (1922). The Court revisited [and left standing] the baseball exemption in Toolson v. New York Yankees, Inc., 346 U.S. 356, 74 S.Ct. 78, 98 L.Ed. 64 (1953), [and] Flood v. Kuhn, 407 U.S. 258, 284, 92 S.Ct. 2099, 2112, 32 L.Ed.2d 728 (1972).

Because the Federal Baseball, Toolson, and Flood cases considered the baseball exemption in very limited contexts, i.e. with regard to baseball's reserve clause and to its league structure, those opinions give little guidance in determining the breadth of baseball's immunity to antitrust liability. The Court has not specifically determined whether the exemption applies to baseball's conduct outside the domain of league structure and player relations. However, the Flood Court stated that the immunity "rests on a recognition and acceptance of baseball's unique characteristics and needs," suggesting that baseball might not be exempt from liability for conduct not touching on those characteristics or needs. Flood, 407 U.S. at 282, 92 S.Ct. at 2111–12.

The Wisconsin Supreme Court endorsed a limited view of the baseball exemption in State v. Milwaukee Braves, Inc., 31 Wis.2d 699, 144 N.W.2d 1, cert. denied, 385 U.S. 990, 87 S.Ct. 598, 17 L.Ed.2d 451 (1966), wherein it rejected a challenge under Wisconsin antitrust law to baseball's decision to move the Milwaukee Braves to Atlanta. The court found that because the issue touched on league structure, application of state antitrust law would conflict with the baseball exemption. Id. 144 N.W.2d at 17. Importantly, however, the court noted:

> We venture to guess that this exemption does not cover every type of business activity to which a baseball club or league might be a party and does not protect clubs or leagues from application of the federal acts to activities which are not incidental to the maintenance of the league structure, but it does seem clear that the exemption at least covers the agreements and rules which provide for the structure of the organization and the decisions which are necessary steps in maintaining it.

Id. at 15.

In apparent agreement with the view of Milwaukee Braves, numerous courts have found that baseball may be subject to antitrust liability for conduct unrelated to the reserve system or to league structure. For example, in Henderson Broadcasting Corp. v. Houston Sports Ass'n, 541 F.Supp. 263 (S.D.Tex.1982), the court explicitly ruled that the exemption did not immunize baseball from liability in a suit brought by a radio station against the owner of the Houston Astros. The court reasoned that "broadcasting is not central enough to baseball to be encompassed in the baseball exemption." Id. at 265.

Other courts have applied the antitrust laws to agreements between baseball entities and third parties without even discussing the possibility that the antitrust exemption might apply. See, e.g., Fleer Corp. v. Topps Chewing Gum, Inc., 658 F.2d 139 (3d Cir.1981) (contract between players association and baseball card manufacturer), cert. denied, 455 U.S. 1019, 102 S.Ct. 1715, 72 L.Ed.2d 137 (1982); Nishimura v. Dolan, 599 F.Supp. 484 (E.D.N.Y.1984) (contract between cable company and New York baseball teams); Twin City Sportservice, Inc. v. Charles O. Finley & Co., 365 F.Supp. 235 (N.D.Cal.1972) (contract between Oakland Athletics and concessionaire), rev'd other grounds, 512 F.2d 1264 (9th Cir.1975), cert. denied, 459 U.S. 1009, 103 S.Ct. 364, 74 L.Ed.2d 400 (1982). See also Steven F. Ross, An Antitrust Analysis of Sports League Contracts with Cable Networks, 39 Emory L.J. 463, 474 n. 52 (1990).

It is thus clear that although the baseball exemption does immunize baseball from antitrust challenges to its league structure and its reserve system, the exemption does not provide baseball with blanket immunity for anti-competitive behavior in every context in which it operates. The Court must therefore determine whether baseball's employment relations with its umpires are "central enough to baseball to be encompassed in the baseball exemption." See Henderson, 541 F.Supp. at 265.

Defendants rely on Salerno [v. American League of Professional Baseball Clubs, 429 F.2d 1003 (2d Cir.1970), cert. denied, 400 U.S. 1001 (1971)] and Moore v. National Association of Professional Baseball Clubs, No. C78–351 (N.D.Ohio filed July 7, 1976), to support their argument that the exemption should apply to antitrust claims brought by umpires. Salerno concerned an antitrust action brought by two umpires alleging wrongful discharge after they attempted to organize umpires for collective bargaining. After expressing concern whether plaintiffs had a valid claim under the antitrust laws, the court ruled without discussion that the baseball exemption applied. Salerno, 429 F.2d at 1004–5. Salerno, however, preceded the decision in Flood, which anchored the baseball exemption to the sport's "unique characteristics and needs." Flood, 407 U.S. at 282, 92 S.Ct. at 2112. Thus, there is a substantial question whether Salerno would be decided similarly after Flood's apparent endorsement of a limited view of the exemption.

In Moore, slip op. at 3, the court stated that because "professional baseball umpires perform an integral function in 'the business of baseball,' " the baseball exemption bars claims brought by umpires against baseball. Moore supports Defendants' position, but, of course, does not bind this Court.

The Court concludes that Defendants have not shown any reason why the baseball exemption should apply to baseball's employment relations with its umpires. Unlike the league structure or the reserve system, baseball's relations with non-players are not a unique characteristic or need of the game. Anti-competitive conduct toward umpires is not an essential part of baseball and in no way enhances its vitality or viability.

Accordingly, because the baseball exemption does not encompass umpire employment relations, application of New York's common law of restraint of trade presents no conflict with the baseball exemption, and Plaintiff's claims are not preempted.

Conclusion

With regard to the Title VII claims: the American League's motion for summary judgment is granted in part and denied in part. With regard to the Human Rights Law claims: BOUD's motion to dismiss is granted, the other Defendants' motions to dismiss are denied. Defendants' motions to dismiss the common law restraint of trade claims are denied.

CLEMONS v. BIG TEN CONFERENCE

1997 WL 89227 (N.D.Ill.1997).

HART, District Judge.

Plaintiff Lorenzo Clemons, brings this action alleging that The Big Ten Conference ("Big Ten") discriminated against him by canceling his contract for the 1994 football season on the basis of his obesity and by treating similarly-situated individuals outside of his protected class differently. Plaintiff seeks damages under the Americans with Disabilities Act, 42 U.S.C. § 12101 et seq. ("ADA"), Title VII of the Civil Rights Act of 1964, 42 U.S.C. § 2000e et seq. ("Title VII"), and 42 U.S.C. § 1981 ("§ 1981"). Presently pending is the Big Ten's motion for summary judgment on all claims.

I. Background

Plaintiff, who is African–American, began officiating football games for the Big Ten in 1988 under a series of one-year contracts. From 1988 through 1993, plaintiff officiated approximately 11 games a year. Each Big Ten football game is staffed by a crew of seven officials and, at all times relevant to this lawsuit, plaintiff was an umpire. Although the position of umpire generally requires the least long-distance running of the seven positions, it nonetheless requires a substantial amount of quick movement and running during the course of the game to maintain a proper position to accurately officiate the game. When plaintiff was initially hired, he weighed 235 pounds.

In 1990, the Big Ten revised its system for rating its officials in order to upgrade officials' accountability and to better quantify their performance. David Parry, who was hired in July 1990 as the Big Ten's

Supervisor of Football Officials, was responsible for nearly all aspects of the supervision of the officiating staff, including the overhaul of the rating system. Parry patterned the new rating system after the National Football League and other major college conference systems. The new system calculated each officials' performance by averaging the ratings given to the official by Parry himself, the coaches at each game and technical advisors. Technical advisors are former, experienced football officials. In order to evaluate the officials, Parry either observed the officials personally or reviewed game tapes, or both.

In 1991, the Big Ten began using its current assessment criteria, comprising five areas of major concern relating to an official's performance: (1) appearance and physical condition; (2) position, coverage and movement; (3) consistency, common sense and judgment; (4) poise, decisiveness and game control; and (5) relationship with the coaches, players and others. Parry testified that the appearance and physical condition of the officials refers to being trim, looking sharp, endurance and the official's ability to cover, move and be in position to make calls. Generally, the better field position an umpire achieves, the greater the probability that the umpire will make the correct call.

In his first year as a Big Ten official, plaintiff was ranked 21st out of 41 officials. In 1990, plaintiff was ranked 36th out of 44 officials and his written evaluation indicated that he should lose 20 pounds. Although plaintiff's ranking placed him in the bottom third of officials, he was selected to officiate the Citrus Bowl in 1990. In 1991, plaintiff was ranked 49th out of 49 officials and his evaluation stated "appearance, gaining weight." Again, plaintiff was selected to officiate a bowl game despite his low ranking. In 1992, plaintiff remained ranked in the bottom third for officials. In April 1992, Parry called plaintiff to discuss his weight. Parry asked plaintiff to report to the August 1992 clinic at 270 pounds. Plaintiff reached his goal weight of 270 pounds in October 1992.

In 1993, plaintiff was ranked 43rd out of 45 football officials. Plaintiff was ranked last out of the six umpires. Plaintiff's written evaluation stated that plaintiff's "[w]eight hinders ratings for appearance and movement. Errors in judgment 12/too many. (Generally on the marginal to technical side.)" Twelve errors was the most of any official for the 1993 season. On February 4, 1994, Parry discussed plaintiff's performance with him, including the negative impact Parry believed plaintiff's weight had on his performance. Plaintiff weighed 277 pounds at the beginning of the 1993 season; at the end of the season he weighed 280 pounds. Parry placed plaintiff on probation and told him he would receive a reduced game schedule for the 1994 season. Parry told plaintiff to lose weight and report to the next clinic in August 1994 at 270 pounds. On February 10, 1994, Parry sent plaintiff a letter confirming that plaintiff was placed on probation:

> As per our visit, February 4, 1994, this letter serves as a reminder regarding your status on our staff.

> Your ratings must be improved and higher. Based upon your ratings for the 1993 season, which you finished forty-three (43) out of forty-five (45) over-all staff ratings and six (6) out of six (6) umpires (last) in your individual position ratings, you are formally put on notice/probation for the 1994 season. If your ratings do not significantly improve, you will be released from the football staff....
>
> During our conversation we discussed your ratings as they related to appearance, movement, and judgments. I suggest you review these concerns.

In April 1994, the Big Ten renewed plaintiff's contract. When plaintiff reported to the clinic on August 5, 1994, however, he weighed at least 285 pounds. Two days later, the Big Ten canceled plaintiff's contract for the 1994 season.

Plaintiff, however, was not left without a job. Plaintiff maintains his regular position as the Inter–Governmental Liaison for the Cook County Sheriff's Office. Prior to this job, plaintiff was a Kimberly–Clark salesperson. Parry was aware of these jobs, as well as that plaintiff was pursuing a career in acting. Both parties agree that plaintiff's weight has no effect on his ability to perform his other jobs.

On January 6, 1996, plaintiff filed this three-count action. In Count I, plaintiff alleges that he was discharged due to his perceived disability of obesity in violation of the ADA. In Count II, plaintiff asserts that the Big Ten violated Title VII by discriminating against him on the basis of his race. In Count III, plaintiff alleges that the Big Ten violated his right to make and enforce contracts on the same terms as white citizens, in violation of 42 U.S.C. § 1981.

II. SUMMARY JUDGMENT

A. Title VII and § 1981 Claims

A plaintiff may establish a discrimination under Title VII or § 1981 either by presenting direct evidence of discrimination or by following the burden-shifting method set out in McDonnell Douglas Corp. v. Green, 411 U.S. 792, 802–04, 93 S.Ct. 1817, 36 L.Ed.2d 668 (1973). Plaintiff has chosen the latter route. Under the McDonnell Douglas burden-shifting analysis, if plaintiff establishes a prima facie case, the burden of production shifts to the defendant to state a legitimate, nondiscriminatory reason for the employment action. Texas Dep't of Community Affairs v. Burdine, 450 U.S. 248, 254, 101 S.Ct. 1089, 67 L.Ed.2d 207 (1981). If the defendant carries this burden, the presumption of discrimination drops from the case, United States Postal Service Bd. of Governors v. Aikens, 460 U.S. 711, 715, 103 S.Ct. 1478, 75 L.Ed.2d 403 (1983), and the plaintiff must demonstrate that the defendant's stated reason for the adverse action is a pretext for an illegitimate, discriminatory reason. McDonnell Douglas, 411 U.S. at 804.

Plaintiff must establish a prima facie case of discrimination in order to withstand summary judgment. Hong v. Children's Memorial Hosp.,

993 F.2d 1257, 1261 (7th Cir.1993). Under the McDonnell Douglas framework, plaintiff may prove a prima facie case of discrimination by showing that (1) he belongs to a protected class; (2) he performed his job satisfactorily; (3) he suffered an adverse employment action; and (4) his employer treated similarly situated employees outside his classification more favorably. Little v. Cox's Supermarkets, 71 F.3d 637, 642 n. 3 (7th Cir.1995). It is not necessary that plaintiff demonstrate that he was replaced by someone outside the protected class. Carson v. Bethlehem Steel Corp., 82 F.3d 157, 158 (7th Cir.1996) (citing O'Connor v. Consolidated Coin Caterers Corp., 517 U.S. 308, 116 S.Ct. 1307, 134 L.Ed.2d 433 (1996)). Rather, "[t]he central question in any employment-discrimination case is whether the employer would have taken the same action had the employee been of a different race (age, sex, religion, national origin, etc.) and everything else had remained the same." Id.

The Big Ten argues that it is entitled to summary judgment because plaintiff has not established he performed adequately as a football official. To show that he was performing adequately on the job, the critical issue is whether plaintiff was performing well at the time of his termination. See Hong, 993 F.2d at 1262. Thus, the only relevant time frame concerning plaintiff's performance is the 1993 season and afterwards. "The fact that an individual may have been qualified in the past does not mean that he is qualified at a later time." Karazanos v. Navistar Intern. Transp. Corp., 948 F.2d 332, 336 (7th Cir.1991) (internal citations omitted).

The Big Ten asserts that plaintiff's performance in the 1993 season was not adequate for numerous reasons. First, plaintiff was rated 43rd out of 45 officials. Plaintiff made the most mistakes of any other official as judged from review of game tapes by coaches, technical advisers, crew chiefs and Parry. In addition, the Big Ten points out that several coaches who evaluated plaintiff were highly critical of his officiating. For the October 23, 1993 Iowa–Michigan State game, Coach Hayden Fry gave plaintiff the lowest marks of the officiating crew and wrote on the back of plaintiff's evaluation form "Don't ever send him to officiate another Iowa game." The head football coach at the University of Minnesota, Jim Wacker, wrote Parry a letter dated November 10, 1993 complaining about plaintiff. Wacker stated that plaintiff "was consistently in poor position during our Illinois game causing our adjusting [Linebackers] and [Strong Safeties] to go around him rather than him moving his position on the field. When asked if he could move his position, he responded in a rather ugly manner and still did not adjust his position. . . ." In February 1994, plaintiff was placed on probation because of his poor ratings and was directed to take steps to improve his performance by losing weight. Plaintiff failed to comply with Parry's directive to lose weight by the August 1994 clinic.

In response, plaintiff argues that he performed adequately because he satisfied all of the expectations contained in a manual distributed by the Big Ten at the annual clinic for officials ("Manual"). Plaintiff asserts that the Manual contains no requirement as to weight. Plaintiff acknowledges that the Manual states that officials should be in good physical condition in order to keep up with the athletes, but argues he cannot be deemed to have failed this requirement because no scale or chart exists to measure this expectation. Plaintiff's argument is without merit. The Big Ten may legitimately expect that its officials maintain themselves in a physical condition such that they are able to move down the field with the football players. The Big Ten's expectations were communicated to plaintiff orally and in his written evaluations. Simply because the Big Ten did not employ height-weight charts does not make the physical condition requirement invalid. Plaintiff has not provided any evidence that an official that cannot keep up with the athletes can nonetheless perform adequately. Plaintiff's evaluations demonstrate that he failed to keep himself in a physical condition that enabled him to keep up with the athletes and place himself in the proper position to make accurate calls.

Plaintiff also argues that satisfactory performance ratings were not a condition of officials' contracts because the Manual does not state that consistently low ratings would result in dismissal. For the purposes of this prong of plaintiff's prima facie case, however, the question is not whether the Manual required that officials achieve satisfactory performance ratings, but simply whether plaintiff was performing adequately at the time of his dismissal. Moreover, it need not have been stated in the Manual that an official's poor performance could lead to dismissal, since plaintiff had been expressly warned (in the February 10, 1994 letter from Parry, for example) of this consequence. Plaintiff admits in his brief that Parry circulated "numerous memoranda" from 1990 through 1994 and "[s]ome of the memoranda state that consistent [sic] low ratings may mean dismissal from the conference." In short, plaintiff's performance ratings represent a valid measuring stick on which to gauge plaintiff's performance. Cf. Hong, 993 F.2d at 1262 (using performance evaluations as evidence of inadequate performance).

Plaintiff, who was ranked 43rd out of 45 officials and received negative comments by several coaches, was not performing adequately. Plaintiff argues, however, that his performance was acceptable because he was only 2.553 points away from the middle third and "[n]o matter how good the scores are for all of the officials there will always be a bottom third with respect to this individual head to head ranking." This argument does not assist plaintiff in making out his prima facie case. Plaintiff must do more than allege that his performance was not far from being satisfactory. He must bring forth some evidence that his performance was adequate. Plaintiff does not assert any facts from which it may be concluded that plaintiff met the expectations of the Big Ten, nor does plaintiff attempt to refute his substandard performance evaluations or the negative comments of his performance from football coaches. Plaintiff's evaluations, which represent a composite of ratings from Parry, coaches and technical advisors, demonstrate that his performance was substandard. Plaintiff has not created an issue of fact as to whether his performance was satisfactory. It was not. Summary judgment will be granted in the Big Ten's favor as to [Counts II and III].

B. ADA Claim

The ADA provides that "[n]o covered entity shall discriminate against a qualified individual with a disability because of the disability of such individual in regard to job application procedures, the hiring, advancement or discharge of employees, employee compensation, job training and other terms, conditions, and privileges of employment." 42 U.S.C. § 12112(a). A plaintiff asserting a claim under the ADA bears the initial burden of establishing a prima facie case. Wernick v. Federal Reserve Bank of New York, 91 F.3d 379, 383 (2d Cir.1996). The Big Ten asserts that summary judgment on plaintiff's ADA claim is proper because plaintiff has failed to establish a prima facie case.

To satisfy this burden, plaintiff must show that (1) he suffers from a disability as defined by the ADA; (2) he is otherwise qualified to perform his job; and (3) he was discharged because of his disability. See id. Plaintiff will be considered disabled if he demonstrates that (1) he has a physical or mental impairment which substantially limits one or more of his major life activities; (2) he has a record of such an impairment; or (3) he is regarded as having such an impairment. 42 U.S.C. § 12102(2).

Plaintiff does not contend that his obesity constitutes a disability or that it substantially limits one of his major life activities. Instead, plaintiff argues that he falls within the third category because the Big Ten regarded him as disabled as a result of his obesity.

To show that the Big Ten perceived him as disabled, plaintiff must demonstrate that the Big Ten believed he had an impairment that substantially limited one or more of his major life activities. See Stewart v. County of Brown, 86 F.3d 107, 111 (7th Cir.1996). The Department of Labor regulations interpreting the ADA ("Regulations") define major life activities as "functions such as caring for one's self, performing manual tasks, walking, seeing, hearing, speaking, breathing, learning and working." 29 C.F.R. § 1630.2(h)(2)(i). With respect to the major life activity of working, the Regulations state as follows:

> The term substantially limits means significantly restricted in the ability to perform either a class of jobs or a broad range of jobs in various classes as compared to the average person having comparable training, skills and abilities. The inability to perform a single, particular job does not constitute a substantial limitation in the major life activity of working.

29 C.F.R. § 1630.2(j)(3)(i). The regulations note that "except in rare circumstances, obesity is not considered a disabling impairment." Id. § 1630 App.

Plaintiff argues that he meets the definition of disabled because the Big Ten regarded him as incapable of performing an entire class of jobs—football officials—as a result of his obesity. The job of a football official, however, does not represent a "class of jobs." It is a single position. Plaintiff cannot demonstrate that he was regarded as disabled on the basis of a specific job of his choosing. See Byrne v. Board of Educ., School of West Allis–West Milwaukee, 979 F.2d 560, 564 (7th Cir.1992) (definition of "major life activity" cannot be interpreted to mean "working at the specific job of one's choice"). "It is well established that an inability to perform a particular job for a particular employer is not sufficient to establish a handicap; the impairment must substantially limit employment generally." Id. at 565; see also Weiler v. Household Finance Corp., 101 F.3d 519, 525 (7th Cir.1996) ("[E]xclusion from one position of employment does not constitute a substantial limitation of a major life activity.").

Both parties agree that plaintiff's ability to work at his other jobs is not limited. Plaintiff has always held down a regular job, first as a Kimberly–Clark salesperson and now with the Cook County Sheriff's Office, during his tenure with the Big Ten. Both parties acknowledge that the Big Ten knew about plaintiff's regular employment, in addition to plaintiff's pursuit of an acting career. Although Parry may have believed that plaintiff's weight prevented him from being an effective football official, plaintiff has offered no support for the contention that he was perceived as being disabled from working generally. In considering whether an individual is substantially limited in the activity of working, the Regulations provide that an individual's "ability to perform in a class of jobs or a broad range of jobs in various classes as compared to the average person having comparable training, skills and abilities" should be examined. 29 C.F.R. § 1603.2(j)(3)(i). Plaintiff possesses skills and abilities in more than one profession. There is nothing in the Regulations to indicate that considering the entire panoply of plaintiff's skills and abilities is impermissible. The relevant "broad range of jobs in various classes" includes plaintiff's other positions. Plaintiff's other occupations, and Parry's knowledge of these occupations, negates any inference that Parry believed plaintiff's weight substantially limited him from working. Cf. Smaw v. Commonwealth of Virginia Dep't of State Police, 862 F.Supp. 1469, 1475 (E.D.Va.1994) (summary judgment granted to defendant because plaintiff's "present position as a dispatcher would seem to negate any argument that she is disqualified from her profession by her weight."). Plaintiff officiated approximately eleven football games annually for the Big Ten and attended a clinic each August. At most, plaintiff has shown that Parry believed that plaintiff's weight hindered him in performing a single job for eleven days a year. This evidence does not demonstrate that plaintiff was perceived as substantially limited in the major life activity of working.

Plaintiff also asserts that Parry regards him as disabled from any job that requires a "modicum of athleticism." Plaintiff has not brought forth any references to the record to support this inference and, here too, plaintiff's other skills doom this argument. Plaintiff's ability to perform other jobs requiring athletic ability are irrelevant to the analysis. The pertinent class of jobs for purposes of analyzing whether plaintiff was perceived as disabled are those jobs for which plaintiff is skilled. The Big

Ten's motion for summary judgment will be granted as to plaintiff's ADA claim.

SOKOLOFSKY v. NATIONAL BASKETBALL ASS'N

495 N.Y.S.2d 904 (App.Div.1985),
aff'd, 496 N.E.2d 222 (N.Y.1986).

PER CURIAM.

Determination of the Commissioner of the State Division of Human Rights, dated February 12, 1985, which, after a hearing, found that petitioner had discriminated against complainant Sokol by refusing to rehire him as an NBA referee on the basis of a disability in violation of Executive Law 296(1)(a) (Human Rights Law), directed that he be offered employment as a referee with back pay to May 23, 1983, the date he was rejected, and awarded $5,000 damages for mental anguish and humiliation, unanimously annulled, on the law, without costs or disbursements, the petition granted and the Commissioner's order vacated.

Complainant Manny Sokolofsky, also known as Manny Sokol, had been a National Basketball Association (''NBA'') referee for 13 years, from 1964 to 1977. Prior to commencement of the 1977–78 basketball season, a standard physical examination disclosed that Sokol had an enlarged heart. As a result, he consulted his personal physician, Dr. Soiefer, who, after a physical examination, certified that he was physically fit to perform as a referee. However, in November 1977, six weeks after the examination, he suffered a myocardial infarction which required a 10–day confinement in intensive care. Under the existing collective bargaining agreement, he received full salary for the 1977–78 season.

In September 1978, Sokol applied for benefits under an NBA disability insurance policy, which afforded disability payments for a 5–year period. As required by the policy, Sokol submitted a physician's certification each year attesting to his inability to work as a referee and declaring his permanent disability from gainful employment. The latest statement by Dr. Schaye, in September 1982, reported his physical impairment as ''Moderate limitation of functional capacity; capable of clerical/administrative (sedentary) activity'' and opined that he was ''totally disabled for gainful activity.'' The NBA also awarded Sokol a discretionary severance pay of $10,000 and a lump sum pension payment, fully liquidating his pension account.

In September 1982, the same month the last certification of disability was filed, Sokol wrote to Darrell Garretson, Chief of Staff of NBA referees, advising that he was ''willing to drop my disability with Guardian Insurance,'' which was about to lapse in any event, and expressing an interest in obtaining ''some opening'' with the NBA, especially since his disability payments were coming to an end. On October 27, 1982, Garretson responded that final decision ''as to any type of employment, if it is available, must come after a review by our legal department."

In March 1983, Sokol was advised that his Social Security disability payments would terminate in May of that year. On April 8, 1983, he was examined by his personal cardiologist, Dr. Allen Unger, who concluded in a letter to then NBA Commissioner O'Brien, that, inasmuch as Sokol was "free of anginal symptoms," he was "physically fit to resume duties as a referee." On May 23, 1983, Scotty Stirling, NBA Vice–President of Operations, advised Sokol: "We have reviewed Dr. Unger's letter and all the other aspects of your case and in our judgment we don't feel it would be appropriate to rehire you for the NBA officiating staff."

Thereafter, on June 16, 1983, Sokol filed a complaint with the Division of Human Rights, charging discrimination in denying reinstatement on account of his disability. At the hearing, Garretson testified that complainant was rejected, not because of any disabling condition but, instead, for his style and manner of officiating when he had been a referee. Garretson claimed that Sokol had been an average referee during his prior tenure with the league and avoided making "unpopular" calls. In addition, he engaged in "histrionics ... on the court"—showboating and antics in making calls, which did not conform to the "low profile" expected of NBA referees in their on-court performance.

At the close of the hearing, the administrative law judge rejected the NBA claim that the decision not to rehire complainant was based upon their evaluation of his prior performance and manner of officiating. In essence, the NBA maintained that his style did not conform to the approved standard by which referees were to maintain a low profile, thus placing principal focus on the skills and talents of the players. It was determined that this was a subterfuge to mask the actual reason for the rejection, namely, complainant's disabling condition, which, it was found, did not prevent him from reasonably performing the duties and activities of an NBA referee. As a result, the Commissioner found that there had been unlawful discrimination in violation of the Human Rights Law.

In a proceeding to review an administrative determination, the court's function is limited to deciding whether there is substantial evidence in the record to support the determination, a question of law for the court. (300 Gramatan Ave. Assocs. v. State Div. of Human Rights, 45 N.Y.2d 176, 179–182, 408 N.Y.S.2d 54, 379 N.E.2d 1183) Where there are charges of discrimination in violation of the Human Rights Law, the initial burden of establishing a prima facie case is upon the complainant. (Matter of Auchenpaugh v. General Electric Co., 92 A.D.2d 680, 460 N.Y.S.2d 200; Matter of Rotterdam–Mohanasen Central School Dist. v. State Div. of Human Rights, 70 A.D.2d 727, 728, 416 N.Y.S.2d 860; Matter of McGrath v. New York State Div. of Human Rights, 52 A.D.2d 1027, 383 N.Y.S.2d 911) Once proof has been adduced of an unlawful discriminatory practice, the burden of going forward shifts to the employer to establish that there existed "some independent legitimate reason which was neither a pretext for discrimination nor was substantially influenced by impermissible discrimination." (Burlington Industries, Inc. v. NYC Human Rights Comm., 82 A.D.2d 415, 417, 441 N.Y.S.2d 821, affd. 58 N.Y.2d 983, 460 N.Y.S.2d 920, 447 N.E.2d 1281; see also Matter of Maloff v. City Comm. on Human Rights [Anilyan], 46 N.Y.2d 908, 910, 414 N.Y.S.2d 901, 387 N.E.2d 1217; Matter of Pace College v. Commission on Human Rights, 38 N.Y.2d 28, 40, 377 N.Y.S.2d 471, 339 N.E.2d 880; City of New York v. Donnaruma, 70 A.D.2d 856, 418 N.Y.S.2d 45) In order to make out a prima facie case, the complainant must demonstrate that (1) he is within the class to be protected; (2) he applied and was qualified for a position for which the employer had sought applicants; (3) despite his qualifications, he was rejected for the position; and (4) the position remained opened and the employer sought other qualified applicants. (McDonnell Douglas Corp. v. Green, 411 U.S. 792, 802, 93 S.Ct. 1817, 1824, 36 L.Ed.2d 668)

In our case, while there is no dispute that complainant, in terms of his disability, was a member of a protected class under the statute and his application to return to his former position had been denied, there is no substantial evidence in the record that his disability did not prevent him from performing in a reasonable manner as an NBA referee. (Executive Law 292[21]) The only proof bearing on the issue is the affirmation of complainant's cardiologist, Dr. Unger, who concluded that his "medical condition would not prevent him from performing the duties of a referee ... in the manner customarily done by other Referees." Dr. Unger, however, did not appear at the hearing and could not be subjected to cross-examination. On petitioner's objection, the administrative law judge ruled that the document would not be received to establish "any ultimate fact by itself."

While the "legal residuum rule" is no longer followed (see Matter of Eagle v. Paterson, 57 N.Y.2d 831, 833, 455 N.Y.S.2d 759, 442 N.E.2d 56; 300 Gramatan Ave. Assocs. v. State Div. of Human Rights, supra, 45 N.Y.2d at p. 180, 408 N.Y.S.2d 54, 379 N.E.2d 1183), under the circumstances of this case, we conclude that the hearsay affirmation of the physician, standing alone, is insufficient to amount to substantial evidence that complainant could reasonably perform the duties of an NBA referee. (See Matter of Eggleston v. Richardson, 88 A.D.2d 750, 451 N.Y.S.2d 470) Other than the statement in the affirmation that complainant underwent an exercise treadmill test, there is no reference to any medical tests sufficient to conclude, with a degree of medical certainty, that the disability was not job-related. While the doctor opined that he could perform in a manner "customarily done by other Referees," the underlying basis for the conclusion is not set forth.

In our view, considering the record as a whole and Sokol's continuous representations through 1982 that he was disabled from employment, it cannot be found that he sustained his burden of proving by substantial evidence that he was physically fit to fully perform as a professional basketball referee. Moreover, there was abundant proof that the NBA's refusal to reinstate him related to grounds other than his physical condition. To the extent his rejection was based upon a determination that his style and manner of officiating did not conform to current standards, in the absence of affirmative proof of discrimination, it was improper for the Commissioner to substitute his judgment for that of the employer as to the qualifications for a particular position. (See Matter of Sperry Rand Corp. v. State Human Rights Appeal Board, 46 A.D.2d 678, 360 N.Y.S.2d 57; Matter of Tony Nuzzo and Sons, Inc. v. State Div. of Human Rights, 45 A.D.2d 921, 922, 357 N.Y.S.2d 570; Matter of New York Tel. Co. v. Wethers, 36 A.D.2d 541, 542, 317 N.Y.S.2d 119).

Notes

1. For other cases in which referees have claimed unlawful discrimination, see *Compton v. National League of Professional Baseball Clubs*, 995 F.Supp. 554 (E.D.Pa.1998) (race), and *Dowling v. United States*, 476 F.Supp. 1018 (D.Mass.1979) (nationality). *See also Beck v. Croft*, 700 P.2d 697 (Or.Ct.App.), *review denied*, 704 P.2d 513 (Or.1985) (whistleblower).

2. Pam Postema eventually settled her lawsuit for an undisclosed amount and a promise she would never again apply for an umpiring position with any league affiliated with MLB. Subsequently, she moved back home to Ohio and found work as a welder inserting tailpipes into muffler housings. *See* Grant Wahl, *Catching Up With ... Baseball Umpire Pam Postema*, Sports Illustrated, Apr. 28, 1997, at 14.

3. In October 1997, the NBA named Dee Kantner and Violet Palmer to its refereeing staff, thereby making it the first major professional men's league to employ women referees. *See* Amy Shipley, *A New Order on the Court; NBA's First Female Referees Ready for Foul Play*, Wash. Post, Oct. 30, 1997, at A1. It is widely believed that the next major professional league to follow suit will be the NHL. *See* Heather Burns & Valerie Lister, *NHL Could Be Next to Cross Gender Line*, USA Today, Nov. 3, 1997, at 3C. In the meantime, the 1999 Women's World Cup will be officiated entirely by women. *See further* Alex Yannis, *Soccer: Women's World Cup*, N.Y. Times, Dec. 22, 1998, at C20.

The vacancies filled by Kantner and Palmer were created by an Internal Revenue Service investigation that forced five referees to resign. In a scheme that took place over many months, the disgraced referees traded in first-class airline tickets provided by the NBA for cheaper tickets and pocketed the difference without reporting the extra income on their tax returns. The scandal is discussed further in *United States v. Armstrong*, 974 F.Supp. 528 (E.D.Va.1997), and *Another NBA Ref Resigns Amid IRS Investigation*, St. Petersburg Times, June 25, 1998, at 8C.

4. While the court in *Clemons* makes no mention of it, the death of John McSherry in April 1996 may have influenced its decision. A major league umpire since 1971, McSherry, who weighed 328 pounds, was calling balls and strikes at the Cincinnati Reds home opener. After just seven pitches, he called time, signalled he needed help, and then suffered a massive heart attack (from which he died later that day at a local hospital). Frightened by McSherry's passing, Eric Gregg and Rocky Roe, two other umpires with weight problems, soon took leaves of absence to get in shape and MLB retained Duke University's famed Diet and Fitness Center to help

all its umpires improve their fitness. *See further* Bill Peterson, *Cinergy Umpires Room Dedicated to McSherry*, Cin. Post, Apr. 2, 1997, at 6C.

5. As *Sokolofsky* reveals, referees are expected to possess a judicial temperament and convey an impartial and professional air. The use of such non-quantifiable criteria was implicitly approved in *Quinn v. National Basketball Ass'n*, 1992 WL 179781 (S.D.N.Y.1992), a case arising from the dismissal of a probationary referee who was let go after being rated in the bottom 30% of the league's referees.

6. Of course, there are times when a referee is selected precisely because he or she does not possess a "judicial" temperament. During his suspension for ignoring referee Mills Lane's warning against biting Evander Holyfield's ears, for example, heavyweight boxer Mike Tyson served as referee at the World Wrestling Federation's "Wrestlemania XIV" extravaganza. The event also featured Pete Rose, suspended baseball gambler, as ring announcer, and Gennifer Flowers, self-proclaimed former mistress of President Clinton, as official timekeeper. *See further* Doug Puppel, *Back in the Ring*, Las Vegas Rev.-J., Mar. 28, 1998, at 1D.

7. Like other labor organizations, referee unions face a host of complex membership, personnel, and bargaining issues. For a useful sampling, see *Collegiate Basketball Officials Ass'n, Inc. v. NLRB*, 836 F.2d 143 (3d Cir. 1987) (athletic conference held to have no duty to bargain with referees due to their status as independent contractors); *Major League Umpires' Ass'n v. American League of Professional Baseball Clubs*, 1997 WL 587357 (E.D.Pa. 1997) (arbitrator's decision that umpires were not entitled to compensation for playoff games lost due to players' strike affirmed); *Jones v. Southeast Alabama Baseball Umpires Ass'n*, 864 F.Supp. 1135 (M.D.Ala.1994) (question of fact existed as to whether umpires union was subject to the Americans with Disabilities Act); *National Ass'n of Basketball Referees v. Middleton*, 688 F.Supp. 131 (S.D.N.Y.1988) (use of mail ballot referendum to decide whether special assessment should be imposed to cover cost of settlement of lawsuit proper under union's by-laws); *National Basketball Ass'n v. National Ass'n of Basketball Referees*, 620 F.Supp. 672 (S.D.N.Y.1985) (removal of union's executive director did not violate his rights); *Strom v. National Ass'n of Basketball Referees*, 564 F.Supp. 250 (E.D.Pa.1983), *aff'd*, 732 F.2d 147 (3d Cir.1984) (referee was entitled to receive written notice of charges against him); *Sorge v. Greater Parma Umpires Ass'n*, 1979 Ohio App. LEXIS 9051 (Ohio Ct.App.1979) (applicant who failed field test was properly rejected as member by umpires union); *Daniels v. Gates Rubber Co.*, 479 P.2d 983 (Colo.Ct.App.1970) (umpires association could not be held liable for member injured while refereeing softball game).

Problem 46

To ensure its referees will be able to handle themselves during altercations, a league has decided it will no longer hire applicants who are shorter than 5'10" or weigh less than 170 pounds. If a candidate who is 5'2" and weighs 129 pounds sues, claiming the requirements are illegal, how should the court rule? *See New York State Division of Human Rights v. New York–Pennsylvania Professional Baseball League*, 279 N.E.2d 856 (N.Y.1972).

C. BAD CALLS

While bad calls, blown calls, late calls, and missed calls are as much a part of sports as home runs and touchdowns, they sometimes also become the stuff of lawsuits. Not surprisingly, courts take a dim view of these actions, reasoning the place to settle such disputes is on the field.

TILELLI v. CHRISTENBERRY

120 N.Y.S.2d 697 (Sup.Ct.1953).

BOTEIN, Justice.

In this Article 78 proceeding the petitioner challenges the power of the respondent, New York State Athletic Commission, to change the vote of one of the judges of a boxing match, in the absence of any explicit statutory or regulatory provision authorizing or prohibiting such action by the Commission.

The facts are substantially undisputed. On December 19, 1952, the petitioner, a professional boxer known as Joe Giardella, fought in a licensed match at the Madison Square Garden against Billy Graham, the second respondent. Two members of the Commission, one of whom was the chairman, were among the large crowd in the hall.

The match lasted for its scheduled ten rounds, and then the referee and two judges assigned by the Commission to officiate at the fight cast their votes to decide which of the contestants was the winner. One judge favored Graham and the referee voted for Giardella. The second judge, named Agnello, voted for Giardella, and the card upon which he tabulated his round-by-round scoring indicated that Giardella had won six rounds to Graham's four. The announcer proclaimed Giardella the winner.

The attending officers of the Commission immediately called for the records kept by the referee and judges. In the words of the Commission Chairman, he and the second Commissioner, who also witnessed the fight, "retired to a separate room and considered all the cards for about a half hour and found * * * that one of the judges, Agnello, had failed to follow the standards set forth in the Boxing Rules of the Commission * * * as to two of the rounds. Accordingly, we directed that such card be corrected to comply with the Boxing Rules, which was done." The Chairman also states that "the commissioners were informed of rumors of a betting coup with which persons surrounding the petitioner were reported to be connected." The effect of the change in Agnello's ruling as to two rounds which he had awarded to Giardella was to reverse the decision. Graham was now declared the victor; and the petition seeks to nullify this action by the Commission.

The petitioner does not "impugn in the slightest degree the high-minded motives and thoroughly honest intentions" of the Commission and acknowledges that "it acted solely for what [it] believed was the best interest of boxing and sports generally." And the respondents make no claim that in reaching his original decision Agnello was animated by any fraudulent, corrupt or other base motive. The correctness, but not the honesty, of his judgment is challenged. Of course, it is not the function of the court, employing the rules for scoring points and credits properly promulgated by the Commission (Boxing Rules, Section III), to now render a third decision as to whether Giardella or Graham won.

Before reaching the fundamental questions presented by this petition, I shall dispose quickly of the respondents' preliminary objection: namely, that Giardella had no standing to sue because, allegedly, he has suffered no injury from the action of the Commission. As in most money-making callings, a boxer's earning capacity is related to his reputation and his reputation is dependent upon his success. In the sports world the interested public follows the detailed records of individual athletes and teams with avidity. It flocks to watch the athletes with winning records; and the earnings of those athletes are related directly to the number of paying spectators they can attract. Spiritually, a professional boxer may emerge greater in defeat than in victory. Materially, however, his prestige and the purses he can command are lowered. Any action which affects his record so prejudicially of necessity impairs economic rights and interests sufficiently to give the petitioner legal standing to sue.

On the merits of the main issue, petitioner cites the statute, which provides that "There shall also be in attendance * * * two duly licensed judges who, with the referee, shall at the termination of each such boxing or sparring match or exhibition render their decision. A majority of the votes cast shall determine the winner." McK.Unconsolidated Laws, § 9123. See to the same effect Rule 23, Rules and Regulations of the Commission. No other persons are explicitly authorized by statute or rule to render a decision in a boxing match which has continued through the scheduled number of rounds. The petitioner therefore argues that the expressed statutory formula for determining a winner is an exclusive one and precludes the action of the Commission.

The Commission's powers, however, are not fathomed so superficially. In the absence of an express grant or denial of authority, the inquiry only begins with the cited provisions. Burstyn, Inc. v. Wilson, 303 N.Y. 242, 245, 251, 101 N.E.2d 665, reversed on other grounds, 343 U.S. 495, 72 S.Ct. 777, 96 L.Ed. 1098. This conclusion is underlined by the stark statutory specification that "the rules and regulations of boxing shall be prescribed by the commission," McK.Unconsolidated Laws, § 9122, and by the promulgation by the Commission of regulations so ample and encompassing in their generality that in appropriate circumstances they could comprehend the Commission's nullification, if not reversal, of the judges' or a referee's decision. See Rules, 48, 67, and 68. The question presented here cannot be resolved by recourse to language alone, without that insight into the underlying purpose and intent of the statute which is so necessary to invest the language with its real meaning. We start with the basic proposition that initially all manner of pugilistic encounters for which admission fees are charged are stamped as illegal and against public policy and any participation therein constitutes a criminal offense, Penal Law, §§ 1710–1716. So vigorous are these penal sanctions that provision is made for the arrest of any person about to participate in a prize fight, § 1715.

Inside these statutory badlands the Legislature, by enactment of the Boxing Law, has carefully charted a rigidly circumscribed area in which prize fighting can be conducted legally. The Boxing Law creates the only legal exception to the penal provisions; and unless it is complied with, all boxing activities are illegal.

The unsavory history of professional boxing in this State reveals why boxing matches and all who participate in them are by legislative policy and enactment made subject to the most inexorable and meticulous regulation, McK.Unconsolidated Laws, Title 25—sometimes referred to herein as the "Boxing Law". The Legislature was plainly apprehensive of the unwholesome influence exerted by gamblers, criminals and other disreputable persons who dominated professional boxing. Since it featured violence, the sport attracted full-blooded patrons who bet heavily on the outcome of the bouts. And since the moral stamina of pugilists, in that era at least, was often weaker than their physical stamina, many were not averse to "fixing" fights at the behest of professional gamblers. Judging from newspaper comment in 1920, the public was revolted by the sordid spectacle presented by professional boxing.

Mr. Justice Seabury, then sitting at Special Term, had this to say about an earlier law: "Two main purposes have prompted such legislation: First, the desire to prevent as far as possible certain brutal and degrading features which have in the past sometimes attended such contests, and, second, to promote and protect such contests when conducted within the legitimate limits of a sport. To achieve those purposes the state has created the Athletic Commission and authorized that Commission to prescribe stringent rules governing the conditions under which such contests can be held." Fitzsimmons v. New York State Athletic Commission, 146 N.Y.S. 117, at page 120. See also: Zwirn v. Galento, 288 N.Y. 428, 430, 43 N.E.2d 474, 475; Baksi v. Wallman, 271 App.Div. 422, 65 N.Y.S.2d 894; Casarona v. Pace, 175 Misc. 269, 22 N.Y.S.2d 726.

Evidently the Legislature decided that the public had manifested sufficient interest in prize fighting to warrant its operation—under close and rigid supervision. But it is clear that the Legislature also decided the spectator was entitled to see a fair fight. With this end in view the statute spells out an elaborate system of bonding, licensing and penalties. Even announcers, ushers, ticket takers, box office employees and special policemen as well as boxers, managers, trainers, seconds and others are included among those required to obtain licenses from the Commission, § 9107. Elaborate provisions are made for fingerprinting every applicant for a license—including officers of a corporation; and a duplicate copy "shall be filed in the office of the division of criminal identification of the department of correction at Albany * * *." § 9111. A license may be revoked upon a finding "that the licensee has, in the judgment of the commission, been guilty of an act detrimental to the interests of boxing * * *." McK.Unconsolidated Laws, § 9117; see also Rules 21 and 63.

To indicate the Legislature's continuing concern lest the criminal element infiltrate professional boxing, the statute was amended as recently as 1952 so as to make consorting with criminals, gamblers, bookmakers, etc. grounds for revocation or suspension of a license, § 9117.

These are no ordinary precautions which the Legislature and the Commission, under its grant of power from the Legislature, have taken in an endeavor to administer professional boxing honestly and cleanly. To appreciate how extraordinary they are one should imagine imposing them upon the average business or industry.

The statutory scheme seeks to insure to the spectator that the participants in a boxing match will strive honestly to the limits of their skill and that they will be judged honestly and competently. It is in this perspective that one should view the Commission's contention that it has the authority and power to change the decision of a judge or referee, to avert, as it asserts, "a fraud upon the public and one of the contestants". Considering such an assertion of power in the generality, and not in the specific setting presented by this petition, I am inclined to agree with the Commission's contention. If, as is concededly not the case here, corruption was found to have influenced a decision, it would seem that the Commission is empowered to take appropriate action, as a reasonable, possibly necessary, implementation of the legislative policy in establishing the Commission.

"Where it is difficult or impractical for the Legislature to lay down a definite, comprehensive rule, a reasonable amount of discretion may be delegated to the administrative officials." Matter of Marburg v. Cole, 286 N.Y. 202, 212, 36 N.E.2d 113, 117, 136 A.L.R. 734.

I believe the Commission has been granted sufficient power by statute to cope with alleged fraud of serious proportions, despite its unexplained failure to deal more specifically by regulation with those situations which foreseeably could arise. Cf. Securities & Exchange Comm. v. Chenery Corp., 318 U.S. 80, 63 S.Ct. 454, 87 L.Ed. 626. Such regulations would seem desirable in this administrative area to dispel any hint of anarchic administration, by advising licensees of their rights, conditioning the public to corrective measures and requiring the Commission to think through its problems in order to formulate the rules.

Given the power in justifiable circumstances, and upon a finding of facts establishing the alleged fraud, the next question is whether it could be exercised in such summary fashion. According to the Chairman, the Commissioners were alerted to a closer scrutiny of this fight by "rumors of a betting coup". Now, a rumor in the boxing world comes close to being a reality—at least in its potentiality for shaking public confidence in the integrity of professional boxing. The sport has been given a bad name because too many of such rumors have been proven true in the past, and public relations have become a real consideration. Other administrative agencies may wait until a rumor dissipates from its own emptiness or achieves some factual dignity; but the Athletic Commission should and must act immediately to destroy or confirm the rumor. A dominant legislative purpose is to secure and maintain the spectator's confidence in the honesty of every aspect of the boxing match. Indeed, the statute appears to contemplate the procedure used here. McK.Unconsol. Laws, § 9105. Rule 48 of the Commission provides: "the Commissioners and deputies * * * shall have full power to act and do all things on behalf of the Commission at any and all exhibitions * * *. Any Commissioner in attendance upon and supervising a contest or exhibition has the full power of the Commission in enforcement of the rules and regulations of the Athletic Commission".

What might be unseemly and dangerous haste by other administrators was justified, might even be required, in this case. First, as just stated, such rumors should be scotched as quickly as possible if unfounded; and prophylaxis should be applied as quickly as possible, if true. Second, it is of the essence of enjoyment of a sporting spectacle that the decision follow the event immediately. Sport followers, unlike lawyers, have no patience with reserved decisions.

The summary method in which the Commissioners acted, while it would be condemned in almost any other area of administrative jurisdiction, was appropriate here.

Finally, assuming the power to act summarily, without notice or hearing, was the action of the Commission unreasonable or arbitrary? Certainly, the existence of an unverified rumor, dark and ominous as it might loom to the future of professional boxing, would not alone justify the Commission's decision. The finding upon which the Commission relies to sustain the reasonableness of its action appears to simmer down to this: Judge Agnello made an honest mistake, which the public might misconstrue as connoting corruption—to the detriment of professional boxing. Setting aside for the moment the serious doubts as to whether the Commission had power to act as it did on this finding, I cannot find any basis in the record from which such a finding could be distilled.

The Commissioners found, on consideration of Judge Agnello's card, that he had failed to follow the standards set forth in the Boxing Rules of the Commission as to two rounds. No amplification of this conclusion is furnished. The corrections which they directed be made on that card changed the overall decision to a victory for Graham.

Again, the conduct of the Commission must be judged by their problems and functions as envisaged and apprehended by the Legislature. The adjectives "arbitrary" and "reasonable", unlike the adjectives "black" and "white", have no set meaning on all occasions. One administrator's arbitrariness may be another administrator's reasonableness, although the two actions are identical. I do not lose sight, too, of the significance of the fact that the two Commissioners personally observed the contest and based their decision on such observation. Such findings, like findings of contempt committed in the presence of the court, are difficult to translate into language, and may not be lightly overridden.

No one, least of all the petitioner, challenges the good faith of the Commissioners. With all the zeal of reformers they sought to spike the disruptive rumor—a spirit which is understandable in the light of the past history of the sport. Unfortunately, the record gives no hint of the norms employed by the Commissioners in changing the results of the two decisive rounds on Agnello's card. The sole reason given by the Commission, it will be recalled, was that Agnello "had failed to follow the standards set forth in the Boxing Rules"; and no amplification whatsoever is furnished of this conclusory statement. Of course, good faith or a well-intentioned personal rationalization of the process by which they shifted the points for those two rounds, are not enough.

The Commissioners were not presumably appointed on the basis of their expertness in judging prize fights, but because of personal stature and administrative capacity. The judges and referees, however, are in turn designated by the Commission on the basis of their specialized skill, experience and integrity in judging boxing bouts.

The scoring of a prize fight is not a routine process, like the scoring of a tennis match. The Commission's rules recite the following factors, among others, which must be taken into account by ring officials in rendering their decisions: damaging effect of blows, aggressiveness, defensive work, ring generalship and sportsmanlike actions. At best, these general standards furnish no chart for a mathematical ticking off of points. A boxing official's judgment reflects not only his perceptiveness and experience, but is inevitably colored by his own sense of prize fighting values. Therefore, a substantial scoring differential among ringside officials ordinarily excites no alarm in boxing circles and split decisions are no rarity. In the very match under discussion the Commission did not see fit to disturb the card of the referee, who like Judge Agnello, had also voted in favor of Giardella.

Therefore, the only reason advanced by the Commission for changing Judge Agnello's card, that "he had failed to follow the standards set forth in the Boxing Rules", becomes so vague as to be meaningless. No facts are furnished to buttress this conclusion; no facts to indicate why the two Commissioners chose to override the decision of their own acknowledged expert.

Even assuming the dubious premise that the Commission had the power to change the decision upon a finding that Agnello had scored honestly but incorrectly in two rounds, there is no reasonable basis in the record for such a finding. Accordingly, the petition must be granted and the action of the respondent, State Athletic Commission, in changing the vote cast by Judge Agnello is annulled.

GEORGIA HIGH SCHOOL ASS'N v. WADDELL

285 S.E.2d 7 (Ga.1981).

PER CURIAM.

On October 23, 1981, a football game was played between R. L. Osborne and Lithia Springs High Schools, members of region 5 AAAA established by the Georgia High School Association. The winner of this game would be in the play-offs, beginning with Campbell High School.

The score was 7 to 6 in favor of Osborne. With 7 minutes, 1 second, remaining in the game, Osborne had the ball on its 47 yard line, 4th down and 21 yards to go for a first down. Osborne punted but "roughing the kicker" was called on Lithia Springs. The referee officiating the game with the approval and sanction of the Georgia High School Association assessed the 15 yard penalty, placed the ball on the Lithia Springs 38 yard line, and declared it was 4th down and 6 yards to go.

The rules of the National Federation of State High School Associations provide that the penalty for roughing the kicker shall be 15 yards and 1st down. There is a dispute as to whether the Osborne coaches properly protested to the referee, before the ball was put in play, the error in the referee's failing to declare a 1st down.

From Lithia Springs' 38, Osborne punted again. Lithia Springs received the punt and drove down the field to score a field goal. Now 2 points behind, Osborne passed. Lithia Springs intercepted and scored again. The final score was Lithia Springs over Osborne, 16 to 7.

On October 26, Osborne filed a written protest with the Executive Secretary of the Georgia High School Association who is charged with making initial decisions of protests. The Executive Secretary conducted an investigation and denied the protest on November 5 on the ground that, notwithstanding the admitted error, no official protest was made to the referee by the Osborne coaches immediately following the play in question.

On appeal by Osborne to the Hardship Committee of GHSA, that committee approved the Executive Secretary's decision on November 8. On appeal, the state Executive Committee of GHSA approved the Hardship Committee's decision on November 11, 1981.

On November 12, suit was filed in the Superior Court of Cobb County by parents of Osborne players against the GHSA. Hearing was held on November 13. The court found that it had jurisdiction, found that the referee erred in failing to declare an automatic first down, and found that a protest was lodged with the proper officials of GHSA. The court found that the plaintiffs have a property right in the game of football being played according to the rules and that the referee denied plaintiffs and their sons this property right and equal protection of the laws by failing to correctly apply the rules.

The court then entered its order on November 13 cancelling the play-off game between Lithia Springs and Campbell High School scheduled for 8 p. m. that evening and ordered "that Lithia Springs High School and R. L. Osborne High School meet on the football field on November 14, 1981 at an agreed upon time between the parties and resume play at the Lithia Springs thirty eight yard line with the ball being in the possession of R. L. Osborne High School and it be first down and ten yards to go for a first down and that the clock be set at seven minutes one second to play and that the quarter be designated as the fourth quarter."

Asserting that the trial court's order was erroneous under Smith v. Crim, 240 Ga. 390, 240 S.E.2d 884 (1977), and would disrupt the play-off games not only between Lithia Springs and Campbell but succeeding play-offs, the GHSA filed a motion for supersedeas in this court on November 13, 1981, and the court entered its order suspending the trial court's order, pending further order of this court.

In Smith v. Crim, supra, we held that a high school football player has no right to participate in interscholastic sports and has no protectable property interest which would give rise to a due process claim. Pretermitting the question of "state action" which is the threshold of the 14th Amendment, we held that Smith was not denied equal protection by the rule of GHSA there involved. Similarly we find no denial of equal protection by the referee's error here. Were our decision to be otherwise, every error in the trial courts would constitute a denial of equal protection. We now go further and hold that courts of equity in this state are without authority to review decisions of football referees because those decisions do not present judicial controversies.

GARDNER v. NEW YORK RACING ASS'N, INC.

525 N.Y.S.2d 116 (App.Div.1988).

PER CURIAM.

Order entered February 2, 1987 (Fingerhood, J.) affirmed, with $10 costs.

"Everybody's got a horse story out there, but the only one worth listening to is the one in which you've cashed a ticket...." (William Murray, The Hard Knocker's Luck, Viking Penguin Inc., p. 263).

The "horse story" underlying this lawsuit is summarized as follows. Plaintiff purchased several combinations of parimutuel tickets on the "daily double" at Saratoga racetrack on August 2, 1986, including a $300 wager coupling Passing Thunder in the first race with Allumeuse, a filly entered in the second race. In fact Passing Thunder did win the first race, and no issue is raised concerning that event. In the second race Allumeuse crossed the finish line first, but was not "officially" declared the winner. Because two horses had fallen and unseated their jockeys during the running of the second race, the three presiding stewards—the individual defendants herein—made an objection immediately following the completion of the race and initiated an inquiry to determine the cause of the mishap. After reviewing a videotape of the race, the stewards disqualified Allumeuse from first place and placed her last for a foul which, defendants apparently now concede, was committed not by Allumeuse, but by a horse named Syntonic. In light of the stewards' determination, no payoff was made to those persons, plaintiff included, who held wagers on Allumeuse. The defendant New York Racing Association ("NYRA") instead distributed the "daily double" and other relevant pools among bettors presenting pari-mutuel tickets on Festivity, the horse (erroneously) declared the "official" winner of the second race. Cold comfort was provided plaintiff later that day when the stewards, having recognized and publicly acknowledged their mistake, awarded the winner's share of the second race purse money to the owner of Allumeuse.

Plaintiff thereafter commenced this action in Civil Court against the NYRA and the stewards presiding over the disputed race. The complaint sets out two causes of action, the first sounding in negligence, and the second founded upon claims of fraud and deceit. Each cause seeks $14,550 in compensatory damages, representing the projected winnings on plaintiff's dishonored pari-mutuel tickets, and punitive damages of $10,000. After joinder of issue, defendants moved to dismiss the complaint for failure to state a cause of action. The court below granted defendants' motion, and we affirm.

Under the rules and regulations of the Racing and Wagering Board, the stewards appointed to supervise a thoroughbred race meeting are accorded broad and varied powers to enforce the "Rules of the Race" (9 NYCRR Part 4035). Among these powers is the authority "to determine the extent of disqualification in case of fouls", and where a foul has occurred to "place the offending horse behind such horses as, in their judgment, it interfered with, or they may place it last. . . ." (9 NYCRR 4039.20; see, 9 NYCRR 4035.2[f]). As the regulation makes plain, the stewards' decision to disqualify Allumeuse, albeit mistaken, necessarily involved the exercise of discretion. Such a quasi-judicial determination cannot form the predicate for a civil suit, "however erroneous or wrong it may be, or however malicious even the motive which produced it." (Rottkamp v. Young, 21 A.D.2d 373, 375, 249 N.Y.S.2d 330, quoting from East River Gaslight Co. v. Donnelly, 93 N.Y. 557, 559; accord, Tango v. Tulevech, 61 N.Y.2d 34, 471 N.Y.S.2d 73, 459 N.E.2d 182; see, Turcotte v. Fell, 84 A.D.2d 535, 443 N.Y.S.2d 169).

Nor may common-law liability properly be fastened upon the defendant NYRA. The racing association is in the nature of a stakeholder responsible for the collection and distribution of the pool and, unlike a bookmaker, does not make or accept a wager or act on personal responsibility (Aliano v. Westchester Racing Assn., 265 App.Div. 225, 38 N.Y.S.2d 741; Holberg v. Westchester Racing Assn., 184 Misc. 581, 53 N.Y.S.2d 490 [AT1]). In any event, defendant NYRA was justified in distributing the "daily double" pool in accordance with the "official" announcement of the winners; indeed, it was obligated to do so. The controlling regulation is found at 9 NYCRR 4008.1, and provides: "When a result is official that word shall be flashed on the result board and shall signify that the placing of the horse is final insofar as the payoff is concerned. If any change be made in the order of finish of a race after the result is so declared official, it shall not affect the payoff...." (see, 9 NYCRR 4008.4).

Although we can readily sympathize with the plaintiff's situation, we do not think it unreasonable to require plaintiff to abide by the decision of the stewards. As the Supreme Judicial Court of Massachusetts stated in a similar context more than forty years ago: "It is common knowledge that at formal horse races there are persons in attendance who are charged with the duty of determining which horses are the winners under the terms and conditions under which a race is being conducted, much as at football or baseball games or other public contests persons are provided to act as referees or umpires. Purchasers of race tickets must be held to know this and to consent to be bound by the judgment of those regularly charged with the duty of decision," (Finlay v. Eastern Racing Association, Inc., 308 Mass. 20, 23, 30 N.E.2d 859, 861).

Notes

1. For a further look at the reluctance of courts to come to the aid of disappointed contestants, see *Crouch v. National Ass'n for Stock Car Auto Racing, Inc.*, 845 F.2d 397 (2d Cir.1988).

2. While everyone in *Tilelli* agreed Judge Agnello honestly believed Giardella had won the fight, there have been instances in which a referee has either taken or been accused of taking a payoff. *See, e.g., White v. Turfway Park Racing Ass'n*, 909 F.2d 941 (6th Cir.1990) (race track stewards), and *People v. Levy*, 128 N.Y.S.2d 275 (App.Div.1954) (professional basketball referee). As a result, a number of states have passed laws that specifically make it a crime to bribe a sports official (or to solicit or receive one while serving in such a capacity). Delaware provides a good example:

> § 703 Bribing official of sporting event.
>
> Whoever directly or indirectly gives or promises to give any money or valuable thing as a bribe, present or reward to any person acting or intending to act as a referee, umpire, judge, timer, measurer or as an official for any purpose, for any amateur or professional athletic or sporting game, match or contest with intent to induce such person to act corruptly in making decisions, rulings, interpretations or adjudications or in the performance of his official duties in connection therewith shall be fined not more than $3,000 or imprisoned not more than 3 years or both.
>
> § 704 Official of sporting event soliciting or receiving bribe.
>
> Whoever acting or intending to act as a referee, umpire, judge, timer, measurer or as an official for any purpose for any amateur or professional athletic or sporting game, match or contest, solicits or receives, directly or indirectly, any money or valuable thing, as a bribe, present or reward to act corruptly in making any decision, ruling, interpretation or adjudication or in any matter in the performance of his official duties in connection therewith shall be

fined not more than $3,000 or imprisoned not more than 3 years or both.

Del. Code Ann. tit. 28, §§ 703–704.

3. Some people, such as noted commentator Frank Deford, are convinced the quality of refereeing, particularly in professional sports, is deteriorating. Whether this is true is debatable. Clearly, as in *Waddell* and *Gardner*, mistakes happen. In addition, referees do give preferential treatment to star players and swallow their whistles at the end of a close game. On the other hand, many types of calls (e.g., deciding where the strike zone is on a particular batter) require referees to exercise their discretion and certain regulations (e.g., the NHL's "in the crease" rule) invite controversy.

4. In the space of two weeks near the end of the NFL's 1998 regular season, referees blew three crucial calls: a mistake in determining the winner of the pre-overtime coin flip allowed the Detroit Lions to beat the Pittsburgh Steelers, a questionable fourth-down catch gave the New England Patriots a win over the Buffalo Bills, and a phantom touchdown handed the New York Jets a victory against the Seattle Seahawks. In response to these gaffes, the NFL changed its coin toss rule and reinstated instant replay for the 1999 season. *See further* Thomas George, *N.F.L. Backs Limited Replay After Complaints of Bad Calls*, N.Y. Times, Mar. 18, 1999, at A1.

5. In an attempt to improve officiating in their respective leagues, in 1998 MLB, bucking more than a century of tradition, decided to transfer umpire supervision to the commissioner's office to assure a uniform strike zone and the NHL began experimenting with a two-referee format to cut down on holding. While the effect of the former change remains to be seen, the latter modification has been heavily criticized for causing too many penalties to be called. *See further* Cammy Clark, *Opinions Vary on Two-Referee System*, Orange County (CA) Register, Nov. 10, 1998, at D4.

6. In addition to the errors listed above, there have been a number of other famous blown calls since the turn of the century. In 1927 in Chicago, for example, boxing referee Dave Barry hesitated for several seconds after Jack Dempsey knocked Gene Tunney to the canvas in their much-publicized championship bout. Aided by the extra time, Tunney was able to get to his feet and went on to win what became known as the "long count" fight. In the 1972 Olympics in Munich, the United States men's basketball team beat the Soviet Union to claim its eighth consecutive gold medal. But then the judges ordered three seconds put back on the clock and the Soviets, using a long pass and a lay up, won the game 51–50. Outraged by the call, the Americans refused to accept their silver medals. In the 1986 World Cup in Mexico City, no official noticed legendary soccer player Diego Maradona had used his fist to score a goal in a quarterfinal game against England. When Argentina went on to win the tournament, the play was dubbed the "hand of God" goal. And in 1996, a hometown fan reached over the wall during the first game of the AL Championship Series and grabbed Derek Jeter's fly ball out of the hands of Baltimore Orioles right fielder Tony Tarasco. Instead of calling an out, the umpire ruled the play a home run, thereby helping propel the New York Yankees into the World Series. *See further* Mark Starr, *Hey! We Wuz Robbed!*, Newsweek, Dec. 21, 1998, at 52.

7. To protect referees from being sued over their calls, a number of states have passed statutes that grant them either partial or complete immunity for official acts taken in good faith. These laws, which often draw a distinction between volunteer and paid referees (as well as between amateur and professional sports), are discussed at length in Shlomi Feiner, *The Personal Liability of Sports Officials: Don't Take the Game Into Your Own Hands, Take Them to Court!*, 4 Sports Law. J. 213 (1997); Scott Parven, *Judgment Calls—Sports Officials in Court*, 9 ABA Ent. & Sports Law. 9 (Fall 1991); Darryll M. Halcomb Lewis & Frank S. Forbes, *A Proposal for a Uniform Statute Regulating the Liability of Sports Officials for Errors Committed in Sports Contests*, 39 DePaul L. Rev. 673 (1990); Kenneth W. Biedzynski, Comment, *Sports Officials Should Only Be Liable for Acts of Gross Negligence: Is That the Right Call?*, 11 U. Miami Ent. & Sports L. Rev. 375 (1994).

Problem 47

With the score tied and two seconds left in the championship game, a referee called a foul against State College. As a result, State lost 81–80. No one took this defeat harder than a novelty store which had laid in a supply of 5,000 t-shirts proclaiming "State College 1998 Basketball Champions." Several weeks later, the official publicly admitted he should not have assessed the penalty and apologized for having made "a stupid mistake." Based on this admission, does the store have a cause of action? *See Bain v. Gillispie*, 357 N.W.2d 47 (Iowa Ct.App.1984).

D. HAZARDS

Because of the contentious nature of their jobs, referees are subject to both physical and emotional abuse. The cases that follow provide examples.

TOONE v. ADAMS

137 S.E.2d 132 (N.C.1964).

Plaintiff appeals from an order striking certain portions of his complaint and sustaining the defendants' demurrer to the complaint as thereafter amended.

The complaint, after the motion to strike had been allowed, alleged the following facts. In June 1960 plaintiff was an umpire for the Carolina League, Inc. The defendant Raleigh Baseball, Inc., was a member of the Carolina League and, under its auspices, operated a baseball club known as the Raleigh Caps of which defendant Kenneth E. Deal was manager. On the night of June 16, 1960 plaintiff was acting as field umpire at a ball game between the Raleigh Caps and the Greensboro Yankees, both teams being members of the Carolina League. The game was being played in Raleigh and the paid attendance was 3,452. During the second inning, plaintiff had to make a decision whether a ball had been caught by a Raleigh outfielder. He ruled that the player had "trapped" the ball between his glove and the ground and thus it had not been caught. When plaintiff made this decision, defendant Deal charged onto the field and engaged in a verbal controversy with plaintiff. During the third inning plaintiff called a player of the Raleigh Caps out at first base. Again Manager Deal rushed onto the playing field and violently protested the decision. He threatened that if plaintiff made another decision with which he disagreed, he would behave in such a manner that plaintiff would be forced to eject him from the game and his ejection would result in extreme hostility towards plaintiff on the part of the partisan fans. Thereafter, during the ninth inning, plaintiff called a batter-runner safe at first base. The Raleigh players began arguing with plaintiff and defendant Deal again "charged on the field" and protested the decision. During the controversy, the Greensboro Yankees scored two runs and the man on first base advanced to second. The Raleigh players were pushing and shoving the plaintiff who requested defendant Deal to control his players. The request was deliberately disregarded. Deal cursed plaintiff and stated that plaintiff would now be forced to "run him out of the game."

Plaintiff promptly informed Deal that he was removed from the game. Before leaving the field, Deal argued and protested for approximately ten minutes. He told plaintiff that he would receive no help from him or his players in getting off the field.

When the game ended fans poured over the right field fence onto the playing field, cursing and challenging plaintiff to fight. Despite these hostile demonstrations plaintiff walked unharmed to home plate where he met his associate umpire. They proceeded to the exit from the playing field where they obtained two policemen to accompany them to the dressing room. On the way, defendant Baxter Adams, without any cause or provocation, and without warning, struck plaintiff a blow on his head thereby causing him injury.

Plaintiff alleged that the defendants Deal and Raleigh Baseball, Inc. owed him the duty to conduct themselves so as not to incite the fans against him and also to provide him with safe passage from the playing field "either by police or by other agents of the corporation" immediately after the game; that their breach of these duties proximately caused his injuries. He averred that defendants should reasonably have foreseen that Deal's arrogant conduct in charging upon the playing field and his threatening manner and attitude toward the plaintiff would incite a partisan crowd against plaintiff and result in an assault upon him by one or more persons. In conclusion, plaintiff alleged that his injuries were proximately caused by the joint "wilful, wanton, and malicious negligence of the defendants" Adams and Deal for which Raleigh Baseball, Inc. was also liable under the doctrine of respondeat superior. He prayed that he recover both compensatory and punitive damages.

In paragraph 6 of his complaint, plaintiff set out certain rules and regulations of the National Association of Professional Baseball Leagues under which the Carolina League operates. Inter alia, these rules provide that the home team shall furnish police protection sufficient to preserve order at a game; they authorize the umpire to remove managers, players, spectators, or employees from the game or field for a violation of the rules or unsportsmanlike conduct; and they declare that his "decisions which involve judgment" shall be final and that players or managers shall not object thereto. Upon motion of defendants, these rules and regulations were stricken from the complaint on the grounds that they were evidentiary. Those portions of the complaint wherein plaintiff referred to the rules were likewise stricken.

The defendant Adams filed no answer and judgment by default and inquiry was rendered against him. He is not a party to this appeal.

When the action came on for trial, defendants Deal and Raleigh Baseball, Inc. demurred ore tenus to the complaint for failure to state a cause of action in that (1) the alleged acts of Deal did not constitute a breach of any legal duty which the defendants owed to the plaintiff; (2) the facts alleged show no causal relation between the conduct of Deal and the assault by Adams; and (3) Deal could not reasonably have foreseen an assault by a spectator. The court sustained the demurrer and the plaintiff appealed.

SHARP, Justice.

The first question raised on this appeal is whether the rules and regulations of the National Association of Professional Baseball Leagues, included in the complaint as paragraph 6, were properly stricken. Plaintiff contends that the rules were properly included in the complaint because they constitute the contract which "governs the relationship between the plaintiff and the demurring defendants."

It is well settled in North Carolina that where a contract between two parties is intended for the benefit of a third party, the latter may maintain an action in contract for its breach or in tort if he has been injured as a result of its negligent performance. Gorrell v. Greensboro Water-Supply Co., 124 N.C. 328, 32 S.E. 720, 46 L.R.A. 513; Jones v. Otis Elevator Co., 234 N.C. 512, 67 S.E.2d 492; Council v. Dickerson's, Inc., 233 N.C. 472, 64 S.E.2d 551. The parties to a contract impose upon themselves the obligation to perform it; the law imposes upon each of them the obligation to perform it with ordinary care and they may not substitute a contractual standard for this obligation. A failure to perform a contractual obligation is never a tort unless such nonperformance is also the omission of a legal duty. Council v. Dickerson's, Inc., supra. The contract merely furnishes the occasion, or creates the relationship which furnishes the occasion, for the tort. Peele v. Hartsell, 258 N.C. 680, 129 S.E.2d 97; Pinnix v. Toomey, 242 N.C. 358, 87 S.E.2d 893; 12 Am.Jur., Contracts § 458; 34 N.C.L. Rev. 253.

The allegation that plaintiff was an umpire for the Carolina League, Inc., of which these defendants were members, remains in the complaint, and establishes the relationship between the parties to this appeal for the purpose of demurrer. Out of this contractual relationship a legal duty developed upon these defendants to use due care to protect the plaintiff and to refrain from endangering his personal safety while he was acting as their umpire. The inclusion of the specific rules of the Baseball League was, therefore, unnecessary to establish the relationship between these parties. Since the plaintiff, having sued in tort, must accept the standard of care prescribed by the common law, any contract provision prescribing a greater, lesser, or the same standard of care is not relevant to the issue of actionable negligence and should be stricken on motion. Pinnix v. Toomey, supra.

Therefore, paragraph 6 of the complaint was properly stricken under the rule that a complaint should not contain irrelevant or evidentiary matter. G.S. § 1–153.

This ruling, of course relates only to the pleadings. It would not necessarily determine the admissibility of the stricken rules as evidence if this case were one for the jury. Rules governing the conduct of games, workmen in industry, and the operation of private business projects have, in proper cases, been held admissible on the theory that they constitute some indication of the care required under the circumstances and are properly considered by the jury in determining whether defendants' conduct measures up to the standard of the reasonably prudent man. See Everett v. Goodwin, 201 N.C. 734, 161 S.E. 316; Annot., 50 A.L.R.2d 16.

The second question presented is whether plaintiff stated a cause of action against defendants for damages proximately caused by their breach of a duty arising out of the contractual relationship between them.

Plaintiff contends (1) that defendants breached the duty which the home team owed him as umpire, to provide adequate protection for his personal safety during and immediately after the game, and (2) that defendant Deal, acting within the scope of his employment by Raleigh Baseball, Inc., deliberately created an attitude of hostility and personal enmity towards plaintiff which aroused the partisan spectators and thereby incited Adams to commit the assault of which plaintiff complains.

For present day fans, a goodly part of the sport in a baseball game is goading and denouncing the umpire when they do not concur in his decisions, and most feel that, without one or more rhubarbs, they have not received their money's worth. Ordinarily, however, an umpire garners only vituperation—not fisticuffs. Fortified by the knowledge of his infallibility in all judgment decisions, he is able to shed billingsgate like water on the proverbial duck's back. Illustrative of this faculty is the storied conversation of three umpires who were discussing matters of mutual interest:

> Balls and strikes, said one, I call them as I see them.
>
> Balls and strikes, said the second, I call them as they are.
>
> They are not balls and strikes until I call them, decreed the third.

It is not necessary for us to decide whether a proper concern for the safety of an umpire today requires the members of the League for which he works to furnish an armed guard to protect him from the baseball public. In this case plaintiff is stymied by his allegation that two policemen and an assistant umpire were escorting him at the time he was assaulted by one irate fan out of an attendance of 3,452. How many policemen would he contend were reasonably required for his adequate protection? Hindsight may indicate that greater vigilance was required of the two who were then acting as plaintiff's escort, but it does not disclose that more were needed to protect plaintiff from the one man who assaulted him. The allegations of the complaint affirmatively disclose that the lack of police protection was not one of the proximate causes of plaintiff's injury.

We come now to the next aspect of the second question. Viewed in the light most favorable to the plaintiff, do the allegations of the complaint justify the inference that Deal's conduct was the proximate cause of Adams' assault upon the plaintiff?

The law imposes upon every person who enters upon an active course of conduct the positive duty to use ordinary care to protect others from harm and a violation of that duty is negligence. It is immaterial whether the person acts in his own behalf or under contract with another. Council v. Dickerson's, Inc., supra. An act is negligent if the actor intentionally creates a situation which he knows, or should realize, is likely to cause a third person to act in such a manner as to create an unreasonable risk of harm to another. Restatement, Torts §§ 302, 303. What is the application of this general statement of the law to the facts of this case?

"Civil liability for an assault and battery is not limited to the direct perpetrator of the act charged; it extends to any person who by any means encourages or incites that act or aids and abets it." 6 Am. Jur.2d, Assault and Battery § 128. Accordingly, all those who participate directly or indirectly in an assault and battery are jointly and severally liable therefor whether or not they were actually present when the assault was committed. However, there can be no joint liability unless there was such procurement, instigation, or incitation as constitutes, in effect, concert of action. 6 C.J.S. Assault and Battery § 27. "One is not responsible for a beating inflicted by another, however wrongful it may be, simply because he thinks the punishment deserved, or is pleased at it, or thinks well of it. He must do something more." Blue v. Christ, 4 Ill.App. 351. Plaintiff makes no allegation that there was ever any personal contact or concert of action between Deal and Adams. Apparently, the theory of plaintiff's case is that Deal attempted to incite mob action but succeeded only in inciting Adams. The allegation of the complaint is that Deal intended that his actions should create an extremely hostile feeling toward the plaintiff. However, it does not follow that he actually intended or should reasonably have anticipated that one or more persons would assault plaintiff as a result.

"One is bound to anticipate and provide against what usually happens and what is likely to happen; but it would impose too heavy a responsibility to hold him bound in like manner to guard against what is unusual and unlikely to happen or what, as it is sometimes said, is only remotely and slightly probable." Hiatt v. Ritter, 223 N.C. 262, 25 S.E.2d 756 (1943).

In Krudwig v. Koepke, 227 Wis. 1, 277 N.W. 670, plaintiff was held entitled to recover against two defendants, master and servant, for an assault by the servant when the master was "miles away." The master, as he had promised to do, paid the servant's fine when he was convicted of assault and battery in the criminal court. The court held both defendants liable in the civil action on the ground that the evidence established a conspiracy. In doing so, it made a distinction between inciting and procuring an assault: "In order that one may incite another, that is, to move another to action, to spur him on, persuade him, it is necessary that he be present at the scene of action; otherwise he is directing, ordering, or procuring. In one instance the initiative is with the actor, in the other the initiative is with the one directing, ordering or procuring. The distinction is a very narrow one * * *." Under these definitions the absent Deal could not have been guilty of inciting, and plaintiff does not contend that he procured the assault.

We have found no case in this jurisdiction or elsewhere which parallels this one, and counsel have cited us to none. The case of Ash v. 627 Bar, Inc., 197 Pa. Super. 39, 176 A.2d 137, is somewhat analogous. There, plaintiff was a patron in defendant's Bar where a shuffle-bowling game was in progress when arguments developed among the players. After plaintiff had bought one round of drinks the bartender demanded that he pay for more. When plaintiff refused, the bartender became furious and shouted, "[I]f you don't get some more money up on the bar, I'm going to beat you up." Plaintiff attempted to leave and the bartender started to run around the bar waving his hands at plaintiff. Plaintiff was knocked unconscious and seriously injured by a blow from behind. The evidence does not reveal whether the blow came from another patron or the bartender. The Court, in holding the 627 Bar, Inc. liable for plaintiff's injuries, said that it had a duty to maintain an orderly place and to protect plaintiff from assaults and insults from employees and patrons both. The court declared that the blow which plaintiff received "was a fruit of the seeds of disorder sown by the bartender" whether it was he or a patron who felled him.

However, that case is clearly distinguishable from the case at hand. There, the injury to the plaintiff occurred almost simultaneously with the violent action of the bartender who, if he did not strike plaintiff himself, surely would have in the next instant had not another done so.

The unsportsmanlike conduct of Deal which plaintiff alleges incited Adams to violence was not contemporaneous with the assault. Indeed, Adams was not present on the field while Deal was protesting the plaintiff's decision and no injury was inflicted upon plaintiff during the course of those altercations, nor was Deal present when Adams struck plaintiff. He knew nothing of Adams' intentions toward plaintiff and an appreciable length of time had elapsed since the altercation which caused plaintiff to eject Deal from the game. To say that Deal's conduct was a proximate cause of the attack on plaintiff would be pure speculation.

No one can say whether Adams' assault on plaintiff was his own reaction to the umpire's ruling, to the "rhubarb" created by Deal, to both, or whether he was merely venting pent-up emotions and propensities which had been triggered by the epithets, dares, or challenges of one or more of the 3,451 other fans attending the game.

In Bird v. Lynn, 10 B. Mon. (Ky.) 422 (1850), the defendant Bird, who lived at the home of defendants Mr. and Mrs. Jouett, "whipped the plaintiff because he was in the habit of saucing Mrs. Jouett." Apparently, in Kentucky in that day, the liability of Mr. Jouett depended on the liability of Mrs. Jouett who was not present at the time of the assault. In exonerating the Jouetts the Court used language appropriate to this case:

> As Mrs. Jouett was not present when the trespass was committed, the word encourage seems to be not sufficiently definite to express the true ground of liability. If Mrs. Jouett had directed Bird to whip or beat the plaintiff, and he had done it in consequence, this would, undoubtedly, have been an encouragement of the trespass, which would make her a party. If she had said in Bird's presence that the plaintiff was a bad boy and deserved a whipping, or that he had mistreated her, and she wished somebody would whip him, in consequence of which Bird had beaten him, this might, in some sense, have been deemed an encouragement of the trespass, and yet, unless she had used this language for the purpose or with the intention of inciting Bird to commit the act and of thus producing or procuring the trespass, we apprehend that Bird, though in fact committing the act, in consequence of what she had said, should be regarded as a mere volunteer, and that she would not be a co-trespasser on the ground of having encouraged the trespass. To make Mrs. Jouett liable as having encouraged the trespass by words used on a prior occasion, those words must have had a direct relation to the trespass, and have been calculated and intended to produce it by stimulating or exciting some person hearing them to do the act or procure it to be done. If it were sufficient that the act was done in consequence of the words spoken, then one person might be made a trespasser and even a felon against his or her consent, and by the mere rashness or precipitancy or overheated zeal of another, and the mere expression of just anger or resentment, or the statement of a fact calculated to excite indignation against an individual, and to create an opinion or desire that he should be chastised, might make the party using such expressions or making the statement liable for the inconsiderate act of another. Under the operation of such a

principle, there would be no safety except in such universal caution and reserve as is neither to be expected nor desired.

In the instant case neither we nor a jury could say that the conduct of Adams was "the fruit of the seeds of disorder" sown by Deal. At the time Adams injured plaintiff he was acting voluntarily and of his own accord. He is legally and morally responsible for his own wrongful acts, and plaintiff has obtained a default judgment against him. The mere fact that both Adams and Deal may have become simultaneously enraged with the plaintiff for the same cause does not establish a concert of action.

It would be an intolerable burden upon managers of baseball teams to saddle them with responsibility for the actions of every emotionally unstable person who might arrive at the game spoiling for a fight and become enraged over an umpire's call which the manager had protested. We hold that Adams' assault upon plaintiff was not so related to the unsportsmanlike conduct of Deal that it may be considered a natural and proximate result of it.

The judgment of the Superior Court sustaining the demurrer is

Affirmed.

WERTHEIM v. UNITED STATES TENNIS ASS'N, INC.

540 N.Y.S.2d 443 (App.Div.),
appeal denied, 547 N.E.2d 101 (N.Y.1989).

PER CURIAM.

Order of the Supreme Court, New York County (Andrew Tyler, J.), entered on or about May 22, 1987, which, inter alia, denied defendant-appellant's motion for an order setting aside the jury finding that defendant was 25% liable, unanimously reversed, on the law, the motion granted, and the complaint dismissed, with prejudice, and without costs.

In this wrongful death action, the decedent, Richard Wertheim, was struck in the groin by a tennis ball that had just been served by a top-ranked player in the U.S. Tennis Open in Flushing, New York, in 1983. At the time, Mr. Wertheim was acting as an umpire whose responsibility it was to call whether a serve was within the boundary set by the center line. He was 61 years of age and had a twenty year history of arteriosclerotic cardiovascular disease.

The fatal serve was an "ace" that landed within the boundary but cut with a spin and struck Mr. Wertheim. Eyewitnesses testified at trial that Mr. Wertheim upon being struck turned to face the backdrop, his knees buckled and his hands reached into the air and to his forehead as he fell backward. His head loudly struck the hard surface of the court. He received immediate medical attention and was hospitalized, but he died four days later. The cause of death was listed as subdural hematoma.

The theory of plaintiff's case was that defendant, the United States Tennis Association, Inc., had unreasonably enhanced plaintiff's risk of injury by requiring line umpires to stand in the "ready position" until the ball was in play. Previously linesmen, as such umpires are called, either sat in elevated chairs or stood at full height. The ready position required the linesman to lean forward with his or her hands placed on or above the knees. The purpose of the ready position was to make the linesmen look more professional and more a part of the game.

We hold that the decedent's injuries and subsequent death were not the proximate result of a breach of duty owed by defendant to the decedent. As a matter of law, a participant in a sporting event assumes the risk of injuries normally associated with the sport. See McGee v. Board of Education, 16 A.D.2d 99, 226 N.Y.S.2d 329, appeal dismissed, 12 N.Y.2d 1100, 240 N.Y.S.2d 165, 190 N.E.2d 537; Dillard v. Little League, 55 A.D.2d 477, 390 N.Y.S.2d 735, lv. to appeal denied, 42 N.Y.2d 801, 396 N.Y.S.2d 1026, 364 N.E.2d 1345. Being hit by a tennis ball is surely a risk normally associated with the sport as far as umpires are concerned. In our view, this case is controlled by the rule of Turcotte v. Fell, 68 N.Y.2d 432, 510 N.Y.S.2d 49, 502 N.E.2d 964.

In that case, the Court of Appeals held that by participating in a sporting event, the plaintiff had consented that the extent of the duty owed to him by the defendant-appellant was no greater than merely to avoid reckless or intentionally harmful conduct. Id. at 437, 510 N.Y.S.2d 49, 502 N.E.2d 964. Here, the decedent was fully aware of the risk of being hit by a ball traveling at a rate of speed in excess of one hundred and twenty miles per hour. Therefore, the claim should have been dismissed as a matter of law. See Maddox v. City of New York, 66 N.Y.2d 270, 496 N.Y.S.2d 726, 487 N.E.2d 553.

We hold as a matter of law that the requirement by defendant-appellant that umpires assume the ready position until the ball is in play was not reckless. Therefore, defendant-appellant did not breach its duty of care owed to the decedent. The "enhanced risk" cases cited by respondent are not controlling on this record. Generally the enhanced risk doctrine in sports injury cases involves fact patterns where a co-participant engages in reckless conduct causing injury to another participant. See Jackson v. Livingston Country Club, 55 A.D.2d 1045, 391 N.Y.S.2d 234. In that situation the duty to avoid reckless conduct is breached. See Turcotte v. Fell, supra. Other factual contexts have given rise to liability for sports injuries under the enhanced risk doctrine where the injury proximately resulted from risk enhancing conduct that was not inherent in the sport. See Stevens v. Central School District No. 1, 21 N.Y.2d 780, 288 N.Y.S.2d 475, 235 N.E.2d 448 (basketball player injured plunging his arm through non-safety glass in window behind net); Cole v. New York Racing Assn., 17 N.Y.2d 761, 270 N.Y.S.2d 421, 217 N.E.2d 144 (jockey thrown from horse and killed by impact with raised concrete footing on metal post along track).

We are of the opinion that if requiring the ready position did enhance the risk of injury to umpires, the degree of enhancement was marginal, and the actions of appellant in setting this requirement did not rise to the level of recklessness. For risk-enhancing conduct to be actionable, the enhancement must be substantial and the culpable conduct unreasonable. See Benitez v. City of New York, 141 A.D.2d 457, 530 N.Y.S.2d 825. The risk-enhancing conduct must also be of such a substantial nature as to constitute a breach of duty for it to be actionable. Here the applicable duty owed to the decedent was to avoid reckless or intentionally harmful conduct. Turcotte v. Fell, supra.

Even if there were a breach of duty under the circumstances presented, we would find it an extremely dubious proposition that the decedent's apparent stroke was the proximate result of the impact of the tennis ball. In light of the severity of the decedent's chronic cardiovascular disease, a condition well known to him in light of his heart attack at age forty and subsequent stroke, we can only view his decision to participate in the sports arena, albeit as a referee but nonetheless in the line of fire of speeding tennis balls, as an assumption of the further risk of aggravation of his delicate medical condition. The eye-witness testimony was consistent with the opinion of appellant's expert that the decedent suffered a stroke upon being hit by the ball.

In light of our determination, it is unnecessary to consider the other issues raised by appellant.

PARKS v. STEINBRENNER

520 N.Y.S.2d 374 (App.Div.1987).

ELLERIN, Justice.

This action for defamation brings into play one of the most colorful of American traditions—the razzing of the umpire.

The plaintiff, Dallas Parks, served as an American League baseball umpire from 1979 through 1982. He alleges that he was defamed by George Steinbrenner, principal owner of the New York Yankees, when Steinbrenner on August 29, 1982, issued a press release, excerpts of which were published in newspapers throughout the United States, criticizing Parks' abilities as an umpire. The press release, which was issued after the Yankees had played a two-game series with the Toronto Blue Jays in Toronto, Canada, on August 27th and 28th, at which Parks officiated, reads as follows:

> Judging off his last two days' performance, my people tell me that he is not a capable umpire. He is a member of one of the finest crews umpiring in the American League today, but obviously he doesn't measure up.
>
> We are making no excuse for the team's play this season, but this weekend our team has had several key injuries and for

umpire Dallas Parks to throw two of our players out of ballgames in two days on plays he misjudged is ludicrous.

This man, in my opinion, has had it in for the Yankees ever since I labeled him and several of the umpires as "scabs" because they worked the American Leagues games in 1979 during the umpires' strike.

Parks must learn that the word scab is a commonly used phrase. It is in no way meant as a personal insult. However, because he worked during the strike for baseball management does not mean he should be protected by them and annually given a job he is not capable of handling.

This less than complimentary critical assessment appears to have been the "final straw" in the rhubarb that had long simmered between the umpire and the owner and resulted in commencement of the instant action, against Steinbrenner and the Yankees, wherein plaintiff seeks damages for defamation on the ground that the press release falsely impugned his ability, competence, conduct and fairness as a baseball umpire.

In subsequently moving, pursuant to CPLR 3211(a)(7), to dismiss the complaint for failure to state a cause of action, defendants argued that the press release represented a nonactionable constitutionally protected expression of opinion. While Special Term found that the statement was "clearly expressed as an opinion", it nevertheless held that the complaint sufficiently pleaded a cause of action in defamation because the press release did not "set forth an adequate statement of facts which would support that opinion". The Court concluded that the only fact contained in the statement—i.e., that Parks expelled two Yankee players from the game—did "not in anyway support the opinions proffered" that plaintiff was incompetent and biased and, further, that no factual basis was set forth for the conclusory assertion that plaintiff misjudged plays.

We disagree with Special Term's assessment of the press release in question and find that it constituted a constitutionally protected expression of pure opinion.

In all defamation cases, the threshold issue which must be determined, as a matter of law, is whether the complained of statements constitute fact or opinion. If they fall within the ambit of "pure opinion", then even if false and libelous, and no matter how pejorative or pernicious they may be, such statements are safeguarded and may not serve as the basis for an action in defamation. (Steinhilber v. Alphonse, 68 N.Y.2d 283, 289, 508 N.Y.S.2d 901, 501 N.E.2d 550; Rinaldi v. Holt, Rinehart & Winston, Inc., 42 N.Y.2d 369, 380–381, 397 N.Y.S.2d 943, 366 N.E.2d 1299, cert. denied, 434 U.S. 969, 98 S.Ct. 514, 54 L.Ed.2d 456.) A non-actionable "pure opinion" is defined as a statement of opinion which either is accompanied by a recitation of the facts upon which it is based, or, if not so accompanied, does not imply that it is based upon undisclosed facts. Alternatively, when a defamatory statement of opinion implies that it is based upon undisclosed detrimental facts which justify the opinion but are unknown to those reading or hearing it, it is a "mixed opinion" and actionable. (Steinhilber v. Alphonse, supra, 68 N.Y.2d at 289–90, 508 N.Y.S.2d 901, 501 N.E.2d 550.) Similarly actionable as a "mixed opinion" is a defamatory opinion which is ostensibly accompanied by a recitation of the underlying facts upon which the opinion is based, but those underlying facts are either falsely misrepresented or grossly distorted. (Silsdorf v. Levine, 59 N.Y.2d 8, 462 N.Y.S.2d 822, 449 N.E.2d 716, cert. denied, 464 U.S. 831, 104 S.Ct. 109, 78 L.Ed.2d 111; Chalpin v. Amordian Press, 128 A.D.2d 81, 515 N.Y.S.2d 434.)

Determining whether particular statements, or particular words, express fact or opinion is ofttimes an exercise beset by the uncertainties engendered by the imprecision and varying nuances inherent in language. While mechanistic rules and rigid sets of criteria have been eschewed as inappropriate vehicles for the sensitive process of separating fact from opinion, reference to various general criteria has been found helpful in resolving the issue. Predominant among these is that the determination is to be made on the basis of what the average person hearing or reading the communication would take it to mean, and that significance is to be accorded the purpose of the words, the circumstances surrounding their use and the manner, tone and style with which they are used. (Steinhilber v. Alphonse, supra, 68 N.Y.2d at 290–291, 508 N.Y.S.2d 901, 501 N.E.2d 550.) An approach which was favorably commented upon in the Steinhilber case is that set forth by Judge Starr in his plurality opinion in Ollman v. Evans (750 F.2d 970 [D.C.Cir.] cert. denied, 471 U.S. 1127, 105 S.Ct. 2662, 86 L.Ed.2d 278), which enunciates four factors which should generally be considered in differentiating between fact and opinion. They are as summarized in Steinhilber, 68 N.Y.2d at 292, 508 N.Y.S.2d 901, 501 N.E.2d 550, as follows: (1) an assessment of whether the specific language in issue has a precise meaning which is readily understood or whether it is indefinite and ambiguous; (2) a determination of whether the statement is capable of being objectively characterized as true or false; (3) an examination of the full context of the communication in which the statement appears; and (4) a consideration of the broader social context or setting surrounding the communication including the existence of any applicable customs or conventions which might "signal to readers or listeners that what is being read or heard is likely to be opinion, not fact" (Ollman v. Evans, supra, at p. 983).

These factors have particular relevance to the statement here in issue which must be evaluated within the broader social context of a baseball club owner versus an umpire, and especial attention should be accorded to whether there exist any customs and conventions regarding the status of an umpire in the great American pastime which would signal to readers that what is being read is likely to be opinion not fact.

A brief historical perspective indicates that there are indeed such relevant customs and conventions. While it was an honor to be selected as the esteemed umpire in the early days of baseball, when it was known as a "gentleman's sport", that position changed markedly with the growth of professionalism in the 1870's, when the position of the umpire concomitantly declined and a lengthy history of abuse took hold. Albert G. Spalding, one of the pioneering promoters of the game, is reported to have said that by harassing umpires fans were exercising their democratic right to oppose tyrants. Baltimore manager Ned Hanlon, one of the leading strategists of the 1890's, observed that "it is impossible to prevent expressions of impatience or actions indicating dissent with the umpire's decision" and advised umpires to accept verbal abuse as part of their role. Thus, a half-century later everyone readily understood the lighthearted acceptance of General Douglas MacArthur's reported statement, on his return to America, that he was proud to have protected American freedoms, like the freedom to boo the umpire.

Since the late nineteenth century, the baseball umpire has had to tolerate extraordinary verbal abuse. Indeed, on occasion he has been the target of unlawful physical attacks by players and fans. For example, in 1940 one fan jumped out of the stands at Ebbets Field to "flatten" umpire George Magerkurth with his fists. When the fan's photograph appeared in the newspaper the next day, it was learned that he had risked more than the exercise of his "right to question the umpire"—the attacker was a paroled felon who was promptly returned to jail for violating his parole. Yet, Magerkurth, perhaps because his assailant had been imprisoned for the attack, never pressed charges for the assault. In the 1985 World Series, Pitcher Joaquin Andujar attacked umpire Don Denkinger on the field of play. Andujar was promptly fined and suspended. As in ordinary life, so in sports, the physical integrity of players, umpires, and fans are protected against unlawful intrusion.

Judges, too, have expressed their acceptance of this American tradition. In dismissing a minor league general manager's defamation action on other grounds, a federal court noted that harsh insults, especially those directed at an umpire, are accepted commonplace occurrences in baseball. (King v. Burris, 588 F.Supp. 1152, 1157, [U.S.D.C. Colorado, 1984].) The contemporary view of a baseball umpire was perhaps best summed up by the Supreme Court of North Carolina in an action brought by a minor league umpire charging a team with failing to provide adequate safety and police protection from a fan who physically assaulted him. (Toone v. Adams, 262 N.C. 403, 137 S.E.2d 132, 136, 10 A.L.R.3d 435.) The court there aptly stated:

> For present day fans, a goodly part of the sport in a baseball game is goading and denouncing the umpire when they do not concur in his decisions, and most feel that, without one or more rhubarbs, they have not received their money's worth. Ordinarily, however, an umpire garners only vituperation—not fisticuffs. Fortified by the knowledge of his infallibility in all judgment decisions, he is able to shed billingsgate like water on the proverbial duck's back (supra, 262 N.C., at 408, 137 S.E.2d 136).

When Steinbrenner's remarks are viewed in this context, it is clear that they would be perceived by the average reader as a statement of opinion, and not fact. The negative characterizations of the plaintiff umpire as "not capable", that "he doesn't measure up", that he "misjudged" plays and that his decision to "throw two of our players out of ball games" was "ludicrous" are readily understood to be the kind of "rhetorical hyperbole" that generally accompany the communication of displeasure at an umpire's "calls". While the subjective and emotional character of such sentiments is commonly recognized and construed as "opinion" rather than fact, that view is expressly emphasized upon a reading of the entire press release with its qualifying phrases of "my people tell me" and "in my opinion". Moreover, on its face, and from its tone, it is immediately evident that the statement represents the view of the owner of an embattled baseball team who is obviously chafing at "the team's [poor] play this season", which has been exacerbated by a weekend of injuries and ejections of players, and who is venting his frustrations in the venerated American tradition of "baiting the umpire". Indeed, even if the assertions in the statement implying that plaintiff was incompetent and biased in performing his duties were to be viewed as statements of fact, it is questionable whether they could be construed as defamatory—i.e., exposing the plaintiff to public contempt, ridicule, aversion and disgrace and inducing an evil opinion of him in the minds of right thinking persons (Rinaldi v. Holt, Rinehart & Winston, Inc., supra, 42 N.Y.2d at p. 370, 397 N.Y.S.2d 943, 366 N.E.2d 1299)—in light of the generally "critical" attitudes which baseball umpires, in any event, ordinarily appear to inspire in both the game's fans and its participants.

Although acknowledging that the statement in issue was "clearly expressed as an opinion", Special Term held that it was actionable because the accompanying underlying facts were found by Special Term not to adequately support the opinions proffered. That one may dispute the conclusions drawn from the specified facts is not, however, the test. So long as the opinion is accompanied by a recitation of the facts upon which it is based it is deemed a "pure opinion" and is afforded complete immunity even though the facts do not support the opinion. The rationale for this broad protection of an expression of opinion accompanied by a recitation of the facts upon which it is based is that the reader has the opportunity to assess the basis upon which the opinion was reached in order to draw his or her own conclusions concerning its validity. (Silsdorf v. Levine, supra, 59 N.Y.2d at pp. 13–14, 462 N.Y.S.2d 822, 449 N.E.2d 716.)

Here the statement appears to set forth the facts upon which defendant Steinbrenner's opinions are based. He notes that plaintiff threw out two Yankee players in two days on plays which he opines, in best partisan tradition, the umpire "misjudged". He also points to his calling Parks a "scab" during a prior umpires' strike as the reason for his belief that the umpire "has had it in for the Yankees ever since". Moreover, and of great significance, is that there is no indication or implication that his opinions as to plaintiff's competence, or the propriety of his calls, are based on some other undisclosed derogatory facts, unknown to the reader, which support those opinions. Even read in a neutral context, dehors the dynamics of the baseball world and its customs, the press release in every respect falls within the orbit of an expression of "pure opinion" which is constitutionally protected (Steinhilber v. Alphonse, supra; Silsdorf v. Levine, supra.)

The reverence which the First Amendment accords to ideas has properly resulted in the determination that, "however pernicious an opinion may seem, we depend for its correction not on the conscience of judges and juries but on the competition of other ideas". (Gertz v. Robert Welch, Inc., 418 U.S. 323, 339–340, 94 S.Ct. 2997, 3007, 41 L.Ed.2d 789.) Those competing ideas about baseball's arbiters will undoubtedly continue to abound aplenty both on the playing fields and in the sports columns, albeit not in the courtroom.

Accordingly, the Order, Supreme Court, Bronx County (Alfred J. Callahan, J.), entered May 9, 1986, which denied the defendants' motion to dismiss the complaint and supplemental complaint for failure to state a cause of action, should be reversed, on the law, and the complaint dismissed, without costs.

Notes

1. Because of attacks like the one in *Toone*, some states now have statutes which make it a crime to assault, injure, or otherwise physically harm a referee. For a discussion of such laws, see Troy Cross, *Assaults on Sports Officials*, 8 Marq. Sports L.J. 429 (1998); Christopher M. Chiafullo, Comment, *From Personal Foul to Personal Attack: How Sports Officials Are the Target of Physical Abuse From Players, Coaches and Fans Alike*, 8 Seton Hall J. Sports L. 201 (1998); Carole J. Wallace, Comment, *The Men in Black and Blue: A Comment on Violence Against Sports Officials and State Legislative Reaction*, 6 Seton Hall J. Sports L. 341 (1996); Robert Lipsyte, *When 'Kill' the Ump is No Longer a Joke*, N.Y. Times, Jan. 19, 1997, § 8, at 1. *See also Carroll v. State*, 620 P.2d 416 (Okla.Ct.Crim.App.1980) (declaring such legislation to be constitutional).

2. As the court in *Wertheim* makes clear, referees generally are thought to assume the same risk as players. This is not always the case, however, especially in suits against insurers. In *Clermont Central Soccer Ass'n v. Cincinnati Insurance Co.*, 676 N.E.2d 1281 (Ohio Ct.C.P.1995), for example, a soccer referee was injured when he ran into a group of players who had turned away from the ball. When he sued, the insurer declined coverage because the policy excluded injuries to "participants." Finding the term to be ambiguous, the court ruled participants included only players.

3. Unlike Dallas Parks, most officials simply ignore criticism. One even has turned it to his advantage. Inspired by the classic children's nursery rhyme, an NHL referee named Paul Stewart in 1991 created a logo featuring three blind mice dressed as hockey referees. Today, his whimsical design appears on a best-selling line of clothing. *See further Three Blind Mice Designs Co. v. Cyrk, Inc.*, 892 F.Supp. 303 (D.Mass.1995).

4. In addition to injuries to their bodies and reputations, officials also sometimes sue for injuries to their pocketbooks. *See, e.g.*, *Barnett v. Topps Co.*, 1998 WL 387593 (E.D.Pa.1998) (suit by MLB umpires for alleged misappropriation of their likenesses by baseball trading card company).

Problem 48

When a referee died as a result of a grueling road trip, his fiancee sued the league for intentionally causing *her* emotional distress. If the defendant moves to dismiss on the ground it owed her no duty of care, how should the court rule? *See Hickey v. National League of Professional Baseball Clubs*, 565 N.Y.S.2d 65 (App.Div.1991).

E. GAME CONTROL

Referees are expected to keep control of the game they are officiating. Although failing to do so usually results in nothing more serious than a sloppy contest and a chorus of boos, it sometimes also clears a path to the courthouse.

KLINE v. OID ASSOCIATES, INC.

609 N.E.2d 564 (Ohio Ct.App.),
appeal denied, 600 N.E.2d 678 (Ohio 1992).

COOK, Judge.

Kevin Kline appeals the lower court's granting of summary judgment in favor of Jack Mercer, OID Associates ("OID"), and Force Fitness Institute ("FFI"). We affirm.

On March 17, 1989, Kline was injured during a co-ed adult indoor soccer game which was held at Springside Racquet and Fitness Center. The two teams were playing aggressively. At one point, with about four minutes left in the game, a physical altercation occurred between some of the players on both teams. Mercer, the referee, ejected the goalie on Kline's team from the game. As a result, Kline took the goalie position. The game continued at high intensity. With less than one minute left, James Moore, a player on the opposing team, attempted to make a goal, which Kline blocked by diving to the side and covering the ball with his body. Moore thereafter attempted either to kick the ball or to intentionally kick Kline. As a consequence of Moore's action, Kline suffered a broken wrist and elbow.

Kline filed a complaint against Moore, Mercer, OID (the owner of the facility where the game was played) and FFI (the organizer of the soccer league), alleging that his injuries were caused by their negligent, intentional or reckless conduct. Mercer, OID, and FFI filed motions for summary judgment. The trial court granted summary judgment in favor of Mercer, OID and FFI, stating that there were no material issues of fact. Kline now appeals.

In a case involving one player against another, the Supreme Court of Ohio determined that before a party may proceed with a cause of action involving injury resulting from a recreational or sports activity, reckless or intentional misconduct must exist. Marchetti v. Kalish (1990), 53 Ohio St.3d 95, 99–100, 559 N.E.2d 699, 702–704. Whether the game is organized, unorganized, supervised or unsupervised, the standard of liability remains the same. Id. at 98, 559 N.E.2d at 702. Such a standard strikes a balance between encouraging vigorous and free participation in recreational or sport activities while ensuring the safety of the players. Id. at 99, 559 N.E.2d at 702. The same logic and standard should apply to nonparticipants involved in the game, unless there is evidence of negligent supervision. To successfully state a cause of action under the theory of negligent supervision, the party must produce evidence such as a defendant allowing a player with a known propensity toward violence to play or allowing a team to play when there was a total absence of management. Brown v. Day (1990), 68 Ohio App.3d 447, 449, 588 N.E.2d 973, 974, citing Hanson v. Kynast (1986), 24 Ohio St.3d 171, 179, 24 OBR 403, 410, 494 N.E.2d 1091, 1098 (Holmes, J., concurring).

In his response to the motion for summary judgment, Kline failed to sufficiently raise the issue that his injuries were a result of the recklessness or intentional acts of the parties, or that the parties were negligent in their supervision of the game. He stated: "* * * a strong argument could be made that [FFI's conduct] amounted to recklessness," but did not make the argument. With regard to OID, Kline stated: "although it has not yet been shown that Defendant OID or its agents had direct knowledge of the extreme aggressiveness of the game, the fact that it occurred on the premises with a manager on duty in charge of supervising the facility indicates that Defendant OID, at least through one of its agents, should have known of it." Once again, there is no evidence of recklessness or intentional misconduct on the part of the defendant. Nor is there a material issue as to negligent supervision because Kline did not present any evidence that OID, FFI, or their agents, knew that Moore or his team members had a propensity for violence or were likely to intentionally cause injury. Brown, supra; Nganga v. College of Wooster (1989), 52 Ohio App.3d 70, 557 N.E.2d 152. Kline argued that Referee Mercer "should have known that the continuation of the game would create an unreasonable risk of harm to the participants," but failed to provide any evidence that Referee Mercer had superior knowledge to Kline's or the other players' and either recklessly or negligently allowed the game to be continued.

From the evidence presented, it appears that Kline, with his thirty years of soccer experience, had at least as much knowledge of any potential for injury in the game as appellees. If it was so obvious that the level of play was too dangerous, Kline could have elected not to play. By continuing to play, Kline assumed the ordinary risks of the game, including the possibility of being injured. Marchetti, supra, 53 Ohio St.3d at 100, 559 N.E.2d at 704. Getting kicked is a common occurrence in soccer, because of the closeness of the players who are also trying to kick or block the ball. See, generally, Thompson v. McNeill (1990), 53 Ohio St.3d 102, 106, 559 N.E.2d 705, 709.

Kline failed to establish that the appellees knew that the game involved any risk greater than the ordinary risk a player assumes when he plays soccer. Nor did he show that his injuries were a result of intentional conduct or recklessness on the part of appellees. Accordingly, his assignments of error are overruled and the judgment of the lower court is affirmed.

SANTOPIETRO v. CITY OF NEW HAVEN

682 A.2d 106 (Conn.1996).

BORDEN, Associate Justice.

This appeal arises out of injuries incurred by a spectator at a softball game. The issues are whether: (1) the plaintiffs' failure to file a motion to set aside the verdict limits the scope of our appellate review to plain error; (2) the trial court improperly directed a verdict in favor of the defendant umpires; and (3) the trial court improperly granted a motion in limine to preclude evidence of bystander emotional distress. We affirm the judgment of the trial court.

Certain facts are not in dispute. On October 16, 1988, the plaintiffs attended a softball game played at East Shore Park in New Haven by teams belonging to an organized league. The defendants David Brennan and Bruce Shepard served as the umpires for that game. The defendant Mark Piombino was a participant in the game.

The plaintiff Raymond Santopietro, Jr., observed the softball game from a position behind the backstop and was not on the field of play. The plaintiff Raymond Santopietro, Sr., was approximately ten to fifteen feet from his son watching another game being played on an adjacent field.

In the sixth inning, Piombino came to bat in the game that Santopietro, Jr., was watching and hit a fly ball. In frustration, he intentionally flung his bat toward the backstop. Somehow the bat passed through the backstop and struck Santopietro, Jr., in the head. As a result, Santopietro, Jr., suffered a fractured skull and other serious injuries.

Both Santopietro, Jr., and Santopietro, Sr., appeal from the judgment of the trial court, Hon. John C. Flanagan, state trial referee, in favor of the defendants rendered following the court's granting of a motion in limine precluding the claim of Santopietro, Sr., for bystander emotional distress, and following a directed verdict in favor of Brennan and Shepard on Santopietro, Jr.'s claim of negligence. Thereafter, the jury rendered a verdict in favor of Santopietro, Jr., against Piombino.

The plaintiffs did not file a postverdict motion, either to set aside the directed verdict in favor of Brennan and Shepard, or in any way raising again the ruling of the court on the motion in limine regarding the claim of Santopietro, Sr., for bystander emotional distress. The trial court rendered judgment for Brennan and Shepard, and for Santopietro, Jr., against Piombino. This appeal followed.

Santopietro, Jr., claims that the trial court improperly directed a verdict for Brennan and Shepard on his claim against them. Santopietro, Sr., claims that the trial court improperly ruled against his claim for bystander emotional distress. We affirm the judgment of the trial court in both respects.

The plaintiffs first challenge the trial court's order directing a verdict in favor of Brennan and Shepard. The plaintiffs argue that the evidence that they produced, viewed in the light most favorable to them, would have permitted a jury reasonably to conclude that Brennan and Shepard had breached a cognizable duty to the plaintiffs, causing them injury.

"The standard of review of directed verdicts is well settled. A directed verdict is justified if on the evidence the jury could not reasonably and legally have reached any other conclusion.... In reviewing the trial court's action in directing a verdict ... we must consider the evidence in the light most favorable to the plaintiff.... This court has repeatedly stated that directed verdicts are not favored." (Citations omitted; internal quotations marks omitted.) Berry v. Loiseau, 223 Conn. 786, 819–20, 614 A.2d 414 (1992).

A review of the evidence in the light most favorable to the plaintiffs indicates that the jury might reasonably have found the following facts. During the course of the game that Santopietro, Jr., was watching when he was injured, there occurred several incidents of unruly behavior by players who were on the same team as Piombino. Some players used vulgar language in a loud and angry manner. Players taunted members of the other team in an attempt to intimidate them. Players threw their gloves and kicked the dirt, and one player kicked a garbage can, upsetting its contents and creating a loud noise. After his turn at bat resulted in an out, another player angrily threw a bat along the ground in the direction of the bats not in use. Another player threw his glove from the pitcher's mound into the dugout. A player inside the dugout repeatedly banged a bat against the dugout, producing a loud noise. Furthermore, the jury could have inferred from the evidence presented that Brennan and Shepard were aware or reasonably should have been aware of these incidents.

After passing a written examination, Brennan and Shepard were both trained and approved to be softball umpires by the Amateur Softball Association (association), a national organization that regulates the conduct of organized amateur softball in the United States. Both Brennan and Shepard possessed years of experience and had umpired hundreds of games. Shepard had received an award honoring him for being the best umpire in New Haven. Brennan testified that, as an umpire, he possesses specialized knowledge about softball and softball rules that is greater than the average person's knowledge. Both Brennan and Shepard were familiar with the association's rules governing the conduct of umpires.

Brennan and Shepard testified that when they observed unsportsmanlike conduct, they would issue a warning and, if the warning was disregarded, they would eject the player from the game. Specifically, they testified that they would have taken such action if they had observed the disruptive behavior described by several witnesses, including taunting, loud swearing, kicking a garbage can, hitting the inside of the dugout with a bat, or throwing a glove from the pitcher's mound into the dugout.

Brennan and Shepard further testified that when they give a warning, it usually has the effect of stopping the disruptive behavior and preventing future improper acts. They testified that any player who tosses a bat should be ejected immediately, and Brennan testified that if he had seen a player toss a bat as described by the witnesses, he would have ejected that player without warning. They testified that such disciplinary action is an effective means by which to control the actions of players.

Shepard testified that, as an umpire, he had the duty to maintain control of the game to prevent harm to spectators, and that warnings constitute the primary means by which to maintain that control. Moreover, Brennan testified that umpires have the authority to suspend the game if necessary to keep order or to prevent harm to spectators.

Brennan and Shepard also testified that the decision of whether to impose discipline in any given instance of unruly behavior is a discretionary matter for the umpire. Brennan testified that the rule against unsportsmanlike conduct gives the umpire authority "at his discretion, to disqualify any player who exhibits unsportsmanlike conduct in the judgment of the umpire." He further testified that decisions whether to take disciplinary action in response to loud swearing, throwing a glove or kicking dirt "are umpire judgment or umpire discretion calls." Shepard testified that the question of whether unruly behavior, such as using loud and abusive language, throwing a glove or kicking a garbage can, constitutes unsportsmanlike conduct will depend on the particular situation. Shepard further testified that the determination of whether unsportsmanlike conduct has occurred sometimes depends upon "the whole tenor of what is going on, the language, plus the gloves, plus whether it's considered taunting or not." Similarly, Brennan testified that "[t]here are a lot of variables that go into" determining whether unsportsmanlike conduct has occurred.

Brennan further testified concerning the subjective nature of the decision whether to discipline a player for unsportsmanlike conduct. Specifically, he stated that "the majority of the time you'll find that umpires are former players, and umpires will use the term unsportsmanlike conduct as some type of action which, had I been a player, I wouldn't like done to me, I wouldn't let another group do it to another player."

We note that this testimony confirms what is the common understanding of the umpire's task. In the absence of exceptional circumstances, a softball umpire, when confronted with unruly behavior by a player that arguably constitutes unsportsmanlike conduct, faces a spectrum of discretionary options. At one end of the spectrum is taking no action; at the other end is ejection of the player or suspension of the game. In between are warnings and other appropriate disciplinary action. The umpire has discretion, within the spectrum, to respond to the offensive behavior in the manner that the umpire finds to be most appropriate in the given circumstances.

The trial court directed a verdict in favor of Brennan and Shepard reasoning, in part, that if a duty exists, expert testimony was required to establish a breach of that duty and that such a breach caused the harm to the plaintiffs. The trial court concluded further that the standard of care applicable to an umpire, whether that standard was breached, and whether that breach caused the plaintiffs' injuries are not matters of common knowledge. We conclude that the plaintiffs were required to establish by expert testimony that the failure of Brennan and Shepard to act in the present case constituted a breach of duty, and that the plaintiffs' evidence did not satisfy that burden.

"A breach of duty by the defendant and a causal connection between the defendant's breach of duty and the resulting harm to the plaintiff are essential elements of a cause of action in negligence." Catz v. Rubenstein, 201 Conn. 39, 44, 513 A.2d 98 (1986); see RK Constructors, Inc. v. Fusco Corp., 231 Conn. 381, 384, 650 A.2d 153 (1994) ("essential elements of a cause of action in negligence are well established: duty; breach of that duty; causation; and actual injury"). A motion for a directed verdict is properly granted if the jury could not reasonably and legally have found that the plaintiff had proved each of these elements. "A directed verdict is justified if ... the evidence is so weak that it would be proper for the court to set aside a verdict rendered for the other party." (Citations omitted.) Boehm v. Kish, 201 Conn. 385, 389, 517 A.2d 624 (1986).

"The existence of a duty is a question of law and [o]nly if such a duty is found to exist does the trier of fact then determine whether the defendant violated that duty in the particular situation at hand. Petriello v. Kalman, 215 Conn. 377, 382–83, 576 A.2d 474 (1990). If a court determines, as a matter of law, that a defendant owes no duty to a plaintiff, the plaintiff cannot recover in negligence from the defendant." (Internal quotation marks omitted.) RK Constructors, Inc. v. Fusco Corp., supra, 231 Conn. at 384–85, 650 A.2d 153.

If the determination of the standard of care requires knowledge that is beyond the experience of an ordinary fact finder, expert testimony will be required. Jaffe v. State Dept. of Health, 135 Conn. 339, 349, 64 A.2d 330 (1949); Sickmund v. Connecticut Co., 122 Conn. 375, 379, 189 A. 876 (1937); Slimak v. Foster, 106 Conn. 366, 368, 138 A. 153 (1927); Matyas v. Minck, 37 Conn.App. 321, 326, 655 A.2d 1155 (1995); see State v. McClary, 207 Conn. 233, 245, 541 A.2d 96 (1988) (expert testimony required in criminal case because nature and cause of victim's injuries "manifestly beyond the ken of the average trier of fact, be it judge or jury").

We note that the plaintiffs' claims in the present case are akin to allegations of professional negligence or malpractice, which we have previously defined as "the failure of one rendering professional services to exercise that degree of skill and learning commonly applied under all the circumstances in the community by the average prudent reputable member of the profession with the result of injury, loss, or damage to the recipient of those services." (Internal quotation marks omitted.) Davis v. Margolis, 215 Conn. 408, 415, 576 A.2d 489 (1990). As Brennan testified, he possesses specialized knowledge as an umpire that is greater than the average person's knowledge. An umpire obtains, through formal training and experience, a familiarity with the rules of the sport, a technical expertise in their application, and an understanding of the likely consequences of officiating decisions. As a result, the umpire possesses knowledge of the standard of care to which an umpire reasonably may be held, and of what constitutes a violation of that standard, that is beyond the experience and ken of the ordinary fact finder.

Moreover, the fact finder's lack of expertise is exacerbated by the highly discretionary nature of the umpire's task. Thus, the fact finder must determine, not just whether in hindsight the umpire erred, but also whether the umpire's error constituted an abuse of his broad discretion. In such cases in which the fact finder's decision requires specialized knowledge, expert testimony is necessary "to assist lay people, such as members of the jury and the presiding judge, to understand the applicable standard of care and to evaluate the defendant's actions in light of that standard." Id., at 416, 576 A.2d 489; see, e.g., Barrett v. Danbury Hospital, 232 Conn. 242, 252, 654 A.2d 748 (1995) (medical malpractice); Davis v. Margolis, supra, at 416, 576 A.2d 489 (legal malpractice); Matyas v. Minck, supra, 37 Conn.App. at 327, 655 A.2d 1155 (negligence of engineer).

In the present case, the plaintiffs do not articulate clearly the umpire's duty upon which they base their claim. The plaintiffs principally rely upon the testimony of Shepard that an umpire's duty is "to maintain control on the field so it does not spill over to spectators." Thus, the plaintiffs appear to postulate a duty owed by the umpires to maintain control of the game in such a way as to prevent harm to others. On appeal, Brennan and Shepard do not concede that such a duty exists, but argue that even if we were to assume its existence, the plaintiffs failed to define the duty. Our research indicates that no other jurisdiction has explicitly considered whether to impose or how to define such a legal duty.

The plaintiffs also rely upon the answer by Brennan and Shepard to the complaint in which they admitted that their "duties at the game at which the plaintiff was injured included preventing disruptive and dangerous behavior, such as throwing of baseball bats." We are not bound, however, by this pleading admission or their testimony concerning their duty to maintain control of the game for two reasons. First, the determination of whether a duty exists to support tort liability is a question of law to be decided by the court. RK Constructors, Inc. v. Fusco Corp., supra, 231 Conn. at 384–85, 650 A.2d 153. Second, umpires cannot, as a matter of law, possibly bear such a duty, taken literally, as this concession suggests, namely, to prevent altogether the occurrence of disruptive and dangerous behavior. The umpires' duty, if it exists, cannot exceed the requirement to take reasonable measures to deter the occurrence of such behavior.

Therefore, for the purposes of this appeal, we assume, without deciding, that umpires such as Brennan and Shepard have a duty, essentially as postulated by the plaintiffs, to exercise reasonable judgment as umpires in order to maintain control of a game so as to prevent an unreasonable risk of injury to others. The breach of this duty, however, must be proved, in the absence of exceptional circumstances, by expert testimony establishing that the allegedly negligent action or failure to act by the umpire constituted an abuse of the umpire's discretion to evaluate the particular circumstances and to take only such disciplinary action as the umpire deems appropriate. Moreover, the expert testimony must establish an abuse of that discretion sufficient to permit a jury to infer that the umpire's action or failure to act constituted such a loss of control of the game as to give rise to an unreasonable risk of injury to the plaintiff.

In fact, in the present case, the plaintiffs concede that expert testimony was required to establish whether the applicable standard of care was breached by Brennan and Shepard. The plaintiffs argue that, through the testimony of Brennan and Shepard, they presented sufficient positive evidence of an expert nature from which the jury could have reasonably concluded that Brennan and Shepard were negligent.

We have previously held that the plaintiff in a medical malpractice action may prove the proper standard of care and its breach through the testimony of the defendant. Console v. Nickou, 156 Conn. 268, 273–74, 240 A.2d 895 (1968); Snyder v. Pantaleo, 143 Conn. 290, 294–95, 122 A.2d 21 (1956). Similarly, in the present case, the record reveals that the testimony of Brennan and Shepard constituted expert testimony through which the plaintiffs might have established negligence. Moreover, Brennan and Shepard, as expert witnesses, were not required specifically to have expressed an opinion that they breached the standard of care in order for the plaintiffs to prevail. Console v. Nickou, supra, at 273–75, 240 A.2d 895; Snyder v. Pantaleo, supra, at 294–95, 122 A.2d 21. Rather, the plaintiffs need only have produced sufficient expert testimony to permit the jury reasonably to infer, on the basis of its findings of fact, that Brennan and Shepard breached the standard of care.

For example, in Console v. Nickou, supra, 156 Conn. at 273, 240 A.2d 895, the defendant physician testified that the applicable standard of care would be breached if a physician left a needle in a patient's body after surgery. Although the physician did not testify that he breached the standard of care, we concluded that his testimony, when applied to the facts of the case, was sufficient to permit the jury reasonably to conclude that the standard of care had been breached. Id., at 273–75, 240 A.2d 895; see also Snyder v. Pantaleo, supra, 143 Conn. at 294–95, 122 A.2d 21 (although plaintiff patient presented no expert opinion that defendant physician was negligent, jury could have found that facts established breach of duty on basis of physician's testimony concerning proper standard of care).

We conclude, in the present case, that the plaintiffs failed to produce sufficient evidence that Brennan and Shepard had breached the applicable standard of care. Brennan and Shepard testified that unsportsmanlike conduct is prohibited and that it is appropriate for an umpire to take action to prevent or stop such conduct. They further testified that the umpire possesses the authority to warn players, eject them or suspend the game if necessary to deter unsportsmanlike conduct or to maintain control of a game. Moreover, when questioned about specific incidents that allegedly had occurred during the game at which Santopietro, Jr., was injured, Brennan and Shepard testified that if they had seen the incidents described by the witnesses, they would have taken some disciplinary action. They also testified, however, that the umpire possesses discretion in the application of the rule prohibiting unsportsmanlike conduct and that the decision whether to take some action against a player is made according to the judgment of the umpire based on the specific circumstances. Neither Brennan nor Shepard testified that, in the specific circumstances of that game, a reasonable umpire would have been required to take action in response to those incidents, or that it would have been unreasonable for an umpire not to have taken such action. In other words, their testimony that, in the exercise of their discretion, they would have taken action does not establish that a failure to act constituted a breach of the standard of care.

The plaintiffs did present evidence that, arguably, would support the conclusion that Brennan and Shepard improperly failed to act in response to two incidents. First, witnesses testified that a player tossed a bat toward other bats after an unsuccessful plate appearance. Brennan and Shepard testified that the local rule required them to eject immediately any player who throws a bat. Brennan further testified that the incident described by the witnesses would "merit an ejection." If we were to interpret this testimony to constitute an expert opinion that a reasonable umpire must have ejected the player in those circumstances, then this evidence would support the conclusion that Brennan and Shepard improperly failed to act with respect to that particular incident. Second, a witness testified that some players taunted members of the other team. Shepard testified that an umpire should take immediate action in response to taunting. Brennan and Shepard do not dispute the plaintiffs' evidence that they did not take any disciplinary action during the game.

The testimony of Brennan and Shepard concerning these two incidents supports a possible conclusion that they failed to exercise their discretion in a reasonable manner on two occasions during the game. The plaintiffs do not contend, however, that these two incidents suffice to establish that Brennan and Shepard breached a duty, which we assume exists, to maintain control of the game in order to prevent unreasonable risk of harm to others. The plaintiffs do not argue, and we do not assume, that Brennan and Shepard possess a duty to make every discretionary call that arises during the course of the game error free. Umpire liability, if it were to exist, must be predicated on facts sufficient to support the conclusion that their unreasonable actions or failure to act led to such a loss of control of the game as to imperil unreasonably the safety of others. We conclude, as a matter of law, that these two incidents of arguably negligent behavior are not sufficient to support such a conclusion.

We conclude, therefore, that the plaintiffs have failed to prove by expert testimony that Brennan and Shepard breached a duty of care to prevent an unreasonable risk of the injuries suffered by Santopietro, Jr. Because the jury could not have reasonably and legally concluded that the plaintiffs had established the elements of a negligence cause of action, a directed verdict was properly granted.

As a result of our conclusion that the plaintiffs did not establish negligence on the part of Brennan and Shepard, we do not reach the claim of Santopietro, Sr., that the trial court improperly precluded his claim for bystander emotional distress.

Notes

1. As explained earlier, some states now have laws which immunize referees from suits based on their official conduct. In *Rolison v. City of Meridian*, 691 So.2d 440 (Miss.1997), for example, such a statute was used to dismiss an action brought by a softball player against umpires who failed to keep another player from throwing a bat at him.

2. Although courts in the United States have been reluctant to hold referees liable for injuries resulting from loss of control, in *Smoldon v. Whitworth* (1996), an unreported case, an English appeals court affirmed a finding of liability against a rugby referee. Within one year of the decision, insurance premiums had increased an average of six percent. *See further* Martin Baker, *Sporting Chance Can Lead to Court*, (London) Daily Telegraph, Aug. 2, 1997, at 13.

Problem 49

During a high school basketball game a player was attacked by a member of the opposing team. As a result, his parents sued the school district, arguing the referees had a duty to protect their son. If the district moves to have the suit dismissed on the ground that it did not hire the officials, how should the court rule? *See Kennel v. Carson City School District*, 738 F.Supp. 376 (D.Nev.1990).

Chapter 9

REPORTERS

A. OVERVIEW

Nearly everything the average fan knows about sports comes from the media. As a result, journalists wield enormous power. This has led to two hotly-debated questions: 1) what right does the press have to obtain information from (and about) sports figures?; and, 2) what standards must it observe when reporting on these individuals?

B. ACCESS

Sports reporters need to be able to speak to a variety of individuals, including players, coaches, and owners. As will be seen, this requirement has led to numerous lawsuits.

1. GRANTED

Sports figures give interviews to curry favor with the public and put their own spin on the news. Of course, things do not always work out as hoped.

VIRGIL v. TIME, INC.

527 F.2d 1122 (9th Cir.1975),
cert. denied, 425 U.S. 998 (1976).

MERRILL, Circuit Judge.

This suit was brought in California state courts by appellee, [Mike] Virgil, complaining of a violation of his right of privacy. It was removed to federal court by appellant, Time, Incorporated, on grounds of diversity. This interlocutory appeal, taken pursuant to 28 U.S.C. § 1292(b), is from an order of the district court denying the motion of appellant for a summary judgment.

The facts are stated by the district court in its memorandum decision as follows:

> The complaint is based upon an article that appeared in the February 22, 1971, issue of Sports Illustrated magazine (owned

by appellant), entitled "The Closest Thing to Being Born." The article concerned the sport of body surfing as practiced at the "Wedge," a public beach near Newport Beach, California, reputed to be the world's most dangerous site for body surfing. The article attempted to describe and explore the character of the unique breed of man who enjoys meeting the extreme hazards of body surfing at the Wedge.

Plaintiff is well known as a constant frequenter of the Wedge and is acknowledged by body surfers there to be the most daredevil of them all. He was extensively interviewed by Thomas Curry Kirkpatrick, the author of the article, and much of the information obtained from these interviews was used in the Sports Illustrated story. Photographs showing plaintiff surfing and lying on the public beach were taken and used to illustrate the article.

Plaintiff admits that he willingly gave interviews to Kirkpatrick and that he knew that his name and activities as a body surfer might be used in connection with a forthcoming article in Sports Illustrated. But plaintiff now alleges that he "revoked all consent" upon learning that the article was not confined solely to testimonials to his undoubted physical prowess.

The article complained of was written by Kirkpatrick, a Sports Illustrated staff writer. In the summer of 1969 he received authorization from the senior editor of the magazine to do a story about the Wedge and the men who surf there. He was supplied with names and information about prominent body surfers, including the plaintiff, by the Beverly Hills bureau of Time, Inc. He began researching the article that summer, and contacted many surfers at the Wedge. Through these sources Kirkpatrick heard about the plaintiff and his daredevil attitude toward body surfing and life in general. He returned to the Newport Beach area the following summer to complete his research. It was during this period that Kirkpatrick first met the plaintiff and conducted several interviews with him.

The photographs complained of were taken by a local free-lance photographer who was commissioned by the defendants to photograph the Wedge and the body surfers. The photographer arranged, through one of the surfers, to have a group of surfers, including the plaintiff, come to the Wedge to have their pictures taken in connection with the article.

Before publication the Kirkpatrick article was checked and researched by another Sports Illustrated staff member. For that purpose the checker telephoned the plaintiff's home and verified some of the information with the plaintiff's wife. The checker also talked to the plaintiff concerning the article, at which point for the first time, the plaintiff indicated his desire not to be mentioned in the article at all, and that he wanted to stop the story. While not disputing the truth of the article or the accuracy of the statements about him which it contained, and while admitting that he had known that his picture was being taken, the plaintiff indicated that he thought the article was going to be limited to his prominence as a surfer at the Wedge, and that he did not know that it would contain references to some rather bizarre incidents in his life that were not directly related to surfing.

In spite of the plaintiff's expressed opposition to the article, the article was published following its approval by the editorial staff and legal counsel for Sports Illustrated. In its published form, the article is eleven pages long and contains approximately 7,000 words. The article refers by name to many people who surf at the Wedge, and concludes in the last two pages with an account of the plaintiff's daredevil feats at the Wedge and a series of anecdotes about him that emphasize the psychological characteristics which presumably explain the reckless disregard for his own safety which his surfing demonstrates.

Along with the photographs of the plaintiff, he complains of these references to incidents in his private, or non-surfing, life. E.g.: "He is somewhat of a mystery to most of the regular personnel, partly because he is quiet and withdrawn, usually absent from their get-togethers, and partly because he is considered to be somewhat abnormal." "Virgil's carefree style at the Wedge appears to have emanated from some escapades in his younger days, such as the time at a party when a young lady approached him and asked where she might find an ashtray. 'Why, my dear, right here,' said Virgil, taking her lighted cigarette and extinguishing it in his mouth. He also won a small bet one time by burning a hole in a dollar bill that was resting on the back of his hand. In the process he also burned two holes in his wrist."

The article quoted a statement Virgil made to the author about a trip to Mammoth Mountain: "I quit my job, left home and moved to Mammoth Mountain. At the ski lodge there one night I dove headfirst down a flight of stairs—just because. Because why? Well, there were these chicks all around. I thought it would be groovy. Was I drunk? I think I might have been."

The article quotes Virgil as saying: "Every summer I'd work construction and dive off billboards to hurt myself or drop loads of lumber on myself to collect unemployment compensation so I could surf at the Wedge. Would I fake injuries? No, I wouldn't fake them. I'd be damn injured. But I would recover. I guess I used to live a pretty reckless life. I think I might have been drunk most of the time."

Again quoting Virgil, the author relates: " 'I love tuna fish. Eat it all the time. I do what feels good. That's the way I live my life. If it makes me feel good, whether it's against the law or not, I do it. I'm not sure a lot of the things I've done weren't pure lunacy.' Cherilee (plaintiff's wife) says, 'Mike also eats spiders and other insects and things.' "

Virgil was further quoted as saying, "I've always been determined to find a sport I could be the best in. I was always aggressive as a kid. You know, competitive, mean. Real mean. I bit off the cheek of a Negro in a six-against–30 gang fight. They had tire irons with them. But that was a long time ago. At the Wedge, there are a lot of individualists."

The articles notes: "Perhaps because most of his time was spent engaged in such activity, Virgil never learned how to read." A photo caption reads: "Mike Virgil, the wild man of the Wedge, thinks it possible his brain is being slowly destroyed."

Respecting the applicable state law, the district court stated:

> California has adopted Dean Prosser's analysis of the tort of invasion of privacy. Kapellas v. Kofman, 1 C.3d 20, 35 n. 16, 459 P.2d 912, 81 Cal.Rptr. 360 (1969). According to that analysis, four separate torts are included within the broader designation of invasion of privacy: 1. Intrusion upon the plaintiff's seclusion or solitude, or into his private affairs; 2. Public disclosure of embarrassing private facts about the plaintiff; 3. Publicity which places the plaintiff in a false light in the public eye; 4. Appropriation, for the defendant's advantage, of plaintiff's name or likeness. Prosser, Law of Torts (4th ed., 1971) 804–14. See also Prosser, Privacy, 48 Cal.L.Rev. 383, 389 (1960).

The district court concluded that of these four separate torts the one alleged by plaintiff was that of public disclosure of embarrassing private facts. We agree.

The most recent definition of this tort and discussion of its elements is that to be found in The American Law Institute Restatement (Second) of Torts (Tentative Draft No. 21, 1975). Section 652D gives a new name to the tort, "Publicity Given to Private Life." The black letter reads:

> One who gives publicity to a matter concerning the private life of another is subject to liability to the other for unreasonable invasion of his privacy, if the matter publicized is of a kind which (a) would be highly offensive to a reasonable person, and (b) is not of legitimate concern to the public.

With respect to "publicity" comment b reads in part:

> "Publicity," as it is used in this Section, differs from "publication," as that term is used in § 577 in connection with liability for defamation. "Publication," in that sense, is a word of art, which includes any communication by the defendant to a third person. "Publicity," on the other hand, means that the matter is made public, by communicating it to the public at large, or to so many persons that the matter must be regarded as substantially certain to become one of public knowledge. The difference is not one of the means of communication, which may

> be oral, written, or by any other means. It is one of communication which reaches, or is sure to reach the public.
>
> Thus it is not an invasion of the right of privacy, within the rule stated in this Section, to communicate a fact concerning the plaintiff's private life to a single person, or even to a small group of persons. On the other hand, any publication in a newspaper or a magazine, even of small circulation, or in a handbill distributed to a large number of persons, or any broadcast over the radio, or statement made in an address to a large audience, is sufficient to give publicity within the meaning of the term as it is used in this Section. The distinction, in other words, is one between private and public communication.

With respect to "private life," comment c reads in part:

> The rule stated in this Section applies only to publicity given to matters concerning the private, as distinguished from the public, life of the individual. There is no liability when the defendant merely gives further publicity to information about the plaintiff which is already public. * * *
>
> Likewise there is no liability for giving further publicity to what the plaintiff himself leaves open to the public eye.

It is argued that by voluntary disclosure of the facts to Kirkpatrick, knowing that he proposed to write an article including information about appellant, appellant had himself rendered public the facts disclosed. We cannot agree.

It is not the manner in which information has been obtained that determines whether it is public or private. Here it is undisputed that the information was obtained without commission of a tort and in a manner wholly unobjectionable. However, that is not determinative as to this particular tort. The offense with which we are here involved is not the intrusion by means of which information is obtained; it is the publicizing of that which is private in character. The question, then, is whether the information disclosed was public rather than private—whether it was generally known and, if not, whether the disclosure by appellant can be said to have been to the public at large.

Talking freely to someone is not in itself, under comment c, making public the substance of the talk. There is an obvious and substantial difference between the disclosure of private facts to an individual—a disclosure that is selective and based on a judgment as to whether knowledge by that person would be felt to be objectionable—and the disclosure of the same facts to the public at large. The former, as the Restatement recognizes, does not constitute publicizing or public communication (see comment b as quoted supra) and accordingly does not destroy the private character of the facts disclosed. See Timperley v. Chase Collection Service, 272 Cal.App.2d 697, 700, 77 Cal.Rptr. 782, 784 (1969); Schwartz v. Thiele, 242 Cal.App.2d 799, 805, 51 Cal.Rptr. 767, 770–71 (1966).

Talking freely to a member of the press, knowing the listener to be a member of the press, is not then in itself making [one's words] public. Such communication can be said to anticipate that what is said will be made public since making public is the function of the press, and accordingly such communication can be construed as a consent to publicize. Thus if publicity results it can be said to have been consented to. However, if consent is withdrawn prior to the act of publicizing, the consequent publicity is without consent.

We conclude that the voluntary disclosure to Kirkpatrick did not in itself constitute a making public of the facts disclosed.

Appellant contends that since Virgil has not denied the truth of the statements made in the article, the publication was privileged under the First Amendment. The law has not yet gone so far. The most recent Supreme Court expression on the subject, Cox Broadcasting Corp. v. Cohn, 420 U.S. 469, 95 S.Ct. 1029, 43 L.Ed.2d 328 (1975), dealt with the same tort as is involved here, characterized by the Court as "the right [of one] to be free from unwanted publicity about his private affairs, which, although wholly true, would be offensive to a person of ordinary sensibilities." Id. at 489, 95 S.Ct. at 1043. The Court noted:

> * * * the appellants urge upon us the broad holding that the press may not be made criminally or civilly liable for publishing information that is neither false nor misleading but absolutely accurate, however damaging it may be to the reputation or individual sensibilities.

Id. The Court refused to reach this broad question "whether truthful publications may ever be subjected to civil or criminal liability consistently with the First and Fourteenth Amendments * * *." Id. at 491, 95 S.Ct. at 1044. It chose instead to deal with a "narrower interface between press and privacy," id., focusing on the protectable area of privacy and excluding from it material to be found in judicial records open to inspection by the public.

The Supreme Court, then, has not held in accordance with the contentions of appellant. Instead it has expressly declined to reach the issue presented. That issue seems to us to be whether, despite California's recognition and the recognition elsewhere given, this tortious violation of privacy is, as a tort to be written out of the law. It seems to us to contemplate the further question whether the private individual is hereafter to be able to enjoy a private life save with leave of the press; whether (at least so far as the press is concerned) the concept of "private facts" continues to have meaning.

To hold that privilege extends to all true statements would seem to deny the existence of "private" facts, for if facts be facts—that is, if they be true—they would not (at least to the press) be private, and the press would be free to publicize them to the extent it sees fit. The extent to which areas of privacy continue to exist, then, would appear to be based not on rights bestowed by law but on the taste and discretion of the press. We cannot accept this result.

To test the validity of such a rule we might start with the public's right to know under the First Amendment. Does the spirit of the Bill of Rights require that individuals be free to pry into the unnewsworthy private affairs of their fellowmen? In our view it does not. In our view fairly defined areas of privacy must have the protection of law if the quality of life is to continue to be reasonably acceptable. The public's right to know is, then, subject to reasonable limitations so far as concerns the private facts of its individual members.

If the public has no right to know, can it yet be said that the press has a constitutional right to inquire and to inform? In our view it cannot. It is because the public has a right to know that the press has a function to inquire and to inform. The press, then, cannot be said to have any right to give information greater than the extent to which the public is entitled to have information.

We conclude that unless it be privileged as newsworthy (a subject we discuss next), the publicizing of private facts is not protected by the First Amendment.

The privilege to publicize newsworthy matters is included in the definition of the tort set out in Restatement (Second) of Torts § 652D (Tentative Draft No. 21, 1975). Liability may be imposed for an invasion of privacy only if "the matter publicized is of a kind which * * * is not of legitimate concern to the public." While the Restatement does not so emphasize, we are satisfied that this provision is one of constitutional dimension delimiting the scope of the tort and that the extent of the privilege thus is controlled by federal rather than state law.

Restatement comment[ary] casts light on the nature of matter that "is not of legitimate concern to the public." The privilege extends to "voluntary public figures," comment c, and to some "involuntary public figures" (those "who have not sought publicity or consented to it, but through their own conduct or otherwise have * * * become news,") comment d. It extends to "all matters of the kind customarily regarded as "news," comment e; and also "giving information to the public for purposes of education, amusement or enlightenment, where the public may reasonably be expected to have a legitimate interest in what is published," comment h.

That this privilege extends to private facts is made clear by comment f. It is emphasized, however, that the privilege is not unlimited. The comment states:

> In determining what is a matter of legitimate public interest, account must be taken of the customs and conventions of the community; and in the last analysis what is proper becomes a matter of the community mores. The line is to be drawn when the publicity ceases to be the giving of information to which the public is entitled, and becomes a morbid and sensational prying into private lives for its own sake, with which a reasonable member of the public, with decent standards, would say that he had no concern. * * *

In our judgment such a standard for newsworthiness does not offend the First Amendment; by the extreme limits it imposes in defining the tort it avoids unduly limiting the breathing space needed by the press for the exercise of effective editorial judgment. See Miami Herald Publishing Co. v. Tornillo, 418 U.S. 241, 94 S.Ct. 2831, 41 L.Ed.2d 730 (1974). Accordingly we accept the Restatement's standard for newsworthiness.

We move, then, to the question whether, with such a standard to be applied, the district court correctly ruled that factual issues remained to be resolved on trial. Here appellant makes a vigorous attack upon the order appealed from. Appellant contends:

> A press which must depend upon a governmental determination as to what facts are of "public interest" in order to avoid liability for their truthful publication is not free at all. * * * [However,] protection of the editor's discretion need not result in a rule which abdicates all responsibility to the press. A constitutional rule can be fashioned which protects all the interests involved. This goal is achieved by providing a privilege for truthful publications which is defeasible only when the court concludes as a matter of law that the truthful publication complained of constitutes a clear abuse of the editor's constitutional discretion to publish and discuss subjects and facts which in his judgment are matters of public interest.

We cannot agree that the First Amendment requires that the question must be confined to one of law to be decided by the judge. Courts have not yet gone so far in other areas of the law involving First Amendment problems, such as libel and obscenity. The testing of facts against a standard founded on community mores does entail judgment of the court itself. But if there is room for differing views as to the state of community mores or the manner in which it would operate upon the facts in question, there is room for the jury function. The function of the court is to ascertain whether a jury question is presented.

The standard against which the evidence must be examined is that of New York Times Co. v. Sullivan, 376 U.S. 254, 285, 84 S.Ct. 710, 11 L.Ed.2d 686 (1964), and its progeny. But the manner in which the evidence is to be examined in the light of that standard is the same as in all other cases in which it is claimed that a case should not go to the jury. If the evidence, so considered, measures up to the New York Times standard, the case is one for the jury, and it is error to grant a directed verdict, as the trial judge did in this case. See also: Alioto v. Cowles Communications, Inc., 519 F.2d 777 (9th Cir.1975), cert. denied 423 U.S. 930, 96 S.Ct. 280, 46 L.Ed.2d 259 (1975).

The final question, then, is whether in application of the standard for newsworthiness taken from the Restatement, jury questions are presented.

We may concede, arguendo, that the privilege to publicize newsworthy matter would, as matter of law, extend to the general subject of the article here in question: body surfing at the Wedge. While not hot news of the day, this subject quite properly can be regarded as of general public interest.

However, accepting that it is, as matter of law, in the public interest to know about some area of activity, it does not necessarily follow that it is in the public interest to know private facts about the persons who engage in that activity. The fact that they engage in an activity in which the public can be said to have a general interest does not render every aspect of their lives subject to public disclosure. Most persons are connected with some activity, vocational or avocational, as to which the public can be said as matter of law to have a legitimate interest or curiosity. To hold as matter of law that private facts as to such persons are also within the area of legitimate public interest could indirectly expose everyone's private life to public view. Limitations, then, remain to be imposed and at this point factual questions are presented respecting the state of community mores.

Among the questions so presented here are: Whether (and, if so, to what extent), private facts respecting Virgil, as a prominent member of the group engaging in body surfing at the Wedge, are matters in which the public has a legitimate interest; whether the identity of Virgil as the one to whom such facts apply is [a] matter in which the public has a legitimate interest. (Additional questions, related not to privilege but to other elements of the tort are: whether, for reasons other than the voluntary and knowing communication to Kirkpatrick, the facts had become matter[s] of public knowledge; if not, whether the publicizing of these facts would prove highly offensive to a reasonable person—one of ordinary sensibilities.)

On these questions the function of the court on motion for summary judgment is to decide whether, on the record, reasonable minds could differ. If in the judgment of the court reasonable minds could not differ, and the answer on which reasonable minds agree favors invocation of the privilege, then summary judgment for the appellant would be proper.

We have no way of knowing whether, in denying summary judgment, the court had in mind matters we have here discussed. We think, on balance, the desirable remand would be one that invites reconsideration of the motion in the light of our views here expressed.

The order denying summary judgment is vacated and the case is remanded for reconsideration of the motion in the light of the views here expressed.

Notes

1. On remand, Sports Illustrated renewed its motion for summary judgment. This time, the district court saw fit to grant it:

> Both parties agree that body surfing at the Wedge is a matter of legitimate public interest, and it cannot be doubted that Mike Virgil's unique prowess at the same is also of legitimate public interest. Any reasonable person reading the Sports Illustrated article would have to conclude that the personal facts concerning Mike

> Virgil were included as a legitimate journalistic attempt to explain Virgil's extremely daring and dangerous style of body surfing at the Wedge. There is no possibility that a juror could conclude that the personal facts were included for any inherent morbid, sensational, or curiosity appeal they might have.

Virgil v. Sports Illustrated, 424 F.Supp. 1286, 1289 (S.D.Cal.1976).

2. The difficulty in striking the appropriate balance between an athlete's right to privacy and the public's right to know resurfaced in dramatic fashion in August 1998. With the effort to break Roger Maris' single season home run record gaining momentum, Associated Press sportswriter Steve Wilstein reported seeing androstenedione, a controversial strength enhancer, in St. Louis Cardinals first baseman Mark McGwire's locker. Believing Wilstein had stepped over the line, the team briefly considered punishing his employer. *See further La Russa: AP Should Be Banned From Clubhouse*, Sacramento Bee, Aug. 24, 1998, at E5. A short time later, Mark Kiszla, a Denver Post columnist, was barred from the Colorado Rockies' locker room after he was caught rifling through slugger Dante Bichette's belongings, looking to see if he was using the drug. *See further Columnist Loses Credentials for Snooping in Locker*, Fort Lauderdale Sun–Sentinel, Aug. 29, 1998, at 4C.

3. Because of incidents like the one involving Mike Virgil, some athletes simply refuse to speak with the press. Claiming he had been misquoted in numerous stories early in his career, for example, Philadelphia Phillies ace Steve Carlton steadfastly declined all requests to be interviewed. For a further look at why some athletes choose not to talk to the media, see David Casstevens, *Yet Another Mouth that Won't Roar*, Dallas Morning News, May 11, 1985, at 1B.

4. In recent years, a number of sports figures have gotten into trouble because of their insensitive public remarks:

> In April 1987, during a nationally-televised program on the 40th anniversary of Jackie Robinson's historic breaking of baseball's color barrier, Los Angeles Dodgers General Manager Al Campanis claimed African–Americans lacked the "necessities" to become baseball managers. Within 24 hours, the team had demanded—and received—his resignation. *See further O'Malley Forces Campanis to Resign*, San Diego Union–Trib., Apr. 8, 1987, at D1.
>
> In January 1988, CBS commentator Jimmy "the Greek" Snyder opined while taping an interview, "The black is a better athlete to begin with because he has been bred to be that way. This goes all the way back to the Civil War, when the slave owner would breed his big black to his big woman so that he could have a big black kid, see." Although he issued a formal apology, insisting he meant no offense, the network quickly fired him. *See further* Steve Pate, *Racial Slurs Cost 'Greek' His CBS Job*, Dallas Morning News, Jan. 17, 1988, at 1B.
>
> In May 1995, CBS commentator Ben Wright told Sports Illustrated women could not play golf as well as men because their

"boobs" got in the way of their backswings. He also maintained the LPGA's difficulty in attracting corporate sponsors was due to the high percentage of lesbians on its tour. After claiming for years that he had been misquoted, Wright reversed himself and charged the network with having ordered a cover-up. *See further* David Ginsburg, *Wright Admits Lesbian Comments: Ex-Golf Analyst Says CBS Told Him to Deny Remarks*, Rocky Mtn. News, May 15, 1998, at 1C.

In March 1997, golfer Tiger Woods was quoted in Gentleman's Quarterly as having made offensive jokes about lesbians and African-Americans. When confronted by the media, Woods sought to brush off the incident by saying his remarks had been made in fun and off-the-record. *See further* Gene Frenette, *Tiger Invited Trouble*, Fla. Times-Union, Mar. 24, 1997, at C1.

In April 1997, golfer Fuzzy Zoeller told reporters he hoped Tiger Woods, who had just won the Masters tournament, would not choose fried chicken and collard greens as the menu for the 1998 Champions Dinner. When Zoeller was accused of being a racist, he insisted he had meant no harm. *See further* Stan Sutton, *Zoeller: Remarks on Woods Weren't Intended to be Racial*, San Antonio Express-News, Apr. 22, 1997, at 2C.

In March 1998, Green Bay Packers defensive end Reggie White insulted Asians, Hispanics, African-Americans, and homosexuals during an hour-long speech to the Wisconsin state legislature. Despite a blizzard of criticism, White, an ordained minister, refused to repudiate his views. *See further* Liz Clarke, *Packers' White Stands by Remarks; His Comments on Races Draw Reaction*, Wash. Post, Mar. 27, 1998, at D1.

In August 1998, former hockey star Bobby Hull was quoted in both Russian and Canadian newspapers as making racial slurs and saying, "Hitler had some good ideas, he just went a little bit too far." When a firestorm of protest erupted, Hull claimed he had been misquoted and sued the papers. *See further Bobby Hull Files Lawsuit for Libel, Slander*, Fort Lauderdale Sun-Sentinel, Nov. 21, 1998, at 8C.

In December 1998, Baltimore Ravens owner Art Modell was castigated for saying if he could, he would hire Adolf Hitler to be the team's new head coach. Modell soon backtracked, calling his comment "a flippant, uncalled for, stupid misspeak." *See further Modell Apologizes for Flippant Hitler Remark*, Ariz. Republic, Dec. 29, 1998, at C6.

In February 1999, Glenn Hoddle, the coach of England's national soccer team, was dismissed after telling The Times of London that disabled people were suffering from bad "karma" from their previous lives. Desperate to save his job, Hoodle claimed he had been misquoted. *See further* Sarah Lyall, *Comments Cost Coach of England His Job*, N.Y. Times, Feb 3, 1999, at D3.

As a result of these and other slips of the tongue, players increasingly are turning to media consultants for assistance in dealing with the press. *See further* Frank Fitzpatrick, *This Coach Gives Professional Athletes Help in Handling Reporters' Questions*, Seattle Times, Aug. 10, 1997, at D6.

5. As the episodes involving Jimmy the Greek and Ben Wright demonstrate, journalists have not protected their own. Indeed, some observers believe the press is more exacting when the sports figure involved is a reporter. *See further* John Gearan, *Sink Your Teeth Into a Foul Topic: Sex, Drugs Rock World of Sports*, Worcester (MA) Sunday Telegram, Sept. 28, 1997, at D1 (pointing out that while sportscaster Marv Albert lost his job after pleading guilty to a misdemeanor, numerous athletes have kept theirs despite committing much more serious crimes), and Carla Hall, *The Foot's in Their Mouths, But It Leaves a Bad Taste in Ours*, L.A. Times, Apr. 17, 1997, at E1 (describing the hostility encountered by announcer David Halberstam after he likened Miami Heat guard John Crotty to one of Thomas Jefferson's slaves).

6. Is sports reporting becoming too focused on non-game issues? Many observers believe the answer is yes and point to the proliferation of sports cable networks and radio call-in shows as the main culprit. *See further* Glenn Dickey, *In Sports News, Rumor Has It*, S.F. Chron., May 9, 1997, at B3 ("There is more sports news available than ever, but the quantity has come at the expense of quality. Too often, rumors and innuendos have replaced facts in reporting. Call it the Gresham's Law of sports.").

Problem 50

In a lengthy story about drug use by the city's professional athletes, a reporter referred to several "unnamed persons." Upon seeing the account, the district attorney initiated an investigation and demanded the writer reveal her sources. If she refuses to turn over the information, will a court order her to do so? *See In re Madden*, 151 F.3d 125 (3d Cir.1998).

2. DENIED

Despite the advantages to be gained by dealing with the media, access is sometimes refused. If the denial is challenged in court, a variety of factors come into play.

WEINBERG v. CHICAGO BLACKHAWK HOCKEY TEAM, INC.

653 N.E.2d 1322 (Ill.App.Ct.), *appeal denied*, 660 N.E.2d 1282 (Ill.1995).

RIZZI, Justice.

Plaintiffs, Mark G. Weinberg and Blue Line Publishing, Inc., brought an action against defendant, Chicago Blackhawk Hockey Team, Inc. (Blackhawks) for violations of the Illinois Antitrust Act (the Act). See 740 ILCS 10/3 (West 1992). Plaintiffs alleged that the Blackhawks violated the Act by (1) refusing to grant plaintiffs media credentials and press access to the Chicago Stadium for the Blackhawks' practices, press conferences and post-game interviews; (2) interfering with an advertising contract between plaintiffs and one of its advertisers; and (3) instigating the arrest of plaintiff Weinberg while he was selling The Blue Line on the streets surrounding the Chicago Stadium. Pursuant to the Blackhawks' motion to dismiss for failing to state a claim, the trial court dismissed the allegations relating to the first and third claims with prejudice, and dismissed the allegations relating to the second claim without prejudice.

On appeal, plaintiffs argue only the dismissal of the allegations relating to the first claim. Accordingly, the sole issue before us is whether the trial court properly dismissed the allegations in plaintiffs' complaint relating to defendant's refusal to grant plaintiffs media credentials and press access to Chicago Blackhawks' practices, press conferences and post-game interviews. We reverse and remand.

A fair reading of plaintiff's complaint reveals the following. The plaintiffs and the Blackhawks publish competing program guides. Plaintiffs publish and sell The Blue Line in the streets surrounding the Chicago Stadium. Each issue of The Blue Line is written for that day's specific game and contains statistical information regarding the Blackhawks and other National Hockey League teams current through the date of publication. The Blackhawks, on the other hand, control and profit from the sale of their game day program, Face Off. The Blue Line and Face Off are the only game day programs published for the Blackhawks' games.

The Blackhawks have exclusive control over the following: (1) the grant or denial of media credentials for Blackhawks' games and practices at the Chicago Stadium; (2) access to the Blackhawks' players and coaching staff during the games and practices; (3) access to the press box and press room at the Chicago Stadium; and (4) access to regularly scheduled press conferences at the Chicago Stadium.

On February 18, 1991, plaintiffs requested media credentials for the remaining home games for the Blackhawks' 1990–91 season. The Blackhawks denied plaintiffs' request stating that the credentials were granted on a first come first served basis and that no credentials remained for the 1990–91 season. On June 6, 1991, one week after the end of the 1990–91 season, plaintiffs made a written request to the Blackhawks for media credentials for the upcoming 1991–92 season. On June 14, 1991, plaintiffs made a second written request. The Blackhawks denied plaintiffs' requests on September 8, 1991. On November 15, 1991, plaintiff again made a written request for media credentials. The Blackhawks did not respond to this request.

The assistant director of public relations of the Blackhawks was quoted as saying that The Blue Line was denied media credentials because, "I don't think we want to set aside credentials for a publication that is conceivably competing against Goal." Goal was the predecessor program of Face Off. Plaintiffs' requests for media packets which the Blackhawks distribute from time to time and which contain statistical information and player photographs have also been repeatedly denied.

Plaintiffs contend that the above allegations of fact establish a violation of the Act. Specifically the above allegations implicate § 3(3) of the Act which states that a person will be deemed to have committed a violation of the Act who shall:

> Establish, maintain, use, or attempt to acquire monopoly power over any substantial part of trade or commerce of this State for the purpose of excluding competition or of controlling, fixing, or maintaining process in such trade or commerce....

740 ILCS 10/3(3) (West 1992). The Illinois Antitrust Act, by its own terms, is to be construed with applicable federal precedent. 740 ILCS 10/11 (West 1992). Specifically, it has been noted that § 3(3) of the Act has been modeled after § 2 of the Sherman Anti–Trust Act, and therefore should be construed with federal cases interpreting § 2 of the Sherman Anti–Trust Act. State of Ill. ex rel. Burris v. Panhandle Eastern (7th Cir.1991), 935 F.2d 1469, 1480.

Plaintiffs refer to two separate theories under which to prove a violation of § 3(3) of the Act. The first theory is known as monopoly leveraging. Monopoly leveraging occurs where a party has monopoly power in one market, and uses this power to extract a competitive advantage in a second market. State of Ill. ex rel. Hartigan v. Panhandle Eastern (C.D.Ill.1990), 730 F.Supp. 826, 923–24, aff'd by State of Ill. ex rel. Burris v. Panhandle Eastern (7th Cir.1991), 935 F.2d 1469. In the present case, plaintiffs allege that the Blackhawks are using their monopoly power in professional hockey in Chicago to gain a competitive edge in the sale of game day programs by illegally refusing to deal with plaintiffs.

In order to state a claim for monopoly leveraging under § 3(3) of the Act, a plaintiff must allege (1) that defendant has monopoly power in one market, (2) that defendant used this power to exact a competitive advantage for itself in a second market, (3) that the competitive advantage was not won on competitive merits, but rather stemmed from a coercive use of the monopoly power in the first market, (4) that the defendant acted with the intent to gain the unwarranted advantage in the second market, and (5) the anti-competitive conduct resulted in a lessening of competition. Panhandle Eastern, 730 F.Supp. at 925.

In the present case, we believe plaintiffs' complaint adequately contains allegations of fact supporting a finding of all the necessary elements. As to the first element, the Blackhawks unquestionably have monopoly power in National Hockey League hockey in Chicago. We note that a professional sports team, like the Blackhawks, is an absolutely unique entity providing the public with an absolutely unique product. The second element, concerning the use of monopoly power to gain an advantage in a second market, is established by the allegations relating to the Blackhawks' refusal to grant plaintiffs media credentials and press access to prevent The Blue Line from competing with Face Off. The same allegations satisfy the third element. The advantage Face Off has acquired was achieved not through procompetitive efficiencies, but rather through denying plaintiffs access to the Blackhawks' games. The fourth element, intent, is supplied by the quote from the assistant director of public relations wherein he stated: "I don't think we want to set aside credentials for a publication that is conceivably competing against Goal."

The only remaining element under the monopoly leveraging theory is whether plaintiffs have sufficiently alleged that the Blackhawks' course of conduct has had an anti-competitive effect. It is this element that the trial court found lacking in plaintiffs' complaint and upon which it dismissed the allegations.

Initially, we note that nowhere in the complaint is it stated that the Blackhawks' course of conduct has had an anti-competitive effect. But such an allegation, being wholly conclusory, is not needed to state a proper claim under the Act. What is required is that the plaintiffs plead sufficient facts which establish either that competition has been harmed, or give rise to the reasonable inference that this is the case.

We believe a fair reading of plaintiffs' complaint gives rise to the reasonable inference that competition has been harmed. The complaint clearly states that the Blackhawks have effectively excluded The Blue Line from the immediate and intimate access to the games and players to which the Blackhawks' own publication enjoys and to which one would reasonably expect any game day program to have. From the very existence of media credentials, press boxes, press rooms and press conferences, we can reasonably infer that a publication without access to these credentials, locations and events is less competitive than it would otherwise be. Through the course of conduct alleged in the complaint, plaintiffs are unable to obtain the quality of photographs, reports and interviews, including answers to plaintiffs' own questions which they would otherwise have. Denying such access necessarily makes The Blue Line less competitive.

It is no answer to argue as the Blackhawks have that The Blue Line easily outsells their own publication. First and foremost, such information is not contained in plaintiffs' complaint and it is to the four corners of plaintiffs' complaint which we look in reviewing a motion to dismiss for failing to state a cause of action. Moreover, an inquiry into whether competition has been harmed is not a mere exercise in bean counting. One of the primary goals of antitrust legislation is to enhance consumer welfare. Accordingly, if The Blue Line cannot put forth its best program due to the monopolistic practices being engaged in by the Blackhawks, then its readers, however many, are suffering an anti-competitive effect. Consumer welfare is measured as much, if not more so, by the quality of a product as it is by the quantity being sold.

The case on which the Blackhawks rely is inapposite. The Blackhawks cite Twin Laboratories, Inc. v. Weider Health & Fitness (2nd Cir.1990), 900 F.2d 566, for the proposition that if sales of a product remain strong after the alleged monopolistic conduct then there is no anti-competitive effect. In that case, the plaintiff was prevented from advertising its nutritional supplements in a magazine whose owner also marketed a nutritional supplement. Despite the advertising ban, the plaintiff continued to post growing sales. The difference in that case and in the case at bar is that the advertising ban there did not lessen the quality of the product. In the present case, the quality of The Blue Line has been adversely affected. For the foregoing reasons, we believe plaintiffs have adequately stated a cause of action under the Act based on monopoly leveraging.

The plaintiffs here prevail for another reason. Plaintiffs' complaint also states a cause of action based on the essential facilities doctrine. The impetus behind this doctrine is the fear that a monopolist will be able to extend monopoly power from one market to another. MCI Communications v. American Tel. & Tel. Co. (7th Cir.1983), 708 F.2d 1081, 1132. Antitrust laws, therefore, require that a party controlling an essential facility provide access to that facility on non-discriminatory terms. MCI Communications at 1132.

To state a cause of action under § 3(3) of the Act based on the essential facilities doctrine, a plaintiff must allege (1) control of the essential facility by a monopolist, (2) a competitor's inability to practically or reasonably duplicate the essential facility, (3) the denial of the use of the facility to a competitor, (4) the feasibility of providing the facility and (5) that denial has had an anti-competitive effect. State of Ill. ex rel. Hartigan v. Panhandle Eastern (C.D.Ill.1990), 730 F.Supp. 826, 925, aff'd by 935 F.2d 1469; see also MCI Communications at 1132–33.

In the present case, plaintiffs have sufficiently alleged facts to support all five elements. First, plaintiffs have alleged that the Blackhawks have exclusive control over the granting of media credentials, access to the players and coaching staff and attendance at games, practices, press conferences and post game interviews. Second, the above allegation gives rise to the reasonable inference that plaintiffs cannot reasonably duplicate the access to the games, players and so forth. Third, plaintiffs have clearly alleged that they have been denied the use of the facility they are seeking. Fourth, the feasibility of providing the facility is demonstrated by the allegations that such access is regularly granted to others. Finally, as stated above, we believe that the complaint gives rise to the reasonable inference that the denial of access complained of has had the anti-competitive effect of lessening the quality of plaintiffs' publication.

The Blackhawks make much out of the fact that the plaintiffs are not seeking the use of a physical facility, but access which they argue is intangible. We fail to see any real significance in this distinction. Moreover, what plaintiffs really sought was use of the Chicago Stadium, which while sadly is no longer standing, certainly was at the time a physical facility.

For the above reasons, we conclude that the trial court erred when it dismissed plaintiffs' complaint for failing to state a cause of action under the Illinois Antitrust Act. Accordingly, the order of dismissal is reversed and the case remanded to the trial court for further proceedings consistent with this opinion.

MILWAUKEE JOURNAL v. BOARD OF REGENTS OF THE UNIVERSITY OF WISCONSIN SYSTEM

472 N.W.2d 607 (Wis.Ct.App.1991).

EICH, Chief Judge.

The University of Wisconsin Board of Regents and other university officials (collectively, "the university") appeal from a judgment ordering them to disclose the names of applicants for the positions of athletic director and football coach at the University of Wisconsin–Madison.

The issue is whether sec. 230.13(2), Stats., which authorizes the secretary of the Department of Employee Relations (DER) to keep records of the "[n]ames of applicants other than those certified for employment" closed to the public, constitutes a mandatory exception to the state's open records law shielding the names of applicants for unclassified positions in the state service from public disclosure. We conclude that it does not and affirm the judgment.

The facts are not in dispute. In 1989, the University of Wisconsin fired its athletic director, reassigned its football coach to other duties and began recruiting to fill both positions. Both are unclassified positions in the state civil service system.

The Milwaukee Journal sought access to the names of applicants for the two positions, filing a written request for the information with the Madison campus chancellor Donna Shalala. Shalala denied the request, taking the position that all records of the applicants' names were closed under sec. 230.13(2), Stats. The Journal then filed a mandamus action seeking release of the information. The university's position remained the same: its answer to the complaint asserted that sec. 230.13(2) "require[d] closure of the records...."

The trial court ruled that sec. 230.13(2), Stats., did not apply to the positions, and that even if it did, the university, in deciding to deny access to the requested information, had failed to exercise the discretion required by the statute's permissive language ("may keep [the] records ... closed to the public").

The university appeals, repeating the arguments made below. Like the trial court, we see sec. 230.13(2), Stats., as inapplicable to the two positions, and we conclude that the statute neither mandates nor authorizes closure of the records.

Wisconsin has a strong public policy of openness in government which is embodied in the state's open records law:

> Declaration of policy. In recognition of the fact that a representative government is dependent upon an informed electorate, it is declared to be the public policy of this state that all persons are entitled to the greatest possible information

> regarding the affairs of government and the official acts of those officers and employees who represent them.
>
> Further, providing persons with such information is declared to be an essential function of a representative government and an integral part of the ... duties of officers and employees.... To that end, [the open records laws] shall be construed in every instance with a presumption of complete public access, consistent with the conduct of governmental business. The denial of public access generally is contrary to the public interest, and only in an exceptional case may access be denied.

Sec. 19.31, Stats.

In light of that policy, "[t]he general presumption of our law is that public records shall be open to the public unless there is a clear statutory exception, unless there exists a limitation under the common law, or unless there is an overriding public interest in keeping the public record confidential." Hathaway v. Joint School Dist. No. 1 of Green Bay, 116 Wis.2d 388, 397, 342 N.W.2d 682, 687 (1984). The university does not claim that any common-law rule limits application of the open records law to the Journal's request, nor does it argue that some "overriding public interest" demands secrecy. As indicated, it bases its refusal to allow access to the information entirely on sec. 230.13(2), Stats., which it claims provides a specific and mandatory public-records-law exemption for the names of applicants for jobs in the unclassified state service.

We begin our consideration of the university's argument with the proposition that any exception to the "general rule" of openness and disclosure must be "narrowly construed." Oshkosh Northwestern Co. v. Oshkosh Library Bd., 125 Wis.2d 480, 482, 373 N.W.2d 459, 461 (Ct.App. 1985).

Exceptions [to openness] should be recognized for what they are, instances in derogation of the general legislative intent, and should, therefore, be narrowly construed; and unless the exception is explicit and unequivocal, it will not be held to be an exception. It would be contrary to general well established principles of freedom-of-information statutes to hold that, by implication only, any type of record can be held from public inspection. Hathaway, 116 Wis.2d at 397, 342 N.W.2d at 687. We see no such "clear," "explicit" or "unequivocal" exception in sec. 230.13(2), Stats.

Chapter 230, Stats., embodies the state's employment relations law. Among other things, it establishes a civil service, provides for the hiring and firing of state employees and generally governs their evaluation and overall treatment. DER, through its secretary, administers the law.

Chapter 230, Stats., divides state employment into two categories: the "classified" service and the "unclassified" service. Sec. 230.08. The unclassified service comprises positions specifically designated in sec. 230.08(2). Generally, the list includes elected officials and officers appointed by the governor, deputy departmental secretaries, division administrators and a variety of other—mostly policy-making or administrative—positions. As for the university, all faculty and academic staff positions—including the athletic director and football coach—are unclassified. Sec. 230.08(2)(d).

The classified service is defined in the statute as: "all positions not included in the unclassified service." Sec. 230.08(3), Stats. Generally, the classified service comprises those labor, clerical, technical and professional positions involved in the day-to-day workings and operations of state government; and the bulk of ch. 230 sets forth in detail the recruitment, application, examination, certification, hiring, promotion and termination processes applicable to such employees.

Appointments to positions in the classified service are made pursuant to a "merit" selection plan based upon competitive examinations. Sec. 230.15(1), Stats. The examinations are part of a process culminating in the "certification" of the top five applicants for a particular position to the appointing authority; and sec. 230.25(2) directs that the final appointment "shall be made ... to all positions in the classified service from among those certified...." Secs. 230.25(1) and (2).

Unlike positions in the classified service, there is no examination or certification process for filling unclassified positions in government. The legislature has given the employing authority—here the university—full discretionary authority to appoint to these positions.

With that background in mind, we turn to sec. 230.13(2), Stats., which, as indicated, allows the DER secretary to keep confidential the names of applicants for state jobs "other than those [who have been] certified for employment."

We believe the statutory language can be read in at least two ways. It can be read to allow the names of all persons applying for state employment—whether in the classified or unclassified service—who have not been certified for employment to be kept confidential. Because the certification process is limited to classified positions no applicants for positions in the unclassified service are ever certified. Thus, reading the statute in this manner would permit withholding the names of all applicants for any unclassified position in state service (including that of athletic director and football coach) as persons "other than those certified for employment."

But the statute may also be read to reach the opposite result. And, mindful of our obligation to construe claimed exceptions to the open records law narrowly, we adopt that reading. We believe the statute's specific reference to applicants who are "certified for employment" would have little meaning if it were intended to encompass two categories of positions, one having a certification process and one not. As we have noted, certification is a means of narrowing the field of applicants for positions within the classified service. It has no application or meaning with respect to unclassified positions. It follows that the legislature's use of such a designation reasonably may be read to limit the application of sec. 230.13(2), Stats., to classified positions.

Thus, as we read the statute, the only names that may be withheld from public scrutiny under its provisions are those of applicants for classified positions who were not certified for employment. The statute simply does not apply to positions in the unclassified service.

So read, the statute reflects what we believe to be a reasonable legislative judgment that while there might be valid reasons to give the secretary some discretion to allow the names of that large group of initial applicants for classified jobs to be kept confidential, the state has no business shielding the names of the finalists for public positions from public view. It makes no sense to us to read the statute, as the university and the dissenting opinion do, to keep secret the names of all applicants who did not survive the first stages of the hiring process for the day-to-day operational jobs in the classified service and also the names of those applicants comprising the group from which the occupants of some of the most influential policy-making positions in government are selected—leaving only those people certified for the day-to-day jobs exposed to public scrutiny.

We decline the university's invitation to construe sec. 230.13(2), Stats., to grant persons applying for these top-level policy-making government positions—persons appointed and paid to serve the public at the highest levels of government—the right to keep secret from the public the very existence of their applications.

The language of sec. 230.13(2), Stats., does not "explicit[ly]" or "unequivocal[ly]" exempt the names of all applicants for positions in the unclassified service from the open records law, and we will not interpret or construe it to do so. Hathaway, 116 Wis.2d at 397, 342 N.W.2d at 687. We agree with the Journal that the absence of any clear direction in sec. 230.13(2)—that secrecy is mandated for applications for high-level government or university positions such as those at issue here—is strong evidence of the legislature's intent that the public interest in an open appointment process must take precedence over whatever public policy considerations might favor secrecy.

Whether, as the university maintains, the names of applicants for university positions—and indeed all unclassified positions in the state service—should be shielded from public view is a question of broad public policy properly directed to the legislature. If the university desires a blanket rule mandating secrecy for the names of job applicants at any level, it should press its case in the legislature, rather than asking the courts to rule contrary to the expressed public policy of the state by creating an exception to the open records law through the interpretation of an ambiguous statute.

Consistent with our obligation to narrowly construe purported exceptions to the state's open records law, we hold that sec. 230.13(2), Stats., neither mandates nor authorizes withholding the names of those persons applying for the positions of athletic director or football coach.

The statute applies solely to classified civil-service positions, and the trial court properly granted judgment in the Journal's favor.

Judgment affirmed.

[The dissenting opinion of Judge Sundby is omitted.]

Notes

1. Alternative player guides, like the one discussed in *Weinberg*, are extremely popular with fans (but not teams) because of their candor, passion, and insights. The first such guide, "Boston Baseball," was produced in 1990 by a Red Sox zealot named Michael Rutstein who had grown tired of the sugary boosterism in the club's official press guide. Since then, diehards in many other cities have taken to publishing their own broadsheets, often quitting their jobs to do so. For a further discussion, see Leslie Kaufman, *Blasts from the Bleachers*, Newsweek, July 20, 1998, at 44.

2. Because of their ability to unlock important doors, press credentials are a much sought after item, particularly for championship games. During the 1998 Super Bowl, for example, the NFL distributed 3,000 credentials, while the NBA, NHL, and MLB each granted more than 1,000 credentials for their 1997–98 finals.

Not surprisingly, the methods used to allocate press credentials have often provoked bitter dissent. When the Washington Sports and Entertainment Group announced which newspapers would be given credentials to cover the grand opening of the MCI Sports Center, many African–American journalists claimed they had been shut out because of their skin color. *See Denying Access to the Black Press*, Wash. Informer, Dec. 10, 1997, at 12.

Similarly, when the NCAA declined to give 1997 Final Four credentials to reporters of on-line sport services, citing a lack of space, many believed the real reason was to prevent competition with its own web service. *See* Steve Outing, *Online Reporters Denied Credentials*, Editor & Publisher, Apr. 12, 1997, at 30. More recently, when it was disclosed 50 credentials would be given to each of the 32 countries in the 1998 World Cup, the tournament's organizers were blasted for failing to distinguish between small countries (like Jamaica) and large ones (like the United States, which had requested 250 credentials). *See* Jeff Rusnak, *French Organizers Get Very Stingy With World Cup Tickets*, Fort Lauderdale Sun–Sentinel, Jan. 18, 1998, at 8C.

3. As *Milwaukee Journal* demonstrates, there is no common law right of access to sports figures (or sports-related information). Thus, to be successful a plaintiff must demonstrate that the denial of access violates some constitutional or statutory right. *See further Matter of Robert M. Jarvis*, N.Y. L.J., Dec. 19, 1995, at 28 (N.Y.Surr.Ct.1995) (petitioner, a professor conducting research for a law review article, failed to establish right to examine sealed adoption records of Babe Ruth's daughters).

Problem 51

To protect the privacy of its players, a women's basketball team bans male reporters from its locker room. No such prohibition applies to female sportswriters. If a newspaper sues, claiming the policy is illegal, how should the court rule? *See Ludtke v. Kuhn*, 461 F.Supp. 86 (S.D.N.Y.1978).

C. DEFAMATION

Members of the press often say or write unflattering things about sports figures. This has led to a number of lawsuits by owners, players, coaches, and others.

1. PUBLIC FIGURE

Defamation law distinguishes between private and public figures and makes it more difficult for the latter to prevail. As a result, defendants in sports cases almost always claim the plaintiff is a public figure.

TIME, INC. v. JOHNSTON

448 F.2d 378 (4th Cir.1971).

RUSSELL, Circuit Judge.

The defendant is the publisher of SPORTS ILLUSTRATED, a weekly periodical devoted to sports and athletics. Annually, it features its selection of "Sportsman of the Year". In 1968, it chose Bill Russell, a star on the professional basketball team of the Boston CELTICS, as its "Sportsman of the Year" and engaged George Plimpton, a well-known writer, especially in the field of sports, to write the feature article.

In developing his article, Plimpton chose to quote from interviews he had had with persons acquainted with Russell and his exceptional talents as a basketball player. In quoting an interview with Arnold Auerbach, the coach of Russell with the CELTICS, Plimpton included in his article the following paragraph:

> That's a word you can use about him—he (Russell) "destroyed" players. You take Neil Johnston—Russell destroyed him. He destroyed him psychologically as well, so that he practically ran him out of organized basketball. He blocked so many shots that Johnston began throwing his hook farther and farther from the basket. It was ludicrous, and the guys along the bench began to laugh, maybe in relief that they didn't have to worry about such a guy themselves.

The "Johnston" referred to in the quoted paragraph is the plaintiff. At the time of the incident referred to, he was an outstanding professional basketball player with the Philadelphia WARRIORS basketball team. He subsequently retired from professional basketball and is now the assistant basketball coach at Wake Forest University in Winston–Salem, North Carolina. Following the publication of the article, he sued the defendant, contending that he had been libeled in the quoted paragraph and had been "damaged in his chosen profession, that of coaching basketball."

After discovery was completed, both parties moved for summary judgment. The District Court, after argument, denied both motions, 321 F.Supp. 837, and both parties have appealed.

Upon application under Section 1292 (b), 28 U.S.C., this Court granted leave to the parties to take an interlocutory cross-appeal. We reverse the denial of defendant's motion for summary judgment and dismiss plaintiff's cross-appeal.

The defendant invoked, in support of its motion, the constitutional rule of privilege, granted under the First Amendment, as applied in New York Times Co. v. Sullivan (1964) 376 U.S. 254, 84 S.Ct. 710, 11 L.Ed.2d 686, and related cases, to publications relating to the public conduct of public officials or public figures or for publications dealing with either public or private persons involved in matters of legitimate public interest.

Specifically, it contends both that the publication in question related to the public conduct of the plaintiff in his character of a public figure and that it fell within the classification of "a matter of legitimate public interest" as enunciated in the recent case of Rosenbloom v. Metromedia, Inc. (1971) 403 U.S. 29, 91 S.Ct. 1811, 29 L.Ed.2d 296, decided June 7, 1971. On either ground, it urges it was entitled to the conditional immunity afforded under New York Times.

There can be no dispute that at the time of the events discussed in the challenged publication the plaintiff met the criteria of "a public figure". "Public figures", within the contemplation of the rule in New York Times, as enlarged by subsequent cases, are "those persons who, though not public officials, are 'involved in issues in which the public has a justified and important interest' " and "include artists, athletes, business people, dilettantes, anyone who is famous or infamous because of who he is or what he has done." Cepeda v. Cowles Magazines and Broadcasting, Inc. (9th Cir.1968) 392 F.2d 417, 419, cert. denied 393 U.S. 840, 89 S.Ct. 117, 21 L.Ed.2d 110.

Consonant with this definition, a college athletic director (Curtis Publishing Co. v. Butts, supra, 388 U.S. 130, 87 S.Ct. 1975, 18 L.Ed.2d 1094), a basketball coach (Grayson v. Curtis Publishing Company (1967) 72 Wash.2d 999, 436 P.2d 756), a professional boxer (Cohen v. Marx (1949) 94 Cal.App.2d 704, 211 P.2d 320), and a professional baseball player (Cepeda v. Cowles Magazines and Broadcasting, Inc., supra, 392 F.2d 417), among others, have all been held to be "public figures". The plaintiff, as he figures in the challenged publication, fits this definition of a "public figure".

Certainly, he was as much a "public figure" as the plaintiff in Cepeda or as the plaintiffs in Grayson and Cohen. He had offered his services to the public as a paid performer and had thereby invited comments on his performance as such. In a sense, he assumed the risk of publicity, good or bad, as the case might be, so far as it concerned his public performance. The publication in question related strictly to his public character. It made no reference to his private life, it involved no intrusion into his private affairs. It dealt entirely with his performance as a professional basketball player; it discussed him in connection with a public event in which the plaintiff as a compensated public figure had taken part voluntarily.

The plaintiff does not seriously question the defendant's premise that he was a "public figure" at the time of the event discussed in the publication; and the District Court apparently assumed in its decision that the plaintiff was such a "public figure". The plaintiff points out, though, that the event, to which the publication related, occurred twelve years before the publication and nine years after the plaintiff had retired as a professional basketball player. It is plaintiff's position that he had, at the time of publication, shed his character of "public figure" and that the New York Times standard was, therefore, inapplicable. This is the basic point of difference between the parties on this aspect of the case. The District Court accepted the plaintiff's view. In so doing, it erred.

The District Court relies for its conclusion primarily on a comment set forth in a note in Rosenblatt v. Baer (1966) 383 U.S. 75, 87, 86 S.Ct. 669, 677, 15 L. Ed.2d 597, note 14: "To be sure, there may be cases where a person is so far removed from a former position of authority that comment on the manner in which he performed his responsibilities no longer has the interest necessary to justify the New York Times rule." This, however, is not such a case as was envisaged by Justice Brennan. The claim that plaintiff had retired as a player in 1958, nine years before the publication, is misleading. While plaintiff did retire as a player in 1958, he, by his own affidavit, "remained in organized professional basketball, until 1966." He thus identifies himself with professional basketball up to approximately two years of the publication in question. And, at the time of the publication itself, he was a college basketball coach, still involved as a public figure in basketball. Perhaps as a college basketball coach, he was not as prominently identified with the sport as in his playing days. Neither was Butts as intimately identified with football as an athletic director as he had been as a coach but that did not make him an anachronism in football history any more than the plaintiff, with his outstanding record, had become a forgotten figure among the many devotees of the game of basketball.

That even the plaintiff did not reckon his career as a professional basketball player forgotten is demonstrated by his claim in this case that a reflection on that career and on his eminence as a player damages him in his present occupation as a college basketball coach. By his claim for damages here, he is contending that his standing as a college basketball coach rests substantially on the public recollection and estimation of his former career as a professional basketball player; and it is for that reason he sues. It is because he is still engaged in basketball and because of the effect that any adverse comment on his record and achievements as a basketball star may have on his present position in basketball that he claims damage herein. It is manifestly inconsistent for him to contend that, when his basis for damage is thus grounded, his "public figure" career has become so obscure and remote that it is no longer a subject of legitimate public interest or comment.

The event to which the publication related remained a matter of public interest not simply because of its relation to plaintiff's own public career; it had an equal or greater interest as marking the spectacular debut of Russell in a career that was still phenomenal at the time of the publication. It was an event that had, in the language of one sports writer reporting it, a "tremendous" "psychological effect on the league". It was an event that was vivid in the memory of Auerbach at the time of the publication and likely in that of other followers of the sport. It is fair to assume that in the memory of basketball fans, the event described was neither remote nor forgotten; nor was it devoid of newsworthiness.

Moreover, mere passage of time will not necessarily insulate from the application of New York Times Co. v. Sullivan publications relating to the past public conduct of a then "public figure". No rule of repose exists to inhibit speech relating to the public career of a public figure so long as newsworthiness and public interest attach to events in such public career. This issue of remoteness as providing a basis for casting a veil about "public figures" in "public events" has often arisen in privacy cases.

There are, it is true, distinctions between actions for an invasion of privacy and suits for defamation but the same considerations it would seem would be present in either case in determining whether mere passage of time will remove the protection afforded by the constitutional privilege created by New York Times for a publication relating to a past event in the career of a "public figure". The vast majority of the reported authorities lend no support to the view urged by the plaintiff and adopted by the District Court. Cohen v. Marx, supra, 211 P.2d at p. 321, where the plaintiff had terminated his career as a professional boxer ten years prior to the offending publication, states convincingly the reasons for denial of remoteness:

> it is evident that when plaintiff sought publicity and the adulation of the public, he relinquished his right to privacy on matters pertaining to his professional activity, and he could not at his will and whim draw himself like a snail into his shell and hold others liable for commenting upon the acts which had taken place when he had voluntarily exposed himself to the public eye. As to such acts he had waived his right of privacy and he could not at some subsequent period rescind his waiver.

To the same effect, among others, are Sidis v. F–R. Pub. Corporation (2d Cir.1940) 113 F.2d 806, 809, cert. den. 311 U.S. 711, 61 S.Ct. 393, 85 L.Ed. 462; Estill v. Hearst Publishing Co. (7th Cir.1951) 186 F.2d 1017, 1022; Werner v. Hearst Publishing Company (9th Cir.1961) 297 F.2d 145, 147; Smith v. Doss (1948) 251 Ala. 250, 37 So.2d 118, 121; Barbieri v. News–Journal Company (Del.1963) 189 A.2d 773, 775–776.

The District Court was, also, in error in concluding that the defendant was not entitled to claim the protection of New York Times on the ground that the offending publication commented on the plaintiff in relation to a matter of legitimate public interest. In its decision, the

District Court in this case anticipated the subsequent decision of the Supreme Court in Rosenbloom v. Metromedia, Inc., supra, which, discarding "the artificiality, * * * of a simple distinction between 'public' and 'private' individuals or institutions", held that First Amendment protection extends "to all discussion and communication involving matters of public or general concern, without regard to whether the persons involved are famous or anonymous", (91 S.Ct., p. 1820) and that a publication, though false, which concerned "a subject of legitimate public interest, even though the target is a 'private' citizen" (Justice White's opinion, 91 S.Ct. p. 1827) is within the orbit of the New York Times privilege. The District Court, while recognizing this extension of the scope of New York Times, held, however, that the subject matter of this publication was not of such legitimate public interest or concern as to qualify for protection thereunder. We disagree.

Rosenbloom, it is true, did not attempt to delineate the exact limits of the phrase, "matter of public or general interest", as used in the plurality opinion, choosing to leave that task, as it put it, "to future cases". It did declare that the term was not "to be limited to matters bearing broadly on issues of responsible government". It cited Time, Inc. v. Hill (1967) 385 U.S. 374, 87 S.Ct. 534, 17 L.Ed.2d 456, by way of illustration, to the effect that the "opening of a new play linked to an actual incident, is a matter of public interest". In so doing, the plurality opinion was substantially restating what the Court had emphasized in Hill that the sweep of the New York Times privilege is not confined to "political expression or comment upon public affairs," nor even matters of social utility or educational value. It embraces the entire range of legitimate public interest. Davis v. National Broadcasting Company (D.C.La.1970) 320 F.Supp. 1070. Such a test clearly is sufficient to cover sports and sports figures, whose "public interest" character is amply demonstrated by the elaborate sports section in every daily newspaper published in this nation and by the numerous periodicals, such as that involved here, exclusively devoted to sports. This "public interest" in sports was the basis for providing First Amendment privilege for the publication involved in Bon Air Hotel, Inc. v. Time, Inc. (5th Cir.1970) 426 F.2d 858, and is at the heart of the Court's identification of the plaintiffs as "public figure(s)" in Butts, Grayson and Cohen. It was applied in Garfinkel v. Twenty–First Century Publishing Co. (1968) 30 A.D.2d 787, 291 N.Y.S.2d 735, where basketball and basketball scouting were stated to be matters of "public interest" in the light of the great attraction the sport has for the public. And, in Sellers v. Time, Inc. (D.C.Pa.1969) 299 F.Supp. 582, 585, aff. 423 F.2d 887, cert. den. 400 U.S. 830, 91 S.Ct. 61, 27 L.Ed.2d 61, an article dealing with the unusual flight of a golf ball in a golf game, taken in connection with the popularity of golf, was deemed a matter of such public interest as to qualify under New York Times.

In summary, we conclude that both because of plaintiff's classification of a "public figure" and because the publication was "speech affecting individuals that is of public interest", the defendant was clearly entitled to invoke the constitutional privilege afforded by the rule in New York Times Co. v. Sullivan and related cases.

Affirmed in part, vacated in part, and remanded with directions that judgment be entered for the defendant.

Note

The advent of the World Wide Web has made private parties more vulnerable to defamation actions because of its spontaneous nature. For a further discussion, see *It's in the Cards, Inc. v. Fuschetto*, 535 N.W.2d 11 (Wis.Ct.App.), *review denied*, 537 N.W.2d 574 (Wis.1995) (comments posted on a sports-related computer bulletin board), and Michael Hadley, Note, *The Gertz Doctrine and Internet Defamation*, 84 Va. L. Rev. 477 (1998) (suggesting traditional defamation standards can be made to work in cyberspace).

Problem 52

In a story which received widespread attention, a reporter claimed the wife of a champion boxer had been a prostitute in her wilder days. If she sues for defamation, will the court treat her as a public or private figure? *See Carson v. Allied News Co.*, 529 F.2d 206 (7th Cir.1976).

2. PROOF

If a plaintiff is deemed a public figure—as most sports figures are—he or she must demonstrate three things: a) the defendant made a false statement of fact, b) which was said with "actual" malice, and, c) caused injury.

a. Fact

Defamation defendants often argue their words should be viewed as "constitutionally-protected opinion" rather than fact. As will be seen, this argument is quite powerful.

STEPIEN v. FRANKLIN

528 N.E.2d 1324 (Ohio Ct.App.1988).

WERREN, Judge.

This cause of action arises as a result of an action for slander and intentional infliction of emotional distress by the appellant, Theodore J. Stepien, against the appellee, Peter J. Franklin, et al. Other appellees in this case are Pacific & Southern Company, Inc., Radio WWWE, Combined Communications Corporations and Gannett Company, Inc.

Theodore J. Stepien ("Stepien") is the former President of the Cleveland Professional Basketball Company, more commonly known as the Cleveland Cavaliers. The Cleveland Cavaliers is a professional basketball franchise operated under the auspices of the National Basketball Association ("NBA"). In addition to his position with the Cavaliers, appellant was also the President and sole shareholder of Nationwide Advertising Service, Inc., the largest personnel recruitment advertising company in the world with offices throughout the United States and Canada. Nationwide was also the principal shareholder of the Cavaliers. Appellant's tenure as President of the Cavaliers began in June 1980 and he remained in that position until the team was sold to George and Gordon Gund in May 1983.

Appellee Peter J. Franklin ("Franklin") is the host of a radio sports talk show known as "Sportsline." During the period in question, Sportsline was regularly broadcast Monday through Friday, 7:00 p.m. to midnight, unless it was pre-empted by a live sports event. Franklin principally employed an audience call-in format—listeners are encouraged to call in and give their opinions and/or solicit Franklin's opinion about sports. Sportsline is entertainment, designed to encourage and capitalize on the considerable public interest in professional sports.

The style of radio and television personalities who host talk shows such as Sportsline varies widely, from the erudite analysis of William F. Buckley to the insults of Joan Rivers. Franklin's style, which is immediately apparent from listening to his show, is an extreme version of the "insult" genre of entertainment. Franklin is often loud, opinionated, rude, abrasive, obnoxious and insulting. In a manner reminiscent of the popular comedian Don Rickles, Franklin frequently hangs up on his callers and/or calls them insulting names.

The period when Stepien was the President of the Cavaliers, June 1980 to May 1983, is also the time period in which the alleged slander and emotional distress took place.

The appellant, after becoming President of the Cavaliers, immediately began an aggressive style of management that involved making numerous player transactions and staff appointments. The appellant went through more than fifty players and six coaches in two and one-half years, including the hiring and firing of one coach twice. This aggressive style of management and the lack of the Cavaliers' success thereafter resulted in appellant's receiving a great deal of unfavorable criticism in the press, nationally and locally.

The factual background specifically relevant to the alleged defamatory statements can be broken down into three general topics: 1. National Basketball Association's moratoriums on trading; 2. The finances of the Cavaliers; and 3. The proposed sale of the team and move to Toronto.

Many of Franklin's alleged defamatory statements complained of herein consisted of those that challenged the appellant's ability to manage an NBA team. These remarks by Franklin involved Cavaliers' player transactions and the league's subsequent reaction to them. In November 1980, the Cavaliers engaged in the above-stated trades that resulted in the team's trading away several first round draft choices. These trades were criticized by most observers and fans as being detrimental to the Cavaliers. In response, the NBA Commissioner imposed a restriction referred to as a "moratorium on trades" involving the Cavaliers. The restriction permitted the team to make trades, but only upon consulting with the league office and obtaining final approval.

After a short while, the moratorium was lifted, but in February 1983, a second moratorium occurred. This restriction required the Cavaliers to give the NBA twenty-four hours to consider any trade and was apparently motivated by the NBA's concern that the Cavaliers' troubles might lead them to make unwise player transactions in order to raise operating capital. The Cavaliers' financial problems were acute. The appellant considered many options to alleviate this problem. Between January and April 1983, the appellant explored several possibilities including selling the team to out-of-town buyers, selling the team to a local buyer, or retaining ownership and moving the team to Toronto. During this period, the media harshly criticized the appellant for not completing the sale and for proposing that the team move away from Cleveland.

There is no question that during the appellant's three-year period of ownership of the Cavaliers, Franklin was a harsh and critical commentator. His descriptions of appellant, extracted from tapes of the show provided to this court, include: "stupid," "dumb," "buffoon," "nincompoop," "scum," "a cancer," "an obscenity," "gutless liar," "unmitigated liar," "pathological liar," "egomaniac," "nuts," "crazy," "irrational," "suicidal," "lunatic," etc.

In May 1984, appellees filed a motion for summary judgment. After extensive discovery and pleadings, the trial court granted summary judgment on July 9, 1986, after considering the case for over a year. The trial court's forty-one page opinion granting summary judgment stated that all of Franklin's statements were protected opinions rather than defamatory factual statements. The opinion also stated that the discussion of sports-related issues on a sports show could not be sufficiently outrageous to provide a legal basis for a claim of intentional infliction of emotional distress.

The appellant appealed the judgment of the trial court and filed the following two assignments of error:

> 1. The trial court erred in dismissing plaintiff's libel action because it failed to correctly apply the 'totality of circumstances' analysis.
>
> 2. The trial court erred in dismissing plaintiff's claim for intentional infliction of emotional distress since reasonable minds could conclude that a three-year, near nightly verbal attack on plaintiff's intelligence, sanity, integrity, and veracity was extreme and outrageous behavior.

The first assignment of error calls upon this court to decide whether summary judgment was properly entered against the plaintiff in a public-figure defamation case. For the reasons which follow, we find that it was.

I

The law of defamation has been given much attention by the federal and state courts. We must begin our analysis with a brief examination of the standard which applies to the underlying defamation proceeding.

In New York Times Co. v. Sullivan (1964), 376 U.S. 254, 84 S.Ct. 710, 11 L.Ed.2d 686, the United States Supreme Court set forth a standard which "prohibits a public official from recovering damages for a defamatory falsehood relating to his official conduct unless he proves that the statement was made with 'actual malice'—that is, with knowledge that it was false or with reckless disregard of whether it was false or not." Id. at 279–280, 84 S.Ct. at 725–726. Appellant admits he is a public figure in the context of Sullivan.

The proof of actual malice must be clear and convincing. Gertz v. Robert Welch, Inc. (1974), 418 U.S. 323, 94 S.Ct. 2997, 41 L.Ed.2d 789. In deciding if the proof is clear and convincing, the focus is upon the defendant's attitude toward the truth or falsity of the published statements, rather than upon the existence of hatefulness or ill will. Garrison v. Louisiana (1964), 379 U.S. 64, 74, 85 S.Ct. 209, 215, 13 L.Ed.2d 125; Herbert v. Lando (1979), 441 U.S. 153, 99 S.Ct. 1635, 60 L.Ed.2d 115; Cantrell v. Forest City Publishing Co. (1974), 419 U.S. 245, 95 S.Ct. 465, 42 L.Ed.2d 419.

The burden is on the plaintiff to show with convincing clarity that the publication of false statements was made with knowledge of their falsity, or with a "high degree of awareness of their probable falsity," Garrison, supra, 379 U.S. at 74, 85 S.Ct. at 216, or "that the defendant in fact entertained serious doubts as to the truth of his publication." St. Amant v. Thompson (1968), 390 U.S. 727, 731, 88 S.Ct. 1323, 1325, 20 L.Ed.2d 262. On appeal, the appellate court must exercise its independent judgment in deciding whether the evidence of the record meets these tests. Bose Corp. v. Consumers Union of United States, Inc. (1984), 466 U.S. 485, 104 S.Ct. 1949, 80 L.Ed.2d 502, rehearing denied (1984), 467 U.S. 1267, 104 S.Ct. 3561, 82 L.Ed.2d 863. This independent review of the record aids in protecting against " 'forbidden instrusion[s] * * * [into] the field of free expression' " and assigns to judges a constitutional requirement that cannot be delegated to the trier of fact, whether the factfinding function be performed in the particular case by a jury or by a trial judge. Id. at 508 and 510, 104 S.Ct. at 1963 and 1964.

On these basic principles, the law of Ohio and federal law are in accord. Grau v. Kleinschmidt (1987), 31 Ohio St.3d 84, 31 OBR 250, 509 N.E.2d 399; Scott v. News–Herald (1986), 25 Ohio St.3d 243, 25 OBR 302, 496 N.E.2d 699; Dupler v. Mansfield Journal Co. (1980), 64 Ohio St.2d 116, 18 O.O.3d 354, 413 N.E.2d 1187, certiorari denied (1981), 452 U.S. 962, 101 S.Ct. 3111, 69 L.Ed.2d 973.

II

Neither this court nor the trial court may weigh the proof or choose among reasonable inferences in deciding whether summary judgment should be granted. As in other civil cases, inferences and questions of credibility must be resolved in plaintiff's (the non-moving party's) favor. Dupler, supra.

Nonetheless, summary judgment procedures are especially appropriate in the First Amendment area. " 'The threat of being put to the defense of a lawsuit brought by a popular public official may be as chilling to the exercise of First Amendment freedoms as fear of the outcome of the lawsuit itself * * *. Unless persons * * * desiring to exercise their First Amendment rights are assured freedom from the harassment of lawsuits, they will tend to become self-censors. And to this extent debate on public issues and the conduct of public officials will become less uninhibited, less robust, and less wide-open, for self-censorship affecting the whole public is hardly less virulent for being privately administered.' " Dupler, supra, 64 Ohio St.2d at 120, 18 O.O.3d at 357, 413 N.E.2d at 1191. See, also, Washington Post Co. v. Keogh (C.A.D.C. 1966), 365 F.2d 965, 968.

In order to withstand a defendant's motion for summary judgment in a defamation action, a public official-plaintiff must produce evidence sufficient to raise a genuine issue of material fact from which a reasonable jury could find actual malice with convincing clarity. Bukky v. Painesville Tel. & Lake Geauga Printing Co. (1981), 68 Ohio St.2d 45, 22 O.O.3d 183, 428 N.E.2d 405. Moreover, only factual disputes that might affect the outcome of the suit under governing law will preclude the entry of summary judgment. Anderson v. Liberty Lobby, Inc. (1986), 477 U.S. 242, 106 S.Ct. 2505, 91 L.Ed.2d 202.

In this case, appellant asserts that summary judgment was inappropriate due to the fact the lower court incorrectly applied the "totality of circumstances" analysis set forth in Scott v. News–Herald, supra. The Scott analysis uses four factors to determine whether a published statement is a constitutionally protected opinion or an actionable defamatory remark. The factors to be considered are: 1. The specific language used; 2. Whether the truth or falsity of the statement is verifiable; 3. The specific context of the statement; and 4. The broader social context in which the statement appeared.

Appellant asserts the trial court erred for two reasons. First, the trial court's general conclusions about the nature of the Sportsline audience are unsupportable in view of the substantial evidence in the record. Second, the statements have not been analyzed accurately with respect to their surrounding context. We disagree.

The trial court, at the time of its decision, had no Ohio case law to detail guidelines for a trial court to follow in making a fact/opinion determination. The trial court found that the United States Court of Appeals for the District of Columbia had "devised a useful framework of analysis" in Ollman v. Evans (C.A.D.C.1984), 750 F.2d 970 (en banc). The Ollman analysis involved the same four factors as the Scott analysis. The Ollman court clearly stated that whether a statement is one of fact or opinion is a question of law for the court, not the jury, to determine, and is therefore an appropriate subject for summary judgment. Id. at 978.

This court finds, as the trial court found, that Franklin's comments were constitutionally protected opinion. As in Scott, the arena of sports is "a traditional haven for cajoling, invective, and hyperbole," and therefore the reasonable reader was on notice that this was a statement of opinion. Scott, supra, 25 Ohio St.3d at 253–254, 25 OBR at 311, 496 N.E.2d at 708–709. The appellant would have us believe that the statistical demographics of Franklin's audience is tantamount to deciding whether his remarks were defamatory. Again, if we are to have a free exchange of ideas, thoughts and discussion, we cannot place on a commentator the burden to protect against listeners who are not reasonable.

The First Amendment militates the protection of unrestricted and hearty debate on issues of concern to the public, including the protection of what "may well include vehement, caustic, and sometimes unpleasantly sharp attacks * * *." New York Times Co., supra, 376 U.S. at 270, 84 S.Ct. at 721. Since this court affirms the lower court's ruling that Franklin's remarks are constitutionally protected opinions, the actual malice standard need not be discussed.

III

The appellant, in his second assignment of error, asserts that Franklin's intensive campaign of verbal harassment over a period of years caused him severe emotional distress.

In Ohio, it is necessary for a party alleging intentional infliction of emotional distress to establish that the alleged culpable conduct so exceeds the bounds of decency that it is considered atrocious, completely outrageous and utterly intolerable in a civilized community. Yeager v. Local Union 20 (1983), 6 Ohio St.3d 369, 375, 6 OBR 421, 426, 453 N.E.2d 666, 671.

Further, in determining whether conduct is culpable, Ohio courts have consistently recognized that it is essential to view such conduct in context. There are situations naturally fraught with antagonism and emotion where a person must be expected to endure the resultant antagonism and mental anguish. Local Lodge 1297 v. Allen (1986), 22 Ohio St.3d 228, 22 OBR 407, 490 N.E.2d 865.

In the cause before this court, the plaintiff is a public figure. Public figures, having thrust themselves into the public eye, cannot prevent others from criticizing or insulting them for their acts or deeds. Scott, supra, 25 Ohio St.3d at 245–246, 25 OBR at 304, 496 N.E.2d at 702. This is especially true when the public figure is a professional basketball team "owner" and the antagonism and criticism is from a member of the media.

Public figures who thrust themselves into the public eye must bear the discomfort of criticisms levied upon their public actions or statements. Baumgartner v. United States (1944), 322 U.S. 665, 64 S.Ct. 1240, 88 L.Ed. 1525. Stepien admitted he made many bold moves in his ownership of the Cleveland Cavaliers. Many of these moves caused heated disputes among fans, media, and the NBA. In this context, Stepien must expect critical commentary. Stepien also considered moving the team to Toronto. This speculative move was also highly controversial. Writers and fans cannot be expected to remain mute when "their" team might leave the Cleveland area. Having engaged in such conduct, the expected response was quite normal, although harsh.

The United States Supreme Court has recently set forth its opinion of intentional infliction of emotional distress in a public-figure context in Hustler Magazine (Flynt) v. Falwell (1988), 485 U.S. 46, 108 S.Ct. 876, 99 L.Ed.2d 41.

In Falwell, a magazine published a parody which, among other things, portrayed Reverend Jerry Falwell as having engaged in a drunken incestuous rendezvous with his mother in an outhouse. Although the lower court found against Falwell on the libel claim, it ruled in his favor concerning the emotional distress claim. The court of appeals affirmed, rejecting Flynt's contention that the "actual malice" standard of New York Times Co., supra, must be met before Falwell can recover for emotional distress. Rejecting as irrelevant the contention that, because the jury found that the parody did not describe actual facts, the parody was an opinion protected by the First Amendment, the court ruled that the issue was whether the parody's publication was sufficiently outrageous to constitute intentional infliction of emotional distress.

The Supreme Court held that in order to protect the free flow of ideas and opinions on matters of public interest and concern, the First and Fourteenth Amendments prohibit public figures and public officials from recovering damages for the tort of intentional infliction of emotional distress without showing in addition that the publication contained a false statement of fact which was made with actual malice. Falwell, supra, 485 U.S. at ___, 108 S.Ct. at 880, 99 L.Ed.2d at 49–50.

Generally, the law does not regard the intent to inflict emotional distress as one which should receive much solicitude, and it is quite understandable that most jurisdictions have chosen to make it civilly culpable where the conduct is sufficiently outrageous. Id. at ___, 108 S.Ct. at 880, 99 L.Ed.2d at 50. But in the world of debate about public affairs, many things done with motives that are less than admirable are protected by the First Amendment. Garrison v. Louisiana, supra (379 U.S. 64, 85 S.Ct. 209).

In Garrison, the court held that a speaker is protected by the First Amendment even if the writer or speaker is motivated by hatred or ill will: "Debate on public issues will not be uninhibited if the speaker must run the risk that it will be proved in court that he spoke out of hatred; even if he did speak out of hatred, utterances honestly believed contribute to the free interchange of ideas and the ascertainment of truth." Id. at 73, 85 S.Ct. at 215.

Thus, while a bad motive may be deemed controlling for purposes of tort liability in other areas of the law, the court ruled the First Amendment prohibits such a result in the area of public debate about public figures. Falwell, supra, 485 U.S. at ___, 108 S.Ct. at 881, 99 L.Ed.2d at 50.

Appellee, Peter J. Franklin, commented about a public figure concerning controversial situations. This court cannot award an emotional distress claim based on Franklin's ill will to Stepien. Therefore, assignment of error number two is not well-taken and the trial court's decision is affirmed.

Notes

1. For a further discussion of the opinion defense, see *Brooks v. Paige*, 773 P.2d 1098 (Colo.Ct.App.1988) (statements on local television program that professional soccer player had "quit" and "backed out" were not actionable because they reflected the opinions of the speakers). *See also* Andrew K. Craig, Comment, *The Rise in Press Criticism of the Athlete and the Future of Libel Litigation Involving Athletes and the Press*, 4 Seton Hall J. Sport L. 527 (1994).

2. Given the incendiary nature of his comments, should the court have ruled against Peter Franklin? If you had been Franklin's employer, would you have told him to tone down his comments? *See further* Leonard Shapiro, *In Miami, Goldberg Has the Words Taken Right Out of His Mouth*, Wash. Post, June 28, 1997, at H10 (reporting on the suspension imposed on radio host Hank Goldberg for criticizing local sports mogul H. Wayne Huizenga).

Problem 53

In a nationally-circulated magazine article, a sportswriter predicted, "Once again, State University's season will be ruined by the incompetence of its head coach. She's always screwed up in the past, and this year will be no different." If the coach sues for defamation, will the reporter's words be treated as protected opinion? *See Washington v. Smith*, 80 F.3d 555 (D.C.Cir. 1996).

b. Actual Malice

Assuming falsity is established, the plaintiff must next show the defendant acted with "actual malice." This is a nearly-impossible task and the reason most public figure defamation lawsuits fail.

BELL v. ASSOCIATED PRESS

584 F.Supp. 128 (D.D.C.1984).

GREENE, District Judge.

On March 29, 1982, the Associated Press moved on its sports wire, and various newspapers subsequently published, a story reading in pertinent part as follows:

> Tampa Bay wide receiver Theo Bell, a member of the National Football League 1979 Champion Pittsburgh Steelers, is being sought on a bench warrant for alleged lewdness at a casino hotel, authorities said Monday.

It later turned out that the person charged was an imposter who had convinced hotel and police officials that he was Theo Bell. Plaintiff brought this action for libel, and defendant has moved for summary judgment. The motion will be granted.

I

It is established that the good faith publication of fair and accurate reports of official actions is privileged. See Binder v. Triangle Publications, Inc., 442 Pa. 319, 275 A.2d 53, 56 (1971). This privilege extends to arrest reports. Restatement (Second) of Torts § 611, comment "n"; see Medico v. Time, Inc., 643 F.2d 134, 138–39 (3d Cir.1981). The issue here is whether, on the facts before the Court, this privilege is a defense to the action.

The facts are as follows. Someone calling himself Theo Bell, football player for the Tampa Bay Buccaneers, was arrested on March 7, 1982, in connection with an incident of lewdness at the Tropicana Hotel in Atlantic City. An official arrest report was prepared (the report was for Theo K. Bell whose employer was listed as the "National Football League, Tampa Bay"), and subsequently a summons and bench warrant were issued when Theo Bell failed to appear in Atlantic City Municipal Court on March 22 as required.

Upon being made aware of this information (the source of the information was the captain of security at the Tropicana Hotel), Robert Wade, a reporter for the Associated Press, made substantial efforts at verification. He contacted the Captain of Detectives James Dooley, the head of the Atlantic City police department's Casino Hotels Investigations Unit, and asked him to "pull the file" on the Tropicana Hotel incident. Captain Dooley advised him that "Theo Bell of the National Football League Tampa Bay Buccaneers had been detained by the police on March 7, 1982 following an incident of lewdness at the Tropicana," and he gave Wade several additional details. Wade went on to contact the Municipal Court Clerk and the Municipal Court Administrator who confirmed that a warrant was outstanding for Theo Bell for failure to answer the charges against him. The vice president for corporate and legal affairs at the Tropicana Hotel likewise confirmed that an incident had occurred at the hotel involving Mr. Bell, and an Atlantic City municipal court judge gave Wade additional information about the charges against Bell.

Wade also contacted a spokesman for the Tampa Bay team who declined comment, and he attempted to contact plaintiff himself, but he was unable to do so because plaintiff was at the time in an alcoholic rehabilitation clinic and the Tampa Bay team would not or could not make his telephone number available.

Except in relatively minor and immaterial respects, plaintiff does not quarrel with these facts. However, he asserts that the AP story was not a report of an official action or proceeding because the arrest report did not result in plaintiff's arrest but in the arrest of the impostor. Memorandum in Opposition at 7. That contention lacks merit.

The point of the privilege is that it covers the reporting of both true and false factual matters. See, e.g., Binder v. Triangle Publications, Inc., supra; Mathis v. Philadelphia Newspapers, Inc., 455 F.Supp. 406 (E.D.Pa.1978); Biermann v. Pulitzer Publishing Co., 627 S.W.2d 87 (Mo.App.1981). In line with this principle, the article must be compared, not with the events as they actually transpired, but with the official reports that the newspaper republished. Mathis v. Philadelphia Newspaper, Inc., supra, 455 F.Supp. at 417; Dameron v. Washington Magazine, 575 F.Supp. 1575 (D.D.C.1983). If the rule were otherwise—that is, if a newspaper would have to verify in the case of every arrest and prosecution that the police had the right suspect—the reporting of criminal proceedings would largely have to cease. Such a result would be entirely at odds with American constitutional and public policy which demands that there be public scrutiny of governmental actions. The considerations underlying that policy are particularly potent when applied to proceedings which result in the arrest or detention of individuals. Where there is no such scrutiny—as is true in some totalitarian countries—individuals sometimes disappear without a trace and without public knowledge or accountability.

Plaintiff has conceded that defendant "thought it was me" (Appendix to defendant's motion at 15.) On that basis, and on the basis of the verifications conducted by Wade, defendant's agent, plaintiff clearly could not carry his burden of proving malice, and the defense based on the reporting of official proceedings is therefore well taken.

II

The same result follows from a "public figure" analysis of the case. Those who, by reason of the notoriety of their achievements or the vigor and success with which they seek the public's attention, are properly classified as public figures, may recover for injury to reputation only upon proof that the falsehood was made with knowledge of its falsity or with reckless disregard for the truth. Gertz v. Welch, 418 U.S. 323, 342, 94 S.Ct. 2997, 3008, 41 L.Ed.2d 789 (1974); Waldbaum v. Fairchild Publications Company, 627 F.2d 1287 (D.C.Cir.1980). The lesser protection public figures have from defamation rests on the proposition that, as the court expressed it in Waldbaum, supra, 627 F.2d at 1291–92,

> ... those who enter the public spotlight have greater access to the media to correct misstatements about them, as shown by their pre-existing media exposure. More important, in 'assum[ing] special prominence in the resolution of public questions,' public figures 'invite attention and comment.' They thus accept the risk that the press, in fulfilling its role of reporting, analyzing, and commenting on well known persons and public controversies, will focus on them and, perhaps, cast them in an unfavorable light.

627 F.2d at 1291–92.

Professional athletes, including football players, have frequently been held to be public figures, especially when they have achieved fame or notoriety. See, e.g., Chuy v. Philadelphia Eagles Football Club, 595 F.2d 1265 (3d Cir.1979); Brewer v. Memphis Publishing Company, 626 F.2d 1238 (5th Cir.1980). It is with these principles in mind that plaintiff's status must be analyzed.

Theo Bell has long been in the public eye. He was a star athlete in high school; he set a number of records at the University of Arizona; and he was a well-known player of the Pittsburgh Steelers from 1976 to 1981. His athletic career received substantial press coverage in Arizona, in Pennsylvania, and elsewhere. In his capacity as a kick-return specialist, he contributed to the Steelers' Superbowl victory in 1979.

Nor has plaintiff's notoriety been confined to the football field. There was a great deal of publicity when he was arrested for trespassing while at Arizona; when he pleaded guilty to disorderly conduct while in Pittsburgh; when, in recent years, he was twice arrested for drunk driving; and when in 1981 he was arrested on charges involving sexual misconduct. In fact, over one hundred newspaper articles have appeared concerning his various activities during the course of plaintiff's career.

For purposes of the law of defamation, there are two classes of public figures (1) "general purpose" public figures, that is, those who have attained such persuasive power and influence or such fame or notoriety that they may be classified as public figures in all situations, and (2) "limited purpose" public figures, that is, those who "voluntarily inject [themselves or are] drawn into a particular public controversy." Gertz v. Welch, supra, 418 U.S. at 351, 94 S.Ct. at 3012; Waldbaum v. Fairchild Publications, Inc., supra, 627 F.2d at 1292. See also, Brewer v. Memphis Publishing Co., 626 F.2d 1238, 1254 (5th Cir.1980) (limited purpose public figure is one who has voluntarily engaged in activities that necessarily involve risk of increased exposure and injury to reputation). It is not necessary here to decide whether a plaintiff is a general purpose public figure under these standards, for, at a minimum, he is clearly a limited purpose public figure.

Plaintiff concedes that he is a public figure for purposes of newspaper stories concerning his role as an athlete, but he claims that the AP story "bore no relationship to [him] as a professional football player." Memorandum in Opposition at 6. That is simply in error.

As a professional athlete, plaintiff willingly assumed the public spotlight. Indeed, his contracts with National Football League teams included an obligation to "cooperate with the news media." App. 164. Those contracts further stipulated that "the success of professional football depends largely on public respect for and approval of those associated with the game," and that if a "player has engaged in personal conduct reasonably judged by [the] Club to adversely affect or reflect" on the Club, it may terminate the contract. App. 164–65. These provisions in the contracts are an accurate reflection of the realities of professional sports.

There is today considerable public interest, concern, and controversy with respect to off-the-field misconduct of professional athletes. Charges of drug abuse and trafficking and other criminal activities are often made and not infrequently sustained.

Since professional sports depends for its financial well-being upon television, other media exposure, and public support, events of this kind have a direct effect on the sports, the teams, and the players.

Plaintiff has recognized the relationship between on-field and off-field activities for he has often talked to the newspapers about his life away from the playing field. Thus, he has given interviews concerning his attitude toward religion, alcohol, drugs, and crime, and he has publicly recognized that his personal problems and his playing career had received widespread public attention "because I'm a public figure." App. 155.

Professional athletes can hardly be permitted to hold themselves out as public figures, seeking a maximum amount of publicity for themselves and their teams with respect to their athletic achievements, while successfully claiming strictly private status when misconduct is charged or proved. Their professional careers and those of other entertainers who seek the public spotlight are so intimately tied to their personal conduct that such a distinction would be entirely unrealistic.

The dissemination of the exploits of professional athletes through the media is responsible in large measure for the enormous financial rewards some of them are reaping. As the court said in Waldbaum v. Fairchild Publications, Inc., supra, 627 F.2d at 1294, "[f]ame often brings power, money, respect, adulation, and self-gratification. It also may bring close scrutiny that can lead to adverse as well as favorable comment."

Just as off-the-field behavior affects the prestige and income of teams and players so does it relate to the status athletes achieve in the community. As Judge Albert V. Bryan, Jr. recently said in sentencing Washington Redskin Tony Peters on a drug charge, "[t]he most tragic aspect of this case, aside from the criminality, ... is that the defendant is a role model in this community.... The youth of this community who are exposed daily to the temptation of drugs ... tend to look upon athletes as larger-than-life."

In short, at least with respect to professional athletes at this particular time, charges of criminal misconduct are a subject of public controversy and those who are the subject of such charges are public figures for that limited purpose.

III

As it turned out, the Associated Press story was in error. However, that error was entirely inadvertent. In view of the peculiar circumstance of an impostor assuming plaintiff's identity, malice or reckless conduct could not possibly be ascribed to defendant. If the Associated Press were to be held liable, therefore, it would have to be on the theory that, even with respect to what appeared to be a public figure involved in an official proceeding, it had a duty not to report on the proceeding as it was reflected in the official police and court records without first conducting a painstaking investigation into the accuracy of the official reports and the identity of the person charged. Such a rule would have the consequence of delaying significantly the publication of news concerning public figures who are charged with criminal offenses, or of halting the publication of such reports altogether. Because such consequences are inconsistent with the values embodied in the First Amendment, the law does not impose such burdens on the press.

Defendant's motion for summary judgment will be granted.

WORLD BOXING COUNCIL v. COSELL

715 F.Supp. 1259 (S.D.N.Y.1989).

CONNER, District Judge.

This bout between boxing heavyweights pits plaintiff, the World Boxing Council (the "WBC"), against defendant, sportscaster Howard Cosell ("Cosell"). In this diversity action, the WBC charges Cosell with libel for a passage in a book he co-authored with writer Peter Bonventre, entitled I Never Played the Game. Cosell counterpunches with a motion for summary judgment under Rule 56, Fed.R.Civ.P., on the ground that the passage in question is constitutionally protected opinion, or, alternatively, that it cannot be demonstrated that he wrote the passage with actual malice. For the reasons articulated below, Cosell's motion for summary judgment is granted.

Background

I Never Played the Game recounts some of Cosell's experiences in professional sports, and expresses his views about the problems afflicting sports in the United States. A significant portion of the book—three chapters—is devoted to boxing. In these chapters, Cosell decries what he perceives to be suspect ratings and dangerous mismatches. He insists that these blemishes on the sport are the product of the concentration of power in unaccountable rating and sanctioning bodies, like the WBC, and powerful individual promoters, like Don King.

The alleged libel occurs in a passage in Chapter 7:

> King derives much of his power through his sway over Jose Sulaiman, the president of the World Boxing Council. The WBC is based in Mexico City, the WBA in Panama, and while each is supposed to be an independent regulator of boxing, both are in reality conspirators in rigging ratings. These organizations are basically instruments of extortion—playing by their own rules, creating their own champions—easily manipulated by the gifts and favors of promoters and managers who are seeking special considerations for their fighters.

H. Cosell, I Never Played the Game at 182–183 (1985). The three allegedly libelous comments contained in the passage are, "conspirators in rigging ratings," "instruments of extortion," and "easily manipulated by the gifts and favors of promoters and managers who are seeking special considerations for their fighters." In these comments, the WBC contends, Cosell accuses it of the crimes of conspiracy, extortion, and bribery, as well as unethical practices such as rating fighters without regard to merit. In response, Cosell first argues that the passage is a constitutionally protected opinion because the language is loose and figurative, consistent with both his outspoken personality and the hyperbolic expression generally associated with boxing commentary. Second, Cosell maintains that, even if his remarks are construed as factual statements, summary judgment is still warranted, because the passage was not written with actual malice.

In boxing, a referee is empowered to end a bout and award the winner a technical knockout if one fighter is no longer able to defend himself. Analogously, in a court of law, a judge may curtail a case and award summary judgment if the evidence is "so one-sided that one party must prevail as a matter of law." Anderson v. Liberty Lobby, Inc., 477 U.S. 242, 251–52, 106 S.Ct. 2505, 2512, 91 L.Ed.2d 202 (1986). I find that, even if Cosell's first legal swing is wide of the target, his second is "on the button;" if the challenged passage was a "low blow," plaintiff was neither deliberately nor recklessly fouled. Therefore, I grant Cosell's motion for summary judgment on the ground that the WBC has suffered a technical knockout on the issue of actual malice.

Discussion

I. Protected Opinion or Unprotected Fact?

It is axiomatic that an expression of opinion, no matter how vituperative, polemical, or obnoxious, is entitled to constitutional protection under the first amendment. See Gertz v. Robert Welch, Inc., 418 U.S. 323, 339–40, 94 S.Ct. 2997, 3006–07, 41 L.Ed.2d 789 (1974); Letter Carriers v. Austin, 418 U.S. 264, 284–86, 94 S.Ct. 2770, 2781–82, 41 L.Ed.2d 745 (1974); Greenbelt Cooperative Publishing Ass'n v. Bresler, 398 U.S. 6, 14, 90 S.Ct. 1537, 1541–42, 26 L.Ed.2d 6 (1970); Mr. Chow of New York v. Ste. Jour Azur S.A., 759 F.2d 219, 224 (2d Cir.1985); Davis v. Ross, 754 F.2d 80, 85 (2d Cir.1985); Cianci v. New Times Pub. Co., 639 F.2d 54, 61 (2d Cir.1980); Hotchner v. Castillo–Puche, 551 F.2d 910, 913 (2d Cir.), cert. denied, Hotchner v. Doubleday & Co., 434 U.S. 834, 98 S.Ct. 120, 54 L.Ed.2d 95 (1977); Rizzuto v. Nexxus Products Co., 641 F.Supp. 473, 481 (S.D.N.Y.) (Weinfeld, J.), aff'd, 810 F.2d 1161 (2d Cir.1986).

It is equally well-settled that whether a statement constitutes fact or opinion is a question of law for the court. See Letter Carriers, 418 U.S. at 282, 94 S.Ct. at 2780; Greenbelt, 398 U.S. at 11–14, 90 S.Ct. at 1540–42; Mr. Chow, 759 F.2d at 224; Davis, 754 F.2d at 85; Rizzuto, 641 F.Supp. at 481; accord Ollman v. Evans, 750 F.2d 970, 979 (D.C.Cir. 1984) (en banc), cert. denied, 471 U.S. 1127, 105 S.Ct. 2662, 86 L.Ed.2d 278 (1985). The court's inquiry must be made from the perspective of an "ordinary" reader of the statement. Mr. Chow, 759 F.2d at 224. What may appear to be a factual question is nevertheless reserved for the court, because of the special interest in enhancing the predictability of decisions in the first amendment area by separating fact from opinion according to announced legal standards, and publishing examples of the manner in which these standards are to be applied. Ollman, 750 F.2d at 978.

Although no bright-line test exists for differentiating opinion from fact, the court's inquiry must include the circumstances surrounding the controversial language. Mr. Chow, 759 F.2d at 226; Ollman, 750 F.2d at 978, 980 n. 17. Cosell argues that, read in the context of the sports world in general, the boxing world in particular, and his own notoriety, his remarks would be understood by an ordinary reader as an expression of opinion.

It is true that language which might be deemed libelous in other contexts has been tolerated and even encouraged in the world of professional sports. Certainly, the sports world is an environment where the kind of 'robust' debate endorsed by the Supreme Court in New York Times v. Sullivan, 376 U.S. 254, 84 S.Ct. 710, 11 L.Ed.2d 686 (1964), has flourished. Even the once fastidious etiquette of Wimbledon has succumbed to the more gross and tawdry vernacular formerly more characteristic of hockey rinks and football stadia. The world of Damon Runyon was not portrayed in the idiom of the church supper. Henderson v. Times Mirror Co., 669 F.Supp. 356, 361 (D.Colo.1987) (citation omitted), aff'd, 876 F.2d 108 (10th Cir.1989).

Nevertheless, Cosell's remarks appear on their face to accuse the WBC of rigging ratings and extorting bribes. Thus, even considering the environment in which they were made, the challenged statements may not clearly be characterized as mere opinion. Other courts have repeatedly recognized the difficulty of distinguishing fact from opinion. Mr. Chow, 759 F.2d at 224; Ollman, 750 F.2d at 978; Rinsley v. Brandt, 700 F.2d 1304, 1309 (10th Cir.1983). Fortunately, in this case, I need not resolve that troublesome question, because I hold that even if Cosell's comments are statements of fact, the WBC is unable to show that Cosell wrote them with actual malice.

II. Actual Malice

A. The Standard

The parties have stipulated that the WBC is a public figure for the purpose of this litigation. Therefore, this matter is controlled by the principles established by the Supreme Court in New York Times v. Sullivan, 376 U.S. 254, 84 S.Ct. 710, 11 L.Ed.2d 686 (1964), and its progeny.

At trial, the WBC would be required to demonstrate, by clear and convincing evidence, that the offending passage was false, and that Cosell wrote it with " 'actual malice'—that is, with knowledge that it was false or with reckless disregard of whether it was false or not." Id. at 279–80, 84 S.Ct. at 726; accord Gertz, 418 U.S. at 327–28, 94 S.Ct. at 3000–01; Contemporary Mission, Inc., et al. v. New York Times, 842 F.2d

612, 621 (2d Cir.1988); Cianci, 639 F.2d at 59; Rizzuto, 641 F.Supp. at 479. More specifically, "[t]he burden of proving 'actual malice' requires the plaintiff to demonstrate with clear and convincing evidence that the defendant realized that his statement was false or that he subjectively entertained serious doubt as to the truth of his statement." Bose Corp. v. Consumers Union of United States, 466 U.S. 485, 511 n. 30, 104 S.Ct. 1949, 1965 n. 30, 80 L.Ed.2d 502 (1984).

The burden of establishing clear and convincing evidence is heavier than the typical civil requirement of proof by a preponderance of the evidence, but lighter than the criminal rule that a trier be convinced beyond a reasonable doubt. Yiamouyiannis v. Consumers Union of the United States, 619 F.2d 932, 940 (2d Cir.), cert. denied, 449 U.S. 839, 101 S.Ct. 117, 66 L.Ed.2d 46 (1980). Under this standard, the evidence presented by plaintiff must be significantly probative and more than merely colorable. Rizzuto, 641 F.Supp. at 479.

The Supreme Court has held that where the clear and convincing evidence standard applies at trial, it governs a summary judgment motion as well. "[T]he inquiry involved in a ruling on a motion for summary judgment ... necessarily implicates the substantive evidentiary standard of proof that would apply at the trial on the merits." Anderson, 477 U.S. at 252, 106 S.Ct. at 2512. This rule continues to be the law of the Second Circuit. Contemporary Mission, 842 F.2d at 621; Herbert v. Lando, 781 F.2d 298, 305 (2d Cir.), cert. denied, 476 U.S. 1182, 106 S.Ct. 2916, 91 L.Ed.2d 545 (1986). The court is compelled to grant summary judgment, and dismiss the case, if it finds that a reasonable jury could not conclude that the WBC had shown, by clear and convincing evidence, actual malice on the part of Cosell. See Liberty Lobby, 477 U.S. at 252, 106 S.Ct. at 2512.

No reasonable jury could find actual malice in this case, because, regardless of the truth of the assertions in Cosell's passage, the WBC is unable to raise an issue of fact regarding Cosell's subjective state of mind when he wrote them. "When the moving party has carried its burden under Rule 56(c), its opponent must do more than simply show that there is some metaphysical doubt as to the material facts." Matsushita Electrical Industrial Co. v. Zenith Radio Corp., 475 U.S. 574, 586, 106 S.Ct. 1348, 1356, 89 L.Ed.2d 538 (1986). It must establish that there is a "genuine issue for trial." Id. at 587, 106 S.Ct. at 1356. Cosell offers substantial, uncontested evidence that, irrespective of the truth of the assertions he makes in the challenged passage, he believed them to be true when he wrote them, and had no reason to doubt their truth. Therefore, he cannot be shown to have written the passage with actual malice.

B. Cosell's Uncontested Evidence

In his affidavit, Cosell swears that promoter Bob Arum told him that he could not get WBC title shots for his fighters unless he gave gifts and favors to its president, Jose Sulaiman. Cosell Aff. p 13. In addition, Cosell's co-author, Peter Bonventre, swears in his affidavit that he, too, heard Arum complain about having to treat Sulaiman lavishly if he wanted fighters rated or fights sanctioned by the WBC. Bonventre Aff. p 12b. Bonventre also recounts an incident where, while interviewing Don King, he commented that King must do a lot of favors for Sulaiman or pay him off, and King joked, without denying it, that he would write it all in a book some day. Bonventre Aff. p 12f. Furthermore, Bonventre swears that he heard Bert Sugar, the former publisher of Ring Magazine, relate a conversation he had with Sulaiman where Sulaiman bragged about receiving expensive gifts from King. Bonventre Aff. p 12a. Both Cosell and Bonventre swear in their respective affidavits that each informed the other of his experiences. Cosell Aff. p 12; Bonventre Aff. p 7. These pieces of evidence support Cosell's contention that, true or not, he believed that the WBC was a "conspirator in rigging ratings," an "instrument of extortion," and "easily manipulated by the gifts and favors of promoters and managers who are seeking special considerations for their fighters."

In its brief, the WBC argues that, "it must be assumed that Cosell fabricated his claim of an admission," because he "wholly failed to identify any particular conversation or circumstance in which Arum made such a statement...." Plaintiff's Brief at 44. Even after drawing reasonable inferences in favor of the WBC, I disagree. The WBC offers no sworn testimony or other evidence contradicting Cosell's affidavit. Indeed, at his deposition, Cosell insisted again that Arum told him about the necessity of bribing Sulaiman. Plaintiff's Exh. 1 at 129. "It is not enough for the plaintiff merely to assert 'that the jury might, and legally could, disbelieve the defendant's denial ... of legal malice.'" Contemporary Mission, 842 F.2d at 621–22 (quoting Liberty Lobby, 477 U.S. at 256, 106 S.Ct. at 2514. "Some facts must be asserted to support the claim that the state of mind existed." Markowitz v. Republic National Bank of New York, 651 F.2d 825, 828 (2d Cir.1981).

Although much of the information supporting Cosell's contention that he believed the remarks in the passage to be true came to him through Bonventre, the WBC offers no evidence suggesting that Cosell had any reason to doubt Bonventre's credibility. Certainly, Cosell is entitled to rely on the research and experience of his co-author, in addition to his own experience, especially when his co-author has worked with him on his television show, Sportsbeat, and is an award-winning journalist who has served as a writer, reporter, and editor for such well-known publications as The New York Times, Newsweek and Inside Sports. Cf. Marcone v. Penthouse International Magazine for Men, 754 F.2d 1072, 1089 (3d Cir.), cert. denied, 474 U.S. 864, 106 S.Ct. 182, 88 L.Ed.2d 151 (1985) (publisher may rely on the professional reputation of an author unless the "allegations are so inherently improbable that only a reckless man would have put them in circulation ... [or] there are obvious reasons to doubt the veracity ... of his reports"); Hotchner, 551 F.2d at 913–14 (publisher may rely on author's allegations where "the evidence does not demonstrate that [the publisher] had cause seriously to suspect that [the author's] opinions ... were without foundation").

The WBC argues that Cosell and Bonventre "cavalierly and summarily dismissed" concerns raised by Richard H. Sugarman, who performed a pre-publication "libel reading" of the book, and Howard Cady, an editor of the book. Plaintiff's Brief at 19–20. However, the WBC concedes that, at a deposition, "[Sugarman] testified that Bonventre reassured him that the statements were true, and if anything, understatements, based on previously published reports, his own experience, and Howard Cosell's experience." Plaintiff's Brief at 20; see also Plaintiff's Exh. 4 at 30. Sugarman's testimony supports Cosell's and Bonventre's contention that they always believed the truth of the assertions made in the book. Sugarman's concerns may bear on whether the publisher believed the comments to be true, but do not reflect on Cosell's state of mind.

Cady, the book's editor, testified at his deposition that he never spoke to either Cosell or Bonventre about the disputed passage, and that his only concern with the book was that certain early portions, relating to professional football, were repetitious. Defendant's Reply Affidavit, Exh. D at 46–47.

C. Reliance on Other Publications

Cosell and Bonventre also claim that they relied on published articles which appeared in the Village Voice and Sports Illustrated. The WBC argues that Cosell distorted the articles in the Village Voice and Sports Illustrated to imply that the WBC was engaging in criminal acts, and seeks to introduce, as evidence of Cosell's alleged misuse of the articles, testimony by an expert witness "in the field of media analysis and communications research." Through a complicated and confusing "scientific/statistical" method of analysis, using "codes" and "labels" and specialized terminology, the expert, Dr. Marilyn Lashner, attempts to offer her view of Cosell's subjective state of mind when he wrote the passage.

Cosell urges the Court to find that Dr. Lashner's testimony would be inadmissible under Rule 702 of the Federal Rules of Evidence. Rule 702 states: "If scientific, technical, or other specialized knowledge will assist the trier of fact to understand the evidence or to determine a fact in issue, a witness qualified as an expert by knowledge, skill, experience, training, or education, may testify thereto in the form of an opinion or otherwise." The Rule excludes Dr. Lashner's testimony, Cosell argues, because the testimony is more confusing than probative, ultimately unhelpful to the trier of fact, and would discourage the factfinder from using his own judgment on an issue for which a factfinder is amply suited to make his own judgment.

I find Cosell's argument persuasive, and would exclude Dr. Lashner's testimony at trial on the grounds he sets forth. A layman is perfectly capable of reading Cosell's book and comparing it with the articles he claims to have relied on, without the "help" of a linguistics expert. Therefore, Dr. Lashner's testimony would waste the time of both the jury and the court. Because it transforms a common sense issue into a technical one, and relies on virtually incomprehensible pseudo-scientific jargon, Dr. Lashner's analysis must be excluded as more apt to confuse than to enlighten, more unfairly prejudicial than probative. Fed.R.Evid. 403 & 702.

Even if Dr. Lashner's testimony were admissible, I find it insufficient to create an issue of fact as to actual malice. No reasonable reader would construe the passage the way Dr. Lashner does. Dr. Lashner states that Cosell deliberately distorted the meaning of the words and phrases borrowed from the articles in a way that converts them into criminal charges against the WBC. Irrespective of Dr. Lashner's conclusions, a reasonable reader would find that Cosell's passage and the articles say virtually the same thing about the same perceived abuses in boxing. Therefore, Dr. Lashner's testimony cannot controvert the evidence that Cosell relied on the articles.

In virtually identical language, and with much more detail, these articles, by other prominent sports journalists, make the same accusations that Cosell makes in I Never Played the Game. For example, correspondent Jack Newfield, in an article in the Village Voice entitled "The Men Who Are Killing A Noble Sport," calls the WBC both a "complicit conniver in rigging ratings," and an "instrument of extortion." Cosell Aff., Exh. C at 1 & 3. A section of another Newfield article in the Voice, "Don King's Boxing Monopoly," contains the heading, "Jose Sulaiman: The Regulator Who Became a Conspirator." Cosell Aff., Exh. B at 5. If anything, the book treats the WBC more gently than the articles.

In Sports Illustrated, Pat Putnam wrote, "[u]pon their sudden elevation, the WBC and WBA found themselves in a position to demand sanctioning fees from fight promoters, plus lavish expenses for title-fight 'observers.' Moreover, they became arrogant panhandlers, exacting tribute." Cosell Aff., Exh. E at 2. The Putnam article also quoted promoter Bob Arum, who complained, "[t]hey demanded that we wine them and dine them or we couldn't get a fight." Id. Newfield, too, repeatedly attacked the integrity of the WBC. In "The Men Who Are Killing A Noble Sport," he wrote, "[i]n contrast, through influence, gifts, gratuities, favors, payoffs, or whatever, stiffs from foreign lands have repeatedly been given chances to compete for world titles." Cosell Aff., Exh. C at 3. He added, "[the WBA and WBC] are both universally regarded as venal vessels easily manipulated by a few promoters and managers." Id. at 4. The language employed by Cosell is so similar to that used in the articles by Putnam and Newfield that Cosell's claim that he relied on them is unusually compelling.

Furthermore, that various journalists throughout the sports world believe that the WBC is manipulated by gifts and favors from promoters supports Cosell's claim that he had no reason to doubt the truth of such an allegation. Cosell is permitted to rely on these articles for the same reason that he is allowed to depend on the reporting of Bonventre: the articles appeared in respected publications, and were authored by reputable journalists, whose allegations were not so improbable that a prudent author would have questioned their accuracy.

Even after "resolving ambiguities and drawing reasonable inferences against [Cosell]," Knight v. U.S. Fire Insurance Company, 804 F.2d 9, 11 (2d Cir.1986), cert. denied, 480 U.S. 932, 107 S.Ct. 1570, 94 L.Ed.2d 762 (1987), a comparison of Cosell's language with the language in the Putnam and Newfield articles reveals that there is no issue of fact as to whether Cosell embellished the charges in the articles with malicious intent.

D. Defendant's Ill–Will and Failure to Investigate

Apart from Dr. Lashner's testimony, the WBC argues that Cosell harbors ill-will towards the WBC, and that Cosell failed adequately to investigate the charges he lodged at the WBC in his book. Even conceding the truth of these factual assertions, it does not follow that Cosell knew or should have known that the allegations in his passage were false. Therefore, the WBC's contentions could not support a finding of actual malice, and a trial is unwarranted as a matter of law.

A factfinder may not find actual malice "on the basis of defendant's hatred, spite, ill will, or desire to injure" the plaintiff. Letters Carriers, 418 U.S. at 281, 94 S.Ct. at 2779–80; accord Greenbelt, 398 U.S. at 10, 90 S.Ct. at 1540 (impermissible for jury to "find liability merely on the basis of a combination of falsehood and general hostility"); Rebozo v. Washington Post Co., 637 F.2d 375, 380 (5th Cir.), cert. denied, 454 U.S. 964, 102 S.Ct. 505, 70 L.Ed.2d 379 (1981) ("Recklessness cannot be inferred, however, from the mere combination of falsehood and the defendant's general hostility toward the plaintiff. . . .").

Standing alone, a defendant's failure to conduct an investigation before publishing his piece is also insufficient proof of actual malice. See St. Amant v. Thompson, 390 U.S. 727, 733, 88 S.Ct. 1323, 1326, 20 L.Ed.2d 262 (1968) ("Failure to investigate does not in itself establish bad faith."); Herbert, 781 F.2d at 308, quoted in Contemporary Mission, 842 F.2d at 621 ("[A] finding of actual malice cannot be predicated merely on a charge that a reasonable publisher would have further investigated before publishing. . . .").

The WBC argues that a failure to investigate may be considered in determining actual malice where the situation does not involve the time pressure attendant on immediately reporting "hot news" items. Whether or not Cosell's book can be characterized as a fast-breaking "hot news" item, I am unable to find support for the WBC's proposition.

The principal case relied on by the WBC, Curtis Publishing Co. v. Butts, 388 U.S. 130, 87 S.Ct. 1975, 18 L.Ed.2d 1094 (1967), allowed a jury to consider a magazine's failure to investigate only after determining that "the editors of the magazine recognized the need for a thorough investigation of the serious charges." Id. at 157, 87 S.Ct. at 1992. The Court allowed the jury to consider the magazine's failure to investigate because the source of defendant's information "had been placed on probation in connection with bad check charges," and was therefore deemed unreliable in the absence of outside support. Id. The Court never held that a failure to investigate may establish bad faith where the situation did not involve "hot news."

Similarly, the WBC's reliance on Golden Bear Distribution Systems v. Chase Revel, Inc., 708 F.2d 944, 950 (5th Cir.1983), is misplaced. In that case, the court noted that the defendant had sufficient time to investigate the activities of the plaintiff, but only after discussing several other grounds supporting the jury's finding that the defendant published its article with reckless disregard for the truth. Id. The evidence adduced at trial showed that both the author and the editor of the article possessed a variety of information indicating that plaintiff was not involved in the fraud detailed in the magazine column. Id. In addition, the defendant refused to print a retraction, despite having been contacted by the plaintiff, which offered to prove it was innocent of any wrongdoing. Id. The defendant's failure to investigate was significant only because the defendant was aware of the substantial likelihood that the plaintiff was not involved in the investment fraud described in the article. In sum, there is no rule that an author must conduct an investigation absent a showing that he had reason to doubt the veracity of his sources, or possessed other information leading him to question the truth of his assertion.

The law is clear that standing alone, neither a defendant's ill-will toward the subject of a derogatory statement, nor a defendant's failure to investigate a defamatory assertion, can establish actual malice. In the absence of precedent, I decline plaintiff's invitation to promulgate a new rule that an author's ill-will toward his subject, combined with a failure to investigate the sources of his information, is enough to establish actual malice, especially where, as here, defendant relied on articles written by investigative journalists in reputable publications, and the WBC provides no evidence suggesting that Cosell's allegations are "so inherently improbable that only a reckless man would have put them in circulation," or, that "there are obvious reasons to doubt the veracity" of his sources. St. Amant, 390 U.S. at 732, 88 S.Ct. at 1326.

E. Evidence of a Subsequent Remedial Change

Lastly, the WBC purports to prove actual malice on Cosell's part by pointing out that the language in the contested passage was altered in a subsequent paperback edition of the book. The WBC argues that, because the language in the paperback edition was modified, Cosell must have known that he lacked support for the passage when he wrote the original hardcover edition.

However, evidence of a subsequent change in an allegedly libelous text is inadmissible for the purpose of proving actual malice. Rule 407 of the Federal Rules of Evidence specifically provides:

> When, after an event, measures are taken which, if taken previously, would have made the event less likely to occur,

> evidence of the subsequent measures is not admissible to prove negligence or culpable conduct in connection with the event.

The primary ground underlying this rule is a social policy of "encouraging people to take, or at least not discouraging them from taking, steps in furtherance of added safety." Fed.R.Evid. 407 advisory committee's note. Courts have applied the broad language of this rule "to exclude evidence of subsequent repairs, installation of safety devices, changes in company rules, and discharge of employees." Id. The principle applies in a libel case as well, because the elimination of defamatory language in a subsequent edition limits the extent of the damage to an individual's reputation by keeping injurious material from the eyes of new readers.

Consistent with this policy, evidence of a subsequent remedial measure is admissible against a defendant if the measure was taken by someone who is not a party to the lawsuit, since admission of the evidence against the defendant would not deter a non-party from taking remedial action. Koonce v. Quaker Safety Products & Mfg. Co., 798 F.2d 700, 719–20 (5th Cir.1986); Dixon v. International Harvester Co., 754 F.2d 573, 583 (5th Cir.1985); Farner v. Paccar, Inc., 562 F.2d 518, 528 n. 20 (8th Cir.1977). Thus, in certain cases, it may be crucial to determine who instituted the remedial change.

In the case at bar, however, it is not important whether Cosell or the non-party publisher was actually responsible for the modification of the paperback edition of I Never Played the Game. Regardless of who altered the text, the subsequent modification does not raise an issue of fact about whether Cosell originally wrote the disputed passage with actual malice. If Cosell altered the text, evidence concerning this act is barred by Rule 407. And if the publisher altered the text, then the subsequent modification is irrelevant, because no inference can be drawn about what Cosell knew or should have known at the time he wrote the hardcover edition based on actions taken by another at a later date with respect to the paperback edition. Overall, none of the grounds asserted by the WBC could support a finding that Cosell wrote the passage in question with actual malice.

F. Further Discovery

In its brief, the WBC asserts that it is currently seeking information from Cosell concerning the identity of alleged confidential sources, tape recordings of conversations between Cosell and Bonventre relating to the book, and the original manuscript of the book. Plaintiff's Brief at 27. However, according to counsel for both sides, all of these discovery issues were resolved by the parties subsequent to the filing of plaintiff's brief.

The issue of Cosell's confidential sources was settled by the Court and the parties, in a stipulation, with Cosell agreeing not to rely on any information derived from unnamed sources. With respect to the audiotapes and the manuscript, counsel for both the WBC and Cosell have represented to the Court that all discoverable materials have been provided to plaintiff. This basis for opposing summary judgment is therefore moot.

CONCLUSION

Acting as the third man in the ring, the Court rules that low or not, Cosell's blow was struck in good faith, and raises his arm in victory.

For the reasons set forth above, Cosell's motion for summary judgment is granted, and the case is dismissed.

Notes

1. As the foregoing cases demonstrate, it is extremely difficult for a public figure to prove actual malice. *See also Silvester v. American Broadcasting Cos.*, 650 F.Supp. 766 (S.D.Fla.1986), *aff'd*, 839 F.2d 1491 (11th Cir.1988) (report about suspicious fire at jai-alai fronton); *Hoffman v. Washington Post Co.*, 433 F.Supp. 600 (D.D.C.1977), *aff'd*, 578 F.2d 442 (D.C.Cir.1978) (article questioning performance claims made by coach selling protein supplements); *Gomez v. Murdoch*, 475 A.2d 622 (N.J.Super.Ct. 1984) (story about under-performing jockey).

2. As *Bell* shows, journalists sometimes have to publish stories before all facts are known. During the 1996 Olympics, for example, the media reported a security guard named Richard Jewell was responsible for the bombing in Centennial Olympic Park. When the FBI later cleared him, Jewell retained a lawyer to restore his reputation. *See further Jewell v. NYP Holdings, Inc.*, 23 F.Supp.2d 348 (S.D.N.Y.1998), and Kevin Sack, *Olympic Bombing Throws Man's Life Into Bitter Tailspin*, Fort Worth Star–Telegram, July 27, 1997, at 1.

3. Besides Howard Cosell, a number of other sports figures have penned "tell-all" accounts. In 1970, for example, New York Yankees pitcher Jim Bouton wrote *Ball Four*, an inside look at life in the major leagues. Despite the passage of nearly three decades, the book remains the genre's seminal work. More recently, New York Jets wide receiver Keyshawn Johnson blasted his coaches and teammates in the peevish *Gimme the Damn Ball* (1997), and Rita Ewing and Crystal McCrary published *Homecourt Advantage* (1998), a novel based on their experiences as NBA wives. For an interesting case concerning a gossip book that did *not* get written, see *Kaplan v. Vincent*, 937 F.Supp. 307 (S.D.N.Y.1996).

Problem 54

At trial, the plaintiff, a professional football player, was able to prove: (a) the defendant, a famous sportswriter, lost $100,000 when the plaintiff missed what would have been the winning field goal in the Super Bowl; (b) following the game, the defendant yelled in a crowded room he "was going to make sure the city rode [the plaintiff] out of town on a rail;" and, (c) six months later, after the defendant had authored more than 30 columns mentioning the missed kick and appeared on numerous talk shows in which he spoke of little else, the plaintiff was released by the team. Given this evidence, has the plaintiff established the defendant acted with actual malice? *See Tavoulareas v. Piro*, 817 F.2d 762 (D.C.Cir.), *cert. denied*, 484 U.S. 870 (1987).

c. Injury

The final element requires the plaintiff to prove the defendant's words injured his or her reputation.

HORNE v. MATTHEWS

1997 WL 598452 (S.D.N.Y.1997).

MARTIN, Judge.

This is an action for libel. Plaintiff John Horne, co-manager of boxer Mike Tyson, alleges that New York Post boxing columnist Wallace Matthews cast disrepute upon Horne's professional reputation in a recent Post column about Mike Tyson. Defendants Matthews and Post publisher N.Y.P. Holdings have moved for dismissal of plaintiff's complaint pursuant to Federal Rule of Civil Procedure 12(b)(6) for failure to state a claim. Because the Court finds that the defendants' published statement is not defamatory as a matter of law, the Court grants the motion and dismisses the complaint.

Background

Horne's complaint alleges a long-running enmity between columnist Matthews and "Team Tyson"—that small group responsible for furthering Tyson's boxing career that includes Tyson himself, promoter Don King, and co-managers Horne and Rory Holloway. Plaintiff blames Matthews for the animosity. Matthews has written several columns claiming that Tyson repeatedly postponed matches for questionable reasons. Team Tyson, in turn, allegedly incurred Matthews' wrath by denying him access to the Tyson training camp.

On April 9, 1997, the day after Tyson postponed his re-match with Evander Holyfield because of a gash above his eye, Matthews wrote a column under the headline: "TYSON DELAYS REMATCH: Maybe 'baddest man' is now Chicken Mike." The lengthy column accuses Tyson of cowardice in postponing the fight and charges that Tyson had never intended to fight Holyfield. As evidence of this latter charge, Matthews wrote that Tyson was partying instead of training. "Rumors filtered out that Richie Giachetti, Tyson's once and future trainer, was disgusted and suggesting the fight be postponed. Even Tyson's co-manager, John Horne, told people that Tyson was 'partying his [butt] off.' "

It is upon this final sentence, the only mention of or allusion to John Horne in the column, that Horne predicates his action. The complaint asserts the statement is false in that Horne had not told people Tyson had been partying. The plaintiff delineates several theories why the allegedly false report defames Horne by impugning his professional character and competence. First, the reader will conclude that Horne breached his fiduciary duty of confidence to Tyson by publicly revealing that Tyson is partying rather than training. The core responsibility of a boxing manager, the plaintiff maintains, is to enshroud the client in a protective garb of secrecy. Horne's violation of this standard would make him, in the eyes of readers, unfit to be a manager. Alternatively, if readers conclude Tyson was not partying and that Horne was simply lying, then Horne is a bad manager for spreading false rumors. Third, again if Tyson was partying, the quote implies Horne is a bad manager because he cannot control Tyson. Fourth, the quotation implies that Horne has perpetrated a fraud upon boxing by promoting a match for which he knows Tyson is unprepared.

Horne maintains that the quotation could ruin Horne's reputation among Tyson and other, potential, boxer-clients, and that it is therefore against this narrower readership that the quotation must be tested. He has pleaded no special damages.

DISCUSSION

" '[W]hether particular words are defamatory presents a legal question to be resolved by the court in the first instance ... and if not reasonably susceptible of a defamatory meaning, they are not actionable and cannot be made so by a strained or artificial construction.' " Golub v. Enquirer/Star Group, Inc., 89 N.Y.2d 1074, 1076, 659 N.Y.S.2d 836, 837, 681 N.E.2d 1282 (1997) (quoting Aronson v. Wiersma, 65 N.Y.2d 592, 593–94, 493 N.Y.S.2d 1006, 1007, 483 N.E.2d 1138 (1985) (ellipsis in Golub)). A quote falsely attributed to a person can amount to libel if its content or its attribution to plaintiff disgraces him. See Mahoney v. Adirondack Publishing Co., 71 N.Y.2d 31, 523 N.Y.S.2d 480, 517 N.E.2d 1365 (1987).

In determining whether the plaintiff has been defamed, the court must test the statement by its effect upon the average and ordinary reader to whom the publication is addressed. Aronson v. Wiersma, 65 N.Y.2d 592, 594, 493 N.Y.S.2d 1006, 1007, 483 N.E.2d 1138 (1985); James v. Gannett Co., Inc., 40 N.Y.2d 415, 419–20, 386 N.Y.S.2d 871, 874, 353 N.E.2d 834 (1976).

Plaintiff argues that the column should be evaluated not through the eyes of the average reader but rather through the eyes of Tyson and potential boxers who might hire Horne in the future. Plaintiff cites no cases supporting the view that this extremely narrow and specialized audience should stand in as the objective interpreter rather than the average reader to whom the publication was addressed. An article on the sports page of a newspaper should be viewed from the perspective of the audience to whom it is addressed, i.e., the understanding of "a sophisticated and sports-conscious reader." November v. Time, 13 N.Y.2d 175, 178, 244 N.Y.S.2d 309, 311, 194 N.E.2d 126 (1963). The decision in November does not suggest, however, that an article about boxing must be judged by the understandings of boxers and other boxing insiders.

New York courts have long recognized that written statements that defame a person in the conduct of or fitness for her profession are defamatory and libel per se. Golub, 89 N.Y.2d at 1076, 659 N.Y.S.2d at 837, 681 N.E.2d 1282; Ben–Oliel v. Press Publishing Co., 251 N.Y. 250, 167 N.E. 432 (1929). The attack must relate to a "matter of significance and importance" to the plaintiff's work. Golub, 89 N.Y.2d at 1076, 659

N.Y.S.2d at 837, 681 N.E.2d 1282. Courts differ in how seriously the defendant's attack must undermine confidence in plaintiff's work. Most recently, the court held that "a defamatory meaning may attach to statements that would cause apprehension about a person's ability to conduct business." Id.; see also, Aronson, 65 N.Y.2d at 594, 493 N.Y.S.2d at 1008, 483 N.E.2d 1138 ("incompatible with proper conduct of [her] business"); Amelkin v. Commercial Trading Co., 23 A.D.2d 830, 831, 259 N.Y.S.2d 396, 398 (N.Y.App.Div.1965) ("ignorant, incompetent, [or] incapable in his calling").

Horne's several theories for liability all fail for the same reason. Given the context in which the statements about Horne appear, the average reader of the New York Post's sports pages would not construe the statements as portraying Horne as "ignorant, incompetent, [or] incapable in his calling." Id. See November v. Time, 13 N.Y.2d 175, 178–79, 244 N.Y.S.2d 309, 312, 194 N.E.2d 126 (1963) ("The words are to be construed not with the close precision expected from lawyers and judges but as they would be read and understood by the public to which they are addressed."); Gannett, 40 N.Y.2d at 420, 386 N.Y.S.2d at 874, 353 N.E.2d 834 (". . . . the court will not strain to place a particular interpretation on the published words.").

The article so single-mindedly focuses on Mike Tyson that—short of the picky analysis of lawyers—no average or even sophisticated sports reader would remotely consider that the statement reflected upon Horne. The column as a whole sets its sights on Tyson's alleged cowardice. The Team Tyson personnel—Horne, Giachetti, and even Don King—play the parts of walk-ons in the drama of a Caesar. These bit players' sole dramatic and thematic purpose is to shed light on the character of Tyson and Tyson alone. There is little if any space for a reader to make inferences about the integrity of these other players. In the eyes of the average sports reader, the remark attributed to Horne is susceptible of this meaning alone—that Tyson has not been preparing for his fight. The remark is not reasonably susceptible to the inference along plaintiff's lengthy and contorted logical chain that Horne has violated some central duty of his profession.

A New York case prominently cited by plaintiff actually highlights the key ingredient Horne's claim lacks. In Mahoney v. Adirondack Publishing Co., defendant published an account of a high school football game that included an extensive portion on the conduct of the coach. 71 N.Y.2d 31, 523 N.Y.S.2d 480, 517 N.E.2d 1365 (1987). That description included a litany of the coach's alleged verbal abuse of players and profanity. The single quotation at issue in the case was " '[c]ome on, get your head out of your & !(!!(& . Play the game.' " Id. at 37, 523 N.Y.S.2d at 482, 517 N.E.2d 1365 (euphemism in original article). The court held that the quote was reasonably capable of having defamatory meaning.

"Although it might be argued that the quoted language is not unexpected or out of character for a football coach, the thrust of the article was to the contrary—that such conduct should be condemned."

Id. at 38, 523 N.Y.S.2d at 482, 517 N.E.2d 1365. The key was that the quote appeared as part of a long list of critical remarks in a portion of the article whose entire thrust was to criticize and even condemn the coach. In other words, the article drew the reader's attention to the character and conduct of the coach. Matthews' article, by contrast, draws the reader's attention to Tyson's character and conduct.

Moreover, even if the reader's attention were somehow to fall upon the character and conduct of Horne instead of Tyson, the average reader would not make the further logical step to conclude that Horne had breached his duties of loyalty and honesty. Plaintiff, citing a legal treatise on agency, has set up a fiduciary standard for a fight manager that is legalistic and complex. It is unlikely in the extreme, however, that the average reader of Matthews' column would consider a fight manager to have the same type of fiduciary duty that one would impose on a trustee. An average reader would not repair to his local law library to evaluate whether Horne has breached some complex fiduciary duty. In short, it would take much more than the brief reference to Horne in Matthews' column to tarnish the reputation of a fight manager in the eyes of a reader of the New York Post.

CONCLUSION

The motion to dismiss is therefore granted and the complaint dismissed.

Notes

1. Even if he had been able to prove injury, John Horne would have had a difficult time quantifying his damages. On the one hand, some believe public figures should never be allowed to collect more than a nominal sum. On the other hand, there are those who believe public figures should always be given extraordinary compensation (due to how hard it is to achieve mass recognition and the greater litigation burdens imposed on such plaintiffs). For a further discussion, see, e.g., T. Michael Mather, *Experience with Gertz 'Actual Injury' in Defamation Cases*, 38 Baylor L. Rev. 917 (1986).

2. In April 1998, a Connecticut woman named Melissa Reed accused Washington Wizards teammates Juwan Howard and Chris Webber of sexually abusing her at a party. Doubting her story, a grand jury declined to indict the players. Howard then filed a defamation suit against Reed seeking $1 in symbolic damages. When Reed, lacking the money to hire a lawyer, did not contest the suit, Howard moved for a default judgment. In November 1998, Montgomery County Circuit Court Judge Durke Thompson granted the motion and, much to the surprise of everyone, tacked on $100,000 in punitive damages. *See further Juwan Howard Awarded $100,000 in Defamation Case*, Jet, Nov. 30, 1998, at 53.

Problem 55

When she saw an unflattering cartoon in a men's magazine, a professional athlete, convinced the joke was directed at her, sued for defamation. If the defendant moves for summary judgment on the ground that a plaintiff's reputation cannot be damaged through spoofing, how will the court rule? *See Flip Side, Inc. v. Chicago Tribune Co.*, 564 N.E.2d 1244 (Ill.App.Ct.1990), *appeal denied*, 571 N.E.2d 147 (Ill.1991).

Chapter 10

GAMBLERS

A. OVERVIEW

From friendly wagers to large-scale bookmaking operations, Americans risk a staggering amount of money on athletic events. This has resulted in three vexing issues: 1) how should such gambling be regulated?; 2) what steps can a sports organization take to protect itself from gamblers?; and, 3) may states use sports to promote their lotteries?

B. RACKETS

Because gambling exists on the fringes of society, most people have only a vague understanding of the "rackets." What follows is an examination of the field's three main constituents: bettors, bookies, and experts.

1. BETTORS

Although most people think of betting as being illegal, numerous types of legitimate wagers can be placed. For a variety of reasons, however, it is often difficult to tell one from the other.

SZADOLCI v. HOLLYWOOD PARK OPERATING CO.

17 Cal.Rptr.2d 356 (Ct.App.1993).

ORTEGA, Acting Presiding Justice.

James Farenbaugh went to Hollywood Park on June 14, 1989, and put down $4,860 on a "Pick–9" ticket. A Pick–9 requires the bettor to pick the winners of the nine races run that day. Picking all nine winners results in a large return.

But Farenbaugh had something else in mind. He cancelled the ticket and bribed the parimutuel clerk to let him keep the worthless ticket. Farenbaugh then set out to sell shares in the ticket to other patrons at the track. The record does not reveal whether this was an ongoing scam by Farenbaugh. In any event, since the chance of hitting a big winner is remote, any shares sold would result in clear profit to Farenbaugh, who, having cancelled the ticket, had none of his own money at risk.

Plaintiffs Jim Szadolci and Daniel Teich bought into the ticket before the first race started. Each paid approximately $240 for a 5 percent share. Teich left the track shortly thereafter. Plaintiff Mardy Loewy apparently bought in for 5 percent after the day's racing program had commenced. The record is not clear at what point Loewy invested (he said probably after the second or third race) or how much he paid for his share (possibly around $300).

But, lo and behold, Farenbaugh (much to his dismay, we assume) picked all nine winners. A valid ticket would have paid $1,380,000. Farenbaugh's cancelled ticket was worth zero.

Szadolci and Loewy (jubilant, we presume, at the prospect of realizing $69,000 each) accompanied Farenbaugh (feigning aplomb, no doubt) to the pay window, only to learn of the ticket cancellation. Unfortunately, the record does not reveal what happened at that moment.

The three plaintiffs sued Hollywood Park, the parimutuel clerk, another track employee, and Farenbaugh for negligence, conspiracy, and negligent hiring. Defendants secured summary judgment and plaintiffs appeal.

Discussion

The trial court's ruling was based on the conclusion that the transactions between plaintiffs and Farenbaugh were illegal bets. Since plaintiffs' complaint relied on a theory which put them in pari delicto, the trial court held, they were barred from recovery. " 'The general rule is that the courts will not recognize such an illegal contract [betting] and will not aid the parties thereto, but will leave them where it finds them. This rule has been rigidly enforced in this state to deny any relief in the courts to parties seeking to recover either their stakes or their winnings under a wagering contract which is in violation of law, . . . [Citations.]' " (Bradley v. Doherty (1973) 30 Cal.App.3d 991, 994, 106 Cal.Rptr. 725.)

Plaintiffs seek to distinguish themselves from the above rule by arguing that the transactions here did not constitute illegal bets. They argue that the trial court found these to be illegal "lay off bets" by erroneously relying on People v. Oreck (1946) 74 Cal.App.2d 215, 168 P.2d 186, which held that a "lay off man" was engaged in illegal bookmaking. What is a lay off bet/man? "If a customer of a bookie bets $5.00 on horse X to win a certain race, and the track odds are 5–1, if that horse wins the bookie must pay the customer $25, while if it loses the bookie wins $5.00. Now, if before the race, the bookie lays off that $5.00 bet with a lay off man, what is the result? If the horse wins, the bookie must pay the customer $25, but he is reimbursed to the extent of $25 by his bet with the lay off man. In a very real sense the bookie has won that bet with the lay off man, and the lay off man has lost. But if the horse loses, the bookie wins $5.00 from his customer, but he must pay the lay off man $2.50. In a very real sense the bookie has lost and the lay off man has won on that transaction...." (Id. at pp. 220–221, 168 P.2d 186.)

But here, argue plaintiffs, unlike in Oreck, Farenbaugh's bet with the track was legal, so their investments did not constitute lay off bets. Farenbaugh possessed, they claim, a chose in action ("a right to recover money or other personal property by a judicial proceeding" (Civ.Code, § 953)), interest in which could be transferred. (See Mattson v. Hollywood Turf Club (1950) 101 Cal.App.2d 215, 225 P.2d 276, which holds there is at least an implied contract between the track and its bettors. Mattson also aptly points out that whether betting on horses "is a game of skill, as some believe, or of chance, as many have learned, it provides a legal method for getting rid of one's money." (Id. at p. 219, 225 P.2d 276.))

We agree that the transactions between Farenbaugh and plaintiffs did not constitute lay off bets, but for a different reason than proffered by plaintiffs. There was no underlying bet between Farenbaugh and any person or entity. Farenbaugh had withdrawn his legitimate bet and had no stake with the track in the outcome of the race, so he was laying nothing off when he fleeced plaintiffs. Farenbaugh had no chose in action. Plaintiffs bought a share of a worthless ticket, which entitled Farenbaugh and them to recover nothing from the track. If there was any kind of implied contract, it was between plaintiffs and Farenbaugh, who impliedly had offered plaintiffs a return if the selected horses won. A lay off bet provides a bookie with a backup. Farenbaugh, who could have used the help, had no backup.

Business and Professions Code section 19595 provides in part: "Any form of wagering or betting on the result of a horse race other than that permitted by this chapter is illegal." The basic approved betting format is for a bettor to give his money to the track, where it is then placed in the parimutuel pool, out of which winning bettors are paid. (See Bus. and Prof. Code § 19594—"Any person within the inclosure where a horse racing meeting is authorized may wager on the result of a horse race held at that meeting by contributing his money to the parimutuel pool operated by the licensee under this chapter....") One of the advantages of this system is that it should eliminate the type of problem that occurred here.

Any way we look at it, plaintiffs laid direct wagers with Farenbaugh, who took their money and impliedly agreed to a 5 percent winner's share for each plaintiff. None of the money involved ended up in the parimutuel pool. So, while these were not lay off bets, they were unauthorized direct bets with Farenbaugh, and illegal.

Plaintiffs argue that these were not bets because Farenbaugh received no compensation, had no interest in the outcome of the races, and was on the same side as plaintiffs. But Farenbaugh had a very real stake in the outcome. For his scam to work, the ticket had to be a loser, because he could then offer his condolences to plaintiffs and walk away with their money. Only when the ticket "won" did Farenbaugh's problems arise. So, Farenbaugh was directly betting against plaintiffs. If their horses won, his scam was revealed and he acquired a measure of grief. If they lost, he kept several hundred dollars of plaintiffs' money without having risked one dime.

Plaintiffs offer the example of friends going to the track and pooling their money, with one of them purchasing the ticket. If the purchaser actually takes his friends' money and hands it to the parimutuel clerk, the bet is legal, plaintiffs argue, because the friends' money has been placed in the parimutuel pool. If he spends his own money and is then reimbursed by his friends, the bet is an illegal lay off bet according to defendants' analysis. This, plaintiffs argue, is illogical. But, since we have a different situation here, we need not analyze whether either of the above situations constitutes legal or illegal betting. Here, no one's money was in the parimutuel pool. There was no lay off bet. The transactions were direct and face-to-face between Farenbaugh and plaintiffs. Plaintiffs laid bets with Farenbaugh. The bets were not as authorized by the Business and Professions Code. They were illegal bets. Plaintiffs have no remedy. Whether the trial court relied on the wrong theory or not, its result was correct.

The judgment is affirmed.

STATE EX REL. HUMPHREY v. GRANITE GATE RESORTS, INC.

568 N.W.2d 715 (Minn.Ct.App.1997), *aff'd*, 576 N.W.2d 747 (Minn.1998).

WILLIS, Judge.

Respondent State of Minnesota filed a complaint against appellants Granite Gate Resorts, Inc., d/b/a On Ramp Internet Computer Services, and Kerry Rogers, individually and as principal officer of Granite Gate Resorts, Inc., alleging that appellants engaged in deceptive trade practices, false advertising, and consumer fraud on the Internet. Appellants challenge the district court's denial of their motion to dismiss for lack of personal jurisdiction. We affirm.

Facts

Rogers, a Nevada resident, is president of Granite Gate, a Nevada corporation that does business as On Ramp. Until August 1995, On Ramp provided Internet advertising on the site located at http://www.vegas.com, which provides Nevada tourist information. Among the sites advertised was WagerNet, an on-line wagering service planned to be available internationally in the fall of 1995, whose page enabled Internet users to subscribe for more information about the service.

The WagerNet site, designed by Rogers, stated:

On–Line sports wagering open to International markets, Fall of 1995

> Global Gaming Services Ltd., based in the country of Belize, is pleased to introduce WagerNet, the first and only on-line sports betting site on the Internet. WagerNet will provide sports fans with a legal way to bet on sporting events from anywhere in the world . . . 24 Hours a Day!
>
> How It Works
>
> First, there is a $100 setup fee, for necessary hardware and software. For security and privacy, all members are issued a card system linked to their personal computer to access WagerNet. Once on-line, the bettor selects the team/s and amount/s they wish to wager. WagerNet then matches your bet with an opposing bettor or bettors to cover your wager. WagerNet charges each bettor a transaction fee of ONLY 2.5% as opposed to the 10% fee charged by most bookmakers.

The website invited Internet users to put themselves on a mailing list for WagerNet information and included a form for that purpose. It gave a toll-free number for WagerNet and also told Internet users to contact On Ramp at a Nevada telephone number for more information. A note on the page advised users to consult with local authorities regarding restrictions on offshore sports betting by telephone before registering with WagerNet.

A linked web page listed the terms and conditions to which an Internet user assented by applying for the private access card and special hardware and software required to access WagerNet's services. This page stated that any claim against WagerNet by a customer must be brought before a Belizian court, but that WagerNet could sue the consumer in his or her home state to prevent the consumer "from committing any breach or anticipated breach of this Agreement and for consequential relief."

On July 5, 1995, Jeff Janacek, a consumer investigator for the Minnesota Attorney General's office, telephoned the toll-free number shown on an On Ramp site that advertised All Star Sports, a sports handicapping service, and asked how to bet on sports events. An On Ramp employee told Janacek to call Rogers directly. Janacek dialed the number he was given, which was the same number that the WagerNet site directed Internet users to call to receive more information, and spoke with an individual who identified himself as Rogers. Janacek identified himself as a Minnesotan interested in placing bets. Rogers explained how to access WagerNet, told Janacek the betting service was legal, and stated that he hoped the service would be up and running by the 1995 football season.

In July 1995, the attorney general filed a complaint alleging that appellants had engaged in deceptive trade practices, false advertising, and consumer fraud by advertising in Minnesota that gambling on the Internet is lawful. In October 1995, Janacek subscribed to the WagerNet mailing list under a fictitious name and received an on-line confirmation stating that he would be sent updates on the WagerNet service. Appellants filed a motion to dismiss for lack of personal jurisdiction. The district court allowed limited discovery to determine the quantity and quality of appellants' contacts with the state. Rogers refused to produce the names of the persons on the WagerNet mailing list, claiming that the information is the sole property of a Belizian corporation. As a sanction, the court found that it is established as a fact for this action that the WagerNet mailing list contains the name and address of at least one Minnesota resident. In December 1996, the district court denied appellants' motion to dismiss for lack of jurisdiction.

Issue

Did the district court err in denying appellants' motion to dismiss for lack of personal jurisdiction?

Analysis

This is the first time a Minnesota court has addressed the issue of personal jurisdiction based on Internet advertising. We are mindful that the Internet is a communication medium that lacks historical parallel in the potential extent of its reach and that regulation across jurisdictions may implicate fundamental First Amendment concerns. It will undoubtedly take some time to determine the precise balance between the rights of those who use the Internet to disseminate information and the powers of the jurisdictions in which receiving computers are located to regulate for the general welfare. But our task here is limited to deciding the question of personal jurisdiction in the instant case, and on the facts before us, we are satisfied that established legal principles provide adequate guidance.

Minnesota's long-arm statute, Minn.Stat. § 543.19 (1996), "permits courts to assert jurisdiction over defendants to the extent that federal constitutional requirements of due process will allow." Domtar, Inc. v. Niagara Fire Ins. Co., 533 N.W.2d 25, 29 (Minn.), cert. denied, 516 U.S. 1017, 116 S.Ct. 583, 133 L.Ed.2d 504 (1995). To satisfy the Due Process Clause of the Fourteenth Amendment, a plaintiff must show that the defendant has "minimum contacts" with the forum state "such that the maintenance of the suit does not offend 'traditional notions of fair play and substantial justice.'" International Shoe Co. v. Washington, 326 U.S. 310, 316, 66 S.Ct. 154, 158, 90 L.Ed. 95 (1945) (quoting Milliken v. Meyer, 311 U.S. 457, 463, 61 S.Ct. 339, 343, 85 L.Ed. 278 (1940)). There must be "some act by which the defendant purposefully avails itself of the privilege of conducting activities within the forum State, thus invoking the benefits and protections of its laws." Hanson v. Denckla, 357 U.S. 235, 253, 78 S.Ct. 1228, 1240, 2 L.Ed.2d 1283 (1958).

Appellants allege that the district court erred in denying their motion to dismiss because a nonresident defendant that places information on the Internet has not purposefully availed itself of the privilege of conducting activities within every state from which that information may be accessed. The assertion of personal jurisdiction in Minnesota, appellants argue, would not comport with the traditional notions of fair play and substantial justice.

A court must consider five factors in determining whether a defendant has established minimum contacts with the forum state: (1) the quantity of the defendant's contacts; (2) the nature and quality of the defendant's contacts; (3) the connection between the cause of action and the defendant's contacts; (4) the state's interest in providing a forum; and (5) the convenience of the parties. Rostad v. On–Deck, Inc., 372 N.W.2d 717, 719–20 (Minn.1985). The first three factors are of primary importance. Land–O–Nod Co. v. Bassett Furniture Indus., Inc., 708 F.2d 1338, 1340 (8th Cir.1983). In close cases, "doubts should be resolved in favor of retention of jurisdiction." Valspar Corp. v. Lukken Color Corp., 495 N.W.2d 408, 411–12 (Minn.1992).

1. Quantity of Contacts.

The quantity of contacts here supports the contention that appellants purposefully availed themselves of the privilege of conducting commercial activities in Minnesota. The district court found that (1) computers located throughout the United States, including Minnesota, accessed appellants' websites, (2) during a two-week period in February and March 1996, at least 248 Minnesota computers accessed and "received transmissions from" appellants' websites, (3) computers located in Minnesota are among the 500 computers that most often accessed appellants' websites, (4) persons located throughout the United States, including persons in Minnesota, called appellants at the numbers advertised on its websites, and (5) the WagerNet mailing list includes the name and address of at least one Minnesota resident.

In Maritz, Inc. v. Cybergold, Inc., 947 F.Supp. 1328 (E.D.Mo.1996), a Missouri federal court exercised personal jurisdiction over the California operator of an Internet site that provided information on a forthcoming service that would charge advertisers for access to a mailing list of Internet users. Id. at 1334. In analyzing the quantity of the defendant's contacts with Missouri, the Maritz court found that the defendant "has transmitted information into Missouri regarding its services approximately 131 times," which allowed an inference that the defendant purposefully availed itself of the privilege of conducting activities in Missouri. Id. at 1333. The quantity of contacts here exceeds that in Maritz.

2. Quality of Contacts.

Even where the quantity of contacts with a state is minimal, the nature and quality of the contacts may be dispositive. Trident Enters. Int'l, Inc. v. Kemp & George, Inc., 502 N.W.2d 411, 415 (Minn.App. 1993); see also Zippo Mfg. Co. v. Zippo Dot Com, Inc., 952 F.Supp. 1119, 1124 (W.D.Pa.1997) (concluding "likelihood that personal jurisdiction can be constitutionally exercised is directly proportionate to the nature and quality of commercial activity that an entity conducts over the internet"). Advertising in the forum state, or establishing channels for providing regular advice to customers in the forum state, indicates a defendant's intent to serve the market in that state. Asahi Metal Indus. Co. v. Superior Court of California, 480 U.S. 102, 112, 107 S.Ct. 1026, 1032, 94 L.Ed.2d 92 (1987).

Appellants argue that they "have not directed their activities at the citizens of Minnesota" because they "only placed information on the internet." An Internet site, however, can be viewed as

> an "advertisement" by which [the foreign corporation] distributes its pictorial images throughout the United States. That the local user "pulls" these images from [the corporation's] computer in [in that case] Italy, as opposed to [the corporation] "sending" them to this country, is irrelevant. By inviting United States users to download these images, [the corporation] is causing and contributing to their distribution within the United States.

Playboy Enters., Inc. v. Chuckleberry Publ'g, Inc., 939 F.Supp. 1032, 1044 (S.D.N.Y.1996).

The Maritz court also rejected the view that Internet advertising is a passive activity:

> [Defendant's] posting of information about its new, up-coming service through a website seeks to develop a mailing list of internet users, as such users are essential to the success of its service. Clearly, [the defendant] has obtained the website for the purpose of, and in anticipation that, internet users, searching the internet for websites, will access [the defendant's] website and eventually sign up on [the defendant's] mailing list. Although [the defendant] characterizes its activity as merely maintaining a "passive website," its intent is to reach all internet users, regardless of geographic location. * * * Through its website, [the defendant] has consciously decided to transmit advertising information to all internet users, knowing that such information will be transmitted globally.

Id. at 1333; see also Inset Sys., Inc. v. Instruction Set, Inc., 937 F.Supp. 161, 165 (D.Conn.1996) (holding that Massachusetts corporation purposefully availed itself of privilege of doing business in Connecticut by advertising its activities and its toll-free number on [the] Internet because [web sites] and toll-free numbers are designed to communicate with people in every state).

Minnesota courts have concluded that defendants who know their message will be broadcast in this state are subject to suit here. See, e.g., Tonka Corp. v. TMS Entertainment, Inc., 638 F.Supp. 386, 391 (D.Minn. 1985) (holding that Minnesota can exert personal jurisdiction over California corporation that produced television program it knew would be broadcast nationwide); BLC Ins. Co. v. Westin, Inc., 359 N.W.2d 752, 755 (Minn.App.1985) (holding that Wisconsin corporation's purposeful behavior in advertising its Wisconsin bar on Twin Cities radio station is such that it should have reasonably anticipated being haled into Minnesota court), review denied (Minn. Apr. 15, 1985); see also A. Uberti & C. v. Leonardo, 181 Ariz. 565, 892 P.2d 1354, 1362 (1995) (concluding that defendant intending to sell its products to any and all United States citizens can be held accountable in any jurisdiction where its products cause injury), cert. denied,516 U.S. 906, 116 S.Ct. 273, 133 L.Ed.2d 194 (1995). Other states have held that direct mail solicitation into the state is sufficient contact to justify personal jurisdiction. See, e.g., State ex rel. Miller v. Baxter Chrysler Plymouth, Inc., 456 N.W.2d 371, 377 (Iowa 1990); Kugler v. Market Dev. Corp., 124 N.J.Super. 314, 306 A.2d 489, 491 (Ch.Div.1973); State v. Colorado State Christian College, 76 Misc.2d 50, 346 N.Y.S.2d 482, 485 (N.Y.Sup.Ct.1973); State v. Reader's Digest Ass'n, Inc., 81 Wash.2d 259, 501 P.2d 290, 302 (1972).

Internet advertisements are similar to broadcast and direct mail solicitation in that advertisers distribute messages to Internet users, and users must take affirmative action to receive the advertised product. Here, the WagerNet site itself stated that it was "open to International markets," indicating an intent to seek customers from a very broad geographic area. The fact that WagerNet had apparently paid for advertising in English on an American commercial site indicates an intent to reach the American market, and by advertising their services with a toll-free number, appellants indicated their intent to solicit responses from all jurisdictions within that market, including Minnesota. A defendant cannot "hide behind the structuring of its distribution system when [the defendant's] intent was to enter the market [in the forum state] and profit thereby." Rostad, 372 N.W.2d at 722. The presence of the disclaimer on the site may be relevant to the merits of the consumer fraud action, but appellants' clear effort to reach and seek potential profit from Minnesota consumers provides minimum contacts of a nature and quality sufficient to support a threshold finding of personal jurisdiction.

3. Connection Between Cause of Action and Contacts.

If the cause of action arises from the nonresident defendant's contacts with the forum state, even a single transaction can be sufficient to establish personal jurisdiction over the defendant. See McGee v. International Life Ins. Co., 355 U.S. 220, 78 S.Ct. 199, 2 L.Ed.2d 223 (1957). Advertising contacts justify the exercise of personal jurisdiction where unlawful or misleading advertisements are the basis of the plaintiff's claims. See Baxter, 456 N.W.2d at 377 (holding that defendants' acts in advertising within forum state are sufficient to render them amenable to suit there in action alleging the advertising is unlawful); Reader's Digest, 501 P.2d at 302–03 (concluding that unfair competition cause of action arose from contacts because mailing sweepstakes entry information constituted illegal lottery within state).

In this case, the state alleges violations of Minn.Stat. §§ 325D.44, subd. 1 (1996) (engaging in deceptive trade practices), 325F.67 (1996) (making false statements in advertisements), and 325F.69, subd. 1 (1996) (engaging in fraud, misrepresentation, or deceptive practices), based on appellants' alleged misrepresentations regarding the legality in Minnesota of the services offered by All Star Sports and WagerNet. Under Minn.Stat. § 8.31, subd. 3 (1996), the attorney general is authorized to seek injunctive relief and civil penalties when satisfied that any of the laws referred to in Minn.Stat. § 8.31, subd. 1 (1996), which include the consumer statutes allegedly violated here, [are] "about to be violated." Thus, the causes of action against appellants arise out of the information that appellants posted on their website inviting Internet users to use the on-line gambling service when it becomes operational, which, as discussed, was directed toward Minnesota and received here. See Maritz, 947 F.Supp. at 1333 (concluding that trademark infringement and unfair competition causes of action result from injuries that arise out of or relate to defendant's website).

4. State's Interest.

Minnesota's interest in providing a forum for a resident plaintiff cannot alone establish jurisdiction, but it can support the exercise of jurisdiction over a nonresident defendant when viewed in light of the first three factors for evaluating whether minimum contacts exist. Trident, 502 N.W.2d at 416. The state has an interest in enforcing consumer protection statutes and regulating gambling. See State v. Alpine Air Products, Inc., 490 N.W.2d 888, 892 (Minn.App.1992) (concluding that consumer fraud statutes were designed to protect and enhance public interests), aff'd, 500 N.W.2d 788 (Minn.1993); see also State v. Brown, 486 N.W.2d 816, 817 (Minn.App.1992) (concluding that Minnesota gambling industry "is highly regulated to prevent its commercialization and to ensure that profits generated from gambling are used for lawful purposes"). The state's interest in providing a forum to enforce its consumer protection laws weighs in favor of exerting jurisdiction over appellants. See Reader's Digest, 501 P.2d at 303 (holding that Washington court had jurisdiction over foreign defendant that advertised there, noting that "[i]f our courts are not open, the state will be without a remedy in any court and the Consumer Protection Act will be rendered useless").

5. Convenience of Parties.

The convenience of the parties is "of minor interest in comparison to the first three factors." Rostad, 372 N.W.2d at 722.

> As technological progress has increased the flow of commerce between States, * * * progress in communications and transportation has made defense of a suit in a foreign tribunal less burdensome.

Hanson, 357 U.S. at 250–51, 78 S.Ct. at 1238.

Appellants argue that the district court placed excessive weight on WagerNet's statement that it reserved the right to sue customers in the customer's home forum or Belize, at WagerNet's option, because WagerNet is not a party to this action. The district court's decision, however, does not rely significantly on WagerNet's claimed choice of forums.

Moreover, appellants do not contest the district court's finding that appellant Rogers "makes all the decisions regarding WagerNet." "Foreign" corporations that seek business in Minnesota and reserve the right to sue Minnesota customers in courts here cannot claim inconvenience as an excuse to avoid personal jurisdiction here, particularly in light of the state's interest in regulating advertising and gambling. Appellants, an American corporation and its officer, who facilitated WagerNet's solicitation of business in Minnesota, have not shown that the inconvenience of defending themselves in Minnesota would be so great, by itself, as to offend traditional notions of due process.

DECISION

Appellants, through their Internet advertising, have demonstrated a clear intent to solicit business from markets that include Minnesota and, as a result, have had multiple contacts with Minnesota residents, including at least one successful solicitation.

The cause of action here arises from the same advertisements that constitute appellants' contacts with the state and implicates Minnesota's strong interest in maintaining the enforceability of its consumer protection laws. Appellants have not demonstrated that submission to personal jurisdiction in Minnesota would subject them to any undue inconvenience. For these reasons, we hold that appellants are subject to personal jurisdiction in Minnesota because, through their Internet activities, they purposefully availed themselves of the privilege of doing business in Minnesota to the extent that the maintenance of an action based on consumer protection statutes does not offend traditional notions of fair play and substantial justice.

Affirmed.

Notes

1. As *Szadolci* demonstrates, courts will not help parties to an illegal bet. Nevertheless, they normally will come to the aid of "innocent" victims. *See, e.g., Webb v. Martin*, 317 S.W.2d 899 (Ky.1958) (because husband had used his wife's property to satisfy his gambling debts without her knowledge or permission, third party had to either return or pay for the goods). *But see Congregation Emunath Israel v. New York City Off–Track Betting Corp.*, 330 N.Y.S.2d 895 (Sup.Ct.1972) (finding that branch office of betting corporation located 38 feet from plaintiff's synagogue did not constitute a legal nuisance).

2. Although the court in *Granite Gate* permitted Minnesota to proceed with its action, no court has yet held internet gambling illegal. This may soon change, however, because numerous prosecutions now are taking place around the country and Congress has before it a bill that would outlaw internet gambling. *See further* Pat Doyle, *Ruling Leaves Question of Web Gambling's Legality Unanswered*, Minneapolis Star–Trib., May 12, 1998, at 1A, and John Maher, *Legislation Offered to Ban Net Betting*, Austin Am.-Statesman, Feb. 8, 1998, at A1.

3. Interestingly, a number of non-gambling statutes contain provisions that affect bettors. First, the tax code permits losses to be deducted only to the extent of winnings. *See* 26 U.S.C. § 165(d) (1994). Second, the Americans with Disabilities Act specifically excludes compulsive gambling from its coverage. *See* 42 U.S.C. § 12211(b)(2) (1994). Third, the bankruptcy code prohibits gambling debts from being discharged if, at the time they were incurred, the person seeking relief had no intention of repaying them. *See* 11 U.S.C. § 523(a)(2)(A) (1994). For a further look at the law's treatment of gambling, see, e.g., Lawrence S. Lustberg, *Sentencing the Sick: Compulsive Gambling as the Basis for a Downward Departure Under the Federal Sentencing Guidelines*, 2 Seton Hall J. Sport L. 51 (1992) (estimating 80% of all Americans engage in some form of gambling and between one and three percent of the population are compulsive gamblers).

Problem 56

To gain valuable publicity, a car manufacturer promised to give a new vehicle to any player who sank a hole-in-one in an upcoming golf tournament. When one of the participants made such a shot, the company refused to pay, claiming the deal was an illegal gambling contract. If she sues, how will the court rule? *See Chenard v. Marcel Motors*, 387 A.2d 596 (Me.1978).

2. BOOKIES

Most sports bets in the United States are placed through "bookies." The following case describes how they operate.

UNITED STATES v. JONES

712 F.2d 115 (5th Cir.1983).

CLARK, Chief Judge.

Under 18 U.S.C. § 1955, a person convicted of operating an illegal gambling business may be imprisoned for up to five years and fined $20,000. This statute makes a gambling business "illegal" only if it "involves five or more persons who conduct, finance, manage, supervise, direct, or own all or part of such business.... " § 1955(b)(1)(ii). This appeal poses a recurring question: How significant must a person's activities be with respect to a gambling business for him to be included in the federal "jurisdictional five"?

A total of eight defendants were tried in the district court for violating section 1955 and related statutes. Six were convicted: Michael Wood Jones, Frank DeLuna, Raymond Arnona, Robert Wilson, Masilea Arnona, and Lester Doming. Biaggio Alfano and Raymond Joseph Palazzolo, Jr., were acquitted.

Jones, DeLuna, and Raymond Arnona candidly admit being partners in a large-scale New Orleans bookmaking operation in violation of Louisiana law. We thus take the liberty of referring to them hereinafter as "the bookies." The bookies' effort below, renewed here, was directed at rebutting the government's position that the other defendants were part of their operation. Of the remaining three who were convicted, only

Wilson appeals. He admits some involvement in the bookies' business but denies that this involvement was sufficient to support his conviction.

We have reviewed the record carefully in light of the challenges made by Wilson and the bookies and conclude that the evidence was sufficient to support the jury's finding that all four were part of an illegal gambling business involving five or more persons. We also find the appellants' other contentions without merit. The judgment entered by the district court upon the jury's verdict is accordingly affirmed.

I. Anatomy of a Bookmaking Operation

For the benefit of the non-gambler, we begin with an outline of the basic principles of bookmaking. United States v. Milton, 555 F.2d 1198 (5th Cir.1977), authored by another member of this panel, provides a good explanation. We borrow from it.

> [A] successful bookmaker is not a gambler but a businessman. He makes his profits not from winning bets, but from collecting a certain percentage of the amount bet that the losing bettors must pay for the privilege of betting. This percentage, usually 10%, is called "juice" or "vigorish." A bookmaker normally has a "line" or "point spread" on each game on which he is taking bets. The calculation is that an equal number of wagered dollars will be attracted to either side of the point spread. Thus, if the line in pro football is Washington by six over Dallas, the bookmaker expects some bettors to wager as much on Dallas to win or to lose by six or fewer points as others will bet on Washington to prevail by more than six points. When this is true, the bookmaker is guaranteed a profit of exactly 10%. When it is not, he may win more than 10% or fail to clear 10%. When the bets placed with a bookmaker are unbalanced, the risk-averse entrepreneur will adopt one of two strategies. The bookmaker may adjust his line up or down until it reaches equilibrium. More likely he will seek to "lay off" a bet to another bookmaker or to a mere bettor. That is, the bookmaker will bet the more popular of the two teams in the amount (ideally) by which bets on that team exceed the sum bet on the disfavored team at a given point spread. If the popular team wins, he will thus pay out to his bettors more than he took in, but will offset this disbursement by his own lay off winnings. By this device the bookmaker seeks to balance his books and assure himself neither more nor less than a 10% profit.
>
> If a bookmaker sets his line badly, he may find it difficult to lay off a sufficient number of bets to offset the risk of loss. Hence accurate "line information" regarding the expectations of his customers proves crucial. Moreover, bookmakers in a relevant market will seek to set a common line. If a particular bookmaker gives the Cowboys 6 points when all others give the Cowboys 3 points, all rational Cowboys fans will bet with the bookie who was out of line, and the rational Redskin fan

> (possibly an oxymoron) with all others. A rational bettor, as opposed to a rational fan, however, will bet equal amounts on the Cowboys plus six and the Redskins minus three. At worst, this cynical but rational bettor will win one bet and lose the other, suffering a net loss of 10% of the losing bet; at best, he will win both wagers.
>
> These hazards of the bookmaking business may be minimized, then, by lay off bets and frequent exchanges of line information among bookmakers. The difficult question in cases of this kind is typically whether lay off wagers and exchanges of line information among individuals or bookmaking operations suffice to create an illegal gambling operation comprising five or more persons.

Id. at 1200–01 (footnotes omitted).

II. Sufficiency of the Evidence

As we have noted, the bookies do not deny their involvement in the gambling operation. The sufficiency objections on appeal relate only to the evidence linking Masilea Arnona, Robert Wilson, and Lester Doming to the operation. For purposes of our decision, we need review only the facts relating to Masilea and Wilson. Because we find the evidence sufficient to support inclusion of the two of them along with the three bookies to make up the requisite jurisdictional five, discussion of the involvement of Lester Doming, who did not appeal, is obviated.

A. *Masilea Arnona*

The evidence connecting Masilea to the bookies' operation was primarily the product of surveillance conducted by the FBI. Government agents testified that Michael Jones regularly went to a phone booth in New Orleans at 4:30 p.m. From there he called Masilea at another pay phone located outside a sports betting facility in Las Vegas. On several occasions Masilea was overheard giving line information to Jones. Jones then shared the information with the other bookies. The betting lines the operation used were very similar to those supplied by Masilea.

Conversations among the bookies demonstrated their reliance on the point spreads Masilea provided. On one occasion, Raymond Arnona asked Jones what the appropriate line was for a particular game. Jones replied, "Well, the [expletive deleted]'s jumping all around, man, I wasn't gonna put it up until I make the call." Later Jones called Raymond back. He said, "This is what she gave me," and proceeded to read off a list of point spreads, including one for the game in question. In several other conversations, the bookies referred to "the lady" and the need to call her and not "leave her stranded."

The conversations were intercepted pursuant to a court-ordered wiretap, the legality of which the appellants do not challenge. Intercepted conversations provided the bulk of the government's case below. The wiretap lasted for nineteen days, from December 14, 1980, to January 1,

1981. In all, more than 2,800 calls were intercepted. The bookies were overheard accepting at least $736,000 in wagers.

The clear inference from this evidence is that Masilea was a regular supplier of line information to the bookies. This is enough to bring her within the broad scope of section 1955, which excludes only "mere bettors." Sanabria v. United States, 437 U.S. 54, 70–71 n. 26 (1978) ("Numerous cases have recognized that 18 U.S.C. § 1955 (1976 ed.) proscribes any degree of participation in an illegal gambling business, except participation as a mere bettor.")

B. Robert Wilson

Robert Wilson conducted a separate New Orleans bookmaking operation that had some dealings with the bookies' business. He and the bookies argue that the dealings between the two are insufficient to support his inclusion in the jurisdictional five.

Two ostensibly separate bookmakers may be linked for purposes of section 1955. Casual conversation between the two is not enough. There must be some showing of interdependence. A frequent exchange of line information or a consistent pattern of layoff betting will suffice. United States v. Avarello, 592 F.2d 1339, 1349 (5th Cir.1979), cert. denied, 444 U.S. 844, 100 S.Ct. 87, 62 L.Ed.2d 57 (1979); United States v. Boyd, 566 F.2d 929, 935 (5th Cir.1978); United States v. Milton, 555 F.2d at 1201.

Here the government attempted to show both. During a nineteen-day wiretap of the bookies' phones, eighteen calls were placed to Wilson. A total of eight wagers were made during these calls. Raymond Arnona placed seven wagers with Wilson, usually for $2,000 apiece. Wilson placed a single wager of $1,000 with Raymond. Of these, only the single bet made by Wilson may fairly be characterized as a layoff bet. In this Circuit a wager is not a layoff wager unless it is placed by a bookmaker for the purpose of ridding himself of excess wagering to achieve a balanced book. Avarello, 592 F.2d at 1351–52 n. 21 (citing United States v. Box, 530 F.2d 1258, 1261–62 (5th Cir.1976)). The bets placed by Raymond uniformly were on the wrong team to achieve this purpose. In other words, Raymond always bet on the team that the majority of the bookies' customers disfavored. Raymond apparently had little faith in the betting abilities of their "mere bettors."

His bets increased the risk by making the book more unbalanced than it was previously. Under our law the wagers placed by Raymond were not layoff bets. Whether Raymond was betting for himself or on behalf of the operation, the evidence shows that he was in fact betting. He was not laying off.

This leaves the single $1,000 wager placed by Wilson. We cannot infer, or allow the jury to infer, a consistent pattern of layoff betting from this single piece of evidence.

Despite this, we find the exchange of line information between the two operations sufficient to support Wilson's inclusion in the jurisdictional five. During the eighteen conversations point spreads were frequently discussed. The shorthand method of comparing lines indicates the exchanges were routine: Raymond and Wilson simply read off a list of numbers to one another with no reference to the games involved. See Avarello, 592 F.2d at 1352 ("the tenor of the conversations themselves suggests that the two men dealt with each other with regularity").

The evidence also shows that the bookies used the line information received from Wilson in establishing their own lines. On at least five occasions during the nineteen-day period, the bookies adjusted point spreads in reliance on advice from Wilson. After a December 14 conversation in which Wilson criticized the bookies' lines on two games, the lines were changed to conform to those Wilson was using. This scenario was repeated on several occasions. We agree with the government that this pattern of behavior supports the inference that Wilson's supply of line information substantially affected the bookies' business. Avarello, 592 F.2d at 1349. It also rebuts the appellants' contention that Wilson provided line information solely for Raymond Arnona's use in making wagers.

C. Conclusion

Section 1955's coverage is broad. All persons providing services that are necessary or helpful to the gambling operation come within its scope. United States v. Colacurcio, 659 F.2d 684, 688 (5th Cir.1981), cert. denied, 455 U.S. 1002, 102 S.Ct. 1635, 71 L.Ed.2d 869 (1982); United States v. Tucker, 638 F.2d 1292, 1295 (5th Cir.1981), cert. denied, 454 U.S. 833, 102 S.Ct. 132, 70 L.Ed.2d 111 (1981). The evidence presented against Masilea Arnona and Robert Wilson was sufficient to support the jury's conclusion that they were part of the bookies' operation. Their activities exceed those of "mere bettors" and thus fall outside section 1955's "sanctuary of bettordom." United States v. Box, 530 F.2d at 1267. We reject the argument that the evidence was insufficient to support the appellants' convictions.

III. Other Contentions

[This portion of the court's opinion, finding that the defendants were not entitled to a new trial, is omitted.]

IV. Conclusion

Our review of the record reveals that the evidence adduced by the government was sufficient to support the appellants' convictions and that the allegations of trial error are without merit.

Notes

1. As explained in *Jones*, bookies make their money from the "vigorish," more commonly known as the "vig." Because of this fact, the odds on a game do not (contrary to popular opinion) indicate which team bookies believe will win. Instead, they reflect how the public is betting. *See further* Reggie Rivers, *Public Sentiment Helps Bookies Draw an Imaginary Line*, Rocky Mtn. News, Jan. 25, 1998, at 8N.

2. Vig is just one of the many words gamblers have made their own. Two others are "push" and "prop." A push refers to a score that exactly matches the point spread (thereby resulting in no profit for the bookie), while a prop is any form of exotic bet. *See further* Jerry Greene, *Bookies Bite the Bullet*, Orlando Sentinel, Jan. 28, 1997, at D2.

3. Most people think of professional criminals, like the ones in *Jones*, when they hear the word "bookie." The typical bookie, however, is actually just an ordinary person trying to make a little extra money. *See further* Gary Rotstein, *You Can Bet On It: Though They Remain Hidden From the Law, Bookies Are a Call Away*, Pitt. Post–Gazette, Jan. 19, 1997, at A1.

4. Although accurate figures do not exist (for obvious reasons), many observers believe illegal bookies may handle up to 97% of the $103 billion that is annually bet on sports in the United States. *See further* Paul Doocey, *Legal Sports Betting*, 17 Int'l Gaming & Wagering Bus. 40–43 (1996).

Problem 57

A state statute defines bookmaking as "accepting bets as a business, rather than in a casual or personal fashion." Under this definition, could a person who coordinates her office's weekly football pool be prosecuted for bookmaking? *See State v. Postema*, 731 P.2d 13 (Wash.Ct.App.), *review denied*, 108 Wash.2d 1014 (1987).

3. EXPERTS

In making their wagers, many bettors rely on professional advice. As will be seen, the law differentiates between research and analysis ("handicapping") and claims of inside information ("touting").

LASKY v. VAN LINDT

453 N.Y.S.2d 983 (Sup.Ct.1982).

MARESCA, Justice.

"I've got a horse right here
his name is Paul Revere
and there's a guy who says
that if the weather's clear
can do, can do
This guy says
the horse can do
If he says the horse can do
can do, can do"

—Frank Loesser's Can Do from Guys & Dolls

On January 25, 1982, respondent New York State Racing and Wagering Board denied petitioner's application for a license as a thoroughbred race horse owner. Respondent based its denial upon its finding that, like the character Nicely–Nicely, who sang the above quoted verse from Guys & Dolls, petitioner was a tout.

Petitioner seeks to annul the determination by the respondent Board and to compel the Board to issue a license to him.

The New York State Racing and Wagering Board has general jurisdiction over all horse racing activities and pari-mutuel betting activities in New York State, both on-track and off-track, and over the corporations, associations and persons so engaged (Unconsolidated Laws, § 7908 and § 8162). In order to compete at any thoroughbred race meeting where pari-mutuel betting is conducted, owners of thoroughbred race horses must be licensed by the Board (Rules and Regulations of the New York State Racing and Wagering Board, 9 NYCRR § 4002.2). The Board is charged with the responsibility for licensing racing participants in accordance with the criteria set forth in Unconsolidated Laws § 7915(2). That section provides, in pertinent part, that the Board: "may refuse to issue or renew a license, or may suspend or revoke a license issued pursuant to this section, if it shall find that the applicant ... is consorting or associating with bookmakers, touts, or persons of similar pursuits, or has himself engaged in similar pursuits ..."

On petitioner's original application for a thoroughbred race horse owner's license, he stated that he was president of the Baltimore Bulletin, and described his business as "direct mail advertising". Upon submission of the application to the Board, a routine inquiry commenced concerning petitioner's financial responsibility. In aid of their inquiry, the Board contacted the Thoroughbred Racing Protective Bureau (TRPB) (an industry information clearinghouse, used by many race-tracks and state racing commissions throughout the country) seeking any files it may have pertaining to petitioner's activities. In addition, representatives of the Maryland Racing Commission were contacted regarding petitioner's status as a licensee, and with the New Jersey Racing Commission regarding his status there as an applicant. Thereafter, petitioner's application was reviewed, together with the TRPB's reports and other accumulated materials.

On January 25, 1982, the Board voted unanimously to deny the application, finding that petitioner is a professional tout. The Board noted that Mr. Lasky's publications frequently convey the impression that he has inside information that would not be available to even the best legitimate handicapper, suggesting that this information involves activity which is, at the very least, contrary to the rules of racing. It was the Board's belief that licensing Mr. Lasky while in his current profession would create an actual or apparent conflict of interest situation that is harmful to the public's perception of racing.

Petitioner contends that he is not a "tout" within the meaning of the Unconsolidated Laws § 7915(2) and the Rules of the New York State Racing and Wagering Board (9 NYCRR § 4002.8) or within the meaning of "tout" as that term is used as a proscribed activity in the context of racing, and that the Board's determination was arbitrary, capricious and an abuse of discretion. In addition, he claims that, given the Board's construction of "tout" in § 7915(2) of the Unconsolidated Laws and implementing regulations, the statute and regulations are overbroad, vague and irrational, and violate petitioner's rights to due process and equal protection of laws as guaranteed by the Fourteenth Amendment to the United States Constitution and Article I, Section 11 of the State Constitution.

Petitioner argues that the Board construed "tout" as a handicapper and that "in the absence of fraud and/or the offering of different selections in the same race to different customers", such construction renders the statute unconstitutional.

A handicapper is "one who rates the entries in a race before post time, who figures out the order of finish of a race beforehand. Factors include distance, weight, track condition, riders, past performances, breeding, idiosyncracies of horses, etc." (A Glossary of Racing Terms, issued by the New York State Racing and Wagering Board).

A "tout" on the other hand is "a person who obtains information on racehorses and their prospects and sells it to bettors" (The American Heritage Dictionary [Houghton–Mifflin Co., 1980 Ed.]; see also, Websters New Twentieth Century Dictionary, Unabridged, Second Edition [1977]). Scarnes New Complete Guide to Gambling (Simon and Shuster, 1974) defines a tout as "a person who makes a living at or away from the track by trying to convince anyone who will listen that he has useful inside information."

In reviewing the various representative publications authored by petitioner, the Board concluded that his publications tend to create the impression that he has inside information as to which horses will win particular races. A perusal of petitioner's publications confirms that the materials do tend to create that impression. The Board's conclusion therefor, that petitioner is a tout as that term is consistently defined in the context of racing, and that his activities are not in the best interests of racing is neither arbitrary, capricious nor an abuse of discretion.

It is important to remember that as a sporting event, horse racing occupies a unique position among the professional sports activities which take place in this state; it is the only sport in which wagering is legal. As such, the state has a vital interest in protecting the integrity of the sport (see, Barry v. Barchi, 443 U.S. 55, 99 S.Ct. 2642, 61 L.Ed.2d 365 [1979]; Hubel v. West Virginia Racing Commission, 513 F.2d 240 [4th Cir., 1975]) and preventing any potential for abuse. The New York State Racing and Wagering Board, having been delegated the responsibility to regulate racing and pari-mutuel betting, reviews many applications such as the one submitted by Mr. Lasky. Its decision in this case to deny Mr. Lasky a license is consistent with its responsibilities to the sport, to the public and to the state.

Petitioner's argument that the statute and implementing regulations are unconstitutionally overbroad, vague and irrational is without merit. A fair reading of the language, as measured by common understanding and practice, clearly gives adequate warning of the type of conduct prohibited. In addition, the legislature, by its enactment of

Unconsolidated Laws, § 7915(2) was of the opinion that licensing touts was inconsistent with the public interest, convenience and necessity and not in the best interests of racing generally, and since owning, training and racing horses is not one of life's "common occupations" (see, Medina v. Rudman, 1st Cir. 545 F.2d 244), it may be subject to the strictest type of regulation.

Petitioner also argues that insofar as the Board reached a determination without affording him the benefit of a hearing, he was denied due process as guaranteed by the Fifth and Fourteenth Amendments to the United States Constitution and Article I, sections 6 and 11 of the State Constitution. This argument was similarly addressed by the Court of Appeals in Fink v. Cole, 1 N.Y.2d 48, 150 N.Y.S.2d 175, 133 N.E.2d 691, where it was stated that the administrative machinery (with respect to processing licenses for thoroughbred racing) "was created for the purpose of determining whether a privilege—a license—should be granted to citizens engaged in the business of horse racing". Since there is no absolute right to a race horse owner's license, petitioner has no "claim of entitlement" that would require the Board to grant him a hearing (see, Perry v. Sindermann, 408 U.S. 593, 92 S.Ct. 2694, 33 L.Ed.2d 570).

Accordingly, the petition is denied.

Notes

1. As *Lasky* points out, handicapping is legal but touting is not. Is this a distinction without a difference?

2. For an interesting article which likens tips on the stock market to tips on gambling, see Lynn A. Stout, *Are Stock Markets Costly Casinos? Disagreement, Market Failure, and Securities Regulation*, 81 Va. L. Rev. 611 (1995).

Problem 58

Before the first week of the football season, a handicapper sent telegrams to 8,000 individuals he did not know. Half were told to bet on Team A and half were told to bet on Team B. When Team A beat Team B, the handicapper sent telegrams to the 4,000 he told to bet on Team A. This time, he told half the recipients to bet on Team C and half to bet on Team D. When Team C lost to Team D, he sent telegrams to the 2,000 he told to bet on Team D. This time, he told half to bet on Team E and half to bet on Team F. When Team E beat Team F, he prepared the following telegram to be sent to the 1,000 people he told to bet on Team E: "As you know, for the past three weeks I have given you three straight winners. If you would like my pick for this week's game, send me $1,000 at the address listed below." Has the handicapper done anything illegal? *See Cohen v. State*, 112 S.E.2d 672 (Ga.Ct.App.1960).

C. CORRUPTION

All sports organizations fear betting, and with good reason. If gamblers are able to infiltrate their operations (or appear to have done so), the public will quickly turn away.

1. BRIBES

Paying an athlete to do less than his or her best ("putting in the fix"), agreeing to take such a payment ("taking a dive"), or conspiring to do either, exposes participants to both civil and criminal actions.

VENZOR v. GONZALEZ

936 F.Supp. 445 (N.D.Ill.1996).

ASPEN, Chief Judge.

Chicago BlackHawk hockey fans at the United Center in downtown Chicago are accustomed to watching minimally talented amateur fisticuffs of short duration. On July 29, 1995, however, the United Center hosted a professional boxing match between Julio Cesar Chavez and Craig Houk which lasted for a shorter period of time than the typical hockey fight. Approximately ninety-six seconds into the first round, Chavez knocked out Houk. According to the plaintiff, who was the fight's promoter, the quick victory was foreordained; Houk took a dive. Jose Venzor brings this action, removed from state court, against Defendants Chavez, Houk, Don King Productions, Don King, and Al Braverman. The seven-count complaint seeks recovery under the Racketeer Influenced and Corrupt Organizations Act (RICO), 18 U.S.C. § 1962, and under various state law theories. Presently before us are motions to dismiss filed by (1) Julio Cesar Chavez, (2) Don King Productions, and (3) Don King and Al Braverman. For the reasons set forth below, we grant in part and deny in part the motions.

Background

According to the complaint, in March 1993 Chavez agreed to fight a June 1993 match in the Chicago area. However, King Productions owned the exclusive right to promote Chavez's fights, and Chavez had failed to obtain a waiver from King Productions before agreeing to the June fight. Venzor, an investor in the June fight, sued Chavez and others in state court to recover his investment. Eventually, Venzor and King began negotiating a settlement, and in February 1995, King Productions' counsel faxed a letter to Venzor's lawyer that generally spelled out the basis for a settlement. Compl. p 10, Ex. B. According to the fax, King agreed to release Chavez from the exclusivity contract for one non-championship fight in Chicago in exchange for Venzor's dismissal of the suit. Id., Ex. B.

On April 20, 1995, the plaintiff met with King in Florida. Id. p 11. King told Venzor that Houk would be Chavez's opponent in the non-title fight. Houk, according to King, "would put up a 'great fight' " and "be a serious and competitive opponent" against Chavez. Id. After the meeting, King Productions' counsel faxed a draft settlement agreement and two subsequent revisions on, respectively, April 25, May 11, and June 28. Id., Exs. C, D, E. The June draft released Chavez to fight in exchange for, among other things, $50,000 to King Productions, a $250,000 purse for Chavez, and a $50,000 purse for Houk. In addition, the May and June drafts named Houk as the opponent.

However, Venzor substituted another boxer's name for Houk's, signed the agreement, and faxed the agreement to Chavez, who then signed and returned the agreement to Venzor by fax. Id. p 16, Ex. F. Later, King called Venzor and insisted that "Chavez would fight nobody but ... Houk." Id. It was not until early July 1995, the plaintiff alleges, that Houk learned that he was Chavez's opponent. Braverman phoned Houk and "instructed ... Houk to go down and to make [Venzor] look bad in doing so." Id. p 17. King Productions promised to pay $10,000 for Houk to throw the fight, and Houk accepted. Id. According to the plaintiff, "[a]s of the date of this phone call, all of the defendants were in agreement that defendant Houk would lose his fight with defendant Chavez." Id.

As the date of the fight—July 29th—approached, King again told Venzor that only Houk would fight Chavez. Id. p 18. Assured of victory, Chavez allegedly failed, starting on July 15, to properly train for the fight; "[h]e consumed substances which were deleterious to his body and which would have otherwise put him at risk in any honest fight at the professional level." Id. p 19. In addition, Chavez "got into at least one bar room fight" and was absent (or tardy) at important meetings, press conferences, and publicity events. Id. Meanwhile, King Productions sent a final fax to Venzor on July 25, confirming the undercard fight and reminding Venzor of his responsibility to pay for Houk's room and dining expenses while in Chicago. Id., Ex. G.

The fight lasted ninety-six seconds; Chavez won by knockout. According to the plaintiff, King Productions and King took possession of the fight's videotapes immediately after the fight ended, and the match was not, contrary to custom, replayed on the United Center's video screens. Id. p 22. However, Venzor obtained an unauthorized videotape of the fight, and claims it shows that the supposed knockout punch, "if contact was made at all, was nothing more than a glancing blow." Id. p 23. Houk "jumped backwards in reaction to the 'knockout' punch and thereafter sat on the ring in the corner until the fight was over." Id.

In addition to the allegations regarding the Chavez–Houk fight, the plaintiff charges that King, King Productions, and Braverman used Houk twice before to throw fights. On January 29, 1994, Houk intentionally lost a match against Meldrick Taylor, a boxer under contract to King Productions, after Houk received a bribe; Taylor " 'needed a win' " because of an upcoming fight between Taylor and Chavez. Id. p 12(a). Also, on September 4, 1994, Houk purposefully lost a fight against Gary Murray, another King Productions boxer. Id. p 12(b).

Based on these allegations, the complaint asserts seven counts: (1) King Productions, King, and Braverman violated 18 U.S.C. § 1962(a), by receiving income from a pattern of racketeering activity and investing or using that income in the establishment or operation of an enterprise, King Productions; (2) King, King Productions, Braverman, Chavez, and

Houk violated § 1962(b) by acquiring or maintaining an interest in or control of an enterprise through a pattern of racketeering activity; (3) King, Chavez, Braverman, and Houk violated § 1962(c) by conducting or participating in the conduct of King Productions' affairs through a pattern of racketeering activity; (4) the defendants violated § 1962(d) by conspiring to violate § 1962(a), (b), and (c); (5) King and King Productions committed promissory fraud by misrepresenting that Houk would be a serious and competitive opponent; (6) Chavez breached an agreement to promote the fight; and (7) the defendants violated the Illinois Professional Boxing and Wrestling Act, 225 ILCS 105/1–26. The defendants move to dismiss, and we now turn to their arguments.

DISCUSSION

A. *Particularity of Fraud Allegations*

Initially, the defendants argue that the allegations of fraud fail to satisfy Federal Rule of Civil Procedure 9(b), which requires that "the circumstances constituting fraud ... shall be stated with particularity." This particularity requirement attempts to serve three purposes: "(1) protecting a defendant's reputation from harm; (2) minimizing 'strike suits' and 'fishing expeditions'; and (3) providing notice of the claim to the adverse party." Vicom, Inc. v. Harbridge Merchant Servs., 20 F.3d 771, 777 (7th Cir.1994). Accordingly, allegations of fraud should report "the who, what, when, where, and how" of the misrepresentation. DiLeo v. Ernst & Young, 901 F.2d 624, 627 (7th Cir.), cert. denied, 498 U.S. 941, 111 S.Ct. 347, 112 L.Ed.2d 312 (1990).

Although the complaint does not always distinguish between defendants as precisely as it could have, e.g., Compl. p 24 (referring broadly to "[o]ne or more Defendants"), we think that the allegations sufficiently spell out the fraud. Principally, the fraudulent scheme comprised inducing Venzor to drop the state court lawsuit against Chavez and to pay King Productions, Chavez, and Houk in exchange for Chavez's release to fight a phony match. The scheme to defraud began with the February 1995 fax from King Productions, in which King represented that he would release Chavez for one fight if Venzor dropped the suit. Compl. pp 10, 24(a). King then furthered the scheme by insisting that Houk serve as the opponent and by misrepresenting that Houk would put up a good fight, id. pp 11, 16, 18, when in fact King and Braverman (acting on King Productions' behalf) paid Houk to lose. And by the time Houk accepted the bribe, all of the defendants agreed that Houk would throw the fight, id. p 17, including Chavez, who trained apathetically for the fight because victory was predetermined, id. p 19. The fight itself provided the final touch, as Houk and Chavez feigned a serious match. Id. pp 21, 23. In sum, the defendants' respective roles and misrepresentations in the fraudulent scheme are sufficiently alleged to satisfy Rule 9(b).

B. *Pattern of Racketeering Activity*

Next, the defendants challenge the complaint's assertion, Compl. p 24(a)-(j), that the following acts constitute a "pattern" of racketeering activity under RICO: (a) On February 21, 1995, sending the fax transmission referenced in paragraph 10 supra in violation of 18 U.S.C. § 1343; (b) On April 25, 1995, sending the fax transmission referenced in paragraph 13 supra in violation of 18 U.S.C. § 1343; (c) On May 11, 1995, sending the fax transmission referenced in paragraph 14 supra in violation of 18 U.S.C. § 1343; (d) On June 28, 1995, sending the fax transmission referenced in paragraph 15 supra in violation of 18 U.S.C. § 1343; (e) Sending the fax transmission [Chavez to Venzor] and making the phone call [King to Venzor] referenced in paragraph 16 supra in violation of 18 U.S.C. § 1343; (f) Making the telephone call [Braverman to Houk] referenced in paragraph 17 supra in violation of 18 U.S.C. § 1343; (g) On July 17, 1995, sending a fax transmission to Plaintiff or his counsel regarding the subject fight in violation of 18 U.S.C. § 1343; (h) Carrying into effect, attempting to carry into effect, conspiring with other persons to carry into effect a scheme in commerce to influence, in any way, by bribery a sporting contest, with knowledge that the purpose of such scheme is to influence by bribery that contest [January 1994 Taylor–Houk fight] as referenced in paragraph 12a supra in violation of 18 U.S.C. § 224; (i) Carrying into effect, attempting to carry into effect, conspiring with other persons to carry into effect a scheme in commerce to influence, in any way, by bribery a sporting contest, with knowledge that the purpose of such scheme is to influence by bribery that contest [September 1994 Murray–Houk fight] as referenced in paragraph 12b supra in violation of 18 U.S.C. § 224; (j) Carrying into effect, attempting to carry into effect, conspiring with other persons to carry into effect a scheme in commerce to influence, in any way, by bribery a sporting contest, with knowledge that the purpose of such scheme is to influence by bribery that contest [July 1995 Chavez–Houk fight] as referenced in paragraphs 17 and 21 supra in violation of 18 U.S.C. § 224.

While RICO's provisions provide scant guidance in giving meaning to "pattern of racketeering activity," the Supreme Court, in H.J. Inc. v. Northwestern Bell T. Co., 492 U.S. 229, 109 S.Ct. 2893, 106 L.Ed.2d 195 (1989), instructed that "to prove a pattern of racketeering activity a plaintiff ... must show that the racketeering predicates are related, [and] that they amount to or pose a threat of continued criminal activity." Id. at 239, 109 S.Ct. at 2900. We think the plaintiff's allegations of racketeering activity meet this "continuity plus relationship" test.

C. Injury

The defendants also argue that Venzor has failed to allege compensable injuries under RICO. Section 1964(c) provides that "[a]ny person injured in his business or property by reason of a violation of section 1962" may sue and recover damages. In order to recover damages, the RICO violation must have proximately caused the damages. Holmes v. Securities Investor Protection Corp., 503 U.S. 258, 268, 112 S.Ct. 1311, 1317–18, 117 L.Ed.2d 532 (1992). Here, the plaintiff alleges that the defendants' scheme caused him to drop the original lawsuit against Chavez, which presumably had some monetary value. Compl. p 24. In addition, the plaintiff alleges that the defendants "deprive[d] the Plaintiff of hundreds of thousands of dollars," id. p 24, presumably including the payments made to the defendants for a sham fight and for any liability the plaintiff may have to disappointed ticket buyers. Significantly, Venzor expressly alleges that he suffered injury to his business and property as a "proximate result" of each RICO violation. Id., Count I p 28 (§ 1962(a)), Count II p 28 (§ 1962(b)), Count III p 28 (§ 1962(c)), Count IV p 31 (§ 1962(d) conspiracy "proximately injured" plaintiff). While proving the claims of damages with evidence may be a different matter, these allegations are sufficient to survive a motion to dismiss.

D. RICO Violations

Next, Chavez and Braverman briefly make individual arguments as to why the complaint fails to allege substantive RICO violations against them. However, none of the arguments are persuasive. First, Chavez protests that the complaint conclusorily alleges that Chavez acquired or maintained an interest in King Productions, see Compl. Count II p 27 (§ 1962(b)), and that Chavez conducted or participated in the conduct of King Productions, see Compl. Count III p 27 (§ 1962(c)). Although Chavez criticizes the allegations as mere factual conclusions, he fails to cite any authority imposing any higher pleading standard. Moreover, the complaint's allegations are consistent with the factual conclusions pleaded, and we thus reject those criticisms as grounds for dismissing those claims as to Chavez.

There exists some authority, however, for Chavez's separate argument that allegations of a RICO conspiracy under § 1962(d) require more than mere conclusions. For example, in Schiffels v. Kemper Fin. Servs., 978 F.2d 344, 352 (7th Cir.1992) the Seventh Circuit stated: "Conclusory allegations of 'conspiracy' are not sufficient to state a claim under § 1962(d); rather, [the plaintiff] must allege facts from which one can infer each defendant's agreement to violate § 1962(c)." Even if such a requirement survives Leatherman v. Tarrant County Narcotics Intelligence and Coordination Unit, 507 U.S. 163, 113 S.Ct. 1160, 122 L.Ed.2d 517 (1993), the complaint here supplies the requisite allegations. According to the complaint, Chavez at the latest entered the conspiracy to fix the fight in early July 1995. We can infer Chavez's agreement with the other defendants from his conduct after early July 1995: improper training, consumption of "deleterious" substances, the bar room brawl, and of course, the feigned fight itself. Compl. p 19.

Lastly, Braverman maintains that the allegations fail to indicate that he agreed to the commission of more than one predicate act. See Gagan v. American Cablevision, Inc., 77 F.3d 951, 961 (7th Cir.1996) (explaining that RICO conspiracy not only requires agreement to violate substantive RICO provision, but also an agreement to the commission of two or more predicate acts). However, the complaint expressly alleges that Braverman participated in the sports briberies of Houk for three different fights, and that Braverman committed wire fraud when he phoned Houk in furtherance of the scheme to defraud Venzor. Accordingly, Braverman's arguments are not grounds for dismissing the RICO claims against him.

E. Promissory Fraud

As for the state law claims, King Productions and King first contend that the fraud claim (Count V) fails to state a claim because the alleged misrepresentation is simply one of opinion, and that the plaintiff fails to allege reliance. Generally, promises to perform future conduct do not constitute fraudulent misrepresentations. Industrial Specialty Chemicals, Inc. v. Cummins Engine Co., 902 F.Supp. 805, 813 (N.D.Ill.1995) (citing HPI Health Care Servs. v. Mt. Vernon Hosp., Inc., 131 Ill.2d 145, 137 Ill.Dec. 19, 29, 545 N.E.2d 672, 682 (1989)). However, the general rule against the viability of "promissory fraud" is subject to an exception " 'where the false promise or representation of intention of future conduct is the scheme or device to accomplish the fraud.' " Bower v. Jones, 978 F.2d 1004, 1011 (7th Cir.1992) (quoting Steinberg v. Chicago Medical Sch., 69 Ill.2d 320, 13 Ill.Dec. 699, 706, 371 N.E.2d 634, 641 (1977)). Specifically, the "scheme exception" applies where the party promises performance in order to induce the other party's reliance, and the other party so relies, but the promisor never intended to keep the promise. Id.

Venzor sufficiently alleges that, in April 1995, King Productions and King misrepresented that Houk would provide a competitive fight against Chavez, Compl. Count V p 24, and that the plaintiff relied on that misrepresentation, id. p 25. For purposes of this motion to dismiss, it matters not that the plaintiff might have doubted Houk's competitiveness against Chavez, or that the plaintiff would have preferred another boxer; the point is that the defendants, by representing that Houk would be competitive, misrepresented that Houk would not throw the fight. In addition, if the plaintiff had known about the bribe, he presumably would not have promoted and staged the match, and thus he has successfully alleged reliance. In sum, the allegations of Count V state a claim for fraud.

F. Breach of Contract

Count VI of the complaint purports to state a claim against Chavez for breach of contract. In Venzor's response brief, the plaintiff states that he withdraws the breach of contract claim. Accordingly, Chavez's motion to dismiss this count is granted.

G. Illinois Professional Boxing and Wrestling Act

Finally, the defendants contend that Count VII, premised on the Illinois Professional Boxing and Wrestling Act, 225 ILCS 105/1–26, fails to state a claim because there exists no private cause of action under the Act. According to the plaintiff, although the Act admittedly does not provide for an express cause of action, an implied cause of action exists. We agree.

Illinois courts "have continually demonstrated a willingness to imply a private remedy where there exists a clear need to effectuate the purpose of an act." Sawyer Realty Group, Inc. v. Jarvis Corp., 89 Ill.2d 379, 59 Ill.Dec. 905, 909, 432 N.E.2d 849, 853 (1982). Under Illinois law,

> [i]mplication of a private right of action is appropriate only if: (1) plaintiff is a member of the class for whose benefit the Act was enacted; (2) it is consistent with the underlying purpose of the Act; (3) plaintiff's injury is one the Act was designed to prevent; and (4) it is necessary to provide an adequate remedy for violations of the Act.

Corgan v. Muehling, 143 Ill.2d 296, 158 Ill.Dec. 489, 496, 574 N.E.2d 602, 609 (1991); see also Sawyer Realty Group, 59 Ill.Dec. at 909, 432 N.E.2d at 853.

In light of the four-factor test employed in Illinois, and the similar licensing schemes in Sawyer Realty Group and Corgan, we hold that there likewise exists an implied cause of action under the Act. First, the provisions specifying the sort of conduct that would subject a licensee (or an applicant for a license) to disciplinary action indicate that Venzor is a member of the class of persons that the Act sought to protect; regulated persons seem to be protected from fellow regulated persons. E.g., 105/16(2), (8)-(10). In addition, although the Act certainly protects spectators of boxing matches, the Act sweeps broader in its protection and imposes duties that go beyond protection of spectators. E.g., 105/13 (promoter must report ticket sales to the Department of Professional Regulation); 105/12 (contestants must be examined by physicians both before and after match). Accordingly, promoters appear to fall within the Act's protected classes.

Moreover, an implied cause of action is consistent with the Act's underlying purpose, which includes protection of properly licensed promoters as well as spectators. Indeed, the Act provides for civil monetary penalties upon the issuance of a cease and desist order by the Department of Professional Regulation, 105/21, and thus a private cause of action for monetary damages will not frustrate the Act. See Sawyer Realty Group, 59 Ill.Dec. at 910, 432 N.E.2d at 854 (existence of limited civil remedies under statutory provisions does not necessarily require rejection of implied cause of action). The third requirement for implication of a private cause of action is also satisfied; given the purposes of the Act, the statutory scheme seeks to prevent Venzor's injuries, including the payments made for a fixed fight, which were caused by the defendants' "sham" boxing match and "dishonorable" conduct. 105/16(2), (10).

Finally, just as an implied cause of action was "necessary to provide an adequate remedy for violations" of the licensing regimes governing real estate brokers, Sawyer Realty Group, 59 Ill.Dec. at 910–11, 432 N.E.2d at 854–55, and psychologists, Corgan, 158 Ill.Dec. at 497, 574 N.E.2d at 610, an implied cause of action provides an adequate remedy for the Professional Boxing and Wrestling Act. The limited monetary recovery available to injured parties and the injunctive relief authorized under the Act, see 105/21 ($10,000 maximum civil penalty may be imposed if Department of Professional Regulation issues cease and desist order), will unlikely make whole those promoters who unwittingly pay for, and are victimized by, sham fights. Cf. Sawyer Realty Group, 59 Ill.Dec. at 910, 432 N.E.2d at 854 (even though injunctive relief and recovery from compensation fund expressly available, implied cause of action necessary to provide adequate remedy); Corgan, 158 Ill.Dec. at 497, 574 N.E.2d at 610 (insufficient incentive to pursue administrative or criminal proceedings "without a potential for a tangible reward"). Thus, we conclude that there exists an implied cause of action under the Act.

Conclusion

For the reasons discussed above, we grant Chavez's motion to dismiss the plaintiff's breach of contract claim (Count VI), but otherwise deny the defendants' motions to dismiss.

Notes

1. Underhanded dealings have a long history in boxing. *See further Kondrath v. Arum*, 881 F.Supp. 925 (D.Del.1995); *Duva v. World Boxing Ass'n*, 548 F.Supp. 710 (D.N.J.1982); Ian Forman, *Boxing in the Legal Arena*, 3 Sports Law. J. 75 (1996). Recently, in an attempt to clean up the sport, Congress enacted the Professional Boxing Safety Act of 1996, 15 U.S.C. §§ 6301–6313 (Supp. II 1996). The statute mandates use of a state-based boxer registration and reporting system, specifies minimum health and welfare standards, prohibits promoters from giving anything of value to boxing commissioners, and subjects violators to fines and prison terms. For a further discussion of the law's provisions, see Kelley C. Howard, *Regulating the Sport of Boxing—Congress Throws the First Punch with the Professional Boxing Safety Act*, 7 Seton Hall J. Sport L. 103 (1997).

2. Despite the passage of eight decades, the most notable fix in American sports history remains the "Black Sox" scandal, which arose when various members of the Chicago White Sox agreed to throw the 1919 World Series in exchange for money. The incident remains a subject of intense study both here and abroad for a number of reasons: (a) it was the impetus for baseball's adoption of a centralized commissioner's office (a model subsequently borrowed by numerous other leagues); (b) it nearly caused the death of baseball (a fate which was avoided by the timely emergence of home run king Babe Ruth); (c) it personified the increasing lawlessness of the country in the wake of World War I; (d) it was orchestrated by a notorious gangster named Arnold Rothstein, better known as "The Brain" and "The Big Bankroll"; (e) it led to a popular legend in which a small boy reportedly begged outfielder Shoeless Joe Jackson to "say it ain't so"; and, (f) it demonstrated the lengths to which underpaid players would go to make extra money. For a further look at the scandal, see Eliot Asinof, *Eight Men Out* (1987), and James R. Devine, *Baseball's Labor Wars in Historical Context: The 1919 Chicago White Sox as a Case–Study in Owner–Player Relations*, 5 Marq. Sports L.J. 1 (1994).

3. Of all team sports, college basketball is the most vulnerable to bribes because many of its athletes are poor (thereby making them easy

targets for gamblers) and only one or two participants are needed to fix a game. *See, e.g.*, *United States v. Burke*, 700 F.2d 70 (2d Cir.), *cert. denied*, 464 U.S. 816 (1983) (explaining how gambler Henry Hill was able to fix Boston College basketball games with the help of a single player). Among the schools to have experienced basketball scandals are Arizona State University, Bradley University, California State University (Fullerton), City College of New York, Long Island University, Manhattan College, Memphis State University, Northwestern University, Seton Hall University, and Tulane University. *See further* Ante Z. Udovicic, *Sports and Gambling a Good Mix? I Wouldn't Bet on It*, 8 Marq. Sports L.J. 401 (1998). *See also* Michael Dobie, *Gambling a Concern*, Bergen County (N.J.) Record, Mar. 25, 1998, at S6 (describing the efforts of the NCAA to prevent fixes during "March Madness," when bets worth $2.5 billion are placed).

4. Some outcomes, although strongly hinting of a fix, are never proven one way or the other. It is widely thought, for example, that the 1958 NFL Championship Game was rigged by Carroll Rosenbloom, owner of the Baltimore Colts, because of a $100,000 wager. *See further* Jim O'Donnell, *Safe Bet We've Seen This Before*, Chi. Sun–Times, Feb. 13, 1997, at 108. Similarly, many people are convinced Sonny Liston, acting on orders from the mob, purposely lost his 1965 heavyweight championship fight with Muhammad Ali (who at the time was known as Cassius Clay). *See further* Robert Rubino, *Critical Link Between JFK and Sonny Liston*, Santa Rosa (CA) Press Democrat, Mar. 1, 1998, at C2 (reviewing at length Ali's so-called "phantom punch"). Likewise, there are those who believe the NBA fixed the 1985 rookie draft lottery to ensure the New York Knicks, whose poor play was dampening interest in the league, would select first. With the pick the team took Georgetown University star center Patrick Ewing. *See further* Jan Hubbard, *Ewing Pick Arrives in the Knick of Time*, San Diego Union–Trib., May 13, 1985, at D1 (pointing out one of the principal clients of the accounting firm that certified the lottery was the corporate parent of the Knicks). More recently, in March 1999, Evander Holyfield and Lennox Lewis' heavyweight title unification bout ended in a controversial draw. Much of the public immediately concluded that promoter Don King had fixed the fight to ensure a lucrative rematch. *See further* Bob Molinaro, *The Shame of Boxing Is That It has None*, Norfolk Virginian-Pilot, Mar. 17, 1999, at C1.

5. Sports bribery cases are not confined to rigging the outcome of games. In December 1998, for example, the International Olympic Committee launched an investigation into allegations that the Salt Lake City Olympic Committee had illegally distributed nearly $400,000 in student scholarships to the families of various delegates as part of its successful bid for the 2002 Winter Olympics. Subsequently, in March 1999, six members of the International Olympic Committee were expelled and a reform commission was created to spearhead changes. *See further* Jere Longman, *Pressed to Purify Games, I.O.C. Ousts 6 Members*, N.Y. Times, Mar. 18, 1999, at C25.

Coincidentally, the biggest scandal in English soccer history began to unfold within days of the start of the IOC's inquiry. Graham Kelly, the chief executive officer of the English Football Association, was forced to resign when it was discovered he had used a $5 million loan to curry favor with the Welsh Football Association in connection with an upcoming vote at the

International Association Football Federation. *See further Bribery Scandal Hits English Soccer*, L.A. Times, Dec. 16, 1998, at D4.

Problem 59

Aliens who commit crimes involving "moral turpitude" are subject to deportation under 8 U.S.C. § 1182(a)(2). In your opinion, would bribing a goalie to throw a game constitute a crime of moral turpitude? *See United States ex rel. Sollazzo v. Esperdy*, 285 F.2d 341 (2d Cir.), *cert. denied*, 366 U.S. 905 (1961).

2. BETTING

To lessen the likelihood of a player taking a dive, all leagues prohibit their members from wagering on their own sport and some forbid bets of any kind. Not surprisingly, these rules have led to a number of bitter disputes.

MOLINAS v. PODOLOFF

133 N.Y.S.2d 743 (Sup.Ct.1954).

JOSEPH, Justice.

Plaintiff brings this action for a permanent injunction to set aside his suspension as a player in the National Basketball Association, to maintain his rights to be a player member in the association and for other relief. The defendant, an unincorporated association, conducts and supervises a professional basketball league consisting of teams owned by nine clubs. The owners of the said clubs comprising the membership of the National Basketball Association (hereinafter designated as N.B.A.) employed professional basketball players known as player members of the association.

A duly-adopted constitution and bylaws regulated the rights, privileges and duties of the members and player members.

The Zollner Machine Works, Inc., of Fort Wayne, Indiana, was the owner of the club known as Fort Wayne Zollner Pistons, a member of the N.B.A.; it entered into a written contract on the form prescribed by the N.B.A. with the plaintiff to play professional basketball in the said league for its club, whereby the club and the plaintiff became bound by the terms of the said agreement, and the constitution and bylaws of the N.B.A.

It is undisputed that on January 9, 1954, the police of Fort Wayne, Indiana, conducted an inquiry as to the Zollner Piston Basketball Team, and the plaintiff, by reason of such investigation, in the late evening of that day, or in the early morning of January 10, 1954, signed a written statement of his having wagered on his team. Specifically the plaintiff admitted:

> I have been a member of the Zollner Piston Basketball Team since October 1953. After being on the team for approximately a month I called a man in New York by the name of Mr. X,

> knowing this man for a long period of time I called him on the telephone and asked him if he could place a bet for me. He said that he could and he would tell me the odds on the game either for or against the Pistons. After hearing the odds or points on the game I either placed a bet on the Pistons or else told him that the odds were too great and I did not want to place the bet. Several times I talked to him over the phone and odds or points were not mentioned and I told him that I thought on some occasions that we could win a particular game and I placed a bet. I did this about ten times. At no time was there a pay off to throw any games made to me by Mr. X. Nor was there any mention of the fact; however, the only reimbursement I received was for my phone calls which I made to him. Also I received approximately $400 for the total times that I have been betting with him. This included the phone bill also.

The plaintiff has admitted, and so testified at the trial, that the statement was a voluntary, free and truthful statement of fact.

Maurice Podoloff, President of the N.B.A., and Mr. Zollner, President of the Fort Wayne Zollner Pistons, arrived at the police station about midnight, and subsequent to being shown plaintiff's statement Mr. Podoloff sent for him. In the conversation that ensued, relating to the wagering situation, and the plaintiff's participation therein, Mr. Podoloff informed the plaintiff that he was "through" as a player, and Mr. Podoloff indefinitely suspended the plaintiff.

The plaintiff predicates his action upon two contentions: (1) that no notice of hearing and charges were given the plaintiff as provided by the contract and the constitution; (2) there was no authority to indefinitely suspend the plaintiff. The defendant contends: (1) that there was due notice and hearing; (2) plaintiff's admissions of wagering constituted a waiver of his rights; (3) plaintiff comes into equity with unclean hands.

The pertinent provisions of the contract and the constitution of the N.B.A. applicable to this matter are as follows: Section 15 of the contract provides:

> It is severally and mutually agreed that any player of a Club, who directly or indirectly bets money or anything of value on the outcome of any game played for any National Basketball Association Club, shall be expelled from the National Basketball Association by the President after due notice and hearing and the President's decision shall be final, binding, conclusive and unappealable; and the Player hereby releases the President and waives every claim he may have against the President and/or the National Basketball Association, and against every Club in the National Basketball Association, and against every director, officer and stockholder of every Club in the National Basketball Association, for damages and for all claims and demands whatsoever arising out of or in connection with the decision of the President of the National Basketball Association.

Section 43 of the constitution of the N.B.A. provides:

> He shall have the power to suspend for a definite or indefinite period or to impose a fine not exceeding $1,000 or inflict both upon any manager, coach, player or officer who in his opinion shall be guilty of conduct prejudicial or detrimental to the association regardless whether the same occurred in or outside of the playing building.

Section 79 of the constitution of the N.B.A. provides:

> Any officer, director, coach or employee of a club, team, corporation or organization operating a franchise in the N.B.A. who or which directly or indirectly wagers money or anything of value on the outcome of any game played by a team of the N.B.A. shall on being charged with such wagering be given a hearing by the President of the Association after due notice, and the decision given by the President shall be final, binding and conclusive and unappealable, and anyone so charged and found guilty shall have no claim against the President and/or N.B.A. or its members or against any club or organization operating a franchise of the N.B.A.

After the plaintiff made his statement to the police, he was peremptorily sent for by Mr. Podoloff and Mr. Zollner. Assuming, but not conceding, that there was no due notice and hearing, as provided by the contract and the constitution of the N.B.A., this court finds that elaboration on plaintiff's contentions is rendered unnecessary because of the conclusions reached by this court in the determination of this matter.

Certain amateur and professional sports, and the athletes participating in such sports, have recently occupied the spotlight of unfavorable public attention. The radio and television have been contributing causes for creating industries out of certain sports. America is sport-minded; we admire the accomplishment of our athletes; we are pleased with the success of our favorite teams and we spend a considerable part of our time rooting, but relaxing nevertheless, with our favorite sports. We inherit from the Greeks and Romans a love for stadia and sport competition.

When the breath of scandal hits one sport, it casts suspicion on all other sports. It does irreparable injury to the great majority of the players, destroys the confidence of the public in athletic competition, and lets down the morale of our youth. When the standards of fair play, good sportsmanship and honesty are abandoned, sporting events become the property of the gamblers and racketeers.

Much has happened in basketball to displease the public. Bribing, fixing and wagering, especially when associated with gamblers and racketeers, are matters of a serious nature. This court need not review the sordid details. It is necessary to recall them to realize the importance of the situations existing in this case.

Courts take cognizance of public interests and public problems; they reflect the spirit of the times and the sentiment and thoughts of the citizens. Laws are promulgated and contracts are made to protect the public and [keep] abreast with the demands, interest and protection of the people. The wagering by player members of the N.B.A. and the contract calling for expulsion is an aftermath of the abuses with which we are concerned. To maintain basketball competition in the N.B.A., to have open competitive sport, the public confidence and attendance, every effort had to be made to eliminate the slightest suspicion that competition was not on an honest, competitive basis.

The player that wagers on games does much to destroy the sport. Unfortunately, in wagering on a basketball game, it is not merely the bet that the team wins, but it is a wager on points, and the wager on the point spread in the manner which this plaintiff made such wagers is censurable. In the light of his knowledge of the basketball scandals, the express prohibitions in wagering and the manner of his betting, I am constrained to say plaintiff's conduct was reprehensible.

This plaintiff wagered, and admitted it, as I have hereinbefore set forth. If there was the slightest suggestion that the statement was involuntary or untrue, or a single suggestion offered to question it, if there was a triable issue, this court would have relegated the defendant to his contractual obligations and ordered a hearing. However, the testimony of the plaintiff before the court that the statement was free, voluntary and true eliminates any question as to the plaintiff's admissions.

The position of the plaintiff, in reality, seems to be one of asserting that he wagered on games, he breached his contract, he violated the constitution of the N.B.A. and was morally dishonest. Nevertheless, he now requests this court to order the defendant to cross all its t's and dot all its i's, and award damages for defendant's suspension without due notice and hearing.

To adjudge the suspension null and void, to bring about a hearing for this plaintiff, that must unquestionably and inevitably result in his expulsion or suspension, would be a mere futile gesture.

It is only by looking at the intent, rather than at the form, that equity is able to treat that as done which in good conscience ought to be done. Camp v. Boyd, 229 U.S. 530, 33 S.Ct. 785, 57 L.Ed. 1317.

There is no doubt that the matter now before this court has evoked a considerable amount of public interest and discussion. While the interest of the public at large in a given case, as an abstract proposition, can never be allowed to influence the court or become determinative, nevertheless, situations arise wherein the decision of the court is made against a background of public interest which is based on public morality. That morality is one which concerns the public desire of honest sport and clean sportsmanship. It necessarily follows, as the day follows the night, that one who has offended against this concept of good morals, and who admits such offense in open court, does not by that very fact satisfy the equitable maxim that he who comes into equity must come with clean hands.

This plaintiff seeks the aid of the chancellor to compel a hearing on charges admitted by him to be true. Such an attitude must constitute its own refutation and condemnation. To compel a hearing, and on that decision to seek damages in salary for the period of time elapsing between plaintiff's suspension and the said hearing, is an affront to the conscience of the chancellor. That equity will not decree such a ludicrous position or the performance of such a useless act is too well-established to require extended argument. See Gueutal v. Gueutal, 113 App.Div. 310, 98 N.Y.S. 1002; Morse v. Miller, Sup., 39 N.Y.S.2d 815, affirmed 267 App.Div. 801, 47 N.Y.S.2d 288, leave to appeal denied 293 N.Y. 936, 56 N.E.2d 311; 30 C.J.S., Equity, § 16.

The maxim of "clean hands" is also expressed in the form "He that hath committed iniquity shall not have equity" (2 Pomeroy Eq.Jur. 5th ed., sec. 397). It applies to unconscientious acts or inequitable conduct. Its application is confined to misconduct in regard to, or at all events connected with, the matter in litigation. Rice v. Rockefeller, 134 N.Y. 174, 186, 31 N.E. 907, 910, 17 L.R.A. 237. Here the admitted misconduct of the plaintiff is most certainly connected with the matter in litigation. An act which would be pronounced wrongful by honest and fair-minded men renders the hands of a moving party unclean.

In the application of this doctrine, whenever a party seeks to set the judicial machinery in motion to obtain some remedy, and has violated conscience or good faith, or other equitable principle in his prior conduct, then the doors of the court will be shut against him; the court will refuse to interfere on his behalf, to acknowledge his right or to award him any remedy (Pomeroy's 5th ed., sec. 397 cases cited).

Accordingly, the complaint is dismissed on the merits and judgment is directed in favor of the defendant.

Notes

1. Following his suspension, Molinas attended Brooklyn Law School, graduated, sued the NBA on the ground its decision violated federal anti-trust laws, lost, continued gambling, served five years of a 15-year jail sentence for fixing college basketball games, moved to Los Angeles following his parole, became involved in the pornographic film industry, collected $500,000 in insurance money after his business partner died under mysterious circumstances, and was killed by the mob just as he was about to go on trial for federal mail violations. *See further* Peter Ephross, *A Would-Be All-Star: Jack Molinas' Tragic Tale*, Forward, Nov. 29, 1996, at 14.

2. Thirty-five years after *Molinas*, MLB began to suspect Pete Rose, the manager and former star player of the Cincinnati Reds, was betting on baseball games. When an investigation turned up evidence of possible wrongdoing, Rose filed a lawsuit challenging Commissioner A. Bartlett Giamatti's authority to discipline him. *See Rose v. Giamatti*, 721 F.Supp. 906 (S.D.Ohio 1989). Eventually, however, Rose dropped his fight in exchange for

an indefinite suspension. As a result of the agreement, no formal findings were made as to whether Rose was guilty. To date, he remains banned from baseball despite numerous pleas for reinstatement. *See further Rose Mulls Lawsuit Against Baseball*, Dayton Daily News, Nov. 19, 1998, at 5C (reporting Rose is planning to sue baseball if his latest request is denied).

3. In addition to Molinas and Rose, other sports figures who have been reprimanded for betting on their own sport include Paul Hornung, Alex Karras, Art Schlichter, and Mike Ditka. *See further* Gary Swan, *Troubles Have Forced Many to Cut Ties*, S.F. Chron., Dec. 3, 1997, at B3.

Problem 60

Because a state law makes it illegal for jai-alai employees to wager at frontons, a player had his wife bet for him. Has he violated the statute? *See Camillo v. State*, 1992 WL 162196 (Conn.Super.Ct.1992).

3. CONSORTING

As a final guard against bribes, sports leagues prohibit their members from "consorting" with unsavory characters.

STEINBRENNER v. ESQUIRE REPORTING CO.

1991 WL 102540 (S.D.N.Y.1991).

SWEET, District Judge.

Defendants in this diversity action, Esquire Reporting Co., Inc. ("Esquire"), Malcolm L. Elvey ("Elvey") and Philip C. Rizzuti ("Rizzuti"), have moved to dismiss the complaint of plaintiff George M. Steinbrenner, III ("Steinbrenner"), or, in the alternative, for summary judgment. For the following reasons, the motion for summary judgment is granted, and the case is dismissed.

The Parties

Steinbrenner, a Florida resident, is a well-known public figure, the principal owner and former Managing General Partner of the New York Yankees Partnership, a limited partnership which owns and operates the New York Yankees Major League Baseball Team ("the Yankees").

Esquire is a Delaware corporation located in New York which provides stenographic services to the legal industry. Elvey, a New York resident, is the principal owner and president of Esquire, and Rizzuti, also a New York resident, is a shorthand or court reporter and licensed notary public who works for Esquire as a stenographer.

Prior Proceedings

This case arises out of an investigation ("the Investigation") undertaken by Francis T. Vincent, Jr., the Commissioner of Baseball ("the Commissioner"), into certain activities of Steinbrenner which were suspected of having been violative of the Major League Agreement ("MLA"), the contract which governs the operation of major league baseball.

As a result of the Investigation, the Commissioner issued a written decision on July 30, 1990 ("the Decision"), which severely curtailed Steinbrenner's activities with respect to the Yankees. Following the Decision, on October 4, 1990 Steinbrenner initiated this action, seeking damages in the amount of $530,000 from the parties responsible for transcribing certain interviews which occurred during the course of the Investigation.

The case was initially assigned to the Honorable John E. Sprizzo, but was transferred to this Court on January 3, 1991 following Judge Sprizzo's recusal.

The defendants filed their motion on October 24, 1990, and oral argument was heard on February 1, 1991.

The Facts

Except as otherwise noted, the following facts are not in dispute.

1. *The Commissioner's Powers.*

Major league baseball is regulated by the MLA, under which all professional baseball clubs, including the Yankees, and the National and American Leagues have delegated certain powers to the Commissioner. These powers include the power to investigate acts and practices that might be "not in the best interests of baseball," and to impose penalties against parties found to have engaged in such acts.

Steinbrenner claims that in exercising any of these powers, the Commissioner is bound by certain rules of procedure promulgated by prior commissioners, which require that all proceedings be conducted "like judicial proceedings and with due regard for all the principals of natural justice and fair play." If the Commissioner directs depositions to be taken, the rules provide that such depositions "will proceed substantially as if the testimony had been taken on an open commission in a judicial proceeding." The defendants dispute the applicability of the rules, claiming that these rules are intended to govern only adversarial proceedings arising out of claims brought before the Commissioner by other parties, rather than unilateral investigations instituted by the Commissioner on his own initiative. In any event, while this may be a factual dispute between the parties, it is simply not material to Steinbrenner's claims against these defendants, who are not parties to the MLA. At most, this issue would be relevant to a claim by Steinbrenner that the Commissioner misused his power by employing the defendants in a manner which violated the rules.

2. *The Investigation.*

In March, 1990, the Commissioner began the Investigation to determine whether certain of Steinbrenner's activities concerning his relationship with a gambler named Howard Spira ("Spira") had been "not in the best interests of baseball." The Commissioner appointed John Dowd ("Dowd") to conduct a preliminary investigation and prepare a report, which the Commissioner would use to decide whether further proceedings were appropriate.

a. The interviews.

The major part of Dowd's Investigation consisted of a series of interviews of Steinbrenner and other Yankee personnel to learn the facts surrounding Steinbrenner's association with Spira. All of these interviews, which took place throughout the month of May 1990, were transcribed by Rizzuti, the Esquire stenographer. Each interview began with Rizzuti swearing the witness in, and the transcripts which Rizzuti produced were each entitled "Sworn Testimony of" the interviewee. In addition, each transcript concluded with a standard certification signed by Rizzuti that the interviewee "was previously sworn and that [this] deposition is a true record of the testimony given by such witness."

Prior to taking any interviews, Dowd established certain procedures to be followed. The interviewees were allowed to have their own counsel present, but Dowd was the only person who would be allowed to examine the interviewee. Copies of the interview transcripts created by Rizzuti were to be provided only to Dowd, for his use in preparing his report to the Commissioner. All of the participants agreed to abide by these procedures.

b. The production of the transcripts.

Rizzuti described the procedure by which the interview transcripts were produced as follows:

> 1) During the interviews, Rizzuti would record keystrokes mechanically on paper and electronically on magnetic tape.
>
> 2) The magnetic tape would be fed into a computer, which would translate the keystrokes into "raw" text, words with no sentence or paragraph structure and no punctuation.
>
> 3) A computer operator would edit the raw text, inserting appropriate punctuation and line breaks and correcting obvious errors, such as the mistranscription of similar sounding words (e.g., "new" for "knew") or typographical errors, and translating Rizzuti's coded keystrokes, such as those used for personal names or other non-standard terms.
>
> 4) The operator would produce a draft transcript for Rizzuti, who would review it and make further corrections based upon handwritten notes recorded on the paper tape and upon his independent recollection of the interview. These corrections would include such things as deleting colloquy which was transcribed but subsequently designated "off the record" by the parties and correcting transcription errors which were detectable only from the context, such as recording the code for one person's name where the conversation had clearly concerned a different person.

At this stage, the transcripts were given to Dowd. Rizzuti stated that after he had turned over the first transcript he received a telephone call from Dowd saying that he had a number of corrections to make to the transcript. As Dowd described the changes to Rizzuti, Rizzuti reported that he understood that they were all "of a stylistic, grammatical nature." While he conceded that he normally would have expected such changes to have been made by means of an "errata sheet" circulated to all of the parties, and especially to the witness, he testified that under the procedures established by Dowd, under which no one else had even received copies of the transcripts, he felt that there was nothing wrong with processing Dowd's changes based solely on Dowd's request. Rizzuti therefore arranged for Dowd to communicate his requests to an Esquire computer operator, who would process the changes. Rizzuti testified that he believed that all of the changes proposed by Dowd did not affect the substance of the transcripts.

Rizzuti also stated that Dowd had never requested that Esquire certify the transcripts as accurate, but that the certification pages were prepared as a matter of routine, despite the fact that the interviewees were not to be given an opportunity to review the transcripts for accuracy.

c. *The Commissioner's hearing.*

On June 4, 1990, after receiving and reviewing Dowd's report, the Commissioner decided to hold his own hearings to investigate further Steinbrenner's relation with Spira. To allow Steinbrenner to prepare for the hearing, the Commissioner provided copies of all of the interview transcripts. In his letter informing Steinbrenner of the decision to hold the hearing, the Commissioner stated

> The sole judgment I have made to date is that, based on the information gathered by [Dowd,] there is a sufficient basis to require a hearing to permit you an opportunity to respond.

The hearing was scheduled for July 5 and 6. At the beginning of the hearing, the Commissioner explained to Steinbrenner that he should not feel bound by any of his prior statements to Dowd, and that if he wished to change any aspect of his story he was free to do so. Steinbrenner was also permitted to submit statements of other witnesses and any other materials which he considered relevant to the matter. During the hearing, the Commissioner introduced as exhibits all of the interview transcripts prepared by Rizzuti.

d. *Steinbrenner's discovery of the changes in the transcripts.*

After the Commissioner's hearing, Steinbrenner's counsel noticed that the interview transcripts which had been provided by the Commissioner seemed not to be entirely accurate records of what had been said at the interviews. On July 19, Steinbrenner inquired of Rizzuti whether any changes had been made in the transcripts. Rizzuti responded by describing how Dowd's changes had been received and processed. Rizzuti testified that at the time of Steinbrenner's initial inquiry, Esquire had in its possession drafts of the interview transcripts which had been marked to indicate Dowd's changes. However, because Rizzuti believed that under Dowd's procedures Esquire was not to supply any material directly to anyone but Dowd, Rizzuti and Esquire gave the marked-up transcripts to Dowd and suggested that Steinbrenner contact Dowd to obtain further information. Rizzuti still had his paper records of the interviews, but by that time the magnetic tapes had been erased.

On the following day, Steinbrenner's counsel notified the counsel for the Commissioner that they had evidence that the transcripts had been altered by Dowd. In response, the Commissioner directed Esquire to cooperate with Steinbrenner to determine what changes had been made. Rizzuti thereupon made his paper notes available to Steinbrenner, who retained an independent stenographic reporting service to transcribe these notes and compare the output to the transcripts produced by Esquire. At no time did Steinbrenner's counsel request the marked-up draft transcripts from Dowd. According to Steinbrenner's counsel, the retranscription and review process began on July 25 and was completed by the evening of July 27. At oral argument, Steinbrenner asserted that at least some of the alterations were not discovered until after the Commissioner's Decision on July 30. Nevertheless, on July 29 Steinbrenner's counsel asserted that the review was completed on July 27.

On July 29, Steinbrenner's counsel sent a letter to the Commissioner's counsel stating that the transcripts were unquestionably not "true and accurate" as certified by Rizzuti, and identifying several examples of discrepancies between Rizzuti's notes of the Steinbrenner interview and the final transcripts which had been produced to the Commissioner. The letter offered no examples of changes from any of the other interviews, but concluded with the assertion that "the evidence that comprises the hearing record is pervasively false" and the demand that the Investigation should be terminated.

e. The Commissioner's decision.

On the morning of July 30, the Commissioner informed Steinbrenner that he was denying the request to terminate the Investigation and advised Steinbrenner of his preliminary decision that, based upon the evidence adduced at the Commissioner's hearing of July 5 and 6 and his review of the record, Steinbrenner would receive a two-year suspension from baseball followed by a three-year period of probation. Steinbrenner and the Commissioner negotiated all day long on the 30th, with the Commissioner ultimately modifying his decision, at Steinbrenner's request, to impose a permanent restriction on Steinbrenner's activity as Managing General Partner of the Yankees, but to avoid the suspension as initially proposed by the Commissioner. Reportedly, Steinbrenner sought to avoid the term "suspension" because he felt that it would adversely affect his membership on the United States Olympic Committee, and therefore consented to a longer term of punishment in exchange for not being suspended. The defendants assert, and Steinbrenner does not dispute, that he did not raise the issue of the alterations in the transcripts at any time during these negotiations.

On the evening of July 30, the Commissioner issued the Decision, and both he and Steinbrenner signed an agreement and resolution ("the Agreement") and an order implementing the Decision ("the Order"). In the eleven-page Decision, the Commissioner set forth the foundation for his conclusion that Steinbrenner's conduct had been "not in the best interest of baseball" and specifically stated

> Mr. Steinbrenner's team of lawyers have also raised assorted objections to the procedures employed and to the purported biases of Mr. Dowd and myself. I have directly and indirectly through my counsel responded to and rejected this posturing. I will not belabor the point other than to state that Mr. Steinbrenner has been afforded a full and fair opportunity to present to me orally and in writing his views and testimony, all of which I have considered with an open mind. In my view, Mr. Steinbrenner's dilemma is not with the procedures I have utilized, but with his inability to rewrite history.

Decision at 8. The Agreement provided that

> Mr. Steinbrenner, recognizing the sole and exclusive authority of the Commissioner and recognizing the benefits to Baseball from a resolution of this matter without further proceedings, agrees to accept the following sanctions imposed by the Commissioner:
>
> 1. Mr. Steinbrenner recognizes, agrees and submits to the sole and exclusive jurisdiction of the Commissioner pursuant to the Major League Agreement * * *
>
> 2. Mr. Steinbrenner acknowledges and accepts the findings of the Decision to which this Agreement is attached and, specifically, that his conduct as described in the Decision was not in the best interests of Baseball. Mr. Steinbrenner further accepts the sanctions imposed on him by the Commissioner and agrees not to challenge the sanctions in court or otherwise. He also agrees he will not institute any legal proceedings of any nature against the Commissioner or any of his representatives, either Major League Baseball or any Major League Club relating to this matter.

Agreement at 2.

Discussion

1. *The Standard for Summary Judgment.*

The standard for summary judgment is familiar. The court is not "to weigh the evidence and determine the truth of the matter but to determine whether there is a genuine issue for trial." Anderson v. Liberty Lobby, Inc., 477 U.S. 242, 249 (1986). In determining whether a genuine issue of fact exists, the court must draw all permissible inferences in favor of the nonmoving party. Branum v. Clark, 927 F.2d 698 (2d Cir.1991).

2. Summary Judgment Based on the Release Contained in the Agreement is Not Warranted.

The defendants argue that summary judgment is appropriate because Steinbrenner's action is contractually barred by the provision of the Agreement with the Commissioner, quoted above, in which Steinbrenner agreed not to "institute any legal proceedings of any nature against the Commissioner or any of his representatives." The defendants claim that they acted as representatives of the Commissioner because they were retained by Dowd to assist him in his preliminary investigation and to transcribe the interviews solely for his benefit. Steinbrenner disputes this contention, asserting that a stenographer is statutorily required by New York C.P.L.R. § 3113(a) to be an independent participant in a deposition. Additionally, Steinbrenner claims that even if the defendants were acting as the Commissioner's representatives, he never intended that the release provision of the agreement would extend to them.

Steinbrenner's reliance on the CPLR is misplaced. Section 101 of the CPLR states that the statute "shall govern the procedure in civil judicial proceedings in all courts of the state and before all judges, except where the procedure is regulated by inconsistent statute." Steinbrenner does not and cannot contend that Dowd's interviews were related to any judicial proceedings in any court, thus the CPLR, including § 3113, do not apply.

The evidence adduced thus far clearly indicates that the proceedings before Dowd were not depositions in the normal sense of the word. Dowd was not only the interrogator, he was also the person in charge of directing the Investigation and the appointed representative of the ultimate decisionmaker, the Commissioner. Dowd established the procedures to be followed, including the rule that only he was to receive copies of the transcripts, procedures which were agreed to by all of the participants. Despite the presence of other counsel, Dowd was the only person to question the interviewees. While a certain amount of colloquy took place between Dowd and the other lawyers, these exchanges were primarily directed at clarifying the information elicited by Dowd, rather than attempting to cut off or obstruct the interrogation. While the record discloses occasional examples of heated or argumentative exchanges, there are also several instances in which the parties professed their mutual interest in cooperating to ensure that all of the information was accurately disclosed to Dowd and the Commissioner.

In light of these obvious differences between the interviews and formal depositions, Rizzuti was justified in regarding Dowd more as having a quasi-judicial role or as an administrative hearing officer than as a mere participant in an ordinary deposition. Therefore, it would not have been unreasonable for Rizzuti to have considered himself and Esquire as representatives of the Commissioner, in much the same way as a courtroom reporter is generally viewed as a representative of the court.

However, Rizzuti's belief, reasonable or not, cannot determine the scope of the release. As the Agreement is a contract between Steinbrenner and the Commissioner, its interpretation naturally depends not on the understanding of potential third party beneficiaries, but rather on the intent of the parties themselves. On this issue, Steinbrenner's affidavit testimony that he did not consider the reporters to have been representatives of the Commissioner is sufficient to create a genuine factual dispute which precludes summary judgment based on the release contained in the Agreement.

3. *Steinbrenner Has Not Established That the Defendants' Behavior Was Improper.*

Summary judgment for the defendants is nevertheless appropriate because Steinbrenner has not carried his burden of establishing a triable factual dispute concerning whether the defendants' actions in connection with the production of the interview transcripts for Dowd were improper.

a. The actual changes to the transcripts were not material.

To the extent that Steinbrenner's claims depend on the falsity of the transcripts, he has failed to present evidence indicating that any of the changes materially altered the substance or tone of the transcripts or that the alterations might reasonably be considered to have affected the Commissioner's Decision.

In the first place, Steinbrenner appears to have misperceived his burden on this motion, asserting that the defendants "have totally failed to make any demonstration that no genuine issue of material fact exists" as to the significance of the transcript alterations. As discussed earlier, a party opposing summary judgment is required to adduce evidence to establish a triable dispute with regard to some material factual issue, particularly as to those issues upon which that party would bear the burden of proof at trial. Steinbrenner cannot prevail based upon a mere assertion that the changes were material; he must identify those particular changes which could reasonably support such a claim.

Rizzuti has testified by affidavit that a number of the changes reported by Steinbrenner were changes made by Esquire personnel, either Rizzuti himself or the computer operator performing the initial transcription, to correct what Rizzuti felt were his own transcribing errors, i.e., places where the transcript did not accurately render what had occurred in the interview. These corrections included both those which were obvious on the face of the transcript, such as clear typographical errors, and those which Rizzuti identified based on his recollection of the proceedings, including those instances in which he had simply keyed in the wrong strokes, and those places where Rizzuti had transcribed material which was later designated as "off the record." The defendants have reviewed Steinbrenner's list of all of the changes identified by his stenographers and, by comparison with the marked-up transcripts which were supplied to Dowd to indicate his changes, have identified those changes made by Esquire and those made by Dowd. However, it is unnecessary to distinguish the source of the changes in order to conclude that Steinbrenner has failed to show that they were material.

The changes identified here range from simple typographical corrections, e.g., the correction of the word "myselfing" to "missing," Steinbrenner Transcript at 449 line 11, to the wholesale deletion and modification of remarks by both Dowd and the interviewees. At most, Dowd's changes appear to have been motivated by a desire to clean up the less-refined language in the interviews and to clarify some of the more confusing and repetitive exchanges. Thus he consistently changed "got," as in "you got to be very careful," to "have," e.g., Steinbrenner Transcript at 87 line 21, corrected "ain't" to "isn't," Kleinman Transcript at 207 lines 2–3, and deleted at least one instance of profanity. He also removed some of the more argumentative colloquy, but left in more than enough such material to indicate that the interviews were conducted in a tense and often contentious atmosphere. Other deletions removed remarks which were not relevant to the scope of the interviews, such as a remark by Dowd relating to the Commissioner's prior involvement in an investigation of Pete Rose, Steinbrenner Tr. at 593. Rizzuti testified that at least some of the simple deletions were based on his handwritten notes as to material which was to be left off the record by agreement of all of the participants.

The only change cited by Steinbrenner which could even arguably be described as substantive was found in the transcript of Dowd's interview of [Philip McNiff, one of Steinbrenner's principal aides]. While trying to determine whether Steinbrenner had promised Spira any type of future consideration in exchange for information, Dowd had a short discussion with a Kevin Hallinan ("Hallinan"), a former New York City policeman who serves as the director of security for Major League Baseball. According to the transcript provided to the Commissioner, Dowd asked Hallinan whether a certain type of statement might be considered a "promise." Rizzuti testified that his own review of his notes indicated that the word used by Dowd was actually "commitment." Both Esquire's computer operator and Steinbrenner's reporters interpreted Rizzuti's keystrokes as indicating that the word was "document." Rizzuti testified that upon review of the draft transcript, he corrected the word to "promise," based on his recollection of the course of the conversation. McNiff testified by affidavit that Dowd had never used the term "promise" in that particular context, although he did not go so far as to state that the correct word was "document." While all of this might barely be enough to create a factual dispute as to which word Dowd really used, there is nothing which even remotely suggests that this casual discussion between Dowd and another of the Commissioner's own representatives, during an interview filled with direct questions to McNiff concerning

Steinbrenner's alleged arrangement with Spira, could reasonably be deemed to have affected the Commissioner's Decision.

In addition, the Commissioner was placed on notice as early as July 20 that the transcripts had been modified, and on July 29 Steinbrenner's counsel reported that the process of identifying all of the changes was complete. Given the day-long negotiations on July 30, Steinbrenner had adequate opportunity to bring any significant changes in the transcripts to the Commissioner's attention prior to the issuance of the Decision. This fact alone would compel the conclusion that none of the changes could have influenced the Commissioner to rule against Steinbrenner.

b. There is no evidence that Rizzuti's certifications of the transcripts was improper.

Not only has Steinbrenner failed to show that the alterations to the transcripts were material, he has not presented evidence sufficient to create a triable dispute on the issue of whether Rizzuti's certification of the transcripts was proper. His evidence on this issue consists of the affidavit of Raymond DeSimone ("DeSimone"), a notary public and court reporter, who asserts that Rizzuti's certification of the transcript after Dowd's changes had been made was a violation of the customs and practices of the shorthand reporting industry. However, a careful reading of DeSimone's testimony reveals that it is not sufficient to create a genuine issue of fact regarding Rizzuti's behavior.

In the first place, DeSimone does not state that it is always improper for a reporter to certify a transcript as accurate after changes have been made, even changes which might render it materially inaccurate as a record of the proceedings, but only states that the reporter should obtain the consent of all of the parties before doing so. Accepting this assertion as true, it is necessary to determine how such consent should have been obtained in the case of the interview transcripts. Unfortunately, DeSimone's testimony is limited to the case of adversarial proceedings, in which all parties, including the primary witness, have access to the transcript and are thus competent to agree with or dispute the proposed changes. DeSimone makes no allowance for the unique procedural rules imposed by Dowd and does not even offer any suggestion as to how his rule of "no ex parte changes" should be applied where there is only one recognized party, particularly where that party is both the examiner and an agent of the ultimate decisionmaker. As Steinbrenner does not dispute that he agreed to Dowd's procedures, his failure to present evidence that under those procedures Rizzuti's behavior was improper is fatal to any claim that the certification of the modified transcripts constituted any type of misconduct.

4. Steinbrenner Has Not Established That His Damages Were Proximately Caused by the Defendants' Acts.

Even if Steinbrenner had demonstrated the existence of a factual dispute as to whether the defendants acted improperly, summary judgment would be appropriate because he has not shown that his damages were proximately caused by the defendants' conduct.

The damages which Steinbrenner seeks to recover are the expenses and legal fees which he incurred in transcribing Rizzuti's original notes of the interviews and comparing those transcripts to the transcripts provided to the Commissioner. When Steinbrenner first raised the issue of the changes in the transcripts, the defendants, in keeping with the rule that all material be provided only to Dowd, turned over to Dowd the marked-up drafts of the transcripts indicating exactly which changes Dowd had made. Steinbrenner was encouraged to obtain these drafts from Dowd in order to find out what the changes were, but he chose instead to follow the more laborious and costly route of retranscribing the original notes and comparing that output by hand with the transcripts which had been provided to the Commissioner.

Steinbrenner asserts that his refusal to follow the simpler course of obtaining the marked-up drafts from Dowd was reasonable in light of the fact that Dowd was the original source of the "tampering," and therefore could not be trusted to provide evidence of his own wrongdoing. However, particularly in light of the preceding finding that none of the alterations was material, Steinbrenner has presented no evidence to support this assertion or to justify his suspicion of Dowd. No proof has been adduced to indicate either that Dowd would not have provided the mark-ups or that they did not in fact identify all of Dowd's changes. While it may be in some respects understandable that Steinbrenner was reluctant to trust Dowd, that reluctance was based on his underlying belief that the Investigation was biased against him, and that belief has not been borne out by the evidence. Particularly with respect to the defendants here, Steinbrenner has simply not created a triable issue as to whether their actions were the proximate cause of his alleged damages.

This conclusion requires the dismissal of each of Steinbrenner's causes of action. Admittedly, there is some authority in New York for the proposition that a plaintiff's failure to establish a proximate relationship between the defendant's acts and the plaintiff's damages is not a grounds for dismissing the plaintiff's claim but only for limiting the amount of recovery. See, e.g., Clearview Concrete Prods. Corp. v. Charles Gherardi, Inc., 88 A.D.2d 461, 453 N.Y.S.2d 750 (2d Dep't 1982) (plaintiff might be entitled to nominal damages for breach of warranty even though actual damages were result of intervening cause and not proximately related to defendant's acts). However, this proposition is inapplicable in the present case because actual damage is a primary element of each of Steinbrenner's claims.

a. Notarial misconduct.

Steinbrenner's first cause of action, for notarial misconduct, is based upon N.Y.Exec.L. § 135:

> For any misconduct by a notary public in the performance of any of his powers such notary public shall be liable to the parties injured for all damages sustained by them.

In order to prevail on such a claim, a plaintiff must show that the notary's conduct resulted in an injury, as the statute clearly imposes liability only for such damages. Where the damages are not causally related to the notary's improper performance of a notarial act, the plaintiff's claim must fail. Cf. Bogensky v. Rosenberg, 202 Misc. 652, 652 (N.Y.Sup.Ct. Suffolk Co. 1952) (notarial misconduct must be predicated on misconduct in acting as notary, rather than harmful behavior by person who happens to be notary).

b. Injurious falsehood.

Similarly, an essential element of the tort of injurious falsehood, upon which Steinbrenner's second cause of action is premised, is that the alleged false statement caused actual injury to the plaintiff. See, e.g., Penn–Ohio Steel Corp. v. Allis–Chalmers Mfg. Co., 7 A.D.2d 441, 444, 184 N.Y.S.2d 58, 61 (1st Dep't 1959) ("If [the false statement] inflicts material harm upon another ... and it results in actual damage to the plaintiff's economic or legal relationships, an action may lie"); Waste Distillation Technology, Inc. v. Blasland & Bouck Engineers, P.C., 136 A.D.2d 633, 634 (2d Dep't 1988); Restatement (Second) of Torts § 623A (1977).

c. Breach of fiduciary duty.

Steinbrenner's third cause of action is based on the defendants' alleged breach of their fiduciary duty toward Steinbrenner. Because the very nature of a fiduciary duty is the requirement the fiduciary act in good faith and candor to avoid harm to the party who is owed the duty, actual damage is a necessary component of this claim as well. See, e.g., Restatement (Second) of Torts § 874 (1977) (fiduciary liable "for harm resulting from" breach).

CONCLUSION

For all of the foregoing reasons, Steinbrenner has not established a genuine dispute concerning the propriety of the defendants' behavior, nor has he shown a triable issue as to whether his damages were proximately caused by the defendants. Therefore, the defendants' motion for summary judgment dismissing the complaint is granted.

Notes

1. The restrictions placed on Steinbrenner were lifted immediately before the start of the 1993 season. Subsequently, he was elected to MLB's Executive Council. One year later, however, he lost this post when he sued baseball over the terms of a marketing deal between the Yankees and Adidas. For a further look at Steinbrenner's often-contentious career, see Hal Bodley, *'Boss' Has Firm Grip on Helm*, USA Today, Mar. 17, 1998, at 1C.

2. The list of sports figures who have been disciplined for consorting with gamblers is very long, and includes, among others, Joe Namath (New York Jets), Leo Durocher (Brooklyn Dodgers), Denny McClain (Detroit Tigers), Willie Mays (New York Mets), Mickey Mantle (New York Yankees), Lenny Dykstra (Philadelphia Phillies), Albert Belle (Cleveland Indians), Billy

Taylor (New York Rangers), and Don Gallinger (Boston Bruins). In addition, some people believe that Michael Jordan's 18–month absence from basketball following the 1992–93 season was in reality a "secret" suspension imposed by the NBA because of his much-publicized association with gamblers. *See further* Armen Keteyian et al., *Money Players: Days and Nights in the New NBA* (1997).

Problem 61

Following a full and fair hearing, the state horse racing commission suspended a jockey for consorting with gamblers. If he appeals on the ground the penalty is excessive, how should the court rule? *See Striker v. Commonwealth*, 383 A.2d 967 (Pa.Cmwlth.Ct.1978).

D. LOTTERIES

Because of the enormous popularity of professional sports leagues, governments occasionally have sought to use their games as the basis of new lottery offerings. As will be seen, such efforts have provoked strong protests.

NATIONAL FOOTBALL LEAGUE v. GOVERNOR OF DELAWARE

435 F.Supp. 1372 (D.Del.1977).

STAPLETON, District Judge.

In August 1976, the Office of the Delaware State Lottery announced a plan to institute a lottery game based on games of the National Football League ("NFL"). Immediately thereafter, the NFL and its twenty-eight member clubs filed suit in this Court against the Governor and the Director of the State Lottery seeking preliminary and permanent injunctive relief barring such a lottery scheme. The State of Delaware intervened, and the complaint was amended to add a request that the Court create a constructive trust on behalf of the NFL clubs of all revenues derived from such a lottery. Finding no threat of immediate irreparable injury to the NFL, the Court denied the prayer for a temporary restraining order.

During the week of September 12, 1976, the football lottery games commenced. Upon defendants' motion, the Court dismissed plaintiffs' claims that the games violated the Equal Protection Clause of the Fourteenth Amendment and the Commerce Clause of the Constitution. With respect to twelve other counts, defendants' motion to dismiss or for summary judgment was denied. The lottery games continued through the season.

In late Fall, a six day trial on the merits was held. That was followed by extended briefing. The matter is now ripe for disposition. This Opinion constitutes the Court's findings of fact and conclusions of law on the questions presented.

Factual Background

The Delaware football lottery is known as "Scoreboard" and it involves three different games, "Football Bonus", "Touchdown" and "Touchdown II". All are weekly games based on regularly scheduled NFL games. In Football Bonus, the fourteen games scheduled for a given weekend are divided into two pools of seven games each. A player must mark the lottery ticket with his or her projections of the winners of the seven games in one or both of the two pools and place a bet of $1, $2, $3, $5 or $10. To win Football Bonus, the player must correctly select the winner of each of the games in a pool. If the player correctly selects the winners of all games in both pools, he or she wins an "All Game Bonus". The amounts of the prizes awarded are determined on a pari-mutuel basis, that is, as a function of the total amount of money bet by all players.

In Touchdown, the lottery card lists the fourteen games for a given week along with three ranges of possible point spreads. The player must select both the winning team and the winning margin in each of three, four or five games. The scale of possible bets is the same as in Bonus and prizes are likewise distributed on a pari-mutuel basis to those who make correct selections for each game on which they bet.

Touchdown II, the third Scoreboard game, was introduced in mid-season and replaced Touchdown for the remainder of the season. In Touchdown II, a "line" or predicted point spread on each of twelve games is published on the Wednesday prior to the games. The player considers the published point spread and selects a team to "beat the line", that is, to do better in the game than the stated point spread. To win, the player must choose correctly with respect to each of from four to twelve games. Depending upon the number of games bet on, there is a fixed payoff of from $10 to $1,200. There is also a consolation prize for those who beat the line on nine out of ten, ten out of eleven or eleven out of twelve games.

Scoreboard tickets are available from duly authorized agents of the Delaware State Lottery, usually merchants located throughout the State. The tickets list the teams by city names, e.g., Tampa or Cincinnati, rather than by nicknames such as Buccaneers or Bengals. Revenues are said to be distributed pursuant to a fixed apportionment schedule among the players of Scoreboard, the State, the sales agents and the Lottery Office for its administrative expenses.

The Parties' Claims

The core of plaintiffs' objections to Scoreboard is what they term a "forced association with gambling". They complain that the football lottery constitutes an unlawful interference with their property rights and they oppose its operation on a host of federal, state and common law grounds. Briefly stated, their complaint includes counts based on federal and state trademark laws, the common law doctrine of misappropriation, the federal anti-gambling laws, the Civil Rights Act of 1871 (42 U.S.C. § 1983), the Delaware Constitution and the Delaware lottery statute.

The defendants deny that the state-run revenue raising scheme violates any federal, state or common law doctrine. Further, they have filed a counterclaim for treble damages under the Sherman and Clayton Acts for federal antitrust law violations charging, inter alia, that the plaintiffs have brought this litigation for purposes of harassment and that they have conspired to monopolize property which is in the public domain.

For the reasons which follow, I have determined that the plaintiffs are entitled to limited injunctive relief, in the nature of a disclaimer on all Scoreboard materials disseminated to the public. The Touchdown II game will also be invalidated. In all other respects, their claims for relief are denied. The defendants' claim for treble damages is likewise denied.

I. Misappropriation

Plaintiffs have proven that they have invested time, effort, talent and vast sums of money in the organization, development and promotion of the National Football League. They have also convincingly demonstrated the success of that investment. The NFL is now a national institution which enjoys great popularity and a reputation for integrity. It generates substantial revenue from gate receipts, broadcasting rights, film rights, and the licensing of its trademarks.

There also can be no dispute that the NFL popularity and reputation played a major role in defendants' choice of NFL games as the subject matter of its lottery. Defendants concede that in making this election they expected to generate revenue which would not be generated from betting on a less popular pastime.

Based on these facts, plaintiffs assert that defendants are misappropriating the product of plaintiffs' efforts or in the words of the Supreme Court, that the State of Delaware is "endeavoring to reap where it has not sown". International News Service v. Associated Press, 248 U.S. 215, 239, 39 S.Ct. 68, 72, 63 L.Ed. 211 (1918) ("INS"). Thus, plaintiffs maintain the lottery must be halted and the ill-gotten gains disgorged.

This Court has no doubt about the continuing vitality of the INS case and the doctrine of misappropriation which it spawned. I conclude, however, that plaintiffs' argument paints with too broad a brush.

The only tangible product[s] of plaintiffs' labor which defendants utilize in the Delaware Lottery are the schedule of NFL games and the scores. These are obtained from public sources and are utilized only after plaintiffs have disseminated them at large and no longer have any expectation of generating revenue from further dissemination. This fact distinguishes the situation in INS.

Plaintiffs insist, however, that defendants are using more than the schedules and scores to generate revenue for the State. They define their "product" as being the total "end result" of their labors, including the public interest which has been generated.

It is undoubtedly true that defendants seek to profit from the popularity of NFL football. The question, however, is whether this constitutes wrongful misappropriation. I think not.

We live in an age of economic and social interdependence. The NFL undoubtedly would not be in the position it is today if college football and the fan interest that it generated had not preceded the NFL's organization. To that degree it has benefited from the labor of others. The same, of course, can be said for the mass media networks which the labor of others have developed.

What the Delaware Lottery has done is to offer a service to that portion of plaintiffs' following who wish to bet on NFL games. It is true that Delaware is thus making profits it would not make but for the existence of the NFL, but I find this difficult to distinguish from the multitude of charter bus companies who generate profit from servicing those of plaintiffs' fans who want to go to the stadium or, indeed, the sidewalk popcorn salesman who services the crowd as it surges towards the gate.

While courts have recognized that one has a right to one's own harvest, this proposition has not been construed to preclude others from profiting from demands for collateral services generated by the success of one's business venture. General Motors' cars, for example, enjoy significant popularity and seat cover manufacturers profit from that popularity by making covers to fit General Motors' seats. The same relationship exists between hot dog producers and the bakers of hot dog rolls. But in neither instance, I believe, could it be successfully contended that an actionable misappropriation occurs.

The NFL plaintiffs, however, argue that this case is different because the evidence is said to show "misappropriation" of plaintiffs' "good will" and "reputation" as well as its "popularity". To a large extent, plaintiffs' references to "good will" and "reputation" are simply other ways of stating their complaint that defendants are profiting from a demand plaintiffs' games have generated. To the extent they relate to a claim that defendants' activities have damaged, as opposed to appropriated, plaintiff's good will and reputation, I believe one must look to other lines of authority to determine defendants' culpability. In response to plaintiffs' misappropriation argument, I hold only that defendants' use of the NFL schedules, scores and public popularity in the Delaware Lottery does not constitute a misappropriation of plaintiffs' property.

In the event a differing analysis is determined to be appropriate in the course of appellate review, I should add that the plaintiffs have not demonstrated that the existence of gambling on its games, per se, has or will damage its good will or reputation for integrity. By this, I do not suggest that an association of the NFL with a gambling enterprise in the minds of the public would not have a deleterious effect on its business. Such an association presupposes public perception of NFL sponsorship or approval of a gambling enterprise or at least confusion on this score, and I treat this subject hereafter. I do find, however, that the existence of gambling on NFL games, unaccompanied by any confusion with respect to sponsorship, has not injured the NFL and there is no reason to believe it will do so in the future. The record shows that extensive gambling on NFL games has existed for many years and that this fact of common public knowledge has not injured plaintiffs or their reputation.

The most prevalent form of such gambling is the illegal form—office pools and head-to-head bets with bookies. Virtually every witness testified that he was familiar with illegal football pools and knew they were available in schools, factories and offices around the country. John J. Danahy, Director of Security for the NFL and a former member of the Federal Bureau of Investigation, estimated that millions of dollars a week are spent for illegal betting on football games and that such gambling provides a major source of income to organized crime.

In addition to the illegal gambling, the evidence shows that there is a substantial volume of legalized sports betting. In Nevada, sports betting, including betting on NFL games, has been legal since 1949. The parties have stipulated that sports betting in Nevada in the fourth quarter of the year, when the betting is primarily on football games, has reached the following levels:

1972	$ 873,318
1973	$ 826,767
1974	$ 3,873,217
1975	$26,170,328

These figures represent both "by event" or "head-to-head" betting and parlay card betting. In addition, pool card gambling on professional football has been legal in Montana since 1974. The NFL has not shown that any of this gambling, legal or illegal, has injured the reputation of professional football or the member teams of the NFL.

Some comment on the plaintiffs' survey evidence on this subject is in order. A market survey was conducted at the direction of the plaintiffs for use in this litigation. One of the questions asked of those surveyed was:

> Suppose there would be legalized betting on National Football League games which was run by a state agency in each of the various states. Do you think that the reputation of the National Football League would be better, stay the same or be worse than before legalized betting?

Those who responded that they thought the NFL's reputation would decline were asked in a follow-up question to explain why they thought so. Fifty percent of those responding in the "National" portion of the survey said that they believed the NFL's reputation would be hurt. Those who conducted the survey broke down the reasons given for that belief into four separate categories:

26%	Will mean more crime
29%	Opposed to betting
19%	Throwing or fixing game
30%	Takes sportsmanship out of the game

While these results do suggest that gambling on NFL games would adversely affect the NFL, there are several reasons why I cannot credit the data. Most importantly, there is the overwhelming evidence already reviewed that, in actual experience, widespread gambling, both illegal and state-authorized, has not hurt the NFL. That evidence is far more persuasive than survey results based on hypothetical questions.

The survey itself bears out the conclusion that those with actual experience with state-run sports betting have far different views than those who are dealing with the question in the abstract. When Delawareans were asked whether the State's football lottery would injure the reputation of the NFL only 22% answered affirmatively.

In addition, there are a number of problems with the form of question used in the survey. It asks the person responding, not whether he or she would think less of the NFL, but rather whether he or she thinks others would have less regard for the NFL. The response is by nature speculation and it is quite conceivable that many who would have no objection to state-run sports betting would assume that others would hold a different view. The question as asked did not elicit relevant information.

Moreover, the question assumed that every state would institute such a program. While it has been suggested that a few other states are considering football lotteries, I have no reason to believe that the Delaware scheme will be imitated by forty-nine other states. In any event, the issue before this Court is whether Delaware's Scoreboard games will injure the NFL's reputation. The question asked in the "national" survey addressed a far broader subject which the plaintiffs have not shown to be relevant.

Finally, the phrasing of the question did not emphasize a proposed system run independently of the NFL. As will be seen, that may have influenced some responses.

II. Trademark and Related Unfair Competition Claims

The Delaware Lottery does not utilize the NFL name or any of plaintiffs' registered service marks for the purpose of identifying, as opposed to describing, the service which it offers. The name utilized for the football related betting games is "Scoreboard" and the individual games are identified as "Football Bonus", "Touchdown" and "Touchdown II". No NFL insignia or the like [is] utilized in the advertising. The cards on which the customers of the Delaware Lottery mark their betting choices, however, identify the next week's NFL football games by the names of the cities whose NFL teams are scheduled to compete against each other, e.g., Philadelphia v. Los Angeles, Washington v. Baltimore, etc. It is stipulated that, in the context in which they appear, these geographic names are intended to refer to, and are understood to refer to, plaintiffs' football teams. It is in this manner that defendants have made it known that the Delaware Lottery offers the opportunity to bet on NFL football.

Undoubtedly when defendants print "Philadelphia v. Los Angeles", the public reads "Philadelphia Eagles v. Los Angeles Rams", and, in this sense, the words utilized by defendants have a secondary meaning. But I do not understand this fact alone to constitute infringement of plaintiffs' registered marks or unfair competition. Defendants may truthfully tell the public what service they perform, just as a specialist in the repair of Volkswagen cars may tell the public of his specialty by using the word "Volkswagen", and just as the manufacturer of a razor blade may advertise the brand names of the razors they will fit. The same rule prevails in the area of comparative advertising which utilizes the trade-names of competing products.

What one may not do, however, is to advertise one's services in a manner which creates an impression in the mind of the relevant segment of the public that a connection exists between the services offered and the holder of the registered mark when no such connection exists. Moreover, this legal prohibition imposes a duty to take affirmative steps to avoid a mistaken impression which is likely to arise from a truthful description of the service even though it does not literally suggest a connection. Potato Chip Institute v. General Mills, 333 F.Supp. 173, 180–81 (D.Neb.1971), aff'd, 461 F.2d 1088 (8th Cir.1972). See also Smith v. Chanel, Inc., 402 F.2d 562 (9th Cir.1968); Cutler-Hammer, Inc. v. Universal Relay, 285 F.Supp. 636 (S.D.N.Y.1968) (particularly the scope of relief granted).

This case presents a novel situation for application of these well established principles. After carefully reading all of the materials disseminated in connection with the Delaware Lottery, I cannot point to any specific statement, symbol, or word usage which tends to suggest NFL sponsorship or approval. At the same time, however, plaintiffs have convinced me that a substantial portion of the present and potential audience for NFL games believes that the Delaware Lottery is sponsored or approved by the NFL.

In what is denominated the "Delaware Special" portion of the market survey referred to above, 19% of the Delaware residents surveyed and 21% of those designated as "fans" either said that, as far as they knew, the legalized betting on professional football was arranged by the State with the authorization of the teams or said that it was conducted by the teams alone. Before answering, some of those questioned were shown a sample lottery ticket and others were not. The results did not vary significantly between the two groups. These figures establish that there is substantial confusion on the part of the public about the source or sponsorship of the lottery.

For purposes of the survey, the plaintiffs designated anyone who had ever seen a professional football game live or on television a "fan".

Using this definition, 85% of those asked about the source of the lottery qualified as "fans". While I do not think that this definition accords with the commonly accepted notion of who are football fans, I think the NFL cogently argues that its universe of "fans" represents fans and potential fans and, that for purposes of this survey the views of both groups are relevant.

Plaintiffs argue that the 26% of the total population and 19% of "fans" who said that they did not know how the football betting was arranged also fall within the class confused or likely to be confused as to the source of the betting. I need not accept this argument to conclude that the plaintiffs have established a significant level of confusion in the marketplace.

This Court perceives only one way to reconcile these survey results with the absence of any affirmative suggestion of sponsorship or approval in the Delaware Lottery advertising and materials. Apparently, in this day and age when professional sports teams franchise pennants, teeshirts, helmets, drinking glasses and a wide range of other products, a substantial number of people believe, if not told otherwise, that one cannot conduct an enterprise of this kind without NFL approval.

While defendants are guilty of no affirmative statements suggesting affiliation and may well not have foreseen that a substantial number of people would infer an association with the NFL, the fact remains that the ultimate result of their promotion of the Delaware Lottery is significant public confusion and the loss to the NFL of control of its public image. I conclude that this fact entitles plaintiffs to some relief.

The only monetary relief sought by plaintiffs—a judgment directing transfer of the proceeds of the Lottery to NFL Charities Incorporated—is inappropriate. These proceeds are not funds that the NFL would have harvested for itself in the absence of the Lottery. Nor is there any reason to believe that the retention by the State of any of these proceeds would result in unjust enrichment. I have previously held that Delaware has a right to profit from a demand for gambling created by NFL games. Relief is appropriate only because of the failure of the defendants to avoid an impression of sponsorship, and this record does not suggest that the proceeds of the Lottery were in any way augmented by any public perception of affiliation. Given the nature of the service provided, I strongly suspect that this limited perception had no effect on revenue.

To eliminate the confusion as to sponsorship, an injunction will be entered requiring the Lottery Director to include on Scoreboard tickets, advertising and any other materials prepared for public distribution a clear and conspicuous statement that Scoreboard is not associated with or authorized by the National Football League.

Officials of the Delaware Lottery volunteered early in this litigation to employ such a disclaimer. The NFL was dissatisfied with the proposal and, as a result, the Lottery Office took no steps to adopt it. Scoreboard tickets were inscribed with the statement, "The 'Scoreboard' Lottery is sponsored solely by the Delaware State Lottery". However, this appeared at the very bottom of the back of the tickets and was not included in defendants' advertising and other promotional materials.

The survey indicates that this approach to the problem was not sufficient to dispel the idea that the NFL was somehow associated with the Lottery. That survey does not suggest to the Court, however, that a prominent statement on all Scoreboard materials disclaiming any affiliation would be insufficient to protect plaintiffs' legitimate interests.

[The remainder of the court's opinion is omitted.]

Notes

1. Despite having prevailed in court, Delaware abandoned "Scoreboard" at the conclusion of the 1976–77 season. Subsequently, in 1984, Canada created "Sport Select," a gambling contest based on MLB scores, to raise money for the 1988 Winter Olympics in Calgary. In response, the major leagues filed a lawsuit in Quebec Superior Court on essentially the same grounds as those relied upon by the NFL. Before a trial could take place, however, the game was discontinued. More recently, in 1989, Oregon created "Sports Action," a lottery involving NBA and NFL teams, to raise money for collegiate sports. While the NFL took no legal action, the NBA filed a 21–count complaint in federal court. The case became moot after the state dropped the NBA portion because of a lack of interest. *See further* Thomas J. Ostertag, *From Shoeless Joe to Charley Hustle: Major League Baseball's Continuing Crusade Against Sports Gambling*, 2 Seton Hall J. Sport L. 19 (1992).

2. In October 1992, Congress passed the Professional and Amateur Sports Protection Act (PASPA). *See* 28 U.S.C. §§ 3701–3704 (1994). Under the Act, sports betting (other than animal pari-mutuel wagering) is now illegal except in those few states which had such betting prior to August 31, 1990: Connecticut (jai-alai), Delaware ("Scoreboard"), Florida (jai-alai), Nevada (sports betting books), Oregon ("Sports Action"), and Rhode Island (jai-alai).

3. Besides grandfathering-in the above states, PASPA also gave New Jersey until December 31, 1993 to decide whether it wanted sports betting. After considering the matter, the state decided it did not. *See further Petition of Casino Licensees for Approval of a New Game, Rulemaking and Authorization of a Test*, 633 A.2d 1050 (N.J.Super.Ct.App.Div.), *aff'd*, 647 A.2d 454 (N.J.1993).

4. During its consideration by Congress, some observers argued PASPA was unconstitutional because of its attempt to regulate intra-state commerce and failure to treat all states equally. For a response to such charges, see Bill Bradley, *The Professional and Amateur Sports Protection Act—Policy Concerns Behind Senate Bill 474*, 2 Seton Hall J. Sport L. 5 (1992).

5. Quite apart from the effort to stop athletic-themed lotteries, many leagues also have asked newspapers and magazines to stop publishing betting lines and to refuse ads from handicappers and bookmakers. On numerous occasions, for example, the NCAA has threatened to bar reporters working for such publications from attending the Final Four, although it has

never made good on this threat. *See further* Arnie Wexler, *Newspapers Fuel National Disease*, Raleigh (N.C.) News & Observer, Sept. 28, 1997, at C2. Along the same lines, since 1990 the NFL's television contract has specifically prohibited broadcasters from discussing the point spreads on its games. *See* Don Pierson, *Tangled Web of Gambling*, Chi. Trib., Dec. 25, 1997, at 1C (pointing out the NCAA's television contract always has contained such a provision).

6. Ironically, the Food and Drug Administration's (FDA) campaign to lower the profile of cigarette manufacturers by banning their ads from billboards and other high-visibility locations is forcing sports leagues to rethink their relationship with gambling enterprises. *See further* Dan Christensen, *Baseball's Big New Gamble*, Palm Beach Daily Bus. Rev., May 7, 1998, at A1. The effect of the FDA's battle against smoking on sports advertising is examined further in Eric D. Brophy, Comment, *Smoking is Dangerous to Your Health: Especially If You Are a Sports Advertiser*, 8 Seton Hall J. Sport L. 261 (1998), and Bradford J. Patrick, Comment, *Snuffing Out the First Amendment: The FDA Regulation of Tobacco Company Advertising and Sports Sponsorships Under the Federal Food, Drug, and Cosmetic Act*, 8 Marq. Sports L.J. 139 (1997).

Problem 62

To increase revenues, a sports league has decided to enter into a licensing agreement with two Las Vegas casinos. Because none of the money generated by this deal will go to them, the players have refused to give their consent (which is needed under the collective bargaining agreement). If they are sued for illegal restraint of trade, how should the court rule? *See Alabama Sportservice, Inc. v. National Horsemen's Benevolent & Protective Ass'n*, 767 F.Supp. 1573 (M.D.Fla.1991).

INDEX

References are to Pages

0-314-23890-5

9 780314 238900

90000